WORLDMARK ENCYCLOPEDIA OF THE NATIONS

Volume 3

ISSN 1531-1635

WORLDMARK
ENCYCLOPEDIA OF THE NATIONS

AMERICAS

Formerly published by Worldmark Press, Ltd.

GALE GROUP

Detroit
New York
San Francisco
London
Boston
Woodbridge, CT

Gale Group Staff

Shelly Dickey, Project Editor
William H. Harmer, Contributing Editor
David Riddle, Jennifer M. York, Assistant Editors
Rita Runchock, Managing Editor

Mary Beth Trimper, Composition and Electronic Prepress Manager
Evi Seoud, Assistant Composition and Electronic Prepress Manager
NeKita McKee, Buyer

Kenn Zorn, Production Design Manager
Michael Logusz, Graphic Artist

ISBN 0-7876-0511-5 (set)
ISBN 0-7876-0512-3 (volume 1)
ISBN 0-7876-0513-1 (volume 2)
ISBN 0-7876-0514-X (volume 3)
ISBN 0-7876-0515-8 (volume 4)
ISBN 0-7876-0516-6 (volume 5)
ISBN 0-7876-4809-4 (volume 6)
ISSN 1531-1635

Printed in the United States of America

10 9 8 7 6 5 4 3 2 1

CONTENTS

For Conversion Tables, Abbreviations and Acronyms, Glossaries, World Tables, Notes to the Tenth Edition, and other supplementary materials, see Volume 1.

GUIDE TO COUNTRY ARTICLES

All information contained within a country article is uniformly keyed by means of small superior numerals to the left of the subject headings. A heading such as "Population," for example, carries the same key numeral (6) in every article. Thus, to find information about the population of Albania, consult the table of contents for the page number where the Albania article begins and look for section 6 thereunder. Introductory matter for each nation includes coat of arms, capital, flag (descriptions given from hoist to fly or from top to bottom), anthem, monetary unit, weights and measures, holidays, and time zone.

FLAG COLOR SYMBOLS

 Yellow Red Green Blue Orange Brown White Black

SECTION HEADINGS IN NUMERICAL ORDER

1 Location, size, and extent
2 Topography
3 Climate
4 Flora and fauna
5 Environment
6 Population
7 Migration
8 Ethnic groups
9 Languages
10 Religions
11 Transportation
12 History
13 Government
14 Political parties
15 Local government
16 Judicial system
17 Armed forces
18 International cooperation
19 Economy
20 Income
21 Labor
22 Agriculture
23 Animal husbandry
24 Fishing
25 Forestry
26 Mining

27 Energy and power
28 Industry
29 Science and technology
30 Domestic trade
31 Foreign trade
32 Balance of payments
33 Banking and securities
34 Insurance
35 Public finance
36 Taxation
37 Customs and duties
38 Foreign investment
39 Economic development
40 Social development
41 Health
42 Housing
43 Education
44 Libraries and museums
45 Media
46 Organizations
47 Tourism, travel, and
    recreation
48 Famous persons
49 Dependencies
50 Bibliography

SECTION HEADINGS IN ALPHABETICAL ORDER

Agriculture	22
Animal husbandry	23
Armed forces	17
Balance of payments	32
Banking and securities	33
Bibliography	50
Climate	3
Customs and duties	37
Dependencies	49
Domestic trade	30
Economic development	39
Economy	19
Education	43
Energy and power	27
Environment	5
Ethnic groups	8
Famous persons	48
Fishing	24
Flora and fauna	4
Foreign investment	38
Foreign trade	31
Forestry	25
Government	13
Health	41
History	12
Housing	42

Income	20
Industry	28
Insurance	34
International cooperation	18
Judical system	16
Labor	21
Languages	9
Libraries and museums	44
Local government	15
Location, size, and extent	1
Media	45
Migration	7
Mining	26
Organizations	46
Political parties	14
Population	6
Public finance	35
Religions	10
Science and technology	29
Social development	40
Taxation	36
Topography	2
Tourism, travel, and recreation	47
Transportation	11

FREQUENTLY USED ABBREVIATIONS AND ACRONYMS

ad—Anno Domini
am—before noon
b.—born
bc—Before Christ
c—Celsius
c.—circa (about)
cm—centimeter(s)
Co.—company
Corp.—corporation
cu ft—cubic foot, feet
cu m—cubic meter(s)
d.—died
e—east
e—evening
e.g.—exempli gratia
    (for example)
ed.—edition, editor
est.—estimated
et al.—et alii (and others)

etc.—et cetera (and so on)
f—Fahrenheit
fl.—flourished
FRG—Federal Republic of
    Germany
ft—foot, feet
ft³—cubic foot, feet
GATT—General Agreement on
    Tariffs and Trade
GDP—gross domestic products
gm—gram
GMT—Greenwich Mean Time
GNP—gross national product
GRT—gross registered tons
ha—hectares
i.e.—id est (that is)
in—inch(es)
kg—kilogram(s)
km—kilometer(s)

kw—kilowatt(s)
kwh—kilowatt-hour(s)
lb—pound(s)
m—meter(s); morning
m³—cubic meter(s)
mi—mile(s)
Mt.—mount
Mw—megawatt(s)
n—north
n.d.—no date
NA—not available
oz—ounce(s)

pm—after noon
r.—reigned
rev. ed.—revised edition
s—south
sq—square
St.—saint
UK—United Kingdom
UN—United Nations
US—United States
USSR—Union of Soviet
    Socialist Republics
w—west

A fiscal split year is indicated by a stroke (e.g. 1998/99).
For acronyms of UN agencies and their intergovernmental organizations, as well as other abbreviations used in text, see the United Nations volume.
A dollar sign ($) stands for US$ unless otherwise indicated.
Note that 1 billion = 1,000 million = 10^9.

ANTIGUA AND BARBUDA

CAPITAL: St. John's.

FLAG: Centered on a red ground is an inverted triangle divided horizontally into three bands of black, light blue, and white, the black stripe bearing a symbol of the rising sun in yellow.

ANTHEM: Begins "Fair Antigua and Barbuda, I salute thee."

MONETARY UNIT: The East Caribbean dollar (EC$) is a paper currency of 100 cents, pegged to the US dollar. There are coins of 1, 2, 5, 10, 25 cents and 1 dollar, and notes of 5, 10, 20, and 100 dollars. EC$1 = US$0.3704 (or US$1 = EC$2.70).

WEIGHTS AND MEASURES: Imperial measures are used, but the metric system is being introduced.

HOLIDAYS: New Year's Day, 1 January; Labor Day, 1st Monday in May; CARICOM Day, 3 July; State Day, 1 November; Christmas, 25 December; Boxing Day, 26 December. Movable holidays include Good Friday, Easter Monday, and Whitmonday.

TIME: 8 AM = noon GMT.

¹LOCATION, SIZE, AND EXTENT

The state of Antigua and Barbuda, part of the Leeward Islands chain in the eastern Caribbean, is approximately 420 km (261 mi) SE of the US Commonwealth of Puerto Rico and 180 km (110 mi) N of the French overseas department of Guadeloupe. The total land area of 440 sq km (170 sq mi) includes Antigua (280 sq km/108 sq mi); Barbuda, 40 km (25 mi) to the N (161 sq km/62 sq mi); and uninhabited Redonda, 40 km (25 mi) to the SW (1.3 sq km/5 sq mi). This total area comprises slightly less than 2.5 times the size of Washington, D.C. The total coastline is 153 km (95 mi). Antigua and Barbuda's capital city, St. John's, is located on the northwestern edge of the island of Antigua.

²TOPOGRAPHY

Partly volcanic and partly coral in origin, Antigua has deeply indented shores lined by reefs and shoals; there are many natural harbors and beaches. Boggy Peak (405 m/1,329 ft), in southwestern Antigua, is the nation's highest point. Antigua's northeastern coastline is dotted by numerous tiny islets; the central area is a fertile plain. Barbuda, a coral island with a large harbor on the west side, rises to only 44 m (144 ft) at its highest point. Redonda is a low-lying rocky islet.

³CLIMATE

Temperatures average 24°C (75°F) in January and 29°C (84°F) in July, with cooling tradewinds from the east and northeast. Rainfall averages 117 cm (46 in) per year; September through November is the wettest period. The islands have been subject to periodic droughts and to autumn hurricanes.

⁴FLORA AND FAUNA

Most of the vegetation is scrub, but there is luxuriant tropical growth where fresh water is available. Many varieties of fruits, flowers, and vegetables are grown. Palmetto and seaside mangrove are indigenous, and about 1,600 hectares (4,000 acres) of red cedar, white cedar, mahogany, whitewood, and acacia forests have been planted. Barbuda is heavily wooded, with an abundance of deer, wild pigs, guinea fowl, pigeons, and wild ducks.

⁵ENVIRONMENT

Water management is the principal environmental concern. A water shortage due to limited freshwater resources is exacerbated by limited rainfall and drought. The existing water supply is threatened by pollution from distilleries, food processing facilities, and other industrial operations. Deforestation resulting from the nation's energy demands, combined with agricultural development, contributes to soil erosion, as rainfall, which is concentrated in a short season, quickly runs off, compounding the water shortage problem on the islands. The nation's main city, St. John's, has developed a problem with waste disposal. Untreated sewage from resort hotels travels in open sewage lines across the land and empties into the sea. Construction of a desalination plant in 1970 relieved some of the water shortage. The government of Antigua and Barbuda created a Historical, Conservation, and Environmental Commission, but little has been done to address the nation's environmental problems.

⁶POPULATION

The population of Antigua and Barbuda in 2000 was estimated at 64,461, the great majority of which live on Antigua. An estimated 4.6% of the population is 65 years of age or older. The projected population for the year 2005 is 65,000, assuming a crude birthrate of 14 per 1,000 population and a death rate of 5, resulting in a natural rate of change of 0.9% for the period 2000–2005.

It was estimated that 37% of the population lived in urban areas in 2000. The capital city, St. John's, had a 2000 population of 24,000. Codrington is Barbuda's only settlement. Antigua and Barbuda's next census was scheduled to take place in 2001.

⁷MIGRATION

The UK has been the historic destination of Antiguan emigrants, but in recent years St. Martin, Barbados, the US Virgin Islands, and the US mainland have been the principal recipients of the outflow. The primary motive for emigration is the search for work. The net migration rate in 1999 was -6.9 migrants per 1,000 population.

[8]ETHNIC GROUPS

Antiguans are almost entirely of African descent. There are small numbers of persons of British, Portuguese, Lebanese, and Syrian ancestry.

[9]LANGUAGES

English is the official and commercial language. An English patois is in common use.

[10]RELIGIONS

The dominant religion is Christianity. St. John's, as capital, serves as the episcopal seat of both the Anglican and Roman Catholic churches. The Church of England claims almost 45% of the population, and other Protestant groups, including Baptist, Methodist, Pentecostal, Seventh-day Adventist, Moravian, and Nazarene, account for some 42%. Roman Catholics make up only 8.7%. Minority religions include Islam and Baha'i.

[11]TRANSPORTATION

There are about 250 km (155 mi) of highways. Total motor vehicle registration was 14,930 in 1995. The railway consists of 77 km (48 mi) of narrow-gauge track, used mainly to haul sugarcane. The islands have no natural deep water harbors; a deep water facility was constructed at St. John's in 1968. The merchant fleet in 1998 consisted of 517 ships (1,000 GRT or over), totaling 2,706,126 GRT. Also in 1998, there were a total of 3 airports, 2 of which had paved runways. Vere Cornwall Bird International Airport, 7 km (4 mi) northeast of St. John's, accommodates the largest jet aircraft; Coolidge Airport, also on Antigua, handles freight. There is also a landing strip at Codrington. The islands' airlines carried 1,250,000 passengers in 1997.

[12]HISTORY

The first inhabitants of Antigua and Barbuda were the Siboney, whose settlements date to 2400 BC. Arawak and Carib Indians inhabited the islands at the time of Christopher Columbus' second voyage in 1493. Columbus named Antigua after the church of Santa Maria de la Antigua, in Sevilla, Spain. Early settlements were founded in 1520 by the Spanish, in 1629 by the French, and in 1632 by the British. Antigua formally became a British colony in 1667, under the Treaty of Breda.

In 1674, Sir Christopher Codrington established the first large sugar estate in Antigua. He leased Barbuda to raise slaves and supplies for this enterprise. In 1834 slavery was abolished, but this was a mere technicality, since no support was provided for the new freemen. In 1860, Antigua formally annexed Barbuda. The Federation of the Leeward Islands served as the governing body of the islands from 1871 to 1956, and from 1958 to 1962, they belonged to the Federation of the West Indies.

Antigua became an associated state with full internal self-government as of 27 February 1967. Opposition to complete independence came from the residents of Barbuda, who sought constitutional guarantees for autonomy in land, finances, and local conciliar powers. With these issues still not fully resolved, Antigua and Barbuda became an independent state within the Commonwealth of Nations on 1 November 1981, with Vere Cornwall Bird as prime minister. (Considered a national hero for his role in leading the nation to independence, when Bird died in 1999, thousands turned out to observe a national moment of silence in his honor.)

Antigua is an active participant in Caribbean affairs. In May 1987, the prime ministers of the members of the Organization of Eastern Caribbean States (OECS) agreed on a merger proposal, creating a single nation out of their seven island states. A national referendum in each of the states was planned for ratification of the accord, but the referendums were defeated and the seven nations remained separate.

By 1999, Antigua and Barbuda had held four general elections as an independent nation.

[13]GOVERNMENT

Universal adult suffrage on the islands dates from 1951, and ministerial government from 1956. The bicameral legislature gained its present form in 1967, and the United Kingdom granted formal independence to Antigua and Barbuda in November 1981. Under the constitution, the British monarch, as head of state, is represented in Antigua and Barbuda by a local governor-general who is appointed on the advice of the prime minister. The bicameral legislature consists of a 17-member House of Representatives, elected from single-member constituencies for up to five years by universal adult suffrage at age 18; and a 17-member Senate, appointed by the governor-general, of whom 11 (including at least 1 inhabitant of Barbuda) are named on the advice of the prime minister, 4 on the advice of the leader of the Opposition, 1 at the governor-general's discretion, and 1 on the advice of the Barbuda council. The governor-general appoints the prime minister, who must have the support of a majority of the House, and the cabinet.

As of the March 1999 elections, the prime minister is Lester Bird. His party, the ALP, won 12 of the 17 seats in the House of Representatives. Bird, in addition to his role as prime minister, hold a number of other governmental posts, including minister of defense; minister of external affairs; minister of legislature, privatization, printing, and electoral affairs; minister of telecommunications and gambling; minister of public works, sewage, and energy; and minister of urban development and renewal.

[14]POLITICAL PARTIES

The Antigua Labour Party (ALP) has held power since 1946, except for a period from 1971 to 1976, when the Progressive Labour Movement (PLM), led at the time by George H. Walter, held a parliamentary majority. Lester Bird, leader of the ALP, has served as prime minister since March 1994. The party's preeminence continued after independence with electoral victories in 1984, 1989, 1994, and 1999. Other active political parties in 2000 include: the United Progressive Party, led by Baldwin Spencer, and the Barbuda's People's Movement, a coalitions of three small opposition political parties.

The ALP grew out of a trade union movement in the 1940s. Under colonial supervision and tutelage, the party became the dominant force in national politics.

[15]LOCAL GOVERNMENT

The island of Antigua has six parishes and two dependencies, Barbuda and Redonda. Twenty-nine community councils, each with nine members, 5 elected and 4 appointed, conduct local government affairs.

[16]JUDICIAL SYSTEM

English common law and local statutory law form the basis for the legal system, which the Eastern Caribbean Supreme Court, based in St. Lucia, administers; it also provides a High Court and Court of Appeal. Final appeals may be made to the Queen's Privy council in the United Kingdom. A court of summary jurisdiction on Antigua, which sits without a jury, deals with civil cases involving sums of up to EC$1500; three magistrates' courts deal with summary offenses and civil cases of not more than EC$500 in value. The Industrial Court, for arbitration and settlement of trade disputes, was reintroduced in 1976. There is currently a plan to establish a regional supreme court with the six other Caribbean Community (CARICOM) member states (Montserrat, Anguilla, Dominica, Grenada, St. Kitts and Nevis, St. Lucia, and

St. Vincent and the Grenadines), but a number of legal and constitutional obstacles will have to be overcome before this can be accomplished.

The constitution prohibits arbitrary arrest and detention. The suspect must be brought before a court within 48 hours of arrest or detention. The constitution prohibits arbitrary interference with privacy, family, home, or correspondence. The government respects these provisions in practice.

17ARMED FORCES

There is a Royal Antigua and Barbuda Defense Force of some 150 active personnel (army 125, navy 25) that forms part of the Eastern Caribbean Regional Security System, established in 1985 with five other countries in the region. The navy has two patrol craft. The military budget in 1998 was $4 million or 0.6% of GDP.

18INTERNATIONAL COOPERATION

Antigua and Barbuda joined the UN on 11 November 1981. It belongs to ECLAC, FAO, ICAO, ILO, IMF, UNESCO, and WHO. It is also a member of the Commonwealth of Nations, CARICOM, CDB, G-77, IADB, OECS, and OAS. The nation is a signatory of the Law of the Sea and a member of the WTO. Two areas totaling about 365 hectares (900 acres) are leased to the US for use as tracking stations for space vehicles and missiles. In May 1987, the prime ministers of Antigua and Barbuda and the six other OECS member-states voted to create a single nation; national referendums on the issue were to be held. The referendums were later defeated and the seven nations remained separate.

19ECONOMY

Throughout most of the island's history, sugar and cotton production were by far the principal economic endeavors. Since the 1960s, however, tourism has been the main industry, accounting indirectly for some 60% of GDP, while the sugar industry has become insignificant and cotton output has declined. From 1988 to 1998, GDP grew by an average 3.1% annually.

During the 1990s, tourism continued to be the dominant activity in the economy, but the combined share in GDP of transport and communications, trade, and public utilities had increased. In addition, increased tourist arrivals helped spur growth in the construction and transport sectors, boosting manufacturing revenues. The dual-island nation's agricultural production is mainly directed to the domestic market; the sector is constrained by the limited water supply and labor shortages that reflect the pull of higher wages in tourism and construction.

20INCOME

The US Central Intelligence Agency (CIA) reports that in 1998 Antigua and Barbuda's gross domestic product (GDP) was estimated at $503 million. The per capita GDP was estimated at $7,900. The annual growth rate of GDP was estimated at 6%. The average inflation rate in 1998 was 2.6%. The CIA defines GDP as the value of all final goods and services produced within a nation in a given year and computed on the basis of purchasing power parity (PPP) rather than value as measured on the basis of the rate of exchange. It was estimated that agriculture accounted for 4% of GDP, industry 12.5%, and services 83.5%.

The World Bank reports that for the same period per capita private consumption (in PPP terms) was $4,600. Private consumption includes expenditures of individuals, households, and nongovernmental organizations. Approximately 36% of household consumption was spent on food, 8% on fuel, 3% on health care, and 18% on education.

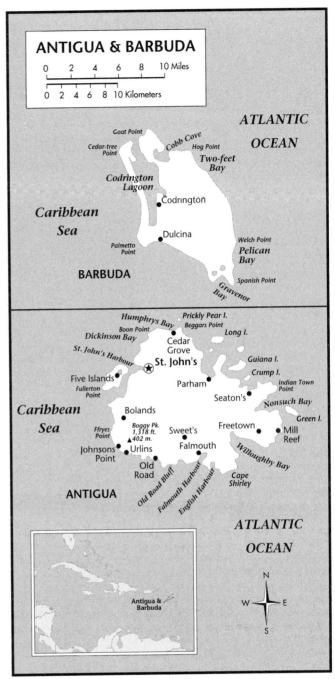

LOCATION: Antigua: 17°9′N; 61°49′W. Barbuda: 17°41′N; 61°48′W.
TOTAL COASTLINE: 153 km (95 mi). **TERRITORIAL SEA LIMIT:** 12 mi.

21LABOR

The total labor force in 1991 was estimated at 20,500. About 82% of the employed labor force worked in occupations connected with tourism or other services; 7% in industry, and 11% in agriculture, hunting, forestry, and fishing.

Unemployment in 1991 officially stood at 5%, although actual unemployment levels among Antiguans are likely to be higher due to high numbers of work permits issued to foreigners. The labor movement is well organized but politically divided.

Workers have a recognized right to strike unless either party to a dispute requests mediation. Employers found guilty of antiunion discrimination are routinely ordered to make compensation payments to an affected worker, although the employer will not be required to rehire the worker. There is a minimum working age of 16, which is entirely enforced by the Labor Ministry. In 1999 the minimum wage ranged from $0.46 per hour for unskilled labor to $1.30 for skilled. However, the vast majority of employed persons earned substantially more than these figures indicate.

The law provides for a maximum 48-hour work week, but most people work 40 hours on the average.

22AGRICULTURE

Some 30% of land on Antigua is under crops or potentially arable, with 18% in use. Sea-island cotton is a profitable export crop. A modest amount of sugar is harvested each year, and there are plans for production of ethanol from sugarcane. Vegetables, including beans, carrots, cabbage, cucumbers, plantains, squash, tomatoes, and yams, are grown mostly on small family plots for local markets. Over the past 30 years, agriculture's contribution to the GDP has fallen from over 40% to 12%. The decline in the sugar industry left 60% of the country's 66,000 acres under government control, and the Ministry of Agriculture is encouraging self-sufficiency in certain foods in order to curtail the need to import food, which accounts for about 25% by value of all imports. Crops suffer from droughts and insect pests, and cotton and sugar plantings suffer from soil depletion and the unwillingness of the population to work in the fields. Agricultural exports, including mangoes, bananas, coconuts, and pineapples, were estimated at us$1.4 million in 1997. Mango production in 1998 was 1,000 tons.

23ANIMAL HUSBANDRY

Livestock estimates in 1998 counted 16,000 head of cattle, 12,000 sheep, and 12,000 goats; there were some 2,000 hogs in the same year. Most livestock is owned by individual households. Milk production in 1998 was an estimated 6,000 tons. The government has sought to increase grazing space and to improve stock, breeding Nelthropp cattle and Black Belly sheep. There is a growing poultry industry. In 1992, the European Development Bank provided us$5 million to the government to help develop the livestock industry.

24FISHING

Most fishing is for local consumption, although there is a growing export of the lobster catch to the US and of some fish to Guadeloupe and Martinique. Antiguans annually consume more fish per capita (46 kg/101.4 lb) per year live weight than any other nation or territory in the Caribbean. The main fishing waters are near shore or between Antigua and Barbuda. There are shrimp and lobster farms operating, and the Smithsonian Institution has a Caribbean king crab farming facility for the local market. The government has encouraged modern fishing methods and supported mechanization and the building of new boats. Fish landings in 1997 were 500 tons; the lobster catch, 65 tons. Exports of fish commodities in 1997 were valued at us$890,000.

25FORESTRY

About 11% of the land is forested, mainly by plantings of red cedar, mahogany, white cedar, and acacia. A reforestation program was begun in 1963, linked with efforts to improve soil and water conservation.

26MINING

Little of the islands' mineral resources, which include limestone, building stone, clay, and barite, were exploited until recently. Some limestone and volcanic stone has been extracted from Antigua for construction purposes, and the manufacture of bricks and tiles from local clay has begun on a small scale. Barbuda

produces a small amount of salt, and phosphate has been collected from Redonda in the past.

27ENERGY AND POWER

Electric power produced in 1998 totaled 90 million kWh, based on a capacity of 26,000 kW. The Antigua Public Utilities Authority, run by the Ministry of Public Works and Communications, operates generating stations at Cassada Gardens and Crabbes Peninsula. Gas is now produced and refined locally. Offshore oil exploration took place during the early 1980s.

As part of the government's energy conservation program, incentives are offered for the manufacture and use of solar-energy units, and there are import surcharges on automobiles with engine capacities exceeding 2,000 cc. Under study as alternatives to fossil fuels are wind power, surplus bagasse from the sugar refinery, and fast-growing tree species. Imports of refined petroleum products in 1994 surpassed 3,000 barrels per day, mostly in the form of jet fuel, distillates, and gasoline. In 1998, all primary energy consumption was petroleum based.

28INDUSTRY

Industrial activity has shifted from the processing of local agriculture produce to consumer and export industries using imported raw materials. Industrial products include rum, refined petroleum, paints, garments, furniture, and electrical components. The government encourages investment in manufacturing establishments, and most industries have some government participation.

Manufacturing—which accounts for 5.5% of GDP—comprises enclave-type assembly for export with major products being bedding, handicrafts, and electronic components. Prospects for economic growth depend on income growth in the industrialized world, especially in the US, which accounts for about half of all tourist arrivals. The industrial park, located in the Coolidge Area, produces a range of products such as paints, furniture, garments, and galvanized sheets, mainly for export.

29SCIENCE AND TECHNOLOGY

Technological services for the fishing industry, such as the introduction of depth finders and hydraulic gear, are provided by the government. An extramural department of the University of the West Indies offers technical courses, as does Antigua State College. The University of Health Sciences at St. John's, founded in 1982, has a school of medicine.

30DOMESTIC TRADE

General business is usually conducted from 8:30 AM to 4 PM, Monday-Saturday, except for Thursday afternoon, when many shops close. Banks are open from 8 AM to noon five days a week, and on Friday additionally from 3 to 5 PM. St. John's is the main commercial center.

31FOREIGN TRADE

Agricultural production is mainly sold domestically. Primary exports include petroleum products (48%), manufactures (23%), and machinery and transport equipment (17%). The country exports mostly to the OECS (26%), Barbados (15%), Guyana (4%), and Trinidad and Tobago (2%).

Imports include food and live animals, machinery and transport equipment, manufactures, chemicals, and oil. Its major providers are the US (27%), the UK (16%), Canada (4%), and the OECS (3%).

32BALANCE OF PAYMENTS

Inward capital movements, of which the largest part is foreign investment (especially for tourism-related construction), compensated for the imbalance in trade and services during the 1980s, but Antigua and Barbuda now maintains a consistently large trade deficit from heavy import dependence, in spite of growing tourism earnings. Export revenues can pay for only one-ninth of import spending.

The US Central Intelligence Agency reports that in 1997 the purchasing power parity of Antigua and Barbuda's exports was $37.8 million while imports totaled $325.5 million resulting in a trade balance of -$287.7 million.

The International Monetary Fund (IMF) reports that in 1996 Antigua and Barbuda had exports of goods totaling $54 million and imports totaling $317 million. The services credit totaled $368 million and debit $155 million. The following table summarizes Antigua and Barbuda's balance of payments for 1996 in millions of US dollars.

Current Account		-40
Balance on goods	-263	
Balance on services	213	
Balance on income	-18	
Current transfers	28	
Capital Account		4
Financial Account		62
Direct investment in Ant. and Bar.	19	
Portfolio investment liabilities	-2	
Other investment assets	36	
Other investment liabilities	9	
Net Errors and Omissions		-37
Reserves and Related Items		11

33 BANKING AND SECURITIES

There were eight commercial banks in 1994, five of which were foreign, including the Bank of Antigua and the Stanford International Bank. The Antigua and Barbuda Development Bank, wholly owned by the government, began operations in 1975. Currency is issued by the Eastern Caribbean Central Bank. The financial industry suffered in Antigua and Barbuda in 1999, due to fears of money laundering by drug cartels. The government passed the Money Laundering Prevention Amendment in order to protect foreign investment in the sector.

34 INSURANCE

There are several life insurance companies on the islands.

35 PUBLIC FINANCE

Since the abolition of the income tax on residents, government revenues have been derived mainly from indirect taxes, principally customs and excise duties and consumption taxes. A major source of revenue is the US's military bases.

The US Central Intelligence Agency (CIA) estimates that in 1997 Antigua and Barbuda's central government took in revenues of approximately $122.6 million and had expenditures of $141.2 million including capital expenditures of $17.3 million. Overall, the government registered a deficit of approximately $18.6 million. External debt totaled $407 million.

36 TAXATION

The income tax, introduced in 1924, was abolished for residents (based on a six-month stay) at the end of 1976. However, a 25% flat tax is levied on an individual's income from trade or business. A property tax is levied at a rate of 7% to 10% for citizens and 14% to 20% for noncitizens. Other taxes include taxes on life and general insurance premiums, property transfers, and a hotel tax. The corporate tax rate is 40%.

37 CUSTOM AND DUTIES

Antigua and Barbuda adheres to the common external tariff schedule of CARICOM; rates (which range up to 35%) are generally ad valorem, based on c.i.f. value, and a wide range of goods is permitted duty-free entry. Additional special rates are applied for tobacco, cement, petroleum products, vans and trucks, and certain types of timber.

38 FOREIGN INVESTMENT

The government's efforts to improve the investment climate have met with some success. Tax holiday periods of 10–15 years are specified under the Fiscal Incentives Act of 1975. Tax rebates of 25–50% are offered to export-oriented industries. Import duty exception for machinery, equipment, spare parts, and raw materials are also granted to approved companies. The offshore financial sector has grown aggressively, offering tax-haven facilities to international business companies, trusts, banks, and insurance companies. In addition, the country has no capital gains or personal income tax. In addition to local tax and duty concessions, manufacturers have access to the US, European, Canadian, and Caribbean markets through the Lome Convention, Caribbean Basin Initiative (CBI), CARICOM, and other agreements

In 1999, the islands' technology sector grew when Internet gaming company Starnet Communications International moved its headquarters to St. Johns.

39 ECONOMIC DEVELOPMENT

Antigua is an excellent location for international business. The country offers a pleasant tropical atmosphere and adequate infrastructure in which to conduct business.

Although only 280 sq km (108 sq mi), Antigua has the largest tourist sector in the Leeward and Windward Islands. Frequent cruise ship arrivals at the St. John's Harbour and the Deep Water Harbour also play a major part in boosting tourism. The opening of the Heritage Quay duty-free shopping complex provides tourists with the opportunity to shop at duty-free prices.

There has been a substantial decrease in agriculture's contribution to the country's GDP, falling from 40% to 4% since the 1960s. However, the Ministry of Agriculture has been implementing policies to encourage farmers to increase output in an effort to decrease imports of agricultural products. The trade imbalance severely endangers the Antiguan and Barbadian economy in the event of decreased tourism revenues.

New hotel construction in 1999 competed with the installment of a completely new telephone system in 2000 for importance to economic development.

40 SOCIAL DEVELOPMENT

Effective from 1973, a social security fund provides for compulsory coverage of all persons between the ages of 16 and 60 years who are engaged in insurable employment. Contributions to the fund amount to 8% of wages (5% from employers and 3% from workers). It provides old age, disability, and survivor benefits. The cost of a medical insurance scheme that includes maternity benefits is shared equally between employers and employees. The government operates day-care centers for children under 5 years of age. The seven-member Board of Guardians meets each month to interview destitute persons who have applied for relief.

Although there are no legal restrictions on women's roles in society, traditions tend to limit their activities outside the home. The Directorate of Women's Affairs provides programs in areas including health, crafts, and business skills to help women advance in the public and private sectors. As of 1999, 3 of 36 members of Parliament were women.

Domestic violence against women is a serious problem, but the legal system is often lenient in addressing this issue. Police are often reluctant to intervene, and many abused women refuse to testify for fear of retaliation. Nongovernmental organizations are increasingly advocating women's rights and providing support to abused women. Domestic violence legislation was passed by the parliament in 1999, and the Directorate of Women's Affairs attempted to educate women about their rights under the new law. Child abuse also appears to be prevalent, but has yet to become a widely recognized social problem.

Human rights are generally respected by the government, although prison conditions are poor.

41HEALTH
Four institutions are maintained for the care of the sick and aged. Holberton Hospital, with 135 beds, is the only public acute care facility. The hospital suffered hurricane damage in 1995, and plans are underway for construction of a new facility. Other facilities include the Fiennes Institute for the aged, with 100 beds, and the Mental Hospital, with 150 beds. In addition, 9 health centers and 18 dispensaries are located throughout the country. In 1995 there were 11 doctors and 218 nurses. The infant mortality rate in 1999 was 21 per 1,000 live births, while the total fertility rate for 1999 was 1.7. The average life expectancy in 1999 was 71 years. As of 1995, 100% of the population was immunized against diphtheria/pertussis/tetanus and 94% against measles, mumps, and rubella. As of 1995, 70 cases of AIDS had been reported.

42HOUSING
The Central Housing and Planning Authority advises on suitable sites, rehabilitates houses in the event of disaster, develops new housing tracts, and redevelops blighted areas. Between 1988 and 1990, 100% of the urban and rural population had access to sanitation services.

43EDUCATION
Education for children between the ages of 5 and 16 years is compulsory. Primary education begins at the age of five years and normally lasts for seven years. Secondary education lasts for five years, three years of lower secondary, followed by two years of upper secondary. The government administers the majority of the schools. As of 2000, there were 72 primary and secondary schools. There were 9,298 students enrolled at the primary schools and 5,845 students at the secondary schools. There currently are three colleges. The University of Health Sciences, Antigua, was founded in 1982. It had, in the 1990s, an enrollment of 46 students and 16 teachers. The University of the West Indies School of Continuing Studies (Antigua and Barbuda) was founded in 1949 and offers adult education courses, secretarial skills training programs, summer courses for children and special programs for women. In 1972, the technical and teacher's training colleges merged and formed the Antigua State College.

The University of the West Indies has campuses in Barbados, Trinidad, and Jamaica, and it maintains extramural departments in several other islands, including Antigua. Those interested in higher education also enroll at schools in the UK, the US, Europe and Canada. Antigua's literacy rate is one of the highest in the Eastern Caribbean.

44LIBRARIES AND MUSEUMS
The largest library is the St. John's Public Library located in St. John's, Leeward Islands, with 50,000 volumes. The library at the University of the West Indies School of Continuing Studies on St. John's has 10,000 volumes. There is an archaeological museum near St. John's.

45MEDIA
The islands' automatic telephone system, operated by the Antigua Public Utilities Authority, has approximately 20,000 telephones. International telephone and telex services are supplied by Cable and Wireless (West Indies), Ltd. Eight broadcasting stations—four AM, two FM, and two television were in operation in 1999.

In 1995 there were some 28,000 radios, and, in 1997, 434 television sets per 1,000 population. There are also two shortwave stations, one coaxial submarine cable, and one Atlantic Ocean INTELSAT earth station.

The *Antigua & Barbuda Herald,* with a circulation of about 2,500, is published biweekly. The *Workers' Voice,* the official organ of the ALP and the Antigua Trades and Labour Union, appears weekly and has a circulation of 6,000. The *Outlet,* published weekly by the Antigua Caribbean Liberation Movement, has a circulation of 5,000. The *Nation,* with a circulation of about 1,500, appears weekly, published by the government.

The constitution ensures the freedom of expression and press, and the authorities are said to generally respect these rights in practice. However, the government dominates all electronic media, thereby restricting to some degree opposing political expression and news.

46ORGANIZATIONS
Four employers' organizations represent workers' interests in Antigua and Barbuda. The Antigua Chamber of Commerce has its headquarters in St. John's. Many missionary and charitable organizations have operations on the islands, including Planned Parenthood, the Inter-American Foundation, the American Bible Society, and the People-to-People Health Foundation.

47TOURISM, TRAVEL, AND RECREATION
Tourism is the main source of revenue in Antigua and Barbuda. Antigua's plethora of beaches—said to number as many as 365—and its charter yachting and deep-sea fishing facilities have created the largest tourist industry in the Windward and Leeward Islands. The international regatta and Summer Carnival are popular annual events. Cricket is the national pastime; local matches are played Thursday afternoons, Saturdays, and Sundays. A wide range of hotels and restaurants served approximately 232,000 tourists in 1998. Receipts from tourism climbed to $269 million in 1997. That year there were 3,185 hotel rooms on these islands. A valid passport is required by all visitors except nationals of the US, Canada and the UK. Visas are not required for short stays.

In 1999 the UN estimated that daily expenditure would average $70 in Barbuda, while daily expenditure in Antigua was estimated at $222. These costs vary greatly according to seasonal demand.

48FAMOUS ANTIGUANS AND BARBUDANS
The first successful colonizer of Antigua was Sir Thomas Warner (d.1649). Vere Cornwall Bird, Sr. (1910–99) was prime minister from 1981–94. (Isaac) Vivian Alexander ("Viv") Richards (b.1952) is a famous cricketer.

49DEPENDENCIES
Antigua and Barbuda has no territories or colonies.

50BIBLIOGRAPHY
Berleant-Schiller, Riva. *Antigua and Barbuda.* Oxford: Clio, 1995.

Coram, Robert. *Caribbean Time Bomb: The United States' Complicity in the Corruption of Antigua.* New York: Morrow, 1993.

Kelly, Robert C. et al., (eds.) *Antigua & Barbuda Country Review 1999/2000.* Houston: Commercial Data International, 1999.

Lazarus-Black, Mindie. *Legitimate Acts and Illegal Encounters: Law and Society in Barbuda and Antigua.* Washington, D.C.: Smithsonian Institution Press, 1994.

ARGENTINA

Argentine Republic
República Argentina

CAPITAL: Buenos Aires.

FLAG: The national flag consists of a white horizontal stripe between two light blue horizontal stripes; centered in the white band is a radiant yellow sun with a human face.

ANTHEM: *Himno Nacional*, beginning "Oíd, mortales, el grito sagrado Libertad" ("Hear, O mortals, the sacred cry of Liberty").

MONETARY UNIT: The peso (A$) is a paper currency of 100 centavos, pegged to the US dollar in 1991. There are coins of 1, 5, 10, 25 and 50 centavos, and notes of 1, 2, 5, 10, 20, 50, and 100 pesos. A$1 = US$1 (or US$1 = A$1).

WEIGHTS AND MEASURES: The metric system is the legal standard.

HOLIDAYS: New Year's Day, 1 January; Labor Day, 1 May; Anniversary of the 1810 Revolution, 25 May; Occupation of the Islas Malvinas, 10 June; Flag Day, 20 June; Independence Day, 9 July; Anniversary of San Martín, 17 August; Columbus Day, 12 October; Immaculate Conception, 8 December; Christmas, 25 December. Movable religious holidays include Carnival (two days in February or March) and Good Friday.

TIME: 9 AM = noon GMT.

¹LOCATION, SIZE, AND EXTENT

Shaped like a wedge with its point in the south, Argentina, the second-largest country in South America, dominates the southern part of the continent. Argentina is slightly less than three-tenths the size of the United States with a total area of 2,766,890 sq km (1,068,302 sq mi); the length is about 3,650 km (2,270 mi) N–S and the width, 1,430 km (890 mi) E–W. To the N Argentina is bounded by Bolivia; to the NE by Paraguay; to the E by Brazil, Uruguay, and the Atlantic Ocean; and to the S and W by Chile, with a total boundary length of 14,654 km (8,106 mi).

Argentina lays claim to a section of Antarctica of about 1,235,000 sq km (477,000 sq mi). Both Argentina and the UK claim the Falkland Islands (Islas Malvinas), with the UK exercising effective occupancy. In 1978, Argentina almost went to war over three Chilean-held islands in the Beagle Channel. The case was referred to papal mediation; on 29 November 1984, the two countries signed a treaty that confirmed Chile's sovereignty over the three islands.

Argentina's capital city, Buenos Aires, is located along the eastern edge of the country on the Atlantic coast.

²TOPOGRAPHY

Except for the mountainous western area, Argentina is for the most part a lowland country. It is divided into four topographical regions: the Andean region, Patagonia, the subtropical plain of the north, and the pampas. The Andean region, almost 30% of the country, runs from the high plateau of the Bolivian border southward into western Argentina. Patagonia comprises all the area from the Río Negro to the southern extremity of the continent, or about 777,000 sq km (300,000 sq mi). Rising from a narrow coastal plain, it extends westward in a series of plateaus. In most places, the altitude range is 90–490 m (300–1,600 ft), although it may rise to 1,500 m (5,000 ft). Patagonia is a semiarid, sparsely populated region. It includes the barren island of Tierra del Fuego, part of which belongs to Chile. A

portion of the Gran Chaco, covering the area between the Andean piedmont and the Paraná River, consists of an immense lowland plain, rain forests, and swampland, little of which is habitable. The most characteristic feature of Argentine topography, however, is the huge expanse of lush, well-watered level plains known as the pampas. Stretching from the east coast estuary, Río de la Plata, the pampas spread in a semicircle from the Buenos Aires area to the foothills of the Andes, to the Chaco, and to Patagonia, forming the heartland of Argentina, the source of its greatest wealth, and the home of 80% of its people.

The major Argentine rivers, which originate in the Andean west or the forested north, flow eastward into the Atlantic Ocean. The Paraná, Uruguay, Paraguay, and Alto Paraná rivers all flow into the Río de la Plata, which reaches a maximum width at its mouth of 222 km (138 mi), between Uruguay and Argentina. The highest peaks in Argentina are Mt. Aconcagua (6,960 m/22,835 ft), also the highest mountain in South America; Mt. Tupungato (6,800 m/22,310 ft); and Mt. Mercedario (6,770 m/22,211 ft). There is a region of snow-fed lakes in the foothills of the Andes in western Patagonia. Many small lakes, some of which are brackish, are found in the Buenos Aires, La Pampa, and Córdoba provinces.

³CLIMATE

Argentina's climate is generally temperate, but there are great variations, from the extreme heat of the northern Chaco region, through the pleasant mild climate of the central pampas, to the subantarctic cold of the glacial regions of southern Patagonia. The highest temperature, 49°C (120°F), was recorded in the extreme north, and the lowest, –16°C (3°F), in the southern tip of the country. Rainfall diminishes from east to west. Rainfall at Buenos Aires averages 94 cm (37 in) annually, and the mean annual temperature is 16°C (61°F). Light snowfalls occur occasionally in Buenos Aires. Throughout Argentina, January is the warmest month and June and July are the coldest. North of the Río Negro, the winter months (May–August) are the driest period of the year. The wide variations of climate are due to the great range in altitude and the vast extent of the country. In the torrid zone of the extreme north, for example, the Chaco area has a mean annual temperature of about 23°C (73°F) and a rainfall of about 76 cm (30 in), whereas Puna de Atacama has a temperature average of 14°C (57°F) and a rainfall of about 5 cm (2 in). The pampas, despite their immensity, have an almost uniform climate, with much sunshine and adequate precipitation. The coldest winters occur not in Tierra del Fuego, which is warmed by ocean currents, but in Santa Cruz Province, where the July average is 0°C (32°F).

4FLORA AND FAUNA

More than 10% of the world's flora varieties are found in Argentina. The magnificent grasslands have figured prominently in the development of Argentina's world-famous cattle industry. Evergreen beeches and Paraná pine are common. From yerba maté comes the national drink immortalized in gaucho literature, while the shade-providing ombú is a national symbol.

Many tropical animals thrive in the forests and marshes of northern Argentina; among them are the capybara, coypu, puma, and various wildcats. In the grasslands and deserts are the guanaco, rhea, and many types of rodents. The cavy, viscacha, tuco tuco, armadillo, pichiciago, otter, weasel, nutria, opossum, various types of fox, and hog-nosed skunk are common. The ostrich, crested screamer, tinamou, and ovenbird are a few of the many species of birds. Caimans, frogs, lizards, snakes, and turtles are present in great numbers. The dorado, a fine game fish, is found in larger streams, and the pejerrey, corvina, palameta, pacu, and zurubi abound in the rivers.

Spanish cattle on the pampas multiplied to such an extent that the role of wild cattle herds in Argentine history was the same as that of the buffalo herds in the US West. Argentina is richly endowed with fossil remains of dinosaurs and other creatures.

5ENVIRONMENT

The principal environmental responsibilities are vested in the Ministry of Public Health and the Environment; the Subsecretariat of Environmental Planning in the Ministry of Transportation and Public Works; and the Subsecretariat of Renewable Natural Resources and Ecology within the Secretariat of State for Agriculture and Livestock. In 1977, the Metropolitan Area Ecological Belt State Enterprise was created to lay out a 150-km (93-mi) greenbelt around Buenos Aires, with controls on emission and effluents as well as on building density.

The major environmental issues in Argentina are pollution and the loss of agricultural lands. The soil is threatened by erosion, salinization, and deforestation. In the mid-1990s, Argentina had 50,900 ha (125,774 acres) of forest and woodland. Air pollution is also a problem due to chemical agents from industrial sources. Per capita industrial carbon dioxide emissions totaled 3.52 m tons in 1992. The water supply is threatened by uncontrolled dumping of pesticides, hydrocarbons and heavy metals. Argentina has a water supply of 166.5 cu mi. Twenty-seven percent of all city dwellers and 83% of people living in rural areas do not have pure water.

Endangered or extinct species in Argentina include the ruddy-headed goose, Argentinian pampas deer, South Andean huemul, Puna rhea, tundra peregrine falcon, black-fronted piping guan, glaucous macaw, spectacled caiman, the broad-nosed caiman, Lear's macaw, the guayaquil great green macaw, and the American crocodile. Of the 255 species of mammals in Argentina, 23 are considered endangered. Fifty-three of the 927 species of birds are threatened. Four species of a total of 204 reptiles are

also threatened. Of the nation's 9,000 plant species, 159 were endangered as of the mid-1990s.

6POPULATION

The population of Argentina in 2000 was estimated at 37,214,757. An estimated 9.5% of the population is 65 years of age or older. The projected population for the year 2005 is 39,626,000, assuming a crude birthrate of 19 per 1,000 population and a death rate of 8, resulting in a natural rate of change of 1.2% for the period 2000–2005. The population rate of change between 1995 and 2000 was 1.3%. The population density in 1998 was 13 per sq km (34 per sq mi).

It was estimated that 89% of the population lived in urban communities of 2,000 or more in 2000, up from 83% in 1980; more than one-third of all Argentines live in or around Buenos Aires. The capital city, Buenos Aires had a 2000 metropolitan population of 12,431,000. Other estimated metropolitan-area populations in 2000 were Córdoba, 1,407,000; Rosario, 1,228,000; Mendoza, 943,000; La Plata, 676,000; and San Miguel de Tucumán, 642,000.

7MIGRATION

Migration to Argentina has been heavy in the past, especially from Spain and Italy. Under the rule of Juan Domingo Perón, immigration was restricted to white persons, exceptions being made for relatives of nonwhites (Japanese and others) already resident. More recently, immigrants from across the border in Paraguay have numbered at least 600,000; Bolivia, 500,000; Chile, 400,000; Uruguay, 150,000; and Brazil, 100,000. Some 300,000 illegal aliens were granted amnesty in 1992. Foreigners, on application, may become Argentine citizens after two years' residence. A total of 16,738 were naturalized in 1991, of which 13,770 were from other American countries. In 1992, Argentina's refugee population was estimated at 11,500. Few Argentines emigrated until the 1970s, when a "brain drain" of professionals and technicians began to develop. In the mid-1980s, some 10,000 of the estimated 60,000 to 80,000 political exiles returned home.

Of much greater significance to Argentina has been the tendency for workers in rural areas to throng to the cities. This had particular political and economic overtones during the Perón regime of 1946–55. Perón's encouragement of workers to move to Buenos Aires and surrounding industrial areas drained rural areas of so many persons that agriculture and livestock raising, the base of Argentina's wealth, suffered severely. Moreover, the inability of the economy to absorb all of the new urban masses led to a host of economic and social problems that still besiege the nation. Both the federal government and provincial governments have since vainly entreated aged workers to return to rural areas.

There has been a significant increase in asylum claims in recent years, beginning the latter half of the 1990s. During 1998, some 600 asylum applications were received from more than 20 different nationalities. As of September 1999, there were 3,000 refugees and asylum seekers, of whom 1,300 received counseling and assistance from UNHCR. Most were from Peru (48%) and Cuba (12%), but there were also more than 30 other nationalities from Latin America, Eastern Europe, Africa, and Asia. In 1999 there were 0.65 migrants per 1,000 population.

8ETHNIC GROUPS

Argentina's population is overwhelmingly European in origin (principally from Spain and Italy); there is little mixture of indigenous peoples. An estimated 85% of the people are of European extraction, and 15% are mestizo, Amerindian, or of other nonwhite groups. The pure Amerindian population has been increasing slightly through immigration from Bolivia and Paraguay.

9 LANGUAGES

The national language of Argentina is Spanish. Argentine Spanish has diverged in many ways from Castilian, showing the effects of the vast influx of foreigners into Buenos Aires, as well as of Spaniards from Andalucía, Galicia, and the Basque provinces. First- and second-generation Italians have added their touch to the language, and French settlers have contributed many Gallicisms.

The outstanding phonetic feature of Argentine Spanish is the yeísmo, in which the *ll* and *y* are pronounced like the *z* in *azure*. The meaning of many Castilian words also has been modified. The Porteños, as the inhabitants of Buenos Aires are called, rely heavily upon a variety of intonations to express shades of meaning.

English has become increasingly popular as a second language, especially in metropolitan areas and in the business and professional community. There are pockets of Italian and German immigrants speaking their native languages. Some Amerindian languages are still spoken, including a version of Tehuelche in the pampas and Patagonia, Guaraní in Misiones Province, and Quechua in some parts of the Jujuy and Salta provinces.

10 RELIGIONS

In 1999, Roman Catholics constituted an estimated 70% of the population with 25,000,000 members. Protestants accounted for 8% with 2,900,000 members, of whom 70% were Pentecostal. There were reportedly 800,000 Muslims, 250,000 Jews, 100,000 Apostolic Armenian Orthodox, and 4,000 Anglicans. The Delegation of Argentine Jewish Associations represents the Jewish community. Supervision of religious bodies is the responsibility of the Ministry of Foreign Affairs and Worship. Argentina retains national patronage, a form of the old Spanish royal patronage, over the Roman Catholic Church. Under this system, bishops are appointed by the president of the republic from a panel of three submitted by the Senate; papal bulls and decrees must be proclaimed by the president and sometimes must be incorporated into an act of the Congress.

Relations between church and state have been relatively free of the conflict that has taken place in other Latin American countries. During the early part of the Perón era, there was no great opposition by the Church, but several of Perón's later actions, especially the legalizing of divorce in 1954, drew strong criticism. In 1955, Perónists pillaged and burned many noted churches of Buenos Aires, and the Church's opposition hardened. After the revolution in 1956, divorce was again made illegal. (It was legalized again in 1987.) The Church made no formal effort to halt the government's program of using terror against left-wing terrorists during the late 1970s. In the early 1980s, however, Church leaders launched a program of national reconciliation, holding meetings with military leaders, politicians, labor and business representatives, and human rights activists. A Roman Catholic revival, especially among the young, was bolstered by the visit of Pope John Paul II in June 1982, the first visit by any pope to Argentina.

11 TRANSPORTATION.

Argentina has the largest railway system in South America, with 37,830 km (23,508 mi) of track as of 1999. Although railroads link all the provinces, the three provinces of Buenos Aires, Córdoba, and Santa Fe contain about one-half the total track and are the destinations of about two-thirds of all goods carried. The seven major railroads and all other lines belong to the state and are administered by Argentine Railways. Until 1947, when Perón

LOCATION: 21°47′ to 55°16′s; 53°38′ to 73°35′w. **BOUNDARY LENGTHS:** Bolivia, 832 km (517 mi); Paraguay, 1,880 km (1,168 mi); Brazil, 1,224 km (761 mi); Uruguay, 579 km (360 mi); Atlantic coastline, 4,989 km (3,100 mi); Chile, 5,150 km (3,200 mi). **TERRITORIAL SEA LIMIT:** 200 mi.

bought them at a price exceeding their real value, the railroads were mainly under the control of British interests. Since then, they have been in decline and have regularly run up large deficits. Gauges are often incompatible, forcing virtually all interregional freight traffic to pass through Buenos Aires. The railroads' share of merchandise transported has declined gradually since 1946, dropping from 12,557 million ton-km in 1973 to 9 million ton-km in 1991

A five-year railroad modernization and rationalization plan was initiated by the military government in 1976, but the general decline of the railway system was not halted, and the number of passengers carried dropped from 445 million in 1976 to about 300 million in 1991. The subway system in Buenos Aires, completely state owned since 1978, consists of five lines totaling 36 km (22 mi).

The continued deterioration of the railroads has resulted in a sharply increased demand for road transportation, which the present highways cannot handle. By 1999, the nation had 208,350 km (129,469 mi) of roads, of which 47,550 km (29,548 mi) were paved. In late 1969, a tunnel under the Río Paraná was opened, connecting Santa Fe with the nation's eastern region. The road system is still far from adequate, especially in view of Argentina's rapidly increasing automotive industry. A total of 285,435 vehicles were produced in 1994, and in the same year the total number registered reached 5,903,466 (including 4,665,329 passenger cars).

The main river system of Argentina consists of the Río de la Plata and its tributaries, the Paraná, Uruguay, Paraguay, and Alto Paraná rivers. There is a total of 10,950 km (6,800 mi) of navigable waterways, offering vast possibilities for efficient water transportation. The river system reaches Paraguay, northeastern Argentina, and regions of Brazil and Uruguay. The La Plata estuary, with its approaches and navigation channels, is the basis of the entire river system. The La Plata ports (Buenos Aires and La Plata) account for more than half of all maritime cargo, including more than two-thirds of all cargo transported on the river system. The Paraná is easily navigable up to Rosario, but the 171-km (106-mi) stretch between Rosario and Santa Fe has considerably less depth and is less suitable for oceangoing vessels. Up-river from Santa Fe, the Paraná rapidly loses depth and is navigable only by small ships.

The port of Buenos Aires handles about four-fifths of the country's imports and exports, and it is the focus of river traffic on the La Plata system. Other major ports are Rosario, Quequén, Bahía Blanca, Campana, and San Nicolás. Most port storage facilities are owned and operated by the government. In 1961, the State Merchant Fleet and the Argentine Overseas Navigation Fleet were merged to form the Argentine Maritime Lines. This state company carries approximately one-half of all Argentine overseas freight. In 1998, the merchant marine consisted of 29 vessels with a total GRT of 233,856.

Buenos Aires is the most important air terminal in South America. The four principal airports include Aeroparque and Ezeiza, both at Buenos Aires, Catarata Iguazu at Iguazu, and El Plumerillo at Mendoza. In 1998, there were 1,374 total airports and landing fields, of which only 141 had paved runways. The government line is Aerolíneas Argentinas; however, there are other major Argentine airlines and many foreign lines operating in the country. In 1997, the total scheduled civil aviation services flew 14,338 million passenger-km (8,910 million passenger-mi) and 220 million freight ton-km (137 freight ton-mi) and carried 8,600,000 passengers on domestic and international flights.

12HISTORY

Before the Spaniards arrived, about 20 Amerindian groups comprising some 300,000 people lived in the region now called Argentina. They were mainly nomadic hunter-gatherers, although the Guaraní practiced slash-and-burn agriculture.

Spaniards arrived in Argentina in 1516. They called the region "La Plata" (literally, "silver") under the mistaken impression that it was rich in silver. Colonists from Chile, Peru, and Asuncion created the first permanent Spanish settlements in Argentina,

including Buenos Aires in 1580. In 1776, Río de la Plata became a vice-royalty, with Buenos Aires as the main port and administrative center.

During the early colonial period, there was little interest in Argentina. The region had no mineral wealth, and Spaniards overlooked the fertile soil and temperate climate of the region. As a result, Buenos Aires had a population of only about 25,000 at the time of the viceroy's arrival. The Spaniards could not afford to ignore Buenos Aires by the late 1700s, when the city was growing rapidly thanks to illegal trade financed by British interests. Goods were smuggled to Brazil and the Caribbean Islands. Spain worried about British and Portuguese expansion and sought to control trade and collect more taxes from the growing commerce.

In May 1810, following the example set by Spanish cities after the capture of King Ferdinand VII by the French, Buenos Aires held an open town meeting (cabildo abierto). A junta was elected, which deposed the viceroy and declared itself in authority. On 9 July 1816, a congress of provincial delegates in San Miguel de Tucumán signed a declaration of independence, and in 1817, Gen. José de San Martín led an army across the Andes to liberate Chile and Perú.

After independence, Buenos Aires was a major force in the region, and strongmen (caudillos) from the surrounding provinces attempted to curb its power. The internal power struggle lasted until Juan Manuel de Rosas became governor of Buenos Aires Province. He imposed order and centralism from 1835 until 1852, when the forces of Gen. Justo José de Urquiza defeated him. A new constitution was adopted in 1853, and Urquiza was elected president in 1854. The struggle for power between Buenos Aires, the hub of commercial activity for the country, and the provinces that provide the raw materials, continued through the late 1800s. It was not until 1880, when the city was named the federal capital, that regional peace was achieved. By then, Argentina was becoming a modern nation, with new railroads and roads under construction. Thousands of European immigrants flocked to the country each year looking for a better life. Buenos Aires alone grew from 90,000 people in 1851 to 1.3 million by 1910, when the city was called the "Paris of South America."

Social conflicts always had been part of Argentina's history, but they intensified during the late 19th century, as the gap between the wealthy classes and the poor widened. The National Party, under the leadership of Gen. Julio Roca (who served two terms as president, 1880–86 and 1898–1904) and supported by the military and landowners, dominated the nation. To combat this powerful coalition, a middle-class party called the Radical Civic Union (Unión Cívica Radical) was formed. The Radicals stressed democratic practices and attempted to expand the political system beyond its elite-restricted boundaries. The Radicals' efforts came to fruition in 1916, when Hipólito Yrigoyen was elected president for a six-year term. But little changed for the working classes. Most workers could barely afford to feed their families during this time, despite the tremendous affluence of the upper class. Workers who sought to improve their working conditions were suppressed. A violent army attack against striking metalworkers in 1919 came to be known as "La Semana Tragica" (The Tragic Week). Yrigoyen sat out for a term, and was reelected president in 1928, but he didn't last long. An economic crisis precipitated by the world depression led to a military coup in 1930.

For the next 13 years, Argentina was ruled by the old Conservative oligarchy. The military-landowner alliance brought both economic recovery and political corruption, as well as the exacerbation of social tensions. Particularly divisive was the matter of Argentina's foreign relations. While opening Argentina to trade with Europe improved the economic picture, many felt that the leadership had sold out to foreign interests. Argentina's careful neutrality toward the Axis powers masked considerable Fascist sympathies, further dividing the nation.

Another military coup in 1943 brought to power an even more Axis-sympathetic group but also launched a new era in Argentine politics. Argentina had undergone an industrial expansion, accelerated by the war. This expansion led to the formation of a large blue-collar workforce, which in 1943 came under the direction of the military head of the Labor Department, Col. Juan Domingo Perón. Perón used his new constituency to build a power base that allowed him in 1946 to be elected president, while his supporters won majorities in both houses of Congress. Perón, it was later reported, allowed many Nazi German leaders to hide in Argentina.

Perón made sweeping political, economic, and social changes. His ideology was an unusual blend of populism, authoritarianism, industrialism and nationalism. His strong personal appeal was buttressed by the charm of his wife Eva ("Evita"), a woman of modest upbringing who captivated the masses with her work on behalf of the poor. Peronist rhetoric stressed the rights of the "descamisados" (literally, "shirtless"), the poor of Argentina.

Perón sought to establish a foreign policy that allied Argentina with neither the West nor East, while acting as protector of weaker Latin American nations against US and British "imperialists." He coined a new word to describe his approach: "justicialismo," roughly the essence of justice. After reelection in 1951, Perón became increasingly dictatorial and erratic, especially after the death of Evita a year later. Economic hardship led to reversals in policy that favored the old oligarchy. Newspapers were shut down and harassed. Perón legalized divorce and prostitution, and began to incite violence against churches. Finally, a military group took over in September 1955.

For the next 20 years, Argentina felt the shadow of Perón. From exile in Spain, Perón held a separate veto power. Under the military's watchful eye, a succession of governments attempted unsuccessfully to create a new political order.

The first of these efforts came from Gen. Pedro Eugenio Aramburu, who repressed Perón's followers and declared their party illegal. After two years of provisional government, elections were held. Rival factions of the old Radical Civic Union competed in a contest won by Arturo Frondizi of the more left-leaning UCRI. With the initial support of the Peronistas, Frondizi attempted to balance that support with the military, which grew nervous at the mention of Peronism. Frondizi curbed inflation through an austerity program and increased Argentina's petroleum production by extending concessions to foreign companies. These economic measures helped increase political tensions, and in the elections of 1961 and 1962, Peronist candidates, running under the banner of the Justicialist Front (Frente Justicialista), won sweeping victories. A military junta removed Frondizi from the presidency in March 1962 and annulled the elections, thus denying governorships to the supporters of Perón. Divisions among the military leaders kept the nation in a state of tension until mid-1964, when new elections were held. Dr. Arturo Illía of the rightist UCRP won the presidency. Illía's administration was beset by rising government debt, inflation, labor unrest, and political agitation, but was most seriously threatened by the military. The chief of the armed forces, Lt. Gen. Juan Carlos Onganía resigned in November 1965, after Illía appointed a Peronist sympathizer as war minister.

In June 1966, following election victories by the Peronist faction, the military leaders installed Onganía as President. Onganía dissolved the nation's legislative bodies and suspended the constitution. Onganía announced a revolutionary program to restore economic prosperity and social stability, saying that only after this restoration would the democratic system be reestablished. Inflation was cut by means of rigid wage controls, and by the end of 1969, the economy was growing at a rate of 7% annually. His economic policies were overshadowed, however, by growing political tension. With the help of the military, strict controls were imposed on the press and all means of mass communication. Students led in denouncing these repressive policies, and in the early months of 1969, violence erupted in Córdoba and Rosario.

Dissatisfaction mounted early in 1970, and acts of terrorism increased. Several groups were active, some of which claimed to be Peronist, others Marxist, still others claiming to be both. The most serious incident was the kidnapping and killing of former President Aramburu by a Peronist group. Although President Onganía stiffened in response to the disorder, it was becoming clear that Argentina would never be stabilized without the participation of the Peronists. For his part, Perón encouraged these groups from abroad.

In June 1970, a junta of high-ranking military officers removed Onganía, and began to move toward democratic reform. Under two ensuing military governments, preparations were made for elections that would include the Peronists, now organized as the Justicialist Liberation Front (FREJULI). In general elections held in March 1973, the winner was Dr. Héctor J. Cámpora, whose unofficial slogan was "Cámpora to the presidency; Perón to power." Cámpora was elected president with 49% of the vote, while FREJULI won a congressional majority and 11 of the 22 provincial governorships. However, Cámpora, who assumed office in May 1973, was no better able than his predecessors to cope with a rising tide of terrorism, much of it from extreme Peronist factions. After a consultation with Perón in Madrid, Cámpora announced his resignation, effective in July.

Perón, who had returned to Argentina in June 1973, ran for the presidency and took 61.9% of the vote in a special election in September. His running mate was his third wife, María Estela ("Isabel") Martínez de Perón, a former exotic dancer. There was no magic left in the elderly Perón. He cracked down on the very terrorist groups he had encouraged, but the economy sagged. When he died in July 1974, his widow succeeded to the presidency.

Isabel had none of Evita's appeal, and her administration plunged Argentina more deeply into chaos. The first year of Isabel Perón's regime was marked by political instability, runaway inflation, and a renewal of guerrilla violence. In September 1975, Perón vacated her office for 34 days, ostensibly because of ill health. During her absence, the military strengthened its position. In March 1976, she was arrested in a bloodless coup, and a military junta consisting of the commanders of the army, navy, and air force took over. The leading member of the junta was Army Commander Lt. Gen. Jorge Rafael Videla, who became president.

The junta dissolved Congress, suspended political and trade union activity, and mounted a concerted campaign against leftist guerrillas. For seven years, the military attempted to "purify" Argentina by imprisoning, torturing and executing leftists, Peronists, trade unionists and members of other political parties deemed divisive. Military officers also kidnapped the babies of the "disappeared" and gave them to officers or released them to adoption agencies. Meanwhile, they attempted a complete liberalization of the economy, including the privatization of banking and industry. However, the military was never able to solve the problem of inflation, which remained in triple digits for most of this period.

In March 1981, Gen. Roberto Viola succeeded Videla as president, and in December, Lt. Gen. Leopoldo Galtieri took over. Troubled by economic woes and lacking any political support from the general populace, the military turned to foreign affairs in an attempt to gain support. In April 1982, Argentina invaded the Falkland Islands, claiming sovereignty over them, but in the ensuing war with the UK, Argentina's armed forces were routed, surrendering in June. The defeat led to Galtieri's resignation, and a new junta was formed in July under Maj. Gen. Reynaldo Benito Antonio Bignone. Liberalization measures during the remainder of 1982 led to strikes and anti-government demonstrations, including a one-day general strike in December in which 90% of the work force reportedly took part. In addition to demands for a return to civilian rule, more and more Argentines demanded to know the fate of at least 10,000 and perhaps as many as 30,000 persons who had "disappeared" during what came to be known as the "dirty war" of 1976–83. Today, official government figures for the "disappeared" stand at 10,000, but human rights groups believe it is much higher.

In elections for a civilian president held in October 1983, the upset winner was a human-rights activist from the UCRP, Dr. Raúl Alfonsín. After taking office in December, Alfonsín called for a new inquiry into the "disappearances" and ordered the prosecution of former junta members. In December 1985, five were convicted, including Lt. Gen. Videla. The legacy of the "dirty war" preoccupied the Alfonsín government. The president saw the need to close the 50-year cycle of military intervention and political instability by building a stable democracy. However, the political reality of Argentina could not be changed by wishes. The human rights trials of leading military officers irked the military, and in April 1987, an abortive military uprising spread to a number of bases. Although Alfonsín refused to yield to the rebels, he soon afterward retreated from his position, getting approval from Congress for a law that would limit the trials to a few superior officers, thereby accepting the defense of "taking orders" for the lower-ranking officers.

The Alfonsín administration also acted to halt rampant inflation with the "Austral Plan" of mid-1985, which froze wages and prices and created a new unit of currency, the austral, to replace the beleaguered peso. The initial success of the plan was weakened by a resurgence of inflation and labor intransigence over wage demands.

With the failure of the Alfonsín administration to stabilize the economy or bring military leaders to justice, Argentines sought change from an old source: the Peronists. In May 1989, Carlos Saul Menem, running under the Justicialist banner, was elected with 47% of the popular vote. Menem was to have taken office in December, but the Alfonsín government was in such dire straits that the president resigned in July and Menem was immediately installed. This was Argentina's first transfer of power between democratically elected leaders in more than 60 years.

Menem, a former soccer player, abandoned his party's traditional support of state enterprises; he cut government spending and generally liberalized the Argentine economy. He also pardoned and released top military leaders. In May 1994, following a first term marked by economic success and political stability, Menem was reelected to a second four-year term. He weathered Argentina's 1995–96 economic recession with the aid of Domingo Cavallo, one-time economy minister and architect of Argentina's anti-inflation plan. Despite the economic successes, many Argentineans grew tired of Menem and alleged corruption in his administration. Menem also couldn't keep his private "playboy" life apart from politics, and began showing the traits of a *caudillo* by pressing for changes to the constitution so he could run for a third term in 1999. His bitter rival and critic, Eduardo Duhalde, prevailed and represented the Justicialists in the 1999 presidential election. For Duhalde and his fellow Peronists, a downturn in the economy came at a bad time. In 1999, Argentina entered a recession and saw its GDP decline by 3%. The economy was affected by downturns in the Russian and Asian economy and devaluation in neighboring Brazil, one of Argentina's biggest trading partners. Unemployment reached 14%. Menem didn't help his party's cause. He seemed more

intent in undermining Duhalde while he actively appeared to be campaigning for a third term in 2003.

In the meantime, Fernando de la Rúa Bruno, the popular mayor of Buenos Aires, had balanced the city's budget and even managed to increase and improve services. A leader of the Unión Cívica Radical, de la Rúa aligned his party with a new political movement called Frente del País Solidario (Frepaso) or Front for a Country in Solidarity, an amalgamation of several center-left parties. Together, they created the Alianza (alliance), and backed de la Rúa for president. De la Rúa's conservatism and successes in Buenos Aires got the attention of voters. He provided a sharp contrast to the excesses of the *bon vivant* Menem. De la Rúa even emphasized his own boring demeanor in political campaigns. A serious president would take the country's problems seriously, his aides stressed. The campaign worked. In October 1999, voters gave de la Rúa 48.5% of the vote. Duhalde received 38.1%. After taking office in December, de la Rúa declared a national economic emergency. By March 2000, he had pushed through Congress a new budget that sliced in half the fiscal deficit. He promulgated new laws to weaken the bargaining power of unions as he continued to push for his plan to make the country more competitive. But he faced many battles. While the Alianza held on to a slim majority in the lower Chamber of Deputies, the Senate remained in control of the Justicialists. In the meantime, the atrocities of the "dirty war" continued to remain a major open wound in Argentina. In 1998, authorities again arrested former dictator Jorge Rafael Videla for investigation of child abductions during the dictatorship. The abductions were not considered to be part of the amnesty, and many more arrests followed. In March 2000, for the first time a former general of the armed forces apologized to the country for crimes committed by the military. Retired General Martín Balza said the military had instituted "state terrorism." Balza shocked Argentineans by publicly confirming the existence of centers of torture and the kidnapping of babies of the disappeared. During the "dirty war," prisoners were buried alive or thrown into the ocean from airplanes and helicopters. Anti-Semitism continued to be a problem in Argentina, despite calls for understanding, and recent government attempts to bring Nazi criminals to justice. The desecration of Jewish cemeteries continued to be a problem.

¹³GOVERNMENT

Argentina's government is ruled by its 1853 constitution, although that document has been suspended many times. The basic structure is federal and republican. In 1949, the Perón government adopted a new constitution, but the subsequent military government expunged that document. Some modifications in the original constitution were subsequently made by a constituent assembly that met in October 1957. In July 1962, a system of proportional representation was adopted.

The constitution provides for a federal union of provinces that retain all powers not specifically delegated to the federal government by the constitution. There is a separation of powers among the executive, legislative, and judicial branches, but the president is powerful within this arrangement. The president can draw up and introduce his own bills in Congress, appoint cabinet members and other officials without the consent of the Senate, and possesses broad powers to declare a state of siege and suspend the constitution. The president is commander-in-chief of the army, navy, and air force and appoints all major civil, military, naval, and judicial offices, with the approval of the Senate in certain cases. The president is also responsible, with the cabinet, for the acts of the executive branch and has the right of patronage (control over appointments) in regard to bishoprics. The president and vice-president are elected by an electoral college for six-year terms. They or their parents must be native-born citizens. Voting is compulsory for all citizens 18 to 70 years of age.

The constitution calls for a National Congress consisting of a Senate and a Chamber of Deputies. The 46 senators are indirectly elected by local legislatures. The term of office is set at nine years, with staggered elections every three years for one-third of the membership. The Chamber of Deputies is the result of direct elections for 254 seats. Seats are allocated to each province in proportion to its population. The deputies' term of office is four years, with one-half of the membership being elected every two years. The Chamber of Deputies is authorized to receive the budget and initiate fiscal legislation and has the exclusive right to impeach officials before the Senate.

The most recent suspensions of the constitution were between 1966 and 1973, and then again from 1976 until 1983. During the most recent suspension, a military junta performed the executive, legislative, and judicial functions. Since the resumption of civilian government in 1983, there has been an uneasy relationship between the military and the government. The controversial trials of military leaders led to serious questions about the credibility of the judiciary, and mild sentences for the accused. Yet, after more than 17 years of democratic government, there appears to be new efforts to bring former military leaders to justice. The latest revisions to the constitution were approved in August 1994.

14POLITICAL PARTIES

Political party activity in Argentina has been sporadic, given the frequency of military takeovers and the many years during which parties have been banned. Still, several parties reformed in the 1980s and continue to be active in the 1990s.

Traditionally, the alignment of Argentine political parties has been along socioeconomic and religious lines. The landowners, the high clergy, and the more conservative lower class supporters have formed an alliance that defends the Church and the status quo. On the other side have been the advocates of change: merchants and professionals who resent the preeminence of the aristocracy and who tend also to be anticlerical. This second group has supported separation of church and state and decentralization. However, in modern times, new parties have emerged to represent the working class, small farmers, and intellectuals.

During the first half of the 20th century, the Radical Party in Argentina was either the governing party or the chief opposition. The Radicals were committed to the expansion of Argentine politics to the middle and lower classes, and a transformation of the nation's economic and social life. This party was as close to a mass-based party as Argentina had ever had. The core was middle class, but the party was also supported by upper- and lower-class elements. Only radical by the standards of Argentine politics, it occupied a middle ground between the Conservatives and the Socialist left. However, with a heterogeneous membership, tensions and schisms were frequent. The party split into the Radical Intransigent Civic Union (Unión Cívica Radical Intransigente—UCRI), which formed the major support for Arturo Frondizi in 1958, and the People's Radical Civic Union (Unión Cívica Radical del Pueblo—UCRP), led by Ricardo Balbín. The UCRP was somewhat more nationalistic and doctrinaire than the UCRI, but shifting policies made the differences difficult to define. Balbín's party survived into the 1980s as the Radical Civic Union (Unión Cívica Radical—UCR). After the military stepped down in 1983, that party was one of the few viable political entities in Argentina, and emerged victorious in the 1983 elections. However, with the failure of the Alfonsín administration, the UCR found itself again in its old role as loyal opposition.

The Conservatives dominated Argentine politics from about 1874 to 1916 and again from 1932 to 1945 when they were known as the National Democrats. This era of Argentine politics was known as the "Concordancia." The Conservatives were the chief spokesmen for the landed interests, from whom they drew their main support. During the Perón regime, the right lost most of its influence. In 1958, conservative parties banded together to form the National Federation of Parties of the Center (Federación Nacional de Partidos del Centro). Years of military rule in the name of conservatism yielded no mass-based conservative parties, mainly because the military professed a disdain for partisan politics. Currently, there are several small right-wing parties, the largest of which is the Union of the Democratic Center (UCD).

Although leftism in Argentina has a long tradition, it was dealt a serious blow during the 1976–83 military governments. Those governments were committed to the extermination of all leftist influences. This meant the jailing and "disappearance" of leaders of the socialist and communist movements. In addition, Peronism preempted much of the ideological appeal of these parties, as well as their traditional working-class constituencies. The earliest leftist party was the Communist Party, founded in 1918 by Juan B. Justo, who split from Yrigoyen and the Radicals. The Communists were never terribly revolutionary, but concentrated instead on the trade union movement.

In the 1970s, Argentine leftism was thrown into confusion by the appearance of several substantial "urban guerrilla" movements. The Trotskyist People's Revolutionary Army (Ejército Revolucionario del Pueblo—ERP), the Montoneros, and the Peronist Armed Forces (FAP), among others, became major players on the Argentine political scene, if only because of the dramatic impact of their actions. Their presence may well have hastened the return of Perón in 1974, but their persistence became a major justification for the military repression that followed. Refusing to make any distinction between a leftist and a terrorist, the government decimated the Argentine left.

Peronism, which defies political classification, is still very much alive in Argentina, in name if not in anything else. Peronism went underground for nearly two decades after the coup of 1955. Operating under the names Popular Union Party, Populist Party and Laborite Party, a variety of Peronist organizations put up candidates wherever possible. The movement was alternately wooed, tolerated, or repressed, depending on the degree to which the military was involved. In 1973, elections were held in which the Peronists were allowed to field a candidate, Hector J. Cámpora, representing a coalition of various Peronist factions and other smaller parties. This coalition, the Justice Liberation Front (Frente Justicialista de Liberación— FREJULI), took 49% of the vote. Under Cámpora's successors, Juan Perón and Isabel Perón, FREJULI remained the governing coalition until the March 1976 coup, after which political activity was suspended until 1980. A "reform" movement led to infighting that crippled the party in the 1983 elections.

In 1989, Carlos Menem's victory was accompanied by solid legislative majorities in both houses of the legislature. The Justicialist Party (JP) had 122 seats in the Chamber of Deputies and 27 seats in the Senate. In the elections of May 1995, the party took 132 of a total 257 seats in the Chamber of Deputies, and 38 of a total 72 Senate seats.

Argentina's party politics have been contentious and vicious over the years, with various sides coalescing in order to defeat rivals. One notable exception was the formation in July 1981 of the Multipartidaria, an alliance among Argentina's five leading parties—FREJULI, the UCR, the Democratic Christian Federation (Federación Demócrata Cristiana), the Movement for Integration and Development (Movimiento de Integración y Desarrollo—MID), and the Intransigent Party (Partido Intransigente). Claiming the support of about 80% of the voters, this opposition alliance began to negotiate with the military concerning a return to constitutional government, and in July

1982, political parties were formally permitted to resume their activities.

In April 1994, the Front for a Country of Solidarity (Frente del País Solidario or Frepaso) was formed. A center-left group, it has won widespread middle-class support by campaigning against government corruption. It defeated the UCR for second place in the 1995 legislative elections when it gained a representation in the Chamber of Deputies of 29 members. In 1999, Frepaso joined the UCR to create the Alianza (alliance) to elect UCR candidate Fernando de la Rúa. He was elected with 48.5% and assumed the presidency in December. The Alianza has a slim majority in the lower house of Congress, but the Justicialists remain in control of the Senate.

15 LOCAL GOVERNMENT

Argentina is a federation of 22 provinces, the federal capital of Buenos Aires, and the territories of Tierra del Fuego, the Antarctic, and the South Atlantic Islands. During the 19th century there was a bitter struggle between Buenos Aires and the interior provinces, and there has long been an element of tension regarding the division of powers between the central government and provincial bodies. The federal government retains control over such matters as the regulation of commerce, customs collections, currency, civil or commercial codes, or the appointment of foreign agents. The provincial governors are elected every four years.

The constitutional "national intervention" and "state of siege" powers of the president have been invoked frequently. The first of these powers was designed to "guarantee the republican form of government in the provinces." Since the adoption of the 1853 constitution, the federal government has intervened over 200 times, mostly by presidential decree. Under this authority, provincial and municipal offices may be declared vacant, appointments annulled, and local elections supervised. Between 1966 and 1973, all local legislatures were dissolved and provincial governors were appointed by the new president. A restoration of provincial and municipal government followed the return to constitutional government in 1973. After the March 1976 coup, the federal government again intervened to remove all provincial governors and impose direct military rule over all municipalities. Since 1983, representative local government has been in force again.

Until 1996, The President appointed the mayor of Buenos Aires, and by law, the President and Congress controlled any legislation that affected the city. Constitutional reforms that year led to an elected mayoral position, and a 60-member Poder Legislativo (legislative power). The members are elected by proportional representation to four-year terms.

16 JUDICIAL SYSTEM

Justice is administered by both federal and provincial courts. The former deal only with cases of a national character or those to which different provinces or inhabitants of different provinces are parties. The Supreme Court, which supervises and regulates all other federal courts, is composed of five members nominated by the president and confirmed by the Senate. Other federal courts include nine appellate courts, with three judges for each; single-judge district courts, at least one for each province; and one-judge territorial courts. The federal courts may not decide political questions. Judges of the lower courts are appointed by the president.

Provincial courts include supreme courts, appellate courts, courts of first instance, and minor courts of justices of the peace (alcaldes) and of the market judges. Members of provincial courts are appointed by the provincial governors. Trial by jury was authorized by the 1853 constitution for criminal cases, but its establishment was left to the discretion of Congress, resulting in sporadic use.

A 1991 law provides a fund for compensating prisoners who were illegally detained during the 1976–83 military dictatorship.

In 1992, a system of oral public trials was instituted in order to speed up the judicial process while improving the protection of procedural rights of criminal defendants.

In practice, there is not a truly independent judiciary. The courts lack power to enforce orders against the executive and federal judges who actively pursue charges of police or military corruption. In 1989, President Menem, in a court-packing maneuver, expanded the number of Supreme Court justices from five to nine.

In 1994, Constitutional amendments provided for a judicial council. The Judicial Council will have power to administrate the federal court and to select and remove judges when Congress passes the necessary enabling act. But as of early 1997, Congress had not passed the legislation. The Constitution prohibits arbitrary interference with privacy, family, home or correspondence. The government respects these provisions.

The Constitution prohibits torture. However, police brutality remains a serious problem. The judicial system is subject to delays, resulting in lengthy pretrial detention.

17 ARMED FORCES

The Argentine armed forces, after being reduced and reorganized, numbered 70,500 in 2000, with 375,000 reserves. To increase efficiency and reduce military influence, the position of commander in chief of each service was replaced by that of a chief of staff. Control of the coast guard was removed from the navy and placed with the Defense Ministry, which also took control of the gendarmerie. Conscription ended on 1 April 1995. The navy (which has air and marine units) numbers 20,000, and there is a national gendarmerie of 18,000, a coast guard of roughly 13,000, and an air force of 10,500. The gendarmerie and coast guard are not considered military, but have military capabilities.

The army of 40,000 is organized into three corps and includes armored, mechanized infantry, engineer and artillery battalions. The navy has 3 submarines, 1 aircraft carrier, 7 frigates, 6 missile-equipped destroyers, and 14 coastal combatants. Defense spending has fallen in the last decade, and the 1998 defense budget was $4.6 billion or 1.4% of GDP. Much of the reduction comes from abolishing internal security forces and unwanted reserves and paramilitary units.

Since the 1930 revolution headed by Gen. José Félix Uriburu, the armed forces have frequently intervened in political affairs; from that year through 1983, 14 of the 18 presidents were military officers. The military remained one of the most potent political forces in Argentina until it suffered the humiliating defeat in the Falklands War in 1982.

Argentina participates in UN Peacekeeping missions in six regions.

18 INTERNATIONAL COOPERATION

Argentina is a charter member of the UN, having joined on 24 October 1945; it belongs to ECLAC and all the non-regional specialized agencies. It is also a member of the OAS and of many other inter-American and intergovernmental organizations, such as G-77, IADB, and LAIA. In 1962, Argentina signed an agreement of cooperation and exchange of information with EURATOM. It led in the attempt to form a Latin American common market, and in 1967, it joined other Latin American nations in claiming an offshore territory extending 322 km (200 mi). Argentina is a signatory to the Law of the Sea and a member of the WTO.

¹⁹ECONOMY

Argentina has one of the most highly developed economies and most advantageous natural resource bases of Latin America, but political instability and conflicts between various sectors of the economy have delayed the realization of its potential. By 1974, the share of GDP from manufacturing amounted to almost a third of revenues; however, manufacturing (including mining) fell to 24.3% in 1986 and to 19% in 1998. The country has to a large degree overcome its dependence on imported machinery and finished products, but in their place there has grown a great external demand for parts and raw materials that are assembled or finished within the country. Basic industries, such as iron and steel, petroleum and petrochemicals, aluminum, plastics, and electrical equipment are being established, but these will continue to require extensive raw material imports for some time, or even permanently, because of the absence of certain minerals, such as bauxite (which is needed for aluminum production).

Economic stagnation during the 1960s was due partly to the tremendous government bureaucracy and partly to political and social unrest, which caused serious work stoppages. Prior to 1970, Argentina suffered serious deficits in trade balance, but with increased exports, favorable trade balances were achieved during the 1970s. In 1974, increases of 7.6% were registered for agriculture, 7.5% for commerce, and 22.3% for construction. However, the average increase of annual GDP registered only 40% from 1977 to 1987. During the period between 1988 and 1999, average annual growth reached 4.4%, due largely to successful economic planning and political stability.

There was widespread inflation in the early 1960s, but rigid controls initiated in 1967 decreased the rate of inflationary growth. From 1973, however, a combination of political instability, massive budget deficits, and union wage demands increased inflation once again. At the time of the March 1976 coup, the annual inflation rate was 444%; it decreased in the late 1970s but rose again to 209% in 1982. The peso had so depreciated by 1982 that the government decided to redenominate the currency in 1983, at 10,000: 1. Also in 1983, Argentina received a stabilization loan from the IMF to compensate for the effects of inflation and recession. As a condition for the loan, the government agreed to reduce the inflation rate to 165% in 1983. By autumn, however, inflation was running at an annual rate of over 900%; the inflation rate for the whole of 1983 was 434%, the highest in the world. Thereafter, it rose without interruption until it reached some 1,200% in mid-1985. At that time, the government introduced the Austral Plan—a bold attempt to halt inflation by freezing wages and prices, revaluing (and redenominating) the currency, and resolving to finance public spending with real assets only (not by printing money); under this plan the annual rate for 1985 was cut to 385%. By the end of 1986, the rate had been cut further to 82%; by early 1987, however, inflation had begun to surge again, and it was expected to exceed 100% by the end of the year.

In July 1989, President Carlos Menem of the Justicialista Party took office at a time when the economy was entangled in a hyper-inflationary spiral. In 1991, President Menem unveiled an innovative stabilization/reform program which was implemented successfully. The cornerstone of the stabilization/reform plan was to link the peso to the dollar at a fixed rate of 0.99 pesos per dollar (under the 1991 "Convertibility Law"), and requiring congressional approval for devaluation. In 1992, economic policy continued to focus on structural adjustment involving a strategy of cleaning up the fiscal accounts. The reforms took on a four-pronged approach: fiscal revenues were strengthened through a broadening of the VAT and an enhancement in revenue enforcement; administrative reforms included a substantial cut in public payroll and revamping of national fiscal accounting; the use of the Central Bank's rediscount window to finance deficits of provincial governments was curtailed; and public enterprises were privatized. Both revenue enhancements and expenditure cutbacks sharply reduced the inflation rate.

After three years of swift growth, the devaluation of the Mexican peso on 20 December 1994 pushed the Argentine economy into a severe recession, but Economy Minister Domingo Cavallo took an austere line and refused to devalue the Argentine currency in 1995, even though the economy shrank by 4.4% in that year. However, the economy began to recover in 1996, and by 1998 the inflation rate held at about 1.0%, one of the lowest rates in the world. Even though inflation was low in 1999, a recession brought the realization that high consumer prices were not the only roadblock to economic development. Mainly due to Brazil's financial crisis, Argentina's main trade partner; negative growth also reflected poor labor policies and a lack of capital in 2000.

²⁰INCOME

The US Central Intelligence Agency (CIA) reports that in 1998 Argentina's gross domestic product (GDP) was estimated at $374 billion. The per capita GDP was estimated at $10,300. The annual growth rate of GDP was estimated at 4.3%. The average inflation rate in 1998 was 1%. The CIA defines GDP as the value of all final goods and services produced within a nation in a given year and computed on the basis of purchasing power parity (PPP) rather than value as measured on the basis of the rate of exchange. It was estimated that agriculture accounted for 7% of GDP, industry 37%, and services 56%.

The World Bank reports that for the same period per capita private consumption (in PPP terms) was $7,820. Private consumption includes expenditures of individuals, households, and nongovernmental organizations. It was estimated that between 1990 and 1998 private consumption grew at an annual rate of 4.0%. Approximately 30% of household consumption was spent on food, 17% on fuel, 15% on health care, and 15% on education.

²¹LABOR

According to the 1970 census, the economically active population of Argentina was 9,011,450; by 1998, it was estimated at over 14,000,000. According to 1996 estimates, the labor force was divided as follows: 18.5% in manufacturing, 2.2% in agriculture and mining, 18.1% in commerce, 10.3% in transport and communications, 9.5% in public administration and defense, and the remainder in other sectors. Unemployment began to rise again in the 1970s, exceeding 7% by 1972; for the rest of the decade, however, Argentina's unemployment rate was among the lowest in Latin America (2.2% in 1978). In the wake of the 1981 recession, unemployment and underemployment rose to about 14%. The unemployment rate was 12% in 1998.

Organized labor has probably had a greater effect on the modern history of Argentina than any other group. Before Perón, unions were poorly organized, few in number, and lacking in political power. Perón used the labor movement as his chief vehicle in achieving and holding dictatorial power. He built the General Confederation of Labor (Confederación General del Trabajo—CGT) from a disjointed membership of about 250,000 into a highly centralized organization of six million workers encompassing every aspect of the Argentine economy. With strong backing from the government, union organization proceeded at a spectacular rate, giving Perón control over landowners and management. In return for their solid support, labor unions won tremendous benefits in the form of higher wages and improved working conditions. These advances, however, were built on a political rather than a sound economic foundation, and the fortunes of the CGT waxed and waned with those of Perón and his followers. In 1999, an estimated 35% of the work force belonged to a union.

Following the 1966 coup, Gen. Onganía attempted to reach an understanding with various factions of the CGT, including the Perónists. Early in 1970, Onganía was successful in negotiating a series of agreements with confederation leaders, but inflationary pressures created a growing dissatisfaction with the economic policies of the government. When Gen. Levingston assumed office in mid-1970, he promised the CGT a stronger voice in labor affairs. The CGT regained much of its former influence under the Cámpora and two Perón governments, pushing for numerous inflationary wage increases. In 1973, an estimated four million workers were organized into 500 trade unions, 45 federations, and three confederations. The CGT, composed of 94 affiliated organizations, had an estimated membership of 2.5 million. All trade union activity was banned after the March 1976 coup, but the ban was rescinded in 1981, and the right to belong to a union was reestablished in September 1982. In December 1982, the unions organized a one-day general strike to protest inflation and human-rights abuses, with about 90% of all workers participating. Another successful one-day general strike, called by the CGT and enlisting about 85% participation, took place in March 1983. The government, which had sought to appease the unions by announcing a 12% wage increase, declared the strike legal.

Shortly after taking office in 1983, the Alfonsín administration attempted to legislate democratic practices into the labor movement. While the bill was defeated in the Senate and the government was forced to water it down, elections were held in most unions in 1984, and a reform movement, known as the Committee of 25, began in the CGT. In 1987, another pragmatic group of reformist union leaders, the Group of 15, called for negotiations rather than the one-day general strikes that the CGT's traditional leadership had been using to bring pressure on the government. The CGT split into two factions in 1989, over the question of whether to support Menem's economic policies. In March 1992, having seen their influence and power diminish, the CGT was reunified.

Through deficit reduction, tight fiscal policy, privatization of inefficient industries, the encouragement of domestic recapitalization and foreign investment, both inflation and unemployment have been reduced under the Menem administration. In late 1991, a deregulation decree and "flexibilization laws" were passed, affecting national union organizations. Under the decree, wage negotiation at the shop-floor level was encouraged, as was linkage of wages to productivity. Also under the deregulation, centralization of the vast union social welfare funds was to occur in the Labor Ministry. The "flexibilization laws" allowed businesses to cut union and pension contributions up to 50% for temporary and training positions, and set ceilings on severance and work-related accident payments. Argentine law specifies that all workers are entitled to a minimum wage (about $200 per month in 1999); family allowances for child care, educational expenses, and special occasions; a minimum paid vacation of 14 days annually; and an annual bonus equal to one-twelfth of an employee's total remuneration for the previous 12-month period. The legal workweek for men and women 18 years and over is 48 hours, with a maximum of eight hours a day. Overtime rates are ordinarily determined through collective bargaining. A minimum of one month's notice is required for dismissal; the employer is obligated to pay full wages during that period and to grant the employee two paid hours a day to seek another job. Provincial laws and regulations provide additional protection for workers. Labor legislation passed in 1998 transferred collective bargaining rights from the local to the national union level, unless the national union chooses to delegate authority to its local affiliate.

There are extensive occupational and health and safety laws but they are not fully enforced because the government has inadequate resources. Cases of very poor labor conditions are known to exist in plants employing illegal aliens.

[22]AGRICULTURE

Agriculture and agro-industry in Argentina focus on the production of cereal, oil grains and seeds, sugar, fruit, wine, tea, tobacco, and cotton. Argentina is one of the greatest food-producing and food-exporting countries of the world, with an estimated 27,200,000 hectares (67,210,000 acres) of arable and permanent cropland. Agriculture and animal husbandry have traditionally supplied the nation with 70–95% of its export earnings, and the landowners have alternated the two activities in accordance with prices on the world market. As of 1998, agriculture made up 7% of the GDP. Agricultural products also account for 70% of exports by value. One of the most important factors in Argentine agriculture is the advanced degree of mechanization; in 1997, an estimated 280,000 tractors and 50,000 harvester-threshers were in use.

The principal agricultural region consists of the humid pampas, one of the world's greatest reaches of arable land. Argentine agriculture is virtually coextensive with this region, although efforts have been made to spread it into other areas. Citrus fruit, tobacco, cotton, and sugarcane are cultivated outside the pampas.

Wheat is the leading crop. Argentina accounted for about 67% of all wheat produced in South America in 1998 and was the world's fifth-leading wheat exporter. The area harvested in 1998 was estimated at 4.6 million hectares (11.4 million acres), and production at 10 million tons. Argentina is the fourth-largest corn-growing country in the world. The area harvested in 1998 was 3.2 million hectares (7.9 million acres), and production was 19.1 million tons. Barley is favored as the grain of greatest yield and resistance to disease; types for feed and beer are grown in the pampas areas having soil unfavorable or a climate too rigorous for wheat. Harvests once amounted to 659,000 tons per season in the early 1970s, but in 1998 production was 500,000 tons.

Rice is a major crop, with a 1998 production of 1,036,000 tons on plantings of 202,000 hectares (499,000 acres). Argentina is one of the world's biggest producers of flaxseed (linseed); production in 1998 was 75,000 tons, down more than 80% from the early 1990s. Most of the crop is exported in the form of linseed oil. The province of Tucumán dominates the sugar-raising industry, which dates from 1646; sugarcane production in 1998 was 19.4 million tons. To control overproduction, the government formed the National Sugar Co. in 1970 and forbade the construction of new sugar mills through the end of the decade.

Cotton growing dates from 1909 and is concentrated in Chaco Province. In 1998 the production of cotton fiber was 300,000 tons, down from 432,000 tons in 1996. Sunflower seed oil is a major industrial plant product; 3.2 million hectares (7.8 million acres) of sunflowers were harvested in 1998, producing 5,400,000 tons of sunflower seeds. Tobacco is raised in several northern provinces, especially Misiones; production in 1998 was an estimated 117,000 tons. Soybean production, only 78,000 tons in 1971–72, increased to 7.1 million tons by 1985–86, and to 18.7 million tons in 1998.

Fruit growing has developed rapidly since the 1940s. Estimates for 1998 fruit production (in tons) were apples, 1,347,000; oranges, 841,000; lemons and limes, 871,000; peaches and nectarines, 280,000; and grapefruit, 230,000. The output of bananas was 400,000 tons in 1974, 10 times the 1961–65 average; it fell to 144,000 tons in 1978 and rebounded to 280,000 tons in 1992 before declining to 170,000 tons in 1998.

The province of Mendoza is the center for the nation's vineyards. In 1998, grape production was two million tons. Argentina is one of the world's leading producers of wine, accounting for 1.26 million tons in 1998, or 4.8% of the world's total production.

23 ANIMAL HUSBANDRY

Argentina is one of the world's preeminent producers of cattle and sheep, possessing approximately 4% of the entire world's stock of the former and 2% of the latter. Livestock and meat exports play an essential part in the nation's international trade. Annual meat exports (including meat extracts) were 598,900 tons in 1978, but fell to 394,900 tons in 1981 and 301,390 tons in 1997. Because of extremely favorable natural conditions, Argentina, with about 54.6 million head of cattle in 1998, is one of the world's leading cattle-raising countries.

Cattle were introduced into Argentina by Pedro de Mendoza in 1536, and these cattle, together with those brought by other explorers, quickly became wild and began to multiply on the lush grasses of the pampas. There was no attempt to control the vast herds; when the inhabitants wanted meat and hides, they would merely kill the animals at random and take the desired parts. The most important single advance was the invention of refrigeration, which enabled ships to transport meat without spoilage. The policy followed by foreign-owned meat-packing firms of purchasing cattle by quality rather than weight led to the introduction of new breeds and selective crossbreeding, which have brought the cattle industry to its present advanced state.

Argentine pastures cover an estimated 142 million hectares (350.9 million acres) and are most productive in the provinces of Buenos Aires, Santa Fe, Córdoba, Entre Ríos, and Corrientes. The most important beef-producing breeds are Shorthorn, introduced in 1823; Hereford, 1858; Aberdeen Angus, 1879; and in recent years, zebu and Charolais.

The dairy industry has shown steady development. In 1998, the following quantities were produced: milk, 9,750,000 tons; cheese, 420,000 tons; and butter, 52,000 tons. The most important dairy breeds are Holstein-Friesian, Jersey, and Holando Argentino. Córdoba, Santa Fe, and Buenos Aires are the three major dairy provinces. Argentina's dairy sector has received the most investments in recent years, especially foreign investments. Egg production was 256,000 tons in 1998. The number of poultry in 1998 reached 55 million.

In sheep raising, Argentina ranks third in South America after Uruguay and Brazil, with an estimated 17,956,000 animals in 1998. Before World War II, Argentina accounted for 14% of the world's wool production, but in the 1970s, its production declined; the wool clip (greasy basis) was 64,000 tons in 1998. In 1998, production of mutton and lamb was 46,000 tons. Patagonia has approximately 40% of all the sheep in Argentina.

Total meat production was 3.16 million tons in 1998, of which 2.25 million tons consisted of beef. Beef exports for 1997 were valued at $622.8 million.

In 1998, Argentina had 3.3 million horses, placing it among the top five countries in the world. Argentine horses, especially favored as polo ponies and racehorses, have won many international prizes. Other livestock in 1998 included 3.2 million pigs and 3.4 million goats. In 1998, Argentina accounted for 4% of the world's production of cow hides. Argentina is South America's largest producer of honey, with an output of 60,000 tons in 1998.

24 FISHING

In a country that is among the world's leaders in meat production, fishing has not been able to develop as an industry of any significance. In recent years, the government has tried with some success to induce the public to eat more fish in order to export more beef, one of the country's largest earners of foreign exchange. Since 1970, the government has offered fiscal incentives to encourage the modernization of the fishing industry. The catch has increased from 475,043 tons in 1982 to 559,777 tons in 1987 to 1,352,948 tons in 1997.

The most favored saltwater fish are the pejerrey, a kind of mackerel; the dorado, resembling salmon but of a golden color; and the zurubí, an immense yellow and black spotted catfish. The principal species in the 1997 catch were Argentine hake (43%), Argentine shortfin squid (30%), and southern blue whiting (6%).

Argentina established a 322-km (200-mi) territorial sea limit in December 1966. In 1982, the government moved to protect Argentina's coastal waters from foreign exploitation, declaring that only 16 foreign vessels would be allowed in Argentine waters at any one time.

25 FORESTRY

Argentina's forests, estimated at some 50.9 million hectares (125.8 million acres), or about 18.6% of the total area, constitute one of its greatest underexploited natural resources. Of the 570 species of trees sold in international commerce, Argentina possesses 370, but of these it exploits only about a dozen species. A major factor in the industry's lack of development is the great distance of most forests from the markets and the resultant high cost of transportation. In the Río Paraná Delta, the woods currently exploited are softwoods, such as the elm and willow, used in the cellulose and container industries; in the Gran Chaco, white quebracho, used as a fuel and in the refining of coal, and red quebracho, from which tannin is extracted; in Misiones Province, several varieties, including cedar for furniture manufacturing; in the Salta-Tucumán region, cedar and oak; and in Patagonia, araucania, pine, cypress, larch, and oak.

The most important tree is the red quebracho, which contains 21% tannin, the extract used for tanning. Argentina possesses four-fifths of the world's supply of this wood. Many quebracho trees now being used are from 200 to 500 years old, and trees younger than 75 years are of little commercial use. Since the trees are not being replaced, it is estimated that the quebracho forests will be largely exhausted by the end of the current century.

Production of roundwood was 13,192,000 cu m in 1997. Exports of forest products totaled $271.2 million that year.

26 MINING

Until relatively recently, Argentina did not produce minerals in significant volume, but the future of the mining industry appears secure. The mountainous northwest, especially the province of Jujuy, is rich in a variety of minerals. New privatization laws were introduced in 1989 to give investors greater guarantees, reduce bureaucratic delays, and attract foreign capital. In 1997, mineral production and trade only contributed 0.3% to the GDP. Metallic and industrial mineral exports amounted to $543 million in 1997, up from $67 million in 1991.

Output of iron ore was 239,400 tons in 1970; it peaked at 1.04 million tons in 1988 but by 1991 had declined to 259,000 tons. In 1994 it was only about 4,000 tons. In 1997 Argentina imported 1.8 million tons of iron ore and concentrate. The largest deposits of iron ore are in Río Negro Province. In 1997, estimated production of important metal concentrates included copper, 30,000 tons; zinc, 29,224 tons; lead, 13,400 tons; cadmium, 74 tons; silver, 54,413 kg; and gold, 2,443 kg. Asphaltite, fluorspar, copper, mica, manganese, gold, silver, and antimony are found mainly in the northwest. There are also deposits of lithium, beryllium, and columbium. There are deposits of varying amounts of industrial minerals such as asbestos, barite, bentonite, clays, celestite, diatomite, feldspar, fluorspar, graphite, gypsum, kaolin, marble, sodium carbonate, and vermiculite. In 1997, Argentina produced 270,000 tons of boron, ranking third in the world after the US and Turkey. The main deposits are in the provinces of Jujuy, Salta, and Catamarca in the Argentine Andes.

27 ENERGY AND POWER

Despite a shortage of energy resources, production of electric power has steadily increased since 1958, after more than a decade of neglect. Installed generating capacity was 21,768,000 kW in 1998, about 40% of which was hydroelectric; in that year, electrical energy production totaled 75.24 billion kWh. The government places great emphasis on the development of hydroelectric projects and nuclear power, even though installed capacity exceeds projected demand. The Yaciretá-Aripe project on the Paraná will add 2,700 MW to Argentina's generating capacity when completed in 1998.

In 1974, Argentina became the first country in Latin America to install a nuclear-powered electric generating plant. The Atucha power station in Buenos Aires Province has a capacity of 357 MW; Embalse (648 MW) in Córdoba Province started up in 1983. In 1980 construction of a second 692-MW reactor at Atucha began, but it was still incomplete in 1999. Nuclear energy accounted for 10.7% of total electricity production in 1998.

The modern petroleum industry dates from 1907; after 1940, it became necessary to supplement domestic production with large-scale imports of foreign fuels. In 1958, ownership of all crude oil and natural gas was taken over by the state, and petroleum was then placed under the control of the state oil corporation, Yacimientos Petrolíferos Fiscales (YPF). Production of crude oil fell from 25.6 million tons in 1982 to 22.3 million tons in 1987 but rose to 37.7 million tons in 1995. Production in 1998 totaled 847,000 barrels per day. In 1978, foreign-owned companies were allowed to drill for oil, after decades of policy changes on the role of foreign companies. In August 1985, the Alfonsín government announced more liberal rules on foreign-company participation; in 1987, YPF's influence was reduced. In July 1993, Argentina privatized YPF via the largest initial stock offering on the New York stock exchange (more than US$3 billion). Large deposits have been found in the San Jorge Gulf near Comodoro Rivadavia. In recent years though, production rates have exceeded the rate at which depleted reserves have been replaced by new discoveries. Proven reserves as of 1 January 1999 were estimated at 2.6 billion barrels.

In conjunction with petroleum extraction, the significant natural gas industry has rapidly expanded. Argentina has the second-largest proven natural gas reserves in South America, exceeded only by Venezuela. Production in 1997 was 27.4 billion cu m, compared with 5.3 billion cu m in 1969 and 9.8 billion cu m in 1982. At the start of 1999, known reserves were estimated at 684 billion cu m. Natural gas is imported from Bolivia (2 billion cu m in 1995). There is a network of over 9,900 km (6,150 mi) of gas pipelines.

A major coal deposit in Santa Cruz Province is estimated to contain 552 million tons of coal, nearly 80% of the nation's total. Production as a whole was reported at 350,000 tons in 1997, down from 505,000 tons in 1988.

28 INDUSTRY

Córdoba is Argentina's major industrial center. It is the center of metalworking, especially for motor vehicle production. Argentina's other principal industrial enterprises are heavily concentrated in and around the city of Buenos Aires. The plants are close to both the many raw materials imported by ship and the vast productive area of the pampas. The major industries in Buenos Aires are food processing, motor vehicles, consumer durables, textiles, chemicals and petrochemicals, printing, metallurgy, and steel. Other industrial areas include Rosario, with important steel-producing plants and oil refineries, tractor and meat-packing plants, and chemical and tanning industries; Santa Fe, with zinc- and copper-smelting plants, flour mills, and dairy industry; San Miguel de Tucumán, with sugar refineries; Mendoza and Neuquén, with wineries and fruit-processing plants; the Chaco region, with cotton gins and sawmills; and Santa Cruz, Salta, Tierra del Fuego, Chubut, and Bahía Blanca, with oil fields and refineries.

During the 1960s, the average annual growth rate of industry was 5.9%; during the 1970s, it fell to only 1.8%. In the early 1980s, industrial production went into recession, declining by 16% in 1981 and by 4.7% in 1982. The sharp cutback in imports due to the foreign debt crisis spurred local manufacturing to growth of 10.8% and 42%, in 1983 and 1984, respectively; 1985 brought a sharp plunge of 10.5%, but 1986 saw a growth of 12.8%, aided by the "Austral Plan." In all, the 1980s saw an average annual growth rate of -1.0%. From 1988 to 1998, manufacturing grew by an annual average of 3.6%, and in 1997 alone by 9.2%, but in 1998 that rate fell to 1.6% and in 1999 was expected to fall even lower.

Packing and processing of foodstuffs is the oldest and most important industry in Argentina. Beginning in the last part of the 19th century, the great frigoríficos, or meat-packing plants, were founded to prepare beef for export to Europe. In recent times, the Argentine government has entered directly into the meat-processing enterprises, which for many years were under British ownership. The textile industry was also developed quite early, making use of wool from the vast herds of sheep and the cotton from Chaco Province. In addition to these traditional products, a variety of synthetic fibers are now produced.

Portland cement is the country's leading construction material. A major chemical industry produces sulfuric, nitric, and other acids and pharmaceuticals. The most important center of this industry is San Lorenzo on the Río Paraná. The petrochemical industry is related to the increasing production of oil and has received special benefits from the government. In 1985, exports of petroleum fuels exceeded imports for the first time, and by 1999 Argentina was self-sufficient in oil and gas. Natural gas annual output growth should reach 3.4% for the next decade. Output of petroleum fuels reached 800,000 barrels per day in 1999; at the same time, new oil reserves were found in Rio Negro Norte.

In 1961, a giant integrated steel mill began production at San Nicolás. Dependent on steel is the automobile industry, which experienced fairly sustained growth during the 1960s and 1970s. Production rose from 33,000 units in 1959 to 288,917 in 1980. Motor vehicle production peaked at 450,000 in 1998, falling back to around 300,000 in 1999. Tractors, motorcycles, and bicycles also are manufactured. Argentina also produces electric appliances, communications equipment—including radios and television sets—motors, watches, and numerous other items.

Industry continues to restructure to become competitive after decades of protection. Capacity utilization rates have increased substantially and companies are now focusing on modernization and expansion of their plants to meet both domestic and foreign demand. New technologies are being adopted, work forces pared, and management is focusing on just what its clients want. Output of cement, trucks, machinery, plastics, petrochemicals and other chemicals all rose, while production of basic metal goods held flat or rose off a low base in the 1990s. The availability of credit as well as continuing strong demand for final products is needed to stimulate growth in Argentina's industries following the 1999 recession.

[29] SCIENCE AND TECHNOLOGY

Argentina has five scientific academies: an academy of agronomy and veterinary science (founded in 1909); an academy of exact, physical, and natural sciences (1874); an academy of medicine (1822); and the National Academies of Sciences of Córdoba (1869) and Buenos Aires (1935). Numerous agricultural, medical, scientific, and technological research institutes exist in Argentina, including, as of 1996, 51 operated by the National Council of Scientific and Technical Research (founded in 1958) and 27 by the National Institute of Industrial Technology (founded in 1957). Research and development expenditures in 1987–97 amounted to 0.4% of GNP. Argentina has 47 universities and colleges offering training in basic and applied sciences. In 1987–97, science and engineering students accounted for 28% of college and university enrollments.

In 1987–97, 147 technicians and 660 scientists and engineers per million people were engaged in research and development.

[30] DOMESTIC TRADE

Many leading mercantile firms have their head offices in Buenos Aires and branches or agents in the other large cities. Department stores, retail shops, and specialty shops in Buenos Aires are on a par with similar establishments in most world capitals. The number of supermarkets and self-service shops is increasing, although most retail trade is still conducted in small specialty shops and grocery stores or in public markets supervised by the municipal governments. Business hours are generally from 9 AM to 6 PM, Monday through Friday, with a one-hour lunch break. Stores are usually open from 9 AM to 9 PM, Monday–Saturday; banks are generally open on weekdays from 10 AM to 3PM. Domestic demand absorbs most of the nation's industrial production. Exports represented less than 10% of Argentina's GDP in 1999.

[31] FOREIGN TRADE

Many industrial products imported prior to 1960 are now produced in Argentina. Argentina removed virtually all non-tariff barriers to trade in 1991 and reduced tariff rates. The only non-tariff barrier is the tariff/quota system applicable to auto and auto parts imports. The Argentina/Brazil auto agreement establishes preferential market access treatment for both countries.

A surge in imports during 1991–92 shifted the trade balance from a large surplus to a deficit position. The strong increase in imports is explained by several factors: first, the dynamic growth of the domestic economy which resulted in greater import demand; second, the reduction of import tariffs and elimination of non-tariff barriers which released pent-up demand for imports; and third, the real appreciation of the peso which made imports much less expensive since the local currency cost of these goods rose by much less than the accumulated inflation since the beginning of the Convertibility Plan. Because exports contributed only 10% to GDP, increased foreign sales had little impact on aggregate growth, skewing the balance of payments report.

The creation of NAFTA was viewed as an extremely positive development and presented Argentina with the possibility of acceding to NAFTA as either a member of MERCOSUR or alone. The government remained fully committed to seeing the creation of MERCOSUR (a common market incorporating Argentina, Brazil, Uruguay, and Paraguay) through its completion (on 1 January 1995). Argentina's exports and imports more than doubled at comparable rates in six years, between 1992 and 1998; but the devaluation of the Brazilian real in 1999 was expected to significantly lower export revenues.

Agricultural products from Argentina; including vegetable oil, animal feed, oil seeds, wheat, and maize; make up the majority of the country's commodity export market (30%). Other important exports are motor vehicles and parts. The top ten exports for 1997 are as follows:

	% OF COUNTRY TOTAL	% OF WORLD TOTAL
Vegetable oils	9.5	17
Crude petroleum	7.4	0.7
Animal feed	7.1	6.6
Oil seeds	4.9	7.8
Wheat	4.6	5.5
Leather	4.4	6.0
Meat	4.0	2.0
Maize	3.2	6.1
Motor vehicle parts and accessories	2.7	0.5
Fish	2.4	2.2

In 1997 Argentina's imports were distributed among the following categories:

Consumer goods	12.5%
Food	4.9%
Fuels	2.9%
Industrial supplies	30.5%
Machinery	29.1%
Transportation	19.8%
Other	0.3%

Principal trading partners in 1998 (in millions of US dollars) were as follows:

COUNTRY	EXPORTS	IMPORTS	BALANCE
Brazil	7,829	7,095	734
United States	2,057	6,104	-4,047
Chile	1,697	710	987
Netherlands	1,111	239	872
Uruguay	828	522	306
Spain	824	1,326	-502
Italy	746	1,597	-851
China (inc. Hong Kong)	745	1,300	-555
Japan	660	1,442	-782
Germany	571	1,897	-1,326
France	320	1,600	-1,280

[32] BALANCE OF PAYMENTS

Until 1952, Argentina's foreign-payments position was excellent, owing mainly to its large exports of basic commodities, principally agricultural products. In that year, however, because of widespread crop failures and unfavorable terms of trade, export value decreased sharply while imports remained high. The Argentine deficit was met by foreign credits, with dollar shortfalls partially covered by large credits from the Export-Import Bank, the IMF, and US banks. Over half of the foreign exchange earned was used during the 1950s and 1960s to service the external debt. The strict economic controls enacted in 1967 helped curb the inflationary trend and thus stabilized the nation's economy. After a decline during the early 1970s because of the international financial crisis, Argentina registered a surplus between 1973 and 1979, but after 1981, the current account was in deficit because of heavy debt-servicing costs.

In view of the liberalization of trade policies and the real appreciation of the peso, the current account deficit has deteriorated sharply since 1990. This has been more than offset by a large influx of foreign capital that was enticed by the government's new economic program. Since 1991, the decline in interest rates internationally and the lack of attractive alternatives for foreign direct investment have helped to generate a massive inflow of foreign capital, much of which was actually owned by Argentines but held abroad. A debt restructuring plan in early 1993 permitted the investment of reserves by eliminating the threat of seizure. Nevertheless, Argentina's external public debt increased in 1995 to almost us$80 billion, due to new borrowing in capital markets and lending from international financial institutions. In 1998, external debt reached $133 billion.

The US Central Intelligence Agency reports that in 1998 the purchasing power parity of Argentina's exports was $26 billion while imports totaled $32 billion resulting in a trade balance of -$6 billion.

The International Monetary Fund (IMF) reports that in 1998 Argentina had exports of goods totaling $26,434 million and imports totaling $29,448 million. The services credit totaled $4,660 million and debit $9,045 million. The following table summarizes Argentina's balance of payments as reported by the IMF for 1998 in millions of US dollars.

Current Account		-14,697
Balance on goods	-3,014	
Balance on services	-4,385	
Balance on income	19,514	
Current transfers	388	
Capital Account		...
Financial Account		18,884
Direct investment abroad	-1,973	
Direct investment in Argentina	6,150	
Portfolio investment assets	-1,068	
Portfolio investment liabilities	10,831	
Other investment assets	402	
Other investment liabilities	4,542	
Net Errors and Omissions		-69
Reserves and Related Items		-4,118

33 BANKING AND SECURITIES

In 1935, the Central Bank of the Argentine Republic was established as a central reserve bank, having the sole right of note issue, with all capital held by the state. The bank acts as the fiscal agent of the state. Its board of directors is appointed by and responsible to the government. The bank administers banking laws, regulates the volume of credit and interest rates, supervises the securities market, and applies government laws and decrees regarding banking and foreign exchange. Legislation in August 1973 increased its control over the commercial banking system. The National Mortgage Bank, founded in 1886, is the most important institution for housing credit. Other institutions include the National Development Bank, the National Bank for Savings and Insurance, and the Cooperative Credit Bank.

The Central Bank took advantage of the recovery in economic activity and relatively high rate of monetary growth in the early 1990s to further the restructure the financial system, and to strengthen it so that it would be able to withstand even severe external stocks. In late 1996, a schedule was implemented gradually to raise Minimum Liquidity Requirements (MLKs) from the current (1997) 17% to 20% by March 1998.

In late 1996, the role of the deposit insurance system (DIS) was broadened to allow support for troubled banks before they went bankrupt. Parallel to these measures, the Central Bank continued to encourage concentration in the financial system through mergers and acquisitions. By 2000, there were 120 financial institutions left, out of a total of 300 existing in 1990. Nine banks in 2000 owned 67% of all deposits, including public sector banks Nacion and Banco de la Provincia de Buenos Aires (accounting for 28% together); foreign owned Banco Rio and Banco Frances; and the privately owned Argentinian Banco Galicia. Total assets in 1999 added up to $15.6 billion, reflecting a growth of 7% from the previous year. Total deposits added up to 25% of GDP.

The Buenos Aires Stock Exchange is one of the 23 markets that form the Buenos Aires Commercial Exchange, which has over 12,000 members and is often confused with the Stock Exchange. The Commercial Exchange, founded in 1854, established the Stock Exchange, which the government subsequently separated from it. The Commercial Exchange now includes a grain market, a foreign currency exchange, a general produce exchange, and the securities exchange. There are also stock exchanges in the cities of Córdoba, San Juan, Rosario, Mendoza, and Mar del Plata, although more than 90% of stock transactions are conducted on the Buenos Aires exchange.

Between late October and early December 1996, Argentine asset prices rose under the influence of a favorable international financial environment, evidence of a recovery in domestic economic activity, and the decision of the government to deepen labor market deregulation. Between 22 October, and 5 December 1996, the Merval Stock index rose 15%, Bocon (peso-denominated) bond prices increased by 8%, and Brady bonds surged 7% (floating rate bond), 8% (discount bond), and 12% (par bond). From 1996 to 1999, while market capitalization rose from $45 million to $115 million, average daily market turnover fell from a high of over $650 million to about $200 million.

34 INSURANCE

In 1984, about 200 insurance companies were in operation in Argentina. Although various legal restrictions have been placed on foreign insurance companies, many retain offices in Buenos Aires. The insurance market is regulated by the Superintendent of Insurance of the nation, which is a branch of the Ministry of Economy.

The Argentine insurance market is characterized by a relatively large number of insurers with no one organization dominating the industry. From 1994 to 1997, there was a reduction in the number of insurers as some closed operations or were liquidated. Observers believe that there will be further reductions in the number of insurance companies as consolidation of the industry and the quest for economies of scale and critical mass continues. Observers expect the Argentine life market to develop significantly, especially under stable currency conditions.

35 PUBLIC FINANCE

Beginning in 1970, Argentina's budget picture steadily worsened. By the late 1970s, deficit spending annually ranged from 10–14% of GDP, and topped 15% in the early 1980s, when public expenditures consumed some 40% of GDP. By the late 1980s, hyperinflation and depletion of reserves necessitated a public finance reform. Since 1991, the government has considerably narrowed the deficit gap through structural reform efforts. Stricter controls on public spending and more efficient tax collection methods resulted in an overall public sector accounts deficit of only about 1% of GDP, compared to a deficit equivalent to 21.7% of GDP in 1989. The deficit grew marginally worse in the late 1990s, reaching 5% of GDP in 1998. Although tax enforcement has improved, evasion is still a major problem. Continued heavy expenditures and low tax revenues threatened to generate a deficit in 1999 and 2000.

The US Central Intelligence Agency (CIA) estimates that in 1998 Argentina's central government took in revenues of approximately $56 billion and had expenditures of $60 billion including capital expenditures of $4 billion. Overall, the government registered a deficit of approximately $4 billion. External debt totaled $148 billion.

The following table shows an itemized breakdown of government revenues and expenditures. The percentages were calculated from data reported by the International Monetary

Fund. The dollar amounts (millions) are based on the CIA estimates provided above.

REVENUE AND GRANTS	100%	56,000
Tax revenue	91.2%	51,091
Non-tax revenue	8.7%	4,860
Capital revenue	0.1%	49
EXPENDITURES	100%	60,000
General public services	9.7%	5,850
Defense	4.5%	2,719
Public order and safety	3.2%	1,945
Education	5.7%	3,438
Health	2.3%	1,409
Social security	52.3%	31,401
Housing and community amenities	2.4%	1,420
Recreation, cultural, and religious affairs	0.4%	228
Economic affairs and services	6.7%	3,993
Other expenditures	0.1%	67
Interest payments	12.8%	7,694
Adjustments	-0.3%	-163

36TAXATION

In 1999, the principal national taxes included personal income tax (ranging between 6% and 30%), wealth tax (0.5%), value-added tax (21%; up from 18% in 1994), and excise taxes on tobacco, alcohol, soft drinks, perfumes, jewelry, precious stones, automobile tires, insurance policies, gasoline, lubricating oils, and other items. There is no inheritance tax. Corporate taxes are levied at 30% for domestic and foreign companies. Provincial and municipal governments impose various taxes.

37CUSTOMS AND DUTIES

The Perón regime abolished in large measure the traditional system of exports and imports. Through the use of multiple exchange rates and through control of Argentine agricultural exports by the Argentine Institute for the Promotion of Exchange, Perón was able to obtain goods from producers at low prices and sell them abroad at great increases, employing the difference to promote the development of industry. In 1959, this cumbersome system of import permits and multiple exchange rates was abolished.

The government employed surcharges on imports to promote the growth of Argentine industries, and special import benefits were allowed to industries and regions regarded as significant contributors to the national economy. The petrochemical, cellulose, and steel industries have shared in these benefits, which include exemption from customs duties and exchange premiums on imports of machinery, spare parts, and raw materials. A special tariff applies to automobiles, which the government plans to dismantle by 2000, when a common MERCOSUR auto policy of a 20% tariff is scheduled to take effect. Duties of 11% were applied to raw materials and medicines, and a duty of up to 30% was applied to electronic appliances. The average Common External Tax rate is 14%. There is a VAT levied on international sales at 21%, and 10% on goods imported for resale.

Argentina, Brazil, Paraguay and Uruguay officially established a customs union (MERCOSUR) on 1 January 1995 with a common external tariff (CET) covering 85% of traded goods, but excluding capital goods, information technology, and telecommunications equipment. Argentina accounts for 27% of MERCOSUR's GDP, while Brazil accounts for 70%.

The government signed the Uruguay Round Agreements in December 1993 and Congress ratified the Agreements at the end of 1994. Argentina was a founding member of the World Trade Organization. Customs procedures are generally extensive and time consuming, thus raising the costs for importers, although installation of an automated system in 1994 eased the burden.

Argentine beef was exported to the US market in 1997 for the first time in 50 years.

38FOREIGN INVESTMENT

During the 19th century, Argentina offered a favorable climate for foreign investment, and the basic development of the nation's transportation system and shipping facilities was financed with British capital. This system placed ownership of extensive properties in foreign hands, arousing the resentment of Argentine nationalists, who advocated a policy of reducing dependence on outside interests. The organization of a national petroleum agency, YPF, in 1922 was one of the first important steps in implementing that policy. The high point in the drive for nationalization came during the Perón era, when railroads were purchased from foreign owners and numerous state-owned enterprises were established. These measures led to substantially reduced foreign investment.

In 1958, President Frondizi negotiated contracts with a number of foreign companies, allowing them to join YPF in the exploitation of Argentine petroleum. In 1958, he promoted a bill designed to attract foreign capital under close government supervision. As a result, foreign companies invested, between 1959 and 1961, over US$387 million, of which more than half came from the US.

Between 1961 and 1966, direct foreign investment declined, with the question of foreign ownership constantly entering the political picture. After the military coup, President Onganía declared that his government would renew an "open door" policy and would provide legal guarantees to investors. The net capital inflow continued through the late 1960s.

In the 1970s, government policies toward investors underwent a significant reappraisal. Restrictions on direct foreign investment, as specified in a foreign investment law enacted in 1973, required specific congressional approval for formation of companies with foreign capital that exceeded 50% of the total. Profit remittances and capital repatriation were limited, and new foreign investments were prohibited in several major areas, including national defense, banking, mass media, agriculture, forestry, and fishing. This restrictive legislation was superseded by a new foreign investment law enacted in 1976 and substantially amended in 1981. As of 1993, foreign companies could invest in Argentina without registration or prior government approval, and the Argentinian-US Bilateral Investment Treaty signed in 1991 came into full effect in 1994. The treaty provided for national treatment in virtually all sectors of the Argentine economy.

Incentives are provided for investments in mining, shipbuilding, iron and steel, petrochemicals, forest industries, silo construction, wine, and maritime fishing, but corporate taxes are equal for foreign- and Argentine-owned companies. Industrial investments within 60 km (37 mi) of the city of Buenos Aires and within the city limits of Córdoba and Rosario are not eligible for extra benefits. Free Trade Zones created in 1994 offer tax-free and duty-free importing and exporting, located at Cordoba, La Plata (opened 1997), Mendoza, Santa Fe, and Comodoro. Capital inflows remain strong. Privatization has generated an enormous source of US dollars with the sale of state-owned enterprises to local and foreign investors. Principal foreign investors include the US, Chile, the EU, and Canada. Foreign direct investment in 1998 totaled $2.4 billion, down from $3.6 billion in 1997.

39ECONOMIC DEVELOPMENT

Argentine economic policy has undergone several cycles of change since the 1940s. During World War II, the demand for Argentine beef and wheat boosted the country's exchange reserves to their highest point in history. Under the Perón regime, however, declining terms of trade and increasing state benefits and subsidies, as well as Perón's attempt to industrialize Argentina at the expense of the agrarian sector, disrupted the nation's economic system. Although inherently a wealthy country, Argentina, with a crushing foreign debt and a shattered economy, was nearly bankrupt.

When Perón fell, steps were taken to fund foreign obligations with long-term provisions for Argentine repayment and to create a climate favorable to private investment. Complicated multiple exchange rates were abolished, and massive financial assistance was extended by the IMF and other foreign agencies. Staggering deficits in the railroads and other state enterprises were a constant problem. The government sought to turn over some of these to private hands, and it also encouraged livestock raising and agricultural production, the chief earners of foreign exchange.

The government abolished many of the state subsidies and at the same time tried to hold wages steady. The austerity program fell hardest on the workers, who saw wages increase sluggishly while prices skyrocketed. They sought political solutions to the economic problems through crippling strikes, which in turn robbed the government of the increased production on which it was relying for a solution to the economic crisis. Between 1960 and 1966, the problems continued, with the government fluctuating between economic nationalism and liberal policies designed to seek foreign investment. Inflation, unemployment, and commercial failures reached new highs. Economic strife formed the backdrop for the military coup of 1966 and the suspension of the constitutional government. Despite widespread opposition, steps were taken in the late 1960s to turn over some state enterprises to private owners; other measures sought to put state-owned businesses on a paying basis.

The 1970s brought a resurgence of economic and political instability. The return to constitutional government—and especially the return of the Perónists to power—brought a period of increased labor influence, extraordinary wage demands, accelerating inflation, and huge government deficits, largely financed through short-term borrowing. The government's Three-Year Plan for Reconstruction and Liberation, announced in December 1973 during Juan Perón's presidency, called for more equitable distribution of income, elimination of unemployment and underemployment, better regional distribution of wealth, and extension of government housing, health, welfare, and education programs and services.

Perón's death in July 1974 and the subsequent political instability aborted this program and led to an economic crisis. In 1978, a medium-term economic adjustment plan, based on free-market principles, was announced. It included regular devaluations of the peso, cuts in public investment, and return of some state enterprises to private ownership; but instead of improving the nation's economic performance, the new policies led to triple-digit inflation and increasing unemployment. In the fall of 1982, the government began to negotiate with the IMF for a standby loan and committed itself to an austerity program, consisting of cuts in government spending, higher interest rates on bank loans to the private sector, and continuing regular devaluations. Additional financial controls, including a temporary ban on the issuance of new import licenses, were imposed the following autumn.

The "Austral Plan," launched in June 1985, was the Alfonsín government's attempt to break out of the stagflation that has characterized the economy since 1982. The combination of a wage-price freeze, a new currency pegged to the dollar, and a commitment to austerity in public spending was initially successful in curbing inflation, although somewhat at the expense of development. Since then, the government has attempted to manage price and wage increases and has offered several public corporations for sale. Multilateral assistance to Argentina totaled $6.3 billion between 1962 and 1986, of which 51% came from the IDB and 41% from the IBRD.

In the 1990s, the industrial sector's performance was excellent, in particular the food processing, construction, and automotive industries. Demand for consumer durable goods was strong as a result of ample credit availability. Construction activity was boosted by infrastructure projects associated with the privatization. Sweeping privatization and a wave of investment, both foreign and local, have modernized old industries and nourished new ones. Farmers have started to plant more profitable products, such as garlic, fruit, and olives. A new mining code has brought foreign investment to a long-neglected sector. Oil and gas output has doubled, attracting investment in petrochemicals, while MERCOSUR has encouraged a boom of car exports. Yet Argentines do not feel as if they are living through an economic boom. A recession in 1999 caused capital flight and high interest rates. Consumption has been slow to pick up, and unemployment remains at around 12%. It is estimated that nearly 40% of the workforce is employed in the black market.

40 SOCIAL DEVELOPMENT

The election of Hipólito Yrigoyen as president of Argentina in 1916 initiated a series of profound changes in the nation's social structure. The Radical-controlled legislature enacted a series of economic and social measures, including a measure to establish retirement funds. Despite differences between Radical leadership and labor, limited social welfare measures were continued until 1930, when Yrigoyen was expelled from office. The Conservative regime in power for the next 13 years took little cognizance of demands for social benefits.

The next major advance in the creation of social and economic benefits was made during the government of Juan Perón, who assumed power in 1946. The 44-hour workweek that had been enacted in 1933 was for the first time put into effect. New provisions established salary increases, paid holidays, sick leave, job tenure, and many other benefits. By 1945, a National Social Security Institute administered social insurance programs and the pension system. In the early 1950s, these measures continued and were extended also to the rural sector. The failure of the Argentine welfare system to live up to Perón's promises helped to bring about his overthrow in 1955. During the 1960s, the pension funds were often diverted for other purposes, and there was a general breakdown in the system. By 1970, many of the persons eligible for welfare payments received none at all, and the secretary of social welfare under the Levingston administration, charged former government authorities with misappropriating millions of pesos.

Most of the social legislation enacted during the Perón years has remained on the statute books. The pension laws, updated in 1993, mandates that workers pay 11% of their wages into a pension fund, and this amount was supplemented by an 16% contribution from the employer. Employees also now have the option of choosing a private pension. Unemployment benefits were introduced for construction workers in 1967 and were expanded to include all employed persons in 1991. Contributions are 1% of earnings of the employed, with an additional 1.5% paid by the employer. Sickness benefits and up to 90 days of paid maternity leave are also provided, funded by 3% of employee earnings and 6% of employer payroll. Both public and private sector employees are covered by workers' compensation, which is being expanded to cover domestic workers and others previously excluded from the system.

Although guaranteed equality under the Constitution, women are fighting for equal advancement and pay in the labor force. The National Women's Council was created in 1991 to coordinate women's policies. President Menem signed a decree in 1993 against sexual harassment in the government. That same year, a decree required that 30% of all political party candidates be female. Despite the government's efforts, discrimination against women in the workplace and sexual harassment continue to be important social problems. A law establishing protection against family violence was passed in 1994. A battered women's shelter and 24-hour hotline are operated by the city of Buenos Aires. A 1998 decree signed by President Menem called for professional equality and equal pay for women in the workforce. As of 1999, 70 of 329 members of parliament were women.

The 1994 Constitution incorporates the UN Convention on Rights of the Child. The National Council on Children and Families is working to develop child protection programs and legislation. Handicapped access to public places is specified in a 1994 law aimed at eliminating barriers to the disabled, and a constitutional amendment the same year recognizes the ethnic and cultural identities of Argentina's indigenous people. Reports of torture and brutality by police persisted in 1999.

41HEALTH

In the field of health and medical care, Argentina compares favorably with other Latin American countries. National health policy is determined by the Department of Public Health, an agency of the Ministry of Social Welfare. Nutritional requirements are comfortably met and, in 1995, 65% of the population had access to safe water and 75% had adequate sanitation. Health and medical services for workers are provided by clinics of unions, and employers are usually required to provide free medical and pharmaceutical care for injured workers. Argentina's total health expenditure from 1990 to 1997 was 9.7% of GDP. In Argentina the private sector takes part in the health services ensuring social security through organizations called Obras Sociales. Funding for health services come from employees payroll taxes and contributions.

There were 2.7 doctors per 1,000 people between 1990 and 1997.

In 1999, the infant mortality rate was 18 per 1,000 live births. Between 1993 and 1996, 7% of all births were classified as low birth weight. Between 1980 and 1993, 74% of married women (ages 15–49) used contraception.

Of the major infectious diseases, smallpox, malaria, and diphtheria have been virtually eliminated, and poliomyelitis has been greatly reduced. The incidence of tuberculosis in 1997 was 56 per 100,000 people, and in 1997, one-year-old children were immunized against the following diseases: tuberculosis (100%); diphtheria, pertussis, and tetanus (85%); and measles (98%). Life expectancy averaged 75 years (79 for females and 71 years for males) in 1999. The death rate in 1999 was 7.6 per 1,000 people. The HIV seroprevalence rate was 0.69 per 100 adults in 1997, when 120,000 people were infected altogether. Argentina reported the second-highest incidence of AIDS cases (41 per million) in South America during the mid-1990s. HIV spread rapidly throughout Argentina via intravenous drug use soon after the first cases of HIV infection were reported.

42HOUSING

Housing in Argentina reflects the Italian and Spanish ethnic backgrounds of the population. Except for marginal rural dwellings and urban shanty towns, concrete, mortar, and brick are favored as the principal construction materials. Wood is generally considered less durable and feared as a fire hazard. In the late 1960s, the Ministry of Social Welfare initiated a program to eliminate the extensive shantytowns in Buenos Aires and other cities. In 1968, the government provided A$50 billion (in old pesos) to finance the construction of 26,000 dwellings, and

private capital totaling A$200 billion (in old pesos) was set aside for an additional 100,000 units. The goal for 1969 was nearly double the previous year's investment, with major attention given to low-cost housing. Various international agencies, including the IBRD and the IDB, cooperated in providing housing funds, as did the US through AID programs. In the 1980s, however, the national housing program languished due to a fiscal policy of austerity, while sources of credit for would-be home buyers practically vanished. The total number of dwellings in the mid-1990s exceeded nine million. Also as of the mid-1990s, there was a housing deficit of roughly 2.5 million houses in Argentina.

A new public credit agency, the National Housing Fund, was established in 1973; the fund is financed by a payroll tax on employers of 5% (as of 1986) on gross earnings.

43EDUCATION

Argentina has one of the lowest illiteracy rates in Latin America, estimated at 3.1% (males, 3.1%; females, 3.1%) for the year 2000. Education is free, secular, and compulsory for all children at the primary level. Secondary education lasts for four to six years depending on the type of course. The general certificate of education lasts for five years; commercial, four or five years; and technical or agricultural lasts for six years. The Ministry of Education supervises the National Council on Technical Education and the National Administration of Middle and Higher Education.

In 1997 there were 22,437 primary schools with 309,081 teachers and 5,153,256 students enrolled. Since 1966, the national universities have been under the supervision of the Ministry of Education. Traditionally, university students have played an active role in campus policy, based in part on the concept of university autonomy established in the Córdoba reform movement of 1918. Student organizations have also been outspoken in national politics, denouncing the policies of the military government in the late 1970s and early 1980s.

Argentina has 46 officially accredited universities with a total of 740,545 students. The largest is the University of Buenos Aires. All institutions of higher learning had a combined total enrollment of 1.7 million students as of the mid-1990s.

Private, foreign, and religious schools are permitted, but they must conform to a nationally prescribed pattern of teaching in the Spanish language.

44LIBRARIES AND MUSEUMS

The National Library was founded in 1810 and has occupied its present site in Buenos Aires since 1902; in 2000 it had about 1.9 million volumes. There are thousands of public and school libraries and innumerable private libraries. The libraries of the University of Buenos Aires have combined holdings of over 2 million volumes. The Catholic University of Argentina, with five campuses, has a combined collection of 90,000 volumes. The National Academy of Medicine has a library with 50,000 volumes in Buenos Aires and the Museum of Ethnography in Buenos Aires has a specialized collection of 100,000 volumes.

The National Museum of Fine Arts in Buenos Aires contains modern Argentine, American, and European works, as well as paintings attributed to old masters, paintings of the conquest of Mexico executed 300–400 years ago, and wooden carvings from the Argentine interior. Also in Buenos Aires are the National Historical Museum; the Isaac Fernández Blanco Museum of Hispanic-American Art, which contains an interesting and valuable collection of colonial art; the Mitre Museum and Library, containing the manuscripts, documents, printed works, and household objects of Gen. Bartolomé Mitre, which constitute a unique record of Argentine political development; the Natural Science Museum; and the Municipal Museum. There are several important historical museums in the provinces, including the Colonial and Historical Museum at Luján and the Natural History Museum of the University of La Plata, which is world-famous for its important collections of the skeletons of extinct pre-Pliocene reptiles (for which the Argentine pampas form one of the richest burial grounds).

45MEDIA

In 1995 there were 4,834,100 telephones (with 12,000 public telephones) in the nationalized system, over half of which were in Buenos Aires and its environs. Internal telegraph facilities and some international circuits to nearby countries are wholly government operated.

As of 1999 there were 260 AM radio stations and 42 TV stations. There were 677 radios, 289 television sets, and 56 mobile phones per 1,000 population.

Buenos Aires is one of the principal editorial centers of the Spanish-speaking world, with more than 50 publishing houses in the 1980s and 1990s. Numerous literary magazines and reviews, as well as books, are published. Press coverage in Argentina is one of the most thorough in the hemisphere. Four news agencies (Noticias Argentinas, TELAM, Diarios y Noticias, and Inter-diarios) were operating in 1995, and the major international news services were also represented. Two of the great dailies of Buenos Aires, *La Nación* and *La Prensa*, enjoy international reputations, and *La Prensa* is probably the most famous newspaper in Latin America. Throughout the early days of the Perón regime, *La Prensa* battled the dictatorship, but it was finally taken over forcibly by Perón and given to the CGT, the dictator's central labor organization. The provisional government of Gen. Eduardo Lonardi returned *La Prensa* to its rightful owner, Alberto Gainza Paz, and it resumed publication in February 1956. In 1969, the Onganía government imposed siege regulations on the press, and in August of that year, two weekly papers were closed down. After the 1976 coup, no formal censorship was introduced, but some journalists were arrested for "subversive" articles. With the restoration of democratic government, harassment of the media stopped.

The largest dailies, with their estimated circulation figures in 1995, are listed in the following table:

	CIRCULATION
BUENOS AIRES	
Clarín	700,000
La Nación	630,000
Diario Popular	150,000
La Prensa	31,500
PROVINCES	
La Voz del Interior (Córdoba)	95,000
La Gazeta (Tucumán)	80,000
El Día (La Plata)	60,000
La Capital (Rosario)	50,000
Los Andes (Mendoza)	60,000
El Litoral (Santa Fe)	40,000

As of 1996, there were an estimated 84,100 personal computers. In 1998 there were 16 Internet hosts per 1,000 population.

46ORGANIZATIONS

Argentine organizations fall into the following main categories: agricultural, business and industrial, and social and cultural. The Argentine Rural Society, established in 1866, with a membership predominantly of owners of large ranches (estancias), occupies itself mainly with the improvement of agricultural and livestock production. The Argentine Association of Cooperatives and the Argentine Agrarian Federation also represent rural interests.

Industrialists and business leaders participate in the Argentine Industrial Union, which originated in 1887 and was reestablished in 1977 through the merger of the Argentine Industrial Confeder-ation and the General Confederation of Industry. The leading chambers of commerce in 1993 were the Argentine Chamber of Commerce; the Chamber of Commerce, Industry, and Production of the Argentine Republic; the Chamber of Foreign Trade of the Federation of Trade and Industry; and the Chamber of Exporters of the Argentine Republic.

Social organizations are found in almost every community of any size. The Athletic and Fencing Club in Parque Palermo, a suburb of Buenos Aires, has extensive recreational facilities. The Argentine capital also sponsors numerous clubs in the delta region. At the other social extreme is the exclusive Jockey Club of Buenos Aires, with a wealthy membership. There are several yacht clubs. The Automobile Club operates a chain of service and rest stations throughout the country, giving travel information and selling gasoline at a slight discount. Many intellectuals belong to the Argentine Writers' Society.

47TOURISM, TRAVEL, AND RECREATION

The government promotes tourism through the National Tourist Bureau, with headquarters in Buenos Aires. In 1998, 4,859,867 foreign tourists visited Argentina, nearly three-fourths of them from other countries in South America, with the greatest number (1,377,288), from Uruguay. Receipts from tourism totaled $5.1 billion in 1997. As of that year, there were 152,326 hotel rooms with 390,072 beds.

Mar del Plata, on the South Atlantic, about 400 km (250 mi) from Buenos Aires, is the most popular ocean resort. The delta of the Río Paraná, forming a series of inland waterways, is a center for pleasure boats and launches. Córdoba, with its fine colonial cathedral, and nearby Alta Gracia attract many visitors. San Carlos de Bariloche, at the entrance to Nahuel Huapi National Park in the Andean lake region of western Patagonia, has become famous as a summer and winter resort, with some of the best skiing in the Southern Hemisphere. The Iguazú Falls, in the province of Misiones, on the border of Argentina and Brazil, is a major tourist attraction. Mendoza, situated in a fertile oasis below the towering Andes, offers such historical attractions as the Cerro de la Gloria, with its monument to San Martín, and the Historical Museum, with its collection on San Martín.

The most popular sport is football (soccer). Tennis, rugby, basketball, and golf are also played. Opportunities for gambling include a weekly lottery, football pools, horse racing at the Palermo and San Isidro tracks (in Buenos Aires), and the casino at Mar del Plata, whose profits go to the Ministry of Social Welfare.

The UN estimated the daily cost of staying in Buenos Aires in 1999 at $214. Expenditure at Chubut, Tierra del Fuego, Mendoza, Rosario, Salta and Jujuy is estimated at $182.

48FAMOUS ARGENTINES

The most famous Argentine is José de San Martín (1778–1850), known as the Protector of the South, who was principally respon-sible for freeing southern South America from the Spanish yoke.

The tyrannical dictator Juan Manuel de Rosas (1793–1877) ruled Argentina from 1829 to 1852. The political tactics and the pen of the statesman and essayist Domingo Faustino Sarmiento (1811–88) did much to undermine him. While in exile, Sarmiento wrote some of his best works, including *Facundo,* the story of a rival caudillo. The most literary of Argentina's statesmen was Gen. Bartolomé Mitre (1821–1906), who was president from 1862 to 1868. Mitre, the founder and owner of the newspaper *La Nación,* wrote several important historical works and biographies. The most famous Argentine political figures of modern times have been Juan Domingo Perón Sosa (1895–1974) and his second wife, Eva Duarte de Perón (1919–52), known as "Evita." Perón's third wife, María Estela ("Isabel") Martínez de Perón, was vice-president during 1973–74 and, after her husband's death, president from 1974 to 1976.

José Hernández (1834–86), one of the first Argentine literary figures to use the uncultured language of the gaucho in his writings, is the author of *Martín Fierro*, considered the greatest of gaucho poems. Ricardo Güiraldes (1886–1927) kept the "gauchesco" spirit alive in his novel *Don Segundo Sombra*, a spiritual study of an Argentine gaucho. A less romantic view of these hardy horsemen of the pampas appears in the writings of Benito Lynch (1885–1951). The works of the poet Leopoldo Lugones (1874–1938) form a panorama of all Argentine life and landscape. José Mármol (1817–71) gave a good description of life in Buenos Aires under the tyrant Rosas in his novel *Amalia*, and Enrique Rodríguez Larreta (1875–1961) wrote the first Latin American novel to win international fame, *La gloria de Don Ramiro*, a reconstruction of Spanish life during the reign of Philip II. The leading contemporary writer of Argentina is Jorge Luis Borges (1899–1986), best known for his essays and collections of tales such as *Historia universal de la infamia*. Other world-famous writers are Julio Cortázar (1914–84) and Adolfo Bioy Casares (b.1914). Outstanding in the visual arts are the sculptor Rogelio Irurtia (1879–1950) and the painters Miguel Carlos Victorica (1884–1955) and Emilio Pettoruti (1892–1971). Argentina's foremost composers are Alberto Williams (1862–1952), founder of the Buenos Aires Conservatory; Juan José Castro (1895–1968); Juan Carlos Paz (1901–72); and Alberto Ginastera (1916–83).

The most famous Argentine scientist, Bernardo Alberto Houssay (1887–1971), was awarded the 1947 Nobel Prize in medicine for his work on diabetes; French-born Luis Federico Leloir (1906–87) won the Nobel Prize for chemistry in 1970. Notable philosophers include Alejandro Korn (1860–1936), whose work marked a reaction against positivism, and Francisco Romero (1891–1962). Carlos Saavedra Lamas (1878–1959), an authority on international law, received the Nobel Prize for peace in 1936. Adolfo Pérez Esquivel (b.1931), a sculptor and professor of architecture, received the Nobel Peace Prize in 1980 for his work in the Argentine human-rights movement.

49 DEPENDENCIES

Argentina continues to claim the Falkland Islands (Islas Malvinas), held by the UK, and a sector of Antarctica as dependencies.

50 BIBLIOGRAPHY

Alexander, Robert J. *Juan Domingo Perón.* Boulder, Colo.: Westview, 1979.

Argentina in Pictures. Minneapolis: Lerner, 1988.

Balze, Felipe A. M. de la. *Remaking the Argentine Economy.* New York: Council on Foreign Relations Press, 1995.

Barnes, John. *Evita—First Lady: A Biography of Eva Perón.* New York: Grove, 1978.

Biggins, Alan. *Argentina.* Oxford, England; Santa Barbara, Calif.: Clio Press, 1991.

Brysk, Alison. *The Politics of Human Rights in Argentina: Protest, Change, and Democratization.* Stanford, Calif.: Stanford University Press, 1994.

Calvert, Susan. *Argentina: Political Culture and Instability.* Pittsburgh, Pa.: University of Pittsburgh Press, 1989.

Corradi, Juan E. *The Fitful Republic: Economy, Society, and Politics in Argentina.* Boulder, Colo.: Westview, 1985.

Crassweller, Robert D. *Perón and the Enigma of Argentina.* New York: Norton, 1987.

Crawley, Eduardo. *A House Divided: Argentina, 1880–1980.* New York: St. Martin's, 1984.

Erro, Davide G. *Resolving the Argentine Paradox: Politics and Development, 1966–1992.* Boulder, Colo.: Lynne Rienner Publishers, 1993.

Fernández, Julio A. *The Political Elite in Argentina.* New York: New York University Press, 1970.

Ferns, Henry S. *The Argentine Republic, 1516–1971.* New York: Barnes & Noble, 1973.

Foster, David W. and Virginia R. *Research Guide in Argentine Literature.* Metuchen, N.J.: Scarecrow, 1970.

Gillespie, Richard. *Soldiers of Perón: Argentina's Monteneros.* New York: Oxford University Press, 1982.

Hastings, Max, and Simon Jenkins. *The Battle for the Falklands.* New York: Norton, 1983.

Horvath, Laszlo. *A Half Century of Perónism, 1943–1993: an International Bibliography.* Stanford, Calif.: Hoover Institution, Stanford University, 1993.

Institute of Latin American Studies. *Argentina in the Crisis Years, 1983–1990: From Alfonsin to Menem.* London: Institute of Latin American Studies, 1993.

Kirkpatrick, Jeane. *Leader and Vanguard in Mass Society: A Study of Perónist Argentina.* Cambridge, Mass.: MIT Press, 1971.

Martínez Estrada, Ezequiel. *X-Ray of the Pampa.* Austin: University of Texas Press, 1975.

Masiello, Francine. *Between Civilization and Barbarism: Women, Nation, and Literary Culture in Modern Argentina.* Lincoln: University of Nebraska Press, 1992.

Norden, Deborah L. *Military Rebellion in Argentina: Between coups and Consolidation.* Lincoln, Nebr.: University of Nebraska Press, 1996.

Peterson, Harold F. *Argentina and the United States, 1810–1960.* Albany: State University of New York, 1964.

Randall, Laura. *An Economic History of Argentina.* New York: Columbia University Press, 1977.

Ranis, Peter. *Class, Democracy, and Labor in Contemporary Argentina.* New Brunswick, N.J.: Transaction Publishers, 1995.

Rock, David. *Authoritarian Argentina: the Nationalist Movement, its History, and its Impact.* Berkeley: University of California Press, 1993.

Sawers, Larry. *The Other Argentina: The Interior and National Development.* Boulder, Colo.: Westview Press, 1996.

Snow, Peter G. *Political Forces in Argentina.* Westport, Conn.: Praeger, 1993.

Solberg, Carl E. *Oil and Nationalism in Argentina: A History.* Stanford, Calif.: Stanford University Press, 1979.

Tella, Guido di and Carlos Rodriguez Braun (eds.). *Argentina, 1946–83: the Economic Ministers Speak.* New York: St. Martin's Press, 1990.

Tella, Guido di, Carlos Rodriguez Braun, and Rudiger Dornbusch (eds.). *The Political Economy of Argentina, 1946–83.* Pittsburgh, Pa.: University of Pittsburgh Press, 1989.

University of Nebraska Press. *Revolution and Restoration: The Rearrangement of Power in Argentina, 1776–1860.* Lincoln, Nebr.: University of Nebraska Press, 1994.

Waisman, Carlos H., and Monica Peralta-Ramos (eds.). *From Military Rule to Liberal Democracy in Argentina.* Boulder, Colo.: Westview, 1986.

Windhausen, Anselm. *Geologia Argentina.* Buenos Aires: Tallares S.A., Casa J. Pueser, 1929.

World Bank, *Argentina: From Insolvency to Growth.* Washington, D.C.: World Bank, 1993.

BAHAMAS

Commonwealth of the Bahamas

CAPITAL: Nassau.

FLAG: Three horizontal stripes of blue, gold, and blue, with a black triangle at the hoist.

ANTHEM: *March on Bahamaland.*

MONETARY UNIT: The Bahamas dollar (B$) of 100 cents has been in use since May 1966; as of June 1972, the Bahamas dollar ceased to be part of the sterling area and was set on a par with the US dollar. There are coins of 1, 5, 10, 15, 25, and 50 cents, and 1, 2, and 5 dollars, and notes of 50 cents and 1, 3, 5, 10, 20, 50, and 100 dollars. B$1=US$1 (or US$1=B$1).

WEIGHTS AND MEASURES: Imperial weights and measures are in use.

HOLIDAYS: New Year's Day, 1 January; Labor Day, 1st Friday in June; Independence Day, 10 July; Emancipation Day, 1st Monday in August; Discovery Day, 12 October; Christmas Day, 25 December; Boxing Day, 26 December. Movable religious holidays include Good Friday, Easter Monday, and Whitmonday.

TIME: 7 AM = noon GMT.

¹LOCATION, SIZE, AND EXTENT

The Commonwealth of the Bahamas occupies a 13,940 sq km (5,382 sq mi) archipelago which extends 950 km (590 mi) SE–NW and 298 km (185 mi) NE–SW between southeast Florida and northern Hispaniola. Comparatively, the area occupied by the Bahamas is slightly larger than the state of Connecticut. There are nearly 700 islands, of which about 30 are inhabited. New Providence, 207 sq km (80 sq mi), although not the largest, is by far the most populous and most densely populated island. The total coastline is 3,542 km (2,201 mi).

The Bahamas occupy a strategic location adjacent to the US and Cuba.

The Bahamas' capital city, Nassau, is located on Nassau Island in the center of the island group.

²TOPOGRAPHY

The Bahamas were formed as surface outcroppings of two oceanic banks, the Grand Bahama Bank and the Little Bahama Bank. The islands are for the most part low and flat, rising to a peak elevation of about 63 m (206 ft), on Cat Island. The terrain is broken by lakes and mangrove swamps, and the shorelines are marked by coral reefs.

³CLIMATE

The climate is pleasantly subtropical, with an average winter temperature of 23°C (73°F) and an average summer temperature of 27°C (81°F). Rainfall averages 127 cm (50 in), and there are occasional hurricanes.

⁴FLORA AND FAUNA

Because of a favorable combination of soil and climate conditions, the islands abound in such tropical flora as bougainvillea, jasmine, oleander, orchid, and yellow elder. Native trees include the black olive, casuarina, cascarilla, cork tree, manchineel, pimento, and seven species of palm. There are 218 species and subspecies of birds, including flamingos, hummingbirds, and other small birds and waterfowl.

⁵ENVIRONMENT

Among the government's priorities in environmental protection are monitoring industrial operations, providing potable water and regular garbage collection throughout the country, maintenance and beautification of public parks and beaches, and the removal of abandoned vehicles. Other significant environmental issues are the impact of tourism on the environment, coral reef decay, waste disposal, and water pollution. The principal environmental agency is the Department of Environmental Health Services. A rookery on Great Inagua affords protection to some 30,000 flamingos as well as to the roseate spoonbill. Land clearing for agricultural purposes is a significant environmental problem because it threatens the habitats of the nation's wildlife.

Endangered species include Kirtland's warbler, Bachman's warbler, green sea turtle, hawksbill turtle, Allen Cays rock iguana, and Watling Island ground iguana. The Caribbean monk seal and American crocodile are extinct. Of 17 species of mammals, two are endangered. Four species of birds are also threatened. Four species of reptiles in a total of 204 are threatened. One amphibian of 124 species is also considered endangered.

⁶POPULATION

The first census was conducted in 1838, and in 1980 a law was passed requiring one to be conducted every ten years. The population in the 1990 census was 255,095, an increase of 22% over the 1980 census figure of 209,505. The population of The Bahamas in 2000 was estimated at 287,548. An estimated 6.5% of the population is 65 years of age or older. The projected population for the year 2005 is 306,000, assuming a crude birthrate of 18 per 1,000 population and a death rate of 5, resulting in a natural rate of change of 1.2% for the period 2000–2005.

It was estimated that 89% of the population lived in urban areas in 2000. Some two-thirds of the people reside on the island of New Providence, the site of Nassau, the capital and largest city. In 2000, Nassau's population was estimated at 195,000. The population of Freeport on Grand Bahama Island (41,035) grew from a few hundred in 1960 to an estimated 24,423 in the 1990s. Population density in 1996 averaged 25.8 persons per sq km (67 per sq mi), but the density on New Providence is over 800 per sq km (2,070 per sq mi).

7MIGRATION

Emigration to the UK, considerable in the past, has fallen off since the mid-1960s. Some Bahamians migrate to the US in search of employment. There is also interisland migration, chiefly to New Providence and Grand Bahama islands.

Located between the US and other Caribbean islands, the country's position has made it a transit point for migrants, including asylum seekers, trying to reach the US. An estimated 100 Cuban nationals seek asylum in the Bahamas each month. As many as 2,000 Haitian nationals are intercepted in Bahamian waters each year. Many illegal immigrants from Haiti take jobs considered menial by Bahamians. The Bahamas presently hosts 75 recognized refugees, who are primarily of Cuban, Haitian, and West African origins. As of September 1999, there has also been an increasing number of asylum-seekers from Europe, Asia, and Africa. The net migration rate of the Bahamas was -1.55 migrants per 1,000 population in 1999.

8ETHNIC GROUPS

Descendants of slaves brought to the Western Hemisphere from Africa make up about 85% of the legal population. About 8% of the total is of mixed origin; the remainder is white, largely of British origin.

9LANGUAGES

English is the spoken and official language of the Bahamas. Haitian immigrants speak French or a Creole patois.

10RELIGIONS

The population is overwhelmingly Christian, with Baptists comprising 32%. Roman Catholics (an estimated 19%) and Anglicans (20%) also have sizable memberships. Methodists (6%) and the Church of God (6%) are represented. Other Protestant denominations account for 12% of the populace; and 5% practice other or no religions. More traditional practices related to witchcraft and known to scholars as voodoo or obeah continue to be observed in some areas.

11TRANSPORTATION

The larger islands have modern road networks. In 1999 there were about 2,693 km (1,673 mi) of highways, of which 1,546 km (961 mi) were paved. There were 70,000 passenger cars and 15,000 commercial vehicles in the early 1990s. About 60% of all vehicles are on New Providence. There are no railways.

The Bahamas established a shipping register in 1976. In 1998, this archipelago nation had a merchant fleet of 1,079 ships of 1,000 GRT or over, with a total volume capacity of 26,631,924 GRT and a deadweight capacity of 41,196,326 tons. Nassau is a major port of call for cruise ships, which visit Freeport as well. Airports in 1998 totaled 62, of which 33 had paved runways. There are international airports at Nassau and Freeport, with frequent connections to the US, Canada, and the UK. In 1997, 704,000 passengers were carried on scheduled domestic and international airline flights. Bahamas Air, a state enterprise, is the national airline.

12HISTORY

Christopher Columbus is believed to have made his first landfall on the island now called San Salvador (formerly Watlings Island) on 12 October 1492, but the Spanish made no permanent settlement there. Spanish traders captured the native Lucayan Indians and sold them as slaves. The first permanent European settlement was established in 1647 by the Eleutherian Adventurers, a group of religious refugees. They and subsequent settlers imported blacks as slaves during the 17th century. The islands were also used as bases for pirates, including the notorious Blackbeard.

The British established a crown colony to govern the islands in 1717. The first royal governor, Captain Woodes Rogers, himself an ex-pirate, drove away the privateers, leaving the slave trade as the main economic enterprise on the islands.

After the end of slavery in 1838, the Bahamas served only as a source of sponges and occasionally as a strategic location. During the US Civil War, Confederate blockade runners operated from the islands. After World War I, prohibition rum-runners used the islands as a base. During World War II, the US used the islands for naval bases.

Like other former British colonies, the Bahamas achieved independence in stages. After self-government was established in 1964, full independence was granted on 10 July 1973. The country's first prime minister was Lynden O. Pindling, leader of the Progressive Liberal Party. Pindling ruled for nearly twenty years, during which the Bahamas benefited from tourism and foreign investment. By the early 1980s, the islands had also become a major center for the drug trade, with 90% of all the cocaine entering the US reportedly passing through the Bahamas. Diplomatic relations were established with Cuba in 1974. A decade later, as increased Cuban immigration to the islands strained the Bahamas' resources, Cuba refused to sign a letter of repatriation.

In August 1992, the Bahamas had its first transfer of political power, when Hubert Ingraham became prime minister. Ingraham was reelected in March 1997 for another four-year term. The principal focus of his administration was economic development and job creation. Under Ingraham's watch, a number of government enterprises were privatized, and a stock exchange was slated to open in two stages in 1999–2000. In September 1999, Hurricane Floyd did extensive damage in the Abacos and Eleuthra, causing a significant dip in tourism revenues, but tourism operations in other parts of the Bahamas were able to resume normal operations days after the Category-4 storm.

13GOVERNMENT

Under the constitution of 10 July 1973, the Bahamas adheres to a republican form of government, formally headed by the British sovereign, who is represented by a governor-general. Executive authority is vested in a prime minister and a cabinet. The bicameral legislature consists of a 16-member Senate, appointed by the governor-general (nine on the advice of the prime minister, four on the advice of the opposition leader, and three at the governor's discretion), and an elected 40-member House of Assembly. The prime minister is the leader of the majority party in the House. The normal span of the elected legislature is five years, but, as in the UK, elections can be called at any time. Suffrage is universal at age 18.

14POLITICAL PARTIES

The Progressive Liberal Party (PLP), a leader in the pro-independence movement, emerged as the Bahamas' majority party in the early 1970s. The Free Progressive Liberal Party, a splinter group formed in 1970, merged with another opposition group, the United Bahamian Party, to form the Free National Movement

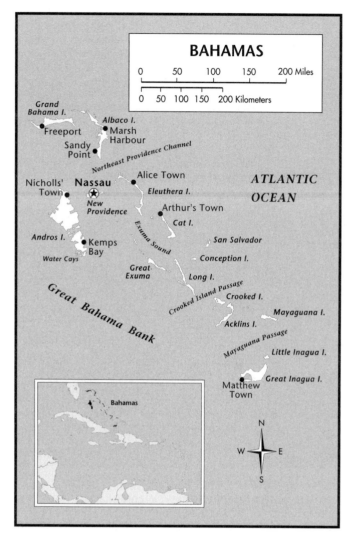

BAHAMAS

| 0 | 50 | 100 | 150 | 200 Miles |

| 0 | 50 | 100 | 150 | 200 Kilometers |

Grand Bahama I.
Freeport
Albaco I.
Marsh Harbour
Sandy Point
Northeast Providence Channel
Nicholls' Town
Nassau
Alice Town
Eleuthera I.
ATLANTIC OCEAN
New Providence
Arthur's Town
Cat I.
Andros I.
Kemps Bay
Exuma Sound
San Salvador
Water Cays
Conception I.
Great Exuma
Long I.
Crooked Island Passage
Crooked I.
Great Bahama Bank
Mayaguana I.
Acklins I.
Mayaguana Passage
Little Inagua I.
Great Inagua I.
Matthew Town

Bahamas

N
W   E
S

LOCATION: 20°50′ to 27°25′N; 72°37′ to 82°32′W. **TOTAL COASTLINE:** 3,542 km (2,201 mi) **TERRITORIAL SEA LIMIT:** 3 mi.

(FNM). After years of loyal opposition, the FNM took power in 1992, winning 32 seats, to 17 for the PLP. In the 1997 elections, the FNM increased its majority to 34 seats, and another seat was added in a by-election later the same year. Meanwhile PLP representation in the House dwindled to six seats, and Lynden Pindling resigned as party leader.

15 LOCAL GOVERNMENT

There are 21 administrative districts, consisting of various islands and groups of islands. Each is headed by a commissioner responsible to the national minister of local government.

16 JUDICIAL SYSTEM

British common law forms the basis of the Bahamas' judicial system. The highest court is the Court of Appeal, consisting of three judges. The Supreme Court is composed of a chief justice, two senior justices, and six justices. High court appointments are made by the governor-general. Ultimate appeals go to the Privy Council of the UK. Lower courts include three magistrates' courts on New Providence and one on Freeport. For other islands, commissioners decide minor criminal and civil cases.

The judiciary is independent. Judges are appointed by the executive branch with the advice of the Judicial and Legal Services Commission.

Long pre-trial detentions are not uncommon in cases involving narcotics. In 1993, new magistrate's courts were established in order to work toward a reduction of backlogs requiring long pretrial detentions. A new Supreme Court was established in Freeport (in addition to the Supreme Court in Nassau).

The lowest level courts are Magistrate's courts which handle crimes with a maximum sentence of five years. The Supreme Court handles most major cases as the trial court. Jury trial is only available for the Supreme Court cases.

Criminal defendants have the right to an attorney, but government appointed counsel is provided only in capital cases. There is also a right to be brought before a magistrate within 48 hours, a right to bail, a presumption of innocence, and a right to appeal.

The Constitution prohibits torture and other cruel punishment. However, in 1991, corporal punishment was reinstated after having been abolished for seven years. Capital punishment is still used despite protests from the United Kingdom, which has requested its former colonies to eliminate the death penalty.

17 ARMED FORCES

The Royal Bahamas Defense Force of 860 sailors is responsible for external security, manning 19 patrol boats and other small craft and four aircraft. Defense expenditures were $20 million (1995–96), or less than 2.7% of gross domestic product.

18 INTERNATIONAL COOPERATION

The Bahamas joined the UN on 18 September 1973 and belongs to ECLAC and all the nonregional specialized agencies except IAEA, IDA, IFAD, and IFC. It is a member of the Commonwealth of Nations, G-77, IADB, and OAS. The Bahamas signed the Law of the Sea and has applied for membership in the WTO.

19 ECONOMY

Tourism, the mainstay of the economy, directly or indirectly involves most of the population. Because of the absence of direct taxation, the Bahamas has also become a financial haven for the activities of a large number of banking and trust companies, mutual funds, investment firms, and offshore sales and insurance companies. Local firms produce a small array of exports, including salt, cement, timber, pharmaceuticals, and petroleum products refined on Grand Bahama and reexported.

In 1998, the country's economy grew by about 4%. This higher growth rate was achieved mainly due to increased tourist arrivals and expenditures, and a boom in the construction of new hotels and resorts. Renewed economic buoyancy follows privatization of major hotels since 1994 and completion of major renovations by the new owners, as well as increased marketing and an improved foreign investment regime. In particular, total tourist arrivals increased by about 25%.

20 INCOME

The US Central Intelligence Agency (CIA) reports that in 1998 The Bahamas's gross domestic product (GDP) was estimated at $5,630 million. The per capita GDP was estimated at $20,100. The annual growth rate of GDP was estimated at 4%. The average inflation rate in 1998 was 2.9%. The CIA defines GDP as the value of all final goods and services produced within a nation in a given year and computed on the basis of purchasing power parity (PPP) rather than value as measured on the basis of the rate of exchange. It was estimated that agriculture accounted for 3% of GDP, industry 5%, and services 92%.

The World Bank reports that for the same period per capita private consumption (in PPP terms) was $10,800. Private consumption includes expenditures of individuals, households, and nongovernmental organizations. Approximately 32% of household consumption was spent on food, 5% on fuel, 3% on health care, and 8% on education.

21LABOR

The total number of workers was estimated at 149,900 in 1999. As of 1995, 40% were employed in tourism-related activities, 30% in government, 10% in business services, and 5% in agriculture. A 1970 Industrial Relations Act, as amended in 1979, requires the registration of trade unions and provides guidelines for labor contracts and job actions. The three leading union federations are the Trade Union Congress, the National Workers Council of Trade Unions and Associations, and the National Congress of Trade Unions. One-quarter of the labor force was unionized as of 1999. Unemployment in 1997 stood at about 14,660, or 9.8%.

Under the Fair Labor Standards Act of 1970, an employee working more than 8.5 hours a day or 48 hours per week is entitled to overtime pay. A minimum paid vacation of one week is also guaranteed, though a minimum of two weeks is standard. In September of 1996, the government established a minimum wage of $4.12 per hour for all public sector workers, but there is no general minimum wage for private sector workers. The Ministry of Labor promulgates minimum health and safety standards. It enforces these standards with routine inspections, and the standards are generally respected by employers.

22AGRICULTURE

Agriculture is carried out on small plots throughout most of the islands. Only about 1% of the land area is cultivated. The nature of the terrain limits the scope of farming, which is mainly a household industry. The main crops are vegetables: onions, okra, and tomatoes, the last two raised mainly for export. Inadequate production has necessitated the import of some 80% of the islands' food supply. Among steps the government has taken to expand and improve agriculture is the reserving of 182,000 hectares (450,000 acres) exclusively for farming, 8,000 hectares (20,000 acres) of which were converted to fruit farming. Export-oriented orange, grapefruit, and cucumber production in Abaco grew in 1992 as export demand expanded. However, on Eleuthera, most agricultural and fishing infrastructure was seriously damaged by Hurricane Andrew. Agricultural products in 1998 included 240,000 tons of sugar cane, 112,000 tons of grapefruit, and 5,000 tons of vegetables. The government is seeking to produce over $100 million annually in food to reduce imports.

23ANIMAL HUSBANDRY

Except for poultry and egg production, the livestock industry is relatively insignificant. In 1998, the livestock population included 1,000 head of cattle, 36,000 sheep, 15,000 goats, 16,000 hogs, and 4,000,000 poultry. About 1,000 tons of cow's milk, 1,000 tons of goat's milk, and 1,000,000 tons of eggs were produced in 1998. Poultry production in 1998 (11,000 tons) accounted for almost all domestic meat production. In December 1991, the government banned foreign chicken, in order to protect local poultry producers from cheaper imports, mainly from the US.

24FISHING

The 1997 catch amounted to 10,508 tons, over 74% of which was spiny lobsters (crayfish). Crayfish and conch exports are commercially important. There is excellent sport fishing for wahoo, dolphin fish, and tuna in Bahamian waters. In 1997,

fisheries exports totaled $60.6 million. Since the Bahamas imports 80% of its food, the government is interested in expanding the role of domestic commercial fishing. Aquaculture and mariculture development are planned to grow into a $150 million annual business by the government, with the anticipation of 15,000 new jobs created.

25FORESTRY

Caribbean pine and cascarilla bark are the major forestry products, but there is no commercial forestry industry. About 32% of the total land area consists of forests and woodlands. Roundwood production in 1997 totaled 117,000 cu m. That year, the Bahamas imported $30.6 million in wood and forest products.

26MINING

Salt, from beds on Great Inagua and Long Island, and aragonite, a component in glass manufacture, are the only commercially important mineral products. Salt and aragonite production were estimated at 900,000 tons and 1,200,000 tons, respectively, in 1997. Limestone sand are produced by Freeport Aggregate Ltd. for the local construction industry.

27ENERGY AND POWER

Most electricity is produced at thermal plants owned by the Bahamas Electricity Corp. Net installed capacity in 1998 was 401,000 kW; production totaled 1,340 million kWh. Electricity consumption in 1996 was one billion kWh. In 1991, a 28,000 kW upgrade was initiated at the Clifton Power Plant on the west end of New Providence Island. Two new gas turbines are scheduled to be built at the Blue Hill Power Station.

28INDUSTRY

Large-scale oil refining began in 1967 with the installation of a large refinery on Grand Bahama with a daily capacity of 500,000 barrels, but by 2000 no oil was being refined. Cement and rum production (Bicardi) are important, and enterprises producing pharmaceuticals (PFC Bahamas) and sea salt (at Great Inagua) have been developed. The Commonwealth Brewery in Nassau produces Heineken, Guinness, and Kalik beers. Rum output declined by almost 45% in 1992 because the only rum producer in the Bahamas, Bicardi, transferred part of its production to another country.

Tax and duty free exemptions are guaranteed until 2054 in the Freeport duty-free zone.

29SCIENCE AND TECHNOLOGY

Agricultural research facilities include the Bahamas Agricultural Research Center, Central Agricultural Station, and the Food Technology Complex.

30DOMESTIC TRADE

Nassau is the principal distribution and import center. Shopping hours are from 9 AM to 5 PM, except Sunday. Banks are open from 9:30 AM to 3 PM, Monday–Thursday, and from 9:30 to 5 PM on Friday.

31FOREIGN TRADE

The US is the Bahama's major trading partner. Canada and the European Community also trade frequently with the Bahamas since several agreements have been signed with these countries. These agreements include the Caribbean Basin Initiative (CBI), the Caribbean-Canada Agreement (CAIBCAN), and the Lome Convention.

Exports include pharmaceuticals, cement, rum, crawfish, and aragonite. Imports are primarily composed of foodstuffs, manufactured goods, crude oil, vehicles, and electronics.

About 55% of imports arrive from the US. Principal trading partners in 1998 (in millions of US dollars) were as follows:

COUNTRY	EXPORTS	IMPORTS	BALANCE
United States	140	891	-751
Switzerland	98	42	56
United Kingdom	94	78	16
Germany	42	104	-62
Singapore	13	75	-62
Italy	3	524	-521
Japan	1	259	-258
Korea	1	228	-227
Russia	1	68	-67
Netherland Antilles		n.a.	85

32 BALANCE OF PAYMENTS

Income from tourism and financial services are vital offsetting factors in the country's balance-of-payments position.

The US Central Intelligence Agency reports that in 1998 the purchasing power parity of The Bahamas's exports was $300 million while imports totaled $1,370 million resulting in a trade balance of -$1,070 million.

The International Monetary Fund (IMF) reports that in 1998 The Bahamas had exports of goods totaling $311 million and imports totaling $1,372 million. The services credit totaled $1,581 million and debit $958 million. The following table summarizes The Bahamas's balance of payments as reported by the IMF for 1998 in millions of US dollars.

Current Account		-594
Balance on goods	-1,061	
Balance on services	623	
Balance on income	-190	
Current transfers	34	
Capital Account		-12
Financial Account		502
Direct investment abroad	-1	
Direct investment in Bahamas, The	235	
Portfolio investment assets	...	
Portfolio investment liabilities	...	
Other investment assets	-4,872	
Other investment liabilities	5,140	
Net Errors and Omissions		222
Reserves and Related Items		-119

33 BANKING AND SECURITIES

Banking started in the Bahamas in 1837, when the first commercial bank opened in New Providence. The Central Bank of the Bahamas, established in 1973, is the central issuing and regulatory authority. Funds for local development are made available through the Bahamas Development Bank.

Low taxation and lenient regulations have encouraged the establishment of about 420 financial institutions in the country in 2000, half of which operate offshore banks, dealing exclusively with nonresidents. The banking sector accounts for more than 20% of GDP. Many of the loans of domestic banks are denominated in foreign currency. Major Bahamian banking institutions include Bank of the Bahamas Limited, Barclay's Bank, British-American Bank, Canadian Imperial Bank of Commerce (CIBC), Citibank, Commonwealth Bank, and the Royal Bank of Canada. Anti-money laundering acts have provided for the security of the banking sector.

The Bahamas International Securities Exchange opened in 2000. It opened in two phases; domestic stocks (from about 20 companies listing an estimated $30 billion in shares) followed by international offerings.

34 INSURANCE

The establishment of a large number of insurance firms in the Bahamas has been encouraged by a 1970 law that permits companies to conduct part or all of their business out of the country, while benefiting from local tax advantages. The government is encouraging the formation of "captive" insurance companies, created to insure or reinsure the risks of offshore companies. In 1997, there were approximately 30 captive insurers in the Bahamas. Supervisory jurisdiction is provided by the Ministry of Finance, Registrar of Insurance Companies.

35 PUBLIC FINANCE

The Bahamian government budget receives revenues primarily from import duties (65%), but Hemispheric Free Trade scheduled for 2005 will greatly reduce revenues. The government is looking for other sources of funds, including a restructuring of the banking system.

The US Central Intelligence Agency (CIA) estimates that in 1997 The Bahamas' central government took in revenues of approximately $766 million and had expenditures of $845 million including capital expenditures of $97 million. Overall, the government registered a deficit of approximately $79 million. External debt totalled $382 million.

The following table shows an itemized breakdown of government revenues and expenditures. The percentages were calculated from data reported by the International Monetary Fund. The dollar amounts (millions) are based on the CIA estimates provided above.

REVENUE AND GRANTS	100%	766
Tax revenue	89.5%	686
Non-tax revenue	10.3%	79
Capital revenue	0.2%	1
EXPENDITURES	100%	845
General public services	13.7%	115
Defense	3.1%	27
Public order and safety	10.6%	90
Education	19.6%	165
Health	15.9%	135
Social security	6.1%	51
Housing and community amenities	1.5%	12
Recreation, cultural, and religious affairs	0.0%	0
Economic affairs and services	17.3%	146
Interest payments	12.3%	104

36 TAXATION

The absence of direct taxation has enabled the Bahamas to attract a substantial number of financial enterprises in search of tax-shelter advantages. The country has no income taxes, capital gains taxes, or profit taxes, and residents are free from succession, inheritance, gift, or estate taxes. The only indirect taxation is a real property tax, ranging from 0.75% to 1% for owner-occupied property and 0.5% to 1.5% on commercial property.

37 CUSTOMS AND DUTIES

Import duties make up approximately 65% of government revenues. Import levies range from 1% to 260% and average 35%. Most duties are applied ad valorem; preferential rates apply to imports from Commonwealth countries. Exemptions are available for many basic commodities. Luxury goods are taxed at separate tariff rates, for example: cigarettes are taxed at 260% with a stamp tax of 7%, pool tables at 100%, bottled water at 70%, automobiles from 45% to 65%, and video tapes at 65%.

38 FOREIGN INVESTMENT

The absence of corporate and personal income taxes acts as a direct inducement to foreign capital. In addition, specific investment incentives include the Industries Encouragement Act, providing total exception from import duties and taxes for development of approved industries; the Hawksbill Act, which provides for tax-free development of the Freeport area; and the Hotel Encouragement Act, which exempts large new hotels from all taxes for 20 years. In 1999, there was a 25% increase in the number of airline seats available to tourists to the Bahamas, and a 26% growth in hotel rooms.

The government actively seeks foreign investment in every sector of the economy. The Bahamas is recognized as an international offshore financial center where the government imposes no tax on income, capital gains or distribution to shareholders, inheritance probate dividends, sales, corporations, or royalties. The absence of most forms of direct taxation together with the benefits of profit repatriation are two of the primary incentives for investing in the Bahamas. The Bahamas has signed an OPIC agreement, and a number of OPIC-financed projects have been approved. Canada also has an investment insurance program in the Bahamas. The country has also become a signatory to the Multilateral Investment Guarantee Agency (MIGA) of the World Bank. In addition, a new International Business Companies Act went into effect in January 1990, simplifying the requirements for incorporation and reducing the cost of forming an offshore company.

Foreign investment remains mainly in the tourism-related sectors, although increased investments have been attracted in offshore banking, shipping registry, and a container terminal. Tourism-related investments are now more diversified both geographically and with regard to the type of product. Since the enactment of the revised foreign landholding act in 1993, investment in the mainly second-home sector has been growing. The government continued efforts to sell off all state-owned hotels in 1996, including sales of the Grand Bahama Beach Hotel, the Lucayan Beach Hotel and Resort, and the Clarion Atlantik Beach Hotel. Major investment in new hotel construction continued into 2000.

39ECONOMIC DEVELOPMENT

The promotion of tourism and financial activity by foreign firms continues as a basic tenet of the Bahamas government. Since the late 1960s, increased emphasis has been focused on development of local industry, with the liberal tax structure remaining the key incentive. In 1976, the government began a series of measures to foster greater participation by Bahamians in the economy. The new ruling included increased working-permit fees for foreigners and sharp rises in property-transfer taxes and business licensing for non-Bahamians. Since late 1979, government permission has been required for the sale of land to non-Bahamians. The Bahamas Development Bank helps provide financing for non-Bahamian entrepreneurs. In 1996, the government implemented an income tax on foreign workers. The government is attempting to diversify the economy and attract new industry, as well as to conserve and develop the country's 800,000 acres of forest.

A number of policy measures were introduced in 1996 that had major repercussions in the Bahamian economy. First, the government modified the customs coding system, in preparation for the eventual Western Hemisphere Free Trade Area in 2005. The number of rates were reduced from 123 to 29, and the rates themselves were lowered as well. Second, the government awarded increases in public sector wages across the board. Third, a minimum public sector wage policy was implemented. Fourth, all temporary civil service workers with at least five years of continuous service were made permanent. The unemployment rate was 9% in 1999.

40SOCIAL DEVELOPMENT

Principal welfare legislation is contained in the National Insurance Act of 1972, as amended most recently in 1999. Workers' compensation and retirement, maternity, survivors', and funeral benefits are provided for, with specific terms set out by the National Insurance Board. Contributions are shared by employers and employees; rates are progressive, depending on weekly wages earned.

Bahamian women are well represented in business, the professions, and government. As of 1997, 11 of 56 members of parliament were women. However, activists are calling for improved child care availability to encourage more women to enter the labor force. As of 1999, the Constitution did not allow foreign-born husbands of Bahamian women to become citizens. Inheritance laws also discriminate against women by mandating that in the absence of a will, a deceased person's estate be passed on the oldest son or nearest male relative. The government has established a Women's Affairs Unit to monitor and promote the rights of women. In 1999 the government authorized establishment of two battered women's shelters and a toll-free hotline to deal with the widespread problem of domestic violence.

Human rights are generally respected by the government, although there are occasional reports of arbitrary arrest and detention and abuse of detainees.

41HEALTH

The government operates the 436-bed Princess Margaret Hospital in Nassau and two other hospitals, the Sandilands Rehabilitation Center and the 82-bed Rand Memorial Hospital. In addition, 57 clinics and 54 satellite clinics are maintained throughout the islands, with emergency air links to Nassau.

In 1995, there were 417 physicians (nearly 15 per 10,000 population) and 80 dentists. In the same year, there were 653 registered nurses. In 1999, the fertility rate was 2.0. In 1999, the infant mortality rate was 18 per 1,000 live births. In 1999, the birth rate was 20 per 1,000 people, and the general mortality rate was 5.4 per 1,000. Average life expectancy in 1999 was 74 years. In 1994, 88% of one-year-old children were immunized against measles and 91% were immunized against diptheria. As of the end of 1996, a total of 2,481 cases of AIDS had been reported. AIDS is the second leading cause of death among the general population and the leading cause among males.

42HOUSING

Overcrowding is a problem on New Providence, and adequate low-cost housing is in short supply. At last estimate, some 70% of housing units were detached houses, nearly 15% were apartments, and more than 10% were single attached dwellings. Over 50% of all homes were stone, concrete and/or brick and over 30% were wood. The Bahamas Housing Authority was established by the government in 1983, with a mandate to develop housing for low-income people.

43EDUCATION

Education is under the jurisdiction of the Ministry of Education and Culture and is free in all government maintained schools. English is the official language. Primary education begins at age 5 and lasts for six years. Secondary education begins at age 11 and consists of two cycles, each of three years duration. Education is compulsory for children aged 5–14. In 1997, 113 primary schools had 1,540 teachers and enrolled 34,199 pupils. Secondary schools had 1,352 teachers and enrolled 27,970 students that same year. In the year 2000, estimates report the adult illiteracy rate to stand at 3.9% (males, 4.6%; females, 3.2%).

Post-secondary training is provided by the government primarily through the College of the Bahamas. The College of Bahamas (founded in 1974) provides a two-year/three-year program which leads to an associate degree. It also offers a Bachelor of Arts degree in education. Other schools of continuing education offering academic and vocational courses include the Bahamas Hotel Training College, the Catholic Continuing Education College of St. Benedicts, and the Industrial Training College. In addition, the Bahamas has been affiliated with the University of the West Indies since 1960.

As of 2000, about 18% of the central government's expenditure is directed to the education sector. An IDB-funded program for the Improvement of Primary and Secondary Education is under way.

[44] LIBRARIES AND MUSEUMS

The Nassau Public Library is the largest of four public libraries on New Providence, with some 80,000 volumes. The Ranfurly Out Island Library, a private institution, distributes free book packages to school libraries throughout the country. The library of the College of the Bahamas in Nassau maintains a collection of 67,000 volumes. Most museums in the Bahamas are archaeological and historical. In Hope Town is the Wyannie Malone Historical Museum. In Nassau there is the Bahamia Museum (1973), featuring ethnology and folklore; the Bahamas Historical Society Museum (1959), a public affairs museum with a Marine Salvage collection; the Nassau Public Library and Museum; the Pompey Museum of Slavery and Emancipation (1992), a historical, ethnological, and folklore museum; and Angelo Roker's Art Centre and Museum.

[45] MEDIA

All telephone, telegraph, and teletype service is provided by the Bahamas Telecommunications Corp. In 1997, 200,000 fully digital telephones were in service, with automatic equipment in use on the major islands. A submarine cable connects New Providence with Florida, and direct dialing to the US has been available since 1971. As of 1999, there were three AM and four FM stations, and one television station, which was established in 1996. In 1997 there were 695,000 radios and 209 television sets per 1,000 population.

The government is said to respect the constitution's provisions for freedom of speech and press.

Three daily newspapers are published in the country. The *Tribune* (Nassau, circulation 12,000 in 1999) appears evenings; the *Nassau Guardian* (13,135), mornings. The daily *Freeport News* has a circulation of 4,000. They are privately owned.

[46] ORGANIZATIONS

Commercial associations include the Bahamas Chamber of Commerce and service groups such as Kiwanis, Rotary, and Lions clubs. Employers' groups include the Bahamas Employers' Confederation and the Hotel Employers' Association. International amateur sports activities are coordinated by the Bahamas Olympic Association.

[47] TOURISM, TRAVEL, AND RECREATION

Tourism in the Bahamas is recovering from a decline which began in 1990, due to the US recession and competition from other Caribbean nations. In 1997, 3.42 million tourists visited the islands. In the same year, tourists spent a total of $1.42 billion in the islands. In 1997 there were 13,288 hotel rooms and 26,576 beds with a 68% occupancy rate.

Visitors are attracted to the Bahamas' excellent climate, beaches, and recreational and resort facilities. Water sports (including excellent deep-sea fishing) are the favorite pastimes. Gambling is legal for non-Bahamians.

Passports are not required for tourists from the UK, Canada, and US for stays of less than three weeks. Passports but not visas are required of most visitors from Western Europe, Commonwealth countries, and Latin America. According to 1999 UN estimates, the cost of staying in the Bahamas varies between seasons. From December until April, estimated daily expenditure was $210, at other times of the year, the cost is $179.

[48] FAMOUS BAHAMIANS

Lynden Oscar Pindling (b. 1930), a lawyer and leader of the PLP, was the Bahamas' first prime minister following independence in 1973 until he was succeeded by Hubert Ingraham (b. 1947) in 1992. Actor Sidney Poitier (b. USA, 1924) was appointed Bahamian ambassador to Japan in 1997.

[49] DEPENDENCIES

The Bahamas has no territories or colonies.

[50] BIBLIOGRAPHY

Boultbee, Paul G. *The Bahamas.* Oxford, England; Santa Barbara, Calif.: Clio Press, 1989.

Craton, Michael. *A History of the Bahamas,* 3d ed. Waterloo, Ontario: San Salvador Press, 1986.

———. *Islanders in the Stream: A History of the Bahamian People.* Athens: University of Georgia Press, 1992.

Evans, F. C., and N. Young. *The Bahamas.* New York: Cambridge University Press, 1977.

Hughes, Colin A. *Race and Politics in the Bahamas.* New York: St. Martin's, 1981.

Johnson, Howard. *The Bahamas: From Slavery to Servitude.* Gainesville: University Press of Florida, 1996.

Keegan, William F. *The People Who Discovered Columbus: The Prehistory of the Bahamas.* Gainesville: University Press of Florida, 1992.

Lewis, James A. *The Final Campaign of the American Revolution: Rise and Fall of the Spanish Bahamas.* Columbia, S.C.: University of South Carolina Press, 1991.

BARBADOS

CAPITAL: Bridgetown.

FLAG: The national flag has three equal vertical bands of ultramarine blue, gold, and ultramarine blue and displays a broken trident in black on the center stripe.

ANTHEM: *National Anthem of Barbados,* beginning "In plenty and in time of need, when this fair land was young. . . ."

MONETARY UNIT: Officially introduced on 3 December 1973, the Barbados dollar (BDS$) of 100 cents is a paper currency officially pegged to the US dollar. There are coins of 1, 5, 10, and 25 cents and 1 dollar, and notes of 1, 2, 5, 10, 20, 50, and 100 dollars. BDS$1 = US$0.50 (or US$1 = BDS$2.00).

WEIGHTS AND MEASURES: The metric system is used.

HOLIDAYS: New Year's Day, 1 January; Errol Barrow Day, 23 January; May Day, 1 May; Kadooment Day, 1st Monday in August; CARICOM Day, 1 August; UN Day, 1st Monday in October; Independence Day, 30 November; Christmas Day, 25 December; Boxing Day, 26 December. Movable religious holidays are Good Friday, Easter Monday, and Whitmonday.

TIME: 8 AM = noon GMT.

¹LOCATION, SIZE, AND EXTENT

Situated about 320 km (200 mi) NNE of Trinidad and about 160 km (100 mi) ESE of St. Lucia, Barbados is the most easterly of the Caribbean islands. The island is 34 km (21 mi) long N–S and 23 km (14 mi) wide E–W, with an area of 430 sq km (166 sq mi) and a total coastline of 97 km (60 mi). Comparatively, Barbados occupies slightly less than 2.5 times the area of Washington, DC.

The capital city of Barbados, Bridgetown, is located on the country's southwestern coast.

²TOPOGRAPHY

The coast is almost entirely encircled with coral reefs. The only natural harbor is Carlisle Bay on the southwest coast. The land rises to 336 m (1,102 ft) at Mt. Hillaby in the parish of St. Andrew. In most other areas, the land falls in a series of terraces to a coastal strip or wide flat area.

³CLIMATE

The tropical climate is tempered by an almost constant sea breeze from the northeast in the winter and early spring, and from the southeast during the rest of the year. Temperatures range from 24° to 29°C (75–84°F). Annual rainfall ranges from about 100 cm (40 in) in some coastal districts to 230 cm (90 in) in the central ridge area. There is a wet season from June to December, but rain falls periodically throughout the year.

⁴FLORA AND FAUNA

Palms, casuarina, mahogany, and almond trees are found on the island, but no large forest areas exist, most of the level ground having been turned over to sugarcane. The wide variety of flowers and shrubs includes wild roses, carnations, lilies, and several cacti. Natural wildlife is restricted to a few mammals and birds; finches, blackbirds, and moustache birds are common.

⁵ENVIRONMENT

Principal environmental agencies are the Ministry of Housing, Lands, and Environment, established in 1978, and the Barbados Water Authority (1980). Soil erosion, particularly in the northeast, and coastal pollution from oil slicks are among the most significant environmental problems. The government of Barbados created a marine reserve to protect its coastline in 1980. As of the mid-1990s, the most pressing environmental problems result from the uncontrolled handling of solid wastes, which contaminate the water supply. Barbados is also affected by air and water pollution from other countries in the area. Despite its pollution problems, 100% of Barbados' urban and rural populations have safe water.

The Barbados yellow warbler, Eskimo curlew, tundra peregrine falcon, and Orinoco crocodile are endangered species. In addition, one plant species is considered endangered.

⁶POPULATION

The population in 1990 was 257,083, an increase of 14.7% over the 1980 census figure of 224,228. By 2000, the population of Barbados was estimated at 259,248. An estimated 10% of the population is 65 years of age or older. The projected population for the year 2005 is 261,000, assuming a crude birthrate of 13 per 1,000 population and a death rate of 8, resulting in a natural rate of change of 0.01% for the period 2000–2005. In 1996, the population density was 597.7 per sq km (1,548 per sq mi), the highest of all American nations.

It was estimated that 50% of the population lived in urban areas in 2000. The capital city, Bridgetown, had a 2000 metropolitan population of 123,000, or over 46% of the island's total. Other major towns are Holetown, Speightstown, and Oistins.

⁷MIGRATION

The net migration rate for Barbados in 1999 was -5.86 migrants per 1,000 population. To meet the problem of overpopulation, the government encourages emigration. Most emigrants now

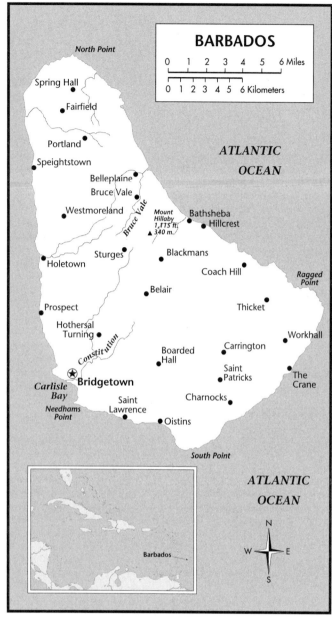

BARBADOS

North Point

Spring Hall

Fairfield

Portland

Speightstown   **ATLANTIC**

Belleplaine   **OCEAN**

Bruce Vale

Westmoreland   Mount   Bathsheba
                              Hillaby   Hillcrest
                              1,115 ft.
                              ▲ 340 m.

Sturges   Blackmans

Holetown   *Ragged*
                     Coach Hill   *Point*

Belair

Prospect   Thicket

Hothersal   Workhall
Turning

            Boarded   Carrington
            Hall
                           Saint   The
                           Patricks   Crane

Bridgetown

Carlisle   Saint   Charnocks
Bay   Lawrence

Needhams   Oistins
Point

                    South Point   **ATLANTIC**

                                                   OCEAN

                                                   N

                                            W   E

                      Barbados   S

LOCATION: 13°2′ to 13°20′N; 59°25′ to 59°39′W.
TOTAL COASTLINE: 101 km (63 mi). **TERRITORIAL SEA LIMIT:** 12 mi.

[10]RELIGIONS

Christianity is the dominant religion. About 67% of the total population is Protestant, with 40% being Anglican, 8% Pentecostal, 7% Methodist, and 12% comprised of various other denominations. Roman Catholics make up approximately 4% of the populace; 17% claim no religious affiliation; and 12% profess other faiths. Minority religions include Islam, Baha'i, and Rastafarianism (Nyabinghi school).

[11]TRANSPORTATION

The highway system had a total length of 1,650 km (1,205 mi) in 1998, virtually all of which (1,582 km/983 mi) was paved; there were 43,711 passenger cars and 2,884 commercial vehicles registered in 1995. Grantley Adams International Airport, situated 18 km (11 mi) southeast of Bridgetown, is the only airport. Barbados is served by one local and 14 international airlines. There is also a deepwater harbor at Bridgetown, with berthing facilities for cruise ships and freighters. In 1998, Barbados had a merchant fleet of 44 ships of 1,000 GRT or over, totaling 641,550 GRT.

[12]HISTORY

Barbados originally supported a considerable population of Arawak Indians, but invading Caribs decimated that population. By the time the British landed, near the site of present-day Holetown in 1625, the island was uninhabited. Almost 2,000 English settlers landed in 1627–28. Soon afterward, the island developed the sugar-based economy, supported by a slave population. Slavery was abolished in 1834, and the last slaves were freed in 1838.

During the following 100 years, the economic fortunes of Barbados fluctuated with alternating booms and slumps in the sugar trade. In 1876, the abortive efforts of the British to bring Barbados into confederation with the Windward Islands resulted in the "confederation riots."

In the 1930s, the dominance of plantation owners and merchants was challenged by a labor movement. Riots in 1937 resulted in the dispatch of a British Royal Commission to the West Indies and the gradual introduction of social and political reforms, culminating in the granting of universal adult suffrage in 1950. In 1958, Barbados became a member of the West Indies Federation, which was dissolved in 1962. The island was proclaimed an independent republic on 30 November 1966. Political stability has been maintained since that time. Barbados helped form CARICOM in 1973, the same year the nation began issuing its own currency. The country was a staging area in October 1983 for the US-led invasion of Grenada, in which Barbadian troops took part. In 1995 it was designated as a center for the Regional Security System, funded by the US, which conducted military exercises in the region.

Laws enacted in the early 1980s led to the development of Barbados as an offshore business center in the 1980s and 1990s, although tourism remained the nation's primary source of revenue. The international recession of the early 1990s negatively affected the economy of Barbados, touching off a decline in tourism and other sectors, and leading to a crisis of confidence in the government. After a no-confidence vote on 7 June 1994, Prime Minister Erskine Sandiford dissolved the House of Assembly, the first time since independence that such an action had been taken, and a new government was installed following general elections in September. Economic recovery in the subsequent years helped Prime Minister Owen S. Arthur lead to BLP to a landslide victory in the 1999 elections, as the country prepared for the launch of a single CARICOM economic market in 2005.

resettle in the Caribbean region or along the eastern US coast. As of September 1999, Barbados did not host any refugees. However, the country's lack of a national refugee law has become a cause for concern as Barbados is expected to receive greater numbers of asylum-seekers in the future due to recent extra-regional migration to and migrant trafficking through the Caribbean.

[8]ETHNIC GROUPS

About 80% of all Barbadians (colloquially called Bajans) are the descendants of former African slaves. Some 4% are white, and other various groups comprise the remaining 16%.

[9]LANGUAGES

English, the official language, is spoken universally, with local pronunciations.

13 GOVERNMENT

The constitution of Barbados, which came into effect on 30 November 1966, provides for a crown-appointed governor-general (who in turn appoints an advisory Privy Council) and for independent executive, legislative, and judicial bodies. The bicameral legislature consists of a Senate and a House of Assembly. The Senate, appointed by the governor-general, has 21 members: 12 from the majority party, two from the opposition, and seven of the governor-general's choice. The 28-member House of Assembly is elected at intervals of five years or less. The voting population is universal, with a minimum age of 18. The governor-general appoints as prime minister that member of the House of Assembly best able to command a majority. The prime minister's cabinet is drawn from elected members of the House of Assembly.

14 POLITICAL PARTIES

The leading political groups grew out of the labor movement of the 1930s. The Barbados Labour Party (BLP) was established in 1938 by Sir Grantley Adams. The Democratic Labour Party (DLP) split from the BLP in 1955. The National Democratic Party (NDP) was formed in 1989 by dissident members of the DLP. The parties reflect personal more than ideological differences.

Errol W. Barrow, the DLP leader, was prime minister from independence until 1976. The BLP succeeded him under J.M.G. ("Tom") Adams, the son of Grantley Adams. In 1981, the BLP retained its majority by 17–10, and Adams continued in that office until his death in 1985. On 28 May 1986, Barrow and the DLP won 24 House of Assembly seats to three for the BLP. After Barrow's death on 2 June 1987, Deputy Prime Minister Erskine Sandiford, minister of education and leader of the House of Assembly, assumed the prime ministership.

Despite the resignation of finance minister Dr. Richie Haynes in 1989, and his subsequent formation of the National Democratic Party, the DLP under Sandiford continued in power, retaining 18 of the now 28 seats in the House of Assembly. The BLP won the remaining 10 seats, leaving the dissident NDP without any representation.

After losing a vote of confidence in the legislature on 7 June 1994, Sandiford dissolved the House of Assembly and scheduled a general election for September. The BLP won by an overwhelming margin, with 19 seats; the DLP won eight, and the NDP, one. The BLP leader, Owen S. Arthur, became the new prime minister. The BLP swept the next elections, held in January 1999, winning 26 of the 28 House seats, while the DLP claimed only two.

15 LOCAL GOVERNMENT

All local governments, including those on the district and municipal levels, were abolished on 1 September 1969; their functions were subsumed by the national government. The country is divided into 11 parishes and the city of Bridgetown for administrative and electoral purposes.

16 JUDICIAL SYSTEM

The Barbados legal system is founded in British common law. The Supreme Court of Judicature sits as a high court and court of appeal; vested by the constitution with unlimited jurisdiction, it consists of a chief justice and three puisne judges, appointed by the governor-general on the recommendation of the prime minister after consultation with the leader of the opposition party. Magistrate courts have both civil and criminal jurisdiction. Final appeals are brought to the Committee of Her Majesty's Privy Council in the UK.

The courts enforce respect for civil rights and assure a number of due process protections in criminal proceedings including a right of detainees to be brought before a judge within 72 hours of arrest. The Judiciary is independent and free from political influence.

17 ARMED FORCES

The Barbados Defense Force was established in 1979, consisting of the former Barbados Regiment and Barbados Coast Guard. In 2000 the armed forces numbered 610 active troops and 430 reserves, of which 500 were in the army and 110 in the navy. The navy was equipped with five patrol boats. The defense budget was $11 million in 1998, or 0.5% of GDP.

18 INTERNATIONAL COOPERATION

Barbados became a member of the UN on 9 December 1966 and belongs to ECLAC and all the nonregional specialized agencies except IAEA and IDA. It is a member of the Commonwealth of Nations, G-77, IADB, and OAS. On 1 August 1973, Barbados joined Guyana, Jamaica, and Trinidad and Tobago as an initial signatory to CARICOM; it had been a member of CARIFTA, CARICOM's forerunner, since 1968. The country also belongs to the Caribbean Development Bank, established in 1970. Barbados is a signatory to the Law of the Sea and a member of the WTO.

19 ECONOMY

The economy has traditionally been dependent on the production of sugar, rum, and molasses. In the 1990s, however, tourism and offshore banking surpassed sugar manufacturing in economic importance.

The Barbadian economy turned in a good overall performance in 2000. GDP grew by 5%, compared to an average 3.4% per annum in 1994–95, driven by the strong performance of the sectors producing traded goods and services. The upsurge in economic activity led to a sharp decline in unemployment (from 24.5% in 1993, to 9.4% in 2000), while the inflation rate was kept at a relatively low 2.2%.

A large increase in public spending resulted in a fiscal deficit of 2.6% of GDP in 1996, in contrast with a 1.3% surplus in 2000. Net international reserves were the equivalent of 18 weeks of imports in 1999.

20 INCOME

The US Central Intelligence Agency (CIA) reports that in 1998 Barbados's gross domestic product (GDP) was estimated at $2.9 billion. The per capita GDP was estimated at $11,200. The annual growth rate of GDP was estimated at 3%. The average inflation rate in 1998 was 2.2%. The CIA defines GDP as the value of all final goods and services produced within a nation in a given year and computed on the basis of purchasing power parity (PPP) rather than value as measured on the basis of the rate of exchange. It was estimated that agriculture accounted for 6% of GDP, industry 15%, and services 79%.

Private consumption includes expenditures of individuals, households, and nongovernmental organizations. It was estimated that between 1990 and 1998 private consumption grew at an annual rate of -3.5%.

21 LABOR

The total labor force as of 1997 was 135,800. In 1997, services accounted for over 75% of the labor force; manufacturing about 9%, agriculture 6%, and mining and construction about 8%. In 1997, the tourism industry accounted for nearly 11% of all employment. Most employees work a 40-hour week. A minimum of a three-week paid holiday each year (four weeks for those employed at least five years) is required by law. There is one major union, the Barbados Workers' Union, and several smaller specialized ones. About 30% of the workforce was organized in 1999. Workers freely enjoy the right to organize and join unions, and unions (except in certain "essential" sector) are not restricted in their right to strike. There was a nine-day strike at the government-operated television station in 1999 over an employee's involvement in a political campaign. Unemployment, traditionally high, was reported at 19.7% in 1995 but fell to 9.4% in 2000. There is a legal minimum work age of 16 which is generally observed. There is also a sector-by-sector government sector minimum wage. In 1999, it proscribed about $0.75 per hour for housekeepers and $2.13 per hour for shop clerks, but most workers make substantially more (sometimes double) than the official minimum.

22 AGRICULTURE

About 16,000 hectares (39,500 acres), or 37.2% of the total land area, are classified as arable. At one time, nearly all arable land was devoted to sugarcane, but the percentage devoted to ground crops for local consumption has been increasing. In 1998, 571,000 tons of sugarcane were produced, down from the annual average of 584,000 tons in 1989–91. In 1997, sugar exports amounted to us$35.6 million, or 12.7% of total exports. Major food crops are yams, sweet potatoes, corn, eddo, cassava, and several varieties of beans. Some cotton is also grown.

23 ANIMAL HUSBANDRY

The island must import large quantities of meat and dairy products. Most livestock is owned by individual households. Estimates for 1998 showed 22,000 head of cattle, 41,000 sheep, 30,000 hogs, 5,000 goats, and 3,000,000 chickens. Poultry production in 1998 included 16,000 tons of meat and 1,000 tons of hen eggs.

24 FISHING

The fishing industry employs about 2,000 persons, and the fleet consists of more than 500 powered boats. The catch in 1997 was 2,764 metric tons. Flying fish, dolphinfish, tuna, turbot, kingfish, and swordfish are among the main species caught. A fisheries terminal complex opened at Oistins in 1983.

25 FORESTRY

Fewer than 20 hectares (50 acres) of original forests have survived the 300 years of sugar cultivation. There were an estimated 5,000 ha (12,350 acres) of forested land in 1997, covering about 12% of the total land area. Roundwood production in 1997 totaled 5,000 cu m, and imports amounted to 3,000 cu m. In 1997, Barbados imported $50.3 million in wood and forest products.

26 MINING

Deposits of limestone and coral are quarried to meet local construction needs. Clay, sand, and carbonaceous deposits provide limited yields. Cement production amounted to 110,000 tons in 1997.

27 ENERGY AND POWER

Supply and distribution of electricity are undertaken by a private firm, Barbados Light and Power, under government concession. Installed capacity in 1998 was 165,000 kW; production that year totaled 672 million kWh. Petroleum accounted for 95% of energy consumption, and natural gas satisfied the remaining energy demand. The world oil crisis of the mid-1970s initiated an active search for commercial deposits of oil and natural gas. Limited pockets of natural gas were discovered, and oil was found in St. Philip Parish. Daily crude oil production in 1998 was about 2,000 barrels, meeting 24% of domestic requirements; natural gas production was 28 million cu m. Reserves of crude oil were estimated at 3.2 million barrels at the end of 1999. As of the beginning of 2000, Barbados was planning to privatize its energy companies, including the National Petroleum Corporation and the Barbados National Oil Company (BNOC).

28 INDUSTRY

In 1999 Barbadian tourism benefited from continued income growth in its major source markets and dynamic marketing efforts by the national authorities, and tourism GDP grew by 6.7%. The UK continued to be the largest market for Barbados, providing about one-third of all overnight visitors to the island, contrasting with declining numbers of visitors from other major markets such as the US and Germany. The construction industry grew by over 3.0% as a result of tourism-related construction projects.

Agricultural manufacturing has lost ground to financial sector services. Offshore banking has become increasingly popular in Barbados, accounting for 18% of GDP in 1998, the largest of all sectors.

Manufacturing GDP, declined by 1.7% in 1996, after three consecutive years of strong growth stimulated by tax concessions which benefited mainly the branches oriented to exports to the CARICOM area. Domestic consumption of manufactured goods fell significantly, due to inflation associated with the implementation of a VAT in 1997. In 1998, manufacturing accounted for only 6% of GDP, a rate which shows little signs of growth.

29 SCIENCE AND TECHNOLOGY

Barbadian learned societies include the Barbados Astronomical Society and the Barbados Pharmaceutical Society, founded in 1956 and 1948 respectively. The Bellairs Research Institute, associated with McGill University in Montreal, is a center for the study of the tropical environment. The Cave Hill Campus of the University of the West Indies has faculties in medicine (located in Bridgetown, Founded in 1963) and, social sciences. Barbados Community College, founded in 1968, offers training in science and technology. The Barbados Museum and Historical Society, in St. Ann's Garrison, established in 1933, has collections illustrating the island's geology, prehistory, natural history, and marine life.

30 DOMESTIC TRADE

There are fish, fruit, and vegetable markets, and stores for all types of shopping. General business is conducted on weekdays from 8 AM to 4:30 PM. Most shops are also open Saturdays from 8 AM to noon. Banks are open from 9 AM to 3 PM, Monday through Thursday, and 8 AM to 5 PM on Friday.

31 FOREIGN TRADE

Sugar and honey, and the products of sugarcane processing (molasses and rum) are the most sought after commodities from Barbados (24%). Electrical equipment, and other small manufactured items make up about a quarter of exports. Other primary exports include soap and cleaning products (4.8%), pesticides and disinfectants (3.6%), and printed matter (3.2%).

In 1997 Barbados's imports were distributed among the following categories:

Consumer goods	20.9%
Food	16.7%
Fuels	8.3%
Industrial supplies	26.0%
Machinery	17.2%
Transportation	10.5%

Principal trading partners in 1998 (in millions of US dollars) were as follows:

COUNTRY	EXPORTS	IMPORTS	BALANCE
United Kingdom	43	77	-34
United States	33	452	-419
Trinidad and Tobago	22	103	-81
Venezuela	18	31	-13
Jamaica	17	9	8
Guyana	9	11	-2
Canada	8	23	-15
Germany	2	21	-19
Brazil	2	18	-16
Japan	1	84	-83

[32]BALANCE OF PAYMENTS

The consistently adverse trade balance is substantially alleviated by foreign currency remittances from various emigrants and by tourist expenditures.

The US Central Intelligence Agency reports that in 1997 the purchasing power parity of Barbados's exports was $280 million while imports totaled $982 million resulting in a trade balance of -$702 million.

The International Monetary Fund (IMF) reports that in 1998 Barbados had exports of goods totaling $257 million and imports totaling $901 million. The services credit totaled $1,024 million and debit $432 million. The following table summarizes Barbados's balance of payments as reported by the IMF for 1998 in millions of US dollars.

Current Account		-57
Balance on goods	-644	
Balance on services	591	
Balance on income	-56	
Current transfers	52	
Capital Account		1
Financial Account		55
Direct investment abroad	-1	
Direct investment in Barbados	16	
Portfolio investment assets	-23	
Portfolio investment liabilities	-26	
Other investment assets	-19	
Other investment liabilities	108	
Net Errors and Omissions		-6
Reserves and Related Items		6

[33]BANKING AND SECURITIES

The bank of issue is the Central Bank of Barbados. In 1972, it replaced the East Caribbean Currency Authority (ECCA). Commercial banks include the Bank of Nova Scotia, Barbados National Bank, Barclay's Bank, Broad Street, Caldon Finance Merchant Bank, Canadian Imperial Bank of Commerce, Caribbean Commercial Bank, Caribbean Financial Services Corporation, Mutual Bank of the Caribbean, and Royal Bank of Canada. Public institutions include the Barbados Development Bank and the Sugar Industry Agricultural Bank. Barbados has begun development of the offshore banking sector, including the Republic Bank of Trinidad and Tobago in 1999.

There is no stock exchange in Barbados, although the Central Bank has established the Barbados Securities Marketing Corp. in anticipation of the future development of a securities exchange. Mutual funds now provide a tax-exempt vehicle for investment in existing shares.

[34]INSURANCE

The regulatory authority is the Supervisor of Insurance of the Ministry of Finance. The General Insurance Association of Barbados is the general trade association. A full range of life and nonlife insurance is available. Barbados Mutual Life Assurance Society and Life of Barbados Limited provided most insurance services in Barbados in 1999.

[35]PUBLIC FINANCE

Revenues are derived mostly from import duties, internal consumption taxes, and income tax. Public sector deficits grew during the 1980s as the economy weakened. The international recession of 1990–91 magnified problems of debt service and debt management. By the end of 1990, the national debt was 9.5% higher than that of 1989. By 1991, the fiscal deficit had become unsustainable; in February 1992, the government began a stabilization program in fiscal policies with assistance from the IMF. By 2000, the deficit problem had been resolved.

The US Central Intelligence Agency (CIA) estimates that in 1997 Barbados's central government took in revenues of approximately $725.5 million and had expenditures of $750.6 million including capital expenditures of $126.3 million. Overall, the government registered a deficit of approximately $25.1 million.

Total revenue was $450 million in 1999, $427 million of which came from taxes. Total expenditure was $495 million.

[36]TAXATION

Tax on individual income as of 1 January 1996 ranged from 25% to 40%. The corporate income tax rate was 40% but companies that improve the national trade position receive special tax rates and exemptions. Other taxes were levied on insurance premiums, property transfers, land value, bank assets, and rental income. A VAT was instituted in 1997, that is levied at 15% generally, and 7.5% on hotel accommodations. Basic commodities are exempt.

[37]CUSTOMS AND DUTIES

Most imports, except those from other CARICOM members, are subject to import duties that include a customs duty, a consumption tax, and a stamp tax. The Common External Tariff (CET) was reduced to 20% in 1999, and the 35% surtax was removed in 2000. Items that carry a higher import duty rate include fruit and vegetables (40%), jewelry (60%), watches (50%), and motor vehicles (45%). The VAT of 15% replaced eleven different taxes, mostly on imports. Import licenses are needed to import many agricultural products, but there are no export controls. Beer and fruit drinks may be imported only from CARICOM countries, but fruit juices may be imported from nonmember states.

Barbados became a signatory to the World Trade Organization agreement in 1994, agreeing to dismantle all non-tariff barriers by the year 2004.

[38]FOREIGN INVESTMENT

Various investment incentives, including exception from custom duties, tax reduction and exceptions, and training grants are available to both domestic and foreign investors. Foreign ownership of Barbadian enterprises or participation in joint ventures must be approved by the Central Bank.

The government favors productive foreign investments, with an emphasis on tourism and banking because of their employment and foreign exchange generating potential. In the mid-1990s, Barbados concluded a Bilateral Double Taxation Treaty; the country has a Tax Information Exchange Agreement with the US, as well as an extensive tax treaty network with other developed countries. Foreign investors are eligible for all available tax incentives, including full exception from all income and withholding taxes for investors in offshore industries.

The offshore sector offers many opportunities, particularly given the island's strong educational base. Some 875 new offshore companies were registered in 1996, bringing the total to

4,137. Offshore banking received considerable foreign interest in 1999.

39 ECONOMIC DEVELOPMENT

The government has been making efforts to relieve the island's economic dependence on sugar by establishing industries and encouraging tourism. Government planning has been in operation since 1951. In 1957, the Barbados Development Board (now the Barbados Industrial Development Corp.) was established. The development plan for 1979–83 called for expansion of the construction sector. During 1962–86, multilateral aid to Barbados totaled US$123.1 million, of which 24% was from the IDB and 57% from the World Bank.

The economy has recovered well since the recession in 1993, with steady growth rates, low inflation, and falling unemployment. Anticipation of a thriving offshore financial sector, and the eventual elimination of excess trade restrictions, has encouraged the government to revamp the economic system, shifting its emphasis from industrial growth to the services sector.

40 SOCIAL DEVELOPMENT

A national social security system began operations in 1937, providing old age and survivors' pensions, sickness, disability, and maternity benefits, and (under a January 1971 extension) employment injury benefits. People between the ages of 16 and 65 are covered. Unemployment insurance was introduced in 1982 and is funded by equal contributions from employers and employees. Sickness and maternity benefits are provided for employed persons, and all government hospitals and clinics maintain public wards for medical treatments, with costs scaled to income.

As of 1999, 10 of 49 members of parliament were women. Although women are well-represented in all aspects of national life, women's rights advocates cite domestic violence as a serious problem. A domestic violence law passed in 1992 requires an immediate police response to reports of violence against women and children. A crisis center staffed by trained counselors is run by the Business and Professional Women's Club. A $190,000 battered women's shelter was opened by the government in 1999. The government has also formed a Child Care Board to monitor and protect the rights of children. In 1997 the Ministry of Labor formed the Disabilities Unit; an advisory committee on disabilities was created in 1998. Human rights are protected under the constitution.

41 HEALTH

Barbados has a national health service. In the mid-1990s, there were 1,100 people per doctor and 84 beds per 10,000 population. There were 355 doctors, 48 dentists, and 898 nurses. As of 1990, 100% of the population has access to health care services. Life expectancy as of 1999 was 75 years. The infant mortality rate was 17 per 1,000 live births. By the mid-1990s, the under-five mortality rate had improved to only 10 per 1,000 from 1960, when it was 90 per 1,000 children under five. In the mid-1990s, the birth rate was 14 births per 1,000 people. As of 1994, 97% of one-year-old children were vaccinated against measles. In 1995, 95 new cases of AIDS were reported.

42 HOUSING

The Barbados Housing Authority is empowered to acquire land, construct housing projects, and redevelop overcrowded areas. At last estimate, 90% of all housing consisted of detached homes and more than 5% of apartments. Over 70% of all homes were owner occupied; more than 15% were rented privately; 5% were occupied rent free; another 5% were rented from the government;

and less than 5% were occupied by squatters or otherwise specified.

43 EDUCATION

The official language in Barbados is English. Primary education begins at the age of five. Secondary education begins at the age of 11 and lasts for six years. The state provides tuition for approximately 86% of the eligible children for primary and secondary education, the latter offering certificate courses equivalent to the general certificate of education in both ordinary and advanced level curricula.

Education is compulsory for children between the ages of 5 and 16. The education program in Barbados is administered by the Ministry of Education and is free in all government-run schools. As of 2000, children in 93 government primary schools numbered 26,900; a small number attend private primary schools. Secondary education was provided in 22 government secondary schools, 15 assisted private schools, and seven senior schools for students ages 14–16. Scholarships are awarded for study in the UK and in Caribbean institutions. The Barbados branch of the University of the West Indies opened at Cave Hill in 1963. It has 266 teachers and 2,264 students. The government pays the fees of all Barbadian students at the Cave Hill Campus of the University of West Indies. The Barbados Community College was established in 1968. Barbados' adult illiteracy rate in 1995 was estimated at 2.6%.

There is also advanced education for adults at the Extramural Center of the University of West Indies, the Erdiston Teachers Training College, and the Samuel Jackman Prescod Polytechnic. There are special schools for the deaf, blind, and mentally retarded, including two residential institutions for disabled persons.

In the mid-1990s, the government allocated approximately 20% of central government expenditure to education.

44 LIBRARIES AND MUSEUMS

A free library (1847) is maintained by the government in Bridgetown. There are seven branches, with bookmobile stops throughout the island. By 2000, the system had 1.6 million volumes. The library of the Barbados branch of the University of the West Indies has 150,000 volumes. There are seven museums in the country in 2000. There are also 17 monuments and historic sites and five zoos and botanical gardens. The Barbados Museum and Historical Society (1933) in Saint Michael is a general museum with collections showing the geology, history, natural history, marine life, and plantation home furnishings of the island, as well as Arawak artifacts. Other museums include the Mallalieu Motor Museum in Christ Church, the Sir Frank Huts on Sugar Museum in Saint James, and a science museum at the Rum Factory and Heritage Park in Saint Phillip.

45 MEDIA

Automatic telephone service is provided by a private firm, the Barbados Telephone Co. Ltd.; there were over 87,000 telephones as of 1995. A wireless telephone service provides overseas communications, and a telex cable connects Barbados with the UK. The Congor Bay Earth Station, opened in 1972, links Barbados with the global satellite communications system. Barbados has a government-controlled television and radio broadcasting service (CBS) and a commercial rediffusion service that broadcasts over a cable network. Altogether, there are two AM and three FM stations and one television station. The Caribbean Broadcasting System (CBS) is government owned. An estimated 227,000 radios were in use in 1995. In 1997, there were 267 television sets per 1,000 population.

There are two daily newspapers (both independently operated, in Bridgetown), the *Advocate* (circulation 15,000 in 1999) and the *Daily Nation* (32,000), as well as some periodicals, including a monthly magazine, the *New Bajan*.

The Constitution of Barbados provides for freedom of expression and the government is said to uphold freedom of speech and press. The government prohibits the production of pornographic materials.

46ORGANIZATIONS

Barbados has a chamber of commerce in St. Michael. Branches of other international organizations include the Lions Club, Rotary Club, 4-H Clubs, Boy Scouts, Girl Scouts, YMCA, and YWCA.

47TOURISM, TRAVEL, AND RECREATION

Barbados, with its fine beaches, sea bathing, and pleasant climate, has long been a popular holiday resort. In 1998, 512,397 tourists visited Barbados, including 186,690 from the United Kingdom. Tourist spending was an estimated $717 million in 1997. There were 6,069 hotel rooms that year with 12,138 beds and a 57% occupancy rate. Cricket is the national sport, followed by surfing, sailing, and other marine pastimes.

A valid passport is required of all visitors except nationals of the US and Canada traveling directly to Barbados with other acceptable identification. The cost of staying in Barbados varies seasonally. According to 1999 UN estimates, the daily cost of staying in Barbados between December and April is $212. At other times of the year, daily costs average $177.

48FAMOUS BARBADIANS

Sir Grantley Adams (1898–1971) was premier of the Federation of the West Indies (1958–62). His son, John Michael Geoffrey Manningham "Tom" Adams (1931–85) was prime minister from 1976 until his death, succeeding Errol Walton Barrow (1920–87). In 1985, Barrow again assumed the office of prime minister until his death. Erskine Sandiford (b. 1938) succeeded Barrow.

Barbados-born Edwin Barclay (1882–1955) was president of Liberia from 1930 to 1944. George Lamming (b. 1927) is a well-known West Indian novelist. Sir Garfield Sobers (b. 1936) has gained renown as the "world's greatest cricketer."

49DEPENDENCIES

Barbados has no territories or colonies.

50BIBLIOGRAPHY

Beckles, Hilary. *A History of Barbados: From Amerindian Settlement to Nation-State*. New York: Cambridge University Press, 1990.

Butler, Kathleen. *The Economics of Emancipation: Jamaica and Barbados, 1823–1843*. Chapel Hill: University of North Carolina Press, 1995.

——. *White Servitude and Black Slavery in Barbados, 1627–1715*. Knoxville: University of Tennessee Press, 1989.

Handler, Jerome S. *The Unappropriated People: Freedom in the Slave Society of Barbados*. Baltimore: Johns Hopkins University Press, 1974.

Hanna, Lewis W. *Land Use Change in the Island of Barbados, 1985–1990*. Newcastle-upon-Tyne, England: University of Newcastle-upon-Tyne, 1990.

Harlow, V. T. *A History of Barbados, 1625–1685*. London: Oxford University Press, 1972.

Hoyos, F. A. *Grantley Adams and the Social Revolution*. London: Macmillan, 1974.

Hunte, George. *Barbados*. London: Batsford, 1974.

Potter, Robert B. *Barbados*. Oxford, England; Santa Barbara, Calif.: Clio Press, 1987.

Puckrein, Gary A. *Little England: Plantation Society and Anglo-Barbadian Politics*. New York: New York University Press, 1986.

Tree, Ronald. *A History of Barbados*. 2d ed. Woodstock, N.Y.: Beekman, 1979.

BELIZE

CAPITAL: Belmopan.

FLAG: The national flag consists of the Belize coat of arms superimposed on a white disk and centered on a blue rectangular field with a narrow red stripe at the top and the bottom.

ANTHEM: *Land of the Free.*

MONETARY UNIT: The Belize dollar (B$), formerly tied to the UK pound sterling and now pegged to the US dollar, is a paper currency of 100 cents. There are coins of 1, 5, 10, 25, 50 cents and 1 dollar, and notes of 1, 1, 5, 10, 20, 50, and 100 dollars. B$1=US$0.50 (or US$1=B$2.00).

WEIGHTS AND MEASURES: Imperial weights and measures are used. The exception is the measuring of petroleum products, for which the US gallon is standard.

HOLIDAYS: New Year's Day, 1 January; Baron Bliss Day, 9 March; Labor Day, 1 May; Commonwealth Day, 24 May; National Day, 10 September; Independence Day, 21 September; Columbus Day, 12 October; Garifuna Day, 19 November; Christmas, 25 December; Boxing Day, 26 December. Movable holidays are Good Friday and Easter Monday.

TIME: 6 AM = noon GMT.

¹LOCATION, SIZE, AND EXTENT

Belize (formerly British Honduras), on the Caribbean coast of Central America, has an area of 22,960 sq km (8,865 sq mi), extending 280 km (174 mi) NNE–SSW and 109 km (68 mi) WNW–ESE. Comparatively, the area occupied by Belize is slightly larger than the state of Massachusetts. Bounded on the N by Mexico, on the E by the Caribbean Sea, and on the S and W by Guatemala, Belize has a total boundary length of 902 km (560 mi).

The capital city of Belize, Belmopan, is located in the center of the country.

²TOPOGRAPHY

The country north of Belmopan is mostly level land interrupted only by the Manatee Hills. To the south the land rises sharply toward a mountainous interior from a flat and swampy coastline heavily indented by many lagoons. The Maya and the Cockscomb mountains (which reach a high point of 1,122 m/ 3,681 ft at Victoria Peak, in the Cockscombs) form the backbone of the country, which is drained by 17 rivers. The coastal waters are sheltered by a line of reefs, beyond which there are numerous islands and cays, notably Ambergris Cay, the Turneffe Islands, Columbus Reef, and Glover's Reef.

³CLIMATE

The climate is subtropical and humid, tempered by predominant northeast trade winds that keep temperatures between 16° and 32°C (61–90°F) in the coastal region; inland temperatures are slightly higher. The seasons are marked more by differences of humidity than of temperature. Annual rainfall averages vary from 127 cm (50 in) in the north to more than 380 cm (150 in) in the south. There is a dry season from February to May and another dry spell in August. Hurricanes occur from July to October.

⁴FLORA AND FAUNA

Most of the forest cover consists of mixed hardwoods—mainly mahogany, cedar, and sapodilla (the source of chicle). In the flat regions there are extensive tracts of pine. The coastal land and the cays are covered with mangrove. Indigenous fauna include armadillo, opossum, deer, and monkeys; common reptiles include iguana and snakes.

⁵ENVIRONMENT

Because of its low population density, Belize has suffered less than its neighbors from such problems as soil erosion and pollution. However, substantial deforestation has occurred, and water quality remains a problem because of the seepage of sewage along with industrial and agricultural chemicals into the water supply. It is estimated that 18% of the country's rural population does not have access to pure water. Pollutants also threaten Belize's coral reefs. Removal of coral, picking orchids in forest reserves, spear fishing, and overnight camping in any public area (including forest reserves) are prohibited. Approximately 14% of Belize's total land area is protected. Natural hazards to Belize's environment include hurricanes and coastal flooding. Belize's national capital was moved 129 km (80 mi) inland from Belize City to Belinopau because of hurricanes. Endangered species in Belize include the tundra peregrine falcon, hawksbill, green sea, and leatherback turtles, American crocodile, and Morelet's crocodile. By 1991, the iguana, Larpy eagle, spoonbill, wood stork, and several types of hawks and parrots were endangered in a total of 121 species of mammals. Of 504 bird species, four are threatened. Thirty-six of 3,240 plant species were also endangered as of the mid-1990s.

⁶POPULATION

The population of Belize in 2000 was estimated at 241,546. An estimated 3.6% of the population is 65 years of age or older. The projected population for the year 2005 is 271,000, assuming a crude birthrate of 26 per 1,000 population and a death rate of 5, resulting in a natural rate of change of 2.1% for the period 2000–2005. The population rate of change between 1995 and 2000 was 2.5%. In 1996, the average population density was 9.6 persons per sq km (25 per sq mi), the lowest in Central America. However, the population density is as high as 360 per sq km (932 per sq mi) on agricultural land.

It was estimated that 47% of the population lived in urban areas in 2000. The largest city is Belize City, with an estimated population of 46,342. The capital city, Belmopan, had a 2000 population estimated at 6,000.

7 MIGRATION

Because of its high emigration rate, Belize encourages immigration. In 1999, the net migration rate was -0.67 migrants per 1,000 population. The population of Belize increased significantly in 1993, with 40,000 Central American refugees and other immigrants, mostly from Guatemala and El Salvador. This offset the heavy Creole emigration to North America. As of 1995, Belize still had 6,000 refugees from El Salvador and 2,000 refugees from Guatemala. UNHCR negotiations with the government produced two significant developments in 1999. First, as of February 1999 refugees are able to apply for naturalization after five years of residence in the country. Second, in May 1999 the government enacted an amnesty program, offering permanent resident status for illegal immigrants and unregistered refugees. By 30 June 1999, some 10,000 families had registered.

8 ETHNIC GROUPS

According to the latest estimates, 44% of the population is Mestizo (mixed White and Maya); some 30% is Creole (of African descent); another 11% is Maya; 6.6% is Garifuna (Carib); and 8% is comprised of various other groups. There are also people of European, Chinese, Asian Indian, and Syrian-Lebanese ancestry.

9 LANGUAGES

The official language is English. At least 80% of the people can speak standard English and/or a Creole patois. Spanish is spoken by approximately 60% of the population; for one-third to one-half it is the first language. Although English is the language of instruction, other languages spoken include Garifuna (Carib), Mayan and other Amerindian languages, and, in the Mennonite colony, Low German.

10 RELIGIONS

In 1998, 58% of inhabitants were Roman Catholic. Only 7% of the populace are Anglicans; another 6% are Pentecostals. Other faiths and denominations have fewer than 10,000 members each. These include Methodists (4.2%), Seventh-Day Adventists (4.1%), and Mennonites (4%). There are approximately 5,000 Hindus and Nazarenes, and smaller numbers of Baha'is, Baptists, Buddhists, Jehovah's Witnesses, Mormons, Muslims, Rastafarians, and Salvation Army members, all of whom are allowed to proselytize freely.

11 TRANSPORTATION

In 1999 Belize had 2,248 km (1,397 mi) of roads, of which 427 km (265 mi) were paved. In the early 1990s, there were about 4,800 motor vehicles. The country had no railways. Belize City is the main port; in the late 1970s, deepwater facilities were constructed through financing from the Caribbean Development Bank (CDB). Other ports and harbors include Big Creek, Corozol, and Punta Gorda. In 1998 Belize's merchant marine was comprised of 403 ships, totaling 1,740,325 GRT. Seven shipping lines provide regular services to North America, the Caribbean, and Europe. Also in 1998, airports totaled 44, only three of which had paved runways. International airports at Belize City (P.S.W. Goldson) and Punta Gorda handle services to the US and Central America. Maya Airways provides domestic service, and there are various international air carriers.

12 HISTORY

Numerous ruins indicate that the area now called Belize was once heavily populated by Maya Indians, whose civilization collapsed around AD 900. Columbus sailed along the coast in 1502, but did not land. The first permanent settlement was established in 1638 by shipwrecked English seamen. Later immigrants included African slaves and British sailors and soldiers.

In its early colonial history the area was a virtual backwater, used only for logging and as a pirate base. A power struggle between England and Spain ensued over possession of the area, with the British prevailing by the 19th century. In 1862 the British organized the area as the colony of British Honduras. For the next century, forestry continued as the main enterprise until eventually supplanted by sugar.

On 1 January 1964, a constitution was promulgated, providing for self-government, although the UK maintained the defense force. That force remained in place partly because of a border dispute with Guatemala, going back to an 1859 treaty. The Guatemalan government pressed territorial claims over the southern quarter of the area. A settlement guaranteeing the country's independence by 1970 seemed to resolve the dispute, but rioting in British Honduras in May 1968 led to the repudiation of the agreement by both the UK and Guatemala.

The country dropped the appearance, if not the reality, of colonial dependence in 1973, adopting Belize as the official country name. The border dispute continued unabated until 1977, when Guatemala and the UK began new negotiations on Belize. The UK, Guatemala, and Belize reached agreement on a solution in March 1981, but disagreement soon followed. Finally, the UK decided to take matters into its own hands and granted Belize independence as of 21 September 1981. Guatemala refused to recognize the new nation, severed diplomatic relations with the UK, and declared the date of independence a national day of mourning. In December 1986, the UK and Guatemala resumed diplomatic ties, but the 1,800-member British garrison remained in Belize. Since independence, control of the government has alternated between the People's United Party (PUP) led by George C. Price, which had dominated Belize's politics since the 1950s, and the United Democratic Party (UDP), led by Manuel Esquivel. The UDP won the elections of 1984 and 1993; in between, the PUP governed from 1989 to 1993.

In 1991 Belize was admitted to the Organization of American States (OAS). The same year, Guatemala's new president, Jorge Serrano, reached an agreement with then-prime minister George Price that led to full Guatemalan recognition of Belize's independence the following year and the signing of a nonaggression pact between the two nations in 1993. The UK withdrew its troops from Belize in 1994.

Belize's tourism industry became a mainstay of the economy in the 1980s and 1990s, growing from 64,000 tourists in 1980 to 247,000 in 1992. By 1995, tourism surpassed all other sectors, including the sugar industry, as a source of foreign exchange, and it continued to grow through the remainder of the decade. Challenges facing Belize in the late 1990s included high unemployment, a growing involvement in South American cocaine trafficking, and increased urban crime, which worsened in 1998 and 1999, prompting new gun control measures.

Negotiations continued with Guatemala over territorial disputes not settled by the 1991 agreement, mainly Guatemalan claims to land in the southern part of the country. Tensions between the two countries continued into the early months of

BELIZE

LOCATION: 15°53′ to 18°31′N; 87°16′ to 89°8′W.
BOUNDARY LENGTHS: Mexico, 251 km (156 mi); Caribbean coastline, 475 km (295 mi); Guatemala, 269 km (167 mi). TERRITORIAL SEA LIMIT: 3 mi.

2000, when Belize's ambassador was expelled from Guatemala, and talks scheduled for February were suspended.

13GOVERNMENT

The independence constitution of 21 September 1981 (based on that of 1 January 1964) vests governmental authority in a governor-general appointed by the UK monarch, a cabinet headed by a prime minister, and a bicameral National Assembly.

The cabinet ministers are appointed by the governor-general on the advice of the prime minister. The National Assembly consists of a 29-member House of Representatives elected by universal adult suffrage, and a Senate of eight members appointed by the governor-general (five on the advice of the prime minister, two on the advice of the opposition, and one on the recommendation of the Belize Advisory Council). Parliamentary elections must be held at intervals of no longer than five years. The voting age is 18.

14POLITICAL PARTIES

The two major parties in Belize are the current majority United Democratic Party (UDP) and the People's United Party (PUP). The UDP, which has been the dominant party since 1993, increased its representation to 26 out of 29 legislative seats in the August 1998 elections, after which Said Musa succeeded Manuel Esquivel as party leader and prime minister. Although it won a sweeping victory in the 1997 municipal elections, the opposition PUP held only three elected seats at the national level as of 1999.

George C. Price dominated Belize's politics after becoming the country's premier in 1964. At independence in 1981, Price became prime minister and ruled for three years. The UDP coalition, under Esquivel's leadership, took 21 House seats in 1984 and ruled until 1989, when the PUP regained control and Price once again became prime minister. He called an early election in June 1993, which his party unexpectedly lost, placing the UDP in its current dominant position.

15LOCAL GOVERNMENT

Belize is divided into six administrative districts: Corozal, Orange Walk, Belize City, El Cayo, Stann Creek, and Toledo. Except for Belize City, which has an elected city council of nine members, each is administered by a seven-member elected town board. Local government at the village level is through village councils.

16JUDICIAL SYSTEM

The independent judiciary is appointed by the crown. The law of Belize is the common law of England, augmented by local legislation. The Judiciary consists of the Magistrate's Courts, the Supreme Court, and the Court of Appeal. The Supreme Court is presided over by a Chief Justice. Appeals are to the court of appeal, established in 1968, and, ultimately, to the UK Privy Council. Six summary jurisdiction courts (criminal) and six district courts (civil) are presided over by magistrates.

The judiciary has protected individual rights and fundamental freedoms. Detainees must be brought before a judge within 72 hours of arrest. Bail is liberally afforded. A jury trial is required in capital cases. The 1981 Constitution provides a wide range of fundamental rights and freedoms. Criminal defendants have rights to presumption of innocence, protection against self-incrimination, counsel, appeal and public trial. The Constitution prohibits torture and other cruel, inhuman, or degrading treatment or punishment. The Constitution also prohibits arbitrary interference with privacy, family, home or correspondence. The government generally respects these provisions.

17ARMED FORCES

The Belize Defense Force, established in 1978 consists of 1,750 men in five regular and three reserve companies and a training organization. The army has three infantry battalions, a maritime wing with two patrol craft, and an air wing with no combat aircraft. The defense budget was $15 million in 1997–98, or 2% of GDP.

¹⁸INTERNATIONAL COOPERATION

Belize was admitted to the UN on 25 September 1981, four days after independence; during the late 1970s, the UN General Assembly had repeatedly supported Belize's rights of self-determination and territorial integrity, in contradistinction to Guatemala's land claims. Belize participates in ECLAC, IBRD, IDA, IFAD, IFC, ILO, IMF, ITU, UPU, UNESCO, and WMO, and is a signatory to the Law of the Sea and a member of the WTO. A member of the Commonwealth of Nations, Belize also belongs to CARICOM and G-77.

¹⁹ECONOMY

The economy is dependent on agriculture and fishing. Sugar, bananas, and citrus fruits are the main cash crops. Until a recent depletion, the country's main export had been forest products, especially mahogany. Belize continues to import most of its consumer goods, including much of its food and all of its petroleum requirements. The tourism industry, fishing industry, and the garment manufacturing industry grew in importance during the late 1990s.

Belize started the decade of the 1990s positively. However, after five years of economic growth averaging 4.3%, the economy decelerated to 1.5% in 1996. This was largely due to a slowdown in tourism, a decline in fisheries production, and cutbacks in public spending and construction. The agricultural sector grew rapidly in that year, with banana and sugar production up by significant amounts, while production of oranges was nearly flat. Fishing was also hurt by corrective measures to overcome the taura virus which affected farmed shrimp production and lower lobster catches. In 1997, the government implemented austerity measures and capital projects that continued the economic depression in the short-run. The agricultural industry experienced a decline of production in 1998, but the fishing, tourism, and garment manufacturing industries gained ground. In 1997 and 1998, GDP growth hovered around 3%, but the forecast for 1999 through 2003 was only 1.5%.

Belize's future economic growth is linked to the improvement of technology and physical infrastructure. The Agency for International Development (USAID), the World Bank, the UK, the EC, the Caribbean Development Bank (CDB), Canada, and Taiwan have provided assistance to Belize for the reconstruction and pavement of major highways, and the construction of houses. Electricity has become dependable, and the telecommunications system is reliable.

²⁰INCOME

The US Central Intelligence Agency (CIA) reports that in 1998 Belize's gross domestic product (GDP) was estimated at $700 million. The per capita GDP was estimated at $3,000. The annual growth rate of GDP was estimated at 0.5%. The average inflation rate in 1998 was -0.5%. The CIA defines GDP as the value of all final goods and services produced within a nation in a given year and computed on the basis of purchasing power parity (PPP) rather than value as measured on the basis of the rate of exchange. It was estimated that agriculture accounted for 22% of GDP, industry 22%, and services 56%.

The World Bank reports that for the same period per capita private consumption (in PPP terms) was $2,890. Private consumption includes expenditures of individuals, households, and nongovernmental organizations. Approximately 27% of household consumption was spent on food, 5% on fuel, 3% on health care, and 13% on education.

²¹LABOR

The labor force in 1997 was estimated at 71,000. About 30% of the labor force was employed in agriculture, forestry, and fishing.

In 1997, unemployment averaged 13%. Although industrial employment tends to be seasonal, Belize City workers rarely accept employment in agriculture.

Labor legislation covers minimum wages, work hours, employment of young persons, and workers' safety and compensation. The National Trades Union Congress of Belize is the major union federation, and the United General Workers' Union is the leading trade union. In 1999, there were 11 independent unions, comprising 11% of the labor force, which represented a cross-section of white-collar, blue-collar, and professional workers (including most civil service employees). There are procedural requirements that a union must meet (mainly the filing of certain documents), but the government freely recognizes the right to join unions and to strike (unions representing "essential" service workers must give an intent to strike notice two days prior to a strike).

There is a minimum work age of 14 (17 to work near hazardous machinery) that is effectively enforced. A minimum wage ranging from $0.87 to $1.12 per hour is also effectively enforced except among undocumented workers, primarily on banana plantations. Workplace safety and health regulations are also effectively enforced by the Ministry of Labor and Public Health, particularly in Belize City.

²²AGRICULTURE

Only 2.5% (57,000 hectares/141,000 acres) of total land area is used for the production of seasonal and permanent crops. Most Mayans still practice the traditional slash-and-burn method of farming, under which at any one time some 80% of the land is left idle. More efficient agricultural colonies have been established by Mennonite immigrants. Sugar and citrus are the leading agricultural exports. Sugarcane production, centered in the northern lowland around Corozal and the town of Orange Walk, totaled 1.208,000 tons in 1998. Citrus production is concentrated in the Stann Creek valley; the 1998 output included 170,000 tons of oranges and 41,000 tons of grapefruit. The US-based Hershey Foods Corp. has invested B$4 million in cacao cultivation in El Cayo.

Because agriculture is not sufficiently diversified, the country relies heavily on food imports. By establishing a marketing board to encourage production of rice, beans, and corn, the government hopes eventually to become self-sufficient in these crops. Rice paddy production, which averaged 9,000 tons annually during 1979–81, fell to a reported 4,000 tons in 1990 but climbed to 17,000 tons by 1998. Corn production, which had been hovering at 18,000 tons per year, rose to a reported 37,000 tons in 1998. Dry bean production was 5,000 tons. Export earnings from sugar in 1997 exceeded us$45.9 million. Belize's sugar industry is heavily dependent on preferential price markets; over 50% of its exports are sent to preferential price markets (principally the European Union). Citrus output (exported in concentrate form), expanded by 170% as new acreage planted in the late 1980s came into production and weather conditions were very favorable. In 1985, a consortium that included Coca-Cola paid b$12 million for 383,000 hectares (946,400 acres) northwest of Belmopan for a citrus farming project. Citrus thus displaced bananas as the country's second most important crop, although banana production went up by 32% following a decline in 1991. Banana production was aided by recent privatization and restructuring in the production and marketing areas, which has acted as a catalyst to improve technology (success in combating sigatoka disease) and infrastructure. Banana production, however, fell from 68,000 tons in 1994 to 45,000 tons in 1995 before rising back to 81,000 tons in 1998. Papaya exports total over 10,000 lb monthly and mango, peanut, pineapple, and winter vegetable exports are also on the rise.

23ANIMAL HUSBANDRY

Mennonite farms account for much of Belize's dairy and poultry output. In 1998, the nation had an estimated 23,000 hogs, 5,000 horses, 4,000 mules, 3,000 sheep, and 1,000,000 chickens. Cattle suited for breeding or crossbreeding with local cattle are Red Poll, Jamaica Black, Hereford, and Brahman (zebu); there were 60,000 head of cattle in 1998. Some 8,000 tons of poultry meat and 8,000 tons of milk were produced in 1998.

24FISHING

Fishing resources and development are good. In 1997, the total catch was 2,620 tons. Lobster is the leading product; of the US$17.9 million in export earnings derived from fishing in 1997, primarily lobster sales. In the mid-1990s, shrimp production increased by 75% as a result of three new shrimp farms opening in 1992. Whiteleg shrimp and spiny lobster are the leading species by volume.

25FORESTRY

Although Belize is still rich in forest resources, the accessible stands of commercial timber have been depleted. Reforestation and natural regeneration in the pine forest (mainly in Cayo, Stann Creek, and Toledo Districts) and artificial regeneration of fast-growing tropical hardwood species are creating a resurgence in forestry. About 92% of Belize's land area is covered with forests and woodlands. Timber cutting is usually done during the short dry season. Total roundwood production in 1997 was 188,000 cu m. The principal varieties of trees cut are mahogany, pine, cedar, and rosewood. Exports of forest produce (including chicle) in 1965 amounted to one-third of total exports; in 1997, however, the export value was $2 million, less than 3% of the total.

26MINING

The Belize, Sibun, and Monkey Rivers, as well as North and South Stann Creeks, were the sites of clay, gravel, and sand operations. Mining accounted for 0.8% of GDP in 1995. In 1997, clay production amounted to 2.6 million tons; dolomite, 30,000 tons; limestone, 310,000 tons; sand and gravel, 350,000 tons; marl, 1.3 million tons; and gold, 5 kg.

27ENERGY AND POWER

Electric power supplied by ten diesel-powered generators is inadequate. A central authority, the Belize Electricity Board, supplies and operates the national power system. In 1998, total installed capacity was 35,000 kW, including power from the Board's generators and additional wattage supplied by private industries and individuals. Production in the same year was 175 million kWh, all from fossil fuels. A 22,000 kW, $50 million hydroelectric power station on the Macal River has been proposed by two US companies. It would be privately owned until 2034, after which the plant would be transferred to the government.

28INDUSTRY

The manufacturing sector is small but has been expanding. Major Industrial activities include textiles and garments, and sugar and citrus processing. The Development Finance Corporation promotes private capital investment in industry.

Aside from the processing of sugar and citrus, the manufacturing sector in Belize continues to be quite small. The manufacturing sector declined in 1998 by 4.4%, partly accountable to low agricultural output. Garment production stabilized and grew in the late 1990s after significant declines in 1994 and 1995 that resulted from heavy competition from Mexico and the US. Other manufacturing products—batteries, beer and beverages—represent a minimal share and are protected by import substitution policies.

Tourism, expanding despite a need for further development, has made an increasing contribution to foreign exchange earnings since 1995; recorded at $105 million in 1998. Offshore business in Belize is a fledgling industry with high growth potential. Attractive incentives to foreign investment have been promoted by the government in order to attract capital.

29SCIENCE AND TECHNOLOGY

University College of Belize and Wesley College, both in Belize City, offer some scientific and technical training, but Belizean students must go abroad for advanced study. The National Library Service operates a Technical/Reference Library in Belize City.

30DOMESTIC TRADE

Except for warehouses and shops in Belize City, open markets still predominate in Belize. Normal business hours in Belize cities are 8 AM to noon and 1 to 5 PM, Monday through Friday. Banks are open from 8 AM to 1 PM, Monday through Thursday, and from 8 AM to noon and 3 to 6 PM on Fridays.

31FOREIGN TRADE

Belize's major partners are NAFTA, the UK, CARICOM and the EC. In 1998, the US imported 37% of Belize's total exports, and supplied 49% of all Belizean imports.

The Belize export market depends mostly upon agriculture, in particular on the sugars, and fruit and nut trade (18% and 52%). There are a few clothing exporters that deal in men's outerwear, and undergarments; accounting for 12% of Belize's exports. Other substantial exports include frozen shell fish (11%), wood (2.1%), and vegetables (1.6%).

In 1997 Belize's imports were distributed among the following categories:

Consumer goods	16.8%
Food	16.0%
Fuels	12.9%
Industrial supplies	27.7%
Machinery	16.6%
Transportation	9.3%
Other	0.7%

Principal trading partners in 1998 (in millions of US dollars) were as follows:

COUNTRY	EXPORTS	IMPORTS	BALANCE
United States	66	160	-94
United Kingdom	51	14	37
Netherlands	13	4	9
Mexico	7	35	-28
Jamaica	5	3	2
Trinidad and Tobago	4	5	-1
Germany	4	2	2
Canada	4	6	-2
Guatemala	1	8	-7
Netherlands Antilles	n.a.	21	

32BALANCE OF PAYMENTS

The visible trade deficit is counterbalanced by overseas aid, British military expenditures, foreign remittances from expatriates, and receipts from tourism.

The US Central Intelligence Agency reports that in 1998 the purchasing power parity of Belize's exports was $95.3 million while imports totaled $149.7 million resulting in a trade balance of -$54.4 million.

The International Monetary Fund (IMF) reports that in 1998 Belize had exports of goods totaling $186 million and imports totaling $291 million. The services credit totaled $141 million and debit $99 million. The following table summarizes Belize's balance of payments as reported by the IMF for 1998 in millions of US dollars.

Current Account		-60
Balance on goods	-105	
Balance on services	42	
Balance on income	-32	
Current transfers	36	
Capital Account		-2
Financial Account		24
Direct investment abroad	-5	
Direct investment in Belize	18	
Portfolio investment assets	...	
Portfolio investment liabilities	13	
Other investment assets	...	
Other investment liabilities	-2	
Net Errors and Omissions		25
Reserves and Related Items		14

33BANKING AND SECURITIES

The bank of issue is the Central Bank of Belize. Two foreign banks, Barclay's Bank, and the Bank of Nova Scotia; and two local banks, the Atlantic Bank, and Belize Bank; conduct commercial banking. The Banking Ordinance was amended in 1996 to authorize offshore banking, with only one in existence in 1999, although over 10,000 offshore financial institutions operate. Anti-laundering legislation was put into effect in 1998, a and small farmers and business bank was created with bilateral aid from Taiwan.

In the fourth quarter of 1996, the Central Bank of Belize was obliged to defend the exchange rate by selling foreign exchange to commercial banks. The quantities involved were not announced, but international reserves fell from $71 million at the end of September 1996, to $65 million at the end of December 1996. However, year-end reserves were still significantly higher than the end-of-June figure of $39 million. Contributing to this rise was the receipt in August of a Taiwanese government loan of $26 million, as well as the proceeds of a bond issue for the new Central Bank building and increased sugar export receipts.

In 1998, the new government led by Said Musa lowered the liquidity and cash reserve requirements of commercial banks, and increased government spending on capital projects, in order to increase funds. Foreign assets had declined even further, from $65 million in 1997 to $51 million in 1998. A $50 million loan from the Taiwanese government was granted for infrastructure development in 1998.

There is no securities exchange in Belize.

34INSURANCE

There are several insurance companies doing business in Belize.

35PUBLIC FINANCE

About half of Belize's recurrent expenditures are financed by customs duties; nearly all capital spending is funded by foreign loans and grants. Since an IMF standby stabilization program was implemented in 1985, fiscal responsibility has improved. The government typically budgets over 50% of projected spending to capital development, and raises 60% of current revenues from trade taxes. Government spending accounts typically for almost one-third of GDP.

The US Central Intelligence Agency (CIA) estimates that in 1997 Belize's central government took in revenues of approximately $140 million and had expenditures of $142 million

including capital expenditures of $58 million. Overall, the government registered a deficit of approximately $2 million.

The following table shows an itemized breakdown of government revenues and expenditures. The percentages were calculated from data reported by the International Monetary Fund. The dollar amounts (millions) are based on the CIA estimates provided above.

REVENUE AND GRANTS	100%	140
Tax revenue	77.4%	108
Non-tax revenue	9.2%	13
Capital revenue	0.7%	1
Grants	12.7%	18
EXPENDITURES	100%	142
General public services	11.4%	16
Defense	5.4%	8
Public order and safety	7.1%	10
Education	20.5%	29
Health	8.2%	12
Social security	5.9%	8
Housing and community amenities	2.6%	4
Recreation, cultural, and religious affairs	1.3%	2
Economic affairs and services	28.1%	40
Other expenditures	1.5%	2
Interest payments	8.0%	11

36TAXATION

Income tax is levied on companies and individuals. Corporate taxes are set at a fixed rate of 35% of the chargeable income; personal income tax is levied on those earning more than $10,000 per year, at a flat rate of 25%. A company granted a development concession has a tax holiday of up to 25 years. The Sales Tax Act of 1999 implemented a 12% tax on alcohol, tobacco, and fuel, and a 8% tax on all other items.

37CUSTOMS AND DUTIES

Customs duties are generally ad valorem. Belize uses the CARICOM Common External Tariff, which ranges from 5% to 45%. There is also a stamp tax (normally 12%) on certain goods. Import duties on industrial products average 20%, and there is a duty of 15% to 25% on luxury items. Certain products require import licenses to protect domestic industry, including sugar and citrus fruits, but these will be removed.

The 1990 Export Processing Zone (EPZ) Act and the Commercial Free Zone (CFZ) Act of 1995 foster the import-export industry with tax incentives. Belize is a CARICOM member state, has free trade agreements with Venezuela and Columbia, and was working on a free trade agreement with Mexico in 1999.

38FOREIGN INVESTMENT

Investments in public projects are coordinated through the Development Finance Corporation and the Office of Economic Development. Private investment is actively encouraged through 25-year development concessions. An Aliens Land-Holding Ordinance governs real estate investment through licensing procedures. Other incentive schemes include the Fiscal Incentives Act, International Business and Public companies Act, Export Processing Zone Act, and the Commercial Free Zone Act. As a whole, low tax rates draw investment to Belize.

Although Belize offers a number of fiscal and other incentives for foreign investment, these concessions must be first be negotiated and evaluated with the government. However, under its designation as a Caribbean Basin Initiative (CBI) beneficiary, investor interest has increased markedly. The government has also begun the sale of Belize citizenship to those willing to pay from $35,000 up to $50,000 for the honor, especially to those from the US, UK, Ireland, and Canada.

The government promotes investment in the fields of agriculture, tourism, light manufacturing, fish processing, and forestry. Certain existing sector investments may require special permits and licenses, such as in the sugar can cultivation industry. Foreign direct investment totaled $26 million in 1998, up from $17 million in 1997, and only $7 million in 1987.

39ECONOMIC DEVELOPMENT

The government has opted to concentrate on developing agriculture, livestock, forestry, fishing, and tourism as foreign exchange earners. The main sources of bilateral aid are the US and the UK; of multilateral aid, the UN, CDB, OAS and IDB. Belize joined the OAS and IDG in 1992 in a move to increase its access to developing financing and external technical cooperation.

Belize undertook several fiscal adjustment measures in 1996, including the retrenchment of the public sector work force and the introduction of a major value-added tax (VAT) of 15%. These two measures caused an increase in annual inflation from 3.2% in 1995 to 4.7% in 1996 and an increase of 1.3% in the rate of unemployment, to 13.8% of the labor force.

The National Development Strategy 1996–2000 drafted by the Ministry of Economic Development stressed fiscal restraint, and identified activities to stimulate private sector development, including physical infrastructure improvement and financial sector reforms.

The inflation rate was at 0.50% in 1998, but unemployment was still at 13%. The VAT was replaced with a lower sales tax, and the financial services industry was reformed to encourage foreign investment. Major capital projects were underway to improve roads and build homes, but were moving at an extremely slow pace.

40SOCIAL DEVELOPMENT

Social security systems were first set up in 1979. Both employers and employees make contributions towards old age pensions, disability, survivor, and health benefits. Retirement is set at age 60 for both men and women, and benefits of 30% of average earnings are paid in addition to 2% of earnings for contributions in excess of 500 weeks. Workers' compensation was introduced in 1981 and covers all employed persons over the age of 14.

Women have access to education and are active in all areas of national life, but face domestic violence and certain types of discrimination in the business sector. As of 1998, five of 37 members of parliament were women. The Women's Bureau of the Ministry of Labor and Social Services develops programs to improve the status of women. Despite these efforts, most women work in low-wage industries and in agriculture. The Families and Children Act, passed in 1998, authorizes the state to legally remove a child from an abusive environment and raises from 16 to 18 the age up to which parents are legally responsible for the care of their children.

The rights of minority groups in Belize are generally well protected, although as of 1996 there have been continued reports of poor treatment of immigrant agricultural workers. The government has generally been cooperative with human rights organizations.

Human rights are generally respected, although there have been reports of extrajudicial killing, use of excessive police force, and other violations.

41HEALTH

Belize is relatively free of endemic diseases; however, since 1976 there has been an increase in the incidence of reported malaria cases. In 1995, 9,413 malaria cases were diagnosed, and Belize was reported as a cholera infected country in 1996, with 25 reported cases during that year. During 1996, 38 cases of AIDS were reported. There are eight public hospitals. The Cayo and Belize districts have two hospitals each, and all the remaining districts have one. There are 40 health centers and 35 rural satellites. As of 1998, there were five physicians per 1,000 population, and 24 hospital beds per 1,000 population.

Life expectancy was 69 years in 1999, and the infant mortality rate in 1999 was 32 per 1,000 live births. The total fertility rate was 4.0. There were 30 births per 1,000 population in 1999. About 90% of one-year-old children had been vaccinated against measles by the mid-1990s. In 1995, 82% of the Belize population had access to safe water, and 57% had access to adequate sanitation.

42HOUSING

Housing is inadequate, and the situation has been aggravated by hurricane devastation. The government has put aside small sums for low-cost housing programs. At last estimate, some 80% of dwellings were detached houses, and more than 15% were apartments. Slightly under 60% were owner occupied; more than 25% were rented privately; over 10% were occupied rent free; and less than 5% were rented from the government. Approximately 70% of houses were wood; more than 10% were concrete; less than 10% adobe; and less than 5% were wood and concrete.

43EDUCATION

Although government statistics claim a 93% literacy rate, the adult illiteracy rate estimated by UNESCO stood at 29.7% in 1995. Primary education is free and compulsory for children between the ages of five and 14. In 1995, there were 51,377 pupils in 277 primary schools, with 1,976 teachers. There were 10,272 students and 758 teachers in secondary schools that same year. Schools are run either by the church or by the government. In 1995, it was estimated that 97% of school age children were enrolled in primary school. Approximately 36% of children (male, 33%; female, 39%) were enrolled in secondary school.

Belize's first university, the University College of Belize, was opened in 1986. The University of the West Indies maintains a School for Continuing Education (SCE) in Belize. There are also several colleges providing specialized training such as the Belize Technical College; the Belize Teachers' College; Belize College of Agriculture; and the Belize Vocational Training Center. There are also two special schools maintained by the government for children with mental and physical disabilities.

In 1996, 19.5% of central government expenditure was allocated to education.

44LIBRARIES AND MUSEUMS

The National Library Service maintains a central library in the Bliss Institute, a children's library, and a branch library in Belize City, as well as branches in all main towns and villages for a total of over 40 service points. The total book stock in 2000 was approximately 150,000 volumes. The remains of the ancient Maya civilization—the best known are at Xunantunich—are being excavated by the government. The Department of Archaeology in Belmopan houses artifacts thus far uncovered.

45MEDIA

Belize is connected by radiotelegraph and telephone with Jamaica, Guatemala, Mexico, and the US. This service, along with cable and telex services, is operated by Cable and Wireless Ltd. An automatic telephone network, covering the entire country, is operated by the Belize Telecommunications, which was fully privatized in early 1992. In 1996, Belize had 29,000 telephones. The Belize National Radio Network, a government station in Belize City, transmits in English and Spanish. The first privately owned commercial radio station began broadcasting in 1990. Altogether, there are one AM and 12 FM radio stations, two television stations, and several cable stations. In 1995, there were 115,000 radios. In 1997, there were 112 television sets per 1,000 population.

There are no daily newspapers. The largest weeklies in 1999 were *Amandala* (circulation 45,000) and *Belize Times* (circulation 6,000), both published in Belize City. The Belize Press Association was formed in 1995.

Though Belize's Constitution assures the freedom of speech and press, there are provisions for the curtailment of these freedoms, including a law forbidding citizens from questioning financial statements submitted by public officials. The Supreme Court has warned journalists that questioning the integrity of the Court or of its members could result in criminal charges. The government makes free use of Belize's largest radio facilities to produce partisan advertisements and party propaganda. The Belize Broadcasting Authority (BBA) asserts its right to delete defamatory or libelous material from political broadcasts.

[46]ORGANIZATIONS

Cooperatives have been actively encouraged. There are 78 agricultural cooperatives, 18 fishing, 7 bee keeper, 5 housing, 3 transport, 3 consumer, 1 arts and crafts, 1 women's, and 5 cooperative societies in the country. The Belize Chamber of Commerce and Industry has its headquarters in Belize City.

[47]TOURISM, TRAVEL, AND RECREATION

Belize is attracting growing numbers of tourists to its Mayan ruins, its barrier reef (the longest in the Western Hemisphere), and its beaches, forests, and wildlife. Tourist arrivals totaled 305,000 in 1997; mostly from the Americas. In the same year, tourist expenditures totaled US$87 million. There were 3,905 hotel rooms with 6,425 beds and an occupancy rate of 27% as of 1997.

In 1999, the UN estimated the cost of staying in Belize City at US$114 and elsewhere at US$99.

[48]FAMOUS BELIZEANS

George C. Price (b. 1919), leader of the PUP, became the country's first premier in 1964. Manuel Esquivel (b. 1940), leader of the UDP, was prime minister from 1984 to 1998.

[49]DEPENDENCIES

Belize has no territories or colonies.

[50]BIBLIOGRAPHY

Ball, Joseph W. *Cahal Pech, the Ancient Maya, and Modern Belize: The Story of an Archaeological Park*. San Diego: San Diego State University Press, 1993.

Bolland, O. Nigel. *Belize: A New Nation in Central America*. Boulder, Colo.: Westview, 1986.

——. *The Formation of a Colonial Society: Belize, from Conquest to Crown Colony*. Baltimore: Johns Hopkins University Press, 1977.

Fernandez, Julio A. *Belize: Case Study for Democracy in Central America*. Brookfield, Vt.: Avebury, 1989.

Grant, Cedric Hilburn. *The Making of Modern Belize: Politics, Society, and British Colonialism in Central America*. New York: Cambridge University Press, 1976.

Kelly, Joyce. *An Archaeological Guide to Northern Central America: Belize, Guatemala, Honduras, and El Salvador*. Norman, Okla.: University of Oklahoma Press, 1996.

McClaurin, Irma. *Women of Belize: Gender and Change in Central America*. New Brunswick, N.J.: Rutgers University Press, 1996.

Merrill, Tim, ed. *Guyana and Belize: Country Studies*. 2nd ed. Washington, D.C.: Government Printing Office, 1993.

Setzkorn, William David. *Formerly British Honduras: A Profile of the New Nation of Belize*. Rev. ed. Athens, Oh.: Ohio University Press, 1981.

Wright, Ronald. *Time among the Maya: Travels in Belize, Guatemala, and Mexico*. New York: Weidenfeld & Nicolson, 1989.

BOLIVIA

Republic of Bolivia
República de Bolivia

CAPITALS: Sucre (legal and judicial capital); La Paz (administrative capital).

FLAG: The flag is a horizontal tricolor of red, gold, and green stripes, representing the animal, mineral, and vegetable kingdoms, respectively, with the coat of arms centered on the yellow band.

ANTHEM: *Himno Nacional,* beginning "Bolivianos, el hado propicio coronó nuestros volos anhelos" ("Bolivians, propitious fate crowned our outcries of yearning").

MONETARY UNIT: The boliviano (B) was introduced on 1 January 1987, replacing the peso at a rate of P1,000,000 = B1. There are coins of 2, 5, 10, 20, and 50 cents and 1 boliviano and notes of 2, 5, 10, 20, 50, 100, and 200 bolivianos. B1 = $0.16529 (or $1 = B6.050) as of 31 March 2000.

WEIGHTS AND MEASURES: The metric system is the legal standard, but some Spanish weights are still used in retail trade.

HOLIDAYS: New Year's Day, 1 January; Labor Day, 1 May; National Festival, 5–7 August; Columbus Day, 12 October; All Saints' Day, 1 November; Christmas, 25 December. Movable holidays include Carnival, Ash Wednesday, Holy Thursday, Good Friday, Holy Saturday, and Corpus Christi.

TIME: 8 AM = noon GMT.

¹LOCATION, SIZE, AND EXTENT

Situated in South America just N of the Tropic of Capricorn, Bolivia has a total area of 1,098,580 sq km (424,164 sq mi), extending about 1,530 km (950 mi) N–S and 1,450 km (900 mi) E–W. Comparatively, the area occupied by Bolivia is slightly less than three times the size of the state of Montana. Completely landlocked, Bolivia is bounded on the N and NE by Brazil, on the SE by Paraguay, on the S by Argentina, on the SW by Chile, and on the W by Peru, with a total boundary length of 6,743 km (4,190 mi).

The capital city of Bolivia, La Paz, is located in the west-central part of the country.

²TOPOGRAPHY

Bolivia has three geographic zones: the Andean highlands in the west, running north to south; the moist slopes and valleys on the eastern side of the Andes, called the Yungas and Valles; and the eastern tropical lowland plains, or Oriente. In Bolivia, the Andes, divided into two chains, attain their greatest width, about 640 km (400 mi), and constitute about one-third of the country. Between the Cordillera Occidental, forming the border with Chile and cutting Bolivia off from the Pacific, and the complex knots of the Cordillera Oriental lies a broad sedimentary plateau about 4,000 m (13,000 ft) above sea level, called the Altiplano, which contains about 28% of Bolivia's land area and more than half of its population. In the north of this plateau, astride the border with Peru, lies Lake Titicaca, 222 km (138 mi) long and 113 km (70 mi) wide; with its surface at an altitude of more than 3,660 m (12,000 ft), it is the highest navigable lake in the world. The lake is drained to the south by the 320-km (200-mi) Desaguadero River, which empties into shallow, salty Lake Poopó. Farther south are arid salt flats. The Cordillera Oriental has high habitable basins and valleys collectively referred to as the Puna. Bolivia's most majestic mountains are in the northern part of the Cordillera Oriental around Lake Titicaca, where the mountain sector is capped with snow; the highest of these is Ancohuma (6,550 m/21,489 ft). Illimani and Illampu, both rising more than 6,400 m (21,000 ft), overlook the city of La Paz, which is protected from cold winds by its position in the spectacular gorge formed by the headwaters of the La Paz River. The three important valleys of this region, Cochabamba, Sucre, and Tarija, are from 1,830 to 3,050 m (6,000 to 10,000 ft) in altitude.

Bolivia's important rivers descend across the Yungas and Valles into the low tropical plains of the Oriente, which comprises three-fifths of the land but only about one-fifth of the population. The Guaporé, the Mamoré, the Beni, and the Madre de Dios rivers cross the often-flooded northern savanna and tropical forests, all converging in the northeast to form the Madeira, which flows into Brazil. The plains become drier in the southeast, forming Bolivia's scrub-covered Chaco. Crossing the Chaco to the southeast, the Pilcomayo River leaves Bolivia to form the border between Paraguay and Argentina.

³CLIMATE

Although Bolivia lies entirely in the tropics, extreme differences in altitude and rainfall give it a great variety in climate. The mean annual temperature of La Paz, at 3,697 m (12,130 ft), is about 8°C (46°F); that of Trinidad, in the eastern lowlands, is 26°C (79°F). In the western highlands, cold winds blow all year round; at night the temperature often drops below freezing, but the sun is intense and the air brilliant during the day. The rainy season lasts from December to February, but during most of the year the high Altiplano plateau is parched and inhospitable. Around Lake Titicaca, rainfall is adequate, but there is less than 5 cm (2 in) a year in the extreme southwest. The fertile valleys in the Cordillera Oriental have a warmer, semiarid Mediterranean climate.

The Yungas and Valles have a semitropical, moist climate that gradually becomes hotter as one descends from the eastern slopes of the Andes to the tropical eastern lowlands. Rainfall is heavy in the northeast, and floods are common in March and April. The lowland plain becomes drier to the south, until it reaches drought conditions near the Argentine border.

4 FLORA AND FAUNA

Bolivia shares much of the wide variety of flora and fauna found in the four countries surrounding it. Because of the wide range in altitude, Bolivia has plants representative of every climatic zone, from arctic growth high in the sierra to tropical forests in the Amazon basin. On the high plateau above 3,050 m (10,000 ft) grows a coarse bunch grass called ichu, used for pasture, thatching, and weaving mats. A reed called totora, which grows around Lake Titicaca, is used for making small fishing boats (balsas). The low bushlike tola and the resinous mosslike yareta are both used for fuel. The Lake Titicaca region is believed to be the original home of the potato.

In the tropical forest, the quinine-producing quina tree grows, as does the Pará rubber tree. There are more than 2,000 species of hardwoods. Aromatic shrubs are common, as are vanilla, sarsaparilla, and saffron plants. Useful native plants include palms, sweet potatoes, manioc, peanuts, and an astonishing variety of fruits. The Chaco is covered with a prickly scrub collectively called monte; tannin-producing quebracho trees also abound there.

On the Altiplano, the most important animal is the llama, one of the most efficient carrier animals known; alpaca and guanaco and several varieties of cavy (guinea pig) are found there, too. Lake Titicaca has several varieties of edible fish. In the tropical Amazon region are the puma, coati, tapir, armadillo, sloth, peccary, capiguara (river hog), and ant bear, as well as several kinds of monkeys. Birdlife is rich and varied. Reptiles and an enormous variety of insects are found below 3,050 m (10,000 ft).

5 ENVIRONMENT

The chief environmental problem in the densely populated Altiplano is soil erosion, resulting from poor cultivation methods (including slash-and-burn agriculture) and overgrazing. Erosion currently affects 30% of the land in Bolivia. Salinity and alkalinization are also a significant problem. Inadequate sanitation and solid-waste disposal, as well as effluents from mining activities, contribute to the Altiplano's declining water quality, which poses a threat both to fish life and to human health. Bolivians have 72.0 cu mi of water supply, but 22% of the city dwellers and 78% of all rural people do not have pure water. The main sources of water pollution are fertilizers, pesticides, and mining. Most environmental legislation dates from the 1970s, when Bolivia enacted the Health Code of 1978 (which contains provisions governing water quality), the National General Forest Act of 1974, and the Law of Wildlife, National Parks, Hunting, and Fishing (Decree Law No. 12,301) of 1975.

In July 1987, the Bolivian government became the first government in history to agree to protect a part of its environment in return for a reduction of its foreign debt, when Conservation International, a US nonprofit group, purchased $650,000 of the debt in return for Bolivia setting aside 1.5 million hectares (3.7 million acres) of tropical lowlands in three conservation areas. As of the mid-1990s, 8.4% of Bolivia's total land area was protected. The Department of Science and Technology, within the Ministry of Planning and Coordination, plans and coordinates all governmental and intergovernmental activities related to the environment.

Endangered species in Bolivia include the puna rhea, South American river turtle, broad-nosed caiman, spectacled caiman, black caiman, jaguar, jaguarundi, margay, ocelot, emperor tamarin, and giant anteater. The llama and the alpaca are also threatened with extinction. In the mid-1990s, out of a total of 267, 21 mammals were considered endangered. There were 34 threatened species of birds in a total of 1,177 species. Four species of reptiles out of 180 and one species of fish were also considered endangered. Of 15–18,000 plant species, 39 were in danger of extinction.

6 POPULATION

The population of Bolivia in 2000 was estimated at 8,139,180. An estimated 3.9% of the population is 65 years of age or older. The projected population for the year 2005 is 8,921,000, assuming a crude birthrate of 27 per 1,000 population and a death rate of 8, resulting in a natural rate of change of 1.9% for the period 2000–2005. The population rate of change between 1995 and 2000 was 2.3%. The population density in 1998 was 7 per sq km (18 per sq mi).

It was estimated that 65% of the population lived in urban areas in 2000, up from 46% in 1980. Three-fourths of the total population lives on the Altiplano or in the western mountain valleys; the southeastern lowlands are sparsely populated. The administrative capital, La Paz, had a 2000 metropolitan population of 1,458,000. Santa Cruz, a departmental capital, had a 2000 metropolitan population of 1,110,000. Sucre, the legal and judicial capital, had 152,000. Other important departmental capitals include Cochabamba, 377,259; Oruro, 195,239; and Potosí, 114,092.

7 MIGRATION

Aside from Spaniards during the colonial period, European immigration has been insignificant. Small numbers of Italians, Poles, and Germans have settled mainly in the vicinity of La Paz and Cochabamba, and some Jewish refugees from Nazi Germany arrived in the 1930s. After World War II, about 1,000 Japanese settled in colonies around Santa Cruz and became successful in truck farming, and several hundred Okinawan families established themselves as rice growers in the same area.

Since the 1950s, migration to neighboring countries has increased: 30,000 left Bolivia in 1950–55; 40,000 left in 1980–85. About 675,000 Bolivians were estimated to reside outside the country in the late 1980s, in search of employment and better economic opportunities. Since the emigrants tend to have basic training or technical skills, a drain of important human resources is occurring. A number of Bolivian braceros (contract agricultural laborers) go to northwestern Argentina to work in rice and sugar harvests. In the 1970s, Brazilian settlers, drawn by improved railroad and highway links, migrated to northeastern Bolivia in growing numbers; these immigrants had a substantial influence on the region, since they continued to speak Portuguese and to use Brazilian currency as their medium of exchange. Within the country, migration is swelling the sparsely populated lowlands, particularly in Santa Cruz and its environs. High unemployment among agricultural laborers and miners has caused significant migration to the cities. The net migration rate for 1999 was -1.5 migrants per 1,000 population.

As of September 1999, the refugee population in Bolivia totaled 351, of whom some 230 benefited from UNHCR programs. Most refugees are from Peru (90%), Cuba (5%), and Colombia (3%) and live in La Paz and Santa Cruz.

8 ETHNIC GROUPS

Estimates of the makeup of the Amerindian population are 30% Quechua and 25% Aymará. Cholos (Bolivians of mixed white and Amerindian lineage) make up another 25 to 30%, and those of wholly European background account for virtually all of the remainder. One reason for the uncertainty of these estimates is that although the distinction between Amerindian, cholo, and white was at one time racial, it has gradually become at least partially sociocultural: Amerindians become cholos when they abandon their native costumes, learn to speak Spanish, and acquire a skill or trade. Not all those classified as whites are without some Amerindian mixture.

The rapidly disappearing Amerindians who populate the tropical plains in the southeast, the Chiriguanos, are believed to be a Guaraní tribe that moved west from Paraguay before the

LOCATION: 9°40′ to 22°53′s; 57°29′ to 69°35′w. **BOUNDARY LENGTHS:** Brazil, 3,125 km (1,942 mi); Paraguay, 756 km (470 mi); Argentina, 742 km (461 mi); Chile, 861 km (535 mi); Peru, 1,048 km (651 mi).

Spanish conquest. The Mojenos, Chiquitanos, and Sirionós inhabit the forest-grassland border in the far east. In all, Amerindians number about 100,000.

⁹LANGUAGES

Spanish, Quechua, and Aymará are all official languages. About 40% of Bolivians speak Spanish as a mother tongue. As spoken by educated Bolivians, it differs less from Castilian than do the dialects of many regions in Spain itself. Approximately 37% of the people still speak Quechua, and 24% speak Aymará,

although an increasing number of Amerindians also speak Spanish.

¹⁰RELIGIONS

The constitution provides for religious freedom, and the government reportedly respects this right in practice. Roman Catholicism is the dominant religion, and the constitution recognizes it as the official religion. The Roman Catholic Church receives support from the State and exercises a certain degree of political influence through the Bolivian Bishops' Conference.

According to 1998 estimates, between 60% and 70% of the population is Roman Catholic. Most of the country's 400 other religious groups are Protestant. Missionary groups include Mennonites, Mormons, Seventh-Day Adventists, Baptists, Pentecostals, and various evangelical groups. There is a small Jewish community with a synagogue in La Paz, as well as a Muslim community with a mosque in Santa Cruz. Korean immigrants also have a church in La Paz. There are small Buddhist and Shinto communities, and a substantial number of Baha'is. Indigenous beliefs and rituals are exercised by the Aymara and Quechua Indians, and many native superstitions persist.

11TRANSPORTATION

Transportation in Bolivia has been seriously impeded both by the geographic configuration of the country and by the concentration of population and mineral wealth in the mountain regions. Railroads and highways twist along the Andean Range, and are often blocked by mudslides during the rainy season. The shortage of transportation facilities is one of the most serious barriers to economic development. Railroads are almost entirely single-track meter gauge, totaling 3,691 km (2,293 mi) in 1999. All of the trackage is government owned. A major portion of the railway system services the Altiplano, the western mountainous region, providing vital international connections with Pacific coast ports. The remaining track connects the eastern city of Santa Cruz with Brazil and Argentina. An important route to Puerto Suárez eventually reaches the Brazilian port of Santos, while the line to Argentina via Villazón continues on to Buenos Aires. The two systems are administered by the government-owned National Railway Co.; two smaller lines (157 km/98 mi) are run by the Mining Corp. of Bolivia and by the Pulacayo mining enterprise.

In 1999, of a total of 52,216 km (32,447 mi) of roads, only about 2,872 km (1,785 mi) were paved, including 27 km (17 mi) of expressways. The Cochabamba-Santa Cruz highway, completed in 1963, was a major achievement in connecting lowland and highland Bolivia. In 1996 there were 547,000 motor vehicles, of which 357,000 were passenger cars, and 189,000 were commercial vehicles.

Airlines are particularly important in view of Bolivia's topography and the underdevelopment of other means of transportation. In 1998, there were an estimated 1,130 airports, only 12 of which had paved runways. The hub of air traffic is El Alto airport near La Paz, the world's highest commercial airport; the other international airport is at Santa Cruz. Lloyd Aéreo Boliviano (LAB), with 50% government capital, services most of the country. In 1997, 2,251,000 passengers were carried on scheduled international and domestic flights. Military Air Transport, operated by the air force, provides some civilian freight and passenger service, and numerous air taxi companies are also in service.

Little use has been made of Bolivia's 10,000 km (6,214 mi) of commercially navigable waterways. The merchant marine had 6 vessels (1,000 GRT or over), totaling 34,948 GRT in 1998. There are no regular riverboat services. Bolivia has free port privileges at Antofagasta and Arica (Chile), at Mollendo (Peru), and at Santos (Brazil).

12HISTORY

By about AD 600, Amerindians (believed to belong to the Aymará-speaking Colla tribe) were settled around the southern end of Lake Titicaca. As they came into contact with coastal tribes, the highly developed classic Tiahuanaco civilization emerged, reaching its peak about AD 900. Lake Titicaca became a place of worship and a great commercial center. Then cultural and political disintegration set in, and by 1300, the Quechua-speaking Incas had conquered the region and had colonized villages in most of what is now Bolivia.

The demise of the Inca empire began in 1527 with the death of the Inca Emperor Huayna Capac. His two sons, Huáscar and Atahualpa, fought a civil war over succession. Francisco Pizarro, taking advantage of the civil war raging between the two heirs, led the Spanish conquest of the Inca Empire in 1532–33. In 1539, Pedro de Anzures established La Plata, subsequently called Charcas and Chuquisaca and now known as Sucre, Bolivia's legal and judicial capital.

The Spaniards did not become interested in the land called Alto Peru, or Upper Peru, until the discovery in 1545 of the fabulously rich silver mine called the Cerro Rico (Rich Hill) de Potosí. Three years later, La Paz was founded on the main silver transport route between Potosí and the coast. In 1559, the audiencia (region under a royal court) of Charcas was established in Upper Peru under the viceroyalty of Lima. The mines continued to produce vast amounts of wealth for the Spanish Empire, and for years the city of Potosí was the largest city in the Western Hemisphere. In 1776, the audiencia was appended to the viceroyalty of La Plata (Buenos Aires).

The independence of Upper Peru came from the revolt of the small, native-born Spanish ruling class. In 1809, a year after Napoleon's invasion of Spain, the Spanish authorities in Chuquisaca (Sucre) were temporarily overthrown, and the local elite proclaimed independence. The movement was quickly put down by Spanish arms. The young government in Buenos Aires showed some interest in the region, having included delegates from Upper Peru when independence was declared at the Congress of Tucumán in 1816. However, independence came from Peru, after Simón Bolívar's victory at the battle of Ayacucho in December 1824. Bolívar then sent his young general, Antonio José de Sucre, to free Upper Peru. On 6 August 1825 a congress at Chuquisaca formally proclaimed the independence of the Republic of Bolívar, a name soon changed to Bolivia. Sucre was chosen as the first president in 1826, and Chuquisaca was renamed Sucre in his honor.

Sucre was driven out of office after only two years. He was succeeded by Gen. Andrés de Santa Cruz, a man with imperial ambitions. In 1836, Santa Cruz conquered Peru and formed the Peruvian-Bolivian Confederation. In 1839, Chilean forces defeated and dissolved the confederation and ended the life term of Santa Cruz.

A period of instability followed, with civilians and army officers succeeding one another, usually by force of arms. The almost constant civil war retarded Bolivia's economic organization and helped bring about the loss of a large part of its land. The first of these losses came after the War of the Pacific (1879–84), pitting Chile against Bolivia and Peru. Chile's superior military force routed the Bolivians and seized what was then the Bolivian port of Antofagasta. The post-war settlement took away Bolivia's only coastal territory, as well as the nitrate-rich coastal area around it. Bolivia was forever after a landlocked country, with only rights of access to the Pacific under a 1904 treaty. Another territorial loss came in 1903 with the cession to Brazil of the Acre region, rich in natural rubber, in exchange for an indemnity and other minor concessions.

The economy was aided in the late 19th century by a silver boom. When prices collapsed, silver production gave way to tin mining. The dominance of mining in Bolivia's economy conditioned the political system. A few wealthy mine and plantation owners, allied with various foreign interests, competed for power. Indians, excluded from the system, found their lot unchanged after almost 400 years.

This arrangement began to unravel with yet another loss of Bolivian territory. In 1932, Bolivia warred with Paraguay over the Chaco, the lowland area believed at the time to be rich in oil. Despite their numerical superiority, the Bolivians were defeated by 1935, and Paraguay controlled about three-fourths of the disputed territory. The formal settlement in 1938 gave most of this land to Paraguay, although Bolivia was promised a corridor to the Paraguay River.

The Chaco war pointed out the weaknesses in Bolivia's political and social structure. Bolivia's loss was in part due to the poor morale of its soldiers, an army of conscripted Indians with no loyalty to the elite officer corps. In 1936 Bolivia's rigid caste system cracked, and Col. David Toro came to power with labor support and a vaguely socialist/nationalist platform. The government expropriated Standard Oil of New Jersey's Bolivian properties in 1937. Toro's government attempted social reform, and its efforts to control mining and banking led to fierce opposition. The tension continued after Toro was forced out of office by Col. Germán Busch. Busch challenged Bolivia's three large tin-mining interests, owned by Patiño, Aramayo and Hochschild. With strong labor backing, Busch arranged for the constitution of 1938, a document guaranteeing the right of labor to organize, universal education, and nationalized subsoil rights. The very next year, Busch died in what was officially ruled a suicide.

World War II brought further strains to Bolivia. As world demand skyrocketed, the tin market boomed, but working conditions remained miserable, and wages remained low. In 1942, protests by tin workers against the "tin barons" and their American financiers was met with force by the government of Gen. Enrique Peñaranda, resulting in the "Catavi massacre." Wishing to retain the strategic materials in mid-war, the United States commissioned a US-Bolivian commission to study working conditions. This report confirmed the workers' grievances, but was completely ignored by Peñaranda. In December of 1943, a coalition of the army and the Nationalist Revolutionary Movement (Movimiento Nacionalista Revolucionario—MNR), which had gained considerable support among the mine workers, engineered a coup, ousting Peñaranda and putting Maj. Gualberto Villarroel into power. The tin market collapsed at the war's end, weakening the government's power base. In 1946, Villarroel was overthrown and hanged, along with others, by a mob of workers, soldiers, and students, and a conservative government was installed.

In 1951, the MNR's candidate, Víctor Paz Estenssoro, a former associate of Villarroel, apparently won the presidential election, but a military junta stepped in, denying the legality of the vote. Paz, representing the left wing of the MNR, became president in 1952 as a result of a party-led uprising. For the next 12 years, Bolivian politics would be dominated by the MNR.

The leadership of the MNR was shared by four men: Paz, Juan Lechín Oquendo, leftist head of the miners' union, Hernán Siles Zuazo, close ally of Paz, and the right-wing Walter Guevara Arze. A pact among the four was to allow them to take turns in the presidency over the next 16 years. The Paz government made dramatic moves in an attempt to transform Bolivian society. The tin holdings of the three dominant family interests were expropriated, and a comprehensive land reform program was begun, along with wide-scale welfare and literacy programs. Industry was encouraged, the search for oil deposits was accelerated, and a new policy gave Amerindians the right to vote and sought to integrate the Amerindian community more fully into the national economy. The right to vote, previously restricted to literate Bolivian males (who constituted less than 10% of the population), was made universal for all Bolivians over 21.

In 1956, as expected, Hernán Siles succeeded to the presidency. But Siles only governed under Paz's watchful eye, and in 1960, Paz challenged the candidacy of Guevara Arze. Guevara went into exile, and Paz again assumed the presidency, with Lechín as his vice-president. Paz became increasingly dictatorial, and the splits within the MNR worsened. Paz conspired to give himself yet another presidential term, complete with rigged elections in June 1964. Siles, now leading the right wing of the MNR, and Lechín, now leading the leftist opposition, conducted a hunger strike protesting Paz's authoritarian designs. Finally, the military defected when it became clear that Paz was without any allies. The military coup occurred in November 1964, with the junta selecting as president Paz's vice-president René Barrientos Ortuño.

Barrientos moved quickly to consolidate his new government, removing Paz's old supporters and sending Lechín into exile. In the following year, a military faction forced Barrientos to allow Gen. Alfredo Ovando Candia to become his "co-president." This odd arrangement was resolved in 1966 with new elections. Barrientos and his newly formed Popular Christian Movement won a resounding victory.

In 1967, an active guerrilla movement with pro-Castro tendencies emerged in southeastern Bolivia. The Bolivian authorities imprisoned the French intellectual Jules Régis Debray, who revealed that the famous comrade of Fidel Castro, Ernesto "Che" Guevara, was leading the guerrilla movement. Later in the year, the Bolivian army apprehended and killed Guevara.

Barrientos died in a helicopter crash in April 1969, and a civilian, Vice-President Adolfo Siles Salinas, became president. Siles was overthrown in September by Barrientos' former rival, Gen. Ovando, who presented himself as a presidential candidate for 1970 but then canceled the election. In October 1970, President Ovando was overthrown by rightist elements of the military, but the next day a leftist faction succeeded in making Gen. Juan José Torres Gonzales the new president.

The Torres regime was marked by increasing political instability. Backed by students and the Bolivian Labor Council, Torres expelled the US Peace Corps, permitted the expropriation of both US and privately owned Bolivian properties, sanctioned the seizure of land by landless peasants, established a labor-dominated People's Assembly, and declared its support for the reestablishment of diplomatic relations with Cuba. In a bloody three-day revolution in August 1971, the Torres government was ousted by a coalition of the armed forces and political leaders from the MNR and the Bolivian Socialist Falange (Falange Socialista Boliviana—FSB), together with other middle-class groups. The leader of the coup was Hugo Banzer Suárez, who was installed as president later in the month. Banzer consolidated his support with the founding of the Nationalist Popular Front, which became the political framework of the new government. Ex-president Paz returned from exile to head the MNR.

The first threats to the Banzer government came from the left. There were reports late in 1971 of renewed activity by the Guevarist National Liberation Army. The government launched a vigorous antiguerrilla campaign and claimed nearly complete success. In 1973, however, Banzer's coalition began to splinter. In 1974, when the MNR threatened to withdraw from the coalition, Paz went into exile again. After two coup attempts had been crushed in the fall of 1973 and two others in the summer of 1974, Banzer formed a new all-military cabinet. In November 1974, the MNR, the FSB, and other political parties were abolished, and trade union meetings were declared illegal.

In response to industrial and political unrest, Banzer announced the restoration of political parties in 1977 and of unions in 1978. He promised to hold new elections in July 1978. Paz again returned from exile to run. The election results were annulled, however, and a new military government came to power in a bloodless coup. Another election took place in July 1979, but because no candidate received a majority and the Congress could not decide whom to select from among the three main candidates, an interim president was named. Another coup followed in November, but constitutional government was restored only two weeks later, in the wake of popular resistance. New presidential and congressional elections in June 1980 again failed to produce a majority winner, and in July there was another coup, staged by Gen. Luis García Meza, who promptly suspended the Congress, banned most political parties and all union activity, and established strict censorship in order to remove the "Marxist cancer" from Bolivia. Paz again went into exile. During the García regime there were frequent reports of arbitrary arrests, use of torture, and other human rights violations. In August 1981, García, who was suspected, along with other top officials in the government, of involvement with the cocaine trade, was deposed in a coup—the 190th in Bolivian history. He went into exile in Argentina in October 1982, and in May 1983, he was ordered arrested on charges of "corruption and economic crimes"—specifically, the fraudulent use of government funds in agricultural, construction, and oil refinery deals. Meanwhile, under two more military governments, political and union rights were gradually restored.

In October 1982, amid a worsening economic situation and increasing labor unrest, the Congress elected Hernán Siles Zuazo to the presidency. Siles, returning to office 22 years after the end of his previous presidency, could still count on electoral support, and had received a plurality of votes in the 1979 and 1980 elections. His shaky coalition faced continued economic problems, including food shortages and rampant inflation, and a right-wing threat from paramilitary groups whose activities were reportedly financed by cocaine smuggling. In November 1983, the Bolivian government announced an austerity program that included a 60% devaluation of the peso and hefty food price increases. By mid-1985, Siles had so mismanaged the economy and the political situation that labor unrest and social tension forced him to call national elections and to agree to relinquish power a full year before the expiration of his term. Banzer won a plurality of the popular vote, but the MNR won more seats in the congressional elections, resulting in a fourth term of office for the 77-year-old Paz. In a departure from the norm, the MNR and Banzer's party agreed to cooperate, allowing a comprehensive economic reform package to pass through the legislature.

Faced with runaway inflation, which reached an annual rate of 14,000% in August 1985, the government abandoned controlled exchange rates, abolished price controls, liberalized external trade, and instituted more restrictive monetary and wage policies. The result was sharply lower inflation and interest rates, and a more stable economy, although the shocks of this liberalization were felt through government layoffs and falling consumer buying power.

More importantly, Paz was able to forge a fundamental consensus among competing political parties in support of a continuing democracy. In 1989, despite a hotly contested presidential race, power passed from the MNR to the left-wing movement of the Revolutionary Left (MIR.) The peaceful transfer of power from one party to another was a milestone in itself. An equally hopeful sign was the fact that the MIR leader, Jaime Paz Zamora, was able to hold together a coalition with the right-wing national Democratic Alliance (ADN) to serve a full four-year presidential term. In Bolivia, this is a major accomplishment.

The elections of 1993 brought the MNR back to power, with Gonzalo Sánchez de Lozada assuming the presidency. Sánchez chose as his running mate Victor Hugo Cárdenas, an advocate for Bolivia's Aymara-speaking Amerindians. While some saw the move as a cynical ploy, others expressed hope that Bolivia's long-suffering native population might be brought into the political system. Sanchez de Lozada's administration embarked on a wide-ranging program of reforms that included decentralization of government, tariff reduction, educational reform, and most notably, a major privatization campaign. State enterprises that were privatized included the national railroad, the state-owned airline, and the nation's electric power generation facilities. Sanchez de Lozada's plans also included privatization of Bolivia's mining sector through joint ventures with foreign investors. In spite of continued economic stabilization and progress, the government's policies drew protests and labor strikes leading to the declaration of a 90-day state of siege in 1995.

In 1997, General Hugo Banzer, the former dictator who had tried unsuccessfully to regain power by legal means since his ouster in 1978, came in first in the June presidential elections and, in the absence of an electoral majority, was chosen by Congress to be the nation's next president. Banzer, a conservative democrat, pledged to halt his predecessor's privatization program while improving basic services and expanding jobs. In March of 2000, after 30 months in power, Banzer faced growing social unrest resulting from an economic crisis and the government's inability to fight corruption and implement an effective anti-narcotics program.

13 GOVERNMENT

Constitutionally, Bolivia is a centralist republic. The constitution of 3 February 1967 (amended in 1994) provides for a representative democracy, with its government divided into an executive branch, a bicameral legislature (a Congress consisting of a Chamber of Deputies and a Senate), and the judiciary.

Bolivia has had a spotty constitutional history. The current constitution is the result of a series of actions begun by the military junta that took control in November 1964. The junta replaced the 1961 constitution with the 1945 constitution, as amended in 1947. At the same time, it retained those sections of the 1961 constitution that dealt with universal suffrage, nationalization of the tin mines, land reform, and compulsory education. The 1967 constitution was further amended to circumscribe the power of militia forces. In practice, the constitution has not been rigorously observed. Coups and states of siege have been frequent. Congress was dissolved by the armed forces from 1969 to 1979 and again between 1980 and 1982. The constitution was amended in 1994 to give more power to the president and recognize indigenous people.

Under the constitution, the president and the vice president are elected by direct popular vote for a four-year term and cannot serve consecutive terms. If no candidate receives a majority in a presidential election, the Congress chooses among the three leading candidates. However, between 1966 and 1978, no presidential elections were held. The president's powers are considerable, and presidential authority often extends beyond the constitution. The president has the prerogative to declare a state of siege and may then rule by decree for 90 days. The Congress consists of 27 senators (three from each department) and 130 deputies. Deputies are elected for four years and senators for six. Bolivia utilizes a form of proportional representation to ensure minority representation in the Chamber of Deputies and an incomplete-list system for the Senate. The regular session of Congress lasts for 90 days.

Universal suffrage, with no literacy or property qualifications, was decreed in 1952 for married persons at 18 years and single persons at 21. The constitution includes a bill of rights, which guarantees the right to express ideas freely, petition the government, and obtain a release under a writ of habeas corpus in case of illegal detention.

14 POLITICAL PARTIES

Bolivia's proportional representation system has encouraged the formation of several political parties. Numerous parties and coalitions have formed and dissolved over the years, usually tied to the personalities of the various leaders.

The Nationalist Revolutionary Movement (Movimiento Nacionalista Revolucionario—MNR) was founded by Víctor Paz Estenssoro, Hernán Siles Zuazo, and others in 1941. Although militant originally, the years have moderated the party's stance.

The MNR came to power in 1952, with the help of the Revolutionary Workers Party, the carabineros (national police), and the miners' and peasants' militias. In the subsequent years, the MNR began to rely increasingly on foreign aid, especially from the US, and became increasingly autocratic and corrupt. Finally, quarreling among the party leadership weakened the party, and by 1964 the MNR's monopoly on power had dissolved. In November 1964, Paz was sent into exile in Peru.

The MNR was then eclipsed by the charisma of President René Barrientos and his Popular Christian Movement. The MNR returned as part of the Nationalist Popular Front, organized by Hugo Banzer Suárez. Banzer then outlawed the MNR in November 1974. In the late 1970s, the MNR reappeared, along with a dissident MNRI (the "MNR of the left") headed by Hernán Siles.

With the restoration of Bolivian democracy, the MNRI won the presidency under Siles along with a coalition of leftist parties that included the Communist Party of Bolivia and the Movement of the Revolutionary Left (Movimiento de la Izquierda Revolucionaria—MIR), headed by Jaime Paz Zamora. MIR was an active partner in the Siles government; Paz Zamora was the vice president, and several MIR officials were in the cabinet. MIR won the presidency in 1989 after an extremely close election, and only after seeking support from the right-wing Democratic Nationalist Alliance (Alianza Democrática Nacionalista—ADN).

The ADN is closely tied to former President Hugo Banzer Suarez. Banzer, a former military officer, came to power in an alliance with the MNR, but eventually ruled as a military dictator. This right-wing party was denied power in 1985 by the MNR/MIR coalition. However, the ADN was instrumental in bringing Paz Zamora to power, and held half the ministerial positions in that government.

In addition to the center-left MNR, the leftist MIR, and the center-right ADN, leading political parties include the Civic Solidarity Union (UCS) and Conscience of the Fatherland (Condepa), both populist parties.

In June 1997 General Hugo Banzer, whose dictatorial regime ruled Bolivia from 1971 to 1978, placed first in the nation's presidential election and, with the backing of Congress, was sworn in in August. Banzer's own party, the ADN, formed a coalition government with the MIR, the UCS, and Condepa. According to preliminary results, the ADN won 13 of 27 contested Senate seats in the June 1997 election.

[15]LOCAL GOVERNMENT
Bolivia is essentially a unitary system, with a highly centralized national government. Bolivia's nine departments—La Paz, Cochabamba, Chuquisaca, Potosí, Oruro, Santa Cruz, Tarija, El Beni, and Pando—are administered by prefects appointed by the president for four-year terms. The departments are subdivided into 94 provinces, each headed by a subprefect recommended by the prefect, appointed by the president, and responsible to him through the minister of the interior. The provinces are further divided into 1,713 cantons, each of which is under the jurisdiction of a magistrate (corregidor). As of 1997, Bolivia had 312 municipalities. There are no local legislatures. Important towns and cities have more self-government. Each has a popularly elected council of from 5 to 12 members, but municipal tax ordinances must be approved by the Senate. Mayors (alcaldes) are also elected. The Amerindian communities, although they are not formal administrative units, are recognized by law.

[16]JUDICIAL SYSTEM
The Bolivian judiciary usually defers to the political direction of the nation's executive. Judicial power is exercised by the Supreme Court, the superior district courts in each department (courts of second instance), and the local courts (courts of first instance).

The Supreme Court, which sits at Sucre, is divided into four chambers: two deal with civil cases, one with criminal cases, and one with administrative, mining, and social cases. The 12 Supreme Court judges, called ministros, are chosen for 10-year terms by a two-thirds vote of the Chamber of Deputies from a list of three names submitted for each vacancy by the Senate. They may be reelected indefinitely.

Most cases that reach the Supreme Court are appellate; its area of original jurisdiction is limited mainly to decisions on the constitutionality of laws and to disputes involving diplomats or important government officials. Each district court judge is elected by the Senate for six years from a list of three submitted by the Supreme Court.

The district courts usually hear appeals from the courts of first instance. Judges of the courts of first instance (tribunales and juzgados) are chosen by the Supreme Court from a list submitted by the district courts. There is also a separate national labor court and an agrarian court, dealing with agrarian reform cases.

Defendants have a right to counsel, to confront witnesses, to present evidence, and to appeal. These rights are generally respected.

[17]ARMED FORCES
Since the 1985 elections, relative political stability and civilian control has reduced the power and cost of the military. In theory there is universal compulsory military training, but only some 20% of the registered youths (22,800 in 1999) are called for service. As of 2000, armed strength totaled 32,500 men (army, 25,000; a navy for lake and river patrol, 4,500; and air force, 3,000), plus a paramilitary police force of 31,100 and a 6,000-member narcotics squad. Defense expenditures in 1998 were $150 million, or 1.8% of the gross domestic product.

[18]INTERNATIONAL COOPERATION
Bolivia is a charter member of the UN, having joined on 14 November 1945, and participates in ECLAC and all the nonregional specialized agencies. It is a signatory of the Law of the Sea. As a member of the International Tin Council, Bolivia retains part of its tin exports to help stabilize prices. Bolivia is also a member of many inter-American and other intergovernmental organizations, notably the Andean Pact, G-77, IADB, LAIA, OAS, and the WTO.

[19]ECONOMY
Bolivia is one of the Western Hemisphere's poorest countries, despite an abundance of mineral resources. Its economy has always been dependent on mineral exports, principally of tin, but these have gradually declined since World War II. Little of the nation's great agricultural and forest potential has been developed; agriculture remains little above the subsistence level, and Bolivia must import large quantities of food. The completion of a natural gas pipeline to Brazil in 1999 may improve the state of the economy.

Bolivian economic production grew at a fairly steady rate of about 5% during the 1960s and 1970s; but in the 1980s, growth was negative. The average growth between 1977 and 1987 was -1.8%, but this improved during the 1990s with an average rate of 4.2%. Inflation, very low by Latin American standards in the 1960s when the average annual rate was 3.5%, began to increase during the 1970s, averaging more than 22% yearly, and reached 14,000% in August 1985, before declining to 10.5% at the end of July 1987.

In August 1985, President Paz implemented a drastic anti-inflationary program; he floated the peso, froze public-sector wages, cut public spending, eliminated controls on bank interest rates, authorized banks to make foreign-currency loans and offer foreign-currency accounts, initiated a comprehensive tax reform, eliminated price controls, established a uniform 20% tariff and removed tariff exemptions, eliminated virtually all import and export restrictions, and modified labor laws to permit greater flexibility in hiring and firing. The immediate result was a jump in capital repatriation and retention as a result of the rise in interest rates. The government also restructured several public-sector institutions, including the Central Bank and COMIBOL, the national mining corporation; the bank closed several branches and reduced staff by 70%, and COMIBOL closed numerous mines and dismissed nearly 20,000 workers.

As of 1999, Bolivia was in its second decade of democratic rule and its thirteenth consecutive year of economic expansion. Market reforms are firmly in place, investment is growing steadily and inflation is under control. Privatization of state-owned industries improved the investment environment of Bolivia. Growth was led by energy, mining, and agriculture; due to completion of the gas pipeline to Brazil, hydrocarbons exploration investments, and soy product investments. Inflation was substantially reduced from the incredible 14,000% in 1985 to only 4.4% in 1998.

20INCOME

The US Central Intelligence Agency (CIA) reports that in 1998 Bolivia's gross domestic product (GDP) was estimated at $23.4 billion. The per capita GDP was estimated at $3,000. The annual growth rate of GDP was estimated at 4.7%. The average inflation rate in 1998 was 4.4%. The CIA defines GDP as the value of all final goods and services produced within a nation in a given year and computed on the basis of purchasing power parity (PPP) rather than value as measured on the basis of the rate of exchange. It was estimated that agriculture accounted for 17% of GDP, industry 26%, and services 57%.

The World Bank reports that for the same period per capita private consumption (in PPP terms) was $1,880. Private consumption includes expenditures of individuals, households, and nongovernmental organizations. It was estimated that between 1990 and 1998 private consumption grew at an annual rate of 3.4%. Approximately 37% of household consumption was spent on food, 11% on fuel, 9% on health care, and 14% on education. The richest 10% of the population accounted for approximately 32% of household consumption and the poorest 10% approximately 2.3%.

21LABOR

The total employment was 1.3 million in 1996. Of these, about 18% were engaged in manufacturing, 2% in agriculture, 20% in commerce, and 8% in construction. Total unemployment was officially estimated at 4.2% in 1996. As of 1999, the monthly minimum wage was $56. As of 1996, approximately 20% of the work force was employed in the informal sector and, therefore, not covered by the minimum wage laws.

In theory, virtually the entire non-agricultural labor force, as well as part of the peasantry, is unionized, but only about one-half of those eligible actually belong to a union. The Central Bolivian Workers' Organization (Central Obrera Boliviana—COB) is the central labor federation, to which nearly all unions belong. The ministries of mines and petroleum, rural affairs, labor, and transportation are nominated by the COB and appointed by the president. Since 1985, the COB has lost influence as the government has pursued policies to stabilize the economic chaos and hyperinflation. The COB has largely abandoned traditional union responsibilities and directed its attention at overthrowing the government's "neoliberal" economic program (largely austerity measures and privatization).

Workers' militias were dissolved by order of the military junta after they had taken control of the mines in May 1965; there was also a purge of pro-Communist trade union leaders. In November 1974, union meetings were declared illegal, but union activity was permitted again in 1978. After the July 1980 coup, trade unions were again suspended, but they were permitted to resume activity in May 1982. In 1993, the COB staged serious work stoppages that resulted in violent confrontations and government concessions. Most recently, COB has not been very effective and has staged few strikes and/or demonstrations during 1996. The public schools were shut down by teachers' strikes for nearly all of February 1999.

22AGRICULTURE

An estimated 5% of Bolivia's land area is devoted to arable farming and permanent crops; another 24% is permanent pasture. Agricultural development has been impeded by extremely low productivity, poor distribution of the population in relation to productive land, and a lack of transportation facilities. Prior to 1953, about 93% of all privately owned land was controlled by only 6.3% of the landowners. The agrarian reform decree of August 1953 was aimed at giving ownership of land to those working it and abolishing the large landholdings (latifundios). By 1980, 30.15 million hectares (74.5 million acres) had been distributed to 591,310 families. By 1996, 60% of Bolivian agriculture was channeled to markets, and 40% was subsistence farming.

Except around Lake Titicaca, about two-thirds of the cultivated land on the Altiplano lies fallow each year. Dry agriculture is the rule, and the most important crops are potatoes, corn, barley, quinoa (a milletlike grain), habas (broad beans), wheat, alfalfa, and oca (a tuber). The potato is the main staple; dehydrated and frozen to form chuño or tunta, it keeps indefinitely. The Yungas and Valles contain about 40% of the cultivated land. The eastern slopes, however, are too steep to permit the use of machinery, and erosion is a serious problem despite the practice of terracing. The most lucrative crop in the Yungas is coca, which is chewed by the local population and from which cocaine is extracted. The net production of coca leaf was estimated at 52,900 tons in 1998, down from 89,800 tons in 1994. Coca leaf production in 1998 represented about 20% of world production. Coffee, cacao, bananas, yucca, and aji (a widely used chili pepper) are also important. In the fertile irrigated valleys, the important crops are corn, wheat, barley, vegetables, alfalfa, and oats. The Tarija area is famous for grapes, olives, and fruit. The region east of Santa Cruz de la Sierra, where most of the nation's unused fertile lands lie, is considered the "promised land" of Bolivian agriculture. Lowland rice production is increasing rapidly and already satisfies domestic need. The sugar grown there is used mostly for alcohol, but in the 1960s, the mills increased their refining capacity, thus meeting internal consumption requirements. In the tropical forests of the northeast, the Indians practice slash-and-burn agriculture.

The leading commercial crops are soybeans, cotton, sugar, and coffee. Area harvested and production in 1998 for selected crops are shown in the following table:

	AREA (HECTARES)	PRODUCTION (TONS)
Soybeans	581,000	1,071,000
Seed cotton	50,000	19,000
Sunflowers	143,000	115,000
Wheat	187,000	164,000
Coffee	25,000	24,000
Sugar	93,000	4,241,000
Rice	143,000	301,000

Droughts and freezing weather in the west during 1992, 1994, and 1995 caused harvests to fall for basic crops like quinoa, potatoes, barley, and garden vegetables.

²³ANIMAL HUSBANDRY

In 1998 there were an estimated 6.3 million head of cattle, 8.4 million sheep, 1.5 million goats, 2.6 million hogs, 631,000 donkeys, and 322,000 horses. Poultry numbered 59 million in 1998.

The main cattle-raising department is El Beni, in the tropical northeast, which has about 30% of the nation's cattle. In 1994, a joint program began with Brazil to eradicate and control hoof and mouth disease in cattle, which had caused exports of beef to fall that year. Cochabamba is the leading dairy center, and improved herds there supply a powdered-milk factory. Genetic development helped increase milk production from an average of 113,000 tons annually during 1989–91 to 205,000 tons by 1998. The Amerindians of the high plateau depend on the llama because it can carry loads at any altitude and provides leather, meat, and dung fuel. Leading animal product exports are hides, alpaca and vicuña wool, and chinchilla fur. Breeding of alpacas and llamas is by and large left to chance; disease is rampant, and production is low, considering the relatively large numbers of animals. Llamas and alpacas are grown for their wool and meat in the Altiplano of La Paz, Potosi, and Oruro. In 1995, the llama population was about two million, and the alpacas numbered 324,336. The UN and the Integrated Association of Camelmen in the High Andes began a program in 1994 to improve the quality of the animals' meat and wool.

²⁴FISHING

Fishing is a minor activity in Bolivia. A few varieties of fish are caught in Lake Titicaca by centuries-old methods and sent to La Paz. The catch was 6,425 tons in 1997. Bolivia has some of the world's largest rainbow trout, and Bolivian lakes are well stocked for sport fishing.

²⁵FORESTRY

Bolivia is potentially one of the world's most important forestry nations. More than half of the total area is held as public land by the state, and more than 40 million hectares (100 million acres) of forest and woodland are maintained as reserves or for immediate exploitation. About 53% of Bolivia's land area consists of forests and woodlands. Trees are mostly evergreens and deciduous hardwoods, with the richest forests on the Andes' eastern slope along the tributaries of the Amazon; humid tropical and subtropical forests account for 37% of Bolivia's forests. More than 2,000 species of tropical hardwoods of excellent quality, such as mahogany, jacaranda, rosewood, palo de balsa, quina, ironwood, colo, and cedar, abound in this area. Sawmills are few, however, and the almost total lack of transportation facilities has made exploitation expensive. Most of the sawmills are in the eastern department of Santa Cruz. Roundwood production in 1997 was 2,315,000 cu m, up from 1,632,000 cu m in 1991. About 50% of Bolivia's exports are derived from forestry. Bolivia is one of South America's leading rubber exporters.

²⁶MINING

Bolivia is the fourth-largest tin-producing nation, after China, Brazil, and Indonesia. Nonfuel mineral exports were valued at $482 million in 1997, constituting about 40% of the nation's exports that year. Zinc became the most valuable export in 1997, producing an income of about $200 million, followed by gold, which earned $110 million.

For two centuries following the discovery of silver at Cerro Rico de Potosí in 1545, the area that is now Bolivia was the world's largest silver producer. Tin production began about 1870 and had surpassed silver in value by the beginning of the 20th century. Before 1952, 80% of the nation's mineral production was in the hands of three mining companies: the Patiño, Hochschild, and Aramayo interests. In that year, they were expropriated and turned over to the Mining Corp. of Bolivia (Corporación Minera de Bolivia—COMIBOL), a government enterprise. The overwhelming problems confronting COMIBOL included falling tin prices, rising production costs, and a shortage of technical personnel. By 1961, one pound of Bolivian tin, worth about $1.00 on the world market, cost $1.30 to produce. Another basic problem facing economic planners was the near exhaustion of the richest tin deposits. To revive the industry, COMIBOL installed equipment to improve recovery from low-grade ores, and the Bolivian government encouraged the export of processed metals, which are more profitable than raw ores. Tin, which used to account for over half the total mineral exports (54.2% in 1968), accounted for only 38.5% by 1973, largely because of the increasing importance of other mineral exports, including crude petroleum. In 1985, tin represented 29% of all export earnings; the collapse of the international tin market in October 1985 was a major blow to the economy. Siglo XX, at Llallague (south of Oruro), was once the world's largest single tin mine, but the mine closed in 1986. Total tin mine production in Bolivia was 12,898 tons in 1997; smelter production was reported at 16,853 tons. COMIBOL is now focusing on the attraction of private firms to operate its mines under joint-venture or operating contracts. Bolivia's tradition of state-owned monopolies is a highly politicized topic among the population; the government's capitalization plan became a way to bring Bolivia the benefits of privatization without entirely turning over state companies to private investors. New mining codes enacted on 3 April 1991 allow foreign firms to operate with fewer restrictions, and also replace royalties with a 30% tax on profits. In May 1994, the government invited bids for exploration and exploitation of all its undeveloped properties. By 1994, privately owned commercial mines became the dominant producer, responsible for 52% of the value of all mine production. COMIBOL has declined in importance relative to national production from 51% in 1985 to 25% in 1997.

Silver, zinc, tungsten, bismuth, lead, copper, gold, asbestos, and other metals are also exported. The nation's first antimony smelter began operations in 1975. Iron deposits have been discovered, and large salt deposits are found near Lake Poopó. Reported mineral output in 1994 was as follows (in tons): zinc, 154,491; tin, 12,898; lead, 18,608; antimony, 5,999; tungsten, 513; and arsenic, 282. Other minerals produced that year include silver, 387,200 kg; gold, 13,292 kg; and rough amethyst, 122 kg.

²⁷ENERGY AND POWER

Installed capacity at Bolivian electric power plants rose from 267,000 kW in 1970 to 971,000 kW in 1998. Total electric power output in 1998 was 2,576 million kWh, of which about 60% was hydroelectric; much of the total was produced by the Canadian-owned Bolivian Power Co., which supplies the cities of La Paz and Oruro. Another large producer is COMIBOL, which operates two plants on its own and also buys power from the government-run National Electricity Co. Bolivia's electricity sector consists of an interconnected system and three main isolated systems. In 1996, the interconnected system accounted for about 90% of national electricity consumption and 77% of installed capacity.

Petroleum production peaked in 1974 but then began to decline because of well depletion; in 1980, Bolivia became a net importer of oil. In 1998, the total average daily production of crude oil was 35,000 barrels, and consumption was slightly higher, at 38,000 barrels per day. Production of natural gas gradually increased from the mid-1980s until the early 1990s; the estimate for 1997 was 3.2 billion cu m. In 1998, natural gas exports accounted for 26% of total exports. The first phase of a pipeline project linking Bolivia to Sao Paulo, Brazil, was completed in February 1999 at a cost of $453 million and went into operation later the same year. Future pipeline plans include a pipeline to northern Chile, and a project to run a pipeline to Asuncion, Paraguay, with a possible extension to Curitiba, Brazil.

28 INDUSTRY

Historically, industrial development has been severely restricted by political instability, the small domestic market, the uncertain supply of raw materials, and the lack of technically trained labor. Domestic industry supplies less than one-fourth of the processed food and manufactured goods consumed. In 1998, manufacturing represented less than 17% of the GDP. Over one-half of output is in nondurable consumer goods—food, beverages, tobacco, and coffee. Handicrafts and hydrocarbons account for much of the remainder.

At their peak, Bolivia's tin mines accounted for 70% of the country's total export earnings, but in 1985 the London Metal Exchange abruptly halved the price of tin, causing economic chaos. The ensuing economic stabilization program was a mixed blessing to industry. The easing of foreign-exchange restrictions, the uniform 20% tariff, and the significant reduction in duties on nonessential consumer goods improved the availability of raw materials and semi-manufactured goods, thereby stimulating industrial growth.

In 1992, growth in the construction industry was a remarkable 15%, sustained both by the larger number of public works projects and by private investment. By 1995, this growth had slowed to 5%. The manufacturing sector grew by 3.8% in 1995, with the largest gains occurring in agriculture-based industries despite the problems resulting from the precarious state of agriculture. The mining and hydrocarbon sector contracted because of the decline in mining output and stagnation in the production of petroleum and natural gas. The drastic reduction of COMIBOL's production resulted from the closing of several mines and frequent labor disputes. The slump in the hydrocarbons subsector was because of the depletion of a number of wells, lack of investment in exploring for new deposits, and the torrential rains that damaged the infrastructure of the state-owned company.

In the late 1990s, Bolivia experienced a renaissance in the mining and hydrocarbons sectors because of privatization of the state-owned interests in these sectors. This attracted foreign interest in developing the energy and minerals potential of the country.

29 SCIENCE AND TECHNOLOGY

The Bolivian National Academy of Sciences was founded in 1960. Notable scientific and technological research institutes and learned societies include the Bolivian Geological Service and Bolivian Petroleum Institute, both in La Paz. Bolivia has eight universities offering courses in basic and applied sciences. In 1987–97, science and engineering students accounted for 30% of college and university enrollments. In 1987–97, Bolivia had 172 scientists and engineers and 154 technicians per million people engaged in research and development.

30 DOMESTIC TRADE

La Paz is the chief marketing center. Oruro is second to La Paz as a market for imported goods and is the main distributing center for mining supplies. Cochabamba distributes its agricultural production to La Paz and the mining districts. Buyers visit agricultural settlements by truck, purchase food for resale at city markets, and sell manufactured goods. Outside the main cities, most buying and selling is carried on at weekly markets and village fairs. In less accessible areas, barter is still common.

Advertising is not highly developed. Newspapers, radio stations, and movie theaters are the main advertising media. Regular retail store hours are weekdays, 9 AM to noon and 2:30 to 6:30 PM. Bank hours are 9 AM to noon and 2 to 4:30 PM.

31 FOREIGN TRADE

Bolivia depends primarily on its mineral exports, especially tin and natural gas. Tin exports, however, have been gradually decreasing since 1946. The 1985 devaluation of tin caused major problems in the Bolivian economy. Exports of natural and manufactured gas and petroleum are expected to surpass those of other minerals in the future.

Bolivia's main attraction, and export commodity, is its natural minerals, including tin, gold, and other ores (10%, 22%, and 19%). Tin exports from Bolivia account for over 8% of the world's total exports. The country also exports natural and manufactured gas (8.0%) to neighboring Brazil through a newly constructed pipeline. Agricultural exports include wood, oil seeds, animal feed, and sugar and honey (7.0%, 4.0%, 3.0% and 2.7%).

In 1997 Bolivia's imports were distributed among the following categories:

Consumer goods	8.7%
Food	8.3%
Fuels	7.3%
Industrial supplies	25.8%
Machinery	26.5%
Transportation	23.3%
Other	0.0%

Principal trading partners in 1998 (in millions of US dollars) were as follows:

COUNTRY	EXPORTS	IMPORTS	BALANCE
United States	303	627	-324
United Kingdom	199	17	182
Peru	140	88	52
Argentina	139	229	-90
Colombia	86	43	43
Ecuador	80	8	72
Chile	34	136	-102
Brazil	30	245	-215
Germany	21	56	-35
Japan	3	472	-469

32 BALANCE OF PAYMENTS

Unlike many nations, Bolivia has no large earnings from tourism or shipping to compensate for trade deficits. After World War II, falling exports and rising imports led to depletion of the nation's gold and foreign currency reserves. By 1969, in part because of increased US aid, the unfavorable balance had been considerably reduced; five years later, thanks to import restrictions and a sharp rise in export earnings, Bolivia had a favorable payments balance of $72.5 million. In the late 1970s, Bolivia's international financial position again began to worsen, and by the end of 1986, the country had accumulated $3.7 billion in foreign debt (perhaps $100 million of it in the private sector), an amount equal to the GDP. External debt equaled $4.1 billion in 1998, only about one-sixth of total GDP for that year.

The US Central Intelligence Agency reports that in 1998 the purchasing power parity of Bolivia's exports was $1.1 billion while imports totaled $1.7 billion resulting in a trade balance of -$600 million.

The International Monetary Fund (IMF) reports that in 1998 Bolivia had exports of goods totaling $1,104 million and imports totaling $1,759 million. The services credit totaled $253 million and debit $441 million. The following table summarizes Bolivia's balance of payments as reported by the IMF for 1998 in millions of US dollars.

Current Account		-673
Balance on goods	-655	
Balance on services	-188	
Balance on income	-160	
Current transfers	330	
Capital Account		10
Financial Account		999
Direct investment abroad	-3	
Direct investment in Bolivia	872	
Portfolio investment assets	...	
Portfolio investment liabilities	-75	
Other investment assets	-106	
Other investment liabilities	310	
Net Errors and Omissions		-234
Reserves and Related Items		-102

33BANKING AND SECURITIES

The Central Bank of Bolivia, established in 1928 and reorganized in 1945, is the sole bank of issue. The 1995 Central Bank Law refined the CBB's controls on the banking sector. The Superintendent of Banks regulates the operations of banks, and the Prudential Norms Financial Committee (CONFIP) regulates finance companies. The Bolivian Development Corp. channels credits from the Inter-American Development Bank into industrial expansion projects.

There are 13 private banks, accounting for over 85% of the deposits and loans of the financial system. Private banks, which had been under strict control since 1953, were largely deregulated in mid-1985. Commercial banks include: Banco Boliviano Americano (BBA), Banco de Credito de Bolivia, Banco de la Nacion Argentina, Banco de La Paz, Banco de la Union, Banco Economico, Banco Industrial SA (BISA), Banco Mercantil, Banco Nacional de Bolivia, Banco Real, Banco Santa Cruz, and Citibank.

The Bolivian Stock Exchange is the main stock exchange, with seven listed companies trading in 1995. There is also the Santa Cruz Stock Exchange.

34INSURANCE

In 1995, there were over 20 insurance companies doing business in Bolivia.

35PUBLIC FINANCE

Many of the expenditures and revenues of autonomous agencies (government development, mining, petroleum corporations, and the universities) do not appear in the central budget. Also, an estimated 15% of revenues come from illegal drug shipments. Since April 1992, comprehensive privatization has helped decrease the need for public sector expenses. In 1996, both current and capital spending had been reduced as a percentage of GDP. On the one hand, state capital spending, in the productive sector, fell overall as the privatization and capitalization programs relieved the state of responsibility for the capital spending of leading industrial enterprises; on the other, social investment rose sharply.

The US Central Intelligence Agency (CIA) estimates that in 1998 Bolivia's central government took in revenues of approximately $1.6 billion and had expenditures of $1.9 billion including capital expenditures of $293 million. Overall, the government registered a deficit of approximately $244 million. External debt totaled $5.4 billion.

The following table shows an itemized breakdown of government revenues and expenditures. The percentages were

calculated from data reported by the International Monetary Fund. The dollar amounts (millions) are based on the CIA estimates provided above.

REVENUE AND GRANTS	100%	1,633
Tax revenue	79.0%	1,290
Non-tax revenue	12.4%	203
Capital revenue	0.8%	13
Grants	7.8%	127
EXPENDITURES	100%	1,877
General public services	11.7%	220
Defense	9.6%	180
Public order and safety	7.2%	135
Education	19.6%	367
Health	3.4%	64
Social security	25.9%	487
Housing and community amenities	1.0%	19
Recreation, cultural, and religious affairs	0.5%	10
Economic affairs and services	13.0%	244
Other expenditures	0.5%	10
Interest payments	7.5%	141

36TAXATION

The Bolivian revenue system contains an unusually large number of taxes, leading to complexity and confusion that make the system difficult to enforce. Income taxes are extremely low, with a flat individual rate of 13%. In December 1994, a 25% tax on corporate income was established which replaced the 3% national income tax on corporations' taxable net worth. Both local and foreign corporations can receive tax holidays, exemptions, and other benefits if they invest in new companies or in production of nontraditional exports. There are taxes on the value of particular assets, such as motor vehicles, boats, and airplanes, which can be deducted from income tax, and taxes of 18–50% on automobiles (18%), alcohol (50%), perfume (20%), cosmetics (30%), and other items classed as luxuries. A VAT of 13%, which can be deducted from income tax, is in effect. The hydrocarbons industry, as outlined in the Hydrocarbon Law, pays an 18% royalty and tax rate for new projects, and a 60% royalty and tax rate on existing projects.

37CUSTOMS AND DUTIES

Export and import duties have traditionally been an important source of government revenue, but in mid-1985, as part of a drive to stimulate the economy, the Paz government established a uniform 20% duty on all imports, eliminated tariff exemptions, removed import restrictions except for those related to health and state security, and eliminated all export controls except those on dangerous substances, endangered species, and cultural treasures. Most import charges end up totaling between 30% and 45%. This is considerably higher than the 20% uniform duty; due to inspection company fees (2%), customs tariffs (2% for publications, 5% for capital goods, and a 10% flat rate), customs warehouse fees, customs fees (2%), and monies for forms and fees. Customs brokers charge up to 20% in fees. There is also a 13% value-added tax on all imports.

The 1990 Investment Law created a number of Free Trade Zones (FTZs), including those in El Alto, Puerto Aguirre, Cochabamba, Santa Cruz, Oruro, and Desaguadero. Bolivia had free trade agreements with MERCOSUR countries (Brazil, Argentina, Paraguay, Uruguay, and Chile) starting in 1997. In 1994, Bolivia signed a free trade agreement with Mexico and continues to lower or eliminate trade barriers.

38FOREIGN INVESTMENT

The Patiño, Hochschild, and Aramayo mining groups, expropriated in 1952, accounted for nearly all the foreign capital in mining at that time. In 1955, Bolivia issued the Petroleum Code, safeguarding foreign investment in the exploitation of petroleum, and US oil companies began large-scale exploration and development. Although the investment law of December 1971 granted substantial benefits to foreign investors; political instability, inadequate infrastructure, and Bolivia's poor debt-repayment record held foreign investments down. The 1990 Investment Law guaranteed basic rights to foreign investors. Subsequent laws governed activities in the mining, hydrocarbon, and banking sectors. Price controls and monopolies still existed in 1999, and only joint ventures with the state were allowed in the major oil, natural gas, and mining industries.

The US has been Bolivia's major foreign investor and trading partner. Most foreign investment in Bolivia is in the hydrocarbons, mining, and electricity generation sectors, and the bulk of that is US-owned. In 1998, half of all foreign direct investment came from the US, approximately $308 million. FDI was equivalent to nearly 8% of GDP in that year. Other major investors included Chile, Italy, Canada, Argentina, and Brazil.

39ECONOMIC DEVELOPMENT

In 1985, Bolivia was one of the first Latin American countries to institute market liberalizations—following the model set by Chile years earlier. In 1993, newly-elected President Lazada, furthered these liberalizations by increasing privatizations, which were called capitalizations in order to deflect criticism, increasing money spent on education and decreasing the federal government's regulatory power.

Privatizations have continued under President Hugo Bonzer, a former military dictator who was elected in 1997. Between 1993 and 1997, growth averaged 4.2% per year, and exports climbed 25% a year. Bolivia's continued economic development appears assured, the only obstacles being the possibility of intensified unrest among the large indigenous population; and failing to adequately—as judged by the US—crack down on cocoa leaf production. If Bolivia meets the conditions of the Heavily Indebted Poor Country (HIPC) debt relief scheme, then $450 million will be knocked off the $4.1 billion external debt by 2003.

40SOCIAL DEVELOPMENT

Social security coverage is compulsory for all workers, and voluntary coverage is available to the self-employed. Those covered by the program receive medical, hospital, dental, and pharmaceutical care for themselves and their families. Old age pensions begin at age 65. A worker's family is eligible for survivors' benefits of 70–80% of the insured person's pension. Maternity benefits cover female workers and workers' wives. Family allowances include cash payments for birth, nursing, and burial and monthly subsidies for each unmarried child. Employers contribute 2% of payroll for workers' compensation and are also required to grant two months' severance pay to dismissed employees.

Although guaranteed equal protection under the Constitution, women by and large do not enjoy the same social status as men due to limited political power and social traditions. In most cases, women earn less than men for doing similar work. Spousal abuse and domestic violence are widespread in Bolivia. In 1995, the Law on Domestic Violence was passed. The government is providing legal services for women and has created a special family protection unit within the police force to deal with these issues. As of 1997, 16 of 157 members of parliament were women.

Although the constitution prohibits sexual discrimination, women are prohibited from working at night and are limited to a shorter work schedule then men. These laws, however, are rarely enforced. A law providing federal protection against sexual harassment was signed in 1999, and the adoption of a new criminal code provided additional protection by classifying sexual harassment as a civil crime.

In 1995, the government launched a national network to prevent and treat child abuse. Government surveys show that nearly one in three children are physically or psychologically abused. Corporal punishment is used widely both at home and in schools. The government is collaborating actively with nongovernmental agencies and the UN to address the issues facing children in need.

Human rights are generally respected by the government, but prolonged detention by police still occurred and the judicial system was plagued by corruption and inefficiency.

41HEALTH

Health conditions have been notably poor, owing to poor hygiene and an insufficient number of doctors and hospitals, especially in rural areas. The most common disorders are acute respiratory diseases, tuberculosis, malaria, hepatitis, and Chagas' disease. In 1996, 134 per 100,000 people were diagnosed with tuberculosis and 618 per 100,000 were diagnosed with malaria. Malnutrition is a serious and growing problem, with 28% of children under five considered malnourished as of 1994. In 1995, only 60% of the population had access to safe water, and 39% of the rural population had adequate sanitation. As of the mid-1990s, there were more than 4,000 physicians and nearly 2,000 nurses. As of 1996, there were 1.6 hospital beds per 1,000 population. The country's public health care expenditures in the mid-1990s equaled 4% of GDP.

There was a birth rate of 31 per 1,000 population in 1999. Approximately 25% of married women (ages 15–49) were using contraception from 1980 to 1993. The government of Bolivia paid 65% of vaccination costs in 1995. In 1997, one-year-old children were immunized at the following rates: diphtheria, pertussis, and tetanus, 82%; polio, 82%; and measles, 98%. The infant mortality rate has declined from 117 per 1,000 live births in 1985 to 62 per 1,000 in 1999. During the period from 1989 to 1995, 13% of all children were suffering from malnutrition.

Life expectancy in 1999 was estimated at 61 years. The overall death rate was 10 per 1,000 people.

Health conditions in Bolivia have improved since the World Health Initiative Program in 1991. The Bolivian government has taken a greater role in the health of its citizens.

In 1995, cholera was reported in 2293 cases. As of 1996, 123 AIDS cases had been identified.

42HOUSING

At last estimate, nearly 70% of all housing units were detached private dwellings; about 25% were detached rooms for rent with common facilities; 5% were huts; and less than 5% were apartments. Although the government intended to provide adequate drinking water systems for all places of 2,000 or more inhabitants and to alleviate the sewage system shortage, water systems remain inadequate. Only about half of the population has access to piped indoor water, and little more than a quarter live in dwellings with adequate sanitary facilities. At last estimate, owners occupied about 70% of all dwellings; less than 15% were rented; and approximately 15% were occupied rent free.

43EDUCATION

Projected adult illiteracy rates for the year 2000 stand at 14.4% (males, 7.9%; females, 20.6%). Primary education, which lasts for eight years, is compulsory and free of charge. Secondary education lasts for another four years. Educational expenditure in 1996 amounted to 4.9% of GNP. In 1990, there were 1,278,775 students enrolled at the primary level with 51,763 teachers; there were also 219,232 secondary students with 12,434 teachers. In 1990, approximately 91% of school age children enrolled in primary schools, while 29% attended secondary school.

Bolivia has 10 state-funded and 23 private universities. The University of San Andrés (founded in 1930) in La Paz is Bolivia's largest university; the University of San Francisco Xavier in Sucre, dating from 1624, is one of the oldest universities in Latin America.

44LIBRARIES AND MUSEUMS

There are a small number of public libraries throughout Bolivia, with a combined collection of 200,000 volumes. The National Library in Sucre (150,000 volumes) also serves as a public library for that city. Another important public library is the Mariscal Andrés de Santa Cruz Municipal Library (80,000 volumes) in La Paz. The most important university libraries are those of the University of San Andrés in La Paz (120,000 volumes) and the University of San Simón in Cochabamba (62,000 volumes). The Department of Culture operates a large library in La Paz with 140,000 volumes, as does the Institute of Bolivian Culture, housing 150,000 volumes. The National Museum of Archaeology (1846) in La Paz is the most prominent museum. Also in La Paz are The National Museum of Art (1961) and the National Museum of Tihuanaca, featuring the art and culture of the indigenous people of Bolivia. There are several provincial museums, including the House of Liberty in Sucre, commemorating Bolivian independence, and the Institute of Anthropology and Archaeology Museum in Cochabamba.

45MEDIA

Bolivia had about 234,400 telephones in 1995. The telegraph system is owned by the Ministry of Communications; remote parts of the country are connected by wireless. There were 177 AM radio stations and 68 television stations as of 1999. In 1997, Bolivia had 672 radio receivers, 115 television sets, and 15 mobile phones per 1,000 population. A government-owned television station broadcasts from La Paz.

In 1995 there were 16 daily newspapers, with a total circulation of 390,000. The most important La Paz daily newspapers, with their estimated circulations in 1999, are *El Diario*, 55,000; *Hoy*, 12,000; and *Última Hora*, 35,000. Important provincial dailies are *Los Tiempos* (Cochabamba), with 19,000 circulation; and *El Mundo* (Santa Cruz), with 20,000.

The Constitution of Bolivia provides for the freedom of speech and press, and the government is said to allow free operation of electronic and print media. However, the Penal Code provides that persons found guilty of slandering government officials may be jailed, though it is said that this law is infrequently enforced.

In 1998, there was less than one Internet host per 1,000 population.

46ORGANIZATIONS

Learned societies include the Institute of Bolivian Sociology, the Society of Geographic and Historical Studies, the Center of Philosophical Studies, the Bolivian Language Academy, the National Academy of Fine Arts, the Archaeological Society of Bolivia, and the Tiahuanaco Institute of Anthropology, Ethnology, and Prehistory. There is a national chamber of commerce, with headquarters in La Paz, as well as departmental chambers of commerce.

47TOURISM, TRAVEL, AND RECREATION

The dry season (May–November) is the best time to visit Bolivia. La Paz and Sucre have many colonial churches and buildings; and there are Inca ruins on the islands of Lake Titicaca, which also offers opportunities for fishing and sailing. The world's highest ski run is located at Chacaltaya, and mountain climbing and hiking are available on the country's "cordilleras" and other peaks.

In 1997 there were 1,109,141 international tourist arrivals in Bolivia with tourism receipts totaling $170 million. There were 14,260 rooms in hotels and other facilities, with 23,649 beds and a 30% occupancy rate.

In 1999, the UN estimated the cost of staying in La Paz at between $132 and $169 per day. Costs in Santa Cruz are an estimated $126 and in Cochabamba are $81. In rural areas, daily expenditure averages $49.

48FAMOUS BOLIVIANS

Pedro Domingo Murillo (1757–1810) was the precursor and first martyr of Bolivian independence. Andrés de Santa Cruz (1792–1865), who considered himself the "Napoleon of the Andes," dominated the early years of the independent nation. The most infamous of the 19th-century Bolivian dictators was Mariano Melgarejo (1818–71). Ismael Móntes (1861–1933), who was president of Bolivia from 1904 to 1909 and from 1913 to 1917, is identified in Bolivian history as the "great president." Simón Patiño (1861–1947), the richest of the "big three" tin barons, began his career as a loan collector and acquired his first mine by chance; he later became one of the world's wealthiest men. Víctor Paz Estenssoro (b.1907), architect of the national revolution of 1952 and founder of the MNR, served as president during from 1952 to 1956 and was reelected in 1960 and 1964; he was deposed shortly thereafter by a military junta but returned to office from 1985 to 1989. Hernán Siles Zuazo (b.1914), also connected with the MNR and later founder of the MNRI, was president in 1956–60 and again in 1982–85. Juan Lechín Oquendo (b.1914?), a leader of the 1952 uprising, led the powerful Bolivian Workers' Federation from its formation in 1952 until 1987.

Bolivia's outstanding literary figure is Gabriel René-Moreno (1836–1909), a historian, sociologist, and literary critic. The highly original poet and philosopher Franz Tamayo (1879–1956), although belonging to the landed aristocracy, was a champion of the downtrodden Amerindian. Tamayo was elected president in 1935, but an army revolt prevented him from taking power. Alcides Argüedas (1879–1946) achieved fame throughout Latin America with his historical works on Bolivia and his novels *Wata wara* and *Raza de bronce*, concerned with the plight of the Indian; his critical sociological study *Pueblo enfermo* provoked an enduring controversy. The archaeologist and anthropologist Arturo Posnansky (1874–1946), born in Austria, did pioneering work in studying the civilization that once flourished at Lake Titicaca. Jaime Laredo (b.1941) is a world-famous violinist.

49DEPENDENCIES

Bolivia has no territories or colonies.

50BIBLIOGRAPHY

Alexander, Robert Jackson. *The Bolivarian Presidents: Conversations and Correspondence with Presidents of Bolivia, Peru, Ecuador, Colombia, and Venezuela.* Westport, Conn.: Praeger, 1994.

Barton, Robert. *A Short History of Bolivia.* Detroit: Ethridge, 1969.

Blair, David Nelson. *The Land and People of Bolivia.* New York: J.B. Lippincott, 1990.

Crandon–Malamud, Libbet. *From the Fat of Our Souls: Social Change, Political Process, and Medical Pluralism in Bolivia.* Berkeley: University of California Press, 1991.

Fifer, J. Valerie. *Bolivia: Land, Location and Politics since 1825.* New York: Cambridge University Press, 1972.

Gallo, Carmenza. *Taxes and State Power: Political Instability in Bolivia, 1900–1950.* Philadelphia: Temple University Press, 1991.

Gill, Lesley. *Precarious Dependencies: Gender, Class, and Domestic Service in Bolivia.* New York: Columbia University Press, 1994.

Heath, Dwight B. *Historical Dictionary of Bolivia.* Metuchen, N.J.: Scarecrow, 1972.

Hudson, Rex A. and Dennis M. Hanratty, *Bolivia, a Country Study.* 3rd ed. Washington, D.C.: Government Printing Office, 1991.

James, Daniel (ed.). *The Complete Bolivian Diaries of Che Guevara and Other Captured Documents.* New York: Stein & Day, 1968.

Klein, Herbert S. *Bolivia: the Evolution of a Multi–ethnic Society.* 2nd ed. New York: Oxford University Press, 1992.

Malloy, James M and Eduardo Gamarra. *Revolution and Reaction: Bolivia, 1964–1985.* New Brunswick, N.J.: Transaction Books, 1988.

Morales, Waltraud Q. *Bolivia: Land of Struggle.* Boulder, Colo.: Westview Press, 1992.

Sanabria, Harry. *The Coca Boom and Rural Social Change in Bolivia.* Ann Arbor: University of Michigan Press, 1993.

Yeager, Gertrude Matyoka. *Bolivia.* Oxford, England; Santa Barbara, Calif.: Clio Press, 1988.

BRAZIL

Federative Republic of Brazil
República Federativa do Brasil

CAPITAL: Brasília.

FLAG: The national flag consists of a green field upon which is imposed a large yellow diamond twice as wide as it is high. Centered within the diamond is a blue globe showing constellations of the southern skies dominated by the Southern Cross. Encircling the globe is a white banner bearing the words *Ordem e Progresso*.

ANTHEM: *Hino Nacional Brasileiro,* beginning "Ouviram do Ipiranga" ("Listen to the cry of Ipiranga").

MONETARY UNIT: The real (R$) is a paper currency of 100 centavos. It was introduced on 1 July 1994 equal to 2750 cruzeiro reais, the currency which had replaced the older cruzeiro in 1986. Until 14 January 1999, the official rate of the real was determined by a managed float, but now floats independently with respect to the US dollar. R$1=US$0.56306 (or US$1=1.7760) as of 31 March 2000.

WEIGHTS AND MEASURES: The metric system is the legal standard, but some local units are also used.

HOLIDAYS: New Year's Day, 1 January; Tiradentes, 21 April; Labor Day, 1 May; Independence Day, 7 September; Our Lady of Aparecida (Patroness of Brazil), 12 October; All Souls' Day, 2 November; Proclamation of the Republic, 15 November; Christmas, 25 December. Movable holidays include the pre-Lenten carnival, usually in February, Good Friday, and Corpus Christi.

TIME: At noon GMT, the time in Fernando de Noronha is 10 AM; Rio de Janeiro, 9 AM; Manaus, 8 AM; Rio Branco, 7 AM.

¹LOCATION, SIZE, AND EXTENT

Situated in east-central South America, Brazil is the largest country in Latin America and the fourth-largest in the world in coterminous area, ranking after Russia, Canada, and China (the US is larger with Alaska, Hawaii, and the dependencies included). Occupying nearly half of the South American continent, it covers an area of 8,511,965 sq km (3,286,488 sq mi), extending 4,320 km (2,684 mi) N–S and 4,328 km (2,689 mi) E–W. Contiguous with all continental South American countries except Ecuador and Chile, Brazil is bounded on the N by Venezuela, Guyana, Suriname, and French Guiana, on the NE, E, and SE by the Atlantic Ocean, on the S by Uruguay, on the SW by Argentina and Paraguay, on the W by Bolivia and Peru, and on the NW by Colombia, with a total boundary length of 22,182 km (13,783 mi). Brazil is divided into 23 states, 3 federal territories, and a Federal District. The Federal District, including the capital of Brasília, inaugurated on 21 April 1960, is surrounded on three sides by the state of Goiás and on the fourth by Minas Gerais.

Brazil's capital city, Brasília, is located in the southeastern part of the country.

²TOPOGRAPHY

The northern part of Brazil is dominated by the basin of the Amazon River and its many tributaries, which occupies two-fifths of the country. The Amazon Basin itself occupies 7,049,975 sq km (2,722,000 sq mi), or about 40% of South America's total area. The Amazon River (Rio Amazonas) is, at 6,280 km (3,900 mi), the world's second-longest river after the Nile, although the Amazon ranks first in volume of water carried; rising in the Peruvian Andes, the Amazon eventually empties into the Atlantic Ocean at an average rate of 200,000 cu m (7 million cu ft) per second. The Amazon lowlands east of the Andes constitute the world's largest tropical rain forest. In the northernmost part of the Amazon Basin lies a series of mountain ranges, known as the

Guiana Highlands, where Brazil's highest mountain, Pico da Neblina (3,014 m/9,888 ft), is located. South of the Amazon Basin is a large plateau called the Brazilian Highlands, ranging in elevation from 300 to 910 m (1,000 to 3,000 ft) above sea level. From the city of Salvador (Bahia) southward to Pôrto Alegre, the highlands meet the Atlantic Ocean in a steep, wall-like slope, the Great Escarpment, which in southeastern Brazil is surmounted by mountain ranges with elevations from 2,100 to 2,400 m (7,000 to 8,000 ft) above sea level.

The Atlantic coast of Brazil has no real coastal plain, but there are stretches of lowlands along the northeast coast, and there are many baylike indentations, where Brazil's principal cities are located. Along the southwest border is a small portion of the upper Paraguay lowlands. The Paraná, Paraguay, and Uruguay rivers flow through southern Brazil; the São Francisco flows 2,915 km (1,811 mi) through northeastern and central Brazil; and the Tocantins (2,699 km/1,677 mi) empties into the Pará and from there into the Atlantic Ocean at an estuary south of the Amazon proper.

³CLIMATE

Brazil is a tropical country but extends well into the temperate zone. The Amazon Basin has a typically hot, tropical climate, with annual rainfall exceeding 250 cm (100 in) in some areas; the Brazilian Highlands, which include roughly half of the total area, are subtropical. The narrow coastal lowland area ranges from tropical in the north to temperate in the south. The cool upland plains of the south have a temperate climate and an occasional snowfall. The coolest period is from May to September, and the hottest is from December to March. October to May is the rainy season. Rainfall is excessive in the lowlands and in the upper Amazon Basin, along the northern coast, at certain points on the east coast, and in the southern interior, while there are periodic droughts in the northeast. The average high temperature in Rio de Janeiro in February is 29°C (84°F); the average low in July is 17°C (63°F).

⁴FLORA AND FAUNA

About one-fourth of the world's known plant species are found in Brazil. The Amazon Basin, the world's largest tropical rain forest, includes tall Brazil nut trees, brazilwood, myriad palms, kapok-bearing ceiba trees enlaced with vines and creepers, rosewood, orchids, and water lilies, and is the home of the wild rubber tree.

South of the vast Amazonian forest is a mixture of semideciduous forest (mata) and scrub forests. The characteristic flora of the northeast interior is the carnauba wax-yielding palm in the states of Ceará and Piauí, and to the east big areas of thorn scrub, the result of generally poor soils and periodic devastating droughts. Along the humid coast are many mango, cajú, guava, coconut, and jack-fruit trees, as well as large sugar and cotton plantations, the latter indigenous. Within the savanna, sparse forests, and "campos cerrados" (enclosed fields) of badly deforested, populous Minas Gerais, are various woody shrubs, lianas, and epiphytes, the staghorn fern, and an abundance of herbs, especially grasses. Brazil has many fair to good pasturage grasses, on which millions of beef cattle graze, not always of high grade, and some dairy cattle in the favored southern states.

In the southern states are exotic flowers, such as papagaias; flowering trees, such as the quaresma, which blossoms during Lent; and the popular ipê tree with its yellow petals, planted on some São Paulo streets. In the southernmost part of the Brazilian plateau forests, where temperate climate prevails, is found a mixture of araucarias (umbrella pines) and broadleaf species. The pampas of Rio Grande do Sul are extensive grasslands. Maté, of economic importance as a beverage, is made from the roasted, powdered leaves of a tree harvested extensively in the southern states.

The Amazon rain forest is host to a great variety of tropical fauna, including hundreds of types of macaws, toucans, parrots, and other brightly colored birds; brilliant butterflies; many species of small monkeys; anacondas, boas, and other large tropical snakes; crocodiles and alligators; and such distinctive animals as the Brazilian "tiger" (onca), armadillo, sloth, and tapir. The rivers in that region abound with turtles and exotic tropical fish, and the infamous "cannibal fish" (piranha) is common; in all, more than 2,000 fish species have been identified.

⁵ENVIRONMENT

As of 1986, it was estimated that the forests of the Amazon were being cleared for colonization, pasturage, timber development, and other commercial purposes at a rate of up to 20 million hectares (50 million acres) a year. As of the mid-1990s, this figure has decreased, although no exact figures are available. A 20-year US-Brazilian project, initiated by the World Wildlife Fund, in Washington, D.C., and the National Institute for Research on Amazonia, in Manaus, has been studying the Amazon forest since 1978 in order to recommend appropriate measures for its protection. A Brazilian law requiring that developers leave 50% of each Amazon land parcel untouched is erratically enforced. Only 3.8% of Brazil's natural areas were protected in the mid-1990s. Federal agencies with environmental responsibilities include the National Environment Council of the Ministry of the Interior, the Brazilian Institute of Forest Development, and the Ministry of Planning. Other environmental problems in Brazil include water pollution and land damage. Rivers near urban industrial centers are polluted by mercury, toxic industrial wastes, and untreated waste. Brazil lacks fertile soil for agriculture, and the existing soils are threatened by erosion from the clearing of the forests.

The damage to the rain forest environment is reflected in the number of endangered species which inhabit the region. Between 1900 and 1950, 60 species of birds and mammals became extinct. Forty species of birds and 318 plant species are currently endangered. The list of endangered species as of 1991 included the Lear's macaw, the guayaquil great green macaw, and the American crocodile. Endangered or extinct species in Brazil include two species of marmoset (buffy-headed and white-eared); three species of tamarin (golden lion, golden-headed lion, and golden-rumped lion); the black saki; the woolly spider monkey; and the maned sloth. In December 1987, the Brazilian senate enacted a law to ban whale hunting within the country's territorial waters.

⁶POPULATION

Brazil is the most populous country in Latin America, as well as one of the most populous in the world. According to the 1991 census, the total population was 146,825,475, an increase of 23% since 1980. By 2000, the population of Brazil was estimated at 173,790,810. An estimated 4.8% of the population is 65 years of age or older. The projected population for the year 2005 is 182,837,000, assuming a crude birthrate of 18 per 1,000 population and a death rate of 9, resulting in a natural rate of change of 0.9% for the period 2000–2005. The population rate of change between 1995 and 2000 was 1.2%. The population density in 1998 was 20 per sq km (52 per sq mi).

The population is concentrated in the Atlantic coastal region, with the states of Rio de Janeiro, São Paulo, and Minas Gerais containing approximately 41% of the total; the states of Bahia, Rio Grande do Sul, Pernambuco, and Ceará have about 23%, and the remaining units about 36%. It was estimated that 81% of the population lived in urban areas in 2000, up from 66% in 1980. The capital city, Brasilia, had a 2000 metropolitan population of 1,985,000. Other major metropolitan areas and their 2000 estimated populations are as follows: São Paulo, 17,711,000; Rio de Janeiro, 10,556,000; Belo Horizonte, 4,160,000; Porto Alegre, 3,699,000; Recife, 3,307,000; Salvador, 3,180,000; Fortaleza, 3,007,000; Curitiba, 2,519,000; Campinas, 1,857,000; Belém, 1,634,000; Manaus, 1,432,000; Santos, 1,257,000; Goiania, 1,103,000; São Luís, 948,000; and São José dos Campos, 949,000.

⁷MIGRATION

Between 1821 and 1945, approximately 5.2 million European immigrants entered Brazil, most of them settling in the south. Brazil has the largest expatriate Japanese colony in the world, numbering more than one million. In recent years, because of the increasing prosperity of Europe and Japan, there has been less desire to migrate to underdeveloped rural Brazil or its inflation-harassed industrial cities. Moreover, immigration is controlled by laws limiting the annual entry of persons of any national group to 2% of the total number of that nationality that had entered in the preceding 50 years. As of September 1999, Brazil was hosting some 2,300 refugees. Some 80% of refugees come from Africa, particularly Angola (57%), the Democratic Republic of the Congo (7%), Liberia (11%), and Sierra Leone (3%). Some 70% of the total refugee population resides in Rio de Janeiro; the remaining 30% live in Sao Paulo and other Brazilian cities. In 1999, the net migration rate was -0.03.

⁸ETHNIC GROUPS

The indigenous inhabitants were Indians, chiefly of Tupi-Guaraní stock, and other small groups in the Amazon Basin and the lowlands of the Paraguay and Paraná rivers. The Portuguese settlers had few taboos against race mixture, and centuries of large-scale intermarriage have produced a tolerant and distinctly Brazilian culture. Within the Brazilian nationality are blended the

LOCATION: 5°16′19″N to 33°45′9″s; 34°45′54″ to 73°59′32″w. **BOUNDARY LENGTHS:** Venezuela, 1,495 km (929 mi); Guyana, 1,606 km (998 mi); Suriname, 593 km (368 mi); French Guiana, 655 km (407 mi); Atlantic coastline, 7,408 km (4,603 mi); Uruguay, 1,003 km (623 mi); Argentina, 1,263 km (785 mi); Paraguay, 1,339 km (832 mi); Bolivia, 3,126 km (1,942 mi); Peru, 2,995 km (1,861 mi); Colombia, 1,644 km (1,022 mi). **TERRITORIAL SEA LIMIT:** 12 mi.

various aboriginal Indian cultures; the Portuguese heritage, with its diverse strains; the traditions of millions of persons of African descent; and European elements resulting from sizable immigration since 1888 from Italy, Spain, Germany, and Poland.

The influx of Japanese and some Arabs during the 20th century has contributed to the complex Brazilian melting pot.

According to the most recent estimates, 55% of Brazil's population are white; 38% are mixed white and black; and 5%

are black. The remaining 1% is comprised of Japanese, Arab, and Amerindian groups.

9LANGUAGES

The official language of Brazil is Portuguese, which is spoken by virtually all inhabitants except some isolated Indian groups. Substantial variations in pronunciation and word meaning, however, distinguish it from the language as it is spoken in Portugal. Spanish is also spoken. A large percentage of the educated have learned either French or English. German, Italian, and Japanese are used in immigrant communities.

10RELIGIONS

Brazil claims no state religion; however, the Catholic Church's National Council of Brazilian Bishops (CNBB) estimates that 75% of the population professes the Roman Catholic faith. The primate is the archbishop of Salvador; Rio de Janeiro and São Paulo are also archdioceses. Based on 1998 estimates, Protestants constitute roughly 20% of the population, the majority of whom (about 85%) are Pentecostal/evangelical; Lutherans and Baptists account for most of the remaining Protestants. Followers of Spiritism and traditional African and syncretic religions—such as Candomble, Xango, Macumba, and Umbanda—make up about 5% of the populace. Immigrants from Arab countries are the primary practitioners of Sunni and Shi'a Islam. Shintoism is practiced among the Brazilian-Japanese community. Missionary groups include The Church of Jesus Christ of Latter-Day Saints and various evangelical groups. The government restricts access of missionary groups to indigenous peoples and requires the groups to obtain permission from the National Indian Foundation to enter official indigenous areas.

11TRANSPORTATION

Roads are the primary carriers of freight and passenger traffic. Brazil's road system totaled 1.98 million km (1.23 million mi) in 1999. The total of paved roads increased from 35,496 km (22,056 mi) in 1967 to 184,140 km (114,425 mi) in 1999. Motor vehicles registered as of 1995 included 12,000,000 passenger cars, and 3,160,689 commercial vehicles. Although the bulk of highway traffic is concentrated in the southern and central regions, important roads have been constructed to link the north-eastern and northern areas with the industrialized south. Roads of all types have been built with federal aid, the most important being the network of more than 14,000 km (8,700 mi) of paved roads south of Brasília; aid is also supplied for their maintenance. In September 1970, construction began on the 5,000-km (3,100-mi) Trans-Amazon Highway, possibly the most ambitious overland road project undertaken in this century, linking Brazil's Atlantic coast with the Peruvian border; when completed, a 4,138-km (2,571-mi) north–south section will link Santarém, on the Amazon River, with Cuiabá. The project has had a profound effect on the Amazon Basin, among the world's last great wilder-nesses. However, a World Bank study in the early 1990s showed that 28% of the country's existing highways were in bad condition, up from only 10% in 1979. Lack of proper road maintenance possibly adds 10–15% to total transportation costs in Brazil.

Brazil's railway system has been declining since 1945, when emphasis shifted to highway construction. The total extension of railway track was 28,862 km (17,935 mi) in 1999, as compared with 31,848 km (19,789 mi) in 1970. Most of the railway system belongs to the Federal Railroad Corp., with a majority government interest; there are also seven private lines.

Coastal shipping links widely separated parts of the country. Of the 36 deep-water ports, Santos and Rio de Janeiro are the most important, followed by Paranaguá, Recife, Vitória, Tubarão, Maceió, and Ilhéus. Bolivia and Paraguay have been given free ports at Santos. There are 50,000 km (31,070 mi) of navigable inland waterways. In 1998, the merchant shipping fleet, which included 179 vessels (1,000 GRT or over), had a total GRT of 4,132,037.

Air transportation is highly developed. In 1997, Brazilian airlines performed 42,385 million passenger-kilometers (26,338 million passenger-miles) of service, transporting 24,307 million passengers. In 1998 there were an estimated 3,265 airports, of which 514 had paved runways. Of the 48 principal airports, 21 are international; of these, Rio de Janeiro's Galeão international airport and São Paulo's Guarulhos International Airport are by far the most active. The main international airline is Empresa de Viação Aérea Rio Grandense (VARIG). Other Brazilian airlines are Transbrasil Linhas Aéreas, Cruzeiro do Sul, (associated with VARIG since 1983), and Viação Aérea São Paulo (VASP), which handles only domestic traffic and is run by the state of São Paulo. All except VASP are privately owned.

12HISTORY

The original inhabitants of Brazil were hunter-gatherers, except in the lower Amazon, where sedentary agriculture developed. There are no reliable population estimates from pre-European times, but probably there were no more than one million.

After the European discovery of the New World, Spain and Portugal became immediate rivals for the vast new lands. Portugal's claim was established by a papal bull of Pope Alexander VI (1493) and by the Treaty of Tordesillas (1494), which awarded to Portugal all territory 370 leagues west of the Cape Verde Islands. On Easter Sunday in 1500, the Portuguese admiral Pedro Álvares Cabral formally claimed the land for the Portuguese crown. Cabral's ship returned to Portugal with a cargo of red dyewood, which had been gathered along the shore, and from the name of the wood, pau-brasil, the new land acquired the name Brazil.

In 1532, the first Portuguese colonists arrived, bringing cattle, seed, and the first slaves from Africa. In 1549, the Portuguese governor-general, Tomé da Souza, founded the city of São Salvador, and established the first Portuguese government in the New World. The same year marked the arrival of the missionary Society of Jesus (the Jesuits) to begin their work among the Indians.

Other Europeans began to move in on the Portuguese colony. In 1555, the French established a settlement in the Bay of Rio de Janeiro. In 1624, the Dutch attacked Bahia and began to extend throughout northeastern Brazil. Under the Dutch, who remained until ousted in 1654, the area flourished economically. Colonists planted sugarcane, and during the 17th century, the large sugar plantations of northeastern Brazil were the world's major source of sugar.

In 1640, Portugal appointed a viceroy for Brazil, with his seat first in Bahia and after 1763 in Rio de Janeiro. The discovery of gold in 1693 and of diamonds about 1720 opened up new lands for colonization in what are now the states of São Paulo, Minas Gerais, Paraná, Goiás, and Mato Grosso. From their base in São Paulo, Brazilian pioneers (Bandeirantes) pushed inland, along with their herds of cattle and pigs, in search of Indian slaves and mineral riches. By the 1790s, when the primitive surface gold and diamond mines were largely exhausted, the Brazilian plateau became thinly populated.

Brazil's first attempt at independence came in 1789 in the mining state of Minas Gerais. A plot, known as the Miners' Conspiracy (Conjuração Mineira) was led by Joaquim José da Silva Xavier, a healer known as Tiradentes ("tooth-puller"). The plot was betrayed and crushed, and Tiradentes was captured and eventually executed, but Tiradentes remains a national hero. In 1807, the invading armies of Napoleon forced the Portuguese royal family and 15,000 Portuguese subjects to flee to Brazil. Rio de Janeiro became the seat of the Portuguese royal family until 1821, when King John (João) VI returned home, leaving his son Pedro to rule Brazil as regent. Meanwhile, Portugal's monopolistic trade practices, the suppression of domestic industry, and oppressive taxation had brought about a strong movement for independence, which Pedro supported.

Pedro proclaimed Brazil's independence on 7 September 1822, and later that year was crowned Emperor Pedro I. In 1831, a military revolt forced him to abdicate. The throne passed to his 5-year-old son, Pedro. In 1840, Pedro was crowned Emperor. Under Pedro II, Brazil enjoyed half a century of peaceful progress. New frontiers were opened, many immigrants arrived from Europe, railroads were built, and the gathering of rubber in the Amazon Basin stimulated the growth of cities, such as Belém and Manaus. The abolition of slavery in 1888 brought about an economic crisis that disrupted the Brazilian Empire. In 1889, a bloodless revolution deposed Pedro II and established the Republic of the United States of Brazil. A new constitution modeled after the US federal constitution, was promulgated by the Brazilian government in 1891. At first, the republic was ruled by military regimes, but by 1894 constitutional stability was achieved.

Meanwhile, empty areas of good soil were settled in the southern plateau by over 2.5 million Italian, Portuguese, German, Polish, and Levantine immigrants. The rapid spread of coffee cultivation in the state of São Paulo transformed Brazil into the world's largest coffee-producing country. By the end of the 19th century, coffee had become the nation's principal source of wealth. Brazil soon entered a period of economic and political turmoil. Malayan and Indonesian rubber plantations had overwhelmed the Brazilian rubber market, while coffee revenues were reduced by falling world prices of coffee. Regionalism and military rivalries contributed to instability, and by 1930, the nation was in a state of unrest. In that year, a military coup with widespread civilian support placed into power Getúlio Vargas, the governor of Rio Grande do Sul.

Vargas' ideology was a blend of populism and corporatism. He sought reforms for Brazil's middle and lower classes, but discouraged dissent and was often repressive. Between 1930 and 1937 Vargas brought a minimum wage and social security to Brazil, but also crushed a leftist uprising in 1935. Vargas formalized his system in 1937, calling it the New State ("Estado Novo"). For eight years, Vargas attempted to industrialize Brazil, while organizing both workers and their employers into state-run syndicates. Vargas was nationalist in foreign policy, although he encouraged foreign investment. He exploited the US-German rivalry over Latin America to get large amounts of aid until joining the allies in 1942.

Conservative elements of the military, convinced that Vargas was a dangerous force, removed him from office, and promulgated a new constitution in 1946. The "Second Republic" was initiated with the presidency of Eurico Dutra. Vargas was returned to the presidency in the election of 1950 and did not attempt to rejuvenate the New State. He did continue to press for industrialization under state control, establishing a National Development Bank and a state petroleum company. Eventually he ran afoul of the military, who demanded his resignation. He committed suicide in August 1954, a few months before his term of office was due to expire.

He was succeeded from 1955 to 1961 by Juscelino Kubitschek de Oliveira. Kubitschek embarked on an ambitious program of development, spending huge amounts of money and attracting large foreign investments in Brazil. Kubitschek's most ambitious program was the building of a new federal capital, Brasília, in the highlands of central Brazil. Inflation and a burdensome national debt proved to be his undoing, and in January 1961 Jânio da Silva Quadros was inaugurated after a campaign promising an end to corruption and economic stability. The situation proved too difficult for Quadros, and he resigned after only seven months. João Goulart, who had been vice-president under both Kubitschek and Quadros, became president only after the conservative Congress combined with the military to reduce his powers and institute an unwieldy form of parliamentary government. In January 1963, in a national plebiscite, Brazil chose to restore presidential powers. But Goulart was caught between pressures from the left, demanding the acceleration of social programs, and the right, increasingly alarmed by trends toward populism.

On 1 April 1964 the military deposed Goulart and arrested 40,000 people, including 80 members of Congress. In the same month, Congress appointed Humberto de Alencar Castelo Branco to the presidency, and in July it approved a constitutional amendment extending Castelo Branco's term of office to March 1967. National elections were postponed, and Brazil entered an era of military supremacy.

In March 1967 Arthur da Costa e Silva, a former army marshal, took office under a new constitution. That constitution was suspended in December 1968, and military hard-liners took the upper hand. Costa e Silva suffered a stroke in September 1969 and died in December. Gen. Emilio Garrastazú Médici, former head of the secret police was chosen to replace him. In March 1974, Gen. Ernesto Geisel, a high official in the Castelo Branco government, became president.

The military governments of the previous 10 years had brought Brazil rapid economic expansion, but there was a dramatic reversal during the oil crisis of 1973–74. Opposition began to mount, encouraged by religious and trade union leaders. President Geisel gradually instituted some degree of political liberalization (abertura), but the military split on the wisdom of this policy.

During the late 1970s, continuing economic difficulties led to labor unrest and numerous strikes, including a strike of 300,000 metalworkers in metropolitan São Paulo in April and May of 1980 that ended only after troops in tanks and trucks occupied the region. Meanwhile, Gen. João Baptista de Oliveira Figueiredo became president in March 1979. That August, Figueiredo continued Geisel's policy of liberalization by signing a political amnesty law that allowed many political exiles to return home. Also in 1979, censorship of the press and the controlled two-party system were abolished. In November 1982, Brazil had its first democratic elections since 1964. Opposition parties won the governorships of 10 populous states and a majority in the lower house of Congress, but the ruling party remained in control of the upper house and the electoral college, which was to choose the next president. Moreover, the military retained broad powers to intervene in political affairs under national security laws.

The 1985 election was indirect, yet the opposition managed to turn the campaign in 1984 into a reflection of popular choice and capture the presidency. The ruling party chose São Paulo governor Paulo Maluf, who proved unable to distance himself from the unpopularity of the military-controlled regime. The opposition capitalized on the groundswell of hostility and coalesced behind the paternal figure of Tancredo Neves, a senator from Minas Gerais who had held office under Vargas and who campaigned as if the ballot were direct. The election went against the government, and in January 1985, the electoral college duly chose Neves as Brazil's first civilian president in a generation. In March, however, just before his inauguration, Neves fell gravely ill, and he died in April without having been formally sworn in. Brazilians feared another military strike, but Vice-President José Sarney was allowed to take office as president. Sarney, who represented a small center-right party allied with Neves' party, consolidated his position after an impressive showing in regional and legislative elections in November 1986.

A new constitution, passed in 1988, was followed by elections a year later. Brazil's first direct presidential elections in 29 years resulted in the victory of Fernando Collor de Mello. Collor received 53% of the vote in the runoff elections. Collor took office in March 1990 and launched an ambitious liberalization program that attempted to stabilize prices and deregulate the economy. Collor was in the process of renegotiating Brazil's huge debt with foreign creditors and the IMF when massive corruption was revealed inside the Collor administration. Allegations implicated Collor himself, who was forced to resign in December 1992. Itamar Franco took over, promising to continue Collor's programs, but long-standing structural problems continued. The nation's chronic inflation was finally brought under control through the Real Plan launched in 1994 by finance minister Fernando Enrique Cardoso (and named for the new currency, linked to the US dollar, that was introduced under the plan).

On the strength of the plan's success, Cardoso, a leading social scientist, was elected to the presidency in October 1994. His policies, which continued to keep inflation under control, reduced tariffs, and included major privatization measures, earned him sufficient support for the passage in January 1997 of a constitutional amendment by the lower house of Congress overturning the nation's ban on consecutive presidential terms and making it possible for Cardoso to seek reelection in 1998. He won reelection in October of 1998 with 53% of the vote in the first round. Worker's Party candidate "Lula" came second with 31.7%. Cardoso also commands the support of a loose center-right coalition of parties that include the Liberal Front Party (PFL) (105 seats in the Chamber and 20 in the senate); Social Democratic Party (PSDB) (99 and 16 seats respectively); Brazilian Democratic Movement (PMDB), (82 and 27 seats respectively); Progressive Renewal Party (PPB), (60 Chamber seats); and Labour Party (PTB) (31 Chamber seats). One of the major challenges tackled by the Cardoso administration was the privatization of the state-owned mining company, Vale de Rio Doce, which drew strong opposition from nationalist, leftist, and religious forces. In May 1997 a $3.2 billion controlling stake in the mining and transport conglomerate was sold to private investors. Cardoso's parties also won a majority of the State Governor races. Shortly after the election, as a result of the economic crisis, Brazil was forced to devalue its *real* currency. Previously pegged to the US dollar, the *real* lost more than 60% of its value in days sending the country into a deeper crisis. Some recovery was observed in late 1998 and in 1999, but social discontent resulting from high unemployment and growing poverty also flourished.

13GOVERNMENT

The Federative Republic of Brazil is a constitutional republic composed of 26 states and the Federal District. This district surrounds the federal capital, Brasília. The constitution of October 1988 (last amended in 1998) establishes a strong presidential system.

The president and vice president are elected to four-year terms and can be reelected once. In 1985, the previous constitution was amended to allow for direct popular election as opposed to an electoral college system. Between 1964 and 1978, presidents were pre-selected by the military. The president is the head of the armed forces and is in charge of the executive branch, assisted in that task by a cabinet of ministers. He also appoints justices to the Supreme Federal Tribunal, the highest court in Brazil.

The Congress consists of the Senate and the Chamber of Deputies. The Senate has 81 members, three for each state plus the Federal District. Senators serve for eight-year terms, with half the members retiring every four years. The 513 deputies (as of 1998) are elected for four-year terms by a system of proportional representation in the states, territories, and Federal District. The constitution stipulates that Congress meet every year from 15 March to 15 December. In practice, from 1964 to 1985, the military used the office of the president to dominate the Congress and the state legislatures, suspending them from time to time.

Voting is compulsory for most men and employed women between the ages of 18 and 65 and optional for persons over 65, unemployed women, those between 16 and 18 years of age, and officers of the armed forces. Illiterates were permitted to vote in 1985. Enlisted servicemen may not vote.

14POLITICAL PARTIES

During the last days of the Brazilian Empire, a group of positivists advocating abolition of the monarchy organized the Republican Party (Partido Republicano—PR) along military lines. After the fall of the empire in 1889, the government was controlled by PR-supported military regimes and opposed locally by the established Conservative and Liberal parties. An opposition group, the Civilian Party (Partido Civilista), organized by Ruy Barbosa, overcame the military regime but was soon absorbed into the Conservative and Liberal groups from Minas Gerais and São Paulo, which instituted a system of alternating the presidency between the two states.

Getúlio Vargas was responsible for the success of three successive parties, one of which survives to this day. In 1930, Vargas formed the Liberal Alliance Movement (Aliança Nacional Liberal—ANL). After Vargas resigned the presidency in 1945 his supporters formed the Social Democratic Party (Partido Social Democrático—PSD). Eurico Dutra, who succeeded Vargas, ran under this party. In 1950, Vargas was elected under the banner of the Brazilian Labor Party (Partido Trabalhista Brasileiro—PTB). Finally, Vargas inspired the National Democratic Union (União Democrática Nacional—UDN) to put up candidates against him. The UDN won the presidency in 1961 for Quadros.

The PSD continued on without Vargas, but formed a coalition with the PTB in 1955. The PSD candidate, Kubitschek, became president, while the PTB's leader, Goulart, became vice-president. In the 1958 congressional elections, however, the PTB broke with the PSD. The PTB survives as a small party, having lost many of its members to other laborite parties.

After the military takeover in 1964, parties disappeared. In 1966, the military allowed the formation of two official parties: the Alliance for National Renewal (Aliança Renovadora Nacional—ARENA) and the Brazilian Democratic Movement (Movimento Democrático Brasileiro—MDB). ARENA was created as the ruling party, with the MDB playing the role of "loyal opposition." ARENA began with two-thirds majorities in both houses of Congress and increased its majorities in the elections of 1970, while also maintaining control of nearly all state legislatures. ARENA scored further gains in the 1972 municipal elections. However, beginning in November 1974, the MDB began to score legislative gains. Moreover, in the 1974 election the MDB was able to raise issues of social justice and civil liberties.

In November 1979, in accordance with the government's liberalization policy, Congress passed a law abolishing ARENA and the MDB and permitting the formation of new parties. Over the next decade, a number of groups emerged. The government created the conservative Social Democratic Party (Partido Democrático Social—PDS) to replace ARENA. The Democratic Workers' Party (Partido Democrático Trabalhista—PDT) is headed by Leonel Brizola, a frequent critic of the military regime and leader of a similar party before 1964. The Party of the Brazilian Democratic Movement (Partido de Movimento Democrático Brasileiro—PMDB) is a moderate successor to the MDB. The Brazilian Social Democracy Party (PSDB) was founded in 1988 by former PMDB members, including future president Fernando Enrique Cardoso. The Workers' Party (Partido dos Trabalhadores—PT) was led by Luis Inacio da Silva, also known as "Lula," the popular leader of the metalworkers' union. In 1989, Lula placed second in the presidential race, running under a coalition of laborite parties called the Popular Front. Lula lost the runoff election to Collor, receiving 47% of the vote. He ran again unsuccessfully in 1994 and 1998. The Brazilian Workers' Party (Partido Trabalhista Brasileiro—PTB) is a populist party with working-class appeal, but is conservative on a variety of economic issues.

In 1985, the Liberal Front Party (PFL) was organized by dissident PDS members. It formed the National Alliance with the PMDB, an alliance that won the 1985 elections. Although the PFL lost the 1989 presidential elections, it soon allied with President Collor, although the scandal of 1992 did little to help its fortunes.

The Communists had been banned since 1957, but were allowed to organize after 1985. The Brazilian Communist Party (Partido Comunista Brasileiro), founded in 1922, is now a Euro-Communist party firmly committed to conventional politics. The Communist Party of Brazil (Partido Comunista do Brasil) is a more radical faction, Maoist in its origins but now expressing solidarity with any socialists who resist reforms.

Fernando Enrique Cardoso of the PSDB was elected president in October 1994, in Brazil's second direct presidential election since 1960, winning 53% of the vote to 26% for the PT candidate, Inacio da Silva ("Lula"), his closest rival. In October 1998 Cardoso won reelection in a first-round election with 53.1% of the vote, defeating "Lula" who came second with 31.7% and socialist Ciro Gomes who placed third with 11%.

15LOCAL GOVERNMENT

Brazil is a highly centralized system, in which local units have very little authority. Each of Brazil's 26 states has its own constitution and popularly elected legislature and governor. The states are divided into 5,507 municipalities, which are, in turn, divided into districts. Each municipality has its own elected council and mayor. The state and municipal legislative bodies are subordinate to the federal government. Municipal authorities are responsible for the construction and maintenance of roads, the creation and upkeep of public parks and museums, and for the program of primary education. As districts increase in population, they, in turn, become municipalities. The large municipalities are important political units and may rival the state in political power. The largest city in each municipality serves as the capital, and usually the largest city in the largest municipality serves as the state capital. The Federal District government in Brasília is appointed by the president with Senate approval.

In 1960, after Brasília became the new capital, the former Federal District, comprising Rio de Janeiro and the 1,165 sq km (450 sq mi) surrounding it, became the state of Guanabara. Eventually this state was amalgamated into the state of Rio de Janeiro. From 1979 on, a few previously unincorporated territories became states.

16JUDICIAL SYSTEM

The legal system is based on continental European principles. Although the jury system has been used in criminal cases for more than 100 years, there is a general tendency away from the use of juries. The Supreme Federal Court is composed of 11 justices, chosen by the president with Senate approval, who serve until age 70. It has final jurisdiction, especially in cases involving constitutional precepts and the acts of state and local authorities. The Federal Appeals Court deals with cases involving the federal government. Immediately below it are federal courts located in the state capitals and in the Federal District, as well as military and labor courts. Codes of criminal, civil, and commercial law are enacted by Congress, but in order to preserve the jurisdiction of state courts, the federal courts will not accept original jurisdiction solely because a law of Congress is involved. Electoral tribunals deal with registration of political parties, supervision of voting, infractions of electoral laws, and related matters.

Each state and municipality has its own judicial system. Justices of the peace and magistrates deal with commercial and other civil cases of the first instance. Decisions from state or municipal courts may be appealed to the federal courts and on up to the Supreme Federal Court.

There is also a system of specialized courts dealing with police, juveniles, and family matters.

The judiciary is independent from the executive and legislative branches. Judges are appointed for life and may not accept other employment.

Criminal defendants have a right to counsel.

17ARMED FORCES

The Brazilian armed forces had a total strength of 291,000 (48,200 conscripts) in 2000. Military service for a minimum of one year is compulsory. Draftees are inducted at the age of 18, but in the event of mobilization, all male citizens up to 45 years of age are liable for service.

The army had 189,000 personnel in 2000; the navy, 52,000 (including 13,900 marines and 1,150 naval airmen); air force personnel totaled 50,000, with 374 combat aircraft; the army, largely armed with Brazilian weapons, has the equivalent of about 60 mechanized, motorized, cavalry, jungle, mountain, artillery, engineers, airborne, coast defense and border patrol brigades. The navy has one carrier and 18 destroyers and frigates, supplemented by 37 patrol and mine warfare craft. Naval aviation forces of 1,400 are equipped with 22 combat aircraft and 54 armed helicopters.

In 1998 Brazil spent $14.7 billion on defense, which was about 1.9% of gross national product.

18INTERNATIONAL COOPERATION

Brazil is a charter member of the UN, having joined on 24 October 1945; it belongs to ECLAC and all the nonregional specialized agencies. The nation contributed a battalion of troops to the UNEF in the Gaza area after the Suez crisis of 1956 and also sent troops to the Congo (now Zaire) in the early 1960s. A signatory of the Law of the Sea, Brazil is also a member of G-77, IADB, LAIA, OAS, WTO, and other inter-American organizations. Brazil participated in the Alliance for Progress program, under which it received US funds for development and stabilization.

19ECONOMY

The history of the Brazilian economy before World War II was characterized by six principal cycles, each centered on one particular commodity: brazilwood, livestock, sugar, gold, rubber, and coffee. At the height of each cycle, Brazil led the world in production of that commodity. Even during the postwar era, variations in price and market conditions for coffee largely determined the degree of national prosperity.

Attempts to diversify the economy through rapid industrialization made Brazil one of the two leading industrial nations of South America, but spiraling inflation thwarted many of the economic advances. The rising inflationary trend of the mid-1960s was due mainly to public budgetary deficits resulting from losses incurred by the government-owned railroads and shipping lines and by official subsidy expenses for imports, such as wheat and petroleum. At the same time, wages increased at a higher rate than productivity; expansion of credit to private enterprises also lagged. The pace of further industrial expansion was determined largely by the availability of foreign exchange, derived chiefly from the sale of coffee, to buy the necessary equipment and raw materials, especially wheat and crude oil.

After the period of what some called an economic miracle (1968–73), during which GDP growth averaged more than 11% annually; the economy cooled to an annual growth rate of 6% between 1974 and 1980, mainly because of increased costs of imported oil. Throughout this period, industrial growth rates outstripped those for the economy as a whole, and industrial products claimed an increasingly large share of GDP.

Inflation was so chronic that in the late 1960s, the government instigated monetary correction, whereby fixed payments were indexed to past inflation. Thus, interest rates, pension payments, mortgage payments, and so forth, kept pace with rising prices, but inflation fed on itself. Even as economic growth surged in the mid-1980s, triple-digit inflation persisted. In February 1986, as the projected inflation rate for the year approached 500%, the government imposed a package of sweeping economic reforms, the Cruzado Plan, which created a new currency (the cruzado), eliminated monetary correction, and froze wages and prices. While inflation plunged to near-zero initially, by mid-1987, it had surged beyond 100%, fueled by increased customer spending due to the price freeze. The government then imposed an austerity program and began negotiations with the IMF for a rescheduling of the staggering foreign debt.

The Brazilian economy was hit by a deep recession and record inflation in 1990. GDP fell by an unprecedented 4%, while inflation hit an all-time high of 2,938%. In March 1990, upon assuming office, President Collor announced sweeping economic reforms designed to stop inflation and integrate Brazil into the developed world economy. In addition, the Collor Plan imposed a price freeze, as well as a freeze on bank deposits, resulting in a precipitated capital flight. Trade barriers were significantly reduced but the attempt to reduce Brazil's large fiscal deficit resulted in the continual resurgence of inflation and a lack of confidence in the government's economic policies.

The Collor Government introduced on 31 January 1991 another package, Collor II, attempting to reduce inflation. The package included wage and price controls and eliminated the overnight market. The economy experienced a lackluster recovery with GDP growth of 1.2%. However, the failure to reduce the structural fiscal deficit, intermittent tightening and loosening of monetary policy, the unfreezing of prices and wages by the third quarter, and the unfreezing of remaining blocked accounts undermined the efforts to reduce inflation.

Under IMF guidance, monetary policy continued to tighten liquidity in 1992. The failure of the government's stabilization efforts produced a new inflationary spiral with monthly inflation rates in the mid-20% range. High real interest rates combined with the acceleration of inflation and the political uncertainty over the outcome of the impeachment proceedings produced another recession with GDP decline of 1.5% for 1992.

Inflation continued to rage in the early 1990s. In 1994 it peaked at 2,700%. That year, the finance minister (who later became president) introduced a new currency, the real, and a new economic plan called the Real Plan. The plan featured privatization of state-owned industries, lowering of tariffs and the abolition of Brazil's unique and counter productive wage-inflation indexing, which had sent prices on a seemingly endless upward spiral. By ending the hyperinflation of the past decades, the government greatly increased the standard of living of millions of Brazilians, allowed businesses to plan for the medium term in an environment of stability, and created a class of economically stable consumers. Inflation had gone down to only 2% by 1998.

From 1988 to 1998, GDP growth averaged 2.4%. The Real Plan suffered in late 1998 due to an international financial crisis, causing the Central Bank to devalue the currency by 8% on 13 January 1999. On 15 January 1999, the Cardoso government announced that the real would no longer be pegged to the US dollar. Immediately, the real lost more than 30% of its value, and subsequent devaluation made the real lose a total of 45% of its value. Despite the devaluation; the economy grew by 1% in 1999, and GDP growth was forecast at 4% for 2000. Inflation rose to 4.9% in 1999 and was expected to reach 8.4% in 2000.

20INCOME

The US Central Intelligence Agency (CIA) reports that in 1998 Brazil's gross domestic product (GDP) was estimated at $1.035 trillion. The per capita GDP was estimated at $6,100. The annual growth rate of GDP was estimated at 0.5%. The average inflation rate in 1998 was 2%. The CIA defines GDP as the value of all final goods and services produced within a nation in a given year and computed on the basis of purchasing power parity (PPP) rather than value as measured on the basis of the rate of exchange. It was estimated that agriculture accounted for 14% of GDP, industry 36%, and services 50%.

The World Bank reports that for the same period per capita private consumption (in PPP terms) was $3,870. Private consumption includes expenditures of individuals, households, and nongovernmental organizations. It was estimated that between 1990 and 1998 private consumption grew at an annual rate of 4.8%. Approximately 22% of household consumption was spent on food, 18% on fuel, 15% on health care, and 34% on education. The richest 10% of the population accounted for approximately 48% of household consumption and the poorest 10% approximately 0.9%.

21LABOR

A 1999 estimate reported the economically active population of Brazil at 75,213,000, or 48% of the total population. In 1997, nearly 20% were engaged in agriculture, 13% in commerce, and 12% in manufacturing.

Generally, there is little unemployment among skilled workers, but there is persistent structural unemployment and high under-employment in rural areas, especially in the northeast. In 1997, 7.8% of the workforce was unemployed. In order to cope with an annual inflation rate that has at times exceeded 2,000%, many Brazilians with fixed income employment have multiple jobs.

Several major schemes have been under way since the 1960s to expand Brazil's industrial work force. The National Industrial Apprenticeship Service provides training for industrial workers; similar training for workers in commerce is provided by the National Commercial Apprenticeship Service. The Center for Technical Education was founded in 1967 in accordance with a plan to improve production in the north and northeast regions. Another national service agency, established in 1976, trains rural workers. Between 1950 and 1993, the economically active female population increased from about 18% of the labor force in 1960 to around 40% by 1999.

Major labor union federations include the Workers' Unitary Central, the Workers' General Confederation (CGT), and the Forca Sindical (FS). A newer federation, the Social Democratic Union (SDS), was founded in 1997. Union financing depends largely on the compulsory checkoff (contribuição sindical) administered by the government, which applies to nearly all workers, except government and domestic employees, irrespective of union affiliation, and amounts to one day's wages per year from each employed worker. Employees who belong to a union must also pay union dues. The union structure in Brazil was created after 1930 by the Getúlio Vargas regime along the "corporative" lines of the syndical organizations of fascist Italy and Portugal. Employee syndicates are paralleled by employer organizations under federal control. The right to strike was outlawed in 1937 but was restored by the 1946 constitution, subject to strict government regulation. Strikes were further limited in the 1964 constitution to disputes in which employers have already rejected arbitration by competent authorities. The right to strike was fully restored in 1984. Strikes in 1999 included those by teachers, truckers, auto workers, and municipal transit workers. Approximately 25% of the workforce is unionized.

The many benefits provided by government legislation have the effect of making workers look to government rather than unions for economic advancement. Comprehensive labor legislation is contained in the consolidated labor laws of 1943 and later amendments. The basic working conditions include provisions for a 44-hour work week, a minimum wage, an annual bonus, paid civil and religious holidays, an annual paid vacation, compensation for overtime work, profit sharing, equal pay for equal work regardless of sex, a family allowance, and severance pay. Special protection is provided for women and minors, as are special benefits for pregnant women. The minimum wage, adjusted annually, varies from region to region. Overtime and night pay must be at least 20% higher than normal hourly wages. These laws generally apply to industrial and commercial workers and, through the Rural Workers' Law, to agricultural workers, but they exclude government employees and domestic workers, who are covered by other regulations. Workers' compensation, provided under the national social security program, was extended to farm workers in 1975. Many labor organizations, which had supported the constitutional revision process begun in 1988, altered their views in 1993. Worries about employment and salaries during the 1992 recession contributed to such opposition.

Enforcement of labor laws is the responsibility of the Ministry of Labor and Social Security through regional delegates of the ministry located in each state. Enforcement, however, is lax. Labor courts are separate from the regular judiciary, and consist of local conciliation and judicial boards, regional labor councils, and a central tribunal. Worker and employer representatives are appointed to each of the labor courts by the president of Brazil, from a list of names submitted by workers and employers. A national mediation service is housed in the Ministry of Labor.

Under the terms of a 1998 constitutional amendment, children under 16 are generally forbidden to work by law except in certain apprentice programs. However, this law is not effectively enforced, and official figures in 1999 put the number of children working at slightly under three million. As of 1999, there was a government set minimum wage of $70 per month, which was only one-fourth of the sum necessary to support a family of four.

22AGRICULTURE

In 1998, 17.9% of Brazil's economically active population worked in agriculture, down from 23.3% in 1990. Total arable and permanent crop area comprises 48.9 million hectares (121 million acres), fifth in the world. Although agriculture's share of exports has declined relative to industrial goods, the value has continued to increase, so that Brazil in 1977 became the world's second-largest exporter of agricultural products. Except for grain (particularly wheat), of which some 6.9 million tons had to be imported in 1997, Brazil is virtually self-sufficient in food. The growth rates for agriculture as a whole averaged 3.0% during 1980–85, 2.3% during 1985–90, and 4.2% for 1991–95. By 1998, agricultural production was 28.7% higher than during 1989–91. In 1998, agriculture accounted for 8% of the total GDP. Export crops are significant— in addition to the traditional exports of coffee and cocoa, Brazil is also a major exporter of soybeans and orange juice. In 1998, Brazil ranked third in the production of cocoa beans (after Côte d'Ivoire and Ghana) at 282,000 tons, or 9.7% of the world's cocoa bean production. In recent years, however, production has been devastated by the effects of the witches-broom fungus.

The Land Statute Law of 1964 was designed to modify the agrarian structure and increase agricultural output in selected regions over a 20-year period. The law empowered the federal government to expropriate unused or underutilized land by offering indemnification in bonds in the case of large properties and cash payment for smallholdings. In redistributing expropriated lands, priority is given to those who work the land under tenancy, sharecropping, or ordinary labor agreements. Responsibility for implementing the law is divided between the Brazilian Agrarian Reform Institute and the National Institute of Agricultural Development. In October 1984, a law was passed to facilitate the distribution of 43.1 million hectares (106.5 million acres) of state-owned land and non-productive private estates to 1.4 million peasant families, primarily in the impoverished northeast, through 1989. The formation of cooperatives was encouraged.

Further agricultural reforms have been carried out under the Carta de Brasília of 1967. The Carta included an incentive program for the construction of storage facilities, to permit farmers to hold products off the market in expectation of better prices. Agricultural research in Brazil is conducted by the Agriculture and Cattle Raising Institute of Research. The expansion of power, transportation, and communications systems during the 1970s further contributed to agricultural development.

Coffee, until 1974 preeminent among export earners, has been declining in importance since the early 1960s, while soybeans, sugarcane, cotton, wheat, and citrus fruits have shown dramatic increases. Brazil led the world in coffee production in 1998, at 1,690,000 tons. Sugarcane production, in which Brazil ranked first in the world in 1998, is grown not only for refined sugar but also as a source of alcohol for fuel. In 1998, production included 22,987,000 tons of oranges, 19,809,000 tons of cassava, and 45,000 tons of cashews. Agricultural production in 1998 (in millions of tons) is shown in the following table:

Sugarcane	338.3
Soybeans	31.4
Rice	7.8
Wheat	2.2
Seed cotton	1.2

23ANIMAL HUSBANDRY

Brazil is a leading livestock-producing country, and 185,500,000 hectares (458,370,000 acres—more than one-fifth of the total national area) are devoted to open pasture. Since World War I, cattle production has become one of the country's major sources of wealth. Hereford and polled angus are raised in the southern states of Rio Grande do Sul and Santa Catarina, and Dutch and Jersey cattle supply dairy products in the uplands of Minas Gerais, Rio de Janeiro, São Paulo, and Paraná. The humped zebu was first introduced in Minas Gerais, where intense crossbreeding produced the Hindu-Brazil breed that is now most common throughout Brazil because it resists tick fever and heat. There were an estimated 161 million head of cattle in 1998, as compared with an annual average of 147.8 million during 1989–91 and 116.6 million during 1979–81.

Hog raising, marked by an improvement in breeds, has doubled since 1935, making Brazil the world's third-largest producer. In 1998 there were an estimated 31.4 million hogs. Berkshires and Poland Chinas have been introduced in quantity, and, since vegetable oils are increasingly replacing lard, the emphasis is on production of pork, ham, and sausages. Brazil is not a major sheep country, since most of the area is too tropical. The bulk of Brazil's 18.3 million sheep are in Rio Grande do Sul. Of the other domestic animals raised commercially in 1998, there were some 12.6 million goats, 6.4 million horses, 2 million mules, and some 900 million chickens. Brazil is the world's third largest exporter of broiler meat; total production in 1998 was 4.6 million tons.

The government encourages production and seeks more efficient methods of conservation and distribution of meat products. Meat production was 11,688,000 tons in 1998, including 5.2 million tons of beef and veal. The dairy industry is most highly developed in the vicinity of large cities. Estimated output of dairy products in 1998 included 21.6 million tons of fresh cow's milk and 1.5 million tons of eggs.

During the years of high inflation, ranchers and farmers looked at their herds and land as assets whose value increased in line with inflation and were less challenged to make investments and increase productivity. With inflation now under control, cattle prices have remained fairly stable, and some meat packers have started turning to the export market.

24FISHING

Although Brazil has a seacoast of some 7,400 km (4,600 mi) and excellent fishing grounds off the South Atlantic coast, the nation has never fully utilized its commercial potential. Traditionally, fishing has been carried on by small groups of individual fishermen using primitive techniques and equipment and seldom venturing out of sight of land. Lack of storage facilities, canneries, and adequate methods of distribution have limited the supply and led to the importation of dried fish. Swordfish is caught in large quantities off the coast of Paraíba and Rio Grande do Norte, and shrimp is caught and dried along the coasts of Maranhão, Ceará, and Bahia. The fish resources of the Amazon River are not exploited, except for the commercial processing of the pirarucú and an aquatic mammal, the sea cow. The annual fish catch is so modest that there has traditionally been a scandalous scarcity during Holy Week, about the only time when Brazilians eat much fish. The total catch in 1997 was 820,480 tons. Exports of fish products were valued at $126.5 million in 1997. Small quantities of lobster are exported.

A fisheries development agency was established in the early 1970s to exploit Brazil's coastal potential. The discovery of large quantities of tuna off the coast of Rio Grande do Sul has interested foreign fishing companies, and Japanese and US concerns have obtained the right to fish in Brazilian waters and to establish storage and canning facilities. Normally, foreign fishing rights are reserved to the Portuguese.

Aquacultural production was valued at $272.4 million in 1997, primarily carp and tilapia.

25FORESTRY

Nearly 58% of South America's forests and woodlands are in Brazil, with an estimated 488 million ha (1,206 million acres). Sylvan areas in Brazil are nearly three-quarters as large as the forests of all African nations combined. Brazil's forests cover 65% of the country's land area and are among the richest in the world, yielding timber, oil-bearing fruits, gums, resins, waxes, essential oils, cellulose, fibers, nuts, maté, and other products. In the rainforest, as many as 3,000 different species per sq mi (2.6 sq km) may coexist. However, only a limited percentage of forestland is being exploited, in part because of a lack of adequate transportation. Brazil is one of the leading producers of tropical hardwood products. Brazilian timber is of fine quality, ranging from wood as light as cork to the wood of the Brazilian pepper tree, with a density one and one-half times that of water. By 1991, rapid deforestation during the previous 30 years in the Amazon (from migration, road building, mining, and tax incentives) had caused the rainforest to shrink by an estimated 8.5% since colonial times. However, the annual rate of deforestation by 1990–95 was 0.5%. The hardwood trees of the Amazon rain forest are of excellent quality, but because of a thriving domestic furniture industry, they are used mainly locally; furniture manufacturing is responsible for 40% of the wood consumption in Brazil. The Paraná pine (Araucaria angustifolia) is in greatest demand. It grows in the southern states in stands that comprise about 420 million trees. A Brazilian ban on log exports has focused exports on value-added products (mostly lumber, plywood, hardboard, and veneers). Policies to develop forest resources have changed recently, and the utilization of native species has become very restricted, mainly in the southern region.

Production of roundwood in 1998 was estimated at 197.8 million cu m; sawn wood production was 18,591,000 cu m in 1998. Production of paper and woodpulp has expanded considerably since 1975; exports of paper intensified between 1981 and 1997, from 337,000 tons to 1,329,000 tons. The total value of Brazilian forest product exports in 1997 reached $2.87 billion. The Amazon region accounted for 40% of the total Brazilian exports of wood products, while the rest of Brazil accounted for 60% (of which Paraná represented 20%). Exports in 1997 (by their total value) included: sawn wood, $411 million; plywood, $264 million; wood pulp, $102 million; fiberboard, $83 million; and veneer, $97 million.

Brazil's production of rubber in 1998 was 54,000 tons; the natural rubber industry, once a world leader, was dealt a strong blow by the development of cheaper synthetics. Forest products like rubber, Brazil nuts, cashews, waxes, and fibers now come from plantations and no longer from wild forest trees as in earlier days.

26MINING

The discovery of gold in Minas Gerais ("general mines") in 1693 made Brazil the world's leading gold producer, but rapid exploitation under the Portuguese colonial system exhausted the mines in less than a century. The dissipation of the nation's gold wealth for the benefit of an overseas power instilled in modern Brazilians a protective attitude toward their mineral reserves, resulting in government control over mining. The 1988 constitution forbids foreign majority participation in direct mining operations. Lack of capital long restricted development by domestic firms, and Brazilian mining laws, as well as adverse geographic conditions, discouraged foreign capital. The majority of the mineral industry is partially or wholly owned by private Brazilian investors, Brazilian corporations, and foreign corporations. In 1995 however, the Brazilian Congress approved constitutional amendments allowing the participation of the private sector (domestic and foreign) in the mining industry through privatization, joint ventures, and by deregulating investment. The state-owned mining giant (Companhia Vale do Rio Doce was privatized in 1997) brought the state $3.3 billion in revenue. Companhia Vale do Rio Doce is now owned by a consortium led by steelmaker Comphania Siderurgica Nacional (CSN). Brazil also has a major petroleum exploration program whose goals are the expansion of its oil reserves and reduction of dependence on foreign oil (it currently imports 60% of its crude oil).

The minerals sector employed about 650,000 persons in 1997. There are also some 500,000 to one million garimpeiros (small-scale independent miners) active in Brazil. In 1997, the total value of minerals produced was about $14.6 billion, or almost 2% of GDP. Brazil is Latin America's leading producer of gold, iron ore, manganese, steel, tin, aluminum, cement, and ferroalloys.

In 1965, the government introduced a 10-year master plan for the evaluation of Brazil's mineral resources. The government also took steps to encourage private capital investment in the development of phosphate reserves, the exploitation of oil-bearing shale, and the expansion of iron ore output. Through the Company for Mineral Resources Research, created in 1969, the government has sought to expand existing mineral industries and to establish new ones. The Amazon region has been a particular focus of the company's efforts. The Carajás mining project in the Amazonian state of Pará, begun in the early 1980s, was expected to lead to the mining there of manganese, copper, tin, silver, gold, nickel, molybdenum, bismuth, and zinc. In 1990–91 investment in mining fell from $1 billion to $400 million. By the mid-1990s, investment was on the rise, due to the government's aggressive economic policies, the diversity of mineral resources, and the constitutional reform that eliminated restrictions on foreign investment in mining.

Brazil's iron ore reserves are known to total 20 billion tons. In 1942, the government-controlled Rio Doce Valley Co. began mining operations in the high-grade deposits of Minas Gerais and increased its activities with the aid of loans from the US Export-Import Bank. Iron ore production for 1974 was 59.4 million tons, more than double the 1969 total; by 1997, output was reported at 187.9 million tons. New deposits in the state of Pará were discovered during the 1970s. In 1981, Brazil became the world's leading exporter of iron ore, 131,000,000 tons were exported in 1995, mostly to Japan and Germany. Output of manganese (mined in Minas Gerais, Mato Grosso, and the territory of Amapá) in 1997 was two million tons. There are important deposits of beryllium, chrome, graphite, magnesite, mica, quartz crystal, thorium, titanium, and zirconium; copper, lead, nickel, tin, and zinc deposits occur in several states. Brazil has become a major exporter of tin in recent years; in 1997, Brazil was the world's third-largest producer of tin following China and Indonesia, at 18,290 tons (down from the peak of 50,200 tons in 1989). Major deposits of high-quality bauxite have been discovered in the Amazon region; output has risen rapidly, from 6.5 million tons in 1987 to 12.5 million tons in 1997. Large phosphate deposits exist in Minas Gerais.

Diamonds and other precious and semiprecious stones are mined in Minas Gerais, Goiás, and Bahia. Gold deposits found at Serra Pelada in 1980 raised gold production to 103,000 kg by 1989, making Brazil the world's sixth-largest producer; production averaged 90,380 kg during 1987–91, but was down to 58,000 kg in 1997. Recent discoveries of platinum indicate that Brazil may have half the world's reserves. There are large supplies of good building stone, as well as sizable deposits of nonmetallic minerals, such as limestone, fluorite, dolomite, and other materials indispensable to the chemical industry.

27 ENERGY AND POWER

Brazil's hydroelectric potential is thought to be one of the world's largest. Great strides are being taken to increase production to keep pace with Brazil's expanding industries. Total installed capacity increased from 4.8 million kW in 1960 to 8.5 million kW in 1968 and to 62.3 million kW in 1998. Production for 1998 was 316.9 billion kWh, of which hydropower contributed 95%. Brazil's hydroelectric potential is estimated at 16.5 billion kW, three times its current capacity. Construction of the Itaipu Dam on the Paraná River took place between 1975 and 1982; this joint Brazilian-Paraguayan project, the world's largest hydro-electric plant, attained its full capacity of 12.6 million kW in 1986, at a cost of $15 billion. About 70% of Brazil's population is served by Itaipu, which generates about 75 billion kWh per year. Each of Brazil's nine turbines (Paraguay controls the other nine) at Itaipu has a capacity of 700,000 kW, which can be transmitted up to 1,000 km (620 mi) away. Brazil regularly purchases a large portion of Paraguay's half of its Itaipu electricity production.

Industrial consumption of electricity has increased rapidly in recent years, especially in highly industrialized areas, such as São Paulo and Minas Gerais, where some 80% of the energy produced is utilized, and where industries are offered generous incentives to convert from fuel oil to electricity. Higher electricity prices since 1993 have permitted electric utilities to invest and improve their financial positions.

Brazil has sharply scaled back its ambitious nuclear power program since 1983. The first nuclear power plant, built with US

help near Rio de Janeiro and known as Angra I, began operations in May 1985. Nuclear generation of electricity only accounted for about 1% of production in 1994. Estimates of uranium reserves were put at 163,000 tons in 1991, the fifth largest in the world.

Brazil's oil reserves are the second largest in South America, surpassed only by those of Venezuela. The government-owned Petróleo Brasileiros (Petrobrás), established in 1953, has had a monopoly over the exploration and development of petroleum reserves; the 1988 constitution guaranteed the maintenance of state monopolies in the petroleum and electricity sectors, despite rampant privatization. In 1995, however, Brazil's Congress and Senate approved a constitutional amendment ending the government's oil monopoly, and allowing foreign companies to drill, prospect, import, export, refine, and transport oil. The government will maintain at least 50% of Petrobras' voting shares plus one. Brazil's government hopes to raise large amounts of money and attract foreign investment through the privatization of the oil sector, in order to pay off the national debt. Foreign participation and investment formerly were forbidden by Brazilian law; however, in the mid-1970s, exploration was opened to foreign companies through risk contracts, and the petrochemicals industry was opened to foreign participation. The National Petroleum Agency (ANP), created in 1997, is charged with opening up the oil industry to both foreign and domestic private interests. Production has traditionally come from the state of Bahia; total production, which amounted to 7.8 million tons in 1968, increased only marginally to nine million tons (or about 186,000 barrels per day) in 1980. By 1998, production totaled 1.2 million barrels per day. Natural gas production was reported at 5.5 million cu m in 1997. In 1975, the government initiated a program to develop alcohol from sugarcane as an energy source. In the 1980s, 80% of the country's cars and light vehicles were powered by alcohol, although slumping oil prices and persistent financial problems within the alcohol industry prompted the government to freeze production at the 1985 level of 11.1 billion liters. By 1995, the production of gasoline-powered vehicles had shifted to 95% from the almost entirely alcohol-powered production of 1989. Alcohol still has an important function to maintain diverse sources of fuel for the transportation sector. Most transportation fuel sold in Brazil is a mixture of 22% ethanol and 78% gasoline. As of 1999, Brazil produced 200,000 barrels per day of ethanol.

The absence of good coking coal is a handicap to industrial plans, and coal production, mainly from Santa Catarina, has been hurt by cutbacks in state investment.

28 INDUSTRY

Major industries include iron and steel production, automobile assembly, petroleum processing, chemicals production, and cement making; technologically based industries have been the most dynamic in recent years, but have not outpaced traditional industries. Peak industrial growth was achieved in 1973, when the manufacturing sector grew by 15.8%; growth rates averaging about 7% were posted during 1978–80, rising to 8.3% in 1985 and 11.3% in 1986. Growth slowed significantly during the 1990s. According to the Brazilian Statistical Institute (IBGE), manufacturing rose an annual average of only 0.7% between 1988 and 1998.

In 1969, 3.7 million tons of crude steel were produced; by 1985, this had reached 20.5 million tons; and by 1998 the total output of processed ore was 190 million tons. Domestic production exceeds domestic needs. Vast reserves of accessible, high-grade ore, plus a rapidly expanding domestic demand for these products, favor continued expansion of the steel industry. The major negative factor is lack of domestic soft coal. Companhia Vale do Rio Doce (CVRD) is the largest Brazilian mining company, responsible for nearly 23% of the mineral output of the country.

Motor vehicle production, Brazil's industrial backbone, experienced a drop of nearly 27% from 1998 to 1999 because of the country's financial difficulties. Production of automobiles went from about two million units in 1997, down to 1.6 million units in 1998. Despite these figures, the automobile industry is expanding rapidly with major sources of foreign investment and the construction of new manufacturing plants.

Brazil mines and refines petroleum products. Because of increased domestic refining capacity during the 1970s, imports of petroleum products were less needed, and by 1979, Brazil was a net exporter of petroleum derivatives. In 1998, Brazil only imported 50% of its petroleum. Brazil's petrochemical industry emphasizes the production of synthetic rubber at Petrobrás' synthetic rubber plant. There are also over 500 pharmaceutical laboratories and plants in Brazil, the majority in São Paulo. Over 80% of the industry is foreign-owned. Increased construction demands boosted Brazil's cement production during the 1980s and 1990s. Brazil's electrical equipment industry manufactures computers, television sets, transistor radios, refrigerators, air conditioners, and many other appliances. Brazil has the largest textile industry in South America in terms of installed capacity and output, with nearly half of the spindles and looms in operation on the continent. The Brazilian pulp and paper sector is also large, consisting of more than 220 companies, which together employ approximately 80,000 people in industrial operations, as well as another 57,000 in forestry work and operations. The pulp and paper sector is almost fully privately-owned. The government allowed foreign investment in vital industries since 1995, and supports the sale of any residual parastatal enterprises.

29 SCIENCE AND TECHNOLOGY

The National Council of Scientific and Technological Development, created in 1951 and headquartered in Brasilia, formulates and coordinates Brazil's scientific and technological policies. The Brazilian Academy of Sciences was founded in 1916 is headquartered in Rio de Janeiro. In 1996 there were 25 specialized learned societies and 52 research institutes covering virtually every area of scientific and technological endeavor. Among the most important scientific institutions are the Oswaldo Cruz Foundation for biological research in Rio de Janeiro and the Butantan Institute in São Paulo, which produces serums for the bites of venomous snakes, a field in which Brazil leads the world. Government expenditures on research and development in 1994 amounted to 1.2 billion reals. In 1987–97, Brazil had 168 scientists and engineers and 59 technicians per million people engaged in research and development.

Brazil entered the space age in 1973, with the launching of the SONDA II rocket as part of a program to determine electron density in the low ionosphere, a question of practical importance for aircraft navigation. Under the government's Amazon development program, Humboldt City, a scientific and technological center, has been established in Mato Grosso. Atomic research is conducted at the Energetics and Nuclear Research Institute of São Paulo; other research reactors are located at Belo Horizonte and Rio de Janeiro. The Nuclear Energy Center for Agriculture was established in 1966. A total of us$550 million was allocated to the nuclear energy program under the 1975–79 development plan, but the program languished in the 1980s.

In 1996, Brazil had approximately 100 universities and colleges offering courses in basic and applied science. In 1987–97, science and engineering students accounted for 27% of college and university enrollments.

30 DOMESTIC TRADE

Rio de Janeiro and São Paulo are the principal distribution centers; the largest numbers of importers, sales agents, and distributors are located in these cities, having branch offices in other areas. Other major commercial centers are Recife and Pôrto Alegre, in the northeast and the south; Belém, which serves as a distribution center for the whole Amazon River Valley; and Salvador, which is the main distribution center for Bahia and the neighboring states.

The Brazilian commercial code permits the exercise of trade by all persons who make trade their habitual occupation and register with the appropriate government body. Goods are sold in department stores, in specialty shops, by street vendors, and in supermarkets in the larger cities, but most commercial establishments have fewer than six employees. There are a number of consumer cooperatives that are generally sponsored by ministries, trade unions, and social security institutes. Producer cooperatives are found mostly in agriculture and fishing. Credit is extended to higher-income customers on open accounts and to lower-income groups on installment payment plans.

Business hours are from 8 AM to 6 PM, Monday through Friday. Banks transact business from 10 AM to 4:30 PM, Monday through Friday. In many smaller cities and towns, stores are closed for over an hour at lunchtime.

Since 1947, the advertising sector (in all the various media) has increased its expenditures many times over. Most advertising agencies maintain headquarters in São Paulo; some major agencies have branch offices in other large cities. Advertisements are presented on television and on all radio stations, with the exception of the special broadcasting system of the Ministry of Education. Newspapers, magazines, periodicals, motion pictures, billboards, posters, and electric signs are used for advertising. Mobile advertising units equipped with loudspeaker systems are common in the larger cities.

31 FOREIGN TRADE

Brazil's long-favorable foreign-trade balance deteriorated substantially between 1958 and 1974 as a result of industrial expansion, which necessitated increased imports of industrial capital goods and petroleum. During 1975–76 and again from 1978 to 1982, the foreign-trade balance was in deficit. Beginning in 1983, Brazil recorded trade surpluses: $5.1 billion in 1983, $11.8 billion in 1984, and $11.3 billion in 1985. This achievement was the result of policies that restricted imports and offered substantial incentives to exporters.

Between 1963 and 1981, exports expanded at an average annual rate of 17%, but they grew by only 9.1% between 1982 and 1985. Coffee has long been Brazil's dominant export, but the proportion of its export earnings declined from 41.3% in 1968 to 5.6% in 1998. As a result of an ambitious energy development program, Brazil's reliance on imported oil dropped from 70% of its needs in 1980 to 45% in 1985.

The notable accomplishment of former President Fernado Collor de Mello to open the Brazilian market remains the cornerstone of Brazil's economic and trade policies. After almost 30 years of import substitution, which initially brought high growth and short-term industrialization in the 1960–70s, this policy was finally recognized in the late 1980s as the principal culprit of Brazil's economic woes, particularly high inflation and industrial decline.

Over the last three years, most of Brazil's non-tariff barriers to trade, which for many years were the hallmark of Brazil's restrictive trade regime, were eliminated or drastically reduced. Import duties were reduced from an average of about 50% in the late-1980s to 14.2% and a maximum of 35%. While the overall level and pervasiveness of non-tariff barriers have been drastically reduced, some import duties remain high in comparison with other countries. While the depression/inflation problems of recent years have reduced purchasing power by about 50% among the working and lower middle classes and further skewed the already highly uneven distribution of income, the Brazilian market remains enormously attractive to US businesses.

Although trade barriers continued to recede with the government of President Itamar Franco who assumed office on 2 October 1992, trade liberalization lost some of its momentum, and there were serious concerns regarding automobile, telecommunications, and informatics sectors. The reforms gained new momentum under President Cardoso's administration.

In 1995, Brazil joined with Argentina, Paraguay, and Uruguay to form the MERCOSUR common market, made up of 200 million people worth over $1 trillion. The agreement covers tariffs for over 85% of 9,000 items with the remainder to be covered by 2001. Brazil has a symbiotic relationship with Argentina, in which the latter supplies natural gas, automobiles, and other products; while the former exports steel, shoes, and paper products.

In 1999, Argentina implemented trade restrictions on certain Brazilian products because prices were ridiculously low from the currency devaluation. Brazil replied by putting its own trade barriers in place. Such measures did not bode well for the MERCOSUR community.

The most popular export commodity from Brazil is coffee. The country also exports a substantial amount of iron ore, steel, and aluminum. The top 10 exports are as follows:

	% OF COUNTRY TOTAL	% OF WORLD TOTAL
Coffee	5.6	18
Iron ore	5.4	29
Animal feed	4.8	11
Iron and steel primary forms	3.7	6.2
Footwear	3.3	4.5
Sugar	3.3	11
Motor vehicle parts and accessories	3.2	1.3
Aluminum	2.9	3.2
Pulp and waste paper	2.6	5.2
Preserved fruit	2.5	9.9

In 1997 Brazil's imports were distributed among the following categories:

Consumer goods	8.1%
Food	8.5%
Fuels	11.5%
Industrial supplies	28.6%
Machinery	29.9%
Transportation	13.4%

Principal trading partners in 1998 (in millions of US dollars) were as follows:

COUNTRY	EXPORTS	IMPORTS	BALANCE
United States	9,899	13,562	-3,663
Argentina	6,747	8,028	-1,281
Japan	2,202	3,599	-1,397
Netherlands	2,744	711	2,033
Germany	3,006	5,239	-2,233
Italy	1,931	3,196	-1,265
Belgium-Luxembourg	2,194	668	1,526
United Kingdom	1,339	1,498	-159
France	1,256	1,987	-731

32BALANCE OF PAYMENTS

After a decline in the mid-1960s, Brazil's reserve holdings grew spectacularly, reaching $6.5 billion by 1974. The prime reason was a steadily rising inflow of long-term capital investment, coupled with trade balances that were favorable or only minimally unfavorable. In 1974, however, a decline in the value of coffee exports and a doubling of import costs (partly attributable to increased oil prices) more than offset a further rise in capital investment, resulting in Brazil's first payments deficit in nearly a decade. Between 1976 and 1978, Brazil had a positive balance of payments, but large deficits were registered in 1979 and 1980. A surplus was achieved in 1981, in part because of Brazil's excellent trade showing. The surpluses in 1984 and 1985 were sufficient to pay all interest on the foreign debt.

During the 1970s and early 1980s, Brazil increasingly came to rely on international borrowing to meet its financing needs. The foreign debt grew rapidly after 1974 as the government pressed for continued economic growth without regard for balance of payments pressures generated by the oil shocks of the later 1970s and without increasing domestic savings or improving the tax base. The huge trade surpluses of 1984 and 1985 halted the upward trend. However, the 1986 surge in consumer spending drained reserves to such an extent that by early 1987, the government was forced to suspend payments on $68 billion of the estimated $108 billion debt, the highest of any developing nation. An agreement was reached in April 1991 on 1989–90 arrears. In 1992, Brazil and the advisory committee representing foreign commercial banks agreed to a debt and debt service reduction for $44 billion. Under the Real Plan, the balance of payments dropped from a surplus of $10.5 billion in 1994 to a deficit of $3.1 billion in 1995, -$5.5 billion in 1996, and -$8.4 billion in 1997.

The US Central Intelligence Agency reports that in 1998 the purchasing power parity of Brazil's exports was $51 billion while imports totaled $57.6 billion resulting in a trade balance of -$6.6 billion.

The International Monetary Fund (IMF) reports that in 1998 Brazil had exports of goods totaling $51,136 million and imports totaling $57,739 million. The services credit totaled $7,631 million and debit $16,676 million. The following table summarizes Brazil's balance of payments as reported by the IMF for 1998 in millions of US dollars.

Current Account		-33,829
Balance on goods	-6,603	
Balance on services	-9,045	
Balance on income	29,445	
Current transfers	1,436	
Capital Account		375
Financial Account		20,063
Direct investment abroad	-2,721	
Direct investment in Brazil	31,913	
Portfolio investment assets	-594	
Portfolio investment liabilities	19,013	
Other investment assets	-5,992	
Other investment liabilities	-21,556	
Net Errors and Omissions		-2,911
Reserves and Related Items		16,302

33BANKING AND SECURITIES

A banking reform enacted in December 1964 provided for the establishment of the Central Bank of the Republic of Brazil (changed in 1967 to the Central Bank of Brazil), with powers to regulate the banking system and the stock market. The Central

Bank serves as the financial agent of the federal government and functions as a depository for the reserves of private banks. The reform also created the National Monetary Council, which formulates monetary policies for the Central Bank.

The Bank of Brazil primarily finances projects in the agricultural sector. The National Economic and Social Development Bank (BNDES) provides long-term financing and administers the privatization program.

There once were about 340 commercial banks in Brazil, with hundreds of branch offices; however, banking reforms reduced that number to 233 in 1998. The largest banks are the federal banks Bank of Brazil, the Federal Savings Bank, and BNDS; private banks Bradesco, Itau, Unibanco, Safra, and Banespa; the Real Bank, and the state bank of Rio Grande do Sul, Banrisul. Since January 1994, banks and other financial institutions must publish constant-currency financial statements. The major banks are considered to be sophisticated and competitive and offer a broad range of financial services, many of them operating on-line.

The 1996 rise in international reserves and the fall of the dollar against the Real falsely portrayed an improvement in the financial market. In an attempt to calm the financial markets' worries about exchange rate risk, the government began issuing bonds indexed to the exchange rate. The bonds were supposed to be a guarantee that exchange rate policy was not going to change. The Central Bank curbed the expansion of the monetary base, thus controlling inflation, while the volume of money controlled by banks increased with the initial relaxation of credit. This enlarged monetary base, which included the stock of federal bonds and deposits at the Central Bank, rose at a faster rate than nominal GDP. At the end of 1996, the enlarged monetary base was equivalent to 23% of GDP compared with 18% of GDP at the end of 1995. The expansion of monetary aggregates resulted from the rise in public debt through bond financing of the fiscal deficit. The relaxation of credit policy after the end of 1995 caused borrowers to overdraw, resulting in liquidity problems during 1996 and 1997. This presented a precarious situation for the Brazilian economy, especially when the 1998 financial crisis occurred. The Central Bank decided to let the real float in relation to the US dollar, severely depreciating the value of the real by about 45%; and the bonds that were supposed to have guaranteed a fixed exchange rate were also devalued. These issues led to a number of bank mergers and closures in 1999 and 2000.

The stock market is a source of financing for all listed companies in Brazil, regardless of ownership. All public issues require the approval of the Securities Commission (CVM). There are nine regional stock exchanges, although over 90% of transactions are carried out in São Paulo and Rio de Janeiro. In 1998, there were 586 companies listed on the Brazilian exchanges. Trading is concentrated in a few stocks. Telebras (the formerly state-owned telecommunications company) accounts for 50% of trade volume. Petrobras, Electrobras, and TELESP; the state-owned petroleum, electric, and Sao Paulo State telecom companies; account for 18% of trade volume altogether.

Brazil opened its market to foreign portfolio investment in 1991. Brazilian tax laws provide incentives for investment in stocks and bonds. Profit and dividend remittances are subject to a 15% income withholding tax. Up to 24% of individual tax liability may be invested annually in share certificates from authorized financial institutions. Furthermore, individuals may deduct from gross income up to 42% of capital subscription in companies or agencies involved in developing the northeastern or Amazon regions, up to 25% of amounts invested in open capital companies, up to 20% of investments in approved forestation or reforestation projects, up to 13.5% of investments in mutual funds, and up to 4% of savings under the National Housing System. Earnings from all the above investments are also excluded from gross income, up to certain limits.

[34]INSURANCE

The operations of insurance companies in Brazil are supervised by the Superintendency of Private Insurance (SUSEP0), the National Private Insurance Council (CNSP), and the Institute of Reinsurance of Brazil (IRB), a company which is 50% owned by the government and 50% by the insurance companies operating in Brazil. The IRB was ready for privatization in the second half of 2000.

With the lifting of restrictions on foreign insurance companies operating in Brazil, several companies made major investments in the market during 1997 and 1998. The US is the top investor, with 40% of the market, with nearly half of insurance policies sold in the state of Sao Paulo.

The Brazilian insurance market is characterized by two large groups of insurance companies. The top five groups had about half of the insurance market, including Sul America, Bradesco, Itau Porto Seguro, and American International Group (AIG-Unibanco). The balance of the market is shared with approximately 80 additional groups.

[35]PUBLIC FINANCE

The Brazilian fiscal year coincides with the calendar year. The budget, prepared under the supervision of the Ministry of Planning and Economic Coordination, represents the government's plans for financing administrative operations and capital expenditures. Budgetary deficits increased considerably in the 1960s. The government's objective—to hold total expenditures fairly constant while raising the share of capital outlays—was achieved by an austerity policy. Although the federal budget deficit was reduced in real terms during the late 1960s, fiscal problems continued to be a major source of inflationary pressure, with revenues hovering between 14.5% and 16.5% of GNP and total government expenditures in the range of 17.5% to 19%. Government revenue increased considerably, and each year the real deficit was reduced below the previous year's level both absolutely and relatively. Public expenditure was stepped up, particularly transfer payments; transfers of capital to decentralized agencies increased, although direct investment by the central government fell off. Thus, more capital was invested in basic infrastructural projects.

Increases in both revenues and expenditures were rapid during the 1970s, but the pattern of decreasing deficits continued. The budgets for 1973 and 1974 actually showed a surplus, although the realized surplus in 1974 fell far short of the budgeted surplus. There was a budget deficit in 1975, but surpluses were recorded annually during 1976–80. One of the principal causes of Brazil's financial instability in the 1980s was the rate at which public spending exceeded revenues. Following another stabilization program in 1990, a budget surplus of 1.4% of GDP was recorded, but deteriorated to a deficit of 1.7% of GDP by 1992. During the 1990s, the budget remained in deficit by about 4.0% of GDP, but in 1999, the budget recorded a deficit equal to 9.5% of GDP due to the devaluation of the real. Public spending accounts for about a third of GDP in Brazil.

The US Central Intelligence Agency (CIA) estimates that in 1998 Brazil's central government took in revenues of approximately $151 billion and had expenditures of $149 billion including capital expenditures of $36 billion. Overall, the government registered a surplus of approximately $2 billion. External debt totaled $212 billion. The following table shows an itemized breakdown of government revenues and expenditures.

The percentages were calculated from data reported by the International Monetary Fund. The dollar amounts (millions) are based on the CIA estimates provided above.

REVENUE AND GRANTS	100%	151,000
Tax revenue	64.8%	97,857
Non-tax revenue	22.1%	33,302
Capital revenue	13.2%	19,880
Grants	0.1%	174
EXPENDITURES	100%	149,000
General public services	8.4%	12,588
Defense	3.1%	4,663
Public order and safety	1.6%	2,402
Education	3.6%	5,417
Health	6.3%	9,338
Social security	30.4%	45,323
Housing and community amenities	0.2%	267
Recreation, cultural, and religious affairs	0.1%	118
Economic affairs and services	5.5%	8,202
Other expenditures	0.2%	269
Interest payments	44.0%	65,612
Adjustments	-3.5%	-5,197

36TAXATION

Brazil's tax structure has been modified repeatedly in recent years, and traditional tax evasion has come under strong attack. A series of income tax reforms, during the 1960s and 1970s closed many loopholes and expanded the roster of taxpayers, mainly through wider use of withholding taxes.

The basic income tax rate on corporations and other legal entities in 2000 was 15%, with an added 10% if profits exceed a certain limit. Firms may effectively reduce income tax liability by investing part of the tax due in government-approved incentive projects or by purchasing quotas in funds that invest in such projects. Corporate income earned overseas is not taxed.

There is a personal income tax of either 15% or 25%. Numerous exclusions from ordinary taxable income include profits on sales of shares, profits from certain real estate sales, and interest on stocks and bonds up to certain limits. Foreigners transferring residence from abroad need not pay income tax on returns from their overseas holdings for the first five years of residence in Brazil.

A value-added tax is payable on sales and transfers of goods at varying rates in accordance with the nature of the production (generally 10% to 15%). All corporations are subject to a social contribution tax at rates ranging from 8% for corporations to 18% for financial institutions. Other taxes include a financial operations levy; taxes on the production and distribution of minerals, fuels, and electric power; a real estate transfer tax; and municipal service and urban real estate taxes. There is a social security tax of 2%, and from 10% to 20% of employee payroll.

37CUSTOMS AND DUTIES

Since the late 1980s, the government has reduced import duties incrementally to encourage trade. Tariffs are assessed on an ad valorem basis, which range from zero to 35%, plus specific duties in some cases. The average tariff rate is 17%. Imported automobiles come with a 70% tax. There is an Industrial Products Tax (IPI) that usually ranges from 0% to 15%, but goes up to 365% on cigarettes and alcoholic beverages. There is also an ICMS tax on goods moved through Brazil, at 18% in Sao Paulo, and 12% in other Brazilian states. All imports and exports are controlled by SECEX, the Foreign Trade Secretariat, with the help of the SISCOMEX computer system.

Certain sectors, including petroleum products and weapons, require departmental or ministerial approval for imports. Importers must pay state and federal value-added taxes at ports, but these may be recovered for goods to be manufactured or sold in Brazil. There are eight free-trade zones, including the oldest one in Manaus, and others in Macapa/Santana, Tabatinga, Guajaramirim, Bonfim, Paracaima, Brasileia, and Epitaciolandia. These zones, and some energy development projects are exempted from import duties, as long as they export at least 90% of production.

Brazil and its MERCOSUL partners implemented a common external tariff in 1995 which increased by 3% in 1997 to 23%, to cover all tariff items by 2006.

38FOREIGN INVESTMENT

Brazilian law gives the same protection and guarantees to foreign capital investments that it gives to investments made by Brazilian nationals. Special incentives are offered for investments in mining, fishing, tourism, shipbuilding, and reforestation and for projects undertaken in the northeast and Amazon regions. The registration of foreign capital and of reinvestment, profit remittance, interest, royalties, and payments, for technical assistance, as well as repatriation of foreign capital, are regulated by Brazil's Foreign Capital and Profit Remittance Law of 1962, as amended. There is no limitation on the repatriation of capital; reinvestment of profits is considered an increase of the original capital for the purposes of the law. In 1995, Brazil statutorily eliminated the distinction between foreign and national capital. Foreign investors have been allowed to trade on the Brazilian stock market since 1991. The petroleum, telecommunications, mining, power generation, and internal transportation sectors were opened up to foreign investment in 1995. These provisions saw foreign portfolio investment go from $760 million the year it was enacted to $30 billion in 1997, but investment fell to $21 billion in 1998.

The growth in the attractiveness of Brazil as a recipient of foreign investment is directly attributable to the economic liberalization implemented under Finance Minister, and later President, Fernando Enrique Cardoso in 1994. He instituted a new currency, reigned in the hyperinflation that had plagued the country for decades, and opened up previously closed industries to private ownership.

Investment comes mainly from the US and EU countries, but investment from the Cayman Islands is thought to represent mainly repatriation of Brazilian capital through FDI. Investment from Spain and Portugal, which does not appear on the 1997 top ten list, increased in 1998 due to investment in telecommunications and the banking sector. The following shows country of origin of foreign direct investment (FDI) in Brazil in 1997: (US millions)

COUNTRY	FDI	PERCENT
US	17,210	26.3
Germany	6,266	9.6
Cayman Islands	4,560	7.5
France	4,341	6.5
The Netherlands	3,186	5.4
United Kingdom	2,441	5.0
Japan	2,426	4.9
Switzerland	2,123	4.6

Prohibitions on remittances for royalty and technical service payments between related parties were removed under the 1992 tax code. In addition, the base tax rate on profits and royalty remittances has been reduced from 25% to 15%.

39ECONOMIC DEVELOPMENT

Economic policy since the late 1960s has had three prime objectives: control of inflation, gradual improvement of the welfare of the poorest sector, and a high economic growth rate. Generally, under the stewardship of finance ministers Roberto de Oliveira Campos and, later, Antonio Delfim Netto (who became minister of planning in 1979), Brazilian policy sought to prevent inflation from eroding economic growth by a process of monetary correction—that is, by the legal revaluation of fixed assets, such as real estate, debits in arrears, and the face value of bonds, to reflect inflation. This technique, which requires extensive government control over the economy, was intended to prevent inflation from distorting the relative values of various types of holdings. It was also disastrously inflationary.

The central stress of the 1975–79 development plan was on economic growth. Economic infrastructure (energy, transportation, and communications) received top priority, with a 25% share of the total investment. A special development plan, known as Palomazonia (the Program for Agriculture, Cattle Raising, and Agrominerals for the Amazon), concentrated on expansion of agriculture, forestry, mineral exploitation, and hydroelectric power in the region. The third national plan (1980–85) placed the greatest emphasis on agricultural development, energy, and social policies. Its main aim was improvement of the public welfare through continued economic growth and more equitable income distribution.

The First National Plan of the New Republic (1986–89), sought to maintain high levels of economic growth, introduce a wide range of basic institutional and fiscal reform in the public sector, and reduce poverty significantly. When inflation continued to mount, however, the Cruzado Plan was introduced; it froze wages and prices for a year, and introduced a new unit of currency, the cruzado. While inflation did drop dramatically, the ensuing consumer spending boom, caused by the desire to take advantage of the price freeze, rekindled inflation. By 1987, Brazil had reverted to orthodox austerity and monetary correction in an attempt to bring the economy under control.

In 1994, finance minister (and later president) Fernando Enrique Cardoso implemented the Real Plan, an economic liberalization named for the newly launched currency, the real. The plan called for the abolition of state control of wages and all indexing to inflation, lowering of tariffs and barriers to international investment, and a massive sell-off of state-owned enterprises in nearly every sector. The plan was almost immediately successful, and attracted huge amounts of international investment while raising the living standards of million of Brazilians. Unfortunately, the 1998 international financial crisis caused the Central Bank to let the real float, devaluating the currency by 45%. Instead of immediately falling into a recession, the economy reported modest gains in 1999 and 2000.

Since the early 1960s, the government has offered special incentives to agricultural and industrial enterprises that further the development of the northeastern and northern regions of the country. The development of these areas is under the supervision of the Development Superintendency of the Northeast, whose activities cover the states of Maranhão, Piauí, Ceará, Rio Grande do Norte, Paraíba, Pernambuco, Alagoas, Sergipe, Bahia, the zone of Minas Gerais located within the Drought Polygon, and the territory of Fernando de Noronha. The Superintendency for the Development of Amazonia, the Superintendency for the Development of the West-Central Region, and the Superintendency for the Development of the Southern Region are the other regional development agencies.

40 SOCIAL DEVELOPMENT

The Organic Social Security Law of Brazil, passed during the Vargas reform years of the 1930s, covered only some four million urban workers by the 1960s, including metallurgical, textile, and other industrial workers and commercial, bank, and store clerks. In 1976, social security laws were consolidated, and in the following year, the National System of Social Security and Welfare was established. Benefits include modest insurance against accidents; old age, invalids', and survivors' pensions; funeral insurance; and medical, dental, and hospital coverage. The social security system is financed by contributions from the employer, the worker, and the government. The maximum rates in 1999 were 8–11% of the monthly salary for employees and 20% of payrolls for employers.

Maternity benefits were introduced under the new Constitution in 1988. However, as a reaction against the maternity leave law, many employers required prospective female employees to present sterilization certificates or tried to avoid hiring women of childbearing age. In 1995, the government passed a law prohibiting employers from demanding sterilization certificates or pregnancy tests.

Perhaps the most significant social challenge facing Brazil is caring for the millions of children who lack sufficient education, housing, health care, and nutrition. It has been estimated that over one-third of all children live in poverty. Thousands of children live and work on the streets in deplorable conditions; some are homeless, but a greater number have homes they return to at night. Many street children abuse drugs and they are often forced to resort to crime and prostitution to make a living. As a result, many shopkeepers have taken action against street children, and there is a widespread tendency to regard the problem as a security concern rather than a human rights issue. Police and security guards have even reportedly been paid by businessmen to execute street children.

Racial discrimination is pervasive in Brazil. Most Afro-Brazilians work in low paid jobs and live in poor housing. They have fewer opportunities for higher education and professional employment. In 1997 the government passed legislation mandating fines and prison sentences for discrimination and other racist acts.

Sexual and domestic violence is common and often goes unreported. A 1998 report noted that women earn, on average, only 56% as much as men do. In the same year, 35 of 594 members of parliament were women.

Indigenous tribes of the Amazon are increasingly being threatened by mining, logging, and ranching, which encroach on their lands.

Serious human rights abuses by the police have been reported, including the beating, torture, and killing of detainees.

41 HEALTH

A health and welfare program, Prevsaúde, introduced by the government in 1981, was intended to double health services by 1987. In 1993, however, Brazil's national health care system came to an end, chiefly due to extensive fraudulent activity by hospitals, physicians, and state and municipal health secretariats. The new Brazilian Minister of Health planned to implement a new system and supported legislation to increase funds for the public health sector. As of 1998, public health services, complemented by private services, covered 75% of the population. The Ministry of Health has made efforts to encourage the federal district and 26 states to participate in some quality of care projects. Initiatives include certification by the International Standards organizations; consulting services; total quality management; patient satisfaction; and development of new technologies to increase efficiency.

Health and sanitary conditions vary widely from region to region. The large cities have competent physicians, generally with advanced training abroad, but there is a dearth of doctors, hospitals, and nurses in most towns in the interior. In 1998, there were 1.26 physicians per 1,000 people and 3.5 beds per 1,000 people.

In 1998, 69% of the population had access to safe drinking water. As part of a pilot program, Brazil is fortifying sugar with vitamin A and is currently investigating the feasibility of fortifying foods with vitamin A or iron. As of 1995, children one-year-old and under were immunized as follows: tuberculosis (87%); diphtheria, pertussis, and tetanus (69%); and measles (78%). In 1995, cholera affected many Brazilians; 15,915 new cases were reported in 1995. The HIV seroprevalence was 0.7 per 100,000 adults in 1994. Two years later in 1996, 79,908 new cases of AIDS were reported.

The infant mortality rate is high, but it has declined over the last 15 years. In 1999, the infant mortality was 35 per 1,000 live births. Many Brazilian women die during childbirth. In 1997, 114 maternal deaths occurred for every 1,000 live births. In 1996, data showed that 70% of married women (between the ages of 15 and 49 years) used contraception. The 1999 death rate was 9 per 1,000 people, while the average life expectancy in 1998 declined to 67 years.

42HOUSING

Despite major urban developments, both the housing supply and living conditions in Brazil remain inadequate. Large, sprawling slums are endemic in the large cities, while most rural dwellers live without amenities such as piped water and electricity. In the mid-1990s, there were nearly 35 million residences. At last estimate, more than 80% of all housing units were detached houses of brick, stone, wood or concrete; less than 10% were apartments; less than 10% were rural dwellings of wood or clay; and less than 5% were semi-private units called "quartes." Roughly 65% of all dwellings were owner occupied; more than 20% were rented; and nearly 15% were issued by employers. Some 30% had sewage facilities, and almost 20% had septic tanks; 80% of all homes had electric lighting.

In 1964, the federal government enacted the National Housing Act and suspended rent controls, with the stipulation that rents could be brought in line with private market levels. The law provided for the establishment of the National Housing Bank (Banco Nacional de Habitação, or BNH), whose main purposes are to stimulate savings to finance home construction through lending institutions, to coordinate the activities of both the public and private sectors, and to introduce financial incentives. The BNH can raise funds through bond issues and may also receive deposits from governmental agencies, public cooperatives, and mixed companies.

Under the National Sanitation Plan, announced in 1971, the government aimed, with the help of us$772 million provided by the IBRD, to provide 90% of urban dwellings with safe water and 65% with sewerage facilities by the end of the 1980s.

43EDUCATION

Education in colonial times was carried on first by the Jesuits and then by a few royal schools. Brazil's public school system, always weak, was under the Ministry of Justice and Interior until 1930, when the Ministry of Education and Health was created by Vargas. Responsibility for public education, as defined by the 1946 constitution and the 1961 directives and standards for national education, is divided between the federal, state, and municipal governments. Public elementary and secondary instruction is almost exclusively a function of the municipalities and states, while higher education is the responsibility of the federal Ministry of Education. Public education is free at all levels and nonprofit private schools also receive public funding. The federal government has been active, however, on all three levels through the Federal Council of Education, established in 1961 to coordinate the implementation of the 1961 directives and to advise the Ministry of Education.

The 1961 directives required the federal government to contribute at least 12% of its tax revenues to education, and state and municipal governments were required to contribute a minimum of 20% of their tax revenues for this purpose. The first National Plan of Education, formulated in 1962, called for the extension of compulsory elementary education to five and, eventually, six years, and by 1980 eight years of schooling was required. The 1988 Brazilian constitution allocates 25% of state and local tax revenues to education. In 1964 there were 10 million students attending school at all levels. Since then, great strides have been made in the Brazilian system of education. In 1998 there were 35,838,372 students enrolled at the elementary level; 6,967,905 at the secondary level; and 1,868,529 at the university level.

There were more than 90 universities in the 1990s, including the Federal University of Rio de Janeiro (founded 1920) and the universities of Minas Gerais (1927), São Paulo (1934), Rio Grande do Sul (1934), Bahia (1946), Recife (1946), Paraná (1946), and Brasília (1961). The federal government maintains at least one federal university in each state. Entrance to a college or university is through an examination called "vestibular"; students may either earn a "bacharel" degree or, with an additional year spent in teacher training, obtain a "licenciado" degree. There are at least 902 institutions at the post-secondary level.

Adult education campaigns have functioned sporadically since 1933, backed by the federal government with some assistance from social, fraternal, Catholic, Protestant, professional, and commercial organizations. Although millions of Brazilians have received literacy training, adult illiteracy estimates for the year 2000 still stood at 14.7% (males, 14.9%; females, 14.6%), according to estimates by UNESCO.

44LIBRARIES AND MUSEUMS

Of Brazil's many hundreds of public libraries, the largest municipal library system is that of São Paulo, with over one million volumes. The National Library in Rio de Janeiro (founded in 1810) houses 1.5 million bound volumes, more than eight million documents, and many rare manuscripts. Included in the collection are 60,000 volumes brought to Brazil by the Royal Family of Portugal in 1808. Various government ministries maintain separate libraries in Brasília. The largest academic library is the São Paulo University Integrated Library System with 2.5 million volumes in 39 libraries.

Brazil has nearly 200 museums. The National Museum (founded in 1818), one of the most important scientific establishments in South America, is especially known for its Brazilian ethnographic collections. Other important museums in Rio de Janeiro include the National Museum of Fine Arts, the Museum of Modern Art, the Historical Museum, the Museum of Mineralogy, the Museum of the Bank of Brazil, the Getúlio Vargas Gallery, and the Indian Museum. The most important museums in São Paulo are the Paulista Museum and the São Paulo Museum of Art. Also in São Paulo is the Museum of Japanese Immigration, detailing Japan's impact on the country. The Goeldi Museum in Belém is famous for exhibits covering every phase of Amazonian life and history and there is a well-known museum of religious art in Vitória.

45MEDIA

The principal telegraph network is operated by the Brazilian Postal and Telegraph Administration, in which the government holds part ownership. National trunk routes and international connections are also operated directly by another mixed corporation, the Brazilian Telecommunications Corp. (EMBRATEL), which inaugurated an earth satellite station in 1969 linking the Brazilian network with member countries of INTELSAT. EMBRATEL has rapidly modernized and extended the domestic telecommunications system with the introduction of microwave networks, including long-distance direct dialing, throughout much of the country. In the Amazon region, the company relies on a tropodiffusion system because of the area's large empty spaces. As of 1995 there were 14,426,673 telephones in use (as compared with 2.4 million in 1973). As of 1999, Brazil had 1,627 AM radio and 251 FM stations and 138 commercial television stations. In 1997 there were 435 radios, 316 television sets, and 28 mobile phones per 1,000 population. Brazil has the fourth-largest television broadcasting system in the world.

As of 1995, there were 373 daily newspapers published in Brazil, with a total circulation of 8,500,000. The following table shows Brazil's leading daily newspapers, with their political orientation and estimated 1999 circulation:

	ORIENTATION	CIRCULATION
RIO DE JANEIRO		
O Globo	Conservative	266,500
Jornal o Dia	Labor	180,000
Jornal do Brasil	Conservative	31,000
SAO PAULO		
O Estado de São Paulo	Conservative	1,230,000
Folha de São Paulo	Independent	286,000
Jornal da Tarde	Independent	709,800
Gazeta Mercantie	NA	104,000
Folha da Tarde	Conservative	90,000
BELO HORIZONTE		
Estado de Minas	Independent	75,000
PORTO ALEGRE		
Zero Hora	NA	727,200
RECIFE		
Diário de Pernambuco	Independent	36,000
BRASÍLIA		
Correio Brasiliense	NA	60,000
Jornal de Brasília	NA	50,000

The largest Brazilian-owned magazine, which competes with the Portuguese-language edition of the *Reader's Digest*, called *Seleções*, is the popular illustrated *Manchete* of Rio de Janeiro (1995 circulation 100,000).

Freedom of the press is guaranteed under the constitution of 1967, and no license is required for the publication of books, newspapers, and periodicals. However, under the newspaper code of 19 September 1972, newspapers were forbidden to publish "speculative" articles on politics or unfavorable reports on the economy. The interests of Brazilian journalists are defended by the Inter-American Press Association and the influential Brazilian Press Association. Newspaper staffs have traditionally enjoyed privileged status and exemption from income taxes; nevertheless, in the early 1970s, reporters were sometimes subject to arrest and alleged brutalities at the hands of the government. In 1979, practically all restrictions on the press were lifted.

In 1996, there were over two million personal computers. In 1998 there were nine Internet hosts per 1,000 population.

46ORGANIZATIONS

Owners of large farms and plantations, particularly coffee plantation owners, usually belong to one or more agricultural associations. The largest of the national agricultural organizations is the National Confederation of Agriculture, but, in general, local member groups of the federation, such as the Paraná Coffee Producers' Association, the Association of Coffee Farmers, and the Brazilian Rural Society, are more powerful than the national organization. Agricultural societies are organized for the primary purpose of promoting favorable legislation toward agriculture in the Congress, and they have become important political units over the years. Other agricultural groups include cattlemen's associations, dairymen's associations, and rice growers' and grain producers' organizations, usually organized on a statewide basis. These are strongest in São Paulo, Minas Gerais, Paraná, Goiás, and Rio Grande do Sul. Chambers of commerce function in every state.

Most international service, social, and fraternal organizations are represented in Brazil. The Rotary International is well organized in the industrial cities of the south, the Boy Scouts of Brazil are active nationwide, and there are Lions clubs and societies of Freemasons. The Catholic Church and the growing number of Protestants maintain various organizations. Catholic Action and the Catholic hierarchy have actively addressed themselves to combating misery and disease, especially in the big-city slums and in the northeast.

47TOURISM, TRAVEL, AND RECREATION

Rio de Janeiro is one of the leading tourist meccas in South America. Notable sights include Sugar Loaf Mountain, with its cable car; the Corcovado, with its statue of Christ the Redeemer; Copacabana Beach, with its mosaic sidewalks; and the Botanical Gardens. Large numbers of visitors are also drawn to the churches of Bahia; the historic city of Ouro Preto in Minas Gerais; and the colorful Amazon Valley cities of Belém and Manaus. Brazil is also famous for its colorful celebrations of Carnival, especially in Rio de Janeiro; neighborhood samba groups rehearse all year for this occasion. Brazil's African heritage can best be savored at the Carnival in Salvador. Eco-tourism attracts growing numbers of visitors to the world's largest rain forest in the North, the Iguacu Falls in the South, and the Mato Grosso wetlands in the Central West region.

No visa is required for tourists from most Western European or Latin American countries entering Brazil, but a valid passport, a tourist card issued by a transportation company, and a round-trip ticket or transportation to another country are required. Citizens of the US and most other countries must secure a visa in advance. Yellow fever vaccination certificates are required if a visitor is from an infected area. A total of 4,818,084 tourists visited Brazil in 1998. Estimated tourism revenues were $2.6 billion in 1997. As of that year, there were 212,580 hotel rooms with 425,160 beds.

Soccer is by far the most popular sport. Brazil hosted the World Cup competition in 1950, and Brazilian teams won the championship in 1958, 1962, 1970, and 1994. The Maracanã soccer stadium in Rio de Janeiro seats more than 180,000 spectators. Other favorite recreations include water sports, basketball, tennis, and boxing.

The UN estimates the daily cost of staying in São Paulo at $128 and Rio de Janeiro at $113. Costs in other cities are significantly lower, with Belo Horizonte at $76, Belém at $72, and Cuiaba at $79.

48FAMOUS BRAZILIANS

Joaquim José da Silva Xavier, also known as Tiradentes (d.1792), led an unsuccessful uprising in 1789 against Portuguese colonial rule. The patriarch of Brazilian independence was José Bonifacio de Andrada e Silva (1763–1838), a geologist, writer, and statesman. Pedro I (Antonio Pedro de Alcántara Bourbon, 1798–1834), of the Portuguese royal house of Bragança, declared Brazil independent and had himself crowned emperor in 1822; he became King Pedro IV of Portugal in 1826 but gave up the throne to his daughter, Maria da Gloria. His Brazilian-born son, Pedro II (Pedro de Alcántara, 1825–91), emperor from 1840 to 1889, consolidated national unity and won respect as a diplomat, statesman, and patron of the arts and sciences. Other famous Brazilians during the imperial period include the Brazilian national hero, Luís Alves de Lima e Silva, Duque de Caxias (1803–80), a patron of the Brazilian army; and Joaquim Marques Lisboa, Marques de Tamandaré (1807–97), a naval hero, soldier, and statesman. In the field of international politics, Joaquim Nabuco (1849–1910) won distinction as a diplomat, journalist, and champion of the abolition of slavery; José Maria de Silva Paranhos, Barão de Rio Branco (1847–1912), was a famous minister of foreign affairs, who represented Brazil at many international conferences; and Ruy Barbosa (1849–1923) was a lawyer, diplomat, statesman, and jurist. A leader of industrial and economic development was Irineu Evangelista de Souza, Barão de Mauá (1813–89). Brazilian aviation pioneer Alberto Santos Dumont (1873–1932) is called the father of flight for his invention of a gasoline-powered airship in 1901. Oswaldo Cruz (1872–1917) founded the Brazilian Public Health Service and helped eradicate yellow fever in Rio de Janeiro. Marshal Cândido Rondon (1865–1957), an explorer of Amazonia, organized the Brazilian Indian Bureau. Dr. Vital Brasil (1865–1950) developed São Paulo's snakebite serum institute at Butantã.

Joaquim Maria Machado de Assis (1839–1908), author of *Memórias Póstumas de Braz Cubas* and other novels and poems, is generally considered the greatest Brazilian literary figure. The poet Euclides da Cunha (1866–1909) wrote *Os Sertões* (1902), one of the foremost works by a Brazilian. Other literary figures include Antônio Gonçalves Dias (1824–64), a romantic poet who idealized the Brazilian Indian; Castro Alves (1847–71), who influenced the abolition of slavery; and contemporary writers such as Gilberto de Mello Freyre (1900–1987), José Lins do Rego (1900–1959), Erico Verissimo (1905–1975), and Jorge Amado (b.1912).

Aleijadinho (Antônio Francisco Lisboa, 1739–1814) was an 18th-century church architect and carver of soapstone religious statues in Minas Gerais. Contemporary artists include the painter Emiliano di Cavalcanti (1897–1976); the painter and muralist Cândido Portinari (1903–62), considered the greatest artist Brazil has produced; and the sculptor Bruno Georgio (b.1905). Lúcio Costa (b. France, 1902–85), regarded as the founder of modern Brazilian architecture, designed the new capital city of Brasília, and Oscar Niemeyer (b.1907) designed most of the government buildings. Robert Burle Marx (1909–94) originated an unusual form of landscaping to complement modern architectural form. Another Brazilian architect of note, Alfonso Eduardo Reidy (b. France, 1909–64), designed the Museum of Modern Art in Rio de Janeiro.

The greatest figure in Brazilian music is the composer and educator Heitor Villa-Lobos (1887–1959), who wrote prolifically in many styles and forms. Other musicians include the composers Carlos Gomes (1836–96), Oscar Lorenzo Fernandez (1897–1948), Francisco Mignone (1897–1987), and Carmargo Guarnieri (b.1907); the concert pianist Guiomar Novaës Pinto (1895–1979); the operatic soprano Bidu Sayao (Balduina de Oliveira Sayao, 1902–99); and the folklorist and soprano Elsie Houston (1900–1943). One of the best-known Brazilians is soccer star Edson Arantes do Nascimento (b.1940), better known as Pelé.

Other noted figures are Getúlio Vargas (1883–1954), president-dictator in the period 1930–45, who increased the power of the central government; Francisco de Assis Chateaubriand Bandeira de Melo (1891–1966), a publisher, diplomat, and art collector; Oswaldo Aranha (1894–1960), president of the UN General Assembly during 1947–49; and Marcelino Candau (1911–83), director-general of WHO during 1953–73. Gen. Ernesto Geisel (1907–96) and his presidential successor, Gen. João Baptista de Oliveira Figueiredo (1918–99), guided Brazil through a period of political liberalization.

⁴⁹DEPENDENCIES

Brazil has no colonies, but three national territories are contiguous with or incorporated within the national domain. The constitution provides for the creation of a territory from part of an established state, the incorporation of a territory into an established state, or the organization of a territory into a new state if that territory can demonstrate its ability to meet the requirements of statehood.

The territories are Amapá, on the French Guiana border; Roraima (formerly Rio Branco), on the Venezuelan border; and the Fernando de Noronha islands, off the northeastern coast. Territorial governors are appointed by the president of the republic, and each territory has one representation in the federal Chamber of Deputies. Territories have no representation in the federal Senate. Trindade and the Ilhas Martin Vaz, small islands in the Atlantic, also belong to Brazil.

⁵⁰BIBLIOGRAPHY

Baaklini, Abdo I. *The Brazilian Legislature and Political System.* Westport, Conn.: Greenwood Press, 1992.

Bacha, Edmar L. and Herbert S. (eds.). *Social Change in Brazil, 1945–1985: the Incomplete Transition.* Albuquerque: University of New Mexico Press, 1989.

Becker, Bertha K. *Brazil: A New Regional Power in the World-economy.* New York: Cambridge University Press, 1992.

Besse, Susan K. *Restructuring Patriarchy: The Modernization of Gender Inequality in Brazil, 1914–1940.* Chapel Hill: University of North Carolina Press, 1996.

Burns, E. Bradford. *A History of Brazil.* 3rd ed. New York: Columbia University Press, 1993.

Chacel, Julian, et al. *Brazil's Economic and Political Future.* Rev. ed. Boulder, Colo.: Westview, 1988.

Erickson, Kenneth P. *The Brazilian Corporative State and Working Class Politics.* Berkeley: University of California Press, 1978.

Fritsch, Winston. *External Constraints on Economic Policy in Brazil, 1889–1930.* Pittsburgh, Pa.: University of Pittsburgh Press, 1988.

Graham, Richard (ed.). *Brazil and the World System.* Austin: University of Texas Press, 1991.

Hartness, Ann. *Brazil in Reference Books, 1965–1989: An Annotated Bibliography.* Metuchen, N.J.: Scarecrow Press, 1991.

Haverstock, Nathan A. *Brazil in Pictures.* Minneapolis: Lerner, 1987.

Kinzo, Maria D'Alva G. (ed.). *Brazil: The Challenges of the 1990s.* New York: St. Martin's Press, 1993.

Levine, Robert M. *Historical Dictionary of Brazil.* Metuchen, N.J.: Scarecrow, 1979.

——*Brazilian Legacies.* Armonk, N.Y.: M. E. Sharpe, 1997.

Macdonald, Norman P. *The Making of Brazil: Portuguese Roots 1500–1822.* Sussex, England: Book Guild, 1996.

Mahar, Dennis J. *Government Policies and Deforestation in Brazil's Amazon Region.* Washington, D.C.: World Bank, 1989.

Page, Joseph A. *The Brazilians. Reading, Mass.: Addison-Wesley Pub. Co., 1995.*

Parkin, Vincent. *Chronic Inflation in an Industrialising Economy: the Brazilian Experience.* New York: Cambridge University Press, 1991.

Payne, Leigh A. *Brazilian Industrialists and Democratic Change.* Baltimore: Johns Hopkins University Press, 1994.

Policymaking in a Newly Industrialized Nation: Foreign and Domestic Policy Issues in Brazil. Austin: University of Texas at Austin, 1988.

Poppino, Rollie E. *Brazil: The Land and People.* New York: Oxford University Press, 1973.

Roett, Riordan. *Brazil: Politics in a Patrimonial Society.* Westport, Conn.: Praeger, 1992.

Selcher, Wayne A. *Brazil's Multilateral Relations Between First and Third Worlds.* Boulder, Colo.: Westview Press, 1978.

CANADA

CAPITAL: Ottawa.

FLAG: The national flag, adopted in 1964, consists of a red maple leaf on a white field, flanked by a red vertical field on each end.

ANTHEM: Since 1 July 1980, *O Canada* has been the official anthem.

MONETARY UNIT: The Canadian dollar (c$) is a paper currency of 100 cents. There are coins of 1, 5, 10, 25, and 50 cents and 1 dollar, and notes of 2, 5, 10, 20, 50, 100, and 1,000 Canadian dollars. Silver coins of 5 and 10 dollars, commemorating the Olympics, were issued during 1973–76. c$1 = us$0.68729 (or us$1 = c$1.455) as of 31 March 2000. US currency is usually accepted, especially in major cities and along the border.

WEIGHTS AND MEASURES: The metric system is the legal standard.

HOLIDAYS: New Year's Day, 1 January; Good Friday; Easter Monday; Victoria Day, the Monday preceding 25 May; Canada Day, 1 July; Labor Day, 1st Monday in September; Thanksgiving Day, 2d Monday in October; Remembrance Day, 11 November; Christmas Day, 25 December; Boxing Day, 26 December. Other holidays are observed in some provinces.

TIME: Newfoundland, 8:30 AM = noon GMT; New Brunswick, Nova Scotia, Prince Edward Island, and Québec, 8 AM = noon GMT; Ontario east of 90° and western Québec, 7 AM = noon GMT; western Ontario and Manitoba, 6 AM = noon GMT; Alberta and Saskatchewan, 5 AM = noon GMT; British Columbia and Yukon, 4 AM = noon GMT.

¹LOCATION, SIZE, AND EXTENT

Canada consists of all of the North American continent north of the US except Alaska and the small French islands of St. Pierre and Miquelon. Its total land area of 9,976,140 sq km (3,851,808 sq mi) makes it the second-largest country in the world (slightly larger than China and the United States), extending 5,187 km (3,223 mi) E–W from Cape Spear, Newfoundland, to Mt. St. Elias in the Yukon Territory and 4,627 km (2,875 mi) N–S from Cape Columbia on Ellesmere Island to Pelee Island in Lake Erie. Canada is bounded on the N by the Arctic Ocean, on the E by Kennedy Channel, Nares Strait, Baffin Bay, Davis Strait, and the Atlantic Ocean, on the S by the US, and on the W by the Pacific Ocean and the state of Alaska. The coastal waters of Canada also include the Hudson Strait and Hudson Bay. The country's total boundary length is 252,684 km (157,602 mi). Canada's capital city, Ottawa, is located in the southeastern part of the country.

²TOPOGRAPHY

Canada's topography is dominated by the Canadian Shield, an ice-scoured area of Precambrian rocks surrounding Hudson Bay and covering half the country. This vast region, with its store of forests, waterpower, and mineral resources, is being increasingly developed. East of the Shield is the Maritime area, separated from the rest of Canada by low mountain ranges pierced by plains and river valleys, and including the island of Newfoundland and Prince Edward Island. South and southeast of the Shield are the Great Lakes–St. Lawrence lowlands, a fertile plain in the triangle bounded by the St. Lawrence River, Lake Ontario, and Georgian Bay. West of the Shield are the farmlands and ranching areas of the great central plains, some 1,300 km (800 mi) wide along the US border and tapering to about 160 km (100 mi) at the mouth of the Mackenzie River. Toward the north of this section is a series of rich mining areas, and still farther north is the

Mackenzie lowland, traversed by many lakes and rivers. The westernmost region of Canada, extending from western Alberta to the Pacific Ocean, includes the Rocky Mountains, a plateau region, the coastal mountain range, and an inner sea passage separating the outer island groups from the fjord-lined coast. Mt. Logan, the highest peak in Canada, in the St. Elias Range near the Alaska border, is 5,951 m (19,524 ft) high. The Arctic islands constitute a large group extending north of the Canadian mainland to within 885 km (550 mi) of the North Pole. They vary greatly in size and topography, with mountains, plateaus, fjords, and low coastal plains.

The central Canadian Shield area is drained by the Nelson-Saskatchewan, Churchill, Severn, and Albany rivers flowing into Hudson Bay. The 4,241-km (2,635-mi) Mackenzie River—with its tributaries and three large lakes (Great Bear, Great Slave, and Athabasca)—drains an area of almost 2.6 million sq km (1 million sq mi) into the Arctic Ocean. The Columbia, Fraser, and Yukon rivers are the principal drainage systems of British Columbia and the Yukon Territory. The Great Lakes drain into the broad St. Lawrence River, which flows into the Gulf of St. Lawrence. Other rivers flow laterally from the interior into Hudson Bay or the Atlantic or Pacific ocean.

³CLIMATE

Most of northern Canada has subarctic or arctic climates, with long cold winters lasting 8 to 11 months, short sunny summers, and little precipitation. In contrast, the populated south has a variety of climatological landscapes. The greatest temperature range is in the Northwest Territories, where the average temperature at Fort Good Hope ranges from –31°C (–24°F) in January to 16°C (61°F) in July.

Cool summers and mild winters prevail only along the Pacific coast of British Columbia. There the mean temperatures range from about 4°C (39°F) in January to 16°C (61°F) in July, the least range in the country. On the prairies there are extreme differences in temperature between day and night and summer and winter. In Ontario and Québec, especially near the Great Lakes and along the St. Lawrence River, the climate is less severe than in western Canada. This region has abundant precipitation that is highly uniform from season to season. The growing season is short, even in the south. Much of the interior plains area does not get enough rain for diversified crops.

East of the Rockies across the flat prairie lies the meeting ground for air from the Arctic, Pacific, and American interior. The mixing of air masses leads to a turbulent atmosphere and the emergence of cyclonic storms, producing most of the rain and snow in the country. The northwest and the prairies, having fewer or weaker storms, are the driest areas, although the prairies are the site of some heavy blizzards and dramatic thunderstorms. The windward mountain slopes are exceptionally wet; the protected slopes are very dry. Thus, the west coast gets about 150–300 cm (60–120 in) of rain annually; the central prairie area, less than 50 cm (20 in); the flat area east of Winnipeg, 50–100 cm (20–40 in); and the Maritime provinces, 115–150 cm (45–60 in). The annual average number of days of precipitation ranges from 252 along coastal British Columbia to 100 in the interior of the province.

4FLORA AND FAUNA

A great range of plant and animal life characterizes the vast area of Canada, with its varied geographic and climatic zones. The flora of the Great Lakes–St. Lawrence region resembles that of the adjacent US section, with white pine, hemlock, sugar and red maples, yellow birch, and beech trees. Coniferous trees—particularly red spruce—predominate in the Maritime region, black spruce in the eastern Laurentian zone, white spruce in the western. In the east are also found the balsam fir, white cedar, tamarack, white birch, and aspen, with jack pine in the drier areas. From the prairie grassland to the Arctic tundra there are aspen, bur oak, balm of Gilead, cottonwood, balsam poplar, white birch, and other deciduous trees. Conifers dominate the northern section. Many types of grasses grow on the interior plains. The wet area along the west coast is famous for its tall, hard conifers: western hemlock and red cedar, Douglas fir, Sitka spruce, and western white pine. Subalpine forests cover the Rocky Mountain area, and here are found such conifers as alpine fir, Engelmann spruce, lodgepole pine and aspen, and mountain hemlock. The great Arctic region is covered with low-growing grasses, mosses, and bushes.

The fauna of the Great Lakes–St. Lawrence region includes deer, black bear, opossum, gray and red squirrel, otter, beaver, and skunk; birds include eastern bluebird, red-winged blackbird, robin, wood thrush, woodpecker, oriole, bobolink, crow, hawk, bittern, heron, black duck, and loon. In the boreal forest area there are moose, caribou, black bear, lynx, timber wolf, marten, beaver, porcupine, snowshoe rabbit, red squirrel, and chipmunk. Typical mammals of the Rocky Mountain area are grizzly bear, mountain goat, moose, wapiti, cougar, and alpine flying squirrel. In the plains are rabbits, gophers, prairie birds, and waterfowl. Abundant on the west coast are deer, Cascade mountain goat, red squirrel, mountain beaver, various species of mice, and Puget striped skunk; common birds include northern Pigmy-owl, band-tailed pigeon, black swift, northern flicker, crow, rufous-sided towhee, and black brant. Over the stretches of the Arctic are the musk ox and reindeer, polar bear, caribou, white and blue fox, arctic hare, and lemming, as well as the snowy owl, ptarmigan, snow bunting, arctic tern, and other birds. Walrus, seals, and whales inhabit Canada's coastal waters.

5ENVIRONMENT

Canada's principal environmental agency is the Department of the Environment, established in 1971 and reorganized in 1979. Responsibilities of this department, also known as Environment Canada, include air and water pollution control, land-use planning, and wildlife preservation. Responsibility for maritime resources was vested in the Department of Fisheries and Oceans under the 1979 reorganization. Air pollution and the resulting acid rain pose a threat to lakes and forests in an area of eastern Canada about 2.6 million sq km (1 million sq mi). Canadian sources estimate that about 14,000 lakes in eastern Canada are acidified and another 300,000 lakes will remain in danger if adequate emission reductions are not implemented. As of the mid-1990s, acid rain had affected a total of 150,000 lakes throughout Canada. Waterfowl populations have already been depleted. About half the acid rain comes from emissions from Canadian smokestacks, but Canada has blamed US industry for 75% of the Ontario pollution.

Canada's rivers and ocean waters have been contaminated by toxic pollutants from agricultural, industrial, mining, and forestry activities. As of the mid-1990s, 50% of Canada's coastal shellfish areas were closed because of the dangerous levels of pollutants. In 1992, Canada ranked ninth in the world for industrial carbon dioxide emissions, with a total of 409.8 million metric tons (14.99 metric tons per capita).

Canada has more than 90 bird sanctuaries and 44 National Wildlife Areas, including reserves in the western Arctic to protect waterfowl nesting grounds. In May 1986, Canada and the US signed an agreement to restore the breeding habitat of mallard and pintail ducks in the midcontinental regions of both countries. The project, which would span 15 years and cost c$1.5 billion, would protect and improve 1,200,000 hectares (3,000,000 acres) of duck habitat. It was hoped that the project would reverse the decline in waterfowl populations, and raise the average annual fall migration to 100 million birds—the level of the 1970s. The project also called for the protection of waterfowl habitats in the lower Mississippi River and Gulf Coast region, and the black duck habitat in eastern Canada and the East Coast of the US.

The annual Newfoundland seal hunt, producing seals for pelts and meat, drew the ire of environmentalists chiefly because of the practice of clubbing baby seals to death (adult seals are shot). Approval by the European Parliament of a voluntary boycott on sealskin imports undercut the market, and the Newfoundland seal catch dropped from about 1,400 in 1981–82 to 360 in 1982–83. In 1987, Canada banned the offshore hunting of baby seals, as well as blueback hooded seals.

Endangered or extinct species in Canada include the Vancouver Island marmot, eastern puma, wood bison, sea otter, right whale, St. Lawrence beluga, Acadian whitefish, mountain plover, piping plover, spotted owl, leatherback turtle, cucumber tree, Furbish's lousewort, Eskimo curlew, Kirtlands warbler, American peregrine falcon, whooping crane, and the southern bald eagle. In a total of 197 mammals, five are on the endangered species list. The list also includes six species of birds which are endangered. Canada is trying to protect its plant resources through the national Green Plan. Out of a total of 3,220 plant species nationwide, 13 are endangered.

6POPULATION

Statistics Canada is the Canadian government bureau that conducts the census; every five years, forms are included with the annual income tax returns that are sent to every mailing address. The population doubled between 1945 and 1993, although the growth rate declined from 12.9% for 1971–81 to 12.1% for 1981–91. The highest growth rates for 1981–91 were in the Northwest Territories (26%), British Columbia (19.6%), and Ontario, 16.9%. By 2000, the population of Canada was

LOCATION: 41°41′ to 83°7′N; 52°37′ to 141°W. **BOUNDARY LENGTHS:** Arctic Ocean coastline, 9,286 km (5,770 mi); Atlantic coastline, including Kennedy Channel, Baffin Bay, Davis Strait, 9,833 km (6,110 mi); US, 6,416 km (3,987 mi); Pacific coastline, 2,543 km (1,580 mi); Alaska, 2,477 km (1,539 mi); Hudson Strait and Hudson Bay shoreline, 7,081 km (4,400 mi). **TERRITORIAL SEA LIMIT:** 12 mi.

estimated at 31,330,255. An estimated 12.2% of the population is 65 years of age or older. The projected population for the year 2005 is 32,855,000, assuming a crude birthrate of 11 per 1,000 population and a death rate of 8, resulting in a natural rate of change of 0.01% for the period 2000–2005. The population rate of change between 1995 and 2000 was 0.9%. The population density in 1998 was three per sq km (eight per sq mi).

The population is unevenly distributed, ranging from 0.02 per sq km (0.045 per sq mi) in the Northwest Territories to 22.8 per sq km (59 per sq mi) on Prince Edward Island. Nearly 85% of the people live within 150 km (93 mi) of the US boundary. All except the Maritime provinces have large areas virtually uninhabited. The population movement has long been from rural to urban areas. It was estimated that 77% of the population lived in urban areas in 2000, up from 76% in 1980. Ontario, with 81.8% of its population classed as urban, was the most urbanized province, followed by British Columbia (80.4%), Alberta (79.8%), and

Québec (77.6%). Only New Brunswick (47.7%), Prince Edward Island (39.9%) and the Northwest Territories (36.7%) have less than half their population in urban areas. The capital city, Ottawa, had a 2000 metropolitan population of 1,085,000. The Toronto metropolitan area had an estimated population of 4,657,000 in 2000; Montréal, 3,401,000; Vancouver, 1,987,000; Edmonton, 913,000; and Calgary, 888,000. Other large cities include Winnipeg, 652,354; Québec, 645,550; Hamilton, 599,760; St. Catherines-Niagara, 364,552; London, 381,522; Kitchener, 356,421; Halifax, 320,521; Victoria, 287,897; Windsor, 262,075; Oshawa, 240,104; and Saskatoon, 210,023. Canada's next census is slated for 2001.

⁷MIGRATION

Canadians of French origin are descendants of about 10,000 settlers who arrived in the 17th century and in the first half of the 18th century. Black slaves were brought to Canada as early as

1608. Later in the 18th century, thousands of British settlers came to Canada from New England and other colonies to the south. By 1850, 500,000 persons had left the British Isles for Canada; between 1846–54, an additional 500,000 arrived, mainly from Ireland. The Underground Railway, a network of people and safe houses that helped runaway slaves reach freedom, operated from 1840–60, and enabled about 30,000 blacks to reach Canada. The peak year for immigration was 1913, when 400,870 people arrived. From 1921–30, there were 1,230,202 immigrants; in 1931–40, 158,562; in 1946–65, 2,504,120. Many reemigrated, mainly to the US; by 1950, Canadian-born persons formed the second-largest group of foreign-born US inhabitants. Between 1951–56, however, the excess of immigration over emigration was almost 600,000. After a lull in the early 1960s, immigration reached a peak of 222,876 in 1967. In 1974, immigration controls were tightened, and between 1975–85, the number of immigrants per year averaged 118,656, and between 1986–93, 193,881. In 1993, total immigration was 252,042. Of these, immigrants from Asia numbered 134,532; from Europe, 50,050; Africa, 19,033; the Caribbean, 19,028; the US, 6,565; and South America, 11,327. Emigration is mainly to the US. In 1990 there were 871,000 Canadian-born people living in the US.

At the end of 1998, Canada hosted some 159,000 refugees recognized in country, refugees resettled from abroad, and asylum-seekers with pending claims. In the same year, some 24,000 requested refugee status. Of the 23,200 cases decided, the Immigration and Refugee Board (IRB) awarded refugee status to 12,880, for an approval rate of 55.5%. Canada is also a major resettlement country, admitting 2,243 refugees in 1998. The government's goal for resettlement in 1999 was 7,300 under government support and 2,800 to 4,000 under private support. During August 1999, two ships carrying hundreds of Chinese "boat people" arrived in British Colombia; most claimed asylum. As of September 1999, more were expected, and the incident has created public controversy.

Interprovincial migration is generally from east to west. During 1990–91 British Columbia gained 37,620 more people from other provinces than it lost, and Alberta 7,502, while Ontario lost 22,301 more than in gained, Saskatchewan 9,941, and Québec, 7,690. In 1999, the net migration rate for Canada was 5.96 migrants per 1,000 population.

8ETHNIC GROUPS

More than 80% of the population is Canadian-born. In general, the percentage of the population born outside Canada increases as one goes westward from Newfoundland to British Columbia. Persons of whole or partial British (including Irish) origin make up 40% of the total population; those of whole or partial French origin (centered mainly in Québec, where they constitute some 80% of the population) make up 27%. Other European groups account for 20% of the total populace. Asian groups, including Chinese and East Indian, form 11.5%.

Amerindians, commonly known as Indians constituted 1.5% in 1998. These Indians were classified into ten major ethnolinguistic groups; the métis, of mixed European and Indian extraction, were recognized as an aboriginal people in the Constitution Act of 1982. Most of the Inuit (Eskimos) live in the Northwest Territories, with smaller numbers in northern Québec and northern Newfoundland (Labrador). Since 1959, Inuit cooperatives have been formed to finance fishing, fish processing, retail, housing, and tourist enterprises, and to promote the graphic arts.

9LANGUAGES

English and French are the official languages of Canada and have equal status and equal rights and privileges as to their use in all governmental institutions. The federal constitution also gives the English and French minorities the right to publicly funded education in their own language at the primary and secondary levels, wherever the number of children warrants it.

The constitution provides for bilingualism in the legislature and courts of Québec, New Brunswick, and Manitoba. Although there are no similarly entrenched constitutional rights in Ontario and Saskatchewan, these provinces have made English and French the official languages of the courts. In 1984, the Northwest Territories Council adopted an ordinance providing for the use of aboriginal languages and establishing English and French as official languages.

English was proclaimed the sole official language of Manitoba in 1890, and French was made the official language of Québec in 1974. However, the 1890 Manitoba legislation was declared unconstitutional in 1979, as was a Québec law passed in 1977 declaring French to be the sole language of the legislature and the courts.

Although Canada is frequently referred to as a bilingual country, only a minority are able to speak both English and French. In Québec, more than 80% of the people speak French as a native language; in the other provinces, most of the people speak only English, although there are sizable proportions of people able to speak French in New Brunswick and parts of Ontario and Manitoba. Some 60% of Canadians report that their only mother tongue is English, and only about 24% say that is French. About 15% report a single mother tongue other than English or French. Italian, German, Chinese, Ukrainian, Portuguese, and Polish are spoken by small numbers of people. There are at least 58 different Indian languages and dialects, in 10 major language groups. Cree is the most common Indian language.

10RELIGIONS

Based on 1998 estimates, 82.1% of the Canadian population belong to Christian denominations. Roman Catholics constitute the largest single group, with 45.2% of the population. Other Catholic groups include Eastern Orthodox (1.4%) and Ukrainian Catholics (0.5%). Protestants make up 36.4% of the populace, including the United Church with 11.5%; Anglicans with 8.1%; Presbyterians with 2.4%; Lutherans with another 2.4%; Baptists with 2.5%; Pentecostals with 1.6%; and various other Protestant denominations with 7.9%. Members of other religions include Jews (1.2% of the population), Muslims (0.9%), Buddhists (0.6%), Hindus (0.6%), Sikhs (0.5%), parareligious faiths— including Scientology, Kabalarianism, and Rastafarianism— (0.1%), and other religions (0.1%). Approximately 12.5% of the population has no religious affiliation.

Freedom of religion has been specifically protected since the enactment of the Canadian Bill of Rights in 1960, now incorporated into the constitution.

11TRANSPORTATION

With such a vast land area, and with most production inland, all forms of transportation are vital. Since 1945, with the rapid growth of road, air, and pipeline services, the trend has been away from railways for carrying both freight and passengers. But because they can supply all-weather transportation in large volume over continental distances, railways are still important. The federal government, through the Canadian Transport Commission, has allowed a few rate rises and has insisted on a slow curtailment of services; nevertheless, the companies have traditionally operated at a deficit or very low margin of profit because of competition and rising costs. There were 67,773 km (42,114 mi) of railways in 1999. Two great continental systems operate about 90% of the railway facilities, the government-owned Canadian National Railways (CNR), which was privatized in 1995, and the privately owned Canadian Pacific Ltd.

(CP). They compete in some areas but cooperate where duplication of service is not profitable. In addition to their railway operations, CNR and CP maintain steamships and ferries, nationwide telegraph services, highway transport services, and hotel chains.

The populated sections are generally well supplied with roads and highways, but because of difficult winter weather conditions, road maintenance is a recurring and expensive task and puts a tremendous strain on road-building facilities. There are about 912,200 km (566,841 mi) of roads, 246,400 km (153,113 mi) of which is paved, including 16,600 km (10,315 mi) of expressways. The 7,820-km (4,860-mi) paved Trans-Canada Highway, a c$500-million project financed jointly by the federal and provincial governments, was completed in 1962. Canada ranks next to the US in per capita use of motor transport, with one passenger car for every 2 persons. Motor vehicles in use in 1995 totaled 16,667,000, including 13,182,000 passenger cars and 3,484,000 trucks, buses, and taxis.

Bounded by water except for the Alaskan and southern land boundaries with the US, and with many inland lakes and rivers that serve as traffic arteries, Canada makes much use of water transport in domestic as well as foreign commerce. Canada's merchant fleet was comprised of 109 ships, totaling 1,489,110 GRT, in 1998. Most overseas commerce is carried by foreign ships. Montréal is Canada's largest port and the world's largest grain port. Others among the many well-equipped ports are Toronto, Hamilton, Port Arthur, and Fort William on the Great Lakes, and Vancouver on the Pacific Coast. The Montréal and lake ports are closed by ice from December to April, during which time Halifax on the Atlantic and Saint John on the Bay of Fundy are the only Atlantic Ocean traffic terminals.

The St. Lawrence Seaway and Power Project, constructed jointly by Canada and the US, and its many canals provide an 8-m (27-ft) navigation channel from Montréal to Lake Superior. The Athabasca and Slave rivers and the Mackenzie, into which they flow, provide an inland, seasonal water transportation system from the end of the railway in Alberta to the Arctic Ocean. The Yukon River is usually open from mid-May to mid-October. All Canadian inland waterways are open on equal terms to the shipping of all nations.

Canada had 1,395 airports in 1998, including 515 with permanent runways. Principal airports include Calgary International at Calgary, Edmonton International at Edmonton, Halifax International at Halifax, Lester Pearson at Toronto, Vancouver International at Vancouver, Winnipeg International at Winnipeg, and Dorval International and Mirabel International at Montreal. International air service is provided by government-owned Air Canada and Canadian Airlines. Regional service is provided by some 570 smaller carriers. Air transport is the chief medium in the northern regions for passengers and freight. Canadian airlines transported 23,981,000 passengers in 1997.

12HISTORY

The first inhabitants of what is now Canada were the ancient ancestors of the Inuit. Exactly where they originated or when they arrived is uncertain, but they probably crossed from eastern Siberia to Alaska, Canada, and Greenland between 15,000 and 10,000 BC. Their descendants, the Dorset people, who inhabited the central Canadian Arctic region from about 700 BC to AD 1300, were primarily hunters of walrus and seal. The shorter-lived Thule culture, which may have assimilated the Dorset, lasted from about 1200 to the first arrival of the Europeans. Although most Inuit lived near the coast, some followed the caribou herds to the interior and developed a culture based on hunting and inland fishing.

Although the Norse had occupied a settlement at L'Anse aux Meadows in Newfoundland by AD 1000, the first fully documented arrival by Europeans was in 1497 by the Italian-born John Cabot, who led an English expedition to the shore of a "new found land" (Newfoundland) and claimed the area in the name of Henry VII. In 1534, the French, under Jacques Cartier, planted a cross on the tip of the Gaspé Peninsula; the following year, his expedition discovered and ascended the St. Lawrence River. By 1604, Pierre du Guast, Sieur de Monts, along with Samuel de Champlain had founded the first permanent French colony, Port Royal (now Annapolis Royal, Nova Scotia). Four years later, Champlain established the town of Québec. The great St. Lawrence waterway led Étienne Brulé and others after him to the Great Lakes and the rivers flowing south through the center of the North American continent. Missionaries and fur traders soon arrived, and an enormous French territory was established. Between 1608 and 1756, about 10,000 French settlers arrived in Canada. In the hope of protecting French settlers and the fur trade, Champlain supported the Huron Indians against their enemies, the Iroquois. When the Iroquois demolished the Hurons, the French colony was almost destroyed.

In the 17th century, England pressed its claim (by virtue of Cabot's expedition) to the rich fur-trading colony, and during the frequent skirmishing between New France and New England the English conquered Québec (1629). Restored to France in 1632, Québec, together with the rest of New France, was placed under the absolute control of a chartered commercial organization, the Company of One Hundred Associates, with the twofold purpose of exploiting the fur trade and establishing settlements. In 1663, New France became a royal province of the French crown. Thereafter, three important officials—the royal governor, the intendant, and the bishop—competed in exercising control of the government. Under the seigneurial system, which had been founded in 1598, large land grants were made to seigneurs, who made other grants to settlers. The actual farmers owed some quasi-feudal dues and could sell the property only by paying a large duty to the seigneur.

The movement of exploration, discovery, commercial exploitation, and missionary enterprise, which had begun with the coming of Champlain, was extended by such men as Jacques Marquette, Louis Jolliet, and Robert Cavelier, Sieur de la Salle, reaching its climax in the last three decades of the 17th century. At that time, French trade and empire stretched north to the shores of Hudson Bay, west to the head of the Great Lakes, and south to the Gulf of Mexico. Meanwhile, a British enterprise, the Hudson's Bay Company, founded in 1670, began to compete for the fur trade.

The European wars between England and France were paralleled in North America by a series of French and Indian wars. The imperial contest ended after British troops commanded by James Wolfe defeated Marquis Louis Joseph de Montcalm on the Plains of Abraham, bringing about the fall of Québec in 1759. The French army surrendered at Montréal in 1760, and the Treaty of Paris in 1763 established British rule over what had been New France. The Québec Act of 1774 established English criminal law but secured seigneurial tenure, a modified oath of office allowing Roman Catholics to serve in the conciliar governments, and the right of the Roman Catholic Church to collect tithes.

These concessions, which reflected the sympathy of the British ruling class for the French upper classes, instituted the separateness of French-speaking Canada that has become a distinctive feature of the country. It also secured the loyalty of the French clergy and aristocracy to the British crown during the American Revolution. Although the poorer French settlers (habitants) sympathized with the Revolutionists, efforts to take Canada by arms for the revolutionary cause failed in the Québec campaign. Some 40,000 Loyalists from the colonies in revolt fled northward to eastern Canada and did much to change the political character of their new country. The Constitutional Act of 1791 divided Lower Canada (now southern Québec) from Upper Canada (now southern Ontario) and provided for elected assemblies with limited powers, the first organs of self-government in the territory.

In the 1780s, the newly organized North West Company began to challenge the Hudson's Bay Company's fur-trade monopoly. The period was one of expansion, marked by Alexander Mackenzie's journey to the Arctic Ocean in 1789 and his overland voyage to the Pacific Ocean in 1793. British mariners secured for Britain a firm hold on what is now British Columbia.

The War of 1812, in which US forces attempting to invade Canada were repulsed by Canadian and British soldiers, did not change either the general situation or the US-Canadian boundary. After amalgamating the North West Company in 1821, the Hudson's Bay Company held undisputed sway over most of the north and west. Eastern border problems with the US were resolved by the Webster-Ashburton Treaty in 1842; in the west, however, US expansionists sought to fix the border at 54°40′N. In 1846, the border was resolved at 49°N, and since then, except for minor disputes, the long border has been a line of peace.

The continuing influx of immigrants stimulated demands for political reforms. In Nova Scotia and New Brunswick the reformers had some early success, but in the two Canadas it was not until groups led by Louis Joseph Papineau in Lower Canada and William Lyon Mackenzie in Upper Canada had conducted separate futile rebellions in 1837–38 that the British government acted. John George Lambton, Earl of Durham, was sent to Canada as governor-general in 1838; he resigned later that year, but in 1839 submitted a report to the crown in which he recommended the granting of some forms of self-government. He also advised the immediate union of the two Canadas for the express purpose of Anglicizing the French Canadians. Union of the two provinces was approved in 1840, but responsible government was not achieved until 1849, after strenuous efforts by leaders in the various provinces. There was, however, no single unified nation—only a string of provinces in the east and the Hudson's Bay Company domain in the west and north.

The movement for Canadian confederation—political union of the colonies—was spurred in the 1860s by the need for common defense and the desire for a common government to sponsor railroads and other transportation. John Alexander Macdonald and George Brown, rival political leaders, agreed in 1864 to unite Upper Canada and Lower Canada under a common dominion government. Already the Maritime provinces were seeking union among themselves; their Charlottetown Conference in 1864 was broadened to admit delegates from the Canadas. After two more conferences, in 1864 and 1866, the dominion government was established under the British North America Act of 1867. The dominion was a confederation of Nova Scotia, New Brunswick, and the two provinces of Canada. There had been much opposition, and Nova Scotia and New Brunswick were brought to accept the union only through the efforts of Sir Charles Tupper and Sir Samuel Leonard Tilley and by the fear and indignation roused by the invasion of Canada by Fenians (militant Irish nationalists) from the US in 1866. Since the name Canada was chosen for the entire country, Lower Canada and Upper Canada became the provinces of Québec and Ontario, respectively.

In 1869, the Hudson's Bay Company relinquished its territorial rights to Rupert's Land and the Northwest Territories. In 1870, the province of Manitoba was established and admitted to the confederation, and the Northwest Territories were transferred to the federal government. In 1871, British Columbia, on the Pacific shore, joined the confederation, largely on the promise of a transcontinental railroad. Prince Edward Island did not join

until 1873. Pushing through the Canadian Pacific (CP) Railway was a main achievement of Macdonald's Conservative administration. The CP was given large grants of land in return for its promise to aid in settling these lands, a policy that is still being carried on. Objection in the west to being taken over by the east led to two métis rebellions, headed by Louis Riel, in 1869–70 and 1885, but the west was opened to settlement nonetheless.

Under the long administration (1896–1911) of the Liberal Party under Sir Wilfrid Laurier, immigration to the prairie provinces was greatly accelerated. The prairie agricultural empire bloomed. Large-scale development of mines and of hydroelectric resources helped spur the growth of industry and urbanization. Alberta and Saskatchewan were made provinces in 1905. In 1921, Manitoba, Ontario, and Québec were greatly enlarged to take in all territory west of Hudson Bay and south of 60°N and all territory east of Ungava Bay. In February 1931, Norway formally recognized the Canadian title to the Sverdrup group of Arctic islands (now the Queen Elizabeth Islands); Canada thus held sovereignty in the whole Arctic sector north of the Canadian mainland. Newfoundland remained apart from the confederation until after World War II; it became Canada's tenth province in March 1949.

Canadian contributions of manpower and resources were immensely helpful to the Allies when Canada joined the British side in World War I; more than 600,000 Canadians served in Europe, and over 60,000 were killed. The war contributions of Canada and other dominions helped bring about the declaration of equality of the members of the British Commonwealth in the Statute of Westminster of 1931. The wartime struggle over military conscription, however, deepened the cleavage between French Canadians and other Canadians. After the war, the development of air transportation and roads helped weld Canada together, and the nation had sufficient strength to withstand the depression that began in 1929 and the droughts that brought ruin to wheat fields. The farmers developed huge cooperatives, especially in Nova Scotia and the prairie provinces, and also took up radical political doctrines, notably through the Social Credit and the Socialistic Cooperative Commonwealth Federation parties.

Canada was again vitally important in World War II, under the premiership of William Lyon Mackenzie King. More than one million Canadians took part in the Allied war effort, and over 32,000 were killed. The nation emerged from the war with enhanced prestige, actively concerned with world affairs and fully committed to the Atlantic alliance.

Domestically, a far-reaching postwar development was the resurgence in the 1960s of French Canadian separatism, symbolized by a series of cultural agreements between France and Québec. In 1970, terrorist acts by the Québec Liberation Front led to the banning of that organization and to the federal government's first invocation in peacetime of emergency powers under the War Measures Act. The emergency measures, imposed on 16 October, were not lifted until 30 April 1971. Although administrative reforms—including the establishment of French as Québec's official language in 1974—helped meet the demands of cultural nationalists, separatism continued to be an important force in Canadian politics. In the 1976 provincial elections, the separatist Parti Québécois came to power in Québec, and its leader, Premier René Lévesque, proposed that Québec become politically independent from Canada, in a relationship termed sovereignty-association. In a referendum on 20 May 1980, in which 82% of those eligible voted, the proposal was defeated, 59.5% to 40.5%. Meanwhile, other provinces had their own grievances, especially over oil revenues. Alberta objected to federal control over oil pricing and to reduction of the provincial share of oil revenues as a result of the new National Energy Program announced in late 1980; the failure of Newfoundland

and the federal government to agree on development and revenue sharing hindered the exploitation of the vast Hibernia offshore oil and gas field in the early 1980s.

Since 1927, when discussions first began on the question of rescinding the British North America Act, disagreements between the provinces and the federal government over constitutional amendment procedures had stood in the way of Canada's reclaiming from the UK authority over its own constitution. In 1980, Liberal Prime Minister Pierre Elliott Trudeau made "patriation" of the constitution a principal priority of his administration. Initially he faced considerable opposition from eight of the 10 provincial premiers, but a compromise on amending procedures and a charter of rights eventually proved acceptable to all but Québec. The Constitution Act, passed in December 1981 and proclaimed by Queen Elizabeth II on 17 April 1982, thus replaced the British North America Act as the basic document of Canadian government. In 1987, Québec was to sign the new constitution, after winning the inclusion of a clause acknowledging that Québec is a "distinct society." The Meech Lake Accord of 1987, however, failed to compel Québec into signing the constitution, and Québec's status has been in limbo ever since. New Brunswick and Manitoba failed to ratify the Accord because of the perceived preferential status Québec would have received. The Charlottetown Accord also proposed recognizing Québec as a "distinct society" in addition to acknowledging aboriginals' inherent right to self-government and converting the senate into an elected and more effective legislative body. On 26 October 1992, however, the majority of Canadians chose not to support the Charlottetown Accord in a national referendum.

Canada joined with the US and Mexico to negotiate the North American Free Trade Agreement (NAFTA), which was built upon the US-Canada Free Trade Agreement (FTA). The three nations came to an agreement in August 1992 and signed the text on 17 December 1992. NAFTA seeks to create a single market of 370 million people with a combined GNP exceeding $6 trillion and was implemented in 1994.

Like the French Canadians of Québec, Canada's native peoples have also challenged the federal government on issues of identity and autonomy. In 1992 the Inuits approved an agreement by which the country's Northwest Territories would be divided in two, with the eastern part comprising the semi-autonomous Nunavut territory, which would serve as an Inuit homeland. Other native groups also advanced land claims.

On 30 October 1995, the province of Quebec held a referendum on secession from Canada; the measure was defeated by the narrowest of margins—a majority of less than 1%. As the 1990s ended, the province remained deeply divided over the secession issue, and the constitutional impasse over the status of Québec persisted. In 1998, Canada's Supreme Court ruled that in order for Quebec to secede from the country, it had to reach agreement with the other provinces and the federal government on issues including a common currency and payment of the national debt.

After ousting the Progressive Conservatives in the 1993 national election, the Liberal party, led by Prime Minister Jean Chrétien, won a second consecutive parliamentary victory for the first time in 40 years in June 1997. However, the party's majority was significantly reduced from its previous size, and the right-wing Reform Party replaced the Bloc Québécois as the leading opposition group, a development that added to the regional fragmentation posing an increasing threat to the national unity of Canada. To overcome regional divisions within their own ranks, Canada's conservatives voted to create the new Canadian Alliance party early in 2000, in an attempt to unite the western-based Reform Party with the Progressive Conservatives.

In the late 1990s, Canada's native peoples achieved two historic milestones in their quest for autonomy. In 1998 the Nisga'a Indians ratified a treaty according them 1930 sq km (745 sq mi) of land in British Columbia. The following year, the Nunavut territory—occupying an area larger than Western Europe—was officially founded as a homeland for the Inuit in the Northwest Territories.

¹³GOVERNMENT

Canada is a federation of 10 provinces and three northern territories (including the Nunavut territory formed in 1999). Under the British North America Act of 1867, which united the four original provinces of Québec, Ontario, Nova Scotia, and New Brunswick into one dominion under the name of Canada, the federation was provided with a powerful central government, which, besides its areas of exclusive authority, held residual authority in matters beyond the powers of local or private concern specifically assigned to the provincial legislatures. The British North America Act—which effectively served, together with a series of subsequent British statutes, as Canada's constitution—could be amended only by the British Parliament. In 1982, the British North America Act was superseded by the Constitution Act (or Canada Act), the principal innovations of which are the Charter of Rights and Freedoms and the provision for amendment. For passage, an amendment requires approval by the federal Parliament and the legislative assemblies of at least two-thirds of the provinces, which must hold an aggregate of at least half the population of all the provinces. However, when an amendment derogates from provincial rights, it will not apply in any province in which the legislative assembly dissented by majority vote. When such an amendment deals with education or other cultural matters, the federal government must pay compensation to any dissenting province, to make up for the funds that would have been transferred had the province accepted the amendment.

Under the Constitution Act, the British sovereign remains sovereign of Canada and head of state; for the most part, the personal participation of Queen Elizabeth II in the function of the crown for Canada is reserved to such occasions as a royal visit. The queen's personal representative in the federal government is the governor-general, appointed by the crown on the advice of the prime minister of Canada; the governor-general is usually appointed for a term of five years. Active executive authority resides in the cabinet, or ministry, headed by the prime minister.

The federal Parliament is made up of the House of Commons and the Senate. A new House of Commons, with 301 members as of 1999, is elected at least once every five years by all Canadian citizens and British subjects 18 years of age or older who have resided in Canada for at least 12 months prior to polling day. Representation by provinces and territories is based on population, ranging from one for the Yukon Territory to 99 for Ontario.

The leader of the party that wins the largest number of seats in a newly elected House of Commons is asked to form the government. The governor-in-council (cabinet), responsible for determining all important government policies and for securing the passage of legislation, financial measures, and administrative provisions, is chosen by the prime minister.

The 105 members of the Senate, or upper house, are appointed for life, or until age 75, by the governor-general on the nomination of the prime minister, with equality of representation for regional divisions. There are equal proportions of senators from the Maritime provinces, Ontario, Québec, and the western provinces. In October 1992, Canadian voters declined a constitutional amendment that would have made the Senate an elected body.

14 POLITICAL PARTIES

Throughout most of the 20th century, national unity has been the primary aim of every Canadian government: leaders of both the English-speaking majority and the French-speaking minority have cooperated to develop a united Canada with a great destiny to which differences arising from national origin were subordinate. In the 1970s, this unity was challenged by a growing demand for French Canadian autonomy. Despite cultural division, national unity has remained a basic factor in Canadian foreign policy. Two elements have contributed to the growth of Canadian nationalism—deliberate government policy and reaction against overidentification with either the UK or the US.

Continuity of policy characterizes party relationships. The Liberal Party (LP), which held office from 1935 to 1957 and again (except for part of 1979) from 1968 to 1984, is nationwide in its representation but has its main strength in Québec. It traditionally emphasizes trade and cultural relationships with the US, while its principal rival, the Progressive Conservative Party (PC), which held power from 1957 to 1968, from May to December 1979, and again since the end of 1984, stresses Canada's relationships with the UK. In economic policy, the Liberals generally champion free trade, while the Conservatives favor a degree of protection; but practical political considerations have modified this distinction.

The Cooperative Commonwealth Federation (CCF) was a farmer-labor party with its main strength in Saskatchewan. Its foreign policy was much like that of the British Labour Party, but with an admixture of traditional Canadian prairie radicalism. It merged with the Canadian Labour Congress to form the New Democratic Party (NDP) in 1961. The Social Credit Party (SCP) has headed governments in Alberta and British Columbia but has not done well nationally. In June 1962, the group collapsed into independent factions, leaving only five representatives in the Commons. In September, the Québec wing of the party united to form the Ralliement des Créditistes, which after the 1965 elections became the new focal point of French Canadian interests.

After 22 years of uninterrupted rule, the Liberals were defeated by the PC in the 1957 elections. This was widely interpreted as a vote of protest against individual Liberal ministers and high taxes, as a reflection of concern over US economic penetration, and as a demonstration of widespread feeling that it was "time for a change." In the general election on 31 March 1958, the PC was returned to power with an unprecedented majority, taking 208 of the 265 seats. The LP was reduced to 49 seats, the smallest number in its history. In the election of June 1962, the PC lost 92 seats. The following February, the PC government lost a vote of confidence, the major issue being defense policy and the refusal of the prime minister to accept nuclear weapons from the US. In the election of April 1963, the resurgent Liberals gained an additional 29 seats for a total of 129 (four short of a parliamentary majority). With some support from the SCP, Liberal leader Lester B. Pearson formed a new government.

In April 1968, the new Liberal Party leader, Pierre Elliott Trudeau, was elected prime minister in a colorful campaign emphasizing personality more than specific issues. In the June general election, which he called for almost immediately, the LP took 155 seats and the PC 72; the SCP lost all five of its seats. In the general elections of 30 October 1972, the Liberals lost their parliamentary majority, winning only 109 seats to the PC's 107. The NDP increased its representation from 22 seats to 31, and the Créditistes, who had resumed calling themselves the SCP in 1971, won 15 seats. When the NDP decided to support the continuance of Liberal rule, Prime Minister Trudeau formed a new cabinet. The Liberal-NDP alliance collapsed on 8 May 1974 when, for the first time in Canadian history, the government

received a vote of no confidence on a budget bill. Elections were called, and the campaign was fought largely on the issue of inflation, with the PC calling for a system of wage and price controls. In the elections of 8 July 1974, the Liberals regained their majority.

In the general elections of 22 May 1979, the Liberals lost to the PC, taking 114 seats of the now 282-seat Parliament to the PC's 136, and were unable to form a government in any province. However, on 13 December 1979, the government of Prime Minister Joe Clark was defeated by a Liberal and NDP coalition on a vote of no confidence on a budget bill that called for an increase of 18 cents a gallon in the excise tax on gasoline. Trudeau, who in November had announced his planned retirement, decided to continue as Liberal leader, and again became prime minister after elections on 18 February 1980 gave the Liberals 147 seats. Four years later, on 29 February 1984, Trudeau again announced his impending retirement, and his party chose John Turner as successor. Brian Mulroney became prime minister following a landslide PC victory in the September 1984 elections, which gave the PC 211 seats, the Liberals 40 (their lowest number ever), the NDP 30, and an independent 1. However, the Liberals regained strength over the next year, and in 1985 won the Québec general election and, in a coalition with the NDP, ended 42 years of PC government in Ontario.

In 1993, the PC fell from power, primarily due to one of the worst Canadian recessions in nearly 60 years and the failure of the PC government to implement constitutional reforms. Brian Mulroney resigned and was succeeded by Kim Campbell. Liberals soundly defeated the PC in the October 1993 election, with 177 of the 295 seats (up from only 80 in 1988). The PC retained only two of their 157 seats. The Liberal party named Jean Chrétien as the new prime minister.

The Liberal Party's majority in Parliament was reduced to 155 in elections called by Chrétien in June 1997. The majority of opposition seats were won by the right-wing populist Reform Party, formed in Alberta in 1988 and led by Robert Manning, which increased its representation to 60 seats, winning broad support in the western provinces. Other party totals were Bloc Québécois, 44; New Democratic, 21; Progressive Conservative, 20; and Independent, 1. In January 2000, members of the Reform Party voted to create a broader conservative grouping called the Canadian Alliance, uniting the western-based, populist Reform Party with the eastern-based Progressive Conservatives in an attempt to eventually unseat the dominant Liberals.

15 LOCAL GOVERNMENT

Canada is made up of 10 provinces and three territories. Each province has a premier and a legislature. They function like those of the central government. However, the provincial parliaments are unicameral. In each province, the sovereign is represented by a lieutenant-governor appointed by the governor-general. The provinces are empowered to regulate their own affairs and dispose of their own revenues. Civil and property rights, civil law, education, health, labor conditions, licenses, management and sale of public land, municipal government, and direct provincial taxation are within the jurisdiction of the provinces. Although the federal government still exercises considerable authority over the northern territories, they now have elected legislative bodies. In the Yukon, the powers of the federal commissioner have been greatly reduced, and the newly formed Nunavut territory, an Inuit homeland, is semi-autonomous.

Each province is divided into municipalities, the number and structure of which vary from province to province. In Prince Edward Island, Nova Scotia, New Brunswick, Ontario, and Québec the first order of municipalities consists of counties, which are further subdivided into cities, towns, villages, and townships, although there are minor variations. In

Newfoundland and the four western provinces there are no counties; municipalities are either rural or urban, the latter being made up of cities, towns, and villages, but again with minor variations. Municipalities are usually administered by an elected council headed by a mayor, overseer, reeve, or warden. Local governments are incorporated by the provinces, and their powers and responsibilities are specifically set forth in provincial laws.

16 JUDICIAL SYSTEM

The civil law follows English common law everywhere except in Québec, where it follows the Napoleonic Code. The main body of criminal law is derived from English sources; most criminal statutes, being federal, are uniform throughout the country. Police magistrates and justices of the peace are appointed by the provincial governments. Civil and criminal courts exist on county, district, and superior levels; all judges of the superior, federal, tax, district, and county courts are appointed for life (but not beyond age 75) by the governor-in-council (the cabinet) and are paid by the federal Parliament. The Supreme Court in Ottawa has appellate, civil, and criminal jurisdiction throughout Canada; its chief justice and eight associate ("puisne") justices (at least three of whom must come from Québec) are appointed by the governor-general. The Federal Court of Canada (formerly the Exchequer Court), organized into trial and appeal divisions, hears cases having to do with taxation, claims involving the federal government, copyrights, and admiralty law. Its appeal jurisdiction includes review of rulings by federal boards and commissions. The Tax Court, with seats in major cities throughout the country, rules on cases involving tax and revenue matters.

The death penalty in Canada was abolished in 1976; that decision was upheld in a vote by the House of Commons in June 1987.

The judiciary is independent of the legislative and executive branches. The Canadian Charter of Rights and Freedoms, part of the 1982 revised Constitution, guarantees a number of individual fundamental rights.

Criminal defendants are afforded a wide range of procedural due process protections including a presumption of innocence, a right to counsel, public trial and appeal.

Canada accepts compulsory jurisdiction of the International Court of Justice with reservations.

17 ARMED FORCES

All service in the armed forces is voluntary. The armed forces were unified in 1968 as functional commands that have land, sea, and air missions, but not separate service headquarters; total forces as of 2000 were 60,600; there were 43,300 reserves. The Land Forces had 20,900 troops; the Maritime Forces had 9,000 and one submarine, 12 frigates, 4 destroyers, and 14 patrol and coastal combatants, deployed in both the Atlantic and Pacific. The air force had a strength of 15,000, with 140 combat aircraft. The coast guard had 4,700 members and some 137 vessels; it was merged with the Department of Fisheries and Oceans, which operated about 90 vessels, including patrol boats and icebreakers. In 2000, 1,380 Canadian troops were stationed with UN peace-keeping troops in Bosnia, and Canadian personnel also partici-pated in peacekeeping operations in seven other regions. Defense expenditures in 1997–98 totaled $7.1 billion or 1.2% of gross domestic product.

The Royal Canadian Mounted Police (RCMP) is a civil force maintained by the federal government, originally to police federal territories. It is the sole police force in the Yukon Territory and the Northwest Territories. However, all the provinces except Ontario and Québec, which have their own police forces, have entered into contracts with the RCMP to enforce provincial laws (under the direction of the provincial authorities). In some munic-ipalities the RCMP also enforces municipal laws. Other urban centers maintain their own police forces or (as in Ontario and Québec) hire the services of the provincial police under contract.

18 INTERNATIONAL COOPERATION

A Commonwealth nation, Canada became a charter member of the UN on 9 November 1945 and participates in ECE, ECLAC, and all the nonregional specialized agencies. A Canadian, Lester B. Pearson, served as president of the General Assembly in 1952/53. Maj. Gen. E. L. M. Burns of Canada was chief of staff of the UN Truce Supervision Organization in the Middle East from August 1954 to November 1956, when UNEF was established, and he served as UNEF commander for the next three years. Canada has also contributed to UN peacekeeping efforts in Kashmir, West Irian (now Irian Jaya, Indonesia), Cyprus, and the Middle East.

Canada is a member of NATO; as part of its contribution to the collective defense of the alliance, Canada has land and air units in the Federal Republic of Germany (FRG). Canada cooperates with the US in North American defense through the North American Air Defense Command (NORAD). Canada also belongs to many inter-American, inter-Commonwealth, and other intergovernmental organizations, including the Asian Devel-opment Bank, IADB, OECD, and the WTO. It is a permanent observer at the OAS. Canada is a signatory to the Law of the Sea. A free-trade agreement with the US signed in 1988 was extended to include Mexico with the 1992 signing of the North American Free Trade Agreement (NAFTA), creating a free trade bloc among the three countries. The agreement was ratified by the govern-ments of all the countries in 1993 and went into effect the following year.

19 ECONOMY

The Canadian economy is the seventh largest among the western industrialized nations. The post-war period has seen a steady shift from the production of agricultural goods toward increased emphasis on manufacturing and services. The service sector employed three-fourths of the workforce in 1999, compared to only half of the workforce in 1960. Canada is a world leader in the production and export of asbestos, nickel, silver, zinc, uranium, cadmium, cobalt, magnesium, gypsum, molybdenum, potash, aluminum, gold, iron ore, copper, fluorspar, and lead. Although no longer the foremost sector of the economy, agriculture is of major importance to the economy as a whole and still is basic in many areas; Canada accounts for approximately 20% of the world wheat trade. Canada is also the world's leading producer of newsprint and ranks among the leaders in other forestry products.

Canada has changed from a country producing and exporting mainly primary products to one that is increasingly producing and exporting manufactured goods. In the 1980s, machinery and equipment joined automotive products among the country's leading exports; at the same time, the importance of natural resource products declined (partly reflecting the 1986 collapse of oil prices).

Canada was hard hit by the recession of the early 1980s, with interest rates, unemployment, and inflation all running higher than in the US. The effects of the recession on minerals and manufacturing were especially severe. By the end of 1982, all mining operations in the Yukon were closed, and throughout the country more than 70,000 of 115,000 miners were unemployed. The economy recovered during the mid-1980s, and Canada's economic growth rate was among the highest of OECD countries during 1984–86. However, differences in prosperity among the provinces increased during the 1980s, with the central provinces relatively robust, the western provinces suffering declines in growth because of lower prices for oil and other natural resources, and the Atlantic provinces depressed. By the second quarter of 1990, the economy had begun to contract, affected by the recession and the central bank's tight monetary policy. Recovery began in the second half of 1991. Although the 1990s were marked by continued high rates of unemployment and restrained domestic spending, the economy posted an average growth rate in GDP of about 3%. Unemployment was rated at a peak of about 12% in 1992 but had gone down to 8% in 1999.

20INCOME

The US Central Intelligence Agency (CIA) reports that in 1998 Canada's gross domestic product (GDP) was estimated at $688 billion. The per capita GDP was estimated at $22,400. The annual growth rate of GDP was estimated at 3%. The average inflation rate in 1998 was 0.9%. The CIA defines GDP as the value of all final goods and services produced within a nation in a given year and computed on the basis of purchasing power parity (PPP) rather than value as measured on the basis of the rate of exchange. It was estimated that agriculture accounted for 3% of GDP, industry 31%, and services 66%.

The World Bank reports that for the same period per capita private consumption (in PPP terms) was $15,645. Private consumption includes expenditures of individuals, households, and nongovernmental organizations. It was estimated that between 1990 and 1998 private consumption grew at an annual rate of 2.0%. Approximately 14% of household consumption was spent on food, 10% on fuel, 4% on health care, and 21% on education. The richest 10% of the population accounted for approximately 24% of household consumption and the poorest 10% approximately 2.8%.

21LABOR

Employment was 14,326,000 in 1998. There were 15,630,000 in the total civilian labor force in the same year. Of those in civilian employment in 1997, 16% were in manufacturing; 3% in agriculture, 5% in construction, and 75% in services. The rate of participation by men in the employed labor force fell from 73.8% in 1992 to 72.4% in 1998 whereas that of women rose from 55.1% to 58.1% during the same period.

Cold weather and consumer buying habits cause some regular seasonal unemployment, but new techniques and materials are making winter construction work more practicable, and both government and many industrial establishments plan as much work as possible during the winter months. Unemployment ranged between 7.5% and 11.8% in the period 1982–95, with the lowest rate occurring in 1989 and the highest in 1983. In 1995, it stood at 9.5%.

In 1999, about 29% of the workforce was unionized. In 1999, nearly all seaports in British Columbia were closed for ten days by strikes. Other strikes that year included those by nurses in Quebec, transit workers in Toronto, grain handlers in Alberta, and, on a rotating basis, doctors in British Columbia. Of this number, about 60% were represented by unions affiliated solely with the Canadian Labor Congress (CLC) and 6% and 4.9% with the Confederation of National Trade Unions and the Canadian Federation of Labor, respectively. All together there were 235 national unions in Canada, and 62 international unions. The public sector is the most highly organized. The largest unions include the Canadian Union of Public Employees, National Union of Public and General Employees, United Food and Commercial Workers International Union, and the Public Service Alliance of Canada.

Federal and provincial laws set minimum standards for hours of work, wages, and other conditions of employment. Minimum wage rates for experienced adult workers in 1999 ranged from c$5.25 in Newfoundland and Prince Edward Island to c$7.20 in the Yukon Territories. Many collective agreements are negotiated

every other year and are concluded without work stoppage, although sometimes with the assistance of government conciliation services. Collectively bargained group health insurance, pension, and unemployment benefit plans supplement payments under the Unemployment Insurance Act, which was reformed in 1990 in order to be funded entirely by employer/employee taxes on insurable earnings. Since 1951, the federal government and the provinces have enacted laws prohibiting discrimination in employment because of race, color, religion, or national origin, as well as laws requiring equal pay for men and women. Safety and health regulations and workers' disability compensation have been established by federal, provincial, and municipal legislation.

Weekly earnings for the industrial aggregate averaged c$605.22 in 1995, up from c$501.08 in 1991.

22AGRICULTURE

Until the beginning of the 1900s, agriculture was the predominant occupation, and farmers and their families made up the majority of the population. Since then, however, the farm population has been shrinking both relatively and absolutely. Even in Saskatchewan, the province with the highest proportion of farm population, farm families account for no more than 25% of the total population. For Canada as a whole, agriculture engaged only 2.5% of the economically active population in 1998. Farm production continues to increase, as have the size of holdings, crop quantity, quality and variety, and cash income. Canada is still one of the major food-exporting countries of the world; agriculture engages about 414,000 people and generates about 2% of GDP. Farm cash receipts for crops totaled c$13.7 billion in 1998.

Of Canada's total land area, about 5% is classified as arable land; another 3% is considered as permanent pasture land. More than 90% of the cultivated area is in the three prairie provinces. The trend is toward fewer and larger farms and increased mechanization and specialization. Ontario and Saskatchewan together account for about half of all farm cash receipts. Sale of field crops provide more than 50% of farm cash income in the prairie region, but less than 10% elsewhere in Canada.

The following table shows the estimated extent and output of principal field crops in 1998:

AREA	YIELD (1,000 HECTARES)	(1,000 TONS)
Wheat	10,768	24,400
Barley	4,269	12,696
Corn	1,118	8,912
Oats	1,592	3,955
Rapeseed (canola)	5,421	7,588

Formerly, Canada imported only such items as could not be grown domestically—coffee, tea, cane sugar, spices, and citrus fruits—while exporting large surpluses of wheat, barley, and livestock. However, food imports have risen sharply in recent years. Nevertheless, Canada remains a significant food exporter; in 1997, Canadian grain exports totaled 26,386,000 tons, third after the US and France.

Federal and provincial departments of agriculture provide guidance and aid to farmers in almost every field of operation. Activities include research and experimentation, protection of animals and crops, irrigation and reclamation, and price stability and farm credit measures. The government can stabilize the price of any agricultural product (except wheat, for which separate provision is made) by outright purchase or by supporting the market with guarantees or deficiency payments.

The departments of agriculture apply fundamental scientific research to soil management and crop and animal production, promote agricultural production, and enact financial measures to ensure greater stability of the farm economy. Long-term and short-term mortgages are made available; other loans are granted for equipping, improving, and developing farms. Various federal acts assist the marketing of produce. Governments, working with product organizations, also set limits on the production of milk, eggs, tobacco, and chicken and turkey meat. Price supports may be given to any designated natural or processed product but are mandatory for cattle, sheep, hogs, dairy products, wheat, oats, and barley. Farmers who have suffered severe crop losses through drought may obtain compensation, and prairie farmers who cannot deliver all their grain to market are given temporary financial assistance. The rail freight rates paid by western farmers to ship their grain to eastern markets, basically unchanged since 1897, increased fivefold between 1983 and 1991. The increase, partially subsidized by the federal government, would pay for improvements in the western rail system.

23 ANIMAL HUSBANDRY

Canada traditionally exports livestock products, producing more than the domestic market can use. Animal production (livestock, dairy products, and eggs) now brings in about half of total farm cash income. Stock raising is the foundation of agricultural economy in the foothills of the Rockies, across northern Alberta and Saskatchewan and southern Manitoba, on the interior plateaus of British Columbia, in the Georgian Bay district of Ontario, in Prince Edward Island, and in western Nova Scotia. One of the great ranching sections is located in the Palliser Triangle of southern Saskatchewan and Alberta.

Livestock on farms in 1998 numbered 13,157,000 head of cattle; 11,843,000 pigs and hogs; 634,000 sheep; and 139,000,000 chickens. In 1998, livestock slaughtered included 3,650,000 head of cattle, and calves, 15,800,000 hogs, and 488,000 sheep. Chicken and turkey production totaled 2,799,000 tons. Milk production in 1998 was 7.7 million tons; butter production amounted to about 95,000 tons, and cheese production to 311,000 tons. Most dairy products are consumed within Canada. In 1998, 342,000 tons of eggs were produced. Cash receipts in 1998 for cattle amounted to C$5,721 million; for dairy products, C$3,844 million; for hogs, C$2,230 million; and for poultry, C$1,345 million.

The wild fur catch, which was important in Canada's early history, is now limited to the northern parts of the provinces, Nunavut, the Northwest Territories, and the Yukon. In 1998, the value of fur production totaled C$47.5 million, with ranch-raised pelts accounting for 64% and wildlife pelts for 36%.

24 FISHING

With a coastline of nearly 29,000 km (18,000 mi) and a lake-and-river system containing more than half the world's fresh water, Canada ranked twenty-second among the world's major fish producers and in 1997 was the world's third-leading exporter of fresh, chilled, and frozen fish by value (after the US and Norway).

Two of the world's great fishing grounds are located off Canada. One lies along the Atlantic coast of the Maritime provinces, and in this region the Grand Banks of Newfoundland constitute the largest area. More than one billion pounds of cod, haddock, halibut, pollock, and other fish are caught every year along the Atlantic in deep-sea and shore operations. Most of the cod and about a third of the total catch is dried and salted for export to Mediterranean and Latin American countries; another third is sold fresh; and the rest is canned. Vast numbers of lobsters and herring are caught in the Gulf of St. Lawrence and the Bay of Fundy. The other great fishing region includes the bays, inlets, river mouths, and fjords of British Columbia. Salmon, the specialty of the Pacific fisheries, is canned for export and constitutes the most valuable item of Canadian fish production. Also exported are fresh halibut and canned and processed herring. Other important export items are whitefish, lake trout, pickerel, and other freshwater fish caught in the Great

Lakes and some of the larger inland lakes. Feed and fertilizer are important by-products.

Canada's total fish and seafood landings were estimated at 1,065,219 tons in 1997, of which all but 45,114 tons were from marine fishing. Pelagic species and other finfish (primarily salmon and herring) accounted for 39% of the 1995 marine catch; shellfish (mostly shrimp, oysters, and crabs), 38%; and groundfish (mostly hake and redfish), 23%. The US imports about 60% of Canada's fish product exports by volume and 50% by value. Japan is the second most important market for fish exports.

Canadian aquacultural production in 1997 was valued at $346.9 million. Canada's aquaculture industry faces many federal and provincial regulatory impediments that restrict its growth, such as regulations on the introduction and transfer policy of new species, salmon tagging, and a moratorium on new aquaculture licenses in British Columbia.

The government protects and develops the resources of both ocean and inland waters and helps expand the domestic market for fish. It extends loans to fishermen for the purchase of fishing craft. Canadian-US action has helped restore Pacific salmon runs and halibut stocks and the Great Lakes fisheries, but pollution represents a threat to freshwater sport fishing, especially in Ontario.

25 FORESTRY

Canada's National Forestry Database (CNFD) reports total forestland area at 417.6 million ha (1,031.9 million acres), equivalent to 42% of the total land area. Only about 6% of Canada's forests are privately owned. Of the 94% under crown (public) control, provincial governments manage 71% and the federal government manages 23%. Some 9.6 million ha (23.7 million acres) of the public forest land are for uses other than timber production, including parks, game refuges, water conservation areas, and nature preserves. Most of the provincial crown forestland is in Québec, British Columbia, and Ontario. The crown forests are leased to private individuals or companies. Each province and territory regulates and controls the harvest rate on crown land through an allowable annual cut.

In 1997, an estimated 191.2 million cu m of roundwood was harvested. Canada ranks as the third-largest producer of coniferous wood products (after the US and Russia), and is the leading supplier of softwood products to world markets. Chief forest products in eastern Canada are pulp and paper manufactures, especially newsprint. Canada leads the world in newsprint production, with 9,205,000 tons in 1997, accounting for 26% of the world's production. Exports of newsprint were valued at over $4.9 billion, with about three-fourths going to the US. In the west, the chief product is sawn timber. Sawn wood production in 1997 totaled 64.7 million cubic m, with exports valued at over $9.3 billion. The manufacture of pulp and paper has been a leading industry for many years. Production (and export value) in 1997 included wood pulp, 24.8 million tons ($5 billion); paper and paperboard, 18.9 million tons, ($8.9 billion); and wood-based panels, 11.3 million tons ($1.6 billion). According to the CNFD, employment in the forestry sector accounted directly for 369,000 jobs in 1996, when exports in the forestry sector totaled C$32.4 billion. About 75% of forestry exports are sent to the US. Exports of wood products contribute about 14% to the value of all Canadian exports.

Other well-known Canadian forestry sector products include Christmas trees and maple syrup. Québec accounts for about 35% of the annual Christmas tree production and 90% of maple syrup production.

With such a large annual forestry output, conservation and reforestation are stressed. Both government and industry promote improvements in management practices and in the use of forest products. New manufacturing methods permit the use of inferior classes of wood.

26MINING

Mining has been conducted in Canada since the 17th century, but the remarkably rapid development of mineral exploitation dates from the end of World War I. Petroleum has been found in the midwest; iron ore deposits in Labrador, Québec, and Ontario; uranium in Ontario and Saskatchewan. The world's largest exporter of metals and minerals, Canada is also the leading producer of uranium and the second-largest producer of mine zinc, and is among the leaders in silver, nickel, aluminum (from imported bauxite), potash, gold, copper, lead, salt, sulfur, and nitrogen in ammonia. Yet the country has only just begun to fully develop many of its most important mineral resources, and resources developed earlier continue to display great growth potential. Beginning in 1981, large new deposits of gold ore were discovered at Hemlo, Ontario, north of Lake Superior; by 1991, more than 50% of Ontario's gold production came from the three mines in the Hemlo district. Gold production has fallen since the peak of 177 tons in 1991; in 1997 it was 169 tons. There are about 50 primary gold mines in Canada, which accounted for roughly 90% of the gold produced.

Based on value of production, the top nonfuel commodities in 1997 were gold ($1.8 billion), copper ($1.49 billion), zinc ($1.36 billion), nickel ($1.28 billion), potash ($1.06 billion), and iron ore ($1.03 billion). The overall value of all mineral production rose slightly to $35.9 billion in 1997. Canada is the world's leading exporter of minerals and metals. Exports of nonfuel minerals in 1997 were valued at $32 billion. Exports of minerals and mineral products represent about 26% of Canada's total exports. Output totals for principal Canadian metals in 1997 are shown in the following table:

	OUTPUT (METRIC TONS)
Iron ore	37,284,000
Copper	654,700,000
Zinc	1,088,968,000
Gold	169
Uranium	14,042
Nickel	190,529
Silver	(1,222,367 kg)
Molybdenum	7,612
Lead	186,180
Platinum group	13,694
Cobalt	5,700

What are believed to be the world's largest deposits of asbestos are located in the eastern townships of Québec, approximately 130 km (80 mi) east of Montréal. Asbestos production in 1997 amounted to 447,000 tons. Other nonmetallic mineral production included salt (13.3 million tons), sand and gravel (214.3 million tons), peat (849,000 tons), and potash (9.3 million tons). An area extending from central Saskatchewan southeast into Manitoba is probably the largest and richest reserve of potash in the world, and at the present rate of consumption it could probably supply all the world's needs for 1,000 years. Steady production began in 1962 and in 1997 known national reserves amounted to 14 billion tons. Known reserves of other minerals in 1997 included (in thousands of tons): iron, 1,310; gypsum, 500; sulfur, 150; sodium sulfate, 91; asbestos, 38; zinc, 13.7; copper, 9.7; nickel, 5.6; lead, 3.47; and molybdenum, 0.14.

27ENERGY AND POWER

Abundantly endowed with fossil fuels and hydroelectric resources, Canada is the world's fifth-leading energy producer. Energy production accounted for 8% of GDP in 1998, exceeded only by manufacturing.

Coal production reached 83.1 million tons in 1998. Although Canada accounted for less than 2% of world coal production in 1995, it exported about 50% of its production, making it the fourth-largest coal-exporting nation. The increase in total output since 1970, especially the increased output from Alberta and British Columbia, is almost entirely due to the growth of the Japanese and South Korean export markets. In eastern Canada, however, domestic coal must be augmented by US coal imports.

In the late 1990s, Canada's oil industry made a strong recovery from low prices in the preceding years. Petroleum production in quantity began in 1947 with the discovery of oil 29 km (18 mi) south of Edmonton. Output of oil in 1999 was 2.6 million barrels per day. Petroleum is now the largest single contributor to mineral output. Natural gas production rose to 170,900 million cubic m in 1998, third in the world after Russia and the US. In early 2000, proved crude oil reserves were estimated at 4.9 billion barrels and natural gas reserves at more than 1.8 trillion cubic m (63.9 trillion cubic ft). There are two major oil pipeline systems, both originating at Edmonton, one extending east to Toronto, and the other southwest to Vancouver and the state of Washington, in the US. As of 1993, the Iroquois pipeline serving the eastern US from Alberta was complete. Between 1998 and 2000, five new pipeline projects, which would pump an additional 30 billion cu m of natural gas to the US, were slated for completion. As of 1996, the Canadian government had an 8.5% stake in the massive $6.3 billion Hibernia oil project off the coast of Newfoundland, which was scheduled to begin production in late 1997. Heavy crude oil is produced entirely in western Canada, with 60% coming form Alberta and 40% from Saskatchewan. There are potentially up to 300 billion barrels of synthetic crude oil available from western Canada's oil sands, which now accounts for 21% of production.

Canada ranks among the top producers of electric power in the world and first in the production of hydroelectricity. In 1998, Canada's total net installed capacity reached 112.5 million kW, of which 59% was hydroelectric, 29% thermal, 12% nuclear, and less than 1% geothermal. The marked trend toward the development of thermal stations, which became apparent in the 1950s, is due in part to the fact that most of the hydroelectric sites within economic transmission distance of load centers have already been developed. When the Churchill Falls project reached completion in 1974, the capacity of the plant was 5,225 MW, making it, at the time, the largest single generating plant of any type in the world. It has since been surpassed by Hydro-Québec's 5,328-MW generator, the first completed station of the massive James Bay project. Total electric power generation in Canada in 1998 was 550,852 million kWh, 60% of it hydroelectric, 27% conventional thermal, 12% nuclear, and 1% from geothermal and other sources. Net exports of electricity amounted to 39,500 million kWh in 1998.

Low-cost electricity generated from waterfalls and fast-flowing rivers has been a major factor in the industrialization of Québec, Ontario, and British Columbia, most significantly in the establishment of metal-smelting industries. In other areas, hydroelectric power is not as abundant, but all provinces have turbine installations. As of 2000, Canada's hydroelectric resources still included substantial untapped potential.

Atomic Energy of Canada Ltd. is responsible for research into reactor design and the application of nuclear power in the electric power field. In 1962, commercial electric power was first generated in Canada by a nuclear reaction when the Nuclear Power Demonstration Station at Rolphton, Ontario, became operative. Canada's first full-scale nuclear power station, completed in 1956 at Douglas Point on Lake Huron, produced its first power early in 1967. In 1999, Canada had 14 nuclear reactors operating at five power facilities. Primary energy consumption in 1997 came from oil, 28.6%; natural gas, 34.2%; hydroelectricity, 20.7%; nuclear energy, 5.1%; and coal, 11.4%.

28 INDUSTRY

Industry accounted for 31% of GDP in 1998, with a 0.80% growth rate, and manufacturing employed 16% of the labor force. The leading industrial sectors are foods and beverages, transport equipment, petroleum and coal products, paper and paper products, primary metals, chemicals, fabricated metals, electrical products, and wood products. During the 1980s the output of manufacturing rose on average by 3.2% per year. Between 1990 and 1995, manufacturing output increased by an average of only 1.7% per year, due to the recession of 1990–92, but increased by 6% in 1999.

Canada's automotive sector produced more than 2.5 million cars and light trucks in 1998. Leading manufacturers include General Motors, Chrysler Corp., and Ford Motor Co. Canada's automotive sector is closely integrated with that of the US.

The production of fabricated metals is one of Canada's leading industries, with about 40 smelters in operation.

Of the total manufacturing output, about half is concentrated in Ontario, which not only is the center of Canadian industry but also has the greatest industrial diversification. Some important industries operate there exclusively.

Québec ranks second in manufacturing production, accounting for more than 25% of the value of Canadian manufactured goods. British Columbia ranks third. Manufacturing is also the leading industry in Manitoba, New Brunswick, Nova Scotia, and Newfoundland.

29 SCIENCE AND TECHNOLOGY

In 1987–97, Canada had 2,719 scientists and engineers and 1,070 technicians per million people engaged in scientific research and development. In the same period, research and development expenditures were estimated at about 1.7% of GNP. Approximately half of this expenditure is carried out by the business sector, much of it by the telecommunication equipment, aircraft, and business machines industries. The federal government accounts for about one-third of the total research and development activity.

The Ministry of State for Science and Technology, established in 1971, is the chief federal policymaking body. In 1986, the National Advisory Board for Science and Technology, chaired by the prime minister, was created, and merged with the ministry. In the following year, a National Science and Technology Policy (NSTP) was approved by ministers of the federal, provincial, and territorial governments. The NSTP has emphasized a strong push linking national research to national needs.

The Royal Society of Canada, founded in 1882 and headquartered in Ottawa, is the most prestigious learned society; there are 53 specialized societies in the fields of agriculture, medicine, science, and technology. The National Research Council of Canada, founded in 1916 and headquartered in Ottawa, coordinates research and development in the country; one of its major facilities is the Dominion Astrophysical Observatory, established in 1918 at Victoria, British Columbia. The Geological Survey of Canada, founded in 1842, is headquartered in Ottawa.

The National Museum of Science and Technology in Ottawa, founded in 1967, shows Canada's role in science and technology. The Ontario Science Centre, established in North York in 1965, has over 800 exhibits. In 1996, Canada had 49 universities offering courses in basic and applied science. In 1987–97, science and engineering students accounted for 16% of college and university enrollments.

30 DOMESTIC TRADE

Wholesalers' and manufacturers' sales branches are the most prominent wholesale and distribution agencies. Wholesaling is particularly prominent in foodstuffs, lumber and building supplies, hardware, coal, clothing, dry goods, automotive equipment, and machinery. In producer goods generally, however, direct relations are often maintained by resident or traveling agents.

Large-volume outlets, including department stores, large mail-order houses, and chain stores, often buy direct from the manufacturer. A wide variety of local and imported goods is available in all major towns and cities. Vast indoor shopping complexes have been developed in the larger cities, including Eaton Centre in Toronto with over 300 stores and the West Edmonton Mall in Alberta.

Because of Canada's size and its regional economic differences, distribution is essentially regional. Toronto and Montréal dominate merchandising, are the headquarters of much of Canada's trade and financial apparatus, and do by far the greatest share of import business. Winnipeg is the business center for grain and agricultural implements. Vancouver is the center of the growing British Columbia market.

There is considerable advertising overflow from the US. Business hours are 9 AM to 5 PM, Monday through Friday. Shopping hours are 9:30 AM to 6 PM, Monday through Saturday; many stores stay open to 9 PM on Thursday and Friday nights. Normal banking hours are from 10 AM to 3:30 PM, Monday through Friday.

31 FOREIGN TRADE

Canada's exports are highly diversified; the principal export groups are industrial goods, forestry products, mineral resources (with crude petroleum and natural gas increasingly important), and agricultural commodities. Imports are heavily concentrated in the industrial sector, including machinery, transport equipment, basic manufactures, and consumer goods. Trade balances are almost invariably favorable. In 1989, the US and Canada signed a free trade agreement; and in 1994 the US, Canada, and Mexico signed the North American Free Trade Agreement (NAFTA). Trade in goods and services between the US and Canada accounts for approximately $1 billion each day.

Cars, trucks, and automobile parts, are the major exports of Canada (totaling 22.1%). Wood and wood products follow Canada's vehicle exports closely (totaling 13%). The top nine exports are as follows:

	% OF COUNTRY TOTAL	% OF WORLD TOTAL
Automobiles	14	11
Paper and paperboard	5.1	14
Wood shaped	4.7	32
Motor vehicle parts and accessories	4.2	6.8
Trucks	3.9	16
Pulp and waste paper	3.6	29
Crude petroleum	3.5	3.3
Gas, natural and manufactured	3.2	16
Aluminum	2.2	9.4

In 1997 Canada's imports were distributed among the following categories:

Consumer goods	12.5%
Food	5.0%
Fuels	4.4%
Industrial supplies	22.2%
Machinery	27.3%
Transportation	25.8%
Other	2.8%

Principal trading partners in 1998 (in millions of US dollars) were as follows:

COUNTRY	EXPORTS	IMPORTS	BALANCE
United States	182,802	135,503	47,299
Japan	4,788	9,434	-4,646
United Kingdom	2,937	4,179	-1,242
China (inc. Hong Kong)	2,030	5,978	-3,948
Germany	1,674	4,161	-2,487
Korea	1,123	2,229	-1,106
France	1,074	3,274	-2,200
Italy	992	2,340	-1,348
Mexico	858	5,023	-4,165
Taiwan	722	2,718	-1,996

[32]BALANCE OF PAYMENTS

Canada's merchandise balances, although fluctuating, showed consistent surpluses between 1961 and 2000, except for 1975. These, however, have been offset by persistent deficits from other transactions. Sources of these deficits include Canada's indebtedness to other countries, travel of Canadians abroad, payments for freight and shipping, personal remittances, migrants' transfers, official contributions, and other Canadian government expenditures abroad.

The US Central Intelligence Agency reports that in 1998 the purchasing power parity of Canada's exports was $210.7 billion while imports totaled $202.7 billion resulting in a trade balance of $8 billion.

The International Monetary Fund (IMF) reports that in 1998 Canada had exports of goods totaling $217,238 million and imports totaling $204,614 million. The services credit totaled $30,922 million and debit $35,677 million. The following table summarizes Canada's balance of payments as reported by the IMF for 1998 in millions of US dollars.

Current Account		-11,213
Balance on goods	12,624	
Balance on services	-4,755	
Balance on income	-19,618	
Current transfers	535	
Capital Account		3,363
Financial Account		11,544
Direct investment abroad	-26,411	
Direct investment in Canada	16,515	
Portfolio investment assets	-14,928	
Portfolio investment liabilities	16,757	
Other investment assets	12,256	
Other investment liabilities	7,355	
Net Errors and Omissions		1,303
Reserves and Related Items		-4,996

[33]BANKING AND SECURITIES

The Bank of Canada, which was established in 1934, is a government-owned institution that regulates the total volume of currency and credit through changes in the cash reserves of eight domestic chartered banks and 45 foreign bank subsidiaries. The Bank of Canada also acts as the government's fiscal agent, manages the public debt, and has the sole right to issue paper money for circulation in Canada. It is empowered to buy and sell securities on the open market, to fix minimum rates at which it will make advances, and to buy and sell bullion and foreign exchange.

The Federal Business Development Bank, established as the Industrial Development Bank in 1944 as a subsidiary of the Bank of Canada, has operated as a separate entity since 1974. It does not engage in the business of deposit banking but supplements the activities of the chartered banks and other agencies by supplying medium- and long-range capital for small enterprises.

The eight domestic chartered banks are commercial and savings banks combined, and they offer a complete range of banking services. Canada's banks were reorganized in 1992 under the Banking Act. Every 10 years the banks' charters are subject to renewal and the Banking Act is revised to keep abreast of changing trends, a practice unique to Canada. The banks were reorganized into Schedule I and II banks. The Schedule I banks are banks whose ownership is public. No one shareholder in Schedule I banks controlled more than 10% of the shares until the law was revised in 2000. Schedule II banks are subsidiaries of foreign or domestic banks that are held privately or semi-privately. In 1999, foreign banks were given the right to operate branches in the full-service and lending sectors. Schedule I banks include the Bank of Montreal, Bank of Nova Scotia, Canadian Imperial Bank of Commerce, Canadian Western Bank, Laurentian Bank of Canada, National Bank of Canada, Royal Bank of Canada, and the Toronto-Dominion Bank of Canada.

Canada's four biggest banks—Royal Bank of Canada (RBC), Canadian Imperial Bank of Commerce (CIBC), Bank of Montréal, and Bank of Nova Scotia—were all among the top 10 in North America in the 1980s. In 1997, only RBC and CIBC qualified. The Canadian banks began in mid-1996 to speak out in favor of liberalized ownership rules if they were to maintain their competitive edge. In October 1996, the bank of Montréal chairman, Matthew Barrett, said domestic banks should have the freedom to merge, and that serious thought should be given to dripping the 10% ownership limit. In 1999, banks with equity of over C$5 billion were allowed to merge, and the ownership limit was raised to 20% on vote-taking shares, and 30% on non-vote taking shares.

The Toronto Stock Exchange (TSE) was founded in 1852 and incorporated in 1878; the Standard Stock and Mining Exchange, incorporated in 1908, merged with it in 1934. Its members have branch offices in principal Canadian cities and in some US financial centers.

The Montréal Stock Exchange was incorporated in 1874. In 1974, it merged with the Canadian Stock Exchange, which was organized in 1926 as the Montréal Curb Market. Other securities exchanges were the Winnipeg Stock Exchange, founded in 1903; the Vancouver Stock Exchange, founded in 1907; and the Alberta Stock Exchange (formerly Calgary Stock Exchange), founded in 1913.

In 1999, the TSE took over all senior equity exchanges from the Montreal market. The Vancouver and Alberta stock exchanges merged to form the Canadian Equities Exchange, handling only junior exchanges. Also, in 2000 the TSE conducted a demutualization, in essence becoming a for-profit organization in order to stimulate growth in the securities sector.

[34]INSURANCE

Of the billions of dollars worth of coverage that Canadians buy every year, most is either life and health insurance or property and casualty insurance. In 1993, Canada had about 900 insurance companies, of which 395 were federally registered and governed by the Insurance Companies Act. Canadians buy more life and health insurance on a per capita basis than any other group except the Japanese (the US is third).

Since 1978 the Canadian property and insurance market has continued to experience underwriting losses. The return on equity fell to 13.1% in 1997, to 6.8% in 1998, and to 5.4% in 1999. Since the industry continues to pay more in claims and expenses than is earns in premium revenue, overall profitability is ultimately determined by revenues generated from investment earnings. A high rate of natural disasters coupled with a low rate of crime in 1999 influenced industry intake. The combined industry ratios were approximately 107.8% in 1998, and

106.8% in 1999, showing an overall unproductive trend. Although the industry continues to be competitive, the pricing structure seems to be inadequate. Price increases must take place to offset continued underwriting losses. In 2000, government restructuring of the financial sector refused to allow bank branches to distribute insurance policies, supporting the insurance industry.

³⁵PUBLIC FINANCE

By far the largest item of expenditure of the federal government is for social services, including universal pension plans, old age security, veterans benefits, unemployment insurance, family and youth allowances, and assistance to disabled, handicapped, unemployed, and other needy persons.

Through the early 1970s, federal budgets remained relatively in balance, fluctuating between small surpluses and small deficits. Since then, however, the budget has been in continuous and growing deficit. The federal debt rose from 18% of GDP in 1974 to 70% of GDP in 1993, and about 65% in 1999. Government options to reduce the deficit are constrained by the high level of non-discretionary spending in the federal budget.

Sources of provincial revenue include various licenses, permits, fines, penalties, sales taxes, and royalties, augmented by federal subsidies, health grants, and other payments. Federal grants and surpluses and federal payments to the provinces under the federal-provincial tax-sharing arrangements constitute a major revenue source of the provinces. Corporation and personal income taxes provide a considerable portion of the revenue of Québec. The largest provincial expenditures are for highways, health and social welfare, education, natural resources, and primary industries. Real property taxes account for more than two-thirds of revenue for municipalities and other local authorities. Almost one-third of their expenditures goes to support local schools.

The US Central Intelligence Agency (CIA) estimates that in 1998 Canada's central government took in revenues of approximately $121.3 billion and had expenditures of $112.6 billion including capital expenditures of $17 billion. Overall, the government registered a surplus of approximately $8.7 billion.

The following table shows an itemized breakdown of government revenues and expenditures. The percentages were calculated from data reported by the International Monetary Fund. The dollar amounts (millions) are based on the CIA estimates provided above.

REVENUE AND GRANTS	100%	121,300
Tax revenue	88.4%	107,267
Non-tax revenue	11.2%	13,643
Grants	0.3%	389
EXPENDITURES	100%	112,600
General public services	5.7%	6,401
Defense	6.1%	6,922
Public order and safety	2.4%	2,723
Education	3.3%	3,684
Health	4.6%	5,233
Social security	42.9%	48,331
Housing and community amenities	1.5%	1,713
Recreation, cultural, and religious affairs	1.4%	1,588
Economic affairs and services	8.5%	9,534
Other expenditures	5.1%	5,769
Interest payments	18.4%	20,702

³⁶TAXATION

The federal government levies direct and indirect taxes, of which the individual and corporation income taxes yield the largest return. Excise taxes (including a general sales tax), excise duties, and customs duties also produce a substantial revenue. Federal inheritance taxes were eliminated as of 1 January 1972. The federal goods and services tax (GST) went into effect on 1 January 1991. It is a 7% value-added tax on most goods and services.

The federal rate structure for personal income tax in 2000 ranged from 17% on the first C$29,590 of taxable income to 29% on taxable income in excess of C$59,180.

The general tax rate payable by corporations on their taxable incomes was 38%. The basic federal tax rate is reduced by a 10% abatement to allow the provinces room to impose provincial corporate income taxes. Nonresident companies are taxed at a basic rate of 25%, and pay an extra 25% of after tax income that was not put back into the business.

³⁷CUSTOMS AND DUTIES

Customs duties, once the chief source of revenue, have declined in importance as a revenue source. The tariff, however, still is an important instrument of economic policy. There is a wide range of duties, progressing from free rates on raw materials to higher duties as goods become more highly processed. Producer goods, including machinery of a kind not made in Canada, are subject to lower rates or are admitted free. Imports from the UK, most Commonwealth countries, and some crown colonies receive a tariff preference on a basis of reciprocity. Imports from nonmembers of the WTO that have not negotiated a trade agreement with Canada are subject to the general or highest duty category. A federal goods and services tax, excise tax, and provincial retail sales tax add to the cost of importation.

In October 1987, Canada and the US reached agreement to establish a free trade area between the two countries which came into force in 1989, with all tariffs being eliminated within 10 years. Canadian commercial policy is generally opposed to the use of quantitative restrictions except as permitted by the WTO, or for sanitary reasons, or in emergencies, or to allocate scarce supplies, or to meet balance-of-payments problems. Canada does not adhere to a general system of import licensing but does require permits for a limited number of products, such as electric power, petroleum, and natural gas and by-products. There are no free ports, but bonded facilities are operated at many ports. Except in grain, for which storage facilities are extremely large, customs warehousing is not extensive.

The United States, Canada, and Mexico signed the North American Free Trade Agreement (NAFTA) in December 1992. Approved by the legislatures of all three countries in 1993, NAFTA replaced the existing free trade agreement between Canada and the United States in 1994 but retained many of its major provisions and obligations.

³⁸FOREIGN INVESTMENT

At the end of 1998, foreign direct investment in Canada, which has increased steadily since the early 1950s, amounted to $142 billion, or almost 24% of GDP. When portfolio investment was added to this figure, total foreign investment accounted for 40% of Canadian GDP. The US is the largest investor in Canada with investments totaling $75 billion or about 71% of the total.

The Foreign Investment Review Agency, empowered to regulate foreign investments in Canada, was disbanded by the Conservative government that took office in 1984. To encourage foreign investment, an agency called Investment Canada was subsequently established. The investment review process has been simplified, and except for certain investments and acquisitions, screening has been abolished. Since 1994, trade between Canada and the US and Mexico has been governed by the North American Free Trade Agreement (NAFTA).

Canada's direct investment abroad reached C$240 billion in 1998. The United States receives roughly 54% of Canada's exported capital, more than any other nation. The UK is second with just under 10% of the total.

39ECONOMIC DEVELOPMENT

Basically, Canada has a free-enterprise economy. However, the government has intervened in times of economic crisis and to accomplish specific social or economic goals. For example, in October 1963, the Canadian government announced a plan, involving tariff rebates, designed to induce US automobile companies to increase the export of vehicles and parts from their plants in Canada; subsequently, US companies markedly increased the scale of their Canadian operations. To dampen speculative buying of the Canadian dollar, the government permitted the dollar to float in the foreign exchange markets as of 31 May 1970; the government's intent was also to make imports cheaper in terms of Canadian dollars, and thereby to dampen domestic inflation. Another attempt at economic intervention, the Canada Anti-Inflation Act, became effective on 16 December 1975. This legislation established an Anti-Inflation Board and an Anti-Inflation Appeal Tribunal to monitor wage and price guidelines, which are mandatory for key sectors of the economy. The act was part of a government program to limit the growth of public expenditures and public service employment, to allow the money supply to increase at a rate consistent with moderate real growth, and to establish new agencies and policies to deal with energy, food, and housing.

A recurrent problem for Canada has been the dominant position of US corporations and investors. Attempts to limit US influence have included tightened tax policies, the Foreign Investment Review Act, and, in 1980, the National Energy Program (NEP), which aimed at reducing foreign ownership of Canada's oil and gas industry, principally through assisting Canadian companies to take over foreign holdings. One beneficiary of the NEP was the government-owned Petro-Canada, created in the mid-1970s; by the end of 1985, Petro-Canada had become the country's second-largest oil company, ranked by assets. However, much of the NEP was eliminated in the mid-1980s by the Conservative government, which sought to encourage foreign investment and to privatize government-owned enterprises. Between 1984 and 1991, the government sold or dissolved over 20 federal corporations, deregulated much of the energy, transportation, and financial sectors, and removed many controls on foreign investment.

In 2000, after more than 10 years of the bilateral trade agreement with the US, Canada's economy was growing at a comfortable pace, unemployment was falling, and inflation was low; but nationals were still dissatisfied with the size of the Canadian economy as compared to US affluence.

40SOCIAL DEVELOPMENT

Welfare needs are met by federal, provincial, and municipal governments as well as by voluntary agencies. Community chests, federated funds, and welfare councils throughout the country, affiliated with the Canadian Welfare Council, provide cooperative planning, financing, and consultative services.

Federal programs include family allowances, old age security, and earning-related disability and survivors' pensions. According to the 1992 Federal Budget, all children under 18 are eligible for small monthly allowances. The amount of these child allowances declines as family net income increases. Persons aged 65 and over receive monthly pensions, supplemented in some provinces on a means-test basis. Under federal-provincial programs, monthly allowances are paid to needy persons aged 65 to 69 and to needy persons aged 18 or over who are blind or totally and permanently disabled. The federal government reimburses each participating province for half the cost of unemployment insurance payments.

The provinces provide allowances to needy mothers and their dependent children, widows, and mothers whose husbands have deserted them, are disabled, or are in mental hospitals. Some provinces provide for divorced, separated, and unmarried mothers, and for mothers whose husbands are in penal institutions. Most provinces reimburse municipalities for part of the costs of aid to transients and to needy residents on the basis of a means test. Municipalities, provinces, and voluntary agencies finance child welfare services. Homes for the aged are generally maintained by municipalities and voluntary organizations.

Since 1941, a contributory scheme of unemployment insurance and a nationwide free employment service have been in operation. As of 1999, workers contribute 2.55% of their earnings, and employers contribute at 1.4 times that rate. In every province, employers are also required to contribute to a workers' compensation insurance fund. Workers are indemnified for accidents or occupational diseases and receive medical aid during the period they do not work. In industries, burial expenses in case of accidental death are included.

Women participate fully in the Canadian labor force, including business and the professions, although government reports show that their average earnings are still less than those of men. A study published in 1995 showed that women earned on average 72 cents for each dollar earned by men. In 1998 the Human Rights Tribunal ordered the Canadian government to pay back wages to mostly female workers in underpaid jobs. As of 1997, 92 of 406 members of parliament were women.

Aboriginal Canadians remain locked in land disputes with the government. Treaty negotiations to transfer land titles to natives or agree to compensation for use of the land have not made much progress. There has been an increase in anti-Semitic harassment in recent years.

41HEALTH

Canada adopted a national health insurance scheme in 1971. Administered regionally, each province runs a public insurance plan with the government contributing about 40% of the cost (mostly from taxes). Government regulations ensure that private insurers can only offer particular types of health care provision. Drug prices are low. Most hospitals and doctors operate privately. Hospitals are paid by allocated budgets and doctors receive fees per treatment. The system offers considerable choice, but there is little competition and the government has used rationing measures to limit health care expenditures. Access to health care and cost containment are good, but there are strains on the budget and an aging population increases the strain. In 1997 the National Forum on Health, created by the government three years earlier, released a report on ways to improve Canada's health system. It recommended several initiatives, including formation of a Health Transition Fund to support provincial and territorial health programs. Major health planning is carried on by provincial governments, most of which offer substantially free care for patients suffering from tuberculosis (1,930 cases reported in 1995), poliomyelitis, and venereal diseases and for certain cancer victims. They also assume responsibility for mental health treatment. Municipalities are responsible for sanitation; communicable disease control; child, maternal, and school health care; public health nursing; health education; and vital statistics. In some cases they supply hospital care and medical service to the poor. The federal government provides consultant and specialist services to the provinces, assists in the financing of provincial programs, provides services to veterans and Indians, exercises control over the standard and distribution of food and drugs, maintains quarantine measures, and is responsible for carrying out certain international health obligations. The federal Department of National Health and Welfare provides financial assistance for provincial health and hospital services through the National Health Program, and for provincial hospital insurance programs through the Hospital Insurance and Diagnostic Services Act of 1957, under which the federal government shares the provinces' costs (since 1977, by means of tax transfers and cash payments). By 1973, this program had been established in all provinces and territories, covering more than 99% of the total population of Canada. Federal and provincial governments contribute toward construction costs of new hospitals. Total health care expenditures for 1995 were US$1,899 per capita. Public insurance pays about 80% of the Canadian population's health bills. The total expenditure on health is second only to the United States, with 9.8% of Gross domestic product going toward health in 1996. The Canadian death rate of 7.1 per 1,000 population in 1995, the maternal death rate (1997) of 5 per 100,000 live births, and the infant mortality rate (1996) of 5.6 per 1,000 live births are among the lowest in the world. In 1998, 6% of all births were low birthweight. Diseases of the heart and arteries account for nearly 40% of all deaths, and cancer accounts for about 28%; the proportion of deaths from causes related to old age is rising. Tobacco consumption, which was 2.8kg a year per adult in 1984–86, was 2.3kg in 1995. Accidents are the leading cause of death in childhood and among young adult males, and rank high for other population groups. In 1998, life expectancy at birth was estimated at 79 years. Canada had a birth rate in 1999 of 11.9 per 1,000. Between 1980 and 1993, 73% of married women (ages 15 to 49) were using contraception. And, in 1997, children up to one year of age were immunized as follows: diphtheria, pertussis, and tetanus (93%); polio (89%); and measles (98%). The HIV seroprevalence was 0.33 per 100 adults in 1997. The latest statistics on AIDS indicate 558 new cases in 1996. From 1990 to 1997, there were 5.1 hospital beds per 1,000 people. In the far eastern part of Canada, hospital beds available in 1993 were as follows: New Brunswick (5,025); Newfoundland (2,900); Nova Scotia (5,357); and Prince Edward Island (675). In 1995, there were 18 doctors per 10,000 population. There were 55,016 physicians, 15,636 dentists, and 232,869 nurses, and 22,197 pharmacists in 1995. As of 1998, there was an oversupply of physicians in Canada.

42HOUSING

There were more than 10 million occupied private dwellings in Canada in the mid-1990s. Single detached homes are the predominant type of housing accommodation, although their relative numbers have gradually declined in favor of multiple dwellings. In 1951, 66.7% of all dwellings were single detached; by the mid-1990s, the proportion had dropped to nearly 60%, while more than 30% were categorized as low density, nearly 10% high rise, and less than 5% mobile dwellings. As of the 1991 Census, almost half of Canada's homes had been built since 1970.

In 1992, the federal government introduced the programs to promote home ownership: the First Home Insurance initiative and the Buyers' Home Plan.

43EDUCATION

Virtually the entire adult population is literate (96.6%). The age limits of compulsory school attendance are roughly from age 6 to age 16. Primary schools lasts for six years and secondary or high school another six years. In 1996, primary schools numbered 12,685. There were 148,565 teachers and 2,448,144 students in primary schools, with a student-to-teacher ratio of 16 to one. The same year, secondary schools had 133,275 teachers and 2,505,389 students.

Each province is responsible for its own system of education. While the systems differ in some details, the general plan is the same for all provinces except Québec, which has two parallel systems: one mainly for Roman Catholics and speakers of French, the other primarily for non-Catholics and speakers of English. Québec, Newfoundland, Alberta, Saskatchewan, and, to a lesser extent, Ontario provide for public support of church-affiliated schools. Primary and secondary education is generally free, although nominal fees are charged for secondary education in some schools or provinces. Public elementary and secondary schools are administered by the provinces and Yukon Territory.

As of the mid-1990s, there were some 60 degree-granting colleges and universities in Canada. There are provincial universities in all provinces; other degree-granting institutions are private or connected with a religious denomination. In 1996, full-time enrollment in all higher level institutions, colleges, and universities was 1,763,105. The federal government operates one military college with degree-granting powers conferred by the province of Ontario. Since 1977, the federal government has contributed to post-secondary education by cash payments and tax transfers, independently of provincial program costs.

Canadian higher education began with the founding of the Collège des Jésuites in Québec City in 1635. The Séminaire de Québec, another Jesuit institution, established in 1663, became Laval University in 1852. Other early institutions on the French collegiate model were the Collège St. Boniface in Manitoba (1827), the University of Ottawa (1848), and St. Joseph's University in New Brunswick (1864). Although many French institutions survive—most notably the University of Montréal, which separated itself from Laval in 1920—most university-level instruction is conducted in English on the Scottish, British, or US model. The first English-language college in Canada was King's College in Halifax, Nova Scotia (1789). Two private universities on the Scottish model are Dalhousie University in Halifax (1818) and McGill University in Montréal (1821). The first state-supported institution, founded in 1827 on the principles of Anglicanism and loyalty to the British crown, was King's College at York in Upper Canada, which became the University of Toronto, the largest and one of the most distinguished of Canadian institutions. Universities in each of the four western provinces—Manitoba, Saskatchewan, Alberta, and British Columbia—founded in the late 19th century, represent a Canadian adaptation of the US state land-grant universities.

Canada also has numerous community colleges, teachers' colleges, technical institutes, nursing schools, and art schools. Adult education is sponsored by universities, colleges, school boards, government departments, and voluntary associations, each of which has some other primary function. The Canadian Broadcasting Corp., the National Film Board, and many museums, art galleries, and libraries engage in adult education as part of their work. Instructors are represented by the Canadian Association of University Teachers, and students by the Canadian Federation of Students.

44LIBRARIES AND MUSEUMS

Municipal public libraries serve the large cities and many small towns and rural areas, and regional units supply library service to scattered population areas. Traveling libraries, operated by provincial governments or university extension departments, also provide mail services for more isolated individuals and communities. Although public libraries are organized and financed by municipalities, in most provinces the provincial government supervises library services and makes grants to the municipal units. Special libraries of various kinds and at various levels serve limited groups. In 2000, Canada had a total of 3,932 libraries, including 1,673 public libraries, 484 academic libraries, 380 government libraries, and a variety of special libraries.

The National Library at Ottawa (6,300,000 volumes) publishes *Canadiana,* a monthly catalog of books and pamphlets relating to Canada, and maintains the National Union Catalogue of books in all major Canadian libraries.

There are about 2,000 museums, art galleries, and related institutions in Canada. Major museums located in Ottawa include the National Arts Center, the National Gallery of Canada (including the Canadian Museum of Contemporary Photography), the Canadian Museum of Nature, and the National Museum of Science and Technology (including the National Aviation Museum and the Agriculture Museum). Other notable Canadian museums include the Royal Ontario Museum in Toronto and the Fine Arts Museum in Montreal. The major museums and art galleries, located in the principal cities, provide valuable educational services to adults and children; many supply traveling exhibitions for their surrounding areas or regions. The National Gallery conducts extension work throughout the country and sends many exhibitions on tour.

45MEDIA

There were 16,470,900 telephones in Canada in 1995. The 10 public and private companies in Telecom Canada provide a major share of the nation's telecommunications services, including all long-distance service, and link regional networks across Canada. Telegraph services are operated by the two transcontinental railroads and by the federal government to outlying districts. All external telecommunication services are operated by the Canadian Overseas Telecommunication Corp., a crown agency. The Post Office became a crown corporation in 1981.

The Broadcasting Act of 1968 entrusted the Canadian Radio-Television Commission with the regulation and supervision of all aspects of the broadcasting system. The publicly owned Canadian Broadcasting Corp. (CBC) provides the national broadcasting service in Canada. Its radio and television facilities extend from the Atlantic Ocean to the Pacific and north to the Arctic Circle. The CBC has broadcasting stations in the principal cities and operates both English- and French-language national networks. Privately owned local stations form part of the networks and provide alternative programs. As of 1999, there were 334 AM broadcasting stations, 35 FM stations, and 80 television stations. In 1997 there were 1,078 radios, 708 television sets, and 139 mobile phones per 1,000 population. Radio Canada International, the CBC's shortwave service, broadcasts in seven languages to Europe, Africa, Latin America, Asia, the Middle East, the South Pacific, and the US.

The Canadian communication satellites play an increasingly significant role in efforts to bring radio and television services to the more remote parts of the country, particularly in the north. Beginning in late 1980, a new television network began broadcasting programs in the Inuit language via satellite, offering viewers the opportunity to "talk back" through their television sets to people in other communities. As of May 1987, radio and television services reached 99% of Canadian homes. A broadcasting policy announced in April 1983 increased the quantity of Canadian content required in programming, established a fund to assist private and independent producers, and relaxed licensing requirements for the use of satellite earth-stations for radio and television reception.

In 1995 there were 106 daily newspapers with a total circulation of 5,815,000. Although some newspapers in Montréal, Québec, Toronto, Winnipeg, and Vancouver have more than local influence, most circulate only on a regional basis and have a limited number of readers. Rural areas are served by over 2,000 monthly and weekly publications. There are many consumer magazines, but only *Maclean's* is truly national. Three large news-gathering organizations are the Canadian Press, a cooperatively owned and operated venture, the British United Press, and United Press International of Canada.

Canada's leading newspapers (with their 1999 daily circulations) include the following:

	LANGUAGE	CIRCULATION
Toronto Star (all day)	English	704,900
Globe and Mail (Toronto, m)	English	381,800
Le Journal de Montréal (m)	French	320,200
Toronto Sun (m)	English	241,100
Vancouver Sun (e)	English	241,100
La Presse (Montréal, m)	French	274,000
Ottawa Citizen (all day)	English	184,600
Province (Vancouver, m)	English	156,700
Edmonton Journal (m)	English	141,600
Gazette (Montréal, m)	English	196,000
Winnipeg Free Press (e)	English	193,500
Calgary Herald (m)	English	116,400
Hamilton Spectator (e)	English	127,400
Le Soleil (Québec, e)	French	122,500

The law provides for freedom of expression, including speech and press, and the government supports these rights. The banning of journalists from reporting on some court cases until after a trial in concluded enjoys widespread public support, in favor of a defendant's right to a fair trial.

As of 1996, there were over 5,600,000 personal computers. In 1998 there were 335 Internet hosts per 1,000 population.

46ORGANIZATIONS

Cooperatives are very important in Canadian agriculture and fishing, and also provide housing, medical insurance, transportation, and other services. The Canadian Red Cross Society, affiliated with the International Red Cross Society, has branches in all 10 provinces. Almost every city has a chamber of commerce, affiliated with the national Canadian Chamber of Commerce. Among organizations active in education are the Canadian Association for Adult Education, the Canadian Association of University Teachers, and the Industrial Foundation on Education, a research organization aiming to promote aid to education by business. The Canada Council is the official national agency for promotion of the arts, humanities, and the social sciences. The Royal Canadian Academy of Arts is the oldest arts organization with national prestige. The Canada Arts Council, a federation of professional cultural organizations, includes the Royal Architectural Institute of Canada, the Canadian Authors' Association, the Canadian Music Council, the Sculptors' Society of Canada, and similar societies. Many voluntary societies are active in the field of health.

47TOURISM, TRAVEL, AND RECREATION

One of Canada's principal attractions for tourists is its extraordinary geographic variety: from the polar ice cap to the mountains, fjords, and rain forests of the west coast, from the lakes, forests, and ranchlands of the interior to the rugged shores and fine beaches of the east, Canada offers a remarkable range of scenic wonders. The excavation of L'Anse aux Meadows in Newfoundland, with its Norse artifacts and reconstructed dwellings, has been designated a world heritage site by UNESCO, as have Nahanni National Park in the Northwest Territories and Dinosaur Park in Alberta's Red Deer Badlands. Among the most spectacular parks are the Kluane National Park in the Yukon and the Banff (with Lake Louise) and Jasper national parks in the mountains of Alberta. Other attractions include the Cabot Trail in Nova Scotia; the Bay of Fundy, between New Brunswick and Nova Scotia; and the Laurentians and the Gaspé Peninsula in Québec.

The arts and crafts of the Dene Indians and the Inuit may be seen in cooperative workshops in Inuvik in the Northwest Territories; and of the North West Coast Indians, at the reconstructed

Indian village Ksan in British Columbia. Québec City is the only walled city in North America; picturesque old fishing villages are to be found in the Atlantic provinces. Fishing and hunting attract many sportsmen to Canada, and ice hockey attracts many sports fans, particularly to the Forum in Montréal. Major league baseball teams play in Montréal and Toronto. In 1992, the Toronto major league baseball team, the Blue Jays, became the first non-American team to both play in and win the World Series.

One of the world's foremost summer theatrical events is the Shakespeare Festival at Stratford, Ontario. Toronto is known for its many theaters, the tower, and a fine zoo; Montréal, the second-largest French-speaking city in the world (after Paris), is famous for its fine French cuisine, its night life, its vast underground shopping and entertainment network, and its excellent subway system.

Montréal in 1967 hosted a major world trade exhibition, EXPO 67; the Summer Olympics took place in that same city in 1976. A world's fair, EXPO 86, was held in Vancouver in 1986, and Calgary was the site of the 1988 Winter Olympics.

In 1998, Canada was the third most popular tourist destination in the Americas after the US and Mexico. In that year, 18,825,100 tourists arrived from abroad, 14,880,400 of them from the US. Gross receipts from tourism were US$8.76 billion in 1997.

Citizens of the US do not need passports but should carry documents attesting to their citizenship, such as birth certificates or voter registration cards. Alien residents should carry their green cards. Nationals of other countries must have valid passports and may require visitor visas; they should check with the nearest Canadian embassy, consulate, or high commission. In 1991, a 7% Goods and Services Tax went into effect; however, it is refundable to foreign tourists.

In 1997, there were 327,383 hotel rooms in Canada with an occupancy rate of 64%. The UN estimated the daily cost of staying in Vancouver at US$176 and US$174 for Toronto in 1999. Montréal was less costly, requiring an average expenditure of US$154.

48 FAMOUS CANADIANS

Political Figures

Because of their exploits in establishing and developing early Canada, then known as New France, a number of eminent Frenchmen are prominent in Canadian history, among them the explorers Jacques Cartier (1491–1557), Samuel de Champlain (1567?–1635), Étienne Brulé (1592?–1633), Jacques Marquette (1637–75), Robert Cavelier, Sieur de la Salle (1643–87), and Louis Jolliet (1645–1700); François Xavier de Laval de Montigny (1623–1708), first and greatest bishop of Québec; Jean Baptiste Talon (1625?–94), first and greatest intendant, who re-created the colony on a sound economic basis; and Louis de Buade, Comte de Palluau et de Frontenac (c.1622–98), greatest of the French royal governors. Great explorers of a later period include Pierre Gaultier de Varennes, Sieur de la Vérendrye (1695–1749), Sir Alexander Mackenzie (1764–1820), David Thompson (1770–1857), Simon Fraser (1776–1871), Joseph E. Bernier (1852–1934), and Joseph Burr Tyrrell (1858–1957). Louis Riel (1844–85), of Indian and French-Irish ancestry, led the métis in rebellion in 1869–70 and 1885, when he was captured and hanged for treason.

Fathers of confederation and other important 19th-century political figures include Louis Joseph Papineau (1786–1871) and William Lyon Mackenzie (1795–1861); Sir John Alexander Macdonald (1815–91), first prime minister of the confederation; George Brown (1818–80), Sir Samuel Leonard Tilley (1818–96), and Sir Charles Tupper (1821–1915). The greatest political leader

at the turn of the century was Sir Wilfrid Laurier (1841–1919), prime minister from 1896 to 1911. The outstanding national leader of the first half of the 20th century was William Lyon Mackenzie King (1874–1950), Liberal prime minister for over 21 years (1921–26, 1926–30, 1935–48), who retired with a record of the longest service as prime minister in Commonwealth history. Charles Vincent Massey (1887–1967), governor-general from 1952 to 1959, was the first Canadian to represent the British crown in Canada. Lester Bowles Pearson (1897–1972), prime minister and Canada's longtime UN representative, won the Nobel Prize for peace in 1957. Pierre Elliott Trudeau (b.1919) served as prime minister from 1968 to 1979 and again from 1980 to 1984, when he was succeeded by Brian Mulroney (b.1939). The best-known French-Canadian separatist was René Lévesque (1922–87), leader of the Parti Québécois, who became premier of Québec in 1976.

Artists

Highly regarded Canadian painters include James Edward Hervey MacDonald (1873–1932), Thomas John ("Tom") Thomson (1877–1917), Frederick Horsman Varley (1881–1969), and Lawren Stewart Harris (1885–1970) of the Group of Seven; James Wilson Morrice (1864–1924); and Emily Carr (1871–1945). Paul-Emile Borduas (1905–60) and Jean-Paul Riopelle (b.1923) both were part of the Montréal School; however, after settling abroad, they probably became better known in France and the US than in their native country. Two other artists of distinction are James W. G. MacDonald (1897–1960) and Harold Barling Town (1924–90). The portrait photographer Yousuf Karsh (b.Armenia-in-Turkey, 1908) is a longtime Canadian resident.

Musicians

Well-known Canadian musicians include the composer Healey Willan (1880–1968); the conductor Sir Ernest Campbell MacMillan (1893–1973); the pianist Glenn Gould (1932–82); the singers Edward Johnson (1878–1959), Jon Vickers (b.1926), and Maureen Forrester (b.1931); the bandleader Guy Lombardo (1902–77); and, among recent popular singers and songwriters, Gordon Lightfoot (b.1938), Paul Anka (b.1941), Joni Mitchell (b.1943), Neil Young (b.1945), and Celine Dion (b.1968).

Actors

Canadian-born actors who are known for their association with Hollywood include Marie Dressler (Leila Koerber, 1869–1934), Walter Huston (Houghston, 1884–1950), Mary Pickford (Gladys Mary Smith, 1893–1979), Raymond Hart Massey (1896–1983), Walter Pidgeon (1897–1984), Norma Shearer (1904–83), Lorne Greene (1915–87), Raymond Burr (1917–93), William Shatner (b.1931), and Donald Sutherland (b.1935). Stage personalities include Beatrice Lillie (1894–1989), Hume Cronyn (1911–96), and Christopher Plummer (b.1929).

Sports

Notable in the world of sports are ice-hockey stars Maurice ("Rocket") Richard (b.1921), Gordon ("Gordie") Howe (b.1928), Robert Marvin ("Bobby") Hull, Jr. (b.1939), Robert ("Bobby") Orr (b.1948), and Wayne Gretzky (b.1961).

Authors

Thomas Chandler Haliburton (1796–1865), author of *Sam Slick*, was the first Canadian writer to attain more than a local reputation. Sir Charles George Douglas Roberts (1860–1943) and Bliss Carman (1861–1929) were widely read poets and short-story writers. Archibald Lampman (1861–99) wrote sensitive poems about nature. Narrative poems about the northwest frontier by Robert William Service (1874–1958) achieved mass popularity, as did the backwoods novels of Ralph Connor (Charles William Gordon, 1860–1937). The animal stories and bird drawings of Ernest Evan Thompson Seton (b. UK, 1860–1946) are still highly regarded. Stephen Butler Leacock (1869–1944), economist and essayist, is regarded as Canada's leading humorist. The *Anne of Green Gables* novels of Lucy Maud Montgomery (1874–1942) have been popular with girls of several generations. Mazo de la Roche (1885–1961) achieved fame for her romantic Jalna novels about an Ontario family. Well-known contemporary novelists include Morley Edward Callaghan (1903–90), Hugh MacLennan (1907–90), Farley McGill Mowat (b.1921), Alice Munro (b.1921), Margaret Lawrence (b.1926), Mordecai Richler (b.1931), and Marian Passmore Engel (b.1933). The novels and plays of Robertson Davies (1913–95), newspaper editor, actor, music critic, and university administrator, crackle with wit. Lorne Albert Pierce (1890–1961) was a prominent editor and literary critic. Herbert Marshall McLuhan (1911–80) was a communications theorist and cultural critic. Herman Northrop Frye (1912–91) was a well-known literary critic, and Margaret Atwood (b.1939) is a noted novelist and poet. The British newspaper publisher William Maxwell Aitken, 1st Baron Beaverbrook (1879–1964), was born in Canada.

The *Histoire du Canada* (1845) of François Xavier Garneau (1809–66) stimulated a great interest in French Canada's heritage. Joseph Octave Crémazie (1827–79) was the first notable French Canadian poet. The poems of Louis Honoré Fréchette (1839–1908) were crowned by the French Academy. Louis Hémon (1880–1913), a French journalist who came to Canada in 1910 and spent only 18 months there, wrote the classic French Canadian novel *Maria Chapdelaine* (1914). Authors of realistic novels dealing with social and economic problems of French Canada include Claude-Henri Grignon (1894–1976), author of *Un Homme et son péché* (1933); Jean-Charles Harvey (1892–1967), author of *Les Démi-civilisées* (1934); Ringuet (Dr. Philippe Panneton, 1895–1960), author of *Trente Arpentes* (1938); Germaine Grignon Guevremont (1900–1968); Roger Lemelin (1919–92), author of *Au pied de la pente douce* (1944); and Gabrielle Roy (Carbotte, 1909–93). Gratien Gélinas (b.1909) is an actor, director, and dramatic satirist. Abbé Félix Antoine Savard (1896–1982) wrote a poetic novel of pioneer life, *Menaud, maître-drayeur*.

Scientists and Inventors

Among the famous Canadian scientists and inventors are Sir Sanford Fleming (1827–1915), inventor of standard time; Sir William Osler (1849–1919), the father of psychosomatic medicine; and Sir Charles Saunders (1867–1937), who developed the Marquis wheat strain, which revolutionized wheat growing in northern latitudes. The codiscoverers of insulin, Sir Frederick Grant Banting (1891–1941) and John James Richard Macleod (1876–1935), were awarded the Nobel Prize for medicine in 1923. George Brock Chisholm (1896–1971) was an eminent psychiatrist and former head of WHO. Gerhard Herzberg (b.Germany, 1904) won the 1971 Nobel Prize for chemistry for his work on molecular spectroscopy. Marius Barbeau (1883–1969), anthropologist and folklorist, was an authority on totem poles and Canadian folk music.

49DEPENDENCIES

Northwest Territories

The Northwest Territories constitute all of Canada north of 60°N except the Yukon and the northernmost parts of Québec and Newfoundland. Also included are certain islands in Hudson Bay, James Bay, and Ungava Bay, plus the vast islands to the north. Total land area is 3,293,020 sq km (1,271,438 sq mi). Most of the people who live in the territories are Inuit or Indians. The estimated population in the mid-1990s was more than 55,000. The Mackenzie River and its tributaries, the Athabasca and Slave, provide an inland transportation route of about 2,700 km (1,700 mi). There is some traffic on Lakes Athabasca, Great Bear, and Great Slave. Most of the settlements in Mackenzie are linked by scheduled air service.

The territory is governed by a commissioner, for whom policy is determined by the governor-general-in-council or the Ministry of Indian Affairs and Northern Development, and by a 22-member elected territorial council. The territorial capital since 1967 has been Yellowknife. Following the approval by voters in April 1982 of a proposal to divide the territory, the federal government has scheduled the division in 1999. The Inuit of the east call their proposed eastern jurisdiction Nunavat; Indians of the west—where opinion on the proposal was sharply split—call their proposed division Deneden. Land claims of Dene Indians and the Inuit overlap.

Northwest Territories' mineral resources include rich deposits of gold, silver, lead, tungsten, and zinc. The Northwest Territories contain some of Canada's total mineral resources. It was the Yukon gold rush in 1897 that triggered a large migration of people northward. In one year 30,000 people from the lower parts of Canada were in the Northwest and Yukon Territories looking for gold.

Today, Canada leads in the production of oil, natural gas and coal. Canada's mining industry contributes US$20 billion annually to the economy and employs 145,000 people. In 1989 Canada's oil and gas industry was valued at US$19 billion with 55% of the revenue coming from oil production. Whitefish and trout are caught in Great Slave Lake; the 100,000 or more lakes of the territories provide an "angler's last frontier" in North America for sport fishermen. Fur production is a sizable industry in the Northwest Territories. A handicrafts industry supplies Inuit-made sculpture and prints to the Canadian Handicrafts Guild.

Yukon Territory

The Yukon Territory, located north of British Columbia and east of Alaska, has a land area of 478,970 sq km (184,931 sq mi) and had an estimated population in the mid-1990s of more than 30,000, of whom some one-fifth were of Indian origin. The principal town is Whitehorse, the capital. An all-weather roadway connects the territory with Alaska and British Columbia, and a railroad connects Whitehorse with ocean shipping at Skagway, Alaska. Air service is available to and from Edmonton, Vancouver, and Fairbanks, Alaska. There are local telephone services in the three chief towns. The territory was separately constituted in June 1898. Since 1978, the Yukon has had a legislative assembly, consisting of 16 elected members. In late 1982, the federal government gave its consent for the Yukon cabinet to call itself the Executive Council and officially to take over some powers hitherto reserved by the federally appointed commissioner, as representative of the governor-general-in-council, or by the minister of Indian affairs and northern development. The Yukon government has recently pressed for provincial status.

Mineral resources include rich deposits of gold, silver, lead, tungsten, and zinc. Mining and tourism are Yukon's principal industries.

50BIBLIOGRAPHY

Balthazar, Louis, *French-Canadian Civilization*. Washington, D.C.: Association for Canadian Studies in the United States, 1996.

Bell, David V. J. *The Roots of Disunity: A Study of Canadian Political Culture*. Rev. ed. Toronto: Oxford University Press, 1992.

Bothwell, Robert. *Canada and Quebec: One Country, Two Histories*. Vancouver: UBC Press, 1995.

Bothwell, Robert. *History of Canada Since 1867*. Washington, D.C.: Association for Canadian Studies in the United States, 1996.

Bumsted, J. M. *The Peoples of Canada*. New York: Oxford University Press, 1992.

Canada. New York: Facts on File, 1993.

Canada in Pictures. Minneapolis: Lerner, 1993.

The Canadian Encyclopedia. 2d ed. Edmonton: Hurtig Publishers, 1988

Clement, Wallace, ed. *Understanding Canada: Building on the New Canadian Political Economy*. Kingston: McGill-Queen's University Press, 1997.

The Community in Canada: Rural and Urban. Lanham, Md.: University Press of America, 1996.

Creighton, Donald. *Canada's First Century, 1867–1967*. New York: St. Martin's, 1970.

Dawson, Robert MacGregor, *Dawson's the Government of Canada*. 6th ed. Toronto: University of Toronto Press, 1987.

Dickey, John Sloan (ed.). *Canada and the American Presence*. New York: New York University Press, 1975.

Driedger, Leo. *Multi-Ethnic Canada: Identities and Inequalities*. Toronto: Oxford University Press, 1996.

Easterbrook, W. T., and Hugh G.J. Aitken. *Canadian Economic History*. Toronto: University of Toronto Press, 1988.

Fenwick, Rudy. *Canadian Society*. Washington, D.C.: Association for Canadian Studies in the United States, 1996

Fox, Annette Baker. *Canada in World Affairs*. Washington, D.C.: Association for Canadian Studies in the United States, 1996

Fry, Earl H. *The Canadian Political System*. Washington, D.C.: Association for Canadian Studies in the United States, 1996

Halpenny, Frances, et al. (eds.). *Dictionary of Canadian Biography*. 7 vols. to date. Toronto: University of Toronto Press, 1972-date.

Inflehart, Ronald. *The North American Trajectory: Cultural, Economic, and Political Ties Among the United States, Canada, and Mexico*. New York: Aldine de Gruyter, 1996.

Ingles, Ernest B. *Canada*. Santa Barbara, Calif.: Clio, 1990.

Joy, Richard J. *Canada's Official Languages: The Progress of Bilingualism*. Toronto: University of Toronto Press, 1992.

Konrad, Victor A. *Geography of Canada*. Washington, D.C.: Association for Canadian Studies in the United States, 1996

Lipset, Seymour Martin. *Continental Divide: The Values and Institutions of the United States and Canada*. New York: Routledge, 1990.

Malcolm, A. II. *The Canadians*. New York: Times Books, 1985.

Pearson, Lester B. *Mike: The Memoirs of the Right Honorable Lester B. Pearson*. 2 vols. New York: Quadrangle Books, 1972–73.

Russell, Peter H. *Constitutional Odyssey: Can the Canadians Become a Sovereign People?* Toronto: University of Toronto Press, 1992.

Simeon, Richard, and Ian Robinson. *State, Society, and the Development of Canadian Federalism*. Toronto: University of Toronto Press, 1990.

Stewart, Gordon T. *The American Response to Canada since 1776*. East Lansing, Mich.: Michigan State University Press, 1992.

Stewart, Gordon T. *History of Canada Before 1867*. Washington, D.C.: Association for Canadian Studies in the United States, 1996

Story, Norah. *Oxford Companion to Canadian History and Literature*. Toronto: Oxford University Press, 1967.

Webber, Jeremy H. A. *Reimagining Canada: Language, Culture, Community and the Canadian Constitution*. Montreal: McGill-Queen's University Press, 1994.

Woodcock, George. *The Canadians*. Cambridge, Mass.: Harvard University Press, 1980.

CHILE

Republic of Chile
República de Chile

CAPITAL: Santiago.

FLAG: The flag, adopted in 1817, consists of a lower half of red and an upper section of white, with a blue square in the upper left corner containing a five-pointed white star.

ANTHEM: *Canción Nacional (National Song)* beginning "Dulce Patria, recibe los votos".

MONETARY UNIT: The peso (P) of 100 centavos replaced the escudo as the nation's monetary unit in October 1975. There are coins of 1, 5, 10, 50, 100, and 500 pesos, and notes of 500, 1,000, 5,000 and 10,000 pesos. P1 = US$0.00194 (or US$1 = P514.50) as of 31 March 2000.

WEIGHTS AND MEASURES: The metric system is the legal standard, but local measures also are used.

HOLIDAYS: New Year's Day, 1 January; Labor Day, 1 May; Navy Day (Battle of Iquique), 21 May; Assumption, 15 August; Independence Day, 18 September; Army Day, 19 September; Columbus Day, 12 October; All Saints' Day, 1 November; Immaculate Conception, 8 December; Christmas, 25 December. Movable religious holidays include Good Friday and Holy Saturday.

TIME: 8 AM = noon GMT.

¹LOCATION, SIZE, AND EXTENT

Situated along the southwestern coast of South America, Chile has an area of 756,950 sq km (292,260 sq mi). Comparatively, the area occupied by Chile is slightly smaller than the state of Montana. A long string of land pressed between the Pacific and the towering Andes, Chile is 4,270 km (2,653 mi) long N–S; it is 356 km (221 mi) wide at its broadest point (just north of Antofagasta) and 64 km (40 mi) at its narrowest point, with an average width of 175 km (109 mi) E–W. It is bordered on the N by Peru, on the NE by Bolivia, on the E by Argentina, on the S by the Drake Passage, and on the W by the Pacific Ocean. At the far SE, at the end of the Strait of Magellan (Estrecho de Magallanes), it has an opening to the Atlantic Ocean. Chile's boundary length is 12,606 km (7,833 mi).

Included in the national territory are the Juan Fernández Islands, Easter Island, and other Pacific islands. A dispute with Argentina over three small islands in the Beagle Channel almost led to war between the two countries in 1978, but papal intervention prevented hostilities. The issue was resolved peacefully by a treaty signed in the Vatican on 29 November 1984 and ratified on 2 May 1985, granting Chile sovereignty over the three islands, giving Argentina rights to waters east of the Strait of Magellan, and dividing the territorial waters south of Cape Horn between the two countries. There is another outstanding boundary problem with Bolivia over its claim for an opening to the sea. Chile also claims the Antarctic Peninsula and other areas of Antarctica, comprising 1,250,000 sq km (482,500 sq mi).

Chile's capital city, Santiago, is located in the center of the country.

²TOPOGRAPHY

Chile is divided into three general topographic regions: the lofty Andean cordillera on the east; the low coastal mountains of the west; and the fertile central valley between. The Andes, occupying from one-third to the entire width of the country, stretch from the Puna de Atacama in the north, a high plateau with peaks averaging 4,600 m (15,000 ft), to middle Chile, where, on the border with Argentina, rises the highest peak in the Western

Hemisphere, Aconcagua (7,265 m/23,834 ft), and then, diminishing in height, run south into the Chilean lake country, with its snow-capped volcanoes and several passes. The coastal range, verging from 300 to 2,100 m (1,000 to 7,000 ft) in height, rises from the sea along most of the coast. In the extreme north, the coastal mountains join with the Andean spurs to form a series of plateaus separated by deep gorge like valleys. In the south, the valleys and the coastal range plunge into the sea and form a western archipelago; fjords reach into the range at about 42°S. The central valley, an irregular alluvial plain 965 km (600 mi) long, 73 km (45 mi) wide at its maximum, and up to 1,200 m (4,000 ft) high, begins below the arid Atacama Desert of the north and ends at Puerto Montt in the south. Fertile between the Aconcagua and Bío-Bío rivers, this valley is the center of agriculture and of population. Although some 30 rivers rise in the Andes and descend to the Pacific, cascades and great waterfalls severely limit navigation; the ocean itself facilitates transportation between the different regions of this narrow country.

The northern side of the Strait of Magellan, part of Patagonia (a region shared by Chile and Argentina), and part of the island of western Tierra del Fuego (divided between Chile and Argentina) is low, glaciated, morainal country.

³CLIMATE

Climatic zones range from the subtropical deserts in the north to the temperate rain forests of Aisén and the tundras of Magallanes in the extreme south. The cold Humboldt Current, traveling northward from the Antarctic, affects the climate of the coastal regions of central and northern Chile. Generally, however, Chile is divided into three climatic regions: (1) The north, which contains the Atacama Desert, one of the driest regions in the world, is characterized by hot and arid weather in the lowlands and occasional summer showers in the Andean highlands. (2) The middle, extending about 1,450 km (900 mi) from 30° to 43°S, has a Mediterranean climate, with mild, wet winters, averaging 11°C (52°F), and long, dry summers, averaging 18°C (64°F). (3) The south, a region of mountains and fjords, has high winds and heavy rains. Annual rainfall ranges from no recorded precipitation in some parts of the north to 50–100 cm (20–40 in) around Concepción, in south-central Chile, to more than 500 cm (200 in) in some southern regions. South of the Bío-Bío River, rains occur all year round. The Andean highlands, even in the tropical north, are cold and snowy.

⁴FLORA AND FAUNA

Chile's botanical zones conform to the topographic and climatic regions. The northernmost coastal and central region is largely barren of vegetation, approaching the most closely an absolute desert in the world. On the slopes of the Andes, besides the scattered tola desert brush, grasses are found. The central valley is characterized by several species of cactus, the hard espinos, the Chilean pine, and the copihue, a red bell-shaped flower, Chile's national flower. In southern Chile, south of the Bío-Bío River, the heavy precipitation has produced dense forests of laurels, magnolias, and various species of conifers and beeches, which become smaller and more stunted to the south. The cold temperatures and winds of the extreme south preclude heavy forestation. Grassland is found in Atlantic Chile (in Patagonia). The Chilean flora is distinct from that of Argentina, indicating that the Andean barrier existed during its formation. Chilean species include the monkey-puzzle tree and the pinelike araucaria, also found in Australia. True pines have been introduced from the Northern Hemisphere.

Chile's geographical isolation also has restricted the immigration of faunal life, and only a few of the many distinctive Latin American animals are found. Among the larger mammals are the puma or cougar, the llamalike guanaco, the Andean wolf, and the foxlike chilla. In the forest region, several types of marsupials and a small deer known as the pudu are found.

There are many species of small birds, but most of the larger common Latin American types are absent. Few freshwater fish are native, but North American trout have been successfully introduced into the Andean lakes. Owing to the vicinity of the Humboldt Current, ocean waters abound with fish and other forms of marine life, which, in turn, support a rich variety of waterfowl, including different penguins. Whales are abundant, and some six species of seals are found in the area.

⁵ENVIRONMENT

The principal responsibility for environmental matters is vested in the environmental programs department in the Ministry of Health and in the National Planning Office, as well as in the ecological advisory office in the Ministry of National Welfare and the department of the environment in the Ministry of Foreign Affairs.

Chile's main environmental problems are deforestation and the resulting soil erosion, and the pollution of its air, water, and land. Air pollution from industry and transportation and water pollution are especially acute in urban centers, where the population has doubled in the last 30 years. In 1992, Chile's industrial carbon dioxide emissions totaled 34.7 million metric tons, or 2.56 metric tons per capita. Untreated sewage poses the major threat to the nation's water quality. As of the mid-1990s, Chile had 112.3 cu mi of water. While 94% of its urban dwellers have pure water, only 39% of its rural dwellers do not.

Endangered or extinct species in Chile include the South Andean huemul, tundra peregrine falcon, puna rhea, Chilean woodstar, ruddy-headed goose, and green sea turtle. As of the mid-1990s, 11 species of mammals in a total of 91 were considered endangered. Of 448 bird species, 15 were threatened with extinction. Also threatened were 27 types of fresh-water fish, and 292 plant species in a total of 5,125.

⁶POPULATION

The population of Chile in 2000 was estimated at 15,155,495. An estimated 6.8% of the population is 65 years of age or older. The projected population for the year 2005 is 15,716,000, assuming a crude birthrate of 15 per 1,000 population and a death rate of 6, resulting in a natural rate of change of 0.9% for the period 2000–2005. The population rate of change between 1995 and 2000 was 1.4%. The population density in 1998 was 20 per sq km (52 per sq mi). However, over 80% of the people live in the central region, between La Serena and Concepción, although this part covers little more than a quarter of the area.

It was estimated that 85% of the population lived in urban areas in 2000, up from 81% in 1980. Santiago, the capital and largest city, had a 2000 metropolitan population of 5,261,000. Other large cities include Viña del Mar, 302,765; Valparaíso, 276,737; Talcahuano, 246,556; Concepción, 329,304; Antofagasta, 226,749; Temuco, 240,880; and Rancagua, 187,134. Chile's next census is slated for April 2002.

⁷MIGRATION

After the Spanish conquest, there were three main waves of immigration: Germans during 1800–50; Spaniards, Italians, Swiss, Yugoslavs, Syrians, Jordanians, and Lebanese around 1900; and Spaniards and European Jews during the 1930s and 1940s. Since World War II, permanent immigration has been minimal.

In the years immediately preceding and after the Allende victory in 1970, about 10,000 political refugees (largely Brazilians, Bolivians, and Argentines) came to Chile. After the military coup of 1973, however, the bulk of them were expelled. The 1970s also witnessed two successive waves of Chilean emigration when, as a reaction to the Allende victory and, later, as a result of the military coup, several hundred thousand Chileans departed the country for political and economic reasons. Many of them later returned. In 1990 a National Office of Refugees was established to facilitate the reincorporation of returning exiles into Chilean society. In its first three years this office assisted more than 13,000 of the 26,000 exiles who returned in this period. In 1996, the UNHCR office closed for Chileans, after 22 years of operation in Chile, as it was determined that the need for asylum for Chileans no longer exists. The net migration rate for Chile in 1999 was zero.

On 5 January 1999, the Chilean Minister of Foreign Affairs signed a resettlement agreement for refugees from the former Yugoslavia. On 16 June 1999, the first group of 26 refugees arrived in Santiago. The project was being implemented by the Vicariate of Social (Catholic Church). As of September 1999, the total refugee population in Chile numbered some 300, 75% from Peru and 12% from Cuba, 240 of the total having benefited from UNHCR programs of assistance.

There is a seasonal pattern of trans-Andean immigration to Argentina by Chilean agricultural workers, and for many years the presence of several thousand Chilean settlers in the Argentine part of Patagonia created a minority problem.

⁸ETHNIC GROUPS

Ethnically, the Chilean population is estimated at nearly 95% white and mestizo (mixed white and Amerindian); 3% Amerindian; and 2% other. Mixtures between the conquering Spaniards, largely Andalusians and Basques, and the Mapuches (Araucanians) produced the principal Chilean racial type. An indigenous population of perhaps as many as 600,000 pure Mapuches live mainly in Temuco and in the forest region south of the Bío-Bío River. Remnants of other small tribal groups are found in isolated oases within the northern desert or live a nomadic existence on the archipelagos and islands of the extreme southern coast. A small minority of Germans and their descendants live in the Valdivia-Puerto Montt area.

9 LANGUAGES

Spanish is the national language. A sizable segment of Mapuche (Araucanian) Amerindians use Spanish in addition to their native tongue. The only other language of any importance is German, spoken mainly in the Valdivia region.

10 RELIGIONS

The Roman Catholic Church was disestablished by the constitution of 1925, but Roman Catholicism remains the principal religion, with about 89% of the population being at least nominally Catholic. The remaining population includes several Protestant denominations, totaling about 11% of the population; and a small Jewish community (about 30,000 members), making up less than 1%. Amerindians still practice an indigenous religion involving shamanism.

11 TRANSPORTATION

In 1999, Chile had 6,782 km (4,214 mi) of railways. Rail lines in the desert area are used mainly for mineral transport. By 1988, cargo transportation by rail had reached nearly 6 million tons annually. There are five international railroads from Chile: a line to Tacna, Peru; two to La Paz, Bolivia; and two to Argentina. In 1975, the first section of a new subway was opened in Santiago; the second section was opened in 1980.

There were 79,800 km (49,588 mi) of roads in 1999, 11,012 km (6,843 mi) of which were paved. The Pan American Highway, extending 3,460 km (2,150 mi) from the Peruvian border to Puerto Montt, is Chile's principal road artery. In 1995 there were about 888,600 passenger cars and 469,000 commercial trucks, buses, and taxis. The Carretera Austral Presidente Augusto Pinochet, a highway, is under construction in the south; when complete it will link Cochrane in Coyhaique with Puerto Montt.

Chile has some 20 ports, 10 of which are used principally for coastal shipping. Valparaíso, the principal port for Santiago, is by far the most important. Arica, Iquique, Tocopilla, Antofagasta, Coquimbo, San Antonio, Talcahuano, and Punta Arenas are other important ports. In 1998, the Chilean merchant marine had 42 vessels over 1,000 tons and a total GRT of 527,201.

Air transportation has become increasingly important. As of 1998 there were 378 airports in Chile, 58 of which had paved runways. Santiago hosts the principal international airport, Arturo Merino. Chile's largest airline is the state-owned National Airlines of Chile (LAN-Chile), which provides both domestic and international service. LAN-Chile's only significant domestic competitor is Copper Airlines (LADECO), a privately owned company In 1997, Chile's airlines carried 4,610,000 passengers on domestic and international flights.

12 HISTORY

Before the Spanish conquest, several small groups of Amerindians lived in Chile. Araucanian Amerindians, who came under the influence of the Incas in the early 15th century, inhabited central and southern Chile. The conquistador Pedro de Valdivia founded Santiago in 1541, and brought Chile north of the Bío-Bío River under Spanish rule. The Araucanians resisted Spanish rule and killed Valdivia in battle. Amerindian resistance continued for 350 years, effectively barring Spanish settlement south of the Bío-Bío. The Araucanians (also known as Mapuches today) were not subjugated until the early 1880s.

During Spanish rule, Chile was subject to the viceroyalty of Peru. Later, the territory was given the status of captaincy-general and was largely administered from Santiago.

Chile had one of Latin America's first independence movements. A cabildo abierto ("town meeting") declared independence in 1810 in response to the French usurpation of the Spanish crown. Rival independence leaders Bernardo O'Higgins and José Miguel Carrera fought each other, then were overcome by Spanish troops. Eventually, Gen. José de San Martín, with O'Higgins as his chief ally, defeated the Spanish in 1817, and in 1818 Chile formally proclaimed independence. O'Higgins ruled from 1818 to 1823, during which time he built a navy and consolidated the Chilean government under his dictatorial regime. However, his anti-clerical and anti-nobility policies proved to be his undoing.

The next few years saw the growth of two political parties, the Conservative and the Liberal. While both were narrow elite factions, they differed in that Liberals favored a parliamentary, secular, federal system, while Conservatives wanted a traditional, religious, centralized system. The two groups fought bitterly, plunging Chile into civil strife until 1830 when Conservative Diego José Victor Portales assumed control of the political system.

Portales ruled as behind-the-scenes dictator from 1830 until his assassination in 1837. He launched a successful three-year war with Peru (1836–39), which destroyed a threatening Bolivian-Peruvian confederation. He also initiated a Conservative rule which was to last until 1861. During that period, Chile's territory expanded with new claims to Patagonia and the island of Tierra del Fuego, and in 1847, the founding of Punta Arenas on the Strait of Magellan.

Between 1861 and 1891, the Conservatives were forced to share power with the Liberals, who had won several legislative victories. A wave of liberal reforms curtailed the power of the Roman Catholic Church and the presidential office. At the same time, both parties suffered a series of splits and realignments. But most notable during this period was Chile's greatest military achievement. In the War of the Pacific (1879–83), Chile again fought Peru and Bolivia, this time over possession of the Atacama Desert and its nitrate deposits. After victories on land and sea, Chilean forces entered Lima in 1881. By a treaty signed in 1883, Peru yielded Tarapacá, while Bolivia surrendered Antofagasta. The disposition of the other contested areas, Tacna and Arica, was not finally settled until 1929, when, with US mediation, Tacna went to Peru and Arica to Chile.

In 1891, Jorge Montt, a naval officer, led a revolt that resulted in eight months of civil war. The triumph of Montt marked the beginning of a 30-year period of stable parliamentary rule. Bolstered by nitrate revenues, Chile's national treasury grew, especially during World War I. But at the same time the seeds of revolt were sown. Miners, farm workers and factory workers, sharing none of this prosperity, began to agitate for change. After the war ended, there was a recession, and the country was on the verge of civil war. In 1920, a coalition of middle and working class groups elected Arturo Alessandri Palma president. Alessandri, the son of an Italian immigrant, found himself in between the left's demands for change and the right's intransigence. He was deposed in a coup in 1924 but recalled in a countercoup in the following year. His second administration lasted only six months, but he left the legacy of a new constitution passed on 18 October 1925. The new system created a strong, directly elected executive to replace the previous parliamentary system.

The military strongman Gen. Carlos Ibáñez del Campo ruled Chile from behind the scenes until 1927, then served formally as president until 1931. US banks loaned large sums to Chilean industry, and efforts were made to salvage the foundering nitrate trade and boost the copper sector. World depression struck, however, bringing an end to foreign loans and a catastrophic drop in world copper prices. A general strike caused Ibáñez to flee in 1931. After two years marked by short-lived juntas and presidencies and a 100-day "socialist republic," Alessandri was again elected.

Chile pulled out of the depression by 1938, but popular demand for social legislation remained unsatisfied. The 1938 election was narrowly won by Radical Party member Pedro Aguirre Cerda, running under the banner of a catchall coalition called the "Popular Front." His ambitious "new deal" program was never enacted, as Aguirre found himself in the crossfire of Chilean politics. His coalition dissolved formally in January 1941, and Aguirre died in November. In 1942, the Radicals won election easily over former dictator Ibáñez.

Juan Antonio Ríos governed moderately amid political conflict aroused by World War II. Ríos at first cooperated with Argentina in toning down the US-sponsored anti-Axis program but later led his country into a pro-Allied position, entering the war on the side of the US in 1944. After World War II, Chile went into an inflationary cycle, and riots and strikes broke out throughout the country. Ríos died in 1946, and a special election brought to power a coalition of Communists and former Popular Front supporters under Gabriel González Videla. González's coalition soon broke down, as the Communists organized demonstrations and strikes. Within months, González fired the three Communists he had appointed to cabinet positions. He then broke off relations with the Soviet Union, and outlawed the Communist party. Strikes and violence grew, and Chile, an example of stability by Latin American standards for so long, seethed with tensions. Chile's pursuit of industrialization, which had started with the Aguirre and Ríos administrations, had led to increasing social problems as the cities bulged with unemployable rural workers. As the cost of living soared, the radicalism of the workers intensified.

The 1952 election brought the 75-year-old Carlos Ibáñez del Campo back to power. The ex-dictator, who had been plotting to return to power for years, defeated González Videla by exploiting a split among the Radicals and the disaffected Communists. Despite his reputation as an authoritarian and his connection with Argentina's Perón, Ibáñez ruled democratically until 1958.

By 1958, the cost of living had soared and Chile's trade balance had moved from a large surplus to a deficit. Evidence of a general discontent could be seen in the 1958 presidential election. A narrow victory was won by Jorge Alessandri Rodríguez (a son of President Arturo Alessandri Palma), who received support from both Liberals and Conservatives. The Socialist Salvador Allende Gossens, supported by his own party and the newly legalized Communist Party, won 29% of the vote (compared with only 5% in 1952), and Eduardo Frei Montalva, candidate of the new Christian Democratic Party (Partido Demócrata Cristiano—PDC), ran third with 20% of the vote.

Aware of popular pressure for reform, Alessandri drew up a 10-year development plan, initiated in 1959 with construction projects, tax reforms, and a token start at agrarian reform. A devastating earthquake and tidal wave in 1960 cut drastically into Alessandri's programs, and his government was unable to regain momentum. In 1964, the traditional parties of the right and center lost strength to a wave of reform sentiment that shifted public attention to a choice between the socialist Allende and the moderate reformer Frei. In September 1964, Frei was elected by an absolute majority, and congressional elections in March 1965 gave the PDC a majority in the Chamber of Deputies and a plurality in the Senate.

The Frei government implemented numerous social and structural reforms. These included educational reform, land reform and a scheme to create a majority Chilean interest in Chile's copper mines. Frei became a cornerstone of the Alliance for Progress, a harsh critic of communism, and a leading exponent of Christian democracy. However, the reforms did not deliver as hoped, and overall economic growth was sporadic. The Frei

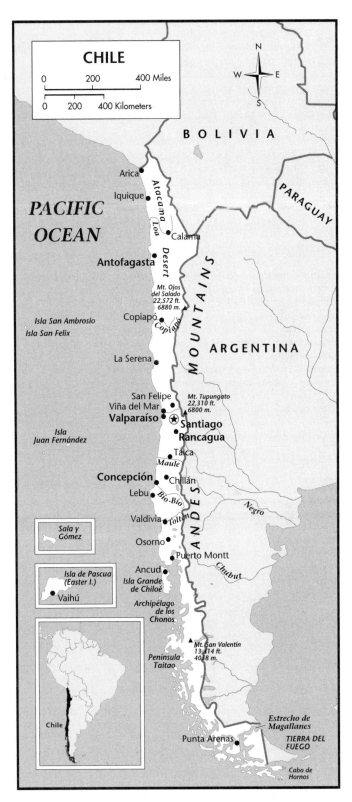

LOCATION: 17°31′ to 56°33′s; 66°25′ to 80°47′w. **BOUNDARY LENGTHS:** Peru, 169 km (105 mi); Bolivia, 861 km (535 mi); Argentina, 5,308 km (3,298 mi); coastline, 5,338 km (3,317 mi). **TERRITORIAL SEA LIMIT:** 12 mi.

administration was not able to control the endemic inflation that had plagued Chile for more than 80 years.

In the 1970 presidential election there were three contenders: Jorge Alessandri, PDC candidate Radomiro Tomic, and the

Socialist Senator Salvador Allende. Allende, who was supported by Popular Unity, a leftist coalition that included the Communist Party, received 36.5% of the total vote. Alessandri followed with 35.2%, and Tomic with 28%, with 0.3% of the ballots left blank as a protest. Since no candidate received a majority of the popular vote, Congress was required by the constitution to select the president from the two leading candidates. The PDC supported Allende in exchange for a promise of full constitutional guarantees. The victory was unique in that for the first time in the Western Hemisphere, a Marxist candidate took office by means of a free election. Dr. Allende, inaugurated on 3 November 1970, called for a socialist economy, a new, leftist constitution, and full diplomatic and trade relations with Cuba, China, and other Communist countries. It was later revealed through US congressional investigations and independent journalistic inquiries that the US, with the help of the International Telephone and Telegraph Corp. (ITT), had secretly worked to thwart the election and confirmation of Allende.

The first full year of rule by Allende witnessed a rise in economic prosperity and employment, as well as an improvement in the standard of living of the poorer elements of the population. Allende expropriated US copper interests, and turned large rural landholdings into peasant communes. By 1972, however, the economy began to lag, and the situation was aggravated by middle- and upper-class resentment over the government's seizures of industrial and agricultural property. In June 1973, against a backdrop of strikes and street brawls beginning in the previous year, an abortive coup attempt was staged by a rightist army contingent. Throughout this period, the US Central Intelligence Agency had secretly supported the 1972 and 1973 strikes and disturbances, especially the truckers' strike, which had caused nationwide shortages of food and consumer goods.

On 11 September 1973, the Allende government was violently overthrown. Allende himself died—officially reported as a suicide. A four-man junta headed by Gen. Augusto Pinochet Ugarte seized power, dissolved Congress, banned all political activities, and declared that Marxism would be eradicated in Chile. At least 3,000 and possibly as many as 10,000 people were killed or "disappeared" without a trace during and immediately after the coup. The military declared a state of siege and assumed dictatorial powers.

During its 16 years in power, the military attempted to eradicate not only Marxism, but all vestiges of leftism, trade unionism, reformism, and, for that matter, any other deviation from the official military line. High on their list of priorities was the privatization of the Chilean economy, which had gradually become more dependent on the state over three decades, a movement that had accelerated dramatically under Allende. This included the attracting of foreign investment, virtually untouched by government regulations or requirements. With unions under siege, workers' rights rapidly eroded under the regime.

This powerful dose of economic liberalization was administered within a continuously authoritarian political system. After the original state of siege was lifted in 1978, Chile continued under a "state of emergency" until another state of siege was declared from November 1984 to June 1985. A third state of siege was in effect from September 1986 to January 1987, after a failed assassination attempt against Pinochet. At each denial of democracy, the Pinochet government insisted that it was not yet done with the task of "redeeming" Chile, and that full political rights could not be restored until then. A constitution that outlawed the advocacy of Marxism and gave Pinochet eight more years of rule was passed by 67% of voters in 1980.

Although forced to operate clandestinely, an opposition nevertheless emerged. A collection of political factions found common cause with the Roman Catholic Church, forming a group called the Civic Union. The Church had become increasingly critical of the Pinochet regime, despite the latter's insistence that Catholicism was the cornerstone of the new Chile. When Pope John Paul II visited Chile in 1987, he brought accusations of torture and other human rights abuses. Finally, in 1988, Pinochet was pressured to call for a plebiscite to determine whether he should become president for another eight years. In February 1988, 16 political parties came together to form the "Coalition for the 'No'." In October 1988, Pinochet was soundly defeated, and in 1989 new elections were held. Christian Democrat Patricio Aylwin, running as the candidate of a 17-party Concert of Parties for Democracy (Concertación de Partidos por la Democracia) received 55.2% of the vote and assumed office in 1990. The election was hailed as a victory for democracy, but Chile remained under the watchful eye of the military. Pinochet, who remained head of the armed forces, retained enormous power.

The general resisted Aylwin's efforts to place the military firmly under civilian control, and threatened a return to military rule if any of his officers were prosecuted for human rights violations. The Truth and Reconciliation Commission, established during the Aylwin administration, recorded 1,102 disappearances and 2,095 executions and death from torture during the dictatorship years. Those figures did not include thousands of others who were detained, tortured, and exiled.

Little could be done to prosecute military abuses. Aylwin's administration was hampered by the constitution approved during the military regime. Pinochet had engineered the constitution to his favor, allowing the regime to appoint eight senators for life in the new government. With eight pro-military senators, the Senate's democratic coalition was unable to reach a majority and make constitutional changes. Military leaders also pushed through an Amnesty Law, which covered human rights abuses between 1973 and 1978. The Supreme Court remained under the control of judges sympathetic to the former military regime.

In the December 1993 presidential elections, The Concert Parties for Democracy, a center-left coalition, backed Christian Democratic Party candidate Eduardo Frei Ruiz-Tagle, the son of former President Eduardo Frei Montalva. With more than 58% of the vote, Frei continued the economic policies of his predecessor, with an even greater emphasis on social spending. It was estimated that about one million Chileans emerged from poverty in the first half of the decade. The Frei regime also emphasized privatization of state-owned enterprises, protection of foreign investment, and trade liberalization. (However, Chile's sought-after admission to NAFTA languished through the mid-1990s, delayed by opposition in the US Congress.) Chile remained the world's leading producer and exporter of copper, but with a greatly diversified export base. By 1997 the nation had achieved 14 consecutive years of economic growth.

While the country's commitment to democratic, representative government appeared secure and stable, Pinochet remained a feared political figure in Chile, and an impediment to real democratic reforms. In 1998, Pinochet retired as head of the military and became a senator for life. Despite eight years of democratic government, relations between the government and the military, which continued to assert its independence, remained tense.

In October 1998, Pinochet traveled to London for back surgery. At the request of Spanish authorities, British police arrested Pinochet, who was recovering at a private hospital. A Spanish judge wanted to take Pinochet back to Spain to try him on charges of torture, kidnapping, genocide, and murder. The arrest became a major international incident, and shocked Chileans, most of whom thought Pinochet was untouchable. Other European countries sought to extradite Pinochet, whose detention strained relations between Chile, England, and Spain. Following a lengthy legal battle that stretched across two continents and three nations, a London court in October 1999 ruled

Pinochet could be extradited to Spain to stand trial on one charge of conspiracy to torture and 34 charges of torturing individual Chileans. Back in Chile, the armed forces remained loyal to Pinochet, and his arrest raised tensions between the military and the government. Yet, in his absence, Chilean politics were changing dramatically. While he languished in detention in England, dozens of military and police officers accused of human rights violations were arrested in Chile. Threatened by Supreme Court actions, the military began to talk directly to human rights lawyers. Some military leaders acknowledged that victims' families had a right to know what happened to the "disappeared."

In March 2000, after 16 months in detention, the 84-year-old Pinochet was released. British authorities cited humanitarian reasons, saying Pinochet was medically unfit to stand trial. Pinochet returned to Chile, where he faced more than 70 criminal charges and efforts to remove him as senator for life. Opponents have vowed to bring him to court.

During his absence, the center-left Concert of Parties for Democracy had backed the Socialist Ricardo Lagos for President. Joaquín Lavín, the conservative candidate, distanced himself from the hard politics of Pinochet and appealed for votes among Chile's poorest. Strains were beginning to show in the center-left coalition, which had ruled the country since 1990. Early in the campaign, Lavín, a former member of Pinochet's government, was not considered a strong candidate against Lagos. But both men finished tied in the December 1999 election, forcing a runoff election a month later. In the second round, Lagos, a member of the Party for Democracy, captured 51.3% to narrowly defeat Lavín, who obtained 48.69% of the vote. With the victory, Lagos became the first Socialist to hold office since Allende. Lagos is a reformed Socialist who distanced himself from Allende's Marxist ideas. More of a social democrat similar in political style to England's Tony Blair, Lagos has promised moderate policies and no changes to the nation's free-market economy. He has promised to spend more on education, health and job training. During the 1999 presidential campaign, the Chilean economy faced its worse recession in 20 years, with unemployment reaching 11%. By 2000, the country showed signs of recovery as Chileans eagerly awaited Lagos' next move.

13 GOVERNMENT

After the restoration of democracy in 1990, Chile continued to feel the legacy of the Pinochet regime. The Constitution of 1980 is still in effect, even though it was created with a different Chile in mind. In 1989, a series of amendments originally planned in 1980 went into effect, restoring the bicameral National Congress. The 1980 constitution, as amended, is the third Chilean constitution. The first two were the original 1833 constitution, and the 1925 amended version. The 1980 constitution was prepared by the Council of State, established in 1975 and included two former presidents, Gabriel González Videla and Jorge Alessandri.

The constitution provides for a strong executive serving a six-year term. The president has the authority to proclaim a state of emergency for up to 20 days. He can dissolve Congress and call for new elections once per term, and he has the power to introduce legislation. There is a bicameral National Congress, consisting of a 120-member Chamber of Deputies and a 46-member Senate. The Senate includes eight appointed members, as well as all ex-presidents, who have life membership. The constitution also provides for an independent judiciary, headed by a 17-member Supreme Court.

The constitution guarantees the active participation of the armed forces in government, establishes limitations on the right to strike and on freedom of information and expression, and institutionalizes a free-market economy.

14 POLITICAL PARTIES

Except for an initial period of political disorder, independent Chile's first century of political life was dominated by the aristocratic Liberal and Conservative parties. Segments of the two parties split, shifted, entered into new alliances, regrouped, and took on new names. Since electoral law permitted the registration of parties with relatively small popular bases, coalitions were usually formed to elect presidents and control the Congress. Many cabinets had a fleeting existence. After 1860, the Radicals emerged from the Liberal party, and over the next six decades, they increased their following with the rise of the middle class. In the meantime, the Liberals became conservative, and moved close to that party. Although the Conservatives and Liberals disagreed over the status of the Roman Catholic Church and over the matter of relative congressional and presidential powers, they were united in opposing the Radicals.

Designation of Chilean parties as being of the right, center, or left has been a function of shifting national political climates. Parties and party alliances have tended to appear and disappear over time. During the 1950s and 1960s, there were fewer, but much larger parties. Before the 1973 military coup there were five major parties in Chile: the Christian Democratic Party, founded in 1957, the Socialist Party, founded in 1931, the Communist Party, founded in 1921 (and outlawed during 1948–58), the National Party, formed in 1966 by members of the Liberal and Conservative parties, and the old Radical Party, which saw its strength greatly diminished after 1964. The ruling Allende coalition of Popular Unity consisted of Socialists, Communists, and several smaller leftist parties. The most radical political group, the Revolutionary Movement of the Left, was not a coalition member.

In September 1973, all the Allende coalition parties were abolished. The other parties were initially suspended and then banned in March 1977.

The reemergence of political parties in the aftermath of Pinochet's ouster was dramatic. In 1990, to ensure that Pinochet's preferred presidential candidate would not take office, several center-left parties came together as the Coalition of Parties for Democracy and backed a single candidate. The coalition includes four major parties: the Christian Democrats (PDC), the Party for Democracy (PPD), the Radical Party (PR), and the Socialist Party (PS). The opposition from the right comes from the Independent Democratic Union (UDI), and the National Renewal (RN), which, bolstered by the eight Senate appointees (who were originally Pinochet holdovers after the 1989 elections), held sway in the Senate until 1994.

15 LOCAL GOVERNMENT

After the military government came to power in September 1973, local authorities yielded power to the armed forces, and the nation was divided into military districts. The traditional 25 provinces, as well as all municipalities, were placed under military control.

The country is divided into 13 regions, including the metropolitan area of Santiago, which is not numbered like the other 12 regions, beginning with Region I at the northern border with Peru and continuing in sequence to Region XII at the southern end. The regions each have a capital and are subdivided into provinces. Provinces and regions are administered by provincial and regional governors. The nation's 340 municipalities, headed by mayors, form the smallest units of local government. Mayors and local councilors are elected every four years from the same roster of candidates, with the mayoral seat going to the candidate with the highest number of votes.

In 1991, a constitutional amendment was passed granting significant autonomy to local areas.

[16]JUDICIAL SYSTEM

The Chilean civil code of 1857, although modified and amended, remained in use until 1973. Although not eliminated by the military in the wake of the 1973 coup, the judicial system had almost all of its major powers removed, with the military code of justice in force as the effective law of the land. In 1975, the junta began to restore some of the traditional powers exercised by the 13-member Supreme Court.

The 1981 constitution, which came into full effect in 1989, provides for an independent judiciary. The Supreme Court, whose 17 members are appointed by the president, would have authority over appellate and lower courts but would not exercise jurisdiction over the seven-member Constitutional Court and the five member Electoral Court, which was to supervise all elections.

Although independent in theory, the judiciary remains subject to criticism for inefficiency and lack of independence. Appointees of the former military regime also dominate the lower courts. By 2000, turnover had diminished the number of pro-Pinochet judges, and some judges were asserting their independence.

Military tribunals have jurisdiction over the military officers. Military courts have also authority to charge and try civilians for defamation of military personnel for sedition. In such cases, appeals can be made to the civilian Supreme Court. Reforms passed in 1991 (the "cumplido" laws) transferred some of the jurisdiction of the military tribunals to the civilian courts

There is no jury trial. The legal system is mainly based on Napoleonic Code. The Constitution provides for the right to counsel.

[17]ARMED FORCES

Chilean males between the ages of 14 and 49 are eligible for military service, but only about 15,000 are called up from a pool of over 100,000 each year. The period of service for conscripts is one to two years. After initial service, Chilean men serve in the reserve (estimated at 50,000 active in 2000). The army had 51,000 (over half conscripts) personnel in 2000, the navy 29,000, and the air force 13,000 regulars and 1,500 conscripts. The army is organized as eight divisions, all with mixed mobile forces and foot infantry armed with European and American heavy weapons and Chilean-made small arms. The navy, which includes aviation and marines, has six destroyers and frigates and four submarines. The air force has a mix of British, American, and French combat aircraft, which number 90, and about the same number of support aircraft. In addition, there is a paramilitary national police force, the carabiñeros, of about 29,500. Defense expenditures were $2.12 billion in 1998, or about 2.79% of gross domestic product.

[18]INTERNATIONAL COOPERATION

Chile is a charter member of the UN, having joined on 24 October 1945, and participates in all the nonregional specialized agencies. Chile supports the Pan American system and in the 1960s began to play a leading role in the OAS. In May 1969, Chile signed the Andean Pact, which now includes Bolivia, Colombia, Ecuador, Peru, and Venezuela. Chile is also a member of G-77 and LAIA, among other intergovernmental organizations. Chile was among those countries that shared in the formation of the IADB. The headquarters of ECLAC and the Latin American office of the FAO are located in Santiago. Chile is also a signatory to the Law of the Sea, and a member of the WTO.

In June 1996, Chile agreed to join the Southern Cone Common Market, known as Mercosur, which includes Brazil, Argentina, Paraguay and Uruguay. The inclusion of Chile, the most economically developed country in the region, gave the Mercosur bloc access to Chile's Pacific Ocean ports.

[19]ECONOMY

The Chilean economy is strongly oriented toward commerce and industry, although minerals, chiefly copper and iron ore, provide most of the country's foreign exchange earnings. Chile's leading industries are engaged in the processing of local raw materials; they include mineral refining, metal manufacturing, food processing, paper processing, and textiles. Chilean agriculture, dwarfed in value by mining and manufacturing, supports less than one-sixth of the population. Arable land is limited, and livestock raising is the dominant rural enterprise.

The economy suffered profound economic disruptions during the Allende period (1970–73). Legal nationalization of industries and expropriation of large agricultural holdings by the military government were accompanied by illegal seizures of property. The chaotic situation was exacerbated by acts of economic sabotage perpetrated by the opposition, by covert destabilization by agents of the US, and by denial of commercial credit by foreign banks and corporations. By the time of the military coup in late 1973, the nation's manufacturing and farm production had fallen by about 10% from 1972 levels, and inflation had soared to 350%.

After the Pinochet coup, the military government attempted to revitalize the economy by emulating the principles of a free marketplace. Subsidies were removed and tariffs were lowered to increase competition. A policy of privatization of industries and utilities was instituted, including the return of companies nationalized under Allende to their previous owners, the sale of government-owned companies to individuals and conglomerates, and the sale of percentages of companies to employees and the public on the stock exchange. The GDP fell by 12% in 1975, but Chile's economic performance began to improve thereafter. The average annual rate of increase in GDP between 1977 and 1981 was 7.8%, and the inflation rate dropped from 174% in 1976 to 9.7% in 1981. In 1982, however, a severe economic slump (caused by the worldwide recession, low copper prices, and an overvalued peso) led to an inflation rate of 20.7% and a drop in the GDP of 14.1% in real terms.

Beginning in 1984, the economy grew moderately, constrained largely by persistently depressed world copper prices. An economic adjustment program introduced in 1985 aimed at strengthening exports other than copper. Civilian rule, starting in 1990, implemented positive monetary policies that continued to lower inflation and attract investment. Inflation was down to 4.7% in 1998, and growth of GDP averaged 7.9% between 1988 and 1998. Unemployment increased from 4.7% in 1995 to an estimated 6.4% in 1998. A temporary downturn in the economy occurred in 1999 due to the world financial crisis and depressed world copper prices, but figures were expected to return to normal in 2000.

In 1999, the Chilean economy completed a decade and a half of strong and sustained expansion. This growth was sustained by high world prices for copper (the principal export) and continued domestic political and social stability. Chile also continued its free market policies and openness to foreign investment. The foreign debt was reduced from 119% of GDP in 1985 to about 17% of GDP in 1998, thus creating a more stable investment market. The immediate economic threat to Chile's prosperity is the high level of domestic spending, which could trigger inflation and cause Chile's central bank to raise interest rates.

[20]INCOME

The US Central Intelligence Agency (CIA) reports that in 1998 Chile's gross domestic product (GDP) was estimated at $184 billion. The per capita GDP was estimated at $12,500. The annual growth rate of GDP was estimated at 3.5%. The average inflation rate in 1998 was 4.7%. The CIA defines GDP as the value of all final goods and services produced within a nation in a given year and computed on the basis of purchasing power parity (PPP) rather than value as measured on the basis of the rate of exchange. It was estimated that agriculture accounted for 6% of GDP, industry 33%, and services 61%.

The World Bank reports that for the same period per capita private consumption (in PPP terms) was $5,575. Private consumption includes expenditures of individuals, households, and nongovernmental organizations. It was estimated that between 1990 and 1998 private consumption grew at an annual rate of 8.7%. Approximately 17% of household consumption was spent on food, 24% on fuel, 20% on health care, and 15% on education. The richest 10% of the population accounted for approximately 46% of household consumption and the poorest 10% approximately 1.4%.

21 LABOR

In 1998, Chile's civilian labor force numbered 5,851,500, or about 39.3% of the population. Of the employed work force in 1995, 48.6% was engaged in professional and white-collar occupations, 16% in agriculture, 16% in manufacturing, 8% in transportation, communications, and utilities, 8% in construction, and 2% in the mining sector. Unemployment and underemployment have plagued successive governments during recent decades, reaching nearly 22% (unofficially) by the end of 1990. It was officially 5.9% in 1994 but had risen to 7.2% by 1998.

Chile's unions, dating from the turn of the century, developed slowly until the 1930s, at which time labor established itself as a political force. Communists, who had played an important role in Chilean labor affairs, were forbidden by law to hold union offices in 1948. Although they were not legally permitted to reenter the labor movement until 1958, they remained a strong influence. In 1953, the government, fearing Communist influence in the unions, formed a confederation of labor unions. About 90% of Chilean unions joined this confederation, the Central Union of Chilean Workers (Central Única de Trabajadores de Chile—CUTCH). By the late 1960s, however, Socialists and Communists had risen to the highest offices in CUTCH and formed a key base of support for Allende's election in 1970. Union membership dropped from about 30% of the labor force in 1975 to about 12% in 1999, or approximately 655,000.

Mining has been the most highly organized sector. Only in recent decades were efforts made to organize agricultural workers. A rural organization law of 1967 doubled the number of rural labor unions and allowed for the organization of 100,000 workers. Many previous provisions, including the right to strike and engage in collective bargaining, were ended with the overthrow of the Allende government in 1973. CUTCH was dissolved, and workers who had formed self-rule and self-defense communities, called cordones industriales, in industrial sections of Santiago bore the brunt of repression by the military.

With the Aylwin administration, a renewed CUTCH worked closely with the government and accepted a market-oriented economic model while encouraging greater social equity. The Aylwin government focused on labor code reforms, professional development and training, freedom of association and collective bargaining, and social welfare program adjustments to increase equity in Chilean society.

As of 1992, CUTCH signed an agreement with the Confederation of Production and Commerce, the largest business association, and the Ministers of Labor, Finance, and Economy to increase the minimum wage rate by 17.1%. This tripartite cooperation marked a significant departure from the antagonistic labor relations of the previous two decades, and showed the government's effort to resolve problems affecting workers' interests. Cooperation between unions and the administration continues to be excellent and important to the success of Chilean economic reforms. In 1998 Congress adopted a measure designed to gradually increase the minimum wage through 2000. As of June 1999, it was approximately $175. There is a minimum work age of 15, provided that the child has the express permission of his or her parents. The law is complied with in the formal economy but is often unenforced in informal economy.

The legal work week is 48 hours and 10 hours per day with limited exceptions. There are also occupational safety and health standards. The government is putting expanded resources into enforcement of these measures and compliance is increasing.

22 AGRICULTURE

Of the total land area of 74.8 million hectares (184 million acres), 4.3 million hectares (10.6 million acres) is arable land and pastures cover 13.5 million hectares (33.4 million acres). Until 1940, Chile was substantially self-sufficient in most basic foodstuffs. Since World War II, serious food deficits have developed, adding to the nation's external payments burden.

Agricultural production of major crops in 1998 (in tons) were as follows:

	TONS
Sugar, raw	490,000
Wheat	1,400,000
Corn	943,000
Oats	250,000
Rice	104,000
Barley	115,000
Rapeseed	52,000

Agriculture was one of the sectors most adversely affected by the recession of 1982, but it quickly recovered by the mid-1980s. Poor results in the traditional agricultural sector inhibit a more rapid expansion in agriculture. One of the areas of most rapid growth is in fresh fruit, with the production of grapes rising by 235% between 1981 and 1985. The fruit harvest in 1998 (in tons) included grapes, 1,665,000; apples, 880,000; peaches and nectarines, 285,000; pears, 250,000; oranges, 115,000; and lemons and limes, 120,000. Avocado production for 1998 was estimated at 60,000 tons, up from 39,000 tons during 1989–91. Most of the avocado orchards are in central Chile, from Region IV to Region VI.

The traditional land system, inherited from colonial times, has retarded maximum use. Chile's first agrarian reform law, passed in 1962 and supplemented by a constitutional reform in 1963, enabled the government to expropriate and subdivide abandoned or poorly cultivated land and compensate the landowner in installments. Another agrarian reform law was passed in 1967 to clarify expropriation and settlement procedures and to permit an increased turnover rate. By the end of the Frei administration in November 1970, some 1,400 agricultural estates, representing 3.4 million hectares (8.4 million acres), had been confiscated and converted to asentamientos (agricultural communities).

The pace of expropriation was accelerated by the Allende government, which by 1972 had doubled the previous administration's figure for land acquisitions. By taking over virtually all of the land subject to redistribution under the 1967 reform act, the Allende government effectively transformed the Chilean land tenure system. In addition, agricultural laborers, often led by militants to the left of the Allende government, illegally seized some 2,000 farms. Following the 1973 coup, the military regime returned almost all farms in the last category to their original owners; the expropriated land was redistributed to 45,000 small-holders. In 1978, the land reform law was replaced by new legislation that removed restrictions on the size of holdings.

23ANIMAL HUSBANDRY

Stock raising is the principal agricultural activity in most rural areas. In 1998 there were an estimated 3.7 million sheep, 3.8 million head of cattle, 1.8 million hogs, 738,000 goats, and 600,000 horses, mules, llamas, and alpacas. The extreme south of Chile is noted for sheep production, while cattle are raised in the central regions. Meat products must be imported from Argentina to fulfill domestic demand. In 1998, 256,000 tons of beef and veal, 235,000 tons of pork, and 11,000 tons of mutton and lamb were produced. In north-central Chile, the hills afford pasturage during the rainy season, and fodder or irrigated pasture provides feed during the dry months. In the south-central regions, natural pasturage is available throughout the year.

The dairy industry is small; milk production totaled 2,080,000 tons in 1998. Production of raw wool in 1998 was an estimated 15,000 tons.

24FISHING

With 1,016 species of fish within Chilean waters, its commercial fisheries have long been important. The low temperatures and Antarctic current supply the purest and most oxygenated marine waters in the world. Since 1959, their growth has been rapid, largely owing to the development of a fish-meal industry, centered around Iquique. Anchovies are predominant along the northern coast, whiting and mackerel in the central waters, and shellfish in the south.

Leading fish and seafood caught commercially are Spanish sardines and yellow jacks, as well as anchovies, whiting, eels, sea snails, mackerel, and mussels. Tuna fishing has increased, as have catches of clams and lobsters. The total fish catch soared from 340,000 tons in 1960 to 1,237,000 tons in 1976 and 6,365,519 tons in 1997. Chile is ranked fourth in the world in total landings of fish. In 1997, Chile contributed 3.4% to the world's exports of fish products, valued at $1.78 billion. Exports of fish and fish meal account for about 9% Chile's total exports. Increasingly, salmon production is playing an important role in Chile's fishing industry, with landings of Atlantic salmon amounting to 96,675 tons in 1997.

25FORESTRY

Chile has extensive forests, estimated at some 11.1 million hectares (27.5 million acres), or about 14.9% of the total land area. Logging operations are concentrated in the areas near the Bío-Bío River. Softwoods include alerce, araucaria, and manio; hardwoods include alamo, laural, lenga, and olivillo. The establishment of radiata pine and eucalyptus plantations, largely as a result of government assistance, has helped Chile to become an important supplier of paper and wood products to overseas markets. Chile is a major source of hardwood in the temperate zone. Native forests are as yet under-utilized and could become an important factor in Chile's growing competitiveness. Radiata pine and eucalyptus are predominant in Regions VI, VII, and VIII; Regions IX and X contain a mixture of both native forests and plantations; and Regions XI and XII mostly contain native forests. Most wood products from Chile are exported as logs, chips, and lumber.

The total roundwood harvest in 1997 was 30,561,000 cu m. About 65% of the roundwood output is used by the forestry industry, and the rest is used as firewood. Commercial uses for roundwood include pulp, wood chips, sawnwood, and lumber

production. At least half of Chile's population uses firewood for heating and cooking.

Government incentives also resulted in an increase of forestry product exports from $36.4 million in 1973 to $468 million in 1980; by 1991, forestry exports rose to $836 million. In 1997, the forestry sector generated exports of $1.43 billion. Export demand has especially strengthened for sawnwood and wood pulp. Production from 1987 to 1991 increased by nearly 60% as a result of maturation of trees planted in the 1970s. Based on current and proposed plantings, Chile's commercial tree production should double over the next 20 years. The major markets for Chilean wood are Japan, South Korea, the US, Taiwan, Belgium, Argentina, and Germany. The Chilean-German Technology Transfer Center in Concepción assists in contributing to the technological development of forestry in the Bío-Bío region.

26MINING

In 1997, mining accounted for more than 8% of Chile's GDP and provided half of its export revenue. About 7% of the Chilean labor force worked in mining, with about 90% of them involved in the metals sector. Traditionally, most of Chile's foreign exchange came from copper alone (75% in 1970, 80% in 1973), but a policy of export diversification reduced copper's share of the total to 42% by 1995. In 1997, about 30% of the world's mined copper was produced in Chile. Copper output totaled 3.39 million tons, up nearly 9% from 1996. Copper earned an estimated $917 million in 1969, $1.1 billion in 1973, and $6.9 billion in 1997.

Legislation passed in 1966 initiated a "Chileanization" policy for the copper industry, which provided for government ownership of a controlling share of the sector; US management of the large mines was permitted to continue. In 1967, the government signed agreements with the three US-owned companies that produced most of Chile's copper. The agreements provided for an increase of Chilean participation, expanded investment to double output by the early 1970s, and a stable tax and exchange rate. The Chilean government was to acquire an equity position in the mines. A law passed unanimously by the Chilean Congress in 1971 provided for the nationalization of the copper holdings of the Kennecott and Anaconda corporations. Copper production grew significantly in the years that immediately followed, despite the emigration—for economic and political reasons—of a large number of trained specialists. The junta subsequently compensated US interests for their expropriated holdings. Foreign investment in copper has since resumed, but by 1997, about 36% of Chile's copper was produced by the state-run Chilean National Copper Corp. (Corporación del Cobre de Chile—CODELCO). The largest single copper mine is the Escondida Mine, opened in late 1990, with an annual capacity of 800,000 tons.

Chile leads the world in natural nitrate production, although world production of synthetic nitrates has sharply reduced Chile's share of total nitrate output. The Salar (salty marsh) de Atacama, which holds significant nitrate reserves, also contains 58% of the world reserves of lithium; in 1997, production of lithium carbonate reached 24,246 tons (second largest after the US). Chile has been an exporter of iron ore since the 1950s, but production, after doubling between the mid-1960s and mid-1970s, fell from 10.3 million tons in 1974 to 6.6 million tons in 1985, but rose to 8.7 million tons in 1991. Following another decrease in 1994–95, production reached this level once again in 1997.

Production totals for 1997 included gold, 49,459 kg; zinc, 33,934 tons; molybdenum, 21,339 tons; and silver, 1,091 tons. Besides copper, Chile's primary export minerals are gold, iodine, iron ore, lithium carbonate, molybdenum, silver, and zinc. Chile is one of the world's leading producers of gold, silver, and molybdenum, as well as iodine, rhenium, lithium, and selenium.

27 ENERGY AND POWER

Electric power generation reached 28.7 billion kWh in 1998, up from 6.9 billion kWh in 1968; about 60% of the power production was hydroelectric. Installed capacity was 7.6 million kW. Within South America, Chile is exceeded only by Brazil in its hydroelectric power potential, much of it located in the heavily populated central part of the country between La Serena and Puerto Montt. The quick descent of Andes-born rivers, together with the narrowness of the country, makes production and transportation of electricity comparatively inexpensive. The Cólbun-Machicura power plant, with a 490,000-kW generating capacity, opened in 1985 on the Maule River.

The state lays claim to all petroleum deposits, and a government agency, the National Petroleum Co. (Empresa Nacional del Petróleo—ENAP), manages oil fields in Region XII. ENAP's oil production only meets 15% of Chile's needs and reserves are decreasing. Production, which began in 1945, is concentrated around the Strait of Magellan, both onshore and offshore; the crude petroleum is transported by sea to the refinery at Concón, north of Valparaíso. A second refinery was completed near Concepción in 1965. In 1998, production totaled 9,670 barrels per day. The production of dry natural gas, as a by-product of petroleum extraction, grew in the 1970s; 1997 production was 2.1 billion cu m (75 billion cu ft), up from 0.8 billion cu m (30 billion cu ft) in 1987. In 1998, Chile imported 197,000 barrels per day of oil, primarily from Nigeria, Gabon, Venezuela, and Ecuador.

Chile's coal reserves have been boosted by recent discoveries in the Bío-Bío area. Reserves are now believed adequate to supply Chile's needs for 100 years. A number of petroleum-fired electric generators have recently been converted to coal.

28 INDUSTRY

Chile ranks among the most highly industrialized Latin American countries. Since the 1940s, manufacturing has contributed a larger share of GDP than has agriculture. About one-third of the value added by manufacturing comes from the production of food, beverages, and tobacco products. During the last decade of the nineteenth century, food product exports soared, with growth of 85% up to 1,000%.

The basic industrial pattern, established in 1914, included food processing, beverage production, sugar refining, cotton and woolen mills, a hosiery mill, a match factory, an iron foundry, and a cement factory. During the next decade, industrial production rose about 85%, but from 1949 to 1958 the level of output was virtually stationary. With the establishment of the Huachipato steel mill in 1950, the groundwork was laid for the development of heavy industry. Chile's first copper refinery was inaugurated in November 1966. The major industrial region is the Santiago-Valparaíso area. Concepción is in the center of an industrial complex. The state-owned firm CODELCO is the worlds largest copper mining company, but the private sector generally produces more copper than the state (two-thirds of the total).

During 1970–73, 464 domestic and foreign-owned plants and facilities were nationalized by the Allende government. These included the copper installations of the Anaconda and Kennecott corporations and other companies owned by US interests. By 1982, the military government had returned most expropriated installations to their original owners. The free-market policies of the junta, together with a worldwide recession, resulted in a 25.5% drop in manufacturing output in 1975. After the mid-1970s, Chilean industry moved away from concentration on import substitution to become more export-oriented. Over 20% of the 1985 value of industrial production came from exports, and in 1998, the value of exports exceeded the value of imports for the first time. Key sectors include textiles, automobiles, chemicals, rubber products, steel, cement, and consumer goods.

The industrial sector grew at an average rate of 7% between 1976 and 1982. Industrial output grew by an average of 3.7% per year between 1980 and 1990, and by 6.6% annually during 1988–98. Manufacturing output grew on average by 3.4% annually during the 1980s, and by 5.8% per year between 1988 and 1998.

29 SCIENCE AND TECHNOLOGY

The Academy of Sciences, which promotes research in the pure and applied sciences, and the Chilean Academy of Medicine, which promotes research and disseminates information in the health sciences, were both founded in 1964 in Santiago and are part of the Institute of Chile. In addition, there were, as of 1996, 64 specialized learned societies in the fields of medicine; the natural, biological, and physical sciences; mathematics and statistics; and technology. The government agency responsible for planning science and technology policy is the National Commission for Scientific and Technological Research. Total expenditures on research and development reached 0.7% of GNP in 1987–97, when 445 scientists and engineers and 233 technicians engaged in research and development.

Chile has 22 institutes conducting research in agriculture, medicine, natural sciences, and technology, as well as the European Southern Observatory. At least 27 colleges and universities offering degrees in basic and applied sciences. In 1987–97, science and engineering students accounted for 42% of college and university enrollments.

30 DOMESTIC TRADE

The best market for manufactured and imported goods is heavily concentrated in central Chile, particularly in Santiago, Valparaíso, and Viña del Mar. Valparaíso, which serves as the shipping outlet for Santiago, is Chile's chief port. Concepción provides direct access to the markets of southern Chile, and Antofagasta to those in northern Chile.

The predominant elements in the pattern of retail merchandising are the independent merchants. They sell their wares in small specialized stores, in municipally owned markets, or in free markets (ferias libres). There is a growing number of chain groceries and supermarkets. Stores are owned primarily by Chileans, although foreign interests are represented in retail merchandising.

The usual retail business hours are from 10:30 AM to 7:30 PM, with half a day on Saturday. Business hours run from 9 AM to 6 or 7 PM, Monday through Friday, with a one hour lunch break at one. Normal banking hours are from 9 AM to 2 PM, Monday through Friday. It is common practice for stores and factories to close for about 15 days sometime between 1 December and 1 April for summer vacation. The business language is Spanish, but most business people also know English.

31 FOREIGN TRADE

Copper remains Chile's largest commodity export (29%), and the country has the highest percentage of the world export market of that mineral (13%). The percentage export of other base metals (13%) gives Chile 10% of world base metal exports. Other significant exports include paper (7.3%), fruit and nuts (6.3%), fish (4.7%), and various wood products (3.6%). Chile claims 10% of the world's wood chip exports.

In 1997 Chile's imports were distributed among the following categories:

Consumer goods	14.4%
Food	5.2%
Fuels	9.9%
Industrial supplies	26.2%
Machinery	28.5%
Transportation	14.6%
Other	1.3%

Principal trading partners in 1998 (in millions of US dollars) were as follows:

COUNTRY	EXPORTS	IMPORTS	BALANCE
United States	2,497	4,384	-1,887
Japan	2,154	994	1,160
Brazil	812	1,125	-313
Germany	712	880	-168
Argentina	654	1,866	-1,212
China (inc. Hong Kong)	610	1,289	-679
Italy	609	700	-91
Korea	608	624	-16
France	583	502	81
Mexico	541	688	-147

32 BALANCE OF PAYMENTS

Between 1982 and 1984, the combination of world recession, slumping copper prices, rising foreign interest rates, and an unexpected rise in imports prompted the Pinochet regime to impose domestic austerity measures in order to meet IMF fiscal and monetary targets. The unrest that followed forced the government to request a 90-day moratorium on some debt repayments and seek rescheduling of $3.4 billion due in 1983–84. The current account balance rose averaged -$2 billion from 1980 to 1995, but fell again to -$4.5 billion in 1998.

The US Central Intelligence Agency reports that in 1998 the purchasing power parity of Chile's exports was $14.9 billion while imports totaled $17.5 billion resulting in a trade balance of -$2.6 billion.

The International Monetary Fund (IMF) reports that in 1998 Chile had exports of goods totaling $14,831 million and imports totaling $17,347 million. The services credit totaled $4,122 million and debit $4,236 million. The following table summarizes Chile's balance of payments as reported by the IMF for 1998 in millions of US dollars.

Current Account		-4,139
Balance on goods	-2,516	
Balance on services	-114	
Balance on income	-1,972	
Current transfers	463	
Capital Account		...
Financial Account		3,181
Direct investment abroad	-2,798	
Direct investment in Chile	4,638	
Portfolio investment assets	-1,420	
Portfolio investment liabilities	591	
Other investment assets	-2,546	
Other investment liabilities	4,716	
Net Errors and Omissions		-1,177
Reserves and Related Items		2,135

33 BANKING AND SECURITIES

During the Allende period, almost all private banks were taken over by the government, mainly through the purchase of stock. The military government reversed its predecessor's policy, and now the financial market is essentially private. In 1999, Chile had, in addition to the Central Bank, 29 banks and 3 finance societies (which have less capital than banks and cannot perform foreign trade operations). There was one state-owned bank; the Banco del Estado is the country's second largest bank, with 13% of loans and 14% of deposits in 1998. Six US banks, twelve Chilean banks, and eleven foreign banks, operated in Chile. The Central Bank and the Superintendent of Banks and Financial Institutions (that reports to the Finance Minister) both regulate the financial industry.

Following government intervention in a number of financial institutions in 1983, the Central Bank introduced three major measures: the issue of $1.5 billion in emergency loans; a provision by which banks could sell their risky portfolios to the Central Bank for 10 years with an obligation to use their profits to buy them back; and the "popular capitalism" program, announced in April 1985, which allowed, among other things, a new share issue for banks in which there had been intervention.

A working group was formed in December 1996 to iron out the remaining technical obstacles to a new banking law so that it might be approved by both houses of Congress before February 1997. Several deadlines have already been missed regarding bank liberalization, which has been under discussion since 1991. The Central Bank kept its main monetary policy instruments unchanged in 1995, but it lifted its target range for interbank rates from 7% to 7.5%. In 1997, a new banking law relaxed some of the restrictions by allowing banks to provide factoring and leasing services.

Securities trading has been traditionally inhibited by the Chilean investors' preference for real estate investment. There is free sale of securities, the largest groups of which are in mining, banking, textile, agricultural, metallurgical, and insurance stocks. All corporations with more than 100 shareholders must register with a stock exchange.

In 2000, some 315 companies were listed on the Bolsa de Comercio de Santiago, (BCS), which was founded on 27 November 1893. It is a private company comprised of 48 shares held by single shareholders. Chile's first stock exchange dates from 1892 and was established in the Port of Valparaiso. It closed in 1982. Stock operations on the Santiago exchange are regulated by the Insurance and Value Superintendency.

In November 1996 the foreign ministry and the Central Bank, together with the superintendencies for banks (SBIF) and for securities and insurance (SVV) completed a draft bill for the launch of an offshore stock market in Santiago. It would operate in foreign currency, not convertible into pesos, and would give access to the local capital and credit markets to all Latin American and other foreign borrowers. The offshore stock market began operations in 2000.

34 INSURANCE

The insurance market is regulated through the Superintendent of Security Markets and Insurance Companies. Accounting practices reflect generally accepted accounting principles, and, in addition, the requirements as established by the Superintendent. These differ from generally accepted accounting principles in the United States in respect to accounting for monetary correction which takes into consideration the changing price levels in Chile.

The Chilean insurance market is characterized by a relatively large number of insurers for its size and a very competitive environment. The market was opened to foreign organizations, the government insurers were privatized, and the market liberalized under the military government. An increasing number of foreign insurers operate in Chile either in association with domestic organizations or independently.

At last estimate, Chile had nearly more than 20 general insurance, more than 15 life insurance, and less than 5 reinsurance companies.

35PUBLIC FINANCE

Chile experienced budget deficits from the early 1960s through the mid-1970s. Expenditures grew steadily with the expansion of public-sector participation in social welfare and economic activities and with increasing government investment in development projects; the resulting deficits were covered by Central Bank loans and foreign borrowing. Budgetary surpluses were recorded from 1975 through 1981, after which the pattern reverted to deficits. From 1985 to 1993, Chile reduced its external debt by $11.3 billion through debt-equity conversions. Of the 1998 government revenue, 75% came from tax revenues. The government announced a package of tax and public works measures designed to stimulate the economy in 1999. The public sector budget is approximately 22% of GDP, and the government generally runs a budget surplus of 1–2% of GDP.

The US Central Intelligence Agency (CIA) estimates that in 1996 Chile's central government took in revenues of approximately $19 billion and had expenditures of $18 billion including capital expenditures of $3 billion. Overall, the government registered a surplus of approximately $1 billion. External debt totaled $32.2 billion.

The following table shows an itemized breakdown of government revenues and expenditures. The percentages were calculated from data reported by the International Monetary Fund. The dollar amounts (millions) are based on the CIA estimates provided above.

REVENUE AND GRANTS	100%	19,000
Tax revenue	83.4%	15,846
Non-tax revenue	16.4%	3,107
Capital revenue	0.2%	47
EXPENDITURES	100%	18,000
General public services	4.1%	736
Defense	8.4%	1,505
Public order and safety	1.7%	305
Education	20.5%	3,688
Health	12.1%	2,179
Social security	34.0%	6,116
Housing and community amenities	5.0%	895
Economic affairs and services	13.9%	2,511
Interest payments	3.1%	554
Adjustments	-2.7%	-488

36TAXATION

Prior to 1920, government revenue was derived largely from export and import taxes, but since then, a more varied tax base has been achieved.

During the Allende period, the Congress, which was strongly influenced by opposition parties, resisted government efforts to introduce redistributive income tax policies. At the end of 1974, the military government eliminated the capital gains tax and established a 15% taxation rate for income from real estate, investments, and commercial activities, which has since been reduced to 10%. Personal income is taxed at rates ranging from 0% for the lowest wage and salary bracket to a maximum of 45%. Corporate income is subject to a basic flat tax of 15% and an additional tax on dividends remitted to nonresidents abroad, bringing the total effective tax rate to 35%. Other principal levies include a VAT (18%), housing tax, inheritance and gift tax, various stamp taxes, and assessments on real estate, entertainment, gasoline, alcoholic beverages, and tobacco. There are withholding taxes on dividends (35%) and royalties (30%).

37CUSTOMS AND DUTIES

The Frei administration (1964–70) imposed extensive import duties and taxes to discourage monetary outflow for nonessential goods and to protect local industries. Imports were curbed by the requirement of advance deposits according to six categories, ranging from 10% for essential goods up to 10,000% for nonessential goods and goods competitive with domestic production. The Allende government reimposed a high tariff schedule meant to discourage the expenditure of scarce foreign reserves on luxury items.

When the military government came to power at the end of 1973, it adopted a policy of liberalizing trade and returning to an open market. Tariffs were removed on foreign goods to force competition on low-efficiency, high-priced local industries. By 1979, tariffs had been reduced to 10%, the only exception to this uniform rate being some car models. In late 1982, the government introduced legislation permitting higher tariffs on some 20 products, including milk, canned fish products, synthetic fibers, and leather footwear.

In 2000, Chile had a set import tax of 9%. Most imported goods are subject to an 18% value-added tax. Automobiles were subject to a luxury tax of 85% on the value above $10,300, and other luxury items were taxed at higher rates. Import and export licenses are mandatory, but easily obtainable. In 1977, free-trade zones were established in Iquique and Punta Arenas. Chile has free trade agreements with Canada, Mexico, Columbia, Venezuela, Ecuador, Costa Rica, and MERCOSUR. Negotiations were underway in 1999 with Bolivia, Peru, the US and NAFTA, and the EU.

38FOREIGN INVESTMENT

Through the Decree Law 600 of 1974 (and its subsequent modifications) and the Chilean Foreign Investment Committee, Chile seeks to encourage foreign direct investment. However, broadcasting, fishing, shipping, and hydrocarbon production usually require majority national control. Foreign investors have purchased many of the assets privatized by the Chilean government over the last decade. From 1993 to 1998, $22 billion of foreign investment went into Chile. Foreign direct investment in 1998 was estimated at $6 billion. That year, total US direct investment was estimated at $1.3 billion. Other principal investors included Canada ($950 million), Spain ($900 million), the United Kingdom, South Africa, Australia, and Japan. Large foreign direct investment projects included projects in the mining, banking, and telecommunications industries.

Chile's net foreign investment abroad increased by more than 50% in 1998 to $3.7 billion.

39ECONOMIC DEVELOPMENT

Chile established two free trade zones: the Free Zone of Iquique (ZOFRI) in the northern tip (Region I), and the Free Zone of Punta Arenas (PARANEZON) in the southern tip (Region XII) during the 1970s to encourage trade. Chile has been negotiating for admission into NAFTA since 1994, but the process has been stalled by the US Congress. Chile also is a member of the South American Mercosur free-trade bloc. Through its concentration on value-added exports and increased foreign direct investment, Chile has become one of Latin America's most developed nations. Economic growth has averaged over 5% annually since 1985, and was 7.9% during 1988–98. Under the Alywin administration, the population living in poverty dropped by 800,000 to 4.5 million, and real incomes of the poorest workers increased by 20%.

Chile's debt management has been very effective. The government negotiated a favorable rescheduling with its creditor banks of its 1991–94 debt maturities. The government's economic policies also kept consumer price inflation limited to an average of 13.6% during 1990–95, down from the annual average of 20.6% during the 1980s, lowering the rate to 4.7% by 1998. Social expenditures, especially those aimed at improving human capital, have risen since 1991 to 15% of GNP (through increased surtaxes). For example, the Program for Youth Labor

Training focuses on the high levels of poverty and unemployment among youth; the program trains 100,000 and includes experience in the private sector. President Lagos, inaugurated in 2000, aimed to bring public accounts into balance by 2001 (after the 1998 financial crisis).

40 SOCIAL DEVELOPMENT

Prior to the 1973 coup, Chile had built one of the most comprehensive social welfare systems in the world, with over 50 separate agencies participating in programs. Following the military's accession to power in 1973, many of the welfare benefits were suspended, and regulations lapsed. From 1974 to 1981, the junta remodeled the welfare system along the lines of private enterprise.

A mandatory private insurance system was introduced in 1981. Pensions are financed exclusively by workers, whose contributions go into individual accounts with Administrators of Pension Funds, which are private social security institutions. Workers must contribute 10% of their taxable income to pension funds monthly, up to a certain limit, 7% of their remuneration for medical care, and about 3% for disability or life insurance, depending on the pension management company chosen. Employers are not required to contribute, and the government provides subsidies for a guaranteed minimum pension. Workers have the option of choosing between the public National Health Service System and a private social security health institute system.

Following the transition to democracy, the chief human rights issues involved redress for abuses committed during the military rule. In 1995, the Supreme Court upheld the murder conviction against General Manuel Contreras, the former chief of the intelligence branch of the army. He was later transferred out of prison to a naval hospital, thus drawing criticism that the government is reluctant to punish military officers to the full extent of the law for human rights abuses.

A 1989 law removed many restrictions on women, although some legal distinctions exist, and divorce is illegal. The National Women's Service (SERNAM) was established in 1991 to fight discrimination against women. In 1996 the group reported that, based on studies of 12,000 domestic violence reports, only one offender in five was punished. In 1997 a total of 61,000 domestic violence reports were filed. The average earnings of women heads of household with university training were only 57% of those of men with equivalent backgrounds in 1997. As of 1997, 15 of 168 members of parliament were women. In 1999 human rights language in the Chilean constitution was amended to refer to "persons" rather than "men."

A 1993 law recognizes ethnic diversity and allows indigenous Mapuche some decision making rights over their land and cultures. Bilingual education is to be introduced in some schools.

Excessive use of force by police has been reported, as well as failure to observe due process of law and other human rights abuses toward detainees.

41 HEALTH

In 1995, Chile's national health expenditure per capita was $331. In the same year, the public health system included 187 hospitals, 230 urban outpatient clinics, 146 rural outpatient clinics, and over 1,000 rural health posts.

The 1998 birth rate was 20 per 1,000 people. Approximately 43% of married women (ages 15 to 49) used contraception according to a study made between 1980 and 1994.

Chile has made considerable progress in raising health standards: the crude death rate per 1,000 was reduced from 12 in 1960 to 5.5 in 1995, and the infant mortality rate declined from 147 per 1,000 live births in 1948 to 11 in 1996. The maternal mortality rate was 25 per 1,000 live births in 1997. There were 29.5 reported cases of tuberculosis per 100,000 people in 1994.

Average life expectancy in 1998 was 75 years. In 1995 the leading causes of death per 100,000 were diseases of the circulatory system (150), cancer (116), injuries or accidents (64), and respiratory diseases (61).

In 1997, there were 11 physicians per 10,000 population. In 1995, there were approximately 3.1 hospital beds per 1,000 people.

An estimated 15% of Chileans, including 10% of children under the age of five, fell below the minimum nutritional requirements established by the FAO. Protein deficiency among the general population has induced an abnormally high rate of congenital mental handicap. In 1995, 85% of the population had access to safe water.

No polio or measles were reported as of 1994. As of March 1996, 1,456 cases of AIDS had been reported.

42 HOUSING

The 1970 housing census enumerated 1,860,111 housing units. The Allende government expanded the housing program. In 1971, 6.5% of the national budget was expended on public housing, mainly for the poor, and the state built 76,079 new housing units. The military government, on the other hand, stressed the role of the private sector in the housing market. In 1974, the number of new units built by the public sector was 3,297, as against 17,084 units built privately; the corresponding figures for 1984 were 276 and 46,493. Construction was one of the hardest-hit sectors in the recession of 1982, but international loans for highway building and maintenance helped offset the losses in housing.

From 1981 through 1985, the number of new units built was 201,244. The number of new dwellings completed jumped from 88,000 in 1991 to 106,000 in 1992. By the mid-1990s, the total housing stock exceeded three million.

43 EDUCATION

Since 1920, primary education has been free, compulsory, and nonsectarian. The adult illiteracy rate, estimated at 50% in 1920, stands at 4.3% in the year 2000, per UNESCO estimates (males, 4.1%; females, 4.5%).

Chile's present educational system stems from a 1965 reform program that called for curriculum modernization (with new texts for all grade levels), teacher training, and professional educational planning and management. There are both state-run and private schools; all state schools provide free education. An eight-year primary and four-year secondary program, with increased emphasis on vocational instruction at the secondary level, was introduced. Proposals are currently being considered to increase the amount of compulsory schooling from eight to ten years. In 1996, enrollment in primary schools totaled 2,241,536 students, taught by 73,960 teachers, with a student-to-teacher ration of 30 to one. Secondary schools had 739,316 students and approximately 52,000 teachers in the same year.

The University of Chile (founded as Universidad Real de San Felipe in 1738) and the University of Santiago de Chile (founded as Universidad Técnica del Estado in 1949) are national universities with branches in other cities. There are numerous institutions which provide vocational and technical education. There are also several Roman Catholic universities. Higher educational enrollment was approximately 380,603 in 1997, compared with 145,497 in 1980.

44 LIBRARIES AND MUSEUMS

Chile's principal libraries and museums are in Santiago. The three most notable libraries are the National Library (1.6 million volumes in 2000), the central library of the University of Chile (41 libraries with an aggregate of over 1,000,000 volumes), and the Library of Congress (700,000). Other significant collections include the Severín Library in Valparaíso (101,000) and the library of the University at Concepción (420,000). The Catholic University of Chile in Santiago has more than a dozen branches holding 500,000 volumes.

Chile's most outstanding museums are the National Museum of Fine Arts, the National Museum of Natural History, and the National Museum of History, all in Santiago, and the Natural History Museum in Valparaíso. The Chilean Museum of Pre-Columbian Art in Santiago has one of the hemisphere's finest collections of indigenous artifacts, including textiles, ceramics, metals and stonework from the Mapuche, Aymara, Tiahuanaco, Atacoma, and Arauconion cultures. There are dozens of historical, public affairs, and ethnographic museums throughout the country.

45 MEDIA

An extensive telegraph service, about three-fourths of which is state-owned, links all the principal cities and towns. Some 90% of Chile's telephone service is provided by Chilean Telephone, formerly a subsidiary of ITT. A total of 1,520,300 telephones were in use in 1995, the majority located in Santiago. International links are supplied by worldwide radiotelephone service and by international telegraph companies. In 1996, Chile also used two Atlantic Ocean satellite and three domestic satellite stations. As of 1999 there were 180 AM and 64 FM radio stations and 63 television stations. In 1997, Chile had 354 radios, 233 television sets, and 28 mobile phones per 1,000 population.

There were 45 daily newspapers as of 1995, the largest of which are in the Santiago–Valparaíso area, where the most important magazines are also published, including the state funded *La Nación*. Among the best-known magazines are *Caras*, (1995 circulation 18,000) and *Qué Pasa?* (20,000). The newspaper *El Mercurio* (founded in 1827) claims to be the oldest newspaper in the Spanish-speaking world. The *El Mercurio* chain includes *La Segunda* and *Las Últimas Noticias* of Santiago, *El Mercurio* of Valparaíso, and *El Mercurio* of Antofagasta.

The names and approximate 1999 circulation figures of the leading daily newspapers of Santiago, Valparaíso, and Concepción were as follows:

	CIRCULATION
SANTIAGO	
La Tercera de la Hora	210,000
La Cuarta	120,000
Las Últimas Noticias	180,000
El Mercurio	150,000
La Nación	50,000
La Segunda	75,000
El Diario Oficial	10,000
VALPARAÍSO	
La Estrella	30,000
El Mercurio	10,000
CONCEPCIÓN	
El Sur	20,000

Many of Chile's newspapers and periodicals were closed for political reasons in the aftermath of the 1973 military coup. The lifting of the second state of siege in mid-1985 brought a significant improvement in the area of the freedom of the press. Opposition magazines resumed publication, and editors were no longer required to submit copy to government censors prior to publication; radio and television programs featuring political debates reappeared in the last half of 1985. The print and broadcast media, as of 1999, is largely independent, and the present government is said to fully support a free press and free speech.

As of 1998, there were over 530,000 personal computers and 15 Internet hosts per 1,000 population.

46 ORGANIZATIONS

The members of many workers' organizations have formed consumer cooperatives. Producer cooperatives also are common, particularly in the dairy industry. The National Society of Agriculture has been politically very influential, and the minister of agriculture has been frequently drawn from its ranks. Representative of the many industrial, commercial, and professional organizations are the National Mining Society, Society of Industrial Development, Commercial Union Society, National Press Association, Medical Society, Chilean Medical Association, Agronomers' Society, Geographical Society of Chile, and Scientific Society.

Among fraternal organizations, the Masonic Order is prominent. The National Council of Sports is the overall confederation of athletic associations. The Chilean Chamber of Commerce, with its headquarters in Santiago, is the central organ for all chambers of commerce and most trade associations. Rotary and Lions clubs are also active among the business community.

Among the more politically potent organizations are the professional middle-class guilds (gremios), which were instrumental in bringing down the Allende government. Social development corporations, comprising mainly business people, have been organized regionally to deal with various welfare problems. The Confederation for Production and Commerce is an official organization representing the country's industrialists and traders.

47 TOURISM, TRAVEL, AND RECREATION

Tourists need a valid passport and visa or tourist card, with exceptions based on reciprocity agreements. Tourist attractions include the Andean lakes of south-central Chile and the famed seaside resort of Viña del Mar, with casinos rivaling those of Monaco. Also popular is Robinson Crusoe Island, in the Pacific. Another Pacific dependency, Easter Island (Isla de Pascua), with its fascinating monolithic sculptures, is a major attraction. The giant Christ of the Andes statue, which commemorates the peaceful settlement of the Chilean-Argentinian border dispute in 1902, is located on the crest of the Andes overlooking the trans-Andean railway tunnel. Santiago is noted for its colonial architecture, as well as the largest library in South America. Popular national parks include Parque Nacional Lanca in the North, the Nahuelbuta Park near Temuco, and Terres del Paine in the far South. Chilean ski resorts, notably Portillo, near Santiago, have become increasingly popular.

The most popular sport in Chile is soccer. Other pastimes include skiing, horseracing, tennis, fishing in the Pacific for marlin and swordfish, and some of the world's best trout fishing in the Lake District.

In 1997, 1,643,640 tourist visits were reported; over half were from Argentina. Tourism receipts totaled $1.02 billion. That year there were 40,829 total hotel rooms with 91,854 beds and an occupancy rate of 29%.

In 1999, the UN estimated the daily cost of staying in Punta Arenas at $177 and staying in Santiago at $199. Hotel charges accounted for 61% to 75% of the daily expenses.

48 FAMOUS CHILEANS

Chile's first national hero was the conquistador Pedro de Valdivia (1500?–53), who founded Santiago in 1541. The Indian leader Lautaro (1525–57), another national hero, served Valdivia as stable boy and then escaped to lead his people to victory against the Spanish. His exploits are celebrated in the great epic poem *La Araucana* by Alonso de Ercilla y Zúñiga (1533?–96), a Spanish soldier. Bernardo O'Higgins (1778–1842), a leader of the fight for independence, was the son of the Irish soldier of fortune Ambrosio O'Higgins (1720?–1801), who had been viceroy of Peru. Diego Portales (1793–1837) helped build a strong central government. Admiral Arturo Prat (1848–79) is Chile's most revered naval hero because of his exploits during the War of the Pacific. Arturo Alessandri Palma (1868–1950), who became president in 1921, initiated modern sociopolitical reform. Salvador Allende Gossens (1908–73), the Western Hemisphere's first freely elected Marxist head of state, served three years as Chile's president (1970–73), initiating a broad range of socialist reforms and dying in the throes of a violent military coup in September 1973. The coup's leader was Gen. Augusto Pinochet Ugarte (b.1915), a former commander-in-chief of the army. Outstanding church figures have been Crescente Errázuriz (1839–1931), archbishop of Santiago, and his successor, José Cardinal Caro (1866–1958). Benjamin A. Cohen (1896–1960) was an undersecretary of the United Nations.

Three distinguished historians, Miguel Luis Amunátegui (1828–88), Diego Barros Arana (1830–1907), and Benjamín Vicuña Mackenna (1831–86), brightened the intellectual life of the second half of the 19th century. José Toribio Medina (1852–1930) gained an international reputation with works ranging from history and literary criticism to archaeology and etymology. Important contemporary historians include Francisco Antonio Encina (1874–1965), Ricardo Donoso (b.1896), and Arturo Torres Rioseco (1897–1971), who is also a literary critic. Benjamín Subercaseaux (1902–73) was a popular historian as well as a novelist.

The first indigenous literary movement was that of the "generation of 1842." One of its leaders was the positivist writer José Victorino Lastarria (1817–88). The novelist and diplomat Alberto Blest Gana (1830–1920) wrote panoramic novels about Chilean society in the tradition of Balzac. Twentieth-century writers include novelist Eduardo Barrios (1884–1963), an explorer of the abnormal psyche; Joaquín Edwards Bello (1887–1968), an author of realistic novels of urban life; the symbolic novelist, poet, and essayist Pedro Prado (1886–1952); and José Donoso (1925–96), perhaps the best-known contemporary novelist.

Poets of note include Gabriela Mistral (Lucila Godoy Alcayaga, 1889–1957), who won the Nobel Prize in 1945; Pablo Neruda (Neftalí Ricardo Reyes, 1904–73), the nation's greatest poet, who was awarded a Stalin Prize as well as the Nobel Prize (1971); and the poet-diplomat Armando Uribe Arce (b.1933).

The nation's first native-born composer was Manuel Robles (1780–1837); Silvia Soublette de Váldes (b.1923) is a leading composer, singer, and conductor; and Gustavo Becerra (b.1925) is a composer and teacher. Claudio Arrau (1903-91) is one of the world's leading concert pianists. Well-known painters are Roberto Matta (b.1911) and Nemesio Atúnez (b.1918), while sculptors include Lily Garafulic (b.1914) and Marta Colvin (b.1917).

49 DEPENDENCIES

Easter Island

About 3,700 km (2,300 mi) w of Chile is Easter Island (Isla de Pascua or Rapa Nui), a volcanic island roughly 24 km (15 mi) long by 16 km (10 mi) wide. Easter Island is inhabited by a mostly Polynesian-speaking population and a few hundred people from the mainland. Easter Island's population exceeded 2,000 in the mid-1990s. The people raise bananas, potatoes, sugarcane, taro roots, and yams. The island is famous for its *moai*, the massive monolithic stone heads of unknown origin, carved from tufa, a soft volcanic stone. The cryptic sculptures have attracted increasing numbers of visitors to the island from both mainland Chile and around the world. In 1975, the government engaged

Spanish consultants to undertake major tourist development on the island. The number of tourist arrivals has been increasing since the 1980s. In 1986, about one-third of the island was a national park.

Easter Island was discovered by Edward Davis, an English buccaneer, in the late 1680s and was named on Easter Day 1722 by Roggeveen, a Dutch navigator. Claimed by Spain in 1770, the island was taken over by Chile in 1888 and is now administered as part of Valparaíso Province.

Diego Ramírez Islands

About 100 km (60 mi) sw of Cape Horn, at 56°30′s and 68°43′w, lies the small, uninhabited Diego Ramírez archipelago.

Juan Fernández Islands

Some 580 km (360 mi) w of Valparaíso, at 33°36′ to 48′s and 78°45′ to 80°47′w, is a group of rugged volcanic, wooded islands belonging to Chile. The two principal islands, about 160 km (100 mi) apart E–W, are Robinson Crusoe, formerly Más a Tierra (93 sq km/36 sq mi), and Alejandro Selkirk, previously Más Afuera (85 sq km/33 sq mi); the smaller island of Santa Clara (or Goat Island) is off the southwest coast of Robinson Crusoe. The chief occupation is lobster fishing. Discovered by Juan Fernández around 1563, the islands achieved fame in 1719, when Daniel Defoe wrote *Robinson Crusoe,* generally acknowledged to have been inspired by the experiences of Alexander Selkirk, a Scottish sailor who quarreled with his captain and was set ashore at his own request on Más a Tierra, where he lived alone until he was rescued (1704–09). The islands are administered by Valparaíso Province.

Sala-y-Gómez Island

About 3,380 km (2,100 mi) w of Chile and some 400 km (250 mi) ENE of Easter Island, at 26°28′s and 105°28′w, lies arid, volcanic Sala-y-Gómez Island. Almost 1,200 m (4,000 ft) long and about 150 m (500 ft) wide, this uninhabited island belongs to and is administered by Valparaíso Province.

San Ambrosio Island

Volcanic San Ambrosio Island, uninhabited, lies 965 km (600 mi) w of Chile, at 26°21′s and 79°54′w, rising to 479 m (1,570 ft).

San Félix Island

Situated 19 km (12 mi) ESE of San Ambrosio Island, at 26°17′s and 80°7′w, is small, uninhabited San Félix Island (about 8 sq km/3 sq mi). Of volcanic origin, the island rises to about 180 m (600 ft). The islet of González is at its southeastern tip. San Félix, along with San Ambrosio, was discovered in 1574.

Chilean Antarctic Territory

Chile claims the section of Antarctica lying between 53°w and 90°w, the Antarctic (or O'Higgins) Peninsula, parts of which are also claimed by Argentina and the UK.

50 BIBLIOGRAPHY

Agosin, Marjorie, *Tapestries of Hope, Threads of Love: the Arpillera Movement in Chile, 1974–1994.* Albuquerque, N.M.: University of Mexico Press, 1996.

Arriaza, Bernardo T. *Beyond Death: the Chinchorro Mummies of Ancient Chile.* Washington, D.C.: Smithsonian Institution Press, 1995.

Bizzarro, Salvatore. *Historical Dictionary of Chile,* 2d ed. Metuchen, N.J.: Scarecrow Press, 1987.

Blakemore, Harold. *Chile.* Oxford, England; Santa Barbara, Calif.: Clio Press, 1988.

Chile Since Independence. New York: Cambridge University Press, 1992.

Collier, Simon. *A History of Chile*. Cambridge: Cambridge University Press, 1996.

Davis, Nathaniel. *The Last Two Years of Salvador Allende*. Ithaca, N.Y.: Cornell University Press, 1985.

Debray, Régis. *Conversations with Allende*. London: NLB, 1971.

Drake, W. and Ivan Jaksic. *The Struggle for Democracy in Chile, 1982–1990*. Rev. Ed. Lincoln: University of Nebraska Press, 1995.

Haverstock, Nathan A. *Chile in Pictures*. Minneapolis: Lerner Publications Co., 1988.

Hojman, D. E. *Chile: The Political Economy of Development and Democracy in the 1990s*. Pittsburgh, Pa.: University of Pittsburgh Press, 1993.

Lavrin, Asuncion. *Women, Feminism, and Social Change in ARgentina, Chile, and Uruguay, 1890–1940*. Lincoln, NB: University of Nebraska Press, 1995.

Loveman, Brian. *Chile: The Legacy of Hispanic Capitalism*, 2nd ed., New York: Oxford University Press, 1988.

Lowden, Pamela. *Moral Opposition to Authoritarian Rule in Chile 1973–90*. N.Y.: St. Martin's Press, 1996.

Oxhorn, Philip. *Organizing Civil Society: The Popular Sectors and the Struggle for Democracy in Chile*. University Park, PA: Pennsylvania State University Press, 1995.

Petras, James F. *Democracy and Poverty in Chile*. Boulder, Colo.: Westview Press, 1994.

Sater, William F. *Chile and the United States: Empires in Conflict*. Athens: University of Georgia Press, 1990.

Spooner, Mary Helen. *Soldiers in a Narrow Land: The Pinochet Regime in Chile*. Berkeley: University of California Press, 1994.

Stewart-Gambino, Hannah W. *The Church and Politics in the Chilean Countryside*. Boulder, Colo.: Westview Press, 1992.

Valenzuela, J. Samuel and Arturo. *Military Rule in Chile: Dictatorship and Oppositions*. Baltimore: Johns Hopkins University Press, 1986.

Zeitlin, Maurice. *The Civil Wars in Chile; or, The Bourgeois Revolutions That Never Were*. Princeton, N.J.: Princeton University Press, 1984.

COLOMBIA

Republic of Colombia
República de Colombia

CAPITAL: Bogotá.

FLAG: The national flag consists of three horizontal stripes; the yellow upper stripe is twice as wide as each of the other two, which are blue and red.

ANTHEM: *Himno Nacional,* beginning "O gloria inmarcesible, júbilo inmortal" ("O unwithering glory, immortal joy").

MONETARY UNIT: The Colombian peso (c$) of 100 centavos is a paper currency. There are coins of 10, 20, and 50 centavos and of 1, 2, 5, 10, 20, and 50 pesos, and notes of 100, 200, 500, 1,000, 2,000, 5,000 and 10,000 pesos. Commemorative gold coins of various denominations also have been minted. c$1 = us$0.00051 (or us$1 = c$1946.00) as of 31 March 2000.

WEIGHTS AND MEASURES: The metric system is the official standard, but Spanish units such as the botella, vara, fonegada, arroba, and quintal are also used.

HOLIDAYS: New Year's Day, 1 January; Epiphany, 6 January; St. Joseph's Day, 19 March; Labor Day, 1 May; Day of St. Peter and St. Paul, 29 June; Independence Day, 20 July; Battle of Boyacá, 7 August; Assumption, 15 August; Columbus Day, 12 October; All Saints' Day, 1 November; Independence of Cartagena, 11 November; Immaculate Conception, 8 December; Christmas, 25 December. Movable religious holidays include Holy Thursday, Good Friday, Holy Saturday, Ascension, Sacred Heart, and Corpus Christi. In addition there are six official commemorative days.

TIME: 7 AM = noon GMT.

¹LOCATION, SIZE, AND EXTENT

Colombia is the only South American country with both Caribbean and Pacific coastlines. The fourth-largest country in South America, it has a total area of 1,138,910 sq km (439,736 sq mi), including insular possessions, and extends 1,700 km (1,060 mi) NNW–SSE and 1,210 km (750 mi) NNE–SSW. Comparatively, the area occupied by Colombia is slightly less than three times the size of the state of Montana. Bordered on the N by the Caribbean Sea, on the NE by Venezuela, on the SE by Brazil, on the SW by Peru and Ecuador, on the W by the Pacific Ocean, and on the NW by Panama, the Colombian mainland is located entirely within the tropics. Its total boundary length is 10,616 km (6,596 mi). Also held by the Republic of Colombia (though claimed by Nicaragua) are the archipelago of San Andrés and Providencia in the Caribbean Sea, about 190 km (120 mi) off the coast of Nicaragua, and the islands of Malpelo, Gorgona, and Gorgonilla in the Pacific Ocean. Colombia also holds the uninhabited Caribbean islands of Quita Sueño Bank, Roncador Cay, and Serrana Bank, to which the US renounced all rights under the Treaty of Quita Sueño, ratified by the US Senate in July 1981; Nicaragua also disputes this claim. Colombia has a dispute with Venezuela over maritime rights in the Gulf of Venezuela. Negotiations have been going on unsuccessfully since 1970, and in August 1987, a Colombian naval vessel entered the disputed region in an apparent attempt to make Venezuela more responsive.

Colombia's capital city, Bogotá is located in the center of the country.

²TOPOGRAPHY

The Andes Mountains divide just north of Colombia's southern border with Ecuador into three separate chains, or cordilleras, known as the Cordillera Occidental (western), the Cordillera Central, and the Cordillera Oriental (eastern). The western and central cordilleras run roughly parallel with the Pacific coast, extending northward as far as the Caribbean coastal lowlands. They are alike in geological structure, both being composed of massive crystalline rocks. The Cordillera Central is the highest range of the Colombian Andes, with several volcanic cones whose snow-covered peaks rise to about 5,500 m (18,000 ft), notably Huila (5,750 m/18,865 ft). The third chain, the Cordillera Oriental, runs northeastward, bifurcating into an eastern branch, the Sierra de los Andes, which slopes down to Venezuela, and a second branch, the Sierra de Perijá, which continues northward to terminate on the border between Venezuela and Colombia just south of the Guajira Peninsula. This range is composed of folded stratified rocks over a crystalline core. On the margin of the Caribbean stands the Sierra Nevada de Santa Marta, an isolated block of mountains composed of a triangular massif of granite, whose highest elevation is Cristóbal Colón (5,797 m/19,020 ft), the tallest peak in Colombia. West of the Cordillera Occidental but not geologically a part of the Andean chain is the low Serranía de Baudó, which skirts the Pacific and extends into the Isthmus of Panama.

Separating the three principal Andean ranges are Colombia's two major rivers, the Cauca (1,014 km/630 mi), which flows northward between the western and central cordilleras, and the Magdalena (1,553 km/965 mi), which divides the central and eastern cordilleras. After emerging from the mountains, the two rivers become one and descend through marshy lowlands to the Caribbean. The area south and east of the Andean ranges is largely composed of river plains divided among the effluents of the Orinoco and Amazon rivers. Open plains immediately adjoin the mountains, but as the distance from the cordillera increases, the plains give way to largely uninhabited and unexplored jungle. The Pacific coastal area is also characterized by jungle vegetation.

Principal rivers on the Pacific coast include the Baudó, San Juan, and Patía.

³CLIMATE

Colombia's climatic variations are determined by altitude, and seasons are periods of lesser or greater rainfall, with little or no temperature change. The country may be divided vertically into four regions. The hot country, or tierra caliente, is the tropical zone, reaching from sea level to roughly 1,100 m (3,500 ft), where the mean annual temperature is 24°C to 27°C (75–81°F); at sea level, temperatures have a mean maximum of 38°C (100°F) and a minimum of 18°C (64°F). Between 1,100 m (3,500 ft) and 2,000 m (6,500 ft) is the temperate zone, or tierra templada, where the average year-round temperature is about 18°C (64°F). Between 2,000 m (6,500 ft) and 3,000 m (10,000 ft) is the cold country, or tierra fría, with temperatures averaging a little over 13°C (55°F). Above the 3,000-m (10,000-ft) level the temperature varies from 13°C to –17°C (55°F to 1°F), according to altitude. The annual mean temperature at the capital, Bogotá (altitude 2,598 m/8,525 ft), is 14°C (57°F). Rainfall is heaviest on the west coast and in the Andean area; rainy and dry seasons, or "winter" and "summer," generally alternate in three-month cycles, as in Bogotá, where precipitation occurs most heavily and consistently during the periods of April to June and October to December. Northern areas have only one long rainy season, from May through October.

⁴FLORA AND FAUNA

More than 45,000 species of plants have been identified in Colombia, and it is predicted that when the region has been thoroughly explored the number may be doubled. At the highest (3,000–4,600 m/10,000–15,000 ft) and coldest level of mountain meadows, called páramos, the soil supports grasses, small herbaceous plants, and dense masses of low bushes. In the intermontane basins some vegetables, European-introduced grains, and corn are found, along with the bushes, trees, and meadow grasses indigenous to the region. The temperate areas support extensive and luxuriant forests, ferns, mosses, trees of the laurel family, Spanish cedars, vegetables, and grain crops. The tropical zone may be divided into four main groups according to the amount of rainfall received: desertlike areas supporting arid plants, deciduous forests, rain forests, and grass plains. Palm trees of various species abound in the tropics, and there are many edible fruits and vegetables.

Animal life is abundant, especially in the tropical area. Among carnivorous species are the puma, a variety of smaller cats, raccoons, and mustelids. Herbivores include the tapir, peccary, deer, and large tropical rodents. Sloths, anteaters, opossums, and several types of monkeys are also found, as well as some 1,665 species and subspecies of South American and migratory birds.

⁵ENVIRONMENT

Colombia's main environmental problems are soil erosion, deforestation and the preservation of its wildlife. Soil erosion has resulted from the loss of vegetation and heavy rainfall, and the soil has also been damaged by overuse of pesticides. Deforestation has resulted from the commercial exploitation of the country's forests which cover approximately 45% of the country. Without a substantial reforestation effort, its timber resources could be exhausted by the year 2000. Approximately 908,000 hectares (2,244,000 acres) of natural forest were lost annually in the 1970s to farming, erosion, and the lumber industry, but only 5,000 hectares (12,000 acres) were reforested each year; between 1981 and 1985, 820,000 hectares (2,260,000 acres) were lost each year, and 8,000 hectares (20,000 acres) were reforested. Between 1983 and 1993, Colombia lost another 5.8% of its forest and woodland. By the mid-1990s, Colombia had the tenth-largest area of mangrove swamps in the world, covering under half a million ha (1,235,500 acres). The nation ranked forty-third globally in industrial carbon dioxide emissions in the early 1990s, with a total of 61.5 million metric tons. Air pollution from vehicle emissions is also a problem, especially in Bogota. Safe drinking water is available to 88% of urban dwellers and 48% of the rural population.

The Colombian government has initiated several programs to protect the environment. By 1959, the Amazon forests, the Andean area and the Pacific coast were protected. In 1973, the government created the National Resources and Environment Code. The main environmental agency is the Institute for Development of Renewable Natural Resources and the Environment (INDERENA), established in 1969. Among other activities, it has undertaken extensive projects in the training of personnel in conservation, fishing, and forestry. The Colombian Sanitary Code, in force since January 1982, establishes pollution control standards. The National Environmental Education Plan for 1991–94 introduces environmental issues in the elementary schools.

Endangered or extinct species in Colombia include the tundra peregrine falcon, Cauca guan, gorgeted wood-quail, red siskin, pinche, five species of turtle (green sea, hawksbill, olive ridley, leatherback, and arrau), two species of alligator (spectacled caiman and black caiman), and two of crocodile (American and Orinoco). By the mid-1990s, 25 of Colombia's 388 species of mammals, 69 in a total of 1,665 bird species, 10 reptile species in a total of 383, and 327 of 45,000 plant species were endangered.

⁶POPULATION

Colombia is the third most populous country in Latin America, following Brazil and Mexico. The population of Colombia in 2000 was estimated at 40,036,927. An estimated 4.5% of the population is 65 years of age or older. The projected population for the year 2005 is 43,662,000, assuming a crude birthrate of 22 per 1,000 population and a death rate of 5, resulting in a natural rate of change of 1.7% for the period 2000–2005. The population rate of change between 1995 and 2000 was 1.7%. The population density in 1998 was 39 per sq km (101 per sq mi), with about 95% of the population residing in the mountainous western half of the country.

A rapid transfer of population to urban centers has taken place since the 1950s; it was estimated that 75% of the population lived in urban areas in 2000, up from 64% in 1980. The capital city, Bogota, had a 2000 metropolitan population of 6,834,000. The populations of other major metropolitan areas in 2000 were as follows: Medellín, 3,831,000; Cali, 2,082,000; and Barranquilla, 1,246,000. Other metropolitan areas include Cartagena (918,000 in 2000), Bucaramanga, and Cúcuta.

⁷MIGRATION

Despite government inducements, such as the granting of agricultural land in the eastern plains, immigration has been insignificant, partly because of the turbulence and violence of the 1940s and 1950s. Emigration is small but significant, since many of those who leave the country are scientists, technicians, and doctors. Between 1951 and 1985, some 218,724 Colombians settled in the US, at an annual rate that surpassed 10,000 by 1981 and rose to 11,802 in 1985. In 1990 there were more persons in the US of Colombian birth—304,000—than of any other South American nationality.

As of May 1997, more than 900,000 people had been internally displaced by the violence between the leftist guerrillas and government forces. By September 1999, estimates of the number of internally displaced persons ranged between 450,000 and 1.6 million. Though estimates varied, studies agree that displacement is pan-national and on the rise. Twenty-seven provinces within

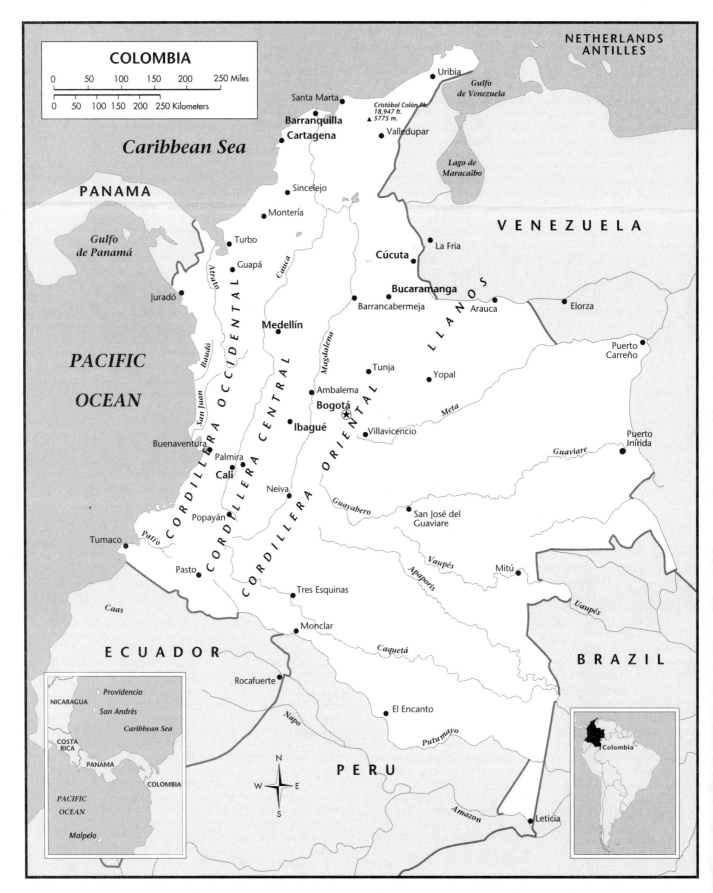

COLOMBIA

0　50　100　150　200　250 Miles

0　50　100 150 200 250 Kilometers

Caribbean Sea

PANAMA

Gulfo de Panamá

PACIFIC OCEAN

NETHERLANDS ANTILLES

Uribia

Gulfo de Venezuela

Santa Marta

Cristóbal Colón Pk.
18,947 ft.
▲ 5775 m.

Barranquilla
Cartagena　Valledupar

Lago de Maracaibo

Sincelejo

Montería

VENEZUELA

Turbo

Cúcuta　La Fria

Guapá

Juradó

Bucaramanga

Barrancabermeja　Arauca　Elorza

Medellín

Puerto Carreño

Tunja

Ambalema　Yopal

Bogotá ✪

Ibagué　Villavicencio

Buenaventura

Puerto Inírida

Palmira

Cali

Neiva

Popayán

San José del Guaviare

Tumaco

Pasto

Mitú

Tres Esquinas

Monclar

ECUADOR

Rocafuerte

BRAZIL

El Encanto

PERU

Leticia

Cordillera Occidental　*Cordillera Central*　*Cordillera Oriental*　*Llanos*

Atrato　*Cauca*　*Magdalena*　*Meta*　*Guaviare*

San Juan　*Baudó*　*Guayabero*　*Vaupés*　*Apaporis*　*Uaupés*

Patío　*Caas*　*Caquetá*　*Napo*　*Putumayo*　*Amazon*

N W E S

Providencia
San Andrés

NICARAGUA

Caribbean Sea

COSTA RICA

PANAMA

COLOMBIA

PACIFIC OCEAN

Malpelo

Colombia

LOCATION: 12°27′46″N to 4°13′30″s; 66°50′54″ to 79°1′23″w. **BOUNDARY LENGTHS:** Caribbean Sea, 1,600 km (994 mi); Venezuela, 2,219 km (1,379 mi); Brazil, 1,645 km (1,022 mi); Peru, 1,626 km (1,010 mi); Ecuador, 586 km (364 mi); Pacific Ocean, 1,300 km (808 mi); Panama, 266 km (165 mi). **TERRITORIAL SEA LIMIT:** 12 mi.

Colombia have been affected by the internal displacement in as far as most of the displaced people have moved to the city of Colombia. According to SISDESC (System of Information on the Families Displaced by Violence in Colombia), in 1997, every two hours, two families were displaced by violence in the country.

While the level of external displacement does not match the level of internal displacement, there is a steady outflow of people fleeing the country. The three neighboring countries most affected by cross-border movements are Panama, Ecuador, and Venezuela. In 1999, about 3,000 Colombians from the north of Santander Department fled to Venezuela in response to the armed conflict in the region. As of 1999, the net migration rate of Colombia was -0.34 migrants per 1,000 population.

⁸ETHNIC GROUPS

The predominant racial strain in Colombia is the mestizo (mixed white and Amerindian), constituting about 58% of the total population in the 1998. An estimated 20% of the inhabitants are of unmixed white ancestry; 14% are mulatto (black–white); 4% are black; 3% are *zambo* (black–Indian); and 1% are pure Amerindian. Blacks and mulattoes are concentrated in the coastal regions and tropical valleys. Pure Amerindians are rapidly disappearing; the remaining few live mainly in inaccessible and barren regions. The principal Amerindian culture of Colombia during the pre-Columbian period was that of the Chibcha, whose descendants are today chiefly concentrated in the departments of Cundinamarca, Boyacá, Santander, and Norte de Santander. The Motilones, one of the few surviving Amerindian groups untouched by civilization in South America, inhabit the region west of Lake Maracaibo and the Venezuelan border; they are famous for their lethal weapon, the black palm bow and arrow. Small, diverse Amerindian groups also inhabit the eastern extremities of the Colombian plains region, the south, and the western coastal jungles.

⁹LANGUAGES

The official language, Spanish, is spoken by all but a few Amerindian tribes. Spanish as spoken and written by educated Colombians is generally considered the closest to Castilian in Latin America.

¹⁰RELIGIONS

Roman Catholicism was the country's official religion until the adoption of the 1991 constitution. The law states that there is no official or state religion but adds that the State is "not atheist or agnostic, nor indifferent to Colombians' religious sentiment." Some observers interpret this to mean that the Roman Catholic Church retains a privileged position; however, a 1994 constitutional court decision declared unconstitutional any official government reference to religious characterizations of the country.

The vast majority of the country is Roman Catholic, 88% in 1996. Between 6 and 7% belong to other Christian denominations, and the remainder belong to other religious faiths or movements, including Judaism, Islam, animism, various syncretic beliefs, agnosticism, and atheism.

¹¹TRANSPORTATION

Transportation lacks integration, owing to the mountainous terrain. For this reason, air transportation has become the most important means of travel for most passengers. Despite the development of roads and railways, river travel has remained the chief mode of transportation for cargo since the trip up the Magdalena River in 1536 by the Spanish conqueror Gonzalo Jiménez de Quesada. Inland waterways navigable by riverboats totaled 14,300 km (8,886 mi) in 1999. The Magdalena, the fourth-largest river in South America, is navigable for 950 km (590 mi); it carries almost all of Colombia's river traffic.

The railroads, which were nationalized in 1954 and deregulated in 1989, had a length of 3,380 km (2,100 mi) in 1999.

Also in 1999 there were about 115,564 km (71,811 mi) of roads, of which only about 13,868 km (8,618 mi) were paved. Many roads are plagued by landslides and washouts. The 2,800-km (1,700-mi) Caribbean Trunk Highway, completed in 1974, links the Atlantic ports of Cartagena, Barranquilla, and Santa Marta with the Pan-American Highway (south of Panama) and the Venezuelan highway system. In the early 1990s, the government proposed a 15-project program, with an estimated cost of $500 million. In 1995 there were 1,150,000 passenger cars and 550,000 commercial motor vehicles.

Owing to inadequate land transport, air service is essential and well developed. A flight from Bogotá to Medellín takes only half an hour, while a truck requires 24 hours over a winding mountain road. In 1998 there were an estimated 1,120 airports, only 89 of which had paved runways. Colombia's airline, Avianca, is the second-oldest commercial airline in the world and one of the largest in Latin America. Avianca handles about two-thirds of the domestic and international movement of passengers. Most of the country's air transportation is handled by the six principal airports at Bogotá, Barranquilla (E. Cortissoz), Medellín, Cali, Cartagena (Rafael Nunez), and San Andreas. In 1997, these airports serviced about 9,189,000 passengers.

Colombia's merchant marine is dominated by the Grand Colombian Merchant Fleet (Flota), a stock corporation owned by the Colombian Coffee Federation. In 1998, merchant marine companies had an aggregate of 14 vessels with 1,000 GRT or over, totaling 64,757 GRT. The nation's chief ports on the Caribbean are Barranquilla, Cartagena, and Santa Marta. Buenaventura is the only important Pacific port.

¹²HISTORY

Archaeological studies indicate that Colombia was inhabited by various Amerindian groups as early as 11,000 BC. Prominent among the pre-Columbian cultures were the highland Chibchas, a sedentary agricultural people located in the eastern chain of the Andes.

The first Spanish settlement, Santa Marta on the Caribbean coast, dates from 1525. In 1536, Gonzalo Jiménez de Quesada and a company of 900 men traveled up the Magdalena River in search of the legendary land of El Dorado. They entered the heart of Chibcha territory in 1538, conquered the inhabitants, and established Bogotá. As a colony, Colombia, then called New Granada, was ruled from Lima, Peru, until it was made a viceroyalty. The viceroyalty of New Granada, consolidated in 1740, incorporated modern Colombia, Panama, Venezuela, and Ecuador. The area became Spain's chief source of gold and was exploited for emeralds and tobacco.

In the late 1700s, a separatist movement developed, stemming from arbitrary taxation and the political and commercial restrictions placed on American-born colonists. Among the Bogotá revolutionaries was Antonio Nariño, who had been jailed for printing a translation of the French Assembly's Declaration of the Rights of Man. Independence, declared on 20 July 1810, was not assured until 7 August 1819, when the Battle of Boyacá was won by Simón Bolívar's troops. After this decisive victory, Bolívar was tumultuously acclaimed "Liberator" and given money and men to overthrow the viceroyalty completely.

After 1819 Bolívar's Republic of Gran Colombia included Colombia, Venezuela, Ecuador and Panama. Venezuela and Ecuador seceded, but Panama remained part of Colombia. In 1831 the country became the State of New Granada. Political and financial order was attained under Francisco de Paula Santander, Bolívar's vice-president, who took office in 1832. During

Santander's four-year term and in the subsequent decade there was intense disagreement over the relative amount of power to be granted to the central and state governments and over the amount of power and freedom to be given the Roman Catholic Church. Characterized by Bolívar as Colombia's "man of laws," Santander directed the course of the nation toward democracy and sound, orderly government.

By 1845, the supporters of strong central government had organized and become known as the Conservatives, while the federalists had assumed the Liberal label. The respective doctrines of the two parties throughout their history have differed on two basic points: the importance of the central governing body and the relationship that should exist between church and state. Conservatism has characteristically stood for highly centralized government and the perpetuation of traditional class and clerical privileges, and it long opposed the extension of voting rights. The Liberals have stressed states' rights, universal suffrage, and the complete separation of church and state. The periods during which the Liberals were in power (1849–57, 1861–80) were characterized by frequent insurrections and civil wars and by a policy of government decentralization and strong anticlericalism.

As effective ruler of the nation for nearly 15 years (1880–94), the Conservative Rafael Núñez, a poet and intellectual, restored centralized government and the power of the church. During his tenure as president, the republican constitution of 1886 was adopted, under which the State of New Granada formally became the Republic of Colombia. A civil war known as the War of a Thousand Days (1899–1902) resulted in more than 100,000 deaths, and the national feeling of demoralization and humiliation was intensified by the loss of Panama in 1903. After refusing to ratify without amendments a treaty leasing a zone across the Isthmus of Panama to the US, Colombia lost the territory by virtue of a US-supported revolt that created the Republic of Panama. Colombia did not recognize Panama's independence until 1914, in exchange for rights in the Canal Zone and an indemnity from the US.

Conservative presidents held power between 1909 and 1930, and Liberals from 1930 to 1942. During World War II, which Colombia entered on the side of the Allies, social and political divisions within the country intensified.

The postwar period was marked by growing social unrest and riots in the capital and in the countryside. Politics became much more violent, especially after the assassination of Jorge Eliécer Gaitán, the leftist Liberal mayor of Bogotá. This extended and bloody period of rural disorder (La Violencia) claimed 150,000 to 200,000 lives between 1947 and 1958. Sporadic guerrilla fighting between Liberals and Conservatives, few of whom understood any ideological implications of their loyalty, ripped Colombia apart. La Violencia convinced Colombia's elite that there was a need to bring the rivalry between Liberal and Conservative under control.

The political system in the 1950s had become irrelevant in the midst of the violence. Three years of Conservative government were followed by a populist military government under Gen. Gustavo Rojas Pinilla. Rojas ruled as an absolute dictator, but could not quell the violence still raging in the field. Overthrown largely by a coalition of Conservatives and Liberals that used newsprint as its weapon, Rojas gave up power in May 1957 to a military junta, which promised and provided free elections.

When the fall of Rojas was imminent, Liberal and Conservative leaders met to discuss Colombia's future. Determined to end the violence and initiate a democratic system, the parties entered into a pact establishing a coalition government between the two parties for 16 years. This arrangement, called the National Front, was ratified by a plebiscite in December 1957. Under the terms of this agreement, a free election would be held in 1958. The parties would then alternate in power for four-year terms until 1974. Thus, Liberals and Conservatives would take turns in the presidency. Parties were also guaranteed equal numbers of posts in the cabinet and in the national and departmental legislatures.

In 1958, the first election under the National Front was won by Liberal Alberto Lleras Camargo. As provided in the agreement, he was succeeded in 1962 by a Conservative, National Front candidate Guillermo León Valencia. In May 1966, Colombia held another peaceful election, won by Carlos Lleras Restrepo, a Liberal economist. Although lacking the necessary two-thirds majority required under the Colombian constitution to pass legislation, Lleras came to power with the firm support of the press and other important public sectors. His regime occupied itself with increasing public revenues, improving public administration, securing external financial assistance to supplement domestic savings, and preparing new overall and sectoral development plans. In April 1970, Conservative Party leader Misael Pastrana Borrero, a former cabinet minister, was elected president, narrowly defeating former President Rojas. The election results were disputed but later upheld.

In August 1974, with the inauguration of the Liberal Alfonso López Michelsen as president, Colombia returned to a two-party system for presidential and congressional elections. As provided by a constitutional amendment of 1968, President López shared cabinet posts and other positions with the Conservative Party. In 1978, another Liberal candidate, Julio César Turbay Ayala, won the presidency, but because his margin of victory was slim (49.5% against the Conservatives' 46.6%), he continued the tradition of giving a number of cabinet posts to the opposition. In June 1982, just before leaving office, Turbay lifted the state of siege that had been in force intermittently since 1948.

Because of a split in the Liberal Party, the Conservatives won the 1982 elections, and a former senator and ambassador to Spain, Belisario Betancur Cuartas, was sworn in as president in August. He continued the tradition of including opposition party members in his cabinet. But Betancur's most immediate problem was political violence, including numerous kidnappings and political murders since the late 1970s by both left- and right-wing organizations. In 1983, it was estimated that some 6,000 leftist guerrillas were active in Colombia. There were at least four guerrilla groups in the field, of which M-19 was the best known. The Betancur government pursued a policy of negotiation with the guerrillas. He offered amnesty and political recognition in exchange for the cessation of activity and the joining of the electoral process. Betancur's last year in office was marred by a seizure by M-19 of the Palace of Justice. Troops stormed the building, and it was completely destroyed by fire, with over 90 people killed.

The 1986 election went resoundingly to the Liberals under the longtime politician Virgilio Barco Vargas, who campaigned on a platform of extensive economic and social reform, focusing on poverty and unemployment. Barco won a significant majority, but the Conservative Party broke from the traditions started by the National Front, refusing cabinet and other government posts offered. President Barco's rhetoric was not matched by policies of any substance, and the economy continued to stagnate. Barco made no progress with drug traffickers, who arranged for the murder of his attorney-general. However, he was able to initiate a plan aimed at bringing guerrilla groups into the political system.

The election of 1990 brought another Liberal, César Gaviria Trujillo, to the presidency. In that election, three candidates were assassinated. Gaviria continued Barco's outreach to the various leftist guerrilla groups, and in 1991 the notorious M-19 group demobilized and became a political party. The other groups chose to remain active. Gaviria responded to their intransigence in November 1992 by announcing new counterinsurgency measures and a hard-line policy against both guerrillas and drug traffickers.

Gaviria also decided to create a new constitution, which occurred on 5 July 1991. It included a number of reforms aimed at increasing the democratization of Colombia's elite-controlled political system.

In the 1994 elections, Colombians continued their preference for Liberal candidates, with Ernesto Samper Pizano winning a runoff election against Conservative TV newscaster Andrés Pastrana. In the general election, only 18,499 votes separated the two candidates. The campaign was again marked by widespread political violence. Samper's government was weakened by charges that he and other senior government officials had accepted money from drug traffickers during the 1994 election campaign. (Congress formally exonerated the president of these charges in 1996.)

The 40 year old campaign by Marxist guerillas to overthrow the Colombian government continued unabated and even escalated in the 1990s. As of 1996, there was a guerilla presence in over half the country's villages and towns, and it was estimated that about a million Colombians had fled their homes between 1987 and 1997 as a result of rural violence. With forces estimated at 10,000, there was no apparent prospect that guerilla groups would succeed in taking over the country, but they continued to thrive, relying heavily on funds from the drug cartels following the collapse of the Soviet union.

By the 1980s Colombian drug traffickers controlled 80% of the world's cocaine trade. In response to a domestic and international crackdown in the mid- and late 1980s, the powerful Medellín cartel stepped up its terrorist attacks, including car bombings and political assassinations. The leaders of the cartel surrendered to the Gaviria government in 1991, but head boss Pablo Escobar escaped from government custody the following year, and was eventually hunted down and killed in 1993. Most top leaders of the Cali cartel, which had taken over much of the Medellín market, were arrested in 1995 and subsequently imprisoned. However, Colombia's lucrative drug trade continued to flourish. In 1998, the Conservative Party came back to power when Andrés Pastrana won the presidential election with 50.5% of the vote, defeating Liberal Horacio Serpa. Upon taking office, Pastrana sought more collaboration from the US to fight the war on drugs and sought to establish peace talks with the guerrillas.

13 GOVERNMENT

Colombia is a unitary republic, organized democratically under the constitution of August 1886, substantially amended in 1910, 1936, 1945, 1957, 1959, 1968, and 1979, and superseded by the constitution of 1991, which included provisions guaranteeing health care, social security, and human rights protection.

The Congress consists of a 161-member Chamber of Representatives and a 102-member Senate. Members of both houses are elected directly for four-year terms. Colombian congressional representation is determined by the size of the population. Some seats are reserved for blacks, Indians, and former guerrillas. The chief executive is granted the initiative in fiscal policies and the power to declare a state of emergency during times of economic and social stress. Under such a declaration, the president may rule by decree for a period of not longer than 90 days in any one year.

The president is elected directly for a four-year term and may not run for immediate reelection. For many years, Colombia used an officer called the designado ("designate"), elected by Congress every two years, who served as a sort of vice president, exercising the executive function in the president's absence. The 1991 constitution introduced a formal vice presidency. The cabinet has 15 members. The Council of State is a consultative body with jurisdiction over administrative conflicts. A comptroller general is elected by the Chamber of Representatives. There is universal suffrage for those 18 years of age and over. Women have had the right to vote since 1954.

14 POLITICAL PARTIES

For many years, the Colombian constitution allowed only two political parties, the Liberal and the Conservative, to participate in the national government. These two parties consistently dominated Colombian politics. Recent changes allow for more parties, and several have emerged, but the Conservative and Liberal parties control a majority of elected offices.

The Liberal Party (Partido Liberal—PL) continues to support religious toleration and a positive response to the social and economic demands of the masses. The Liberals theoretically support separation of church and state, though in practice a strong church is accepted. Federalism, while important in theory, has been abandoned in practice by Liberal leaders. Liberals have been far more successful electorally than the Conservatives, having won all but one post-National Front presidential elections, and enjoy majority support in both houses. In 1998, the Liberal Party lost the presidency but retained control of both Chambers.

The policy of the Conservative Party (Partido Conservador Social—PCS) has been characterized by close cooperation with the Roman Catholic Church, a lack of tolerance for non–Roman Catholic religious beliefs, maintenance of class privileges, and highly centralized government, with local authority strictly subservient to national rule. Before universal suffrage, the Conservatives sought to allow only heads of families to vote. Under the leadership of Andrés Pastrana, the son of former Conservative president Misael Pastrana, the PCS regained the presidency in 1998.

Despite the spread of suffrage and the rise of industrialization and a middle class, both parties continue to be dominated by a wealthy oligarchy. Both are controlled at the national level by a convention and a directorate, and congressional discipline is strong. Since the National Front agreement of 1958, the two parties have become increasingly similar ideologically.

Congressional and presidential elections from 1958 through 1982 primarily constituted votes of confidence in the National Front. Perhaps as a means of protest, 60% of eligible voters abstained from the presidential election in 1978, and 80% of the electorate abstained from the municipal and local elections of March 1980. In 1982 and 1986, however, Colombian voters turned out in record numbers, with 55% of the electorate participating in the presidential ballot in 1982 and 57% in 1988.

The Colombian Communist Party (Partido Communista de Colombia—PCC), a traditional, Marxist-oriented party, combined with the nation's largest guerrilla group, the Colombian Revolutionary Armed Forces (Fuerzas Armadas Revolucionarias de Colombia—FARC, to form the Patriotic Union (UP); the group has not become major force in electoral politics.

There is considerable independent party activity in Colombia, and it has been increasing. Traditionally, the third force in Colombian politics was provided by former dictator Rojas Pinilla, whose National Popular Alliance (Alianza Nacional Popular—ANAPO), now defunct, was a strong party movement. The election of 19 April 1970 gave rise to the extremist rebel group M-19, which stood for the April 19th Movement. After over two decades of military actions against the government, M-19 demobilized in 1991 and fielded candidates in the 1990 elections. Currently, M-19 is part of a coalition of leftist parties and other dissident groups, called Democratic Alliance M-19.

Several militant leftist groups remain outside the political system, including the National Liberation Army (Ejército de Liberación Nacional—ELN) and the Revolutionary Armed Forces of Colombia. Although officially a member of the Patriotic Union, the FARC also refuses to demobilize. The People's Liberation Army (EPL) began to demobilize in 1993, but a dissident faction refused orders to lay down arms, and returned to the field.

Ernesto Samper Pizano of the Liberal party was elected president in 1994 with 50.4% of the vote, defeating PSC Andrés Pastrana. Following the 1994 elections, 59 Senate seats were held by the Liberal Party, 31 by conservative groups, and 12 by other parties; in the House of Representatives, the liberals had 89 seats, conservatives 53, AD/M-19 had 2, and other parties had 17. In 1998, Pastrana obtained 52% of the vote and became Colombia's first Conservative president in more than a decade. The Liberal Party retained control of the Senate and the Chamber of Deputies with 98 of 161 seats in the Chamber and 51 out of 102 seats in the Senate.

15 LOCAL GOVERNMENT

Colombia is divided into 32 departments (states) and the Bogotá federal district, and subdivided into 1,011 municipalities. Departments control their own finances, as well as administration, within the limits set by the constitution. Governors of departments, once appointed by the president, are now elected. Each departmental assembly meets yearly for a session of two months. Assembly members are elected by universal suffrage, one for each 40,000 inhabitants.

The departments have the power to establish municipal districts and to review the acts of the municipal governments to determine their constitutionality. Each municipality has a popularly elected municipal council. Another reform from the 1991 constitution is the direct election of mayors, where previously mayors were chosen by the president and were directly under the control of their respective governors. Mayors are elected by direct vote to a two-year term.

16 JUDICIAL SYSTEM

The judicial system comprises a Constitutional Court, Supreme Court of Justice, Council of State, the Higher Judiciary Council, and superior and municipal courts. The Supreme Court in Bogotá is composed of 24 magistrates selected for lifetime terms by justices already in office. The Supreme Court reviews state and municipality laws, frames bills to be submitted to Congress, and proposes reforms. It acts as an advisory board to the government and can veto decrees. It has original jurisdiction in impeachment trials and constitutional interpretation and appellate jurisdiction in ordinary judicial matters. The court is divided into four chambers—civil cassation, criminal cassation, labor cassation, and constitutional procedure.

There is a superior court of three or more judges in each of the judicial districts and a number of municipal courts. A judge of minors in the capital of each department has jurisdiction throughout the department. There are also special labor courts. In criminal cases, the judge chooses a five-member jury; jury duty is obligatory. There is no capital punishment; the maximum penalty for crimes is 20 years in prison. Although the right of habeas corpus is guaranteed by the constitution, suspects in security cases have been detained incommunicado for 10 days or longer.

The 1991 Constitution extensively revises the judicial system. It establishes an independent prosecution system and a national people's defender office to investigate human rights cases. Traditional courts on Indian reservations are validated. A Constitutional Court reviews the constitutionality of proposed legislation.

The judiciary is independent both in theory and in practice from the executive and legislative branches. In 1991, the government set up five regional jurisdictions to handle narcotics, terrorism, and police corruption cases in which anonymous judges and prosecutors handle the major trials of narcotics terrorists. The government implemented significant reforms to the system of regional jurisdiction in 1999, but they have yet not been fully implemented.

The procedures in the new regional courts have raised concerns over defendants' rights. In 1993, the constitutional court invalidated provisions of the regional court law under which detainees could be held without right to bail.

Criminal defendants have a right to an attorney, although indigents have difficulties in obtaining effective counsel. In some cases, inability to post bail and backlogs in processing result in the accused serving the applicable sentence for the crime charged before the case goes to trial.

17 ARMED FORCES

Colombia's total armed forces in 2000 amounted to 144,000 personnel. All adult males (18–30) are obliged by the constitution to serve if called, for one or two years, then retain reserve service obligations until age 45. Most conscripts serve in the army (121,000, 63,800 conscripts), but all services have token conscript contingents.

The army is organized in five divisions of 17 infantry brigades, stationed on a regional basis. Special mobile forces, counterinsurgency forces, rangers, commandoes, and mechanized guard forces number an additional 17 battalions, armed with American and European weapons. The army controls 54,700 of 60,700 reservists.

Air force personnel numbered 8,000 in 2000; combat aircraft numbered 72, armed helicopters 72. The navy had 15,000 personnel, including 8,500 marines and coast guard personnel. Naval ships included four frigates, four submarines, and 104 patrol craft and gunboats. There is also a 87,000-member national police force.

Colombia's defense forces are frequently occupied in opposing rural violence, often stemming from militant guerrilla groups and drug lords' armies. Guerrilla forces number perhaps 20,000. The military supplies peasants with arms and instruction in self-defense tactics. Defense expenditures in 1998 amounted to around $4 billion, or 4.2% of gross domestic product.

18 INTERNATIONAL COOPERATION

Colombia is a charter member of the UN, having joined on 5 November 1945, and participates in ECLAC and all the nonregional specialized agencies. It was the only Latin American country to participate actively in the Korean War and the Suez Canal crisis. In Korea, a regiment of 1,000, three times relieved, was continuously in action. Colombia has been active in the OAS since its formation at Bogotá in 1948.

The Andean Pact, signed by five countries in May 1969, has opened up new marketing possibilities for Colombian products, in addition to those already existing in the US and Europe. Colombia also participates in G-77, the IADB, and the WTO, and it is a signatory to the Law of the Sea.

19 ECONOMY

With the expansion of the manufacturing sector, Colombia's economy has become more dependent upon industry than agriculture. Coffee was by far the most important crop: its share of total exports ranged from about 40% to 65% of the annual total between 1964 and 1986, depending on crop yields and international commodity prices. In 1997, this share had dropped to only 21%. Colombia decided to reduce its dependence on coffee exports because of widely fluctuating world market conditions, and to encourage other agricultural exports, especially sugar, bananas, rice, potatoes, and cotton. The government also attempted to attract investment in manufacturing and mining projects. Mining has been the area of the most impressive growth; Colombia became a net exporter of petroleum in 1986, and coal became a major export as well. New oil output from the Cusiana field and other fields will play an important role in the coming years; oil production continues to be a significant source of foreign investment. The Trade Development Bureau (PROEXPO) was established in 1967 to increase the volume of non-traditional exports and to provide a flexible exchange rate and special tax incentives.

During the 1970s, Colombia's economy struggled with an inflationary spiral that rose from a rate of 15.4% in 1972 to 25% during the following decade. Inflation was kept close to 20% annually through the 1980s and much of the 1990s. After 1983, however, the economy improved significantly, and growth rates rose above the world and hemispheric averages—an average of 4% between 1988 and 1998. In 1998 GDP increased by only 0.20%, down from 3.1% in 1997. Estimates for 1999 indicated a negative growth rate for the first time since 1931. Industrial production fell by 20% in the first four months of 1999, but regained a positive rate by 2000.

In 1990, President Cesar Gaviria instituted an economic restructuring plan known as apertura (opening). The program was essentially in line with international liberalizations that have dominated national economies during the 1990s: trade expansion through tariff reduction and privatization of state-owned enterprises. In the initial stages of the program, Colombia signed free trade agreements and has long supported hemisphere-wide free trade agreements. The government also began privatizing an array of industries and resources, including banks, power plants, airports, seaports, roads and telecommunications networks; but privatization slowed after the initial excitement of the plan.

In 1995, domestic political considerations constricted Colombia's economic liberalization. In 1996, US President Bill Clinton announced that Colombia would be decertified as a country that fully cooperated with US narcotics policy. The move was taken in response to continued narco-guerilla unrest in the countryside and, perhaps more seriously, allegations that President Samper had solicited and received campaign contributions from the drug cartels. This made it difficult for US companies to further invest in the country, and halted the growth of trade; but despite the uncertainties in Colombian investment, the US remained the biggest foreign investor in the country. The 1995 Social Pact for Productivity, Prices, and Wages was also dismissed as a result of suspected government corruption in 1997.

In 1999, due to economic instability in 1998, Colombia signed its first agreement with the IMF for a $3 billion approved standby line of credit. The government also unveiled plans to renew the privatization many state-owned enterprises to revitalize the economy. Nevertheless, guerilla warfare put off potential investors.

20 INCOME

The US Central Intelligence Agency (CIA) reports that in 1998 Colombia's gross domestic product (GDP) was estimated at $255 billion. The per capita GDP was estimated at $6,600. The annual growth rate of GDP was estimated at 0.2%. The average inflation rate in 1998 was 17%. The CIA defines GDP as the value of all final goods and services produced within a nation in a given year and computed on the basis of purchasing power parity (PPP) rather than value as measured on the basis of the rate of exchange. It was estimated that agriculture accounted for 19% of GDP, industry 26%, and services 55%.

Private consumption includes expenditures of individuals, households, and non-governmental organizations. It was estimated that between 1990 and 1998 private consumption grew at an annual rate of 3.9%. The richest 10% of the population accounted for approximately 46% of household consumption and the poorest 10% approximately 1.1%.

21 LABOR

In 1970, 50% of the 5,100,000-member labor force worked in agriculture; by 1993, 23% of the labor force of about 11,500,000 held jobs in agriculture and 27% in industry. An average of 350,000 people joined the labor force annually during the 1970s and early 1980s, creating a demand for new positions that could not be met. To alleviate the problem, the government undertook an extensive program in which export production and foreign investments figure prominently. In 1997, the labor force was estimated at 16.8 million.

The largest confederation, the Unitary Workers Central (CUT), represented 50% of the organized labor movement in 1999. The second-largest union, the Maoist/Social Christian Columbian Democratic Workers' Confederation accounted for about 30%, and the General Confederation of Democratic Workers represented about 20% of organized labor. About 7% of the workforce was unionized in 1999.

The 1991 constitution guarantees the right to strike except in public utilities, equal rights for women workers, workers' participation in management, universal education, expanded social insurance coverage, and the incorporation of ratified international labor conventions into the labor code. The basic source of Colombian labor legislation is the Substantive Labor Code of 1950, as amended. Colombia's basic labor law covers all inhabitants, regardless of nationality, and guarantees individual and collective rights. Maximum daily and weekly hours are 8 and 48, respectively, except in agriculture, stock breeding, and forestry, in which they are 9 and 54, respectively. There are overtime rates, annual vacations, sick benefits, and a compulsory twice-yearly bonus. Social security is compulsory, with the employer paying one-half and the employee and the government one-quarter each. Firms located more than a mile from a school must maintain primary schools for the children of the workers. In 1999, the minimum wage was $125 per month.

Urban unemployment is a major problem and has nearly doubled since 1994, when the average urban unemployment rate was 7.6. By 1998, it had risen to 15%.

22 AGRICULTURE

Agriculture, despite an endemic problem of poor productivity, remains the most important segment of the Colombian economy. In 1998, agriculture accounted for 19% of the GDP.

Only about 5% of Colombia's land area is cultivated, most of it in elevated regions of the temperate zone. The small area of cultivation is due in part to the rugged Andean terrain and in part to lack of irrigation. In 1996, irrigated districts covered only about 340,656 ha (841,761 acres), while private irrigation watered 710,000 ha (1,754,000 acres). The flat, fertile valleys are generally devoted to livestock, limiting cultivation to the slopes, an uneconomical practice that is gradually being changed. Hand cultivation, especially by machete and hoe, predominates, but mechanization is making headway on the larger farms. Fertilizer is expensive and not sufficiently used. The small size of farms is another constraint on agricultural growth: in the mid-1980s, farms of less than 20 hectares (50 acres) accounted for 80% of all agricultural land.

Coffee, by far the most important crop, is grown mainly on the Andean slopes at altitudes of 1,300–1,800 m (4,200–6,000 ft). Colombia, the world's second-largest coffee grower, contributes 13–16% of the total world production each year. In 1998, coffee-growing farms, many under six hectares (15 acres), accounted for about 1,085,000 hectares (2.6 million acres), over two-thirds of the land under permanent crops. In 1992, despite a severe drought, the amount of coffee exported increased by over 30% as a result of a successful strategy for expanding the external markets. In 1993, coffee production increased to 1,080,000 tons, but dwindled to only 678,000 tons in 1994.

Production in 1998 was 732,000 tons. In 1997, coffee accounted for 61% of agricultural exports, and for 21% of Colombia's total exports.

Sugar, also important, is grown chiefly in the Cauca Valley, with its center at Cali. Many varieties of bananas are grown; bananas for export are produced in the Uraba and Santa Maria regions. Colombia is the world's third-largest banana exporter (after Ecuador and Costa Rica) and supplies about one-sixth of the world export market. Corn, yucca, plantains, and, in high altitudes, potatoes have been traditional food staples since before the Spanish conquest. Beans, rice, and wheat, introduced in the 19th century, are also important in the diet. Other export crops include fresh-cut flowers, cotton, and tobacco. Cocoa is produced in limited amounts for domestic consumption. Colombia produces much of its domestic food requirements, but it has to import wheat, barley, fats, oils, and cocoa.

Since 1940, the government has taken an increasing part in the control, organization, and encouragement of agriculture. Through the Colombian Institute of Agrarian Reform (Instituto Colombiano de la Reforma Agraria—INCORA), farmers are given financial support, technical aid, and social assistance for better housing, education, and health facilities. INCORA acquires land for equitable distribution to farmers and helps to develop potentially valuable but uncultivated land and to increase agricultural productivity. The production-oriented Rural Development Program, begun in 1976, gave technical assistance and credit to about 30,000 small landholders. Farmers have also benefited from the us$150-million rural electrification program, introduced in 1981, and from a program to extend irrigation and drainage systems, initiated in the early 1980s.

Agricultural production (in thousands of tons) for major crops in 1998 was as follows:

	1998
Sugar, raw	2,160
Plantains	2,597
Potatoes	2,818
Rice	1,850
Cassava	1,845
Bananas	2,200
Corn	1,200
Sorghum	339
Cotton	40
Palm oil	438
Cocoa	45
Dry beans	139

Marijuana, coca leaf, and opium are also grown for the production of illicit drugs. In 1998, Colombia produced and estimated 81,400 tons of coca leaf and 61 tons of opium.

23ANIMAL HUSBANDRY

Occupying about 40 million hectares (99 million acres) of pasture, livestock farming, especially cattle breeding has long been an important Colombian industry. Of this total area, about 19 million hectares (46.9 million acres) are actually used for livestock production. The Ministry of Agriculture maintains experimental stations in Antioquia and Bolívar departments to improve breeds, but the quality of livestock is still low. Cattle are driven to market by truck. This practice often entails crossing high mountains, with much wastage; accordingly, there has been a movement to construct slaughterhouses and meat-packing plants near the ranges. Dairy farming, not important in the past, expanded in the 1970s, especially near the big cities. Colombian sheep produce about one-third of the wool used by the country's textile industry. The government maintains an experimental station for sheep in Cundinamarca and for goats in Norte de Santander. In 1998 there were 28.2 million cattle, 2.4 million

sheep, and 2.5 million pigs. The production of beef and veal decreased from a 1989–91 average of 713,000 tons a year to 690,000 tons in 1998.

24FISHING

Colombia has an abundance of fish in its Caribbean and Pacific coastal waters and in its innumerable rivers. Lake Tota in Boyacá and Lake La Cocha in Nariño abound in trout, as do the artificial reservoirs of Neusa and Sisga in Cundinamarca. About half of the annual catch consists of freshwater fish. Tarpon are caught in the delta waters of the Magdalena, and sailfish, broadbills, and tuna in the Caribbean. The 1994 fish catch was 122,708 tons. The development of crustacean aquaculture has expanded since the mid-1980s, especially for Penaeid shrimps. In 1997, aquaculture production was valued at $189.8 million, primarily tilapia and rainbow trout by volume.

25FORESTRY

Colombia's forested area is some 50 million hectares (123.6 million acres), or nearly 50% of the total area. Although much timberland is inaccessible or of limited value, the nation is self-sufficient in lumber. Roundwood production was 21,486,000 cu m in 1997; exports of roundwood were valued at $1.5 million that year. The soft tropical woods that predominate are also suitable for plywood production, for paper pulp, and for furniture manufacture; the wood pulp, paper and paperboard, and wood-based panels outputs in 1997 were 176,000 tons, 704,000 tons, and 109,000 tons, respectively.

26MINING

The new Constitution of 1990 replaced the 1866 Constitution; under the new article 332, the state retains the rights to all surface and subsurface nonrenewable and natural resources. The government grants concessions for exploration and production. In 1989, the new mining code became law. The mining act was written to encourage mineral exploration and development by expediting the processing of claims, by improving the security of mineral occupancy and tenure, and by providing financial aid to small- and medium-scale miners. The government planned to privatize 28 state-owned companies, including the coal producer Carbones de Colombia S.A. (CARBOCOL) and the nickel producer Cerro Matoso S.A. In 1997, mining (including the petroleum sector) accounted for $1.7 billion of the total foreign investment of $5.3 billion in Colombia. In 1996, the petroleum sector accounted for 27% of total exports, or $2.86 billion; coal accounted for 10%, or $1.06 billion. Expansion of the mining sector was hampered by ongoing tourist activity, including sabotage of mining and pipeline facilities.

Colombia is the third-largest coal producer in the Western Hemisphere (after the US and Canada); proven reserves, the largest in Latin America, are sufficient for the next millennium at current extraction rates. Colombia began a modest export program in the mid-1970s; exports are projected to reach 49 million tons per year by 2001. It is also one of the few countries that is self-sufficient in coking coal for its steel industry. In the early 1980s, Carbones de Colombia (CARBOCOL), a state agency, began to expand coal-mining operations in conjunction with Spain, Romania, Brazil, and the International Resources Corp. (INTERCOR), an Exxon affiliate. ECOCARBON, a state-owned company that manages and regulates Columbia's coal resources, was formed in 1993.

Colombia is one of the world's largest producers of precious metals and stones; in 1990, production of emeralds surpassed three million carats. The production and sale of emeralds is a joint private-government venture administered by Mineralco, the government-administered mining agency. Colombia is South

America's only producer of platinum, and it ranks second in the region in gold production. Colombia is also a leading producer of nickel; in 1997, production amounted to 31,230 tons.

A large copper deposit, with reserves estimated at 625 million tons, was discovered at Pantanos, Antioquia, in 1973. The country's substantial copper, iron, nickel, and lead reserves are of major importance to the future development of the economy. Colombia also has a variety of quarried resources, such as limestone, sand, gravel, marble, gypsum, clay, and feldspar, as well as minor deposits of sulfur, asbestos, bauxite, mercury, zinc, and dolomite, among others. Salt production is a government monopoly; the production of marine salt in 1995 was 182,000 tons, and of rock salt, 144,000 tons.

The production of principal minerals (excluding petroleum and natural gas) in 1995 and 1997 (preliminary) included the following:

	1995	1997
Coal (tons)	26,020,000	32,362,000
Gold (kg)	21,160	18,810
Iron ore (tons)	734,000	737,000
Silver (kg)	5,913	3,510
Platinum (kg)	973	409
Emeralds (carats)	6,304,000	6,688,000
Feldspar (tons)	58,100	66,845

27ENERGY AND POWER

Colombia's mountainous terrain and network of rivers offer one of the highest potentials in the world for the generation of hydro-electric power. These resources remain largely undeveloped, despite intensive government efforts. Installed capacity was 14,614,000 kW in 1998. In the same year, production was 45,020 million kWh. The expansion of electrical capacity in Colombia has benefited significantly from financial support by the IBRD. About 80% of Colombia's current capacity is based on hydropower (mainly the newly completed Guavio facility), which is scarce in times of drought.

Colombia's proved petroleum reserves were estimated at 2.6 billion barrels in 2000. Production of oil has rapidly risen from 7.4 million tons in 1982 to 19.6 million tons in 1987 to 30.1 million tons in 1995. As of 1998, it was 743,000 barrels per day. In 1976, Colombia was forced to start importing oil. It was thus a source of considerable pride to Colombians when petroleum exports recommenced late in 1986. Guerrillas have made the export pipeline a target, however, and outflow has been disrupted occasionally. Between 1986 and 1995, there were 375 attacks on oil facilities, but there has been a general decrease in guerilla activities since 1992. The Colombian government plans to invest $27 billion to improve national infrastructure over the next several years. Empresa Colombiana de Petróleo (ECOPETROL), a state agency, was attempting to attract more foreign investment to the country's oil and gas sector as of 1996.

The production and consumption of natural gas have grown since the mid-1970s. Proved reserves in early 2000 were 195 billion cu m. In 1998, production totaled 7 billion cu m.

28INDUSTRY

The National Association of Manufacturers (Asociación Nacional de Industriales—ANDI) represents firms engaged in some 40 different branches of manufacturing. ANDI was founded in 1944 to assist both large and small businesses. Since 1940, the Industrial Development Institute (Instituto de Fomento Industrial—IFI), a government-operated finance corporation, has been investing in enterprises that otherwise might not be undertaken because of high risk or lack of capital. It provides direct financing for construction, acquisition of essential machinery and equipment installation services, and working capital. Most of the industrial activity is concentrated in and around Bogotá, Medellín, Barranquilla, and Cali. Industries in Medellín produce textiles, clothing, chemicals, plastic, and printed materials.

Manufacturing accounted for 15% of GDP in 1950, 24% at its peak in 1977, and 14% in 1998. Colombia is almost self-sufficient in consumer products, which represent about half of total industrial production. The 1970s witnessed a shift in industrial development policies from import substitution to expansion of exports. While the pace of industrial growth declined slightly in the mid-1970s, it increased by 2.5% between 1977 and 1987. This growth continued into the early 1990s, but slowed by mid-decade. Industry declined by 2.3% in 1998.

Export-oriented industries include coal and oil derivatives, chemicals, porcelain, and glass. In 1995, mining and hydro-carbons grew by 17%; the highest growth sector in the Colombian economy. That the rest of the industrial economy has been sluggish in recent years is due to a cluster of factors, including the lack of infrastructure, labor difficulties, and most significantly, the civil unrest in the countryside caused by bands of paramilitaries loyal to drug traffickers and political extremists. The decline in industry also reflects an ebb in the country's construction boom. The construction sector grew by nearly 10% a year through the early part of the 1990s, but fell to just 5.3% in 1995. While this was a significant growth rate, it was a 50% fall from preceding years.

29SCIENCE AND TECHNOLOGY

The government of President Turbay Ayala (1978–82) emphasized research in farming, in order to help raise agricultural production. The Academy of Exact, Physical, and Natural Sciences (founded in 1933) and the National Academy of Medicine (founded in 1890), are both located in Bogotá. As of 1996, there were 24 specialized agricultural, medical, scientific, and technical learned societies, and 13 scientific research institutes in Colombia, and the country had 43 universities offering degrees in basic and applied sciences. In 1987–97, science and engineering students accounted for 28% of college and university enrollments.

30DOMESTIC TRADE

There are four primary marketing areas: the Caribbean coast region, the Antioquia region, the Cauca Valley region, and the Bogotá region. Firms desiring distribution of their products to all important national markets generally appoint agents in the leading city of each of the four regions (Barranquilla, Medellín, Cali, and Bogotá, respectively). Most small purchases are made for cash, but many stores offer installment credit facilities.

Small, individually owned retail establishments predominate, although chain stores are increasing. Variety stores on the pattern of those in the US are becoming popular, and food supermarkets are increasing in larger cities. Local farmers' markets, however, are still more generally patronized even in the cities, and in rural areas they are often the only trading centers.

Business hours vary largely with climatic conditions; however, the usual workday is from 8 AM to noon and from 1 to 5 PM. Most businesses close on Saturday afternoons, Sundays, and on state or religious holidays. Banking hours are from 9 AM to 3:30 PM.

The principal advertising media are newspapers, magazines, radio, and television; in motion picture theaters, it is also customary to display advertisements on the screen between features. There are a number of advertising and public relations firms.

31FOREIGN TRADE

Beginning in 1990, Colombia opened up its economy to greater international trade and investment. The program of liberalization resulted in mass privatizations and lifting of restrictions on foreign investment; and substantially reduced import tariffs while eliminating most import licensing requirements. The government also signed the Andean Free Trade Agreement (ANCOM) with Venezuela, Peru, Ecuador, and Bolivia; the Latin American Integration Association (LAIA) with Argentina, Bolivia, Brazil, Chile, Ecuador, Mexico, Paraguay, Peru, Uruguay, Venezuela, El Salvador, Costa Rica, Guatemala, Nicaragua, and Honduras; a Bilateral Free Trade Agreement with Chile; and an agreement with Mexico and Venezuela called the Group of Three (G-3).

Colombia also has several free-trade zones, the largest of which is Barranquilla, on the Caribbean. Other free-trade zones providing benefits for importers and exporters, as well as for manufacturers located within the zone boundaries, are the Buenaventura Harbor, Cúcuta, Palmaseca (near Cali's international airport), and the Caribbean port of Santa Marta. The illicit trade in marijuana and cocaine, especially to the US, is known to be substantial, but there are no reliable estimates of its volume or its value. The Columbian government estimated in 1999 that drug traffickers smuggled $5 billion annually in contraband into the country.

Columbia exports 14% of the world's coffee, and coffee is this country's largest commodity export (21%). Fuels contribute to the export market as well, including crude and refined petroleum (16%); and coal, lignite, and peat (5.9%). Agricultural exports like fruit, nuts, vegetables, sugar and honey account for 12% of Columbia's exports. The country also exports gold, silver, platinum, and emeralds (4.6%).

In 1997 Colombia's imports were distributed among the following categories:

Consumer goods	9.7%
Food	7.8%
Fuels	2.9%
Industrial supplies	36.9%
Machinery	27.1%
Transportation	13.2%
Other	2.4%

Principal trading partners in 1998 (in millions of US dollars) were as follows:

COUNTRY	EXPORTS	IMPORTS	BALANCE
United States	4,491	5,298	-807
Venezuela	958	1,647	-689
Germany	746	748	-2
Ecuador	517	397	120
United Kingdom	314	322	-8
Italy	303	404	-101
France	291	454	-163
Japan	284	1,052	-768
Spain	161	494	-333
Mexico	151	493	-342

32BALANCE OF PAYMENTS

When President Carlos Lleras Restrepo took office in August 1966, the economy of Colombia was unstable; inflation was spiraling, and there was a lack of centralized economic planning. Lleras embarked on an austerity program that included trade and exchange controls, tight credit policies, tax reforms, a balanced budget, and the determination of priorities in the field of public investment. The cutback in imports had repercussions in the industrial sector, but controls were then loosened and business activity stepped up rapidly.

Colombia succeeded in building up a national account surplus during the 1970s, 1980s and early 1990s. Emphasis on export expansion, import substitution, and continuation of foreign assistance led to further progress. The second half of the 1990s, though, brought a consistently negative balance of payments of about 5% of GDP. The Pastrana government implemented austerity measures through an IMF $2.7 billion loan in the hopes of cutting the fiscal deficit to 3.6 by 2000, and 1.5% by 2003.

The US Central Intelligence Agency reports that in 1998 the purchasing power parity of Colombia's exports was $11.3 billion while imports totaled $14.4 billion, resulting in a trade balance of -$3.1 billion.

The International Monetary Fund (IMF) reports that in 1998 Colombia had exports of goods totaling $11,363 million and imports totaling $14,008 million. The services credit totaled $2,115 million and debit $3,509 million. The following table summarizes Colombia's balance of payments as reported by the IMF for 1998 in millions of US dollars.

Current Account		-5,908
Balance on goods	-2,645	
Balance on services	-1,394	
Balance on income	-2,349	
Current transfers	480	
Capital Account		...
Financial Account		4,741
Direct investment abroad	-529	
Direct investment in Colombia	3,038	
Portfolio investment assets	801	
Portfolio investment liabilities	903	
Other investment assets	-294	
Other investment liabilities	822	
Net Errors and Omissions		-230
Reserves and Related Items		1,397

33BANKING AND SECURITIES

The Bank of Bogotá, founded in 1879, was the first Colombian credit establishment. The Bank of the Republic was established in 1923 as the semi-official central bank. This bank is the sole note-issuing authority. The notes must be covered by a reserve in gold or foreign exchange of 25% of their value. The Bank of the Republic also operates the mint for the government. It rediscounts and makes loans to official and semiofficial institutions. In 1963, the Monetary Board was set up to assume from the bank the responsibility for setting required reserve rates for managing general monetary policy; this board, which formulates monetary, credit, and exchange policy, is thus the most influential financial agency in Colombia. The government supervises the banking system by means of a special governmental body, called the Superintendency of Banks.

In 1999, the Colombian financial system included 27 commercial banks (five of them state-owned), the Columbian Export Promotion Bank (BANCOLDEX), 35 foreign bank offices, eight savings and loans corporations (CAV's), 23 development banks, and a state-owned mortgage bank. The Bank of the Republic and the commercial banks supply mainly short-term loans, and investment corporations make long-term loans.

In 1982, in the wake of a scandal that led to the liquidation of a commercial bank and a finance company, the government moved to reform the banking sector by placing limits on the equity any individual (or his family) could hold in a financial institution and on the credit any lending institution could extend to any individual or entity. Several more crises in the ensuing years shook public confidence in the financial system, but tight government control over the sector has brought it back to a state of partial recovery.

Beginning in 1989, the government began to privatize the banks. Several bank liquidations took place in 1999, including

Pacifico, Andino, and Selfin. Two government owned banks merged (Estado and Uconal), while the largest government bank, Caja Agraria, was liquidated and replaced by the new Banco Agrario. The goal of the Superintendency was to reduce the number of banking institutions to about 17. The Central Bank devalued the peso by 9% in 1998, and by 10% in 1999, in an effort to stimulate economic growth. Manufacturing exports had increased by 57% in 2000.

The Bogotá Stock Exchange, organized in 1928, is the largest official stock exchange in the country. The Medellín Exchange was established in 1961, and the Occidente Stock Exchange in Cali was established in 1983 and began operations in 1993. Trading of stocks and fixed-income securities rose 41% in 1996 over the previous year. The three public exchanges reported a total volume of $36 billion in 1998; the Bogota exchange accounted for 57%, the Medellin 28%, and the Cali exchange 15%.

34INSURANCE

The government regulates the insurance industry through the Insurance Section of the Superintendency of Banks. A social insurance system, the Institute for Social Insurance (Instituto para Seguros Sociales-ISS) established by law in 1946, was organized by the Ministry of Labor to provide life and disability insurance, a pension plan, and a health program for employees in the modern private subsector. In 1999, there were 27 insurance companies in operation, two of which were governmental.

During 1995, regulations were issued which require insurance companies to adjust investments to market or equity values and to account for such changes through the income statements. Prior to 1995, any such unrealized adjustments were adjusted directly to policy holders' surplus funds. The Colombian market is characterized by a relatively modest number of insurers, a competitive environment, and a few dominant companies in terms of market share. A number of foreign insurers operate in Colombia, but foreign insurance companies may not establish local branch offices in lieu of opening major offices.

35PUBLIC FINANCE

Much of Colombia's foreign debt has been accumulated by financing infrastructural rather than industrial projects, the latter being more common among Latin American nations during the 1970s and 1980s. Considerable sums were spent in the 1990s to stimulate the development of industry, and higher than normal military expenditures were necessitated by the continuing and disruptive guerrilla activity. The inflationary conditions that prevailed from 1961 into 2000 also stimulated government expenditures. For political reasons, the national government was unable to raise tax revenues sufficient to cover sharply expanding investment outlays. Loans from external financial agencies (including the IMF, IDB, and IBRD) were substantial, but insufficient to permit a buildup in the level of public investment operations. The recession of the early 1980s brought another round of deficits as spending increased far more rapidly than revenues. By the 1990s, reforms in the public sector had greatly improved the efficiency of public expenditures.

The US Central Intelligence Agency (CIA) estimates that in 1998 Colombia's central government took in revenues of approximately $26 billion and had expenditures of $30 billion including capital expenditures of $3.7 billion. Overall, the government registered a deficit of approximately $4 billion. External debt totaled $18 billion.

The following table shows an itemized breakdown of government revenues and expenditures. The percentages were calculated from data reported by the International Monetary Fund. The dollar amounts (millions) are based on the CIA estimates provided above.

REVENUE AND GRANTS	100%	26,000
Tax revenue	87.8%	22,828
Non-tax revenue	12.2%	3,172
EXPENDITURES	100%	30,000
General public services	5.9%	1,770
Defense	14.4%	4,320
Public order and safety	6.0%	1,800
Education	21.0%	6,300
Health	8.8%	2,640
Social security	10.8%	3,240
Housing and community amenities	5.3%	1,590
Recreation, cultural, and religious affairs	0.7%	210
Economic affairs and services	8.2%	2,460
Interest payments	17.4%	5,220
Adjustments	1.5%	450

36TAXATION

In addition to income taxes, Colombia levies a 15% VAT, and municipal and property taxes. Many stamp taxes are imposed on legal documents. Personal income tax rates vary from 10% to 35%. There is a flat tax on corporate income of 35%. Indirect taxes include a tax on exported goods and services, a 5% surcharge on imports, a gasoline tax, and local taxes on vehicles and property.

The 1960 tax law began the process of modernizing Colombia's tax structure. Recognizing that Colombia's fiscal problems stemmed from insufficient revenues rather than excessive spending, the Lleras Restrepo administration (1966–70) introduced legislation to curb tax evasion and instituted a system of withholding income tax at the source. After President López took office in August 1974, a new series of fiscal measures was put into effect, including a revision of income, property, and sales taxes, removal of tax exemptions for government companies, and a reduction in tax incentives for exporters. The principal objectives of the tax reform were more progressivity in tax assessment scales, promotion of economic stability, and a reduction in the incidence of tax evasion. A clampdown on tax avoidance and evasion was also the motivation behind the reform measures of December 1982, which, like those under López, came amid a budgetary crisis. As part of an emergency package, a special amnesty was declared so that taxpayers who had omitted assets or declared nonexisting liabilities were allowed to make corrections in their tax returns and pay the tax due without additional penalty. The measure was reportedly targeted at those who had profited from the drug trade. During the 1990s, tax evasion was still quite common, and the government was considering raising tax levels in 1999 to help stimulate the economy.

37CUSTOMS AND DUTIES

Colombian import tariffs have been significantly reduced and simplified. There are four tariff levels: 5% for raw materials, intermediate and capital goods not produced in Columbia; 10% and 15% for goods in the first category but with domestic production in Columbia; 20% for finished consumer goods; and 35% for automobiles, and other luxury items. The average tariff lies between 11% and 14%. The four-tariff system also acts as the CET for the Andean Community, which became effective for Columbia in 1995. VAT is 16%, but automobiles sales tax ranges from 16% to 45%. Legislation was being planned in 1999 to reduce the sales tax to 12%.

Non-tariff barriers to trade include restrictions on poultry parts, powdered milk, wheat, and other agricultural products. Tariff rates for some of these selected basic commodities ranged up to 119% in 1999. Import and export licenses are required for most items.

Colombia maintains free trade agreements with Venezuela, Ecuador, Bolivia, and Mexico. There are also international agreements for preferential duty rates with the Caribbean Common Market and the Central American Common Market. Several free trade zones are in operation.

38 FOREIGN INVESTMENT

The government has been increasing its promotion of foreign investment in recent years. The former Gaviria Administration implemented an aggressive economic liberalization program, known as apertura or opening, and foreign companies were put on an equal legal footing with local ones. In order to continue boosting the economy, the government has negotiated free trade agreements with several countries. A free trade pact among Colombia, Venezuela and Central America (except Costa Rica) came into operation on 1 July 1993. In addition, an agreement was signed between Colombia, Venezuela, and Mexico (G-3) on establishing a free trade zone in 1994. In 1993, Colombia, Venezuela, Ecuador and Bolivia achieved a customs union, with free trade between the four countries under the auspices of the Andean Pact. Effective 1 January 1994, Pact members implemented a common external tariff (CET) based on a four-tier tariff range.

The industry most heavily invested in by foreigners is the petroleum industry, which saw international investment grow from $458 million in 1993 to $890 million in 1997. In 1996, the Council on Economic and Social Policy (CONPES) eliminated the requirement of government authorization for investment in public services, mining, and hydrocarbons. Despite this allowance, investment in the hydrocarbons sector requires an association contract with the state-owned oil company ECOPETROL. Due to the opertura program, the sectors that have seen the largest growth in international investment have been infrastructural. Investment in the utilities sector (electricity, gas, and water) leapt from $145 million in 1996 to $2.3 billion in 1998. The transportation and communications sectors, which have been mostly privatized in recent years, grew from $5.7 million in 1993 to $360 million in 1997. Columbia ended its monopoly over telecommunications in 1998, but foreign ownership of such companies was limited to 70%.

In 1998, foreign direct investment declined from $5.6 billion in 1997, to $3.2 billion, due to political uncertainty. US businesses represent Colombia's largest international investors by far. The following table shows major foreign direct investment in Colombia by country, in millions of dollars (excluding portfolio and petroleum):

COUNTRY	STOCK 1995	% TOTAL
US	4,330,452	28.1
Panama	2,501,993	16.2
Spain	2,176,921	14.1
Virgin Islands	634,816	4.1

39 ECONOMIC DEVELOPMENT

In 1974, President López outlined to Congress a long-range development plan with a major objective of achieving maximum growth while raising the living standards of the poorer half of the population. Efforts were to be concentrated in four main areas: exports, agriculture, regional development, and industry. An economic program published in 1980, during the administration of Turbay, listed investment in energy, economic decentralization, regional autonomy, improvements in communications and transportation, mining development, and social improvement as its principal aims. A national development plan for the years 1981–84 provided for acceleration of public works. In 1982, during the Betancur presidency, economic emergencies were declared so that decrees to revise banking and fiscal policies could be issued without the need of congressional approval. The Barco administration formulated an economic program similar to that proposed in 1974 by López, whose objectives were to attack unemployment and poverty while encouraging growth.

In 1990, President Cesar Gaviria instituted a national system of economic liberalization known as apertura, or opening. The system called for greatly increased international investment, a lowering of trade barriers, and massive state sell-offs. These began in earnest in the early 1990s as the government sold off seaports, airports, power plants, telecommunications networks, banks—even roads. In addition to these measures, the government aggressively pursued the creation of regional trading blocs and became a major voice in support of a hemispheric free trade area. Colombia became a member of ANCOM, LAIA, a bilateral free-trade pact with Chile and the G-3.

Liberalizations secured Colombia as a reliable regional market. The country saw positive growth every year for over two decades and was one of the only Latin American countries not to default on its international loans during the 1980s. Impeding further development are domestic political scandals, poor infrastructure, and narco-terrorism. In 1998, growth slowed, and even turned negative in 1999.

A $2.7 billion IMF loan in 1999 was needed in order to save the shrinking economy, which improved from the inflow and austerity measures during the next year. In 2000, the US government gave $1.3 billion in aid to Colombia's government and army, chiefly to help the war against drugs, but guerilla armies continued to operate in at least two-fifths of the country.

40 SOCIAL DEVELOPMENT

According to legislation enacted in 1971, social security coverage extends to salaried and nonsalaried people alike, including small business people, and other self-employed workers in both rural and urban areas. In 1994, a private insurance system was introduced. Employees may choose between public or private pension systems, and may also select from among many privately run pension management systems. Both employers and employees contribute to the program, while the government guarantees a minimum pension. A comprehensive medical program was implemented in 1995, and coverage is being extended gradually to all inhabitants, regardless of their contributions. Employees contribute 4% of earnings and employers 8% of payroll, while the government funds low earners. A worker's compensation program is funded fully by employers and provides benefits in proportion to the degree of incapacity.

In 1975, measures were enacted to end discrimination against women under the law. However, there is still discrimination against women, especially in rural areas. They earn 30–40% less than men for doing similar work, and occupy few of the top positions in government. As of 1998, 32 out of 263 members of parliament were women. Rape and other acts of violence against women are widespread, and traditionally the law has not provided strict penalties for offenders. However, a 1996 law provided penalties for acts of domestic violence, and legislation the following year modified the penal code.

Urban Colombia, and especially Bogotá, has acquired a reputation for street crime: pickpockets and thieves are a common problem. Drug trafficking flourishes on a large scale, despite government efforts to suppress cocaine smuggling and to eradicate the coca and marijuana crops. Kidnapping, both for political reasons and for profit, is widespread.

Human rights excesses by security forces declined under the Samper government, but remained at roughly the same level in the late 1990s, when reports of extrajudicial killings and disappearances continued. Human rights abuses are committed by many groups, including guerillas, narcotics traffickers, paramilitary groups and the military. Prison conditions are harsh, but international monitoring of conditions is allowed by the government. As of 1999, the government was still struggling to maintain order in the country.

The constitution provides for special rights and protection for Colombia's many indigenous minorities, but these are not always respected in practice.

41 HEALTH

Health standards have improved greatly since the 1950s, but malaria is still prevalent up to 1,100 m (3,500 ft) in altitude, and many Colombians suffer from intestinal parasites. Malnutrition, formerly a very serious problem, with nutritional goiter, anemia, scurvy, and pellagra frequent, had become less severe by the early 1980s, when the per capita calorie supply was estimated at 102% of requirements. In 1995, 8% of children under five years old were considered to be malnourished. As of 1996, there was a cumulative total of 7,776 reported cases of AIDS. In 1995, 80% of the population had access to safe water.

Colombia's population was expected to rise to 39 million by the end of the century, overtaking Argentina as the third most heavily populated country of the region (after Brazil and Mexico). Health care provisions (doctors and beds) do not compare favorably with other countries of the region.

In 1997, there were 12 physicians for every 10,000 people. According to a study made 1995, 87% of the population (34 million population in 1993) had access to health care services. In 1993, Colombia departed from its older health care system to one of payment by capitation and structured competition among integrated health care service delivery systems; five million people in the poorest groups, previously excluded from the medical system, now have access to health services.

Average life expectancy in 1998 was 71 years. The infant mortality rate decreased from 99.8 per 1,000 live births in 1960 to 24 in 1997. In 1998 there were 23 births per 1,000, with 72% of married women (ages 15 to 49) using contraception in 1995. In 1997, children up to one year of age were immunized against the following: tuberculosis (96%); diphtheria, pertussis, and tetanus (81%); polio (82%); and measles (89%). Colombia's death rate for 1990–95 was 6.6 per 1,000 inhabitants. Between 1986 and 1992, there were approximately 22,000 civil war-related deaths. In the mid-1990s, malaria was at epidemic numbers with nearly 130,000 cases reported. Tuberculosis was also present at nearly 9,000 cases.

42 HOUSING

Colombia's housing shortage is largely a result of the rapid growth of the urban population. With the annual urban population growth rate at over 5%, the housing deficit was estimated to be around 800,000 units in the early 1980s and is expanding annually. Total housing units numbered approximately 7 million in the mid-1990s. At last estimate, more than 85% of all housing units were detached houses, ranches, and huts; less than 15% were apartments, and the remainder were mobile units, natural shelters, and non-residential housing. Roughly 70% were owner occupied, and 25% were rented. Three-fourths of all dwellings were made of bricks, adobe, mud or stone; nearly 15% had external walls of wattle or daub; 7% were wood; and 3% were mostly cane. Public resources are channeled into urban housing through the Central Mortgage Bank, whose mortgages, because of interest rates, down-payment requirements, and repayment terms, have usually been accessible only to upper-middle-income groups; and the savings and loan corporations, whose interest rates are pegged to inflation through daily monetary correction factors known as units of constant purchasing power value (UPACs). In addition, through AID, substantial private funds from US investors have been used for various housing programs. A us$2.6-billion government program for the rehabilitation and construction of new housing in the 1987–90 period was announced by the Barco government, with 131,000 units to be constructed and 258,000 units to be improved.

Rural housing problems in Colombia are dealt with primarily by the Credit Bank for Agriculture, Industry, and Mining, and by the Colombian Institute of Agrarian Reform.

43 EDUCATION

Education is free and compulsory for five years in Colombia. Illiteracy is declining, having dropped from an estimated 90% at the end of the 19th century to an estimated 8.2% in 2000 (males, 8.2%; females, 8.2%). The constitution provides that public education shall not conflict with the doctrines of the Roman Catholic Church; courses in the Roman Catholic religion are compulsory, and the Church is in virtual control of the public schools. Private schools have freedom of instruction, and there are a number of Protestant schools, principally in Bogotá. The national government supports secondary as well as university education and maintains a number of primary schools throughout the country.

By law, Colombia must spend at least 10% of its annual budget on education. In 1996, the education budget was 19.0% of total government expenditure. Financing and supervision of public education is the joint responsibility of the Ministry of Education, the departments, and the municipalities. Secondary and technical education and universities are administered by the Ministry of Education. The central government also pays teachers' salaries.

In 1996 there were 4,916,934 students enrolled in 48,933 primary schools, with 193,911 teachers. Secondary schools had 3,317,782 students and 169,816 teachers in the same year. Although schooling is compulsory for children in the 6-12 age group, dropout rates are high at the primary level, particularly in rural areas, where the students frequently live at considerable distances from their schools. Almost all secondary schools are in the larger cities; thus, little educational opportunity is open to rural children, except those reached by educational radio and television broadcasting. The government has established two basic programs for improving secondary education—the integration of practical training into high-school academic curricula and the training of agricultural experts at the secondary level—so that students who do not go on to college (relatively few do) are prepared to receive further technical training or to earn a living. The National Apprenticeship Service offers technical and vocational training in fields that contribute to national development; the program is financed by compulsory contributions from private enterprises and employees.

As of 1996 there were 644,188 students enrolled in higher education in Colombia; post-secondary teachers numbered 66,538. The National University in Bogotá, founded in 1572, is one of the oldest in the Western Hemisphere. Other important universities include the Universidad Javeriana (founded 1622), which is operated by the Jesuits; the Universidad de los Andes, a private institution based on a US model; and the Universidad Libre, a private university with active liberal leanings. In 1964, the Colombian Overseas Technical Specialization Institute (ICETEX) was formed to coordinate scholarship and fellowship funds for Colombians wishing to study abroad. Graduates of foreign schools who return to Colombia reimburse ICETEX from their subsequent earnings.

44 LIBRARIES AND MUSEUMS

The National Library, founded in 1777 in Bogotá, has over 680,000 volumes. It also acts as a public library and maintains a small circulating collection and a children's room. The cities have municipal libraries and the towns have village libraries, which are under the control of the Colombian Institute of Culture. There are two valuable private libraries in Bogotá, established by Dr. Luis Agusto Cuervo and Dr. Antonio Gómez Restrepo, respectively; each contains about 50,000 volumes. The Bank of the Republic maintains the Luis Angel Arango Library, an important cultural center holding some 400,000 volumes. The library of the National University in Bogotá has approximately 183,000 volumes. The University of the Andes in Bogotá has 210,000 volumes. The Library of Congress holds 140,000 volumes. There are over 1,000 local branches of the public library.

The most notable of Bogotá's museums are the National Museum, which concentrates on history and art since the Spanish conquest, the founding of Bogotá, and the colonial period; the National Archaeological Museum, which exhibits indigenous ceramics, stone carvings, gold objects, and textiles; the Museum of Colonial Art, formerly part of the National University, which specializes in art of the 16th, 17th, and 18th centuries; and the Gold Museum, located in the Bank of the Republic. There are more than 50 provincial museums, including many archeological and anthropological sites.

45MEDIA

Telephone and telegraph networks link all provincial capitals and connect these centers with surrounding rural areas. Each local system is independent; most are municipally owned, but a few are in private hands. Long-distance service is provided by the national government and is based on an agreement among local and departmental systems. In the early 1980s, the National Telecommunications Enterprise (TELECOM) had one of the largest automatic telephone service networks in Latin America. Its high-capacity microwave system connected the 40 largest cities in the country. In 1995, over 3,220,700 telephones were in service.

Most of the nation's 498 (463 AM, 35 FM) radio stations were privately owned in 1999. In 1997 there were 60 television stations. In the same year, there were 565 radio receivers, 217 television sets, and 35 mobilephones per 1,000 population. All television is owned and operated by the national government, but there are some commercial programs. Color television was introduced in 1979. Colombia launched its own communications satellite in 1985.

Almost every town publishes at least one daily newspaper. The press varies from the irregular, hand-printed newspapers of the small towns of the interior to such national dailies as *El Tiempo*, one of the most influential newspapers of the Spanish-speaking world. The country's principal newspapers and their 1999 daily circulations are as follows:

	ORIENTATION	CIRCULATION
BOGOTÁ		
El Tiempo (m)	Liberal	245,000
El Espectador (m)	Liberal	190,900
El Espacio (e)	Liberal	170,000
El Nuevo Siglo (m)	Conservative	68,000
CALI		
El País (m)	Conservative	75,000
Occidente (m)	Conservative	25,000
MEDELLÍN		
El Colombiano (m)	Conservative	110,000
BARRANQUILLA		
El Heraldo (m)	Liberal	70,000
BUCARAMANGA		
El Vanguardia liberal (m)	Liberal	42,000
MANIZALES		
La Patria (m)	Conservative	33,000

In general, the authorities are said to respect free speech and free press; most media are able to resist pressure from the government concerning sensitive issues, though censorship has been exercised occasionally in times of national emergency, and journalists exercise some self-censorship.

As of 1997, there were some 550,000 personal computers, and three Internet hosts per 1,000 population.

46ORGANIZATIONS

The National Federation of Coffee Growers, organized in 1927, is a semiofficial organization partly supported by tax revenue. The organization carries great weight as the representative of Colombia's leading industry, and its influence is felt in many spheres. Other trade associations include the National Association of Manufacturers, the People's Association of Small Industrialists of Colombia, and chambers of commerce in the larger cities. The Bank Association is an association of both national and foreign banks in Colombia. The Colombian Livestock Association, the National Federation of Cotton Growers, and the National Association of Sugar Growers serve their respective industries. Most farmers belong to the Agricultural Society of Colombia.

Learned societies include the Academy of History, the Colombian Academy of Language, the Colombian Academy of Exact, Physical, and Natural Sciences, the Academy of Medicine, the Colombian Academy of Jurisprudence, the Colombian Geographical Society, the Colombian Institute of Anthropology, and a number of regional bodies. The National Association of Colombian Writers and Artists includes most of the country's writers, painters, sculptors, and composers. Journalists have national and local organizations.

47TOURISM, TRAVEL, AND RECREATION

The tourist industry in Colombia developed greatly in the late 1970s but declined in the 1980s. Spurred by the government's economic liberalization program, earnings from tourism rose from $755 million in 1993 to $955 million in 1997. In that year the country had 52,340 hotel rooms with an occupancy rate of 42%. Colombia has mountains, jungles, modern and colonial cities, and resorts on both the Pacific and the Caribbean, all of which the Colombian Government Tourist Office (CORTURISMO) has aggressively promoted.

Soccer is the most popular sport, followed by basketball, baseball, boxing, and cockfighting; there are also facilities for golf, tennis, and horseback riding, and bullrings in the major cities.

Tourists from Western countries generally require no visa, but all visitors need a valid passport and a return ticket for entry. No vaccinations are required.

In 1999, the UN estimated the cost of staying in Cartagena at $115 per day, $108 in Bogotá, $115 in Cali, and $96 in Medellin.

48FAMOUS COLOMBIANS

Outstanding political and military figures in Colombian history include Francisco de Paula Santander (1792–1840), who served as a general in the war of independence and was the first president of independent Colombia, and José María Córdoba (1800?–1830), a brilliant young soldier of the war of independence, who was made a general at 22 by Simón Bolívar.

Colombia, famous for its literary figures, has produced three outstanding novelists widely read outside the country: Jorge Isaacs (1837–95), whose most famous work, *María*, is a novel in the Romantic tradition; José Eustacio Rivera (1880–1929), whose outstanding novel, *La Vorágine (The Vortex)*, written after World War I, is a drama of social rebellion; and Gabriel García Márquez (b.1928), a Nobel Prize winner in 1982, who is best known for *Cien años de soledad (One Hundred Years of*

Solitude). Colombia has had a number of noteworthy poets. The 19th-century Romantic school included Julio Arboleda (1814–92), José Eusebio Caro (1817–53), Gregorio Guitiérrez Gonzales (1826–72), and Rafael Pombo (1834–1912). Caro, who was influenced by the English poets, is generally rated as the most important Colombian Romantic. José Asunción Silva (1865–96) is regarded as the father of Latin American symbolism; his *Nocturnos* are among the finest poems in the Spanish language. Guillermo Valencia (1873–1945), the author of *Anarkos*, was a polished poet of the classical school, and León de Greiff (b.1895) is a well-known modern poet. Miguel Antonio Caro (1843–1909) and Rufino José Cuervo (1844–1911) were philologists and humanists of great erudition who influenced scholars and students in the 19th century. The Instituto Caro y Cuervo in Bogota is devoted to the study and publication of their works. Well-known literary critics include Baldomero Sanín-Cano (1861–1957) and Antonio Gómez-Restrepo (1868–1951).

Colombia's most notable painter was Gregorio Vázquez Arce y Ceballos (1638–1711), whose drawing and coloring have been compared to the work of the Spanish painter Murillo. Francisco José de Caldas (1770–1816) was a brilliant botanist who discovered a system for determining altitude by the variation in the boiling point of water and began the scientific literature of the country. Guillermo Uribe-Holguín (1880–1971) and José Rozo Contreras (b.1894) are noted composers. The works of the contemporary historian Germán Arciniegas (b.1900) are well known to the English-speaking world through translation.

49 DEPENDENCIES

The archipelago of San Andrés and Providencia, administered as an intendancy, is located 729 km (453 mi) from the Caribbean coast northwest of Cartagena and about 190 km (118 mi) off the Nicaraguan coast. Grouped roughly around the intersection of longitude 82°w and latitude 12°N, the archipelago consists of the islands of San Andrés and Providencia and 13 small keys. The population is mostly black. Both English and Spanish are spoken. The principal towns are San Andrés, San Luis, and Loma Alta on the island of San Andrés and Old Town on Providencia.

50 BIBLIOGRAPHY

Bruhns, Karen Olsen. *Archaeological Investigation in Central Colombia.* Oxford: Tempus Reparatum, 1995.

Bushnell, David. *The Making of Modern Colombia: a Nation in Spite of Itself.* Berkeley: Univ. of California Press, 1993.

Cohen, Alvin, and Frank R. Gunter. *The Colombian Economy: Issues of Trade and Development.* Boulder, Colo.: Westview Press, 1992.

Colombia in Pictures. Minneapolis: Lerner, 1987.

Davis, Robert H. *Colombia.* Oxford, England; Santa Barbara, Calif.: Clio Press, 1990.

———. *Historical Dictionary of Colombia,* 2d ed. Metuchen, N.J.: Scarecrow Press, 1993.

Giraldo, Javier. *Colombia: The Genocidal Democracy.* Monroe, Maine: Common Courage Press, 1996.

Harding, Colin. *Colombia: A Guide to the People, Politics, and Culture.* London: Latin American Bureau, 1995.

Hartlyn, Jonathan. *The Politics of Coalition Rule in Colombia.* New York: Cambridge University Press, 1988.

Kline, Harvey F. *Colombia: Democracy Under Assault.* Boulder, CO: Westview, 1995.

McFarlane, Anthony. *Colombia Before Independence: Economy, Society, and Politics under Bourbon Rule.* New York, NY, USA: Cambridge University Press, 1993.

Pearce, Jenny. *Colombia: the Drugs War.* New York: Gloucester Press, 1990.

Political Violence in Colombia: Myth and Reality. London: Amnesty International Publications, 1994.

Randall, Stephen J. *Colombia and the United States: Hegemony and Interdependence.* Athens: University of Georgia Press, 1992.

COSTA RICA

Republic of Costa Rica
República de Costa Rica

CAPITAL: San José.

FLAG: The national flag consists of five horizontal stripes of blue, white, red, white, and blue, the center stripe being wider than the others.

ANTHEM: *Himno Nacional,* beginning "Noble patria, tu hermosa bandera" ("Noble native land, your beautiful flag").

MONETARY UNIT: The colón (c) is a paper currency of 100 céntimos. There are coins of 1, 5, 10, 25, and 50 céntimos and of 1, 2, 5, 10, and 20 colones, and notes of 5, 10, 20, 50, 100, 500, and 1,000 colones. c1 = $0.00336 (or $1 = c297.25) as of 31 March 2000.

WEIGHTS AND MEASURES: The metric system is the legal standard, but local measures also are used.

HOLIDAYS: New Year's Day and Solemnity of Mary, 1 January; Day of St. Joseph (Costa Rica's patron saint), 19 March; Anniversary of the Battle of Rivas, 11 April; Labor Day, 1 May; Day of St. Peter and St. Paul, 29 June; Anniversary of the Annexation of Guanacaste, 25 July; Feast of Our Lady of the Angels, 2 August; Assumption (Mother's Day), 15 August; Independence Day, 15 September; Columbus Day, 12 October; Immaculate Conception, 8 December; Abolition of Armed Forces Day, 1 December; Christmas, 25 December. Movable religious holidays include Holy Thursday, Good Friday, Holy Saturday, and Corpus Christi.

TIME: 6 AM = noon GMT.

¹LOCATION, SIZE, AND EXTENT

The third-smallest country in Central America, Costa Rica has an area of 51,100 sq km (19,730 sq mi), including some small islands. Comparatively, the area occupied by Costa Rica is slightly smaller than the state of Virginia. Its length is 464 km (288 mi) N–S, and its width is 274 km (170 mi) E–W. Costa Rica is bordered on the N by Nicaragua, on the E by the Caribbean Sea, on the SE by Panama, and on the SW and W by the Pacific Ocean; the total boundary length is 1,929 km (1,199 mi). Costa Rica's capital city, San Jose, is located in the center of the country.

²TOPOGRAPHY

Costa Rica has three main topographic regions. The central highlands, extending from northwest to southeast, reach elevations of more than 3,660 m (12,000 ft) south of San José; the highest point in the country is Chirripó Grande (3,810 m/12,500 ft). Four volcanoes, two of them active, rise near the capital city; one of these volcanoes, Irazú (3,432 m/11,260 ft), erupted destructively during 1963–65. Nestled in the highlands is the Meseta Central, with an elevation of 900–1,200 m (3,000–4,000 ft), covering some 2,000 sq km (770 sq mi) of fairly level, fertile terrain. Half of the population, the centers of culture and government, four of the six main cities, and the bulk of the coffee industry are found on the plateau. The Atlantic coastal plain, on the Caribbean side of the highlands, comprises about 30% of Costa Rica's territory and is low, swampy, hot, excessively rainy, and heavily forested. The Pacific slope, some 40% of the country's area, resembles the Caribbean lowlands, but to the northwest is a dry area producing cattle and grain. Fifteen small rivers drain Costa Rica.

³CLIMATE

Costa Rica has only two seasons: the wet season, from May to November, and the dry season, from December to April. There are three climatic zones. The torrid zone, which includes the coastal and northern plains to an altitude of 900 m (3,000 ft), is characterized by heavy rains, almost continuous on the Atlantic watershed, and by a temperature range of 25–38°C (77–100°F). The temperate zone, including the central valleys and plateaus, has altitudes ranging from 900 to 1,800 m (3,000 to 6,000 ft), with regular rains from April through November and a temperature range of 15–25°C (59–77°F). The cold zone, comprising areas higher than 1,800 m (6,000 ft), has a temperature range of 5–15°C (41–59°F) and is less rainy but more windy than the temperate regions. The average annual rainfall for the country is more than 250 cm (100 in).

⁴FLORA AND FAUNA

Costa Rica supports varied flora and fauna. From the coast to an altitude of about 900 m (3,000 ft) are tropical forests and savannas; oaks and chaparrals are found between 2,070 and 3,050 m (6,800 and 10,000 ft); and subandean and subalpine flora characterizes the highest mountains. The dense tropical forests contain rich stands of ebony, balsa, mahogany, oak, laurel, campana, and cedar. Plant life is abundant, and the country has more than 1,000 species of orchids.

Most of the wild mammals common to South and Central America, such as jaguar, deer, puma, and varieties of monkeys, are found in Costa Rica. There are over 790 species of birds and 130 species of snakes and frogs; fish and insects are plentiful.

⁵ENVIRONMENT

Nearly all of Costa Rica was once covered by forests, but deforestation for agricultural purposes and cattle ranching has reduced virgin forest to only 25% of the total area. Between 1983 and 1993, the country lost an additional 5.2% of its forests and woodlands. Most of the wood is wasted by burning or rotting, and there is little incentive for conservation or reforestation. The result has been soil erosion and the loss of soil fertility. Another serious problem, according to the UN, has been contamination of the soil by fertilizers and pesticides used in growing important cash crops, such as bananas, sugarcane, and coffee. Costa Rica's use of pesticides is greater than that of all the other countries in Central America added together. Under the General Health Law of 1973, the Ministry of Health has broad powers to enforce pollution controls, and the Division of Environmental Health has attempted to set standards for air and water quality. However, trained personnel and equipment are lacking. Carbon dioxide emissions from industrial sources totaled 3.8 million metric tons in 1992, a per capita level of 1.21 metric tons. As of the mid-1990s, Costa Rica has 22.8 cu mi of water with 89% of the total used for farming activity. Of the nation's urban dwellers 88% have safe drinking water, as well as 99% of the rural population. The coastal waters are threatened by agricultural chemicals and lowlands often flood at the beginning of the rainy season.

Costa Rica's national park system is among the most extensive and well developed in Latin America. The system, covering nearly 4% of the total land area, includes 12 parks, six nature reserves, four recreation areas, the Guayabo National Monument archaeological site in the Turrialba region, and the International Peace Park established jointly by Costa Rica and Panama on their common border. Altogether, 12.7% of Costa Rica's total land area is protected. Although Costa Rica protects some 80 animal species by law, the IU recognizes only nine species as being endangered: the red-backed squirrel monkey, tundra peregrine falcon, spectacled caiman, American crocodile, four species of sea turtle (green sea, hawksbill, olive ridley, and leatherback), and golden toad. Of 203 mammal species in Costa Rica, 10 are threatened. Fourteen species of birds in a total of 796 are also threatened. Two types of reptiles in a total of 218 and 418 plant species in a total of 8,000 are considered endangered.

6 POPULATION

The population of Costa Rica in 2000 was estimated at 3,743,677. An estimated 4.9% of the population is 65 years of age or older. The projected population for the year 2005 is 4,084,000, assuming a crude birthrate of 21 per 1,000 population and a death rate of 4, resulting in a natural rate of change of 1.6% for the period 2000–2005. The population rate of change between 1995 and 2000 was 2.1%. The population density in 1998 was 69 per sq km (179 per sq mi).

It was estimated that 52% of the population lived in urban areas in 2000, up from 43% in 1980. The capital city, San Jose, had a 2000 metropolitan population of 1,063,000. Other large cities are Limón, 67,784; Alajuela, 158,276; Puntarenas, 92,360; Cartago, 108,958; and Heredia, 67,387.

7 MIGRATION

In 1995, 24,600 refugees were in Costa Rica. Of these, 4,200 were from El Salvador and 19,500 were from Nicaragua. Large numbers of Nicaraguans migrate seasonally to Costa Rica seeking employment opportunities. Illegal migration is a major national concern, with estimates of 300,000 to 500,000 in 1999, mostly from Nicaragua. In the aftermath of Hurricane Mitch, Costa Rica declared an amnesty, which expired on 31 July 1999. While intended primarily for aliens from Belize and Panama, UNHCR secured a provision that extended the amnesty to refugees. Under the amnesty, some 160,000 people applied for permanent residence. As of 1999, most new asylum-seekers have been coming from Cuba, Peru, and Colombia, with smaller numbers coming from outside of the Americas. The net migration rate in 1999 was 0.63 migrants per 1,000 population.

8 ETHNIC GROUPS

The population is fairly homogeneous, primarily of European (mainly Spanish) descent. Whites and mestizos (mixed white and Amerindian) account for 96% of the total population. The remainder are blacks (2%), Chinese (1%), and Amerindians (1%). The blacks for the most part are of Jamaican origin or descent, and some mulattoes live mainly in the Limón port area. Most of the Amerindians reside on isolated reservations.

9 LANGUAGES

Spanish is the national language, but English is also spoken around Puerto Limon and among the middle class. Descendants of the Jamaican blacks speak an English dialect.

10 RELIGIONS

Roman Catholicism, the predominant religion, is the official religion of the state, but the constitution guarantees religious freedom. Some 76% of the population in 1997 was Roman Catholic. San José is an archbishopric; there are four other bishops in the country. The remaining 14% of the populace belonged to smaller evangelical churches. Of these churches, mainstream Protestant denominations, including Methodist, Baptist, and Episcopalian, accounted for less than 1%. Likewise, the Jewish population made up less than 1%. Jehovah's Witnesses constituted 1%. Seventh-Day Adventists, the Unification Church, and Hare Krishnas had small numbers of adherents in the country. Quakers, Mennonites, and other pacifist religious groups also had small communities.

11 TRANSPORTATION

San José is linked to both coasts by railroad and by highway. The Inter-American Highway, 687 km (427 mi) long, connects Costa Rica with Nicaragua and Panama. Another major highway runs from San José to the Caribbean coast beyond Limón. As of 1999 there were 35,597 km (22,120 mi) of roads, of which 6,051 km (3,760 mi) were paved. Motor vehicle registrations in 1995 included 57,400 passenger automobiles and 73,240 commercial vehicles.

Of the three railroad lines, the Atlantic Railway between Limón and San José and the government-owned Pacific Electric Railway between San José and Puntarenas are interconnected; in 1974, the government nationalized the Northern Railway, taking ownership away from the British. A railway line operated by the Banana Company of Costa Rica (246 km/153 mi) is used mainly for company business. Some 27% of the total 950 km (590 mi) of railway was electrified as of 1999.

Principal ports are Puerto Limón on the Caribbean Sea and Puntarenas, Caldera, and Golfito on the Pacific. As of 1998, Costa Rica had no merchant vessels of more than 1,000 GRT. There are about 730 km (454 mi) of seasonally navigable waterways.

There were 156 airports in 1998, 28 of which had paved runways. Líneas Aéreas Costarricenses, S.A. (LACSA), the national airline, provides domestic and international services centered at Juan Santamaria International Airport near San José. In 1997, 992,000 passengers were carried on scheduled domestic and international flights.

12 HISTORY

There were about 25,000 Amerindians in the region when Columbus landed in 1502. He named the area Costa Rica ("rich coast"), probably because he saw gold ornaments on some of the Indians. Costa Rica was organized as a province by the Spanish in 1540 and was eventually placed under the provincial administration in Guatemala. Cartago, the colonial capital, was founded in 1563.

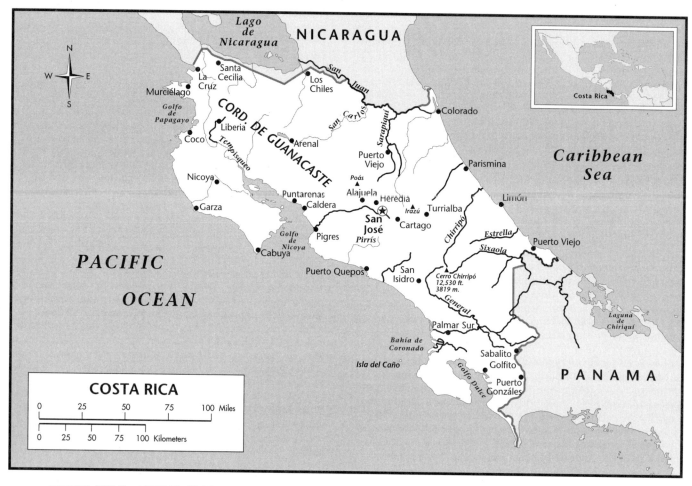

LOCATION: 8°2′26″ to 11°13′12″N; 82°33′48″ to 85°57′57″w. **BOUNDARY LENGTHS:** Nicaragua, 300 km (186 mi); Caribbean coastline, 212 km (132 mi); Panama, 363 km (226 mi); Pacific coastline, 1,016 km (631 mi). **TERRITORIAL SEA LIMIT:** 12 mi.

When independence came to Central America in 1821, Costa Rica had fewer than 70,000 inhabitants. In the following year, it was absorbed into the short-lived Mexican Empire proclaimed by Agustín de Iturbide. Following the collapse of Iturbide's rule, Costa Rica became a member of the United Provinces of Central America in 1823. At the same time, the provincial capital of Costa Rica became San José. The United Provinces fell apart in 1838, and in 1848, the Republic of Costa Rica was established. The new state was threatened by William Walker, a US military adventurer who invaded Central America in 1855, but his troops were repelled in 1857, and in 1860 Walker was captured and executed. In 1871, General Tomás Guardia, a dictator, introduced the constitution that, though frequently modified, remained Costa Rica's basic law until 1949.

In the late 19th and early 20th centuries, there was a series of boundary disputes with Panama and Nicaragua, in the course of which Costa Rica annexed Guanacaste Province from Nicaragua. In World Wars I and II, Costa Rica was a US ally, but not a military participant.

Meanwhile, the success of coffee cultivation, introduced in the early 1800s, had encouraged rapid population growth, progress in education, and the beginnings of modern economic development, through the construction of a coast-to-coast railroad from Limón on the Caribbean through San José to the Pacific. Banana cultivation was started in 1871, and the United Fruit Co. (now United Brands) made Costa Rica a major producer of bananas.

A period of relative political stability that began with the turn of the century ended after World War II, when President Teodoro Picado Michalski annulled the 1948 elections in order to impose Rafael Ángel Calderón Guardia as president rather than the legally elected Otilio Ulate Blanco. José Figueres Ferrer led a civilian uprising, installed his own junta for 18 months, and restored democratic government, turning over the presidency to Ulate. In 1949, a new constitution, based on the constitution of 1871, reinstated free elections and banned a standing army.

Figueres was elected president by an overwhelming majority in 1952 (with women voting for the first time), and under his leadership, Costa Rica was one of the most democratic and prosperous countries in Latin America. Figueres was strongly opposed to all dictatorships, and Costa Rica proceeded to sever diplomatic relations with several Latin American countries. Border skirmishes with Nicaragua in 1955 were resolved through OAS mediation.

In 1958, the candidate of the opposition National Unification Party, Mario Echandi Jiménez, was elected by a bare majority vote. He was unable to enact his program of minimizing the government's role in social and economic matters because the legislature was dominated by other parties. In 1962, Francisco J. Orlich Bolmarich, a candidate of Figueres's National Liberation Party (Partido de Liberación Nacional—PLN), won the elections and continued Figueres's progressive program. Costa Rica joined the Central American Common Market (CACM) in 1963 and has benefited from Central American economic integration, especially through increasing industrialization. Figueres served as president again from 1970 to 1974 and was succeeded by the PLN candidate, Daniel Oduber Quirós. A conservative, Rodrigo Carazo Odio, was elected president in 1978, and Luis Alberto Monge Álvarez of the PLN became president in 1982.

During the 1980s, Costa Ricans were confronted with a severe economic crisis and with increasing political violence in the region, including sporadic terrorist activities in San José. The Monge government introduced an austerity program to help economic recovery and also tried to avoid being drawn into the war in neighboring Nicaragua between the insurgents known as "contras" and the Sandinista government. Nevertheless, the government resisted pressure from the US to support the contras or to accept US aid toward the building of a military establishment.

In February 1986, the PLN won the presidential election, with Oscar Arias Sánchez defeating Rafael Ángel Calderón Fournier. An important factor in the PLN victory was the popularity of the incumbent, President Monge. In August 1987, a peace plan for Central America outlined by Arias was signed in Guatemala by Nicaragua, Guatemala, Costa Rica, El Salvador, and Honduras. Among the provisions were free elections in all countries, a guarantee of basic democratic freedoms in Nicaragua, a cease-fire by both Sandinistas and contras, an end to outside aid to the contras, amnesty for the contras, repatriation or resettlement of refugees from all countries, and an eventual reduction in the armed forces of all countries. Arias won the Nobel Prize for peace later in that year.

In 1990, amid continued economic troubles, Calderón Fournier was elected, and his Social Christian Unity Party (PUSC) won a paper-thin majority in the Legislative Assembly. Although he campaigned on a platform of liberalization and the reduction of Costa Rica's social welfare system, little change was accomplished. The economy nevertheless rebounded, with peace settlements easing some of Costa Rica's demographic problems.

On 6 February 1994, Costa Ricans returned the PLN to power, as José María Figueres Olsen, son of former president Figueres, was elected president of Costa Rica. In response to the nation's weakening economy, Figueres introduced an economic reform package in 1995 that focused on government-spending cuts and the privatization of state-owned enterprises. These measures, which represented a reversal of the traditional policies of Figueres's PLN ruling party, drew stiff opposition from labor leaders, who feared cutbacks in Costa Rica's large public sector, and touched off a month-long strike by the nation's teachers. Although the government responded by modifying some of its proposed plans, public support for Figueres plummeted as the nation's economy continued to slip, officially entering a recession in 1996. In December 1996 Figueres announced plans to raise taxes, privatize parts of the state-owned banking and telecommunications systems, and end the state insurance monopoly.

Elections were held in February of 1998 and Social Christian leader Miguel Angel Rodríguez won with 46.9% of the vote, narrowly defeating National Liberation Party candidate José Miguel Corrales who obtained 44%. Rodríguez's party also won 29 of out 49 seats in the unicameral Congress. The sweeping Social Christian Union Party victory was attributed to popular discontent with Figueres' National Liberation Government between 1994 and 1998.

13 GOVERNMENT

For the most part, Costa Rica has held to a tradition of orderly, democratic rule. The nation is a republic organized under the constitution of 1949, based on the constitution of 1871. A president, two vice presidents, and a unicameral congress (the Legislative Assembly) of 57 members (in 1999), apportioned by provinces, are all directly elected for four-year terms. The cabinet (composed of 17 members in 1997) is appointed by the president, who may also remove any of its members. For each three assembly deputies, one substitute deputy (suplente) is elected to obviate any subsequent need for by-elections. After each population census, the Supreme Electoral Tribunal proportions the number of deputies for each province. This body, consisting of three magistrates elected by the Supreme Court for six-year terms, also supervises all other aspects of the electoral process. Suffrage is universal and obligatory for all persons of 18 years or more.

The constitution bars all high government officials from running for the legislature or the presidency while already in office. The president, cabinet ministers, and all government employees are forbidden to interfere with or to participate in election campaigns or to hold party office. The constitution guarantees equality before the law, as well as freedom of speech, assembly, press, and organization. In addition, it guarantees foreigners the same rights as Costa Rican citizens. However, foreigners may not participate in political affairs, nor may members of the clergy.

14 POLITICAL PARTIES

The largest political grouping is the PLN (Partido de Liberación Nacional—National Liberation Party), a reformist party that has been the nation's leading party since its formation in 1948. The other major party is the more conservative Social Christian Unity Party (Partido Unidad Social Cristiana—PUSC), which held the presidency during 1978–82, 1990–1994, and is in power in the 1998–2002 period. The PUSC has ties to Christian Democratic parties in the Western Hemisphere and Europe. There are also several minor parties. In the 1994 elections, José María Figueres of the PLN was elected president with 49.7% of the vote, to 47.5% for PUSC candidate Miguel Angel Rodriguez. In 1998, Rodríguez became president with 46.9% of the vote, defeating PLN's José Miguel Corrales. The PSUC also won a majority in Congress with 29 seats, followed by the PLN with 22, the remaining six seats went to small and provincial parties.

15 LOCAL GOVERNMENT

Costa Rica is divided into seven provinces, which are further subdivided into 81 cantons and 429 districts. The governor of each province is appointed by the president and is responsible to the minister of government. There are no provincial assemblies. The chief city of each canton elects a council (municipalidad), which possesses legislative powers and cooperates with a presiding officer appointed by the national executive. A police agent appointed by the national government oversees each district.

16 JUDICIAL SYSTEM

The judiciary consists of justices of the peace, lower courts, labor courts, a court of cassation, two civil courts of appeal, two penal courts of appeal, and the Supreme Court, the highest court in the land. The Supreme Court is composed of 22 justices chosen for eight-year terms by the Legislative Assembly. Justices are automatically reelected for an additional eight-year term unless the Legislative Assembly votes to the contrary by a two-thirds majority. The Assembly also names 25 alternates from a list of 50 names submitted by the Supreme Court, and vacancies on the court are then filled by lot from the list of alternates. Relatives of incumbent justices are ineligible for election. The Supreme Court, by a two-thirds majority, can declare legislative and executive acts unconstitutional. Justices of lower courts are appointed by the Supreme Court, but justices of the peace are appointed by the minister of government acting for the president. Capital punishment has been abolished. The judiciary is independent of the legislative and executive branches and assures fair public trials. Public security forces generally observe procedural safeguards established by law and the 1949 constitution. The constitution prohibits arbitrary interference with privacy, family, home, or correspondence. Judges may approve use of wiretaps in limited cases, primarily to combat narcotics trafficking.

17ARMED FORCES

The 1949 constitution prohibits armed forces. A 4,400-member (in 2000) Civil Guard, a 2,000-member Rural Assistance Guard, and a 2,000-member Border Security Police, all operating under the Ministry of Public Security, perform security and police functions. An antiterrorist battalion serves as the presidential guard. Small coast guard and air units (11 planes and helicopters) patrol the coast for revenue purposes. The security budget was $72 million in 1999 with no significant arms imports.

18INTERNATIONAL COOPERATION

Costa Rica is a charter member of the UN, having joined on 2 November 1945, and participates in ECLAC and all the nonregional specialized agencies. It also belongs to CACM, G-77, IADB, and WTO. Costa Rica signed the Rio Pact and Law of the Sea.

Costa Rica is the home of the Inter-American Institute of Agricultural Science, a specialized agency under the OAS, founded in 1944 for the advancement of agriculture, with its main campus at Turrialba. There is also a Graduate School of Public Administration for Central America, organized by the UN and financed by Central American governments. San José is the seat of the Inter-American Human Rights Court.

In November 1974, Costa Rica participated in an unsuccessful move to repeal the OAS sanctions against Cuba. Costa Rica resumed trade relations with Cuba in January 1975, and in July it participated in the successful action on the resolution to lift OAS sanctions. In May 1981, however, Costa Rica severed diplomatic relations with Cuba to protest the latter's support of leftist subversion in Central America. In August 1987, a peace plan for Central America proposed by Costa Rica was signed by Costa Rica, El Salvador, Guatemala, Honduras, and Nicaragua.

19ECONOMY

The economy of Costa Rica, like that of all other countries in Central America, was originally based on the production of tropical agricultural commodities for export. There is some forestry in Costa Rica but very little mining, although steps have been taken to exploit bauxite, sulfur, and petroleum. Since about 1961 there has been a significant expansion of manufacturing activity, but most industrial plants remain small, concentrating on simple consumer goods to displace more expensive imports. Government efforts to promote diversification of agricultural production have resulted in notable expansion of cattle and dairy farming, second in value only to coffee among agricultural sectors. The opening of an Intel chip-making factory in 1998 spurred high growth rates and an influx of high technology companies, and increasing tourism revenues supported the growing economy.

Through the 1960s, prospects for economic expansion were promising, particularly in view of progress toward economic integration in Central America. However, in the 1970s, increases in import prices for raw materials and finished goods caused an inflationary spiral (100% in 1982), to which certain internal factors, such as credit expansion and wage increases, also contributed significantly. Chiefly because of a decline in coffee prices in 1978 and the doubling of oil import costs in 1979, the economic growth rate fell sharply from 8.9% in 1977 to –8.8% in 1982. Costa Rica normally spends the whole of its export revenues from coffee on importing petroleum.

Positive growth rates averaging 3.8% resumed in 1983 and continued through 1985, largely due to government-imposed austerity in return for IMF standby agreements. Unemployment declined from an official high of 9.1% in 1982 to 6.7% in 1986. The annual inflation rate dropped as well, from 90% to 11.8% in the same period. The foreign debt, rescheduled in 1983 and 1985, remained high at $3.67 billion at the end of 1985. The overall growth rate between 1978 and 1988 was 4.1%.

Although per capita income slipped in the early 1990s, Costa Ricans still enjoyed the highest per capita income in Central America. Following a structural adjustment period, real GDP grew by 7.3% in 1992. In 1993, however, economic growth slowed to 4.5%; continually declining until the rate hit –0.8% in 1996. This was the result of lingering negative expectations in the private sector, adverse effects of increasing international competition, and unfavorable climatological conditions. Tight fiscal and monetary policy contributed to the mild recession. Annual inflation stood at 12% in 1998, a significant improvement on the 22.5% recorded in 1995. Unemployment was down to only 5.6% in 1998, but underemployment remained a problem.

By 1997, the growth rate had recovered to a healthy 3.7%, and 6.2% in 1998, in part due to increased tourist and export trade, and new investment activity. The GDP growth rate for 1999 was estimated at over 7.5%, mainly due to the Intel corporation's activities in the country, but estimates placed the rest of the country's growth rate at 3%. There were fears that the growth rate would fall rapidly in 2000 when the Intel plant finished its growth period, but the company has stimulated other high technology investment projects.

20INCOME

The US Central Intelligence Agency (CIA) reports that in 1998 Costa Rica's gross domestic product (GDP) was estimated at $24 billion. The per capita GDP was estimated at $6,700. The annual growth rate of GDP was estimated at 5.5%. The average inflation rate in 1998 was 5.5%. The CIA defines GDP as the value of all final goods and services produced within a nation in a given year and computed on the basis of purchasing power parity (PPP) rather than value as measured on the basis of the rate of exchange. It was estimated that agriculture accounted for 15% of GDP, industry 24%, and services 61%.

Private consumption includes expenditures of individuals, households, and nongovernmental organizations. It was estimated that between 1990 and 1998 private consumption grew at an annual rate of 3.1%. The richest 10% of the population accounted for approximately 35% of household consumption and the poorest 10% approximately 1.3%.

21LABOR

In 1998, the labor force amounted to 1,376,500, or 41.2% of the total population. About half the total work force is concentrated in San José and Alajuela provinces. The structure of civilian employment in 1996 was as follows: industry and commerce, 23%; agriculture, 21.6%; government and services, 55.1%. Public sector employment grew from 159,794 in 1991 to 169,371 in 1992, mostly in central government. Unemployment was 5.6% in 1998.

A labor code governs labor-management relations. Minimum wages are set for two-year periods by a mixed labor-management commission. The Supreme Court ruled in 1998 that most public sector employees have the right to strike. Conciliation systems and labor courts function effectively.

Unionization was about 15% of the total work force in 1999, and included some 420 unions and 167,000 workers. Union membership is almost entirely public sector workers. In recent years, Solidarismo, a Costa Rican alternative to traditional trade unions, has grown popular and probably now outnumbers union membership, comprising 18–20% of the total work force. Solidarismo promotes cooperative labor/management relations by offering workers practical benefits (like credit unions), in exchange for which workers renounce their striking and collective bargaining rights. Solidaristas are established with mutual contributions from the employer and the workers, so that the fund serves as savings plan, benefits, and severance pay.

The minimum wage in July 1999 varied from $132 per month for domestic servants to $640 for certain professionals. The workweek is set at 48 hours during the day or 36 hours at night. Overtime pay is required for work in excess of that. Occupational health and safety standards are inconsistently enforced, especially outside of San José.

22AGRICULTURE

About 10.3% (530,000 hectares/1,310,000 acres) of the total land area is used for crop production, and 2,340,000 hectares (5,782,000 acres) in use as permanent pasture. Nearly half of all farms average less than 10 hectares (25 acres) in size. Over 326,000 persons, or about 23% of the economically active population, were engaged in farming in 1998.

Corn and sugar crops are usually sufficient to meet domestic needs, but beans and rice must be imported from time to time. Agriculture accounted for about 15% of the GDP in 1998. The principal cash crops are coffee, bananas, cocoa, and sugar. Coffee and bananas together accounted for 31% of exports in 1997, with values of $402.5 million and $503.2 million, respectively.

Over 85% of coffee properties belong to Costa Ricans. The banana industry has been producing more than one million tons of bananas annually since the 1970s. The principal marketer of Costa Rica's bananas is Standard Fruit Co. Corn, rice, potatoes, beans, sisal, cotton, citrus fruits, pita (used to make hats, baskets, and mats), yucca, vegetables, pineapples and other fruits, tobacco, abaca (hemp), and vegetable oils (especially African and coconut palms) are produced primarily for domestic consumption. Estimated crop production in 1998 (in tons) was sugar (raw), 300,000; bananas, 2,200,000; rice, 200,000; coffee, 138,000; corn, 33,000; dry beans, 14,000; and cocoa, 4,000. In 1998, the value of agricultural output was 28% higher than the annual average during 1989–91.

23ANIMAL HUSBANDRY

About 46% of Costa Rica's total land area was devoted to livestock raising in the early 1990s as the result of a major conversion of land to pasturage during the 1970s. In the past, Costa Rica had to import meat, but recent improvements in animal husbandry have made the country self-sufficient and provided a surplus for export. However, low productivity, low international prices, and high domestic interest rates affected profitability of the beef cattle sector in 1993 and 1994. National milk production in 1998 was an estimated 600 tons, enough to permit exports of excess production. Exports of beef were worth $27.3 million in 1997. In 1998, there were an estimated 1,527,000 head of cattle, 280,000 hogs, 115,000 horses, and 17,000,000 chickens.

24FISHING

Fish abound in Costa Rican waters, particularly in the Pacific Ocean, where 89% of the annual harvest is caught. Tuna, herring, and shrimp are the most valuable commercial fish; they are caught, processed, and shipped abroad by US firms. A small native fishing industry contributes to the domestic food supply and exports shark, mollusks, and live lobsters. Pearl fishing, once an important industry on the Pacific coast, has declined. In 1997, the total volume of fish landed was an estimated 33,613 tons.

25FORESTRY

Costa Rica's forestland has declined from about 75% of the total land area in 1940 to 24% in 1995. About 18% of the area still forested is lightly exploited, while 82% is virgin forest. Varieties of commercial woods include laurel, cedar, oak, quina, espavel, campana, cristobal, pochote, maca wood, cedro macho, cedar, and caoba (mahogany). In the Golfo Dulce rain forest of the southern Pacific coast, 135 families of trees embracing some 1,315 species in 661 genera have been identified. Forest products include rubber, chicle, ipecac, roots, medicinal plants, seeds, and other plant products. Although lumber exports have declined, overall timber output increased to 5,167,000 cu m of roundwood cut in 1997, of which about 68% was used for fuel. Roundwood and sawn wood exports in 1997 totaled $1,005,000 and $1,558,000, respectively.

26MINING

The production of minerals contributes less than 1% to the GDP. Mineral production in 1997 included cement, 850,000 tons; common clay, 412,000 tons; limestone, 1,500,000 tons; and marine salt, 37,000 tons. Diatomite, lime, pumice, silver, sandstone, and sand and gravel were also mined in 1997. Except for clays, fertilizers, and lime, most mineral commodities were produced for domestic use. Gold-mining activity plunged in the early 1980s but recovered in 1985 due to the Central Bank's establishment of a support price. The government encourages the mining industry by allowing duty-free importation of machinery and tools.

27ENERGY AND POWER

Costa Rica depends upon imports for an overwhelming proportion of its petroleum needs; this dependency has contributed greatly to the inflationary trends of recent years. Because of a scarcity of fuels, Costa Rica depended on hydro-electric energy for about 86% of its light and power in 1999. Installed capacity as of 1998 was 1,415,000 kW, more than double the 1973 total. Production of hydroelectricity totaled 5,742 million kWh in 1998. In February 1999, construction of the 55-MW geothermal station at Miravalle was completed. Preliminary work for the 90-MW Toro hydroelectric complex is now underway. Two other installations include the 157-MW Arenal and the 174-MW Corobisi plants.

Most of the nation's electricity is generated by the Instituto Costarricense de Electricidad (ICE), an autonomous government corporation, which owns and operates the central transmission network. In the early 1960s, the IBRD helped finance construction of a 30,000-kW hydroelectric plant on the Río Macho, about 50 km (30 mi) from San José, the installation of 9,000 kW of diesel generating capacity at Colima and Limón, and the extension of the central transmission network. These facilities provided a 40% increase in generating capacity in Costa Rica's central zone. In 1991, Costa Rica's hydroelectric potential was estimated at 25,450,000 kW.

28INDUSTRY

Costa Rica is one of the most industrialized countries in Central America, although industries are predominantly small-scale and primarily involve assembling or finishing imported semifinished components. Of the few larger-scale manufacturing enterprises, the majority are in chemical fertilizers, textiles, coffee and cocoa processing, chemicals, plastics, and computer chips. The Intel corporation opened a chip-manufacturing plant in 1998. Other manufacturing projects include aluminum processing, a petro-chemical plant at Moin, a tuna-processing plant at Golfito, and an oil refinery at Puerto Limon. Industry represented 24% of GDP in 1998, and had a growth rate of almost 8%.

29SCIENCE AND TECHNOLOGY

The principal scientific policymaking body in Costa Rica is the General Directorate of Geology, Mining, and Petroleum (founded in 1951). Several institutes specialize in tropical sciences, including the Organization for Tropical Studies in San Pedro, the Tropical Science Center in San José, and the Tropical Agronomy Center in Turrialba, as well as medicine, nuclear energy, technology, geology, agriculture, and meteorology. The University of Costa Rica in San José, founded in 1843, has faculties of agronomy, science, pharmacy, engineering, medicine, microbiology, and dentistry. The National University in Heredia, founded in 1973, has faculties of exact and natural science, earth and sea sciences, and health sciences. The Technological Institute of Costa Rica in Cartago, founded in 1971, has numerous attached research centers. In 1987–97, science and engineering students accounted for 20% of college and university enrollments. In the same period, there were 532 scientists per million people engaged in research and development.

30DOMESTIC TRADE

San Jose is the commercial center, and most importers, exporters, and manufacturers' agents operate there. San Jose importing and exporting firms handle more than 75% of the country's total trade. Most trading is carried on by small merchants in the public markets. Cooperative societies produce, buy, and sell food, clothing, machinery, and other items. There are no formal commercial credit companies as such, but installment buying at high interest rates is becoming widespread.

Shops are open on weekdays from 8:30 to 11:30 AM and from 2 to 6 PM, and on Saturday in the morning only. Business hours are from 8 AM to 12 PM, and 2 to 6 PM, Monday through Friday. Normal banking hours are 8 to 11 AM and 1:30 to 3 PM, Mondays through Friday, and 8 to 11 AM on Saturday. Advertising agencies in Costa Rica, all located in San Jose, offer advertising services through newspapers, radio, television, and direct mail.

31FOREIGN TRADE

Among Costa Rica's major exports are coffee, bananas, sugar, cocoa, and cattle and meat products—all commodities vulnerable to world market prices. The major markets for Costa Rican exports are the US, Benelux, Germany, Italy, Guatemala, El Salvador, the UK, and France.

Imports consist mainly of raw materials for industry and mining, followed by consumer goods and capital goods for industry, mining, and transportation. Major suppliers include US, Japan, Mexico, Venezuela, Guatemala, and Germany.

In 1996, falling terms of trade due to lower international prices for coffee, beef, and sugar, and the drop in banana production, caused traditional exports to perform less well than in previous years. However, the growth of non-traditional exports picked up part of the slack, despite some adverse effects from much-enhanced competitiveness of competing Mexican exports. Despite the economic recession, the value of imports of goods increased by 16% in 1996, well above the 8% for the previous year. A major factor was the substantial increase in international fuel prices and a relatively strong local currency. As a result, the trade deficit worsened from 1995 by almost 117% to $76 million.

The value of imports continued to rise into 1998, by after 1997 the value of imports as compared to exports was balanced. Exports after 1998 were expected to climb above imports because of the sale of computer chips.

Costa Rica relied mostly on agriculture to sustain its commodity export market in 1996. Fruits and nuts made up almost a third of exports (30%), and coffee was the second-largest export (15%). Other agricultural exports included non-

edible vegetable oils (4.6%), fruit (2.5%), edible vegetables (2.4%), meat (2.0%), and sugar (1.5%). A small percentage of medicinal and pharmaceutical products, and gold were exported from Costa Rica (2.1% and 1.7%).

In 1996 Costa Rica's imports were distributed among the following categories:

Consumer goods	14.6%
Food	10.0%
Fuels	9.4%
Industrial supplies	37.2%
Machinery	16.0%
Transportation	9.9%
Other	3.0%

Principal trading partners in 1998 (in millions of US dollars) were as follows:

COUNTRY	EXPORTS	IMPORTS	BALANCE
United States	2,674	3,138	-464
United Kingdom	220	52	168
Germany	215	131	84
Netherlands	204	48	156
Guatemala	173	145	28
Italy	138	88	50
El Salvador	113	115	-2
Canada	88	85	3
Mexico	83	326	-243
Japan	64	385	-321

32BALANCE OF PAYMENTS

Costa Rica has traditionally experienced balance-of-payments difficulties because of the vulnerability of its main sources of exchange earnings to fluctuations in world markets. The nation's payments problems in the late 1970s were aggravated by domestic inflationary policies and rising trade imbalances, despite increases in foreign capital receipts. The deficit on capital accounts declined in the mid-1980s due to increases in capital investment from foreign loans and credits and favorable renegotiation of the foreign debt. During the early 1990s, an unfavorable trade balance resulted from fluctuating coffee prices and high oil prices, but the balance of payments leveled out by 1999.

The US Central Intelligence Agency reports that in 1998 the purchasing power parity of Costa Rica's exports was $3.9 billion while imports totaled $4.5 billion resulting in a trade balance of -$600 million.

The International Monetary Fund (IMF) reports that in 1998 Costa Rica had exports of goods totaling $5,547 million and imports totaling $5,791 million. The services credit totaled $1,330 million and debit $1,183 million. The following table summarizes Costa Rica's balance of payments as reported by the IMF for 1998 in millions of US dollars.

Current Account		-460
Balance on goods	-245	
Balance on services	147	
Balance on income	-468	
Current transfers	105	
Capital Account		...
Financial Account		192
Direct investment abroad	-8	
Direct investment in Costa Rica	559	
Portfolio investment assets	...	
Portfolio investment liabilities	-90	
Other investment assets	-29	
Other investment liabilities	-240	
Net Errors and Omissions		-237
Reserves and Related Items		505

33BANKING AND SECURITIES

The Central Bank (Banco Central de Costa Rica), an autonomous governmental body established in 1950, issues currency, holds the nation's gold reserves, formulates general banking policy, and regulates commercial banks. Three commercial state banks, which dominate the banking system, are operated as autonomous government corporations: the Banco Nacional de Costa Rica, Banco de Costa Rica, and Banco Crédito Agrícola de Cartago. The banking monopoly was surrendered in 1995. There are also over 50 private banks and financial groups operating in Costa Rica. Total bank assets at the end of 1998 were approximately $6.3 billion, of which the three public banks held $3.5 billion. The top three private commercial banks had assets between $185 to $220 million.

Monetary variables reflect the cautious monetary policy followed by the Central Bank. However, a slight relaxation of stringency took place after 1995 in an effort to counter the recessionary trend in the economy. Year-end inflation fell from 22.6% in 1995, to 13.9% in 1996, and 11.7% in 1998. The Central Bank's basic rate, which had been rising since 1993, peaked at 33% in June 1995 before falling to a low of 21.9% in 1996. The lack of efficiency of the financial system has been the main culprit of persistently high nominal rates.

Costa Rican residents can own and deal in gold, own foreign securities and foreign currencies, maintain foreign bank balances, import and export national bank notes, and import goods from abroad, but they must repatriate export earnings. Costa Ricans traditionally put their savings into real property rather than securities, but on several occasions during the 1960s and 1970s, the government successfully floated bond issues within the country.

Stock sales and foreign currency transactions are handled by the Bolsa Nacional de Valores in San José. The Superintendency of Financial Markets (SUGEVAL) is in charge of the stock exchange.

34INSURANCE

Only the government's National Insurance Institute (Instituto Nacional de Seguros), founded in 1924, may write insurance in Costa Rica. It handles all types of insurance, the most important being life, fire, automobile, and workers' compensation. One of the more popular features of life insurance policies is that the holder may borrow up to the full face value of the policy after paying premiums for only two years. In 1996, the insurance monopoly was reformed to allow private agents to sell policies, while the INS continued to hold all underwriting rights. The INS does, however, reinsure its risks with private, foreign insurers.

35PUBLIC FINANCE

The central government budget is passed upon by the Legislative Assembly. Municipal budgets are of minor importance, and local government funds are mainly grants from the national government. The financial range of the public sector extends to a large number of publicly owned entities.

The US Central Intelligence Agency estimates that, in 1991, government revenues totaled approximately $1.1 billion and expenditures $1.34 billion, including capital expenditures of $110 million. External debt totaled $3.2 billion in 1996.

The following table shows an itemized breakdown of government revenues and expenditures. The percentages were calculated from data reported by the International Monetary Fund. The dollar amounts (millions) are based on the CIA estimates provided above.

REVENUE AND GRANTS	100%	1,100
Tax revenue	87.9%	967
Non-tax revenue	12.1%	133

EXPENDITURES	100%	1,340
General public services	4.9%	66
Public order and safety	6.6%	88
Education	16.8%	225
Health	22.1%	296
Social security	20.5%	274
Housing and community amenities	0.3%	4
Recreation, cultural, and religious affairs	0.9%	12
Economic affairs and services	8.1%	109
Interest payments	19.9%	267
Adjustments	-0.1%	-1

Costa Rica faces macro-economic problems because of serious fiscal deficits exacerbated by pressures to increase government spending. The deficit is compounded by a bloated public sector, unsustainable wage and pensions increases, mushrooming internal debt, and the lack of effective competition due to remaining public sector monopolies. The fiscal deficit grew from 1% of GDP in 1993 to about 8% in 1994, but was cut to 3.8% in 1995. In 1997, the figure was down to 2.2%, but rose to 4.3% in 1998.

36TAXATION

Indirect taxes, such as import duties, contribute about three-quarters of government revenues.

Both individuals and businesses residing in Costa Rica are subject to income tax only on income derived from sources within the country. The corporate tax rate is 30%; incentives are available for new industries and for engaging in the export of nontraditional products. Personal income taxes range from 10%–15% for employed persons and 10%–20% for self-employed persons. There is a 13% VAT, a property tax, a franchise tax, a real estate transfer tax, and a selective consumption tax levied on luxury items, with rates ranging from 10% to 75%.

37CUSTOMS AND DUTIES

Initially, the import tariff was primarily for revenue-raising purposes, but in 1954 it was increased to protect Costa Rican industry. In 1962, tariffs were raised so high that they virtually prohibited foreign competition in certain fields. Import duties usually include a specific duty on the gross weight in kilograms and ad valorem duties of varying percentages of the c.i.f. value of the imported goods.

Since Costa Rica's entry into GATT, tariffs have been lowered. As of 1996, customs duties range from 1% to 28%. However, food tariffs were between 14% and 19%. Import duties on raw materials, bulk grains, and oilseeds were reduced to 1% in 1996. Capital goods and most finished products have a tariff of 1% and 10% to 15% respectively. There is a 13% VAT. Excise tax ranges between 5% and 75%, applying to about half of all products imported. For example, arms and munitions are taxed at 75%; costume jewelry, fireworks, and whiskey at 50%; wine and beer at 40%.

Costa Rica has a bilateral free trade agreement with Mexico, and was planning future agreements in 1999 with Dominican Republic, Panama, Chile, and Trinidad and Tobago. Costa Rica is also a member of the Central American Common Market (CACM) with El Salvador, Guatemala, Honduras, and Nicaragua. The CACM has a CET of 5% to 20% for most products.

38FOREIGN INVESTMENT

Foreign investment, which is welcomed in Costa Rica, is concentrated in manufacturing (45%) and agriculture (25%, mainly banana and coffee interests). Other investments are placed in the railways, tobacco, communications, airlines, government bonds, and real estate. The US, Costa Rica's major foreign investor (78% in 1998), has interests chiefly in computer chip manufacturing, agriculture, petroleum refining and distribution, utilities, cement, and fertilizers. The continued high level of trade with the US has been conductive to private foreign investment, especially in export industries. Investment incentives include constitutional equal treatment guarantees and free trade zones. Foreign direct investment in Costa Rica in 1998 was $530 million, or 5% of GDP.

Liberalization of Costa Rica's trade and investment regimes, resolution of the internal debt problem, and passage of legislation expanding private sector investment in energy, telecommunications, roads, ports, and airports have boosted opportunities for foreign and local investors and increase Costa Rica's prosperity. In 1998, the Public Concessions Law defined the ways in which foreigners could invest in Costa Rica's public sector. Still, in the energy sector, foreign ownership may not exceed 65%, and a long list of activities are reserved for the state. The government had no privatization programs in 1999, but in 2000 investment was promoted by the government in the electricity and telecommunications parastatals.

Costa Rica has sought to widen its economic and diplomatic ties, including outside the region. Costa Rica has maintained connections with the US, EU, along with the other Central American states, through periodic ministerial consultations. The country is a founding member of the WTO and has actively participated in the follow-up to the Summit of the Americas to bring about the Free Trade Area of the Americas by the year 2005.

39ECONOMIC DEVELOPMENT

Despite trying to remain neutral, Costa Rica was affected adversely by regional political turmoil in the late 1970s and the 1980s. Instability in neighboring Nicaragua and Panama discouraged new investment and tourism in Costa Rica. Many displaced Nicaraguans and Salvadorans sought refuge in Costa Rica, further burdening the country's educational and health facilities. An oil shock and debt crisis also made economic recovery difficult.

Following an economic crisis in the early 1980s, Costa Rica made significant progress toward macroeconomic stability, structural adjustment, and growth through increasingly diversified exports. GDP growth averaged 4% from 1988 to 1998. Nontraditional exports and tourism have increased rapidly and account for almost 60% of foreign currency earnings; official unemployment declined to 5.6%, and inflation declined to 12% in 1998. Impressive growth after 1998 was recorded, in part due to the investments of the Intel Corporation.

40SOCIAL DEVELOPMENT

The national Social Security Fund administers social insurance and pension programs. Most of the population is covered by these social services, which have been extended throughout the country and include workers' compensation and family assistance benefits. In 1974, a family allowance program established pensions for persons, employed or not, that are not covered under the national social insurance system. The social security program is compulsory for all employees under 65 years of age. Pensions are generally set at 60% of average earnings during the last five years of coverage.

Women have equal rights under the law. The 1990 Law for the Promotion of the Social Equality of Women further obligates the government to promote political, economic, social, and cultural equality. Although women remain underrepresented in senior government positions, progress has been made. In 1998, 11 Legislative Assembly members were women. In 1997, women occupied 45% of all management, executive, and technical positions. In 1996, the government adopted a three-year plan to promote equal opportunities for women, based in large part on the platform enacted by the 1995 world conference on women in Beijing. The law stipulates that women receive equal pay for equal work, but men usually have higher earnings. The Women's Council and the Women's Delegation, two government agencies, act as advisors and advocates for women who have suffered abuse or harassment.

Prisons are overcrowded, but conditions are generally considered to be humane.

41HEALTH

Health standards have steadily improved in Costa Rica. The crude death rate per 1,000 population decreased from 22.1 in the early 1930s to four in 1995. The infant mortality rate, 166.7 per 1,000 live births in 1927, was 62.3 in 1968, and 13 in 1995. The decreases in mortality rates were attributed to improvements in sanitary and medical facilities under the national health program administered by the Ministry of Health. The fertility rate was 3.1 in 1994, a 1.3% yearly reduction since 1984. The use of contraceptives is one of the highest in Latin America and the Caribbean. In the mid-1990s, 75% of married females aged 15–49 were using a form of contraception. During 1998, life expectancy at birth was an average of 76.9 years.

Hospitals are located in the principal cities, and about 95% of the hospital beds are in urban areas. In 1993, Costa Rica had 1.4 physicians per 1,000 people.

Health services for the rural population are generally inadequate, and the refugee problem has severely taxed urban services. However, there are sanitary units and dispensaries to care for the health needs of the poor. During the 1980s, the greatest health problem was protein-calorie malnutrition, particularly among infants and children. Diseases of the circulatory system are the leading cause of death. As of 1995, 100% of the population had access to safe water, and in 1997, Costa Rica immunized children up to one year old as follows: diphtheria, pertussis, and tetanus (91%); measles (99%); polio (93%); and tuberculosis (91%).

There were 947 new cases of AIDS reported in 1996. The HIV seroprevalence in 1994 was 0.5 per 1,000 adults. The incidence of tuberculosis was 19 per 100,000 in 1996.

42HOUSING

Sources for housing mortgages include private funds, the Central Bank, the Social Security Fund, and the national banking system. The National Institute of Housing and Urban Affairs, established in 1954, administers a national low-cost housing program. At last estimate, approximately 30% of all housing had no electricity.

43EDUCATION

Costa Rica has one of the most literate populations in Latin America; by the year 2000, adult illiteracy dropped to 4.4% (males, 4.5%; females, 4.3%) (UNESCO). Approximately 22.8% of the government's expenditure went toward education in the latter half of the 1990s. Primary education lasts for six years followed by three years of secondary education. This again is followed by a two-year highly specialized course. Primary and secondary education is free, and primary-school attendance is compulsory. In 1998, enrollment in 3,711 primary schools totaled 529,637 students, with 19,235 teachers. Student-to-teacher ratio stood at 28 to one. Also in 1998, 202,415 students were taught by 10,943 teachers in secondary schools.

The country has 39 universities, including an open university. The University of Costa Rica (founded in 1843) is supported by the government and enrolls about 28,000 students. The Open University (1977), in San José, operates 28 regional centers for all students who apply. There are also the Autonomous University of Central America (1976), in San José, and the National Autonomous University of Heredia (1973), among others.

44LIBRARIES AND MUSEUMS

The National Library at San José, founded in 1888, is a reference library containing about 270,000 volumes in 2000. Other important libraries in San José are the National Archives, with 8,500 volumes, and the library of the University of Costa Rica, which contains about 403,000 volumes. The Inter-American Institute of Agricultural Sciences, in Turrialba, has a library of over 90,000 volumes. The Legislative Assembly maintains a library of 35,000 volumes and the Indigenous Museum (1890) holds 40,000 volumes.

The National Museum of Costa Rica in San José, founded in 1887, is a general museum with collections of pre-Columbian, colonial, republican, and religious art, a herbarium, and bird displays. The Museum of Costa Rican Art was founded at San José in 1977. There are several other art museums in the capital as well, including the Indigenous Museum, the Museum of Gold, and the Museum of Jade.

45MEDIA

Costa Rican telephone, telegraph, and radio systems are owned and operated by both governmental and private firms. In 1995 there were over 346,100 telephones in use. There are 71 AM radio stations and six television stations in Costa Rica. In 1997 there were 271 radios, and 403 television sets, and 19 mobile phones per 1,000 population.

The major daily newspapers, all published in San José, (with 1999 circulations) include *La Nación,* an independent morning paper (113,200); *La Prensa Libre,* an independent evening paper (56,000 each edition); *La República,* an independent morning journal (67,500); and *Diario Extra,* also an independent morning paper (100,000). There are several periodicals and magazines available, the most popular of which is the general interest weekly *Esta Semana,* with a 1995 circulation of 27,000.

Freedom of speech and the press is guaranteed by the constitution and observed in practice. Print and electronic media are largely privately owned. As of 1998, there were eight Internet hosts per 1,000 population.

46ORGANIZATIONS

The government stimulates the formation of cooperatives, but the movement is limited. Consumer cooperatives purchase, sell, and distribute goods among the membership. The cooperative credit societies procure loans for agriculture, stock raising, and industrial development, and cooperative housing associations provide low-cost housing facilities.

There are chambers of commerce and of industry in San José, in addition to some 50 employers' and industrial organizations. Church-sponsored groups have a sizable membership. An unusual organization, combining features found in credit unions, company unions, and building and loan societies, is the Movimiento Solidarista, which advocates harmony between employers and workers.

47TOURISM, TRAVEL, AND RECREATION

Visitors to Costa Rica must have passports. US citizens may travel on a tourist card available at consulates and transportation companies. In 1998, Costa Rica received 942,778 tourists, of whom 347,442 were from the US. Revenues from tourism reached $719 million in 1997. There were 13,437 hotel rooms with a 47% occupancy rate that year.

Popular tourist sights in San José are the National Museum, National Theater, and the Central Bank's gold exhibition. Other attractions include the Irazú and Poás volcanoes, brief jungle excursions, and the Pacific beaches. Popular recreations are bird-watching, mountain climbing, swimming, water skiing, and deep-sea fishing. Football (soccer) is the national sport, and there are matches every Sunday morning in San José from May through October. Horseback riding is widely available.

In 1999 the UN estimated the daily cost of staying in San José at $139. Costs elsewhere averaged $83.

48FAMOUS COSTA RICANS

José María Castro was Costa Rica's first president (1847–49, 1866–68). Juan Rafael Mora Porras, the second president of the republic (1849–59), successfully defended the country against the invasion of US military adventurer William Walker. General Tomás Guardia (1832–82) led a revolt against the government in 1870, became a dictator, and in 1871 introduced the constitution that remained in force until 1949. José Figueres Ferrer (1906–90), president during 1953–58 and 1970–74, is regarded as the father of the present constitution. Oscar Arias Sánchez (b.1940), president since 1986, won the Nobel Prize for peace in 1987 for his plan to bring peace to Central America. Ricardo Fernández Guardia (1867–1950) is regarded as Costa Rica's greatest historian. Joaquín García Monge (1881–1958) founded the literary review *Repertorio Americano.*

49DEPENDENCIES

Cocos Island—26 sq km (10 sq mi), about 480 km (300 mi) off the Pacific coast, at 5°32′N and 87°2′w—is under Costa Rican sovereignty. It is mainly jungle, with a maximum elevation of 850 m (2,788 ft). There is no permanent population, but the island is popular with transient treasure hunters. Cocos Island has two harbors and is of strategic importance because of its position along the western approach to the Panama Canal.

50BIBLIOGRAPHY

American University. *Area Handbook for Costa Rica.* Washington, D.C.: Government Printing Office, 1970.

Ameringer, Charles. *Don Pepe: A Political Biography of José Figueres of Costa Rica.* Albuquerque: University of New Mexico Press, 1978.

Barry, Tom. *Costa Rica: a Country Guide.* Albuquerque, NM: Inter-Hemisphere Education Resource Center, 1990.

Bell, John P. *Crisis in Costa Rica: The 1948 Revolution.* Austin: University of Texas Press, 1971.

Bension, Alberto et al. *Costa Rica and Uruguay Studies.* New York: Oxford University Press, 1993.

Costa Rica and Uruguay. New York: Oxford University Press, 1993.

Costa Rica in Pictures. Minneapolis: Lerner, 1987.

Creedman, Theodore S. *Historical Dictionary of Costa Rica, 2nd ed.* Metuchen, N.J.: Scarecrow Press, 1991.

Denton, Charles F. *Patterns of Costa Rican Politics.* Boston: Allyn & Bacon, 1971.

Dorn, Marilyn April. *The Administrative Partitioning of Costa Rica: Politics and Planners in the 1970s.* Chicago: University of Chicago, 1989.

Fernández Guardia, Ricardo. *Costa Rica en el siglo XIX.* San José: Gutenberg, 1929.

Gudmundson, Lowell. *Costa Rica Before Coffee: Society and Economy on the Eve of the Export Boom.* Baton Rouge: Louisiana State University Press, 1986.

Herrick, Bruce, and Barclay Hudson. *Urban Poverty and Economic Development: A Case Study of Costa Rica.* New York: St. Martin's, 1980.

Honey, Martha. *Hostile Acts: U.S. Policy in Costa Rica in the 1980s.* Gainesville: University Press of Florida, 1994.

Jones, Chester L. *Costa Rica and Civilization in the Caribbean.* New York: Gordon, 1976 (orig. 1935).

Longley, Kyle. *The Sparrow and the Hawk: Costa Rica and the United States During the Rise of José Figueres.* Tuscaloosa: University of Alabama Press, 1997.

Rolbein, Seth. *Noble Costa Rica.* New York: St. Martin's Press, 1988.

Rovinski, Samuel. *Cultural Policy in Costa Rica.* New York: UNESCO, 1978.

Seligson, Mitchell A. *Peasants of Costa Rica and the Development of Agrarian Capitalism.* Madison: University of Wisconsin Press, 1980.

Stansifer, Charles L. *Costa Rica.* Oxford, England; Santa Barbara, Calif.: Clio Press, 1991.

Williams, Philip J. *The Catholic Church and Politics in Nicaragua and Costa Rica.* Pittsburgh, Pa: University of Pittsburgh Press, 1989.

Winson, Anthony. *Coffee and Democracy in Modern Costa Rica.* New York: St. Martin's Press, 1989.

CUBA

Republic of Cuba
República de Cuba

CAPITAL: Havana (La Habana).

FLAG: The flag consists of five alternating blue and white horizontal stripes penetrated from the hoist side by a red triangle containing a white five-pointed star.

ANTHEM: *Himno de Bayamo (Hymn of Bayamo),* beginning "Al combate corred bayameses" ("March to the battle, people of Bayamo").

MONETARY UNIT: The Cuban peso (c$) of 100 centavos is a paper currency with one exchange rate. There are coins of 1, 2, 3, 5, 20, 40, and 100 centavos and notes of 1, 3, 5, 10, 20, 50, and 100 pesos. c$1 = us$1 (us$1 = c$1).

WEIGHTS AND MEASURES: The metric system is the legal standard, but older Spanish units and the imperial system are still employed. The standard unit of land measure is the caballería (13.4 hectares/133.1 acres).

HOLIDAYS: Day of the Revolution, Liberation Day, 1 January; Labor Day, 1 May; Anniversary of the Revolution, 25–27 July; Proclamation of Yara, 10 October. Celebration of religious holidays falling during the workweek was prohibited by a 1972 law.

TIME: 7 AM = noon GMT.

¹LOCATION, SIZE, AND EXTENT

The Republic of Cuba consists of one large island and several small ones situated on the northern rim of the Caribbean Sea, about 160 km (100 mi) south of Florida. With an area of 110,860 sq km (42,803 sq mi), it extends 1,223 km (760 mi) E–W and averages about 89 km (55 mi) N–S. Cuba is the largest country in the Caribbean, accounting for more than one-half of West Indian land area. Comparatively, the area occupied by Cuba is slightly smaller than the state of Pennsylvania. It is separated from Florida by the Straits of Florida, from the Bahamas and Jamaica by various channels, from Haiti by the Windward Passage, and from Mexico by the Yucatán Channel and the Gulf of Mexico. Cuba's total coastline is 3,764 km (2,339 mi). The largest offshore island, the Isle of Youth (Isla de la Juventud), formerly known as the Isle of Pines (Isla de Pinos), lies southwest of the main island and has an area of 2,200 sq km (849 sq mi); the other islands have a combined area of 3,715 sq km (1,434 sq mi).

Cuba's capital city, Havana, is located on its northeastern coast.

²TOPOGRAPHY

Cuba's spectacular natural beauty has earned it the name Pearl of the Antilles. The coastline is marked by bays, reefs, keys, and islets. Along the southern coast are long stretches of lowlands and swamps, including the great Zapata Swamp (Ciénaga de Zapata). Slightly more than half the island consists of flat or rolling terrain, and the remainder is hilly or mountainous, with mountains covering about a quarter of its total area. In general, eastern Cuba is dominated by the Sierra Maestra, culminating in Pico Real del Turquino (1,974 m/6,476 ft); around Camagüey are rolling plains and low mountains; central Cuba contains the Trinidad (Escambray) Mountains in addition to flat or rolling land; and the west is dominated by the Sierra de los Órganos. The largest river, the Cauto, flows westward for 370 km (230 mi) north of the Sierra Maestra but is little used for commercial navigation purposes.

³CLIMATE

Except in the mountains, the climate of Cuba is semitropical or temperate. The average minimum temperature is 21°C (70°F), the average maximum 27°C (81°F). The mean temperature at Havana is about 25°C (77°F). The trade winds and sea breezes make coastal areas more habitable than temperature alone would indicate. Cuba has a rainy season from November to April. The mountain areas have an average precipitation of more than 180 cm (70 in); most of the lowland area has from 90 to 140 cm (35–55 in) annually; and the area around Guantánamo Bay has less than 65 cm (26 in). Droughts are common. Cuba's eastern coast is often hit by hurricanes from August to October, resulting in great economic loss.

⁴FLORA AND FAUNA

Cuba has a flora of striking richness, with the total number of native flowering species estimated at nearly 8,000. The mountainous areas are covered by tropical forest, but Cuba is essentially a palm-studded grassland. The royal palm, reaching heights of 15 to 23 m (50–75 ft), is the national tree. Pines like those in the southeastern US grow on the slopes of the Sierra de los Órganos and on the Isla de Juventud (Isle of Youth). The lower coastal areas, especially in the south, have mangrove swamps. There is a small area around Guantánamo Bay where desert plants grow.

Only small animals inhabit Cuba. These include tropical bats, rodents, birds, and many species of reptiles and insects.

⁵ENVIRONMENT

The Cuban government has formed several agencies to protect the environment. Among them are the National Parks Service, the National Commission of Environmental Protection and Rational Use of Natural Resources (1977), the National Environmental Education Program, the Academy of Sciences of Cuba, and the National Commission for the Protection of the Environment and for Conservation of Natural Resources. As of 1994, Cuba's most pressing environmental problems were deforestation and the preservation of its wildlife. The government has sponsored a successful reforestation program aimed at replacing forests that had gradually decreased to a total of 17% of the land area by the mid-1990s. Another major environmental problem is the pollution of Havana Bay. In 1994, Cuba had the seventh-largest mangrove area in the world. Altogether, 89% of the country's water is used for agricultural purposes. Eighty-eight percent of Cuba's city dwellers and 99% of its rural people have pure water. In 1992 Cuba emitted 28.6 million metric tons of industrial carbon dioxide, a per capita level of 2.64 metric tons. Endangered or extinct species in Cuba include the Cuban solenodon, four species of hutia (dwarf, Cabera's, large-eared, and little earth), two species of crocodile (American and Cuban), the Cuban tree boa, and the ivory-billed woodpecker. In 1994, 11 mammal species in a total of 39 were considered threatened. Fifteen bird species in a total of 286 were also threatened. Four types of reptiles of 100 were endangered, along with 860 plant species out of a total of 8,000.

[6]POPULATION

The population of Cuba in 2000 was estimated at 11,139,412. An estimated 9.1% of the population is 65 years of age or older. The projected population for the year 2005 is 11,314,000, assuming a crude birthrate of 12 per 1,000 population and a death rate of 8, resulting in a natural rate of change of 0.01% for the period 2000–2005. The population rate of change between 1995 and 2000 was 0.4%. The estimated population density in 1996 was 99 per sq km (256 per sq mi).

It was estimated that 78% of the population lived in urban areas in 2000. The capital city, Havana, had a 2000 metropolitan population of 2,302,000. Other important cities are Santiago de Cuba (405,354), Camagüey (283,008), Holguín (228,053), Santa Clara (194,354), and Guantánamo (200,381).

[7]MIGRATION

Before independence, there was a large migration from Spain; the 1899 census reported 129,000 Spanish-born persons living in Cuba. The 1953 census reported about 150,000 persons of foreign birth, of whom 74,000 were Spaniards. From 1959 through 1978, Cuba's net loss from migration, according to official estimates, was 582,742; US figures indicate that during the same period a total of 669,151 Cubans arrived in the US.

During the 1960s, Cuban emigrants were predominantly of the higher and middle classes, but in the 1970s urban blue-collar workers and other less educated and less wealthy Cubans came to predominate. The flow of emigrants declined in the late 1970s, but beginning in April 1980, Cubans were allowed to depart from Mariel harbor; by the end of September, when the harbor was closed, some 125,000 Cubans in small boats (the "freedom flotilla") had landed in the US. Of that number, 2,746 were classified as "excludable aliens" and were being held in prisons or mental institutions. According to an agreement of December 1984, Cuba agreed to accept the 2,746 back; repatriation began in February 1985, but in May, Cuba suspended the agreement. Some Cubans have combined to make it to the US in small boats and rafts. A total of 3,656 did so in 1993 and 3,864 in the first half of 1994. By the mid-1980s, well over 500,000 Cuban exiles were living in the Miami area. In 1990 there were 751,000 Cuban-born persons in the US. Large numbers have also settled in Puerto Rico, Spain, and Mexico.

Since 1979, the Cuban government has been providing education to a number of students from developing countries. Due to events making return to their homelands difficult, many have become refugees sur place. Sporadically, Cuba receives groups of Haitians who generally return to their homeland voluntarily. Between 1991 and 1994, UNHCR worked with the government to protect and assist more than 1,500 Haitians during a temporary stay in Cuba. In 1995, Cuba was harboring 1,500 refugees from the Western Sahara; in 1999, the government was still working with UNHCR to return them to their country of first asylum. UNHCR was assisting a total of 1,014 refugees in Cuba in 1999, the majority of whom were students recognized as refugees. Cuba has recently seen an increase in asylum applications from non-Spanish-speaking countries. The net migration rate for Cuba in 1999 was -1.52 migrants per 1,000 population.

[8]ETHNIC GROUPS

According to the 1998 estimates, mulattos constitute 51% of the total Cuban population. Whites (primarily of Spanish descent) make up about 37% of the total; blacks account for 11%; and Chinese for 1%. Virtually the entire population is native-born Cuban.

[9]LANGUAGES

Spanish is the national language of Cuba.

[10]RELIGIONS

The Roman Catholic Church has never been as influential in Cuba as in other Latin American countries. In the 1950s, approximately 85% of all Cubans were nominally Roman Catholic, but the Church itself conceded that only about 10% were active members.

From the early-1980s into the 1990s, Roman Catholics represented about 40% of the population. Other religions in Cuba include Santería (a group of cults that meld African beliefs with Christian dogma), Jehovah's Witnesses, several Protestant churches, including Baptist, Methodist, and Presbyterian, and a very small Jewish population. Since the Castro revolution, the number of people who attend churches has diminished, and it is estimated that half of the population has no religion. A resurgence of religious practice beginning in 1992 has raised church-state relations to a new level of interest.

[11]TRANSPORTATION

In 1999, Cuba had about 60,858 km (37,817 mi) of roads, of which 29,820 km (18,530 mi) were paved, including 638 km (396 mi) of expressways. The first-class Central Highway extends for 1,223 km (760 mi) from Pinar del Río to Guantánamo, connecting all major cities. An extensive truck and bus network transports passengers and freight.

Nationalized railways connect the east and west extremities of the island by 4,807 km (4,808 mi) of standard-gauge track. In addition, large sugar estates have 9,630 km (5,984 mi) of lines of various gauges.

Cuba first began to develop a merchant marine under the revolutionary government. The USSR had supplied oceangoing vessels and fishing boats and, in the mid-1960s, built a huge fishing port in Havana Bay to service Cuban and Soviet vessels. By 1998, the Cuban merchant fleet had 18 vessels of at least 1,000 GRT, totaling 89,091 GRT. Cuba's major ports—Havana, Cienfuegos, Mariel, Santiago de Cuba, Nuevitas, and Matanzas—are serviced mainly by ships of the former Soviet republics, with ships from Spain, the UK, and Eastern Europe making up the bulk of the remainder.

In 1998 there were an estimated 170 airports, 77 of which had paved runways. The principal airport is Jose Marti at Havana. There are daily flights between Havana and the major Cuban cities, and weekly flights to Spain, Mexico, Moscow, Prague, and Jamaica. Cubana Airlines is the national air carrier. The number of air passengers increased from 140,000 in 1960 to 1,117,000 in 1997. Between 1975 and 1980, airports at Havana and Camagüey were renovated, and new airports were built at Bayamo, Manzanillo, and Las Tunas.

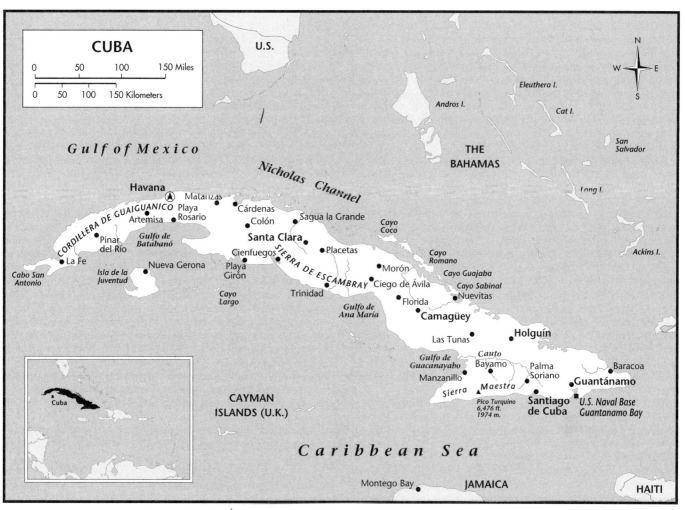

CUBA

Gulf of Mexico

Nicholas Channel

THE BAHAMAS

Eleuthera I.

Andros I.

Cat I.

San Salvador

Long I.

Ackins I.

U.S.

Havana
Matanzas
Cárdenas
Playa Rosario
Artemisa
Colón
Sagua la Grande
CORDILLERA DE GUAIGUANICO
Santa Clara
Cayo Coco
Pinar del Río
Gulfo de Batabanó
Cienfuegos
Placetas
Cayo Romano
La Fe
Nueva Gerona
Playa Girón
SIERRA DE ESCAMBRAY
Morón
Cayo Guajaba
Cabo San Antonio
Isla de la Juventud
Trinidad
Ciego de Ávila
Cayo Sabinal
Cayo Largo
Florida
Nuevitas
Gulfo de Ana María
Camagüey
Las Tunas
Holguín
Gulfo de Guacanayabo
Cauto
Bayamo
Palma Soriano
Baracoa
Manzanillo
Sierra Maestra
Guantánamo
Pico Turquino 6,476 ft. 1974 m.
Santiago de Cuba
U.S. Naval Base Guantanamo Bay

CAYMAN ISLANDS (U.K.)

Caribbean Sea

Cuba

Montego Bay
JAMAICA
HAITI

LOCATION: 74°8′ to 84°57′w; 19°49′ to 23°17′N. **TERRITORIAL SEA LIMIT:** 12 mi.

12 HISTORY

Cuba was originally inhabited by about 50,000 Ciboney and Taíno, agricultural Amerindians related to the Arawak peoples, who died from disease and maltreatment soon after the Spanish arrived. Christopher Columbus made the European discovery of Cuba in 1492 on his first voyage to the Americas. The African slave trade began about 1523 as the Amerindian population declined, and grew thereafter, especially with the development of coffee and sugar on the island. During the early colonial years, Cuba served primarily as an embarkation point for such explorers as Hernán Cortés and Hernando de Soto. As treasure began to flow out of Mexico, Havana became a last port of call and a target for French and English pirates. In 1762, the English captured Havana, holding Cuba for almost a year. It was ceded to Spain in exchange for Florida territory in the Treaty of Paris (1763). Spanish rule was harsh, and intermittent rebellions over the next century all ended in failure.

Cuba's first important independence movement came in 1868, when Carlos Manuel de Céspedes, a wealthy planter, freed his slaves and called for a revolution against Spain. For the next 10 years, guerrillas (mambises), mainly in eastern Cuba, fought in vain against the Spanish colonial government and army. Although eventually subdued, Céspedes is nevertheless viewed as the father of Cuban independence. A second hero was added in the 1890s when poet and journalist José Martí founded the Cuban Revolu-

tionary Party during exile in the US. The call to arms (Grito de Baire) on 24 February 1895 initiated a new war. After landing with a group of recruits gathered throughout the region, Martí was killed at Dos Ríos, in eastern Cuba. The Spanish had the insurrection under control within a year.

In the end, the Cubans had to rely on the US to defeat the Spanish. Anti-Spanish sentiment, fueled by US newspapers, erupted after the battleship Maine mysteriously blew up in Havana harbor on 15 February 1898. The US declared war on Spain on 25 April, and in a few months, the Spanish-American War was over. The Treaty of Paris (10 December 1898), established Cuban independence. During the interim period 1899–1902, the US army occupied Cuba. It instituted a program that brought about the eradication of yellow fever, but it was more fundamentally concerned with the establishment of US political and commercial dominance over the island.

On 21 February 1901, a constitution was adopted, and Cuba was nominally a free nation. But the US insisted that Cuba include in its constitution the Platt Amendment, which gave the US the right to intervene in Cuban affairs and maintain a naval base at Guantánamo.

For the next 30 years, Cuba lived through a succession of governments, constitutional and otherwise, all under the watchful eye of the US. American companies owned or controlled about half of Cuba's cultivated land, its utilities and mines, and other natural resources. The US Marines intervened in 1906–9, in 1912, and again in 1920. The period culminated in the brutal dictatorship of Gerardo Machado y Morales (1925–33).

Cuba entered another unstable phase in 1933. A nationalist uprising chased Machado from office. After the US attempted to install a regime, a "sergeants' revolt" headed by 32-year-old Fulgencio Batista y Zaldívar assumed power and named Ramón Grau San Martín provisional president. Grau, a physician and university professor noted for his nationalist zeal, was never recognized by the US, and his regime lasted only four months. From 1934 until 1940, Batista ruled through a series of puppet presidents. During these years, Batista made two major contributions to Cuba. In 1934, President Franklin D. Roosevelt allowed Cuba to abrogate the Platt Amendment, although the US retained its naval base at Guantánamo Bay. Batista also allowed the drafting of a new constitution, passed in 1940 under which he became president. In 1944, Batista permitted Grau San Martín, now his political enemy, to take office. The eight years of rule by Grau and his ally, Carlos Prío Socarrás, were ineffective and corrupt, and in 1952, a reform party was expected to win election.

That election was subverted, however, on 10 March 1952, when Batista seized power in a military coup. During the seven years of Batista's second administration, he used increasingly savage suppressive measures to keep himself in office. Under the Batista regime, the US dominated the economy, social services suffered, poverty and illiteracy were widespread, and the bureaucracy was flagrantly corrupt. It was at this point that Fidel Castro came on the scene.

Castro's insurrection began inauspiciously on 26 July 1953 with an abortive raid on the Moncada Army Barracks in Santiago. Captured, jailed, and then exiled, Castro collected supporters in Mexico, and in 1956 landed in Cuba. Routed by Batista's troops, Castro escaped into the Sierra Maestra with a mere dozen supporters. The force never grew to more than a few thousand, but clever use of guerrilla tactics evened the score with Batista's poorly trained army. Moreover, there was almost no popular support for Batista, and in 1958 the US ended its military aid to the falling government. On 1 January 1959, the Batista regime collapsed, and Batista and many of his supporters fled the country. Castro's 26th of July Movement took control of the government, and began to rule by decree. The revolutionary government confiscated property that had been dishonestly acquired, instituted large-scale land reforms, and sought to solve Cuba's desperate financial and economic problems by means of a bold revolutionary program.

After June 1960, Cuban-US relations deteriorated at an accelerated pace. Largely in retaliation for the nationalization of about $2 billion in US-owned property in Cuba, the US severed diplomatic relations with the Castro government. Tensions increased when the revolutionary regime nationalized US oil refinery companies for refusing to process Soviet crude oil. The US response was to eliminate Cuba's sugar quota. In April 1961, a group of 1,500 Cuban exiles—financed, trained, organized, and equipped by the CIA—invaded Cuba at the Bay of Pigs on the southern coast. The brigade was defeated within 72 hours, and the 1,200 surviving invaders were captured. They were eventually released after US officials and private sources arranged for a ransom of $50 million in food and medical supplies.

Meanwhile, Communist influence was growing in the Cuban government. Castro declared Cuba to be a Socialist country in late 1960, and the following year declared himself to be a Marxist-Leninist and a part of the Socialist world. All major means of production, distribution, communication, and services were nationalized. Soviet-style planning was introduced in 1962, and Cuba's trade and other relations turned from West to East. In October 1962, US planes photographed Soviet long-range-missile installations in Cuba. The US blockaded Cuba until the USSR agreed to withdraw the missiles, in exchange for a US government pledge to launch no more offensive operations against the island.

However, the US did continue its attempt, through the OAS and other international forums, to isolate Cuba politically and economically from Latin America and the rest of the non-Communist world. All Latin American governments were pressured to break off diplomatic relations with Cuba. Castro responded with an attempt to destabilize certain Central and South American governments. Inspired by the Sierra Maestra campaign, guerrilla movements became active throughout the region, often with Cuban support. However, by 1967, when Ché Guevara was killed in Bolivia, these movements had collapsed. The US was only slightly more successful in its campaign of isolation. The OAS suspended Cuba in 1962, but in July 1975 passed the "freedom of action" resolution allowing countries to deal with Cuba as they pleased.

During the Carter administration, there were moves to normalize relations with Cuba. In 1977, the US and Cuba resumed diplomatic contacts (but not full relations) and concluded fishing and maritime rights agreements. However, the advent of the Reagan administration brought increased tensions between the two countries. Citing Cuban involvement in Angola, Ethiopia, Nicaragua, and Grenada, the US took up a more intransigent stance toward Cuba.

Domestically, Castro's administration has had its successes and failures. A strong social welfare system, including free health care and subsidized housing, was implemented in the 1960s and 1970s. However, an attempt to produce 10 million metric tons of sugar by 1970 seriously crippled the island's economy. Other mismanaged projects have led to economic stagnation or chaos. Cubans live frugally under a highly controlled system of rationing.

Cuba was dealt a serious blow in the late 1980s with the collapse of the Soviet Union, which meant a cutoff of economic and military aid on which Cuba had come to rely heavily over the years. The USSR had been Cuba's most important trading partner and provided the major market for Cuban sugar. The few consumer goods the USSR had supplied in the past were no longer available.

About three-quarters of a million Cubans have fled Cuba since Castro came to power. Most have settled in southern Florida, and many still have hope of returning to a Castro-free Cuba. There have been sporadic attempts to reunite families broken up by the emigration, but political circumstances often curtail these programs. For example, in February 1985 the repatriation of 2,746 "undesirables" from the US began, but after Radio Martí (sponsored by Voice of America) began broadcasting in Spanish in May 1985, Cuba abrogated the agreement.

Just as the Cuban economy began to show signs of a rebound from the collapse of the Soviet Union, the US tightened its embargo with the Cuban Democracy Act of 1992. This led to another wave of emigration in 1994, as thousands of Cubans left the island on rafts and other small vessels bound for Florida. To stem this tide of illegal immigration, the US in 1995 reached an agreement with Cuba under which the US would admit 20,000 Cuban immigrants per year. Cuba, in turn, was to take steps to prevent future "boat lifts."

US-Cuba relations deteriorated further, and Cuba's weakened economy was hampered anew in 1996 when the US Congress passed the Helms-Burton Act, another embargo-strengthening measure. The act met with harsh international criticism, and Canada and the World Trade Organization moved to fortify trade ties with the Castro government as a rebuff to the US. Prior to the passage of Helms-Burton, Cuba had renewed its crackdown on the pro-democracy movement. In February 1996, Cuban air force planes shot down two civilian aircraft over international waters, killing the four persons aboard. The planes had left the US carrying computer and medical supplies.

In late 1999 and early 2000, tensions between Cuba and the US returned to the international spotlight with the highly publicized custody dispute surrounding Elian Gonzalez, a six-year-old Cuban boy who was the sole survivor of an attempted boat crossing to the US in which his mother and 10 other Cuban refugees drowned. The dispute between the boy's father in Cuba and his expatriate relatives in Florida, who wanted him to stay in the US, became a rallying point for both the Castro regime in Cuba and the anti-Castro Cuban community in southern Florida.

Despite its acquiescence to some economic reforms—dollar transactions and limited self-employment in the agricultural sector— the Castro regime retains its commitment to socialism. Its economy, still recovering from the collapse of the Soviet Union, has been buoyed by increased tourism, mining, and cigar and fish exports. But economic growth has not translated into an improved quality of life for most Cubans, and Castro has continued to blame poverty and harsh living conditions on the US embargo.

In January 1998 Cuba held its second direct election to the National Assembly. Participation was limited to a "yes" or "no" vote for a list of candidates approved by the Communist Party. A month later, the Assembly appointed Fidel Castro Chairman of the Council of State for five more years. The approach of a new century marked four decades of rule by the aging leader.

13 GOVERNMENT
After he became premier on 16 February 1959, Fidel Castro was the effective source of governmental power. The juridical basis for this power rested on the Fundamental Law of the Revolution, which was promulgated on 8 February 1959 and was based on Cuba's 1940 constitution. To regularize government functions, a 10-member Executive Committee, with Castro as premier, was formed on 24 November 1972.

A new constitution, first published on 10 April 1975, then approved by the first congress of the Cuban Communist party in December, and ratified by a 97.7% vote in a special referendum in February 1976, established the National Assembly of People's Power as the supreme state organ. The deputies, originally elected by municipal assemblies and directly elected in national elections since 1993, serve five-year terms. The National Assembly elects the Council of State, whose president is both head of state and head of government. There are six vice-presidents in the Council of State, and 23 other members.

In January 1998, the second direct election to the National Assembly took place; all 610 candidates approved by the Communist Party received the required 50% of the vote necessary for election to the Assembly. One month later, the Assembly reelected Castro as president of the state council. He remains the key figure in domestic and foreign policy making. The constitution recognizes the Communist party as the "highest leading force of the society and of the state," which effectively outlaws other political parties.

Suffrage is universal for citizens age 16 and over, excluding those who have applied for permanent emigration.

14 POLITICAL PARTIES
Fidel Castro came to power through a coalition group known as the 26th of July Movement. Along with it, in 1959, the Student Revolutionary Directorate (Directorio Revolucionario Estudiantil) and the Communist Party (Partido Socialista Popular—PSP) were permitted to function.

Castro's relationship with the PSP was at first uneasy. The PSP condemned his early attempts at insurrection as "putschism," and did not support the 26th of July Movement until it had

reached its final stages in 1958. After June 1959, Castro began to refer to anti-Communists as counterrevolutionaries, and used the PSP as an organizational base and as a link to the USSR. In December 1961, Castro declared his complete allegiance to Marxism-Leninism.

By 1962, the 26th of July Movement, the Student Revolutionary Directorate, and the PSP had merged into the Integrated Revolutionary Organization (Organización Revolucionaria Integrada), which, in turn, gave way to the United Party of the Socialist Revolution (Partido Unido de la Revolución Socialista) and, in 1965, to the Cuban Communist Party (Partido Comunista Cubano—PCC).

On 17 December 1975, the PCC convened its first congress, which ratified a 13-member Politburo; Fidel Castro was reelected first secretary of the PCC. The second congress of the PCC took place in December 1980. The third congress, in February and November-December 1986, witnessed a massive personnel change when one-third of the 225-member Central Committee and 10 of 24 Politburo members were replaced, with Fidel Castro reelected first secretary. The Young Communist League and the José Martí Pioneer Organization for children up to 15 years of age are mass political organizations closely affiliated with the PCC. As of 1999, the PCC remained Cuba's only authorized political party. Its fifth congress took place in Havana in October 1997.

15 LOCAL GOVERNMENT
The country is divided into 14 provinces and 169 municipalities. The Isla de la Juventud is a special municipality. The 1976 constitution provides for a system of municipal assemblies to be elected for 2½-year terms by direct universal suffrage at age 16. Municipal assemblies choose delegates to provincial assemblies and deputies to the National Assembly. The most recent municipal elections were held in January 1998.

16 JUDICIAL SYSTEM
The 1976 constitution establishes the People's Supreme Court, consisting of a president, vice-president, and other judges, as the highest judicial tribunal. All members of the court are elected by the National Assembly, as are the attorney general and deputy attorneys general. Through its Governing Council, the court proposes laws, issues regulations, and makes decisions that must be implemented by the people's courts, whose judges are elected by the municipal assemblies. There are also seven regional courts of appeal, as well as district courts with civil and criminal jurisdiction. Military tribunals assume jurisdiction for certain counterrevolutionary cases.

Although the constitution provides for an independent judiciary, the courts are subordinate to the National Assembly and the Council of State.

There are no jury trials. Most trials are public. The legal system is based on Spanish and American law influenced with communist legal theory.

17 ARMED FORCES
The Castro government has maintained conscription since 1963, and it now requires two years of military service from men between the ages of 16 and 50. Two-year service is voluntary for women. Total armed strength in 2000 was estimated at 65,000 on active duty and 39,000 reserves. The army had 45,000 personnel. One armored division and an airborne brigade are always combat-ready. The army is equipped with 1,500 Russian tanks and other combat vehicles. Russian equipment dates back to the 1960s.

The navy has 5,000 personnel and four operational flotillas, including 1 submarine. The air force has 10,000 personnel and 130 combat aircraft and 45 armed helicopters. Paramilitary forces included 20,000 state security troops, 6,500 border guards, 50,000 civil defense forces, the 65,000-member youth labor army, and the million-member territorial militia. Except for small military training missions, Cuba has withdrawn its troops from Africa and Central America. Cuban arms imports were estimated to amount to an average of $1.5 billion a year in the 1980s until Russia cut its aid to around $500 million in 1991. Cuba's key military ally and supporter for decades, Russia cut off nearly all military assistance by 1993. In 2000, an estimated 810 Russian troops and advisers remained in Cuba. Cuba's 1998 defense budget was estimated at $750 million, or about 5.4% of GDP.

The US maintains a naval base at Guantánamo Bay in southeastern Cuba, under a 1934 leasing treaty. The US government considers the base to be of some strategic and training significance in the Caribbean and has refused to give it up, despite demands by the Castro regime that it do so. About 2,000 military personnel are stationed at Guantánamo.

[18]INTERNATIONAL COOPERATION

Cuba is a member of the UN, having joined on 24 October 1945, and belongs to ECLAC and all the nonregional specialized agencies except the IBRD, IDA, IFC, and IMF. The nation participates in G-77 and became a full member of the now disbanded CMEA on 11 July 1972. According to Western estimates, there were 6,000–8,000 Soviet civilian advisers in Cuba in the mid-1980s.

Cuba's charter membership in the OAS was suspended at the second Punta del Este meeting, in February 1962, through US initiative. The isolation of Cuba from the inter-American community was made almost complete when, at Caracas, on 26 July 1964, the OAS voted 15–4 for mandatory termination of all trade with the Castro government. However, relations with Latin America and the US improved markedly during the early 1970s, and at the San José, Costa Rica, meeting of the OAS on 29 July 1975, each member country was left free to determine its own stance toward Cuba. By the end of the year, most OAS members had restored relations with Cuba, which rejoined as a nonparticipating member.

Since the 1960s, Cuba has been very active in the Nonaligned Movement, and held its chairmanship between 1979 and 1983. The sixth summit conference of nonaligned countries took place in Havana on 3–9 September 1979; at the conference, President Castro denounced the US and described Cuba as a friend of the USSR. Cuba is a signatory of the Law of the Sea and a member of the WTO.

[19]ECONOMY

One of the world's cane sugar producers, Cuba is primarily an agricultural nation; sugar is the leading earner of foreign exchange, representing about 6% of world output. Tourism revenues outstripped sugar revenues in 1992.

After 1959, the revolutionary government, following policies espoused by Ernesto "Che" Guevara, attempted to liberalize the sugar economy in order to achieve agricultural diversification and industrialization. When this policy proved disastrous to the sugar crop, in 1962 Castro reversed the Guevara program and announced a goal of 10-million-ton crop by 1970. Despite a severe drought in 1968–69, Cuba did achieve a record 7.6-million-ton output of refined sugar in 1970. Efforts to diversify foreign trade during the early 1970s were aided by record high prices for sugar. Between 1971 and 1975, the Cuban economy grew by about 10% annually, and moderate growth continued through most of the 1980s. Commercial agreements with Argentina, Canada, Spain, France, the UK, Italy, and the FRG indicated Cuba's keen desire to move away from nearly exclusive reliance on the Socialist countries for both imports and exports.

Nevertheless, trade with the then-USSR and other CMEA members still made up the bulk of Cuba's foreign commerce, and Soviet aid remained essential to the economy.

In 1986 and 1987, GDP growth was approximately 1.7%; the declining rate of growth was the result of a depressed world sugar market, a falling dollar, and prolonged drought. The situation worsened when the Soviet Union collapsed and its control of the Eastern bloc countries ended, the resulting cutoff of Soviet assistance led to the near demise of traditional markets for Cuban exports. Therefore, the Cuban economy slowed significantly, losing 35% of GDP between 1989 and 1993.

As measures for economic recovery, the Castro government restricted public expenditure as well as restructured the economy. It allowed trading with market economies and developed new sources of foreign currency. The government placed special emphasis on the promotion of foreign investment and the development of sugar and tourism.

In the late 1990s, the government experimented with limited market-economy mechanisms, such as pay incentives and bonuses, in a bid to improve productivity. Tourism established new records in 1996, with arrivals increasing by 35% to 1,001,739, and gross revenues rising by 18% to $1.3 billion. In that year growth leapt to 7.8%, but it slowed during the following years. In 1998, Cuba's economy grew by 1.2.%, led by tourism. Annual inflation was almost nonexistent in 1998, down from 19.0% in 1995.

[20]INCOME

The US Central Intelligence Agency (CIA) reports that in 1998 Cuba's gross domestic product (GDP) was estimated at $17.3 billion. The per capita GDP was estimated at $1,560. The annual growth rate of GDP was estimated at 1.2%. The CIA defines GDP as the value of all final goods and services produced within a nation in a given year and computed on the basis of purchasing power parity (PPP) rather than value as measured on the basis of the rate of exchange. It was estimated that agriculture accounted for 7.4% of GDP, industry 36.5%, and services 56.1%.

[21]LABOR

All Cuban workers belong to a trade union, under the central control of the Confederation of Cuban Workers (CTC), which is affiliated with the Communist-oriented World Federation of Trade Unions. Independent unions are explicitly prohibited. Those who attempt to engage in independent union activities face government persecution and harassment. Strikes are not legally permitted. Unemployment, which the Castro government estimated at 33% of the work force in 1958, was practically abolished, but a limited unemployment scheme, in which redundant workers received 70% of their former wages until rehired, was introduced in the early 1980s to rationalize certain sectors of the economy. Underemployment is a chronic problem, and has been exacerbated by the idling of thousands of industrial workers whose jobs rely on foreign imports. Labor has been shifted to agriculture to compensate for fuel and machinery shortages affecting food and production.

The minimum wage varies, depending on the type of employment. As of 1999, it was $8.25 for a maid, $9.50 for a bilingual office clerk, and $10.75 for a gardener. The minimum wage is supplemented by social security consisting of free medical care and education and subsidized housing and food; a worker must still earn significantly more than minimum wage to support a family. The eight-hour workday, a weekly rest period, an annual paid vacation of one month, and workers' compensation are guaranteed by the constitution. The workweek is 44 hours, with shorter workdays for hazardous occupations.

In June 1990, the state labor force of 3,600,000 was distributed as follows: industry, 22%; agriculture, forestry, and fishing, 20%; education and culture, 13.3%; trade, 11%; services, and government, 16.7%; construction, 10%; transportation and communications, 7%. Women constituted 38% of the work force, up from 27% in 1975.

22AGRICULTURE

The state owns about 3 million hectares (7.4 million acres) of arable land, and 750,000 hectares (1.8 million) of permanent crops. About 14.9% of economically active population was engaged in the agricultural sector in 1998. An agrarian reform law of June 1959 made the government proprietor of all land in Cuba, created the National Institute of Agrarian Reform (INRA) as administrator, and set a general limit of 30 caballerías (400 hectares/990 acres) of farmland to be held by any one owner. A second agrarian reform, of October 1963, expropriated medium-size private holdings; there remained about 170,000 small private farms, with average holdings of over 16 hectares (40 acres). By 1985 there were 1,378 farm cooperatives. Almost a third of cultivated land is irrigated.

Sugarcane, Cuba's most vital crop and its largest export, is grown throughout the island, but mainly in the eastern half. The government regulates sugar production and prices. Sugar output reached 7.6 million tons in 1970, but that fell short of the 10 million tons projected. Subsequent targets were lowered, and the output was 7.9 million tons in 1979, 6.7 million in 1980 (when crop disease reduced production), 8 million in 1985, and 3.5 million in 1998. Cuba has pioneered the introduction of mechanical cane harvesters, and by 1994 there were 7,400 harvester-threshers (up from 5,717 in the early 1980s). Cuba and Russia signed several finance and investment accords in 1992 and 1993 whereby Russia will supply fuel, spare parts, fertilizer and herbicide in exchange for Cuba's sugar harvest, with Russia annually importing a minimum of 2 million tons of Cuban sugar. The sugar industry also has diversified into exporting molasses, ethyl alcohol, rum and liquor, bagasse chipboard, torula yeast, dextran, and furfural. Tobacco, the second most important crop, is grown on small farms requiring intensive cultivation. In the late 1970s, the average annual production was about 35,000 tons, but crop disease in 1979 resulted in a drop in production to 8,200 tons in 1980; production was 42,000 tons in 1995. Other crops in 1998 included (in tons) oranges, 340,000; lemons and limes, 36,000; grapefruit, 420,000; rice, 388,000; bananas, 325,000; potatoes, 326,000; sweet potatoes, 220,000; and coffee, 21,000. Other Cuban products with export potential include: mangoes, pineapples, ginger, papayas, and seeds.

23ANIMAL HUSBANDRY

In the state sector, milk production in 1998 amounted to 660,000 tons (431,000 during 1989–91) and egg production reached 56,000 tons (120,000 tons during 1989–91). Livestock in 1998 included an estimated 4.6 million head of cattle, 1.5 million hogs, 620,000 horses, 310,000 sheep, 118,000 goats, and 12 million chickens. The populations of most livestock species have declined since 1990, as a result of input shortages from the worsening economy. Honey production in 1998 was an estimated 5,000 tons, the highest in the Caribbean.

24FISHING

The territorial waters of Cuba support more than 500 varieties of edible fish. The catch in 1997 was 122,904 tons, compared with 244,673 tons in 1986. Tuna, lobster, and shellfish are the main species caught. The Cuban Fishing Fleet, a government enterprise, supervises the industry.

The former USSR aided in the construction of a fishing port in Havana to service the Cuban and former-Soviet fleets as well as to process and store fish. Seafood exports are an important source of foreign exchange; in 1997, fish and fish products exports amounted to $97.6 million.

25FORESTRY

Much of the natural forest cover was removed in colonial times, and cutting between the end of World War I and the late 1950s reduced Cuba's woodland to about 14% of the total area and led to soil erosion. Between 1959 and 1985, about 1.8 billion seedlings were planted, including eucalyptus, pine, majagua, mahogany, cedar, and casuarina. State forests cover 2,608,000 hectares (6,444,000 acres), or about 23.7% of the total land area. Roundwood production in 1997 amounted to 3,152,000 cu m; sawn wood, 130,000 cu m.

26MINING

Nickel is Cuba's leading mineral commodity, with 61,500 tons produced in 1997. Production has been boosted by a joint venture between Sherritt Inc. of Canada and Compañía General del Níquel. Nickel deposits and plants are located in eastern Cuba at Nicaro, Moa, and Punta Gorda, all in Holguín Province. Cuba is also a significant producer of cobalt, with 8% of world mine production in 1997. Copper is extracted in the provinces of Pinar del Río and Santiago de Cuba. The Matahambre mine is the primary source of copper; national copper production in 1997 was 1,000 tons (metal content), a substantial decline from prerevolutionary days. Chromite production was 44,000 tons; cobalt, 2,500 tons. In 1997, Cuba produced 180,000 tons of salt from seawater. High-quality marble is also produced.

27ENERGY AND POWER

Cuba has no coal, and its hydroelectric potential is slight. Bagasse (sugarcane waste) has traditionally supplied most of the sugar industry's fuel. In 1998, Cuba's net installed capacity was 4,325,000 kW; total production that year was 15,274 million kWh. A 1,650-MW nuclear plant, built with Soviet assistance in Cienfuegos, was to have been operational by 1993, supplying 15% of Cuba's annual electrical output. On 6 September 1992, however, President Castro announced that work on the plant had been indefinitely stopped, since Russia was demanding hard currency payment.

Crude oil was first produced in Cuba in 1942. The domestic petroleum industry was nationalized in July 1960, and all subsoil deposits were also nationalized; domestic and foreign holdings (mostly US) were expropriated or confiscated after foreign-owned refineries refused to process oil from Eastern Europe. Crude oil production dropped from 52,000 tons in 1959 to 10,000 tons in 1961, but rose to 104,000 tons in 1968 and to 868,000 tons by 1985. As of 1991, production totaled less than 700,000 tons. As a result of energy shortages following the collapse of the Soviet Union, Cuba attempted to increase oil production in the 1990s. Production in 1999 was estimated to have increased 23% from the previous year, when it came to 31,000 barrels per day. In 1991, Union de Petroleo de Cuba (a state-owned company) granted two French companies a six-year oil exploration contract in an approximately 1,800 sq km (700 sq mi) concession off Cuba's north coast. Natural gas production in 1994 amounted to 34 million cu m.

28INDUSTRY

All Cuban industrial production was nationalized by March 1968. The industrial production growth rate was 6% in 1995.

Cuba had 156 sugar mills in 1985, and at that time, about 10% of exports from the then-USSR to Cuba consisted of machinery for the sugar industry. Other food processing plants produced cheese, butter, yogurt, ice cream, wheat flour, pasta, preserved fruits and vegetables, alcoholic beverages, and soft drinks. Light industry comprises textiles, shoes, soap, toothpaste, and corrugated cardboard boxes.

In 1996 construction expanded by 31%, agriculture by 17%, mining by 12%, and manufacturing by 8%. An influx of foreign investment followed the passage of new investment laws after 1993. Industrial production continued to grow into 2000.

29SCIENCE AND TECHNOLOGY
In 1987–97, total expenditures for research and development amounted to 0.8% of GNP; 1,121 technicians and 1,612 scientists and engineers per million people were engaged in research and development. Emphasis fell on agricultural research, new technologies for the recovery of nickel and cobalt, and a joint Soviet Cuban spaceflight research program. The Academy of Sciences of Cuba, founded in 1962, is Cuba's principal scientific institution; it, as well as the Ministry of Agriculture, operates numerous research centers throughout Cuba. Institutions offering higher education in science and engineering include the University of Havana (founded in 1928), the University of Oriente at Santiago de Cuba (founded in 1947), the Central University of Las Villas in Villa Clara (founded in 1952), the University of Camagüey (founded in 1967), and the University Center of Pinar del Rio (founded in 1972). In 1987–97, science and engineering students accounted for 16% of college and university enrollments.

30DOMESTIC TRADE
Havana is Cuba's commercial center. Provincial capitals are marketing and distribution centers of lesser importance. Camaguey is a cattle and sugar center, Santa Clara lies in the tobacco belt, and Santiago is a major seaport and mining city. Holguin has been transformed into a major agricultural and industrial center.

By May 1960, the National Institute of Agrarian Reform was operating about 2,000 "people stores" (tiendas del pueblo), and by the end of 1962 all retail and wholesale businesses dealing in consumer essentials had been nationalized. In 1984 there were 27,301 retail establishments in Cuba.

Because of the US-organized trade boycott and the inability of production in the then-USSR and Cuba to meet Cuban demands, rationing was applied to many consumer goods in the 1960s and 1970s. By the mid-1980s, rationing had been reduced and accounted for about 25% of individual consumption. Allocation of major consumer items after 1971 was by the "just class" principle, with the best workers receiving priority. The availability of basic consumer items increased noticeably after 1980, when the smallholder's free market (mercado libre campesino) was introduced. Under this system, small-scale private producers and cooperatives could sell their surplus commodities directly to consumers once their quotas had been filled. However, the peasant markets were abolished in May 1986, allegedly because they led to widespread speculation and profiteering.

31FOREIGN TRADE
Cuba has established or reestablished trade relations with many countries in Latin America, the Caribbean, Africa, Asia, and Europe. The sudden rupture of trade with the former Soviet Union and the Eastern bloc nations in 1989 after 30 years of interrelationship caused severe trauma to the Cuban economy. However, there remains a clear political will on the part of the former Soviet republics to maintain economic relations with Cuba with a certain degree of preference. Nevertheless, Cuba has diversified its trading partners in recent years.

Almost half of Cuba's commodity export market (46%) is taken up by sugar and honey, representing 6.3% of the world's export sales in these commodities. Nickel is the second most lucrative exported commodity (14%), followed by medicinal and

pharmaceutical products (9.1%). Other exports, in the agricultural sector, include tobacco (7.5%), shell fish (7.0%) and fish (2.7%). Primary imports include petroleum, food, machinery, and chemicals.

Russia buys 27% of Cuba's exports; Canada, 18%; and Spain, 8%. Imports come from Spain (17%), France (9%), and Canada (9%). Principal trading partners in 1998 (in millions of US dollars) were as follows:

COUNTRY	EXPORTS	IMPORTS	BALANCE
Russia	374	77	297
Netherlands	230	47	183
Canada	227	263	-36
Spain	122	603	-481
China (inc. Hong Kong)	93	156	-63
France	55	285	-230
Germany	26	83	-57
United Kingdom	24	61	-37
Italy	12	213	-201
Venezuela	6	144	-138

32BALANCE OF PAYMENTS
Since the US stopped trading with Cuba in 1963, Cuba's dollar reserves have dropped to virtually nothing, and most trade is conducted through barter agreements. In 1997, Cuba's debt to the former Soviet Union was estimated at $20 billion. With the demise of the USSR, Cuba has focused on trading with market-oriented countries in order to increase foreign currency reserves, notably by promoting sugar exports and foreign investment in industry. Remittances from Cuban workers in the US (totaling approximately $800 million annually), tourism dollars, and foreign aid help to cover the trade deficit.

The US Central Intelligence Agency reports that in 1998 the purchasing power parity of Cuba's exports was $1.4 billion while imports totaled $3 billion resulting in a trade balance of -$1.6 billion.

33BANKING AND SECURITIES
All banks in Cuba were nationalized in 1960. The National Bank of Cuba, established in 1948, was restructured in 1967. Commercial banks include Banco Financiero International (1984). Savings banks include Banco Popular dul Ahorro. A number of foreign banks offer limited services in Cuba. The Grupo Nuevo Banco was set up in 1996. There are no securities exchanges.

Hard-currency reserves have been depleted by import growth in excess of export growth. In the domestic economy, the attempt to reduce enterprise subsidies caused an increase in demand for working capital which the state was unable to meet. A combination of price and direct rationing systems is operating.

34INSURANCE
All insurance enterprises were nationalized by January 1964. Although insurance never accounted for more than 1% of national income, new opportunities began to emerge throughout the insurance sector as a result of the changes in economic structure. Seven insurance companies and two reinsurers had offices in Cuba in 1997. They concentrated on freight insurance, but there was interest in development and diversification.

Cuba's domestic state insurance company, Esen, appeared to be preparing to compete with foreign companies in the domestic market in 1997. It launched a major marketing drive with an expanded sales force of 3,500 to persuade Cubans to take out new personal insurance policies. Apparently, they were having some success, despite the lack of a private insurance tradition. The volume of premiums was 30% higher in 1995 than in 1990. New products include not only travel and medical insurance, but also pensions and life insurance policies. Although limited foreign penetration into the Cuban market would help to develop the sector, the authorities will foster the development of Cuban insurers before the sector is fully opened. Private insurance schemes will not replace state social security provision.

35 PUBLIC FINANCE

Under the Economic Management System, developed during the 1970s and approved by the PCC Congress in 1975, state committees for statistics and finances have been established, and formal state budgets, abandoned in 1967, have been reintroduced. State revenues come from the nationalized enterprises, income tax, social security contributions, and foreign aid.

The US Central Intelligence Agency (CIA) estimates that in 1998 Cuba's central government took in revenues of approximately $12.3 billion and had expenditures of $13 billion. Overall, the government registered a deficit of approximately $700 million. Total external debt is estimated at $30 billion with two-thirds of that amount owed to Russia.

36 TAXATION

A 1962 tax code instituted a sharply progressive income tax as well as a surface transport tax, property transfer tax, documents tax, consumer goods tax, and a tax on capital invested abroad.

37 CUSTOMS AND DUTIES

In December 1990, Cuba introduced new tariff regulations to standardize product descriptions. The regulations have a general tariff and a most-favored-nation tariff.

38 FOREIGN INVESTMENT

In February 1960, Fidel Castro announced that foreign investment in Cuba would be accepted only if delivered to the government to be used as it saw fit. The enterprises in which this capital would be invested were to be "national enterprises," so that Cuba would not be dependent on foreigners. Any new foreign investment were to be controlled by the Central Planning Board. From mid-1960s, US holdings in Cuba were systematically seized, partly for political reasons and partly because US corporations refused to accept Cuba's terms of nationalism. Some of the investments of other foreign nationals were left operating under stringent governmental regulation.

Between 1960 and the early 1970s, foreign investment activities were restricted to limited technical and economic assistance from East European countries and the then-USSR with which Cuba concluded over 40 cooperation agreements between 1963 and 1983. Limited investments from the non-Communist world were sought, with some success, in the mid 1970s. In 1982, in a further effort to attract investors from Western Europe, Canada, and Japan, Cuba passed its first foreign investment law, permitting foreign companies to form joint ventures with the Cuban government but to own no more than 49% of the stock. In 1985, however, direct investment in Cuba by OECD countries totaled only $200,000.

Since 1990, the Cuban government has seen the necessity to open its recessed economy to foreign investment, either via joint ventures or other forms of association. In 1992, Cuba further intensified its efforts to attract foreign investment in several key areas of its economy, including sugar, tourism, textiles, tobacco, pharmaceuticals, nickel, and shipping. In 1995, full repatriation of profits and 100% foreign ownership was allowed in Cuba.

As of 1998, there were 322 joint ventures in force, with partners from over fifty different countries, totalling over $5 billion. In addition, many foreign contracts were sought for oil drilling. Principal foreign investors include Spain, France, Italy, the Netherlands, and Latin America.

Investment in the tourism sector increased dramatically after 1996. Sherritt International, the Canadian mining company which produces half of Cuba's nickel exports, planned to expand its operations by $440 million in 1997. As of late 1997, Mexico's Grupo Domos was seeking a partner to take a stake in a major project to update the telecommunications system. Two free trade zones were inaugurated in May 1997 and another two were planned. French companies were to invest in power and sugar, and South Africa signed a trade agreement.

39 ECONOMIC DEVELOPMENT

Until 1959, the Cuban government followed a policy of free enterprise; government ownership was largely limited to local utilities. When the Castro government came to power in 1959, it proceeded to create a centrally planned economy. By means of nationalization and expropriation, all producer industries, mines, refineries, communications, and export-import concerns were brought under government control by 1968.

Planning in the 1960s vacillated on the question of whether Cuba should concentrate on the production of sugar, on industrialization, or on a balance between the two. After 1963, sugar predominated. But the effort that went into the 1970 harvest diverted enormous resources from other sectors of the economy. At the same time, there was growing absenteeism, and low productivity in the labor force, attributed to the policy of eliminating material incentives. Under the Economic Management System, pay was again tied to production though the introduction of a system akin to piecework.

The 1975–80 development plan, approved by at the PCC Congress in December 1975, set specific production goals for Cuban industry and projected an overall economic growth rate of 6% annually; it was announced in 1980 that the actual growth rate was 4%. The 1981–85 plan introduced new incentive schemes and gave more freedom to market forces; it also eased restrictive hiring regulation. One of the major aims of the plan was to increase industry's share of gross social product to 50%, but industry accounted for only 45.3% in 1985. The 1986–90 plan envisioned a 5% annual growth and aimed particularly at an increase in exports. In December 1986, 28 austerity measures were approved by the National Assembly, including increases in transport and electricity prices and rationing of kerosene.

Under several finance and investment accords signed by Cuba and Russia in 1992 and 1993, Russia agreed to supply fuel, tires and spare parts for mechanical harvesters and other vehicles, fertilizers, and herbicides for Cuba's sugar harvest. In addition, Russia agreed to import a minimum of 2 million tons of Cuban sugar. Russia also agreed to extend a $350 million credit to Cuba to complete and further develop a number of oil, energy, and nickel mining projects that had previously been backed by the Soviet Union.

Cuba continued to apply timid market reforms while actively seeking foreign investment. Economic growth in the late 1990s was projected to come from an expansion of manufacturing, tourism, mining, and services. Other positive factors include the improved tourist industry and a sharp recovery of the cigar industry. The creation of a new Central Bank completed financial sector reforms begun in 1995. These reflected the increased role of the private sector in financial transactions. In 2000, the Cuban economy continued its growth through the generous investment of foreign countries, but the US trade embargo held fast in the face of opposition from key US political leaders.

40 SOCIAL DEVELOPMENT

Although there was no unified social insurance program during the Batista regime, laws were enacted setting up more than 50 retirement and disability pension plans in various industries, trades, and professions. A single system of social security covering almost all workers and protecting them against the risks of old age, disability, and survivorship was enacted in 1963.

Contributions to pension programs are made by employers (10% of earnings for self-employed persons), with the government making up the deficit. Pensions are set at a rate of 50% of average earnings. The national health care system covers all citizens. The Maternity Law provides 18 weeks of maternity leave.

The Family Code of 1975 proscribes all sex discrimination. Women receive equal access to education and are found in most professions. As of 1998, 166 of 601 members of Parliament were women. Legislation provides for the equal rights of illegitimate and legitimate children, and specifies the obligations of parents. Following a dramatic increase in prostitution, the government instituted a crackdown in 1998 and 1999, deploying police to neighborhoods frequented by prostitutes.

There were reports of serious human rights abuses in 1999, although there were no substantial reports of deaths from excessive police force, as there had been in 1998. Prison conditions are harsh: medical care is inadequate and abusive treatment is not uncommon. Human rights activists have been targeted for arbitrary arrest and detention. The government does not allow international organizations to monitor the condition of prisons and the treatment of prisoners.

41HEALTH

Sanitation is generally good, and health conditions greatly improved after the 1959 revolution. However, with the dissolution of the Soviet Union, Cuba no longer receives the same level of foreign support and has fallen behind in many of its social services. In spite of this, in 1993, 100% of the population was reported to have access to health care; safe water was available to 95% in 1995.

Infant mortality declined from more than 60 per 1,000 live births before 1959 to 7 in 1997. About 9% of babies born in 1993 were considered low birth weight. Studies show that as of 1998, 79% of married women (ages 15 to 49) used contraception. The government claims to have eradicated malaria, diphtheria, poliomyelitis, tuberculosis, and tetanus. In 1997, children up to one year of age were immunized as follows: tuberculosis (99%); diphtheria, pertussis, and tetanus (99%); polio (97%); and measles (99%).

Life expectancy was an average of 76 years for women and men in 1998, and the overall death rate was 7 per 1,000 people in 1999. In 1996, major causes of death were recorded as follows: circulatory system diseases (311 per 100,000); malignant neoplasms (141 per 100,000); and infectious diseases (51 per 100,000). There were 13.3 reported cases of tuberculosis per 100,000 in 1996. The incidence of TB decreased steadily from 1979 to 1991 (503 cases), but there was a reversal in the following years. By the end of 1996, 534 cases of AIDS had been reported.

In 1997, there were 5 doctors for every 1,000 people. In 1995, there were 60 hospital beds per 1,000 population. Medical services are now more widely distributed in rural as well as urban areas. All doctors are obliged to work for the rural medical service in needy areas for two years after graduation. All health services are provided free of charge.

42HOUSING

Cuban housing has not kept pace with the population increase. All large cities have slum problems, despite the construction of over 600,000 housing units between 1959 and 1985. In the 1980s, over half of all housing units were detached houses. The remainder were apartments, palm huts called hohios, and cuarterias, housing units in buildings composed of a number of detached rooms where occupants share some or all facilities. More than half of all dwellings were concrete and brick, about one-third were solid wood, and a smaller number were constructed with palm planks. Water was piped indoors to roughly half of all homes and outside to one-fifth; about half had private bath facilities.

43EDUCATION

Education has been a high priority of the Castro government. In 1959 there were at least 1 million illiterates, and many more were only semiliterate. An extensive literacy campaign was inaugurated in 1961, when 100,000 teachers went out into the countryside. For the year 2000, UNESCO estimated the illiteracy rate of persons aged 15 years and over to be 3.6% (males, 3.5%; females, 3.6%). Education is free and compulsory for six years (6–11 years of age). In 1997, Cuba's 9,926 primary schools enrolled 1,094,868 students and employed 92,820 teachers. Student-to-teacher ratio stood at 12 to one. Secondary education lasts six years beyond the primary level. In 1997, 712,897 secondary students were instructed by 70,628 teachers. An innovation of the Castro government was the addition of agricultural and technical programs to the secondary-school curriculum; the work-study principle is now integral to Cuban secondary education. Students in urban secondary schools must spend at least seven weeks annually in rural labor. The first junior high schools, based on the work-study concept, were introduced in 1968. Catholic parochial schools were nationalized in 1961.

Cuba has five universities: the University of Havana (founded 1728), Oriente University at Santiago de Cuba (1947), the University of Las Villas at Santa Clara (1952), University of Camagüey (1974), and the University of Pinar Del-Rio. Workers' improvement courses (superación obrera), to raise adults to the sixth-grade level, and technical training schools (mínimo técnico), to develop unskilled workers' potentials and retrain other workers for new jobs, were instituted after 1961. Today, special worker-farmer schools prepare workers and peasants for enrollment at the universities and for skilled positions in industrial and agricultural enterprises. In 1997, tertiary education enrolled 111,587 students, with 22,574 teachers.

44LIBRARIES AND MUSEUMS

The José Martí National Library in Havana, founded in 1901, had a collection of 1 million volumes in 2000. Besides acting as the National Library, it provides lending, reference, and children's services to the public. Other sizable collections in Havana are found at the Havana University Library (203,000 volumes), the Library of the Institute of Literature and Linguistics (98,000) the José Antonio Echevarría Library of the House of the Americas (120,000), and the University of the East in Santiago (535,000 volumes).

Although libraries of private institutions disappeared in the 1960s and many collections were transferred to the National Library, the number of special and research libraries increased, especially with the creation of many departments of the Academy of Sciences. A national library network was established by the Department of Libraries of the National Cultural Council.

The National Museum of Fine Arts in Havana contains classical and modern art from around the world as well as Cuban art from the colonial period to the present day. The Colonial Municipal Museum and the Felipe Poey Natural History Museum in Havana, the Bacardi Municipal Museum in Santiago, the Oscar Rojas Museum in Cárdenas, and the Ignacio Agramonte Museum in Camagüey are also noteworthy.

45MEDIA

All telephone service is free; about 95% of the telephones are automatic. In 1995 there were 344,200 telephones in use. As of 1999 there were 150 AM and 5 FM radio broadcasting stations and 58 television stations operating throughout the country. In

1997 there were 351 radios and 241 television sets per 1,000 population.

Like the radio and television stations, the press is controlled and owned by the government. Cuba's major newspapers are all published in Havana and include *Granma,* established in 1965 (with an estimated 1999 circulation of 675,000), the official organ of the Communist party. The party also publishes weekly editions in Spanish, English, and French. The weekly *Juventud Rebelde* is the publication of the Union of Young Communists, and had a 1999 circulation of 250,000.

Magazines published in Havana include *Bohemia* (weekly, 20,000, general articles and news) and *Mujeres* (monthly, 250,000, women's-interest news). *Prensa Latina,* the Cuban wire service, covers international affairs and distributes its coverage throughout Latin America.

The constitution states that print and electronic media are state property and cannot be made private. Media operate under strict guidelines and reflect government views. The government is said to intimidate journalists through the penal system and the threatening of jobs.

Online access is extremely limited, with less than one Internet host per 1,000 population in 1998.

46ORGANIZATIONS

Most of the leading mass organizations in Cuba were founded shortly after the revolution. The Committees for the Defense of the Revolution were founded on 28 September 1960 to combat counterrevolutionary activities. The Federation of Cuban Women was established 23 August 1960. The National Association of Small Farmers, the leading peasants' organization, was established 17 May 1961; in 1989 it had 167,461 members, both private farmers and members of cooperatives. The Confederation of Cuban Workers, the principal trade union federation, antedates the revolution. Founded in 1939, it had a total membership of 3,060,838 workers in 1990.

47TOURISM, TRAVEL, AND RECREATION

Before 1959, tourism, especially from the US, was a major source of revenue. Foreign tourism declined in the 1960s, and Cuba's ornate and expensive hotels were used mainly by visiting delegations of workers and students. Renewed emphasis on international tourism characterized the 1976–80 development plan, under which 25 new hotels were opened. Today, the Cuban government actively promotes tourism as a means of offsetting the financial decline brought on by the collapse of the Soviet bloc. In 1998, 1,415,832 foreign visitors arrived in Cuba. Revenue from tourism was $1.35 billion in 1997, compared with $145 million in 1987.

Among Cuba's attractions are fine beaches; magnificent coral reefs, especially around the Isle of Youth; and historic sites in Old Havana (where some buildings date from the 17th century); Trinidad, and Santiago de Cuba. Passports and visas are required for nationals of countries that do not have visa-free agreements with Cuba. In June 1992, Cuba was admitted to the Caribbean Tourism Organization.

In 1999, the UN estimated the cost of staying in Havana at $192. Santiago de Cuba is slightly less expensive than the capital, requiring an estimated $150 in daily expenses.

48FAMOUS CUBANS

José Martí (1853–95), poet, journalist, and patriot, was the moving spirit behind the revolution that liberated Cuba from Spain. Antonio Maceo (1848–96), the mulatto general known as the "Titan of Bronze," became famous both as a guerrilla fighter and as an uncompromising advocate of independence. Carlos J. Finlay (1833–1915) gained lasting recognition for his theory regarding the transmission of yellow fever.

Cuban literature is most famous for its poetry and essays. The influential Afro-Cuban tradition has been explored by Cuban scholars, most notably by Fernando Ortiz (1881–1916), jurist and ethnographer. Another leading writer was José Antonio Saco (1797–1879), author of a six-volume history of slavery. Ernesto Lecuona (1896–1963) was a composer of popular music, and Juan José Sicre (b.1898) is Cuba's outstanding sculptor.

The major heroes of the revolution against Batista are Fidel Castro Ruz (b.1926); his brother, Gen. Raúl Castro Ruz (b.1931); Argentine-born Ernesto "Che" Guevara (1928–67), who was killed while engaged in revolutionary activities in Bolivia; and Camilo Cienfuegos (d.1959). Cubans notable in literature include poet Nicolás Guillén (1902–89) and playwright and novelist Alejo Carpentier y Valmont (1904–80). Alicia Alonso (b.1921), a noted ballerina, founded the National Ballet of Cuba.

49DEPENDENCIES

Cuba has no territories or colonies.

50BIBLIOGRAPHY

Balfour, Sebastian. *Castro.* New York: Longman, 1990.

Brune, Lester H. *The Cuba-Caribbean Missile Crisis of October 1962.* Claremont, Calif.: Regina Books, 1996.

Cardoso, Eliana A. *Cuba After Communism.* Cambridge, Mass.: MIT Press, 1992.

Chayes, Abram. *The Cuban Missile Crisis.* New York: Oxford University Press, 1974.

Cuba After the Cold War. Pittsburgh: University of Pittsburgh Press, 1993.

Cuba and the Caribbean: Regional Issues and Trends in the Post-Cold War Era. Wilmington, Del.: Scholarly REsources, 1997.

Cuba and the Future. Westport, Conn.: Greenwood Press, 1994.

Cuba: a Short History. New York: Cambridge University Press, 1993.

Foner, Philip S. *The Spanish-Cuban-American War and the Birth of American Imperialism, 1895–1902.* 2 vols. New York: Monthly Review Press, 1972.

Halebsky, Sandor, and John M. Kirk (eds.). *Cuba: Twenty-Five Years of Revolution, 1959–1984.* New York: Praeger, 1985.

Haverstock, Nathan A. *Cuba in Pictures.* Minneapolis: Lerner Publications Company, 1987.

Matibag, Eugenio. *Afro-Cuban Religious Experience: Cultural Reflections in Narrative.* Gainesville: University Press of Florida, 1996.

Mesa-Lago, Carmelo. *The Economy of Socialist Cuba: A Two-Decade Appraisal.* Albuquerque: University of New Mexico Press, 1981.

Newsom, David D. *The Soviet Brigade in Cuba: a Study in Political Diplomacy.* Bloomington: Indiana University Press, 1987.

——. *Cuba: Between Reform and Revolution.* New York: Oxford University Press, 1988.

Preeg, Ernest H. *Cuba and the New Caribbean Economic Order.* Washington, D.C.: Center for Strategic and International Studies, 1993.

Rudolph, James D. (ed.). *Cuba, a Country Study,* 3d ed. Washington, D.C.: Government Printing Office, 1985.

Ruffin, Patricia. *Capitalism and Socialism in Cuba: a Study of Dependency, Development, and Underdevelopment.* New York: St. Martin's Press, 1990.

Schroeder, Susan. *Cuba: A Handbook of Historical Statistics.* Boston: G.K. Hall, 1982.

Simons, Geoffrey Leslie. *Cuba: From Conquistador to Castro.* Houndmills, Basingstoke, Hampshire, England: Macmillan Press, 1996.

Toward a New Cuba?: Legacies of a Revolution. Boulder, Colo.: L. Rienner Publishers, 1997.

DOMINICA

Commonwealth of Dominica
Dominica

CAPITAL: Roseau.

FLAG: On a green background appears a cross composed of yellow, black, and white stripes; in the center is a red disk with 10 yellow-bordered green stars surrounding a parrot.

ANTHEM: *Isle of Beauty, Isle of Splendor.*

MONETARY UNIT: The East Caribbean dollar (EC$) of 100 cents is the national currency and is pegged to the US dollar. There are coins of 1, 2, 5, 10, and 25 cents, and 1 dollar, and notes of 5, 10, 20, and 100 East Caribbean dollars. EC$1 = US0.3704 (US$1 = EC$2.70).

WEIGHTS AND MEASURES: The metric system is being introduced, but imperial measures remain in common use.

HOLIDAYS: New Year's Day, 1 January; Labor Day, 1 May; Caricom Day, 2 July; Bank Holiday, 1st Monday in August; National Days, 3–4 November; Christmas, 25 December; Boxing Day, 26 December. Movable religious holidays include Carnival, Good Friday, Easter Monday, and Whitmonday.

TIME: 8 AM = noon GMT.

¹LOCATION, SIZE, AND EXTENT

Although usually classified as one of the Windward Islands, Dominica, located between Guadeloupe to the N and Martinique to the S, marks the midpoint of the Lesser Antilles. To the E lies the Atlantic Ocean, to the W the Caribbean Sea. The island has an area of 750 sq km (290 sq mi) and is 47 km (29 mi) long by 26 km (16 mi) wide, with a coastline of 148 km (92 mi). Comparatively, the area occupied by Dominica is slightly more than four times the size of Washington, D.C.

Dominica's capital city, Roseau, is located on the southwest coast of the island.

²TOPOGRAPHY

The most rugged island of the Lesser Antilles, Dominica is a mass of peaks, ridges, and ravines. Several mountains are over 1,200 m (4,000 ft), of which the highest is Morne Diablotins, with an altitude of 1,447 m (4,747 ft). The whole land mass is of recent volcanic formation, and the mountain peaks are cones of volcanoes with lava craters and small lakes of boiling water. The coastal rim of the island is a thin strip limited by the mountainsides, which extend directly down to the shore.

³CLIMATE

The climate of Dominica is mildly tropical; in the winter months the temperature averages 25°C (77°F); in the summer, 28°C (82°F). The spring months are the driest; the heaviest rains fall during late summer. The average yearly rainfall ranges from about 200 cm (80 in) on the drier Caribbean coast to 635 cm (250 in) in mountainous inland areas. Destructive hurricanes coming in from the Atlantic Ocean can be expected during the late summer months. Dominica was devastated by hurricanes in 1979 and 1980; the cost of restoring agricultural production was estimated at $68.5 million, more than double the 1978 GNP.

⁴FLORA AND FAUNA

Since few plantations could be established on Dominica's rugged terrain, the island is still covered with forests, some of which have never been cut except by the destructive winds of a hurricane. On one 4-hectare (10-acre) plot in the rain forest as many as 60 species of trees may be identified. Some of the most common are chataignier, gommier, carapite, breadfruit, white cedar, and laurier.

There are no large wild animals, but the agouti and manicou can be found. Some 135 species of birds inhabit Dominica, the coastal waters of which abound in fish.

⁵ENVIRONMENT

As a member of the Organization of Eastern Caribbean States (OECS) formed in 1981, Dominica shares environmental problems common to the area's island countries. Water shortages are among the most significant. Other areas of concern are pollution from chemicals used in farming and untreated sewage. The nation's forests are endangered by the expansion of farming activities.

Pollution of the nation's coastal waters threatens the tourist trade in the area. Two extensive areas have been set aside as nature reserves. The southern reserve, which constitutes Morne Trois Pitons National Park, covers an area of 6,500 hectares (16,100 acres). In it are the nesting places of the red-necked and imperial parrots, both endangered species of Dominica; the tundra peregrine falcon and the green sea and hawksbill turtles are also classified as endangered. Hurricanes are the most destructive natural threat to the environment.

⁶POPULATION

The population of Dominica in 2000 was estimated at 63,944. An estimated 11% of the population is 65 years of age or older. The projected population for the year 2005 is 61,000, assuming a crude birthrate of 15 per 1,000 population and a death rate of 7, resulting in a natural rate of change of 0.8% for the period 2000–2005. The population density of Dominica in 1996 was 110 persons per sq km (286 per sq mi), one of the lowest in the West Indies.

It was estimated that 71% of the population lived in urban areas in 2000. The capital city, Roseau, had a 2000 metropolitan population of 21,000. Dominica's next census is scheduled to take place in 2001.

7 MIGRATION

There are no restrictions on foreign travel, emigration, or repatriation. In 1999 the net migration rate was -24.65 migrants per 1,000 population.

8 ETHNIC GROUPS

Up-to-date statistics on racial or ethnic origins are not available. In 1981, the vast majority of Dominicans (91%) were descendants of African slaves brought to the island in the 17th and 18th centuries. Some 6% of the population was of mixed descent, and a small minority of about 0.5% was of European origin. Dominica is the only island of the Caribbean on which descendants of the Carib Indian population still make up a community of significant size. Isolation and the establishment of a 1,500-hectare (3,700-acre) reserve have enabled the Caribs, who number about 3,000 people, to preserve their identity.

9 LANGUAGES

English is the official language of Dominica. Nearly all Dominicans also speak a French patois, based on a mixture of African and French grammar and consisting mostly of French words, with some English and Spanish borrowings. Some islanders speak French as their first language.

10 RELIGIONS

The dominant religion is Christianity, but religious freedom for all faiths is provided for in the constitution. About 77% of the population are Roman Catholic. Various Protestant denominations constitute 15% of the populace, including Methodists with 5%, Pentecostals with 3%, Seventh-Day Adventists with 3%, Baptists with 2%, and others with 2%. Other minority religions comprise the remaining 6%, including Islam, Baha'i and Rastafarianism.

11 TRANSPORTATION

A paved road circles the northern two-thirds of the island, connecting the two main towns, Roseau and Portsmouth, with Melville Hall Airport in the northeast. Much of the road system was severely damaged by the 1979 hurricane; reconstruction has averaged about 16 km (10 mi) a year. There were about 780 km (485 mi) of roadways in 1999, of which 393 km (244 mi) were paved. There are 2,770 passenger cars and 2,830 commercial motor vehicles on the island. A deepwater harbor has been completed near Roseau on Woodbridge Bay, and both Roseau and Portsmouth also receive ships. Dominica Air Transport and other small airlines connect the main airport with Martinique, Guadeloupe, Antigua, and Barbados. There is a 760-m (2,500-ft) airstrip at Canefield, about 5 km (3 mi) north of Roseau.

12 HISTORY

The first island sighted by Christopher Columbus on his second voyage to the New World was Dominica at which he arrived Sunday (dies dominica), 3 November 1493. Carib Indians, whose ancestors originally had come from the Orinoco Basin in South America and, during the 14th century, had driven out the indigenous Arawaks, inhabited the island. The Caribs resisted conquest, and the Spaniards soon lost interest in the island, which had no apparent mineral wealth.

In 1635, France claimed Dominica, and French missionaries visited the island seven years later, but strong Indian resistance to further contact prevented either the French or the English from settling there. In 1660, England and France declared Dominica a neutral island and left it to the Caribs. Within 30 years, however, Europeans began to settle on the island, and in 1727 the French

took formal possession. Under the Treaty of Paris in 1763, however, France ceded the island to Great Britain, which then developed fortifications for its defense. French colonist established coffee plantations during the nearly forty years they held the island. The British introduced sugar production later, but the large slave plantations that characterized other West Indian islands never developed on Dominica. When Great Britain abolished slavery in the West Indies in 1834, 14,175 Dominican slaves obtained their freedom.

Dominica became the first and only British Caribbean colony to have a Black-controlled legislature in the 19th century, but blacks lost most of their political power when the British government, acceding to the wishes of Dominican planters, diluted the strength of the Legislative Assembly and, in 1896, reduced Dominica to a crown colony. Great Britain governed Dominica as part of the Leeward Islands from 1871 until 1939, and in 1940 transferred governance to the Windward Islands administration. From 1958 to 1962, the island belonged to the Federation of the West Indies. Dominica became an associated state of the Commonwealth of Nations in 1967 and on 3 November 1978 became an independent republic.

In its first years of independence, Dominica had several problems. Hurricanes, especially Hurricane David in 1979, brought great destruction to the island, but the corrupt, tyrannical administration of Premier Patrick John led to numerous severe difficulties. Dominicans ousted John in June 1979, and, after a year of interim rule, Mary Eugenia Charles became prime minister in July 1980.

Charles, the first female prime minister in the Caribbean, remained in office for 15 years. Her Dominica Freedom Party received parliamentary majorities in 1985 and 1990, partly because of an improved economic picture. Charles fully supported and sent a token force to participate in the US-led intervention of the island of Grenada in October 1983.

In the early 1990s, controversy flared over the practice of granting "economic citizenship" to Asian nationals who invested $35,000 or more in the country. In response, the government implemented stiffer requirements, including licenses, waiting periods, and additional financial outlays.

Prime Minister Charles's DFP lost its majority in the 1995 elections, and Edison James, leader of the United Workers' Party, formed a new government. Under James, Dominica's economy improved, but charges of corruption concerning the continued sale of Dominican citizenship to foreigners, allegedly including gangsters and smugglers, seriously undermined his creditability. On 31 January 2000 the James government lost an early election to Rosie Douglas and the Dominica Labour Party, which won a plurality of seats in the parliament and formed a coalition with the DFP. Douglas has pledged to reform or abandon the economic citizenship program. In April 2000, he introduced plans for Dominica to become a full fledged member of the European Union.

13 GOVERNMENT

Under the independence constitution of 3 November 1978, Dominica has a unicameral parliament, the House of Assembly, with 21 members elected by universal adult suffrage (at age 18) and 9 appointed members (5 named on the advice of the prime minister, 4 the advice of the leader of the opposition). The life of the Assembly is 5 years. The Prime Minister and Leader of the Opposition nominate the President, though Parliament officially elects the head of state, who in turn appoints the prime minister and cabinet from the majority party in the assembly.

14 POLITICAL PARTIES

Dominica's major political parties are the Dominica Freedom Party (DFP), the Dominica Labour Party (DLP), and the United

DOMINICA

Dominica Passage

0   2   4   6   8Miles

0   2   4   6   8 Kilometers

Vielle Case

Portsmouth

Glanvillia

Wesley

Caribbean Sea

Marigot

Toulaman

▲ Morne Diablatins
4,747 ft.
1447 m.

Salibia

Colihaut

Morne Raquette

Castle Bruce

Salisbury

Layou

Saint Joseph

Pont Cassé

Rosalie

Massacre

Laudat

La Plaine

Roseau ⊛ *Roseau*

Pointe Michel

Berekua

Soufrière

Grand Bay

Caribbean Sea

N
W   E
S

Dominica

LOCATION: 15°N; 16°W. **TOTAL COASTLINE:** 148 km (92 mi).
TERRITORIAL SEA LIMIT: 12 mi.

Workers' Party (UWP). The DFP held power from 1980 to 1995, led by Eugenia Charles, the first woman prime minister in the Caribbean region. (Party leadership was transferred to Brian Alleyne in 1993, but Charles remained prime minister.) The UWP dominated the 1995 elections, winning 11 of the 21 elected seats in the National Assembly. (The DFP and DLP, led by Rosie Douglas, each won 5.) Following the elections, UWP leader Edison James became prime minister. The DLP won 10 of the 21 elected seats in the 2000 election and formed a coalition government with the DFP, now led by Charles Savarin, which captured 2 seats.

15 LOCAL GOVERNMENT

In contrast to other English-speaking islands in the Caribbean, Dominica has a well-developed local government system. There are 25 village councils, made up of both elected and appointed members. Both Roseau and Portsmouth have town councils. There are also 10 parishes, which are administrative divisions for the national government.

16 JUDICIAL SYSTEM

Dominica's judicial process derives from English common law and statutory acts of the House of Assembly. The courts of first instance are the four magistrates' courts; at the second level is the Court of Summary Jurisdiction. The highest court is the Eastern Caribbean Supreme Court, based in St. Lucia, and one of its six judges must reside in Dominica and preside over the Court of Summary Jurisdiction. In exceptional cases, appeals may be carried to the Judicial Committee of the UK Privy Council. Patrick John, who had been convicted in lower courts of planning to overthrow the constitutional government, made such an appeal, and the Privy Council dismissed the charges in 1982. (In 1985, however, he was retried, convicted, and sentenced to 12 years' imprisonment for treason.)

The law provides for public trial before an independent, impartial court. Criminal defendants have the right to legal counsel, and to appeal.

17 ARMED FORCES

A police force of 300 is in charge of law and order. Dominica, along with Antigua and Barbuda, Grenada, St. Kitts and Nevis, St. Lucia, and St. Vincent and the Grenadines, is a member of the Regional Security System, established in 1985. Defense from foreign attack would come from the US or UK.

18 INTERNATIONAL COOPERATION

Dominica became a member of the UN on 18 December 1978 and belongs to ECLAC and all the nonregional specialized agencies except IAEA, ICAO, and WIPO. Dominica also belongs to the Commonwealth of Nations, as well as the Caribbean Development Bank, CARICOM, G-77, OAS, and the Organization of Eastern Caribbean States (OECS). In May 1987, the prime ministers of the member-states of the OECS agreed to create a single nation of the seven island states. The accord was subject to a national referendum in each of the states. The referendums were defeated by the OECS countries and they remained separate. The nation is a member of the WTO and a signatory of the Law of the Sea.

19 ECONOMY

Virtually the entire economy is based on agriculture, fishing, and forestry. Bananas are the main crop, employing one-third of the labor force, although farming methods are often described as inefficient. Coconuts, from which copra is extracted for export, are also important. Tourism is a potential source of income but it is relatively underdeveloped; still lacking are a jet airport, a good system of roads, and luxury hotels. Cruise liners began dropping anchor at Dominica in 1999. The government is promoting industrial development involving agroprocessing and light industry, and hopes to build an airport.

20 INCOME

The US Central Intelligence Agency (CIA) reports that in 1997 Dominica's gross domestic product (GDP) was estimated at $216 million. The per capita GDP was estimated at $3,300. The annual growth rate of GDP was estimated at 1.8%. The average inflation rate in 1997 was 3.2%. The CIA defines GDP as the value of all final goods and services produced within a nation in a given year and computed on the basis of purchasing power parity (PPP) rather than value as measured on the basis of the rate of exchange. It was estimated that agriculture accounted for 20% of GDP, industry 16%, and services 64%.

The World Bank reports that for the same period per capita private consumption (in PPP terms) was $3,010. Private consumption includes expenditures of individuals, households, and nongovernmental organizations. Approximately 33% of household consumption was spent on food, 11% on fuel, 3% on health care, and 6% on education.

21 LABOR

The labor force in 1997 was estimated at 25,000. About 40% of the labor force is employed in agriculture, fishing, and forestry, 32% in industry and commerce, and 28% in services. Labor unions include the Dominica Trade Union, established in 1945; the Dominica Amalgamated Workers' Union, which originated as a banana workers' union; and the Waterfront and Allied Workers' Union. Other unions represent civil servants and teachers. Unemployment was officially 15% in 1992. Unions represented less than 10% of the workforce in 1996.

Unions have the right to strike, organize, and engage in collective bargaining. The minimum working age is 15 and this is generally observed without government enforcement. The minimum wage is set by the government and varies from sector to sector. Last revised in 1989, it mostly averages between $.74 and $1.11 per hour. New recommendations were made by an advisory board in 1998 but had not been implemented as of 1999.

The work week is 40 hours, and the law provides for a minimum of two weeks of paid vacation per year. Occupational safety and health standards are not generally enforced by the government, but most employers comply with them.

22 AGRICULTURE

About 22.6% of the total land area is arable. Agricultural production was on the decline even before the 1979 hurricane disaster. The main crop of Dominica is bananas, output of which had fallen to 29,700 tons in 1978. As a result of Hurricane David, production hit a low of 15,700 tons in 1979. Agriculture suffered a further blow from Hurricane Allen in August 1980. However, after outside financial support began to rehabilitate the sector, production rose to 27,800 tons in 1981 and totaled 30,000 tons in 1998.

Agriculture accounts for about 20% of GDP and employs 40–50% of the labor force. Agricultural exports amounted to $21.8 million in 1997. Most crops are produced on small farms, the 9,000 owners of which are banded together in about 10 cooperatives; there are also several large farms that produce mostly bananas for export. Coconuts and citrus fruits are grown in commercial quantities. Production for 1998 included coconuts, 17,000 tons; grapefruit, 21,000 tons; lemons and limes, 1,000 tons; and oranges, 8,000 tons. Fruits and vegetables are produced mostly for local consumption.

23 ANIMAL HUSBANDRY

There are about 2,000 hectares (4,900 acres) of pastureland, comprising 2.7% of the total land area. The island does not produce sufficient meat, poultry, or eggs for local consumption. In 1998 there were an estimated 13,000 head of cattle, 10,000 goats, 8,000 sheep, and 5,000 hogs. In 1998, production of meat totaled 1,000 tons; and milk, 6,000 tons.

24 FISHING

Before Hurricane David, some 2,000 persons earned a living fishing in coastal waters, producing about 1,000 tons of fish a year and meeting only about one-third of the local demand. The hurricane destroyed almost all of the island's 470 fishing boats;

afterward, only about a dozen vessels could be reconstructed for use. In 1997, the catch was only 855 tons.

25 FORESTRY

Dominica has the potential for a lumber industry. Some 50,000 hectares (123,600 acres) are classified as forest and woodland, representing 67% of the total land area. In 1962, Canadian experts produced a study indicating that over a 40-year period the island could produce a yearly output of 800,000 cu ft of lumber. Before Hurricane David, annual output had reached about 265,000 cu ft. There are some 280 hectares (700 acres) of government land allocated to commercial forestry and about 38 hectares (94 acres) of forestland in private hands. Commercially valuable woods include mahogany, blue and red mahoe, and teak. In 1997, Dominica imported 8,000 cu m of roundwood. Total imports of forest products that year amounted to $5.6 million.

26 MINING

Commercial mining is limited. Pumice is the major commodity extracted from the island for export. Dominica produces clay, limestone, volcanic ash, and sand and gravel primarily for the construction industry.

27 ENERGY AND POWER

Of the numerous short streams on Dominica, at least 30 might be sources of hydroelectric power on a small scale; about 50% of the power supply already comes from hydroelectric sources. In 1991, the Trafalgar Hydroelectric Power Station came onstream, making the island nearly self-sufficient in energy. The island also has thermal power potential in the volcanic Boiling Lake, the temperature of which has been recorded in the range of 82–92°C (180–198°F). In 1998, 40 million kWh of electricity were produced.

28 INDUSTRY

Dominica has only light industry, most of it is connected with the processing of agricultural products. Industrial establishments include a plant for processing coconuts into oil and copra for export; four plants to process limes and other citrus fruits; two bottling plants; two distilleries; four small apparel plants; and four small furniture factories. Dominica exports water to its Caribbean neighbors; soap and toiletries are also exported. Home industries produce some leather work, ceramics, and straw products.

In the 1990s, the small manufacturing sector has been expanding at a modest pace, including electronic assembly, rum, candles, and paints. The Trafalgar Hydro Electric Power Station is now operational, making the island virtually energy self-sufficient. In 1998, the manufacturing growth rate was 21%, but accounted for only about 9% of the total GDP.

29 SCIENCE AND TECHNOLOGY

Late in 1980, Dominica created a Council for Science and Technology, under the Ministry of Education. However, without a budget and a clear directive of purpose, the council had accomplished little by 1986. The Caribbean Agricultural Research Development Institute has been active in more than a half-dozen projects.

30 DOMESTIC TRADE

Local produce markets exist in all the small villages and towns. Commercial activity is concentrated in the morning hours, since tropical rains impede afternoon travel. Banks are open from 8 AM to 1 PM, Monday–Friday, with additional hours from 3 to 5 PM on Friday. There is no commercial activity on Saturday afternoon and Sunday.

31FOREIGN TRADE

Dominica is well known for its exports of bananas, which reflect about half of the country's commodity export revenues (49%). Soap and cleaning products account for a full third of exports. Other exports include vegetables (3.3%), paint (2.7%), and perfume (2.6%).

In 1996 Dominica's imports were distributed among the following categories:

Consumer goods	12.5%
Food	21.9%
Fuels	6.3%
Industrial supplies	37.9%
Machinery	13.3%
Transportation	7.9%
Other	0.1%

Principal trading partners in 1998 (in millions of US dollars) were as follows:

COUNTRY	EXPORTS	IMPORTS	BALANCE
Jamaica	16	2	14
United Kingdom	15	20	-5
Trinidad and Tobago	4	21	-17
France	4	6	-2
United States	3	57	-54
Barbados	3	6	-3
St. Lucia	2	3	-1
Japan	n.a.	8	
Korea	n.a.	6	
China (inc. Hong Kong)	n.a.	51	

32BALANCE OF PAYMENTS

The increasingly unfavorable balance of trade produces a current-account deficit and boosts the foreign debt. Recurrent hurricanes add to the debt burden. Dominica hopes to be able to offset the trade deficit with tourism revenues.

The US Central Intelligence Agency reports that in 1997 the purchasing power parity of Dominica's exports was $50.4 million while imports totaled $104.2 million resulting in a trade balance of -$53.8 million.

The International Monetary Fund (IMF) reports that in 1996 Dominica had exports of goods totaling $53 million and imports totaling $101 million. The services credit totaled $61 million and debit $45 million. The following table summarizes Dominica's balance of payments for 1996 in millions of US dollars.

Current Account		-40
Balance on goods	-48	
Balance on services	16	
Balance on income	-19	
Current transfers	10	
Capital Account		25
Financial Account		10
Direct investment abroad	...	
Direct investment in Dominica	18	
Portfolio investment assets	...	
Portfolio investment liabilities	-	
Other investment assets	-10	
Other investment liabilities	1	
Net Errors and Omissions		7
Reserves and Related Items		-2

33BANKING AND SECURITIES

The principal national banks are the National Commercial and Development Bank of Dominica and the Dominica Agricultural Industrial and Development (AID) Bank. Private commercial banks include Barclays (UK), the Royal Bank of Canada, and the Banque Française Commerciale. Dominica is a member of the Eastern Caribbean Central Bank, which issues a common currency. Dominica has no stock market.

34INSURANCE

Representatives of British, Canadian, and US insurance companies do business in Dominica.

35PUBLIC FINANCE

Operating revenues come mostly from customs duties, excise taxes, and other taxes and fees for government services. The leading areas of expenditure are education, health, public services, housing, and defense.

The US Central Intelligence Agency (CIA) estimates that in 1997 Dominica's central government took in revenues of approximately $72 million and had expenditures of $79.9 million including capital expenditures of $11.5 million. Overall, the government registered a deficit of approximately $7.9 million. External debt totaled $153 million.

36TAXATION

Taxes levied by the Dominican government include a progressive personal income tax ranging from 0% to 40%; a business income tax of 35%; social security taxes; a 3% gross receipts tax on retail sales; and taxes on land transfers and land-value appreciation. There is no capital gains tax except the land-value appreciation tax.

37CUSTOMS AND DUTIES

Specific import duties apply to food, and ad valorem duties to other items. The government levies export duties on principal agricultural products; the charge is heavy on rum and cigarettes but lighter on bananas and coconuts. Under a 1992 Caribbean Community agreement, Dominica eliminated import licensing. Dominica has adopted CARICOM's CET, which ranges up to 35%.

38FOREIGN INVESTMENT

The amount of foreign investment in Dominica is limited, in large part because the island lacks the infrastructure to support an industrialization program. Investment increased in the early 1990s under the Charles government, particularly in agriculture. The marketing of banana production is monopolized by European multinational corporations. Tax holidays and import-duty exemptions are offered as investment incentives. The area near the Canefield airstrip is industrial estate and export processing zone. The government agency for industrial development has had some success in attracting capital investment funds for the island. The introduction of an offshore financial industry may attract investment, as well as increased tourism.

Other investment incentives include repatriation of profits, alien's landholding license fee, factory building/industrial estates, residence/work permits.

39ECONOMIC DEVELOPMENT

Dominica seeks to foster private enterprise. However, the Charles government was willing to intervene in the economy where it perceived a need. In 1986, for example, it created an export-import agency and announced a land-reform program, both to stimulate agriculture. Under the latter, the government purchased 800 hectares (2,000 acres) of land in prime growing areas and then guaranteed a minimum holding with security of tenure, as well as services and equipment, to small farmers and landless farm workers.

As of 1994, the government encouraged agriculture expansion by a program of diversification. This program was aimed at improving the marketing of production and providing income guarantees for farmers diversifying into new crops. There was still serious concern at the implication of the restructuring of formerly protected European markets, despite the EC's implementation of favorable banana terms on 1 July 1993.

The economy is dependent on agriculture and thus is highly vulnerable to climatic conditions. Agriculture accounts for about 30% of GDP and employs 40% of the labor force. Development of the tourist industry remains difficult because of the rugged coastline and the lack of an international airport, but the government bought land for the construction of an airport in 1999.

40 SOCIAL DEVELOPMENT

Until the early 1980s, a high rate of unemployment, a markedly high rate of emigration, and very limited resources hindered the development of social service programs in Dominica. In 1976, the government established the Social Security Scheme, which covers all workers from 14 to 60 years of age, including apprentices. Under this plan, both workers and employers contribute specific amounts to a government fund, which provides pensions for workers reaching retirement age, compensation for workers who become incapacitated, and survivor benefits. There are also sickness and maternity benefits.

As of 1999, the social security system is supported by worker contributions of 3% of earnings (7% self-employed) and a 7% employer payroll tax. Retirement is set at age 60, with benefits of 30% of average earnings plus 2% for every 50 weeks of contributions in excess of 500.

Apart from the constitution, there is no specific legislation in force to protect women from sex discrimination. A hotline manned by volunteers is available for battered women, and the Welfare Department often helps them find temporary quarters. In 1995, two women were voted into Parliament. The existing law governing sexual offenses, which required either medical evidence or witness corroboration, was replaced by a new law in 1998.

Indigenous Carib minorities face minimal discrimination, and most live on a 3,700-acre reservation set aside for them by the government in 1903. Human rights are generally respected in Dominica. However, instances of excessive police force have been documented, and prison conditions are poor.

41 HEALTH

In 1995 there were 47 physicians, 312 nurses, and 8 dentists per 100,00 population in public sector jobs. The one general hospital on Dominica is in Roseau, the 195-bed Princess Margaret Hospital. There are 7 health centers and 44 clinics scattered across the island. Serious tropical diseases such as yaws and malaria have been eradicated, but owing to the high humidity and rainy conditions, tuberculosis and other respiratory diseases continue to be a problem. Intestinal parasites afflict particularly those in the early years of life. There were 2,000 births in 1994. Only 7% of newborns were low birth weight between 1992 and 1995. In 1996, the infant mortality rate was 21 per 1,000 live births. Average life expectancy in 1998 was 77 years. In 1997, 99% of the country's children were immunized against measles, and the same percentage for DPT, tuberculosis, and polio. Some 31 new cases of AIDS were reported in 1996, and 12 new cases of tuberculosis were reported in 1994. Polio and measles were absent from the island in 1994.

42 HOUSING

Hurricane David in 1979 destroyed the homes of over four-fifths of the population. Under an emergency housing program, construction supplies were brought into the island, and shelters were built for most of the population. In the early 1980s, the last period for which information is available, about four-fifths of all dwellings were detached houses and fewer than one-fifth were apartments. Over two-thirds were owner occupied, one-fifth were rented privately, and about 10% were occupied rent free. A small number were rented from the government. Over half of all housing units were wooden, while smaller percentages were either concrete or wood and concrete.

43 EDUCATION

Much of Dominica's school system had to be rebuilt after the 1979 hurricane. In 1995 there were 64 primary schools, with 641 teachers and 12,627 students enrolled. Education is compulsory between the ages of 5 and 16. In secondary schools, there were approximately 6,500 students enrolled. Technical and vocational studies offer practical training in technical and electrical engineering, auto mechanics, plumbing, general business, construction, and agriculture. Transportation to secondary schools is a problem for students in rural areas.

Higher educational facilities include a teacher training institute, a technical college, a nursing school, and a local center maintained by the University of the West Indies. In higher level institutions, there were 34 teaching staff and 484 students in 1993.

44 LIBRARIES AND MUSEUMS

A library system maintained by the government includes branches in five of the leading villages; there is also a mobile library unit for rural areas. No information is available on museums in Dominica.

45 MEDIA

In 1997 there were 703 radios and 81 television sets per 1,000 population. As of 1999, there were 3 AM and 2 FM radio stations and one (cable) television station. Dominicans also receive TV and radio broadcasts from neighboring islands. Two weekly newspapers are published in Roseau, the *New Chronicle* (circulation in 1999, 4,500) and the government-published *Official Gazette* (550), among other journals and periodicals. Dominica had 13,700 digital telephone lines in operation in 1995.

The constitution provides for the right of free expression, and the government is said to respect free speech and a free press. Independent print and electronic media operate without restrictions by the government authorities.

46 ORGANIZATIONS

There are many cooperatives and credit unions in Dominica. A chamber of commerce and a small Rotary Club also function.

47 TOURISM, TRAVEL, AND RECREATION

Dominica's tourism industry is expanding gradually with government support. However, development of tourism has been slow compared with that on neighboring islands, but Dominica expects to benefit from the growth of ecotourism. Its principal attraction is the rugged natural beauty of its volcanic peaks, forests, lakes, and waterfalls, and over 365 rivers. Day trips to Dominica from Barbados, Guadeloupe, and Martinique have gained increasing popularity. Cricket is the national sport.

In 1997, 65,446 tourists arrived in Dominica. Revenues from tourism reached US$40 million. Hotel rooms numbered 623 that year. In 1999, the UN estimated the cost of staying in Dominica at $184 per day.

48 FAMOUS DOMINICANS

Maria Eugenia Charles (b.1919), cofounder of the Dominica Freedom Party, became prime minister in 1980.

49 DEPENDENCIES

Dominica has no territories or colonies.

⁵⁰BIBLIOGRAPHY

Baker, Patrick L. *Centring the Periphery: Chaos, Order, and the Ethnohistory of Dominica.* Montreal: McGill-Queen's University Press, 1994.

Caribbean and Central American Databook, 1987. Washington, D.C.: Caribbean/Central American Action, 1986.

Honeychurch, Lennox. *The Dominica Story: A History of the Island.* London: Macmillan, 1995.

Investing in Dominica. Washington. D.C.: Caribbean/Central American Action, 1986.

Myers, Robert A. *Dominica.* Santa Barbara, Calif.: Clio Press, 1987.

Trouillot, Michel-Rolph. *Peasants and Capital: Dominica in the World Economy.* Baltimore: Johns Hopkins University Press, 1988.

DOMINICAN REPUBLIC

Dominican Republic
Republica Dominicana

CAPITAL: Santo Domingo.

FLAG: The national flag, adopted in 1844, consists of a white cross superimposed on a field of four rectangles, the upper left and lower right in blue, the upper right and lower left in red. The national seal is at the center of the white cross.

ANTHEM: *Himno Nacional,* beginning "Quisqueyanos valientes, alcemos nuestro canto" ("Valiant Dominicans, let us raise our song").

MONETARY UNIT: The Dominican peso (RD$) of 100 centavos is a paper currency. There are coins of 1, 5, 10, 25, and 50 centavos and 1 peso, and notes of 1, 5, 10, 20, 50, 100, 500, and 1,000 pesos. RD$1 = US$0.06329 (US$1 = RD$15.80) as of 31 March 2000.

WEIGHTS AND MEASURES: The metric system is the legal standard, but US and Spanish weights are widely used in commercial transactions.

HOLIDAYS: New Year's Day, 1 January; Epiphany, 6 January; Altagracia Day, 21 January; Duarte Day, 26 January; Independence Day, 27 February; Labor Day, 1 May; Restoration of Independence, 16 August; Day of Our Lady of Las Mercedes, 24 September; All Saints' Day, 1 November; Christmas, 25 December. Movable religious holidays include Good Friday and Corpus Christi.

TIME: Eastern Daylight Savings Time is maintained throughout the year; 8 AM = noon GMT.

¹LOCATION, SIZE, AND EXTENT

The Dominican Republic occupies the eastern two-thirds of the island of Hispaniola (Española) and includes the islands of Beata, Catalina, Saona, Alto Velo, and Catalinita in the Caribbean Sea, and several islets in the Atlantic Ocean. It has an area of 48,730 sq km (18,815 sq mi), with a length of 386 km (240 mi) E–W, extending from Cape Engaño to the Haitian border, and a width of 261 km (162 mi) N–S, extending from Cape Isabela to Cape Beata. Comparatively, the area occupied by the Dominican Republic is slightly more than twice the size of the state of New Hampshire. Bounded on the N by the Atlantic Ocean, on the E by the Mona Passage (which separates it from Puerto Rico), on the S by the Caribbean Sea, and on the W by Haiti, the Dominican Republic has a total boundary length of 1,563 km (971 mi).

The Dominican Republic's capital city, Santo Domingo, is located on its southern coast.

²TOPOGRAPHY

The Dominican Republic is generally mountainous, with deserts in the extreme western regions. The principal mountain range, the Central Cordillera, running from east to west and extensively pine-forested, bisects the republic. Between the Central Cordillera and the Northern Cordillera (and their associated plains) lies the famous Cibao (La Vega Real) Valley (225 km/140 mi long, with an average width of 23 km/14 mi), noted for the excellent quality of its soil. Fertile valleys also abound in the central and eastern areas. The country contains both the highest mountain in the West Indies, Mt. Duarte (3,175 m/10,417 ft), and the lowest-lying lake, Lake Enriquillo (40 m/131 ft below sea level). The Yaque del Norte, the Yaque del Sur, and the Yuna are the principal rivers.

³CLIMATE

Climate and rainfall vary with region and altitude. Generally, however, average minimum and maximum temperatures range from 18° to 29°C (64° to 84°F) in the winter and from 23° to 35°C (73° to 95°F) in the summer. The coastal plain has an annual mean temperature of 26°C (79°F), while in the Central Cordillera the climate is temperate and the mean is 20°C (68°F). Rainfall varies from an annual average of 135 cm (53 in) in the eastern regions, with an extreme of 208 cm (82 in) in the northeast, to a mean of 43 cm (17 in) in the western areas. The rainy season generally extends from May to November and the dry season from December to April. The nation lies within the hurricane belt, and tropical storms constitute a major weather hazard.

⁴FLORA AND FAUNA

Plants and animal life vary by region. Dense rain forests are common in the wetter areas; scrub woodland thrives along the drier slopes; and savanna vegetation is found on the open plains. Dominican mahogany and highly resinous pine trees grow in the high mountains. The rare hutia (a small rodent) and herds of wild boar are found in the mountainous areas. Ducks, doves, and several varieties of pigeons are seasonal visitors. Lake Enriquillo is the natural habitat of large flocks of flamingos. Spanish mackerel, mullet, bonito, and yellowtail snapper are found in the surrounding waters.

⁵ENVIRONMENT

The main agencies responsible for environmental protection are the Department of National Parks and the Department of State for Agriculture. The Dominican Republic has environmental problems in the areas of deforestation, water supply, and soil erosion, and as the eroding soil enters the sea, it damages the nation's coral reefs as well. UN sources report that, as of 1993, the nation was losing 20,000 hectares per year of its forest lands largely due to commercial interests. The felling of trees was prohibited in 1967 to remedy the ill effects of indiscriminate cutting by commercial producers and farmers and the destruction by fire of large stands of timber. However, many farmers continue to cut trees surreptitiously to make more land available for cultivation. Soil erosion results from a combination of rainfall and the use of land in mountainous areas. As of 1994, the Dominican Republic has an inadequate water supply. The country has 4.8 cu mi of water with 89% used for farming. Only 74% of all urban dwellers and 67% of rural inhabitants have pure water. Water pollution results from the effects of mining along with industrial and agricultural sources.

Endangered species in the Dominican Republic include the tundra peregrine falcon, Haitian solenodon, three species of sea turtle (green sea, hawksbill, and leatherback), and American crocodile. In 1994, one of the country's mammal species and five bird species were considered endangered, and four types of reptiles were also threatened. As of 1993, 62 plant species in a total of 1,600 were threatened with extinction.

6POPULATION

The population of the Dominican Republic in 2000 was estimated at 8,261,536. An estimated 4.2% of the population is 65 years of age or older. The projected population for the year 2005 is 8,937,000, assuming a crude birthrate of 24 per 1,000 population and a death rate of 5, resulting in a natural rate of change of 1.8% for the period 2000–2005. The population rate of change between 1995 and 2000 was 1.7%. The population density in 1998 was 171 per sq km (443 per sq mi).

It was estimated that 65% of the population lived in urban areas in 2000, up from 51% in 1980. The capital city, Santo Domingo, had a 2000 metropolitan population of 3,601,000. Other important cities are Santiago de los Caballeros (1,540,000 in 2000), La Romana, San Pedro de Macorís, San Francisco de Macorís, and Concepción de la Vega.

7MIGRATION

Four overseas immigration movements have taken place in recent decades: approximately 5,000 refugees from the Spanish Civil War in the late 1930s; a Jewish refugee group, which arrived in 1940; a continuous flow of Japanese, mainly farmers, since 1950; and 600 Hungarian refugees invited by the government in 1957. These are dwarfed, however, by the influx of Haitians, some seasonal, others permanent. The number of Haitians living in the Dominican Republic has been estimated at 500,000 to 1,000,000.

Emigration became significant for the first time during the 1960s, when 93,300 Dominicans legally entered the US; during 1971–80, the figure rose to 148,100, and during 1981–85, it was 104,800. In 1990 there were 357,000 Dominican-born people living in the US, mostly along the eastern seaboard. This census total may have been an undercount, for estimates of the Dominican population in the US ranged as high as 1,000,000, including 200,000 in Puerto Rico.

An estimated 35,000 Haitians entered the Dominican Republic after the military coup that overthrew Haiti's president, Jean-Bertrand Aristide, in September 1991. By May 1997, 20,000 Haitians had returned to their homeland, voluntarily or by deportation. The majority of Haitian refugees live outside the capitol, Santo Domingo. The Dominican Republic government initiated a program to deport illegal migrants back to Haiti. However, this program does not affect recognized refugees or asylum seekers, as they receive temporary residence permits. As of September 1999, there were 630 Haitian refugees in the Dominican Republic, all of whom had been living in the country for several years. The net migration rate in 1999 was -4.14 migrants per 1,000 population.

8ETHNIC GROUPS

Ethnic divisions have been estimated at 16% white, 11% black, and 73% mulatto. Descendants of early Spanish settlers and of black slaves from West Africa constitute the two main racial strains.

9LANGUAGES

Spanish is the official language. Some English is spoken in the capital, and a Creole dialect is used along the Haitian border.

10RELIGIONS

Religious freedom is protected by law, and there is no state religion. However, the Roman Catholic Church, which signed a concordat with the government in 1954, is extended special privileges not granted to other religions. In 1998, professing Roman Catholics represented an estimated 68.1% of the population. Protestants, including Baptists and Seventh-day Adventists, and other Christians accounted for another 11.3%. As many as 20.4% declared no religious affiliation whatsoever.

11TRANSPORTATION

The national highway system is the dominant means of inland public transportation. Three main highways emanate from Santo Domingo: the Carretera Sánchez (connecting with Elias Piña on the Haitian border), the Carretera Mella (to Higüey in the extreme southeast), and the Carretera Duarte (to Monte Cristi on the northwest coast). In 1999 there were 12,600 km (7,830 mi) of roadways, of which 6,224 km (3,868 mi) were paved. In 1995, 120,000 passenger cars and 80,000 commercial vehicles were licensed. During the same year, 757 km (470 mi) of railways in four different gauges were in service.

The Santo Domingo, Andrés, and Haina harbors, all in the Santo Domingo area, handle the vast majority of imports. Other large ports include Puerto Plata in the northwest; La Romana, Boca Chica, and San Pedro de Macorís in the southeast; and Barahona in the southwest. The Dominican merchant fleet had one ship of 1,587 GRT in 1998.

Also in 1998 there were an estimated 36 total airports, 14 of which had paved runways. Dominicana de Aviación provides international service from Las Americas International Airport at Punta Caucedo, 29 km (18 mi) east of Santo Domingo. Cargo and mail service to the US mainland, Puerto Rico, and the US Virgin Islands is provided by Aerolíneas Argo. Alas del Caribe provides domestic passenger service, as does Aerovías Quisqueyanas. There are also international airports at Puerto Plata and La Romana. In 1997 34,000 passengers were carried on regularly scheduled domestic and international flights.

12HISTORY

The eastern part of the island of Hispaniola was originally known as Quisqueya, meaning "mother of all lands." It was first settled by the nomadic and warlike Carib Amerindians and later by the agricultural and peace-loving Arawaks. Christopher Columbus made the European discovery of the island and claimed it for Spain in 1492. Santo Domingo, the oldest city in the New World, was founded four years later by Bartholomew Columbus, the explorer's brother. By 1517, Hispaniola had become the springboard for Spanish conquest of the Caribbean and of the American mainland. As with other Caribbean islands, the Amerindian population dwindled, and were replaced by African slaves.

The importance of Hispaniola waned during the 16th and 17th centuries. In 1697, by the Treaty of Ryswick, Spain was forced to recognize French dominion over the western third of the island, an area now known as Haiti. In 1795, under the Treaty of Basel, Spain ceded to France the eastern two-thirds of the island, which by then had been renamed Santo Domingo. The island then came under the rule of the rebellious ex-slave Toussaint L'Ouverture. After Haiti received independence in 1804, the French retained the rest of the island until 1809. After a brief

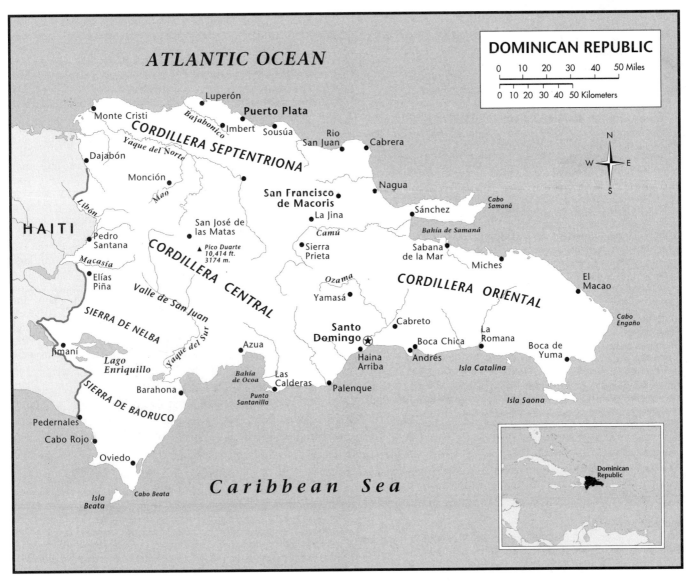

LOCATION: 17°36′22″ to 19°56′9″N; 68°19′24″ to 72°0′48″W. **BOUNDARY LENGTHS:** Total coastline, 1,288 km (799 mi); Haiti, 275 km (170 mi).
TERRITORIAL SEA LIMIT: 6 mi.

attempt at independence, the Dominicans fell under the control of Spain, which regained the eastern section of the island under the Treaty of Paris (1814).

In 1821, the Dominicans, led by José Múñez de Cáceres, proclaimed their independence. The Dominicans sought to become part of Simón Bolívar's newly-independent Republic of Gran Colombia, but in 1822, the Haitians conquered the entire island. For 22 years, the Haitians ruled with an iron fist. A civil war in 1843 gave the Dominicans the opportunity to try again for independence, and, under Juan Pablo Duarte, they established the Dominican Republic as an independent state.

Between 1844 and 1916, the new republic alternated among personalist leaders, who sought foreign protection against Haiti. The most prominent among these were Pedro Santana and Buenaventura Baez, who dominated Dominican politics until 1882. Santana restored the Dominican Republic to the Spanish Empire during 1861–65. Baez in 1869 negotiated a treaty providing for US annexation, but the US Senate refused to ratify it.

After a 17-year dictatorship, the Dominican Republic entered a turbulent period characterized by general political instability and increasing debt to US interests. In 1905, US President Theodore Roosevelt appointed an American receiver of Dominican customs, and a subsequent treaty provided for repayment of the debt. This first application of the "Roosevelt Corollary" to the Monroe Doctrine was followed in 1916 by the US establishment of a military government under Marine Capt. H. S. Knapp. It ruled the Dominican Republic until 12 July 1924, when sovereignty was restored. US customs control continued until 1941.

In 1930, Rafael Leonidas Trujillo Molina was elected president. For the next 31 years, he ruled the Dominican Republic either directly or indirectly. Trujillo had himself reelected in 1934, 1940, and 1947, then arranged for his brother to become president in 1952 and 1957, and then installed Joaquín Balaguer in 1960. Under Trujillo, the Dominican Republic achieved some economic progress, removing its foreign debt. But Trujillo brutally suppressed fundamental human rights. Only one party was allowed, the press was totally controlled, and constant purges weeded out all but his most servile supporters. His most dubious achievements were a result of his own megalomania. In the capital city of Santo Domingo, which he renamed Ciudad Trujillo (Trujillo City), there were 1,870 monuments to Trujillo, who gave himself the title "The Benefactor of the Fatherland." He also amassed a personal fortune estimated at $900–$1,500 million.

Trujillo was assassinated on 30 May 1961. In July 1961, the Balaguer cabinet resigned as street rioting broke out. The opposition agreed to an interim coalition government under Balaguer that September, with Rafael Trujillo, Jr., as head of the armed forces. In November, the US sent warships just outside Dominican waters to prevent the armed forces chief and his two uncles from a staging a rumored coup. They went into exile immediately.

After rule by an interim Council of State, Juan Bosch of the Dominican Revolutionary Party was elected president in 1962. He assumed office in February 1963 but remained in power for only seven months, during which time very little of the promised social and economic reform could be accomplished. The military, which overthrew Bosch in September 1963, proceeded to install a three-man civilian junta, called the Triumvirate, which was in turn overthrown by the supporters of Juan Bosch in April 1965. With anarchy threatening—and, according to US allegations, Communists deeply involved in the pro-Bosch insurrection—the US sent 23,000 troops into the Dominican Republic, ostensibly to protect the lives of US citizens. Within weeks, the OAS had set up an Inter-America Peace Force in the country. This controversial set of arrangements eventually brought order to the country. After the 1966 elections, all US and OAS troops left the island.

In the general elections of June 1966, Balaguer, returned from exile, campaigned vigorously throughout the country, while Bosch, his chief opponent, remained home, apparently fearful of an attempt on his life. Balaguer won with 57.2% of the vote. Four years later, Balaguer ran essentially without opposition, as most parties withdrew from the campaign in response to rising political violence.

Events in 1974 followed a similar pattern. Two days before the election, an opposition coalition announced their withdrawal from the contest. The opposition's principal candidate, Silvestre Antonio Guzmán Fernández of the PRD (Dominican Revolutionary Party), called for general abstention from the election, charging Balaguer with fraudulent practices. Only one candidate—Adm. Luis Homero Lajara Burgos, a former chief of police under Trujillo—remained in the race. The results gave Balaguer an overwhelming majority, with 924,779 votes to Lajara Burgos's 105,320.

Following the 1974 elections, the opposition coalition, an amalgam of widely divergent political elements, decided to disperse in anticipation of the 1978 campaign. Despite their lack of representation in the legislature and in municipal councils as a result of the election boycott, the major opposition parties, aided by a large degree of press freedom, remained active and vocal. In the 1978 elections, the main presidential candidates were Balaguer and the PRD's Guzmán. Guzmán won with a 158,000-vote plurality, and his party gained a majority in the Chamber of Deputies. Numerous other parties, including the newly legalized Dominican Communist Party, participated in the elections. A right-wing military attempt to prevent Guzmán from assuming office was foiled, partly because of US government pressure.

During Guzmán's term, political prisoners were freed, press censorship was practically abolished, and political parties engaged in open activity. At the same time, however, there were mounting economic difficulties, aggravated by two hurricanes in 1979, which together left 1,300 people dead, 500 missing, and 100,000 homeless. In May 1982, a left-wing PRD senator, Salvador Jorge Blanco, was elected president. On 4 July, six weeks before his term was due to expire, Guzmán committed suicide, after several close associates were accused of fraud. Power was transferred peacefully to Vice President Jacobo Majluta Azar, and, in August 1982, to Blanco.

Whatever plans President Blanco may have had were soon overtaken by the country's burgeoning foreign debt. Blanco turned to the IMF for assistance. The resultant restrictive economic policy raised production costs and reduced industrial output. A cut in the US sugar quota, as well as a generally low world price for the commodity, was a further blow to the economy.

In presidential elections held 16 May 1986, former president Joaquín Balaguer was returned to office with 857,942 votes (41.6%). Jacob Majluta Azar of the PRD took 814,716 votes (39.5%), and Juan Bosch of the PLD (Dominican Liberation Party) won 379,269 votes (18.4%). Balaguer embarked on an ambitious program of public works that created employment for nearly 100,000 people. But by 1988, inflation was on the rise, and the peso had become unstable. Nationwide strikes in 1989 suggested that the country was headed for further crisis.

In 1990, Balaguer stood for reelection, and won a narrow, hotly contested victory amid claims of fraud by the opposition. Officially, Balaguer received 35.7% of the vote to Juan Bosch's 34.4%. Balaguer was nevertheless inaugurated, but immediately created controversy by suggesting a set of IMF-style liberal reforms. This brought national strikes in August and November of 1990, and demands for resignation. In the Chamber of Deputies, where Bosch's PLD held a plurality of seats, Balaguer faced serious opposition.

The results of a large portion of the May 1994 presidential vote, won, once again, by Balaguer, were voided by the electoral board, and Balaguer agreed to shorten his term to two years, scheduling a new election for May 1996. In that contest, no candidate won a majority, but a second round of voting on 30 June produced a victory for Leonel Fernández of the PLD, who took office in August.

Although economic reforms introduced in late 1994 helped improve growth and lower inflation, unemployment remained high, spurring substantial emigration to the US and Puerto Rico. In March and June 1995, riots occurred in response to unauthorized increases in public transportation fares. During his four years in office, Fernández successfully privatized several state-owned enterprises and utilities. The economy expanded at an average of 5% annually, unemployment fell, and inflation was low. Fernández successfully fought government corruption and consolidated democratic institutions. In spite of his popularity, however, he was constitutionally prevented from seeking reelection in the polling scheduled for May 2000.

13 GOVERNMENT

The constitution of 28 November 1966 established a unitary republic consisting of 26 (currently 29) provinces and a single National District. The government is effectively controlled by the chief executive, a president directly elected for a four-year term and eligible for reelection. Cabinet ministers (called secretaries of state) are appointed by the president, who must be at least 30 years of age.

The National Congress consists of a Senate, composed of 30 members, and a 149-member Chamber of Deputies, apportioned on the basis of population. Members of the two houses are elected for four-year terms and must be at least 25 years of age. Bills for legislative action may be introduced by the president, by the National Congress, or by the Supreme Court. Voting is by universal suffrage of citizens 18 years or older, although younger citizens, if married, may also vote. Presidential and congressional elections are not held simultaneously. Presidential elections are scheduled for 2000 and parliamentary elections for 2002.

14POLITICAL PARTIES

Although the Dominican Republic has 3 major parties and more than 10 minor parties, two men, Joaquín Balaguer Ricardo and Juan Bosch Gavino, dominated its political system for decades, but starting in 1996 a new cadre of politicians emerged.

Joaquín Balaguer, a former president under Trujillo, was elected to the presidency six times, most recently in 1994. He founded the Social Christian Reform Party (Partido Reformista Social Christiano—PRSC) while living in exile in New York in 1963. The party, which Balaguer still led in the mid-1990s, is tied to the Christian Democratic political movement, and relies principally on peasant and middle-class support. Currently, it holds 2 of 30 Senate seats and 17 of 149 seats in the Chamber of Deputies.

Juan Bosch, who held the presidency for seven months in 1963 before the Dominican crisis, remained a major voice in Dominican politics into the 1990s. Bosch founded the Dominican Revolutionary Party (Partido Revolucionario Dominicano—PRD) in 1939. After withdrawing from the PRD, Bosch created his own party, the Dominican Liberation Party (Partido de la Liberación Dominicana—PLD) in 1973. In the second round of voting in the 1996 presidential elections, the PLD's Leonel Fernandez was elected president with just over 51% of the vote. The party gained 4 seats in the Senate and 49 seats in the Chamber of Deputies.

The PRD continues on without Bosch, and with far more success than Bosch was ever able to achieve. The PRD won the presidential elections of 1978 and 1982, although it was unable to achieve a majority in either house of Congress in 1982. Headed by Jose Francisco Peña Gomez, the PRD has an association with the Socialist International, and a "Eurosocialist" ideological thrust of moderate economic and social change. The party draws support from landless peasants and urban workers. Peña Gomez received 23% of the vote in 1990 and 48.75% in 1996. The PRD won 83 seats in the Chamber of Deputies and 24 Senate seats. Peña Gómez's unexpected death in 1998 forced the PRD to find a new presidential candidate. Hipólito Mejía emerged as the PRD leader and he is running ahead in the polls for the May 2000 elections.

The Independent Revolutionary Party (PRI) was the vehicle for Jacobo Majluta Azar, who served as president briefly in 1982. A former PRD member, Majluta received only 7% of the vote in 1990. The party, now led by Arturo Martinez, holds no seats in the Chamber of Deputies or the Senate.

15LOCAL GOVERNMENT

The Dominican Republic is divided into 29 provinces and a National District, encompassing Santo Domingo. The provinces are further subdivided into 31 municipal districts and 95 municipalities. The president appoints the provincial governors. Municipal districts must have at least 5,000 inhabitants and produce sufficient revenue to finance their own administrative agencies. The municipalities and the National District are governed by mayors and municipal councils of at least five members, elected by popular vote.

16JUDICIAL SYSTEM

The judicial system is headed by a Supreme Court with nine judges, which rules on constitutional questions and serves in the last instance on appeals. Supreme Court judges are elected by the Senate and cannot be removed from office. The Supreme Court appoints the judges of the lower courts and of the special courts. All judges are required to hold a law degree.

There are 26 provincial courts, as well as one court of first instance in the National District. The judicial system also includes one judge or court of justice for each of the country's 72 municipal districts, three courts of appeal, a court of accounts, and a land tribunal. There are also justices of the peace. The death penalty was abolished in 1924. Although the constitution provides for an independent judiciary, in practice the executive branch as well as public and private entities exert pressures on the courts. The constitution guarantees public trials, and indigent defendants have a right to a court-appointed attorney at state expense.

Military courts try military personnel charged with extrajudicial killings. The 1994 constitutional reforms mandated a National Judicial Council. The National Judicial Council has seven members including the president and legislators from both houses of Congress, the president of the Supreme Court, and a second Supreme Court justice.

17ARMED FORCES

The army of 15,000 is organized into 4 infantry brigades and 5 independent battalions. The air force has 5,500 personnel and is equipped with 10 combat aircraft of US and UK origin. The navy of 4,000 mans 17 coast defense ships and 4 auxiliaries. The national police numbers 15,000, including 1,000 special operations officers. In 1998, the armed forces were allocated $180 million or about 1.1% of GNP.

18INTERNATIONAL COOPERATION

The Dominican Republic is a charter member of the UN, having joined on 24 October 1945, and participates in ECLAC and all the nonregional specialized agencies except WIPO. It also belongs to G-77, IADB, and OAS, as well as the International Bauxite Association and the International Coffee Organization. The Dominican Republic is a member of the WTO and a signatory of the Law of the Sea. The nation's application to join CARICOM was blocked by Grenada in July 1983.

19ECONOMY

The economy is based primarily on agriculture, which accounts for about 19% of the GDP, half of the labor force, and a major share of total exports. By the 1990s, services had overtaken agriculture as the main employer and GDP component. Tourism accounts for about $1 billion annually, as do remittances from Dominicans working in the US. The government encourages investment in industry and tourism, seeking to diversify the economy and reduce the nation's dependence on sugar production.

Between 1968 and 1974, the average annual growth of GDP was 10.5%. The improved political climate during that period stimulated public and private investment, both domestic and foreign, and the development of tourism. A sugar boom also contributed to rapid growth. During the second half of the 1970s, the growth rate slowed, in part because of rising oil prices and a weakening of the sugar market; damage from two 1979 hurricanes cost an estimated $1 billion.

The GDP declined by 2.2% in 1985, reflecting low world prices for the country's exports, declining US sugar quotas, and IMF imposed austerity. Unemployment soared to 26%, and inflation reached 37.5% the same year. The economy recovered somewhat in 1986 and 1987, due to the government's capital spending program and an increase in foreign investment.

Overall economic performance was positive during the 1990s. Although GDP declined in both 1990 and 1991; in 1992 real GDP increased by 7%. The high inflation prevailing in the late 1980s and early 1990s was finally tamed in 1993, as a result of an austerity program that brought the annual inflation rate from 53.9% in 1992 to only 4.6% in 1993. However, very tight monetary and fiscal policies caused the economy to decline by 1.7% in 1994. Boosted by the continuous expansion of tourism, mining, and the export processing zones, the country posted a real GDP growth of 8.3% in 1999, up from 4.7% recorded in

1995. This was the highest growth rate in the world for that year. Inflation continued at low levels. The rate of inflation fell from 14.3% in 1994 to 6% in 1999.

20 INCOME

The US Central Intelligence Agency (CIA) reports that in 1998 the Dominican Republic's gross domestic product (GDP) was estimated at $39.8 billion. The per capita GDP was estimated at $5,000. The annual growth rate of GDP was estimated at 7%. The average inflation rate in 1998 was 6%. The CIA defines GDP as the value of all final goods and services produced within a nation in a given year and computed on the basis of purchasing power parity (PPP) rather than value as measured on the basis of the rate of exchange. It was estimated that agriculture accounted for 19% of GDP, industry 25%, and services 56%.

Private consumption includes expenditures of individuals, households, and nongovernmental organizations. It was estimated that between 1990 and 1998 private consumption grew at an annual rate of 4.3%. The richest 10% of the population accounted for approximately 38% of household consumption and the poorest 10% approximately 1.6%.

21 LABOR

The labor force in 1999 consisted of about 3.6 million persons. In 1997, 20% were engaged in agriculture, 18% in industry, 20% in commerce, and 5.7% in construction. Unemployment is a persistent problem, affecting an estimated 16% of the work force in 1997. Underemployment was also widespread.

In 1999, about 10% of the Dominican work force was unionized. Major labor confederations include the National Confederation of Dominican Workers, and the Unitary Workers Confederation. The 1992 labor code grants employees in nonessential public services the right to strike and eliminates the prohibition against general, political, or sympathy strikes. The code also specifies steps for union registration, entering into collective bargaining pacts, and calling strikes. But widespread intimidation of union organizers and members has been reported. Strikes may be called if arbitration is unsuccessful and notice is given 10 days in advance.

The labor code prohibits employment of children under 14. However, economic and social conditions have forced many children to work to help support their families. The minimum wage, $125 per month in 1999, covers only a fraction of a family's costs.

Workers have reported forced and coerced overtime in factories in free trade zones and on sugar cane plantations. Occupational health standards are not enforced and working conditions, especially on sugar plantations, can be particularly harsh.

22 AGRICULTURE

With almost 30% of the total land area suitable for crop production and about 20% of the labor force engaged in farming, agriculture remains the primary occupation, accounting for 12% of GDP in 1998. Value of agricultural output grew at an average annual rate of 7.1% during 1968–73, but since 1975 the sector has been hampered by droughts (1975, 1977, and 1979), hurricanes (in 1979 and 1980), and slumping world prices and quota allocations for sugar (since 1985). In 1998, agricultural production was 4% higher than during 1989–91. The fertile Cibao Valley is the main agricultural center. In 1997, arable land totaled 1,020,000 hectares (2,520,000 acres); with land under permanent crops at 480,000 hectares (1,186,000 acres).

After Cuba, the Dominican Republic is the second-largest Caribbean producer of sugarcane, the nation's most important commercial crop. The State Sugar Council (Consejo Estatal de Azúcar—CEA) operates 12 sugar mills and accounts for more than half of total production. Other large producers are the privately owned Vicini, with three mills, and Gulf & Western, whose largest mill is at La Romana. In 1998, sugar cane production was 509.7 million tons, down from 638.5 million tons in 1990. Output of sugar has declined annually since 1982, and land is gradually being taken out of sugar production and switched to food crops. Production of raw sugar rose from 636,000 tons in 1990 to 813,000 tons in 1997 but fell to 510,000 tons in 1998. The Dominican Republic has the largest single allocation of the US sugar import quota. In 1997, exports of sugar and related products (such as molasses, inverted syrups, and furfural) generated US$128 million.

Another leading cash crop is coffee. Part of the crop was destroyed by hurricanes in 1979 and 1980, and 1979/80 production was only 670,000 bags (40,200 tons). Although production was usually about 57,000–59,000 tons annually in the 1980s, the acreage harvested declined from 157,000 hectares (388,000 acres) in the early 1980s to 139,000 hectares (363,000 acres) in 1998, indicating a greater yield per acre. Coffee production in 1998 was estimated at 57,000 tons; exports of coffee in 1997 generated $58.5 million. Cocoa and tobacco are also grown for export. In 1998, production of cocoa beans was 143,000 tons and of tobacco, 43,000 tons. Banana production in 1998 was 359,000 tons. Production of other crops in 1998 (in thousands of tons) included rice, 475; coconuts, 160; cassava, 126; tomatoes, 198; pulses, 56; dry beans, 24; eggplants, 7; and peanuts, 2.

Under a land reform program initiated in 1962, a total of 178,602 hectares (441,333 acres) had been distributed to 36,480 farmers by the end of 1977. The government encourages fuller use of the nation's arable land through extensive land-clearing and irrigation projects and diversification of crops. Some mechanization has taken place on the large plantations, but primitive techniques are generally used. In 1973, the first stage of the Integrated Agricultural and Livestock Development Plan was initiated, calling for an investment of RD$38.1 million, to be financed by the IDB. The plan was designed to provide credit and technical aid to 45,000 small farmers, improve side roads, and study the country's water resources. The second stage of the plan, in the early 1980s, included extension of farm credits, reforestation, manpower training for irrigation projects, and reorganization of the Dominican Agrarian Institute.

Agricultural exports, mostly in the form of sugar, coffee, cocoa, tobacco, and cigars generated $395.6 million in 1997 and directly employed 11% of the labor force. Another 30% of the labor force is indirectly involved with agriculture. The government and private sector are emphasizing diversification to nontraditional agricultural crops such as fresh fruits, vegetables, and flowers.

23 ANIMAL HUSBANDRY

In 1998, Dominican livestock included 570,000 goats and 135,000 sheep. There were also about 2.5 million head of cattle, 60% for beef and 40% for dairy. The hog population was decimated by African swine fever, decreasing from 400,000 in 1978 to 20,000 in 1979; by 1998, however, it had risen to 960,000. Poultry is the main meat source because it is cheaper than beef or pork. Poultry production relies on imports of feed grain from the US. In 1998, 169,000 tons of poultry meat were produced, along with 77,000 tons of beef and 358,000 tons of milk.

24 FISHING

Although the waters surrounding the Dominican Republic abound with fish, the fishing industry is comparatively undeveloped, and fish for local consumption are imported. In 1997, the total marine catch was 13,504 tons, up from 13,169 tons in 1984. Marlin, barracuda, kingfish, mackerel, tuna, sailfish, and tarpon are found in the Monte Cristi Bank and Samaná Bay, which also supports bonito, snapper, and American grouper. The inland catch amounted to 1,772 tons in 1997.

25FORESTRY

About 12.4% of the total land area consisted of forests and woodlands in 1997. Roundwood production in 1997 totaled 982,000 cu m. Virtually all the timber cut is for land clearing and fuel.

26MINING

The Dominican Republic has a variety of mineral resources, and mining was long an important asset to the economy. Production, however, has stagnated since a slump began in the mid-1980s, and it remained modest as of 1997, accounting for 2.5% of the GDP. The mineral industry primarily produces small quantities of cement, gold and silver, gypsum, nickel, and salt.

The Aluminum Co. of America (Alcoa) mined bauxite, traditionally the principal product of the mining sector, between 1959 and 1983, when it turned its concession over to the state; it ceased operations in 1985. Production of bauxite in 1991 dropped to 7,000 tons (down 92% from the previous year) and ceased in 1992. In 1991, mining operations were suspended at the largest mine by presidential decree, in response to increasing fears of deforestation, even though reforestation of mined areas was in progress. Currently, nickel is the country's most important mining product; 32,558 tons were produced in 1997, amounting to 4.8% of total world production and making the Dominican Republic the world's seventh leading nickel producer.

A gold and silver mine and a processing plant were opened at Pueblo Viejo, on the north coast, in 1975. The plant, initially owned by New York and Honduras Rosario Mining, was nationalized in October 1979. By 1980, the mine had become the largest gold producer in the Western Hemisphere. Production was declining by the mid-1980s, so mining of the sulfide zone of the gold ore body has commenced; such mining, however, requires more extensive processing facilities than currently exist. Production of gold was estimated at 2,349 in 1997 (down from 7,651 kg in 1987) and of silver, 12,406 kg (down from 39,595 kg in 1988).

The country is one of the few sources of amber in the Western Hemisphere. Salt Mountain, a 16-km (10-mi) block of almost solid salt about 37 km (23 mi) west of Barahona, is the largest known salt deposit in the world. Gypsum (of which there are large deposits near Salt Mountain) is quarried by Loma de Sa y Yeso C. por A.; the Dominican Republic, Cuba, and Jamaica are the only sources of gypsum in the Caribbean. Gypsum and limestone are exported primarily to Puerto Rico. There is also some iron mining, and substantial lignite deposits were found in the early 1980s.

27ENERGY AND POWER

With no coal and little petroleum, the country has depended upon imported diesel oil for its electrical energy, although a substantial development of hydroelectric potential took place during the 1970s and early 1980s. Net installed public capacity was 1,642,000 kW in 1998, when 8.48 billion kWh were produced. The Dominican Electric Corp. (Corporación Dominicana de Electricidad), purchased for us$15 million from US interests in 1972, is responsible for all public production, sale, and distribution of energy. As of 1994, the Dominican Electric Corp. supplied electricity only ten hours per day, with frequent blackouts. Power cuts for both commercial and residential customers remained a problem as of 1999. A new 300 MW, $260 million gas turbine project was slated for completion in 2000.

Steam thermal units supply about 70% of the nation's energy needs; hydroelectric power is used mainly for irrigation. The Tavera Dam, with a capacity of 60,000 kW, was completed in 1972. The Sabana Yegua hydroelectric and irrigation complex, begun in 1974, opened in 1980. The Habo I coal-fired plant at Haina was inaugurated in 1984.

Under the terms of an agreement with Venezuela and Mexico, the Dominican Republic buys one-third of its oil at discount prices. A petroleum deposit in Haina had an estimated potential output of 30,000 barrels per day in 1991.

28INDUSTRY

The manufacturing industry, responsible for 17% of GDP, expanded by 5% in 1998, and 6.7% in 1999. The total industrial sector accounted for one-third of GDP, growing by 8.6% in 1998.

Including the processing of sugar, food processing represents more than half of the total industrial production. Dominican agriculture was hard hit during the late 1990s by droughts in 1996 and 1997, and a hurricane in 1998; but little effect was seen on the manufacturing sector. Small plants produce powdered and condensed milk, ceramics, aluminum furniture and fittings, concrete blocks, pipes and tiles, air conditioners, barbed wire, and other products.

Since 1990, free assembly zones have contributed more than 3.5% of the GDP. The most active sectors in this industry were related to the processing of clothes and textiles, tobacco, electronics, and shoes.

29SCIENCE AND TECHNOLOGY

The Dominican Medical Association and the Dominican Sugar Institute have their headquarters in Santo Domingo. Ten colleges and universities offer degrees in engineering, basic sciences, medicine, and agriculture. In 1987–97, science and engineering students accounted for 35% of college and university enrollments.

30DOMESTIC TRADE

Santo Domingo is the principal port and commercial center, while Santiago de los Caballeros is the market and distribution center for the Cibao Valley. Most importing and exporting firms are located in Santo Domingo. Importers ordinarily represent numerous foreign manufacturers.

Department stores and supermarkets are increasing in number, but most retail stores are specialty shops. Groceries, meat, and fish are sold in most cities through a large central market, by neighborhood stores, and by street vendors. Retail credit is granted by larger stores and automobile dealers.

Usual business hours are from 8:00 AM to noon and from 1:00 to 5:00 PM, Monday through Friday, and from 8 AM to noon on Saturday. Government offices are open weekdays from 7:30 AM to 2:30 PM. Banks are open from 8:30 AM to 4:00 PM, Monday through Friday. Advertising media include television, radio, newspapers, magazines, and outdoor displays. Most businessmen speak English, but Spanish is preferred.

31FOREIGN TRADE

Numerous free trade zones make the Dominican Republic attractive to export-import businesses. Some FTZ businesses moved to Mexico after the NAFTA agreement.

Clothing production brings in the majority of export monies (32%), but the commodity market also supports the export of pig iron (7.8%), medical instruments (7.7%), sugar (5.6%), and electrical parts (5.1%). Dominican Republic imports include food, petroleum, cotton and fabrics, chemicals, and pharmaceuticals.

Principal trading partners in 1998 (in millions of US dollars) were as follows:

COUNTRY	EXPORTS	IMPORTS	BALANCE
United States	525	2,209	-1,684
Germany	59	98	-39
France	33	102	-69
Italy	28	112	-84
Korea	26	163	-137
Japan	24	274	-250
Spain	23	193	-170
Mexico	13	270	-257
Brazil	4	141	-137
Venezuela	3	838	-835

[32]BALANCE OF PAYMENTS

For more than 20 years prior to 1961, the Dominican Republic had no internal or external debt. In 1961, however, about US$70 million was taken out of the country by the Trujillo family and others. Political instability induced further net outflows of private capital throughout the 1960s. The nation's current accounts position worsened during the 1970s, as trade deficits grew. Declines in export earnings in the 1980s brought shortages of foreign exchange. Large increases in imports and a sharp drop in commodity exports pushed the merchandise trade deficit to over $1.6 billion by the end of 1992, and $1.4 billion in 1998. Tourism, expatriate remittances, and earnings from the free trade zones help to finance the trade deficit.

The US Central Intelligence Agency reports that in 1997 the purchasing power parity of the Dominican Republic's exports was $997 million while imports totaled $3.6 billion resulting in a trade balance of -$2.6 billion.

The International Monetary Fund (IMF) reports that in 1998 the Dominican Republic had exports of goods totaling $4,981 million and imports totaling $7,597 million. The services credit totaled $2,502 million and debit $1,320 million. The following table summarizes the Dominican Republic's balance of payments as reported by the IMF for 1998 in millions of US dollars.

Current Account		-336
Balance on goods	-2,617	
Balance on services	1,182	
Balance on income	-887	
Current transfers	1,987	
Capital Account		...
Financial Account		696
Direct investment abroad	...	
Direct investment in Dom. Rep.	700	
Portfolio investment assets	-18	
Portfolio investment liabilities	-4	
Other investment assets	-66	
Other investment liabilities	84	
Net Errors and Omissions		-351
Reserves and Related Items		-10

[33]BANKING AND SECURITIES

The Central Bank of the Dominican Republic (Banco Central de la República Dominicana—BCRD) is the sole bank of issue. The state-owned Banco de Reservas, established in 1941, is the largest commercial bank in the country and acts as the fiscal agent and depository for the government. The Agricultural and the Industrial Credit Bank promotes the development of agriculture as well as industry by granting medium-term and long-term credit. The National Housing Bank (Banco Nacional de Vivienda) is a primary investor in low-cost housing. Other commercial banks include the Bank of Nova Scotia, Citibank, Banco Nacional de Credito, Banco Intercontinental, Banco Metropolitano, Banco Mercantil, Bancy Gerencial y Fiduciario, Banco Osaka, Banco Global, Banco BHD, and Banco Popular Dominicano.

At the end of January 1996, the central bank tightened reserve requirements for lending based on new deposits and imposed limits on new lending to the commercial sector. The prime lending rate, which had fallen from 24% in December 1995 to 17% in 1996, was 18% in 1999. The exchange rate was devalued 9% in 1998, and continued to devalue through that year, but stabilized in 1999.

Securities are traded on the Santo Domingo Securities Exchange, founded in 1991.

[34]INSURANCE

Insurance firms are government-supervised and are required to furnish a bond to guarantee their obligations. Net premiums on life insurance are taxable, and the law requires that a certain proportion of the premiums collected must be invested locally. The insurance market is regulated by the Superintendent of Insurance of the nation. In relation to the North American and European markets, the Dominican insurance industry has very low penetration and is among the lowest in Latin America, the result of relatively low per capita income and general lack of insurance awareness.

[35]PUBLIC FINANCE

Between 1968 and 1975, dependence on foreign loans and grants to finance the budget was substantially decreased, and by 1975 tax revenues amounted to about 12% of the GNP. In the late 1970s, this trend was reversed, with rising expenditures and increased assistance from abroad. Legislation was passed in 1997 to allow the privatization of state-owned enterprises, including public utilities, the country's largest bank, an insurance company, and a number of factories. The government receives almost one-third of its revenues from taxes on imports, but the increasing use of the free trade zones diminishes indirect tax returns.

The US Central Intelligence Agency (CIA) estimates that in 1999 the Dominican Republic's central government took in revenues of approximately $2.3 billion and had expenditures of $2.9 billion including capital expenditures of $867 million. Overall, the government registered a deficit of approximately $600 million.

The following table shows an itemized breakdown of government revenues and expenditures. The percentages were calculated from data reported by the International Monetary Fund. The dollar amounts (millions) are based on the CIA estimates provided above.

REVENUE AND GRANTS	100%	2,300
Tax revenue	90.8%	2,089
Non-tax revenue	8.1%	187
Capital revenue	0.7%	17
Grants	0.3%	8
EXPENDITURES	100%	2,900
General public services	11.7%	339
Defense	4.7%	136
Public order and safety	3.9%	113
Education	14.3%	414
Health	11.2%	326
Social security	5.6%	163
Housing and community amenities	13.2%	382
Recreation, cultural, and religious affairs	1.2%	34
Economic affairs and services	30.2%	875
Interest payments	3.1%	90
Adjustments	0.9%	27

[36]TAXATION

Personal income tax rates in 1995 ranged upward from 0% to 26%. As of January 1995 business income was taxed at a flat rate of 25%. Other taxes include a selective consumption tax ranging from 5% to 80%, a value-added tax at a flat rate of 8%, and a technical education tax.

³⁷CUSTOMS AND DUTIES

The customs tariff is primarily a revenue-raising instrument, although it is occasionally used to protect local industry. In the 1960s and early 1970s, import duties constituted the greatest single source of government revenue (accounting for 40–45% of the annual total during 1964–70), but by 1986 the share of import duties in government income had fallen below 30%. Export duties provided only about 5% of government revenues in 1986. In September 1990, a government decree simplified the tariff schedule to 6 categories, with 7 tariff rates, ranging from 5% to 35%.

As of 1999, the Dominican Republic had agreed to eliminate non-tariff trade barriers, and the maximum tariff rate for agricultural goods stood at 40%. Nevertheless, quotas were put in place for rice, sugar, garlic, poultry meat, beans, onions, and milk. Import tariffs ranged from 0% to 35% for other goods, and taxes for nonessential goods ranged between 10% and 60%. The consumption tax for luxury items was 30%, and the tax on industrialized goods and services was 8%.

There are no free ports, but at least 19 industrial free zones have been established at locations including La Romana, San Pedro de Macorís, Santiago de los Caballeros, Baní, and Puerto Plata.

In 1998, the Dominican Republic helped to establish the Central American-Dominican Republic Free Trade Area (CADRFTA). The country also has an agreement with CARICOM, and Western Hemisphere governments for a free trade area by 2005.

³⁸FOREIGN INVESTMENT

In August 1996, the Dominican Congress passed the Multilateral Investment Guarantee Agreement (MIGA) and in September 1996, President Leonel Fernandez signed the accord. The program was designed to encourage the flow of foreign private investment to less developed countries by mitigating political risks associated with a project. It also provides guarantees to foreign investors against the risk of transfer restriction, expropriation, and war and civil disturbance in the host country. In 1997, the government established the Office for Investment Promotion (OPI).

Major foreign investors include GTE and Bank of Nova Scotia of Canada; Shell of Holland/England; and Central Romana, Philip Morris, Citibank, Esso, Texaco, and Colgate Palmolive of the US. The bulk of foreign investment came from those countries listed above.

³⁹ECONOMIC DEVELOPMENT

Caribbean Basin Initiative (CBI) and Generalized Systems of Preferences—government programs that allow the import of raw materials, equipment, and goods for reexport duty-free—benefit the economy. Tax exempt status for up to 20 years is also available. Duty-free access to the EC market was granted by joining the Lome Convention in 1989, which also provides inexpensive financing for economic development projects. The addition of free trade zones greatly improved the level of industry in the country, but the NAFTA agreement transplanted some manufacturers to Mexico.

The 1998 hurricane caused at least $1.2 billion in damage; analysts estimated that the Dominican Republic's emergency aid would amount to 25% of its annual budget. The US offered $47 million, and the EU offered $50 million. Foreign aid may have successfully saved the small economy, and even improved it in 1999. Still, the state has a number of parastatals to privatize, and

the fairly strict tariff regime has driven most investment capital into the free trade zones.

⁴⁰SOCIAL DEVELOPMENT

Social assistance is administered by the Dominican Social Insurance Institute, which operates benefit programs dealing with sickness, disability, survivors' and workers' compensation, occupational disease, maternity, incapacity, and old age. The social insurance program is funded, in principle, by compulsory contributions from employees (2.5% of earnings), employers (7.5% of payroll), and the government (2.5% of employee earnings and any remaining deficit). Retirement is set at age 60 for both men and women.

An Institute for the Development of Women was created in 1975, but women still have lower economic and social status than men. They are often paid less for similar work and occupy few top leadership positions. Employers avoid hiring pregnant women, and some administer pregnancy tests to job applicants. Divorce is easily obtainable by either spouse. Pending legislative proposals to strengthen women's rights remained stalled in Congress as of 1995. Women held 26 legislative seats in 1998. Domestic violence and sexual harassment are common. In 1998 the government established a facility for the forensic examination of abused women.

Haitian immigrants, many of whom are low paid agricultural workers, face considerable discrimination. An estimated half million live under harsh conditions in special camps for sugar cane workers. Some persons of Haitian ancestry with rights to Dominican citizenship may have been expelled along with undocumented Haitians. Reports of mistreatment of Haitian migrant workers continue.

Documented human rights violations include police brutality, arbitrary detention, and mistreatment of suspects in custody. Killings by police doubled between 1998 and 1999. Nongovernmental human rights organizations are permitted to operate.

⁴¹HEALTH

In 1998 average life expectancy was 71 years; the infant mortality rate in 1996 was 45 per 1,000 live births; and overall mortality was estimated at 5.5 per 1,000 people for 1995–2000. As of 1998, studies indicated that 64% of women with partners (ages 15 to 49) used contraception.

Modern aqueducts, drainage systems, and garbage disposal plants have been constructed in the principal cities. The National Water Supply and Sewerage Institute was established in 1962, and the National Rural Water Service was formed in 1964. From 1988 to 1994–95, an estimated 79% of the population had access to safe water, compared with 37% in 1970, and 85% had adequate sanitation. In 1989–95, however, approximately 10% of children under 5 years of age were considered to be malnourished, and 9% of all births in 1990–95 were low birth weight. As access to health care has improved, so has the under-5 mortality rate, which in 1996 was 56. In 1980 it was 94. As of 1998 tuberculosis accounted for 15% of all deaths from communicable diseases.

In 1997 there were 22 doctors per 10,000 people. Between 1985 and 1995, statistics indicate that 80% of the population had access to health care services. As of 1995, the incidence of deaths from AIDS was 5 per 100,000 population.

In 1997 the country immunized children up to 1 year of age against tuberculosis (88%); diphtheria, pertussis, and tetanus (80%); polio (81%); and measles (47%). Major causes of death between 1990 and 1994 were: communicable diseases (27 per 100,000); malignant neoplasms (28 per 100,000); and injuries (30 per 100,000). Total per capita health care expenditure in 1995 was $77 million.

42HOUSING

Rapid population growth and migration to urban areas have combined to create an increasingly serious housing shortage. The National Housing Institute and the National Housing Bank, both established in 1962, have made modest efforts to ease the problem, between them constructing nearly 10,000 units during 1966–72. During 1975–78, construction activity slowed down, but the 1979 hurricanes prompted a construction boom—not, however, to create new housing but to replace units that had been destroyed by the storms. The Guzmán government promoted the building of low-cost housing at a rate of about 6,000 units a year. President Jorge Blanco pledged in 1982 that 25,000 low-cost houses would be built annually during his administration, and President Balaguer, after he returned to office in 1986, also built low-cost housing, though at a far slower pace than announced. In the 1980s, roughly four-fifths of all housing units were detached houses; other units included single rooms and apartments. Roughly 65% of dwellings obtained water through a public system, while 20% used wells. Concrete, wood, and palm were the most frequently used construction materials for dwellings, and they were used about equally.

43EDUCATION

For the year 2000, the estimated adult illiteracy rate stood at 16.2% (males, 16%; females, 16.3%). The foremost educational objective in recent years has been the enrollment of the entire population in the 5–14 age range. Nine years of education is compulsory. Primary education lasts for eight years followed by four years of secondary education.

In 1997 there were 1,360,044 students enrolled in primary schools. In 1998 secondary school enrollment numbered 329,944 students, with approximately 13,000 teachers. Teacher training has been expanded dramatically with aid from UNESCO, UNICEF, and other agencies.

The state-run Autonomous University of Santo Domingo, founded in 1538 and the oldest in the hemisphere, has suffered from a lack of resources. There are four private universities, one technological institute, four colleges, and seven schools of art and music. In 1997, about 176,995 students were enrolled in the university and higher level institutions, with 9,041 teachers.

44LIBRARIES AND MUSEUMS

There are about 130 libraries located throughout the country, of which the library of the University of Santo Domingo is the most important, with over 105,000 volumes. The National Library, founded in Santo Domingo in 1970, had a collection of over 154,000 volumes in 2000. In general, public library collections are few and small, mostly containing only a few hundred books. Exceptions are the public library in Santo Domingo, with holdings of about 35,000 volumes, and in Baní with 38,000 volumes.

The leading museums are in and around Santo Domingo. The Museum of Dominican Man (formerly the National Museum) houses 19,000 pre-Columbian, colonial, and contemporary exhibits relating to the country's history. The Gallery of Modern Art promotes the music, painting, sculpture, and poetry of both Dominican and foreign artists and writers. A new complex at the Plaza of Culture houses several museums, the National Library, and the National Theater. The Alcázar de Colón is the 16th-century home of the Columbus family; the reputed tomb of Christopher Columbus is in the Cathedral of Santa María la Menor. The zoological and botanical garden in Santo Domingo is unique because of its natural setting and grottoes. Ponce de Leon's fort was declared a historic site in 1972 and is maintained as a museum.

45MEDIA

The Dominican Telephone Co. operates the domestic telephone system, and the government controls domestic telegraph service. The larger cities have automatic telephone exchanges, and about 90% of the telephones are on an automatic dial system. In 1995 there were some 552,200 telephones, most of which were in the capital. International cable service is provided by All America Cables and RCA. The same year there were 120 AM radio stations and 25 television stations, of which the government-owned Radio-Televisión Dominicana is the most important. In 1997 there were 177 radios, 84 television sets, and 16 mobile phones per 1,000 population.

The newspapers of the Dominican Republic are rated by the Inter-American Press Association as among the freest in Latin America. The leading daily is El Caribe, an independent morning daily, published in Santo Domingo (circulation 32,000 in 1999). Two other papers of importance, also published in the capital, are El Nacional (circulation 56,000), and the Listín Diario (about 88,000). Of the four dailies published outside the capital, La Información of Santiago (circulation 15,000) is the best known.

The legally provided freedom of speech and the press are said to be generally supported in practice by the government. Many privately owned radio and TV stations broadcast differing political points of view, as do the many independent newspapers and periodicals. A 1971 law prohibits the broadcast of foreign-language programming.

In 1998 there were 6 Internet hosts per 1,000 population.

46ORGANIZATIONS

Consumer associations, mainly for low-income groups, deal in basic foods such as rice, plantains, potatoes, and beans. The Confederation of Employers of the Dominican Republic and the National Council of Businessmen are the principal employers' organizations. There are chambers of commerce in Santo Domingo and other large towns.

47TOURISM, TRAVEL, AND RECREATION

Although the Dominican Republic offers fine beaches and historical sites as well as good hotel facilities, it had no organized tourist industry to speak of until 1967, and received no more than 45,000 visitors per year. Increased political stability made the country more attractive to tourists, and by 1973 the number of foreign visitors had grown to 182,036. By 1997 the Dominican Republic had 38,585 hotel rooms with an occupancy rate of 76%, and tourism was a mainstay of its economy. That year receipts from tourism amounted to $2.1 billion with 2.21 million tourists arrivals. The Ministry of Tourism has conducted a vigorous campaign to promote such resort centers as La Romana, Puerto Plata, Samaná, and Playa Grande. Visitors require valid passports. Short-stay visitors may not require visas or may require only tourist cards, depending on nationality.

Baseball is the national sport. Other popular pastimes include basketball, boxing, tennis, golf, hunting, fishing, and scuba diving. The Juan Pablo Duarte Olympic Center is one of the best-equipped sports facilities in the Caribbean.

In 1999 the UN estimated the daily cost of staying in Puerto Plata at $84 and in Santo Domingo at $116. Expenses in smaller towns are estimated at only $67 per day.

48FAMOUS DOMINICANS

Juan Pablo Duarte (1813–76), national hero of the Dominican Republic, was the leader of the famous "La Trinitaria," along with Francisco del Rosario Sánchez (1817–61) and Ramón Matías Mella (1816–64), which proclaimed and won independence from Haiti in 1844. Emiliano Tejera (1841–1923) and Fernando Arturo de Merino (1833–1906), first archbishop of the Dominican Republic, were noted statesmen.

Rafael Leonidas Trujillo Molina (1891–1961) was the dominant figure in the political life of the country from 1930 until his assassination on 30 May 1961. He served four times as president and was commander-in-chief of the armed forces. Since his appointment as president in 1960, Joaquín Balaguer (b.1909) has continued to be a prominent political figure in the Dominican Republic. Juan Bosch (b.1909), founder of the leftist PRD and later of the PLD, who served for seven months as president in 1963, is another important politician.

Juan Bautista Alfonseca (1810–75), the father of Dominican music, was the first composer to make use of Dominican folklore. José Reyes (1835–1905), musician and soldier, wrote the music for the national anthem. José de Jesús Ravelo (1876–1954) composed the oratorio *La Muerte de Cristo*, which has been performed yearly since 7 April 1939 at the Basílica de Santa María la Menor on Good Friday. Other prominent Dominican musicians are Juan Francisco García (1892–1974), Luis Emilio Mena (1895–1964), and Enrique de Marchena (b.1908). Juan Marichal (b.1938) achieved fame in the US as a baseball pitcher.

[49]DEPENDENCIES

The Dominican Republic has no territories or colonies.

[50]BIBLIOGRAPHY

Atkins, G. Pope. *Arms and Politics in the Dominican Republic.* Boulder, Colo.: Westview, 1981.

Baud, Michiel. *Peasants and Tobacco in the Dominican Republic, 1870–1930.* Knoxville: University of Tennesee Press, 1995.

Black, Jan K. *The Dominican Republic: Politics and Development in an Unsovereign State.* Winchester, Mass.: Allen Unwin, 1986.

Calder, Bruce J. *The Impact of Intervention: The Dominican Republic During the U.S. Occupation of 1916–1924.* Austin: University of Texas Press, 1984.

Crassweller, Robert D. *Trujillo: The Life and Times of a Caribbean Dictator.* New York: Macmillan, 1966.

Dominican Republic and Haiti: Country Studies. 2nd ed. Washington, D.C.: Library of Congress, 1991.

Gleijeses, Piero. *The Dominican Crisis: The 1965 Constitutional Revolt and American Intervention.* Baltimore: Johns Hopkins University Press, 1979.

Gordon, Raul (ed.). *Image of the Dominican Republic: The Dominican Miracle.* New York: Gordon, 1978.

Grasmuck, Sherri, and Patricia R. Pessar. *Between Two Islands: Dominican International Migration.* Berkeley: University of California Press, 1991.

Haverstock, Nathan A. *Dominican Republic in Pictures.* Minneapolis: Lerner Publications Co., 1988.

Landau, Luis. *Dominican Republic: Its Main Economic Development Problems.* Washington, D.C.: IBRD, 1978.

Lowenthal, Abraham F. *The Dominican Intervention.* Cambridge, Mass.: Harvard University Press, 1972.

Moya Pons, Frank. *The Dominican Republic: A National History.* New Rochelle, N.Y.: Hispaniola Books, 1995.

Munro, D. G. *Intervention and Dollar Diplomacy in the Caribbean, 1900–1921.* Princeton, N.J.: Princeton University Press, 1964.

Pacini Hernandez, Deborah. *Bachata: A Social History of a Dominican Popular Music.* Philadelphia: Temple University Press, 1995.

Palmer, Bruce. *Intervention in the Caribbean: the Dominican Crisis of 1965.* Lexington, Ky.: University Press of Kentucky, 1989.

Plant, Roger. *Sugar and Modern Slavery: Haitian Migrant Labor and the Dominican Republic.* Totowa, N.J.: Biblio Dist., 1986.

Safa, Helen Icken. *The Myth of the Male Breadwinner: Women and Industrialization in the Caribbean.* Boulder, Colo.: Westview Press, 1995.

Schoenhals, Kai P. *Dominican Republic.* Santa Barbara, Calif.: Clio Press, 1990.

Vedevato, Claudio. *Politics, Foreign Trade and Development: A Study of the Dominican Republic.* New York: St. Martin's, 1986.

Wiarda, Howard J., and Michael J. Kryzanek. *The Dominican Republic, a Caribbean Crucible.* 2nd ed. Boulder, Colo.: Westview Press, 1992.

ECUADOR

Republic of Ecuador
República del Ecuador

CAPITAL: Quito.

FLAG: The flag consists of three horizontal stripes, the yellow uppermost stripe being equal to the combined widths of the blue center stripe and the red lower stripe; coat of arms superimposed at center of the flag.

ANTHEM: *Salve, O Patria (Hail, O Fatherland).*

MONETARY UNIT: The sucre (s/) of 100 centavos is a nonconvertible paper currency. There are coins of 10, 20, and 50 centavos and 1 sucre, and notes of 50, 100, 500, 1,500, 5,000, and 10,000 sucres. s/1 = $0.00004 (or $1 = s/24900.00) as of 31 March 2000.

WEIGHTS AND MEASURES: The metric system is the legal standard, but local and old Spanish units are also used.

HOLIDAYS: New Year's Day, 1 January; Epiphany, 6 January; Labor Day, 1 May; Battle of Pichincha, 24 May; Simón Bolívar's Birthday, 24 July; Quito's Independence Day, 10 August; Guayaquil's Independence Day, 9 October; Columbus Day, 12 October; All Saints' Day, 1 November; All Souls' Day, 2 November; Cuenca's Independence Day, 3 November; Foundation of Quito, 6 December; Christmas Day, 25 December. Movable holidays include Carnival and Holy Week.

TIME: Mainland, 7 AM = noon GMT; Galápagos Islands, 6 AM = noon GMT.

¹LOCATION, SIZE, AND EXTENT

The fourth-smallest country in South America, Ecuador is located on the west coast of the continent and is crossed by the Equator (the country gets its name from the Spanish word for "Equator"). It has a length of 714 km (444 mi) N–S and a width of 658 km (409 mi) E–W. Ecuador borders Colombia on the N, Peru on the E and S (it has lost about two-thirds of the territory it once claimed to these countries), and the Pacific Ocean on the W, with a total boundary length of 4,247 km (2,639 mi).

The Galápagos Islands, a province of Ecuador with an area totaling 8,010 sq km (3,093 sq mi), are approximately 1,130 km (700 mi) off the coast on the Equator at 89° to 92°W. The total area of the republic and its territory is estimated at 283,560 sq km (109,483 sq mi). Comparatively, the area occupied by Ecuador is slightly smaller than the state of Nevada. Ecuador also claims about 200,000 sq km (77,000 sq mi) of land awarded to Peru under the 1942 Protocol of Rio de Janeiro. Armed hostilities flared along a still undemarcated stretch of the border in January 1981, but by 20 February, a 14-km (9-mi) demilitarized zone had been arranged along the disputed line. Official maps of Ecuador show the entire region as Ecuadoran territory. Ecuador's capital city, Quito, is located in the north central part of the country.

²TOPOGRAPHY

Ecuador is characterized by three distinct regions: the coast; the highlands, or Sierra; and the eastern interior jungles, or Oriente. The coast, except for a hilly area west of Guayaquil, is a low alluvial plain from 32 to 185 km (20 to 115 mi) wide, comprising about one-quarter of the national territory. It extends from sea level to the base of the Cordillera Real of the Andes, at an elevation of about 460 m (1,500 ft). The Guayas in the southwest and the Esmeraldas in the northwest form the principal river systems and serve as important arteries of transportation in their respective regions.

The highlands constitute another fourth of the country. This region is formed by two parallel ranges of the Andes, from 110 to 290 km (70 to 180 mi) wide, and the intervening narrow central plateau, nearly 640 km (400 mi) long. This inter-Andean plateau is divided into 10 basins at altitudes from 2,400 to 2,900 m (7,800 to 9,500 ft), some draining east and some west. The Andes are studded with massive snow-capped volcanoes, the highest of which are Chimborazo, 6,267 m (20,561 ft); Cotopaxi, 5,948 m (19,514 ft), the world's third-highest active volcano; Cayambe, 5,790 m (18,996 ft); Antisana, 5,705 m (18,717 ft); Altar, 5,320 m (17,454 ft); Iliniza, 5,266 m (17,277 ft); Sangay, 5,230 m (17,159 ft); and Tungurahua, 5,016 m (16,457 ft).

The Oriente, forming part of the upper Amazon Basin, begins at the base of the Andes at about 1,200 m (4,000 ft). The land at first drops quickly and is segmented by rushing torrents escaping from the cold highlands. At about 260 m (850 ft), the jungle becomes almost level, and the streams suddenly widen into sluggish, meandering rivers as they begin their journey down the Amazon system to the Atlantic.

³CLIMATE

The climate varies with the region. Most of the coast consists of wet, tropical forest, increasingly humid toward the north. The cold Humboldt Current, which flows northward along the coast of Peru and then heads out into the Pacific off the coast of central Ecuador, limits the rainfall on a strip of the coast extending from as far north as the Bay of Caráquez and widening to include most of the coastal lowlands south of Guayaquil. In the Guayaquil area there are two seasons: a hot rainy period, lasting from January to May; and a cooler dry season, during the rest of the year, when sea breezes modify the equatorial heat. The tropical jungles of the Oriente, east of the Andes, are more humid than the coast; there, temperatures are high, and rain falls all year round.

The climate of the central plateau is governed mainly by the altitude. The capital, Quito, at 2,850 m (9,350 ft), has perpetual spring, with an average temperature of 13°C (55°F) and about 127 cm (50 in) of rainfall annually. The highlands are cut by numerous deep valleys, which bring subtropical climates to within a few miles of the more temperate areas. Cold and wind increase as the slopes surrounding the central plateau ascend to form the páramo, or highland meadow. The higher areas rise to peaks with perpetual snow above 5,200 m (17,000 ft). Exceptionally heavy rains in late 1982 caused extensive flooding, affecting about 4.5 million people and causing widespread crop and property damage.

[4] FLORA AND FAUNA

The arid savanna strip along about half of Ecuador's coast, with occasional low shrubs and isolated ceiba trees, contrasts sharply with the northern coast and the inner portion of the southern coast. In these humid regions, the typical dense growth of the tropical jungle abounds, extending as wet mossy forests up the Andean slopes to over 2,400 m (8,000 ft) in some places. Beyond the moisture barrier formed by the Western Cordillera, the high mountain slopes above 3,000 m (10,000 ft) are covered with wiry páramo grass and, in the northern province of Carchi, with a mulleinlike plant, the fraylejón (espeletia).

The highland valleys, at an altitude between 2,400 and 3,000 m (8,000 and 10,000 ft), support most of the temperate-zone plants; potatoes and corn, for example, have been raised there for thousands of years. There are few native trees in the highlands; eucalyptus was introduced in the 1860s and has been widely planted. The Oriente has little that is unique to tropical flora except for the delicious naranjilla, a small green orange used in making a conserve.

Ecuadoran jungles support the usual smaller mammals, reptiles, and birds. In the highlands, the condor and a few other species of birds are found. There is relatively little wild game because of the density of the population and the intensive use of the land. The Amerindians still make some use of the llama in southern Ecuador. Throughout the highlands, Amerindians and some mestizos raise cavies (guinea pigs) in their homes as an important source of meat.

[5] ENVIRONMENT

As of 1994, Ecuador's major environmental problems were erosion in the highland areas; deforestation, especially in the Oriente; and water pollution. The Ecuadoran Institute of Water Resources estimated that the amount of arid land increased by 31.5% between 1954 and 1979, when 7.5% of the coastal lowland and Sierra were classified as arid. Between 1981 and 1985, 340,000 hectares (840,000 acres) of land were deforested annually. By the 1990s, Ecuador had lost over 30% of the original mangrove area, which covered over 117,000 hectares.

As of 1994, it was estimated that, at current deforestation rates, coastal forests will be completely eliminated within 15 years and the Amazon forests will be gone within 40 years. Traditional farming practices have been blamed for most of these problems, but oil development has also played a role in the clearing of forests. A program for reforestation and maintenance of existing forests was initiated in 1979, but only 4,000 hectares (10,000 acres) were reforested annually during the early 1980s. Ecuador's principal environmental agency is the Ministry of Natural Resources and Energy. Land erosion is accelerated by deforestation.

Flooding and desertification are related problems which have damaged or eliminated valuable soil, particularly in the western coastal region. As of 1993, 10,000 hectares of land were affected. Water pollution is a problem due to the influx of domestic, industrial, and agricultural contaminants.

Ecuador's cities produce 1.2 million tons of solid waste per year. The nation has 75.3 cu mi of water with 90% used for agricultural purposes. Some 18% of all urban dwellers and 56% of the rural population do not have pure water.

The expansion of Ecuador's population centers threatens its wildlife. Twenty-one species of mammals in a total of 280 are currently endangered. Sixty-four of 1,447 bird species and eight of 345 reptile species are also endangered. Of the 10,000–20,000 plant species in Ecuador, 256 are threatened with extinction. An extensive wildlife protection system was established in 1970. As of 1994, 39.2% of Ecuador's total land area was protected. Endangered or extinct species on the Ecuadoran mainland include the tundra peregrine falcon, yellow-tailed woolly monkey, five species of turtle (green sea, hawksbill, olive ridley, leatherback, and South American river), and three species of crocodile (spectacled caiman, black caiman, and American).

Endangered species in the Galápagos Islands include the dark-rumped petrel, Galápagos dark-rumped petrel (a subspecies), black petrel, African ass, two species of turtle (green sea and hawksbill), and the Galápagos giant tortoise and 11 of its subspecies. A subspecies of Galápagos giant tortoise is extinct, and another may be.

Ecuador's natural attractions could lead to increased tourism, benefiting the economy. However, environmental problems, including further endangerment of native plants and animals, could be exacerbated without careful management of the areas attractive to tourists.

[6] POPULATION

The population of Ecuador in 2000 was estimated at 12,782,161. An estimated 4.4% of the population is 65 years of age or older. The projected population for the year 2005 is 13,837,000, assuming a crude birthrate of 19 per 1,000 population and a death rate of 5, resulting in a natural rate of change of 1.4% for the period 2000–2005. The population rate of change between 1995 and 2000 was 2.0%. The population density in 1998 was 44 per sq km (114 per sq mi).

It was estimated that 62% of the population lived in urban areas in 2000, up from 47% in 1980. The capital city, Quito, had a 2000 metropolitan population of 1,556,000. Guayaquil, the major port, had 2,127,000 metropolitan inhabitants in 2000. Other large cities were Cuenca (194,981), Machala (144,197), and Portoviejo (132,937).

[7] MIGRATION

Ecuador has had no large-scale immigration since the colonial period, and emigrants have generally outnumbered newcomers. There was an influx of European refugees in the late 1930s. In 1959, a modest attempt was made to colonize the northern coastal province of Esmeraldas with Italian families.

Within Ecuador, the largest migration is from rural areas to the cities, as urban employment opportunities widen. There is also a growing movement from the overpopulated highlands to the virgin lands of the Oriente and the coast.

As of May 1997 there were around 14,500 persons who concerned UNHCR in Ecuador. Most of these people were from Cuba and Colombia, living and working in the capital, Quito. There were also a number of rural refugees from Colombia, living in the provinces of Esmeraldes, Corchi, and Sucumbios, near the Colombian border. In 1999, there were 277 refugees under UNHCR's program in Ecuador, mostly from Colombia and Peru. However, Ecuador—like other Latin American countries—was beginning to experience an increasing number of asylum seekers from outside the Americas in 1999, particularly from Africa, Asia, and the Middle East. The net migration rate for Ecuador in 1999 was 0.55 migrants per 1,000 population.

ECUADOR

0　　100　　200 Miles

0　　100　　200 Kilometers

PACIFIC OCEAN

COLOMBIA

Esmeraldas

Tulcán

Guayllabamba
Ibarra
Putumayo

Santo Domingo
de los Colorados
Quito ★
Aguarico

Boca de Cojimíes
Chone
Blanco
Napo

Manta
Quevedo
Nuevo
Rocafuerte

Portoviejo
Latacunga
Curaray

Jipijapa
Chimborazo
20,702 ft.
6310 m.▲
Ambato

Daule
Riobamba
Pindoyacu

La Libertad
Babahoyo
Pastaza

Guayaquil
Milagro
Macas

Isla Puná
Cuenca
ANDES MTS.

Gulfo de
Guayaquil
Machala

PERU

Santa Rosa
Zamora

Loja

Ecuador

Isla Pinta
Isla Marchena
GALAPAGOS ISLANDS
Isla
Fernandina
Isla San Salvador
Isla Santa Cruz
Isla Isabela
Isla San
Cristóbal
Isla
Santa Maria
Isla
Espanola

LOCATION: 1°26′30″N to 5°1′S; 75°11′44″ to 81°1′W. **BOUNDARY LENGTHS:** Colombia, 590 km (368 mi); Peru, 1,420 km (887 mi); Pacific coastline, 848 km (527 mi). **TERRITORIAL SEA LIMIT:** 200 mi.

⁸ETHNIC GROUPS

The population of Ecuador is about 55% mestizo (mixed Amerindian and Spanish). About 25% are Amerindian; 10% are Spanish; and another 10% are black. There are only a few groups of unassimilated Amerindians on the coast, notably the Colorados and Cayapas. The blacks live mainly in the northern coastal province of Esmeraldas. The Amazon Basin is inhabited by many primitive tribes, including the Jívaros, once famous for their shrunken-head war trophies, and the Záparos, Aucas, Secoyas, and Cofanes. In the early 1980s, the tribes were organized in the Federación Shuar, which seeks to preserve their cultural identities.

⁹LANGUAGES

The official language of Ecuador is Spanish, spoken by about 93% of the population. The Spanish of the coastal areas is similar to that of the other lowland areas of Latin America, maintaining something of the Andalusian characteristics, especially the dropping or slurring of the consonants represented by *s* and *d*. In the isolated highlands, a more precise Castilian pronunciation is found, but many words and even some of the singsong intonations of Quechua, the Amerindian language, have crept into the Spanish.

Nearly 7% of the total population speak only Quichua, a dialect of the Quechua language, while another 6% speak it in addition to Spanish. Quechua was imposed on the Amerindians of Ecuador by the conquering Incas in the 15th century, supplanting a number of unrelated languages. Remnants of these forgotten languages are retained in many modern place names. There has been little detailed study of the languages of the jungle tribes of the Oriente.

¹⁰RELIGIONS

Approximately 1,000 different religious groups, churches, cults, societies, Christian fraternities, and foundations coexist in Ecuador. However, introduced by the Spaniards with the conquest in 1540, Roman Catholicism is by far the dominant religion. According to 1998 estimates, some 90% of the population identifies themselves as Roman Catholics. Protestants, including Anglicans, Baptists, and Methodists, make up less than 2% of the population. Buddhists, Baha'is, Hindus, Jews, and members of the Church of Scientology have small communities. Animistic religions survive among the jungle Amerindians of the Oriente. Freedom of worship is guaranteed by the constitution.

¹¹TRANSPORTATION

The topography and climate of Ecuador have greatly hindered the development of adequate means of land transportation. In 1999 there were 42,874 km (26,642 mi) of highways, including 5,752 km (3,574 mi) of asphalted roads. The Pan American Highway (1,076 km/669 mi in Ecuador) extends the length of the highlands from Tulcán on the Colombian border to Loja in the south and on to Peru. In 1970, the five-nation Bolivarian Highway was undertaken, as were east-west routes linking the Oriente with the Sierra, and Guayaquil with its hinterland. The most important lateral route connecting the highlands and the coast runs from Latacunga, crossing a pass in the Cordillera Real over 3,650 m (12,000 ft) high, to Quevedo in the lowlands. In 1995 there were 200,000 passenger cars and 280,000 commercial vehicles.

Modern port facilities to serve Guayaquil were opened in 1963 on an estuary 10 km (6 mi) from the Guayas River. The Guayas River basin is important for transportation in the coastal provinces. Other international ports are Esmeraldas, Puerto Bolívar, and Manta; La Libertad and Balao can accommodate oil tankers. In 1998, Ecuador's merchant marine consisted of 23 ships of at least 1,000 GRT, with a total gross registered tonnage of 99,078.

Railways, all government owned, are of decreasing importance because of their poor condition and competition from highways. The three railroad networks total 965 km (600 mi); the most important line runs between Guayaquil and Quito. Floods in 1983 damaged much of the system, and by 1986 service had been restored on only some of the sections.

Ecuador's rugged topography has hastened the growth of air travel. There were some 183 airports and airfields in 1998, 56 of which had paved runways; those of Guayaquil (Simon Bolivar) and Quito (Mariscal Sucre) are international. In 1997, total scheduled airline traffic amounted to 2,035 million passenger-kilometers (1,265 million passenger-miles), and 1,791,000 passengers were carried on scheduled domestic and international airline flights. The government-run Ecuatoriana de Aviación provides service between Ecuador and the rest of Latin America.

¹²HISTORY

Archaeological explorations indicate that the coastal regions of present-day Ecuador supported corn-cultivating communities as early as 4500 BC. In the first few centuries AD, the population was divided into dozens of small isolated tribes. By AD 1000, the highland groups had formed a loose federation, the Kingdom of

Quito, but they were absorbed into the Inca Empire in the late 15th century. Atahualpa, son of the conquering Inca Huayna Capac and a Quito princess, later became emperor, but by then the Spanish forces under Francisco Pizarro were gaining a foothold on the coast.

Pizarro's pilot, Bartolomé Ruiz, the first European to see the Ecuadorian coast, arrived in 1526 on a scouting expedition. The actual conquest reached Ecuador in 1531. Except for a few emeralds, from which their first landing place took its name (the city and province of Esmeraldas), the Spanish found those shores valuable only as a stopping place on their way to the riches of the Incas in Peru. Sebastian de Belacázar, a lieutenant of Pizarro, extended Spanish dominion northward from Peru after the conquest of the Incas. He found the northern capital of the Inca Empire left in ashes by the retreating Amerindians, and on that site in 1534, he founded the city of San Francisco de Quito, later to become the capital of the republic.

The Spanish governed the region as the Audiencia of Quito, part of the Viceroyalty of Peru. Quito, in the cool highlands, was soon steeped in culture and rich in ornately decorated churches and monasteries. Guayaquil, the principal seaport, grew slowly because of its unhealthy tropical climate, and would not become a major city until much later. The Spanish colonial period was a time of ruthless exploitation of the Amerindians and bickering and bloodshed among the Spanish in the struggle for power and riches.

The early stirrings of Ecuadorian independence were spread, in part, through the writings of the 18th-century satirist Francisco Javier Eugenio de Santa Cruz y Espejo. Abortive revolts against Spanish rule came in 1809 and in 1811. The decisive struggle began on 9 October 1820, with the proclamation of an independent Guayaquil. Finally, on 24 May 1822, with the Battle of Pinchincha, the Spanish were defeated. This victory unified the liberation movements of the continent. Simón Bolívar and José de San Martín met in Guayaquil in 1822 to consider the future of newly freed areas. Liberated Ecuador became part of Bolívar's dream, the Republic of Gran Colombia, consisting of modern Ecuador, Colombia, Venezuela, and Panama. In 1830, when this union collapsed, the traditional name Quito was dropped in favor of La República del Ecuador, "The Republic of the Equator."

Republic of Ecuador

The Republic's first president was Juan José Flores, one of Bolívar's aides. The 15-year period of Flores's domination was noted for iron-handed conservative rule. In 1832, he occupied the Galápagos Islands in a comic-opera invasion witnessed only by the giant tortoises native to the islands. Then, from 1845–60, Ecuador went through 11 presidents and juntas. The nation was split between pro-clerical Conservatives and the more secular Liberals, and regional strongmen vied for power.

From 1860 to 1875, Ecuador was ruled by the fervently religious Conservative Gabriel García Moreno, Ecuador's first great statesman. He sought peace and consolidation for his torn country through a rigid, theocratic government. His administration granted special privileges to the Roman Catholic Church, even dedicating the Republic to "The Sacred Heart of Jesus" by act of congress in 1873. Beyond his religious zeal, García Moreno was also known for developing roads and public education, beginning the Guayaquil-Quito railway, and putting Ecuador on a firm financial footing. However, his relentless conservatism caused bitter strife, culminating in the dictator's assassination in 1875. In the ensuing period of confusion, the Conservatives were not able to carry on the program of García, nor could the opposition take command until the emergence of Gen. Eloy Alfaro, who ushered in the Radical Liberal era with the revolution of 1895. He and the succeeding Liberal presidents were able to counteract much of García's program. Church and state were carefully separated, and liberty of thought, worship, and the press was established. The Guayaquil-Quito railway was completed, uniting the coast and the highlands commercially.

The Liberal era continued until 1944, with numerous interludes of violence and crisis. The economy rose and fell with world prices on such commodities as cocoa. Territory was lost to Brazil in 1904, Colombia in 1916, and finally Peru in 1942. The border dispute with Peru, originating in the colonial period, came to a climax when Peru invaded Ecuador's southern and Oriente (Amazon Basin) provinces. The Rio de Janeiro Protocol awarded to Peru the greater part of the Amazon Basin territory claimed by Ecuador

In 1944 José María Velasco Ibarra came to power as a nationalist denouncing the Rio agreement. Velasco, who had served as president during 1934–35, ruled for three years until he was sent into exile. After three ineffective presidents in less than one year, Galo Plaza Lasso (1948–52) was elected to the presidency. Plaza, later chief of the OAS, ruled for four years. In 1952, Velasco Ibarra returned to office for four years, and was again elected in 1960. In his inaugural address, Velasco formally renounced the Treaty of 1942, and embarked on an economic program of "growth through inflation."

By 1961, with Ecuadorian currency in a slump and consumers heavily taxed, the air force revolted and sent Velasco into exile, thus ending Ecuador's unprecedented streak of elected governments. Vice President Carlos Julio Arosemena Monroy assumed the presidency on 7 November 1961. Arosemena lasted less than two years, and in July 1963, he was arrested by the military for "drunkenness" (a charge that could have been substantiated throughout his presidency) and sent into exile.

Military governments

A four-man military junta headed by Capt. Ramón Castro Jijón took over and ruled until March 1966. Elections were scheduled and held in October 1966 for a constitutional assembly. Otto Arosemena Gómez, cousin of Arosemena Monroy, became provisional president. In 1968, new elections were held for the presidency, won yet again by Velasco. On 22 June 1970, following a fiscal crisis, Velasco suspended the 1967 constitution and assumed dictatorial power. He dissolved Congress, reorganized the Supreme Court, and proceeded to rule by executive decree.

In June 1971, Velasco promised new presidential and congressional elections, which were scheduled for the following June. However, on 15 February 1972, Velasco was overthrown in a bloodless coup after he refused demands by senior army officers to postpone the elections. On the following day, Gen. Guillermo Rodríguez Lara was installed as head of a new military government. Velasco, deported to Panama, was granted asylum by Venezuela.

Return to elected government

The regime of General Rodríguez lasted for four years, and then he was ousted on 12 January 1976. A three-member Supreme Council assumed power, promising a return to civilian government within two years. Presidential elections took place in July 1978, but because none of the candidates received the required majority, a runoff election was held in April 1979. The winner was Jaime Roldós Aguilera, a populist running under the banner of the Concentration of Popular Forces. Christian Democrat Osvaldo Hurtado was made vice-president. Both were inaugurated on 10 August 1979, the day Ecuador's current constitution went into effect. Roldós was killed in a plane crash on 24 May 1981, whereupon Hurtado became president until 1984.

Hurtado's term was marked by modest gains in the economy, but by 1984, a flagging economy, caused in part by widespread flooding, led to calls for change. The 1984 election was won by

León Febres Cordero Rivadeneira, a conservative Social Christian who advocated a free-enterprise economic policy. Febres formed a coalition government and pressed his platform of reducing state intervention in the economy and making it more responsive to market forces.

Economic recovery falters

Just as it appeared that Febres's fiscal policies were about to bring widespread benefits to the populace, Ecuador was dealt two staggering blows: the 1986 plunge in world oil prices cut revenues by 30%, and a devastating earthquake in March 1987 cut off oil exports for four months and caused more than $1 billion in damage. The government had already suspended repayment of the $11 billion foreign debt in January 1987, but after the earthquake repayment was further postponed. Febres's fortunes took a turn for the worse with the decline in oil prices. His coalition partners were defeated in elections held on 1 June 1986, and the leftist parties opposed to him gained control of parliament.

In presidential elections held 31 January 1988, Rodrigo Borja Cevallos of the Democratic Left (ID) Party and Abdalá Bucaram Ortiz of the Roldista Party (honoring ex-President Roldós) won the most votes in a field of 10 candidates. Borja won the runoff election, and took office along with a strong contingent in congress. The government made improvements in Ecuador's human rights record, and reached an accord with the terrorist group Alfaro Vive, Carajo (literally, "Alfaro [Eloy] lives, damn it!"). However, economic troubles, particularly inflation, continued, and the ID lost half its congressional seats in midterm elections in 1990. In 1992, voters elected a conservative government, headed by President Sixto Durán-Ballén of the Republican Unity Party (PUR) and Vice President Alberto Dahik of the Conservative Party (CP). Durán-Ballén imposed severe economic measures to try to improve Ecuador's situation. These measures proved economically successful, but socially unpopular. Support for Durán-Ballén began to decline.

However, on 26 January 1995, the longstanding border dispute with Peru sprang to life once again when Ecuadorian troops attacked a Peruvian post. A full-fledged war began, which lasted until March 1, causing some 80 casualties and leaving 200 wounded. Although the war created further economic difficulties for Ecuador, it also stirred national pride, and Durán-Ballén's popularity rose on the tide of fervent patriotism. By the fall of 1995, however, Durán-Ballén had once again fallen from favor due to charges of political corruption against himself and Vice President Alberto Dahik. Dahik fled the country, and Durán-Ballén served the remainder of his presidential term with little support.

In July 1996, Abdalá Bucaram was elected president of Ecuador. A showy and eccentric populist, Bucaram quickly alienated most of the political establishment. Under Bucaram, US Ambassador Leslie Alexander told Ecuadorians, the country was gaining a reputation for pervasive corruption. Bucaram had come to describe himself as "El Loco," or the madman, and citizens began to believe that he was indeed crazy. By February 1997, they had had enough. More than 2 million Ecuadorians marched, calling for his ouster during a one-day strike. On February 6, Congress declared Bucaram mentally incompetent, charged him with corruption and ousted him from office. During the presidential crisis, Bucaram at first refused to leave office, and sought refuge in Guayaquil. Vice President Rosalia Arteaga and Fabian Alarcon, leader of Congress, claimed the presidency. Bucaram finally fled to Panama, while Arteaga agreed to briefly become president until Congress could establish right of succession. Alarcon emerged as interim president, and held office until the next presidential election in 1998. Bucaram was accused of absconding with $100 million to $300 million in public funds during his brief presidency. This sum was a significant one for a country in deep financial crisis. Through most of the 1990s, Ecuador suffered double-digit inflation as high as 50% to 60% a year. By 1999, the economy had contracted by 7.5%, and only one in three Ecuadorians had a full-time job. By 2000, over 62% of Ecuadorians lived in poverty, some with virtually nothing to their names.

Many of the country's Pacific Coast communities were battered by El Niño storms during early 1998, causing millions of dollars in damage. In this atmosphere of economic uncertainty, presidential elections were held in May 1998, with Harvard-educated Jamil Mahuad facing Alvaro Noboa, a banana tycoon and reputedly the richest man in the country. With promises for political stability and economic recovery, Mahuad prevailed at the polls and took office in July 1998. The next month, extensive constitutional reforms approved by a National Constituent Assembly took effect. Reforms gave unprecedented new rights to the country's indigenous peoples, who had become more vocal about their rights during the 1990s.

In 1996, the leaders of 11 indigenous groups joined with women, ecologists, and human rights workers to found the Pachakutik ("change" or "revolution" in Quichua) political movement. Under this new political umbrella, native peoples urged massive social changes, and won several seats in Congress by 2000. In the meantime, Mahuad was unable to bring the economy under control and was making political enemies. In May 1999, Mahuad and Peruvian president Alberto Fujimori formally ended their border dispute. Ecuador gained a small sliver of land, and navigation rights on some Peruvian rivers. The peace accord was seen as a defeat within Ecuador, where the military resented its loss of power and resources and was embarrassed by territorial concessions to Perú. By late 1999, native peoples had grown disenchanted with Mahuad. Amerindian leaders accused him of lacking sympathy for native peoples' economic problems. Mahuad also had overseen a $1.2 billion bailout of 18 corrupt banks. The financial scandal only widened after a jailed banker claimed he had given $3.1 million to Mahuad's presidential campaign.

In January 2000, Mahuad announced plans to replace the sucre, the national currency, with the US dollar. Mahuad wanted to stabilize the economy and end chronic inflation, but native peoples grew angry at the plan because they believed they would lose their savings. The sucre had been pegged at about 8,000 per dollar only a year earlier, but now stood at 25,000 per dollar. On January 21, thousands of native peoples marched to Quito to protest "dollarization" of the economy and called for Mahuad's ouster. With the aid of the military, they occupied the empty Congress building and Supreme Court. Mahuad fled the government palace. Gen. Carlos Mendoza took power and declared that a three-man junta would lead the country. The junta was composed of Antonio Vargas, leader of the Confederation of Indigenous Nationalities of Ecuador, Carlos Solorzano, a former Supreme Court justice, and Col. Lucio Gutierrez. The junta only lasted a few hours. Under intense international pressure, including US threats to end economic aid, Mendoza dissolved the junta. Congress named the 62-year-old vice president, Gustavo Noboa Bejarano, as president of the country despite protests by Mahuad. Noboa, a respected former rector and law-school dean at the Catholic University, said he would not abandon plans to "dollarize" the economy. By giving up its currency, Ecuador turned itsmonetary policy to the US Federal Reserve. Noboa's government has attempted to assure Ecuadorians that the new currency will stabilize the nation. With a "Get to Know the Dollar" campaign, the government plans to convert all sucres in circulation, about $450 million, before the end of 2000.

¹³GOVERNMENT

Since 1860, Ecuador has had 17 different constitutions. The most recent constitution came into force in August 1998. The previous constitution was approved on 10 August 1979, in preparation for a return from military to civilian rule. That document was amended in 1984 and again in 1996, but many Ecuadorians believed their needs were not reflected by that document. In 1998, a 70-member elected National Constituent Assembly rewrote the constitution. Unprecedented rights granted to native populations and blacks were among key reforms. The constitution gave them equal rights, additional rights that guaranteed their lands, protected their culture and customs. Native peoples were allowed to use their own languages and teach their children in their native languages at schools, although Spanish remained the official language of the nation. The constitution also emphasized unity in diversity. Eradicating poverty was a key component written into the new constitution, which also prohibits granting amnesty to human rights violators. The constitution also prohibits the death penalty.

The unicameral Chamber of Representatives (or Congress) consists of 125 provincial and national members. Twenty members are elected at large by proportional representation to five-year terms. The chamber meets in full session for two months a year, leaving the rest of its business to four permanent committees. The president and vice-president are elected for a four-year term, and are not allowed to seek consecutive terms. As is traditional in Ecuador, the president initiates the budget and appoints the cabinet, as well as provincial governors, many administrative employees, and diplomatic representatives. Under the 1998 constitutional reforms, the chamber may no longer remove cabinet ministers (it forced the finance minister out of office late in 1986, and ousted the president of Ecuador in February 1997). The president also controls the armed forces and can declare a state of siege. Voting is compulsory for literate people aged 18 to 65, and optional for illiterates.

¹⁴POLITICAL PARTIES

The constitution guarantees the right of democratic activities of political parties. A party must gain a minimum of five percent of the vote to remain in the electoral registry and retain its legal standing. The 1998 constitution also allows candidates without party affiliation or party backing to run for office. It also makes it the responsibility of the government to promote equal participation of men and women in politics. There are currently 20 parties active in Ecuadorian politics.

Two major parties played dominant roles prior to the 1960s. The Conservative Party (Partido Conservador—PC), which held sway during the first half of the republic's history, was the political representative for the Roman Catholic Church, and its support came from the large landowners of the highlands. The principal opposition, the Radical Liberal Party (Partido Liberal Radical—PLR), which rose to power in the revolution of 1895, was supported by businessmen and the newer city elite. It sought scrupulous separation of church and state, especially in public education, and called for the development of industry and the attraction of foreign capital.

Modern parties on the right include the Social Christian Party (PSC), the Republican Unity Party (PUR), and the Ecuadorian Conservative Party (PCE). On the left are the Democratic Left (ID), linked to the Social Democratic Movement; the Popular Democracy Party (DP) of former President Hurtado; the traditional Ecuadorian Radical Liberal Party (PLRE); and the Radical Alfarista Front (FRA).

Ecuador's populist tradition has given rise to many parties, organized along highly personalist lines, such as the Roldista Party (PRE), headed by Abdalá Bucaram, the Popular Revolutionary Action (APRE), and the Concentration of Popular Forces (CFP).

The far left in Ecuador has been beset by factionalism and governmental intrusion. In the 1920s, the original Socialist Party of Ecuador split into the Socialist Party and the Communist Party. Further splits occurred with the advent of the Cuban revolution. Currently, the Popular Democratic Movement (MPD), the Ecuadorian Socialist Party (PSE), and other parties vie for the non-Communist vote. Communists are divided between the Communist Party of Ecuador (PCE), which is identified as a pro-North Korean faction; and the Communist Party of Ecuador/Marxist-Leninist (PCMLE), which is identified as Maoist.

In the 1996 national elections, an indigenous electoral movement called Pachakutik (Quichua for "cataclysmic change") sponsored candidates for offices on the national, provincial, and local levels. Pachakutik candidates won eight seats in Congress as well as several mayoral positions in cities throughout the country. Their successes, although small on the overall national scale, increased the voice of indigenous peoples in Ecuadorian politics and prodded the traditional political parties to give more attention to long-neglected indigenous concerns.

¹⁵LOCAL GOVERNMENT

The three levels of local government—province, canton, and parish—are controlled by the central government in a fundamentally unitary system. Ecuador has 20 continental provinces, plus the insular Galápagos Islands. The provincial governors, who are appointed by the president, are responsible to the interior ministry. Each province is divided into cantons, which in urban areas are administratively subordinate to the municipality with which they coincide. A municipal council is popularly elected and in turn elects its officers. In the larger towns, a mayor is popularly elected. The municipality is unique in that it lies somewhat outside the unitary pattern and is less subject to national control than are the other units of local government. The rural canton, of little importance in the sparsely populated Oriente and northern coast, is significant in the more developed regions of the highlands and the coastal provinces of Guayas and Manabí. The highest official of the canton, the political chief, is appointed by the president on the recommendation of the provincial governor.

¹⁶JUDICIAL SYSTEM

Traditionally, the judicial function has been carried out by five levels of tribunals. The parochial judge, the political lieutenant appointed by the president to supervise the affairs of the parish, handles only minor civil cases. Cantonal courts, at least one in each canton, try minor civil and criminal actions. Provincial courts handle all but a few of the criminal cases and the more serious civil and commercial suits. Superior courts handle appeals from the lower courts and have other administrative duties in the district; they may try original cases only if these relate to the affairs of their district. The Supreme Court has 31 justices and three alternates chosen by the National Chamber of Representatives for six-year periods.

Although citizens are afforded a wide range of freedoms and individual rights, there remain some shortcomings in the functioning of the judicial system, which is susceptible to political pressure. Police officers are tried only in closed session before police courts so that convictions for abuse or other violations are rare. Despite laws restricting arbitrary arrest and detention, such violations continue to occur in practice. Modernization of the court system began in 1993. In 1998, a new Judicial Council, with the power to administer the court system and discipline judges, began operations. In November of that year, the council's disciplinary committee fired two judges and two court employees for improperly releasing suspected drug traffickers. Because Ecuadorians continued to distrust the judicial system, reports of citizens taking the law into the own hands by lynching or burning criminal suspects continued into the year 2000.

[17]ARMED FORCES

The armed forces of 57,100 are designed for internal security more than external defense. In 1998, Ecuador spent $720 million on defense or around 3.4% of GNP. Since 1933, the law has mandated 1-year conscription. In recent decades the army has built roads and bridges and, through the Military Geographic Institute, has mapped uncharted areas of the country.

As of 1995, the navy of 4,100 (including 1,500 marines) mans 2 submarine and 11 small surface combatants. The air force of 3,000 (with 78 combat aircraft) also provides air defense and transport services. The coast guard numbers 270.

[18]INTERNATIONAL COOPERATION

Ecuador is a charter member of the UN, having joined on 21 October 1945. It belongs to ECLAC and all the nonregional specialized agencies. Ecuador is also active in the OAS and its various commissions, as well as in G-77, IADB, and LAIA. Ecuador received full membership in OPEC in 1973. As of September 1987, the nation, which claims a 200-mi territorial sea limit, had declined to sign the Law of the Sea. Ecuador is a member of the WTO.

Under the US-backed Alliance for Progress program, Ecuador financed its private industry, improved and expanded the Quito sewerage system, promoted housing development, increased production of foodstuffs and raw materials, moved toward eradication of foot-and-mouth disease, implemented a mapping program, purchased selected Australian sheep, and implemented the land settlement program. In the early 1970s and again in the early 1980s, relations with the US were strained because of Ecuadoran seizures of US tuna-fishing boats. In mid-1983, the US lifted its prohibition on the importation of Ecuadoran tuna, and the tension between the two countries over tuna fishing eased.

In 1965, Ecuador and Colombia established a permanent Colombian-Ecuadoran economic integration commission. In May of that year, Ecuador signed the Andean Pact, thereby becoming a member of the Andean Common Market.

[19]ECONOMY

Ecuador's average annual GDP growth rate exceeded 9% in the 1970s, due largely to an oil-driven economy. As oil prices fell in the early 1980s, debt began to increase. Furthermore, a major earthquake in 1987 interrupted oil production and exports. The average annual GDP growth rate between 1988 and 1998, however, was 2.9%. Growth stemmed mainly from increased petroleum production and expansionary fiscal policy.

The administration of President Ballén, elected in July 1992, raised petroleum derivatives taxes and electricity tariffs, while cutting public expenditures and freezing public sector employment. As a result, the 1992 public sector deficit fell from 7% to 2.8% in 1995. The inflation rate, which stood at 60% at the end of 1992, fell to 25% by 1995. Although the Ballén administration's reforms were relatively successful in stabilizing the economy and encouraging foreign investment, key sectors like petroleum, utilities, and aviation still experienced heavy government involvement.

The late 1990s brought a border dispute with Peru, shortages of electric power, and high interest rates that combined to restrain growth in the GDP. Large parastatals put off the interest of foreign investment. The growth rate was only 1% in 1998, the inflation rate soared to 43%, and government corruption was rampant. The 1999 growth rate was a discouraging -7%, inflation had ballooned to 63%, and the unemployment rate was over 20%. Economic revival and austerity measures were well overdue in 2000.

[20]INCOME

The US Central Intelligence Agency (CIA) reports that in 1998 Ecuador's gross domestic product (GDP) was estimated at $58.7 billion. The per capita GDP was estimated at $4,800. The annual growth rate of GDP was estimated at 1%. The average inflation rate in 1998 was 43%. The CIA defines GDP as the value of all final goods and services produced within a nation in a given year and computed on the basis of purchasing power parity (PPP) rather than value as measured on the basis of the rate of exchange. It was estimated that agriculture accounted for 12% of GDP, industry 37%, and services 51%.

The World Bank reports that for the same period per capita private consumption (in PPP terms) was $1,810. Private consumption includes expenditures of individuals, households, and nongovernmental organizations. It was estimated that between 1990 and 1998 private consumption grew at an annual rate of 2.4%. Approximately 26% of household consumption was spent on food, 15% on fuel, 13% on health care, and 10% on education. The richest 10% of the population accounted for approximately 34% of household consumption and the poorest 10% approximately 2.2%.

[21]LABOR

In 1998, there were 3,151,200 employed wage earners. In the same year, 7.3% were engaged in agriculture, 30% in commerce and hospitality, 15% in manufacturing and mining, 5.8% in construction, and 6.2% in transportation. The unemployment rate officially stood at 11.5% in 1998.

In 1999, only 12% of the economically active population was affiliated with labor unions. The largest concentration of unions has been in the Guayas and Pichincha provinces. The dominant groups are the Ecuadoran Confederation of Class Organizations (Confederación Ecuatoriana de Organizaciones Clasistas—CEDOC), the Ecuadoran Confederation of Workers (Confederación de Trabajadores del Ecuador—CTE), and the Ecuadoran Confederation of Free Trade Union Organizations (Confederación Ecuatoriana de Organizaciones Sindicales Libres—CEOSL). These three confederations form the United Front of Workers (Frente Unido de Trabajadores—FUT).

The labor code provides for a 40-hour work week. Special permits are necessary for women and minors and for workers in certain hazardous industries. There are minimum wages, two-week paid vacations, overtime pay, social security, and severance pay. The minimum monthly wage was about $55 in 1999. Fringe benefits include three bonuses and paid vacation of 15 days a year, plus a seniority bonus of one day for each year of service in excess of five years, up to a 30-day maximum. Benefits typically can double the basic salary.

[22]AGRICULTURE

Although Ecuador's main economic activity has long been agriculture, only about 11% of the land is arable or under permanent crops, and another 18% is permanent pasture. Throughout the 1970s, agricultural development was neglected because of the emphasis on oil exploitation, and the sector showed negative rates of growth, declining by 5.4% in 1978, 2.8% in 1979, and 2% in 1980. During 1985–90, however, agriculture (along with fishing and forestry) showed an average annual increase of 4.8%. By 1998, agricultural production was 51.6% greater than the annual average during 1989–91. Agriculture employed 27.2% of the labor force in 1998 and contributed 13% to GDP.

The land census of 1974, which covered a much larger area than the previous census of 1954, showed that during the intervening period the number of agricultural units had grown by 172,810. This increase was the result of agrarian reform and colonization, initiated in 1964. Ceilings imposed on the maximum size of holdings ranged from 800 hectares (2,000 acres) of arable land plus 1,000 hectares (2,500 acres) for pasture in the Sierra region to 2,500 hectares (6,200 acres) plus 1,000 hectares (2,500 acres) of pasture in the coastal region. The 1975 plans of the Ecuadoran Land Reform and Colonization Institute called for the redistribution of 80,000 hectares (198,000 acres) of land in the coastal region.

Traditionally, agricultural products have included bananas, coffee, tea, rice, sugar, beans, corn, potatoes, and tropical fruit. Exported products of more recent prominence include roses and carnations, strawberries, melons, asparagus, heart of palm, and tomatoes. The major crops of the highlands are corn, barley, wheat, kidney beans, potatoes, horsebeans, peas, and soybeans, all for domestic consumption. Agriculture on the coast is largely oriented toward the export market. Increased acreage and improved yields, as well as the government's price-support program, have caused rapid growth in agriculture. Most of the cacao crop is produced on plantations of 60 hectares (150 acres) or larger, but the more important banana and coffee crops are grown mainly on small landholdings by independent farmers. Banana exports rose from less than 5% of total exports after World War II to 62.2% in 1958; in 1974, they were 10.8%, and in 1997, 25.2% ($1.3 billion). Ecuador is the world's leading banana exporter, selling over 4.5 million tons abroad in 1997. Cacao became a valuable export in the mid-1970s, but low prices and declining harvests had a negative impact on revenues until the early 1980s, when they began to rise again. In 1978 and 1979, coffee brought high export earnings ($281.2 million and $263.1 million, respectively), but with lower world prices, coffee export earnings fell to $106 million in 1981, despite an increase in production. Revenues rose steadily during the 1980s, reaching $290 million in 1986, but fell to $75 million in 1992. Coffee revenues in 1997 amounted to $86.3 million.

Principal commodities in 1998 (in tons) were sugar, 4,800,000; bananas, 7,494,000; corn, 688,000; plantains, 894,000; palm oil, 208,000; potatoes, 602,000; cocoa beans, 35,000; and coffee, 120,000. The production of paddy rice reached 1,072,000 tons in 1998.

The agricultural sector of the economy presents potential for further development and growth. Crops for domestic consumption, particularly rice, barley, maize, African palm, and potatoes, continue to show growth due to increased area planted and improved yields. Other segments likely to experience growth are nontraditional agricultural products such as flowers, fresh fruit, and vegetables, and processed foods. The government's agricultural policy focuses on integration into the World Trade Organization, import tariffs, and the lack of credit in the agricultural sector.

23ANIMAL HUSBANDRY

The dairy industry is located in the most fertile valleys of the highland plateau from Ibarra to Riobamba, where irrigation is available. The beef cattle industry is an important part of the agricultural economy, as exports to Colombia and Peru have become more profitable; there were 5,329,000 head of cattle in 1998. Nearly all the sheep (2,056,000 in 1998) are in the highlands; most are raised by Amerindians and are pastured at over 2,700 m (9,000 ft). The wool is of poor quality. Hogs and goats, found throughout the country, are frequently diseased and poorly fed; in 1998 there were an estimated 2,795,000 hogs and 310,000 goats. The use of bananas as hog feed has made hog farming more attractive economically. Poultry production has been steadily growing—135,000 tons in 1998, up from an annual average of 69,000 tons during 1989–91. Beef production totaled 153,000 tons in 1998. Milk production in 1998 totaled 1,950,000 tons, and eggs, 58,000 tons.

24FISHING

In the waters around the Galápagos Islands, Ecuador has some of the world's richest fishing grounds, particularly for tuna. In the past, these waters were exploited mainly by foreign companies, but in recent years, Ecuadoran enterprises have participated more fully. Shifts in ocean currents can cause great variance in the annual catch. Ecuador is a leading producer of canned tuna. Shrimp farming occupies some 110,000 hectares (over 270,000 acres). Ecuador produces more shrimp than any other nation in the Americas, and exports more than 35,000 tons annually, mostly to the US. Rainbow trout aquaculture is being developed in the Andean highlands. The total catch in 1997 was 688,297 tons, down from 1,003,380 tons in 1986. Exports of fish and fish products in 1997 totaled $1,179 million.

Ecuador proclaimed sovereignty over its coastal waters to a limit of 200 km. In 1952, along with Peru and Chile, Ecuador signed the Declaration of Santiago (joined later by Colombia) to enforce these rights.

25FORESTRY

One of Ecuador's vast untapped resources is its forestland. Forests, half of which are government owned, cover 15,600,000 hectares (38,548,000 acres), or 56.3% of the total mainland area. The tropical jungles contain more than 2,240 known species of trees. Some of the denuded highlands have been planted with eucalyptus trees, which prevent soil erosion and provide both fuel and rough lumber. Total roundwood production in 1997 was 11,808,000 cu m. About 50% of the wood cut was burned as fuel.

Ecuador is the world's largest producer and exporter of balsa. Several varieties of hardwoods, including species of mahogany, are used in cabinetmaking. Other forest products having some importance are the fiber for Panama hats (toquilla palm), vegetable ivory (tagua palm), kapok (ceiba tree), quinine (cinchona bark), and rubber.

26MINING

Aside from petroleum, Ecuador's known mineral resources include gold, silver, copper, bismuth, tin, lead, zinc, clays, kaolin, limestone, marble, and sulfur. A mining law of 1991 offers incentives for exploration, allows foreign individuals and companies access to mining rights, attempts to curtail corruption and unnecessary bureaucracy in the mining sector, and requires environmental impact statements to be filed before any mining activity starts. In 1997, production of nonfuel minerals contributed 1.4% to the GDP and employed 60 workers, or 2% of the active labor force. Export revenues from nonfuel mineral output totaled $26 million in 1997. Production of gold in 1997 was around 15 tons. The most important producer was Bira S.A., which produced 9 tons in the Portovelo-Zaruma district. Other production totals for 1997 include silver, 2,134 kilograms; copper, 100 tons; lead, 200 tons; zinc, 100 tons; kaolin, 7,300 tons; limestone, 4,261 tons; and marble, 1,089 tons.

27ENERGY AND POWER

In recent years, an increasingly important percentage of Ecuador's national income has come from the petroleum industry. Initially, this industry was slow in developing, and production actually declined from 2,849,000 barrels of crude oil in 1965 to a low of 1,354,000 barrels in 1971. Starting in the 1970s, however, output increased dramatically, from 28,579,000 barrels in 1972 to 77,052,000 barrels in 1981, and to 109,400,000 barrels in 1991. After leaving OPEC in 1992, Ecuador's daily crude oil production rose from 321,000 barrels in 1992 to nearly 400,000 barrels by the end of 1995. Production in 1998 was 377,000 barrels per day. The value of petroleum exports was $1.6 billion in 1995, accounting for 39% of total exports. Net oil exports in 1998 were 236,000 barrels per day.

Extensive oil fields have been found in the Oriente; proved oil reserves were estimated at 2.1 billion barrels in 1999. At the rate of current extraction, known reserves will be depleted by around 2010. A 1969 agreement between the government and a Texaco-Gulf oil company consortium provided for the construction of a 480-km (300-mi) pipeline with a capacity of 250,000 barrels a day; the pipeline, which carries petroleum across the Andes, was partially destroyed in the March 1987 earthquake and was unusable for five months. Most oil comes from the Oriente Province (the Amazon jungle region) and is transported via the 502-km (312-mi) Trans-Ecuador pipeline to the tanker-loading port of Esmeraldas.

In the early 1970s, most of the oil industry was managed by foreign companies, which were granted concessions by the government; in 1996, Petroecuador, the state oil agency, controlled all production, exploration, and marketing. Production of natural gas is relatively small, totaling 4 billion ft (113 million cu m) in 1997.

Installed capacity rose from 93,000 kW in 1958 to 357,000 kW in 1972 and 3,119,000 kW in 1998. Total production of electric power in that year amounted to 9,657 million kWh, 83% of it hydroelectric. In order to conserve oil, energy requirements were increasingly being covered by hydroelectricity, by large projects, and by small-scale decentralized stations. In 1987, a 156 MW station at Agoyan was completed. As of 1992, recently opened plants were capable of producing another 600,000 kWh per year. In 1995, a serious drought affected hydroelectric generating capacity, and daily blackouts became common. In January 1996, electricity workers protesting the government's privatization plans commandeered Ecuador's seven hydroelectric plants and drastically cut production.

28INDUSTRY

Ecuador enjoyed a period of prosperity in the 1970s, due in large part to a boom in oil. A decline in international oil prices, an earthquake in 1987, and political difficulties hampered industrial development during the 1980s. During 1988–98, manufacturing output increased by an annual average of 2.5% per year. According to official estimates, in 1998 manufacturing contributed an estimated 22% GDP, but achieved only minimal growth during that year, and negative growth in 1999.

The most promising sectors, outside of oil, are linked to agriculture and natural resources. In the agricultural sector, expansion has come from processed foods and nontraditional agricultural products, such as flowers and fresh tropical fruits (mango, babaco, and passion fruit) and vegetables (asparagus and heart of palm). Other major manufactured items include canned seafood, automobiles, processed coffee, and cocoa.

29SCIENCE AND TECHNOLOGY

In 1996, Ecuador had 20 agricultural, medical, scientific, and technical learned societies and research institutes, most notably the General Directorate of Hydrocarbons, the Institute of Nuclear Sciences, the Ecuadoran Institute of Natural Sciences, and the National Institute of Agricultural Research, all in Quito; the Charles Darwin Research Station in the Galapagos Islands; and the Naval Oceanographic Institute In Guayaquil. Ecuador has 19 colleges and universities offering degrees in basic and applied sciences. In 1987–97, science and engineering students accounted for 27% of college and university enrollments. In 1987–97, Ecuador had 146 scientists and engineers and 42 technicians per million people engaged in research and development.

30DOMESTIC TRADE

In the mountains, businesses are generally open from 8 AM to 6 PM, with a two-hour midday break; lunch hours are longer along the coast during the hottest months (December–April). Banks are usually open from 9 AM to 1:30 PM and from 2 to 6 PM during the week. Urban and suburban factories typically operated from 7 AM to 4 PM. Rural domestic trade among the *camposinos* (indigenous peoples) is limited by frequent deep levels of poverty and underdevelopment. The (mostly urban) middle class is relatively moderate in size, and suffered major declines in purchasing power during the 1980s and 1990s, when economic growth faltered. Unemployment and underemployment have stimulated the growth of informal domestic economic activity.

31FOREIGN TRADE

Ecuador's trade balance is generally positive, due overwhelmingly to its oil exports. Ecuador's oil reserves and refineries account for over a third of the country's commodity exports (34%). Agricultural exports include bananas (19%), shrimp (15%), coffee and cocoa (11%), and fish (5.0%). In 2000, the government raised the price of Ecuadorian petrol by 60% in order to forge an economic recovery. Ecuador exports about half of its petroleum to the US, 60% of its shrimp, 26% of its bananas, 57% of its coffee, and 70% of its cut flowers. The US supplied 31% of Ecuador's imports in 1997.

In 1997 Ecuador's imports were distributed among the following categories:

Consumer goods	14.1%
Food	7.6%
Fuels	7.6%
Industrial supplies	34.9%
Machinery	22.7%
Transportation	12.9%
Other	0.2%

Principal trading partners in 1998 (in millions of US dollars) were as follows:

COUNTRY	EXPORTS	IMPORTS	BALANCE
United States	1,808	1,855	-47
Colombia	378	569	-191
Japan	324	494	-170
Chile	242	182	60
Germany	229	227	2
Italy	192	178	14
Spain	151	104	47
Korea	96	121	-25
Venezuela	37	284	-247
Brazil	33	224	-191

32BALANCE OF PAYMENTS

Ecuador's balance of payments showed repeated deficits on current accounts until the vast increases in petroleum exports during the 1970s; only in 1974 did the net balance finally register a surplus of $26.7 million. International reserves rose steadily from $57.3 million in 1967 to $64.7 million in 1971, increased dramatically (with the rise in oil exports) from $143.4 million in 1972 to $1 billion by December 1980, and then dropped (as the oil market softened) to $304 million at the end of 1982, but were up to $500 million by 1987.

In 1992, currency appreciation caused a narrowing in the trade surplus, which pushed down international reserves. In 1994, increased production in the petroleum, banana, construction, and manufacturing sectors generated growth of 4%, up from 3% the year before, helping Ecuador post a merchandise trade surplus of $435 million. The surplus, however, was offset by a deficit on the services account resulting in a current account deficit of $807 million. Increased exports in 1995 were partially offset by increased military imports due to the conflict with Peru. The current account deficit in 1997 also showed an increase of military imports with a deficit of $734 million (according to the US embassy in Ecuador). The 1998 peace agreement with Peru assuaged the balance of payments deficit, but by that time the flight of private capital due to the unstable political situation had precipitated a negative turn in the economy.

The US Central Intelligence Agency reports that in 1997 the purchasing power parity of Ecuador's exports was $3.4 billion while imports totaled $2.9 billion resulting in a trade balance of $500 million.

The International Monetary Fund (IMF) reports that in 1998 Ecuador had exports of goods totaling $4,203 million and imports totaling $5,198 million. The services credit totaled $804 million and the debit $1,211 million. The following table summarizes Ecuador's balance of payments as reported by the IMF for 1998 in millions of US dollars.

Current Account		-2,169
Balance on goods	-995	
Balance on services	-407	
Balance on income	-1,543	
Current transfers	776	
Capital Account		15
Financial Account		2,040
Direct investment abroad	...	
Direct investment in Ecuador	831	
Portfolio investment assets	...	
Portfolio investment liabilities	...	
Other investment assets	44	
Other investment liabilities	1,165	
Net Errors and Omissions		-456
Reserves and Related Items		570

33BANKING AND SECURITIES

The Central Bank of Ecuador, founded as a private bank in 1927, was declared an organ of the state in 1948 by the Monetary Board. The Central Bank issues and stabilizes currency, holds and manages foreign-exchange reserves, issues import and export permits, and regulates international transactions. The Monetary Board supervises government monetary, financial, and exchange policies. In 1997, there were 41 private banks operating in Ecuador with combined assets of 15.2 billion. The five largest banks, with half of these assets, included Banco Popular, Filanbanco, Banco del Progreso, Banco del Pichincha, and Banco del Pacifico.

The government-owned National Development Bank (BNF) was founded in 1928 to provide credit for agricultural and industrial development. Other major government-owned financial institutions are the Bank of the State (BEDE), the National Finance Corporation (CFN), the Ecuadorian Housing Bank (BEV), and the Development Bank of Ecuador (BEDE).

On 1 December 1996, president Abdalá Bucaram anchored the fully convertible sucre to the dollar. In July 1997 the sucre was pegged at a fixed exchange rate of 4 new sucres (4,000 old sucres) per dollar. Bucaram was dismissed from the government for incompetency, and his plan was abandoned by the Alarcon government, which introduced a currency auction system to minimize fluctuations between the sucre and the dollar. The sucre depreciated by almost 200% in 1999. In 2000, President Mahuad decided to dollarize the economy at 25,000 sucres per dollar. He was also ousted in a coup d'etat on an anti-dollarization platform, but the incumbent President Naboa went ahead with the plan anyway. IMF-backed recovery plans for 2001 included massive amounts of foreign assistance.

Trading in securities is relatively minor. Ecuador has two stock exchanges, one in Quito and the other in Guayaquil, both established in 1969. Purchase and sale of government and some private securities are functions of the National Financial Corp., which, along with several hundred business people, owns the two stock exchanges. This autonomous agency, founded in 1964,

deals in mortgage bonds issued by banks for agricultural and industrial development and in general seeks to mobilize funds for technical assistance to industry.

34INSURANCE

The principal branches of insurance are fire, marine, and vehicular, with some growth in aviation and aircraft. Other branches, including life, are still undeveloped. In the mid-1980s, there were some 30 insurance companies in Ecuador.

Insurance is closely governed by legal provisions determining necessary reserves and security funds and requiring a percentage of investments in government securities. The Superintendency of Banks periodically examines insurance operations and authorizes the formation of new companies. In accordance with the General Insurance Law of 1965, all insurance companies must apply to the Bank Superintendency for authority to operate.

It has been proposed (as of 1997) to privatize the management of pension funds in the state security system, the Instituto Equatoriano de Seguridad Social (IESS). This will be made possible by separating the IESS into three sectors: health, pensions, and rural social security.

35PUBLIC FINANCE

The central government, 20 provincial and some 100 municipal governments, and a large number of decentralized autonomous agencies constitute the public sector of the Ecuadoran economy. Central government budgets in the late 1970s and early 1980s grew expansively from one year to the next, with oil being the key source of income. Economic reforms instituted in 1992 rose domestic fuel prices and utility rates, eliminated subsidies, and brought the government budget into balance. These changes helped eliminate the budget deficit by 1994. The government was able to maintain budgetary control in 1995 when faced with increased military expenditures because of the boarder conflict with Peru, with a deficit of only 1.4% of GDP. However, the 1996 balance ran a deficit of 3% due to increased public spending. A growing fiscal deficit in the late 1990s due to declining oil prices, El Nino damage, and the inefficiencies of the public sector, caused the removal of several political leaders. The extreme financial crisis during 1999 and 2000 caused the total public debt to rise from 64% in 1997 to 116% in 1999. The fiscal deficit was 5% of GDP in 2000.

The US Central Intelligence Agency (CIA) estimates that in 1999 Ecuador's central government took in revenues of approximately $5.1 billion and had expenditures of $5.1 billion. External debt totaled $16 billion.

The following table shows an itemized breakdown of government revenues and expenditures. The percentages were calculated from data reported by the International Monetary Fund. The dollar amounts (millions) are based on the CIA estimates provided above.

REVENUE AND GRANTS	100%	5,100
Tax revenue	88.3%	4,501
Non-tax revenue	11.7%	599
EXPENDITURES	100%	5,100
General public services	7.1%	364
Defense	13.1%	669
Public order and safety	4.3%	219
Education	18.4%	939
Health	11.2%	570
Social security	1.9%	99
Housing and community amenities	0.6%	30
Recreation, cultural, and religious affairs	0.4%	21
Economic affairs and services	11.9%	609
Other expenditures	3.4%	171
Interest payments	23.2%	1,183
Adjustments	4.5%	227

36TAXATION

Taxation provides the government with most of its income. Levies include the income tax, 12% VAT, stamp tax, real estate tax, transfer tax, municipal taxes, and inheritance and gift taxes.

The basic tax on corporate income after the 1990 tax reform was 25% on undistributed profits and 36% on profits paid to foreign stockholders residing abroad. The basic corporate tax rate for oil companies with risk service contracts is 44%. The basic personal income tax rate starts at 25%. Additional rates and surcharges are applicable to certain classes of income. A stamp tax is levied on almost all commercial and legal documents. Estate, inheritance, and gift taxes vary according to the amount involved and the closeness of family relationship between donor and recipient. Municipal real estate taxes range from 0.3% to 2%. A special consumption tax is imposed on cigarettes, alcoholic beverages, and soft drinks at rates ranging from 20.6% to 103%.

A new tax reform package was slated for September 2000.

37CUSTOMS AND DUTIES

Import duties range from 0% to 30%. The average tariff rate is 13% ad valorem. Importers also pay a 1% service charge, a 2% special tax, and a 12% value-added tax. Ecuador has a CET with Colombia and Venezuela, ranging from 5% on raw materials and capital goods, 10% or 15% for intermediate goods, and 20% for consumer goods. Agricultural products and equipment are duty free. The automobile tax of 35% was repealed in 2000, but the tariff levels increased between 2% and 5% to help finance the public debt. Excise taxes on imported and locally manufactured cigarettes, soft drinks, alcoholic beverages, and other luxury items were reduced in 1997.

Comparatively few non-tariff trade barriers remain following measures taken in the 1990s to liberalize trade. Ecuador is a member of the Andean Pact, and the Latin American Integration Association (LAIA). Ecuador also has bilateral free trade agreements with Colombia, Bolivia, Venezuela, Chile. All accord preferential duty treatment. Five free trade zones were established in 1991, including the Zona Franca de Esmeraldas, Zona Franca del Pacifico S.A., Zona Franca Centro Ecuatoriana C.A., Zona Franca Manabi, and Parque Industrial de Cuenca C.E.M.

38FOREIGN INVESTMENT

The government welcomes foreign investment and has substantially decreased regulatory barriers in recent years. As a member of the Andean Pact, Ecuador's foreign investment policy is governed largely by the parameters of Andean Pact Decisions 291 and 292 of May 1991, which provide for equal treatment of foreign and domestic investors, and unrestricted remittance of profits overseas. As of 8 January 1993, foreign investment was allowed without previous authorization in virtually all sectors of the economy that were open to domestic private investment, with total remittance permitted. Foreign oil companies must work with Petroecuador, the state oil company. Investment in mining, fishing, and media require government approval. Mining companies must deal with the Ministry of Energy and Mines, while fishing operations are mainly restricted to about half ownership, and media investments are limited to 25%. Investment in telecommunications and electricity were closed to foreigners until 2000, when the government announced plans to sell half of the rights in each sector.

Total foreign direct investment in Ecuador amounted to $577 million in 1997, of which Switzerland accounted for $26 million; The Netherlands, $15 million, and the US, $14 million. These figures do not include investments made in the petroleum sector, which are estimated at $446 million.

39ECONOMIC DEVELOPMENT

In 1992/93, a major macroeconomic adjustment program was introduced, featuring a sizable currency devaluation (35%) and substantial increases in domestic fuel and electricity prices. Free trade agreements with Colombia, Venezuela, and Bolivia were signed, and new investment regulations were adopted to open up the economy to foreign investment and eliminate previous bureaucratic impediments. In April 1993, Ecuador qualified for Andean Trade Preference Act benefits, and has officially submitted an application to join the GATT.

High debt service obligations and external payments arrears to commercial banks impaired Ecuador's economic growth during the rest of the 1990s. The economy basically fell apart in 1999, despite aid throughout the decade from multilateral donors. In 2000, Ecuador accepted a $600 million loan from the IMF, IBD, and the Andean Development Corporation; while it rescheduled loan payments on $600 million with the Paris Club. This was part of a total $2 billion package from multilateral aid agencies to take place over a period of three years. In order to receive the money, the government was required to undertake a privatization program, and increase the price of petrol by 60%. Total external debt in 2000 reached $13.6 billion, most of which was in default.

40SOCIAL DEVELOPMENT

The Social Welfare and Labor Ministry is active in a number of programs dedicated to the public welfare, participating in such cooperative efforts as the Andean Indian Mission of the UN.

Ecuador's social security program is administered through the Ecuadorian Social Security Institute. This program, based on the Compulsory Social Insurance Law of 1988, is operated through three agencies: the Social Security Fund, the Pension Fund, and the Social Insurance Medical Department. All workers in industry and commerce are covered. The benefits, for those who fulfill the requirements, consist of health and maternity insurance with free medical service, accident and occupational disease insurance, old age pensions, survivors' pensions, funeral expenses, and unemployment insurance. In 1999, workers' contributions to the pension system ranged from 6% to 8% of earnings, depending on the type of employment; employers contributed 2.39% of payroll. Unemployment benefits are given as a lump sum payable after at least 60 days of unemployment.

Despite equal legal status, women have fewer educational and employment opportunities than men. There are fewer women in the professions, and salary discrimination is common. As of 1998, 18 of 123 members of Parliament were women. In 1995, a law was passed that criminalized spousal abuse. Social, economic, and cultural change is promoted by the Ecuadorian Women's Permanent National Forum, founded in 1994.

Indigenous peoples in the Amazon area are increasingly demanding that the government take into account their interests before making decisions that affect their land. In 1999 major demonstrations were held to protest the government's economic austerity measures.

Human rights organizations reported cases of mistreatment of detainees and incommunicado detention. The judicial system is slow and pre-trial detention may be lengthy.

41HEALTH

Malnutrition and infant mortality are the country's two basic health problems. In 1996, children under 5 years old had a 48% mortality rate. Food production has risen slightly, while the population has been increasing by 2% a year.

Other health problems are largely being controlled. Yellow fever was eliminated by the efforts of the Rockefeller Foundation. Two antituberculosis organizations have helped reduce the mortality from that disease, which earlier was responsible for one-fifth of the nation's deaths. As of 1995, 70% of the population had access to safe water.

Health facilities are largely concentrated in the towns and are both too expensive and too distant to be used by most of the highland Amerindian population. Hospitals are operated by agencies of the national government, the municipalities, and private organizations or persons. In 1995 health care personnel for 10,000 population included 13 physicians, 2 dentists, and 5 nurses. The country spent a total of $71 per capita in 1995 on health care.

The 1998 birthrate was 25.4 per 1,000 people. Studies show that from 1990 to 1998, 57% of married women (ages 15 to 49) used contraception. The infant mortality rate in 1996 was 39 per 1,000 live births. Life expectancy at birth in 1998 was estimated at an average of 69.9 years. In 1997, Ecuador immunized large numbers of children up to 1 year old: tuberculosis (99%); diphtheria, pertussis, and tetanus (76%); polio (77%); and measles (75%). The overall death rate in 1999 was 5 per 1,000 people. As of 1994, major causes of death were cited as follows: communicable diseases (116 per 100,000); neoplasms (78 per 100,000); injuries (83 per 100,000), and circulatory system diseases (142). Malaria, which as recently as 1942 caused about one-fourth of the deaths in Ecuador, is still a problem; 12,011 cases were reported in 1996. There were 7,938 reported cases of tuberculosis in 1996. In 1996, 40 cases of measles were reported. Cholera still persists; however, fewer than 1% of the 1,060 cases accounted for died of cholera in 1996.

In 1997, the HIV seroprevalence was low at 0.3 per 100 adults. Some 186 new cases of AIDS were reported in 1996, when the cumulative total since 1984 was 1,279.

[42] HOUSING

The 1974 housing census counted 2,747,800 housing units in the country. Almost all rural homes and many city dwellings on the coast are made with split bamboo siding and a palm thatch or corrugated iron roof. A housing development bank, Banco de la Vivienda, was established in 1961. In the late 1970s, the Institute of Sanitary Works initiated a program of well digging and latrine construction in rural areas. In 1990, 64% of all housing units were private houses with sanitary facilities; 12% were mediagreas, substandard one-story dwellings; 8% were apartments; 8% were cuartes, or semi-private units, and 7% were ranchos or covachas, dwellings of wood, stone, or brick covered with palm leaves, straw or other vegetation. Owners occupied 68%; 23% were rented; 6% were occupied rent free; and 3% were rented in exchange for services. Half of all dwellings had private toilet facilities and 40% had private baths.

[43] EDUCATION

The illiteracy rate for persons 15 years of age and over declined from 11.7% in 1990 to 8.1% in the year 2000 (males, 6.4%; females, 9.8%). A five-year plan (1963–68) was implemented to teach 450,000 adults to read and write. A distinctive feature of the program was its goal of functional literacy, whereby adults not only learned how to read and write but also received further school training to develop their capacities and skills. The Ministry of Education is the principal authority for all educational programs except higher education, which is supervised by a national technical council. Education received 13.0% of the national budget in the latter part of the 1990s.

Education is free and compulsory from ages 6 to 14. At the primary level, in 1997 there were 74,601 teachers and 1,888,172 students enrolled in 17,367 primary schools. The student-to-teacher ratio stood at 25 to one. Secondary level schools had 814,359 students and approximately 63,000 teachers in 1993.

The Central University of Ecuador dates from 1594. There are three Catholic universities, in Quito, Guayaquil, and Cuenca. The National Polytechnic School in Quito offers degrees in industrial science and mechanical engineering, while the Polytechnical School of the Littoral in Guayaquil provides training in naval and petroleum engineering and in the natural sciences. At the universities and all higher level institutions, there were 206,541 students enrolled and 12,856 teaching staff in 1991.

[44] LIBRARIES AND MUSEUMS

The oldest and most important library in Ecuador is the Central University Library in Quito. It was founded in 1586 and has 170,000 volumes. Other important collections are maintained at the Cuenca University Library (more than 63,000 volumes) and at the National Library in Quito (over 70,000 volumes). Libraries are also maintained by the other universities; the municipalities of Quito, Guayaquil, Cuenca, and Riobamba; the Ecuadoran Culture House; the Central Bank of Ecuador (100,000 volumes); and other organizations, including the Ecuadoran Culture House, which holds the Laura de Crespo room of National Authors.

A number of museums in Ecuador preserve and display paintings, sculpture, coins, records, and artifacts of historic and scientific interest. One of Ecuador's best collections of Inca and pre-Inca objects is found in a privately owned museum near Cuenca. Quito has the National Museum and Archives, the Museum of Modern Art, the Archaeological Museum and Art Galleries of the Central Bank of Ecuador, the Jijón and Caamaño Archaeological and Historical Museum, and the museum of the Ecuadoran Culture House, as well as other smaller collections in schools and government agencies. There are municipal museums in many smaller cities, as well as ethnographic and historical museums.

[45] MEDIA

In 1995 there were 598,300 telephones in use; telephone service is operated by the government. Between the main cities and towns there are radiotelephone links. Quito is connected by telegraph with Colombia and Peru, and there are telephone and cable connections with all parts of the world. Ecuador had 272 AM radio stations and 15 television stations as of 1999. In addition to the numerous local stations, there was one central government network, Radio Nacional del Ecuador. In 1997, there were 342 radio receivers, 294 television sets, and 13 mobile phones per 1,000 population.

The leading newspapers, with their political tendencies and estimated daily circulations in 1999, were as follows:

	ORIENTATION	CIRCULATION
QUITO		
El Comercio (m)	Independent	100,000
Últimas Noticias (e)	Independent	90,000
Diario Hoy (a)	Independent	58,600
GUAYAQUIL		
El Universo (m)	Independent	203,300
La Razón (e)	Independent	28,000
CUENCA		
El Mercurio (m)	Conservative	20,000

The government requires all mass periodicals to participate in literacy and adult education campaigns. There is no censorship of newspapers or of radio and television stations, as ensured by Ecuador's constitution.

In 1996 there were 43,758 personal computers. Online access is extremely limited, with 1 Internet host per 1,000 population in 1998.

46ORGANIZATIONS

The outstanding contemporary learned society is the Ecuadoran Academy, founded in 1875, the second academy in Spanish America. It is a correspondent of the Royal Spanish Academy. The Ecuadoran Culture House prints works of contemporary Ecuadoran writers, encourages the investigation of scientific and social problems, and conducts discussions on cultural matters.

Fraternal organizations and service clubs in Ecuador include the Masons, Rotary clubs, and Lions clubs. The International Red Cross is also active. Social and charitable organizations are sponsored by the Roman Catholic Church. In addition, there are about seven chambers of commerce and industry and at least 10 employers' organizations.

47TOURISM, TRAVEL, AND RECREATION

Tourists may enter Ecuador with tourist cards in place of visas if they are citizens of other Western Hemisphere countries. Visitors need a yellow-fever inoculation certificate if arriving from infected areas. Tourist facilities on the coast include modern resort hotels and fine beaches. Ecuador's highlands, reached by air or by the spectacular railroad or highway, are rich in natural beauty. Quito, the second-highest capital in the world, has modern hotels and transportation. Its churches and monasteries, with their delicately carved doors and altars, and an abundance of exquisite paintings and sculptures, make Quito, in the words of a 1979 UNESCO citation, a "cultural patrimony of mankind."

An important part of Ecuador's cultural life is the feria, or market day, which takes place weekly in many towns. The town of Otavalo, about 56 km (35 mi) north of Quito, is well known for its colorful Saturday fairs. The Galápagos Islands, world-famous for their unusual wildlife, have become a popular site for ecotourism.

In 1997, there were 529,492 tourist arrivals in Ecuador, over half from other countries in South America. Tourism receipts totaled $290 million. There were 42,358 hotel rooms with 88,4019 beds that year.

Tourism has the potential to experience significant growth in Ecuador, given the natural attractions and architectural and historical sights. Further development of ecotourism must be carefully managed to avoid a negative impact on Ecuador's environment. In 1999, the UN estimated the cost of staying in Guayaquil was $148 per day and daily expenses in Quito were estimated at $146.

48FAMOUS ECUADORANS

Ecuadorans claim Atahualpa (1500?–33), the last emperor of the Incas, as the first renowned figure in their country's history; during the civil war between him and his half-brother, Huáscar, his administration of the Inca empire was based in what is now Ecuador. The 16th-century Amerindian general Rumiñahui is remembered for his heroic resistance to Spanish conquest. During the colonial period, Quito produced notable artists and sculptors. Among these were Miguel de Santiago (d.1673) and the Amerindians Manuel Chile (Caspicara) and Pampite. Francisco Javier Eugenio de Santa Cruz y Espejo (1747–95), the national hero of Ecuador, inspired much of the independence movement through his political writings. Espejo advocated complete emancipation from Spain, autonomous government for each colony, and nationalization of the clergy. Although he did not live to take part in the War of Independence (he died in prison for his political activities), he was an important figure in its philosophical development.

Vicente Rocafuerte (1783–1847), an early president, made significant contributions to the development of the republic. Another president, Gabriel García Moreno (1821–75), was the first to achieve national consolidation; he also contributed to the literary development of the nation. Juan Montalvo (1823–89)

bitterly and brilliantly opposed conservatism in his essays and other works. Eloy Alfaro (1841–1912), another outstanding president, was noted for the honesty of his administration.

Among Ecuador's literary figures were Numa Pompilio Llona (1832–1907), a poet-philosopher, and Juan de León Mera (1832–94), a poet and novelist. Outstanding Ecuadorans of the 20th century include the poets Gonzalo Escudero (1903–71), Jorge Carrera Andrade (1903–78), César Dávila Andrade (1918–67), and Benjamín Carrión (1897–1979); the novelist Jorge Icaza (1906–78); the painter Oswaldo Guayasamin Calero (b.1919); José María Velasco Ibarra (1893–1979), who served five times as president of his country; and Galo Plaza Lasso (1906–87), a former president of Ecuador and of the OAS.

49DEPENDENCIES

Ecuador's only territory, administered as a province since 1973, is the Archipelago of Columbus (Archipiélago de Colón), more commonly known as the Galápagos Islands, after the Spanish name for the large land tortoise found there. The six largest islands of the group (with their earlier names in parentheses) are Isabela (Albemarle), Santa Cruz (Indefatigable), Santiago (San Salvador or James), Fernandina (Narborough), Floreana (Santa María or Charles), and San Cristóbal (Chatham). Lying on the equator, this cluster of 60-odd islands is scattered over nearly 60,000 sq km (23,000 sq mi) of ocean and has a total land area of 8,010 sq km (3,093 sq mi). The center of the group lies at about 90°w, some 1,130 km (700 mi) from the coast of Ecuador and about 1,600 km (1,000 mi) southwest of Panama.

Most of the islands are small and barren. The largest, Isabela, which is 121 km (75 mi) long and makes up half the land area of the group, has the highest volcano (now only slightly active), reaching 1,689 m (5,541 ft). The climate of these tropical islands is modified by the cold Humboldt Current, which keeps the mean annual temperature as low as 21°c (70°F). Desertlike low-lying areas contrast with mist-shrouded heights at 240 m (800 ft) and higher elevations that have considerable rainfall.

Charles Darwin visited the islands in 1835 during his voyage on the *Beagle*, and his observations there made an important contribution to the development of his theories of evolution and natural selection. The unique forms of plant and animal life found on the various islands include 15 species of giant tortoise, considered to be the longest-lived creatures on earth, with a life span of about 150 years and a maximum weight of more than 225 kg (500 lb). In the mid-1980s, their number was estimated at 10,000. The Galápagos have 85 species of birds. In 1959, Ecuador declared the Galápagos a national park to prevent the extinction of the wildlife. The islands have since become one of the world's most noted focal points for naturalist studies and observations. About 21,000 visitors come to the islands each year.

Early Amerindian navigators, traveling on balsa rafts, frequently went to the Galápagos for the excellent fishing, but there is no evidence of any permanent settlement. Bishop Tomás de Berlanga of Panama landed at the Galápagos in 1535; he was the first of a series of Spaniards to visit the islands. In 1832, the first president of Ecuador, Juan José Flores, declared the islands a national territory. Several were used from time to time for penal colonies, but the practice was discontinued in 1959. The administrative seat is San Cristóbal. Only four of the islands are inhabited, and the estimated population numbers 6,000.

50BIBLIOGRAPHY

Conaghan, Catherine M. *Restructuring Domination: Industrialists and the State in Ecuador.* Pittsburgh, Pa.: University of Pittsburgh Press, 1988.

Corkill, David. *Ecuador.* Santa Barbara, Calif.: Clio Press, 1989.

Cueva, Augustín. *The Process of Political Domination in Ecuador.* New Brunswick, N.J.: Transaction Books, 1981.

Darwin, Charles. *Voyage of the Beagle.* Garden City, N.Y.: Natural History Press, 1962 (orig. 1840).

Development Centre of the Organization for Economic Cooperation and Development. *The Political Feasibility of Adjustment in Ecuador and Venezuela.* Paris: Development Centre of the Organization for Economic Cooperation and Development, 1994.

Ecuador in Pictures. Minneapolis: Lerner Publications Co., 1987.

Fitch, John S. *The Military Coup d'Etat as a Political Process: Ecuador, 1948–1966.* Baltimore: Johns Hopkins University Press, 1977.

Hanratty, Dennis M. (ed.). *Ecuador, a Country Study.* 3rd ed. Washington, D.C.: Library of Congress, 1991.

Hassaureck, Friedrich. *Four Years Among the Ecuadorians.* Carbondale: Southern Illinois University Press, 1967.

Hidrobo Estrada, Jorge. *Power and Industrialization in Ecuador.* Boulder: Westview Press, 1992.

Hurtado, Osvaldo. *Political Power in Ecuador.* Albuquerque: University of New Mexico Press, 1981.

Indigenous Peoples and Democracy in Latin America. New York: St. Martin's Press, 1994.

Isaacs, Anita. *Military Rule and Transition in Ecuador, 1972–92.* Pittsburgh, Pa.: University of Pittsburgh Press, 1993.

Martz, John D. *Ecuador: Conflicting Political Culture and the Quest for Progress.* Boston: Allyn and Bacon, 1972.

———. *Regime, Politics and Petroleum: Ecuador's Nationalistic Struggle.* New Brunswick, N.J.: Transaction, 1986.

Newson, Linda A. *Life and Death in Early Colonial Ecuador.* Norman: University of Oklahoma Press, 1995.

Pineo, Ronn F. *Social and Economic Reform in Ecuador: Life and Work in Guayaquil.* Gainesville: University Press of Florida, 1996.

Radcliffe, Sarah A. *Remaking the Nation: Place, Identity and Politics in Latin America.* London: Routledge, 1996.

Salomon, Frank. *Native Lords of Quito in the Age of the Incas.* New York: Cambridge University Press, 1986.

Schodt, David W. *Ecuador: An Andean Enigma.* Boulder, Colo.: Westview Press, 1987.

Spindler, Frank MacDonald. *Nineteenth Century Ecuador: A Historical Introduction.* Fairfax, Va.: George Mason University Press, 1987.

Van Aken, Mark J. *King of the Night: Juan Jose Flores and Ecuador, 1824–1864.* Berkeley: University of California Press, 1989.

Whitten, Norman E., Jr. *Sicuanga Runa: The Other Side of Development in Amazonian Ecuador.* Urbana: University of Illinois Press, 1985.

EL SALVADOR

Republic of El Salvador
República de El Salvador

CAPITAL: San Salvador.

FLAG: The national flag consists of a white stripe between two horizontal blue stripes. The national coat of arms is centered in the white band.

ANTHEM: *Saludemos la Patria Orgullosos (Let us Proudly Hail the Fatherland)*.

MONETARY UNIT: The colón (c), often called the peso, is a paper currency of 100 centavos. There are coins of 1, 2, 3, 5, 10, 25, and 50 centavos and 1 colón and notes of 1, 2, 5, 10, 25, 50, and 100 colónes. c1 = $0.11416 (or $1 = c8.760) as of 31 March 2000.

WEIGHTS AND MEASURES: The metric system is the legal standard, but some old Spanish measures also are used.

HOLIDAYS: New Year's Day, 1 January; Labor Day, 1 May; Independence Day, 15 September; Columbus Day, 12 October; All Souls' Day, 2 November; First Call for Independence, 5 November; Christmas, 25 December. Movable religious holidays include Good Friday, Holy Saturday, Easter Monday, and Corpus Christi; there is a movable secular holiday, the Festival (1st week in August).

TIME: 6 AM = noon GMT.

¹LOCATION, SIZE, AND EXTENT

El Salvador, the smallest Central American country, has an area of 21,040 sq km (8,124 sq mi), extending 269 km (167 mi) WNW-ESE and 106 km (66 mi) NNE-SSW. Comparatively, the area occupied by El Salvador is slightly smaller than the state of Massachusetts. Bounded on the N and E by Honduras, on the S and SW by the Pacific Ocean, and on the NW by Guatemala, El Salvador has a total boundary length of 852 km (529 mi). It is the only Central American country without a Caribbean coastline.

El Salvador's capital city, San Salvador, is located in the west central part of the country.

²TOPOGRAPHY

El Salvador is a land of mountains and once-fertile upland plains. It is divided into three general topographic regions: (1) the hot, narrow Pacific coastal belt, 260 km (160 mi) long and 16–24 km (10–15 mi) wide; (2) the central plateau, at an altitude of about 610 m (2,000 ft), crossing from east to west, between two mountain ranges; and (3) the northern lowlands, formed by the wide Lempa River Valley, bounded by a high mountain range ascending to the Honduran border.

The central plateau, north of the Pacific coastal belt, is an area of valleys endowed with rich volcanic soil. This is the agricultural, industrial, and population center of the country; the capital, San Salvador (682 m/2,237 ft above sea level), is in this region. Almost surrounded by active volcanoes—Santa Ana (2,381 m/7,812 ft), San Vicente (2,173 m/7,129 ft), San Miguel (2,132 m/6,995 ft), San Salvador (1,967 m/6,453 ft), and Izalco (1,965 m/6,447 ft)—the region is a zone of recurrent earthquakes and volcanic activity; Izalco is known as the Lighthouse of the Pacific. El Salvador has several lakes, the largest being Ilopango, Güija, and Coatepeque. The Lempa, the most important of some 150 rivers, rises in Guatemala and runs south into El Salvador, eventually reaching the Pacific.

A major earthquake occurred in the San Salvador area in October 1986, leaving 1,500 dead and 329,165 homeless.

³CLIMATE

Located in the tropical zone, El Salvador has two distinct seasons: the dry season, from November to April, when light rains occur, and the wet season, from May to November, when the temporales, or heavy rains, fall. The coastal plain receives the heaviest rainfall. Some interior areas are relatively dry most of the year, necessitating irrigation and a selection of crops suited for arid land cultivation. The average annual rainfall is 182 cm (72 in). Temperatures vary with altitude, from the hot coastal lowlands to the semitropical central plateau; in general, the climate is warm, with an annual average maximum of 32°C (90°F) and an average minimum of 18°C (64°F). The average temperature at San Salvador is 22°C (72°F) in January and 23°C (73°F) in July.

⁴FLORA AND FAUNA

Indigenous trees include the mangrove, rubber, dogwood, mahogany, cedar, and walnut; pine and oak are found in the northern mountainous region. Varieties of tropical fruit, numerous medicinal plants, and balsam, a medicinal gum, grow in the country. Native fauna (greatly reduced in recent decades) includes varieties of monkey, jaguar, coyote, tapir, and armadillo, along with several kinds of parrots and various migratory birds. Fish, both freshwater and saltwater, turtles, iguanas, crocodiles, and alligators abound. Both venomous and nonvenomous snakes, the latter including the boa constrictor, are common in El Salvador.

⁵ENVIRONMENT

Because of heavy cutting, the forest resources of El Salvador had been reduced to about 6% of the total area by 1996. Forty-five percent of the wood taken from the forests is used for fuel. Peasant farmers burn the small trees and other growth on the hillsides to plant corn and beans, thus hastening the erosion of the topsoil. Seventy-five percent of the land area in El Salvador is threatened by erosion and desertification at a rate of 20 tons per hectare per year. The government enacted forestry conservation measures in 1973, but they have had little effect on the rate of deforestation. Among the environmental consequences of forest depletion, in addition to loss of soil fertility, are diminution of groundwater resources and drastic loss of native flora and fauna. Pollution is widespread and restrictions on waste disposal, including disposal of toxic waste, are lax. El Salvador's cities produce 0.5 million tons of solid waste per year. Water quality is deteriorating. By 1993, 90% of El Salvador's rivers were polluted. Safe drinking water is available to 78% of the urban population and 37% of the rural dwellers. Eighty-nine percent of the nation's 4.5 cu mi of water is used for agricultural purposes. There is no comprehensive national law controlling environmental protection, and the legislation that is on the books is poorly enforced. The National Environmental Protection Committee, established by decree in 1974, has had little impact.

The pollution of the environment in El Salvador is a serious threat to the survival of its plants and wildlife. In 1994, only 0.2% of its total land area was protected. As of 1994, six mammal species in a total of 129 were threatened. Two types of birds in a total of 432 and one type of reptile in 92 are also threatened. Of 2,500 plant species, 26 are considered endangered. Endangered or extinct species in El Salvador include the tundra peregrine falcon, four species of turtle (green sea, hawksbill, leatherback, and olive ridley), American crocodile, ocelot, spectacled caiman, jaguar, giant anteater, and Central American tapir.

6POPULATION

The population of El Salvador in 2000 was estimated at 5,925,374. An estimated 4.6% of the population is 65 years of age or older. The projected population for the year 2005 is 6,383,000, assuming a crude birthrate of 23 per 1,000 population and a death rate of 6, resulting in a natural rate of change of 1.8% for the period 2000–2005. The rate of population change between 1995 and 2000 was 2.2%. El Salvador, with an estimated population density in 1998 of 292 per sq km (756 per sq mi), is the most densely populated country in Central America.

It was estimated that 47% of the population lived in urban areas in 2000, up from 42% in 1980. The capital city, San Salvador, had a 2000 metropolitan population of 1,415,000. Other major cities are Santa Ana (202,337) and San Miguel (182,817).

7MIGRATION

Until the early 1980s, emigration and immigration were negligible in El Salvador, except for migration of Salvadorans seeking economic advantages in Honduras, a trend that inflamed tensions between the two nations and was an underlying cause of their 1969 war. At that time, 300,000 Salvadorans were estimated to have settled in Honduras; following the war, as many as 130,000 Salvadorans may have returned from Honduras.

While the US granted temporary asylum to thousands of Salvadoran refugees under the Carter administration, the Reagan administration began returning them to El Salvador in 1981. Of the 1 million Salvadorans estimated to be in the US in 1988, an estimated 550,000 had entered the country illegally, about 500,000 of them since 1979. Their remittances to their families in El Salvador are an important component of the stagnant economy, and their absence from the Salvadoran labor force has kept local unemployment lower than it would otherwise have been. Migration from rural to urban areas also is heavy. An estimated 550,000 people were displaced from their homes by warfare between 1979 and 1992.

In 1989, Belize, Costa Rica, El Salvador, Guatemala, Honduras, Mexico, and Nicaragua adopted a five-year plan called CIREFCA to solve the problems of uprooted people. Between 1989 and 1994, this plan helped repatriate 30,000

Salvadorians to their homeland. Thousands of more Salvadorians who decided not to go home were integrated into asylum countries. As of 30 June 1999, there were only 33 refugees, almost all Nicaraguans, benefiting from UNHCR assistance in El Salvador. The net migration rate for El Salvador in 1999 was -4.66 migrants per 1,000 population.

8ETHNIC GROUPS

The population of El Salvador is racially and culturally homogeneous, with about 94% mestizo (mixed white and Amerindian), 5% Amerindian (mainly the Pipil tribes), and 1% white.

9LANGUAGES

The official language of the country is Spanish. A few Amerindians continue to speak Nahua.

10RELIGIONS

The constitution of 1962 guarantees religious freedom and exempts churches from property taxes. The constitution specifically recognizes the Roman Catholic Church, granting it legal status; however, it also provides that other churches may register for such status according to the law. About 56.7% of the population identifies themselves as Roman Catholic; San Salvador is an archbishopric. Church officials and clergy have been active in the movement for human rights and social justice in El Salvador and have consequently been the targets of right-wing death squads and government security forces. In March 1980, Archbishop Oscar Arnulfo Romero y Galdames was killed by a sniper as he said mass at a hospital chapel in San Salvador. US aid was temporarily suspended after the murder of three US nuns and a social worker the following December.

About 17.8% of the population are members of various Protestant churches, including Baptist and Lutheran denominations. There are also many active Protestant missions throughout the country. Approximately 2.3% of the populace are associated with other churches and religious groups, including the Church of Jesus Christ of Latter-day Saints (Mormons), Seventh-day Adventists, Jews, Muslims, and Amerindian tribal religionists, among others. As many as 23.2% of inhabitants have no religious affiliation whatsoever.

11TRANSPORTATION

As of 1999 there were 1,986 km (1,234 mi) of paved highways and a total of 10,029 km (6,232 mi) in the road network. The Pan American Highway links El Salvador with Guatemala in the northwest and Honduras in the southeast. The Cuscatlán Bridge, where the Pan American Highway crosses the Lempa River, was the main thoroughfare for travel between eastern and western El Salvador at the time of its destruction by guerrillas in January 1984. In 1995, registered passenger vehicles numbered about 24,600, and commercial vehicles numbered 36,800.

El Salvador had 602 km (374 mi) of public-service railroad tracks in 1999. The major domestic rail lines are operated by the National Railway of El Salvador, which was formed in 1975 by a merger of the Railways of El Salvador and the US-owned International Railways of Central America. There are rail connections to Puerto Barrios, Guatemala, which, under an agreement with the government of Guatemala, provides El Salvador with a port on the Caribbean. Another line runs west from La Unión/Cutuco to the El Salvador Guatemala border, providing a rail link to Mexico. The entire rail system is narrow gauge and single track.

The country's three ports—La Unión/Cutuco, La Libertad, and Acajutla—are located on the Pacific coast. Inland waterway traffic is negligible.

In 1998 there were an estimated 86 airports, only 4 of which had paved runways. El Salvador is linked with the entire Western Hemisphere, Europe, and the Far East through international air

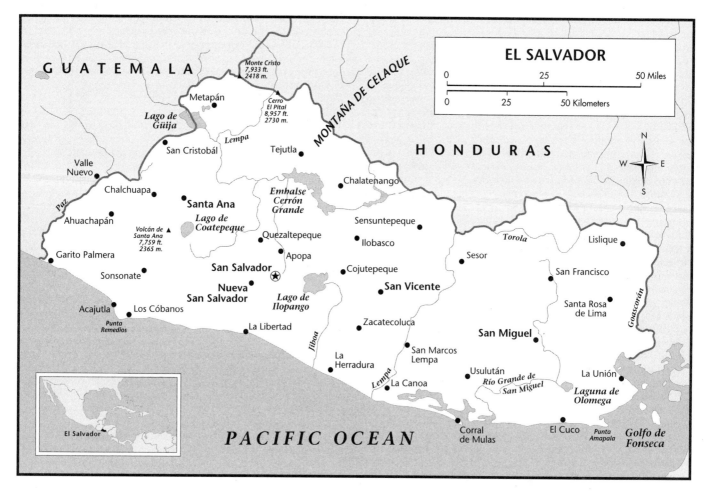

LOCATION: 13°9′ to 14°26′N; 87°41′ to 90°08′W. **BOUNDARY LENGTHS:** Honduras, 335 km (208 mi); Pacific coastline, 304 km (189 mi); Guatemala, 203 km (126 mi). **TERRITORIAL SEA LIMIT:** 200 mi.

services provided by Transportes Aéreos Centroamericanos (TACA) and other transportation companies. The principal airport, El Salvador International, is near San Salvador. In 1997, 1,698,701 passengers were carried on scheduled domestic and international airline flights.

12HISTORY

About 3000 BC, nomadic Nahuatl Amerindians, originally from present-day Mexico, migrated to Central America. The Pipil Amerindians were living in the region now known as El Salvador at the time of the Spanish conquest. They were an agricultural people, with a civilization similar to that of the Aztecs, except that the Pipil had abolished human sacrifice. In addition to the Pipil, two smaller groups, the Pocomans and the Lenca, lived in the area.

In 1524, Pedro de Alvarado, a Spanish conquistador sent by Hernán Cortés from Mexico, invaded El Salvador. After being forced to retreat by Amerindian resistance, he returned in 1525, defeated the Pipil and founded Sonsonate and San Salvador. During Spanish colonial period, San Salvador was one of six administrative regions under the captaincy-general of Guatemala. Spanish settlement consisted of a few cattle ranchers and some farmers.

The first call for independence from Spain, still commemorated as a national holiday, was made on 5 November 1811 by Father José Matías Delgado from the church of La Merced in San Salvador. However, independence did not come until 15 September 1821, when Guatemala led a movement for the independence of all of Central America. In 1822 the Mexican Emperor Agustín de Iturbide annexed all of Central America, but a year later he was deposed. El Salvador joined the United Provinces of Central America, which dissolved in 1838–39.

The republic was formally proclaimed on 25 January 1859. Turbulence, political instability, and frequent presidential changes characterized Salvadoran history during the second half of the 19th century. This period also saw the growth of coffee as El Salvador's leading product. The Salvadoran elite, known as the "14 families" or simply "the 14," created large coffee plantations, often on the land of displaced Indians. There followed a period of relative stability during 1900–30, but the seizure of power in 1931 by Gen. Maximiliano Hernández Martínez brought a period of constant military rule for almost 50 years. Hernández ruled for 13 years. Known for his mysticism, he also presided over the brutal suppression of a peasant uprising in 1932, with about 30,000 people killed. Few of the governments after Hernández even tried to reduce the gap between the landowners and the landless classes, and those who did were doomed to failure.

Landless Salvadorans found land available in neighboring Honduras. During the 1960s the influx of Salvadorans increased, provoking countermeasures from the Honduran government. Tensions rose between the two nations, and on 14 July 1969, they went to war for four days. The immediate occasion of the conflict was the Central American soccer championship (which El

Salvador won over Honduras on a disputed referee's call), leading US journalists to dub it the "Soccer War." A total of 3,000–4,000 people on both sides were killed. After an OAS-sponsored cease-fire, the two sides worked out a peace settlement, which was signed on 30 October 1980. A leftover border dispute was settled by the International Court of Justice (ICJ) in 1992.

In 1972, the military candidate for president was opposed by José Napoleón Duarte of the Christian Democratic Party (PDC). Duarte was denied election by fraud and sent into exile. Pressure for reform now came from the armed resistance from several leftist factions. The right unleashed "death squads" whose function was to intimidate and eliminate any who attempted to introduce change to the country.

By the late 1970s, the situation had become a civil war. The guerrillas had consolidated under the Farabundo Martí National Liberation Front (FMLN), and right-wing violence escalated. The military had not distinguished itself in its response to the violence, having engaged in widespread repression against suspected rebels. In 1979, a coup brought to power a set of reformist officers, who found common cause with such civilian leaders as Duarte. The junta liberalized the political system, setting legislative elections for 1982. The junta nationalized banks and the coffee export trade, while launching an ambitious and controversial land-reform program. Attacked by both left and right, the junta was unable either to suppress left-wing guerrillas or to control its own security forces, which began their own vigilante campaigns even as the angry landowners hired "death squads" to suppress opposition among peasants, students, clergy, and other groups.

In December 1980, José Napoleón Duarte of the Christian Democratic Party was installed by the junta as president—El Salvador's first civilian head of state since 1931—and a state of siege was proclaimed. Human rights groups could scarcely keep up with the number of violations occurring. In 1980, Archbishop Romero was assassinated while celebrating mass. In January 1981, the guerrillas launched their unsuccessful "final offensive," and throughout the rest of the year the bloodshed continued unabated. It is estimated that at least 62,000 people died between October 1979 and April 1987, most of whom were civilian noncombatants murdered by death squads and government security forces.

The junta headed by Duarte oversaw the drafting of a new constitution, adopted on 20 December 1983 by a constituent assembly that had been elected in March 1982. An interim president, Álvaro Alfredo Magaña, served through the March 1984 presidential election. In 1984, Duarte defeated Roberto D'Aubuisson Arrieta of the National Republican Alliance in a runoff election in May. Duarte thus became the first constitutionally elected president in over 50 years.

Duarte's regime was a difficult balancing act between right and left, in the midst of attempts to bring about reform. The Christian Democrats won a majority in the National Assembly in the March 1985 legislative elections, but Duarte's overriding problem was the ongoing civil war. Eventually, economic dislocation brought on by Duarte's austerity measures and charges of corruption led to the election in 1989 of ARENA's (National Republican Alliance) Alfredo Félix Christiani Burkard. As Christiani came to office, many feared the worst, for ARENA had been tied to former candidate D'Aubuisson, an extreme anticommunist who had frequently been accused of plotting against the government and supporting the death squads.

Christiani allayed these fears, and then some others. He called for direct dialogue between the government and the guerrillas. Although the process was rocky, and punctuated by military escalations, on 31 December 1991 the government and the FMLN signed an agreement, the Chapultepec Accord, which supplied the long hoped-for political solution to the civil war. A cease-fire took effect 1 February 1992, and held until 15 December 1992, when the FMLN officially laid down its arms.

The accord calls for reforms throughout the military, including the purge of officers linked to human rights abuses, and a reduction by 50% of the force. While the former has been a slow process, the latter goal was achieved ahead of schedule. In addition, paramilitary groups were to be banned, and land reforms were to be initiated.

New elections were held in 1994, and voters returned ARENA to power, with Armando Calderón Sol winning the presidential runoff election. Calderón embarked on an ambitious economic liberalization plan, cutting tariffs, privatizing banks and pensions, and attracting foreign investment. However, in spite of healthy economic growth of 4–5% a year, underemployment and low wages continued for much of the nation's workforce, accompanied by an upswing in violent crime. In the countryside, marauding bands robbed agricultural workers, while urban dwellers fell prey to organized gang activity, imported by Salvadorans returning to the country from the United States in the early 1990s. In spite of a 1996 12-point government plan that included investment in infrastructure and social services, the electorate voiced its discontent with the ruling ARENA party in the March 1997 parliamentary and local elections by giving the leftist FMLN its first significant legislative boost since the 1992 peace accords and effectively legitimizing the former guerrillas as a major political force. FMLN representation in the 84-member legislature increased from 14 to 27 seats, while ARENA's share fell from 42 to 28 seats. In addition, FMNL candidates made significant gains in local elections throughout the country.

Presidential elections were last held on 7 March 1999. The ruling ARENA party retained control of the presidency. ARENA's Francisco Flores won with 51.4% of the vote. In the March 2000 parliamentary election, ARENA only obtained 36% in the Assembly, securing 29 out of 84 seats in the legislative body. The strong showing by the FMLN made them the largest party in the Assembly, with 31 seats.

13 GOVERNMENT

The constitution adopted on 20 November 1983 defines El Salvador as a republic. The constitution vests executive power in the president, who is to be elected by direct popular vote for a term of five years. The president, who must be native-born, over 30 years of age, the offspring of native-born parents, and a layperson, is not eligible for immediate reelection. The president is commander-in-chief of the armed forces, enforces the laws, formulates an annual budget, draws up international treaties and conventions (which must be ratified by the National Assembly), appoints diplomatic and consular officials, and supervises the police. Every two years, the National Assembly elects three substitutes (designados), who can, in order of designation, assume the presidency when the president and vice-president are not available.

Legislative power is exercised by a unicameral National Assembly composed of 84 deputies apportioned among the various departments according to population. Deputies are elected for a three-year term and must be at least 25 years of age. The Assembly levies taxes, contracts loans and arranges for their payment, regulates the money supply, approves the executive budget, ratifies treaties and conventions, declares war, and suspends or reestablishes constitutional guarantees in national emergencies. The deputies, the president's ministers, and the Supreme Court all may propose legislation. The Assembly approves legislation and is technically empowered to override a presidential veto by a two-thirds vote.

Universal male and female suffrage was inaugurated in 1950. However, voting in El Salvador has been a source of controversy. During the 1980s, the government made voting compulsory, while the guerrillas insisted the citizens should not collaborate with the system. Thus, the Salvadorans were confronted with a dilemma: vote, and face the wrath of the guerrillas, or refuse to vote, and immediately become suspected of leftist sympathy. At times, voting was not secret. Current practices suggest a more confidential and voluntary system is developing.

[14] POLITICAL PARTIES

The leading party of the right in El Salvador is the National Republican Alliance (Alianza Republicana Nacionalista—ARENA), organized in 1982 by Roberto D'Aubuisson. ARENA controlled the National Assembly until 1985, and its next leader, Alfredo Christiani, was elected to the presidency in 1989. Five years later, ARENA candidate Armando Calderón Sol became president. In the March 1997 parliamentary elections, ARENA's representation was reduced from 42 seats in the 84-member legislature to 28. In 1999, ARENA recovered and won the presidency again with 51.4% of the vote, but a year later its support fell to 36% in the National Assembly elections of March 2000.

The Chapultepec Accords introduced a new force into El Salvador's electoral system: the Farabundo Martí National Liberation Front (Frente Farabundo Martí de Liberación Nacional—FMLN). Named for an insurgent leader of the 1930s, the FMLN was originally a paramilitary group in armed rebellion against the government. As part of the 1992 accords, the FMLN is now a legal party after having ceased its military operations. The FMLN-backed candidate, Ruben Zamora, was the runner-up in the 1994 presidential election, winning 24% of the vote. In the March 1997 legislative elections, the FMLN made significant gains, nearly doubling its representation in the Legislative Assembly, from 14 to 27 seats, and winning municipal elections in half the departmental capitals. In the March 2000 elections, the FMLN won 31 seats, shy of a majority but more than any other political party.

The moderate Christian Democratic Party (Partido Demócrata Cristiano—PDC) was formed in 1960. For three decades, it was associated with its leader and founder, José Napoleón Duarte. Damaged by many splits over the years, and suffering after Duarte's unsuccessful presidency (1984–1989), the centrist PDC has lost strength among the electorate. In the most recent National Assembly elections in March 2000, it obtained 7.2% of the votes and 6 seats in the 84-member Assembly. The National Conciliation Party (PCN), which was founded by the military in 1961, obtained 8.8% of the votes in the election and secured 13 seats, enough to give a majority to either ARENA or the FMLN. Therefore, the PCN has gained an important negotiating role in Salvadorian politics.

In March 2000, the Centro Democrático Unido (United Democratic Centre, social-democratic) and Partido Acción Nacional (National Action Party) secured 2 and 3 seats, respectively, in the National Assembly.

[15] LOCAL GOVERNMENT

El Salvador is divided into 14 departments, each with a governor and alternate governor appointed by the executive power through the corresponding ministry. The country's 262 municipalities (cities, towns, and villages) are administered by mayors and municipal councils elected by popular vote. Traditionally independent in their local functions, municipalities may be limited in their activities by the departmental governor.

[16] JUDICIAL SYSTEM

The court system includes justices of the peace, courts of the first instance, intermediate level appellate courts, and the Supreme Court made up of 13 justices selected by the National Assembly. Other than justices of the peace, judges are appointed to renewable three-year terms. An 11-member National Council of

the Judiciary, appointed by the National Assembly, is an independent body charged with screening judicial candidates for nomination.

According to the constitution, the Supreme Court is the court of last appeal; it passes on writs of habeas corpus, constitutionality of the laws, jurisdiction and administration of lower courts, and appointment of justices below the appellate level. There are also special courts, appointed by the National Assembly, and military tribunals, selected by the Supreme Court. The 1995 legislation provides for oral trials and establishes family and juvenile courts. The 1996 Criminal Procedure code replaces a criminal system based on civil law with one in which oral argument is the norm.

Under the constitution, defendants have the right to a presumption of innocence, to representation by legal counsel, to be present in court and to confront witnesses.

El Salvador accepts compulsory jurisdiction of the International Court of Justice with reservations.

[17] ARMED FORCES

The armed forces have a prescribed minimum strength of 3,000 men, set by the National Assembly. All Salvadoran males between 18 and 30 years of age are eligible for military service. In 2000, 24,600 personnel were in service, 22,300 of whom were in the army, 700 in the navy and marine corps, and 1,600 in the air force. The air force has 31 combat aircraft and 17 armed helicopters. National police and village militia forces number an additional 12,000. In 1998, $105 million, or about 0.9% of the gross domestic product was budgeted for national defense.

US military assistance during the civil war (1979–92) reached over $1 billion. In 1992 the US spent $200 million in El Salvador.

El Salvador maintains observers as part of an international peacekeeping force in Western Sahara.

[18] INTERNATIONAL COOPERATION

El Salvador is a founding member of the UN, having joined on 24 October 1945, and participates in ECLAC and all the nonregional specialized agencies except UNIDO. It is also a member of the CACM, of which it was a principal advocate, as well as G-77, IADB, OAS, and the WTO. As of 1987, El Salvador was a signatory of the Law of the Sea. El Salvador signed a peace plan for Central America outlined by Costa Rican President Oscar Arias Sánchez. Many of its principles, such as amnesty for rebels and repatriation or resettlement of refugees, applied to El Salvador.

[19] ECONOMY

The economy has largely recovered from the civil strife of the 1980s. Agriculture (mostly coffee) is the foundation of El Salvador's economy, providing about two-thirds of the nation's exports and employing over one-third of its labor force. The industrial sector is based in Salvador and has been oriented largely to the domestic and Central American markets. El Salvador enjoys one of the lowest levels of indebtedness in the region, with the bulk of foreign financing provided on a concession basis.

In the 1970s, El Salvador was the most industrialized nation in Central America, although a dozen years of civil war eroded that position. The Crisitani administration, which came into power in 1989, began a comprehensive economic reform plan oriented toward a free market economy. A market-based currency exchange rate was adopted. Price controls were eliminated, as were the sugar, coffee, and cotton marketing monopolies. The nationalized banking system was largely privatized beginning in 1989. However, due to increased credit availability and public services prices, inflation doubled to around 20% in 1992.

Bolstered by peace, El Salvador's economy experienced brisk growth, with yearly GDP growth averaging 6.5% from 1990 to 1995. But the currency remained rocky as the country's inflation rates fell to 12% in 1993 and 8.9% in 1994, but rose to 11.4% in 1995. The latter increase was explained by the increase in VAT and one-off increases in charges for telephone, electricity and water services. Different from the rest of Latin American economies, El Salvador eluded the aftershocks of the "Tequila Effect" based on a combination if solid macro-economic management and low external debt. The government slowed down economic growth to 3% in 1996 to rein in inflationary pressures, via tight monetary and fiscal policies and a stable exchange rate. El Salvador ended 1996 with a record low inflation rate of only 7.4%, one of the lowest rates among all Latin American countries. The government was successful in subduing inflationary pressures, mainly a demand pull inflation due to a tight monetary policy scenario. In 1996, the overall economic expansion was slowed down as the government applied the monetary brakes in order to curb import demand and avoid balance-of-payments pressures. Higher interest rates resulting in very expensive borrowing costs and pessimistic expectations combined to drive down domestic investment.

Economic growth between 1988 and 1998 averaged approximately 5%, but only 2.7% growth was forecast for 1999 to 2003. These figures reflected continued low world market prices for commodities that were exported from El Salvador, as well as the international financial problems of 1998. The inflation rate was only 2.6% in 1998.

20 INCOME

The US Central Intelligence Agency (CIA) reports that in 1998 El Salvador's gross domestic product (GDP) was estimated at $17.5 billion. The per capita GDP was estimated at $3,000. The annual growth rate of GDP was estimated at 3.7%. The average inflation rate in 1998 was 2.6%. The CIA defines GDP as the value of all final goods and services produced within a nation in a given year and computed on the basis of purchasing power parity (PPP) rather than value as measured on the basis of the rate of exchange. It was estimated that agriculture accounted for 15% of GDP, industry 24%, and services 61%.

Private consumption includes expenditures of individuals, households, and nongovernmental organizations. It was estimated that between 1990 and 1998 private consumption grew at an annual rate of 5.9%. The richest 10% of the population accounted for approximately 41% of household consumption and the poorest 10% approximately 1.2%.

21 LABOR

The civilian labor force was estimated at three million in 1998. Unemployment in 1997 was estimated at 8%, down from 40–50% in 1985.

The first official recognition of labor came in 1946, when a minister of labor and social welfare was added to the cabinet. In 1950, labor was permitted to organize. By 1972, about 4% of all wage and salary earners were unionized, and the proportion had increased to about 20% by in 1999. At that time, there were about 150 active unions and other workers' organizations, with a total of over 300,000 members. Technically only private sector workers may strike, nevertheless, many public sector workers carry out strikes that are treated as legitimate.

The workday is fixed at eight hours, and the workweek at 44 hours. Because of severe rural underemployment, many workers receive far less than the official minimum agricultural wage, which in 1999 was equivalent to $3.57 per day (the minimum wage was $4.81 per day for industrial and service workers). Compulsory social security provisions cover enterprises employing five or more persons but exclude agricultural, domestic, and government workers.

22 AGRICULTURE

Arable land in 1997 consisted of 565,000 ha (1,396,000 acres) planted with annual crops, and 251,000 ha (537,266 acres) with permanent crops. Irrigation covered 120,000 ha (297,000 acres) in 1997, half of it in the Sonsonate and Sensunapan region. In 1998, agriculture represented 12% of GDP and 40% of employment.

Coffee, El Salvador's major crop (30% of total agricultural output), is grown principally in the west and northwest at elevations of 460 to 1,520 m (1,500 to 5,000 ft). Primarily as a result of the civil war, coffee production declined in the 1980s. In June 1993, the Ministry of Economy certified the first shipment of organic coffee; the agrarian reform cooperative that produced the coffee had not used chemicals or pesticides for over four years. Production in 1998 amounted to 137,000 tons (down from 156,000 tons in 1990). Exports of coffee in 1997 amounted 165,621 tons, valued at to $514.8 million. Coffee export earnings were boosted by high international prices that year. The coffee industry is a major employer in El Salvador, generating about 82,000 jobs.

Sugar production fell between 1979 and 1981 but later recovered; cane production in 1998 was 5.5 million tons, and the sugar industry contributed $55.7 million to the country's foreign exchange earnings in 1997. Sugar is the most important agricultural product after coffee, and is grown mostly by independent producers. Investment has increased, as has the area under cultivation (in contrast to the other two major export crops). The world price has, however, been in decline for several years, and this decline has cut export earnings; the government secured a $30.4 million loan from Venezuela to divert some production to gasohol.

Traditional grains grown in El Salvador include white corn, sorghum, rice, and edible beans. These crops make up the fundamental diet for most Salvadorans and are produced on virtually all small farms. Production amounts in 1998 included corn, 552,000 tons; sorghum, 217,000 tons; rice, 72,000 tons; and beans, 73,000 tons. An additional 325,000 tons of corn were imported in 1997 to meet local demand.

Land that was originally planted for cotton is now being used for sugar cane, pasture, and nontraditional crops. El Salvador has steadily been shifting agricultural exports towards nontraditional items such as jalapeño peppers, marigold flowers, okra, and pineapples. Traditional coffee areas are also being absorbed by urbanization projects.

23 ANIMAL HUSBANDRY

Cattle and hogs are the predominant livestock in El Salvador. Cattle are of the "criollo" type and are used for production of both meat and milk. The dairy sector continues to suffer from inefficient production methods, poor animal genetic quality, and diseases. There are over 100 slaughterhouses operating illegally and without sanitary control. The government plans to rebuild the livestock sector through financial and technological assistance.

The poultry industry is one of El Salvador's most organized and efficient agri-businesses, divided into smaller family farms and large commercial operations. The poultry industry directly generates roughly 6,000 jobs (60% of which are in rural areas), with an additional 20,000 secondary jobs. Commercial production accounts for 80% of poultry meat and about 75% of egg production.

In 1998 there were 1,157,000 head of cattle. The hog population rose from 390,000 in 1950 to 560,000 in 1979 but then declined to 314,000 in 1998. Other livestock included

96,000 horses, 24,000 mules, 15,000 goats, and 8,000,000 chickens. In 1998, milk production was 405,000 tons. A total of 45,000 tons of eggs were produced during the same year.

24 FISHING

The fishing industry, which centers on shrimp, has undergone significant development since it first gained commercial importance in 1957. The best coastal fishing grounds are off the southeastern sector. Scaled fish include freshwater robalo, sea bass, mullet, mackerel, swordfish, and redmouth; a tuna industry has been operating since 1963. The total fish catch was 10,987 tons in 1997.

25 FORESTRY

Forests and woodlands covered 104,000 hectares (256,000 acres) in the mid-1990s, representing only 5% of the total land area. Virgin forests once covered 90% of El Salvador. Almost all of the lumber used in building and in other Salvadoran industries must be imported, mainly coming from neighboring Guatemala, Honduras, and Nicaragua. Roundwood production in 1997 was 4.5 million cu m. Forest products include dye woods and lumber, such as mahogany, walnut, and cedar, for furniture and cabinet work. El Salvador is the world's main source of balsam, a medicinal gum; between Acajutla and La Libertad in the southwest is the so-called Balsam Coast, which supports a species of balsam tree unique to El Salvador.

26 MINING

Geologically, about 90% of the country is of volcanic origin and is less well endowed with mineral resources than any other Central American country. Although gold, silver, copper, lead, zinc, and sands that contain titanium and ilmenite are found in El Salvador, there is little commercial mineral production. Gold and silver mining were halted in the 1980s due to political unrest, but gold trade and mining activity were reported in 1994 in the San Sebastian area (near Santa Rosa de Lima by the Honduran border). In 1997, industrial minerals, especially limestone mined for domestic cement plants, were the primary commodities of the Salvadoran mineral industry. Limestone production totaled 3,000 tons, and cement production totaled 960,000. Production of other mineral commodities (in tons) included secondary steel (45,000) and marine salt (32,000).

27 ENERGY AND POWER

El Salvador has no exploitable fossil fuels. Electric power production is controlled by the government's autonomous agency, the Executive Hydroelectric Commission of Río Lempa (CEL), created in 1945 to plan and develop the country's electric power facilities. The total installed power capacity rose from 171,000 kW in 1965 to 962,000 kW in 1998. Production increased from 582 million kWh in 1965 to 3,291 million kWh in 1998. Of that total, hydroelectric sources supplied 62%; petroleum plants contributed 22%; and the remainder was supplied by geothermal resources. Hydroelectric generation alone rose from 1.66 billion kWh in 1990 to 2.3 billion kWh in 1995.

Geothermal energy sources have been explored to determine the possibility of tapping volcanically produced underground steam for power. At the end of 1975, CEL opened a 30,000-kW geothermal plant at Ahuachapán, at a cost of $25 million. This and subsequent projects were expected to reduce Salvadoran dependency on imported fuels, a goal frustrated by the civil war.

28 INDUSTRY

The leading industrial region is the department of San Salvador. Other industrial centers are La Libertad, Santa Ana, San Miguel, Usulutan and San Vicente. There are coffee-processing plants, sugar mills, bakeries; and plants making petroleum products, vegetable oils, fats, confectionery, dairy products, tobacco, soap, candles, matches, shoes, cement, and organic fertilizers.

Large-scale industry was introduced in the 1960s, relying mostly on imports of crude materials. In 1963, an oil refinery at Acajutla began processing Venezuelan crude oil; most of the output is consumed locally. During the early 1970s, the greatest increase in value of manufacturing occurred in chemicals and textiles. Civil war during the 1980s hurt industrial production, with an average annual rate of -6% between 1977 and 1987.

Following the attainment of civil peace in the 1990s, the Salvadoran economy boomed. This growth was sustained by the recovery of the agricultural sector, and expansion of the construction and manufacturing sectors. Boosted by the rapid growth and development of its MAQUILA Zones, the economy became the most industrialized and best-performing in the Central American region.

Growing at a rate of 8%, the manufacturing sector provided 22% of the GDP in 1998. The same basic problems persist from decade to decade: the low purchasing power of the local population, and the difficult financial and political situation of other Central American countries on which El Salvador depends for export markets. Nevertheless, El Salvador received substantial amounts of foreign direct investments in the industrial sector in 1999.

29 SCIENCE AND TECHNOLOGY

El Salvador has research institutes devoted to the study of seismology and geology, meteorology and hydralogy, agriculture (including the Salvadoran Institute for the Study of Coffee), and medicine. The principal learned society in the country is the El Salvador Academy, headquartered in San Salvador. In the same city are museums devoted to natural history and zoology. Nine colleges and universities offer degrees in basic and applied sciences. In 1987–97, science and engineering students accounted for 59% of college and university enrollments. In 1992, research and development expenditures totaled 1.08 billion colones; in 1987–97, 356 technicians and 20 scientists and engineers per million people were engaged in research and development.

30 DOMESTIC TRADE

San Salvador is the chief commercial and marketing center. However, following the end of the civil war, thousands of Salvadorans returned from the US and made San Miguel and Santa Ana one of the most industrialized cities in Central America.

Food is generally produced in small, scattered plots in the vicinity of urban areas and taken to market by traders (mostly women), either on their heads or by pack animals. Residents of remote rural areas usually consume most of what they produce exchanging the remainder for other commodities. In urban areas, the business units are mainly small shops, while in rural regions, individual traders conduct their business at town marketplaces, where agricultural\ produce, meats, fruit, handicrafts, ceramics, and flowers are sold.

The usual business hours in the major cities are from 8 AM to noon and from 2 to 6 PM on weekdays and from 8 AM to noon on Saturday. Banking hours are from 9 to 11:30 AM and from 2:30 to 4 PM on weekdays, with a half day on Saturday.

31 FOREIGN TRADE

The main export continues to be coffee, although El Salvador has long sought to diversify its exports into other agricultural products such as cotton, as well as manufactures. One of the country's greatest weaknesses remains its trade deficit. The deficit is sustained in part by huge inflows of remittances from Salvadoran workers in the US, estimated at $1.34 billion in 1998.

El Salvador depends upon its coffee growers for more than a third of its commodity exports revenues (36%). Other exports include paper (4.8%), sugar (4.4%), medicinal and pharmaceutical products (4.2%), and shrimp (2.9%).

In 1997 El Salvador's imports were distributed among the following categories:

Consumer goods	15.3%
Food	12.5%
Fuels	11.3%
Industrial supplies	34.7%
Machinery	15.7%
Transportation	10.3%
Other	0.2%

Principal trading partners in 1998 (in millions of US dollars) were as follows:

COUNTRY	EXPORTS	IMPORTS	BALANCE
United States	1,345	1,667	-322
Guatemala	229	351	-122
Germany	151	77	74
United Kingdom	127	34	93
Costa Rica	105	124	-19
Nicaragua	67	68	-1
Honduras	62	71	-9
Mexico	25	240	-215
Japan	21	139	-118
France	20	239	-219

32BALANCE OF PAYMENTS

El Salvador's positive trade balances in the late 1970s changed into deficits after 1980. The main reasons for this development were declines in cotton, sugar, and coffee export earnings, civil war, and the virtual collapse of the CACM market. Capital inflow, principally in the form of remittances, transfers, donations, and credits from the US, has helped cover the deficit.

The US Central Intelligence Agency reports that in 1997 the purchasing power parity of El Salvador's exports was $1,960 million while imports totaled $3.5 billion resulting in a trade balance of -$1,540 million.

The International Monetary Fund (IMF) reports that in 1998 El Salvador had exports of goods totaling $2,451 million and imports totaling $3,718 million. The services credit totaled $290 million and debit $549 million. The following table summarizes El Salvador's balance of payments as reported by the IMF for 1998 in millions of US dollars.

Current Account		-84
Balance on goods	-1,267	
Balance on services	-259	
Balance on income	-66	
Current transfers	1,507	
Capital Account		1
Financial Account		636
Direct investment abroad	...	
Direct investment in El Salvador	872	
Portfolio investment assets	...	
Portfolio investment liabilities	-221	
Other investment assets	-83	
Other investment liabilities	67	
Net Errors and Omissions		-249
Reserves and Related Items		-303

33BANKING AND SECURITIES

The Central Reserve Bank of El Salvador, established in 1934, was nationalized in 1961. It is the sole bank of issue and the fiscal agent for the government. The entire banking system was nationalized in March 1980, but was later privatized. By 1989, the financial system was practically broke; destroyed by mismanagement and political conflict. In 1991, as part of economic reforms, the government privatized six commercial banks and seven savings and loan institutions. In 1994, the government

created the Banco Multisectorial de Inversiones (BMI) to promote private sector development. The Banking Law was modified in 1995 to encourage foreign banks to enter the country. There are at least 19 commercial banks, including the Banco Cuscatlan, Banco Salvadoreno, Banco Agricola Comercial, Banco de Desarrollo e Inversion, Banco Hipotecario, Bancasa, Grupo Capital, Citibank, Unibanco, Dresdner Bank Lateinamerika, BAC Florida, Bank Santander, Banco Ahorromet, and the Commercial Bank of El Salvador.

A stock exchange was established in San Salvador in 1993, with five government issues of long-term bonds. In the first 12 months of activity, stock market transactions were nearly $100 million; the rate of growth in 1993–95 was rapid, and by the end of 1995 transactions reached an estimated $2.4 billion. The market trades almost exclusively in government bonds and short-term commercial paper, but private companies were expected to put shares on the market in the late 1990s.

34INSURANCE

By 2000, El Salvador had at least 19 insurance companies in operation. The 1995 Insurance Law provided national treatment for foreign insurance firms.

35PUBLIC FINANCE

Most current public revenues come from taxes, fees, and fines. Municipal taxes and fees are subject to approval by the Ministry of the Interior. Until the early 1980s, government fiscal operations had generally shown surpluses; these enabled the government to sustain a growing volume of capital expenditures, resulting in a higher government share in total investments. Improved tax collection in 1998 resulted in approximately 56% of government revenues being attributed to the VAT.

The US Central Intelligence Agency (CIA) estimates that in 1997 El Salvador's central government took in revenues of approximately $1.75 billion and had expenditures of $1.82 billion including capital expenditures of $317 million. Overall, the government registered a deficit of approximately $70 million. External debt totaled $3.5 billion.

The following table shows an itemized breakdown of government revenues and expenditures. The percentages were calculated from data reported by the International Monetary Fund. The dollar amounts (millions) are based on the CIA estimates provided above.

REVENUE AND GRANTS	100%	1,750
Tax revenue	95.1%	1,663
Non-tax revenue	4.6%	81
Capital revenue	0.3%	5
Grants	0.2%	3
EXPENDITURES	100%	1,820
General public services	13.6%	248
Defense	7.1%	129
Public order and safety	16.3%	297
Education	19.6%	357
Health	10.3%	187
Social security	5.4%	99
Housing and community amenities	1.8%	33
Recreation, cultural, and religious affairs	1.7%	31
Economic affairs and services	17.1%	311
Interest payments	11.9%	217
Adjustments	-4.9%	-89

36TAXATION

Residents of El Salvador, whether citizens or not, are subject to progressive taxation on both domestic and foreign income ranging from 10% to 30%. Amounts received from insurance policies, interest on savings accounts, gifts, and inheritances are tax exempt. Taxes on corporate income are levied at 25% for amounts over the first $75,000, which are exempt. Other levies include a 13% value-added tax, and a real estate transfer tax (3% only if real estate has a market value over $250,000). There are no local taxes.

³⁷CUSTOMS AND DUTIES

El Salvador's import tariff, formerly used primarily to raise revenues, has in recent years been employed to protect certain industries. As a member of the CACM, El Salvador operates under a common tariff classification system, as well as a common code and regulations. As part of President Christiani's free market economic policies during the 1990s, import licenses were eliminated and tariffs were lowered. However, tariffs on some luxury items such as automobile and alcoholic drinks, are subject to rates up to 30%. In 1996, El Salvador eliminated its import tariff on capital goods. In 1999, the tariff on intermediate goods and raw materials was reduced to 5% and 10%, respectively. Final goods have a tariff of 15%. There are six Free Trade Zones: San Bartolo, El Progreso Industrial Park, El Pedregal, Exportslava, San Marcos Free Zone, and American Park. El Salvador has special trade relations with Mexico, Spain, Venezuela, the Dominican Republic, Guatemala, Honduras, and Colombia.

³⁸FOREIGN INVESTMENT

The Salvadoran government has fostered foreign investment since the 1988 Foreign Investment and Promotion Law came into force. Incentives include unrestricted remittance and reinvestment of profits; and for firms located in the Free Zones, the government offers up to a 20-year income tax holiday, and duty-free importation of materials needed for production. Major foreign investors include Coastal Technologies (power generation), Kimberly Clark (paper products), Texaco (fuel storage and distribution), Esso and Shell (petroleum refining), Bayer (pharmaceuticals), Sara Lee (clothing assembly), Xerox (sales), AIG (insurance), and British American Tobacco. El Salvador received approximately $250 million in direct investments in 1999, the majority from the US.

³⁹ECONOMIC DEVELOPMENT

Prior to 1950, the government, with moderate success, followed a policy of stimulating national economic development indirectly by building roads, developing power facilities, establishing credit facilities, and extending tariff protection to some industries. The prosperity and advantageous international position of Salvadoran coffee masked the long-term need for further diversification.

During the 1950s, it became apparent that El Salvador's primary problems were the growing population and lack of uncultivated arable land. The government therefore embarked on a program to encourage intensification of agriculture and expansion of small industry. The National Council for Economic Planning and Coordination (CONAPLAN), established in 1962, drafted a comprehensive five year plan (1965–69) embodying general objectives proclaimed by the government in line with the aims of the US-inspired Alliance for Progress. The objectives included an increase of the GNP; decrease in illiteracy; expansion of education, health, and housing programs; extension of social security benefits to areas not yet covered; and implementation of an integrated program of agrarian reform. The stimulus for the development program was to be provided by a small group of wealthy Salvadorans, with a minimum of government participation.

In early 1973, CONAPLAN drafted a development plan for 1973–77, concentrating on production, labor, and social welfare. The basic objectives of the plan were improvement in income distribution, employment, health, nutrition, housing, and education; stimulation of the agricultural, industrial, and construction sectors; acceleration of regional development; and

export diversification. The plan called for adoption of a government-sponsored investment and financing program, institutional and financial reforms, and policies to stimulate private investment.

The economic reforms adopted in 1980 included a land redistribution program, nationalization of the banking system. After the civil war was over, the country received substantial influx of economic aid and private remittances. As part of the economic reform program, initiated in 1989 by newly elected President Christiani, the country's economy has been recuperating at a fair pace. After the signing of the Chapultepec Peace Accords in January 1992, El Salvador has boosted business confidence and stimulated private investment.

In January 1986, a comprehensive stabilization program was announced. Among its most important measures were unification of the exchange rate at C5=$1 (a 50% devaluation), raising of fuel prices and public transportation fares, imposition of price controls on consumer staples (food, medical supplies, and clothing), tariff hikes on nonessential imports, and a rise in commercial interest rates. Because of the continuing costs from the civil war, and also from a drought the program fell short of its objectives.

In 1990, the IMF approved a standby agreement, which was followed by another one in January 1992 and another one in May 1993. The World Bank extended a $75 million structural adjustment loan in1991, and the Inter American Development Bank provided additional sectoral adjustment financing. Aided by the government's economic reforms and the IMF and World bank supported macroeconomic programs, the country's economy continued to prosper. The rising influx of private remittances, official transfer, and the return of local capital boosted domestic demand as well as construction activity, especially in transportation infrastructure and other public projects. The industrial sector also benefited from this upturn.

El Salvador's external debt decreased sharply in 1993, chiefly as a result of an agreement under which the US forgave about $461 million of official debt. Debt still stood at around $2.4 billion in 1999, despite US forgiveness. In 1998, significant aid came from the World Bank for agricultural reform ($40 million) and structural adjustment ($52.5); from the Central American Bank for Economic Development ($20 million) for road repair; and from the Inter-American Development Bank ($60 million) for poverty alleviation. Total non-US government aid reached $600 million in 1998.

⁴⁰SOCIAL DEVELOPMENT

The Salvadoran Social Security Institute was created in 1949 as an autonomous institution to provide national insurance for health, accidents, unemployment, invalidism, old age, and death. A basic social security law was passed in 1953; its program is supported by compulsory contributions from workers, employers, and the government. Employees contribute 2%–5.5% of earnings for pensions, sickness, maternity, and work-injury benefits; employers contribute 5.5% of payroll. Most social security participants reside in urban areas, as agricultural labor is exempt from coverage. The Ministry of Public Health and Social Welfare supervises institutions and hospitals for the infirm and aged, as well as child welfare and maternal care services.

Women have the same legal rights as men, but in practice face discrimination in employment, salaries, and access to credit. The new Family Code, implemented in 1994, removes previous provisions that discriminated against women and grants spousal rights to unmarried couples living together for at least 3 years. Domestic violence against women is pervasive. The incidence of child abandonment and abuse and the use of child labor appear to be on the increase as of 1999. The government is working with the United Nation's Children's Fund to improve the welfare of children.

Very few Salvadorians claim indigenous status; most have been assimilated into the general population. Indigenous groups live in poor rural areas. Most lack titles to their land and therefore lack the collateral necessary to access credit from a bank. The foremost indigenous association is the National Association of Indigenous Salvadorians (ANIS).

Human rights violations reported in 1999 include use of excessive force and extrajudicial killings by police. New criminal and sentencing codes decreased violations of due process.

41 HEALTH

Health standards have improved considerably since 1930. Average life expectancy in 1998 was 69.6 years. The infant mortality rate, 139.4 per 1,000 live births in 1930 to 1934, declined to 40 by 1996. The crude death rate, 23 per 1,000 in 1930 to 1934, dropped to 7 in 1990–1995. From 1979 to 1991, there were approximately 75,000 war-related deaths. The fertility rate has dropped from 5.3 in 1980 to 3.2 in 1997. Malnutrition persisted in 23% of children under 5 from 1992–97.

However, immunization rates for children up to one year old were quite high in 1997: tuberculosis (93%); diphtheria, pertussis, and tetanus (97%); polio (96%); and measles (97%). The contraceptive prevalence for women in couples was 53% from 1990–98.

In 1997, there were 10 physicians per 10,000 people. In 1995, there were 15 hospital beds per 1,000 inhabitants. The Ministry of Public Health and Social Welfare coordinates mobile health brigades, professional medical delegations, field offices, clinics, laboratories, and dispensaries. UNICEF, the US Institute of Inter-American Affairs, the Rockefeller Foundation, and other foreign organizations have assisted health campaigns. Total health care expenditures in 1995 were $158 per capita.

The principal causes of death remain gastroenteritis, influenza, malaria, measles, pneumonia, and bronchitis, caused or complicated by malnutrition, bad sanitation, and poor housing. Statistics show that from 1994 to 95, only 62% of the population had access to safe water, and 73% had adequate sanitation. In 1996, tuberculosis declined markedly, with an incidence of 67 per 100,000. In 1994, major causes of death were noted as communicable diseases and maternal/perinatal causes (202 per 100,000); noncommunicable diseases (385 per 100,000); and injuries (201 per 100,000). There were 1,416 new cases of AIDS reported in 1996 and 2,798 cases of malaria in 1994. Much of the progress since the 1930s was undermined by the country's civil war, which overtaxed health care facilities while, in real terms, expenditures on health care declined. The National Medical School was shut down in 1980.

42 HOUSING

Inadequate housing, most critically felt in cities and towns, is endemic throughout El Salvador. More than half of all urban dwellings have earthen floors and adobe walls, and many have straw roofs. In the early 1990s, an estimated 47% of all households did not have easy access to drinking water, and 59% lacked plumbing. Housing problems have been exacerbated by the civil war, which has created hundreds of thousands of refugees. In the late 1980s, total housing units numbered 1,100,000, with 5.1 people per dwelling.

43 EDUCATION

In 1930, 72% of Salvadorans over ten years of age were illiterate; by the year 2000, the figure had been reduced to about 21.3% (males, 18.4%; females, 23.9%). Primary education is free and compulsory through elementary school, and the public school system is government controlled. Enforcement of primary-school attendance is difficult, however, and truancy is high in rural areas. Primary education lasts for nine years, followed by three years of secondary education, on completion of which students can obtain the "Bachillerato," which is equivalent to a high school diploma.

In 1997 there were 1,191,052 students enrolled in primary schools. In the same year, secondary schools had 152,474 students and approximately 9,300 teachers.

In 2000, an institutional reform process for education has been initiated under a Basic Education Modernization Project, and the government is seeking international funding support for improvements in the quality and coverage of secondary education.

Twelve private and three public universities offer higher education. In 1996, 112,266 students were enrolled and 5,919 teachers taught at the universities and other higher level institutions. The University of El Salvador in San Salvador, authorized in 1841 and with enrollments averaging 30,000, was a base for antigovernment agitation during the 1970s. The university was stormed and ransacked by government troops on 26 June 1980; at least 50 students and the rector were killed, and the university did not reopen for several years.

44 LIBRARIES AND MUSEUMS

The National Library in San Salvador is the largest in the country, with 150,000 volumes. The library at the University of El Salvador has 91,000 volumes. The Central American University José Simeón Cañas in San Salvador has 150,000 volumes. In addition, there are three governmental libraries attached to the ministries of Education, Economics, and Foreign Affairs and a few small private and college libraries. The Ministry of Education maintains a mobile library with a total of 25,000 volumes.

The David J. Guzmán National Museum in San Salvador, founded in 1883, is a general museum housing historical documents and pre-Columbian artifacts. The Natural History Museum of El Salvador was founded in 1976. The National Zoological Park in San Salvador, established in 1961, maintains a natural science museum.

45 MEDIA

Ownership of domestic telephone and telegraph services has been transferred from the government to a semiautonomous agency. In 1997, there were 350,000 telephones in use. There is an automatic telephone system in San Salvador. As of 1999 there were 18 AM and 80 FM radio stations and 5 commercial television stations, including the government-owned Radio Nacional. Radios in use increased from 398,000 in 1968 to about 2,230,000 in 1995. In 1998 there were 461 radios, 250 television sets, and 7 mobile phones per 1,000 population.

The principal newspapers are published in San Salvador. They are, with 1999 circulations, *La Prensa Gráfica*, 97,300; *El Diario de Hoy*, 99,000; *El Mundo*, 58,000; *Diario Latino*, 20,000; and *La Noticia*, 30,000.

The constitution of El Salvador provides for freedom of expression, including that of speech and press, and the government is presently said to respect these rights in practice. Print and broadcast journalists are said to freely and regularly criticize the government without censure.

As of 1996, there were 39 Internet hosts in El Salvador. Online access is extremely limited, with approximately one Internet host per 1,000 population in 1998.

46 ORGANIZATIONS

Of prime importance is the Salvadoran Coffee Association, founded in 1930 to promote coffee production, distribution, and consumption; to improve quality; and to provide information and advice to growers. Its membership includes all native and foreign coffee growers in El Salvador, and it receives financial support from the government export tax on coffee. Other prominent management organizations include the National Coffee Institute, Chamber of Commerce and Industry, Salvadoran Association of Industrialists, Cattle Raisers' Association, El Salvador Sugar Cooperative, National Sugar Institute, Salvadoran Cotton Growers' Cooperative, and National Federation of Small Salvadoran Enterprises. In the early 1970s, the Salvadoran Communal Union was formed to improve peasant farming methods and to campaign for agrarian reform. In 1986, the union claimed 100,000 members.

[47]TOURISM, TRAVEL, AND RECREATION

A valid passport and visa are required for entry into El Salvador by all visitors except other Central American nationals, who need only a passport. After the 1989 installation of the Christiani regime, tourism rebounded, rising from 130,602 visitors in 1989 to 541,863 in 1998. By that year, El Salvador had 3,750 hotel rooms and 7,500 beds with a 70% occupancy rate. In 1997 receipts from tourism totaled $75 million.

El Salvador's best-known natural wonder is Izalco, an active volcano often referred to as the Lighthouse of the Pacific because its smoke and flames are a guide to ships. Noteworthy are the cathedrals and churches of San Salvador, Santa Ana, and Sonsonate; the parks, gardens, and architecture of San Miguel; and the colonial atmosphere of San Vicente. Archaeological ruins of pre-Columbian origin are found in many parts of the country. Among the most striking are those at Tazumal, near Santa Ana, which include large pyramids and buildings with ancient carvings and inscriptions; there are more than 100 pyramid sites in El Salvador, many still unexcavated. The Pacific coast contains excellent beaches, and there is large-game fishing in the Gulf of Fonseca and in the ocean. Football (soccer) is the national sport.

In 1999 the UN estimated the cost of staying in San Salvador at $155 per day. Outside the capital, daily expenses are an estimated $46.

[48]FAMOUS SALVADORANS

The national hero of El Salvador is Father José Matías Delgado (1768–1833), who raised the first call for independence. A renowned political leader was Manuel José Arce (1786–1847), who fought against the Mexican empire of Iturbide and was the first president of the United Provinces of Central America. Gerardo Barrios Espinosa (1809–65) was a liberal president during the 19th century.

Prominent Salvadoran literary figures of the 19th century were Juan José Cañas (1826–1912), a poet and diplomat and the author of the Salvadoran national anthem, and Francisco E. Galindo (1850–1900), a poet and dramatist.

Writers of note in the 20th century include Alberto Masferrer (1865–1932), an essayist and poet; Juan Ramón Uriarte (1875–1927), an essayist and educator; and Salvador Salazar Arrué (b.1899). Juan Francisco Cisneros (1823–78) is a nationally recognized painter.

Key figures in Salvadoran politics of the 1970s and 1980s are José Napoleón Duarte (1926–90) and Roberto D'Aubuisson Arrieta (1943–92). The assassinated Roman Catholic Archbishop Oscar Arnulfo Romero y Galdames (1917–80) was well known as a defender of human rights.

[49]DEPENDENCIES

El Salvador has no territories or colonies.

[50]BIBLIOGRAPHY

Brockman, James R. *The Word Remains: A Life of Oscar Romero*. Maryknoll, N.Y.: Orbis Books, 1982.

Browning, David. *El Salvador: Landscape and Society*. Oxford: Clarendon, 1971.

Byrne, Hugh. *El Salvador's Civil War: A Study of Revolution*. Boulder, Colo.: Lynne Rienner Publishers, 1996.

Doggett, Martha. *Death Foretold: the Jesuit Murders in El Salvador*. Washington, D.C.: Georgetown University Press, 1993.

El Salvador's Decade of Terror: Human Rights Since the Assassination of Archbishop Romero. New Haven: Yale University Press, 1991.

Haggerty, Richard A. (ed.) *El Salvador, a Country Study*. 2d ed. Washington, D.C.: Library of Congress, 1990.

Haverstock, Nathan A. *El Salvador in Pictures*. Minneapolis: Lerner, 1987.

Johnstone, Ian. *Rights and Reconciliation: UN Strategies in El Salvador*. Boulder, Colo.: Lynne Reinner Publishers, 1995.

Lindo-Fuentes, Hector. *Weak Foundations: the Economy of El Salvador in the Nineteenth Century*. Berkeley: University of California Press, 1990.

Little, Michael R. *A War of Information: The Conflict Between Public and Private U.S. Foreign Policy on El Salvador, 1979-1992*. Lanhan, M.D.: University Press of America, 1994.

Montgomery, Tommie Sue. *Revolution in El Salvador: Origins and Evolution*. Boulder, Colo.: Westview, 1982.

Parkman, Patricia. *Nonviolent Insurrection in El Salvador: the Fall of Maximiliano Hernandez Martinez*. Tucson: University of Arizona Press, 1988.

Webre, Stephen. *José Napoleón Duarte and the Christian Democratic Party in Salvadoran Politics, 1960–1972*. Baton Rouge: Louisiana State University Press, 1979.

Woodward, Ralph Lee. *El Salvador*. Santa Barbara, Calif.: Clio, 1988.

FRENCH AMERICAN DEPENDENCIES

FRENCH GUIANA

Located on the northeast coast of South America, and extending from 1°30′ to 5°30′N and from 51°4′ to 54°3′W, French Guiana (Guyane Française) has an Atlantic shoreline of about 320 km (200 mi) and a total area of some 91,000 sq km (35,000 sq mi). It is separated from Brazil by the Oyapock River in the E and the Tumuc-Humac Mountains in the S (440 km/273 mi); and from Suriname by the Maroni River (398 km/247 mi) on the W. Its length is about 400 km (250 mi) N–S, and its width is 300 km (190 mi) E–W. Several islands offshore are part of French Guiana including: the Îles du Salut (Devil's Island, Royale, and Saint-Joseph).

French Guiana consists of a small, low swampy coast called "terres basses," varying from 10 to 30 km (6–19 mi) in width, and a vast, partly unexplored interior, the "terres hautes," with grassy plateaus, equatorial forests (which cover 90% of the land area), and mountains. The mean annual temperature along the coast is 26°C (80°F) year-round. There is a rainy season from January to June; annual rainfall has a range of 350–400 cm (140–160 in). Average humidity is 85%. Endangered species in 1987 included the tundra peregrine falcon, three species of turtle (South American river, olive ridley, and leatherback), and the black caiman.

The population was estimated at 167,982 in mid-1999. Four-fifths of the inhabitants live in the coastal lowlands, and about 55% of the total live in Cayenne, the capital city. About 66% of the population is either black or mixed-raced, 12% is white, 12% is either of East Indian, Chinese, or Amerindian origin, and 10% belongs to other ethnic origins. In the interior are six tribes of aboriginal Indians; descendants of fugitive black slaves from Dutch Guiana (now Suriname) have settled along the rivers. Roman Catholicism is the dominant religion. The official language is French.

Amerindian tribes inhabited the region from ancient times, but their numbers probably did not exceed 25,000 on the eve of European colonization. The land now known as French Guiana was first settled by Frenchmen in 1604 and was awarded to France by the Peace of Breda in 1667. Since 1946, it has been an overseas department, sending, in 1986, two deputies and one senator to the French parliament and one representative to the French Economic and Social Council. The old penal settlements to which French prisoners were once deported have been completely liquidated. Devil's Island, the most famous of the offshore penal colonies, operated from 1851 until 1951. French Guiana consists of Cayenne and St.-Laurent-du-Maroni, each of which has the status of an arrondissement. The French commissioner is assisted by a popularly elected 19-member general council and a 31-member regional council.

Arable land and labor both being scarce, agriculture in French Guiana is still in a primitive state. Trade is mainly with France. The territory's exports, mainly shrimp, fish, and timber, totaled US$148 million in 1997; imports totaled US$600 million. The total fisheries catch was 7,541 tons in 1994; exports of fish products were valued at $36,255,000 that year. Timber exports totaled $2.6 million in 1995. Gold, which has been mined since 1853, and large deposits of bauxite are the chief mineral resources. An estimated 2,500 kg of gold were extracted in 1995.

The European Space Agency launches communications satellites from Kourou.

Education for French Guiana's children is compulsory and provided by the government, which has constructed 66 primary and 19 secondary schools. The Pasteur Institute, five hospitals, and other health units provide public health services. The infant mortality rate in 1999 was estimated at 12.93 per 1,000 live births, down from 14.6 per 1,000 live births in 1996.

GUADELOUPE

The French overseas department of Guadeloupe, situated among the Lesser Antilles, extends 15°52′ to 18°7′N, and 61° to 63°5′W. The length of Guadeloupe proper is 67 km (42 mi) E–W, and its width is 60 km (37 mi) N–S; its total coastline amounts to 656 km (408 mi). A narrow channel, Rivière Salée, divides Guadeloupe proper into two islands: Basse-Terre (848 sq km/327 sq mi) and Grande-Terre (585 sq km/226 sq mi). Outlying islands include Marie-Galante and La Désirade, and the Les Saintes and Petite Terre island groups, near the main islands; St. Barthélémy, about 120 km (75 mi) to the NW; and St. Martin, about 175 km (110 mi) to the NW, the northern two-thirds of it French, the southern third Dutch. Total area, including the outlying islands, is 1,780 sq km (687 sq mi). Basse-Terre is volcanic; its highest peak, La Soufrière (1,484 m/4,869 ft), erupted in the 18th and 19th centuries and is still active. Annual rainfall ranges from 99 cm (39 in) on La Désirade to between 500 and 1,000 cm (200–400 in) on the mountains of Basse-Terre. Ferns, bamboo, mangrove, and tropical hardwoods are abundant. Endangered species include the Guadeloupe wren, green sea turtle, and leatherback turtle.

The estimated population in mid-1999 was 420,943. About 90% of the inhabitants are blacks or a mixture of blacks and descendants of Normans and Bretons who first settled the island in the 17th century. Some 95% of the people are Roman Catholic. French is the official language, but a Creole dialect is widely spoken.

Guadeloupe was first settled by Arawak Indians from Venezuela about AD 200. Carib Indians, also from Venezuela, overran this agricultural and fishing community around AD 1000. Discovered by Columbus in 1493 and occupied by the French in 1635, Guadeloupe has, except for short periods during the Napoleonic wars, been French ever since. In 1648, St. Martin was shared with the Dutch. Guadeloupe became an overseas department in 1946. It is represented in the French parliament by three deputies and two senators. Local administration is similar to that of regions and departments in metropolitan France. The appointed commissioner is assisted by a 41-member general council, elected by universal suffrage, and by a newly created regional council.

There are about 2,082 km (1,300 mi) of highways, of which about 1,752 km (1,089 mi) are paved. There are no railways except for privately owned plantation lines. Marine traffic is concentrated at Pointe-à-Pitre and Basse-Terre. Steamships connect Guadeloupe with other West Indian islands, with North and South America, and with France. Air France and other airlines serve the international airport at Pointe-à-Pitre.

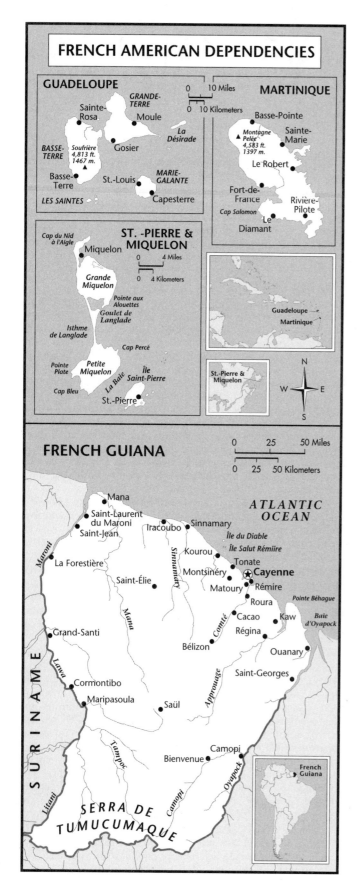

Sugar, traditionally the primary agricultural crop, is slowly being replaced by bananas, eggplant, and flowers. About 64% of import and 75% or export trade is with France. In 1997, exports yielded US$133 million; imports totaled US$1.7 billion. Sugar refining and rum distilling are the traditional industries. The total fisheries catch in 1994 was 8,676 tons. Cement and natural pumice are produced primarily for local construction.

In 1994/95, elementary school enrollment totaled 38,332; secondary schools, a total of 41,656 students. Two teaching and research units—one for law and economics, the other for liberal arts and the sciences—provide higher education at the Université Antilles-Guyane in Pointe-à-Pitre. Several hundred scholarship holders study in French universities. The infant mortality rate was an estimated 8.54 per 1,000 live births in 1999, down from 17 in 1985.

MARTINIQUE

The island of Martinique is situated from 14°26′ to 14°53′N and 61°W among the Lesser Antilles in the Caribbean Sea, between the islands of Dominica and St. Lucia. It has an area of 1,110 sq km (429 sq mi), with a length of 75 km (47 mi) SE–NW and a maximum width of 34 km (21 mi) NE–SW. Its total coastline is about 350 km (220 mi). Most of the island is mountainous. The two highest peaks, Pelée (1,397 m/4,583 ft) and Carbet (1,196 m/3,923 ft), are volcanoes. On 8 May 1902, Mt. Pelée erupted, completely destroying the city of St. Pierre and killing 30,000 inhabitants. About 25% of the land is wooded, with both European and tropical trees represented. Average temperature is about 26°C (80°F) and average annual rainfall about 190 cm (75 in).

The mid-1999 estimated population was 411,539. The population, composed mostly of descendants of black Africans, Carib Indians, and Europeans, is predominantly Roman Catholic. French is the official language, but a Creole dialect is widely spoken and English is understood in tourist areas.

There are 2,724 km (1,703 mi) of roads and no railways. Steamer service connects Martinique with North and South America and France. Air France and other airlines provide air service from Lamentin Airport near Fort-de-France.

First inhabited by Carib Indians, Martinique was discovered by Columbus in 1502, and colonized by the French in 1635. Except for the periods 1762–63, 1793–1802, and 1809–15, the island has remained in French hands ever since. It is represented in the French parliament by four deputies and two senators.

Martinique's economy is agricultural. Sugarcane and bananas are the leading crops; pineapples, citrus fruit, mangoes, avocados, coffee, and cacao are also grown. Sugar refining, rum distilling, and fruit processing are the chief industries. Bananas, petroleum products, and rum are the principal exports; foodstuffs and oil are the main imports. Martinique produced about 4.8 million barrels of refined petroleum products in 1994 from imported crude oil. Timber production was 12,000 cu m in 1995, and the fish catch in 1994 was 5,905 tons. In 1997, exports totaled US$200 million; imports totaled US$1.6 billion. Trade is mainly with France, which heavily subsidizes the budget. Tourism has become more important than agriculture as a source of foreign exchange.

Education is compulsory through the primary and secondary levels. There is a branch of the Centre Universitaire Antilles-Guyana. Martinique has 16 hospitals. The infant mortality rate in 1999 was estimated at 6.76 per 1,000 live births, down from 14 in 1985. Life expectancy was 79.3 years in 1999.

ST. PIERRE AND MIQUELON

The French territorial collectivity of St. Pierre and Miquelon (Territoire des Îles Saint-Pierre et Miquelon) is an archipelago in the North Atlantic Ocean, between 46°45′ and 47°10′N and 56°5′ and 56°25′W, located about 24 km (15 mi) W of Burin Peninsula on the south coast of Newfoundland. It consists of three main islands, St. Pierre, Miquelon, and Langlade—the two latter linked by a low, sandy isthmus—and several small ones. The length of the group is 43 km (27 mi) N–S, and it measures 22 km (14 mi) E–W at its widest extent. The total area is 242 sq km (93 sq mi). The islands were the focus of a maritime boundary dispute between Canada and France, but in 1992 an arbitration panel awarded the islands an exclusive economic zone area of 12,348 sq km (4,768 sq mi) as a settlement. Although the archipelago is volcanic in origin, the highest point, Morne de la Grande Montagne, is only 393 m (1,289 ft). The temperature varies between an average daily low of –15°C (5°F) in winter and an average daily high of 22°C (72°F) in summer. The spring and autumn are very windy, and fogs are frequent throughout the year; annual precipitation averages 130 cm (51 in). Vegetation is scanty, except on Langlade, where several species of trees are found. Animal life includes seabirds, foxes, rabbits, and deer. The population in mid-1999 was estimated to be 6,966. Most of the people are descendants of Basque, Breton, and Norman settlers and are Roman Catholics.

The first permanent French settlement dates from 1604, and, except for several periods of British rule, the islands have remained French ever since. They became a French overseas territory in 1946, an overseas department in 1976, and a territorial collectivity in 1985. The economy has traditionally centered around fishing and by servicing the fishing fleets operating off the coast of Newfoundland, but the number of ships stopping at St. Pierre has been declining in recent years. The annual cod catch declined from 13,000 tons in 1991 to 86 tons in 1994. Total exports in 1996 amounted to US$1.2 million, while imports totaled US$60.5 million, requiring heavy subsidies from France.

GRENADA

Grenada

CAPITAL: St. George's.

FLAG: The national flag consists of a red border surrounding a rectangle divided into two gold and two green triangles. There are seven yellow stars—three on the upper and three on the lower red border, and one large star at the apex of the four triangles—representing the six parishes and the island of Carriacou. A yellow nutmeg is represented on the hoist triangle.

ANTHEM: National Anthem beginning "Hail Grenada, land of ours, we pledge ourselves to thee."

MONETARY UNIT: The East Caribbean dollar (EC$) is a paper currency of 100 cents, pegged to the US dollar. There are coins of 1, 2, 5, 10, 25, and 50 cents, and 1 dollar, and notes of 5, 10, 20, and 100 East Caribbean dollars. EC$1 = US$0.37037 (or US$1 = EC$2.70).

WEIGHTS AND MEASURES: The metric system is in use.

HOLIDAYS: New Year, 1–2 January; Independence Day, 7 February; Labor Day, 1 May; Thanksgiving, 25 October; Christmas, 25 December; Boxing Day, 26 December. Movable holidays include Good Friday, Easter Monday, and Emancipation Day, 1st Monday in August.

TIME: 8 AM = noon GMT.

¹LOCATION, SIZE, AND EXTENT

Located about 160 km (100 mi) N of Trinidad and 109 km (68 mi) SSW of St. Vincent, Grenada, which includes the inhabited islands of Grenada, Carriacou, and Petite Martinique, has an area of 340 sq km (131 sq mi). Comparatively, the area occupied by Grenada is slightly less than twice the size of Washington, D.C. Grenada island extends 34 km (21 mi) NE–SW and 19 km (12 mi) SE–NW, and has a coastline of 121 km (75 mi).

Grenada's capital city, Saint George's, is located on the island's southwestern coast.

²TOPOGRAPHY

Volcanic in origin, Grenada is very hilly, with the highest peak, Mt. St. Catherine, in the Central Highlands, rising to 840 m (2,756 ft). The coastline is indented with many beaches and small bays. Several short streams cross the terrain. Lake Grand Etang is formed in the crater of a volcano at 530 m (1,740 ft) above sea level.

³CLIMATE

The tropical climate is tempered by almost constant sea breezes; the prevailing wind is from the northeast. Temperatures range from 21° to 29°C (70–84°F). Annual rainfall varies from about 150 cm (60 in) in the northern and southern coastal belts to as much as 380 cm (150 in) in the Central Highlands. There is a wet season from June to December, but rain falls periodically throughout the year.

⁴FLORA AND FAUNA

The Central Highlands support a wide variety of forest trees, and many types of tropical flowers and shrubs grow throughout the island. Characteristic wildlife includes the hummingbird, egret, dove, and wild pigeon; also to be found are armadillo, agouti, and monkeys.

⁵ENVIRONMENT

As a member of the Organization of Eastern Caribbean States (OECS) formed in 1981, Grenada shares the advantages and disadvantages of island nations in the area. Water supply is limited and, in some areas, polluted by agricultural chemicals and sewage. Forests are threatened by the expansion of farming activities and the use of wood for fuel. The nation's coasts are affected by industrial pollution which threatens the nation's tourist trade. Environmental responsibilities are vested in the Ministry of Health and Housing. Endangered or extinct species include the Grenada hook-billed kite, tundra peregrine falcon, the green sea and hawksbill turtles, the spectacled caiman, and the Orinoco crocodile.

⁶POPULATION

The population of Grenada in 2000 was estimated at 97,913. An estimated 3.8% of the population is 65 years of age or older. The projected population for the year 2005 is 104,000, assuming a crude birthrate of 26 per 1,000 population and a death rate of 4, resulting in a natural rate of change of 2.2% for the period 2000–2005. Due to high fertility rates and substantial emigration, Grenada has an increasingly young population, with about half its population under age 21. Population density in 1996 was an estimated 280 persons per sq km (726 per sq mi).

It was estimated that 38% of the population lived in urban areas in 2000. St. George's, Grenada's capital city and port, had a 2000 metropolitan population of 33,000. Grenada's next census is slated for 2001.

⁷MIGRATION

Grenadians have always emigrated, mainly to the UK and Canada. Emigration increased after the 1979 coup. As of 1999, Grenada hosted no refugees or asylum-seekers. However, the country's lack of a national refugee law is a cause for concern as Grenada is likely to see an increase in the number of asylum-seekers due to escalating extra-regional migration and migrant trafficking through the Caribbean. In 1999, the net migration rate was -13.74 migrants per 1,000 population.

8ETHNIC GROUPS

The descendants of former African slaves, together with mixed black and white racial strains, make up about 91% of the population. The remainder consists of small groups of Asian (largely Indian) and European descent.

9LANGUAGES

English is the official and common language. A French-African patois also is spoken.

10RELIGIONS

The dominant religion is Christianity, but religious freedom is provided for all groups in the constitution. According to 1998 estimates, 53% of the population is Roman Catholic. Other main groups include Anglicans, Presbyterians, and Methodists. Minority religions are Islam and Baha'i.

11TRANSPORTATION

In 1999, Grenada's road system of 1,040 km (646 mi) included 638 km (396 mi) of paved roads. The country's major port is St. George's. A new international airport, Point Salines, built largely with Cuban assistance, and scheduled for completion in 1984, was repeatedly cited by the US as posing a possible military threat to the Caribbean region. After the US-led invasion in 1983, the airport was completed with funding mainly from the US. Airline flights began in October 1984, and in 1997, the airport served 322,000 arriving and departing passengers. In 1998 there were 3 airports, 2 of which had paved runways. The smaller airports are at Pearls and on Carriacou.

12HISTORY

Grenada was inhabited by Arawak Indians when first discovered on 15 August 1498 by Christopher Columbus, who named it Concepción. By the 18th century, the island was known as Grenada. The origin of that name is unknown, possibly a corruption of the Spanish city of Granada. A secure harbor (at St. George's) attracted traders and some French settlers during the 16th century. After a few failed French private ventures in 1650 and 1657, the French government annexed Grenada in 1674. The island remained under French control until 1762, when Admiral George Rodney captured it for Great Britain. The French regained Grenada in 1779, but the Versailles treaty of 1783 returned Grenada to Britain.

Sugar was Grenada's main product until the 19th century. At that time, the development of spices, especially nutmeg, coupled with the emancipation of slaves in 1834, led to a new economic base for the island. The economy flourished during the second half of the 19th century, and the cultivation of nutmeg, cloves, ginger, and cinnamon, earned Grenada the name Isle of Spice. Grenada's colonial status ended in 1958 when it joined the ill-fated Federation of the West Indies. In 1962, the federation dissolved, and in 1967, Grenada became an associated state of the UK.

On 28 February 1972, general elections resulted in the victory of Eric Matthew Gairy, who ran under the banner of the pro-independence Grenada United Labour Party (GULP). A constitutional conference was held in London during May 1973, and independence was set for the following February. Independence came on 7 February 1974, in spite of widespread strikes and demonstrations protesting Gairy's secret police force, actions that

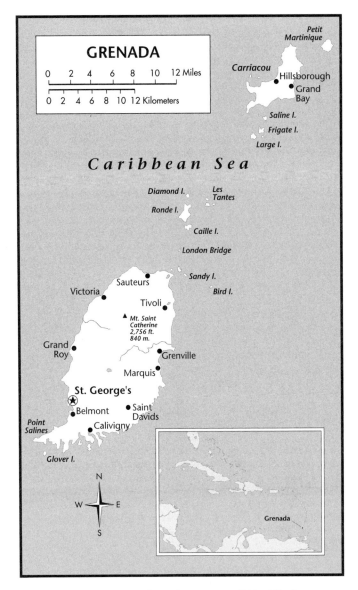

LOCATION: 12°7′N and 61°40′W. **COASTLINE:** 121 km (75 mi).
TERRITORIAL SEA LIMIT: 12 mi.

were supported by trade unions in neighboring Barbados and Trinidad and Tobago. Prime Minister Gairy ruled for five years.

On 13 March 1979, the opposition party, the New Jewel Movement, seized power, and Maurice Bishop became prime minister of the People's Revolutionary Government (PRG). Bishop suspended the constitution, jailed opposition leaders, and shut down independent newspapers. The PRG was drawn toward Cuba and its allies in the Caribbean region, as relations with the US and some of Grenada's more conservative Caribbean neighbors deteriorated.

On 19 October 1983, in the course of a power struggle within the PRG, Bishop and several followers were shot to death, and a hard-line Marxist military council, headed by Gen. Hudson Austin, took over. Six days later, thousands of US troops, accompanied by token forces from seven other Caribbean nations, invaded the island, ostensibly to protect the lives of American students there. Nearly all of the 700 Cubans then in Grenada were captured and expelled. In spite of the UN General Assembly's condemnation of the invasion, Gen. Austin was placed in detention, and the governor-general, Sir Paul Scoon, formed an interim government to prepare for elections. US combat troops were withdrawn in December 1983, but 300 support troops and 430 members of Caribbean forces remained on the island until September 1985.

Elections were held in December 1984, and Herbert Blaize and his New National Party (NNP) won 59% of the popular vote and 14 of the 15 House of Representatives seats. Prime Minister Blaize died in December 1989, and Ben Jones formed a government until the elections of 1990. Those elections elevated the National Democratic Congress (NDC) to majority status and Nicholas Brathwaite became prime minister. By 1993, ten years after the US invasion, tourist arrivals in Grenada had more than tripled, and the Point Salines airport, begun by the ousted Cubans and completed in 1984, was a modern facility servicing international flights.

In his 1994 budget, Brathwaite reintroduced the personal income tax, which had been abolished in 1986. Controversy over the tax helped carry the NNP to victory in the June 1995 election, and Keith Mitchell, who had promised to rescind the tax once again, became the new prime minister.

In November 1998, Mitchell's government lost its parliamentary majority when two members crossed over to the opposition, forcing early elections. In spite of allegations of government corruption, Mitchell's NNP swept the polling, winning all 15 seats in the House of Representatives in the January 1999 elections—the fourth peaceful electoral contest since the 1983 US intervention. Mitchell received credit for bolstering the country's economy and increasing foreign investment.

In August 1998, Fidel Castro arrived in Grenada for his first state visit since 1983. Mitchell's government has pursued economic cooperation with Cuba, and Mitchell had visited Cuba the previous year. During the Castro visit, an economic agreement was signed by the two countries. In spite of steady economic growth and low inflation, the IMF issued a warning in 1999 about the state of Grenada's public finances, especially the nation's growing budget deficit, which was partially caused by tax cuts.

13GOVERNMENT

The independence constitution, effective in 1974 but suspended after the 1979 coup, was reinstated after the US invasion. It provides for a governor-general appointed by the British crown and for a parliamentary government comprising independent executive, legislative, and judicial branches. Under this constitution, the bicameral legislature consists of a Senate of 13 members appointed by the governor-general, acting on the advice of the prime minister and the leader of the opposition, and a 15-seat House of Representatives. The governor-general appoints as prime minister the majority leader of the House. The cabinet, which comprises the prime minister, four senior ministers, and four ministers of state, is the executive arm of the government and is responsible for making policy. In 1996, a portfolio for women's affairs was created.

14POLITICAL PARTIES

The New National Party (NNP), formed from a coalition of moderate parties and headed by Prime Minister Keith Mitchell, has been the majority party since the 1995 elections when it won 8 out of 15 seats in the House. In early elections called in January 1999, the party won 62% of the vote and all 15 House seats. The National Democratic Congress (NDC), a moderate party, took 5 of 15 seats in the House of Representatives in the 1995 elections but won no seats in 1999 (although garnering 25% of the vote).

The Grenada United Labour Party (GULP) was under the leadership of Sir Eric Gairy, who founded it in 1950, until Gairy's death in 1997. Right-wing and populist in its approach, the group won no seats, but 12% of the vote, in the 1999 elections. The moderate National Party (NP), organized in 1989 by former prime minister Ben Jones, did not sponsor any candidates in 1999. On the left, the Maurice Bishop Patriotic Movement (MBPM) has never won legislative representation.

15LOCAL GOVERNMENT

For administrative purposes, the main island is divided into six parishes and one dependency.

16JUDICIAL SYSTEM

The Grenada Supreme Court, in St. George's, consists of a High Court of Justice and a two-tier Court of Appeals. The Court of Magisterial Appeals hears appeals from magistrates' courts, which exercise summary jurisdiction; the Itinerant Court of Appeal hears appeals from the High Court.

On joining the Organization of Eastern Caribbean States (OECS) in 1991, the Grenada Supreme Court became the Supreme Court of Grenada and the West Indian Associated States. Under the OECS system, appeals may be taken from this court to the Privy Council in London.

The judiciary is independent. There are no military or political courts. The law provides for the right to a fair public trial, to a presumption of innocence, to remain silent, and to seek the advice of an attorney.

17ARMED FORCES

A UK- and US-trained 550-man Royal Grenada Police and Coast Guard provides internal defense. A US-trained Special Services Unit participates in the East Caribbean Regional Security System, established in 1985 jointly with Antigua and Barbuda, Dominica, St. Kitts and Nevis, St. Lucia, and St. Vincent and the Grenadines.

18INTERNATIONAL COOPERATION

Grenada became a member of the UN on 17 September 1974 and participates in ECLAC and all the nonregional specialized agencies except IAEA, IMO, WIPO, and WMO. Grenada joined the OAS on 13 May 1975. It is also a member of the Commonwealth of Nations, CARICOM, and G-77. Grenada is a signatory of the Law of the Sea and a member of the WTO.

19ECONOMY

Grenada's economy is highly dependent on international trade and finance for its development. Exports of nutmeg, cocoa, spices and banana are the main earners of foreign exchange, with tourism close behind. The economy is essentially agricultural and centers on the traditional production of spices and tropical plants. Agriculture accounts for about 10% of GDP and 80% of exports and employs 24% of the labor force. Tourism is the leading foreign exchange earner, followed by agricultural exports. Manufacturing remains relatively undeveloped, but is growing due to a favorable private investment climate. The economy achieved an impressive average annual growth rate of 5.5% in 1986–91 but has slowed since 1992. Grenada's economy grew by approximately 5% in 1998.

20INCOME

The US Central Intelligence Agency (CIA) reports that in 1998 Grenada's gross domestic product (GDP) was estimated at $340 million. The per capita GDP was estimated at $3,500. The annual growth rate of GDP was estimated at 5%. The average inflation rate in 1998 was 1.4%. The CIA defines GDP as the value of all final goods and services produced within a nation in a given year and computed on the basis of purchasing power parity (PPP) rather than value as measured on the basis of the rate of exchange. It was estimated that agriculture accounted for 9.7% of GDP, industry 15%, and services 75.3%.

The World Bank reports that for the same period per capita private consumption (in PPP terms) was $3,620. Private consumption includes expenditures of individuals, households, and nongovernmental organizations.

21LABOR

Grenada's labor force is estimated at 40,000 (1991), including a large supply of unskilled and semiskilled workers. Unemployment was estimated in 1991 at 28% of the labor force. The distribution of the employed labor force in 1991 was agriculture, 24%; construction, 8%; industry, 5%; services, 31%; and other sectors (including self-employed), 32%. In 1999, there were no minimum wage laws in effect.

Approximately 35% of the labor force is unionized. There are several major trade unions in the country, including civil service unions. All major unions belong to one major federation, the Grenada Trade Unions Council (GTUC). The GTUC is somewhat connected to the government organizationally and receives subsidies from the government for its operating budget. Grenada has one of the largest per capita public sector work forces in the eastern Caribbean region. Civil servant salaries consume a large percentage of government revenues and exceed all export earnings from Grenada's agricultural fishing and manufacturing sectors combined.

Workers are free to strike and employees who claimed to have been dismissed for union activism may seek redress through formal governmental procedures.

The minimum working age is 18. This minimum age is respected and enforced in the formal economy, but enforcement is somewhat lax in the informal economy.

22AGRICULTURE

Numerous spices, fruits, and vegetables are grown in Grenada. The principal crops for export are nutmeg and mace, bananas, cocoa beans, and other fresh fruits and vegetables. Production in 1998 included bananas, 4,000 tons; cocoa, 1,000 tons; and avocados, 2,000 tons. Banana production decreased in the 1980s due to the appearance of Moko disease. There are small scattered plots of cotton, cloves, limes, nutmeg, cinnamon, and coffee. Both cotton and lime oil are produced on Carriacou. Food crops consist of yams, sweet potatoes, corn, peas, and beans. Grenada is especially known for its nutmeg production, earning it the nickname "Spice Island." Prices for nutmeg, however, have been rather low in recent years due to a soft market and the collapse of the Grenada/Indonesia cartel in 1990. Late in 1991, Grenada and Indonesia (the world's largest nutmeg producer) signed a new cartel agreement which aims to constrict production, thereby driving up world prices for the spice. In 1997, exports of agricultural products amounted to US$13 million.

23ANIMAL HUSBANDRY

There is very little dairy farming in Grenada. Most livestock is raised by individuals for their own use. In 1998 there were an estimated 4,000 head of cattle, 20,000 sheep and goats, and 1,000 donkeys. Some 250,000 poultry were raised to supply local needs.

24FISHING

Fishing is mostly coastal. The 1997 catch was 1,408 tons, predominantly tuna and scad.

25FORESTRY

There are approximately 3,000 hectares (7,400 acres) of rain forest, about 75% of which is government owned. Since 1957, some 320 hectares (800 acres) of forest, primarily of Honduras mahogany, blue mahoe, and teak, have been introduced. The Forestry Development Corp. was established in 1979 to develop forest resources and woodworking industries. Imports of forestry products totaled $6.2 million in 1997,

26MINING

There are no reported mining operations in Grenada except for open-face red gravel deposits for the local construction industry.

27ENERGY AND POWER

The government and the Commonwealth Development Corp. jointly operate a private company, Grenada Electricity Services, Ltd., for the supply and distribution of electricity throughout the island. In 1998, net installed capacity of electric generating plants was about 9,000 kW; output that year totaled 105 million kWh.

28INDUSTRY

Industry is small scale, mainly producing consumer products for local use. Local firms produce food and beer, oils, soap (from copra), furniture, mattresses, clothing and a number of other items. In 1996, Grenada expanded its production of flour, animal feed, chemicals, paints and tobacco.

In 1985, the government established the Industrial Development Corporation, which built a 7.3 hectare (19.5 acres) industrial park near Point Salines airport. New industries that had located there by mid-1987 included data entry, protective clothing, and tire retreading. The manufacturing sector maintained a consistent rate of growth of about 5% between 1988 and 1998, and 14% in 1998 alone.

29SCIENCE AND TECHNOLOGY

St. George's University School of Medicine was founded in 1976. A school of agriculture is located in Mirabeau. The Grenada National Museum, at St. George's, maintains exhibits on technology and native fauna and flora.

30DOMESTIC TRADE

There are meat, fish, fruit, and vegetable markets, in addition to other types of small retail shops, all over the island. St. George's is the import and merchandising center. A widespread network of cooperatives exists for the distribution and sale of agricultural products.

Shopping hours are usually from 8 to 4 PM on weekdays and 8 AM to 1 on Saturdays. Banks are open from 8 AM to 2 PM, Monday through Friday, and 2:30 PM to 5 PM, on Fridays.

31FOREIGN TRADE

Annual trade deficits are caused by the large flow of imports, including motor vehicles and other consumer goods, fuels, and fertilizer. Virtually all exports are agricultural products.

The spice trade supports Grenada, with the largest percentage of commodity exports, including nutmeg and mace (22%). Other important exports include fruits (like bananas) and nuts (18%), cocoa (17%), fish (13%), hats (4.0%), and alcoholic beverages (1.8%).

In 1996 Grenada's imports were distributed among the following categories:

Consumer goods	17.2%
Food	25.3%
Fuels	9.7%
Industrial supplies	25.7%
Machinery	13.2%
Transportation	8.9%
Other	0.1%

Principal trading partners in 1998 (in millions of US dollars) were as follows:

COUNTRY	EXPORTS	IMPORTS	BALANCE
United States	12	62	-50
Germany	4	2	2
St. Lucia	4	4	0
Trinidad and Tobago	3	84	-81
Netherlands	3	2	1
Barbados	2	8	-6
United Kingdom	1	15	-14
Venezuela	1	3	-2
Japan	n.a.	9	
China (inc. Hong Kong)	n.a.	2	

32BALANCE OF PAYMENTS

The adverse trade balance is generally offset by a flow of remittances from migrant groups abroad and by tourist expenditures.

The US Central Intelligence Agency reports that in 1997 the purchasing power parity of Grenada's exports was $22 million while imports totaled $166.5 million resulting in a trade balance of -$144.5 million.

The International Monetary Fund (IMF) reports that in 1996 Grenada had exports of goods totaling $25 million and imports totaling $148 million. The services credit totaled $107 million and debit $46 million. The following table summarizes Grenada's balance of payments for 1996 in millions of US dollars.

Current Account		-58
Balance on goods	-123	
Balance on services	61	
Balance on income	-16	
Current transfers	19	
Capital Account		29
Financial Account		26
Direct investment abroad	...	
Direct investment in Grenada	18	
Portfolio investment assets	...	
Portfolio investment liabilities	-1	
Other investment assets	9	
Other investment liabilities	...	
Net Errors and Omissions		3
Reserves and Related Items		-

33BANKING AND SECURITIES

Local financial institutions include the National Commercial Bank of Grenada, the Grenada Bank of Commerce, the Grenada Development Bank, and the Grenada Cooperative Bank. Foreign banks include Barclays Bank and the Bank of Nova Scotia. In 1992, Republic Bank Limited of Trinidad and Tobago bought 51% of the National Commercial Bank. There is no stock exchange.

Grenada is a member of the Organization of Eastern Caribbean States (OECS), and a member of the Eastern Caribbean Central Bank (ECCB), which is headquartered in St. Christopher and Nevis. Grenada's finances are bound by the ECCB's general guidelines on money supply and bank regulation

and the currency is the Eastern Caribbean dollar, which is pegged to the US dollar at a constant exchange rate of EC$2.70:$1.

34INSURANCE

There are a number of international firms (mainly UK, US, and Canadian) and some local interests doing business in Grenada. A full range of life and nonlife insurance is available. There were at least nine insurance companies operating in Grenada in 2000.

35PUBLIC FINANCE

Main sources of revenue are export and import duties, income tax, estate duties, and various internal rates, licenses, and taxes. The 1986 Fiscal Reform Program replaced a number of taxes, including a personal income tax, with a VAT of 20% on certain consumer goods. In 1999, the government decided to double its expenditure on infrastructure projects, including airport expansion, the creation of a new port, and road construction.

The US Central Intelligence Agency (CIA) estimates that in 1997 Grenada's central government took in revenues of approximately $85.8 million and had expenditures of $102.1 million including capital expenditures of $28 million. Overall, the government registered a deficit of approximately $16.3 million. External debt totaled $78 million.

The following table shows an itemized breakdown of government revenues and expenditures. The percentages were calculated from data reported by the International Monetary Fund. The dollar amounts (millions) are based on the CIA estimates provided above.

REVENUE AND GRANTS	100%	85.8
Tax revenue	76.0%	65
Non-tax revenue	7.1%	6
Capital revenue	7.3%	6
Grants	9.5%	8
EXPENDITURES	100%	102.1
General public services	12.3%	13
Defense	0.0%	0
Public order and safety	10.0%	10
Education	16.8%	17
Health	10.4%	11
Social security	8.6%	9
Housing and community amenities	2.1%	2
Recreation, cultural, and religious affairs	2.1%	2
Economic affairs and services	28.4%	29
Other expenditures	2.1%	2
Interest payments	7.0%	7

36TAXATION

Corporate taxes are levied on net profits at a rate of 30% on the first US$50,000 and 40% on the remainder. A debt service levy is payable on salaries over US$12,000 per year at a rate of 10%. VAT ranges from 5% on most services to 15% on locally manufactured products.

37CUSTOMS AND DUTIES

All imports are subject to a general or preferential tariff, as well as a fixed package tax. Grenada adopted the CARICOM community CET in 1991, which ranged up to 35% in 2000. Capital equipment is exempt from tariffs.

38FOREIGN INVESTMENT

Since independence, the government has sought to attract foreign investment for industrial development, especially the processing of local agricultural commodities for export. Grenada offers incentive competitive with other Caribbean nations and gives high priority to foreign investment that is either 100% foreign owned or joint venture with nationals.

There are no free trade zones in the country, but generous investment incentive packages are available, including a tax holiday of up to 15 years. There has been a considerable amount of foreign investment in the country's hotel sector. The government planned to issue 10 additional licenses for the telephone industry by year end 1997. In addition, a $75 million hotel was being built by the famous Ritz chain. Most foreign investment during the 1990s came in the form of infrastructure construction projects related to the tourism industry.

39ECONOMIC DEVELOPMENT

Government policy has aimed toward sustained development of agriculture and tourism as the prime sectors of the economy, with respect to both employment and foreign exchange earnings. Import substitution has been the focal point of the agricultural development plan. The PRG is committed to nationalizing agriculture and turned the large estates that had belonged to former Prime Minister Gairy into cooperative farms.

Following the 1984 election, the Blaize government reversed the trend toward state control and embarked on an economic policy that encouraged private sector participation and modified the fiscal system to encourage economic growth. The establishment of the Industrial Development Corporation and of the National Economic Council early in 1985 were essential components of the new policy, as was the privatizing of 18 state enterprises. The tax structure was modified in 1986 to offer incentives to the private sector.

Economic growth is expected to remain at around 5%, based on new foreign investment. Tourism is expected to pick up as new hotels are built. The government is expanding its cargo ports to handle the growing volume of cargo.

40SOCIAL DEVELOPMENT

A National Insurance Scheme, introduced on 4 April 1983, provides old age, disability, survivor, health, and maternity benefits to workers; it is financed by wage contributions of 5% from employers and 4% from workers. The retirement age is 60 for both men and women, and pensions equal 30% of average earnings. Survivor pensions total 75% of the pension of the insured. A funeral grant is also provided, amounting to E.C. $2,000 in 1999.

A National Child Care Committee coordinates services for children. An increase in child abuse cases was reported in 1999, in addition, many cases go unreported. The law mandates harsh penalties for both child and spousal abuse. Although Grenadian law imposes a 15-year sentence for rape, women's rights advocates claim that most cases of rape and abuse go unreported. Working women also earn less than men on average. As of 1999, 4 of 15 members of Parliament were women.

Human rights organizations operate freely in Grenada. Flogging is a legal form of punishment, although it is rarely used in practice. There were no reports of police brutality in 1999.

41HEALTH

Grenada is divided into 7 medical districts, each headed by a medical officer. Grenada General Hospital in St. George's and two other general hospitals (one on Carriacou and one in St. Andrews) have a combined total of 340 beds (1998). Other hospital facilities include an 80-bed mental hospital (rebuilt after being severely damaged in the 1983 invasion) and a nursing home with 120 beds. There are 36 health centers, which provide primary care. In 1998, there were 50 doctors and 173 nurse/midwives.

In 1996, the infant mortality rate was 14 per 1,000 live births, and life expectancy averaged 71 years for both women and men in 1998. The total fertility rate was 3.2 children per woman during her childbearing years. In 1997, 92% of the country's children were immunized against measles. Malaria has virtually been eradicated and a program to eradicate yellow fever mosquito is making progress.

In 1996, there were 76 new cases of AIDS reported.

42HOUSING

The Grenada Housing Authority is a government agency empowered to acquire land and construct low-income housing projects. All main population centers have been supplied with sewerage and piped-water facilities; in the mid-1980s, about three-fourths of the population had access to potable water. In the early 1980s, the latest point for which information is available, some 90% of all dwellings were detached houses. Nearly 75% of all housing units were owner occupied, 14% were rented, and 9% were occupied rent free. The most common construction material for homes was wood (70%), followed by concrete (12%), and wood and brick combined (7%).

43EDUCATION

Grenada's educational system is modeled largely on the British educational system. Education is free and compulsory for children between the ages of 5 and 16. Primary education lasts for seven years and secondary education for five years. In 1993, there were 22,345 students and 963 teachers at the primary level, with a student-to-teacher ratio of 23 to one. Secondary schools had a total of 10,213 students and 377 teachers in that same year.

Postsecondary institutions include T.A. Marryshow Community College, Grenada National College, Technical and Vocational Institute, the Teacher Training College, and the Institute for Further Education. St. George's University Medical School, a private US institution founded in 1977, provides medical training for students from other countries, the majority from the U.S. Illiteracy is low in Grenada, with an adult literacy rate at an estimated 91%.

44LIBRARIES AND MUSEUMS

The Grenada Public Library is headquartered in St. George's and has three other branches with a total, in 2000, of 60,000 volumes. The St. George's University Medical School maintains a collection of 6,000 volumes. There is also a mobile library that visits the island's schools. The Grenada National Museum, founded in 1976, is located in St. George's and focuses on the history and archeology of the island.

45MEDIA

A local automatic telephone system covers the island, with connections to Carriacou. In 1995, there were about 20,100 telephone lines. Radio and television services are provided by Radio Grenada and Grenada television. There is 1 AM radio station, no FM station, and 2 television stations as of 1999. In 1997, there were 817 radios and 306 television sets in use per 1,000 population.

There are four weekly newspapers and several newspapers publishing irregularly. The most popular weeklies are *The Informer* (1995 circulation, 5,000), *Grenada Today* (4,500), and *The Grenadian Voice* (3,500).

The constitution provides for free speech and press, and the government is said to uphold these rights.

[46]ORGANIZATIONS

Grenada has chapters of a number of international social and professional organizations, including a Chamber of Industry and Commerce, Lions Club, and Rotary Club. Boy Scouts and Girl Guides are available to youths.

[47]TOURISM, TRAVEL, AND RECREATION

Tourism, although modest in relation to that of other Caribbean islands, was a major enterprise for Grenada before the 1979 coup and 1983 invasion. Since 1984, it has recovered rapidly, and the government is emphasizing development of the tourist infrastructure. There has also been substantial foreign investment in the hotel sector. Since 1989, American Airlines nonstop service to Grenada has boosted tourism significantly. Tourist arrivals numbered 111,000 in 1997 and tourism revenues were US$59 million. There were 1,175 hotel rooms with a 62% occupancy rate as of that year. Grenada offers the visitor a wide array of white sand beaches and excellent sailing. Two yacht harbors provide port and customs facilities. A valid passport is required for entry into Grenada, except for citizens of the UK, the US, and Canada who have two documents proving citizenship. Visas are not required by visitors from North America, the UK, France, Germany, and certain other countries.

In 1999, the UN estimated the cost of staying in Grenada at $296 per day between December and April. At other times of the year daily expenses were approximately $226.

[48]FAMOUS GRENADIANS

Theophilus Albert Marryshow (1889–1958) is known throughout the British Caribbean as "the Father of Federation." Eric Matthew Gairy (b.1922), a labor leader, became the first prime minister of independent Grenada in 1974. Maurice Bishop (1944–83) ousted Gairy in 1979 and held power as prime minister until his assassination. After the US-led invasion, the task of choosing an interim government fell to the governor-general, Sir Paul Scoon (b.1935). Herbert A. Blaize (1919–89) was elected prime minister in 1984; he was Grenada's first chief minister (1957) and its first premier (1967).

[49]DEPENDENCIES

Carriacou (34 sq km/13 sq mi), Petit Martinique, and several other islands of the Grenadines group are dependencies of Grenada.

[50]BIBLIOGRAPHY

Beck, Robert J. *The Grenada Invasion: Politics, Law, and Foreign Policy Decision Making*. Boulder, Colo.: Westview, 1993.

Brizan, George. *Grenada, Island of Conflict—From Amerindians to People's Revolution, 1498–1979*. London: Zed Books, 1984.

The Grenada Documents. London: Sherwood Press, 1987.

Heine, Jorge (ed.). *A Revolution Aborted: The Lessons of Grenada*. Pittsburgh, Penn.: University of Pittsburgh Press, 1990.

Lewis, Gordon K. *Grenada: The Jewel Despoiled*. Baltimore: Johns Hopkins University Press, 1987.

MacDonald, Scott B., Harald M. Sandstrom, and Paul B. Goodwin, Jr. (eds.) *The Caribbean after Grenada: Revolution, Conflict, and Democracy*. New York: Praeger, 1988.

Meeks, Brian. *Caribbean Revolutions and Revolutionary Theory: An Assessment of Cuba, Nicaragua, and Grenada*. London: Macmillan Caribbean, 1993.

Schoenhals, Kai P. *Grenada*. Santa Barbara, Calif.: Clio, 1990.

GUATEMALA

Republic of Guatemala
República de Guatemala

CAPITAL: Guatemala City.

FLAG: The national flag consists of a white vertical stripe between two blue vertical stripes with the coat of arms centered in the white band.

ANTHEM: *Himno Nacional*, beginning "Guatemala feliz" ("Happy Guatemala").

MONETARY UNIT: The quetzal (Q) is a paper currency of 100 centavos. There are coins of 1, 5, 10, and 25 centavos, and notes of 50 centavos and 1, 5, 10, 20, 50, and 100 quetzales. Q1 = $0.12788 (or $1 = Q7.820) as of 31 March 2000. US notes are widely accepted.

WEIGHTS AND MEASURES: The metric system is the legal standard, but some imperial and old Spanish units are also used.

HOLIDAYS: New Year's Day, 1 January; Epiphany, 6 January; Labor Day, 1 May; Anniversary of the Revolution of 1871, 30 June; Independence Day, 15 September; Columbus Day, 12 October; Revolution Day, 20 October; All Saints' Day, 1 November; Christmas, 25 December. Movable religious holidays include Holy Thursday, Good Friday, and Holy Saturday.

TIME: 6 AM = noon GMT.

¹LOCATION, SIZE, AND EXTENT

Situated in Central America, Guatemala has an area of 108,890 sq km (42,043 sq mi), with a maximum length of 457 km (284 mi) NNW–SSE and a maximum width of 428 km (266 mi) ENE–WSW. Comparatively, the area occupied by Guatemala is slightly smaller than the state of Tennessee. It is bounded on the E by Belize, Amatique Bay, and the Caribbean Sea, on the SE by Honduras and El Salvador, on the S by the Pacific Ocean, and on the W and N by Mexico, with a total boundary length of 2,087 km (1,297 mi).

Guatemala has long laid claim to territory held by Belize (formerly known as British Honduras). In 1821, upon achieving independence, Guatemala considered itself the rightful inheritor of this former Spanish possession and continued to regard Belize as an administrative adjunct of Guatemala. In 1859, British rights to the area were defined in a treaty with Guatemala, but, alleging that the UK had not fulfilled its obligations, Guatemala subsequently refused to recognize the British title. In mid-1975, Guatemala demanded the cession of one-fourth of the territory of Belize as a condition for recognizing that country's sovereignty. When Belize did become independent in September 1981, Guatemala refused to recognize the new nation. In January 1983, the Guatemalan government announced that it would drop its sovereignty claim and would press instead for the cession of the southernmost fifth of Belize's territory. Guatemala's claim has been rejected not only by the UK and Belize but also by the UN General Assembly and, in November 1982, at the CARICOM heads of government conference. In mid-1986, Guatemala and the UK reestablished consular and commercial relations.

Guatemala's capital city, Guatemala City, is located in the southcentral part of the country.

²TOPOGRAPHY

A tropical plain averaging 48 km (30 mi) in width parallels the Pacific Ocean. From it, a piedmont region rises to altitudes of from 90 to 1,370 m (300 to 4,500 ft). Above this region lies nearly two-thirds of the country, in an area stretching northwest and southwest and containing volcanic mountains, the highest of which is Mt. Tajumulco (4,211 m/13,816 ft). The larger towns and Lake Atitlán are located in basins at elevations of about 1,500 to 2,400 m (5,000 to 8,000 ft). To the north of the volcanic belt lie the continental divide and, still farther north, the Atlantic lowlands. Three deep river valleys—the Motagua, the Polochic, and the Sarstún—form the Caribbean lowlands and banana plantation area. North of it, occupying part of the peninsula of Yucatán, is the lowland forest of Petén, once the home of the Mayas. The largest lakes are Izabal, Petén Itza, and Atitlán.

Of some 30 volcanoes in Guatemala, 6 have erupted or been otherwise active in recent years. A catastrophic earthquake in February 1976 left nearly 23,000 dead, 70,000 injured, and 1 million people whose homes were partially or completely destroyed.

³CLIMATE

Temperature varies with altitude. The average annual temperature on the coast ranges from 25° to 30°C (77° to 86°F); in the central highlands the average is 20°C (68°F), and in the higher mountains 15°C (59°F). In Guatemala City, the average January minimum is 11°C (52°F) and the maximum 23°C (73°F); the average minimum and maximum temperatures in July are, respectively, 16°C (61°F) and 26°C (79°F). The rainy season extends from May to October inland and to December along the coast, and the dry season from November (or January) to April. Because of its consistently temperate climate, Guatemala has been called the "Land of Eternal Spring."

⁴FLORA AND FAUNA

Flowers of the temperate zone are found in great numbers. Of particular interest is the orchid family, which includes the white nun *(monja blanca)*, the national flower. There is also an abundance of medicinal, industrial, and fibrous plants.

Indigenous fauna includes the armadillo, bear, coyote, deer, fox, jaguar, monkey, puma, tapir, and manatee. The national bird is the highland quetzal, the symbol of love of liberty, which reputedly dies in captivity. Lake Atitlán is the only place in the world where a rare flightless waterbird, the Atitlán (giant pied-billed) grebe, is found; this species, classified as endangered, has been protected by law since 1970. There are more than 900 other species of native birds, as well as migratory varieties. Reptiles, present in more than 204 species, include the bushmaster, fer-de-lance, water moccasin, and iguana.

[5]ENVIRONMENT

Guatemala's main environmental problems are deforestation—over 50% of the nation's forests have been destroyed since 1890—and consequent soil erosion. As recently as 1993, the nation obtained 90% of its energy from wood, losing 40,000-60,000 hectares of forest per year. Between 1965 and 1990, Guatemala also lost over 30% of its mangrove area, which totaled 16,000 hectares in the early 1990. The nation's water supply is at risk due to industrial and agricultural toxins. Guatemala has 27.8 cu mi of water with 74% used for agriculture and 17% used in farming activity. Fifty-seven percent of the people living in rural areas do not have access to pure water, compared with 8% of urban dwellers. Guatemala's cities produce 0.7 million tons of solid waste per year, which, together with thousands of tons of fertilizer annually, contribute to the pollution of the nation's soil. United Nations sources show that environmental contamination is responsible for a significant number of deaths due to respiratory and digestive illnesses. Despite the establishment in 1975 of a ministerial commission charged with conserving and improving the human environment, coordination of antipollution efforts remains inadequate, and Guatemala still suffers from a lack of financial resources and well-trained personnel to implement environmental control programs.

In 1994, 12.2% of Guatemala's total land area was protected. In the same year, 10 of Guatemala's 174 animal species and 10 in a total of 900 bird species were considered endangered. Four types of reptiles in a total of 204 and 282 plant species of 8,000 were threatened with extinction. Endangered or extinct species in Guatemala include the horned guan, Eskimo curlew, California least tern, green sea turtle, hawksbill turtle, olive ridley turtle, spectacled caiman, American crocodile, and Morelet's crocodile.

[6]POPULATION

The population of Guatemala in 2000 was estimated at 12,669,576. An estimated 3.4% of the population is 65 years of age or older. The projected population for the year 2005 is 14,423,000, assuming a crude birthrate of 33 per 1,000 population and a death rate of 6, resulting in a natural rate of change of 2.7% for the period 2000–2005. The population rate of change between 1995 and 2000 was 2.8%. The population density in 1998 was 100 per sq km (259 per sq mi).

Most of the people live in the southern third of the country. It was estimated that 40% of the population lived in urban areas in 2000, up from 37% in 1980. The capital and largest city, Guatemala City, had a 2000 metropolitan population of 2,697,000.

Other large cities are Escuintla, 63,471, and Quezaltenango, 93,439. Guatemala's next census is scheduled to take place in 2003.

[7]MIGRATION

Because of persecution and civil war, Amerindian peasants began emigrating across the Mexican border in 1981. Under the CIREFCA plan (International Conference on Central American Refugees), 18,000 Guatemalans repatriated between 1989 and 1994. In 1995, 9,500 repatriated from Mexico, and in 1996, another 3,974 repatriated from Mexico. As of May 1997, there were still 40,000 in Mexico and Belize. Between 1984, when the first repatriation movements took place, and July 1999, a total of 43,663 refugees had returned to more than 160 communities throughout Guatemala. The Guatemalan government spent some $30 million on 36 farms purchased for collective returns. In 1999, the net migration rate was -1.93 migrants per 1,000 population.

[8]ETHNIC GROUPS

Guatemala has a larger proportion of Amerindians in its total population than any other country in Central America. In 1998 this figure was estimated at 44%. About one-half of this number were members of various communities descended from the Maya-Quiché ethnolinguistic group. Persons of mixed Amerindian and Spanish ancestry, called mestizos, constituted about 56% of the national total. Amerindians who have become assimilated and no longer adhere to a traditional Amerindian life-style are also called ladinos, but this term is sometimes used to refer to mestizos. Blacks and mulattoes inhabit the Caribbean lowlands. The white population is estimated at less than 1% of the total.

[9]LANGUAGES

Spanish, spoken by some 60% of the population, is the official and commercial language. Amerindians speak some 28 dialects in five main language groups: Quiché, Mam, Pocomam, and Chol—all of the Mayan language family—and Carib. Amerindian languages are spoken by about 40% of the populace.

[10]RELIGIONS

The constitution guarantees religious freedom. Roman Catholicism is the predominant religion (60%), with an archbishopric at Guatemala City and bishoprics at Quezaltenango, Verapaz, and Huehuetenango. Many inhabitants combine Christian beliefs with traditional Amerindian rites.

Protestant churches were estimated to have fewer than 500,000 adherents in 1980, but rapidly growing fundamentalist groups increased the number of Protestants to some 40% of the population in 1998, most of whom belong to Assembly of God churches. During the civil war in the early 1980s, the government allied itself with conservative Protestant groups and accused the Catholic Church of helping the leftist guerrillas. The regime's relationship with the Church worsened when Gen. José Efraín Ríos Montt refused to listen to the Vatican's plea for clemency for six alleged subversives condemned to death by secret tribunals in March 1983 and let them be executed a few days before the visit of Pope John Paul II to Guatemala. While in Guatemala, the Pope explicitly referred to the discrimination and injustice the Amerindians had suffered.

Minority groups and religions with small communities include Mormons, Jehovah's Witnesses, Jews, and Muslims.

[11]TRANSPORTATION

In 1999, the total length of Guatemala's road system was estimated at 13,100 km (8,140 mi), of which 3,616 km (2,247 mi) was paved, including 140 km (87 mi) of expressways. In 1995, about 102,000 passenger cars and 96,800 commercial vehicles were registered. Two international highways cross Guatemala: the 824-km (512-mi) Franklin D. Roosevelt Highway (part of the Pan American Highway system) and the Pacific Highway. Guatemala Railways operates 90% of the 884 km (549 mi) of narrow-gauge railway.

Few of the rivers and lakes are important to commercial navigation. Puerto Barrios and Santo Tomás on the Caribbean

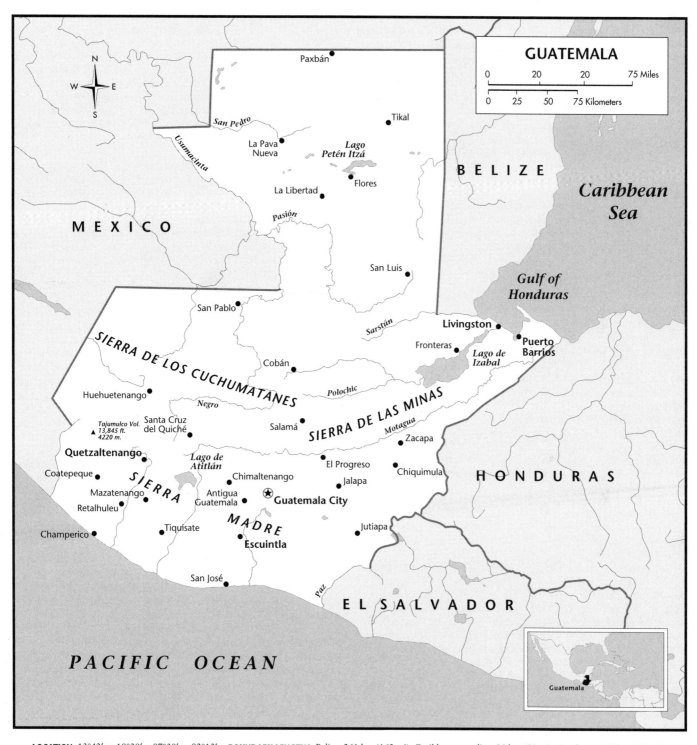

GUATEMALA

MEXICO

BELIZE

Caribbean Sea

Gulf of Honduras

HONDURAS

EL SALVADOR

PACIFIC OCEAN

Paxbán

Tikal

La Pava Nueva

Lago Petén Itzá

Flores

La Libertad

San Pedro

Usumacinta

Pasión

San Luis

San Pablo

Sarstún

Livingston

Fronteras

Puerto Barrios

Lago de Izabal

Cobán

Polochic

SIERRA DE LOS CUCHUMATANES

Huehuetenango

Negro

Tajumulco Vol. ▲ *13,845 ft. 4220 m.*

Santa Cruz del Quiché

Salamá

SIERRA DE LAS MINAS

Motagua

Zacapa

Quetzaltenango

Lago de Atitlán

El Progreso

Chiquimula

Coatepeque

SIERRA

Chimaltenango

Jalapa

Mazatenango

Antigua Guatemala

⊛ **Guatemala City**

Retalhuleu

MADRE

Champerico

Tiquisate

Jutiapa

Escuintla

San José

Paz

Guatemala

LOCATION: 13°42′ to 18°30′N; 87°30′ to 92°13′W. **BOUNDARY LENGTHS:** Belize, 261 km (162 mi); Caribbean coastline, 85 km (53 mi); Honduras, 248 km (154 mi); El Salvador, 167 km (104 mi); Pacific coastline, 245 km (152 mi); Mexico, 925 km (575 mi). **TERRITORIAL SEA LIMIT:** 12 mi.

coast are Guatemala's chief ports; the Pacific coast ports are Champerico and San José. In 1998, Guatemala had no registered cargo ships.

There were an estimated 478 airports in 1998, but only 12 had paved runways. La Aurora Airport at Guatemala City, the first air terminal in Central America, serves aircraft of all sizes, including jumbo jets. The government-owned Aviateca has a monopoly on scheduled domestic service and also flies to other Central American countries, Jamaica, Mexico, and the US. In

1998, 508,000 passengers were carried on scheduled domestic and international flights.

12HISTORY

Three distinct stages—Mayan indigenous, Spanish colonial, and modern republican—have left their mark on the history of Guatemala. These separate ways of life persist, but are slowly merging.

Guatemala includes much of the old Mayan civilization, which may date back as early as 300 BC. The classical Mayan period lasted from about AD 300 to 900 and featured highly developed architecture, painting, sculpture, music, mathematics (including the use of zero), a 365-day calendar, roads, and extensive trade. This great pre-Columbian civilization seems to have collapsed around AD 900, and by the 12th century, the Mayas had disintegrated into a number of separate Amerindian groups. The Amerindians offered resistance to the Spanish expedition sent by Hernán Cortés from Mexico and led by Pedro de Alvarado during 1523–24, but by the end of that time, their subjugation to Spain was virtually complete.

Alvarado founded the first Guatemalan capital, Santiago de los Caballeros de Guatemala, in 1524. Because of several earthquakes, the capital was moved a number of times until it became permanently established at Guatemala City in 1776. From 1524 until 1821, Guatemala (City and Province) was the center of government for the captaincy-general of Guatemala, whose jurisdiction extended from Yucatán to Panama. Economically, this was mainly an agricultural and pastoral area in which Amerindian labor served a colonial landed aristocracy. The Roman Catholic religion and education regulated the social life of the capital. Spanish political and social institutions were added to Amerindian village life and customs, producing a hybrid culture.

In 1821, the captaincy-general won its independence from Spain. After a brief inclusion within the Mexican Empire of Agustín de Iturbide (1822–23), Guatemala, along with present-day Costa Rica, El Salvador, Honduras, and Nicaragua, formed the United Provinces of Central America in 1824. This federation endured until 1838–39. Guatemala proclaimed its independence in 1839 under the military rule of Rafael Carrera, an illiterate dictator with imperial designs. None of his ambitions were realized, and he died in 1865.

Guatemala then fell under a number of military governments, which included three notable administrations: Justo Rufino Barrios (1871–85), the "Reformer," who was responsible for Guatemala's transition from the colonial to the modern era; Manuel Estrada Cabrera (1898–1920), whose early encouragement of reform developed later into a lust for power; and Jorge Ubico (1931–44), who continued and elaborated on the programs begun by Barrios.

Guatemalan politics changed with the election of reform candidate Juan José Arévalo Bermejo in 1945. Arévalo's popularity marked one of the first mass-based movements in Guatemalan politics. In 1951, Jacobo Árbenz Guzmán was elected. Following Arévalo's approach to land reform, Árbenz expropriated holdings of the United Fruit Co., a US firm. The US alleged communist influence within the Árbenz government, and began mobilizing opposition against him. In the summer of 1954, Col. Carlos Castillo Armas and an army of Guatemalan exiles, backed by the CIA, invaded Guatemala from Honduras and toppled Árbenz. Castillo took over, restored expropriated properties, and ruled by decree until he was assassinated by a presidential palace guard in July 1957.

After a period of confusion, Gen. Miguel Ydígoras Fuentes became president in January 1958. His administration was essentially a military dictatorship, even though he claimed to follow democratic principles. He was particularly hard on his domestic critics, denouncing them as communists. He was equally bombastic on the international stage, denouncing the US, quarreling with Mexico over fishing rights, and challenging the UK over Belize. He was also contemptuous of Fidel Castro, and allowed Guatemala to be a training area for the exiles in the abortive US invasion of the Bay of Pigs in April 1961.

In March 1963, Ydígoras was overthrown by Defense Minister Col. Enrique Peralta Azurdia, who declared a state of siege. For two years, Peralta ruled dictatorially, and continued to assert Guatemala's claims on Belize. In September 1965, the Peralta regime announced a new constitution and elections, and in March 1966, Dr. Julio César Méndez Montenegro was elected president. He was the first civilian president since Árbenz, and would be the last for some time. During his term, the army and right-wing counterterrorists proceeded to kill hundreds of guerrillas, who were believed to be sponsored by Cuba, and claimed destruction of the guerrilla organization by the end of 1967. Uprooted from the countryside, the guerrillas concentrated their efforts on the capital, where, in 1968, guerrillas assassinated US Ambassador John G. Mein.

Guatemala returned to military rule as Col. Carlos Arana Osorio was elected president in 1970. He instituted the country's first comprehensive development plan, but the plan was upset by guerrilla violence, which now engulfed the country. Ambassador Karl von Spreti of the Federal Republic of Germany (FRG) was murdered in April 1970 by leftists. Many prominent Guatemalans were killed or held for ransom. In response to the violence, Arana suspended civil liberties from November 1970 to November 1971. In 1974, Arana's candidate, Gen. Kjell Laugerud García, was confirmed by Congress as president, after an election marred by charges of fraud. Laugerud followed a centrist policy and obtained a measure of popular support. During his tenure, guerrilla violence decreased, and some political liberties were restored. The principal challenge to Laugerud's administration was the need to rebuild Guatemala after the catastrophic earthquake of February 1976.

A militant rightist, Gen. Fernando Romeo Lucas García, was elected president in 1978. As guerrilla violence continued, there was also an upsurge of activity by right-wing "death squads," which, according to unofficial Guatemalan sources, committed over 3,250 murders in 1979 and even more during 1980. In addition, hundreds of Amerindians were reportedly massacred during antiguerrilla operations. The Carter administration objected to Guatemala's deteriorating human rights record, whereupon the military charged that communist influence had reached the White House.

In January 1981, the main guerrilla groups united and escalated while the government went into crisis. The elections of March 1982 were won by Laugerud's handpicked candidate, Gen. Angel Aníbal Guevara. Three weeks later, a coup placed in power a "born-again" Protestant, Gen. José Efraín Ríos Montt. After his month-long amnesty offer to the guerrillas was rejected, he declared a state of siege in July, and the antiguerrilla campaign intensified. The government's counter-insurgency killed between 2,600 and 6,000 in 1982, and drove up to a million Guatemalans from their homes by the end of 1983. In March 1983, Ríos lifted the state of siege and announced that elections for a constituent assembly would be held in July 1984. But Ríos, who had fought off some 10 coup attempts during his administration, was overthrown in August 1983.

The new government of Brig. Gen. Oscar Humberto Mejía Victores declared that the coup was undertaken to end "abuses by religious fanatics" and pledged continued efforts to eradicate the "virus of Marxism-Leninism." Elections for a constituent assembly were held, as promised, in July 1984. In May 1985, the assembly promulgated a constitution for a new government with an elected Congress. The general elections of November 1985 were followed by a runoff election in December. The overwhelming winner was Mario Vincio Cerezo Arévalo of the Guatemalan Christian Democratic Party (DCG). He also brought a majority into Congress.

Political violence decreased under Cerezo, who withstood two attempted coups. But he was unable to make any progress on human rights in Guatemala, and was unwilling to risk prosecution of military personnel who had been the most serious violators. As the economy worsened, political instability increased, including violence.

The elections of 11 November 1990 necessitated a runoff election, which was won by Jorge Serrano of the Movement for Solidarity and Action (Movimiento para Acción y Solidaridad—MAS). Serrano's inauguration in January 1991 marked the first transition in memory from one elected civilian government to another. Serrano promised to negotiate with insurgents and bring to justice both corrupt former officials and human rights violators.

But Serrano overplayed his hand politically. On 25 May 1993 Serrano declared a state of emergency and suspended the constitution. A week later, the military intervened and removed Serrano from office. It then restored the constitution and allowed Congress to select Serrano's successor. This unusual service of the military in defense of democracy led to the naming of Ramior de León Carpio as president on 5 June. De León, a human rights advocate, promised to bring to justice those responsible for the dismal state of human rights in Guatemala. He also proposed reductions in the military, which predictably were not well-received by the officer corps.

On 29 December 1996, under the government of Alvaro Arzu, the Guatemalan government signed a peace accord with the guerilla Guatemalan National Revolutionary Unity. This signaled the end of Central America's longest-running guerilla war. Peace came in phases beginning with an informal ceasefire in March 1996, along with the signing of the socioeconomic accord. The latter had taken a year to negotiate and called for the government to raise its tax revenues from 8% to 12% of GDP and increase its spending in health, education, and housing. The last accord, signed in Mexico City in September 1996, called for legislative and judicial reforms. It also included a reassessment of the military's role, as the parties agreed to remove the army from public security functions and to annul the law that provided for the Civil Defense Patrols established in the 1980s to fight guerillas in the highland villages.

In February 1999, the country's Historical Clarification Commission blamed the army for more than 90% of the deaths or disappearances of more than 200,000 Guatemalans during the 36-year civil war. In many instances, the army committed genocide against entire Mayan villages, the report concluded. The three-member commission blamed the United States government for supporting right-wing regimes even though it knew about the atrocities being committed by the army. An earlier report by the Catholic Church revealed similar findings. During a short visit to Guatemala in March 1999, US President Bill Clinton said his country had been wrong for supporting the Guatemalan army. He pledged to support the peace process. In May, the peace process suffered a setback when Guatemalans rejected 50 key constitutional reforms that would have diminished the role of the army and given protection and recognition to Amerindian languages and traditional customs, in a vote in which only about 20% of Guatemalans took part. In November of 1999, Alfonso Portillo, a populist lawyer, captured 47.8% of the vote in the presidential election, not enough to prevent a runoff election, held a month later. Portillo, a member of the conservative Guatemalan Republican Front (FRG), was a controversial candidate. During his campaign, he confirmed reports that he had killed two men in the Mexican state of Guerrero and had fled to avoid prosecution in 1982. Portillo said the killings were in self-defense and that he left because he could not have gotten a fair trial. He was also criticized for close ties to former dictator Gen. José Efraín Ríos Montt, whose 17-month regime in 1982–83 was blamed for some of the worst atrocities against Amerindians. Ríos Montt, as FRG's secretary general, worked closely with Portillo. The populist attorney built support with promises to reduce crime, one of the worst problems facing the nation after

the war. Crime was rampant throughout the nation, with dramatic increases in murders, kidnappings, and armed robbery. Portillo also promised to aid the poor and curb unemployment, a message that did not go unheard in a nation where 64% of Guatemalans are unemployed or underemployed. In the December runoff election, Portillo captured 68.3% of the vote to win the presidency. His party captured 63 of 113 seats in Congress, while the conservative PAN won 37 seats. A leftist coalition captured 9 seats.

13 GOVERNMENT

Constitutionally, the Guatemalan government is defined as democratic and representative, and the new constitution that took effect on 14 January 1986 reaffirms that definition. Since the 1950s, however, civil disorder has often prompted the suspension of constitutional guarantees.

Guatemala is a republic. The president, who must be a native-born lay person at least 40 years old, is elected by direct vote for a four-year term and may not be reelected. The constitution calls for a popularly elected vice-president. The office of vice-president provides a guarantee of presidential succession in case of the death or disability of the chief executive. There is a five-member court of constitutionality, which officially advises the president. Its members are appointed, one each by the Supreme Court, Congress, the president, the University of San Carlos, and the bar association. The president, who has broad powers, appoints and is assisted by a cabinet. The cabinet members traditionally resign at the end of each year so that the president may choose a new cabinet. The president, who is also commander-in-chief of the armed forces, appoints most military officers, the 22 governors, and other important public and diplomatic officials. Presidential duties include preserving public order, proposing laws, and making an annual presentation of the budget.

The unicameral National Congress has 113 members elected to four-year terms. Ninety-one members are elected from departmental constituencies, while 22 are elected by proportional representation. In districts with a population over 200,000, an additional deputy is elected to represent each additional 100,000 inhabitants or fraction exceeding 50,000. In addition, at-large representatives are elected by proportional representation from lists submitted by each political party. Under the constitution, Congress imposes taxes, enacts the national budget, declares war and makes peace, and ratifies treaties and conventions proposed by the president. Congress elects the president of the judiciary and judges of the Supreme Court and courts of appeals. The president may veto congressional bills, but Congress may override by a two-thirds vote. All public officials must declare the amount of their incomes and property holdings before assuming their posts and after they leave office.

Citizenship is acquired at the age of 18. Voting is obligatory for literate men and women 18 years of age and older and optional for nonliterate citizens.

14 POLITICAL PARTIES

Political power in Guatemala has been largely a matter of personal, rather than party, influence. Although parties have generally developed along conservative or liberal lines, political periods are commonly identified with the names of important leaders.

Under President Carlos Castillo Armas (1954–57), the Guatemalan Communist Party and other leftist parties were dissolved, and all other parties were temporarily suspended. To prevent further party proliferation, the membership necessary for party certification was raised from 10,000 to 50,000 in 1963. Only three parties were able to meet this requirement in time for the March 1966 elections: the Revolutionary Party (Partido Revolucionario—PR), a center-left party, the conservative Institutional

Democracy Party (Partido Institucional Democrático—PID), formed in 1965, and the militantly anticommunist National Liberation Movement (Movimiento de Liberación Nacional—MLN).

During the 1970s, these parties remained dominant. The MLN won the presidency in 1970, and an MLD-PID coalition took the 1974 election (which was ultimately decided in Congress), defeating Gen. José Efraín Ríos Montt, representing the leftist National Opposition Front, a coalition of the several parties, including the Christian Democrats (Partido de Democracía Cristiana Guatemalteca—DCG). In 1978, the PR and PID formed a center-right coalition. In the congressional voting, the MLN won 20 seats, the PID 17, the PR 14, the DCG 7, and other parties 3. In the presidential elections of March 1982, a coalition of the PR, PID, and the National Unity Front (Frente de Unidad Nacional—FUN), an extreme right-wing party formed in 1977, won a plurality of 38.9% of the vote. Congress endorsed the PR-PID-FUN candidate, Gen. Ángel Aníbal Guevara, as president, but he was deposed in a coup later in March. All parties were suspended by the new ruler, Gen. Ríos, but political activity resumed in March 1983. In the 1980s, the Christian Democrats grew significantly, winning the 1985 presidential and congressional elections. In addition, a host of new parties entered the political arena. Many had hopeful names suggesting national reconciliation, moderation, and solutions to Guatemala's problems. Among these were the National Union of the Center (Unión del Centro Nacional—UCN), the Democratic Party for National Cooperation (Partido Democrático de Cooperación Nacional—PDCN), the Solidarity Action Movement (Movimiento para Acción y Solidaridad—MAS), the National Advancement Plan (Plan por el Adelantamiento Nacional) and the National Authentic Center (Centro Auténtico Nacional).

The left-wing guerrilla movement is represented by the Guatemalan National Revolutionary Unity (Unidad Revolucionaria Nacional Guatemalteca—URNG). Founded in 1982, these groups consist of the Guerrilla Army of the Poor (Ejército Guerrillero de los Pobres—EGP), the Guatemalan Workers' (Communist) Party (Partido Guatemalteco del Trabajo—PGT), the Rebel Armed Forces (Fuerzas Armadas Rebeldes—FAR), and the Organization of the People in Arms (Organización del Pueblo en Armas—ORPA). During the 1999 elections, the leftists won nine seats in Congress. The main political parties in 1999 were the conservative Frente Republicano Guatemalteco and Partido de Avanzada Nacional; Frente had 63 seats in Congress and PAN had 37 seats.

15LOCAL GOVERNMENT
Guatemala is divided into 22 departments, plus Guatemala City, each with a governor appointed by the president. Municipalities are governed by a mayor and independent municipal councils whose officials are popularly elected for two-year terms.

16JUDICIAL SYSTEM
The Constitution of 1985 established an independent judiciary and a human rights ombudsman. Courts of ordinary jurisdiction are the nine-member Supreme Court, 10 courts of appeals, 33 civil courts of first instance, and 10 penal courts of first instance. There is also a Constitutional Court. Judges of the Supreme Court and courts of appeals are elected for four-year terms by the National Congress from lists prepared by active magistrates, the Bar Association and law school deans. Judges of first instance are appointed by the Supreme Court. Courts of private jurisdiction deal separately with questions involving labor, administrative litigation, conflicts of jurisdiction, military affairs, and other matters. An independent tribunal and office of accounts supervises financial matters of the nation, the municipalities, and state-supported institutions, such as the National University. A new

criminal procedural code affording stronger due process protections took effect in July 1994. Trials are public. Defendants have the rights to counsel, to be presumed innocent, and to be released on bail.

Because military courts retain control of military personnel who commit crimes while on official business, it has been difficult to pursue actions in civil court cases involving human rights abuses by the military.

17ARMED FORCES
The national armed forces (31,400 active and 35,000 reserves) are combined for administrative purposes, and the army provides logistical support to the navy and air force. A conscription law (30 months service) encourages recruitment. In 2000 the armed forces numbered 29,200 in the army, 1,500 in the navy, and 700 in the air force. The navy had 15 coastal patrol craft, and the air force had 10 combat aircraft and 12 armed helicopters of low readiness. The national police force of about 7,000 supplements the army in a national emergency. Defense expenditures amounted to $124 million (1998) or 0.7% of gross domestic product. A decree promulgated in December 1983 authorized military service for women.

To curb human rights abuses, the United States reduced its military assistance in the 1980s, sending no aid in 1983 and 1984. While the US ban was in effect, Israel emerged as an important supplier of arms to Guatemala.

18INTERNATIONAL COOPERATION
Guatemala is a charter member of the UN, having joined on 21 November 1945, and participates in ECLAC and all the nonregional specialized agencies. It is also a member of G-77, IADB, OAS, and the WTO, as well as the International Coffee Organization and many other inter-American and intergovernmental organizations. Guatemala was one of the countries that formed the Union of Banana-Exporting Countries in 1974, and it was the first country to ratify the agreement establishing the CACM. In August 1987, Guatemala signed the Central American peace plan outlined by Costa Rican President Oscar Arias Sánchez.

19ECONOMY
Since the Spanish conquest, the economy of Guatemala has depended on the export of one or two agricultural products. During the colonial period, indigo and cochineal were the principal exports, but the market for them was wiped out by synthetic dyes in the 1860s. Cocoa and essential oils quickly filled the void. Coffee and bananas were introduced later, and in 1999, the chief exports were coffee, sugar, and bananas. Guatemala's economy, the largest in Central America, is dominated by the private sector, which generates nearly 90% of GDP.

Since World War II, the government has encouraged light industrial production (such as tires, clothing and pharmaceuticals). Nevertheless, in 1995, agricultural pursuits occupied 58% of the national labor force and accounted for some two-thirds of Guatemalan foreign exchange earnings. Living standards and personal income remain low, and no significant domestic market exists, except for subsistence crops.

The economy boomed from 1971 thorough early 1974. Then, as a result of inflation (21.2% in 1973), the world energy crisis, and an annual population growth of 2.9%, the economic growth rate slowed from 7.6% for 1973 to 4.6% for 1974. During the second half of the 1970s, Guatemala's economic performance slowed further; during 1974–80, the average annual growth rate was 4.3%. By the early 1980s, the civil war, coupled with depressed world commodity prices, had led to decreases in export earnings and to foreign exchange shortages. The GDP dropped by 3.5% in 1982, the first decline in decades, and the GDP declined or was stagnant through 1986. The annual inflation rate, which averaged 11% during 1979–81, dropped to no more than 2% in 1982. It rose thereafter, reaching 31.5% in 1985 and about 40% in the first half of 1986.

In the 1990s the Guatemalan economy grew at a healthy pace, propelled by nontraditional exports and investment. Inflation was reduced through fiscal and monetary policies to an average of 12% in 1993. Economic growth accelerated to an estimated 5.0% in 1993 compared with 4.6% in 1992. In a sudden shift that was perceived as a recession by the private sector, GDP growth decelerated in 1996 to 3.1%. The slowdown reflected a combination of factors: windfall profits from coffee exports; a slowdown in most Central American countries causing a significant decline in Guatemalan exports, and a severe competition of domestic products by Mexican imports. In addition, domestic demand cooled off as private sector credit demand ran out of steam, and tax increases were designed to strengthen the fiscal situation ahead of the signing of the peace accords. Growth for 1997 had improved to 4% thanks to greater domestic and trade liberalization; despite Hurricane Mitch, which destroyed a large portion of the country's agricultural produce for the year, GDP growth reached 5% in 1998.

20INCOME

The US Central Intelligence Agency (CIA) reports that in 1998 Guatemala's gross domestic product (GDP) was estimated at $45.7 billion. The per capita GDP was estimated at $3,800. The annual growth rate of GDP was estimated at 5%. The average inflation rate in 1998 was 6.4%. The CIA defines GDP as the value of all final goods and services produced within a nation in a given year and computed on the basis of purchasing power parity (PPP) rather than value as measured on the basis of the rate of exchange. It was estimated that agriculture accounted for 24% of GDP, industry 21%, and services 55%.

Private consumption includes expenditures of individuals, households, and nongovernmental organizations. It was estimated that between 1990 and 1998 private consumption grew at an annual rate of 4.4%. The richest 10% of the population accounted for approximately 47% of household consumption and the poorest 10% approximately 0.6%.

21LABOR

Most of Guatemala's Amerindian population engages in subsistence agriculture and self-employed handicraft activity. In 1999, the economically active population numbered 3,489,000. As of 1995, it was divided among the following sectors: agriculture, 58%; industry, 14%; services, 14.4%; trade, 7%; construction, 4% and transportation and communications, 2.6%. As of 1995, some 1,400 persons were registered as unemployed.

The trade union movement was born at the end of World War II. Directed in part by foreign communist labor leaders and cultivated by a sympathetic administration, the labor movement grew in the next 10 years to a force claiming nearly 500 unions with 100,000 members. With the overthrow of the Árbenz government in 1954, however, the unions were dissolved. After slow reorganization, the trade unions numbered about 110 by 1974, but in 1979 and 1980, trade union activity was severely restricted. In 1992, the Labor Code of 1947 was amended to facilitate freedom of association, to strengthen the rights of working women, to increase penalties for violations of labor laws, and to enhance the role of the Labor Ministry and the courts in enforcement. There were approximately 1,300 registered unions with 2% of the work force as members in 1999. There were also about 400 company-sponsored "solidarity" organizations, with a total of approximately 170,000 members. Unions are independent of government and political party domination. Former President Cerezo was reputed to be an advocate of workers' rights, but in 1987, he enacted a new tax code without suggested modifications from the business community, whereupon he quickly lost the confidence of the private sector and attempted to blame retailers for the price increases caused by these policies. The labor code and social security system effectively cover less than one-fourth of the economically active population.

Workers have the right to strike, but it is weakened by legal restrictions and the force of tradition in a country where strikes were illegal until recently. Generally, the government has not intervened in strikes which it has declared illegal; it did not do so for strikes that were called in April and May of 1996 which the government denounced as illegal. But more forceful antistrike legislation passed in June of 1996 may encourage more active intervention by the government against illegal strikes.

Additionally, labor organizers report receiving telephone and mail threats and employers actively suppress union organization. Workers dismissed for union activity have little legal or administrative redress.

The workweek is statutorily recognized as being 44 hours long, but most workers work longer hours out of economic necessity. The minimum wage as of January 1999 was $2.53 per 8-hour day for industrial workers and $2.29 per day for agricultural workers.

22AGRICULTURE

In 1997, only about 17.5% of the total land area of Guatemala was used for the production of annual or perennial crops, although almost two-thirds is suitable for crop or pasture use. Agriculture contributes about 25% to GDP, makes up 75% of export earnings, and employs 50% of the labor force. The principal cash crops are coffee, sugar, bananas, and cotton, followed by hemp, essential oils, and cacao. Coffee is grown on highland plantations; most of the bananas are produced along the Atlantic coastal plain. Cash crop output in 1998 included 18,189,000 tons of sugarcane, 183,000 tons of coffee, 1,000 tons of cotton, and 720,000 tons of bananas. Subsistence crop production included 997,000 tons of corn and 84,000 tons of dry beans, along with rice, wheat, and fruits and vegetables. Nontraditional agricultural exports have greatly increased in recent years; such products include: lychee, rambutan, melon, papaya, mango, pineapple, broccoli, okra, snow peas, celery, cauliflower, asparagus, garlic, spices and nuts, and ornamental plants. Guatemala's trade surplus in agricultural products was $946.2 million in 1997.

An agrarian reform law of 1952 provided for government expropriation of unused privately owned agricultural lands, with the exception of farms of 91 hectares (225 acres) or less and those up to 273 hectares (675 acres) if two-thirds of the acreage was under cultivation. By 1954/55, 24,836 hectares (61,371 acres) had been distributed to 10,359 farmers. The law of 1952 was supplemented by an agrarian reform law of 1956, which aimed to distribute state-owned farms (fincas nacionales) to landless peasants. From 1954 to 1962, the government distributed 17,346 land titles. In 1962, the National Agrarian Improvement Institute was created to provide assistance to the new landowners and to improve their living standards. The government requires plantation owners to set aside land for the raising of subsistence crops for their tenants. An agrarian credit bank provides loans to small farmers. Some of the land farmed by Amerindians is held in common by groups of families and is never sold.

23ANIMAL HUSBANDRY

Consumption of dairy products and meat is low, despite improvements in stock raising and dairying. The wool industry in the western highlands supplies the famed Guatemalan weavers. Hog and poultry production is ample for domestic consumption. In 1998, there were 2,130,000 head of cattle, 826,000 hogs, 551,000 sheep, 118,000 horses, and 24,000,000 chickens.

Guatemala exports poultry, with 120,000 tons of poultry meat and 109,000 tons of eggs produced in 1998. Total cattle numbers continue to fall despite increased illegal imports from Honduras and a decline in illegal exports to Mexico. Depressed beef prices and rising production costs are the main causes of this trend.

24FISHING

Guatemalan waters are rich in fish, including shrimp, snapper, and tuna. The total catch in 1997 was 11,303 tons (up from 7,344 tons in 1991), nearly 40% of which came from inland waters.

25FORESTRY

Forests are among Guatemala's richest natural resources; they covered some 54% of the total land area in 1994, up from 43% in 1979. The forests in the Petén region yield cabinet woods, timber, extracts, oils, gums, and dyes. Mahogany, cedar, and balsam are important export products, and chicle for chewing gum is another important commodity. In 1997, 13,529,000 cu m of roundwood were produced, with 98% burned for fuel. Sawn wood production was 355,000 cu m that year. Imports of forestry products exceeded exports by $69.5 million in 1997.

26MINING

The principal commercial minerals are antimony, gold, iron ore, and lead. Limited mineral production was reported in 1997, including antimony and gold mined in the Huehuetenago District. Guatemala was the 3d largest producer of antimony in Latin America, after Bolivia and Mexico. Production, however, has steadily declined since the 1980s, totaling 600 tons in 1994 but rebounding to 880 tons in 1997. Large nickel deposits in the area of Lake Izabal, with an annual production capacity of 9,000 tons in 1997, have been developed by Exploraciones y Explotaciones Mineras Izabel S.A. (Eximbal). A nickel plant opened in 1977 but was closed down in 1981 because of falling sales, rising fuel costs, and burdensome taxation. Gold, which was mined from the colonial period until the early 20th century, is no longer a major export item, but is still mined; in 1997, about 30 kg was produced. Reported deposits of coal, iron, gold, copper, quartz, marble, manganese, sulfur, uranium, mica, and asbestos await exploitation. Marble is exported to Mexico and other nearby countries.

27ENERGY AND POWER

In 1998, net installed capacity was 974,000 kW; total production in that year reached 3,085 million kWh. Installations remain inadequate for the country's growing consumer needs. Guatemala City and more than 60% of the remainder of the country are supplied by a formerly US-owned firm, the Electric Co. of Guatemala, which was purchased by the government in 1972 for $17 million. Most of the capacity elsewhere is provided by the government-owned Electrification Institute. A major 300 MW hydroelectric plant on the Chixoy River, which came on stream late in 1985, accounts for about 60% of the total electrical capacity. The remainder is produced primarily by thermal plants, with the exception of a 15,000 kW geothermal plant at Zunil. The 1988 National Electrification Plan called for another 252,000 kW of capacity from hydroelectric plants to be built on the Bobos, Grande, Samala, and Serchil Rivers. The 120 MW San Jose power station, completed in 1999, is Central America's first coal-fired power plant.

Guatemala's principal petroleum resources lie in Alta Verapaz, Petén, Lake Izabal, and Amatique Bay, where much recent exploration has taken place. An intensive search for petroleum was carried out in 1975 near the Mexican border, and new deposits were discovered in 1981 in Alta Verapaz and the Petén basin. A pipeline between Rubelsanto and the Caribbean coastline was opened in 1981, but was attacked 17 times in 1991 by guerrillas. Production averaged 24,000 barrels per day in 1999. A combination of difficult geological conditions, guerrilla activity, poor infrastructure, and the low quality of Guatemala's oil have dissuaded most oil companies from investment. A Bahamian company, Basic Resources International, was the only company producing crude oil in 1991. Since 1983, however, oil legislation has been liberalized, and exploration activity has increased.

28INDUSTRY

Manufacturing and construction account for about one-fifth of GDP. Industry as a whole grew by an average 4%, and manufacturing by 2.8% annually between 1988 and 1998; compared to an annual average decline of 0.70% and 0.30% respectively between 1978 and 1988. Guatemalan factories produce beverages, candles, cement, pharmaceuticals, chemicals, cigarettes, foodstuffs, furniture, matches, molasses, rubber goods, shirts, shoes, soap, sugar, textiles, and apparel. More recently established firms produce electrical machinery, refined petroleum products, metal furniture, instant coffee, pasteurized milk, plastic, plywood, aluminum and tires. Handmade woven and leather goods are sold to tourists and exported.

Most of the country's industrial enterprises operate on a very small scale. A small domestic market has traditionally limited Guatemala's industrial potential, although the CACM temporarily broadened the market for the country's exported manufactures. The value of Guatemala's exports more than tripled between 1972 and 1978. During the 1980s, however, the industrial sector declined, partly because of the collapse of the CACM but also because of a shortage of the foreign exchange necessary to purchase basic materials. In the mid-1980s, Guatemalan firms turned to export production as internal demand contracted. The 1986 devaluation of the quetzal raised the cost of imported industrial inputs. During the 1990s, the value added by manufacturing remained at a steady pace, except for during 1996. The manufacturing sector suffered from increased competition from Mexico, often unregistered and untaxed, while export to major neighboring markets was hampered in 1996 by the slowdown in Costa Rica and El Salvador.

In 1998, the manufacturing sector represented 14% of GDP, and had a growth rate of 3.5%. Major manufactures included sugar, clothing and textiles, furniture, chemicals, petroleum, metals, and rubber. Heavy industry included a small steel mill located in Escuintla, and an oil refinery that had a capacity of 20,000 barrels per day. The pharmaceutical industry shrank by 53% in 1998 because several manufacturing companies had moved their businesses to Mexico. Construction, very dynamic during the first half of the 1990s, was affected by falling demand in 1996 and 1997, but grew by about 25% annually in 1998 and 1999. Electricity generation and telephone services continued to grow strongly, while oil production, thanks to a very active development policy, increased by 250% between 1992 and 1998.

29SCIENCE AND TECHNOLOGY

In 1987–97, total Guatemalan expenditure on research and development amounted to 0.2% of GNP, with 112 technicians and 104 scientists and engineers per million people engaged in research and development. The Academy of Medical, Physical, and Natural Sciences, headquartered in Guatemala City, dates from 1945. In 1996, Guatemala had learned societies devoted to natural history, pediatrics, and engineering, and research institutes concerned with nuclear energy, industry, and earth sciences. The Institute of Nutrition of Central America and Panama founded in 1949 and administered by the Pan American Health Bureau Organization and the World Health Organization, conducts research and disseminates scientific and technical information. Five universities offer degrees in basic and applied sciences. The National Museum of Natural History is located in Guatemala City.

30 DOMESTIC TRADE

Outside the capital city, markets are held on appointed days, and local fairs are held annually. Traders bring their wares on large racks atop buses or by mule, herding animals ahead of them. Prices are not fixed. Although there are some modern, tourist-oriented shops, traditional methods of commerce, with modifications, also prevail in Guatemala City. Business hours are weekdays, 8 AM to 6 PM; shops also open on Saturday mornings. Normal banking hours in Guatemala City are weekdays, 9 AM to 3 PM.

31 FOREIGN TRADE

The Guatemalan commodity export market is dominated by coffee (25%) and sugar (12%). Other main exports are fruit (bananas) and nuts (8.6%), medicinal and pharmaceutical products (4.0%), vegetables (2.6%), and cardamom (2.4%). Most exports go to the US. Nontraditional exports, such as cut flowers, fruits and berries, shrimp, and textile assembly, are of growing importance to the Guatemalan economy.

In 1997 Guatemala's imports were distributed among the following categories:

Consumer goods	13.5%
Food	10.4%
Fuels	10.5%
Industrial supplies	35.2%
Machinery	17.3%
Transportation	13.0%
Other	0.1%

Principal trading partners in 1998 (in millions of US dollars) were as follows:

COUNTRY	EXPORTS	IMPORTS	BALANCE
United States	2,011	2,135	-124
El Salvador	340	213	127
Costa Rica	132	190	-58
Germany	117	149	-32
Canada	106	45	61
Mexico	81	650	-569
Japan	76	241	-165
Korea	60	293	-233
Venezuela	14	190	-176
China (inc. Hong Kong)	n.a.	171	

32 BALANCE OF PAYMENTS

Guatemala generally finances its trade deficit through capital inflows. Capital flight caused by regional instability during the 1980s led to large deficits on the overall payments balance and brought foreign exchange reserves down from $709.6 million at the end of 1978 to $112.2 million at the end of 1982. In 1991 and 1992, with inflation lowered, private capital inflows were large enough to offset public capital outflows and the current account deficit. As a result, foreign reserves expanded during the 1990s, growing by $559 million. Foreign exchange reserves were over $1 billion from 1997 into 1999. Exports increased by 7.2% in 1997, and by 20.7% in 1998. National income reports do not include the export value added by the textile assembly industry (as they are generally located in the Free Trade Zones), and remittances from Guatemalans living abroad, which help finance the trade deficit.

The US Central Intelligence Agency reports that in 1997 the purchasing power parity of Guatemala's exports was $2.9 billion while imports totaled $3.3 billion resulting in a trade balance of -$400 million.

The International Monetary Fund (IMF) reports that in 1998 Guatemala had exports of goods totaling $2,847 million and imports totaling $4,256 million. The services credit totaled $640 million and debit $792 million. The following table summarizes Guatemala's balance of payments as reported by the IMF for 1998 in millions of US dollars.

Current Account		-1,039
Balance on goods	-1,409	
Balance on services	-152	
Balance on income	-184	
Current transfers	705	
Capital Account		71
Financial Account		1,137
Direct investment abroad	...	
Direct investment in Guatemala	673	
Portfolio investment assets	-12	
Portfolio investment liabilities	66	
Other investment assets	242	
Other investment liabilities	168	
Net Errors and Omissions		67
Reserves and Related Items		-235

33 BANKING AND SECURITIES

The Bank of Guatemala (BANGUAT) is the central bank and the bank of issue. The Monetary Board, an independent body, determines the monetary policy of the country. Associated with the Bank of Guatemala are four other government institutions: The National Mortgage Credit Institute (the official government mortgage bank); two development banks, the National Bank of Agricultural Development and the National Housing Bank; and the National Finance Corp., organized in 1973 to lend funds to industry, tourism, and mining to provide technical assistance. BANGUAT intervenes in the foreign exchange market to prevent sharp deviation in the exchange rate. In 1998, the Central Bank spent over $500 million to support the exchange rate, but the currency depreciated by 15% anyway that year.

As of 1999, the formal banking system consisted of 34 private commercial banks, three state banks, and several financial houses. Over 18 international banks are represented in one form or another. The five largest banks control approximately 40% of total assets. Several financial institutions collapsed in 1998 and 1999, prompting the government to bring banks into line with the Basle convention on minimum capital requirements. The government also hopes to make credit more available.

When the Bank of Guatemala was established the Fund for the regulation of the Bond Market was created to encourage security issues. Nevertheless, Guatemalans still tend to prefer tangible investments, and there is no fully developed securities market. The National Stock Exchange of Guatemala (the Bolsa Nacional de Valores-BNV) opened in 1989 where shares from private companies in the country and other securities are traded. It is the largest of Guatemala's stock exchanges. The other two main exchanges, the Bolsa Nacional Global and the Bolsa Agrícola, merged to form the Corporación Bursatil in 1994. Three government bonds are traded on the exchanges, including CENIVACUS, CERTIBONO, and CDP. The volume traded in 1999 was $5.9 billion.

34 INSURANCE

In 1999 there were at least 15 registered insurance companies operating in Guatemala. In addition, the National Mortgage Credit Institute, a government corporation, dealt in both life and nonlife insurance policies.

35 PUBLIC FINANCE

Fiscal policy loosened after the 1985 elections, but tax reforms in 1987 failed to generate additional income, and governmental expenditures continued to grow. By 1990, the public sector deficit was 4.7% of GDP. The Serrano administration transformed the deficit of 1990 to a slight surplus in 1991 and a virtually balanced budget in 1992. The consolidated public sector deficit amounted to 1.2% in 1991 and 1.0% in 1992. Guatemala's public sector is among Latin America's smallest, and the tax burden is one of the lightest, at 8% of GDP. The budget deficit grew to 2.5% of GDP in 1998, from only 0.50% in 1997, forcing the government to reevaluate its taxation and customs practices. Continued privatization and trade liberalization should boost public finances.

The US Central Intelligence Agency (CIA) estimates that in 1998 Guatemala's central government took in revenues of approximately $1.87 billion and had expenditures of $2.1 billion including capital expenditures of $477 million. Overall, the government registered a deficit of approximately $230 million. External debt totaled $4.6 billion.

The following table shows an itemized breakdown of government revenues and expenditures. The percentages were calculated from data reported by the International Monetary Fund. The dollar amounts (millions) are based on the CIA estimates provided above.

REVENUE AND GRANTS	100%	1,868
Tax revenue	97.3%	1,818
Non-tax revenue	7.8%	145
Capital revenue	0.3%	5
Grants	0.8%	15
EXPENDITURES	100%	2,113
General public services	14.8%	314
Defense	15.2%	321
Public order and safety	0.0%	0
Education	19.0%	401
Health	10.6%	223
Economic affairs and services	16.0%	339
Other expenditures	-10.0%	-211
Interest payments	10.0%	211

[36]TAXATION

The personal income tax rate ranges from 15% to 30%. Only income earned from Guatemalan sources is taxed. Capital gains are taxed at a flat rate of 15% and real estate is taxed at 25%. Corporate income is taxed at 30%, and dividends at 12.5%. An industrial development law provides tax exemptions for new industries. Other levies include a value-added tax of 10%, a 3.5% tax on foreign exchange transactions, a 3% sale tax levied on businesses, and excise taxes on beverages, cigars, tobacco, gasoline, vehicles, and airline tickets.

[37]CUSTOMS AND DUTIES

Guatemala requires licenses for the importation of restricted goods, including pharmaceuticals, basic food grains, milk, coffee beans, and armaments. As a member of the CACM, Guatemala adheres to a common tariff classification system as well as a common customs code and regulations. Duties are stated as both specific and ad valorem. Import duties are generally minimal, ranging from 0–15%. Imports of agricultural products that exceed the quota have higher rates. Textile tariffs and shoe tariffs are scheduled to be phased out by 2005. There is also a 10% VAT.

[38]FOREIGN INVESTMENT

There is no general requirement for local participation nor any restriction on repatriation of capital. Guatemala's major diplomatic interests are regional security and, increasingly, regional development and economic integration. Guatemala participates in several regional groups, particularly those related to trade and environment. Foreign investor interest in Guatemala picked up with the signing of peace accords in 1996, and deregulation of the electric and telecommunications sectors. Structural reforms, such as the privatization program and trade liberalization measures,

will add to investor appetite, but substantial investment in infrastructure and training the work force is needed. As of the first quarter of 1997, the government had invited bids for 12 oil exploration and production contracts. Oil production increased by 250% between 1992 and 1998.

In 1998, Guatemala passed the Foreign Investment Law, reducing the barriers to foreign investment. But investment was still restricted to minority ownership of domestic airlines and ground transport. Incentives are available for the forestry, mining, tourism, and petroleum sectors. There are also eight Free Trade Zones.

[39]ECONOMIC DEVELOPMENT

Guatemala's economic development policy is to create rural employment through the provision of investment incentives. Such enticements include inexpensive financing by government institutions, free assistance and technical support, and preferential treatment to use government facilities and institutions for guidance. The government has initiated a number of programs aimed at liberalizing the economy and improving the investment climate. After the signing of the final peace accord in December 1996, Guatemala was well-positioned for rapid economic growth. Growth in the late 1990s was led by development of petroleum mining and refining.

The country's economy is commanded by the private sector which generates about 85% of GDP. The public sector is small and shrinking, with its business activities limited to transportation, and several development oriented institutions. Problems hindering economic growth include illiteracy and low levels of education; inadequate and underdeveloped capital markets; and lack of infrastructure, particularly in the transportation, communications and electricity sectors. The distribution of income and wealth remains skewed. The wealthiest 10% of the population receives almost one half of all income, the top 20% receives two-thirds of all income.

[40]SOCIAL DEVELOPMENT

Social security was established in 1945, and the Guatemalan Institute of Social Security (Instituto Guatemalteco de Seguridad Social) began to function three years later. At first, only accidents were covered; then maternity and hospitalization allotments for widows and orphans were provided. Finally, general medical insurance and pensions for the disabled, aged, widows, and minors were added to the system. In 1977, the program began operating on a national level and including agricultural workers. Contributions are made by employers (3.0% of payroll in 1999), workers (1.5% of earnings), and the state (25% of cost of the benefits paid). Pensions are set at 50% of average monthly earnings. Free medical care is provided for those receiving pensions.

The Office of Women's Affairs was created within the Ministry of Labor in 1981. After the March 1982 coup, women were appointed to several important posts, including, for the first time, the Supreme Court. Despite legal equality, women are paid significantly less than their male counterparts and are generally employed in low-wage jobs. Some domestic laws also discriminate against women. Women can be charged with adultery, while men can only be charged with a lesser crime. Sexual violence, including domestic violence, is widespread, and most cases go unreported. However, the number of complaints for both rape and spousal abuse has risen in recent years. In 1997 the National Women's Forum was established to promote women's issues. As of 1999, 10 of 113 members of Parliament were women.

Guatemala's indigenous peoples were the targets of serious human rights abuses by security forces during the civil war. An estimated 100,000 died during the internal conflict, and an additional 40,000 disappeared. The human rights situation has since improved. The government has made efforts to establish peace and respect human rights. However, reports of police mistreatment of detainees continued in 1999, and an amnesty law passed in late 1996 made it unlikely that those responsible for human rights violations in the past would be punished. As of 2000, it was estimated that indigenous people made up over half the population but were still mostly excluded from the political, economic, and cultural mainstream.

41 HEALTH

Health coverage has been estimated to be low, with more than 40% of the population receiving no access to health care services. There were 9 physicians per 1,000 population in 1997. In 1995, 42% of the gross domestic product went to health expenditures. Among the chief causes of death are heart disease, intestinal parasites, bronchitis, influenza, and tuberculosis. In 1994, major causes of death were pneumonia and influenza (16.5%), perinatal conditions (13.8%), intestinal infectious diseases (8.9%), and nutritional deficiencies (5.7%). Malnutrition, alcoholism, and inadequate sanitation and housing also pose serious health problems. From 1990 to 1995, 62% of the population had access to safe water, and 60% had adequate sanitation. Malaria rates are high. In 1995, there were 23,608 new cases. Cholera was reported in 7,970 people in 1995. In 1995 there were 17 reported cases of tuberculosis per 100,000 inhabitants. Guatemala does attempt to vaccinate its children, and figures from 1997 are as follows: tuberculosis (88%); diphtheria, pertussis, and tetanus (83%); polio (83%); and measles (74%). All routine vaccinations are paid for by the government. It is estimated that the poorest half of the population gets only 60% of the minimum daily caloric requirement. Some steps have been taken to fortify foods with daily vitamin requirements. Currently sugar is being fortified with vitamin A and wheat flour will be fortified with iron. Data collected from 1990 to 1998 indicates that 32% of married women (ages 15 to 49) were using contraception.

The total fertility rate was 4.5 in 1997, a dramatic reduction from 6.5 in 1980. By 1997 the maternal mortality rate had fallen to 55 deaths per 1,000 live births, down from 200 in 1990. In 1996, the infant mortality rate was 38 per 1,000 live births, and the overall mortality rate in 1994 was 7.4 per 1,000 people. The average life expectancy was 67.4 years in 1998. From 1966 to 1992, there were about 140,000 war-related deaths.

The HIV-1 seroprevalence in 1997 was 0.52 per 100 adults; 1,371 cumulative cases of AIDS were reported between 1984 and 1996.

Political violence and problems associated with poverty have left more than 200,000 Guatemalan children orphaned. Many suffer from psychological problems and malnutrition.

42 HOUSING

Many of the nation's urban housing units and most of its rural dwellings have serious structural defects and lack electricity and potable water. In the early 1980s, the last period for which information is available, nearly three-fourths of all dwellings were detached houses, 10% were palomars (units without water and private bath facilities), another 10% were improvised dwellings, and 6% were apartments. Over 50% of all housing was owner occupied, 30% was rented, and 12% was occupied rent free. Only 48% of the urban population and 28% of the rural population had sewer service. A public housing program is supervised by the National Housing Bank. The Ministry of Public Health and Welfare is charged with the improvement of rural dwellings.

43 EDUCATION

In the year 2000, the adult illiteracy rate was estimated at 31.3% (males, 23.8%; females, 38.9%). Elementary education is free and compulsory for six years although enforcement is lax in rural areas. In 1990, an estimated 56.7% of children aged 6–11 attended school. In 1997, there were 1,544,709 students in primary schools. In that same year, secondary schools had 384,729 students and approximately 23,000 teachers. Among Guatemala's six universities, the Universidad de San Carlos, in Guatemala City, is the most important center of higher learning. The others include Universidad del Valle de Guatemala, Universidad Francisco Marroquin, Universidad Mariano Galvez, Universidad Rafael Landivar, and Universidad Rural. In 1995, all post-secondary institutions had a combined enrollment of 80,228 students.

The education budget accounted for 15.8% of the central government budget in the latter half of the 1990s.

44 LIBRARIES AND MUSEUMS

There are three notable libraries in Guatemala City. The National Library, with about 160,000 volumes, has collections of Guatemalan and other Central American books and newspapers. The General Archives of Central America has a 100,000-item collection of documents for the three-century colonial period, when Guatemala was the administrative center for the Central American area. The library of the Geographical and Historical Academy of Guatemala (30,000 volumes) is of special value to researchers. The Central American Industrial Research Institute maintains the largest technical library in Central America (36,000 volumes). The Institute of Nutrition in Central American and Panama in Guatemala City maintains an important collection of public health documents. The University of San Carlos library has 205,000 volumes. There are small public library branches in Quetzeltenanyo.

The Museum of Archaeology and Ethnology (1948) in the capital has an excellent collection of Mayan artifacts, and the Colonial Museum in Antigua contains colonial paintings, wood carvings, iron and leather work, and sculpture. Also in the capital are the National Museum of Fine Arts, the National Museum of History, and the Center for Conservation Studies, founded in 1981.

45 MEDIA

Except for a few privately controlled facilities, the government owns and operates the postal, telephone, and telegraph services. In 1995 there were 231,100 telephones, all of them automatic. The Guatemalan Telecommunications Enterprise provides international radiotelegraph and radiotelephone service. As of 1999 there were 91 AM radio stations and 6 television stations. In 1997 there 73 radios, 126 television sets, and 6 mobile phones per 1,000 population.

There were, in 1999, six daily newspapers, all published in Guatemala City. Their names and orientations with 1999 circulations are as follows:

	ORIENTATION	CIRCULATION
Prensa Libre (m)	Moderate liberal	120,000
El Gráfico (m)	Moderate conservative	60,000
Siglo Veintiuno	Moderate	50,000
Diario la Hora (e)	Moderate liberal	20,000
La Republica	Moderate	NA
Diario de Centro América (e)	Official (government)	15,000

The constitution provides for free speech and a free press, though journalists admit that in certain cases fears of reprisals or government pressure lead to self-censorship.

Online access is extremely limited, with less than one Internet host per 1,000 population in 1998.

46 ORGANIZATIONS

Artisans', consumers', service, and savings and credit cooperatives are grouped in four federations. The major employers' organizations are the General Farmers' Association, the Chamber of Commerce, the Chamber of Industry, and the National Coffee Association.

47 TOURISM, TRAVEL, AND RECREATION

All visitors need a passport and may need a visa depending on nationality. Tourism has rebounded since Guatemala's return to civilian rule in 1986. In 1998, 636,278 foreign tourists entered the country. Tourist expenditures totaled $325 million in 1997. That year there were 13,854 rooms with 35,707 beds and an occupancy rate of 63%. Guatemala's main tourist attractions are Mayan ruins, such as Tikal; the numerous colonial churches in Guatemala City, Antigua Guatemala, and other towns and villages; and the colorful markets and fiestas.

In 1999, the UN estimated the cost of staying in Guatemala City at $129 per day. Costs elsewhere average $79 per day.

48 FAMOUS GUATEMALANS

The *Rusticatio Mexicana*, by Rafael Landívar (1731–93), represents the height of colonial Guatemalan poetry. Outstanding figures of the romantic period were philologist Antonio José de Irisarri (1786–1868); José Batres y Montúfar (1809–44), the author of *Tradiciones de Guatemala* and many poetical works; and José Milla y Vidaurre (1822–82), a historian and novelist and the creator of the national peasant prototype, Juan Chapín. Justo Rufino Barrios (1835–85) became a national hero for his liberal, far-reaching reforms between 1871 and 1885. Enrique Gómez Carillo (1873–1927), a novelist and essayist, was perhaps better known to non-Spanish readers during his lifetime than any other Guatemalan author. Twentieth-century novelists include Rafael Arévalo Martínez (1884–1975), Carlos Wyld Ospina (1891–1956), and Flavio Herrera (1895–1968). The novelist and diplomat Miguel Ángel Asturias (1899–1974) was awarded the Nobel Prize for literature in 1967.

Mario Cardinal Casariego (b.Spain, 1909–83) became the first Central American cardinal in 1969. Among the better-known Guatemalan political personalities of the 20th century are Col. Jácobo Árbenz Guzmán (1913–71), president during 1951–54, and Gen. Miguel Ydígoras Fuentes (1896–1982), president during 1958–63.

49 DEPENDENCIES

Guatemala has no territories or colonies.

50 BIBLIOGRAPHY

American University. *Guatemala: A Country Study*. Washington, D.C.: Government Printing Office, 1983.

Benz, Stephen Connely. *Guatemalan Journey*. Austin: University of Texas Press, 1996.

Dosal, Paul J. *Power in Transition: The Rise of Guatemala's Industrial Oligarchy, 1871-1994*. Westport, Conn.: Praeger, 1995.

Guatemala in Pictures. Minneapolis: Lerner, 1987.

Hendrickson, Carol Elaine. *Weaving Identities: Construction of Dress and Self in a Highland Guatemala Town*. Austin: University of Texas Press, 1995.

Immerman, Richard H. *The CIA in Guatemala*. Austin: University of Texas Press, 1982.

Jonas, Susanne. *The Battle for Guatemala: Rebels, Death Squads, and U.S. Power*. Boulder, Colo.: Westview Press, 1991.

Jones, Oakah L. *Guatemala in the Spanish Colonial Period*. Norman: University of Oklahoma Press, 1994.

Maya Cultural Activism in Guatemala. Austin: University of Texas Press, 1996.

Perera, Victor. *Unfinished Conquest: The Guatemalan Tragedy*. Berkeley: University of California Press, 1993.

Schlesinger, Stephen C., and Stephen Kinzer. *Bitter Fruit: The Untold Story of the American Coup in Guatemala*. Garden City, N.Y.: Doubleday, 1982.

Sexton, James D. *Campesino: The Diary of a Guatemalan Indian*. Tempe: University of Arizona Press, 1985.

Stoll, David. *Between Two Armies in the Ixil Towns of Guatemala*. New York: Columbia University Press, 1993.

VanKirk, Jacques. *Remarkable Remains of the Ancient Peoples of Guatemala*. Norman: University of Oklahoma Press, 1996.

Woodward, Ralph Lee. *Guatemala*. Santa Barbara, Calif.: Clio, 1992.

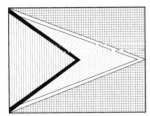

GUYANA

Cooperative Republic of Guyana

CAPITAL: Georgetown.

FLAG: A red triangle at the hoist extending to the flag's midpoint is bordered on two sides by a narrow black stripe; extending from this is a golden arrowhead pointing toward the fly and bordered on two sides by a narrow white stripe. Two green triangles make up the rest of the flag.

ANTHEM: Begins "Dear land of Guyana, of rivers and plains."

MONETARY UNIT: The Guyanese dollar (G$) of 100 cents is a paper currency tied to the US dollar. There are coins of 1, 5, 10, 25, 50, and 100 cents, and notes of 1, 5, 10, 20, and 100 Guyanese dollars. G$1 = US$0.00554 (or US$1 = G$180.50) as of 31 March 2000.

WEIGHTS AND MEASURES: Guyana officially converted to the metric system in 1982, but imperial weights and measures are still in general use.

HOLIDAYS: New Year's Day, 1 January; Republic Day, 23 February; Labor Day, 1 May; Caribbean Day, 26 June; Freedom Day, 7 August; Christmas, 25 December; Boxing Day, 26 December. Movable religious holidays include Good Friday, Easter Monday, Phagwah, 'Id al-'Adha, Yaou-Mun-Nabi, and Dewali.

TIME: 9 AM = noon GMT.

¹LOCATION, SIZE, AND EXTENT

Situated on the northeast coast of South America, Guyana is the third-smallest country on the continent, with an area of 214,970 sq km (83,000 sq mi), extending 807 km (501 mi) N-S and 436 km (271 mi) E-W, including disputed areas. Comparatively, the area occupied by Guyana is slightly smaller than the state of Idaho. Bounded on the N by the Atlantic Ocean, on the E by Suriname, on the S and S-W by Brazil, and on the NW by Venezuela, Guyana has a total boundary length of 2,921 km (1,815 mi).

Neither Guyana's western border with Venezuela nor its eastern border with Suriname has been resolved. Venezuela claims all territory west of the Essequibo River, an area of more than 130,000 sq km (50,000 sq mi), or over three-fifths of Guyana. Suriname claims a largely uninhabited area of 15,000 sq km (5,800 sq mi) in the southeast, between two tributaries of the Corentyne River.

Guyana's capital city, Georgetown, is located on the country's Atlantic coast.

²TOPOGRAPHY

Guyana has three main natural regions: a low-lying coastal plain, extending for about 435 km (270 mi) and ranging from 16 to 64 km (10–40 mi) in width, much of which is below high-tide level and must be protected by sea walls and drainage canals; a region of heavily forested, rolling, hilly land, about 160 km (100 mi) in width, which contains most of the mineral wealth and comprises almost five-sixths of Guyana's land area; and in the south and west, a region of mountains and savannas. There are several large rivers, including the Essequibo, Demerara, and Berbice, but few are navigable for any distance above the plains because of rapids and falls.

³CLIMATE

The climate is subtropical and rainy. The average temperature at Georgetown is 27°C (81°F); there is little seasonal variation in temperature or in humidity, which averages 80–85%. Rainfall

averages 230 cm (91 in) a year along the coast, falling in two wet seasons—May to July and November to January—and 150 cm (59 in) in the southwest, where there is a single wet season, extending from April through August.

⁴FLORA AND FAUNA

The flora varies with the rainfall and soil composition. The coastal area, originally swamp and marsh with mangrove and associated vegetation, has long been cleared for farming. In inland areas of heavy rainfall there are extensive equatorial forests, with green-heart a major species; varieties of trees may number as many as 1,000. Local fauna includes locusts, moth borers, acoushi ants, bats and other small mammals. There may be more than 728 species of birds. Northwestern coastal beaches are an important breeding ground for sea turtles.

⁵ENVIRONMENT

Because over 80% of Guyana is still wilderness, the country has so far sustained little serious environmental damage. The air is clean, but water supplies are threatened by sewage and by agricultural and industrial chemicals. One potential problem for the nation's water supply is the pollution of its wells by salt water from the ocean. Guyana has 57.8 cu mi of water with 99% used for farming purposes. Ninety percent of the nation's city dwellers have pure water, but 49% of people living in the rural areas do not. The nation's cities produce 0.1 million tons of solid waste per year. Since 1985, the nation has experienced an increase in diseases related to water and food consumption. Kaieteur National Park is the only specifically designated conservation area. In 1994, 12 of Guyana's 198 mammal species and nine of its 728 bird species were endangered. Three types of reptiles in a total of 137 and one freshwater fish were also endangered. Sixty-eight of Guyana's 6–8,000 plant species were threatened with extinction. Endangered or extinct species in Guyana include the tundra peregrine falcon, the black caiman, and four species of turtle (green sea, hawksbill, olive ridley, and leatherback).

6POPULATION

The population of Guyana in 2000 was estimated at 703,399. An estimated 3.7% of the population is 65 years of age or older. The projected population for the year 2005 is 709,000, assuming a crude birthrate of 18 per 1,000 population and a death rate of 13, resulting in a natural rate of change of 0.01% for the period 2000–2005. The population rate of change between 1995 and 2000 was 1.0%.

More than 90% of the people live on 5% of the land along the Atlantic coast; the interior is practically uninhabited. It was estimated that 38% of the population lived in urban areas in 2000, up from 36% in 1995. The capital and chief port, Georgetown, had a 2000 population of 254,000. Linden had an estimated 35,000 inhabitants, and New Amsterdam had about 25,000. Guyana's next census is slated for 2001.

7MIGRATION

Although specific figures are not available, there is known to have been significant outward migration in the 1980s, creating shortages of skilled workers and managers. Unofficial estimates put the number at 10,000 to 30,000 a year in the late 1980s, chiefly persons of Asian Indian extraction. Their destination was chiefly the US and Canada. According to 1999 estimates, about 50,000 Guyanese citizens live in the Venezuelan territory that borders Guyana and are fully integrated into the local population.

Guyana has traditionally had only a very small number of asylum-seekers, mainly from Cuba and Angola. Statistics, as of September 1999, indicated that only one asylum-seeker, a Liberian national, has been granted refugee recognition in the country in recent years. In 1999 the net migration rate was -12.43 migrants per 1,000 population.

8ETHNIC GROUPS

An estimated 49% of the population is of East Indian descent and 32% of African descent. Those of mixed ancestry constitute 12%; Amerindians account for 6%; white and Chinese peoples make up the remaining 1%.

9LANGUAGES

English is the official language and is used in government, the schools, the press, and commerce. Also spoken are Chinese, Portuguese, Amerindian languages, and a patois used mainly by those of African descent.

10RELIGIONS

Christians constitute approximately 50% of the total population, of whom about one-third are Anglicans, one-quarter are Roman Catholics, and 15% are Pentecostals. There are smaller groups of Baptists, Methodists, Seventh-Day Adventists, and Jehovah's Witnesses. Hindus make up some 41% of the population, and Sunni Muslims about 9%. Substantial numbers of the populace also practice Rastafarianism and the traditional Caribbean religion known as Obeah, either exclusively or in conjunction with the practice of other faiths.

11TRANSPORTATION

About 88 km (55 mi) of rail track are in service, originally built for the government-owned mining companies. The two government-owned passenger railway systems, however, have been scrapped: the Georgetown to New Amsterdam line in 1972, and the Georgetown to Parika line in 1974. Waterborne passenger and cargo service between these cities is now carried out by a government-owned transport service via the Essequibo and Berbice rivers. Georgetown is the main port, while New Amsterdam accommodates coastal and small oceangoing vessels. Springlands, on the Corentyne River, is the main port for service with Suriname. Waterfalls and rapids near the coast have prevented the development of river transportation to the interior, which contains 6,000 km (3,700 mi) of navigable waterways.

Roadways measured an estimated 7,970 km (4,953 mi) in 1999, of which only 590 km (367 mi) were paved. As of 1995, Guyana had about 24,000 passenger cars, and 9,000 commercial taxis, trucks and buses. There were an estimated 48 airports in 1998, only 4 of which had paved runways. Georgetown's Timehri International Airport is served by several international carriers. Guyana Airways Corp., a government company, operates domestic and international air service. In 1997, 126,000 passengers were carried on scheduled domestic and international flights.

12HISTORY

The coastline was first charted by Spanish sailors in 1499, at which time the area was inhabited by Amerindians of the Arawak, Carib, and Warrau language groups. By 1746, the Dutch had established settlements on the Essequibo, Demerara, and Berbice rivers, and had withstood French and English attempts to capture and hold the area. The English occupied the settlements in 1796 and again in 1803, and gained formal possession at the Congress of Vienna in 1815. The three main settlements were united into the Colony of British Guiana in 1831. Slavery was abolished in 1834, and many blacks settled in cooperative villages or moved into the towns. Under pressure from planters, indentured servants were brought in from India to work on the sugar plantations. As a result, most of the sugar workers still are of Asian Indian origin, while the urban population is predominantly black. This division into ethnocultural groupings later became an important factor in Guyana's politics.

The change in British imperial policy after World War II was reflected in a new constitution introduced in 1953, providing for a bicameral legislature and universal adult suffrage. Elections were held in the same year. However, the British balked after the People's Progressive Party (PPP) captured 18 of the 24 elected seats. Six months after the elections, the UK suspended the constitution, charging Communist subversion of the British Guiana government. The colony was governed on an interim basis until 1957, when general elections again were held. Again, the PPP won, with 47.9% of the votes, and Cheddi Jagan, leader of the PPP, was named chief minister.

The colony was granted full internal self-government in 1961, following four years of continued economic and social progress. In elections held under a new constitution introduced that year, the PPP won 20 of the 35 seats in the newly established Legislative Assembly. In October 1961, Jagan, who had been named prime minister, went to Washington, D.C., to ask President Kennedy for US aid. Classified documents released in the mid-1990s reveal that, following Jagan's visit, Kennedy gave the CIA orders to destabilize Jagan's government. Kennedy also urged Britain to withhold full independence from Guyana until Jagan was removed from power. Through covert operations, the CIA incited a general labor strike and racial violence between Jagan's Asian Indian followers and his opponents, mainly of African descent. British troops were called upon to restore order, but the situation did not calm until July.

In the elections of December 1964, the PPP again emerged as the strongest party, but due to US efforts to undermine its power, it was unable to form a government alone. As a result, the British governor called upon the leader of the People's National Congress (PNC), Forbes Burnham, to establish a government.

The following November, an independence conference held in London approved the present constitution, and on 26 May 1966, Guyana became a sovereign and independent nation. Guyana was proclaimed a cooperative republic on 23 February 1970, the 207th anniversary of a Guyanese slave revolt led by Cuffy, still a national hero. The PNC ruled as majority party between 1968 and 1992, although not without controversy.

Guyana became known to the US public in 1978 in the wake of the Jonestown massacre. The government of Guyana, in an attempt to colonize the nation's wilderness regions, had in 1977 allowed an American, James Warren "Jim" Jones, to establish the People's Temple commune at what became known as Jonestown, in the northwest. Many in the US had become concerned with developments in the commune, and US representative Leo J. Ryan had gone to Jonestown to investigate. He and four other US citizens were murdered at a nearby airstrip by Jones's followers. Then, on 18 November 1978, Jones and more than 900 of his followers committed suicide by drinking poisoned punch.

Between 1980 and 1985, relations between the PNC and opposition parties deteriorated sharply, as opposition parties charged harassment and fraud. The assassination in 1980 of Dr. Walter Rodney, a leading opposition figure, escalated the conflict. Under the administration of Forbes Burnham (1980–1985), human rights declined steadily. Burnham died in 1985 and was succeeded by First Vice-President and Prime Minister Desmond Hoyte. The new president sought to improve Guyana's relations with non-Socialist nations, particularly the US, and attempted the liberalization of the Guyanan economy.

However, by 1992 the country had grown tired of the PNC, and elected Cheddi Jagan of the PPP to the presidency in what was considered to be the first free and fair election since 1965. Jagan, who had been minority leader for years, received an impressive mandate with 53.4% of the vote, to 42.3% for the PNC. This translated to a solid 36 PPP seats in the National Assembly. Jagan had mellowed in the three decades since his ouster by the CIA, and in an ironic twist of history he was elected this time with the full support of the US. Jagan served effectively as president until his death in March 1997 at age 78. Under Jagan's administration, Guyana was able to consolidate its massive foreign debts and began to enjoy sustained economic growth. Jagan's widow, Janet Jagan, was elected to succeed him in general elections held on 15 December 1997, but the opposition PNC challenged the legitimacy of the election. In spite of a Caricom audit that deemed the election fair, the opposition PNC, led by former prime minister Hoyte, continued to protest the presidency of Jagan throughout the early months of 1998, and there were demonstrations and other forms of civil unrest, as well as a 55-day strike by civil servants. On August 14, the 78-year-old, U.S.-born Jagan, suffering from a heart condition, stepped down, naming as her successor finance minister Bharrat Jagdeo, who, at age 35, became one of the world's youngest heads of state. The next national elections were expected to be held in 2001.

13 GOVERNMENT

As of 23 February 1970, Guyana became a cooperative republic. Guyana's first president was elected by the National Assembly on 17 March 1970, and the post of governor-general was abolished. Proclamation of the cooperative republic also entailed the provision of mechanisms for the takeover of foreign enterprises.

Guyana's basic parliamentary structure dates from the constitution negotiated prior to independence in 1966. Under a new constitution approved in 1980, the unicameral National Assembly consists of 53 members elected by secret ballot under a system of proportional representation for a five-year term, plus 10 members elected by 10 regional councils, and 2 members elected by the National Congress of Democratic Organs. The latter, which is composed of deputies from local councils, together with the National Assembly, constitutes the Supreme Congress of the People of Guyana, which may be summoned or dissolved by the executive president. This office, created by the 1980 constitution, is filled by the leader of the majority party as both chief of state and head of government. The president appoints a cabinet includ-

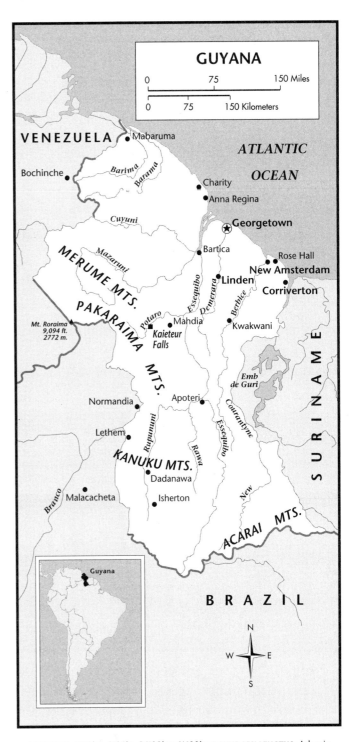

LOCATION: 1°12′ to 8°34′N; 56°29′ to 61°23′W. BOUNDARY LENGTHS: Atlantic coastline, 459 km (285 mi); Suriname, 600 km (372 mi); Brazil, 1,119 km (694 mi); Venezuela, 743 km (461 mi). TERRITORIAL SEA LIMIT: 12 mi.

ing a prime minister, who also holds the title of first vice-president.

The voting age and age of majority are 18 years, and suffrage is universal. However, electoral irregularity is the rule, rather than the exception. A British-led team of observers pronounced the 1980 vote "fraudulent in every respect." The 1992 election was considered by most observers to be the first fair poll since 1965. Boycotts both before and after elections have been frequent as a result of fraud charges, but the net effect of these boycotts has been to enhance the power of the majority party.

14POLITICAL PARTIES

Guyana's political parties are generally committed to socialism or some variant of it, but differ in the groups they represent and especially the ethnic groups that support them. A schism between the black and Asian Indian communities defines the major political division in the country.

In 1950, Cheddi Jagan and his wife organized the People's Progressive Party (PPP), which was anticolonial in nature, claimed to speak for the lower social classes, and cut across racial lines. Early in 1955, Forbes Burnham, who had been minister of education in Jagan's government, led a dissident PPP wing in the formation of the People's National Congress (PNC), which became the predominant political vehicle of Guyanese blacks, with Asian Indians remaining in the PPP.

Until 1992, the PNC had dominated Guyana's politics since independence. It draws its members primarily from urban blacks, and was in the majority from its first government, formed after the 1964 elections, until 1992 when the PPP returned to power. The PNC ideologically defines itself as socialist, but stresses the importance of a mixed economy in which the private sector is encouraged.

The PPP had been the opposition party since the 1960s, after dominating Guyanan politics in the 1950s. Appealing to Asian Indian rice farmers and sugar workers, the PPP nevertheless claims to be primarily an ideological party. Over the years, the PPP has taken an orthodox socialist position along the lines of international Communism. However, Jagan has at times called for increased foreign investment, and introduced conservative economic measures during his tenure as premier in the early 1960s. PPP opposition has been both loyal and otherwise. After the 1973 elections, the PPP boycotted the National Assembly, charging electoral fraud. In 1976 the representatives took their seats. In the 1980s the party appeared to be waning, but the 1992 elections gave a boost to this long-standing party.

Because Guyana uses a proportional representation system, small parties are accommodated within the system. In preparation for the 1992 elections, Guyanan citizens formed nearly 20 new parties. One such group is the Working People's Alliance (WPA), a multi-ethnic independent party professing its own brand of Marxism. The WPA, founded in 1979, boycotted the 1980 elections on the grounds that they were bound to be rigged. In June 1980, its leader, Walter Rodney, was killed in a bomb blast. The party took one seat in the 1985 elections, and 2 seats in the 1992 elections.

The United Force (TUF) was organized by Peter D'Aguilar, a wealthy brewer of Portuguese extraction, in the early 1960s. Its program, called economic dynamism, was based principally on close ties with the West, encouragement of foreign enterprise, and the acquisition of foreign loans. It helped the PNC form the first non-PPP government in Guyana in 1964, but in 1968 the PNC formed a government by itself. In 1973, TUF lost the four seats it had won in 1968. In 1980, TUF won two seats, which it held until 1992, when it lost one of the two.

The 1992 elections brought the PPP and Cheddi Jagan back to power. Jagan served as president until his death in March 1997. In the general elections of December 1997, his widow, Janet Jagan, was elected to succeed him, and the PPP remained in power with 36 seats, while the PNC held 26, the Alliance for Guyana 1, the TUF 1, and the Guyana Democratic Party 1. However, following extended challenges by the PNC over the validity of the election, Jagan resigned the following August, naming finance minister Bharrat Jagdeo to succeed her. The next elections were expected to take place in 2001.

15LOCAL GOVERNMENT

Guyana's system of local government was restructured after independence. Guyana is divided into 10 regions, each of which is administered by a chairman and council. City and village councils administer the local communities.

16JUDICIAL SYSTEM

The Supreme Court has two divisions: the high court, which consists of the chief justice of the Supreme Court and 10 puisne justices and has both original and appellate jurisdiction; and the court of appeal (established 30 July 1966), which consists of a chancellor, the chief justice of the Supreme Court, and as many justices as the National Assembly may prescribe. The chancellor of the court of appeal is the country's chief judicial officer. Magistrates' courts exercise summary jurisdiction in lesser civil and criminal matters. The constitution of 1980 provides for an ombudsman to investigate governmental wrongdoing. English common law is followed. Although there is an ombudsman, he lacks the authority to investigate allegations of police misconduct. There is no independent body charged with responsibility for pursuing complaints of police brutality or abuse.

The constitution provides for an independent judiciary. Delays in judicial proceedings are caused by shortages of trained personnel and inadequate resources.

17ARMED FORCES

The Combined Guyana Defense Force numbered 1,600 full-time officers and troops (including a women's army corps) in 2000. Reserves and paramilitary forces numbered 1,500. Army personnel numbered 1,400; the navy and air force numbered 100 each. The armed forces also manage a national service corps (1,500) for community development projects. Defense expenditures in 1998 were US$8 million or 1% of GDP. Only the army has modern weapons.

18INTERNATIONAL COOPERATION

Guyana became a member of the UN on 20 September 1966 and belongs to ECLAC and all the nonregional specialized agencies, except IAEA. Guyana is also a member of the Commonwealth of Nations, CARICOM, G-77, IDB, and the WTO. It holds permanent observer status with the OAS, and is a signatory to the Law of the Sea.

19ECONOMY

Guyana's economy is dominated by the production and processing of primary commodities, of which sugar, gold and bauxite are the most important. Much of the country is undeveloped, with more than 90% of the population and almost all of the agriculture concentrated in the narrow coastal plain. The interior is sparsely settled, and communications are poor. The bulk of the population is engaged in agriculture, either as laborers on sugar plantations or as peasant cultivators of rice. Although sugar and rice continued to be important export earners, bauxite and gold share comparable percentages of national exports. The government plays a direct role in the sugar industry; the nation's leading sugar producing company was nationalized in 1976.

Beginning in the late 1970s, Guyana's economy suffered a severe decline, attributable both to the increasingly high costs of imported oil and petroleum products (39% of Guyana's merchandise imports in 1983) and to sagging production and prices of Guyana's exports. In 1982 there were serious shortages of basic commodities, foreign exchange reserves dwindled, and Guyana was forced to reschedule its debts. In 1985, the IMF declared Guyana ineligible for further loans because of noncompliance with fund conditions and high arrears.

However, Guyana's economy improved dramatically under the Economic Recovery Program (ERP) launched by the government in April 1989. The program, which was designed with the assistance of International Monetary Fund (IMF) and World Bank officials; was supported by Canada, the UK, and the US. It marked a drastic reversal in government policy away from a predominantly state-controlled, socialist economy towards a more open, free market system. The government reformed its monetary and fiscal policy establishing a free market in foreign currency, which was designed to stabilize the exchange rate and put an end to runaway inflation. The exchange rate remained stable at G$125 to the dollar and inflation dropped from a 1989–91 annual average of 60–100% to only 14% in 1992. The growth rate reached 6% in 1991, after 15 years of decline. The government also eliminated price controls, removed import restrictions, promoted foreign investment, and divested itself of 15 of 41 state-owned enterprises by 1997.

Real GDP growth of 6.2% registered in 1997 marked the seventh consecutive year of strong recovery, with all of the key sectors demonstrating significant increases in production. Growth was particularly strong in the major export industries, including rice and sugar. However, a severe drought and political turmoil due to the 1997 elections brought the growth rate down by -1.8% in 1998. Privatization was scheduled to continue in 1999, but foreign investment lost momentum due to political instability.

20INCOME

The US Central Intelligence Agency (CIA) reports that in 1998 Guyana's gross domestic product (GDP) was estimated at US$1.8 billion. The per capita GDP was estimated at US$2,500. The annual growth rate of GDP was estimated at -1.8%. The average inflation rate in 1998 was 4.1%. The CIA defines GDP as the value of all final goods and services produced within a nation in a given year and computed on the basis of purchasing power parity (PPP) rather than value as measured on the basis of the rate of exchange. It was estimated that agriculture accounted for 37% of GDP, industry 22%, and services 41%.

Private consumption includes expenditures of individuals, households, and nongovernmental organizations. The richest 10% of the population accounted for approximately 32% of household consumption and the poorest 10% approximately 2.4%.

21LABOR

The total work force in 1993 was about 278,090; unemployment reached 12.9% during the same year. The sugar industry is on the rebound, with higher wages and 6,000–7,000 new jobs added after 1990. The sugar industry employed 24,000 people in 1993. The bauxite industry has declined in recent years; production fell by 40% in 1992 due to the deterioration of the mines at Linden. The central government employs about 18,000 people, and 46,000 more work in the public sector. Another 58,000 people work in the growing private sector. The total number of employed was registered at 121,861 in 1992. About 25% of the work force is formally organized. The public sector employs 53% of the labor force. Wages and conditions of work are increasingly regulated by government action and by collective bargaining. The Trades Union Congress is the national labor federation, and consist of 22 unions. Approximately 34% of the workforce is unionized.

Many Guyanese leave Guyana to find work abroad, mostly in the US; this is especially true of educated Guyanese.

No person under 14 is allowed to work except in nonhazardous occupations or a family business. However, this regulation is not effectively enforced. The Labor Ministry promulgates minimum wages in various sectors of private employers. The minimum public-sector wage was US$63 per month in 1999.

22AGRICULTURE

Agriculture, the main economic activity, provides nearly half the total value of exports and a large part of domestic food needs. Because the narrow strip of rich, alluvial soil along the coast lies in part below the high-tide mark of the sea and rivers, and because of heavy seasonal rainfall, agricultural expansion requires heavy expenditures for flood control, drainage, and irrigation. About 2.5% of the land is used for temporary and permanent crop production.

Guyana has two sugarcane harvests per year, and there are currently eight sugar mills in operation. About 90% of all cane is grown on land owned or leased by Guysuco, the government-owned sugar monopoly. Guysuco is managed under contract by the British firm Booker Tate. Independent farmers contributed only 8.3% to total cane production in 1995. Guyana is not an efficient producer of sugar and can not compete on the world market; it depends on preferential export markets for its sugar trade. Sugar production in 1998 was 2,600,00 tons, up from the 395,000 tons produced in 1971; sugar accounted for 29% of exports in 1980 and about 23% in 1997. Rice production in 1998 (532,000 tons) has more than doubled since 1991. Agricultural exports in 1997 totaled US$226.4 million, up from US$175.8 million in 1992. Other crops, grown for domestic consumption, include bananas, citrus, cassava, and yams.

23ANIMAL HUSBANDRY

Livestock in 1998 included 220,000 head of cattle, 130,000 sheep, 79,000 goats, 20,000 hogs, and 12,000,000 chickens. Other important domestic animals are goats, horses, mules, and donkeys. Extensive work is carried on to improve cattle productivity by importing breeding stock and providing artificial insemination and veterinary services.

24FISHING

Efforts are being made to increase the fish catch in order to improve the local diet and reduce imports of fish. The catch was 57,409 tons in 1997. The principal species caught that year were Atlantic seabob (18,391 tons) and tilapia (150 tons). Fish exports amounted to US$28.3 million in 1997. The Demerara Fish Port Complex, built near Georgetown with Japanese aid, includes a fish-processing plant and office facilities.

25FORESTRY

Forests cover about 16,500,000 hectares (40,770,000 acres), or 84% of the total land area. Commercial exploitation, however, is confined to a relatively small section in the northeast. The government-operated timber plant buys lumber from private sawmills and processes it with a view to standardizing and raising the quality of timber for export. Only about 20% of the forest area is reasonably accessible for timber exploitation. Green-heart is the most important timber produced and exported. Timber production was about 516,900 cu m in 1997. Exports of forestry products amounted to US$38.8 million that year.

26MINING

Mineral production is second only to agriculture in importance. Guyana was the fifth-largest bauxite producer in Central and South America in 1997, following Brazil, Jamaica, Venezuela, and Suriname. Production has recovered from the 1988–90 decline; in 1997, about 2.5 million tons were produced, up from 1.4 million tons in 1990 and 2.1 million in 1995. Gold, diamonds, and crushed stone also are mined. In 1997, gold mine output was 14,308 kg, and an estimated 50,000 carats of diamonds were mined. Bauxite and gold accounted for roughly one-fifth of the country's GDP.

Guyana's bauxite-mining industry came fully under state control on 1 January 1975, when the government nationalized Reynolds Guyana Mines Ltd., a subsidiary of the US Reynolds Metals. The government agreed to pay compensation totaling us$10 million in 13 annual installments. Guyana's largest bauxite producer, Demerara Bauxite Co. (owned by Aluminium Co. of Canada), was nationalized in July 1971 and renamed the Guyana Bauxite Co. All mineral rights were vested in the state, but the government encouraged foreign investment through joint ventures or outright foreign ownership of Guyanese companies; mining concessions were negotiated with government agencies. The Bauxite Industry Development Co., Ltd. (BIDCO) oversaw the entire bauxite industry in Guyana, but the government planned to privatize the two state-owned bauxite companies in 1998.

27ENERGY AND POWER

Net installed electric generating capacity was 114,000 kW in 1998, all of it but 2% in conventional thermal plants. Total electric energy produced was 325 million kWh. Frequent power failures have hampered production and thus impeded economic growth. The lack of reliable electricity in and around Georgetown has prompted many businesses to utilize imported small diesel-operated generators, further increasing total fuel demand.

A Canadian company found very high grade oil in the Essequibo region, also claimed by Venezuela, but further exploration was suspended when the company, unable to find the necessary financing, shut down its operations. In 1986, the government reached agreement with Venezuela on the barter of 500,000 tons of bauxite per year for 10,000 barrels of oil a day, half of which is used by the bauxite industry. In 1991, there were four oil concession holders for the Takutu Basin.

28INDUSTRY

Industry is limited chiefly to processing gold, bauxite, sugar, and rice for export and food and beverages for the local market. Manufacturing accounted for about 11% of GDP in 1998, when output decreased by 8.9% over the previous year.

In 1993 the government announced a policy move toward total privatization, joint ventures, public share offers, employee and management buyouts, and leased management contracts. The government has been following a serious program of privatization of key state enterprises, such as the telephone utility—80% of which is now owned by the U.S. Virgin Islands firm Atlantic Telenetwork. In 1996, six companies were offered for privatization, including the state-owned Guyana Electricity Corporation (GEC), Guyana Airways Corporation, the Linmine and Bermine bauxite mines, Guyana National Printers, Guyana Stores, the Guyana Pharmaceutical Corporation, Versailles Dairy Complex, and the Wauna Oil Palm Estate. The government continues its hold on the state monopoly Guyana Sugar Corporation (Guysuco). Following privatization of the government-owned rice mills and the transfer of rice transactions to the common market for foreign currency, the rice industry recovered and its production increased. In 1996, rice output increased 6.8% and sugar production increased 7.7%.

29SCIENCE AND TECHNOLOGY

The University of Guyana, founded in 1963 at Georgetown, has faculties of agriculture, health sciences, technology, and natural sciences. The Guyana School of Agriculture Corporation was founded in 1963. The Inter-American Institute for Cooperation on Agriculture, founded in 1974 at Stabroek and operated by the Organization of American States, aims to stimulate and promote rural development as a means of achieving the general devel-

opment and welfare of the population. The Pan-American Health Organization has maintained an office in Georgetown since 1949. The Guyana Zoo, an adjunct of the Guyana Museum in Georgetown, specializes in the display, care, and management of South American fauna.

30DOMESTIC TRADE

Domestic trade is conducted largely through small retail establishments scattered throughout the settled areas, and by cooperatives. There are also traditional informal markets for the sale of agricultural products. Normal business hours are 9:30 AM to 6 PM, Monday–Friday, and 8 to 11:30 AM on Saturday. Banks are open weekdays from 8 AM to 12:30 PM and 3 to 5 PM.

31FOREIGN TRADE

Leading exports are sugar, bauxite, rice, gold, shrimp, rum, timber, and molasses. In 1968, bauxite replaced sugar as Guyana's single most important export. From the 1970s to mid-1980s, however, world markets for Guyana's export commodities weakened while oil import costs rose, leading to chronic trade deficits. As a result of Guyana's economic reform program, import restrictions have been removed, and import licenses are granted routinely by the Ministry of Trade, Tourism, and Industry.

Guyana's biggest exports are sugar (25%) and gold (24%). The mining industry also produces a large amount of bauxite/alumina exports (16%). Foodstuffs account for substantial amounts of commodity export percentages, including rice (11%), shrimp (2.3%), and rum (2.0%).

In 1992 Guyana''s imports were distributed among the following categories:

Consumer goods	8.0%
Food	6.2%
Fuels	10.7%
Industrial supplies	22.9%
Machinery	37.0%
Transportation	14.9%
Other	0.2%

Principal trading partners in 1998 (in millions of US dollars) were as follows:

COUNTRY	EXPORTS	IMPORTS	BALANCE
United States	141	157	-16
Canada	137	7	130
United Kingdom	109	43	66
Netherlands Antilles	61	82	-21
Trinidad and Tobago	14	121	-107
Netherlands	13	12	1
Barbados	10	10	0
France	9	10	-1
Japan	7	19	-12
Cuba	6	17	-11

32BALANCE OF PAYMENTS

Guyana generally runs a deficit on current accounts, which became increasingly severe in the 1980s. Since 1989, the government has sought a policy of a free market in foreign currency and the removal of import prohibitions. Still, over half of the annual budget went to debt servicing during the 1990s. In 1996, Guyana's debt with Paris Club creditors was reduced by 67%; bringing total external debt to us$1.5 billion, or, slightly less than 100% of GDP.

The US Central Intelligence Agency reports that in 1997 the purchasing power parity of Guyana's exports was us$5,394 million while imports totaled us$641.6 million resulting in a trade balance of us$4,752.4 million.

The International Monetary Fund (IMF) reports that in 1995 Guyana had exports of goods totaling us$496 million and imports totaling us$537 million. The services credit totaled us$134 million and debit us$172 million. The following table summarizes Guyana's balance of payments for 1995 in millions of US dollars.

Current Account		-135
Balance on goods	-41	
Balance on services	-38	
Balance on income	-118	
Current transfers	62	
Capital Account		10
Financial Account		71
Direct investment abroad	...	
Direct investment in Guyana	74	
Portfolio investment assets	...	
Portfolio investment liabilities	3	
Other investment assets	-9	
Other investment liabilities	2	
Net Errors and Omissions		11
Reserves and Related Items		43

33BANKING AND SECURITIES

The Bank of Guyana is the central bank. In addition to the Bank of Guyana, seven commercial banks operate in the country. Three of them are foreign-owned, namely, Bank of Baroda, Bank of Nova Scotia, and The National Bank for Industry and Commerce (NIBC). In April 1994, the government sold its shares in the Guyana Bank for Trade and Industry (GBTI). In November 1994 the Demerara Bank (a private, domestic bank) and the Citizen's Bank started operations. Further liberalization of the financial sector occurred in April 1995 when Parliament approved the Financial Institutions Act of 1995. The new legislation aimed to tighten the supervisory and regulatory framework of the financial system. The NIBIC, one of Guyana's largest banks, was offered for privatization in 1996. By 1999, only one state-owned bank remained: the Guyana National Cooperative Bank (GNCB).

While a number of firms with publicly issued share capital are active, no large-scale securities market has developed.

34INSURANCE

As of 1995, there were at least eight insurance companies operating in Guyana.

35PUBLIC FINANCE

The budget follows the calendar year. Taxes finance the current account budget, with net surpluses or deficits being added to or subtracted from a general revenue balance. Nearly half of government revenue is derived from customs and excise receipts. Divestment of state enterprises, elimination of price controls and subsidies, and a reform of fiscal and monetary policy have led to debt restructuring and forgiveness. Nevertheless, in 1998, Guyana's debt was about 100% of GDP, and government expenditure reached 40% of GDP in 1998.

The US Central Intelligence Agency (CIA) estimates that in 1997 Guyana's central government took in revenues of approximately us$253.7 million and had expenditures of us$304.1 million including capital expenditures of us$108.8 million. Overall, the government registered a deficit of approximately us$50.4 million. External debt totaled us$1.5 billion.

36TAXATION

Income taxes are the major source of direct tax revenue. Personal income taxes are levied at a rate of 0%, 20%, and 33.33%. The corporate tax rate is 45% for commercial companies (generally nonmanufacturing companies) and 35% for all other companies. Other taxes include property tax and consumption tax on locally manufactured goods, a withholding tax of 15%, and stamp taxes. Local government authorities derive their revenues primarily from land, building, and service taxes. Tax evasion is a constant problem.

37CUSTOMS AND DUTIES

Customs revenues are traditionally a main source of government income. Guyana uses the common external tariffs of CARICOM. Intra-CARICOM trade is free of tariffs. The CET on imports is 5–20%. Consumption taxes are also levied on imports, based on c.i.f. value, but some items are exempted to encourage development. Export taxes range from 0.5% of value to 10%. There is an 80-acre gold Export Processing Zone in Linden.

38FOREIGN INVESTMENT

Investment by foreign firms accounted for the bulk of capital formation prior to the establishment of Guyana's cooperative republic in 1970. After Guyana became a cooperative republic, the government did little to attract foreign private investment. The Hoyte government, however, began efforts to obtain foreign investments for the rehabilitation of the bauxite industry and for oil prospecting and gold mining. New legislation to simplify foreign investment procedures was written in 1987.

The implementation of the Economic Recovery Program and the strong interest of the government in privatization attracted many foreign investors. In 1988, the government permitted foreign ownership of businesses operating in Guyana. In addition, the government is prepared to implement arrangements designed to facilitate investors' derivation of tax benefits in their home territories as well as tax credits in Guyana. Other investment incentives include: tax holidays, export allowances, accelerated depreciation, an Export Processing Zone, and special provisions for agribusiness, mining, and tourism.

39ECONOMIC DEVELOPMENT

A continuing theme of Guyanese economic development policy has been the attempt, without great success, to expand agriculture and to diversify the economy. A seven-year development program (1966–72) aimed to move the country's economy away from its heavy dependence on sugar, rice, and bauxite and to increase funds for scientific, vocational, and technical training and agricultural education. A key feature of the 1972–76 development plan was its emphasis on improving Guyana's health and housing standards.

A decisive change in economic orientation was marked by the proclamation on 23 February 1970 of a cooperative republic. The government embarked on a policy of cooperative socialism by nationalizing the bauxite industry, seeking a redistribution of national wealth, and fostering the establishment of cooperative enterprises for agricultural production, marketing, transportation, housing and construction, labor contracting, services, and consumer purchases. Within a decade, about 80% of the economy was in the public sector.

As economic conditions declined in the late 1970s and early 1980s, the government instituted such austerity measures as import restrictions, foreign exchange controls, cutbacks in planned government spending, and layoffs of government employees.

From 1953 through 1986, Guyana received us$115.5 million in nonmilitary loans and grants. Multilateral assistance during the same period equaled us$265.4 million, of which 42% came from the IDB and 30% from the IBRD. The 1985 declaration by the IMF that Guyana was ineligible to receive further assistance until outstanding debts with the fund had been repaid was an indication of how severe the nation's financial crisis had become. In 1983, the US had vetoed aid from US and IDB sources, and late in 1985 a barter agreement with Trinidad and Tobago was suspended because of Guyana's failure to repay outstanding loans. As a result, the Hoyte government sought a rapprochement with international lending agencies: a delegation from the IMF, the World Bank, and the IDB visited Guyana late in 1986, and early in 1987 the Guyana dollar was devalued by 56%.

In the late 1990s, primarily as a result of economic reforms, agricultural output grew at a stable rate. Manufacturing output also grew because of improvements in electricity generation and distribution and improved incentives for private investments. These factors combined made continued recovery with real growth rates in excess of 5% per year possible until 1997. Drought and political instability threatened the a decade of economic development.

The continuation of sound macroeconomic policies and public sector reform, together with multilateral and bilateral assistance, is crucial to sustaining growth. The fiscal situation is expected to continue improving in the short and medium term, largely as a result of increased current revenues. The inflation rate is likely to stay low, while the medium-term external position of Guyana will remain clouded by the large external debt outstanding, so that the search for debt relief and preferred lending from international donors remains essential.

40 SOCIAL DEVELOPMENT

A National Insurance Scheme covering all employed persons between the ages of 16 and 59 was introduced in September 1969. In April 1971, the scheme was broadened to include self-employed persons in the same age bracket. Social welfare benefits include workers' compensation, maternity and health insurance, death benefits, disability, and old age pensions. In 1999, workers contributed 4.8% of earnings, and employers made a 7.2% payroll contribution. Retirement pensions are 40% of average weekly earnings, disability pensions are 30%, and survivor benefits are 50% of the payable old age or disability pension.

The 1990 Equal Rights Act which was intended to end sex discrimination has proven difficult to enforce because it lacks a specific definition of discrimination. An antidiscrimination act passed in 1997 was intended to strengthen enforcement of the 1990 law. There is no legal protection against sexual harassment in the workplace or dismissal on the grounds of pregnancy. Legislation passed in 1990 strengthened women's property rights in cases of divorce. A 1996 law defined and criminalized domestic violence. As of 1997, 12 of 65 members of Parliament were women.

Amerindians are regulated by the Amerindian Act which was initially introduced during colonial times. Although the Act is not usually enforced, it limits the rights of indigenous peoples by banning the sale of alcohol to Amerindians, and requiring them to obtain government permission prior to accepting a job.

In the late 1990s, Guyana continued to have serious human rights problems, including police abuses, pretrial detention, and poor prison conditions.

41 HEALTH

In 1997, there were 2 doctors per 10,000 population. Some 90% of the population of Guyana had adequate sanitation and 65% had access to safe water in 1994–95. In 1998 the average life expectancy was 64.6 years. The total fertility rate was 2.5 in 1994. About 20,000 births were reported in that same year. Infant mortality in 1996 was 32 per 1,000 live births, and the overall mortality rate in 1999 was 9 per 1,000 people. A high incidence of malaria was present in 1997 with 34,075 new cases, and malaria was the country's second leading cause of death. Of the 6,506 cholera cases in 1995, 565 died. The incidence of filariasis, enteric fever, helminthiasis, nutritional deficiencies, and venereal diseases still is significant. Yellow fever remains a constant threat. In 1997, 82% of Guyana's children were vaccinated against measles, roughly a 28% increase from 1988.

In 1995, there were 96 new AIDS cases reported and 132 deaths from the disease.

42 HOUSING

Housing is a critical problem, as is the lack of adequate water supplies and of effective waste disposal and sewage systems. Urban development plans have been prepared for Georgetown and New Amsterdam, and a number of schemes, including the construction of low-cost rental housing, have been inaugurated. Loans are made through the Guyana Cooperative Mortgage Finance Bank, founded in 1973. To spur housing development, the government established the Guyana Housing Corp. in 1974. The government provides supervision by trained personnel for those willing to build their own homes. Housing is provided by some firms for their employees. In the 1980s, over two-thirds of all housing units were detached houses and under one-fourth were apartments. Owners occupied over half of all dwellings, while about one-quarter were rented, and one-tenth were occupied rent free. Three-fourths of all dwellings were wooden, with a smaller proportion made either of wood and concrete, or concrete.

43 EDUCATION

The adult illiteracy rate for the year 2000 was estimated at 1.5% (males, 1.0%; females, 1.9%), among the lowest in South America. Although educational standards are high, educational development has suffered in recent years from shortages of teachers and materials. School attendance is free and compulsory for eight years for children between the ages of 5 and 14. All schools in Guyana are public, as church and private schools were taken over by the government in 1976. While primary education lasts for six years, secondary education has five years. In 1997, there were 420 schools at the primary level with 102,000 students and 3,461 teachers. The student-to-teacher ratio stood at 29 to one. Also in 1997, secondary schools had 62,043 students and approximately 2,200 teachers.

The first students completed the one-year course at the Government Training College for Teachers in 1960. Teachers also are trained in the UK and at the University of the West Indies in Jamaica. The University of Guyana was established in 1963, and awarded its first degrees in 1967. The university has faculties in agriculture, the arts, health sciences, social sciences, education, and technology. The Kuru Kuru Cooperative College was established in 1970 to equip the Guyanese people both technically and philosophically for cooperative socialism and nation building. There were 8,965 students enrolled at universities and all higher level institutions in 1997.

44 LIBRARIES AND MUSEUMS

The National Library in Georgetown, with holdings of more than 198,000 volumes, also functions as a public library and has 37 branches. The Guyana Society Library (formerly the Library of the Royal Agricultural and Commercial Society) is the oldest in the country and has a collection of rare books dealing with the Amerindians of Guyana. Other important libraries include the British Council Library, the Caribbean Community Secretariat, and the library of the US Information Agency. The University of Guyana, founded in 1963, maintains a library which has holdings of over 200,000 volumes.

The Guyana Museum in Georgetown has a collection of flora and fauna, archaeological findings, and examples of Amerindian arts and crafts. It also has an aquarium and a zoological and botanical park.

45 MEDIA

In 1991, Atlantic Tele-Network (ATN) purchased 80% of the Guyana Telephone and Telegraph Company. In that year there were 33,000 telephones in use. In 1995, there were 44,100 telephones in use. A public corporation runs the postal system. Overseas radiotelephone and cable services are provided by Cable and Wireless (W.I.), a private firm. An international telex service was inaugurated in 1967. Broadcasting is carried on by the government-owned Guyana Broadcasting Corp. As of 1999, there were 4 AM and 3 FM radio stations and 3 television stations (one public, two private). There were 817 radios and 306 TV sets in use per 1,000 population in 1997.

That same year there were two daily newspapers in Guyana, the state-owned *Guyana Chronicle* (circulation 18,600) and the *Stabroek News* (18,000), an independent newspaper. *The Mirror* (circulation 25,000) is an evening paper published by the People's Progressive Party.

In the late 1980s there were reports of government harassment of independent and opposition media. Presently, the government is said to generally respect the constitutional provisions for freedom of speech and the press.

46ORGANIZATIONS

Cooperative societies cover virtually every aspect of the economy. At the end of 1960, 588 societies were registered, with a total membership of 38,597; by October 1988 there were 1,459 societies, with a membership of some 100,000. There is a chamber of commerce in Georgetown.

47TOURISM, TRAVEL, AND RECREATION

Guyana's scenery varies from the flat marshy coastal plain to the savannas, plateaus, and mountains of the interior; the 226-m (740-ft) Kaieteur Falls, four times as high as Niagara, is the country's most outstanding scenic attraction. Riding, hunting, fishing, and swimming are available in the southern savanna of the Rupununi. Cricket is the national sport.

Visitors from Commonwealth countries and the US need valid passports and return or onward tickets. Visitors from most other countries need both a passport and a visa. In 1997, there were 76,000 tourist arrivals in Guyana, and tourism receipts totaled US$60 million. In 1999, the UN estimated the cost of staying in Georgetown at US$41 per day. Elsewhere in Guyana, daily expenses are approximately US$46.

48FAMOUS GUYANESE

Citizens of Guyana who have established literary reputations abroad include the novelists Edgar Mittelholzer (1909–65), Edward Ricardo Braithwaite (b.1912), and the poet and novelist Jan Carew (b.1925). Linden Forbes Sampson Burnham (1923–85), former leader of the PNC, dominated Guyanese politics from 1964 until his death. Cheddi Berret Jagan, Jr. (1918–97), founder of the PPP, was chief minister from 1957 to 1961 and premier from 1961 to 1964, and was the main opposition leader after returning to office in 1992. Hugh Desmond Hoyte (b.1930) served as president from 1985 to 1992.

49DEPENDENCIES

Guyana has no territories or colonies.

50BIBLIOGRAPHY

Chambers, Frances. *Guyana*. Santa Barbara: Clio, 1989.

Daly, Vere T. *A Short History of the Guyanese People*. London: Macmillan Education, 1975.

Flanery, Michael. *The Why of Jonestown*. Pittsburgh: First Edition Books, 1980.

Guyana in Pictures. Minneapolis: Lerner, 1988.

Hintzen, Percy C. *The Costs of Regime Survival: Racial Mobilization, Elite Domination, and Control of the State in Guyana and Trinidad*. New York: Cambridge University Press, 1989.

Mangru, Basdeo. *A History of East Indian Resistance on the Guyana Sugar Estates, 1869–1948*. Lewiston, N.Y.: Edwin Mellen Press, 1996.

Merrill, Tim (ed.). *Guyana and Belize: Country Studies*. 2d ed. Washington, D.C.: Library of Congress, 1993.

Premdas, Ralph R. *Ethnic Conflict and Development: The Case of Guyana*. Brookfield, Vt.: Avebury, 1995.

Singh, Chaitram. *Guyana: Politics in a Plantation Society*. Stanford, Calif.: Hoover Institution Press, Stanford University, 1988.

Spinner, Thomas J. *A Political and Social History of Guyana, 1945–1983*. Boulder, Colo.: Westview, 1984.

Williams, Brackette F. *Stains on my Name, War in my Veins: Guyana and the Politics of Cultural Struggle*. Durham: Duke University Press, 1991.

HAITI

Republic of Haiti
République d'Haïti

CAPITAL: Port-au-Prince.

FLAG: The upper half is blue, the lower half red; superimposed in the center is the national coat of arms with the motto *L'Union Fait la Force* ("Union makes strength").

ANTHEM: *La Dessalinienne (Song of Dessalines).*

MONETARY UNIT: The gourde (G) is a paper currency of 100 centimes. There are coins of 5, 10, 20, and 50 centimes and notes of 1, 2, 5, 10, 50, 100, 250, and 500 gourdes. Silver (5, 10, and 25 gourdes) and gold (20, 50, 100, 200, 1,000 gourdes) coins have also been minted. US paper currency also circulates freely throughout Haiti. G1 = $0.051 (or $1 = G19.49) as of 31 March 2000.

WEIGHTS AND MEASURES: The metric system is official for customs purposes, but French colonial units and US weights are also used.

HOLIDAYS: Independence and New Year's Day, 1 January; Forefathers Day, 2 January; Pan American Day, 14 April; Labor Day, 1 May; Flag and University Day, 18 May; National Sovereignty Day, 22 May; Assumption, 15 August; Anniversary of the Death of Dessalines, 17 October; UN Day, 24 October; All Saints' Day, 1 November; Commemoration of the Battle of Vertières and Armed Forces Day, 18 November; Discovery of Haiti, 5 December; Christmas, 25 December. Movable religious holidays include Carnival (three days before Ash Wednesday) and Good Friday.

TIME: 7 AM = noon GMT.

¹LOCATION, SIZE, AND EXTENT

Occupying the western third of the island of Hispaniola, Haiti has an area of 27,750 sq km (10,714 sq mi) including the islands of Tortuga (La Tortue), Gonâve, Les Cayemites, and Vache. Comparatively, the area occupied by Haiti is slightly larger than the state of Maryland. Extending roughly 485 km (300 mi) ENE-WSW and 385 km (240 mi) SSE-NNW, Haiti is bounded on the N by the Atlantic Ocean, on the E by the Dominican Republic, on the S by the Caribbean Sea, and on the W by the Windward Passage and the Gulf of Gonâve, with a total boundary length of 2,046 km (1,271 mi). Haiti claims Navassa Island, an uninhabited US possession about 50 km (31 mi) west of Hispaniola.

Haiti's capital city, Port-au-Prince is located on Hispaniola's west coast.

²TOPOGRAPHY

The coastline of Haiti is irregular and forms a long southern peninsula and a shorter northern one, between which lies the Gulf of Gonâve. Rising from the coastal plains to a peak height at La Selle of 2,680 m (8,793 ft) and covering two-thirds of the interior, three principal mountain ranges stretch across the country; one runs east and west along the southern peninsula, while the others stretch northwestward across the mainland. Once-fertile plains run inland between the mountains: the Plaine du Nord, extending in the northeast to the Dominican border, and the Artibonite and Cul-de-Sac plains reaching west to the Gulf of Gonâve. Of the many small rivers, the Artibonite (237 km/147 mi), which empties into the Gulf of Gonâve, and L'Estère (45 km/28 mi) are navigable for some distance.

³CLIMATE

The climate is tropical, with some variation depending on altitude. Port-au-Prince ranges in January from an average minimum of 23°C (73°F) to an average maximum of 31°C (88°F);

the range in July is 25–35°C (77–95°F). The rainfall pattern is varied, with rain heavier in some of the lowlands and on the northern and eastern slopes of the mountains. Port-au-Prince receives an average annual rainfall of 137 cm (54 in). There are two rainy seasons, April–June and October–November. Haiti is subject to periodic droughts and floods, made more severe by deforestation. Hurricanes are also a menace.

⁴FLORA AND FAUNA

Tropical and semitropical plants and animals are characterized more by their variety than by their abundance. In the rain forest of the upper mountain ranges, pine and ferns as well as mahogany, cedar, rosewood, and sapin are found. Coffee, cacao, and coconut trees and native tropical fruits such as avocado, orange, lime, and mango grow wild. Many species of insects abound, but there are no large mammals or poisonous snakes. Ducks, guinea hens, and four varieties of wild pigeons rare elsewhere are plentiful, and egrets and flamingos live on the inland lakes. Reptile life includes three varieties of crocodile, numerous small lizards, and the rose boa. Tarpon, barracuda, kingfish, jack, and red snapper abound in the coastal waters.

⁵ENVIRONMENT

According to an AID report, Haiti "is suffering from a degree of environmental degradation almost without equal in the entire world." The virgin forests that once covered the entire country have now been reduced to 4% of the total land area. According to United Nations sources, Haiti loses 3% of its forests every year. Deforestation has had a disastrous effect on soil fertility, because the steep hillsides on which so many Haitian farmers work are particularly susceptible to erosion. The nation loses 1.35 tons of soil per square kilometer yearly. Agricultural chemicals, such as DDT, are widely used in Haiti. These pollutants plus the use of oil with high lead content are a significant source of pollution. Not only has much of the topsoil been washed away, but the eroded slopes retain little rainfall and are vulnerable to flooding. The chief impediment to reforestation is the fact that Haiti is so intensely cultivated that allocation of land for forests means a reduction in the land available for crop growing and grazing. Foreign organizations have attempted to alleviate these problems. In 1981, an $8 million Agroforestry Outreach Project, funded primarily by the US, helped farmers plant trees throughout Haiti—over 4.5 million seedlings by 1983. The government also agreed to set up the nation's first two national parks with funding from the US Agency for International Development. However, as of 1994, only 0.3% of Haiti's total land area was protected. Water quality is also a serious environmental problem. Haiti has 2.6 cu mi of water with 68% used for farming activity. Sixty-three percent of the nation's city dwellers and 77% of the rural population do not have pure water.

As of 1994, six species of mammals, one bird species, and four types of reptiles were endangered. Endangered or extinct species in Haiti include the tundra peregrine falcon, Haitian solenodon, green sea turtle, hawksbill turtle, and American crocodile.

6 POPULATION

In 2000, Haiti's population was estimated at 6,991,589. An estimated 3.6% of the population is 65 years of age or older. The projected population for the year 2005 is 7,584,000, assuming a crude birthrate of 31 per 1,000 population and a death rate of 13, resulting in a natural rate of change of 1.8% for the period 2000–2005. The population rate of change between 1995 and 2000 was 1.9%. Haiti is the most densely populated country in the Western Hemisphere; population density in 1998 was 277 per sq km (717 per sq mi).

It was estimated that 35% of the population lived in urban areas in 2000, up from 24% in 1980. The capital and largest city, Port-au-Prince, had a 2000 metropolitan population of 1,791,000. Other major cities are Jacmel (216,600) and Les Cayes (214,606). Haiti's next census is slated for September 2001.

7 MIGRATION

Emigration from Haiti has been mainly to Cuba, other Caribbean states, Canada, and the US; illegal emigration to the US has been substantial since the 1960s. Between 1972 and 1981 more than 55,000 Haitian "boat people"—and perhaps over 100,000—arrived in Florida. During 1981–85, 43,312 Haitians were admitted legally to the US. In September 1981, the US and Haitian governments agreed to work together to halt the flow of refugees, and these efforts apparently met with success. Over the next 10 years only 28 of the 22,716 Haitians intercepted at sea were admitted to the US.

Several thousand Haitian migratory workers travel to the Dominican Republic each year during the cane-harvest season; many more change their residences permanently.

Following the 1991 coup, which overthrew President Jean-Bertrand Aristide, many Haitians left for the Dominican Republic, Jamaica, Suriname, Cuba, Panama, Honduras, Venezuela, Colombia, and Mexico. Between 1991–93, 43,000 Haitians tried to reach the US by boat, but were interdicted and held at Guantanamo Bay, the US naval base in Cuba. In October 1994, President Aristide was returned to power thanks to a US-led multinational force into Haiti that entered in September of 1994. Soon after Aristide's return to power, Haitians began repatriating, and the UNHCR helped repatriate 8,052 persons from various countries. From the US, 16,500 repatriated voluntarily. The UNHCR office in Haiti was closed in April 1996. In 1999, the net migration rate was -3.26 migrants per 1,000 population.

8 ETHNIC GROUPS

For the vast majority of Haiti's people, the African ethnic influence is dominant. About 95% of the inhabitants are black; mulattos and whites make up the remaining 5% of the population.

9 LANGUAGES

The official languages of Haiti is French; however, it is only spoken by about 20% of the population. Virtually all the people speak Creole, a mixture of early 17th-century provincial French and African tongues, with infusions of English, Spanish, and Amerindian words. English is used in the capital and to a lesser extent in the provincial cities, and along the Dominican border a Spanish Creole is spoken.

10 RELIGIONS

For many years Roman Catholicism was the official religion of Haiti. Its official status was repealed with the enactment of the 1987 constitution; however, neither the government nor the Vatican has renounced the 1860 Concordat that serves as a basis for relations between the two. In many ways Roman Catholicism retains a position of honor, but Haitians are guaranteed the freedom to practice all religions by the constitution. According to 1998 estimates, Roman Catholics represent about 80% of the population. Most of the remainder belong to various Protestant denominations, the largest being the Baptist (10%) and Pentecostal (4%) churches. Other significant non-Catholic Christian groups include Methodists, Episcopalians, Jehovah's Witnesses, Mormons, Adventists, and Orthodox. Non-Christian groups include Jews, Muslims, Rastafarians, and Baha'is. Voodoo, a traditional religion partially derived from West African beliefs, is still widely practiced, often in tandem with Christianity. There are associations of voodoo practitioners and priests, but there is no established hierarchy or church.

11 TRANSPORTATION

In 1999, Haiti had 4,160 km (2,585 mi) of roads, 1,011 km (628 mi) of which were paved. Farm-to-market roads are few, and most produce for the local market is transported by burro or carried on foot by women. In 1980, a new highway linking Port-au-Prince with Les Cayes was opened, and several road improvement projects have been completed; overall, however, road conditions continue to deteriorate because of flooding. There were some 32,000 passenger cars and 21,000 commercial vehicles in 1995. Also in 1995, Haiti had a ratio of 127 inhabitants per registered vehicle, the highest ratio of any country in the Western Hemisphere. Two railroad systems, the National Railroad of Haiti and the Cul-de-Sac Railroad, with a combined trackage of 301 km (187 mi), originally operated lines from Port-au-Prince to Verrettes and to Léogâne, and from Cap-Haïtien south to Bahon. By 1982, however, most of the system had become inoperative; the 40 km (25 mi) of lines that remained in 1999 were being used only for sugarcane transport.

The commercial shipping fleet consists of a few hundred small sailing vessels engaged in coastal trade and a few motorized vessels of light tonnage. The island depends chiefly on foreign shipping. During the early 1980s, the IBRD sought to stimulate intercoastal trade by building port facilities at Jérémie, Port-au-Prince, and Port-de-Paix. Other ports and harbors include Cap-Haitien, Gonaives, Jacmel, Les Cayes, Miragoane, and Saint-Marc.

In 1998 there were an estimated 13 airports, three of which had paved runways. Domestic air service is supplied by the privately owned Air Haiti, which connects principal cities on regular scheduled flights and also serves as an international carrier. Haiti Air Inter also provides domestic service. A jet airport at Port-au-Prince opened in 1965.

LOCATION: 18°1′42″ to 20°5′44″N; 71°38′ to 74°28′45″W. **BOUNDARY LENGTHS:** Dominican Republic, 275 km (171 mi); total coastline, 1,771 km (1,098 mi). **TERRITORIAL SEA LIMIT:** 12 mi.

¹²HISTORY

In 1492, Christopher Columbus made the European discovery of the island of Hispaniola and established a settlement near the present city of Cap-Haïtien. Within 25 years, the native Arawak Amerindians, a peace-loving, agricultural people, were virtually annihilated by the Spanish settlers. Bishop Bartolomé de las Casas, a missionary to the Amerindians, who had originally come to Hispaniola as a planter in 1502, proposed that African slaves be imported for plantation labor. Some time after 1517, a forced migration of Africans gave Haiti its black population.

About 1625, French and English privateers and buccaneers, preying on Spanish Caribbean shipping, made the small island of

Tortuga their base. The French soon also established a colonial presence on nearby mainland coasts and competed with the Spaniards. In the Treaty of Ryswick (1697), Spain ceded the western third of the island (Haiti) to the French. Under French rule it became one of the wealthiest of the Caribbean communities. This prosperity, stemming from forestry and sugar-related industries, came at a heavy cost in human misery and environmental degradation.

The French Revolution in 1789 outlawed slavery in France, which inspired Haiti's nearly half million black slaves to revolt. In a series of violent uprisings, slaves killed white planters and razed estates. Although they suffered cruel reprisals, they fought on under the direction of Toussaint L'Ouverture, an ex-slave who had risen to the rank of general in the French army. By 1801 Toussaint controlled the entire island, and promulgated a constitution, which abolished slavery. The emperor Napoleon did not accept this move, and sent 70 warships and 25,000 men to suppress the movement. Toussaint was captured, and died in a French prison.

Jean Jacques Dessalines, another black general risen from the ranks, continued the struggle, and in 1803, the disease-decimated French army surrendered. On 1 January 1804, Dessalines proclaimed Haiti's independence. Dessalines, after assuming the title of emperor in 1804, was assassinated in 1806, and Haiti was divided into a northern monarchy and a southern republic. Under both regimes, the plantations were distributed among former slaves, and Haiti became a nation of small farmers. Haiti was reunited by Jean Pierre Boyer in 1820, and in 1822 the Haitian army conquered Santo Domingo (now the Dominican Republic). For 22 years there was one republic for the entire island. In 1844, however, one year after Boyer was overthrown, the Dominican Republic proclaimed its independence from Haiti. In 1849, the president of Haiti, Faustin Elie Soulouque, proclaimed himself Emperor Faustin I. He was dethroned by a revolution headed by Nicholas Fabre Geffrard, who reestablished the republic and became president. In 1860, Geffrard negotiated a concordat with the Holy See that established Roman Catholicism as the national religion, although freedom of worship was retained.

A long period of political instability between 1843 and 1915, during which time Haiti had 22 dictators, culminated in the assassination of President Vilbrun Guillaume Sam and was followed by US military occupation. The occupation, which lasted 19 years, terminated in 1934 during the administration of President Sténio Vincent (1930–41), who in 1935 proclaimed a new constitution.

After World War II, another period of political instability culminated in 1950 in a coup d'etat that brought Gen. Paul Magloire to power. Magloire's economic policies led to a serious depression. In December 1956 a national sit-down strike, organized jointly by business, labor, and professional leaders, forced Magloire into exile. A period of chaos ensued, with seven governments trying to establish control.

In a September 1957 election filled with irregularities François Duvalier, a middle-class black physician known to his followers as Papa Doc, became president. He began to rule by decree in 1958, and in May 1961, he had himself elected for another six years. On 22 June 1964, Duvalier was formally elected president for life. Despite several attempted revolts, he consolidated his position, ruling largely through his security force, the Tontons Macoutes ("bogeymen"). Political opposition was ruthlessly suppressed, and thousands of suspected dissidents "disappeared." Also murdered were some 3,000 supporters of Daniel Fignolé, leader of the Peasant Workers Movement (Mouvement Ouvrier Paysan) and Duvalier's most effective opponent.

Political life under the Papa Doc regime was characterized by plots against the government and governmental counterterrorism, the latter entrusted to the Tontons Macoutes and to other thugs known as cagoulards. Opposition leaders went into hiding or exile. The Haitian Revolutionary Movement (Mouvement Révolutionnaire Haïtien), led by Haitian exiles Luc B. Innocent and Paul G. Argelin, began operations in Colombia in February 1961.

The National Democratic Union (Union Démocratique Nationale) was founded in Puerto Rico in April 1962 by former Ambassador Pierre Rigaud, with a branch in Venezuela organized by Paul Verna and an underground movement operating in Haiti. Invasions in 1964, 1969, and 1970 met with no success. Haitian exiles in New York, Montreal, Chicago, and Washington mounted an influential anti-Duvalier campaign during the 1960s.

Throughout this period, no party operated openly in Haiti except the Duvalierist Party of National Unity (Parti de l'Unité Nationale).

On 22 January 1971, Duvalier named his son Jean-Claude as his successor. Papa Doc died on 21 April 1971, and Jean-Claude, at the age of 19, became president for life the following day. The younger Duvalier sought to ease political tensions, encouraged tourism and foreign investment, and contributed to the beginnings of an economic revival. However, political arrests did not wholly cease, and there were severe economic reverses in the mid- and late 1970s.

In February 1979, elections to the National Assembly took place amid allegations of government fraud. Opposition groups were then arrested, tried, and convicted of subversion, but later released. In January and March 1982, two small exile groups tried unsuccessfully to overthrow the government by staging armed invasions. The first municipal elections of the Duvalier period were held in spring 1983. The voting resulted, for the most part, in victories for the government, partly because several opposition figures had been arrested during the campaign.

Jean-Claude proved to be an ineffectual leader, and tensions mounted as the economy stagnated after 1980. When civil disorder began to break out in the mid-1980s, the president became increasingly reclusive, occasionally attempting repression. In February 1986, following a series of demonstrations and protests, Jean-Claude and his family fled to France, and the National Governing Council (Conseil National de Gouvernement—CNG), led by Lt.-Gen. Henri Namphy, seized power.

The immediate aftermath of the CNG's takeover was euphoric. Political prisoners were released, and the dreaded Tontons Macoute, Duvalier's clandestine secret police, were disbanded. Namphy's declared purpose was to provide a transition to the inauguration of a democratically elected government. A constituent assembly, convened in October 1986, drafted a new constitution that was approved by referendum in March 1987.

Hopes for the restoration of democracy soon faded. The presidential election scheduled for November 1987 was postponed as gangs of thugs and soldiers killed at least 34 persons. The CNG attempted new elections and a new government, but those governments had no legitimacy at home or abroad. In December, 1990 a Roman Catholic priest, Jean-Bertrand Aristide, was elected with 67.5% of the votes cast.

Aristide had an ideology, a sort of egalitarian Catholic doctrine, and a political coalition of 15 parties, the National Front for Change and Democracy (FNCD), but he did not have the confidence of the military. Upset by his popularity and his foreign policy, which favored stronger hemispheric relations at the expense of US-Haitian relations, the military under General Raoul Cédras ousted him in October 1991. From exile, Aristide did not relent, and appealed to international organizations for help. The UN and OAS forged an agreement between Cédras and Aristide that was to return Aristide to the presidency in October 1993, but the military balked. Aristide promptly appealed to the Clinton administration, even as he criticized US policy, and the Clinton administration responded with sanctions against the Haitian regime in May and June of 1994. However, the impasse persisted.

In September 1994, as a last resort, the Clinton administration secured international support for a military invasion of Haiti to force Cédras from power. A US invasion force was assembled and war seemed imminent. However, at the 11th hour, Clinton sent a special delegation, headed by former US president Jimmy Carter, to negotiate a peaceful solution to the crisis. As US fighter planes were about to take off for Haiti, the Carter team reached an agreement with Cédras and war was diverted. American forces peacefully took control of the country, and in October 1994, restored Aristide to power.

Returning to the country after a three-year absence, Aristide faced two major challenges: rescuing the country's economy, which was in dire straits following the international embargo that had been imposed on it, and curbing the rampant violent street crime, gang activity, and vigilantism that had developed in the absence of an adequate justice system. To cope with the security vacuum created by the departure of the military regime, UN peacekeeping forces arrived in March of 1995. In June, elections for local and legislative office, although marred by mismanagement and requiring additional rounds of voting, remained free of state-sponsored violence and were generally regarded as a sign of success for the nation's fledgling democracy. Although there was strong sentiment among many Haitians in favor of having Aristide remain in office beyond the end of his designated single term as president (most of which had been usurped by military rule), US support remained contingent on adhering to the terms of the 1987 constitution, which barred the president from seeking a second consecutive term. Aristide himself wavered about honoring this provision but ultimately stepped down, endorsing a close associate, René Préval, to succeed him in office. Préval was elected on 17 December 1995, with 88% of the vote. In February 1996 he took office, becoming Haiti's second democratically elected president in the country's 191-year history as an independent nation. The presence of both a UN peacekeeping force of over 1,000 and several hundred US troops was extended through November 1997. In July 1997 Haiti became a member of the Caribbean Community (CARICOM).

Even under relatively stable political conditions, Haiti's economic and security problems proved intractable. Poverty and unemployment—estimated at 80%—remained endemic. In May 1996 Préval agreed to economic reforms demanded by the International Monetary Fund, including privatization of state-owned enterprises, a measure previously resisted by his government. However, former president Aristide opposed the privatization plans and in 1997 formed a new political grouping of his own. After failing to win parliamentary approval for three nominees for prime minister in 1998, President Préval dissolved parliament in January 1999 and unilaterally appointed a new prime minister, provoking civil unrest in the streets. Through the rest of 1999 and early 2000, Préval repeatedly postponed promised legislative elections, leaving the country without a fully operating government, as a wave of violence escalated, eventually claiming the life of the country's most prominent radio journalist, Jean Leopold Dominique, who was murdered in April 2000 murder. An election date of May 2000 was set, but observers predicted that Préval would continue to delay beyond the mid-June electoral deadline after which any new parliament could not be installed until January 2001. It was also widely predicted that Aristide would run again in the presidential elections scheduled for December and probably retake the presidency.

13 GOVERNMENT

Under Article 197 of the 1964 constitution, François Duvalier was appointed president for life, with the stipulation that this article be approved in a nationwide plebiscite. On 14 June, the voters were declared to have "almost unanimously" given their consent. He was granted power to dissolve the Legislative Assembly and the cabinet, and to govern by decree in case of grave conflict. A constitutional amendment in January 1971 allowed the president to choose his successor. Jean-Claude Duvalier became president for life in April 1971 and was chief of state and head of government until early 1986.

The constitution adopted in March 1987 established a president elected to a five-year term as head of state and restricted to no more than two nonconsecutive terms in office. The head of

government was to be the prime minister, appointed by the president from the party holding the majority in both houses of the legislature, made up of a 27-member Senate and a Chamber of Deputies with 83 members. Supporters of the Duvaliers were barred from holding political office for 10 years. Senators are elected for six years and deputies for four.

Since its passage, the constitution was suspended in June 1988, and reinstated in March 1989. The leaders of the coup of October 1991 claimed to be observing the constitution, and Marc Bazin was named head of a caretaker government. But to all observers, nothing approaching a political system was present in Haiti until the restoration of the democratically elected Aristide government in late 1994. Because of an agreement with the US, Aristide was unable to seek a second term and endorsed René Préval to succeed him in office. He was elected on 17 December 1995 as the country's second democratically elected president.

14 POLITICAL PARTIES

From the mid-19th to the mid-20th century, two major political parties, the Liberals and the Nationalists, were predominant. The Liberals, composed mainly of the wealthier and better-educated mulatto minority, advocated legislative control of government, while the Nationalists, composed mainly of the lower- and middle-class black majority, favored a strong executive. The traditional mulatto hegemony, whose wealth was inherited from the departed French colonists, was ended by Duvalier, who used the mulattoes as a scapegoat.

After Jean-Claude Duvalier became president in 1971, some political activity was allowed, but by 1982 most dissidents had again been silenced. In 1979, an opposition Haitian Christian Democratic Party (Parti Démocratique Chrétien d'Haïti—PDCH) was founded, but its leader, Sylvio Claude, was arrested in October 1980. In the 1979 legislative elections only one antigovernment candidate won a seat; he resigned in July 1981. The PDCH dropped out of the municipal election campaign in 1983 following the arrest of several party members on national security charges.

Dozens of parties emerged after the CNG ousted Jean-Claude Duvalier in February 1986, most prominently, the National Front for Change and Democracy (FNCD), which backed Jean-Bertrand Aristide in the 1990 elections, but from which he later disassociated himself. Other groups include the National Congress of Democratic Movements (CONACOM), the Rally of Progressive National Democrats (RDNP), the Revolutionary Progressive Nationalist Party (PANPRA), and the Movement for the Installation of Democracy in Haiti (MIDH), under former prime minister Marc Bazin.

By 1995 the dominant party, and the one associated with Aristide, was the Lavalas Political Platform, an alliance of the Lavalas Political Organization (OPL) and the Movement for the Organization of the Country (MOP). Backed by Aristide and Lavalas, René Préval was elected president in the December 1995 elections with 88% of the vote. In the mid-1995 legislative elections, all but one of the 18 vacated Senate seats were won by Lavalas candidates, and the party also swept the election in the lower house, with 12 seats going to candidates of other groups, including independents. In 1997, former president Bertrand Aristide formally registered a new party, called the Lavalas Family movement, which was expected to challenge the existing Lavalas government party in the next elections. Legislative elections, initially scheduled for June 1999, were postponed repeatedly throughout the rest of 1999 and the first half of 2000. Presidential elections were scheduled for December 2000.

15 LOCAL GOVERNMENT

As of 1999, Haiti was divided into 9 departments and subdivided into arrondissements and communes. Each department is headed by a prefect appointed by the central government. Under the constitution, a commune is headed by an elected mayor, whose powers are strictly circumscribed. Local government is limited, and all taxes collected by the communes are paid directly into the national treasury. The first open municipal elections in 26 years took place in 1983. Local mayoral and council elections were held in December 1995. In January 1999 President René Préval began appointing mayors and other local officials because political violence and instability had resulted in the delay of local elections.

16JUDICIAL SYSTEM

The judiciary consists of four levels: the Court of Cassation, courts of appeal, civil courts, and magistrates' courts. Judges of the Court of Cassation are appointed by the president for 10-year terms. Government prosecutors, appointed by the courts, act in both civil and criminal cases. There are also land, labor, and children's courts. Military courts function in both military and civilian cases when the constitution is suspended. The legal system is based upon the French Napoleonic Code.

Until 1995, the Haitian armed forces controlled law enforcement and public security even though the Constitution called for separation of the police and military. The 1987 Constitution was put into effect in 1995. Although the Constitution also calls for an independent judiciary, all judges since 1986 have been appointed and removed at the will of the government and political pressures affect the judiciary at all levels. The justices of peace issue warrants and adjudicate minor infractions. The Supreme Court deals with questions of procedure and constitutionality. Haiti accepts compulsory jurisdiction of the International Court of Justice.

17ARMED FORCES

In 1994, a civilian administration replaced the military government. The armed forces and police were disbanded and they were replaced with a security force of 3,000 personnel. The air force was disbanded in 1995. Security is currently entrusted to the National Police Force, which has an estimated 5,300 members. A small coast guard mans patrol craft only. In addition, a civilian police force of about 285 is operated by the United Nations Civilian Police Mission (MIPONUH). Security expenditures in 1998 were $48 million or 2.4% of GDP.

18INTERNATIONAL COOPERATION

Haiti is a charter member of the UN, having joined on 24 October 1945, and belongs to ECLAC and all the nonregional specialized agencies. It is also a member of IADB, OAS, the WTO, and other inter-American organizations, as well as of G-77 and the International Coffee Organization. Haiti is a signatory of the Law of the Sea.

19ECONOMY

Haiti is one of the world's poorest countries; 75% of the population lives in abject poverty. The economy is basically agricultural: coffee, mangoes, sugar, rice, corn, sorghum, and wood are the main products. Some cottage industries were developed in the mid 1940s, and in the late 1950s and early 1960s the mining sector, particularly bauxite and cooper, grew to provide important export items. By the early 1980s, however, mining was losing its importance, and light export-oriented industry, based on cheap labor, was the main growing area. The black market transshipment of cocaine is prevalent in the Haitian economy.

Haiti has suffered a series of natural and political setbacks. Hurricanes have often destroyed substantial parts of the coffee and sugar crops. During the 1960–70, the real GDP declined annually by 0.2%. The accession of Jean Claude Duvalier in 1971 improved the economy, and between 1970 and 1979, the average annual growth of the GDP was 4%. The economy took a downward turn in the early 1980s, growing by only 0.90% between 1977 and 1987.

On 30 September 1991 a military coup headed by General Cedras deposed the democratically elected government of President Jean Bertrand Aristide. The OAS and the US imposed several economic sanctions following this military coup. The accumulated contraction in the economy from 1991–94 amounted to about 30%. A UN-mediated agreement called for President Aristide's return to power, which occurred in 1994.

With considerable external assistance, Haiti's administration implemented measures aimed at improving the preconditions for economic stability and growth through fiscal policy and structural reforms. Only an incipient recovery was registered: real GDP grew by only 2% in 1996, which was disappointing after the 4.5% growth posted in 1995. After Aristide was voted out of office in 1996, the Prime Minister resigned in 1997, and the legislature broke up in 1999; all these factors contributed to a cessation of economic reforms. Growth in 1997 only reached 1.4%, but was up again to 3.1% in 1998, and was expected to be 2% in 1999. Donors pledged hundreds of millions of dollars in order to support the country and alleviate poverty, but foreign aid was frozen in 1999 due to the lack of a federal budget.

20INCOME

The US Central Intelligence Agency (CIA) reports that in 1998 Haiti's gross domestic product (GDP) was estimated at $8.9 billion. The per capita GDP was estimated at $1,300. The annual growth rate of GDP was estimated at 3%. The average inflation rate in 1998 was 8%. The CIA defines GDP as the value of all final goods and services produced within a nation in a given year and computed on the basis of purchasing power parity (PPP) rather than value as measured on the basis of the rate of exchange. It was estimated that agriculture accounted for 42% of GDP, industry 14%, and services 44%.

21LABOR

In 1998, the labor force was estimated at 3 million. Agriculture employed 66%; industry, 9%; and services, 25%. Unofficially, the unemployment rate in 1996 was put at 50%.

Because the proportion of wage earners is relatively small, the labor movement is weak. In 1999 there were six small union federations, representing about 5% of the total labor force, and 2–3% of the industrial sector. In 1999, teachers struck for several months over a pay increase that had not been implemented. In industry and service organizations, the eight-hour day and the two-week paid vacation are standard. A revised pre-coup minimum wage applies to private sector workers, but is not enforced for agricultural employees. In 1999, the minimum daily wage was $2.18. Since the majority of Haitians work in subsistence agriculture, they are not covered by the minimum wage.

22AGRICULTURE

With 66% of the laboring population deriving its living exclusively from the soil, farming is the mainstay of the Haitian economy. Although only about one-third of the country's land is considered suitable for cultivation because of the rugged terrain, over 33% of the land was actually being used for crop and feed production in 1994; permanent pasture land amounted to 18% of the total land area. Nevertheless, population growth outstripped agricultural growth during the 1970s, and a drought in 1985 affected the production of such important staple crops as rice, maize, and beans. Consequently, foodstuffs have had to be imported in increasing quantity.

Haitian agriculture is characterized by numerous small plots averaging slightly over 1 hectare (2.5 acres) per family, on which peasants grow most of their food crops and a few other crops for cash sale; few farms exceed 12 hectares (30 acres). Haiti employs an unusual form of farming called arboriculture. Combinations of fruit trees and various roots, particularly the manioc plant, the traditional Haitian bread staple, replace the grain culture of the usual subsistence-economy farming. Crops are cultivated with simple hand tools; the plow or animal power is only rarely employed, except on sugarcane plantations. Coffee is grown on humid mountain slopes, cotton on the semiarid plateaus and sea-level plains, and bananas as well as sugar on the irrigated plains, which covered about 17,000 hectares (42,000 acres) in 1998. Rice has become a basic staple for Haitians, but local production only meets a little more than 20% of demand.

Production of coffee in 1998 totaled 27,000 tons, as compared with the record high of 43,600 tons in 1962. Sugarcane is the second major cash crop, but production has been declining; in 1976, Haiti became a net importer of sugar. Sugarcane production in 1998 was 1,000,000 tons. Other agricultural production figures for the 1998 growing season (in thousands of tons) were bananas, 288; corn, 206; rice, 101; sorghum, 95; dry beans, 35; and cocoa beans, 5.

23 ANIMAL HUSBANDRY

Stock raising is generally a supplementary activity on small farms. In 1998 there were 1,300,000 head of cattle, 800,000 hogs, 1,618,000 goats, 290,000 mules and burros, 138,000 sheep, and 6,000,000 poultry. The hog population was decimated by African swine fever in 1979, and careful efforts at replacement have been unsuccessful. In the mid-1990s, the poultry industry contracted from over 100 commercial producers to less than ten. In addition to the embargo and political uncertainty, the industry is under competitive pressure of low cost poultry imports from the US. Poultry production has not risen enough to fill the vacuum in the rural diet. Extension work directed by the Department of Agriculture's educational center at Damien has helped to stabilize animal husbandry. Poultry production slowly increased from about 6,000 tons per year in the mid-1990s to 8,000 tons by 1998. Native stock has been upgraded by the introduction of hogs and cattle from abroad, particularly the zebu, which does well in the hot, dry plains. Two major stock-feeding centers operate at Port-au-Prince and Cap-Haïtien. Livestock products in 1998 included 80,000 tons of meat, 20,000 tons of goat's milk, 37,000 tons of cow's milk, and 4,000 tons of eggs.

24 FISHING

While the proximity of Haiti to the Windward Passage and the north-flowing currents off the Venezuelan coast place it in the path of major fish migrations, including tuna, marlin, bonito, and sardines, the commercial fishing industry is not developed. Reef fish, including giant grouper and rock lobster, are important food sources because deep-sea fishing is limited. Fisheries have been successfully developed in the small ponds and in the irrigation and drainage ditches of the Artibonite Plain. Carp and tertar, a native fish, are abundant, but lack of transport and other facilities limits this important food source to local consumption. The catch was estimated at 5,643 tons in 1997, including 1,000 tons of Caribbean spiny lobster and 380 tons of conch.

25 FORESTRY

Originally, Haiti was endowed with abundant forest resources. Excellent stands of pine were located in the mountain rain forests of La Hotte Massif and in the Massif du Nord. (Haitian pine is high in turpentine and rosin content, making it suitable for naval stores.) Major stands of mahogany grew in the Fer à Cheval region, and small stands occurred in the island's lower mountain ranges. Tropical oak, cedar, rosewood, and taverneaux also were widespread; hardwoods included lavan (mahogany), narra,

tindalo, and ipil. The intensive use of the forests for fuel, both in colonial times and in the modern era, and the clearing of woodlands for agriculture resulted in a decline of Haiti's forestland from over 2.7 million hectares (6.7 million acres) before the coming of Columbus to about 140,000 hectares (346,000 acres) by 1994, the majority of which was privately owned. Such deforestation has created a problem with soil erosion. Reforestation efforts have been more ambitious in design than successful in execution, although the Agroforestry Outreach Project oversaw the planting of 4.5 million seedlings between 1981 and 1983. Of the estimated 6,601,000 cu m of wood cut in 1997, almost 96% was used for fuel.

26 MINING

All subsoil rights belong to the state. The Mining Law of 1976 and the creation of the Ministry of Mining and Energy Resources in 1978 made relations between the government and private investment possible, so that mining companies may be privately owned. Haiti possesses undeveloped resources of lignite, copper, gold, silver, antimony, tin, sulfur, coal, nickel, gypsum, and porphyry. Manganese deposits are found in the Morne Macat section of the Massif du Nord; bauxite, near Miragoâne; lignite deposits in the Plateau Central; and copper deposits, both sedimentary and in veins, in the Massif du Nord. Mining is limited, and mineral exploration has generally been conducted by foreign enterprises. Production of bauxite, which peaked at 613,000 tons in 1979, and exports of which were worth $14.9 million in 1982, ceased with the 1985 closing of the Reynolds mine. Private gold mining is permitted, but the metal must be sold to the National Bank. Copper mining was suspended in 1971 because it became uneconomical. The Haitian marble industry is being developed for export possibilities; clay, limestone, gravel, salt, and stone are also produced for the domestic market. Production in 1997 included 750,000 cubic meters of gravel, 250,000 cubic meters of sand, and 100 tons of marble.

27 ENERGY AND POWER

Net installed electrical capacity totaled 155,000 kW in 1998. Output increased from 118 million kWh in 1970 to 728 million kWh in 1998. More than half of the nation's electricity was generated by petroleum-burning plants in 1998. The Péligre Dam on the Artibonite River, financed by a $30-million loan from the US Export-Import Bank, was opened in 1971, and the Gaillard Dam on the same river was opened in 1985. Power represented the government's top investment priority in the early 1970s, but a decade later the electricity supply was still erratic and inadequate. Most industrial plants have standby generators. In 1971, the government took over the foreign-owned electric company and established the Haitian Electrical Co. as a government enterprise. By 1990, however, only 10% of the population had access to electricity.

Oil exploration and drilling operations have been conducted in the Plateau Central, Gonâve Island, and the Cul-de-Sac region, but there was no commercial production as of the mid-1990s. During the trade embargo on Haiti, gasoline and other petroleum products were regularly smuggled in through the Dominican Republic.

28 INDUSTRY

Industry is primarily devoted to the processing of agricultural and forestry products. During 1970–78, the industrial sector grew by 8.3% annually; between 1977 and 1987, growth was null; and between 1988 and 1998 the sector declined by 3.1% annually. The parastatal flour refinery and cement factory were sold to foreign interests in 1999. The flour refinery had been out of service for five years before it began operations again in 1998. The cement factory was undergoing restructuring in 1999, and thus was closed. Other industries produce aluminum, enamelware, garments and hats, essential oils, plastic, soap, pharmaceuticals, and paint. A steel plant commenced operations in 1974, converting imported scrap into steel sections. Haitian plants also assemble US-made components to create electronic devices, toys and leather goods. In 1986, before the trade embargo, some 140 export assembly firms employed about 40,000 people. The figure was only 400 in 1994. In 1999, 25,000 people were employed in such firms.

In 1998 aggregate demand was boosted by continued growth in domestic investment and a moderate increase in consumption. Industry grew by 6% annually in 1997 and 1998. However, a growing trade imbalance preempted a more robust recovery. Construction has been consistently more dynamic than agriculture and manufacturing, which realized only moderate output increases.

29SCIENCE AND TECHNOLOGY

The National Council for Scientific Research, founded in 1963, coordinates scientific activities in Haiti, especially in the public health field. Four colleges and universities, including the University of Haiti, offer degrees in basic and applied sciences.

30DOMESTIC TRADE

Port-au-Prince, a free port, is the commercial center of Haiti, with Cap-Haitien second in importance. Most Haitian products are sold in regional markets, which meet on traditional established days, once or twice a week. Women peddlers comb the countryside for comestibles, traveling great distances to and from markets. The Croix-de-Bossales market in Port-au-Prince is the largest market in the country, handling about two-thirds of the food and manufactures used in the capital.

Imported goods usually are sold in small stalls (boutiques), but there are some modern supermarkets. Specialty goods and articles for the tourist trade are offered by merchants who are generally franchised to handle specific brands. Although foreign imports, motion pictures, and soft drinks are advertised in newspapers, radio is the principal advertising medium.

Stores are generally open on weekdays from 8 AM to 5 PM in the winter. In summer, closing time is set by law at 4 PM; on Saturdays, stores close at noon. Banks are open from 9 AM to 1 PM, Monday through Friday.

31FOREIGN TRADE

Coffee has been supplanted as the main export by manufactured articles assembled in Haiti for export. The high deficit in the trade balance, with a marginal increase in exports and continued high import buoyancy in the late 1990s, reflects pent-up aggregate demand that is not satisfied by domestic production. Narrowing the trade deficit will therefore require a policy mix that prioritizes export-oriented productive sectors.

The light manufacture of clothes in Haiti accounts for the majority of commodity exports (44%). Other exports include coffee (9.6%), perfume (5.7%), fruit and nuts (5.6%), toys, and sporting goods (3.8%). Haiti's biggest export market is, by far, the US. Principal trading partners in 1998 (in millions of US dollars) were as follows:

COUNTRY	EXPORTS	IMPORTS	BALANCE
United States	256	603	-347
France	8	35	-27
Canada	3	15	-12
Germany	2	17	-15
United Kingdom	1	15	-14
Japan	1	44	-43
Netherlands	1	22	-21
Dominican Republic	n.a.	38	
Columbia	n.a.	29	

32BALANCE OF PAYMENTS

The current account deficit peaked in 1995 at 17% of GDP due to a rush of imports after sanctions were lifted, but gradually decreased to about 6% of GDP in 1998. The US Central Intelligence Agency reports that in 1997 the purchasing power parity of Haiti's exports was $110 million while imports totaled $486 million resulting in a trade balance of -$376 million.

The International Monetary Fund (IMF) reports that in 1998 Haiti had exports of goods totaling $299 million and imports totaling $641 million. The services credit totaled $180 million and debit $381 million. The following table summarizes Haiti's balance of payments as reported by the IMF for 1998 in millions of US dollars.

Current Account		-38
Balance on goods	-341	
Balance on services	-201	
Balance on income	-12	
Current transfers	516	
Capital Account		...
Financial Account		193
Direct investment abroad	...	
Direct investment in Haiti	11	
Portfolio investment assets	...	
Portfolio investment liabilities	...	
Other investment assets	87	
Other investment liabilities	96	
Net Errors and Omissions		-121
Reserves and Related Items		-35

33BANKING AND SECURITIES

The national bank of the Republic of Haiti (Banque Nationale de la République d'Haïti—BRH), the sole bank of issue and government depository, was founded in 1880 and acquired from US interests in 1934 and became the fiscal agent of Haiti in 1947. As the nation's principal commercial bank, it participates in the national lottery, the national printing office and plant, the National Archives, banana development, the tobacco and sugar monopolies, the Agricultural and Industrial Development Institute, and the Agricultural Credit Bureau; it is also a depositor with the IMF and IBRD.

The first private Haitian bank, the Bank of the Haitian Union, opened in 1973. In 1999, 11 other commercial banks were in operation; including one of them Haitian (Banque Industrielle et Commerciale d'Haiti), one US (Citibank), and one Canadian (Bank of Nova Scotia). There are two state-owned banks, Banque Nationale de Crédit and Banque Populaire Haitienne. Other banks included Promobank, Unibank, Sogebank, Socabank, Inter-Continental, and Capital Bank.

There is no securities exchange in Haiti. Trading in Haitian corporations that make public offerings of their bonds or equity shares is conducted on the New York over-the-counter market.

34INSURANCE

Major world insurance companies maintain agencies or branches in Haiti, the most prominent being Sun Life of Canada, the first to enter into life insurance. The insurance classes covered are life, accident, sickness, fire, and motor.

35PUBLIC FINANCE

The US Central Intelligence Agency (CIA) estimates that in 1997 Haiti's central government took in revenues of approximately $323 million and had expenditures of $363 million. Overall, the government registered a deficit of approximately $40 million. External debt totaled $1.13 billion.

36TAXATION

Income tax is the most important direct tax. Corporate and personal income taxes are progressive from 9% to 30%. Since

1951, new corporations, if placed on the government's list of recommended new industries have benefited from special tax concessions, including customs duties exemption and a five-year corporate income tax exemption. In 1985, the VAT on many consumer goods was raised from 7% to 10%.

37CUSTOMS AND DUTIES

In February 1987, a new tariff structure replaced all remaining specific duties with ad valorem tariffs and introduced new rates of between zero and 40% except for higher rates on rice, maize, millet, flour, and gasoline. The average tariff rate was set at 20%, with rates of 10% on equipment and raw materials. The Haitian government is considering a proposal to lower tariff rates as much as 50%. All imports are subject to a 10% VAT.

Haiti has been invited into CARICOM, but had not agreed to membership as of 1999. The country is also a part of the CBI, allowing duty-free entry of exports to the US; and is a signatory to the Lome Convention allowing mostly free exporting to the EU.

38FOREIGN INVESTMENT

The government welcomes foreign investment, granting important concessions to new industries not competing with local production. Such enterprises are exempt from import and export duties for the life of the enterprise and enjoy a full tax exception for the first five year of operation. Companies locating in the industrial park are entitled to tax exception for a further three years. For companies that locate outside Port-au-Prince metropolitan area the 100% income tax exemption for 5 to 15 years with 15% to 20% of the income tax payable thereafter. Additionally, for export and import oriented business, there is an exemption without time limit from customs duties on imported machinery, equipment, raw materials, and accessories needed for production. Foreign capital enjoys equal status treatment with Haitian capital. The National Office for Investment Promotion is in charge of foreign investment.

Substantial foreign investment in Haiti began during World War II as a means of stimulating production goods considered essential to the US war effort. Agricultural development was financed largely by the US Export-Import Bank and the World Bank, supplemented with private foreign capital.

In October 1996, the IMF approved a $131 million loan to Haiti. The credit, to be provided over a three-year period, is aimed at supporting a national economic reform program. The international donor community committed $2 billion in concessional loans and grants to Haiti for the 1995–99 period, including $390 million from the World Bank. Unfortunately, the political impasse of 1999 caused a freeze on international donations.

Foreign direct investment since the lifting of the trade embargo in 1995 has increased only moderately; most investment comes from petroleum companies. Other major foreign investors include American Airlines, American Rice Corporation, Citibank, Compagnie Tabac, Continental Grain, Seaboard Marine, and Western Wireless, from the US; and Royal Caribbean and Scotiabank.

39ECONOMIC DEVELOPMENT

Although its annual national revenue covers basic necessities, the government supports development programs by encouraging loans and by requiring private enterprises to finance development projects. Aided by the US and various international aid organizations, the government has supported the construction of tourist facilities, public works, and irrigation and the creation of monopolies in cement, sugar marketing, tobacco and lumbering.

The framework for economic policy in 1996 was determined mainly by the passage of a structural reform program and the agreement signed between the Central Bank and the Ministry of Finance to curtail financing of the fiscal deficit by the Central Bank. Passage of the structural reform program (which forms the basis for international financial support and includes Civil Service Reform and Modernization of Public Enterprises), proved slow and difficult. The Civil Service Reform prescribes the modalities for a reduction of the civil service by 7,500 employees over a period of 18 months. The Modernization of Public Enterprises program established a legal framework for private sector participation in the state-owned enterprises, in the form of either concession, management contract, and/ or capitalization.

About 75% of the population lives in abject poverty. Nearly 70% of all Haitians depend on the agriculture sector, which consists mainly of small-scale subsistence farming and employs about two-thirds of the economically active work force. The country has experienced only moderate job creation since President Aristide was returned to power in October 1994. Failure to reach agreement with multilateral lenders in late 1995 led to rising deficit spending and subsequently increasing inflation and a drop in the value of the Haitian currency in the final months of 1995. Potential investors, both foreign and domestic, have been reluctant to risk their capital, planning to "wait and see" what happens. The government will have to grapple with implementing necessary, although unpopular, economic reforms in order to obtain badly needed foreign aid and improve Haiti's ability to attract foreign capital if the Haitian economy is to gain momentum. Haiti will continue to depend heavily on foreign aid in the medium term.

Macroeconomic stability, structural and institutional reforms, and poverty alleviation are still the main objectives in Haiti's agenda for the future. The administration has demonstrated its commitment through an ESAF program with the IMF; the passage of laws pertaining to structural reforms; coordinated efforts with multilateral and national institutions to design the modernization of the state program; and continuation of programs for poverty alleviation such as the Economic and Social Assistance Fund. Political difficulties in 1999 undermined most plans for furthering economic development.

40SOCIAL DEVELOPMENT

Public social insurance programs are limited, but there is a pervasive tradition of self-help and personal charity. The national lottery is the principal source of welfare funds, while an employer tax provides workers' compensation for occupational accidents for the relatively small number of industrial workers. Old age, disability, and survivor benefits are funded by 2%–6% of employee wages and an equal percentage of the employer's payroll. As of 1999, pensions were set at one third of average earnings during the last ten years of employment.

A social services law enacted in 1961 required every factory, enterprise of regional importance, and "foreign colony" to endow its neighborhood with social services such as dispensaries, schools, low-cost housing, and artesian wells. The law, however, contained no precise definitions of the enterprises affected, no specifications as to the extent of the services to be rendered, and no details on control, enforcement, or penalties. A health and maternity insurance law of 1967 had not been implemented as of 1995.

The status of women varies, ranging from restriction to traditional occupations in rural areas to prominent positions in the public and private sectors in urban areas. As of 1995, 3 of 83 seats in the lower house of Parliament were occupied by women. Domestic abuse is widespread.

In 1994, the government signed the International Convention on the Rights of the Child. Many children in Haiti are forced to work as domestic servants in the homes of middle and upper class families, a practice that has been cited as "20th-century slavery" in a UN report.

Levels of violence by Haiti's military government were high in 1993 and the first half of 1994, causing thousands of refugees to flee the country, many in small boats made unsafe by overcrowding. Under the government of Aristide, however, the human rights situation improved. In 1997, austerity measures led to strikes and antigovernment demonstrations. Human rights violations by police were reported in 1999.

41HEALTH

In general, sanitation facilities in Haiti are among the poorest in Latin America. Haiti lacks water in both quantity and quality, with only 29% of the urban population having access to safe water in 1995. City sewerage systems are inadequate, and business and residential areas often make use of septic tanks. In 1995, only 27% of Haiti's population had access to adequate sanitation.

The number of physicians increased from 412 in 1972 to 887 in 1988 and, in 1997, there was approximately one doctor per 10,000 people. Half the doctors are in Port-au-Prince, and a fourth are in other principal towns, leaving a minimum of medical services for the rural population. In 1995, there were eight hospital beds per 1,000 people.

Malaria and yaws have been combated by WHO, while other health programs have been conducted by the Rockefeller Foundation and the American Sanitary Mission. Tuberculosis has long been a serious health problem, and in 1991, there were about 155 reported cases of tuberculosis per 100,000 inhabitants. Malnutrition and gastrointestinal diseases are responsible for more than half of all deaths. Children may receive vaccinations, but the statistics are very low. As of 1995, Haiti's government did not pay for routine vaccines. In 1997, children up to one year old were vaccinated against tuberculosis (40%); diphtheria, pertussis, and tetanus (35%); polio (32%); and measles (30%). Goiter was present in 12.4% of school age children in 1996. Some 27% of children were underweight between 1989 and 1995. In the early 1980s, Haitians were named among the groups that had high risk factors for contracting acquired immune deficiency syndrome (AIDS), but as of late 1987, it had not been ascertained what those risk factors are. Haiti has one of the highest HIV infection rates in the Americas. The HIV-1 seroprevalence rate was 5.17 per 100 adults in 1997. Almost 5,000 new cases of AIDS were reported in 1996.

The fertility rate has declined from 6.3 in 1960 to 4.4 children per woman in 1997. Some 15% of all births between 1993 and 1996 were considered low birth weight. Haiti has the highest maternal mortality rate in the Americas region: 457 maternal deaths per 1,000 live births occurred in 1997. The infant mortality rate fell from 182 per 1,000 live births in 1960 to 74 in 1996, and the general mortality rate was 11.9 per 1,000 in 1990–95. During 1998, the average life expectancy was 54.5 years. The 1999 birth rate was 32.5 per 1,000 people. In 1997 contraception among women (ages 15 to 49) was used at the rate of 18%. In 1993, still only about half the population (45%) had access to health care services. Total health care expenditures for 1995 were $19 per capita.

42HOUSING

Although housing projects have been constructed in Port-au-Prince and in Cap-Haïtien, there is an increasing shortage of low-cost housing. Migration to the major cities has compounded the urban housing problem. Outside the capital and some other cities, housing facilities are generally primitive and almost universally without sanitation. Wooden huts are the prevalent standard for the countryside. There is as yet no official low-cost housing program. By presidential decree, the National Housing Office

was established in 1966. Housing built in the 1970s in Port-au-Prince for about 18,000 people merely replaced demolished units. A new cooperative project, supervised by the National Housing Office and financed by UNDP, was initiated in 1979 in St. Martin, on the outskirts of Port-au-Prince. Housing construction is reported to have proceeded at a steady pace since that time. According to the latest available information, total housing units numbered 890,000, with 6.1 people per dwelling.

43EDUCATION

Although 80% of the students speak Creole and have only rudimentary knowledge of French, educational programs are mostly conducted in French. The Office of National Literacy and Community Action has the major responsibility for literacy programs throughout the country. The adult literacy rate for the year 2000 was estimated at 51.4% (males, 49.0%; females, 53.5%).

Although education is compulsory between the ages of six and 12, the majority of children do not attend school. It was estimated that in the early 1990s only 26% of primary school aged children were enrolled in school. In 1991, Haiti had 7,306 primary schools, with 555,433 pupils and 26,208 teachers. In general secondary schools there were 184,968 students and 9,470 teachers. The Université d'État d'Haïti (Port-au-Prince), dating from 1920, offers the following schools: administration and management, agronomy, economics, ethnology, law, medicine and pharmacy, odontology, science, and surveying. There are about two dozen other universities in Haiti, including the Universite Jacques Theodore Holly. There are also several vocational training centers and trade schools.

44LIBRARIES AND MUSEUMS

The library of the Brothers of St.-Louis de Gonzage, the finest in Haiti, includes bound newspaper collections covering the 19th and 20th centuries and many rare works of the colonial and republican eras. The Bibliothèque Nationale contains about 23,000 volumes. Le Petit Séminaire, a parochial college, has an excellent library. The government has a wealth of library material dating back to colonial Saint-Domingue in the National Archives and rare papers on the Napoleonic expedition in Haiti in the famous Rochambeau Collection. Private libraries, notably the Mangones Library in Pétionville, make important contributions to Haitian scholarship. There is a French Institute and an American Institute library in Port-au-Prince. The University of Haiti has an important agricultural collection.

The National Museum in Port-au-Prince dates from 1938. The Museum of the Haitian People, also in the capital, has anthropological and folklore collections, and the College of St. Pierre houses the Museum of Haitian Art, which opened in 1972. There is a historical and public affairs museum in the capital as well.

45MEDIA

The government owns and operates domestic telephone and telegraph communications. In 1995 there were 45,000 telephone lines, with automatic transmission in Port-au-Prince, Cap-Haïtien, Jacmel, and Les Cayes, and a new 30,000-line network was nearing completion. All America Radio and Cables, RCA Global Communications, and Western Union International provide international telephone and telegraph service. As of 1999 there were 33 AM radio stations, no FM stations, and 2 TV stations, providing commercial and government broadcast services. In 1997 there were 55 radios and 5 television sets per 1,000 population. Télé Haïti is a commercial cable station; it has also been given exclusive rights to import and sell television parts and receivers. National Television of Haiti, the official station, began broadcasting in 1985.

The principal Haitian newspapers (all published in Port-au-Prince) are the three dailies, *Le Matin*, (1999 circulation, 5,000), *Le Nouvelliste*, (6,000), and *L'Union*, (7,000). *Le Moniteur*, the official gazette, is published three times a week.

The constitution guarantees free speech and a free press, and the government is said to uphold these freedoms with few exceptions. There are generally no reports of censorship, nor do the media appear to practice self-censorship.

46 ORGANIZATIONS

Organizational activity in Haiti is limited. The Credit Cooperative of Les Cayes, the only cooperative of any significance, has maintained a sizable membership. Branches of the Red Cross, Rotary, Boy Scouts, and Girl Scouts function, as does the Masonic Order. The Centre d'Art, an informal artists' cooperative founded in 1944, has exhibited Haitian artists locally and internationally. There is a chamber of commerce in Port-au-Prince.

47 TOURISM, TRAVEL, AND RECREATION

For entry to Haiti, visitors generally are required to have passports. Nationals of the US, UK and its possessions, France, and Germany do not need visas. In the 1980s, tourism was adversely affected by the island's generally depressed economy and political turbulence and by the alleged link between Haitians and AIDS. Tourism had declined in the mid-1990s, falling from 143,700 tourist arrivals in 1990 to 70,200 in 1994, but rebounded to 149,000 by 1997. Tourists spent $57 million in that year. There were 1,758 hotel rooms in 1997.

The average daily cost of staying in Port-au-Prince, according to 1999 UN estimates, was $174. Elsewhere the average cost estimate was $57 per night.

Port-au-Prince is a free port for a variety of luxury items. Tourist attractions include white sand beaches, numerous colonial buildings in Port-au-Prince and other cities, and the early 19th century Citadelle and Sans Souci Palace in Cap-Haïtien. Rapid divorces—granted in 24 to 48 hours—and casino gambling are among the attractions for US residents. Football (soccer) is the national sport, and cockfighting is very popular. Tourist resorts offer facilities for water sports and tennis.

48 FAMOUS HAITIANS

The national heroes of Haiti include Pierre Dominique Toussaint L'Ouverture (1743–1803), the Precursor; Jean Jacques Dessalines (1758–1806), who defeated Napoleon's army and proclaimed Haitian independence; Alexandre Sabès Pétion (1770–1818), first president of the republic established in southern Haiti; and Henri Christophe (1767–1820), king of Haiti (1811–20), who built the famous Citadelle and Sans Souci Palace. François Duvalier ("Papa Doc," 1907–71), originally trained as a physician, was elected president in 1957 and in 1964 became president for life. His son Jean-Claude Duvalier (b.1951) inherited his father's title in 1971 but was ousted in 1986. Leslie F. Manigat (b.1930) was president in 1988.

John James Audubon (1785–1851), an artist and ornithologist, was born in Haiti. The writers Éméric Bergeaud (1818–58), Oswald Durand (1840–1906), Philippe Thoby-Marcelin (1904–75), Jacques Roumain (1907–44), and Jean Fernand Brierre (b.1909) have won international literary recognition. Noted poets include the dramatist Pierre Faubert (1803–68), Corolian Ardouin (1812–35), Alibée Féry (1819–96), and Charles-Seguy Villavaleix (1835–1923). Haitian artists include the sculptor Edmond Laforestière (1837–1904); the primitive painter Héctor Hippolyte (1890–1948), leader of the Afro-Art Renaissance in the Caribbean; Wilson Bigaud (b.1929); and Enguérrand Gourge (b.1931). Haitian composers include Occide Jeanty (1860–1936) and Justin Elie (1883–1931); Ludovic Lamothe (1882–1953) used voodoo music in his compositions.

49 DEPENDENCIES

Haiti has no territories or colonies.

50 BIBLIOGRAPHY

Abbott, Elizabeth. *Haiti: The Duvaliers and their Legacy*. New York: Simon and Schuster, 1991.

Dayan, Joan, *Haiti, History, and the Gods*. Berkeley: University of California Press, 1995.

DeWind, Josh. *Aiding Migration: the Impact of International Development Assistance on Haiti*. Boulder, Colo.: Westview Press, 1988.

Dupuy, Alex. *Haiti in the New World Order: The Limits of the Democratic Revolution*. Boulder, Colo.: Westview Press, 1997.

Greene, Anne. *The Catholic Church in Haiti: Political and Social Change*. East Lansing: Michigan State University Press, 1993.

Haggerty, Richard A. (ed.) *Dominican Republic and Haiti: Country Studies*. 2d ed. Washington, D.C.: Library of Congress, 1991.

Haiti: Dangerous Crossroads. Boston, Mass.: South End Press, 1995.

Heinl, Robert Debs. *Written in Blood: The Story of the Haitian People, 1492–1995*. Lanham: University Press of America, 1996.

Laguerre, Michel S. *The Military and Society in Haiti*. Knoxville: University of Tennessee Press, 1993.

Nicholls, David. *From Dessalines to Duvalier: Race, Colour, and National Independence in Haiti*. New Brunswick, N.J.: Rutgers University Press, 1996.

Plummer, Brenda Gayle. *Haiti and the United States: the Psychological Moment*. Athens: University of Georgia Press, 1992.

HONDURAS

Republic of Honduras
República de Honduras

CAPITAL: Tegucigalpa.

FLAG: The national flag consists of a white horizontal stripe between two blue horizontal stripes, with five blue stars on the white stripe representing the five members of the former union of Central American provinces.

ANTHEM: *Himno Nacional,* beginning "Tu bandera es un lampo de cielo" ("Thy flag is a heavenly light").

MONETARY UNIT: The lempira (L), also known as the peso, is a paper currency of 100 centavos. There are coins of 1, 2, 5, 10, 20, and 50 centavos, and notes of 1, 2, 5, 10, 20, 50, and 100 lempiras. L1 = $0.06784 (or $1 = L14.74) as of 31 March 2000.

WEIGHTS AND MEASURES: The metric system is the legal standard; some old Spanish measures are still used.

HOLIDAYS: New Year's Day, 1 January; Day of the Americas, 14 April; Labor Day, 1 May; Independence Day, 15 September; Birthday of Francisco Morazán, 3 October; Columbus Day, 12 October; Army Day, 21 October; Christmas, 25 December. Movable religious holidays include Holy Thursday, Good Friday, and Holy Saturday.

TIME: 6 AM = noon GMT.

¹LOCATION, SIZE, AND EXTENT

Situated in Central America, Honduras has a total area of 112,090 sq km (43,278 sq mi), with a length of 663 km (412 mi) ENE-WSW and 317 km (197 mi) NNW-SSE. Comparatively, the area occupied by Honduras is slightly larger than the state of Tennessee. It is bounded on the N and E by the Caribbean Sea, on the S by Nicaragua and the Gulf of Fonseca, on the SW by El Salvador, and on the W by Guatemala, with a total boundary length of 2,340 km (1,454 mi). Under the terms of an arbitration award made by Alfonso XIII of Spain in 1906, Honduras received a portion of the Mosquito (Miskito) Coast, or La Mosquitia, north and west of the Coco (Segovia) River. Citing Honduras's failure to integrate the territory, Nicaragua renewed its claim to the entire Mosquito Coast in the 1950s and brought the case to the International Court of Justice (ICJ). In February 1957, Honduras created the new Department of Gracias a Dios, made up of the former Mosquitia territory. The ICJ determined in 1960 that Nicaragua was obligated to accept the 1906 arbitration ruling concerning that country's boundary with Honduras. The judges ruled, by a vote of 14–1, that once a valid arbitration award was made in an international dispute, it became effective, and remained so, despite any lapse of time in carrying it out.

The two tiny Swan Islands (Islas del Cisne), lying at 17°23′N and 83°56′w in the west Caribbean Sea some 177 km (110 mi) NNE of Patuca Point, were officially ceded by the US to Honduras on 20 November 1971. For administrative purposes, they are included under the Department of Islas de la Bahía, whose capital is Roatán on Roatán Island. The Swan Islands had been effectively held by the US, which asserted a claim in 1863 to exploit guano, and had housed a weather station and an aviation post.

The capital city of Honduras, Tegucigalpa, is located in the south central part of the country.

²TOPOGRAPHY

Honduras is mountainous, with the exception of the northern Ulúa and Aguán river valleys on the Caribbean Sea and the southern coastal area. There are four main topographic regions: the eastern lowlands and lower mountain slopes, with 20% of the land area and no more than 5% of the population; the northern coastal plains and mountain slopes, with 13% of the land and about 20% of the population; the central highlands, with 65% of the area and 70% of the population; and the Pacific lowlands and their adjacent lower mountain slopes, with 2% of the area and 5% of the population.

The width of the Caribbean coastal plain varies from practically no shore to about 120 km (75 mi), and the coastal plain of the Gulf of Fonseca is generally narrow. The highest elevations are in the northwest (almost 3,000 m/10,000 ft) and in the south (over 2,400 m/8,000 ft). Many intermontane valleys, at elevations of 910 to 1,370 m (3,000 to 4,500 ft), are settled. The old capital city, Comayagua, lies in a deep rift that cuts the country from north to south. Tegucigalpa, the modern capital, is situated in the southern highlands at about 910 m (3,000 ft). There are two large rivers in the north, the Patuca and the Ulúa. Other important features include the Choluteca, Nacaome, and Goascorán rivers in the south, Lake Yojoa in the west, and Caratasca Lagoon in the northeast.

³CLIMATE

The northern Caribbean area and the southern coastal plain have a wet, tropical climate, but the interior is drier and cooler. Temperature varies with altitude. The coastal lowlands average 31°C (88°F); from 300 to 760 m (1,000 to 2,500 ft) above sea level the average is 29°C (84°F); and above 760 m (2,500 ft) the average temperature is 23°C (73°F). There are two seasons: a rainy period, from May through October, and a dry season, from November through April. Average annual rainfall varies from over 240 cm (95 in) along the northern coast to about 84 cm (33 in) around Tegucigalpa in the south. The northwest coast is vulnerable to hurricanes, of which the most destructive, Hurricane Fifi in September 1974, claimed some 12,000 lives, caused $200 million in property damage, and devastated the banana plantations.

⁴FLORA AND FAUNA

Honduras has a rich and varied flora and fauna. Tropical trees, ferns, moss, and orchids abound, especially in the rain forest areas. Mammal life includes the anteater, armadillo, coyote, deer, fox, peccary, pocket gopher, porcupine, puma, tapir, and monkeys in several varieties. Fish and turtles are numerous in both freshwater and marine varieties. Among the reptiles are the bushmaster, coral snake, fer-de-lance, horned viper, rattlesnake, and whip snake, caiman, crocodile, and iguana. Birds include the black robin, hummingbird, macaw, nightingale, thrush, partridge, quail, quetzal, toucanet, wren, and many others.

⁵ENVIRONMENT

The major environmental problems are soil erosion and loss of soil fertility (in part because of traditional slash-and-burn cultivation) and rapid depletion of forests for lumber, firewood, and land cultivation. In the mid-1980s, deforestation had claimed 347 square miles; that figure was projected to increase dramatically later in the decade as a result of the construction of a charcoal-burning steel mill and a pulp and paper mill. According to the World Environment Center, Honduras was predicted to be completely deforested by the year 2000.

Enforcement of anti-pollution laws has been weak, and Honduras also lacks an integrated economic development and land-use policy. Rivers and streams in Honduras are threatened by pollution from mining chemicals. The nation has 24.5 cu mi of water with 91% used in farming activities. Nineteen percent of city dwellers and 47% of people living in rural areas do not have pure water. Honduras' cities produce 0.5 million tons of solid waste per year. Air pollution results from a lack of pollution control equipment for industries and automobiles. The Secretariat of Planning, Coordination, and Budget (Secretaría de Planificación, Coordinación, y Presupuesto—SECPLAN), the Ministry of Natural Resources, and several other agencies are vested with environmental responsibilities.

In the mid-1990s, 7.7% of the total land area in Honduras was protected. In the same year, one of Honduras' 179 species of mammals was threatened. Eleven bird species in 672 and three reptiles in a total of 161 were also threatened. Forty-three plant species of 5,000 are endangered. Endangered or extinct species in Honduras include the tundra peregrine falcon, jaguar, three species of turtle (green sea, hawksbill, and olive ridley), and three species of crocodile (spectacled caiman, American, and Morelet's).

⁶POPULATION

The population of Honduras in 2000 was estimated at 6,130,135. An estimated 3.2% of the population is 65 years of age or older. The projected population for the year 2005 is 6,750,000, assuming a crude birthrate of 27 per 1,000 population and a death rate of 8, resulting in a natural rate of change of 1.8% for the period 2000–2005. The population rate of change between 1995 and 2000 was 2.8%. The population density in 1998 was 55 per sq km (142 per sq mi), compared with 13 per sq km (33 per sq mi) in 1950.

It was estimated that 47% of the population lived in urban areas in 2000, up from 35% in 1980. The capital city, Tegucigalpa, had a 2000 metropolitan population of 1,241,000. San Pedro Sula, the second-largest city, had an estimated population of 450,000; La Ceiba, 71,600; and El Progreso, 63,400.

⁷MIGRATION

Before 1969 there was a steady flow of immigrants from El Salvador. The steps taken by the Honduran government in 1969 to curb this influx were a contributing cause of the "soccer war" with El Salvador during the same year. When the Sandinistas took over in Nicaragua in 1979, former National Guard members began to arrive in Honduras, and by 1983 there were 5,000–10,000 of them along the border. In addition, at least 25,000 Miskito Amerindians from Nicaragua and about 21,000 Salvadorans had fled to Honduras by the end of 1986. Many of them later returned, but by the end of 1992 about 100,000 citizens of Central American nations had taken refuge in Honduras.

As a result of the Central American refugee problem of the 1990s, Honduras has adopted a restrictive policy toward refugees. As of 30 June 1999, there were only nine recognized refugees in Honduras, eight of whom were from Haiti. Also as of 1999, delays in the reconstruction process after the severe damage inflicted by Hurricane Mitch have caused an increase in Honduran emigration to North America. In 1999, the net migration rate was -1.46 migrants per 1,000 population.

⁸ETHNIC GROUPS

The vast majority (90%) of the Honduran people are mestizo, a mixture of white and Amerindian. About 7% of the population is Amerindian, the largest proportion being in the Copán area near the Guatemalan border. Blacks, about 2% of the population, live mostly along the north coast. Perhaps 1% of the population is white, chiefly of Spanish origin.

⁹LANGUAGES

The official language is Spanish. However, English is used widely, especially in northern Honduras. The more important Amerindian languages include Miskito, Zambo, Paya, and Xicaque.

¹⁰RELIGIONS

Religious freedom is guaranteed by the constitution of 1982. The Roman Catholic Church reports a membership that comprises slightly more than 80% of the country's total population. However, according estimates based on a 1999 poll of citizens 18 or older, only 60.3% of the population identify themselves as Roman Catholic. Approximately 28.7% report themselves to be evangelical Christians, and 6.8% designate themselves as belonging to other religious groups. The remaining 4.2% polled were either undecided or provided no answer. The primary faiths include Roman Catholicism, Judaism, Greek Orthodox, Episcopalian, Lutheran, Jehovah's Witnesses, Mennonite, the Church of Jesus Christ of Latter-Day Saints, the Union Church, and about 300 evangelical Protestant churches.

¹¹TRANSPORTATION

In 1998 there were 14,173 km (8,807 mi) of highways, about 3,126 km (1942 mi) of which were paved. The Pan American Highway virtually bypasses Honduras, entering from El Salvador and running to the eastern Nicaraguan border. The 362-km (225-mi) Inter-Ocean Highway is the only surface connection between the Pacific and the Caribbean that includes in its path both Tegucigalpa and San Pedro Sula. In 1971, a paved highway was opened between Tegucigalpa and San Pedro Sula and west to the Guatemalan border. Tegucigalpa is served by secondary roads to the north and east, while San Pedro Sula is connected both to the important Caribbean ports of Puerto Cortés, Tela, and Trujillo and to the western Mayan shrine site of Copán. Road improvements near the Nicaraguan border were undertaken with US military aid beginning in 1983.

Rail service exists only in the north, connecting the industrial and banana-growing northeastern coastal zone with the principal ports and cities. National Railway of Honduras, owned and operated by the government, maintains all 595 km (370 mi) of track.

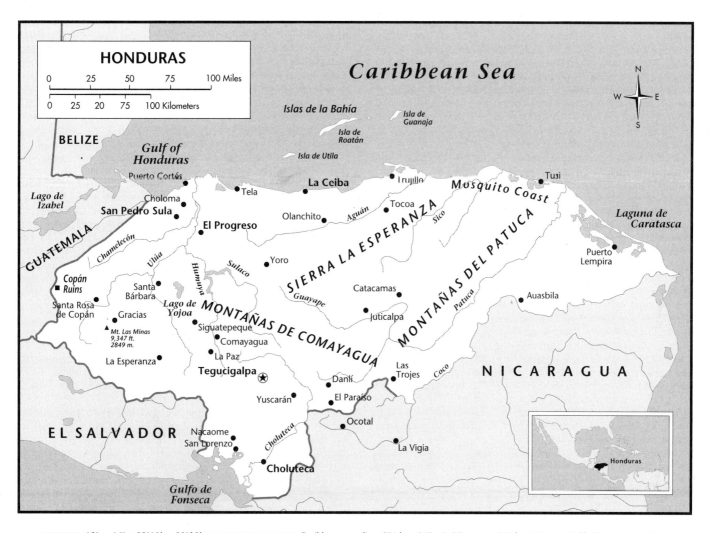

HONDURAS

| 0 | 25 | 50 | 75 | 100 Miles |
| 0 | 25 | 20 | 75 | 100 Kilometers |

Caribbean Sea

Islas de la Bahía

Isla de Guanaja

Isla de Roatán

Isla de Utila

BELIZE

Gulf of Honduras

Puerto Cortés

Lago de Izabel

Choloma

San Pedro Sula

El Progreso

La Ceiba

Tela

Trujillo

Tocoa

Olanchito

Aguán

Mosquito Coast

Tusi

GUATEMALA

Chamelecón

Ulúa

Yoro

Sico

Laguna de Caratasca

Puerto Lempira

Copán Ruins

Santa Bárbara

Humuya

Sulaco

SIERRA LA ESPERANZA

Catacamas

Guayape

MONTAÑAS DEL PATUCA

Patuca

Auasbila

Santa Rosa de Copán

Gracias

Lago de Yojoa

MONTAÑAS DE COMAYAGUA

Juticalpa

▲ Mt. Las Minas 9,347 ft. 2849 m.

Siguatepeque

Comayagua

La Esperanza

La Paz

Tegucigalpa ★

Danlí

Las Trojes

Coco

NICARAGUA

Yuscarán

El Paraíso

EL SALVADOR

Nacaome

San Lorenzo

Choluteca

Ocotal

La Vigia

Choluteca

Gulfo de Fonseca

Honduras

LOCATION: 13° to 16°N; 83°10′ to 89°20′W. **BOUNDARY LENGTHS:** Caribbean coastline, 591 km (367 mi); Nicaragua, 922 km (573 mi); Gulf of Fonseca coastline, 74 km (46 mi); El Salvador, 335 km (208 mi); Guatemala, 248 km (154 mi). **TERRITORIAL SEA LIMIT:** 12 mi.

Four principal ports—Puerto Cortés, Tela, La Ceiba, and Puerto Castilla—serve the country on the Caribbean side. Another Caribbean port, Roatán, is offshore, in the Bay Islands; and Puerto de Henecán, on the Pacific coast, opened in 1979, replacing Amapala as a port facility, although the latter retains a naval base. La Ceiba and Tela are primarily banana-trade ports; Puerto Castilla (completed in 1980) serves the Olancho forestry project; and Puerto Cortés and Puerto de Henecán handle general traffic. River traffic is negligible. In 1998, the Honduran merchant fleet comprised 247 vessels, totaling 555,534 GRT.

Air service is important in the transportation of passengers and cargo. In 1998 there were 122 airports in Honduras, 11 of which had paved runways. The two principal airports are Ramon Villeda, at San Pedro Sula, and Toncontín, about 6.4 km (4 mi) from Tegucigalpa. Toncontín is served by Transportes Aéros Nacionales de Honduras/Servicio Aéreo de Honduras (TAN/SAHSA), Líneas Aéreas Costarricenses (LACSA), Challenge, and TACA airlines and the domestic carrier Lineas Aéreas Nacionales (LANSA). TAN/SAHSA flies to the US, Mexico, and other Central American countries and also provides domestic passenger service. In 1997, 333,000 passengers were carried on scheduled domestic and international flights at Toncontín; 370,000 were carried on scheduled domestic and international flights at Ramon Villeda.

12 HISTORY

Before the Spaniards entered the land now called Honduras, the region was inhabited by the warlike Lencas and Jicaques, Mexican Amerindian traders, and Paya hunters and fishermen. The Mayan ceremonial center at Copán in western Honduras flourished about the 8th century AD but was in ruins when Columbus reached the mainland on his fourth voyage in 1502. He named the region Honduras, meaning "depths."

Colonization began in 1524 under Gil González de Ávila. In 1536, Pedro de Alvarado, who came from Guatemala at the bidding of Hernán Cortés in Mexico, founded San Pedro Sula, and another faction founded Comayagua in 1537. After the treacherous murder by the Spaniards of an Amerindian chieftain named Lempira in 1539, his followers were subjugated. In that year, Honduras was made part of the captaincy-general of Guatemala, and for most of the period until 1821, it was divided into two provinces, Comayagua and Tegucigalpa. Some silver was produced in the mines of Tegucigalpa, but the area was otherwise ignored by the Spanish empire.

Honduras joined other provinces of Central America in declaring independence from Spain in 1821. It came under the Mexican empire of Agustín de Iturbide in 1822–23. Honduras was a member of the United Provinces of Central America from 1824 to 1838. During that time, a liberal Honduran, Francisco Morazán, became president and struggled unsuccessfully to hold the federation together. He was exiled in 1840 and assassinated in 1842.

After Honduras declared itself independent on 26 October 1838, conservatives and liberals fought for political control. From 1840 to 1876, conservative leaders held power either as presidents or as army leaders. The second half of the 19th century brought the development, by US companies, of banana growing in northern Honduras. During the administration of liberal president Marco Aurelio Soto (1876–83), there was a "golden age" in Honduran letters and education.

US corporate interests, especially the United Fruit Co. (now United Brands), and military dictators dominated Honduran political and economic life during the first half of the 20th century. Honduran politics was dominated by the conservative Gen. Tiburcio Carías Andino (1932–48). In 1948, his handpicked successor, Juan Manuel Gálvez, took office. Gálvez proved to be more than a mere puppet, but was conservative nonetheless. When the election of 1954 produced no presidential candidate with a majority vote, he transferred the presidency to the vice-president, Julio Lozano Díaz, who governed for almost two years. After an abortive attempt to have himself elected president, Díaz was deposed in 1956 by high army officers, who set up a junta. Democratic elections were held in 1957, and José Ramón Villeda Morales of the Liberal Party was elected president.

In 1963, just before completing the final months of his six-year term, Villeda was turned out of office by a coup. The liberal government was succeeded by a conservative coalition of military, Nationalist Party, and Liberal Party leaders under an air force officer, Col. Oswaldo López Arellano. This government was legalized almost two years later by an elected constituent assembly, which adopted a new constitution and proclaimed López president in June 1965.

During López's second term, a bitter and destructive four-day war broke out in July 1969 between Honduras and El Salvador. Although the immediate cause of the war was animosity arising from a World Cup elimination-round soccer match between the two countries, the underlying causes were a long-standing border dispute and the long-term migration of some 300,000 Salvadorans in search of land, which the Honduran government made it illegal for Salvadoran immigrants to own. Salvadoran troops won the ground war, but Honduran planes controlled the air. Out of this stalemate and with the help of the OAS, a compromise cease-fire was arranged. In June 1970, the two nations accepted a seven-point peace plan, creating a "no-man's-land" demilitarized zone along their common frontier. In the fall of 1973, Honduras and El Salvador began bilateral talks to resolve their differences. Progress was slow, and it was not until October 1980 that Honduras and El Salvador signed a treaty settling the dispute.

In the 1970s, López and the military continued to dominate Honduran politics. A civilian, Ramón Ernesto Cruz Uclés, was elected president in 1971, but lasted only briefly. By 1972, Gen. López was back in power. Gen. López assumed the title of chief of state, and suspended the National Congress and all political party activities. It was later discovered that in 1974 officials in the López administration had accepted a $1.25-million bribe from United Brands in exchange for a 50% reduction in the banana tax. A Honduran investigative commission insisted on examining López's Swiss bank account, and the scandal came to be known as "Bananagate" in the US. Finally, in April 1974, López was overthrown by a group of lieutenant colonels.

This military group was something of a reformist group, seeking social reforms and the removal of the senior officer corps. Political activity continued to be banned following the coup of 1975. Meanwhile, a significant grassroots movement, the National Front of United Peasants, had come to the fore and was pressuring the successive military governments to enact a program of large-scale land redistribution.

There followed two more military governments led by Col. Juan Alberto Melgar Castro (1975–78) and Gen. Policarpo Paz García (1978–83). This period saw strong economic growth and the building of a modern infrastructure for Honduras. At the same time, there was a gradual movement toward the democratization of the system.

Elections to a constituent assembly took place in April 1980, followed by general elections in November 1981. Under a new constitution in 1982, Roberto Suazo Córdova of the Liberal Party became president. The armed forces retained broad powers, including veto power over cabinet appointments and responsibility for national security. The military continued to grow in response to domestic instability and the fighting in neighboring Nicaragua and El Salvador. By 1983, several thousand anti-Sandinista guerrillas (popularly known as "contras") in Honduras were working for the overthrow of the Sandinista government, while the Honduran army, backed by the US, was helping Salvadoran government forces in their fight against leftist guerrillas.

The Suazo government worked closely with the US on matters of domestic and foreign policy. US military presence in Honduras grew rapidly. Several joint military maneuvers took place during 1983–87, and the US CIA used Honduras during that time as a base for covert activities against the Sandinista regime. In exchange, the US sent large amounts of economic aid to Honduras. Suazo also worked closely with the Honduran military, allowing it to pursue its anticommunist agenda freely. This arrangement led to an unprecedented political stabilization in Honduras.

This stability became apparent in November 1985, when Hondurans elected José Simón Azcona Hoyo to the presidency in the first peaceful transfer of power between elected executives in half a century. Azcona was elected with only 27% of the vote, due to a peculiarity of Honduran electoral laws. Azcona attempted to distance himself from the US in foreign policy and was critical of US contra policy. He signed the Central American peace plan outlined by President Oscar Arias Sánchez of Costa Rica; however, he did not move to close down contra bases as promised.

In 1989, Rafael Leonardo Callejas of the National (conservative) Party was elected. With the Nicaraguan issue fading after the Sandinistas' electoral loss, Callejas focused on domestic issues, applying a dose of both conservative economics and IMF austerity measures to the Honduran economy. Callejas moved to reduce the deficit and allow for a set of market adjustments, which in the short term produced a good deal of dislocation but led to higher rates of growth thereafter. Most significantly, Callejas maintained good relations with the military. In an unprecedented show of restraint, the military sat on the sidelines as voters went to the polls in November 1993.

The voters themselves showed a good deal of resentment toward the Callejas reforms. The Liberal Party returned to power in the person of Carlos Roberto Reina. While it was unlikely that its economic problems would be solved quickly, Honduras nevertheless had achieved a level of political stability that few could have anticipated in decades past. Reina, known for his support of human rights and clean government, called for a "moral revolution" to combat crime, poverty, and widespread corruption in both the public and private sectors. In late 1994 corruption charges were filed against former president Callejas and other top government officials. Reina also took steps to further reduce the influence of Honduras's powerful military, most notably the abolition of the draft, including the notorious press-gang conscription by which young men were seized off the streets and forced into military service. The liberal administration also dismantled the military-controlled Public Security Forces (FUSEP), replacing them with a new civilian force.

Reina proved less successful in dealing with the economic problems of his nation, long considered the poorest in Central America. An already difficult situation was exacerbated by the 1994 drought that slashed production of hydroelectric power, creating an energy crisis that drove up food and fuel prices and caused chronic power outages. The struggle to improve economic conditions continued through 1996, with the government caught between an international financial community demanding tough structural reforms and a beleaguered population unwilling to tolerate the sacrifices entailed by such programs. In November of 1997, Carlos Roberto Flores of the Liberal Party won the presidential elections with 52.8%. His party also won 62 out of 128 seats in the unicameral National Assembly. But the fury of Hurricane Mitch destroyed Honduras' economy and placed an even heavier burden on President Flores' challenges. The subsequent economic crisis of 1999 further worsened the economic situation of that country making it the worst performing nation in Latin America in the last two years.

13GOVERNMENT

The constitution of 1965, suspended following the 1972 coup, was superseded by a governing document adopted in November 1982. It defines Honduras as a democratic republic headed by a president who must be a native-born civilian. The president is elected by direct popular vote for a four-year term. The executive branch also includes a cabinet of 14 ministers. A constitutional change approved by the legislature in November 1982 deprived the president of the title of commander-in-chief of the armed forces, transferring that responsibility to the army chief of staff.

The 1982 constitution provides for the popular election of deputies to the unicameral National Assembly, consisting of 128 deputies. The deputies, who are directly elected for four-year terms, must be natives or residents of the constituencies they represent. All men and women 18 years of age and older are eligible to vote.

14POLITICAL PARTIES

The two major parties in Honduras are the Liberal Party (Partido Liberal—PL) and the National Party (Partido Nacional—PN). Both descend from the old Liberal and Conservative Parties from the 19th century. Although generally the National Party remains more conservative in nature, the two parties are very close ideologically.

The National Party was in power from 1932 to 1954 under Carías and Gálvez. In 1965, a PN-backed constituent assembly promulgated a new constitution, designated its membership as the National Congress for a six-year term, and proclaimed Gen. Oswaldo López Arellano as president. In the 1971 elections, the PN candidate, Gen. Ramón Ernesto Cruz, received about 52% of the vote and was elected president. Their most recent success came in 1989, when Rafael Leonardo Callejas became president. In the 1997 elections, its presidential candidate was Alba Gunera, the first woman to seek Honduras' presidency. She gained 42% of the vote. The National Party won 54 seats in the National Assembly in 1997.

The Liberals rely on their following in urban areas and among the laboring classes and have had some successes over the last half-century. In 1957, José Ramón Villeda Morales was elected to the presidency, and governed until 1963, when he was removed by a coup. The next successes came in 1981 with the election of Suazo, and then in 1985 with the election of José Simón Azcona Hoyo, in 1993, Carlos Roberto Reina and in 1997 Carlos Flores, who became president with 52% of the vote. The Liberal Party also won 67 out of the 128 seats in the National Assembly.

Two minor parties occupy mildly leftist positions: the Christian Democratic Party, under Efraín Díaz, and the National Innovation and Unity Party, led by Germán Leitzelar. Each of those parties won one seat in the National Assembly in the last election. In 1997, a Social Democratic party made its debut. The Partido de Inovación y Unidad-Social Democracia (Party for Innovation and Unity-Social-Democracy, social-democratic) won five seats in the National Assembly.

In the December 1996 primaries preceeding the November 1997 presidential elections, the Liberal Party nominated Carlos Roberto Flores, and Nora Gúnera de Melgar won the National Party nomination with backing of both the "Callejistas" (supporters of former president Callejas) and the "Oswaldistas" (backers of defeated 1993 presidential candidate Oswaldo Ramos Soto). Flores went on to win the election and his party won 62 of 128 seats in the National Assembly.

15LOCAL GOVERNMENT

Honduras is divided into 18 departments, each with a governor popularly elected for a two-year term. Departments are divided into municipalities (283 in 1997) governed by popularly elected councils. Localities with populations between 500 and 1,000 have a mayor, a legal representative, and a council member. A council member is added for each additional 1,000 residents, but the total is not to exceed seven. A special law governs the Central District of Tegucigalpa and Comayagüela.

Under the jurisdiction of the local government, municipal land is granted or lent to peasants in the district in sections known as ejidos. The ejido system is designed to aid landless peasants and has become an important function of local administration.

16JUDICIAL SYSTEM

Judicial power is exercised by the nine-member Supreme Court (with seven substitutes) and 10 courts of appeal, as well as by 67 courts of first instance and 325 justice of the peace courts of limited jurisdiction. The Supreme Court appoints the judges of the courts of appeal and the courts of first instance, who, in turn, appoint local justices of the peace. The justices of the Supreme Court are elected by the National Assembly and serve for four-year terms. The Supreme Court has the power to declare laws unconstitutional.

There is a military court of first instance from which appeals can be taken to the civilian judicial system. In practice, the civilian courts are not independent. Because of underfunding and corruption, the formal resolution of legal disputes in courts is often the product of influence and political pressure.

The constitution provides for an independent judiciary and the right to a fair trial. A public defender program provides services to indigent defendants. There are 106 public defenders and 196 public prosecutors assigned nationally.

Honduras accepts jurisdiction of the International Court of Justice with reservations.

17ARMED FORCES

The Honduran military establishment consists of an army, an air force, a small navy, and a special security corps. Two years of compulsory peacetime military service was terminated in 1995. Reserve status is open to men between 32 and 55 years of age (60,000 registered). The regular forces consisted of 8,300 personnel in 2000; there were 5,500 in the army, 1,800 in the air force, and 1,000 in the navy. Paramilitary police forces numbered 6,000 personnel. The defense budget in 1998 was $33 million or 0.6% of GDP.

The armed forces are equipped with US and NATO weapons that allow the army to field 4 infantry brigades and a ground attack air force (49 combat aircraft). The armed forces are also structured for internal defense.

US military aid to Honduras increased from $3.9 million in 1980 to $81 million in 1986 and then dropped to $61 million in 1987 and $20 million in 1991. During the 1980s, the US-built

Regional Military Training Center at Puerto Castilla trained anti-Sandinista rebels, contras from Nicaragua, as well as counterinsurgency forces from El Salvador. About 400 US troops maintain bases in Honduras.

[18]INTERNATIONAL COOPERATION

Honduras is a charter member of the UN, having joined on 17 December 1945, and it participates in ECLAC and all the nonregional specialized agencies except IAEA. It also belongs to G-77, IADB, OAS, WTO, and various other inter-American and intergovernmental organizations. In 1982, Honduras joined with Costa Rica and El Salvador to set up the Central American Democratic Community to promote economic development and safeguard democracy in the region. In August 1987, Honduras and four other Central American countries signed the peace plan for Central America outlined by Costa Rican President Oscar Arias Sánchez. Honduras is a signatory to the Law of the Sea.

[19]ECONOMY

Honduras is one of the poorest and least developed countries in Latin America. The economy is based mostly on agriculture, which accounted for 27% of GDP and over 40% of the workforce in 1998. About 16% of the land is arable, located mostly along the coastal plains. Coffee and bananas account for 65% of total Honduran export revenues. The vast majority of banana holdings are controlled by two US companies, United Brands and Standard Fruit, and most other profitable agricultural enterprises are owned by a small number of private citizens. With its economy enormously dependent on banana production, the country is vulnerable to weather and world market price variations. Honduras also has extensive forest, marine and mineral resources, although widespread slash-and-burn agricultural methods continue to destroy forests. Hondurans, however, are becoming more concerned about protecting their environmental patrimony, in part because of the benefits of ecotourism.

In 1995, the Honduran economy rebounded from the severe recession experienced in 1994. Real GDP growth in 1995 was 3.6%. It was led by a solid expansion in agricultural production spurred by soaring world coffee prices, excellent basic grains harvests, and a resurrected banana industry as well as a growing maquila (Free Trade Zone) sector that employed 65,000 people by year's end. Honduras also received abundant rainfall which replenished the nation's dams and enabled the country to generate adequate hydroelectric energy, thus avoiding the drought-related power cuts which adversely affected economic performance in 1994. In 1996, Honduran GDP grew about 3.5%. However, inflation for 1996 reached 24.9%, a disappointment to GOH economic policy-makers who hoped to bring that figure down to 16% for the year. The government succeeded in reducing inflation to that level in 1997, and down to 14% in 1998. Unfortunately hurricane Mitch destroyed 20% to 80% of the 1998 coffee and banana crops, and an estimated $3 billion in damages equal to half of the annual GDP. This caused a rise in inflation to 16%, a higher fiscal deficit, and a low GDP of 3%. The economic crisis of 1999 worsened the economic situation of that country making it the worst performing nation in Latin America in 1999 and 2000.

[20]INCOME

The US Central Intelligence Agency (CIA) reports that in 1998 Honduras's gross domestic product (GDP) was estimated at $14.4 billion. The per capita GDP was estimated at $2,400. The annual growth rate of GDP was estimated at 3%. The average inflation rate in 1998 was 15%. The CIA defines GDP as the value of all final goods and services produced within a nation in a given year and computed on the basis of purchasing power parity (PPP) rather than value as measured on the basis of the rate of exchange. It was estimated that agriculture accounted for 20% of GDP, industry 19%, and services 61%.

Private consumption includes expenditures of individuals, households, and nongovernmental organizations. It was estimated that between 1990 and 1998 private consumption grew at an annual rate of 3.3%. The richest 10% of the population accounted for approximately 42% of household consumption and the poorest 10% approximately 1.2%.

[21]LABOR

In 1998, the economically active population totaled 2,135,000 (excluding the armed forces). In 1996, agriculture engaged 37%; services, 39%; and industry, 24%. The unemployment rate in 1998 was 3.9%.

About 14% of the labor force was unionized in 1999. The principal labor organizations in 1999 were the Confederation of Honduran Workers (CTH), the General Workers' Central (CGT), and the Unitary Confederation of Honduran Workers.

Honduras did not have effective labor legislation until 1954. It joined the ILO in 1955 and subsequently adopted several labor codes, most notably that of 1959, which established the Ministry of Labor. The code also provided for union organization, collective bargaining, arbitration, social security, and fair labor standards, including an 8-hour day, a 44-hour week, 6-hour night shifts, and overtime, holiday, vacation, maternity, and severance pay. Because of high unemployment and a lack of government enforcement, however, these regulations are often not enforced.

The labor code disallows children under 16 from working; however, in actuality, economic necessity and a lack of government enforcement mean that many children do work, especially on small farms in rural areas and as street vendors in cities. As of 1999, the minimum wage ranged from $2.27 to $3.79.

[22]AGRICULTURE

Over 16% of the national territory is agriculturally productive; because of the uneconomical system of land use, much arable land has not been exploited. Agriculture is the primary sector of the economy, accounting for about 20% of GDP and 37% of employment in 1998. Farming methods are inefficient, and crop yields and qualities are low. The principal export crops are bananas and coffee; the major subsistence crops are corn, sorghum, beans, and rice. In 1998, agricultural production was 20% higher than during 1989–91. In 1985, the sector grew by 2.6%; in 1992, 2.1%, and in 1995, 6.9%. The trade surplus in agricultural products totaled $129.8 million in 1997. Crop production for 1998 included sugarcane, 3,779,000 tons; bananas, 947,000 tons; sorghum, 99,000 tons; dry beans, 76,000 tons; rice, 53,000 tons.

Since 1972, agrarian reform has been an announced priority of the national government. In January 1975, plans were made for the distribution of 600,000 hectares (1,483,000 acres) of land among 100,000 families over a five-year period. The program was suspended in 1979 because of lack of funds and pressure from landowners; by that time, only about one-third of the goal had been met. The reform program was revived in the early 1980s, and in 1982, lands totaling 27,960 hectares (69,090 acres) were distributed to 4,000 peasant families. By 1986, however, land reform was at a virtual standstill; peasant groups, demanding immediate land distribution, staged "land invasions" and seized the offices of the National Agrarian Institute in San Pedro Sula. The agricultural modernization law eliminated subsidized credit to small farmers, while high commercial interest rates squeezed small farmers from the credit market.

23ANIMAL HUSBANDRY

Honduran consumption of milk and meat is traditionally low. However, pastures account for 13.8% of the total land area. Poor transportation facilities are a barrier to the development of stock raising and dairying, two potentially profitable economic activities. Honduras has nearly 100,000 livestock operations, mostly small or medium-sized producers. About 50% of all cattle ranches are 50 ha (124 acres) or smaller, and 95% of all ranches have less than 100 head. In 1998, the cattle population was estimated at 1,945,000 head; hogs, 700,000; horses and mules, 244,000; and chickens, 54,000,000. That year, 605,000 tons of raw milk and 45,000 tons of eggs were produced. Exports of beef were valued at $3.2 million in 1997, nearly all of it sent to the US. By 1998, livestock and poultry production had increased 24% since 1989–91.

24FISHING

There is commercial fishing in Puerto Cortés, and other areas are served by local fishermen. A small local company operates a cannery for the domestic market on the Gulf of Fonseca. There is a commercial fishing concern on the island of Guanaja, and a large refrigeration-factory ship is engaged in freezing shrimp and lobster near Caratasca. In 1997, the total catch was 23,585 tons. Shrimp accounted for about 45% of the total catch, taken mostly from southern shrimp farms. Exports of fish products amounted to $50.4 million in 1997.

25FORESTRY

About 54% of Honduras is covered by forests, including stands of longleaf pine and such valuable hardwoods as cedar, ebony, mahogany, and walnut. Total roundwood production in 1997 amounted to 6.92 million cu m, and forest products exports were valued at $22.7 million. The National Corporation for Forestry Development (Corporación Hondureña de Desarrollo Forestal), established in 1974, is charged with the overall preservation, exploitation, and exportation of Honduran forest resources. The privatization of government-owned woodlands is expected to intensify the use of forestry resources. A restriction on the export of raw wood also is causing growth in the woodworking industry for semifinished wood products.

26MINING

The mineral resources of Honduras consist of coal, copper, gold, gypsum, lead, salt, silver, zinc, and some marble. Lead and zinc and small amounts of cadmium, copper, silver, and gold are commercially important. The nonmetallic minerals extracted in Honduras are cement, marble, and salt. Inadequate transportation continues to hamper full development of mineral resources. In the mid-1990s, the El Mochito Mine in the Santa Bárbara Department was the only large operating base metal mine in Honduras. Lead and zinc concentrates from the mine contributed less than 2% to GDP. Under 0.3% of the labor force was employed in the mining sector.

Between 1882 and 1954, the New York and Honduras Rosario Mining Co., the oldest mining company in the republic, produced over $60 million worth of gold and silver from the Rosario mines near Tegucigalpa. By the mid-1960s, these mines had become virtually nonproductive, but a mine situated west of Lake Yojoa remains active. In 1975, the government granted Industrial Alliance a lease on the Tatumbla gold and silver mines. In 1991, a study determined that the Yuscarán gold and silver deposit in El Paraíso Department would be economical for production operations. As of 1997, the San Andres Mine southwest of San Pedro de Sula—the second-largest gold mine in Honduras—had not yet reached full production. In 1997, production of zinc was 25,500 tons; lead, 3,400 tons; silver, 35,000 kg; and gold, 150 kg.

27ENERGY AND POWER

Much of Honduras' total energy consumption is derived from the burning of wood; about 25% is provided by imported crude oil and petroleum products, supplied mainly by Mexico and Venezuela. Hydroelectricity provided 88% of Honduras' electricity generation in 1998. Net installed capacity was 635,000 kw that year, and production totaled 2,904 million kWh.

The government is playing a significant role in the development process, through the National Electric Co. The 290-MW El Cajón hydroelectric project, financed by the IBRD, IDB, Central American Bank for Economic Integration (CABEI), OPEC, and Japan, was completed in March 1985. The $58-million Nispero hydroelectric project, financed by the IBRD and CABEI, and the rural electrification program in Aguán Valley, financed by AID at a cost of $13 million, have helped boost energy production by an average annual rate of 9% since 1981. Moreover, increased domestic hydroelectricity production has reduced the consumption of petroleum (all of which must be imported). About 60% of the country's power supply was knocked out by a fire at the El Cajou dam in early 1999, resulting in power rationing that was still in effect at midyear.

Petroleum explorations have been carried on by US companies since 1955. A Texaco refinery at Puerto Cortés began producing in 1968, and petroleum derivatives are exported to the US and Belize.

28INDUSTRY

Industry as a whole has continually supplied almost 25% of Honduras' GDP, with manufacturing accounting for 15% of the total. Manufacturing has traditionally been limited to small-scale light industry supplying domestic requirements.

Assembly plant operations developed in the 1970s, especially after a free-trade zone was established in Puerto Cortes in 1975. San Pedro Sula is the center for matches, cigars, cigarettes, cement, meatpacking, sugar, beer and soft drinks, fats and oils, processed foods, shoes and candles. Tegucigalpa has plants for the manufacture of plastics, furniture, candles, cotton textiles, and leather. The country has also established a well-known apparel assembly industry in the maquiladora sector, which employed 110,000 workers in 1999.

Production in the manufacturing industry, mainly of nondurable goods, rose 5.8% in 1998. The largest growth was seen in the construction sector, at 17%, which was expected to grow by 50% in 1999 due to reconstruction projects following the hurricane. The electric, gas and water sectors gained almost 9%. However, in 1999 a fire temporarily closed the Cajon hydroelectric plant that had supplied 40% of the country's electricity. The electronic distribution system was privatized in 2000.

29SCIENCE AND TECHNOLOGY

The Honduran Academy (founded in 1949), the Honduran Coffee Institute, and the National Agriculture Institute are all located in Tegucigalpa. The José Cecilio del Valle University (founded in 1978) has engineering and computer science departments, and the National Autonomous University of Honduras (founded in 1847) has faculties of medicine, pharmacy, dentistry, and engineering. The Pan-American Agricultural School (founded in 1942) has students from 20 Latin American countries. The National Museum in Tegucigalpa has natural-history exhibits. In 1987–97, science and engineering students accounted for 24% of college and university enrollments.

30DOMESTIC TRADE

The principal distribution centers include Puerto Cortes and San Pedro Sula; Tegucigalpa is a leading center of retail trade. In major cities, shops are comparable to those in Central American towns. In the countryside, small markets and stores supply staple needs.

Business hours are generally from 8 AM to noon and 1:30 or 2 to 5 or 6 PM on weekdays and 8 to 11 AM on Saturdays. Banks in Tegucigalpa are open from 9 AM to 3 PM, Monday through Friday.

31 FOREIGN TRADE

Honduras remains at the forefront of Central American economic integration efforts. In May 1992, Honduras signed several trade agreements with its neighbors, including a Honduran/Guatemalan Free Trade Agreement, a Honduran/Salvadoran Free Trade Agreement, and a Honduran/Salvadoran/Guatemalan Northern Triangle Accord, with the intent of accelerating regional integration. Honduras is also a member of the WTO, and the CACM. Free trade agreements were under discussion with Chile, Panama, Mexico, the Andean Community, Taiwan, and the Dominican Republic in 1999.

The most important export from Honduras is coffee (42%), followed by the cultivation of fruits and nuts (23%). Other exports include shrimp and lobster (8.6%), wood and logging products, including paper (7.7%), and meat (4.2%).

In 1997 Honduras's imports were distributed among the following categories:

Consumer goods	16.7%
Food	12.4%
Fuels	10.2%
Industrial supplies	34.6%
Machinery	15.2%
Transportation	10.6%
Other	0.3%

Principal trading partners in 1998 (in millions of US dollars) were as follows:

COUNTRY	EXPORTS	IMPORTS	BALANCE
United States	591	n.a.	
Germany	124	34	90
Belgium	70	17	53
Nicaragua	70	201	-131
Japan	67	117	-50
El Salvador	64	68	-4
Spain	44	27	17
Mexico	6	121	-115
Canada	6	1,166	
Trinidad and Tobago	2	119	-117

32 BALANCE OF PAYMENTS

Since 1973, trade balances have been negative. Investment income repatriated by foreign companies in Honduras is an endemic burden on the local economy. The Honduran authorities have generally adhered to the policies of fiscal and monetary restraint that were introduced early in 1959, following a period of exceptional strain on the country's international reserves. The fall in reserves resulted from a decline in income from the banana industry and reduced international prices for other major exports. Political instability in the region in the late 1970s to the mid-1980s, together with low commodity prices and high oil prices, had an adverse effect on the balance of payments. The 1990s brought a continuation of the negative trade balance (averaging 7% of GDP), especially after the increase of imports after hurricane Mitch. However, the current account deficit was forecast to fall to 6% of GDP in 2000 due to an increase in agricultural and clothes exports. International reserves reached $700 million in 1999 due, in part, to increased remittances from abroad, and international aid following the hurricane ($300 million from the US alone).

The US Central Intelligence Agency reports that in 1996 the purchasing power parity of Honduras's exports was $1.3 billion

while imports totaled $1.8 billion resulting in a trade balance of -$500 million.

The International Monetary Fund (IMF) reports that in 1998 Honduras had exports of goods totaling $2,017 million and imports totaling $2,340 million. The services credit totaled $370 million and debit $396 million. The following table summarizes Honduras's balance of payments as reported by the IMF for 1998 in millions of US dollars.

Current Account		-333
Balance on goods	-323	
Balance on services	-26	
Balance on income	-176	
Current transfers	192	
Capital Account		48
Financial Account		261
Direct investment abroad	...	
Direct investment in Honduras	84	
Portfolio investment assets	...	
Portfolio investment liabilities	264	
Other investment assets	-62	
Other investment liabilities	264	
Net Errors and Omissions		23
Reserves and Related Items		2

33 BANKING AND SECURITIES

In 1950, the Central Bank of Honduras (Banco Central de Honduras), the sole bank of issue, was established to centralize national financial operations and to replace foreign currencies then in circulation. In 1999, there were 23 commercial banks in Honduras with an estimated $3 billion in assets. In addition, there are some 150 non-bank financial institutions, many of them associated with the major banks. The Banco Atlántida, the most important commercial bank, accounts for over one-half of the total assets of private banks. US banks play a significant role in the commercial system: the Atlántida is affiliated with Chase Manhattan, and the second-largest commercial bank, the Banco de Honduras, is affiliated with Citibank of New York.

The government-controlled banks, including the National Development Bank, the National Agricultural Development Bank, and the Municipal Bank, provide credit for development projects. The National Development Bank extends agricultural and other credit—mainly to the tobacco, coffee, and livestock industries—and furnishes technical and financial assistance and other services to national economic interests. The Municipal Bank gives assistance at the local level.

In 1990, the Central Bank devalued the lempira and let it float freely until 1994, when a currency auction was created. The year of 1995 saw the Financial Sector Reform Law, which created a modern Banking Commission. Elements of Central Bank reforms in 1997 included the abolition of the government's right to borrow at below-market rates of interest.

In 1990, a stock exchange opened in San Pedro Sula to raise short-term bond finance for local businesses.

34 INSURANCE

The oldest insurance company in Honduras is Honduras Savings (Ahorro Hondureño), established in 1917. Five other companies deal with life insurance and other types of policies. The number and the role of foreign companies in the insurance sector have decreased because of government incentives to domestic under-writers.

35 PUBLIC FINANCE

The US Central Intelligence Agency (CIA) estimates that in 1997 Honduras's central government took in revenues of approximately $655 million and had expenditures of $850 million including capital expenditures of $150 million. Overall, the government registered a deficit of approximately $195 million. External debt totaled $5 billion.

36TAXATION

Honduran tax rates are progressive. The basic rate on net income begins at 12% on incomes of over L50,000 and rises to 40% on those of more than L1,000,000; a surcharge of 10% is levied on amounts over L100,000, and a surcharge of 15% is applied to incomes over L500,000. No distinction is made for tax purposes between individuals and businesses. Agricultural activities and industries classified as "basic" receive favorable depreciation rates.

The corporate tax rate is 15% on the first L100,000 of taxable income and 35% on the excess. The government also levies a value-added tax at a normal rate of 7% (10% for alcohol and tobacco products) and social security taxes. In addition, there are excise taxes, mainly on beer and cigarettes, but also on imported matches, soft drinks, imported sugar, and new motor vehicles. New industries are exempted from income and production taxes and import duties for up to 10 years.

District and municipal governments obtain their revenues from taxes on amusements and livestock consumption and from permits, licenses, registrations, certifications, storage charges, transfers of real estate, and fines.

37CUSTOMS AND DUTIES

Most imports from outside the CACM are subject to a CET ranging from 0%–15%. Duties are levied ad valorem over the cost, insurance, and freight value of goods. Honduras also imposes a sales tax (12% on most goods, 15% for alcohol and tobacco) and consumption tax on selected imports: 20% on alcoholic beverages, 35% on motor vehicles, and 55% on cigarettes. Capital goods are admitted at a tariff rate of only 1%.

In June 1992, the Central Bank of Honduras eliminated the need for most import permits and foreign exchange authorizations.

38FOREIGN INVESTMENT

Traditionally, the Honduran attitude toward foreign enterprise has been favorable. Foreign capital is treated in the same way as domestic capital; however, firms in the distribution, health services, telecommunications, fishing and hunting, mining, insurance and financial services, or lumber business must have 51% Honduran ownership. Honduran economic development has been powerful influenced by foreign investment in agriculture, industry, commerce, and other economic sectors.

Since 1910, the Standard and Fruit and Steamship Co. and United Brands (formerly the United Fruit Company) have developed railroads, ports, plantations, cattle farms, lumber yards, breweries, electric power, housing, and education. All contracts, aside from commodity exports, were canceled on 15 September 1975; plans to convert banana-marketing operations into a joint venture fell through, however, and in 1976, the government instead expropriated large tracts of land from the banana producers. Mines have been developed by the New York and Honduras Rosario Mining Co.

The United States has historically been, and remains today, Honduras' largest investor, accounting for at least three-quarters of the estimated $1 billion in foreign direct investment in Honduras, and more than 100 American companies operate there. Seventy-five of those companies produce apparel, but the largest US investment in Honduras is in the agribusiness sector. Other important sectors include petroleum products marketing, electric power generation, banking, insurance, and tobacco. US franchises have substantially increased their presence in recent years, mostly in the fast food sector. Other major investors include Japan, El Salvador, Korea, Hong Kong, and Taiwan.

Opportunities for foreign investment include machinery and equipment, automotive parts and service equipment, tourism, medical equipment, electrical power systems, and construction equipment and products. Best prospects for agricultural products are corn, milled rice, wheat, soybean meal, and consumer-ready products.

39ECONOMIC DEVELOPMENT

During the administration of President Callejas, between 1990 and 1993, economic policy was mostly based on neoliberal ideas. This included a move from an inward-oriented policy to an export-oriented one. In addition, privatization was deeply emphasized. During that period, GDP was characterized by consistent growth. At the same time the country's galloping inflation was reduced to single digits. Government corruption, however, prompted citizens to vote Callejas out of office.

The November 1993 elections gave birth to a new political era in Honduras. President Reina of the Liberal Party was expected to slow down the pace of market-oriented reforms, but to continue privatization. Strong growth in nontraditional exports and the prospects for an improvement in coffee prices helped to finance the current account deficit. The continuation of foreign aid and investment was essential to closing the Honduras trade gap.

With the election of President Flores in 1998, reforms were focused on alleviating the lot of the poorest citizens in Honduras (unemployment and underemployment reached 36% in 1997), and improving international competitiveness. Hurricane Mitch caused some setbacks, but altogether the economy was heading towards greater stability and prosperity in 1999.

Honduras is a participating member of the following international financial institutions: the World Bank, the Inter-American Development Bank (IDB), the International Monetary Fund (IMF) and the Central American Bank of Economic Integration (CABEI).

40SOCIAL DEVELOPMENT

The present Honduran Social Insurance Law covers accidents, illness, maternity, old age, occupational disease, unemployment, disability, death, and other circumstances affecting the capacity to work and maintain oneself and one's family. Effective coverage, however, has been limited mainly to maternity, sickness, and workers' compensation. Social security services are furnished and administered by the Honduran Social Security Institute and financed by contributions from employees, employers, and the government. In 1999, workers contributed 1% of their earnings toward retirement, disability, and survivor insurance, while employers paid 2% of their payroll. Old-age and disability benefits equal 40% of basic monthly earnings and an increment for contribution beyond 60 months. These programs exclude domestic and agricultural workers.

Traditional attitudes prevent women from obtaining full access to the educational and economic opportunities guaranteed by law. As of 1997, there were 12 female deputies in Congress out of 128. In 1999 women accounted for 51% of the work force and were represented in most professions, although their career opportunities were often limited. The penal code was amended in 1997 to criminalize domestic violence and sexual harassment.

The government committed 32% of its budget to public education and health care in 2000. Many Honduran children, however, remain severely disadvantaged. There is a growing problem of child abuse resulting in many homeless children.

The government's human rights record has improved since 1995, but serious abuses still occur, including torture and killing by police. Human rights groups have challenged the existence of organized death squads.

[41]HEALTH

Health conditions in Honduras are among the worst in the Western Hemisphere, and health care remains inadequate. In the mid-1990s there was one physician per 1,266 people and 1.1 hospital beds per 1,000 inhabitants. The Inter-American Cooperative Public Health Service, created in 1942 under the joint sponsorship of Honduras and the US, has contributed to public health through malaria control, spraying, construction of water systems and sewage disposal plants, personnel training, and the establishment of a national tuberculosis sanatorium. US Peace Corps volunteers help train personnel for urban and rural clinics. Nearly 20% of children under five years of age were considered malnourished in the mid-1990s. Honduras started fortifying sugar with Vitamin A in 1996. Total health care spending between 1990–95 was 5.6% of the total gross domestic product.

Major causes of illness and death are diseases of the digestive tract, intestinal parasites, accidental homicide and suicides, influenza, pneumonia, cancer, and infant diseases. Malnutrition, impure water, poor sewage disposal, and inadequate housing are the major health problems. Cholera was reported in 4,717 cases of which 77 turned fatal in 1995. In 1995, there were 1,022 malaria cases per 100,000 population. Honduras has been hard hit by AIDS. The HIV-1 seroprevalence in 1997 was 1.4 per 100 adults. As of 1997, 43,000 Hondurans have been infected with HIV since 1985, and the mortality rate from AIDS is unusually high. In 1994–95, about 70% of the population had access to safe water, and 68% had adequate sanitation. Immunization rates for children up to one year old in 1997 were as follows: tuberculosis (99%); diphtheria, pertussis, and tetanus (94%); polio (93%); and measles (89%). The government pays 79% of routine immunization bills (1996). In 1999, the birth rate was 31 per 1,000 people, with about 50% of married women (ages 15 to 49) using contraception in 1997. The total fertility rate was 4.3 children per mother during her childbearing years in 1997. The infant mortality rate in 1999 was 41 per 1,000 live births, and the general mortality rate in 1999 was 7 per 1,000 people. Life expectancy in 1999 was an average of 65 years.

[42]HOUSING

Many urban dwellings—and most rural dwellings—lack running water, electricity, and indoor plumbing. Estimates of the shortage in housing units grew from 173,000 in 1961 to 320,700 in 1973 and to 500,000 in 1985. The most recent estimate indicates that 26% of all households had piped water, 23% had flush toilets, and 38% had electric lighting. Projects under way during the include a $30-million low-cost housing program sponsored by the Housing Finance Corp. and a $19-million venture undertaken by the National Housing Institute.

[43]EDUCATION

The rate of illiteracy among adults in the year 2000 was estimated at 27.8% (males, 27.8% and females: 27.5%). Public education is free and compulsory for children ages 7 to 13 in primary school and ages 14 to 19 in secondary school. As of 1998 there were 1,032,595 students enrolled in primary schools and 169,430 enrolled in secondary schools. Primary school lasts six years, followed five years of secondary education.

In 1994, the number of students enrolled in all institutions of higher learning amounted to 54,106 with 4,078 teaching staff. The major university is the National Autonomous University of Honduras, founded at Tegucigalpa in 1847, with branches at San Pedro Sula and La Ceiba. There are several other universities, as well as technical and agricultural schools.

[44]LIBRARIES AND MUSEUMS

Although the National Archive of Honduras was established in 1880 to conserve and maintain the records of the republic, no great attention has been shown to government documents and other records in modern times. The National Archive (40,000 volumes) includes land titles dating from 1580, historical documents dating from the 17th century, a newspaper collection from 1880 onward, a civil registry, and a collection of laws since 1880. The Ministry of Education has charge of the National Archive, as well as of other libraries and museums. Another noteworthy institution is the National Library in Tegucigalpa (70,000 volumes). The National University's library in Tegucigalpa contains over 160,000 volumes. In Tegucigalpa, the National Museum exhibits historical and archeological works and the Miguel Paz Baraona Historical Museum highlights the personal effects of the national hero as well as the country's history. There are regional museums in Omoa, Comayagüela and Copán, and the government continues to uncover the Mayan ruins of Copán and other sites.

[45]MEDIA

The government owns and operates postal, telephone, and telegraph services. Tegucigalpa and San Pedro Sula are linked by a multiplex radio relay network. The Tropical Radio Co. provides international radiotelegraph and radiotelephone service. In 1995, there were 117,100 telephones. As of 1999, Honduras had 176 AM radio stations, no FM stations, and 11 television stations. In 1997, there were 409 radios, 90 television sets, and 2 mobile phones per 1,000 population.

The country's principal newspapers (with 1999 circulation) were *La Tribuna* (60,000), *Tiempo* (42,000), and *El Heraldo* (45,000), all published in Tegucigalpa, and *La Prensa* (62,000), published in San Pedro Sula.

The constitution provides for freedom of speech and press, and the government is said to generally respect these rights. The media itself, however, is said to be subject to a high degree of politicization and corruption.

In 1996, there were 82 Internet sites in Honduras. Online access is extremely limited, with less than one Internet host per 1,000 population in 1998.

[46]ORGANIZATIONS

The Chamber of Commerce and Industries has its headquarters in Tegucigalpa; chambers of commerce also function in San Pedro Sula, La Ceiba, and other towns. Various producers' and professional associations, as well as social and cultural groups, are also active.

[47]TOURISM, TRAVEL, AND RECREATION

A valid passport is needed for entry into Honduras. Visitors also need visas, except for nationals of the US, Canada, Western Europe, Japan, Australia, and New Zealand.

Honduran governments have attempted to attract foreign visitors. After a period of stagnation, tourism experienced modest growth in the late 1980s. In 1998, there were an estimated 321,149 tourist arrivals, up from the previous year by 17%. In 1997 tourists spent $146 million and there were 11,428 hotel rooms with 19,542 beds. The main tourist attraction is the restoration at Copán, the second-largest city of the ancient Mayan Empire. There are also beaches on the northern coast and good fishing in Trujillo Bay and Lake Yojoa.

In 1999, the UN estimated the cost of staying in Tegucigalpa at $151 per day, with hotel charges accounting for 66% of this expenditure. Daily costs in San Pedro Sula are estimated at $138.

[48]FAMOUS HONDURANS

José Cecilio del Valle (1780–1834), a member of the French Academy of Sciences, was an intellectual, a political leader, and the author of the Central American declaration of independence. Francisco Morazán (1799–1842) was the last president of the

United Provinces of Central America, which lasted from 1823 to 1839. Father José Trinidad Reyes (1797–1855) founded an institute in 1847 that became the National University. Outstanding literary figures were Marco Aurelio Soto (1846–1908), an essayist and liberal president; Ramón Rosa (1848–93), an essayist and biographer; Policarpo Bonilla (1858–1926), a politician and author of political works; Alberto Membreño (1859–1921), a philologist; Juan Ramón Molina (1875–1908), a modernist poet; Froilán Turcios (1875–1943), a novelist and writer of fantastic tales; and Rafael Heliodoro Valle (1891–1959), a historian and biographer.

⁴⁹DEPENDENCIES

Honduras has no territories or colonies.

⁵⁰BIBLIOGRAPHY

Anderson, Thomas P. *The War of the Dispossessed: Honduras and El Salvador.* Lincoln: University of Nebraska Press, 1981.

Barry, Tom. *Honduras: A Country Guide.* Albuquerque, N.M.: Inter-Hemispheric Education Resource Center, 1990.

Cline, William R. (ed.). *Economic Integration in Central America.* Washington, D.C.: Brookings Institution, 1978.

Durham, William H. *Scarcity and Survival in Central America: Ecological Origins of the Soccer War.* Stanford, Calif.: Stanford University Press, 1979.

Euraque, Dar'io A. *Reinterpreting the Banana Republic: Region and State in Honduras, 1870–1972.* Chapel Hill: University of North Carolina Press, 1996.

Honduras: A Country Study. 3rd ed. W. Va.: Department of the Army, 1995.

Honduras in Pictures. Minneapolis, Minnesota: Lerner Publications Company, 1987.

Howard-Reguindin, Pamela F. *Honduras.* Santa Barbara, Calif.: Clio, 1992.

Karnes, Thomas L. *The Failure of Union: Central America, 1824–1975.* Rev. ed. Tempe: Arizona State University, Center for Latin American Studies, 1976.

Kelly, Joyce. *An Archaeological Guide to Northern Central America: Belize, Guatemala, Honduras, and El Salvador.* Norman, Okla.: University of Oklahoma Press, 1996.

MacCameron, Robert. *Bananas, Labor, and Politics in Honduras: 1954–1963.* Syracuse, N.Y.: Syracuse University Press, 1983.

MacLeod, Murdo J. *Spanish Central America: A Socioeconomic History, 1520–1720.* Berkeley: University of California Press, 1973.

Meyer, Harvey Kessler. *Historical Dictionary of Honduras.* 2d ed. Metuchen, N.J.: Scarecrow Press, 1994.

Peckenham, Nancy, and Annie Street (eds.). *Honduras: Portrait of a Captive Nation.* New York: Praeger, 1985.

Ronfeldt, David F. *U.S. Involvement in Central America: Three Views from Honduras.* Santa Monica, Calif.: RAND, 1988.

Rosenberg, Mark B., and Philip L. Shepherd (eds.). *Honduras Confronts Its Future: Contending Perspectives on Critical Issues.* Boulder, Colo.: Lynne Rienner, 1986.

Schulz, Donald E. and Deborah S. Schulz. *The United States, Honduras, and the Crisis in Central America.* Boulder, Colo.: Westview Press, 1994.

Woodward, Ralph Lee, Jr. *Central America: A Nation Divided.* 2d ed. New York: Oxford University Press, 1985.

JAMAICA

CAPITAL: Kingston.

FLAG: Two diagonal yellow gold bars forming a saltire divide the flag into four triangular panels. The two side panels are black, and the top and bottom panels are green.

ANTHEM: First line, "Eternal father, bless our land..."

MONETARY UNIT: The Jamaican dollar (J$) of 100 cents was introduced on 8 September 1969. There are coins of 1, 5, 10, and 25 cents, and 1 dollar, and notes of 2, 5, 10, 20, 50, and 100 dollars. J$1 = US$0.02389 (or US$1 = J$41.850) as of 31 March 2000.

WEIGHTS AND MEASURES: Both metric and imperial weights and measures are used.

HOLIDAYS: New Year's Day, 1 January; Labor Day, 23 May; Independence Day, 1st Monday in August; National Heroes' Day, 3rd Monday in October; Christmas, 25 December; Boxing Day, 26 December. Movable religious holidays include Ash Wednesday, Good Friday, and Easter Monday.

TIME: 7 AM = noon GMT.

¹LOCATION, SIZE, AND EXTENT

Jamaica is an island in the Caribbean Sea situated about 160 km (90 mi) S of Cuba. It has a total area of 10,990 sq km (4,243 sq mi) and extends, at maximum, 235 km (146 mi) N-S and 82 km (51 mi) E-W. Comparatively, the area occupied by Jamaica is slightly smaller than the state of Connecticut. The total coastline is 1,022 km (634 mi).

Jamaica's capital city, Kingston, is located on the country's southeastern coast.

²TOPOGRAPHY

The greater part of Jamaica is a limestone plateau, with an average elevation of about 460 m (1,500 ft). The interior of the island is largely mountainous, and peaks of over 2,100 m (7,000 ft) are found in the Blue Mountains, which dominate the eastern part of the island; the highest point on the island is Blue Mountain Peak, at 2,256 m (7,402 ft) above sea level.

The coastal plains are largely alluvial, and the largest plains areas lie along the south coast. The island has numerous interior valleys. There are many rivers, but most are small, with rapids and falls that make navigation virtually impossible for any distance.

³CLIMATE

The climate ranges from tropical at sea level to temperate in the uplands; there is relatively little seasonal variation in temperature. The average annual temperature in the coastal lowlands is 27°C (81°F); for the Blue Mountains, 13°C (55°F).

The island has a mean annual rainfall of 198 cm (78 in), with wide variations during the year between the north and south coasts. The northeast coast and the Blue Mountains receive up to 760 cm (300 in) of rain a year in places, while some parts of the south coast receive less than 75 cm (30 in), most of it falling between May and October. The rainy seasons are May to June and September to November. The period from late August to November has occasionally been marked by destructive hurricanes.

⁴FLORA AND FAUNA

The original forest of Jamaica has been largely cut over, but in the areas of heavy rainfall along the north and northeast coasts there are stands of bamboo, ferns, ebony, mahogany, and rosewood. Cactus and similar dry-area plants are found along the south and southwest coastal area. Parts of the west and southwest consist of grassland, with scattered stands of trees.

The wild hog is one of the few native mammals, but there are many reptiles and lizards. Birds are abundant. Jamaican waters contain considerable resources of fresh- and saltwater fish. The chief varieties of saltwater fish are kingfish, jack, mackerel, whiting, bonito, and tuna; freshwater varieties include snook, jewfish, gray and black snapper, and mullet.

⁵ENVIRONMENT

Among the government agencies charged with environmental responsibilities are the Ministry of Health and Environmental Control, the Ministry of Agriculture, and the Natural Resources Conservation Authority. The major environmental problems involve water quality and waste disposal. Jamaica has 2.0 cu mi of water with 86% used for agriculture and 7% used for industrial purposes. Fifty-four percent of the people living in rural areas and 5% of the city dwellers do not have pure water. Coastal waters have been polluted by sewage, oil spills, and industrial wastes. Another major source of water pollution has been the mining of bauxite, which has contaminated the ground water with red-mud waste. Another environmental problem for Jamaica is land erosion and deforestation. Forest and woodland decreased 4.5% between 1983 and 1993. Jamaica's coral reefs have also been damaged. The nation's cities produce 0.3 million tons of solid waste per year. Kingston has the waste disposal and vehicular pollution problems typical of a densely populated urban area.

In the mid-1990s, five of Jamaica's mammal species were endangered, and two bird species and 10 plant species were threatened with extinction. Endangered or extinct species in Jamaica include the tundra peregrine falcon, homerus swallowtail butterfly, green sea turtle, hawksbill turtle, and American crocodile.

⁶POPULATION

The population of Jamaica in 2000 was estimated at 2,668,740. An estimated 6.4% of the population is 65 years of age or older. The projected population for the year 2005 is 2,764,000, assuming a crude birthrate of 17 per 1,000 population and a death rate of 5 resulting in a natural rate of change of 1.2% for the period 2000–2005. The population rate of change between 1995 and 2000 was 0.9%. The population density in 1998 was 238 per sq km (616 per sq mi).

It was estimated that 56% of the population lived in urban areas in 2000, up from 47% in 1980. The parishes of Kingston and St. Andrew, which comprise the capital city and its suburbs, had a 2000 population of 621,000. Other leading cities are Spanish Town (about 92,383), Portmore (90,138), and Montego Bay (83,466). Jamaica's next census is scheduled to take place in 2001.

⁷MIGRATION

Jamaica's net loss from emigration totaled 145,800 between 1891 and 1921; after a net gain of 25,800 during 1921–43, losses of 195,200 were recorded from 1943 to 1960, and 265,500 from 1960 through 1970. Until the UK's introduction of restrictions on immigration from Commonwealth countries in 1962, a large number of Jamaican workers emigrated to Great Britain. In 1964, in an effort to curb increasing migration, Jamaica passed the Foreign Nationals and Commonwealth Citizens (Employment) Act, providing Jamaicans with easier access to the island's employment market; however, domestic unemployment continued to plague Jamaica through the 1970s. During this period, Jamaica suffered from a "brain drain," losing perhaps as much as 40% of its middle class. From 1971 through 1980, 276,200 Jamaicans left the island, 142,000 for the US. In the mid-1990s, there were 350,000 Jamaican-born people in the US.

The great disparity between rural and urban income levels has contributed to the exodus of rural dwellers to the cities, where many of these migrants remain unemployed for lack of necessary skills. In 1999, the net migration rate was -8.39 migrants per 1,000 population.

Jamaica is a transit point for migrants, including asylum-seekers, trying to reach the US. As of September 1999, Jamaica was hosting 25 recognized refugees, most from Cuba, and had granted humanitarian status to a number of others, notably five nationals of Sierra Leone. Asylum-seekers continue to arrive from Cuba, Haiti, and other parts of the world.

⁸ETHNIC GROUPS

About 97.7% of the population is of partial or total African descent. This population is comprised of blacks, mulattos, and black-East Indians or black-Chinese. Other ethnic groups include East Indians (1.3%), Chinese (0.2%), Europeans (0.2%), and other (0.6%). Nearly the whole population is native-born Jamaican. Black racial consciousness has been present in Jamaica at least since the beginnings of the Rastafarian sect, founded in 1930 and based on the ideas of Marcus Garvey.

⁹LANGUAGES

Jamaica is an English-speaking country, and British usage is followed in government and the schools. Creole is also often used.

¹⁰RELIGIONS

There is freedom and equality of religion in Jamaica. The Protestant Church is dominant, with its various denominations comprising 61.3% of the total population. The Church of God now claims the largest number of adherents, with 21.2% of the Protestant populace. Seventh-Day Adventists rank second, with 9%. Baptists rank third, with 8.8%. The Pentecostal Church

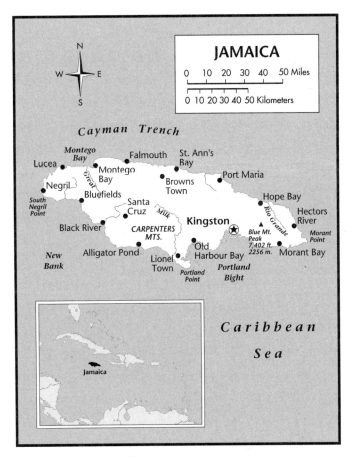

LOCATION: 17°43′ to 18°32′N; 76°11′ to 78°21′W. **TOTAL COASTLINE:** 1,022 km (634 mi). **TERRITORIAL SEA LIMIT:** 12 mi.

claims 7.6% of the Protestant population. The Church of England (Anglican), formerly the dominant religion in Jamaica, now ranks fifth, with 5.5%. The Methodist and United Churches each comprise 2.7%. Jehovah's Witnesses claim 1.6%; the Brethren and Moravian account for 1.1% each. The Roman Catholic Church is also significant, constituting 4% of the total population. The Pope visited Jamaica in August 1993. Other religious groups, including some spiritual cults, make up the remaining 34.7%. The Rastafarian movement continues to grow and is culturally influential in Jamaica and abroad. Rastas regard Africa (specifically Ethiopia) as Zion and consider their life outside Africa as a Babylonian captivity; use of marijuana, or ganja, plays an important role in the movement.

¹¹TRANSPORTATION

Jamaica has an extensive system of roads; in 1999 there were 18,700 km (11,620 mi) of roads, including 13,100 km (8,140 mi) of paved roads. In 1995 there were 104,000 licensed passenger cars and 21,600 commercial vehicles on the island. Motorbus service, which has greatly facilitated travel, is operated by the government-owned Jamaica Omnibus Services Co.

The standard-gauge rail system totals 370 km (230 mi) of track. Of that total, 207 km (129 mi) belong to the government-owned Jamaica Railway Corp. (JRC) in common carrier service but are no longer operational. The remaining track is privately owned and used to transport bauxite.

Kingston, the main port, handles nearly all of the country's foreign imports but only a small percentage of its exports, by weight. The remaining exports are shipped through 18 other ports, which tend to specialize in particular commodities: Montego Bay and Port Antonio in bananas and sugar, for instance, and Port Esquivel and Ocho Rios in bauxite. More than 30 shipping companies provide passenger and cargo service. The port facilities of Kingston harbor are among the most modern in the Caribbean. Jamaica's merchant marine has a small fleet, including as of 1998, 2 ships totaling 3,478 GRT.

Air service is the major means of passenger transport between Jamaica and outside areas. In 1998 there were an estimated 36 airports, 11 of which had paved runways. Control of the two modern airports, Norman Manley International Airport (Kingston) and Sangster International Airport (Montego Bay), was assigned to the Airports Authority of Jamaica in 1974. About a dozen airlines provide scheduled international air transportation. Air Jamaica, the national airline, operates internationally in association with British Airways and British West Indian Airways. The government owns a controlling interest in Air Jamaica and has also invested in a domestic air carrier, Trans Jamaican Airlines. In 1997, 1,400,000 passengers were carried on scheduled domestic and international flights.

12HISTORY

Jamaica was discovered by Christopher Columbus in 1494 and was settled by the Spanish in the early 16th century. The Spanish used the island as a supply base and also established a few cattle ranches. The Arawak Indians, who had inhabited the island since about AD 1000, were gradually exterminated, replaced by African slaves. In 1655, the island was taken over by the English, and the Spanish were expelled five years later.

Spain formally ceded Jamaica to England in 1670 by the Treaty of Madrid. The island became a base for English privateers raiding the Spanish Main. A plantation economy was developed, and sugar, cocoa, and coffee became the basis of the island's economy. The abolition of the slave trade in 1807 and of slavery itself in 1834 upset Jamaica's plantation economy and society. The quarter million slaves were set free, and many became small farmers in the hill districts. Freed slaves were replaced by East Indians and Chinese contract workers. The economy suffered from two developments in mid-century: in 1846 the British rescinded favorable terms of trade for Jamaica, and the union blockade during the US Civil War limited commercial options for the island. Bankruptcies and abandonment of plantations followed, and dissension between the white planters and black laborers led to a crisis. An uprising by black freedmen at Morant Bay in 1865 began a struggle which necessitated the imposition of martial law. Parliament established a crown colony government in 1866, and Jamaica's new governor, Sir John Peter Grant, introduced new programs, which included development of banana cultivation, improvement of internal transportation, and reorganization of government administration. Advances in education, public health, and political representation pacified the island.

These measures did not resolve Jamaica's basic problems, stemming from wide economic and social disparities, and social unrest came to the surface whenever economic reverses beset the island. The depression of the 1930s, coupled with a blight on the banana crop, produced serious disruption and demands for political reform. A royal commission investigated the island's social and economic conditions, and recommended self-government for Jamaica. A Jamaica legislative council committee concurred, and in 1944, Jamaica had its first election. The contenders in that election were two recently formed political parties, the People's National Party (PNP), led by Norman W. Manley, and the Jamaica Labour Party (JLP), founded by Manley's cousin, Sir Alexander Bustamante.

During the 1950s, the bauxite industry and the tourist trade assumed prominent roles in the economy. The economic gains from these enterprises did little to solve Jamaica's underlying economic problems. Jamaica joined with other British Caribbean colonies in 1958 to form the Federation of the West Indies, but in a referendum in 1961 a majority of Jamaicans voted for withdrawal from the federation. The governments of the UK and Jamaica accepted the decision of the electorate, and Jamaica became an independent state on 6 August 1962, with dominion status in the Commonwealth of Nations. The PNP had supported the federation concept, so the JLP became the independence party, and Bustamante became the nation's first prime minister.

The JLP held power through the 1960s. Donald Sangster became prime minister in 1965 and was succeeded by Hugh Shearer, also of the JLP, two years later. In February 1972, the PNP regained a majority in Parliament, and the late Norman Manley's son, Michael, headed a new democratic socialist government.

Manley moved to nationalize various industries, and expanded Jamaica's programs in health and education. Manley placed price controls on a number of key products and provided consumer subsidies for others. Internationally, Manley established friendly relations with Cuba, which the US decried. Deteriorating economic conditions led to recurrent violence in Kingston and elsewhere during the mid-1970s, discouraging tourism. By 1976, Jamaica was faced with declining exports, a critical shortage of foreign exchange and investment, an unemployment rate estimated at 30–40%, and rampant currency speculation.

The PNP nevertheless increased its parliamentary majority in the December elections that were held during a state of emergency. Tourism suffered another blow in January 1979 with three days of rioting in Kingston, at the height of the tourist season. Meanwhile, Manley quarreled with the IMF. The IMF responded to Jamaica's request for loan guarantees by conditioning acceptance on a set of austerity measures. Manley refused to initiate many of the market-oriented measures the IMF was demanding.

Manley called for elections in the fall of 1980. The campaign was marred by somewhere between 500 and 800 deaths, and was further inflamed by PNP claims that the CIA was attempting to destabilize its government. The opposition JLP won a landslide victory, and Edward Seaga became prime minister and minister of finance. He announced a conservative economic program that brought an immediate harvest of aid from the US and the IMF. In October 1981, Jamaica broke off diplomatic relations with Cuba, and two years later it participated in the US-led invasion of Grenada.

In December 1983, Seaga called for elections, which the PNP boycotted, leaving the JLP with all 60 seats in the House of Representatives. Seaga then implemented an IMF plan of sharp austerity, pushing the economy into negative growth for two years. In May 1986, Seaga turned away from the IMF, announcing an expansionary budget. The JLP nevertheless suffered a sharp loss in July parish elections, with the PNP taking 12 of 13 municipalities. By January 1987, a new IMF agreement was in place, but their political position continued to slide.

The 1989 elections were a good deal less tumultuous than expected. The two parties reached an agreement to control their respective partisans, and election violence was minimal. The rhetoric was also considerably less inflammatory, as the PNP's Manley ran as a more moderate candidate. Citing the deterioration of social services under Seaga, and promising to attract foreign capital, Manley was returned to the prime ministership as the PNP took a powerful 45-seat bloc in the House of Representatives. Manley reversed many of Seaga's policies, but by 1992, inflation was on the rise and the economy slowed. Unemployment hovered around 20%. Manley retired in 1992, leaving the government to Percival J. Patterson.

Patterson moved further to the right from Seaga, encouraging more market-oriented reforms. Within a year of taking office, he called for elections, in which violence erupted anew and 11 died in campaign-related killings. The PNP increased its parliamentary margin to 52–8, a small consolation for a government besieged by serious political, social, and economic problems.

Political violence resurged in 1996, following the establishment in 1995 of two new political parties, the Jamaica Labour Party and the rival National Democratic Movement. Clashes between party regulars in Kingston and Spanish Town led to 10 deaths in a six-month period. Vigilante killings in response to a high crime rate were also the norm in 1995 and 1996, with police reporting 22 such killings in that span.

In March 1997, former prime minister and PNP founder Michael Manley died. In the December elections that year, the PNP remained the dominant party, the first time a Jamaican political party had won a third consecutive legislative victory. The ruling party also swept local elections in September 1998. However, it presided over an increasingly troubled country, with continued economic contraction and an escalating crime wave, much of it attributable to rival gangs that had begun as armed militias created by the major political parties in the 1970s and later evolved into highly powerful organized crime networks engaged in international drug smuggling and other illicit activities. In the first half of 1999 alone, an estimated 500 Jamaicans had been killed in gang-related violence. In addition, rioting following the announcement of a 30% gasoline tax increase in April. With export revenues driven down by low prices and high costs, and tourism hurt by rising violence, an economic recovery was seen as unlikely before 2001.

13 GOVERNMENT

The 1962 constitution provides for a governor-general appointed by the crown, a cabinet presided over by a prime minister, and a bicameral legislature.

The Senate, the upper house, consists of 21 members appointed by the governor-general, 13 on the advice of the prime minister and 8 on the advice of the leader of the opposition. The popularly elected House of Representatives consists of 60 members (increased from 53 in 1976). The House is by far the more important of the two. The governor-general appoints both the prime minister and the leader of the opposition. The normal term of office in Parliament is five years, but elections can be called at any time. Suffrage is universal at age 18.

The cabinet consists of the prime minister and at least 11 additional ministers, appointed by the governor-general on the advice of the prime minister.

14 POLITICAL PARTIES

Two political parties, the Jamaica Labour Party (JLP) and the People's National Party (PNP), dominate Jamaican politics. Their fortunes have risen and fallen dramatically over the past thirty years. Both parties have held more than three-fourths of Parliament. The JLP, founded in 1943 by Sir Alexander Bustamante, is the more conservative of the two parties. Its original political base was the Bustamante Industrial Trade Union, which Bustamante organized in 1938. The JLP held a parliamentary majority during the first 10 years of independence, and again from 1980–89 under Edward Seaga, who remains opposition leader.

The PNP, founded by Norman W. Manley in 1938, held to a moderate socialist program and from its foundation sought responsible government and independence for Jamaica. The party formed its first government in 1972 under Michael Manley. In 1976, the PNP remained in power, increasing its majority by 10 seats in a House that had been enlarged by 7. After losing in 1980, the PNP refused to participate in the parliamentary

elections called by Prime Minister Seaga for December 1983, two years ahead of schedule. The PNP draws much of its support from the National Workers' Union, Jamaica's largest trade union, and is primarily an urban, middle-class party that has moved toward the political center since its defeat in the 1980 elections. Both the JLP and PNP stand for a broad program of social reform and welfare, and economic development with the participation of foreign capital. The PNP was returned to power in the 1989. In 1992, its founder and longtime leader Michael Manley retired and was succeeded by Percival (P.J.) Patterson, who led the party to a second parliamentary victory in 1993.

A third political party, the National Democratic Movement (NDM), was formed in October 1995 by Bruce Golding, who was the former chairman of the JLP. In December 1997, Patterson led the PNP to a third consecutive parliamentary victory in national elections. The PNP won 50 seats (a loss of only 2 seats from its previous majority), and the opposition JLP won 10.

15 LOCAL GOVERNMENT

Local government is patterned on that of the UK, and the unit of local government is the parish. Responsibility for local government is vested in 12 parish councils and the Kingston and St. Andrew Corporation, which represents the amalgamation of two parishes. Since 1947, all of the councils (called parochial boards until 1956) have been fully elective, although the members of the House of Representatives from each parish are ex-officio members of the councils. Elections are normally held every three years on the basis of universal adult suffrage.

Local government authorities are responsible for public health and sanitation, poor relief, water supply, minor roads, and markets and fire services. Revenues come largely from land taxes, supplemented by large grants from the central government.

16 JUDICIAL SYSTEM

The judicial system follows British practice, with some local variations. Cases may be brought in the first instance before a lay magistrate (justice of the peace), a magistrate, or a judge in the Supreme Court, according to the seriousness of the offense or the amount of property involved. The Supreme Court also has appellate jurisdiction. Final appeal rests with the seven-member Court of Appeals, appointed on the advice of the prime minister in consultation with the leader of the opposition. The attorney general, who need not be a member of Parliament, is appointed by the governor-general on the advice of the prime minister. The Constitution gives power to the Court of Appeal and the Parliament to refer cases to the Judicial Committee of the Privy Council in the United Kingdom.

A special "gun court" considers cases involving the illegal use or possession of firearms or ammunition.

The judiciary is independent but is overburdened and backlogged because of a lack of trained personnel. Recent increases in salaries, training programs for judicial personnel, and improvement in court facilities may eventually serve to improve efficiency and processing of cases. In 1995, to reduce the backlog of cases, the government initiated a night court.

17 ARMED FORCES

The Jamaica Defense Force assumed responsibility for the defense of Jamaica following the withdrawal of British forces in 1962. The total defense force in 2000 numbered 3,780 personnel, including 950 reserves. Designed for minimal defense missions, the armed forces have three ground force battalions, an air wing of 140 patrol and administrative aircraft, and a coast guard of seven patrol boats. In 1997–98, Jamaica spent $47.9 million on defense.

18INTERNATIONAL COOPERATION

Although Jamaica remains a member of the Commonwealth of Nations, the country's political, social, and economic ties have shifted toward participation in Latin American, Caribbean, and third-world international organizations. Jamaica was admitted to UN membership on 18 September 1962 and is a member of ECLAC and all the nonregional specialized agencies except IDA. The nation belongs to CARICOM, G-77, IADB, and OAS, as well as the International Bauxite Association. Jamaica also participates in a number of common services with other West Indian islands, including support of the University of the West Indies; the West Indies Shipping Co., which maintains an interisland shipping service; and the West Indian Meteorological Service. Jamaica is a signatory of the Law of the Sea and member of the WTO, and has been chosen as the site of the International Seabed Authority.

19ECONOMY

The structure of the Jamaican economy has undergone extensive changes since 1945, when it was primarily dependent on tropical agricultural products such as sugar, bananas, coffee and cocoa. The island has since become one of the world's largest producers of bauxite, though the industry suffered severely in the 1980s from high local costs and low world prices. It has also developed into a major tourist center for North Americans. Since 1983, tourism has been Jamaica's primary foreign exchange earner.

The underlying weaknesses of Jamaica's economy (including unemployment, underemployment, and unequal distribution of income) have revealed themselves as the market for bauxite has weakened. During 1972–80, production and foreign sales of bauxite, sugar and bananas declined; tourism dropped because of rising social unrest; investor confidence waned; and consumer prices (1975–81) increased by 325%. With the change of administration in both Jamaica and the US during 1980–81, more than $1 billion in IMF and other credits became available. This was enough to extricate the country from its immediate payments crisis, but weak growth continued through 1986, when per capital income was 5.6% less than in 1981.

This trend of declining growth performance continued in the 1990s as the country experienced negative growth, for the first time in nearly a decade, declining by 1.5% in 1996. Underlying this performance was a marked deterioration in manufacturing and construction which declined by 2% and 3%, respectively, and the surfacing of severe problems in the financial sector. Significant among industries showing decline was the apparel industry, second only to bauxite and aluminum in terms of export earnings, resulting in a 5% drop in apparel exports in January–October 1996, compared to the same period of 1995. This marked a reversal of the progress for this sector, which experienced 22% growth during the same period of 1995. Competition from NAFTA caused many garment manufacturers to close, and thousands of workers to go jobless. In 1996, prices rose by only 15.8% (inflation peaked at 80% in 1992), continuing a trend of declining inflation. The decline in inflation was attributable to several factors, including the 12% appreciation of the Jamaican currency between April and June, 1996, and the contractionary conditions prevailing in the economy. Growth declined by 2.1% in 1997; and 0.70% in 1998, when the inflation rate was down to 9.9%. The exchange rate for the Jamaican currency continued to decline in 1999.

20INCOME

The US Central Intelligence Agency (CIA) reports that in 1998 Jamaica's gross domestic product (GDP) was estimated at $8.8 billion. The per capita GDP was estimated at $3,300. The annual growth rate of GDP was estimated at -2%. The average inflation rate in 1998 was 9.9%. The CIA defines GDP as the value of all final goods and services produced within a nation in a given year and computed on the basis of purchasing power parity (PPP) rather than value as measured on the basis of the rate of exchange. It was estimated that agriculture accounted for 7.4% of GDP, industry 42.1%, and services 50.5%.

The World Bank reports that for the same period per capita private consumption (in PPP terms) was $1,980. Private consumption includes expenditures of individuals, households, and nongovernmental organizations. It was estimated that between 1990 and 1998 private consumption grew at an annual rate of -0.3%. Approximately 24% of household consumption was spent on food, 3% on fuel, 1% on health care, and 9% on education. The richest 10% of the population accounted for approximately 29% of household consumption and the poorest 10% approximately 2.9%.

21LABOR

The labor force in 1998 was estimated at one million. The total unemployment rate in 1996 was 16%. Of those employed, 21% worked in agriculture, forestry, and fishing; 9% in manufacturing; 6% in transport and communications; and 6% in financial services.

The two major trade unions are closely identified with the country's two main political parties: the National Workers' Union with the PNP and the Bustamante Industrial Trade Union with the JLP. The Trade Union Congress is a third major union. The combined membership of unions in 1999 amounted to 15% of those employed. The ability to strike is neither authorized nor prohibited by law and strikes do occur. The government rarely interferes with union organizing or bargaining efforts and it effectively enforces laws which prohibit discriminating against workers for their union activities.

Labor legislation covers such items as national insurance, employment of nationals, hours of work, minimum wages, employment of women and youths, apprenticeship, and welfare (workers' compensation and factory conditions). The industrial workweek is generally 8 hours a day for 5 days with mandatory overtime pay for work in excess of 8 hours. Hours in agriculture and some of the service industries vary, but are usually longer. The minimum wage was raised to $30 per week in August 1999, but most salaried workers earn more than the minimum.

22AGRICULTURE

Jamaican agriculture accounts for about 8% of GDP, less than in most developing countries. Agriculture (together with forestry and fisheries) is the third largest foreign exchange earner and the second largest employer of labor. Attempts to offset the serious price and production problems of traditional agricultural exports by encouraging production of winter vegetables, fruits, and flowers have had limited success. Vegetable and melon production in 1998 amounted to 362,000 tons; principal varieties include pumpkin, carrot, cabbage, tomato, callaloo, and cucumber. Production of other crop groups (with leading varieties) in 1998 included: pulses (red peas, peanut, gungo peas), 5,000 tons; condiments (scallion, hot pepper, onion), 8,000 tons; fruits (papaya, pineapple, watermelon), 1,410,000 tons; cereals (corn, rice), 3,000 tons; and roots and tubers (yams, potatoes, plantains), 307,000 tons.

Sugar, the leading export crop, is produced mainly on plantations organized around modern sugar factories that also buy cane from independent growers. Sugar has suffered badly from low world prices and cuts in US buying quotas. Raw sugar production in 1998 was estimated at 179,000 tons, down from 290,000 tons in 1978. As a result of heavy rains in early 1993, the Sugar Manufacturers' Corporation announced a lowering in estimated production levels for the year by nearly 10%. Sugar is Jamaica's largest agricultural export, earning $103.1 million in 1997. The government is in the process of privatizing all four of its sugar estates. Banana production in 1998 was 130,000 tons. Other major export crops in 1998 included cocoa, and coffee. Blue Mountain coffee, which is primarily exported to Japan, brings in some $12 million annually in foreign exchange earnings. Jamaica also exports coconuts, pimientos, citrus fruits, ginger, tobacco, yams, papayas, dasheens, peppers, and cut flowers. Jamaica exported $292.9 million and imported $362.7 million in agricultural products during 1997.

The island's food needs are met only in part by domestic production, and foodstuffs are a major import item. The main food crops, grown primarily by small cultivators, are sweet potatoes and yams, rice, potatoes, manioc, tomatoes, and beans. Jamaica is a major producer of marijuana, which, however, remains illegal. The government participates in a US-funded campaign to eradicate marijuana trading.

23 ANIMAL HUSBANDRY

Livestock has long been important in Jamaica's agricultural life, providing both fertilizer and protein for the local diet. Despite increases in the livestock population and in the production of meat, milk, and poultry, increased demand has resulted in continued imports of livestock products. Livestock holdings in 1998 included some 400,000 head of cattle, 440,000 goats, and 180,000 hogs. Livestock products in 1998 included 82,000 tons of meat (72% poultry) and 53,000 tons of cow's milk.

24 FISHING

The fishing industry grew during the 1980s, primarily from the focus on inland fishing. Whereas the inland catch in 1982 was 129 tons, by 1997 it had risen to 3,680 tons. Nevertheless, substantial imports have been required to meet domestic needs. The total catch in 1997 was 11,458 tons.

25 FORESTRY

By the late 1980s, only 185,000 hectares (457,000 acres) of Jamaica's original 1,000,000 hectares (2,500,000 acres) of forest remained. Roundwood production increased from 55,000 cu m in 1981 to 220,000 cu m in 1988 and to 355,000 cu m in 1997. About 88% of the timber cut in 1997 was used as fuel wood. The Forestry Department began a reforestation program in 1963 that was scheduled to last for 30 years; the target was to plant 1,200 hectares (3,000 acres) of timber a year. During the 1980s, reforestation averaged 1,000 hectares (2,500 acres) a year, but deforestation continued at twice that rate.

26 MINING

Jamaica is the world's fourth-leading producer of bauxite (1997 production was 11,875,000 tons) and the third leading producer of alumina, accounting for roughly 7% of world production; alumina production came to 3,414,000 tons in 1997. Mining and quarrying contributed 8.6% to GDP in 1995, with 98% coming from bauxite and alumina. Firm bauxite and alumina demand coupled with strong prices have the government and private sector cooperating to increase production; in the 1980s, a global glut of alumina had severely hurt the Jamaican bauxite and alumina industries. The alumina decrease was partly the result of labor strikes at all refineries.

In 1997, Jamaica produced 263,662 tons of gypsum and an estimated 196,000 tons of lime. Good-quality marble is found in the Blue Mountains, and silica and clays are also exploited.

27 ENERGY AND POWER

Jamaica has no coal deposits and very little hydroelectric potential. Oil and gas exploration begun in 1981 had produced no results as of 1995. Electricity is the main source of power and is almost all generated by steam from oil-burning plants. In 1998, the total amount of electricity generated by public and private sources was 6,386 million kWh, and installed capacity was 1.2 million kW. In 1977, the government granted the Jamaica Public Service Co. (JPS) a 40-year franchise as the sole supplier of public power. In 1993, however, JPS entered into a $23.2 million contract with a US firm to build a 35,000–kW generator, whose ownership would be transferred to the private sector under the Energy Sector Privatization Program of the World Bank and the Inter-American Development Bank. Some large enterprises, such as the bauxite companies, and the sugar estates generate their own electricity.

As of 1991, imports of fuels accounted for about 19% of total imports. Jamaica has made a few ventures into alternative sources of energy, but these are still minor relative to overall demand. A large solar water-heating plant was opened in 1981, and the Agency for International Development (AID) has helped finance a $33.3-million power plant, also using solar energy. In 1985, Tropicana Petroleum of California and Shell invested US$23 million in an ethanol plant (mostly for export to the US) at Kingston, using sugarcane as raw material.

28 INDUSTRY

Since 1945, when Jamaican manufacturing was confined largely to processing agricultural products and making beer, clothing and furniture, the industrial sector has grown and diversified considerably. The island now produces a wide range of goods, including mineral fuels and lubricants, fertilizers, steel, cement, and agricultural machinery, along with footwear, textiles, paints, building materials, and processed foods. In the 1980s, the government emphasized manufacturing for export, rather than for import substitution alone. The textile industry was specifically an export business, but the 1996 NAFTA agreement forced the closure of most garment factories in Jamaica. A lime processing factory was slated for operation in 1999.

In 1996, the production of bauxite and aluminum, the leading export commodities, bounced back from a sharp decline in 1995, but the growth of earnings was dampened by soft conditions in aluminum markets. While bauxite and aluminum output grew by 8.9% and exports of ore and aluminum grew by 9.5%, the value added of mining and quarrying, which consists overwhelmingly of these products, grew by only 2%. In 1998, the bauxite and alumina industry produced at the highest level in a decade; 12.6 million tons. However, the manufacturing sector growth rate actually declined in 1998 by 4.2%, in part due to the high cost of production and low world prices. Also, an explosion at Jamaica's main export destination in 1999 reduced efficiency.

29 SCIENCE AND TECHNOLOGY

Learned societies include the Jamaica Institution of Engineers and the Medical Association of Jamaica, both in Kingston, and the Jamaican Association of Sugar Technologists, in Mandeville. Research institutions include the Caribbean Food and Nutrition Institute, in Kingston, and the Sugar Industry Research Institute, in Mandeville. The Scientific Research Council, located in Kingston and founded in 1960, coordinates research efforts in Jamaica. The University of the West Indies, with a campus in Mona, has faculties of medical sciences and natural sciences. An agricultural college is located in Portland. The College of Arts, Science and Technology, founded in 1958, is located in Kingston, and the College of Agriculture, founded in 1982, is located in Portland. In 1986, the Scientific Research Council had 18 scientists and engineers and 15 technicians engaged in research and development. In 1987–97, science and engineering students accounted for 64% of college and university enrollments.

³⁰DOMESTIC TRADE

Imports normally account for about one third of the goods distributed, and importing is in the hands of a relatively small number of firms. Competition is limited by the acquisition of import licenses, and profit margins are high. Many importers function as wholesalers and also have retail outlets. Locally produced consumer goods often are marked through the same firms.

Retail outlets range from supermarkets and department stores, in the urban areas, to small general stores and itinerant merchants, in the rural regions. Purchases tend to be made in small quantities, and credit was extended freely until 1961, when the government instituted on retail credit and on profit margin.

Shops are open weekdays between 8 and 9 AM; large stores generally close at 4:30 or 5 PM, with one early closing one day a week. Food stores, drugstores, and family enterprises, however, often remain open until 9 PM or later. Banks are normally open on weekdays from 9 AM to 2 PM. Newspapers, radio, and television are the main advertising media.

³¹FOREIGN TRADE

Since the discovery of bauxite deposits in the 1950s, Jamaica has become increasingly active in international trade and has gradually loosened its ties to the Commonwealth and increased commercial contacts with North America and the Caribbean. On the supply side, the Jamaican government is committed to attracting foreign investment; and on the demand side, Jamaica is a consumer oriented country, that produces very little of its major necessities. The US supplies at least 50% of Jamaica's food needs, but two-thirds of all tourists come from the US. Jamaica has never recorded a visible trade surplus. In February 1991, the government implemented the CARICOM Common External Tariff (CET), creating the first customs union in the Caribbean.

This island's most lucrative export is alumina and bauxite (51%), while the garment industry comes second (19%). Sugar (6.4%), fruits (bananas) and nuts (4.5%), and rum (2.6%) are the important agricultural products.

In 1996 Jamaica's imports were distributed among the following categories:

Consumer goods	18.9%
Food	12.1%
Fuels	15.2%
Industrial supplies	24.4%
Machinery	14.6%
Transportation	11.9%
Other	2.9%

Principal trading partners in 1998 (in millions of US dollars) were as follows:

COUNTRY	EXPORTS	IMPORTS	BALANCE
United States	524	1,534	-1,010
United Kingdom	159	115	44
Canada	151	95	56
Netherlands	123	23	100
Russia	92	1	91
Norway	77	10	67
France	49	17	32
Japan	16	200	-184
Trinidad and Tobago	16	230	-214
China (inc. Hong Kong)	6	57	-51

³²BALANCE OF PAYMENTS

Balance-of-payments deficits in the 1960s and early 1970s were directly related to the growth of the Jamaican economy and to increased imports of capital goods and raw materials. Later in the 1970s, however, the continued deficits were symptomatic of a weakened economy, declining exports, and the flight of capital. The payments picture brightened somewhat in the first half of the 1980s (despite rising debt payments and the downturn of bauxite exports), as income from tourism and remittances from Jamaicans abroad rose, while substantial international assistance enabled Jamaica to meet its payments obligations. In the 1990s, a favorable balance of payments was aided by increased tourism inflows, reduced capital outflows, significant improvement in the agricultural sector, stability in the foreign exchange rate, and the improved economic strength of the US, Jamaica's major trading partner.

The US Central Intelligence Agency reports that in 1997 the purchasing power parity of Jamaica's exports was $1.7 billion while imports totaled $2.8 billion resulting in a trade balance of -$1.1 billion.

The International Monetary Fund (IMF) reports that in 1998 Jamaica had exports of goods totaling $1,613 million and imports totaling $2,710 million. The services credit totaled $1,770 million and debit $1,260 million. The following table summarizes Jamaica's balance of payments as reported by the IMF for 1998 in millions of US dollars.

Current Account		-255
Balance on goods	-1,097	
Balance on services	510	
Balance on income	-304	
Current transfers	635	
Capital Account		16
Financial Account		327
Direct investment abroad	-82	
Direct investment in Jamaica	369	
Portfolio investment assets	-4	
Portfolio investment liabilities	11	
Other investment assets	-39	
Other investment liabilities	72	
Net Errors and Omissions		-44
Reserves and Related Items		-44

³³BANKING AND SECURITIES

The Bank of Jamaica, the central bank, acts as the government's banker and is authorized to act as agent for the government in the management of the public debt. It also issues and redeems currency, administers Jamaica's external reserves, oversees private banks, and influences the volume and conditions of the supply of credit. Financial institutions in Jamaica in 1999 included 6 commercial banks, 13 merchant banks, 3 development banks, and 67 credit unions. Total assets of commercial banks amounted to $4.75 billion; assets of merchant banks, finance and trust companies equaled $300 million. Commercial banks include the Bank of Nova Scotia, Citibank, Union Bank, CIBC, National Commerce Bank, and Trafalgar Commercial Bank.

Various measures were introduced to restructure the liquidity profile of the banking system. In July 1992, in an attempt to reduce domestic credit and curb inflation, the minimum liquid assets ratio of the commercial banks was raised to 50% (it had been 20% in April 1991). The measure appeared to have been successful and the inflation rate fell until May 1993. However, the first half of 1994 saw a rise in the inflation rate, reflecting the government's price liberalization policies. This was contained by sustained tight monetary and fiscal policy. Reduced interest rates stimulated rapid growth in domestic credit, however, and in 1995 money supply grew by 38.5%.

Economic instability which emerged during 1995–96 brought into focus the relationship between the central bank and the government, and in particular, the destabilizing impact of the government's drawdown of its deposits. The government has since recommended that the central bank be given greater autonomy, and transferred its operational revenue and expenditure accounts from the central bank to commercial banks. It also froze the aggregate balance in the Bank of Jamaica at the

September 1995 level in an attempt to minimize any expansionist effect of fiscal operations on money supply.

The lack of confidence in the financial sector was underlined in October 1996, when further rumors of a liquidity crisis lead to a run on Jamaica's fourth largest financial institution, the Citizen's Bank. Despite the bank's relatively healthy assets position, hundreds of depositors were prompted to withdraw their assets over a three-day period. Following the announcement of record losses of $24.6 million at the National Commercial Bank (NCB) group in the nine months prior to June 1996, it was confirmed that the National Security Bank (NSB) and Mutual Security Bank (MSB), both subsidiaries of the NCG group, were to merge their operations, thus creating the island's largest commercial bank. The extent of the drain upon public finances caused by the precarious state of the financial sector became clear in mid-February 1997, when it was reported that net advances by the Bank of Jamaica to financial institutions had risen by $17.4 million in January alone. Several financial institutions had become dependent upon the government to solve their liquidity problems.

In January 1997, the government established the Financial Sector Adjustment Company (FINSAC) to rescue the ailing financial sector. By 1998, FINSAC had already spent $2.3 billion on the restructuring project, with annual debt financing amounting to approximately $170 million. In order to pay for its operations, FINSAC sold shares in the Canadian Imperial Bank of Commerce, and merged Citizens, Eagle, and Island Victoria commercial banks into one entity called Union Bank. Laws were instituted to improve the solvency of Jamaican banks.

In September 1968 the Jamaican Stock Exchange was incorporated. Jamaica's security market merged with the stock markets in Barbados and Trinidad and Tobago in 1989.

34INSURANCE

Insurance companies in Jamaica are regulated by law, through the Superintendent of Insurance of the Ministry of Finance. Three major life and general insurance companies operating in Jamaica in 1996 were the Insurance Co. of the West Indies, Jamaica International Insurance Co., and Life of Jamaica.

35PUBLIC FINANCE

Debt servicing accounts for about 62% of the fiscal budget, which limits economic expansion. Privatization of public entities has been one of the strategies used by the government to reduce the budget deficit.

The US Central Intelligence Agency (CIA) estimates that in 1998 Jamaica's central government took in revenues of approximately $2.27 billion and had expenditures of $3.66 billion including capital expenditures of $1.27 million. Overall, the government registered a deficit of approximately $1.39 billion. External debt totaled $4 billion.

36TAXATION

In 1996, there was a single income tax of 25% on all income over J$50,544. Income tax deductions include allowances for social security, retirement fund contributions, and charitable contributions. Personal allowances and deductions for medical expenses, insurance premiums, and mortgage interest are no longer applicable.

There is a single 33.33% tax on all companies except banks, which pay an additional tax of 6%. Special depreciation allowances, income tax incentives, and other benefits are still available. Other taxes include business licenses, document taxes, duties on estates, excise taxes, consumption duties, import duties, tonnage taxes, wharfage charges, retail sales taxes, fees on betting and gambling, a motor vehicle tax, and a hotel accommodations tax.

The main source of local revenue is a property tax based on the unimproved value of the land.

37CUSTOMS AND DUTIES

The importance of customs duties as a major source of government income is declining, and most imports are duty free. The remaining duties on imports from non-CARICOM nations range from 0% to 20%. In addition, a stamp duty is levied on motor vehicles, alcohol, and tobacco of 25% to 56%; as well as a special consumption tax of 5% to 39.9%. Most imported items are subject to a 15% general consumption tax (15%). Special rates or exemptions on dutiable imports apply to goods from members of CARICOM and signatories of the Lomé Convention.

Licenses are required for imports of certain durable and nondurable consumer goods. License applications are reviewed by the Trade Board. Most capital goods and raw materials do not require import licenses. Jamaica has three Free Trade Zones; the Kingston Export Free Zone, the Montego Bay Export Free Zone, and Garmex.

38FOREIGN INVESTMENT

Foreign investment in Jamaica has accounted for a large part of the capital formation of the post-1945 period. Until the early 1960s, new US and Canadian capital was invested heavily in the bauxite industry. Capital investment in bauxite and aluminum then tapered off, but investment increased in other industries as a result of a vigorous campaign by the government. Starting in 1972, however, capital investments in the private sector fell substantially. After 1980, the JLP government of Prime Minister Seaga had some success attracting foreign capital, but then the economic downturn of the mid-1980s again produced a decline in foreign investment. By early 1987, when 120 US companies operated in Jamaica, cumulative US investment, excluding the bauxite industry, was over $1 billion. There are no statuary restrictions on sectors open to foreign investment, but in practice most service industries are reserved for Jamaicans.

Increased investment, particularly in the private sector, has been identified by the government as an essential factor in the strategy for reviving and sustaining the economy. Government has therefore continued and initiated actions that are intended to encourage investment in a number of areas such as those that generate foreign exchange, utilize domestic raw materials, and generate employment. The government offers a wide range of incentives, including tax holidays up to a maximum of 10 years and duty-free concessions on raw materials and capital goods for approved incentive periods. There are in existence several acts that provide major benefits for foreign investors, such as the Industrial Incentives Act, the Export Industries Encouragement Act, and the Hotel Incentives Act. Additionally, since the liberalization of exchange controls in September 1991, investors are free to repatriate without prior approval from the Bank of Jamaica.

The US continues to play a leading role in foreign investment. A US firm acquired control of Jamaica's only flour manufacturer, Jamaica Flour Mills, for $35 million in late 1996. In 1997, the Financial Sector Adjustment Company privatized a large number of companies in order to support the country's financial sector. Investment in the late 1990s was modest; foreign direct investment between 1996 and 1998 amounted to about $72 million. Half was in agriculture, 20% in films, 8% in manufacturing, 7% in the garments and textiles industry, and 5% each in tourism and information processing. Major investors included the US, Colombia, Canada, and the UK.

39ECONOMIC DEVELOPMENT

Since assuming office in 1992, Prime Minister Patterson has consolidated the market-oriented reforms initiated by his predecessor, Michael Manley, to make Jamaica a regional leader in economic reform. Patterson has eliminated most price controls, streamlined tax schedules, and privatized government enterprises. Tight monetary and fiscal policies under an IMF program have helped slow inflation and stabilize the exchange rate, but, as a result, economic growth has slowed down and unemployment remains high. Jamaica's medium-term prospects depend largely on its ability to continue to attract foreign capital and limit speculation against the Jamaican dollar.

Inevitably, the contraction of economic output impacted adversely on the employment situation. The reduced performance of the traditionally labor-intensive apparel industry contributed significantly to rising unemployment as some 7000 jobs, amounting to 25% of the employment in the industry, were lost. Along with job losses in the financial sector and other sectors, 1996 witnessed overall losses of employment amounting to 10% of the labor force and raising unemployment above the 20% mark. The unemployment rate was 16.5% in 1997. Problems in the financial sector continued into the new millennium, disturbing economic development.

40 SOCIAL DEVELOPMENT

Jamaica has pioneered in social welfare in the West Indies since 1938. Successful community development programs, which draw on local sources of leadership and use self-help methods, have long been in operation throughout the country. The Jamaica Social Welfare Commission, founded in 1937, is one of the most important voluntary agencies; it receives support from government and industry.

Government assistance is provided to those in need, and rehabilitation grants and family allowances are made. A National Insurance Scheme (NIS) came into effect in April 1966, providing benefits in the form of old age and disability health and maternity coverage, pensions, workers' compensation, widows' and widowers' pensions, and grants. The program is financed by contributions from employers and employees. Employers are required by law to provide 12 weeks maternity leave at 66.6% of pay. Social security provides for partial reimbursement of maternity benefits to some exporters whose labor force is 75% female.

Jamaican women are guaranteed full equality under the constitution and the 1975 Employment Act, but cultural traditions, economic discrimination, and workplace sexual harassment prevent them from achieving it. Women participate actively in politics. In 1995, 30% of senior civil service positions, and 13% of political offices were held by women. As of 1997, however, only 13 of 81 members of Parliament were women. A 1995 domestic violence law that took effect in 1996 provides for restraining orders and other measures to combat spousal abuses.

Children's rights are protected by the 1951 Juvenile Act which sets restrictions on the employment of minors and provides for the protective care of abused children. A lack of resources, however, prevents this law from being applied fully.

While Jamaica's human rights record has improved in recent years, serious abuses continue to occur. A major problem is lack of police accountability for human rights violations. Prison conditions are poor, but are open to inspection by international human rights organizations.

Crime is a serious social problem, with 900 reported homicides in 1996. The murder rate nearly equals that of New York, a city with three times the population of Jamaica.

41 HEALTH

The central government provides most medical services in Jamaica through the Ministry of Health. In 1996, the island had 364 government-operated primary health centers offering five levels of service. There were 23 public hospitals in 1995. There were also nine small private hospitals. In 1995 there were 417 doctors and 1,836 registered nurses. In 1997 there were 14 doctors per 10,000 people. In 1995 5% of the total gross domestic product went to health expenditures.

The government conducts a broad public health program, involving epidemic control, health education, industrial health protection, and campaigns against tuberculosis, venereal diseases, yaws, and malaria. In 1995, 84% of the population had access to safe drinking water.

Public health programs have brought about a significant decrease in the death rate. The death rate was 6.2 per 1,000 people in 1990–95, and the infant mortality rate was 24 per 1,000 live births in 1996. Tuberculosis, hookworm, and venereal diseases remain the most prevalent diseases. Immunization programs are conducted against poliomyelitis and diphtheria, with 1997 vaccination rates for children up to one year of age as follows: tuberculosis (97%); diphtheria, pertussis, and tetanus (90%); polio (90%); and measles (88%). In 1989–95, 10% of Jamaica's children under five years old were considered malnourished, and 10% of births were low birthweight in 1993–96.

Life expectancy averaged 74.7 years for both men and women in 1998. The maternal mortality rate was 100 per 100,000 live births in 1997.

The adult HIV-1 seroprevalence rate was 0.9 per 100 adults in 1997. There were 1,533 AIDS cases reported between 1982 and 1996. Since 1987 the annual AIDS case rates have doubled every two years. Heterosexual transmission predominates.

42 HOUSING

Housing is one of the government's most pressing problems. While middle- and upper-income housing is comparable to that in neighboring areas of North America, facilities for low-income groups are poor by any standard. The problem has been aggravated by constant migration from the rural areas to the cities, causing the growth of urban slums. Most new urban housing is built of cinder block and steel on the peripheries of the cities. Rural housing is primarily built of wood and roofed with zinc sheeting. Squatter settlements surround the major cities of Jamaica. According to the latest available information, total housing units numbered 597,000 with 3.9 people per dwelling.

43 EDUCATION

Jamaica's estimated illiteracy rate for the year 2000 stands at 13.3% (males, 17.5%; females, 9.3%). In the latter half of the 1990s, the government devoted approximately 12.9% of its budget to education. In 1997 there were 293,863 primary school students and 9,512 teachers, with a student-to-teacher ratio of 31 to 1. Secondary students numbered 235,071 and teachers totaled 10,931 in 1993. Education is compulsory for six years of primary education. At the secondary level, there are two stages, one of three years and one of four.

The University of the West Indies, founded in 1948 as the University College of the West Indies, achieved full university status in 1962 and serves all British Commonwealth Caribbean territories. There are faculties of arts, natural sciences, education, general studies, medicine, law, library studies, management studies, public administration, and social work at Jamaica's Mona campus; arts, natural sciences, social sciences, agriculture, engineering, international relations, and management studies at St. Augustine in Trinidad; and arts and natural sciences in Barbados. Higher technical education is provided at the College of Arts, Science, and Technology. Jamaica also has a school of agriculture, several teacher-training colleges and community colleges, and an automotive training school. At the university level, there were a total of 8,434 students enrolled in 1997.

The Jamaica Movement for the Advancement of Literacy Foundation, known as JAMAL (formerly the National Literacy

Board), has reached more than 100,000 students since its founding in 1972.

44 LIBRARIES AND MUSEUMS

The Jamaica Library Service provides free public library programs throughout the island and assists the Ministry of Education in supplying books to primary-school libraries. The book stock of the Public Library Service totals 2,666,000 volumes, 1,473,000 in schools and 1,193,000 in parish libraries. There are 696 service points, including parish and branch libraries, book centers, and 14 bookmobiles. There are 474,000 volumes at the Mona campus of the University of the West Indies. The National Library in Kingston holds over 46,000 volumes.

The Institute of Jamaica in Kingston, has a notable collection of artifacts and materials relating to the West Indies, as well as a museum and exhibition galleries focusing on natural history, military, and maritime studies. The National Gallery of Art, the African-Caribbean Institute, and Jamaica Memory Bank are also part of the Institute of Jamaica. Spanish Town houses the Jamaican's People's Museum of Craft and Technology and the Old Kings House Archaeological Museum. There is a botanical garden and zoo at Hope, on the outskirts of Kingston.

45 MEDIA

The Post and Telegraphs Department provides daily postal deliveries to all parts of the island and operates Jamaica's internal telegraph service. Jamaica International Telecommunications (JAMINTEL) is 51% government-owned and provides five major international services: telephone, telegraph, television, telex, and leased circuits. Telephone service is provided by the privately owned Jamaica Telephone Co. In 1997, 350,000 telephones were in use. Telephone communications between Jamaica and other countries were improved in 1963 by a 1,370-km (850-mi) submarine telephone cable linking Jamaica and Florida and in 1971 by the addition of a satellite communications system. All telephone exchanges are automatic.

Jamaica has two major broadcasting companies. The privately owned Radio Jamaica Rediffusion broadcasts 24 hours a day over both AM and FM bands; it also owns an extensive wire network. The government-owned Jamaica Broadcasting Corp., with similar transmitting facilities, broadcasts FM radio and television programs. As of 1999 there were 1 AM and 7 FM radio stations and 7 television stations. In 1997, there were 482 radio sets, 323 TV sets, and 22 mobile phones per 1,000 population.

As of 1999, there were three daily newspapers, all privately owned. The morning *Daily Gleaner* (circulation about 50,000 in 1999) and the evening *Daily Star* (circulation 45,000) are published by the Gleaner Co., which also publishes the *Sunday Gleaner* (100,000) and the *Thursday Star* (60,000), an overseas weekly. There are also a number of weeklies and monthlies, and in addition, several papers are published by religious groups.

The Constitution of Jamaica provides for free expression, including the rights of free and press, and the government is said to respect these rights in practice.

As of 1996 there were 187 Internet hosts in Jamaica. Online access is extremely limited, with less than one Internet host per 1,000 population in 1998.

46 ORGANIZATIONS

The producers of the main export crops are organized into associations, and there are also organizations of small farmers. The Jamaica Agricultural Society, founded in 1895, is concerned with agricultural and rural development and works closely with the government. The cooperative movement has grown rapidly since World War II. All cooperatives must register with the government and are subject to supervision. Savings and credit groups are the most numerous, followed by marketing organizations. Consumer cooperatives have had little success.

Outside the agricultural sector, the chambers of commerce have long been the most important business groups. There is a wide range of professional and cultural organizations, including a women's federation, 4-H clubs, and an automobile association.

46 ORGANIZATIONS

The producers of the main export crops are organized into associations, and there are also organizations of small farmers. The Jamaica Agricultural Society, founded in 1895, is concerned with agricultural and rural development and works closely with the government. The cooperative movement has grown rapidly since World War II. All cooperatives must register with the government and are subject to supervision. Savings and credit groups are the most numerous, followed by marketing organizations. Consumer cooperatives have had little success.

Outside the agricultural sector, the chambers of commerce have long been the most important business groups. There is a wide range of professional and cultural organizations, including a women's federation, 4-H clubs, and an automobile association.

47 TOURISM, TRAVEL, AND RECREATION

Immigration regulations require the possession of a valid passport, but visitors from the US, Canada and other Commonwealth countries, Japan and parts of Europe may stay up to six months without other valid identification. All visitors must have an onward ticket.

Jamaica is firmly established as a center for tourists, mainly from North America. Greatly expanded air facilities, linking Jamaica to the US, Canada, and Europe, were mainly responsible for the increase in tourism during the 1960s. Rising fuel costs and a weak international economy, as well as intermittent political unrest, contributed to a slowdown in the growth rate of the industry in the 1970s; between 1980 and 1986, however, the number of tourists increased by 68%, and tourism has continued to grow in the 1990s. In 1998, 12,353,914 tourists visited the island. Receipts from tourism in 1997 totaled US$1.13 billion. There were 19,359 hotel rooms and 40,437 beds with a 56% occupancy rate that year. Major tourist areas are the resort centers of Montego Bay and Ocho Rios. Cricket is the national sport, and excellent golf and water-sports facilities are available.

The UN estimates the cost of staying in Kingston in 1999 at $160.

48 FAMOUS JAMAICANS

Names associated with Jamaica's early history are those of Europeans or of little-known figures such as Cudjoe, chief of the Maroons, who led his people in guerrilla warfare against the English in the 18th century. George William Gordon (1820–65), hanged by the British as a traitor, was an advocate of more humane treatment for blacks. Jamaica-born Marcus Garvey (1887–1940), who went to the US in 1916, achieved fame as the founder of the ill-fated United Negro Improvement Association. In the mid-20th century, Jamaicans whose names have become known abroad have been largely political and literary figures. Sir (William) Alexander Bustamante (1894–1977), trade unionist, political leader, and former prime minister of Jamaica, and his cousin and political adversary, Norman Washington Manley (1893–1969), a Rhodes scholar and noted attorney, were leading political figures. More recently, Norman Manley's son Michael (1923–97), prime minister during 1972–80, and Edward Seaga (b.US, 1930), prime minister from 1980-89, have dominated Jamaica's political life. The novelists Roger Mais (1905–55), Vic Reid (1913–87), and John Hearne (b.1926) have built reputations in England, and the poet Claude McKay (1890–1948) played an important role in the black literary renaissance in the

US. Performer and composer Robert Nesta ("Bob") Marley (1945–81) became internationally famous and was instrumental in popularizing reggae music outside Jamaica.

⁴⁹DEPENDENCIES

Jamaica has no territories or colonies.

⁵⁰BIBLIOGRAPHY

American University. *Area Handbook for Jamaica*. Washington, D.C.: Government Printing Office, 1976.

Bakan, Abigail B. *Ideology and Class Conflict in Jamaica: The Politics of Rebellion*. Montreal: McGill-Queen's University Press, 1990.

Barrow, Christine. *Family in the Caribbean: Themes and Perspectives*. Kingston, Jamaica: I. Randle, 1996.

Bryan, Patrick E. *The Jamaican People, 1880–1902: Race, Class and Social Control*. London: Macmillan Caribbean, 1991.

Butler, Kathleen Mary. *The Economics of Emancipation: Jamaica & Barbados, 1823-1843*. Chapel Hill: University of North Carolina Press, 1995.

Campbell, Mavis Christine. *The Maroons of Jamaica, 1655–1796: A History of Resistance, Collaboration & Betrayal*. Granby, Mass.: Bergin & Garvey, 1988.

Dawes, Hugh N. *Public Finance and Economic Development: Spotlight on Jamaica*. Lanham, Md.: University Press of America, 1982.

Floyd, Barry. *Jamaica: An Island Microcosm*. New York: St. Martin's, 1979.

Hall, Douglas. *Free Jamaica, 1838–1865: An Economic History*. New Haven, Conn.: Yale University Press, 1966.

Holt, Thomas C. *The Problem of Freedom: Race, Labor, and Politics in Jamaica and Britain, 1832–1938*. Baltimore: Johns Hopkins University Press, 1992.

Hurwitz, Samuel J. and Edith F. *Jamaica: A Historical Portrait*. New York: Praeger, 1971.

Jamaica in Pictures. Minneapolis: Lerner, 1987.

Kaufman, Michael. *Jamaica under Manley: Dilemmas of Socialism and Democracy*. London: Zed Books, 1985.

Keith, Nelson W. *The Social Origins of Democratic Socialism in Jamaica*. Philadelphia: Temple University Press, 1992.

LaFont, Suzanne. *The Emergency of an Afro-Caribbean Legal Tradition: Gender Relations and Family Courts in Kingston, Jamaica*. San Francisco: Austin Winfield, 1996.

Levi, Darrell E. *Michael Manley: The Making of a Leader*. Athens: University of Georgia Press, 1990, 1989.

Looney, Robert E. *The Jamaican Economy in the 1980s: Economic Decline and Structural Adjustment*. Boulder, Colo.: Westview Press, 1987.

Norris, Katrin. *Jamaica: The Search for an Identity*. London: Oxford University Press, 1962.

Payne, Anthony. *Politics in Jamaica*. New York: St. Martin's, 1988.

Stone, Carl. *State and Democracy in Jamaica*. New York: Praeger, 1986.

Waters, Anita M. *Race, Class and Political Symbols: Rastafari and Reggae in Jamaican Politics*. New Brunswick, N.J.: Transaction Books, 1985.

MEXICO

United Mexican States

Estados Unidos Mexicanos

CAPITAL: Mexico City (México).

FLAG: The national flag is a tricolor of green, white, and red vertical stripes; at the center of the white stripe, in brown and green, is an eagle with a snake in its beak, perched on a cactus.

ANTHEM: *Mexicanos, al grito de guerra (Mexicans, to the Cry of War).*

MONETARY UNIT: The peso (P) is a paper currency of 100 centavos. There are coins of 1, 5, 10, 20, 50, 100, 500, 1,000 and 5,000 pesos and notes of 2,000, 5,000, 10,000, 20,000, 50,000 and 100,000 pesos. As of 1 January 1993, a new unit of currency (the new peso) was issued, worth 1,000 of the pesos that were used until 31 December 1992. P1 = $0.10661 (or $1 = P9.380) as of 31 March 2000.

WEIGHTS AND MEASURES: The metric system is the legal standard, but some old Spanish units are still in use.

HOLIDAYS: New Year's Day, 1 January; Constitution Day, 5 February; Birthday of Benito Juárez, 21 March; Labor Day, 1 May; Anniversary of the Battle of Puebla (1862), 5 May; Opening of Congress and Presidential Address to the Nation, 1 September; Independence Day, 16 September; Columbus Day, 12 October; Revolution Day (1910), 20 November; Christmas, 25 December. Movable religious holidays include Holy Thursday, Good Friday, and Holy Saturday. All Souls' Day, 2 November, and Our Lady of Guadalupe Day, 12 December, are not statutory holidays but are widely celebrated.

TIME: 6 AM = noon GMT.

¹LOCATION, SIZE, AND EXTENT

Situated south of the US on the North American continent, Mexico has an area of 1,972,550 sq km (761,606 sq mi), including many uninhabited islands off the E and W coasts, which have a combined area of 5,073 sq km (1,959 sq mi). Comparatively, the area occupied by Mexico is slightly less than three times the size of the state of Texas. Mexico extends about 3,200 km (2,000 mi) SSE–NNW and 1,060 km (660 mi) ENE–WSW. Bordered on the N by the US, on the E by the Gulf of Mexico (including the Bay of Campeche), the Caribbean Sea, Belize, and Guatemala and on the S and W by the Pacific Ocean, Mexico has a total boundary length of 13,868 km (8,617 mi), including the narrow peninsula of Baja California, which parallels the W coast of the mainland.

Mexico's capital city, Mexico City, is located in the south-central part of the country.

²TOPOGRAPHY

Mexico's dominant geographic feature is the great highland central plateau, which occupies most of the width of the country, extending from the US border to the Isthmus of Tehuantepec. It averages 900 to 1,200 m (3,000–4,000 ft) in elevation in the north and 2,100 to 2,400 m (7,000–8,000 ft) in the central part of the country. The plateau is enclosed by two high cordilleras (mountain chains), the Sierra Madre Oriental on the east and the Sierra Madre Occidental on the west, each separated from the coast by lowland plains. The ranges rise to over 3,000 m (10,000 ft), and some volcanic peaks exceed 5,000 m (16,400 ft); Pico de Orizaba, or Citlaltépetl (5,639 m/18,501 ft), Popocatépetl (5,465 m/17,930 ft), and Ixtaccíhuatl (5,230 m/17,159 ft) are the highest. The plateau falls to the low Isthmus of Tehuantepec and then rises again to Chiapas Highland to the south. The lowlands of Tabasco, Campeche, and Yucatán lie north and east of Chiapas.

There are no important inland waterways. Except for the Rio Grande (known as the Río Bravo del Norte in Mexico), which extends for about 2,100 km (1,300 m) of the boundary with the US, and the Papaloapan, an important source of waterpower, the other rivers are short; they are the Lerma, Santiago, Usumacinta (part of the boundary with Guatemala), Grijalva, Balsas, Pánuco, and the Soto la Marina. The largest lake in Mexico is Lake Chapala, in Jalisco State, covering about 1,680 sq km (650 sq mi).

³CLIMATE

The climate varies according to altitude and rainfall. The tropical and subtropical zone (tierra caliente), ranging from sea level to about 900 m (3,000 ft), consists of the coastal plains, the Yucatán Peninsula, and the lower areas of southern Mexico. These areas have a mean temperature of 25–27°C (77–81°F), with a minimum of 16°C (61°F) and a maximum of almost 49°C (120°F). The temperate zone (tierra templada), at elevations of 900 to 1,800 m (3,000–6,000 ft), has a temperate-to-warm climate and a mean temperature of 21°C (70°F). Mexico City and most other important population centers are in the cool zone (tierra fría), starting at about 1,800 m (6,000 ft), with a mean annual temperature of 17°C (63°C). The highest mountain peaks are always covered with snow.

Most of Mexico is deficient in rainfall, but two coastal belts covering about 12% of the total area—from Tampico south along the Gulf of Mexico and from the state of Colima south along the Pacific—receive an average of from 99 to 300 cm (39–118 in) per year. Annual rainfall may exceed 500 cm (200 in) in Tabasco and Chiapas, while in parts of Baja California, virtually no rain falls. Precipitation is adequate in central Mexico except at altitudes above 1,800 m (6,000 ft), while the northern states are semidesert or desert. Most of the country receives its heaviest rainfall during the summer months.

[4]FLORA AND FAUNA

Plant and animal life differs sharply with Mexico's varied climate and topography. The coastal plains are covered with a tropical rain forest, which merges into subtropical and temperate growth as the plateau is ascended. In the northern states there is a dry steppe vegetation, with desert flora over much of the area. Oaks and conifers are found in mixed forest regions along the mountain slopes. The Yucatán Peninsula has a scrubby vegetation.

Among the wild animals are the armadillo, tapir, opossum, puma, jaguar, bear, and several species of monkey, deer, and boar. Poisonous snakes and harmful insects are found, and in the coastal marshes, malarial mosquitoes pose a problem. The only remaining elephant seals in the world are on Guadalupe Island west of Baja California.

[5]ENVIRONMENT

The Secretariat for Urban Development and Ecology (SEDUE) has the principal environmental responsibility. One of Mexico's most widespread environmental problems is soil erosion; slash-and-burn agricultural practices, especially in the tropical zones, have also contributed to deforestation. Mexico loses its forest at a rate of 2,375 sq mi annually due to agricultural and industrial expansion. Mexico has the fourth most extensive mangrove area in the world, covering approximately one million hectares. Mexico City, located more than 2,250 m (7,400 ft) above sea level and surrounded by mountains, has chronic smog, aggravated by the presence in the metropolitan region of thousands of factories, more than two million motor vehicles, and by open burning of garbage by slum dwellers in an attempt to dispose of the 30% of the city's refuse that is not regularly collected. Cities along the US-Mexican border also suffer from serious air pollution. In 1992, Mexico had the world's 13th highest level of industrial carbon dioxide emissions, totaling 332.8 million metric tons, a per capita level of 3.77 metric tons. Transportation vehicles are responsible for 76% of the air pollution. Water pollution results from the combined impact of industrial, agricultural, and public waste. Mexico's cities produce 12.9 million tons of solid waste per year along with 164 million tons of industrial waste. Mexico has 85.8 cu mi of water. In the north, fresh water resources are scarce and polluted; in the central southeast region they are frequently inaccessible and of poor quality. Thirty-eight percent of the nation's rural dwellers do not have pure drinking water. An environmental protection statute adopted in 1971 has not been widely enforced; however, SEDUE, which was created in 1982, is fostering a more coherent approach to environmental issues.

In 1994, 25 of the nation's mammal species and 35 bird species were endangered. Endangered or extinct species in Mexico include the volcano rabbit, Mexican grizzly bear (possibly extinct), Lower California pronghorn, Sonoran pronghorn, imperial woodpecker, southern bald eagle, American peregrine falcon, tundra peregrine falcon, horned guan, masked bobwhite quail, whooping crane, light-footed clapper rail, California least tern, maroon-fronted parrot, ridge-nosed rattlesnake, Bolson tortoise, five species of turtle (green sea, hawksbill, Kemp's ridley, olive ridley, and leatherback), bighead pupfish, blackfin skiffia, San Estebán Island chuckwalla, spectacled caiman, two species of crocodile (American and Morelet's), and totoaba.

[6]POPULATION

The 1990 census showed a total population of 81,249,646, more than double the 1960 census total of 34,923,129. During 1970–80, annual population growth was 3.1%, one of the highest rates in the world, but during the 1980s, the growth rate declined to 2.1%, aided by government promotion of family planning.

However, the mid-1996 population estimate of 95,722,000 by the US Bureau of the Census indicated a higher rate of growth than the official one. By the year 2000, the population of Mexico was estimated at 102,026,691. An estimated 4.4% of the population is 65 years of age or older. The projected population for the year 2005 is 110,574,000, assuming a crude birthrate of 22 per 1,000 population and a death rate of 5, resulting in a natural rate of change of 1.8% for the period 2000–2005. The population rate of change between 1995 and 2000 was 1.6%. The population density in 1998 was 50 per sq km (130 per sq mi).

It was estimated that 74% of the population lived in urban areas in 2000, up from 66% in 1980. Approximately 32% of the entire population lived in 14 urban areas, including the Federal District of over 500,000 persons. The capital city, Mexico City, had a 2000 metropolitan population of 18,131,000. Other major cities (with their metropolitan populations in 2000) were Guadalajara, 3,908,000; Monterrey, 3,416,041; Puebla, 1,968,000; León, 1,050,000; Ciudad Juárez, 1,168,000; Tijuana, 1,167,000; San Luis Potosi, 931,000; Toluca, 1,184,000; and Torreon, 953,000.

[7]MIGRATION

As of 1990, the US Census Bureau estimated that 13,496,000 persons of Mexican ancestry were living in the US, up from 8,740,000 in 1980. Formerly, under an agreement between the US and Mexico, there was a large annual movement of Mexican agricultural laborers (braceros) into the US. The US has since banned such border crossings, and the 1986 Immigration Act imposes stiff penalties on employers who hire illegal aliens. Nevertheless, hundreds of thousands of illegal crossings still take place annually.

In the 1970s, there was substantial internal migration to the frontier areas, especially to the northern border states, to Quintana Roo and Guerrero in the south, and to government colonization projects such as Papaloapan, Veracruz, where the construction of irrigation, flood control, and hydroelectric projects attracted many people. Most notable, however, is the migration of rural inhabitants to Mexico's already overcrowded cities, creating huge urban slums, especially in Mexico City. Guadalajara and Monterrey, although growing rapidly, are attempting to use Mexico City's experience to plan urban and industrial growth. The great disparity between rural-zone, low-income, marginal groups producing only for their own consumption and highly developed urban and industrial sectors has produced acute social problems.

Mexico has long had a liberal asylum policy; the most famous exile in Mexico was probably Leon Trotsky, a revolutionary exiled from the USSR in 1929 who lived in Mexico City from 1937 until his assassination in 1940. In the 1930s and 1940s, Spanish republican refugees in the tens of thousands settled in Mexico, as did thousands of refugees from World War II. In the 1970s and 1980s, many victims of Latin American military regimes fled to Mexico. By the end of 1993, the number of persons from Guatemala, El Salvador, and other Central American countries living in Mexico was about 400,000, not counting 45,000 Guatemalan refugees living in camps. Over 13,000 Guatemalans repatriated in 1995 and 1996. By 30 June 1999, 42,652 Guatemalan refugees had returned to Guatemala from Mexico. At that time, about 22,500 Guatemalan refugees remained in the southeastern states of Campeche (7,100), Quintana Roo (2,900), and Chiapas (12,500). These refugees were in the process of gaining full legal and socioeconomic integration under the Mexican government's Migratory Stabilization Plan, enacted in August 1996. Nearly 2,200 in Campeche and Quintana Roo had already been naturalized in September

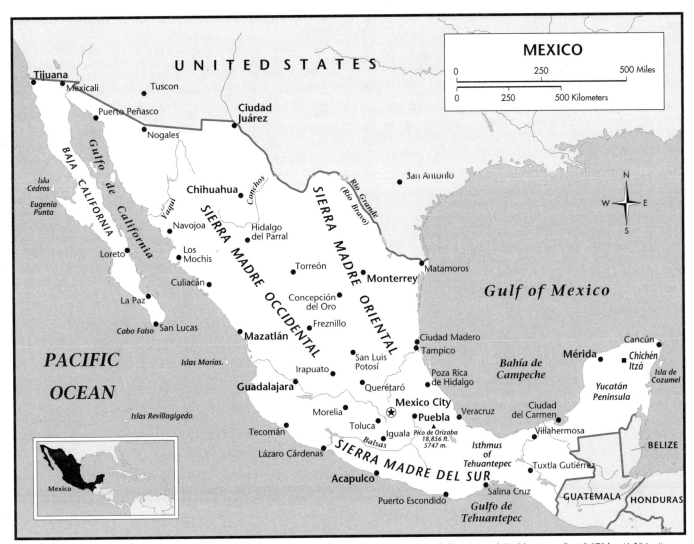

MEXICO

0 250 500 Miles

0 250 500 Kilometers

UNITED STATES

Tijuana
Mexicali
Tuscon
Puerto Peñasco
Nogales
Ciudad Juárez

BAJA CALIFORNIA
Gulfo de California
Isla Cedros
Eugenia Punta

San Antonio

Chihuahua
Conchos
Yaqui
Navojoa
Hidalgo del Parral
Los Mochis
Torreón
Monterrey
Matamoros

SIERRA MADRE OCCIDENTAL
SIERRA MADRE ORIENTAL

Rio Grande (Rio Bravo)

Gulf of Mexico

Loreto
Culiacán
La Paz
Cabo Falso San Lucas

Concepción del Oro
Freznillo
Mazatlán
San Luis Potosí
Ciudad Madero
Tampico

PACIFIC OCEAN

Islas Marías
Irapuato
Poza Rica de Hidalgo

Bahía de Campeche

Cancún
Mérida
Chichén Itzá
Isla de Cozumel

Guadalajara
Querétaro
Mexico City
Puebla
Veracruz
Ciudad del Carmen

Yucatán Peninsula

Islas Revillagigedo

Morelia
Toluca
Iguala
Balsas
Pico de Orizaba 18,856 ft. 5747 m.

Villahermosa

BELIZE

Tecomán
Lázaro Cárdenas

SIERRA MADRE DEL SUR

Isthmus of Tehuantepec
Tuxtla Gutiérrez

Mexico

Acapulco
Puerto Escondido
Salina Cruz
Gulfo de Tehuantepec

GUATEMALA
HONDURAS

N W E S

LOCATION: 14°32′ to 32°43′N; 86°42′ to 118°22′W. **BOUNDARY LENGTHS:** US, 3,326 km (2,067 mi); Gulf of Mexico and Caribbean coastline, 2,070 km (1,286 mi); Belize, 251 km (156 mi); Guatemala, 871 km (541 mi); Pacific coastline (including Baja California), 7,339 km (4,560 mi). **TERRITORIAL SEA LIMIT:** 12 mi.

1999; another 1,800 applications for naturalization were being processed.

As of September 1999, Mexico was host to some 2,500 urban refugees, most of whom had remained from the Central American conflict of the 1980s. Also, the largest community of US citizens living outside the US, estimated at 200,000, is found in Mexico. Mexico has also been receiving increasing numbers of asylum-seekers from outside the Americas.

Many Mexicans migrate to the urban areas from rural areas that lack job opportunities. In 1999, the net migration rate was -2.84 migrants per 1,000 population.

8ETHNIC GROUPS

The people of Mexico are mostly mestizos, a mixture of indigenous Amerindian and Spanish heritage. There are small numbers of persons of other European heritages, and small numbers of blacks are found in Veracruz and Acapulco. At last estimates, 60% of the population was mestizo, 30% pure Amerindian, 9% pure white, and 1% other. Amerindian influence on Mexican cultural, economic, and political life is very strong.

9LANGUAGES

Spanish, the official language, is spoken by nearly the entire population, thus giving Mexico the world's largest Spanish-speaking community; more Mexicans speak Spanish than Spaniards. Only a small number of inhabitants, about 1% of the population according to last estimate, speak only indigenous Amerindian languages or dialects. A larger percentage, some 7.5% at last estimate, speak some Amerindian language. There are at least 31 different Amerindian language groups, the principal languages being Nahuatl, Maya, Zapotec, Otomi, and Mixtec.

10RELIGIONS

According to the latest estimates, 89% of the Mexican population is at least nominally affiliated with the Roman Catholic Church, and about 6% are Protestant. About 50,000 officially follow indigenous Amerindian religions; however, more than 2% of the population, while professing the Roman Catholic faith, include strong Amerindian elements in their religion. The Jewish population was an estimated 35,000, and there were some 25,000 Buddhists and 25,000 Muslims.

Following an amendment to the constitution adopted in 1991, ecclesiastical corporations now have legal rights and can acquire property. All church buildings, including schools, however, remain national property. Priests now have political rights, and religious control over both public and private education prohibited earlier under the 1917 constitution has been restored. Roman Catholicism has increased greatly in activity since the 1940s; there have been religious processions and considerable construction of new churches in major cities. The bitter anticlericalism of the Mexican Revolution, of the 1917 constitution, and of the administration of President Plutarco Elías Calles (1924–28) had lessened by the 1960s. In 1992, full diplomatic relations with the Vatican were established.

11TRANSPORTATION

The local, state, and federal Mexican road system amounted to 252,000 km (156,593 mi) in 1999, of which 94,248 km (58,566 mi) were paved; most roads are engineered for year-round service. In 1995 there were an estimated 12,150,000 registered vehicles (as compared with 7,499,320 in 1986), including 8,400,000 passenger cars and 3,750,000 commercial vehicles.

The major railroad system is the National Railway of Mexico. In 1998, the total route length was 31,048 km (19,293 mi), consisting of six integrated lines. A railway improvement program was carried out during 1975–79, but in the mid-1980s, the network was still in disrepair. The Mexico City subway system, totaling 120 km (75 mi), suffers from overcrowding. The system's technology, however, is being exported to other developing countries.

Mexico's inland waterways and lakes are not important for transportation, but ocean and coastal shipping is significant. Of Mexico's 102 ocean ports, the most important are Tampico, and Veracruz, on the Gulf of Mexico; Mazatlan and Manzanillo, on the Pacific coast; and Guayamas, on the Gulf of California. These five ports together handle about 80% of total general cargo tonnage for Mexico. Most Mexican ships are operated by the government-owned Maritime Transport of Mexico. The merchant marine in 1998 had 52 vessels totaling 852,004 GRT. The oil tanker fleet, owned and operated by Mexican Petroleum (Petróleos Mexicanos—PEMEX), the government oil monopoly, included 28 tankers.

Air transportation in Mexico has developed rapidly. In 1998 there were an estimated 1,805 airports and airfields, 232 with permanent-surface runways. Principal airports include Juan N. Alvarez at Acapulco, Cancun International at Cancun, Cozumel International at Cozumel, Miguel Hidalgo at Guadalajara, Gen. R. Buelna at Mazatlan, Manuel C. Rejon at Merida, Benito Juarez at Mexico City, Gral. Escobedo at Monterrey, and G. Diaz Ordaz at Puerto Vallarta. Mexican commercial aircraft performed 23,668 million passenger-km (14,707 million passenger-mi) of service in 1997, carrying 17,266,000 passengers on scheduled domestic and international flights. The main airline company is the newly privatized Aeroméxico.

12HISTORY

The land now known as Mexico was inhabited by many of the most advanced Amerindian cultures of the ancient Americas. The Mayan civilization in the Yucatán Peninsula began about 2500 BC, flourished about AD 300–900, and then declined until its conquest by the Spanish. The Mayas had a well-developed calendar and a concept of zero; skillful in the construction of stone buildings and the carving of stone monuments, they built great cities at Chichen Itzá, Mayapán, Uxmal, and many other sites. About 1200–400 BC the Olmecs had a civilization with its center at La Venta, featuring giant carved stone heads and the first use of pyramids for worship among the Amerindians. In the early 10th century AD the Toltecs, under Ce Acatl Topiltzin, founded their capital of Tollan (now Tula) and made the Nahua culture predominant in the Valley of Mexico until the early 13th

century. At that time, the Aztecs, another Nahua tribe, gained control.

The Aztec Empire, with its capital at Tenochtitlán (now Mexico City), founded in 1325, was essentially a confederation of allied and tributary communities. Skilled in architecture, engineering, mathematics, weaving, and metalworking, the Aztecs had a powerful priesthood and a complex pantheon dominated by the sun god and war god Huitzilopochtli, to whom prisoners captured from other tribes were sacrificed.

The empire was at its height in 1519, when the Spanish conquistadores, under Hernán Cortés, having set out from Cuba, landed at modern Veracruz; with superior weapons and the complicity of local chieftains, the Spaniards had conquered Mexico by 1521. First, Cortés imprisoned the emperor Montezuma II, who was wounded by stoning when he was released in an attempt to quell an uprising against the Spanish. Then Montezuma's nephew, Guatemotzin, drove the Spanish from Tenochtitlán on 30 June 1520, now called "la noche triste" ("the sad night"), during which Montezuma died, probably at the hands of the Spaniards. Eventually, Cortés returned to Tenochtitlán and defeated Guatemotzin.

The Spaniards brought Roman Catholicism to Mexico, imposed their legal and economic system on the country, and enslaved many of the inhabitants. The combination of Spanish oppression and the smallpox, influenza, and measles the conquistadores brought with them reduced the Amerindian population from an estimated 5 million in 1500 to 3.5 million a century later; not until late in the 18th century did Mexico match its pre-Columbian population. Gradually, the Spaniards extended their territory southward, to include, for a time, the captaincy-general of Guatemala, and northward as far as California, Nevada, and Colorado.

Spain ruled Mexico as the viceroyalty of New Spain for three centuries. Continued political abuses and Amerindian enslavement combined with the Napoleonic invasion of Spain in 1807 and consequential political uncertainty to produce a movement for independence. In 1810, a revolt against Spain was begun by a priest, Miguel Hidalgo y Costilla, and a captain, Ignacio José Allende. Both were captured and shot by loyalists in 1811, but the revolt was continued by another priest, José María Morelos y Pavón, who proclaimed Mexico an independent republic in 1813. Morelos and his followers were defeated and he was shot in 1815, but a swing toward liberalism in Spain in 1820 altered the political picture, leading Mexico's conservative oligarchy to favor independence as a way of preserving its power. In 1821, under the leadership of a rebel, Vicente Guerrero, and a former loyalist, Agustín de Iturbide, independence was again proclaimed and this time secured. Iturbide proclaimed himself emperor in 1822 but was deposed in 1823, when a republic was established; when he returned in the following year, he was captured and shot.

In the next 25 years, there were at least 30 changes of government. Gen. Antonio López de Santa Anna, who had participated in the overthrow of Iturbide, become the dominant figure in the 1830s and 1840s and attempted to centralize the new government. Texas gained its independence from Mexico in 1836 as a result of the defeat of Santa Anna at San Jacinto; in 1845, after a period as the Republic of Texas, it joined the US. Mexico lost the subsequent war with the US (1846–48), which began over a dispute about the border of Texas; under the Treaty of Guadalupe Hidalgo, Mexico recognized the Rio Grande as the boundary of Texas and ceded half its territory (much of the present western US) in return for $45 million. In 1853, the US purchased a small portion of land from Mexico for another $10 million, which was widely regarded as further compensation for the land lost in the war.

A reform government was established in 1855 after a revolt against Santa Anna, and a new liberal constitution was adopted in 1857. Included in the reforms were laws abolishing military and clerical immunities. Article 27 prohibited corporations from holding land, and Article 123 established federal authority in matters of worship and religious discipline. Benito Juárez, the leader of the reform movement, became president in 1858. In 1861, during a period of civil strife, French troops under Emperor Napoleon III intervened in Mexico, ostensibly because Mexico had not paid its debts; in 1863, they captured Mexico City and installed Archduke Maximilian of Austria as emperor, with his Belgian wife, Carlota, as empress. After the French troops withdrew in 1866, partly because the US protested their presence and partly because Napoleon needed them in France, forces loyal to Benito Juárez and led by José de la Cruz Porfirio Díaz regained control of the country. Maximilian was executed and the republic restored in 1867; Carlota, who had returned to Europe to plead with Napoleon to protect her husband, was driven mad by his death.

Díaz twice ran for president, in 1867 and 1871, each time leading an abortive military uprising after his electoral defeat. Finally, in 1876, Díaz seized power and assumed the presidency, a position he held (except for 1880–84, when a subordinate exercised nominal power) until 1911. Under his dictatorship, Mexico modernized by opening its doors to foreign investors and managers. At the same time, the so-called Pax Porfiriana meant suppression of all dissent, by persuasion or by force, and a complete lack of concern with improving the life of the Mexican peasant; an elite corps of mounted police, the Rurales, held the rural areas in check. As the president's aging circle of associates, called Científicos (Scientists), clung tenaciously to power, resentment among the middle classes and the peasantry continued to grow.

After Díaz was once again reelected to the presidency in 1910, the Mexican Revolution erupted. This revolution, which by 1917 had claimed perhaps one million lives, was, on the one hand, a protest by middle-class political liberals against the stultifying Díaz regime and, on the other, a massive popular rebellion of land-hungry peasants. The interests of these two groups sometimes coincided but more often clashed, accounting for the turmoil and confusion of those years. The spark that touched off the revolution was the proclamation on 5 October 1910 of the Plan of San Luis Potosí, in which the liberal politician Francisco Indalecio Madero, who had lost the vote to Díaz, called for nullification of the election. Riots in Mexico City forced Díaz to resign and leave the country in 1911, and Madero was elected president later in that year. Meanwhile, popular revolts led by Emiliano Zapata and Pancho Villa, who refused to submit to Madero's authority, led the country into chaos. Madero, accused by the Zapatistas of not giving land to the peasants, was ousted and murdered in 1913 by Gen. Victoriano Huerta, who had conspired with the rebels. When Huerta, a corrupt dictator, was driven from power by Venustiano Carranza and Álvaro Obregón in July 1914, a full-scale civil war broke out. This phase of the revolution ended in February 1917, when a new constitution was proclaimed; this nationalistic, anticlerical document, considered by some to be the world's first socialist constitution, embodied the principle of the one-term presidency in order to prevent the recurrence of a Díaz-type dictatorship. Article 3 established government rather than church control over schools; Article 27 provided for public ownership of land, water, and minerals; and Article 123 ensured basic labor rights. Carranza was elected president in 1917, but for the next decade Mexico was still beset by political instability and fighting between various revolutionary groups. Most of the revolutionary leaders met with violent deaths. Zapata, still regarded by many as a revolutionary hero,

was assassinated in 1919, and both Carranza and Obregón (who was president during 1920–24) lost their lives in military coups.

Political stability at last came to Mexico with the formation in 1929 of an official government party that incorporated most of the social groups that had participated in the revolution; it has been known since 1945 as the Institutional Revolutionary Party (Partido Revolucionario Institucional—PRI). Although its main pillars were, at least in theory, the peasants, workers, and other popular movements, it has also been closely allied with business since the 1940s. The most outstanding political leader of the post-1929 era was Lázaro Cárdenas, president during 1934–40, who sought with some success to realize the social goals of the revolution. His reforms included massive land redistribution, establishment of labor unions with strong bargaining positions, extension of education to remote areas of the country, and in 1938, the expropriation of foreign petroleum holdings, mostly US-owned. A compensation agreement with the US was reached in 1944, when the two nations were World War II allies.

The postwar years have been marked by political stability, economic expansion, and the rise of the middle classes, but also by general neglect of the poorest segments of the population. One serious political disturbance came in 1968, the year the Summer Olympics were held in Mexico City, when the army and police clashed with students protesting political repression and human rights abuses. The number of students shot and killed has never been revealed. Yet, for many Mexicans, the murder of the students marked the unraveling of the authoritarian PRI, which could no longer hold on to power without resorting to extreme violence.

An economic boom during the late 1970s, brought about by huge oil export earnings, benefited a small percentage of the people, but millions of peasants continued to be only slightly better off than in 1910. Declining world oil prices in 1981 led to a severe financial crisis in 1982, a year of presidential elections. Mexico's new president, Miguel de la Madrid Hurtado, immediately introduced a series of austerity measures and promised a crackdown on corruption, which has long been a problem in Mexico. After the arrest of two government officials for misuse of public funds and fraud, the anticorruption drive appeared to languish; furthermore, public resentment of austerity increased. In 1985, when the PRI was accused of electoral malpractice in local and congressional elections, resentment boiled over in violent public protest. In October 1987, the PRI named Carlos Salinas de Gortari, a 39-year-old economist, as its candidate to succeed President de la Madrid in December 1988. In September 1993, changes in federal electoral law and practices were designed to make future elections more tamperproof.

Mexico City was devastated by a major earthquake in September 1985. The official death toll was 7,000, although unofficial estimates were as high as 20,000; in addition, 300,000 were left homeless. There was widespread protest over the fact that many of the buildings destroyed had been built in violation of construction regulations and claims that foreign emergency aid had been misappropriated by the government.

In August 1992, formal negotiations regarding the North American Free Trade Agreement were concluded, whereby Mexico would join the US and Canada in the elimination of trade barriers, the promotion of fair competition, and increased investment opportunities. NAFTA went into effect on 1 January 1994.

In January 1994, within hours after the NAFTA agreement went into effect, a primarily Amerindian group calling itself the Zapatista Army of National Liberation resorted to an armed uprising against the government. They initially took control of four municipalities in the State of Chiapas to protest what it regarded as government failure to effectively deal with regional social and economic problems. Two months after the Zapatista uprising, the nation witnessed its first high-level political assassination in over 60 years when PRI presidential candidate Luis Donaldo Colosio was murdered in Tijuana. His replacement, Ernesto Zedillo, was elected at the end of the year in a closely monitored campaign.

The devaluation of the peso in late December of 1994 threw the nation into economic turmoil, triggering its worst recession in over half a century. Over a million Mexicans lost their jobs, and the country's gross domestic product plummeted 10.5% in the first months of 1995. The US responded to its neighbor's distress with a multimillion-dollar bailout that averted even worse damage to the economy.

The discontent bred by this economic crisis, together with continued high levels of poverty, rising crime and corruption, and political instability, led in 1997 to a rejection of Mexico's nearly 70-year-old system of one-party rule. In June of that year, the PRI lost its majority in the lower house of the National Congress, its control superseded by the combined power of the leftist Party of the Democratic Revolution (PRD) and the conservative National Action Party (PAN), as well as two smaller parties. The PRD obtained one of its most important victories in Mexico City, where former presidential candidate Cuauhtémoc Cardenas Solórzano was elected mayor. Both parties, especially the PAN, went on to win important gubernatorial seats throughout the country.

The 1997 elections shocked the PRI, and party loyalists began to push for change. Traditionally, the president selected his successor from the PRI ranks, a practice known as the "dedazo," which means pointing the presidential finger at the new candidate. But in 1999, with the PRI celebrating its 70th anniversary, Zedillo said there would be no "dedazo," and replaced the practice with a presidential primary. By late 1999, party loyalist Francisco Labastida Ochoa had earned the party's ticket, and even led some presidential polls in early February 2000. But leading to the July 2 presidential election, Labastida was facing increasing competition from PAN candidate Vicente Fox Quesada. A former Coca-Cola executive and governor of Guanajuato, Fox was gaining a wide following by openly attacking the PRI, even discussing sensitive issues that others would not touch, including the PRI's connections to illegal drug trafficking. In the meantime, Cardenas, who resigned as mayor of Mexico City in September 1999, was losing support in his third try at the presidency. Cardenas had some successes as mayor, but could not bring crime under control. Many Mexicans believe the PRI defrauded Cardenas from a presidential victory in 1988. The country now has an autonomous Federal Electoral Institute. Following the 1997 elections, when the PRI lost its supremacy at the polls, more Mexicans came to believe in their electoral system.

Yet, even with assurances of clean elections, Mexico faced many problems. Political violence continued in Chiapas, Oaxaca and Guerrero in 2000. In late 1999, the government proposed a new peace initiative in Chiapas. In the late 1990s, the country was also facing an unprecedented crime wave that affected every facet of society. Even the historically respected military had been tainted by the arrests of high-ranking military leaders accused of being involved in the drug trade.

On 2 July 2000, after over seven decades of PRI rule, Fox was elected president in an upsetting victory over Labastida. Although he did not receive a majority of the votes, Fox won by a 7% margin. The vote was the cleanest in Mexico's history, passing standards of freedom and fairness, as well as remaining peaceful. Fox drew support from beyond his conservative PAN party, indicating voter support for his commitment to tackling government corruption and economic reform. He is scheduled to be sworn in on 1 December 2000.

13 GOVERNMENT

Mexico is a federal republic consisting of 31 states and the Federal District. Its basic political institutions are defined in the constitution of 1917.

The president, elected for a six-year term (by universal adult suffrage beginning at age 18) and forever ineligible for reelection, appoints the attorney-general and a cabinet, which may vary in number. Although the constitution established separation of powers, in practice the Mexican chief executive dominates the legislative and judicial branches. Since the president is head of state, head of government, and commander-in-chief of the armed forces, and since his party, the PRI, has enjoyed a clear majority in Congress since it was created, it has been said that the only limit placed on the power of a president of Mexico is that of time—six years in office. With the approval of Congress, the president may intervene in the states, restricting their independence; also, under congressional authorization, he has certain legislative authority, especially in the regulation and development of commerce and industry. There is no vice-president. If the president dies or is removed from office, Congress is constitutionally empowered to elect a provisional president.

The bicameral Congress, also elected by direct universal suffrage, is composed of a Senate (Cámara de Senadores), expanded from 64 to 128 members in 1994 (four from each state and four from the Federal District), and a Chamber of Deputies (Cámara de Diputados) made up of 500 members; one deputy (and one alternate) represents each 250,000 people or fraction above 100,000, with a minimum of two deputies from each state, and 200 members are allocated by proportional representation from minority parties. Senators are elected for six years (half the Senate is elected every three years) and deputies for three years, and both groups are ineligible for immediate reelection. Congress meets from September through December; for the other eight months of the year there is a permanent committee consisting of 14 senators and 15 deputies. The Congress may legislate on all matters pertaining to the national government and the Federal District.

In an effort to unite various interest groups within the government party, a National Consultative Committee, composed of living ex-presidents of Mexico, was formed in 1961 by President Adolfo López Mateos (1958–64). In the final 1962 congressional session, legislation was passed to reform the 1954 electoral law. The bill was designed to give minority parties a greater chance for representation in the Chamber of Deputies by allowing them five seats if they received 2.5% of the total vote and one additional seat for each 0.5% of the vote beyond that. Under this measure, a small party could obtain up to 20 seats without winning in a single district. A new electoral reform, introduced in 1977, stipulated that the minimum number of members must be 65,000 for a party to be registered and that the party must receive 1.5% of the popular vote to have its registration confirmed. In 1986, Congress stipulated that 200 deputies would be elected by a system of proportional representation within multimember constituencies, while 300 deputies would be elected by majority vote within single-member electoral districts.

14 POLITICAL PARTIES

From 1929 to 1997, the majority party and the only political group to gain national significance was the Institutional Revolutionary Party (Partido Revolucionario Institucional—PRI), formerly called the National Revolutionary Party (Partido Nacional Revolucionario) and the Party of the Mexican Revolution (Partido de la Revolución Mexicana). The PRI includes only civilians and embraces all shades of political opinion. Three large pressure groups operate within the PRI: labor, the peasantry, and the "popular" sector (such as bureaucrats, teachers, and small business people).

In the July 1997 elections, the PRI, for the first time in nearly 70 years, failed to retain a majority of seats in the 500-member lower house of Congress, the Chamber of Deputies. Following the election, the PRI had 239 seats; the Party of the Democratic Revolution (PRD) had 125; 122 seats were controlled by the National Action Party (PAN); the Green Ecological Party (PVEM) had 8; and the Workers Party (PT) had 6.

Of the major opposition parties, the PRD advocates active government intervention in economic matters and questions close relations with the United States, while PAN favors a reduced government role in the economy, backs close ties with the US, and is closely linked to the Catholic Church.

Vicente Fox, of the conservative PAN party, was elected on 2 July 2000, thereby ending over 70 years of PRI control. He will be sworn in on December 1.

15 LOCAL GOVERNMENT

Twenty-nine states of Mexico were created as administrative divisions by the constitution of 1917, which grants them those powers not expressly vested in the federal government; Mexico's two remaining territories, Baja California Sur and Quintana Roo, achieved statehood on 9 October 1974, raising the total to 31. Each state has a constitution, a governor elected for six years, and a unicameral legislature, with representatives elected by district vote in proportion to population. An ordinary session of the legislature is held annually, and extraordinary sessions may be called by the governor or the permanent committee. Bills may be introduced by legislators, by the governor, by the state supreme court, and by municipalities (a unit comparable to a US county). In addition to the 31 states, there is also one federal district comprising Mexico City, whose governor serves as a member of the cabinet. Many state services are supported by federal subsidies. Until 1997, the president appointed the mayor of Mexico City. Political reforms allowed the first open elections in 1997. PRD candidate Cuauhtémoc Cardenas Solórzano was elected mayor. When he resigned to run for the presidency in 1999, Rosario Robles Berlanga became the first woman mayor of Mexico City.

The principal unit of state government is the municipality. Mexico's 2,378 municipalities are governed by municipal presidents and municipal councils. State governors generally select the nominees for the municipal elections. Municipal budgets are approved by the respective state governors.

16 JUDICIAL SYSTEM

Mexico's judiciary, both federal and state, has been a separate branch of government since independence. Federal courts include the Supreme Court, with 21 magistrates; 32 circuit tribunals, and 98 district courts, with one judge each. Special courts include a fiscal tribunal and boards of conciliation and arbitration.

Supreme Court magistrates are appointed for life by the president, with the approval of the Senate, and can be removed only by a guilty verdict after impeachment. The other justices are appointed for six years by the Supreme Court magistrates. The Supreme Court has both original and appellate jurisdiction in four divisions: administrative, civil, labor, and penal. Circuit courts hear appeals from the district courts.

The jury system is not commonly used in Mexico, but judicial protection is provided by the Writ of Amparo, which allows a person convicted in the court of a local judge to appeal to a federal judge. Capital punishment, except in the army for crimes against national security, was abolished by the penal code of 1 January 1930.

Although the judiciary is constitutionally independent and judges are appointed for life (unless dismissed for cause), there have been charges that judges are sometimes partial to the executive. Low pay and high caseloads contribute to a suscepti-bility to corruption in the judicial system. In unprecedented moves in 1993, the government issued an arrest warrant for obstructing justice and for bribery against a former Supreme Court Justice and three federal judges were dismissed for obstructing justice.

In 1995, Congress passed a judicial reform law. The judicial reform law provides for a competitive examination for selecting most lower and appellate federal court judges and law secretaries. The Supreme Court has the authority to strike down a law for unconstitutionality. The judicial reform law provides that the Supreme Court may declare a law unconstitutional when one-third of the congress, one-third of a state congress, or the Attorney General asks the Supreme Court to review the constitutionality of the law.

The judicial trial system is based on the Napoleonic Code and consists of a series of fact-gathering hearings. The record of the proceeding is not available to the public.

17 ARMED FORCES

Total full-time strength of the armed forces was 178,770 in 2000. The army had 130,000 personnel. Regular army units included the presidential guard (a mechanized brigade group), 2 infantry brigades, 4 armored brigades, an airborne brigade, and support units. The navy, including naval air force and marines, had 37,000 personnel; naval vessels included 3 destroyers, and 105 patrol and coastal combatants. The air force had 11,770 personnel, 125 combat aircraft, and 95 armed helicopters. Paramilitary forces included 14,000 rural defense militia; military reserves number 300,000. Defense expenditures in 1998 amounted to $6 billion or about 1.3% of gross domestic product.

Under the required military training program, all 18-year-old males must complete one year of part-time basic army training. In 2000, 60,000 conscripts were on active duty, drawn by lottery.

18 INTERNATIONAL COOPERATION

Mexico is a charter member of the UN, having joined on 7 November 1945, and participates in ECLAC and all the non-regional specialized agencies. Mexico was host to the Inter-American Conference on War and Peace in 1945, which established the Latin American basis of the UN Conference. Luis Padilla Nervo of Mexico served as president of the UN General Assembly's sixth regular session (1951–52), and Jaime Torres Bodet was first director-general of UNESCO. In May 1972, at the UNCTAD sessions in Santiago, Chile, President Luis Echeverría Álvarez proposed the Charter of Economic Rights and Duties of States, defining the relationship between developed and developing nations. The charter was approved by the UN General Assembly in 1974. The UN International Conference on Women was held in Mexico City in mid-1975. During the de la Madrid administration, Mexico joined the Contadora Group (with Colombia, Panama, and Venezuela) in an effort to bring about a negotiated settlement to the conflict in Central America. Mexico also joined the Five Continents Initiative for Peace and Disarmament, to promote a nuclear test ban and stop the spread of the arms race into outer space.

Mexico, which for many years was the only Latin American nation to recognize Fidel Castro's Cuba, has based its foreign policy on the principles of nonintervention and self-determination of peoples, which it helped incorporate into the charter of the OAS in 1948 (Articles 15–17). Mexico was a leading proponent of the OAS resolution in July 1975 that gave member nations the right to exercise freedom of action in restoring diplomatic and commercial relations with Cuba. During President Echeverría's visit to Cuba in August 1975, the two nations signed an economic cooperation agreement.

Mexico belongs to such inter-American organizations as the IADB and LAIA, in addition to the OAS. As a member of G-77,

Mexico has been prominent among nonaligned nations. Particularly during the presidency of José López Portillo y Pacheco (1977–82), Mexico assumed a leading role among the third-world countries; in October 1981, it hosted "North-South" talks among the leaders of 8 industrialized and 14 developing countries. Mexico is also a signatory of the Law of the Sea and a member of the WTO. In 1992, Mexico signed the North American Free Trade Agreement (NAFTA), creating a free-trade zone comprising the US, Mexico, and Canada. The agreement was ratified by all three governments in 1993 and took effect the following year.

[19]ECONOMY

Although Mexico's economy is predominantly agricultural (with more than 24.3% of its economically active population employed in primary production), commerce and industry have long been the chief sources of revenue. Mexico is self-sufficient in most fruits and vegetables and in beans, rice, and sugar, and it is approaching self-sufficiency in meat and dairy products; marginal subsistence, however, is still the lot of much of Mexico's rural population. A great mining nation, Mexico is the world's leading producer of silver and is well endowed with sulfur, copper, manganese, iron ore, lead, and zinc. Exports from manufacturing plants in Mexico account for at least 90% of the country's GDP.

Since 1960 there has been a gradual improvement in the social and economic integration of Mexico, but because of a population increase, the marginal sector is still very large. The birth rate fell from 3.2% in 1970 to 1.6% in 1999, but about half of the population was under 20 years old. Large-scale migration from countryside to city occurred with industrialization. Mexico City's enormous population growth has been accompanied by mass poverty. The top 20% of income earners account for 55% of all income.

The oil discoveries of the early 1970s led to a boom, and in the second half of the 1970s, Mexico's economy was one of the fastest growing in the world. During 1978–81, the GDP increased by 8% annually and the government embarked on an ambitious public spending program, to a great degree financed by external borrowing. About three-quarters of all export earnings were brought in by crude oil. This dependency contributed to the financial crisis of 1982, when falling world oil prices, together with rising interest rates and the overvaluation of the peso, resulted in a surging foreign debt and, by August, an acute foreign exchange shortage. The annual inflation rate, which had hovered around 30% during 1979–81, reached almost 100% in 1982.

In December 1987, the Pact for Stability and Economic Growth (PECE), a series of price and wage restraint agreements, was implemented. The agreements between government, labor, and the private sector combined austere fiscal and monetary restraints with price/wage controls and freer trade possibilities. The PECE helped curb inflation to 51.6% in 1988 without incurring a recession. Gradual recovery saw the inflation rate fall to 20% in 1991, 11.9% in 1992, and to around 10% in 1993.

The North American Free Trade Agreement (NAFTA), in effect as of 1 January 1994, opened the domestic market to foreign trade by eliminating trade barriers between Mexico, the US, and Canada over the next 15 years.

In 1995, Mexico's economy was in a serious recession. The government reported that the GDP fell by 6.9% that year. The problem began with a massive devaluation of the peso in December 1994, which brought on a financial crisis and exposed certain vulnerabilities in the economy, such as excessive trade and current accounts deficits and heavy reliance on short-term capital to finance deficits. As a result, both inflation and interest rates soared. The financial problems raised concerns in other Latin American economies and discouraged foreign investment, which

only exacerbated Mexico's problem. An international assistance package organized by the US provided $50 billion in loans (including $20 billion from the US). However, the government only used about half of this amount for its recovery the following year; GDP grew by an estimated 4.2% in 1996. The depreciation of the peso had the effect of making Mexican goods less expensive and thus more competitive on world markets.

In 1997, because of the increase in exports, Mexico had a GDP growth rate of 6.8%. The National Program for Development Finance (PRONAFIDE) of 1997 outlined the government's economic policy framework for the period 1997 to 2000. It supported further privatization and deregulation of the economy. The GDP growth rate dropped to 4.8% in 1998; due to the Russian debt default, the Brazilian currency crisis, and general international financial difficulties. The PRONAFIDE plan envisioned a 5% growth rate annually after 2000, while the actual rate in 1999 was only approximately 3%.

[20]INCOME

The US Central Intelligence Agency (CIA) reports that in 1998 Mexico's gross domestic product (GDP) was estimated at $815 billion. The per capita GDP was estimated at $8,300. The annual growth rate of GDP was estimated at 4.8%. The average inflation rate in 1998 was 19%. The CIA defines GDP as the value of all final goods and services produced within a nation in a given year and computed on the basis of purchasing power parity (PPP) rather than value as measured on the basis of the rate of exchange. It was estimated that agriculture accounted for 6% of GDP, industry 26%, and services 68%.

The World Bank reports that for the same period per capita private consumption (in PPP terms) was $5,455. Private consumption includes expenditures of individuals, households, and nongovernmental organizations. It was estimated that between 1990 and 1998 private consumption grew at an annual rate of 1.6%. Approximately 30% of household consumption was spent on food, 4% on fuel, 2% on health care, and 7% on education. The richest 10% of the population accounted for approximately 43% of household consumption and the poorest 10% approximately 1.4%.

[21]LABOR

Mexico's civilian labor force of 39,507,000 in 1998 was distributed as follows: services, 28.8%; agriculture, 24.3%; commerce, 17.1%; industry, 16.1%; building, 5.2%; transportation and communications, 4.1%; public administration and the military, 4.4%. Underemployment, Mexico's major labor problem, affected mainly those engaged in agriculture. According to official figures, unemployment was 13.4% in 1985; that percentage was reported as 2.3% in 1998, but was indicative of only the largest metropolitan areas. Rural unemployment was believed to be significantly higher. There is no general unemployment compensation system.

The constitution of 1917 provides that all labor disputes be submitted to boards of conciliation and arbitration consisting of an equal number of workers and employers and one government representative. Under the federal labor law, completely revised in 1970 and subsequently amended, every employee is entitled to one paid day of rest after every 6 days of work, 7 paid holidays, and at least 6 days of vacation after a year of employment and at least 8 days after two years. An annual bonus equal to 15 days' pay is required to be paid to all employees before Christmas, and vacation pay carries a 25% premium. Labor by women and children is limited. The workday is generally eight hours, and double or triple pay must be paid for overtime.

The minimum wage varies by geographical area; there is no national minimum wage. In April 1996, the minimum wage in southeast Veracruz state, including Mexico City, was $3.99 per day (including a "negative" income tax subsidy that in effect brought it up to $4.55 per day). Only about 16% of workers earn the minimum wage. Many workers earn less, while those employed by prosperous industrial enterprises can earn three to four times more. Since 1963, nearly every enterprise in Mexico has been required to distribute a percentage of annual profits to its employees. Under the revised regulations effective 15 October 1974, workers are entitled to about 10% of employers' gross profits, subject to certain exemptions and limitations.

About 25% of the labor force was unionized in 1996. The Confederation of Mexican Workers (CTM, founded in 1936) is the largest union federation. The second largest trade unions confederation is the Federation of Government Employee Unions (FSTSE), consisting exclusively of federal workers. The Revolutionary Workers and Peasants Confederation (CROC) is considered to be the rival of the FSTSE, a rivalry encouraged by the government in order to discourage a monopoly of power by the FSTSE.

Children as young as 14 may work, but with severe restrictions as to the conditions and hours of employment. Child labor provisions are well-enforced among medium and large companies, but many children work in smaller companies, in agriculture, or in the informal economy, usually in family enterprises.

22 AGRICULTURE

Agriculture's contribution to GDP fell from 15.1% in 1960 to 10.7% in 1970 and 5% in 1998—yet agriculture employs about 23% of the labor force. Only about 13% of Mexico's total land area is suitable for cultivation, and only 6% is cultivated with permanent crops; over 6.1 million hectares (15 million acres) are irrigated.

In 1960, Mexico became self-sufficient for the first time in corn; it continues to be self-sufficient in beans, rice, sugar, and most fruits and vegetables and fluctuates between being either a net importer or self-sufficient with wheat and corn. During the late 1960s, Mexico almost tripled the investment allocated for agriculture. The government continues to protect agriculture and to ensure domestic consumption through import and export duties and controls. The government supports the prices of corn, wheat, beans, and fresh eggs and then sells these and other farm products at minimal prices through retail stores operated by the National Corporation for Public Subsidies. In 1977, the government introduced a new program called the Mexican Alimentary System, seeking to foster food production through subsidized credit, cheap raw materials, guaranteed prices, and crop insurance. Because of a record harvest in 1981, the agricultural sector grew by 6% overall. The program was terminated in December 1982 because of what the government called its limited contribution to rural welfare and incomes.

In 1998, the principal crops' production totals (in tons) were as follows: sugarcane, 48,895,000; corn, 18,411,000; sorghum, 6,386,000; wheat, 3,241,000; dry beans, 1,475,000; soybeans, 180,000; rice, 483,000; and barley, 497,000. Principal exports are coffee, cotton, fresh fruit, sugar, tobacco, and tomatoes. In 1997, the value of agricultural exports amounted to $6,292 million, with coffee exports accounting for $923.9 million; tomatoes, $523.4 million, and cotton, $110.7 million.

At the time of the Mexican Revolution, an estimated 830 landowners held 97% of the land. The principles of land reform were incorporated into Article 27 of the constitution of 1917, which provided for division of large landholdings into small farms, communally owned by villages, known as ejidos (one individual may only own 100 hectares/247 acres of irrigated land). Much of the arable land has been expropriated for the establishment of ejidos. The Agrarian Reform Law of April 1972 formally recognizes two types of landholdings, private and ejidal

(in the form of lifetime land grants, which cannot be disposed of by sale or transfer). The proportion of ejidal-owned land rose from 7.5% in 1930 to 26.3% in 1960 and 47% in 1970. By 1986, 61.1% of the farm population belonged to the ejidal system, but the system yielded only about 33% of total agricultural output, and an estimated four million peasants remained landless. Beginning in the late 1970s, the government sought to group together ejidal holdings into larger collectives to increase production.

23 ANIMAL HUSBANDRY

More than one-third of the total land area is suitable for pasture. Livestock produced in the central, southern, and southeastern states are mostly native breeds of general-purpose cattle; in the northern and northwestern states, Herefords and other improved breeds are raised for export, mainly to the US.

In 1998, the livestock population was estimated at 25.6 million head of cattle, 15.5 million hogs, 8.6 million goats, 6.5 million sheep, 6.25 million horses (third in the world), 3.25 million donkeys, 3.27 million mules, and 409 million chickens. Output of livestock products in 1998 included 8,494,000 tons of cows' milk, 123,000 tons of goats' milk, 1,380,000 tons of beef and veal, 1,590,000 tons of poultry meat, 961,000 tons of pork, and 1,422,000 tons of eggs. In 1996, cattle inventories declined due to lower birth rates of calves, high slaughter rates, and increased exports. One of the worst droughts in decades in northern Mexico (combined with unfavorable weather in southern Mexico) was also responsible for the decline in livestock inventories.

24 FISHING

Mexico's principal commercial catches are shrimp, sardines, bass, pike, abalone, Spanish mackerel, and red snapper. Coastal fishing is important. The 1997 catch was 1,571,898 tons. The leading species caught by volume that year were California pilchard, 325,659 tons; yellowfin tuna, 140,286 tons; jumbo flying squid, 120,877 tons; and tilapia, 83,132 tons.

The fishing industry is largely handled by cooperative societies, which are granted monopolies on the most valuable species of fish. Most fish processed in Mexico's canneries are consumed domestically. Ensenada, in Baja California, is Mexico's most important fisheries center. It produces most of the canned fish and virtually all of Mexico's abalone and spiny lobster exports. Mexico's first fisheries college, the Higher Institute of Marine Sciences, is located in Ensenada. In 1997, Mexico's exports of fish products were valued at over $825.1 million.

25 FORESTRY

About 48.7 million hectares (120.3 million acres) are classified as forestland. Palms are found at elevations up to 500 m (1,600 ft), while mahogany, cedar, primavera, and sapote are found from 500 to 1,000 m (1,600–3,300 ft). Stands of oak, copal, and pine grow from 1,000 to 1,500 m (3,300–4,900 ft), and conifers predominate in higher elevations. Mexico has 72 species of pine, more than any other country; pine accounts for 85% of annual forestry production. About 90% of Mexico's forestry production comes from temperate forests, which are mainly found in the states of Chihuahua, Durango, Jalisco, Michoacán, Oaxaca, Chiapas, and Guerrero. Tropical forests account for only 10% of forestry production, and exist in the states of Chiapas, Quintana Roo, Yucatan, Campeche, Tabasco, and Oaxaca.

Mexico's forestry policy is designed to protect and renew these resources, so that forests may fulfill their soil-protection functions and timber reserves may be exploited rationally and productively. Only about 30% of all forests are exploited, mostly in Chihuahua, Durango, and Michoacán. Timber is often located in mountainous regions with rough terrain and few all-season roads. As a result, wood production costs are 35–40% higher than the world average. Moreover, most roundwood comes from ejido (communally owned) forests; this system has greatly inhibited the development of an integrated forest industry. Mexico's ability to supply its own wood products needs are severely restricted by the limited timber available. Roundwood production in 1997 was estimated at 23,213,000 cu m by the FAO; forestry imports exceeded exports by $1.02 billion. Over 90% of the hardwood demand is for the manufacture of furniture.

There are also many other useful products found in Mexico's forests other than wood. Annual forestry production also includes an estimated 100,000 tons of resins, fibers, oils, waxes, and gums. The indigenous peoples living in Mexico's rain forests are estimated to utilize up to 1,500 species of tropical plants to manufacture 3,000 different products such as medicines, construction and domestic materials, dyes, and poisons.

²⁶MINING

In 1997, Mexico was one of the world's leading mineral producers, ranking first in the production of silver, bismuth, and celestite (strontium mineral); second in fluorspar; among the top five in white arsenic and graphite; and among the top ten in barite, cadmium, copper, gypsum, lead, molybdenum, manganese, salt, sulfur, and zinc. Metallic deposits are principally in the Sierra Madre ranges. Copper, gold, and manganese are mined mainly in the northwest; lead, zinc, and silver in central Mexico; and coal and petroleum in the east. Silver and gold are often found together. Output of principal minerals in 1997 included silver (metal content of ore), 679,090 kg; gold, 26,001 kg; iron ore, 10,467,000 tons; cadmium, 1,327 tons; zinc, 379,252 tons; barite, 236,606 tons; lead, 174,661 tons; and copper, 342,319 tons.

Mexico ranked high in reserves of graphite and silver, with about 15% (3.1 million tons) and 13% (37,000 tons) of total world reserves, respectively. The country was among the top reserveholders of cadmium (35,000 tons); mercury (5,000 tons); and selenium (4,000 tons). Lead reserves totaled one million tons, zinc reserves six million tons, molybdenum, 90,000 tons, and copper and manganese 14 million and four million tons, respectively. Sulfur is found in the salt domes of the Isthmus of Tehuantepec; reserves of all forms amounted to 75 million tons in 1997. Uranium and similar deposits were discovered in the states of Chihuahua, Durango, Sonora, and Querétaro in 1958. In 1969, the country's first uranium ore smelting plant was installed at Aldama, Chihuahua, with a processing capacity of 60 tons per day. By 1990, however, Mexico was importing uranium from Germany and France for its domestic needs. An area in Baja California potentially rich in gold, silver, copper, lead, and zinc was discovered by a sensor on board the US space shuttle *Columbia* in November 1981.

By 1997, nearly all formerly state-owned mines had been privatized. Although low prices for base metals (except copper) and precious metals have hurt the industry, the North American Free Trade Agreement (NAFTA) was expected to have a significant role in attracting foreign investment to the Mexican mineral sector.

²⁷ENERGY AND POWER

Nationalization of the electricity supply industry, begun in 1960, was completed in 1975. Net installed generating capacity as of 1998 was 38,114,000 kW, compared with 27,338,000 kW in 1988. The amount of electricity produced in 1998 was 176,055 million kWh, of which about 20% was hydroelectric and about 5% was nuclear power. The possibilities for geothermal electrical production are extensive, with over 100 thermal springs available for exploitation. Geothermal sources provided 740 MW of electricity in 1994, and generated 5,322 million kWh. Petroleum accounts for about 66% of Mexico's energy consumption.

Oil seeps were first documented in Mexico in 1543; the first oil wells were drilled in 1869. The first major discovery was the La Paz No. 1 well in the Ebano-Panuco Field in 1904. The petroleum industry was nationalized in 1938 and has since been operated by a government-owned institution, Mexican Petroleum (Petróleos Mexicanos—PEMEX). In 1961, the final compensation payment of the $18 million owed to a British concern (Mexican Eagle Oil Co.) ended Mexico's expropriation debt. The Petroleum Law of 1958 permitted PEMEX to take over all concessions held by private firms and granted it a monopoly in the petroleum industry. The company was a special target of the de la Madrid administration's crackdown on corruption in 1983. In 1999, PEMEX was the largest civilian employer in the country, and the single most important entity in the Mexican economy. PEMEX is also the world's sixth-largest oil company. As of 2000, PEMEX was developing offshore basins in the Gulf of Mexico and constructing a new natural gas processing plant.

Although the government restricts exploration and exploitation of petroleum deposits, some foreign and private exploratory drilling has been permitted. Producing fields are along the Gulf of Mexico coastline from the state of Tamaulipas to the state of Tabasco, with the richest concentrations around Tampico and in Veracruz and Tabasco. In 1974, extensive new discoveries were made in the Chiapas-Tabasco region and in Baja California. A 1975 discovery in the state of Veracruz was estimated to have reserves exceeding those of Chiapas and Tabasco combined. Estimated oil reserves as of 1999 were 28.4 billion barrels, second in the Western Hemisphere after Venezuela.

Crude oil production first reached one million barrels per year in 1907. Mexico's production rose rapidly during the 1970s, peaking at 3,015,000 barrels per day in 1985. It stayed at about 2.9 million barrels per day through the late 1980s and then rose to around 3.1 million barrels per day in the early 1990s. Production in 1999 was 3.4 million barrels per day. Mexico exports about half the oil it produces, mostly crude oil to the US, Spain, and the Far East. In 1999, petroleum export revenues amounted to $8.6 billion. The majority of oil production comes from the Villahermosa District in the State of Tabasco and the offshore wells of the Bay of Campeche. Average production per well is about 220 barrels per day, except for wells in the Bay of Campeche, which produced about 16,000 barrels daily in 1989. The same two regions dominate in the production of natural gas; in 1998, Mexico produced 36 billion cu m of natural gas (mostly from offshore sources). Proven reserves of natural gas were estimated at 30.1 trillion cu ft (852 billion cu m) in early 2000.

²⁸INDUSTRY

Mexico has one of the best-developed manufacturing sectors in Latin America. In the 1980s, the Mexican government retreated from its position of dominance over the economy, and the private sector was given an expanded role. Manufacturing output increased on average by 2.3% per year during the 1980s and by 3.9% annually during 1988–98. In 1998, manufacturing contributed an estimated 22.1% to GDP, and had a growth rate of 7.4%.

The principal manufacturing industries include food and beverages, tobacco, chemicals, iron and steel, petroleum, textiles, clothing, and motor vehicles. The soft drink industry produces 8 million bottles per year. Mexico's refinery capacity was 1.5 million barrels per day in 1999. In 1998, Mexico produced 1.5 million motor vehicles. Leading manufacturers are Ford, Chrysler, General Motors, and Volkswagen.

Manufacturing has been focused around the reexport processing industry. These so-called *maquiladoras* are usually located near the US border and owned by a foreign corporation; they contract to assemble or process imported goods brought in from the US and then reexport them duty free. In 1999, there were some 3,300 maquiladora factories employing 494,721 workers. Baja had the most export industries in 1999, at over 1,100; other leading states included Sonora, with 244; and Tijuana, which hosts the majority of electronic-related assembly plants, at 782.

29SCIENCE AND TECHNOLOGY

The National Academy of Science, founded in 1884, is the principal scientific organization. Among Mexico's 36 scientific and technological learned societies and 26 scientific research institutes, the natural sciences and medicine predominate. Especially well known is the International Maize and Wheat Improvement Center, founded in Mexico City in 1966; its director, Norman Ernest Borlaug, received the Nobel Peace Prize in 1970 for his work in advancing the "green revolution." More than 60 universities and colleges in Mexico offer courses in basic and applied sciences. In 1987–97, science and engineering students accounted for 32% of college and university enrollments.

The primary science and technology policymaking body is the National Council for Science and Technology, a decentralized public body created in 1970 composed of researchers, scientists, academicians, and government officials. They formulate, study, evaluate, and execute national science and technology policies. In 1989, the Consultative Council on Sciences was created to advise directly the President of Mexico on science and technology. In 1993, Mexico's expenditures totaled 3.6 billion pesos; 8,595 scientists and engineers and 2,477 technicians were engaged in research and development.

30DOMESTIC TRADE

Mexico City is the commercial hub of the country and is the principal distribution point for all types of commodities. Other large cities, such as Guadalajara, Monterrey, and Puebla, serve as distribution points for their respective regions. Regional marketing is dominated by the open market, with its small stalls or shops, where business is transacted on an individual bargaining basis. There are also chain stores, supermarkets, department stores (some selling by mail), and a government-operated chain of more than 2,000 discount-priced food and clothing stores.

Although most sales are for cash, the use of consumer credit is increasingly extensive, especially for automobiles, furniture, household appliances, and other expensive items. The withdrawal of large amounts of foreign capital in late 1994 and 1995 and the ensuing peso devaluation plunged Mexico into its worst economic crisis since the 1930s. Domestic commerce declined by 14.9% in 1995. Due to the high amount of private debt per capita, consumer spending fell by 11.7% in 1995, the most severe decline ever reported in Mexico.

Normal business hours are from 9 or 9:30 AM to 7 PM Monday through Friday, with one or two hours for lunch. Banks are open from 9 AM to 1:30 PM. Products are advertised through newspapers, radio, television, outdoor signs, and motion picture shorts and slides.

31FOREIGN TRADE

Not including exports from the maquiladoras, the most important export commodities from Mexico are crude oil and automobiles. Mexico also exports seven percent of the world's vegetables. The top ten exports are:

	% OF COUNTRY TOTAL	% OF WORLD TOTAL
Crude petroleum	10	3.6
Passenger motor vehicles	9.0	2.9
Electrical distributing equipment	4.5	13
Electrical machinery	4.0	4.1
Television receivers	4.0	13
Telecoms equipment	3.8	2.6
Engines	3.6	5.0
Motor vehicle parts and accessories	3.4	2.1
Switchgears	2.8	3.4
Vegetables	2.2	7.0

Mexico formerly imported mainly consumer goods, but in 1997 consumer goods accounted for only 14.6% of imports. The main bulk of imports that year were machinery and equipment, and industrial supplies. In 1997 Mexico's imports were distributed among the following categories:

Consumer goods	13.7%
Food	5.3%
Fuels	2.5%
Industrial supplies	30.7%
Machinery	32.1%
Transportation	12.3%
Other	3.5%

Principal trading partners in 1998 (in millions of US dollars) were as follows:

COUNTRY	EXPORTS	IMPORTS	BALANCE
United States	103,306	93,252	10,054
Canada	1,521	2,292	-771
Germany	1,152	4,558	-3,406
Japan	856	4,553	-3,697
Spain	715	1,257	-542
United Kingdom	655	1,056	-401
France	403	1,430	-1,027
Italy	182	1,581	-1,399
China (inc. Hong Kong)	106	2,034	-1,928
Korea	73	1,951	-1,878

32BALANCE OF PAYMENTS

Mexico's balance of payments, in deficit throughout much of the 1960s, turned favorable in the 1970s, as inflows of foreign funds rose fast enough to offset the worsening visible trade balance. However, during the 1980s a steep rise in imports due to trade liberalization led to a growing imbalance. Mexico's external position had so deteriorated by 1986 that the IMF and World Bank coordinated a financial rescue package of $12 billion and commercial banks agreed to reschedule $44 billion in foreign debt; an innovative feature of the agreement was that repayment was effectively tied to Mexico's oil export earnings. Mexico began running a current account deficit in 1988, that remained through the 1990s. Following the 1994 devaluation of the peso, international lenders provided $40 billion in economic aid, half from the US. This influx of capital resulted in bringing the current account deficit to less than 1% of GDP in 1995, from at least 7% in 1994. In 1998, the deficit had risen back to almost 4%.

The US Central Intelligence Agency reports that in 1998 the purchasing power parity of Mexico's exports was $117.5 billion while imports totaled $111.5 billion resulting in a trade balance of $6 billion.

The International Monetary Fund (IMF) reports that in 1998 Mexico had exports of goods totaling $117,459 million and imports totaling $125,374 million. The services credit totaled $12,064 million and debit $13,067 million. The following table summarizes Mexico's balance of payments as reported by the IMF for 1998 in millions of US dollars.

Current Account		-15,960
Balance on goods	-7,915	
Balance on services	-1,003	
Balance on income	-13,056	
Current transfers	6,014	
Capital Account		...
Financial Account		17,308
Direct investment abroad	...	
Direct investment in Mexico	10,238	
Portfolio investment assets	-768	
Portfolio investment liabilities	1,294	
Other investment assets	1,531	
Other investment liabilities	5,013	
Net Errors and Omissions		1,845
Reserves and Related Items		-3,193

33BANKING AND SECURITIES

The Bank of Mexico (established 1925), in which the government owns 51% of the capital stock, is also the central bank and bank of issue. Together with the National Banking and Insurance Commission and the Secretariat of Finance, it supervises commercial, savings, trust, mortgage, capitalization, and investment institutions. National institutions for economic development extend agricultural and long-term industrial credit and finance and develop public works, international trade, cooperatives, and the motion picture industry; they also operate savings accounts. The National Financing Agency (founded in 1934) acts as a financing and investing corporation; it also regulates the Mexican stock market and long-term credits.

There are a number of state development banks, including Nacional Financiera (Nafin, mainly for small and medium-sized businesses), Banco Nacional de Comercio Exterior (Bancomext, foreign trade), Banco Nacional de Obras y Servicios Públicos (Banobras, public works and services), Financiera Azucarera (sugar industry), Banco Nacional de Comercio Interior, and Banco Nacional de Crédito Rural. Nafin and Bancomext are by far the most important.

In September 1982, in order to stop the flight of capital, the government nationalized all 57 private banks; their combined assets were estimated at $48.7 billion. After the inauguration of President de la Madrid in December 1982, it was announced that 34% of the shares of the nationalized banks would be sold to bank workers and users and to federal, state, and municipal agencies. No single shareholder would be allowed to purchase more than 1% of the stock, and the federal government would retain a 66% controlling interest. The government had consolidated the commercial banking system into 19 financial institutions by the end of 1986. In November 1986 the government introduced a plan that would privatize 18 of Mexico's 19 state owned commercial banks. The sale of the banks began in 1987. In 1990 the government began allowing foreigners to buy up to 30% of the state's banks. By July 1992 the banking system was completely private. The only foreign bank permitted to operate within Mexico as of 1993 was Citibank; another 100 foreign banks had representatives in Mexico, however.

The 1990s brought fundamental change to the financial sector. Apart from liberalization of interest rates and credit terms and the elimination of obligatory lending to the public sector, there was the creation of new financial instruments and institutions. At the end of 1994, there were around 50 commercial banks in operation compared with just 19 two years earlier. The newly privatized commercial banks had problems almost from the outset. The principal cause was poor asset quality which manifested itself in an increasingly serious burden of non-performing loans.

Faced with the prospect of a wholesale banking collapse, the government came up with a succession of different measures to deal with the problem of bad debts. There has been a scheme to enable bank loans to be rescheduled using index-linked *Unidades de Inversión* (UDIs) and a program of support for bank debtors (*Apoyo a Deudores*, ADE) designed to help as many as eight million people reschedule debts of up to $26,000. In May 1996, the government announced a further scheme to help mortgage debtors under which it was to assume 30% of monthly payments due during the year, the proportion falling progressively to 5% over 10 years.

Apart from providing relief for debtors, the government also set up a program to enable banks to meet capital and loan loss provisions (*Programa Temporal de Capitalización Temporal*), as well as a fund (*Fondo Bancario de Protección de Ahorro-Fobaproa*) to take over banks' bad debts in exchange for new capital injections by shareholders. Nevertheless, it has had to step in and take control of a number of institutions. The reserve package cost the government a considerable sum. However, limited the damage by selling off banks in its control, mainly to foreign investors. Foreign investors also helped to capitalize banks which were in private hands. By 1999, there were $61 billion of unpaid debts that the Mexican government had bought from banks in order to keep them from collapsing, adding to the public debt. These bank loans equaled 20% of GDP in 1999.

In mid-March 1997, after two years of preparation, the government introduced measures to curb money laundering. Anywhere between $4 billion and $30 billion of drug money is laundered in Mexico every year. Starting in 1998, banks, brokerages, and large foreign exchange houses had to report all cash transactions involving $10,000 or more to the central bank.

The National Securities Commission (founded in 1946) supervises stock transactions. The Stock Exchange of Mexico (Bolsa Mexicana de Valores), the largest stock exchange in Latin America, was organized in its present form in 1933. It lists the stocks of the most important industrial companies, as well as a few mining stocks. Two smaller exchanges at Monterrey and Guadalajara were absorbed in 1976 by the Mexico City exchange. Trading on the exchange increased tenfold between 1976 and 1981, but dropped thereafter with the prolonged recession. It recovered to its 1979 level by 1986 and rose 124% in 1987 despite a spectacular crash in October and November of that year tied to the Wall Street's crash. The greatest part of the trading is in fixed-interest, high-yield bonds and bank deposit paper. Under new rules, which came into force in November 1989, foreigners are allowed to purchase almost any stock through a "neutral" trust, although as of 1997 they still did not have voting rights. In 1992, the market behaved erratically, largely because of sensitivity to the political and economic situation in the US and uncertainty about NAFTA.

In 1996, the recovery in the stock market strengthened as the economy began to pull out of recession, inflation and interest rates fell, and the currency held steady. As confidence grew, so foreign investment flowed back into the market. By mid-year, the total value of foreign investment in the stock exchange was $33.8 billion compared with $27.8 billion at the end of 1995, $34.4 billion at the end of 1994, and $54.6 billion at the end of 1993.

34INSURANCE

Since 1935, all life, fire, marine, automobile, agriculture, accident and health, and other insurance companies have been Mexican operated. Insurance companies must be authorized by the National Banking and Insurance Commission. In recent years, regulation has changed from rates and forms to solvency requirements. The effect of this change has been to increase product and price competition to the advantage of the consumer. The Mexican market has been divided into general and life insurers (including composites) and surety companies for purposes of regulation and government oversight. At year-end 1995, there were approximately 55 insurers, including three mutuals, two reinsurers, and two government companies. In addition, there were approximately 20 surety organizations with a total premium volume exceeding $115 million.

The Mexican insurance market is characterized by a relatively small number of insurers, with the top five insurers enjoying 70% of the market in terms of premiums. Thereafter, the size of insurers drops very rapidly. During 1996, two of the top five insurance organizations were expected to complete a merger, with the resulting company having 30% of the 1995 market. With the liberalization of the insurance market, a number of foreign insurance organizations have established or strengthened their presence in Mexico. In 1995, the insurance market in Mexico totaled approximately $3 billion, with very low penetration when compared to North America and Europe, especially for life products.

35PUBLIC FINANCE

Major sources of revenue are income taxes, a VAT, and public enterprise revenues. Among regular government departments, education receives the largest budget allocation, but outlays for debt service, subsidies to federal enterprises, and capital expenditures for highways, irrigation, and hydroelectric projects have exceeded regular departmental expenditures in recent years. The public-sector deficit usually increases sharply in the last year of a presidential term as the outgoing administration strives to complete its public works program.

During the 1960s, government revenues rose at a faster rate than GDP, with revenues from income taxes (including surcharges) increasing by 170% in the 1960–69 period. Budgets in the 1970s and early and mid-1980s continued to show current-account "surpluses," or minimal apparent deficits; the fact that borrowings and transfers are built into the budget structure masked the true magnitude of annual deficits. In the late 1970s and the early 1980s, real budget deficits increased substantially, reaching nearly 18% of the GDP by 1982. By slashing public spending, the government was able to bring the deficit down to 8.9% of the GDP in 1983 and 7.1% in 1984, but the collapse of the world oil price sent it up to 16.3% in 1986. By the early 1990s, however, public finances were strengthening, and a surplus (on a cash basis) of P35,054 million was recorded in 1992, equivalent to 3.4% of GDP in 1991. Nonrecurrent revenues amounted to P30,123 million, mainly derived from the sale of shares of the state-owned telephone company and bank privatization. Excluding privatization revenues, the surplus in 1992 was equivalent to 1.5% of GDP in 1992, as opposed to a deficit of 1.5% in 1991. Public revenues policy in 1992 sought to widen the tax base and simplify and enforce tax administration. At the same time, public expenditures have been reoriented to provide basic infrastructure and services. In 1997 and 1998 there was a current account deficit equaling 0.70% and 1.3% respectively.

The US Central Intelligence Agency (CIA) estimates that in 1998 Mexico's central government took in revenues of approximately $117 billion and had expenditures of $123 billion including capital expenditures of $6.6 billion. Overall, the government registered a deficit of approximately $6 billion. External debt totaled $159.9 billion.

The following table shows an itemized breakdown of government revenues and expenditures. The percentages were calculated from data reported by the International Monetary Fund. The dollar amounts (millions) are based on the CIA estimates provided above.

REVENUE AND GRANTS	100%	117,000
Tax revenue	88.4%	103,439
Non-tax revenue	11.5%	13,440
Capital revenue	0.1%	121
EXPENDITURES	100%	123,000
General public services	7.0%	8,594
Defense	3.5%	4,365
Public order and safety	0.9%	1,148
Education	22.1%	27,203
Health	3.4%	4,233
Social security	18.1%	22,210
Housing and community amenities	3.4%	4,187
Recreation, cultural, and religious affairs	0.6%	748
Economic affairs and services	17.6%	21,601
Other expenditures	15.4%	18,969
Interest payments	13.7%	16,848
Adjustments	-5.8%	-7,106

36TAXATION

The main sources of tax revenue in Mexico are income tax, VAT, and local levies on real property. The federal government also imposes excise taxes on alcohol and cigarettes, as well as production taxes on mining.

A new income tax law, effective 1 January 1987, retained the 1981 division of taxpayers into four groups: resident corporations; resident individuals; nonresident corporations and individuals taxed only on their Mexican-source income; and nonprofit organizations, which, though paying no taxes, are still required to file annual returns. Corporate income tax rates range from 17% to 34%, depending on the type of business. Under the new code, interest on business-related loans is no longer deductible, but most business investments henceforth may be deducted in one year instead of several. The individual tax rate ranges from 3% of the first Ps1,796 of taxable income to 35% on incomes in excess of Ps118,565.94.

The value-added tax (VAT), in effect since 1980, is presently 15% on goods and services, except in border zones in which a 10% VAT applies. Medicine and food products are zero rated. VAT-exempt goods and services include sales of animals, vegetables, and fruit for other than industrial use; sales of tractors, fertilizers, and pesticides; rentals of agricultural machinery; international freight; and international air passenger service.

37CUSTOMS AND DUTIES

In February 1960, Mexico joined with six other Latin American nations in signing a treaty establishing LAFTA, which was superseded by LAIA on 1 January 1981.

Under the terms of a trade policy agreement with the IBRD, Mexico's import tariffs were lowered substantially in 1988. In general, ad valorem duties range from 0% for basic consumption goods and raw materials to 20% for consumer goods and luxury items. The average tariff in 1999 was about 11%, and most goods were subject to a 15% value-added tax.

Since mid-1985, Mexico has undertaken a major liberalization of its trade restrictions, departing from the import-substitution approach that had been followed since the 1940s. In the second half of 1985, the need for many import licenses were abolished, and Mexico joined GATT in July 1986. Until June 1985, a license was required for 4,513 of the 8,077 items on the Import Tariff Schedule. Trade protected in this manner represented 75% of total import value. By 1991, less than 2% of all imports (14% of total import value) were subject to licensing requirements, and in 1999 there were hardly any licensing requirements. Businesses may receive reductions of up to 100% on duties for certain industrial imports in Mexico's free trade zones.

Mexico gives preferential treatment to some imports from the ten other member nations of the Latin American Integration Association and has signed a free-trade agreement with Chile. The North American Free Trade Agreement (NAFTA) entered into force on 1 January 1994. It further lowered tariffs on US and Canadian goods to 0–10%. Under NAFTA, tariffs will be phased out by 2005, however, many US goods already enter Mexico duty-free.

38 FOREIGN INVESTMENT

Federal law aims at attracting foreign investment without placing the nation "at the mercy of interests that are not those of Mexico and its citizens." Under Mexico's basic foreign investment law, adopted in 1973, capital profits and dividends may be transferred to and from Mexico. Mexico encourages the inflow of foreign funds by allowing foreigners to make bank deposits without revealing the identity of the depositors. The 1993 Foreign Investment Law opened the economy to further foreign investment. Investment in high-technology and export-oriented industries is particularly welcome.

Specific investment limits include a general limit of up to 49% in many industries, and a maximum of 40% for secondary petrochemical products. Sectors from which foreigners are excluded are petroleum and hydrocarbons, basic petrochemicals, radioactive minerals and nuclear energy, electricity, telegraphic communications, rail and sea transportation, and coin minting. Land and water within 100 km (62 mi) of Mexico's borders or 50 km (31 mi) of the coastline may not be foreign owned. Foreign investment is supervised by the National Foreign Investment Commission. Investment trends have shifted in recent years with the service sector now the largest recipient of direct foreign investment.

The US is the leading source of direct foreign investment in Mexico, with about 60% of the accumulated total in 1999. The total amount of US foreign investment in Mexico was $25.4 billion in 1997, concentrated largely in manufacturing and finance. Other prominent sources of direct foreign investment included the UK, Germany, Canada, Japan, and the Netherlands.

Foreign portfolio investment (capital inflows that are used to purchase stocks, bonds, and treasury bills) in Mexico increased from $493 million in 1989 to $7,500 million in 1991 but fell to $4,800 million in 1995 as the country entered a recession. Portfolio investment, potentially more volatile than direct investment, increased in Mexico because of growing confidence since debt renegotiation, increased issues of international securities, and changes in regulations to facilitate foreign purchase of most Mexican debt and equity instruments.

39 ECONOMIC DEVELOPMENT

Modern Mexican economic policy derives in principle from the constitution of 1917, which, in Article 27, proclaims national ownership of subsoil rights, provides for expropriation of property needed for national purposes, and provides for the breaking up of large estates and the establishment of village communal landholdings (ejidos). The property of foreign oil companies was expropriated in 1938, and production, refining, and distribution were placed under the government-controlled PEMEX. The government has also nationalized the railway and banking systems, owns most electric power plants, and partly owns some industrial establishments. Majority Mexican ownership was required in virtually all sectors until early 1984, when restrictions on foreign investment were relaxed somewhat.

The government encourages local industry by giving financial support, customs protection, and tax exemption to approved or new enterprises. The National Financing Agency has supported new industries by purchasing their stock and then reselling it to the public when the firm is established. The executive branch of government may set ceiling prices on foodstuffs, drugs, and other basic necessities, such as workers' rents.

Major development projects in the 1970s included an attempt to increase agricultural productivity, modernization of the nation's railroads, expansion of the fishing fleet, and resettlement of some 50,000 families from the northern states to the southern states Campeche, Yucatán, and Quintana Roo.

When the exploitation of huge oil deposits began in the mid-1970s, the Mexican government embarked on an expansionist economic policy, which included an ambitious public-spending program financed to a great degree by foreign borrowing. A 17-point development program announced in 1978 created about three million new jobs by 1981, but it was not fully implemented because of the drop in world oil prices and the subsequent financial crisis. The crisis reached its climax in August 1982, when the government suspended all payments of foreign debt principal and had to resort to emergency credits to avoid default.

New credits from the IMF were conditional upon Mexico's acceptance of an austerity program that entailed reduction of the budget deficit from 17.9% of the GDP in 1982 to 8.5% in 1983. Other austerity measures included tax increases, increases in the prices of controlled commodities, such as bread and salt, and steps to decrease tax evasion and reduce inflation. The de la Madrid administration simultaneously pursued policies to reduce the inflated value of the peso and to generate massive trade surpluses; indicative of their effectiveness were the 1983 and 1984 surpluses, over $13 billion in each year. The government, moreover, pursued rescheduling of its foreign debt, winning agreements in 1983 ($14 billion) and 1986 ($43.7 billion). In 1985 and 1986, however, the earthquake and the fall in world oil prices undermined the recovery; export revenues plunged, and inflation soared. The 1986 rescheduling was conditional upon Mexico's agreement to increase development of the export sector and encourage efficient import-substitution policies, as well as foreign investment.

Since Mexico joined GATT in 1986, trade barriers have been eliminated and tariffs reduced. Privatizations since 1989 include: the telephone company, Telmex; Mexico's 18 commercial banks; the airlines, Aeromexico and Mexicana; two large copper mines, Cananea and Mexicana de Cobre; and two large steel companies, Sicartsa and AHMSA. Privatizations have produced large one-time revenues for the government, while simultaneously reducing the government's role in the economy thus garnering savings by reducing its transfers to inefficient enterprises. Furthermore, these new profit-making private sector companies have widened the tax base.

The North American Free Trade Agreement (NAFTA), ratified in 1992 and implemented in 1994, culminated several years of trade liberalization efforts begun in 1986. NAFTA's goal is the creation of a market of 360 million consumers with $6 trillion in annual output. Tariffs on most industrial and agricultural goods will be eliminated or phased out within 15 years. NAFTA trading benefits are only given to goods produced wholly or principally in NAFTA countries. NAFTA also eliminates trade barriers and investment restrictions on participating countries autos, trucks, buses and auto parts within 10 years. NAFTA also proposes to safeguard domestic agricultural production of the dairy, egg, poultry, and sugar sectors. NAFTA also opens up foreign investment possibilities in the Mexican energy sector. NAFTA also has provisions for the textiles and services sectors, banking, investment, and intellectual property rights. Labor and environmental impacts are also addressed. Mexico has also established free trade agreements with Venezuela and Colombia as a member of the Group of Three, and with several other Central American nations. Mexico also signed a free trade agreement with Chile in 1991.

40 SOCIAL DEVELOPMENT

Mexico's basic social insurance program was enacted on 30 December 1942. The social security system includes old age pensions, disability, medical, and work injury benefits. Pensions are financed by contributions from employees, employers, and the government. Retirement is set at age 65, and benefits are determined by length of employment. Insurance for occupational accidents is financed by employer contributions, and provides for 100% of earnings for temporary disability, and 70% of salary for those permanently disabled.

Insured workers and their families receive medical and maternity benefits. During pregnancy and childbirth and for a period thereafter, insured women receive obstetrical care, nursing aid, a cash subsidy, and a layette

Government employees are covered by the Security and Social Services Institute for Civil Workers. Various decentralized enterprises and government departments provide their own social security and health services. Programs for children, including a primary-school breakfast program, are overseen by the National Institute for Child Protection. The Mexican Institution for Child Welfare provides care for neglected, abandoned, or sick children.

An amendment to the 1917 constitution states that men and women are equal before the law, but the traditional concept of women as homemakers is widely accepted. However, this traditional role is beginning to change albeit slowly. Women have held top political and union leadership roles; as of 1997, 113 of 628 members of Parliament were women. Women have the right to file for separation or divorce, and the right to own property in their own name. However, human rights abuses have been committed by employers attempting to keep pregnant women off their payrolls to avoid providing the costly maternity benefits required by law. These abuses include mandatory pregnancy testing, firing women, and inducing them to quit by imposing unpleasant or hazardous working conditions. Domestic violence is a serious problem, and in 10 states, legislation allows men "the right to correct their wives."

Indigenous peoples have full protection under the law, but in practice they face discrimination and experience severe economic deprivation. Numerous nongovernmental organizations in Mexico are working to protect and promote the rights of indigenous peoples. The 1996 San Andres Accords, which addressed the demands voiced in the 1994 Chiapas uprising, expanded indigenous rights.

The human rights of citizens are generally respected, although in 1999 there were reports of extrajudicial killings, torture, illegal arrests and arbitrary detention.

41 HEALTH

Mexico has made slow but measurable progress in public health. The Health Sector Reform Program, launched in 1995, has aimed at reorganizing the healthcare system to expand coverage and increase efficiency of services. Mexico had a birth rate of 24.6 per 1,000 people in 1998. About 67% of the married women (ages 15 to 49) were using contraception in 1996. The infant mortality rate, which was 101.7 per 1,000 live births in 1948, was reduced to 23 by 1996. The general mortality rate was 4.7 per 1,000 in 1995. Average life expectancy, meanwhile, rose from 32.4 years in 1930 to 57.6 in 1965; by 1998, average life expectancy was estimated at 72.6 years for men and women. Maternal mortality was 48 per 100,000 live births in 1997. Cholera, yellow fever, plague, and smallpox have been virtually eliminated, and typhus has been controlled. There were 6,293 malaria cases reported in 1998. Permanent campaigns are waged against malaria, poliomyelitis, skin diseases, tuberculosis, leprosy, onchocercosis, and

serious childhood diseases. In the mid-1990s, 83% of the population had access to safe water, and 50% had adequate sanitation. Immunization rates for children up to one year of age were as follows in 1997: tuberculosis (99%); diphtheria, pertussis, and tetanus (93%); polio (94%); and measles (84%). In 1997, the National Social Security System operated 14,978 outpatient clinics and 372 general hospitals. In 1995, there was one bed per 1,000 people. In 1997, there were 116,000 physicians and 17 doctors per 10,000 inhabitants. Total health care expenditures were $160 per capita in 1995. Major causes of death in 1994 were noted as follows: communicable diseases (63 per 100,000); neoplasms (57 per 100,000); injuries (73 per 100,000); and circulatory diseases (111).

The HIV-1 seroprevalence in 1997 was 0.4 per 100 adults. As of January 1997, 29,962 AIDS cases had been diagnosed.

42 HOUSING

Mexico's public housing program dates from 1938. A 1946 law permitted credit institutions to finance low-rent projects and create a housing bank. Each of two large projects built during the 1940s and 1950s—the President Alemán Urban Center (completed in 1950) and the President Juárez Urban Center (completed in 1952), both in Mexico City—contains a school, a playground, and stores. In 1992, Mexico had 15,100,000 dwellings, of which 49.9% had piped water, 51% had flush toilets, and 87.5% had electric lighting.

Government agencies that have fostered the development of low-income housing include the Fund for Housing Operations and Bank Discounts, the National Public Works and Services Bank, the Housing Credit Guarantee and Support Fund, and the National Housing Institute. In 1974, the National Workers' Housing Fund Institute (Instituto del Fondo Nacional de la Vivienda para los Trabajadores—INFONAVIT) was created to provide housing for workers. With funds provided by employers (equal to 5% of the total salary of each worker), INFONAVIT makes direct loans to employees and provides short-term loans to finance the construction of approved multi-unit projects, which are then sold to employees covered by the program. All these efforts, however, have not come close to eradicating Mexico's housing shortage, which had been exacerbated by accelerated population growth in the 1980s. The government allocated us$1.93 billion in 1989 to build 250,000 low-cost housing units, and expected to receive an additional us$700 million from the World Bank to build more. The 1990 National Housing Plan predicted a shortage of 6.1 million homes, to be felt most severely in the outskirts of urban areas, including Mexico City, Guadalajara, Monterey, and cities in the northern states.

43 EDUCATION

Primary schooling is compulsory and free. Except in the Federal District, where education is administered by the federal government, schools are controlled by the states.

In 1971, children of the age for obligatory schooling (between 6 and 14) numbered 13,159,000; however, only 74% attended school. Between 1960 and 1965, for each 100 pupils enrolled in the first grade, only 23 completed the sixth, making an attrition rate of 77%. The attrition rate is estimated at 48%. At the other end of the educational cycle, only 12,000 graduated from institutions of higher education. Approximately 97% of Mexico's youth between the ages of 16 and 25, a 1968 government report stated, were unprepared to participate in the country's development. Significant improvement had been recorded by the late 1970s, when an estimated 92% of eligible boys and 90% of eligible girls were actually in primary school; the figures for secondary school in 1984 were 56% and 53%, respectively. Recent estimates indicated that 33% of the total Mexican population was in school.

During 1965, the government established 7,000 new literacy centers, raising the total to 11,000. The literacy program helped reduce Mexico's adult illiteracy rate from 37.8% in 1960 to 10.4% in 1995 (males: 8.2% and females: 12.6%).

In 1997, Mexico had 524,927 teachers and 14,650,521 students in 95,855 primary schools, with a student-to-teacher ratio of 28 to one. At the secondary level, there were 485,059 teachers and 7,914,165 students in that same year.

Major universities include the National Autonomous University (founded in 1551), the National Polytechnic Institute, and Iberoamericana University (private), all in Mexico City, and Guadalajara University, the Autonomous University of Guadalajara, and the Autonomous University of Nuevo León. In each state there are other state and private institutions. There were 170,350 teaching staff and 1,612,318 students in all institutions of higher learning in 1997.

The government provides extracurricular education through cultural and motorized missions, community-development brigades, reading rooms, and special centers for workers' training, art education, social work, and primary education.

⁴⁴LIBRARIES AND MUSEUMS

The Mexican public library system has over 4,800 branches holding in total almost 20,000,000 volumes and servicing over 72,000,000 registered library users as of 1993. The National Library, now affiliated with the National University of Mexico, has about 2,000,000 volumes. Other important collections include the Library of Mexico, the Library of the Secretary of the Treasury, and the central library of the National Autonomous University in Mexico City. In total, there are over 1,000 libraries affiliated with institutions of higher education.

The National Museum of Anthropology in Mexico City, founded in 1825, has over 600,000 anthropological, ethnological, and archaeological exhibits and a library of 300,000 volumes. Among its exhibits are the famous Aztec calendar stone and a 137-ton figure of Tlaloc, the god of rain. The National Historical Museum, attached to the National Institute of Anthropology and History, has more than 150,000 objects ranging in date from the Spanish conquest to the constitution of 1917. The National Museum of Art exhibits Mexican art from 17th century to present, while several other art museums exhibit the works of leading European artists, including the Museum of Modern Art and the Museum of Popular Art. Also in Mexico City is the Frida Kahlo Museum in the former home of Frida Kahlo and Diego Rivera, featuring the works of the latter, considered to be Mexico's finest artist. (There is another museum featuring Rivera's work in Guanajuato.) Many public buildings in Guadalajara and elsewhere display murals by famous Mexican painters.

⁴⁵MEDIA

National and international telegraphic service is furnished by the government-owned National Telegraph Co. The government also owns and operates the international radiotelegraph and radiotelephone facilities. A privately owned telephone company provides supplemental facilities in outlying areas. The largest utility is the government-owned Telephones of Mexico. The number of telephones in service in 1995 was 7,620,900.

The national microwave network, now complete, cost more than ₱650 million; facilities by 1968 included the central telecommunications tower in the Federal District and a land station for artificial satellite communications at Tulancingo, Hidalgo, with one of the largest antennas in the world. The network serves most of the country's larger cities.

As of 1999 there were 824 AM and 500 FM radio television stations and 236 television stations. In 1997, Mexico had 324 radios, 251 television sets, and 18 mobile phones per 1,000 population.

Leading newspapers (with their estimated average daily circulations in 1999) include the following:

MEXICO CITY	CIRCULATION
Esto (m)	400,000
El Heraldo (m)	373,600
La Prensa (m)	208,000
Ovaciones (m)	130,000
El Universal (m)	93,800
Excélsior (m)	200,000
El Nacional (m)	210,000
Novedades (m)	190,000
MONTERREY	
El Norte (m)	133,800
La Tribuna (m)	23,000
TAMPICO	
El Heraldo de Tampico (m)	95,000
El Sol de Tampico (m)	77,000
GUADALAJARA	
El Occidental (m)	49,400
Ocho Columnas (d)	48,000

Freedom of the press is guaranteed by law and to a large extent exercised in practice. However, by controlling the supply of newsprint and by providing advertising, indirect subsidies, and outright payoffs to the press, the government exerts an indirect form of press censorship. Mexico's libel and slander laws were made more restrictive in 1982.

As of 1996, there were some 239,750 personal computers. In 1998, there were 8,075 Internet hosts per 1,000 population.

⁴⁶ORGANIZATIONS

The Mexican government supervises and promotes producer and consumer cooperatives, which are exempt from profits and dividends taxes and are given customs protection. Producer cooperatives are active in agriculture, fishing, forestry, and mining. Consumer cooperatives buy, sell, and distribute clothing, foodstuffs, and household articles.

Chambers of commerce and of industry are located in most cities, and merchants and manufacturers are required to join either or both. Headquarters for the national chamber of commerce and industry are in Mexico City. In 1993, 62 industrial chambers and 32 industrial associations represented the major economic sectors. The principal employers' organization is the Employers' Confederation of the Mexican Republic, which dates from 1929.

⁴⁷TOURISM, TRAVEL, AND RECREATION

In 1998, Mexico was the second most popular tourist destination in the Americas after the US. That year 19,810,000 tourists entered Mexico, over 18 million from the United States. Receipts from tourism in 1997 were $7.8 billion. That year there were 382,364 hotel rooms and 764,728 beds with a 56% occupancy rate.

Mexico's tourist attractions range from modern seaside resort areas, such as Tijuana, Acapulco, Puerto Vallarta, Punta Ixtapa/Zihuatanejo, Cozumel, and Cancún, to the Mayan ruins of Chiapas State and the Aztec monuments of the south-central regions. Mexico City, combining notable features from the Aztec, colonial, and modern periods, is itself an important tourist mecca. Veneration of the patron saints plays an important role in Mexican life, and the calendar is full of feast days (fiestas). These predominantly Roman Catholic celebrations include many ancient Amerindian rites and customs and, invariably, bands of mariachi musicians playing Mexican folk songs. Tourists from the US and Canada may enter Mexico with a tourist card stamped with a Mexican visa. All other visitors need a passport and a visa. Business travelers require non-immigrant visas and business permits.

Mexico was host in 1968 to the Summer Olympics and in 1970 and 1986 to the World Cup soccer championship; the World Cup helped tourism recover from the effects of the earthquake, which kept many visitors away in 1985 and 1986. Mexico's most popular sports are baseball, soccer, jai-alai, swimming, and volleyball. Bullfights are a leading spectator sport; the Mexico City arena, seating 50,000 persons, is one of the largest in the world, and there are about 35 other arenas throughout the country.

The cost of traveling in Mexico varies considerably from city to city. According to 1999 UN figures, daily expenses are estimated at $222 for Cozumel, $202 for Cancún, $195 for Mexico City, $106 for Tijuana, and $54 for Ciudad Lazaro.

[48]FAMOUS MEXICANS

The founder of Spanish Mexico was Hernán Cortés (1485–1547), a daring and clever Spanish conquistador. One of the great heroes in Mexican history is Guatemotzin (Cuauhtémoc, 1495?–1525), the last emperor of the Aztecs, who fought the Spanish after the death of his uncle, Montezuma II (Moctezuma or Motecuhzoma, 1480?–1520). Bartolomé de las Casas (1474–1566) and Junípero (Miguel José) Serra (1713–84) were Spanish-born missionaries who tried to improve the conditions of the Amerindians in the colonial period. Two heroes of the War of Independence were the liberal priests Miguel Hidalgo y Costilla (1753–1811) and José María Morelos y Pavón (1765–1815). The first 25 years of independence were dominated first by Manuel Félix Fernández, known as Guadalupe Victoria (1786?–1843), and then by Antonio López de Santa Anna (1794–1876). Austrian-born Maximilian (Ferdinand Maximilian Josef, 1832–67) and Belgian-born Carlota (Marie Charlotte Amélie Augustine Victoire Clémentine Léopoldine, 1840–1927) were emperor and empress from 1864 to 1867, ruling on behalf of the emperor of France. Benito Juárez (1806–72), the great leader of the liberal revolution, attempted to introduce a program of national reform. The dictator José de la Cruz Porfirio Díaz (1830–1915) dominated Mexico from 1876 to 1911. He was overthrown largely through the efforts of Francisco Indalecio Madero (1873–1913), called the Father of the Revolution. Revolutionary generals and politicians included Venustiano Carranza (1859–1920) and Álvaro Obregón (1880–1928). Two other revolutionary leaders—Doroteo Arango, known as Pancho Villa (1877?–1923), and Emiliano Zapata (1879?–1919)—achieved almost legendary status. The foremost political leader after the revolution was Lázaro Cárdenas (1895–1970). Luis Echeverría Álvarez (b.1922), who held the presidency during 1970–76, made Mexico one of the leading countries of the developing world in international forums. Miguel de la Madrid Hurtado (b.1934) became president in 1982. The diplomat Alfonso García Robles (1911–91) shared the 1982 Nobel Peace Prize for his work on behalf of disarmament.

Painters Diego Rivera (1883–1957), José Clemente Orozco (1883–1949), and David Alfaro Siqueiros (1898–1974) are renowned for their murals. The Spaniards Bernal Díaz del Castillo (1496?–1590?) and Bernardino de Sahagun (1499?–1590) wrote historical accounts of the Spanish conquest. Mexican-born Juan Ruiz de Alarcón y Mendoza (1580?–1639) became a playwright in Spain. Juana Inés de la Cruz (1651–95), a nun, was a poet and proponent of women's rights. Outstanding novelists include José Joaquín Fernández de Lizardi (1776–1827), author of *El periquillo sarniento*; Mariano Azuela (1873–1952), author of *Los de abajo*; Martín Luis Guzmán (1887–1976),

author of *El águila y la serpiente*; and Gregorio López y Fuentes (1897–1966), author of *El indio*. Well-known contemporary authors include Augustín Yáñez (1904–80), Octavio Paz (b.1914), Juan Rulfo (1918–86), and Carlos Fuentes (b.1928). Poets include Salvador Díaz Mirón (1853–1928), Manuel Gutiérrez Nájera (1859–95), and Amado Nervo (1870–1919). The outstanding figure in recent Mexican literary life is the diplomat, dramatist, poet, essayist, and critic Alfonso Reyes (1889–1959). Anthropologist Carlos Castaneda (b.Brazil, 1931) is widely known for his studies of mysticism among the Yaqui Amerindians. Well-known Mexican composers include Manuel Ponce (1882–1948), Silvestre Revueltas (1899–1940), Carlos Chávez (1899–1978), and Agustín Lara (1900–70). Significant figures in the motion picture industry are the comedian Cantinflas (Mario Moreno, 1911–93), Mexican-born actor Anthony Rudolph Oaxaca Quinn (b.1916), and directors Emilio Fernández (1904–86) and Spanish-born Luis Buñuel (1900–83).

Notable Mexican sports figures include Fernando Valenzuela, (b.1960), a pitcher for the Los Angeles Dodgers who won the Cy Young Award as a rookie.

[49]DEPENDENCIES

Mexico has no territories or colonies.

[50]BIBLIOGRAPHY

Aspe, Pedro, and Paul E. Sigmund. *The Political Economy of Income Distribution in Mexico*. New York: Holmes & Meier, 1984.

Bailey, John J. *Governing Mexico: The Statecraft of Crisis Management*. New York: St. Martin's Press, 1988.

Bancroft, Hubert Howe. *History of Mexico*. 8 vols. San Francisco: Bancroft, 1883–88.

Barkin, David. *Distorted Development: Mexico in the World Economy*. Boulder, Colo.: Westview Press, 1990.

Barry, Tom (ed.). *Mexico: A Country Guide*. Albuquerque, N.M.: Inter-Hemispheric Education Resource Center, 1992.

Bazant, Jan. *A Concise History of Mexico*. New York: Cambridge University Press, 1977.

Brading, D. A. (ed.). *Caudillo and Peasant in the Mexican Revolution*. New York: Cambridge University Press, 1980.

Camp, Roderic Ai. *Entrepreneurs and Politics in Twentieth-century Mexico*. New York: Oxford University Press, 1989.

Carmichael, Elizabeth. *The Skeleton at the Feast: The Day of the Dead in Mexico*. Austin: University of Texas Press, 1992.

Changing Structure of Mexico: Political, Social, and Economic Prospects. Armonk, N.Y.: M. E. Sharpe, 1996.

Cross, Harry E., and J. A. Sandos. *Across the Border: Rural Development in Mexico and Recent Migration to the United States*. Berkeley: Institute of Government Studies, University of California, 1981.

Cypher, James M. *State and Capital in Mexico: Development Policy since 1940*. Boulder, Colo.: Westview Press, 1990.

Diaz del Castillo, Bernal. *The Discovery and Conquest of Mexico*. New York: Da Capo Press, 1996.

Fuentes, Carlos. *A New Time for Mexico*. New York: Farrar, Straus and Giroux, 1996.

Grayson, George W. *The North American Free Trade Agreement*. Ithaca, N.Y.: Foreign Policy Association, 1993.

———. *The Politics of Mexican Oil*. Pittsburgh: University of Pittsburgh Press, 1981.

Hamilton, Nora. *The Limits of State Autonomy: Post-Revolutionary Mexico*. Princeton, N.J.: Princeton University Press, 1982.

Hart, John M. (John Mason). *Revolutionary Mexico: The Coming and Process of the Mexican Revolution*. Berkeley: University of California Press, 1987.

"History in Mexico." *The Economixt.* 8 July 2000, vol. 356, no. 8178, p. 17.

Johnston, Bruce F. (ed.). *U.S.-Mexico Relations: Agriculture and Rural Development.* Stanford, Calif.: Stanford University Press, 1987.

MacLachlan, Colin M., and Jaime E. Rodriguez. *The Forging of the Cosmic Race: A Reinterpretation of Colonial Mexico.* Berkeley: University of California Press, 1980.

Maxfield, Sylvia. *Governing Capital: International Finance and Mexican Politics.* Ithaca: Cornell University Press, 1990.

Mexican Politics in Transition. Boulder, Colo.: Westview Press, 1987.

Mexico in Pictures. Minneapolis: Lerner, 1988.

Meyer, Michael C. *The Course of Mexican History.* 5th ed. New York: Oxford University Press, 1995.

Morris, Stephen D. *Political Reformism in Mexico: An Overview of Contemporary Mexican Politics.* Boulder, Colo.: L. Rienner, 1995.

Nord, Bruce. *Mexican Social Policy: Affordability, Conflict and Progress.* Lanham, Md.: University Press of America, 1994.

North American Free Trade Agreement: Final Text. CCH International, 1992.

Ortiz-Martínez, Guillermo. *Capital Accumulation and Economic Growth: A Financial Perspective on Mexico.* New York: Garland, 1984.

Oster, Patrick. *The Mexicans: A Personal Portrait of a People.* New York: W. Morrow, 1989.

Padgett, L. Vincent. *The Mexican Political System.* 2d ed. Boston: Houghton Mifflin, 1976.

Prescott, William Hickling. *History of the Conquest of Mexico.* New York: Harper, 1843.

Quirk, Robert E. *The Mexican Revolution and the Catholic Church, 1910–1929.* Bloomington: Indiana University Press, 1973.

Ratt, W. Dirk. *Mexico and the United States: Ambivalent Vistas.* Athens, Ga.: University of Georgia Press, 1996.

Reed, John. *Insurgent Mexico.* New York: Simon & Schuster, 1969 (orig. 1916).

Ruiz, Ramón Eduardo. *The Great Rebellion: Mexico, 1905–1924.* New York: Norton, 1980.

———. *Triumphs and Tragedy: A History of the Mexican People.* New York: W.W. Norton, 1992.

Semo, Enrique. *The History of Capitalism in Mexico: Its Origins, 1521–1763.* Austin: University of Texas Press, 1993.

Shafer, Robert Jones. *Mexican Business Organizations: History and Analysis.* Syracuse, N.Y.: Syracuse University Press, 1973.

Stevens, Evelyn P. *Protest and Response in Mexico.* Cambridge: MIT Press, 1974.

Turner, Frederick C. *The Dynamic of Mexican Nationalism.* Chapel Hill: University of North Carolina Press, 1968.

Weintraub, Sidney (ed.). *U.S.-Mexican Industrial Integration: The Road to Free Trade.* Boulder, Colo.: Westview Press, 1991.

———. *Mexican Trade Policy and the North American Community.* Washington, D.C.: Center for Strategic and International Studies, 1988.

Wilkie, James W. (ed.). *Society and Economy in Mexico.* Los Angeles, Calif.: UCLA Latin American Center Publications, 1990.

NETHERLANDS AMERICAN DEPENDENCIES

NETHERLANDS ANTILLES

The five islands of the Netherlands Antilles are divided geographically into two groups: the Leeward Islands (Benedenwindse Eilanden) and the Windward Islands (Bovenwindse Eilanden). The Windward group, off the north coast of South America, comprises the islands of Curaçao, with an area of 444 sq km (171 sq mi), and Bonaire, 288 sq km (111 sq mi). Aruba, another Windward island, seceded from the Netherlands Antilles in 1986. The Leeward group, more than 800 km (500 mi) to the northeast, consists of the southern part of St. Martin (Sint Maarten), 34 sq km (13 sq mi); Saba, 13 sq km (5 sq mi); and Sint Eustatius, 21 sq km (8 sq mi). The islands total 800 sq km (309 sq mi).

All the Windward Islands have volcanic bases, partly covered with coral reefs; they are semiarid and flat, with little vegetation. The Leeward Islands are more mountainous and receive enough rainfall to enable crops and vegetation to flourish. Saba, the most fertile, is an extinct volcano with luxuriant vegetation in its crater, on its sides, and leading down to the sea. Temperatures average between 25° and 31°c (77° and 88°F); annual rainfall averages 107 cm (42 in) on the Windward Islands and 51 cm (20 in) on the Leeward Islands. In 1987, the tundra peregrine falcon and the American crocodile were endangered species. The entire population of the Netherlands Antilles was estimated at 207,827 in mid-1999. The estimated population of the Windward Islands in the mid-1990s was 158,000, consisting of Curaçao, 142,000, and Bonaire, 16,000. The Leeward Islands had 35,000 residents, consisting of Sint Eustatius, 2,000; St. Martin, 32,000; and Saba, 1,000. Most of the inhabitants were born on the islands. Persons of mixed African origins account for 85% of the population, but over 40 ethnicities are represented, including Dutch, Surinamese, British, Latin Americans, French West Indians, Carib Amerindians, and US emigrants.

The official language is Dutch. Papiamento, a lingua franca evolved from Dutch and English with an admixture of French, Spanish, Portuguese, Arawak, and African words, is also common, principally in the Leeward Islands. English is spoken, mainly in the Windward Islands. Spanish is also widely spoken. Roman Catholicism has the most adherents on the Leeward Islands and Saba, but Protestantism is dominant on St. Martin and Sint Eustatius.

Buses, private automobiles operating as small buses on fixed routes, and taxicabs provide the only public transportation. There are no rivers or railroads. Each island has a good all-weather road system. The most important port is on Curaçao, where there is a natural harbor at Willemstad. Airline connections to nearby islands and countries are provided by Dutch Antillean Airlines (Antilliaanse Luchtvaart Maatschappij—ALM), Royal Dutch Airlines (Koninklijke Luchtvaart Maatschappij—KLM), and other international carriers.

The European discovery of the Windward Islands was made by Columbus in 1493, and that of the Leeward Islands (including Aruba) by a young Spanish nobleman, Alonso de Ojeda, who sailed with Amerigo Vespucci in 1499; hence the claim went to Spain. The Dutch fleet captured the Windward Islands in 1632 and the Leeward Islands in 1634. Peter Stuyvesant was the first

governor. In 1648, St. Martin was peacefully divided between the Netherlands and France; this division still exists. During the colonial period, Curaçao was the center of the Caribbean slave trade. For a period during the Napoleonic wars (1807–15), Great Britain had control over the islands. Slavery was abolished in 1863.

Under a 1954 statute, the Netherlands Antilles is a component of the Kingdom of the Netherlands, with autonomy in internal affairs. A governor, appointed by and representing the crown, heads the government, with a Council of Ministers as the executive body. The ministers are responsible to the Staten, a 23-member legislature (15 from Curaçao, 3 each from Bonaire and St. Martin, and 1 each from Saba and Sint Eustatius). Members are elected by general suffrage of Dutch nationals aged 18 or older. A 1951 regulation established autonomy in local affairs for each of the then-existing island communities—Aruba, Curaçao, Bonaire, and the Leeward Islands—with responsibilities divided between an elected island council, an executive council, and a lieutenant-governor. By agreements made in 1983, St. Martin, Saba, and Sint Eustatius have separate representation in the Staten, elect their own separate councils, and have their own lieutenant-governors and executive councils. Cases are tried in a court of first instance and on appeal in the Joint High Court of Justice, with justices appointed by the crown. Defense is the responsibility of the Netherlands; a naval contingent is permanently stationed in the islands, and military service is compulsory. The Netherlands Antilles is an associate member of the EU.

The prosperity of Curaçao is inseparably linked with its oil refineries. These were built there, beginning in 1918, chiefly because of the favorable location of the islands, their good natural ports and cheap labor, and the political stability of the territory. Tankers bring crude oil from Venezuela. The economic significance of the refineries is great, not only because of their output, but also because they provide employment and stimulate other economic activities, such as shipbuilding, metal industries, shipping, air traffic, and commerce in general. The government controls the price of basic foodstuffs and participates in the setting of rates to be charged for transportation and by privately owned utilities.

The currency unit is the Netherlands Antilles guilder, or florin (NAf) of 100 cents; NAf1 = $0.55866 (or $1 = roughly NAf1.79). The GDP for 1997 was estimated at us$2.1 billion, or us$11,500 per capita. The unemployment rate (including Aruba) was 14.9% in 1998, and 60–70% of the work force was organized in labor unions. The principal agricultural products are sorghum, orange peel, aloes, groundnuts, yams, divi-divi, and some assorted vegetables. The fish catch in 1994 was 1,100 tons. Curaçao's favorable position at the crossing of many sea-lanes has stimulated commerce since the earliest days of European settlement. Transit trade benefits from Curaçao's improved harbors; Willemstad is a free port, as are the islands of Saba and Sint Eustatius. In 1997, exports were estimated at us$268.2 million and imports at us$1.4 billion. Refined petroleum products are exported to the Netherlands and other countries from a refinery on Curaçao. Petroleum shipments dominated the country's

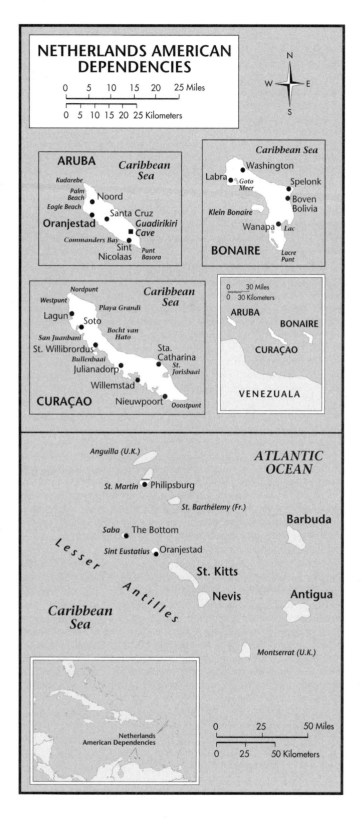

The Bank of the Netherlands Antilles (Bank van de Nederlandse Antillen) issues currency, holds official reserves, regulates the banking system, and acts as the central foreign exchange bank. There are 14 authorized commercial banks and several savings and loan institutions that also handle financial matters. The Netherlands Antilles Development Bank was created in 1981 to stimulate foreign investment in service industries. Tax treaties with the US have encouraged US individuals and businesses to shelter their funds in the islands. Development aid from the Netherlands totaled about $97 million in 1996.

There are 74 nursery schools, 86 primary schools, 55 secondary schools, 1 teacher-training college, and the University Institute of the Netherlands Antilles, on Curaçao (all excluding Aruba); all schools are government-supported. The language of instruction is Dutch in the Leeward Islands, except in the International School, where classes are taught in English; English is also used in the Windward Islands. The literacy rate is more than 95%, although education is not compulsory. There are six hospitals on Curaçao and four on the other islands.

All the islands have cable, radiotelegraph, or radiotelephone connections with one another and, via the central exchange at Curaçao, with international systems. There are 9 AM, 4 FM, and 3 TV stations on the islands. Broadcasts are in Papiamento, Dutch, Spanish, and English. In 1992 there were about 205,000 radios and 64,000 televisions (including Aruba). Two daily newspapers in Dutch and four in Papiamento are published in the Netherlands Antilles, along with several weekly and monthly periodicals.

Tourism is a significant source of revenue. Annually, more than 469,000 cruise passengers visit the islands; total visitors to the islands amount to over 1,000,000.

ARUBA

The island of Aruba is located off the north coast of South America, NW of Curaçao. It has an area of 193 sq km (75 sq mi). The land is basically flat and is renowned for its white-sand beaches. The temperature is almost constant at 27°C (81°F); the annual rainfall averages 60 cm (24 in). The mid-1999 population was estimated at 68,675. The official language is Dutch, but Papiamento, English, and Spanish are also spoken. The religion of the majority is Roman Catholic.

There are no rivers or railways. The road system connects all major cities. There are three deepwater harbors, at San Nicolas, Oranjestad, and Barcadera. Airline connections are provided by Dutch Antillean Airlines (Antilliaanse Luchtvaart Maatschappij—ALM), Royal Dutch Airlines (Koninklijke Luchtvaart Maatschappij—KLM), and other international carriers.

In March 1983, at the Hague, the governments of the Netherlands and Netherlands Antilles agreed to grant Aruba the status of a separate state. On 1 January 1986, Aruba seceded from the Netherlands Antilles, becoming a separate member of the kingdom. In 1990, Aruba requested and received from the Netherlands a cancellation of the agreement that would have granted independence in 1996.

The head of government is a governor appointed by and representing the crown. A Council of Ministers, led by a prime minister, has executive power. The ministers are responsible to the Staten, a legislative body of 21 members elected by universal adult suffrage for four-year terms. Cases are tried in a court of first instance and on appeal in the Joint High Court of Justice, with justices appointed by the crown. Defense is the responsibility of the Netherlands; a naval contingent is stationed on the island, and military service is compulsory.

The two principal sources of revenue for the island are tourism and oil refining. Coastal Aruba Refining Co., a subsidiary of Coastal Corp. of Houston, produces asphalt, diesel fuel,

foreign trade—refined petroleum accounted for about 98% of exports in 1993, while crude oil made up 64% of imports that year. In 1996, the US was the market for 28.6% of exports; Honduras, 6.4%; Belgium-Luxembourg, 6%; Italy, 4.9%; Guatemala, 4.5%, and Costa Rica, 4%. Venezuela provided 34% of imports in 1996, followed by the US (16.4%), Mexico (15.5%), Netherlands (5%), Italy (3.5%), and Brazil (2.8%).

feedstock for other refineries, kerosene, and residual fuel oil at the Lago refinery. Since the refinery reopened in 1993, economic growth has surged, as the refinery provides a major source of employment and foreign exchange earnings. The currency unit is the Aruban florin (Af) of 100 cents, with a fixed exchange rate of Af1 = $0.5587 (or $1 = Af1.79) since 1986. The GDP for 1997 was US$1.5 billion, or US$22,000 per capita. The unemployment rate was 0.6% in 1996, leading to a large number of unfilled job vacancies despite recent sharp increases in wage rates.

In 1997, Aruban exports were valued at US$1.73 billion (mostly refined petroleum products), and imports at US$2.12 billion. The US and the EU are Aruba's major trading partners. There is a Central Bank of Aruba, and there are six commercial banks. The Aruba Development Bank was created in 1982 to stimulate foreign investment in service industries.

Medical care is entirely subsidized by the government; there is a modern hospital. There were 26 preprimary schools, 33 primary schools, 23 secondary schools, and 1 teacher-training college. Although education is not compulsory, the literacy rate is high (over 90%). There are 4 AM and 6 FM commercial radio stations and one television station in Aruba. There is one daily newspaper published in Dutch, one in English, and one in Papiamento. There were an estimated 22,922 telephones on the island in 1993.

Tourism is the major source of revenue. Over 500,000 tourists annually visit the island, with about half coming from the US.

NICARAGUA

Republic of Nicaragua
República de Nicaragua

CAPITAL: Managua.

FLAG: The national flag consists of a white horizontal stripe between two stripes of cobalt blue, with the national coat of arms centered in the white band.

ANTHEM: *Salve a ti, Nicaragua (Hail to You, Nicaragua).*

MONETARY UNIT: The gold córdoba (c$) is a paper currency of 100 centavos. There are coins of 5, 10, 25, and 50 centavos and 1 and 5 córdobas, and notes of 1, 2, 5, 10, 20, 50, 100, 500, 1,000, 5,000, 10,000, 20,000, 50,000, 100,000, 200,000, 500,000, 1,000,000, 5,000,000, and 10,000,000 córdobas. c$1 = us$0.07994 (or us$1 = c$12.510) as of 31 March 2000.

WEIGHTS AND MEASURES: The metric system is the legal standard, but some local units are also used.

HOLIDAYS: New Year's Day, 1 January; Labor Day, 1 May; Liberation Day (Revolution of 1979), 19 July; Battle of San Jacinto, 14 September; Independence Day, 15 September; All Saints' Day, 1 November; Christmas, 25 December. Movable religious holidays include Holy Thursday and Good Friday.

TIME: 6 AM = noon GMT.

¹LOCATION, SIZE, AND EXTENT

Nicaragua, the largest of the Central American countries, has an area of 129,494 sq km (49,998 sq mi), which includes the area covered by the waters of Lake Nicaragua (about 8,000 sq km/ 3,100 sq mi) and Lake Managua (about 1,000 sq km/390 sq mi). Comparatively, the area occupied by Nicaragua is slightly larger than the state of New York. The country has a length of 580 km (360 mi) NE-SW and a width of 494 km (307 mi) NW-SE. Bounded on the N by Honduras, on the E by the Caribbean Sea, on the s by Costa Rica, and on the w by the Pacific Ocean, Nicaragua has a total boundary length of 2,141 km (1,330 mi).

In 1980, Nicaragua unilaterally abrogated its 1928 treaty with Colombia, confirming that nation's sovereignty over the Caribbean archipelago of San Andrés and Providencia, about 190 km (120 mi) off the Nicaraguan coast. Nicaragua also disputes the Treaty of Quita Sueño, ratified by the US Senate in July 1981, according to which Colombia received the uninhabited islands of Quita Sueño Bank, Roncador Cay, and Serrana Bank.

Nicaragua's capital city, Managua, is located in the southwestern part of the country.

²TOPOGRAPHY

The Caribbean coast, known as the Mosquito (or Miskito) Coast or Mosquitia, consists of low, flat, wet, tropical jungle, extending into pine savannas 80–160 km (50–100 mi) inland. The coastal lowland rises to a plateau covering about one-third of the total area. This plateau is broken by mountain ranges extending eastward from the main cordillera to within 64–80 km (40–50 mi) of the Caribbean coast. The mountainous central area forms a triangular wedge pointed southeast, rising at its highest to some 2,000 m (6,600 ft). The plains and lake region, in a long, narrow structural depression running northwest to southeast along the isthmus, contains a belt of volcanoes rising to 1,500 m (5,000 ft) and extending from the Gulf of Fonseca to Lake Nicaragua. In this region is located Lake Managua, at 41 m (136 ft) above sea level, which drains through the Tipitapa Channel into Lake Nicaragua, at 32 m (106 ft) above sea level, which, in turn, drains

through the San Juan River eastward into the Caribbean. Lake Nicaragua is about 160 km (100 mi) long and 72 km (45 mi) wide at the widest point, while Lake Managua is 56 km (35 mi) long by 24 km (15 mi) wide.

The principal waterways are the Coco (or Segovia) River, navigable up to 240 km (150 mi) inland from the eastern Mosquito Coast, and the San Juan, navigable to within a few miles of the Caribbean, where a series of rapids halts transportation.

Nicaragua lies in an earthquake zone. The last major earthquake, which occurred on 23 December 1972, claimed an estimated 10,000 lives and demolished a 70-square-block section of central Managua. A major volcanic eruption was that of Cerro Negro (977 m/3,205 ft), northwest of Managua, in 1968.

³CLIMATE

Except in the central highlands, the climate is warm and humid. Average humidity in Managua in June, the most humid month, is 84%; in April, the driest month, 62%. The mean temperature, varying according to altitude, is between 20° and 30°C (68° and 86°F). In Managua, monthly average temperatures range from a minimum of 23°C (73°F) and a maximum of 30°C (86°F) in January to a minimum of 26°C (79°F) and a maximum of 31°C (88°F) in July. There are two seasons: a wet season, from May to December, and a dry season, from January through April. Rainfall, however, varies according to region, and the rainy season in the eastern area may extend 9 or even 12 months. Average annual rainfall along the Mosquito Coast reaches 254–635 cm (100–250 in) as a result of the easterly trade winds blowing in from the Caribbean; the highlands also have heavy rainfall. Managua receives 114 cm (45 in), while the Pacific coast averages over 200 cm (80 in) a year.

⁴FLORA AND FAUNA

The central highlands region has extensive forests of oak and pine on the slopes, but lower valley elevations show damage from fire and agricultural activities. The largest pine savanna in the rainy tropics stands on the lowlands behind the Mosquito Coast. The wet and humid Caribbean coastal plain has an abundance of tropical forest, with wild rubber, cedar, ebony, mahogany, and rosewood attracting some exploitation.

Wildlife includes the puma, deer, monkey, armadillo, alligator, parrot, macaw, peccary, and several species of snakes (some poisonous). Lake Nicaragua contains the only freshwater sharks in the world, owing to a prehistoric geological movement that separated the lake from the Pacific Ocean, gradually changing the ocean water into fresh water.

[5]ENVIRONMENT

Nicaragua's major environmental problems are soil erosion, caused in part by cultivation of annual crops on steep slopes, and depletion of upland pine forests for lumber, fuel, and human settlement. The nation lost 24% of its forest and woodland between 1983 and 1993. One contributing factor is the use of wood for fuel. Excessive or ineffective use of pesticides to control malaria, along with widespread agricultural use, has resulted in some environmental contamination. Nicaragua's cities produce 0.5 million tons of solid waste per year. Industrial pollutants have contaminated the lakes and rivers. The nation has 42.0 cu mi of water. Fifty-four percent is used for farming and 21% in industrial activity. As of 1995, 19% of Nicaragua's city dwellers and 67% of its rural population did not have access to safe drinking water. Dumping of sewage and chemical wastes has made Lake Managua unsuitable for swimming, fishing, or drinking. Primary responsibility for resource conservation is vested in the Nicaraguan Institute of Natural Resources and Environment (Instituto Nicaragüense de Recursos Naturales y del Ambiente—IRENA), established in October 1979.

In the mid-1990s, eight of the nation's mammal species were endangered. Seven bird species and 68 plant species were threatened with extinction. Endangered or extinct species in Nicaragua include the tundra peregrine falcon, four species of turtle (green sea, hawksbill, leatherback, and olive ridley), the spectacled caiman, and the American crocodile.

[6]POPULATION

The population of Nicaragua in 2000 was estimated at 4,850,976. An estimated 3.0% of the population is 65 years of age or older. The projected population for the year 2005 is 5,522,000, assuming a crude birthrate of 30 per 1,000 population and a death rate of 5, resulting in a natural rate of change of 2.5% for the period 2000–2005. The population rate of change between 1995 and 2000 was 2.6%. The population density in 1998 was 40 per sq km (104 per sq mi).

It was estimated that 65% of the population lived in urban areas in 2000, up from 53% in 1980. The capital city, Managua, had a 2000 metropolitan population of 1,319,000. Other major cities are León, 100,982; Granada, 88,636; Masaya, 74,946; Chinandega, 67,792; Matagalpa, 36,983; Esteli, 30,653; Tipitapa, 30,078; Chichigalpa, 28,889; and Juigalpa, 25,625.

[7]MIGRATION

During the 1980s, Nicaragua hosted more than 10,000 refugees, mainly from El Salvador and Guatemala. Most have since repatriated. Those who chose to remain have been naturalized or granted permanent resident status.

After the Sandinista takeover in 1979, thousands of Nicaraguans left the country. It was estimated in 1987 that 24,000 had fled to Honduras, 16,000 to Costa Rica, and over 200,000 to the US, chiefly to Florida. After the defeat of the Sandinistas in the 1990 elections, some 200,000 Nicaraguans returned from abroad. Under the CIREFCA plan, 1989-94, 70,000 Nicaraguans repatriated. In 1999, the net migration rate was -1.06 migrants per 1,000 population.

[8]ETHNIC GROUPS

The Nicaraguan population is basically mestizo, a mixture of white and Amerindian. There are no census data on racial composition, but estimates place the mestizo component at 69% and the white population at 17%; blacks account for 9%, and Amerindians for the remaining 5%.

Traditionally, the Atlantic littoral has been inhabited mainly by blacks from Jamaica, Belize, and various present and former British possessions in the Caribbean. The more densely populated Pacific coast highland has long been basically mestizo in composition. Most Amerindian groups in Nicaragua have been assimilated, but Miskito Amerindians, as well as Sumus, make their traditional homes on the Mosquito Coast and neighboring areas.

[9]LANGUAGES

Spanish is the official language and is spoken by the overwhelming majority of the population. Some Nahuatl and other Amerindian words and phrases are in common use. English is often spoken as a second language at professional levels.

[10]RELIGIONS

Roman Catholicism is the predominant religion, claiming the allegiance of about 79.2% of the population. The country comprises one archbishopric (with its seat at Managua) and five bishoprics (León, Granada, Bluefields, Matagalpa, and Estelí). Relations between the Sandinista government and the Roman Catholic Church deteriorated in 1982–83. There were assaults on individual churches and members of the clergy, and several antireligious incidents occurred during the visit by Pope John Paul II in March 1983. Relations began to improve in 1987, aided by the presence of a new papal nuncio, Pablo Giglio.

Approximately 15.1% of the populace are members of evangelical churches. Another 1.5% are members of the Moravian Church, and 0.1% belong to the Episcopal Church. An additional 1.9% claim membership in other churches or religious groups; 8.5% profess no religion or are atheistic. There are also small communities of Jews, Muslims, Mormons, Mennonites, Jehovah's Witnesses, and the Church of Scientology. Amerindian tribal religionists and spiritists also practice, sometimes combining elements of Christianity and African religions.

[11]TRANSPORTATION

Main transportation arteries are concentrated in the more densely populated Pacific region. The national road network in 1999 totaled 16,382 km (10,026 mi), of which 1,818 km (1,130 mi) were paved. The Inter-American Highway from Honduras to Costa Rica was completed in 1972. The Pacific Highway begins in Granada and passes through Managua, León, and Chinandega to Corinto. In 1995 there were 72,000 passenger cars and 75,000 commercial vehicles registered. Pacific Railways of Nicaragua, government-owned, with a length of 373 km (231 mi), was shut down in 1993.

The Naviera Nicaragüense provides regular services to Central America, the US, and Europe. As of 1998, Nicaragua had no merchant fleet. Corinto is Nicaragua's only natural harbor on the Pacific coast and the major port, handling about 60% of all waterborne trade. Other ports include Puerto Sandino and San Juan del Sur on the Pacific and Puerto Cabezas on the Atlantic coast. In 1983, Bulgaria pledged to help Nicaragua build a deepwater port at El Bluff, on the Atlantic; the port now allows ships from Europe, Africa, and the Caribbean to deliver goods to Nicaragua without passing through the Panama Canal. Inland waterways total 2,220 km (1,380 mi), including Lake Nicaragua and the San Juan River.

Air transportation is important because of limited road and railway facilities. In 1998 there were an estimated 184 airports, only 13 of which had paved runways. A new state-owned airline,

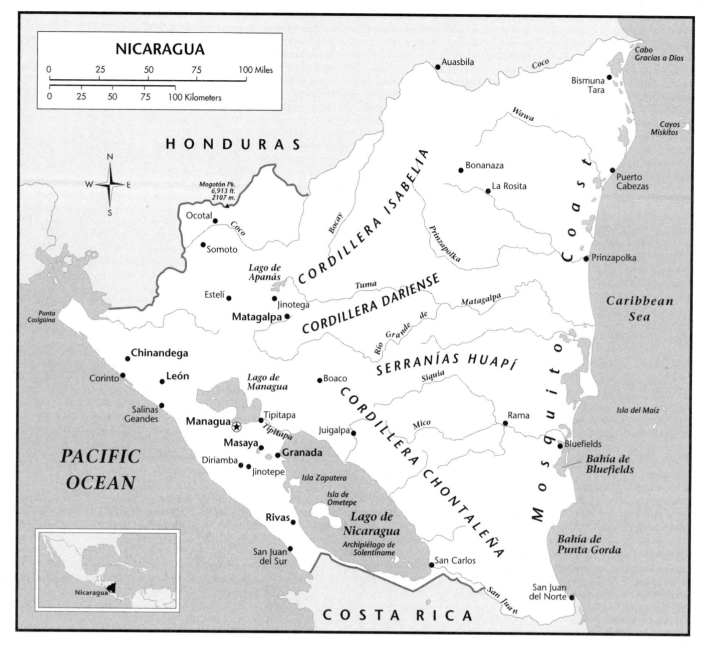

NICARAGUA

HONDURAS

Cabo
Gracias a Dios

Auasbila

Coco

Bismuna
Tara

Wawa

Cayos
Miskitos

Mogotón Pk.
6,913 ft.
2107 m.

Ocotal

Coco

Somoto

Bonanaza

La Rosita

Puerto
Cabezas

Lago de
Apanás

Estelí

Jinotega

Matagalpa

Tuma

CORDILLERA ISABELIA

Prinzapolka

Prinzapolka

CORDILLERA DARIENSE

Matagalpa

Río Grande de

Caribbean
Sea

Chinandega

León

Corinto

Salinas
Geandes

Lago de
Managua

Boaco

SERRANÍAS HUAPÍ

Siquia

Isla del Maíz

Managua

Tipitapa

Tipitapa

Masaya

Granada

Juigalpa

Mico

Rama

Bluefields

Bahía de
Bluefields

PACIFIC
OCEAN

Punta
Cosigüina

Diriamba

Jinotepe

Isla Zapatera

CORDILLERA CHONTALEÑA

Isla de
Ometepe

Rivas

Lago de
Nicaragua

Archipiélago de
Solentiname

San Carlos

Bahía de
Punta Gorda

San Juan
del Sur

San Juan
del Norte

San Juan

COSTA RICA

Mosquito Coast

Nicaragua

LOCATION: 10° to 15°N; 83° to 87°W. **BOUNDARY LENGTHS:** Honduras, 922 km (573 mi); Caribbean coastline, 478 km (297 mi); Costa Rica, 300 km (186 mi); Pacific coastline, 346 km (215 mi). **TERRITORIAL SEA LIMIT:** 200 mi.

Aerolíneas de Nicaragua (AERONICA), provides services to El Salvador, Costa Rica, Panama, and Mexico. The principal airport is Augusto Sandino, an international terminal at Las Mercedes, near Managua. In 1997, 51,000 passengers were carried on scheduled domestic and international flights.

12HISTORY

Nicaragua derives its name from that of the Amerindian chief Nicarao who once ruled the region. The first European contact came with Columbus in 1502. At that time the northern part of the country was inhabited by the Sumo Amerindians, the eastern by the Miskitos, and the region around Lakes Nicaragua and Managua by agricultural tribes.

The first Spanish settlements in Nicaragua were founded by the conquistador Gil González de Ávila in 1522. The cities of

Granada and León were founded in 1524 by Francisco Hernández de Córdoba. During the next 300 years—most of the colonial period—Nicaragua was ruled as part of the captaincy-general of Guatemala. On 15 September 1821, the independence of the five provinces of Central America, including Nicaragua, was proclaimed. After a brief period under the Mexican empire of Augustín de Iturbide (1822–23), Nicaragua joined the United Provinces of Central America. On 30 April 1838, Nicaragua declared its independence from the United Provinces, and a new constitution was adopted.

Nicaragua did not immediately consolidate as a nation. The Spanish had never entirely subdued Nicaragua, and the Mosquito Coast at the time of independence was an Amerindian and British enclave, especially around the Bluefields area. Britain occupied the Mosquito Coast during the 1820s and 1830s, and maintained a significant presence thereafter. Beyond that, Nicaragua was torn apart by a bitter struggle between liberals, based in León, and conservatives, based in Granada.

Yet another factor impeding Nicaragua's development was constant foreign intervention focusing on the trade route through the country. Commodore Cornelius Vanderbilt competed with the British for control of the transisthmian traffic, a rivalry settled by the Clayton-Bulwer Treaty of 1850. In 1853, liberals led by Máximo Jérez and Francisco Castellón revolted and invited the US military adventurer William Walker to help their rebellion. Walker invaded Nicaragua in 1855, capturing Granada and suppressing Jérez, and had himself elected president in 1856. He lasted only one year, and was captured and executed in Honduras in 1860. Conservatives seized control in 1863 and ruled until 1893.

The 30-year conservative reign brought increases in coffee and banana production. Liberals successfully revolted in 1893, and José Santos Zelaya became president. Zelaya's dictatorship lasted 16 years, during which he incorporated most of the Mosquito territory into Nicaragua, developed railroads and lake transportation, enlarged the coffee plantations, and stirred up revolts among his Central American neighbors. In 1901, by the Hay-Pauncefote Treaty, Great Britain gave the US the undisputed right to build a Central American canal. Zelaya was finally deposed in 1909, after a conservative revolt.

From 1909 until 1933, the US grew in influence in Nicaragua. Conservatives immediately asked for help from Washington. The US placed an American agent in the customhouse in 1911, and US banks extended considerable credit to the bankrupt Treasury. US marines and warships arrived in 1912 in support of president Adolfo Díaz. US forces remained active in Nicaraguan politics and administered the country directly or through handpicked rulers until August 1925. During this period, the Bryan-Chamorro Treaty of 1914 allowed the US to build a canal across Nicaragua. After the marines withdrew, the liberals revolted against the US-backed conservative government of Diego Manuel Chamorro and established a government on the Mosquito Coast. The marines returned in 1926 to reimpose Díaz.

In November 1928, the marines supervised the electoral victory of the liberal José María Moncada, with whom the conservatives had made peace. The guerrilla hero Gen. Augusto César Sandino began organizing resistance to the marine occupation force in 1927, and fought the US troops to a standstill. With the inauguration of US President Franklin D. Roosevelt's "good neighbor" policy in 1933, the marines were pulled out for the last time. But the marines left a legacy, having built the Nicaraguan National Guard, headed by Anastasio ("Tacho") Somoza García.

In the following year, the liberal Juan B. Sacasa was elected to office. Also during 1934, officers of the National Guard shot Sandino after offering to negotiate a settlement with his forces. The National Guard was now unchallenged in Nicaragua, and three years later, Somoza unseated Sacasa and assumed the presidency. Somoza and his family were to rule Nicaragua directly or indirectly for the next 42 years.

Somoza was president until 1947, making constitutional changes as necessary to prolong his term. Although he retired in 1947, he returned in 1950, and was assassinated in 1956. "Tacho's" son, Luis Somoza Debayle, was president of Congress, and immediately became president under the constitution. The next year, he was elected by a rather suspicious 89% of the vote.

In 1962, a law was passed prohibiting relatives within four generations from immediately succeeding Luis Somoza as president. Accordingly, in February 1963, René Schick Gutiérrez of the National Liberal Party was elected president for a four-year term. Schick died in office in August 1966 and was succeeded by his first vice-president, Lorenzo Guerrero. The presidential election of February 1967 returned the Somozas to power with an overwhelming victory for Anastasio Somoza Debayle, the younger brother of Luis.

According to Nicaraguan law, Anastasio's term in office was due to end in May 1972. But by March 1971, Somoza had worked out an agreement allowing him to stand for reelection in 1974, ruling in the interim with a three-man coalition government. Anastasio and his triumvirate drew up a new constitution, signed by the triumvirate and the cabinet on 3 April 1971. Then, after declaring nine opposition parties illegal, Somoza easily won the September 1974 elections.

While Somoza consolidated his hold on Nicaragua, an insurgent organization, the Sandinista National Liberation Front (Frente Sandinista de Liberación Nacional—FSLN), began to agitate against his rule. At first, the group was small and confined to the foothill and mountain regions of Nicaragua. But domestic opposition to Somoza mounted, driven by the family's monopolistic and corrupt economic practices. One powerful example of the corruption was the disappearance of half the US relief aid extended to Nicaragua after a devastating 1972 earthquake. Most of the rebuilding of Managua was done by Somoza-controlled firms on Somoza's land. Throughout the 1970s, Somoza's opposition grew, and US support began to dissipate.

In December 1974, guerrillas kidnapped 13 prominent political personalities, including several members of the Somoza family. The group secured a ransom of US$1 million and the release of 14 political prisoners. Somoza responded by declaring a martial law and unleashed the National Guard. The Guard's repressive tactics created even more enemies of the Somoza regime. Repression continued throughout the 1970s, and climaxed in January 1978 with the assassination of Pedro Joaquín Chamorro, editor and publisher of the opposition newspaper *La Prensa*. The assassins were never found, but most felt that Somoza and the National Guard were behind the killing of this moderate leader from a prominent family.

By 1979, loss of support from the Church and the business community left Somoza without domestic allies. He had become isolated diplomatically, and after the Carter administration cut off military aid, his ability to remain in power further weakened. In May, 1979, the Sandinistas launched a final offensive. By July, Somoza had fled the country (he was assassinated on 17 September 1980 in Asunción, Paraguay). By this time, an estimated 30,000–50,000 people had died during the fighting.

Nicaragua was now ruled by a coalition Government of National Reconstruction, made up of various religious and political leaders, but dominated by the Sandinista leadership. That coalition had unraveled by mid-1980, when Alfonso Robelo and Violeta Barrios de Chamorro, widow of Pedro Chamorro, resigned from the government. Chamorro continued publishing *La Prensa* and preserved the paper's reputation for independence, while Robelo went into exile and supported the resistance. The Sandinistas dissolved the National Guard, and in 1982 a number of anti-Sandinista guerrilla groups (broadly referred to as the "contras") began operating from Honduras and Costa Rica. These groups consisted of former Guard members and Somoza supporters ("Somocistas") who engaged in guerrilla-style offensives, aimed at disrupting Nicaragua's agriculture and oil supplies.

The Sandinistas engaged in an ambitious program to develop Nicaragua under leftist ideals. They nationalized Somoza's land and commercial interests. They also initiated agrarian reform, and announced a series of social programs, including literacy and public health campaigns. Politically, they professed democratic ideals, but delivered only sporadically. A Statute on Rights and Guarantees was adopted, but elections were postponed. As antigovernment activity increased, the government became increasingly authoritarian. A state of emergency, proclaimed in

March 1982 and extended into 1987, introduced prior censorship, particularly felt by *La Prensa*. Daniel Ortega emerged as the leader of the Sandinistas, and became president when elections were finally held in 1984. However, in that election, the major opposition groups withdrew from the election, making it a rather hollow victory.

In April 1981, the Reagan administration cut off aid to Nicaragua and, citing the Sandinistas' support for leftist guerrillas in El Salvador, began aiding the contras with funds channeled through the CIA. The Reagan administration sent military aid to Honduras and Costa Rica and sought increases in funding for the contras. Despite some overtures from the Sandinistas, including the expulsion of 2,200 Cuban advisors, the US continued to support the contras.

Internationally, the Sandinistas made some gains. In 1986, the World Court ruled that the US had violated international law by mining the harbors in Nicaragua. The rulings made little difference because the US refused to recognize the decision. In the US, Congress proved reluctant to fund the Nicaraguan resistance. In 1986, it was revealed that US government funds derived from covert arms sales to Iran had been secretly diverted to provide aid to the contras in violation of a US congressional ban on such aid.

On the domestic scene, the Sandinistas were less successful. Their economic policies had not produced impressive results. The inflation rate reached 33,000% in 1988 and reserves dwindled. Price controls had led to serious shortages in basic foodstuffs. Lacking any capital for investment, the situation was becoming hopeless. Attempts to pin the economic woes on the civil war fell on deaf ears as the economic situation worsened.

The Sandinistas continued to seek negotiated settlements for their internal strife. In 1986, they signed an accord with leaders of the Miskito Amerindians, granting autonomy to their region. In August 1987 Nicaragua signed the Arias peace plan for Central America. Nicaragua promised guarantees of democratic rights, and a reduction of hostilities with the contras, including a cease-fire, a reduction in the armed forces, repatriation or resettlement of refugees, and amnesty for the rebels. In exchange, the Nicaraguans were to receive guarantees of nonintervention by outside powers. Implementation was sporadic, but elections were held in 1990. The US, for its part, pledged $9 million in support of free elections, and urged all other outside donors to tie aid to the holding of elections.

The 1990 elections had a surprise winner—Violeta Chamorro. Heading a 10-party alliance called the National Opposition Union (UNO), Chamorro received 54% of the vote to Daniel Ortega's 41%. UNO also took a majority in the National Assembly. Chamorro moved to liberalize the Nicaraguan economy, but found it sluggish. Austerity measures led to dislocations and political disquiet. The US delivered miniscule amounts of economic aid, to the disappointment of hopeful Nicaraguans. Nevertheless, Chamorro's government succeeded in driving down hyperinflation that had reached 13,500% to an acceptable single-digit level, and obtaining relief of much of the country's $10 billion foreign debt, as well as achieving stable economic growth of around 4% from 1994 to 1996.

Politically, Chamorro's situation was tenuous. With the Sandinistas still in control of the military, Chamorro had a difficult time achieving a reduction in force. Sandinista organizations and syndicates remained, often striking against the Chamorro government. Meanwhile, the resettlement and repatriation of the contras moved slowly. Some former contras took to the field again, resuming their previous attacks on civilian installations. Chamorro's own coalition, UNO, proved shaky, withdrawing support from her government in 1993 after she attempted to call for new elections. The beleaguered government persisted, but by 1994 the outlook for further progress in

unifying the country and implementing democratic and free-market reforms was bleak.

The prospect of a peaceful political transition in the politically polarized country were considered so shaky that international observers were called in for the October 1996 elections, as they had been in 1990. Although the results were later contested, and some irregularities found, the elections proceeded peacefully and without incident. With 80% of the electorate voting, Arnoldo Alemán, the conservative former mayor of Managua, and leader of the Liberal Constitutionalist Party (PLC) defeated Sandinista leader Daniel Ortega in Nicaragua's first peaceful transition of power in 100 years. The Liberal Party took 41 of the 93 seats Chamber of Deputies, while the Sandinistas took 38; the remaining seats were won by leftist and conservative groups. Challenges facing Alemán included the privatization of government-owned enterprises, reduction of underemployment, and the return of (or restitution for) property appropriated by the Sandinistas.

Arnoldo Alemán Lacayo was born on 23 January 1946 in Managua to the Minister of Education during the Somoza dictatorship. He attended the Universidad Nacional Autónoma in Léon to study law, which he practiced upon his graduation in 1967 until 1979. Alemán opposed the Sandinista revolution and became politically active to illustrate this. He was supportive of the Somoza regime and vehemently opposed the Sandinista desire to convert Nicaragua into a communist state after the 1979 revolution. His links to the Cuban-American contingency in the United States as well as with exiled Nicaraguans helped further establish him politically in Nicaragua.

President Arnoldo Alemán Lacayo, and Vice-President Enrique Bolanos Geyer, were inaugurated into office on 10 January 1997. Though the elections were plagued with allegations of corruption, Alemán began his term in office positively. His close ties with right-wing groups and American entrepreneurs helped establish Nicaragua's market economy, and he worked hard to instill strict economic reforms focused on economic growth. Throughout Alemán's term, the GDP has steadily increased. Until 1998, Alemán's efforts paid off—reforms were reaping some success, even amidst the muddied waters the legacy of civil war and years of financial mismanagement had left behind. Then came Hurricane Mitch in 1998, devastating Nicaragua and neighboring Honduras and leaving Nicaragua, already the poorest country in Central America, with $1 billion worth of damage. Worst hit was the agricultural sector, which the country depends on for the majority of its exports. By 1999, Alemán was forced to deal with a trade deficit approaching $900 million. However, despite the destruction caused by Hurricane Mitch, Nicaragua's economy has continued to grow slightly. Aid and debt relief have contributed to this and thus helped stabilize the economy, but the hand of President Alemán and his commitment to free market reforms and economic growth have no doubt played a role as well. Alemán has increased talks with the Sandinistas during his term, and the two parties have indeed found common ground in one area: scandal allegations. In 1998, Daniel Ortega, the Sandinista former president faced accusations from his stepdaughter of sexual abuse dating back to her childhood. Meanwhile, Alemán faced charges that the presidential plane he had been using was actually reported stolen in the United States and that it had been used throughout Central America and Colombia to carry cocaine. Both Ortega and Alemán denied all charges against them.

Alemán has also faced border disputes during his term: in March 2000, it coupled with Costa Rica to continue an ongoing battle over its border with Honduras, each claiming sovereignty over the Gulf of Fonseca. Other challenges during Alemán's presidency have been land reform and the land distribution process (favoring Sandinistas and their supporters), as well as growing poverty and migration issues.

13 GOVERNMENT

Although constitutionally defined as a democracy, Nicaragua, between 1934 and 1979, was ruled by the Somoza family, who did not hesitate to suppress political opponents violently. The last of the constitutions promulgated during the Somoza period, effective 3 April 1974, provided for a bicameral Congress and a president elected for a six-year term, and guarantees of political rights. After the FSLN took power as the Government of National Reconstruction in July 1979, this constitution was abrogated and Congress dissolved. From July 1979 until November 1984, executive power was vested in a junta composed of five members (three members after April 1980).

The 1984 electoral reforms created an executive branch with a president elected for a six-year term by popular vote and assisted by a vice president and a cabinet. (The presidential term was shortened to five years in 1995.) Legislative power is vested in a 93-member unicameral National Constituent Assembly elected under a system of proportional representation for six-year terms. The electoral process in Nicaragua is said to be one of the most complicated in the Americas as it forces voters to select candidates for the office of president, National Assembly posts, and local municipalities from a vast number of political parties. Further, vote count is still a tedious, manual process.

The Sandinista constitution of 1987 is still in effect; it preserves the previous institutional structure. President Arnoldo Alemán's Liberal Alliance, a conservative group that supported the Somoza dictatorship, also supported the National Opposition Union (UNO) candidate and its candidate former President Violeta Chamorro during her six-year reign. Alemán's support diminished when Chamorro failed to control the UNO coalition; Aleman thus switched to the Liberal Party to launch his presidential campaign in 1996. The disbanded UNO party forced Chamorro to link with the Sandinistas in Congress to maintain control of her office; she thus maintained the Sandinista control over the Revolutionary Army. Alemán's main purpose as the National Liberal Party representative was to overturn Chamorro and try to reverse some of the economic policies of her regime.

President Alemán pledged to increase collaboration between his ultraconservative Liberal Party and the Sandinistas. Alemán, who has been commended for his efforts to achieve some consensus with his political opponents, renewed collaboration talks in 1999—much to the approval of the numerous aid agencies working in the aftermath of Hurricane Mitch.

14 POLITICAL PARTIES

Nicaragua's traditional two parties were the National Liberal Party (Partido Liberal Nacionalista—PLN) and the Nicaraguan Conservative Party (Partido Conservador Nicaragüense—PCN). The PLN favored separation of church and state, some social legislation, no foreign interference in the political process, and limited land reform. It was supported by government employees, the National Guard, and large segments of the middle and lower classes. The PCN desired government cooperation with the Catholic Church (but also advocated freedom of religion), less government interference in private business, and a regressive tax structure.

When the leftist Sandinista National Liberation Front (FSLN), which was founded in 1962, came to power in July 1979, all political parties except those favoring a return to Somoza rule were permitted. Since the Somozas had all been liberals, the PLN was specifically banned.

Under the Sandinistas, Nicaragua's governing political coalition, the Patriotic Front for the Revolution (Frente Patriótico para la Revolución—FPR), formed in 1980, consisted of the FSLN, the Independent Liberal Party (Partido Liberal Independiente—PLI), the Popular Social Christian Party (Partido Popular Social Cristiano—PPSC), and the Moscow-oriented Nicaraguan Socialist Party (Partido Socialista Nicaragüense—PSN). Opposition parties included the Conservative Democratic Party (Partido Conservador Demócrata—PCD), the Nicaraguan Social Christian Party (Partido Social Cristiano Nicaragüense—PSCN), and the Social Democratic Party (Partido Social Demócrata—PSD).

The National Opposition Union (UNO), under which Violeta Chamorro was elected president in 1990, was a 10-party coalition that included both the Conservatives and the Liberals, as well as several parties formerly aligned with the Sandinistas, including the PLI and the PSD. The PLI was also the party of Vice President Virgilio Godoy. Others included the Christian Democratic Union (UDC), the National Democratic Movement (MDN), the National Action Party (PAN), and the Neo-Liberal Party (PALI).

By the mid-1990s, the UNO coalition had disbanded. Nicaragua had numerous parties ranging across the political spectrum, although the country was dominated by two principal opposed groups, the Liberal Constitutionalist Party (PLC), a right-wing successor to the traditional liberal party, and, on the left, the still-active FSLN. In the October 1996 presidential election, Arnoldo Alemán, former mayor of Managua and leader of the PLC, was elected with 51% of the vote, supported by a coalition of parties and factions called the Liberal Alliance (AL). Daniel Ortega, the FSLN candidate, won 38% of the vote, with the rest going to candidates from smaller parties. In the legislative elections, 42 of the 93 seats in the National Assembly were won by the National Alliance, with the FSLN winning 36, and the remaining 15 going to candidates from nine other parties. These included the Christian Way (Camino Cristiano), the Conservative Party of Nicaragua (PCN), the center-right Nicaraguan Resistance Party (PRN), the center-left Sandinista Renovation Movement (MRS), and the center-right Independent Liberal party (PLI). Altogether, 24 political parties and popular organizations participated in the 1996 elections. The next national elections were scheduled for the year 2000.

15 LOCAL GOVERNMENT

In July 1982, the nation's departments were consolidated into six regions and three special zones, each to be administered by an official directly responsible to the central government. However, under the Chamorro government, Nicaragua has returned to the old system, with 15 departments and two autonomous regions along the Atlantic coast.

Local elections for mayoralties accompany national elections.

16 JUDICIAL SYSTEM

At the head of the judicial branch is the Supreme Court in Managua whose justices are appointed by the National Assembly for six-year terms. The Supreme Court consists 12 judges and has administrative, criminal, civil, and constitutional matters divisions.

The judicial system consists of both civilian and military courts. Military courts investigate, prosecute and try crimes committed by or against the police or armed forces. Therefore, the military courts have jurisdiction over citizens involved in security-related offenses. In a controversial 1993 decision, a military court exercised jurisdiction to convict a former member of the EPS (Sandinista Popular Army).

17 ARMED FORCES

In 2000, the regular armed forces, a fusion of the Sandinista and Contra armies, numbered 16,000. The army had 14,000 personnel, the navy 800, and the air force 1,200 (with no combat aircraft and 15 armed helicopters). A reorganization of the army was under way as of 1999. The navy operated five patrol boats and two minesweepers. Weapons remain Russian, but foreign advisors are gone as are foreign subsidies. Nicaragua spent $26 million for defense in 1998 or 1.2% of GDP.

[18]INTERNATIONAL COOPERATION

Nicaragua is a charter member of the UN, having joined on 24 October 1945, and belongs to ECLAC and all the nonregional specialized agencies. It also participates in CACM, G-77, IADB, and OAS, as well as the International Coffee Agreement and other inter-American and international organizations. Nicaragua is a signatory to the Law of the Sea.

The Sandinistas enjoyed considerable international support even before the July 1979 revolution. Not only Cuba, but also Panama and Venezuela backed the guerrillas, and by mid-June 1979, Brazil, Costa Rica, Ecuador, and Mexico had cut diplomatic ties with the Somoza regime. Later in that month, the OAS called for "immediate and definitive replacement" of Somoza with a broadly based democratic government. During the 1980s, relations with the US and other Western governments deteriorated, the borders with Honduras and Costa Rica grew tense, and the Sandinista government found its firmest support in Mexico and in the Communist-bloc countries. In August 1987, Nicaragua signed the Central American peace plan outlined by Costa Rican President Oscar Arias Sánchez.

[19]ECONOMY

Nicaragua has long had, in effect, two economies: an export segment, producing mainly cotton, meat, coffee, and sugar; and a subsistence segment, tying a majority of both urban and rural Nicaraguans to an impoverished existence. Agriculture and forestry remain the mainstays of the Nicaraguan economy, employing nearly half of the labor force. During 1960–64, the GDP increased by an annual average of 8.1%, the highest rate in Latin America. Annual growth ranged from 4% to 6% during 1965–73, largely because of favorable world prices for Nicaraguan commodities. The 1972 earthquake that struck Managua caused material losses estimated at $845 million, but the agricultural sector was left largely unscathed.

The civil war of the late 1970s disrupted the economy. During this era, 80% of the economy was nationalized. In 1978, the GDP fell by 7.9%; in 1979, the year of the Sandinista takeover, by 25%. Massive public spending resulted in a GDP growth of 10.4% in 1980 and 7% in 1981. However, because of floods in May 1982, a weak international market for export crops, the virtual collapse of the CACM, continuing political uncertainty, mounting economic pressure by the US, and disruption by the contras, the economy suffered a GDP decline of 1.4% in 1982, and continued to decline through 1986 (with the exception of 1983, when high world prices and a bumper harvest boosted GDP by 4.6%). The average annual inflation rate during 1980–82 was 35%, but by 1984, it had risen to 50%; in 1985 it soared to 334%, and the 1986 rate was 778%. Because of shortages, rationing of soap, flour, and cooking oil was introduced in 1982.

In response to both domestic and international pressure, the Sandinista regime entered into negotiations with the Nicaraguan Resistance and agreed to nation-wide elections in February 1990. Nicaraguan voters elected as their president the candidate of the National Opposition Union (UNO), Violeta Barrios de Chamorro. President Chamorro instituted the first democratic government in more than 50 years when she took office in April 1990. She inherited a country with a totally controlled economy and the highest per-capita foreign debt in the world. Inflation was ascending uncontrollably and the economy was in shambles. During President Chamorro's nearly seven years in office, her government achieved major progress toward consolidating

democratic institutions, advancing national reconciliation, stabilizing the economy, privatizing state-owned enterprises, and reducing human rights violations.

Nicaragua began free market reforms in 1991 after 12 years of economic free-fall under the Sandinista regime. Despite some setbacks, it has made dramatic progress: privatizing 351 state enterprises, reducing inflation from 13.5% to 12.1%, and cutting the foreign debt in half. As a result of the strong decline in foreign debt, the country's current account balance declined as a percentage of GDP from 60.0% in 1992 to 38.3% in 1996. In addition, the government's budget deficit in 1996 stood at 13.6% of GDP, down considerably from 20.3% in 1990. The economy began expanding in 1994 and grew at a rate of 5.5% in 1996 (its best performance since 1977). The election of Arnoldo Alemán in 1996 served to continue the social and economic reforms perpetuated by the Sandinista regime. Damage caused by Hurricane Mitch in 1998 reduced the GDP to 4% for that year, but improved estimates for 1999 ranged from 5% to 6.3%. The government planned to reduce taxes and further liberalize trade in 1999.

[20]INCOME

The US Central Intelligence Agency (CIA) reports that in 1998 Nicaragua's gross domestic product (GDP) was estimated at $11.6 billion. The per capita GDP was estimated at $2,500. The annual growth rate of GDP was estimated at 4%. The average inflation rate in 1998 was 16%. The CIA defines GDP as the value of all final goods and services produced within a nation in a given year and computed on the basis of purchasing power parity (PPP) rather than value as measured on the basis of the rate of exchange. It was estimated that agriculture accounted for 32% of GDP, industry 24%, and services 44%.

Private consumption includes expenditures of individuals, households, and nongovernmental organizations. It was estimated that between 1990 and 1998 private consumption grew at an annual rate of 3.4%. The richest 10% of the population accounted for approximately 40% of household consumption and the poorest 10% approximately 1.6%.

[21]LABOR

In 1998, the official estimate of the total economically active population was 1,630,000. In 1995, the labor force was distributed as follows: services, 54%; agriculture, 31%; and industry, 15%. However, according to some estimates, more than 50% of the work force remains unemployed or underemployed. Officially, unemployment was at 13.3% in 1998.

Nicaragua became a member of the ILO in 1919, withdrew in 1938, and rejoined in 1957. The former labor code, effective January 1945, was patterned on Mexican labor legislation. In establishing and protecting the rights of workers, emphasis was placed on law rather than collective bargaining. A new code, effective as of 1996, allows all public and private sector employees to form and join unions and legally recognizes cooperatives, as well as the right to strike. The maximum legal work week is 48 hours, with one day of rest per week.

As of 1999, less than 50% of the labor force was organized.

Children may not work until the age of 14 but this regulation is not effectively enforced and many children work in agriculture and in cities as urban street-peddlers.

The minimum wage varies from sector to sector throughout the formal economy. In 1999, the monthly minimum wage was $37.50 in agriculture, $10.00 in construction, and $50.00 in manufacturing.

[22]AGRICULTURE

Nicaragua's economy is predominantly agricultural. Land under cultivation amounted to 1,270,000 ha (3,138,000 acres), or about 10.5% of the total land area. Some 88,000 hectares (217,400 acres) were under irrigation in 1994. The harvest season begins in November and lasts through January; during the rest of the year, most rural laborers are unemployed. Plantings begin in May immediately before the wet season.

The main agricultural exports are coffee, cotton, sugar, and bananas. Nontraditional exports are growing and include: honeydew melons, cantaloupe, sesame seed, onions, baby corn, asparagus, artichokes, and cut flowers. Sorghum, cacao, yucca, tobacco, plantains, and various other fruits and vegetables are produced on a smaller scale for the local markets. Bananas were once nearly totally decimated by Panama disease. By the late 1960s, however, production had begun a slow recovery, reaching 135,000 tons in 1992 (up from 29,000 tons in 1970). Banana production in 1998, however, was just 80,000 tons. Cottonseed production has expanded from virtually zero prior to 1950 to 105,700 tons in 1985, before falling to 3,000 tons by 1998. During the 1980s, coffee was severely threatened by contra activities; production of 64,000 tons in 1998 was an improvement over the 28,000 tons produced in 1990. In 1998, 370,000 tons of processed sugar from 3,843,000 tons of cane were produced, largely for export. Major food crops in that year were corn, 296,000 tons; rice, 212,000 tons; sorghum, 111,000 tons; and dry beans, 85,000 tons.

During the Somoza era, most of the titled land was held by large landowners (with farms of 140 hectares/346 acres or more), who owned some 60% of the land while representing only 5% of the farming population. About 36% of the farm population controlled individual holdings of less than 3.5 hectares (8.6 acres). The Sandinista government expropriated almost one million hectares (2.5 million acres) of land, of which over two-thirds became state farms and 280,000 hectares (692,000 acres) were turned into peasant cooperatives. Agriculture was severely disrupted in 1979 and 1980 because of the revolution, but by 1981 it had recuperated. In May 1982, severe floods caused damages estimated at $180 million; the withdrawal of the Standard Fruit Co. in the following October caused losses of $400,000 per week in foreign exchange earnings. Bad weather continued to plague the sector through 1984. An estimated 450,000 hectares (1,111,500 acres) of land were redistributed in 1985. From 1983 to 1987, the contras sought to destabilize Nicaraguan agriculture by damaging agricultural machinery, destroying crop storage sheds, and intimidating farm workers. After eight years of steady decline, the agricultural sector grew by a modest 1–2% in 1992, mostly due to the largest coffee harvest since 1984.

23ANIMAL HUSBANDRY

Nicaragua, the second largest cattle-raising country of Central America (after Honduras), had 1,688,000 head of dairy and beef cattle in 1998. There were also 245,000 horses, 400,000 hogs, and 55,000 mules and donkeys. Total beef production in 1998 was 47,763 tons. Meat exports, perennially one of Nicaragua's most important trade commodities, were valued at US$23 million in 1981 but had fallen to US$7 million by 1987, but have increased since then to $42.4 million in 1998. The primary markets for Nicaraguan beef are the US, El Salvador, and Puerto Rico. In 1990, Nicaragua was given back access to the US beef products market, and since then the livestock industry has been a profitable business and a key economic indicator for the country. Milk production in 1998 totaled 215,000 tons.

24FISHING

Commercial fishing in the lakes and rivers and along the seacoasts is limited. In 1997, the total catch amounted to 16,130 tons, over 93% of which came from marine waters. About 80% of the marine catch comes from the Atlantic coast. Shrimp and

lobster catches in 1997 amounted to 6,437 and 3,690 tons, respectively. Exports of shrimp and lobster expanded after the 1960s and by 1980 had reached an export value of US$25.9 million. In 1997, exports of fish products nearly reached $81.2 million. Commercial fishing is now trying to diversify its catch to include more red snapper, grouper, and flounder.

After the Sandinistas took over, the fishing industry was nationalized. After an agreement made in 1982, the former USSR expanded the fishing port at San Juan del Sur to service its tuna fleet. In late 1991, the government privatized the Atlantic seafood packaging plants, causing seafood production to rise by 19.8% in 1992.

25FORESTRY

About 26% of Nicaragua is still forested. The country has four distinct forest zones: deciduous hardwood, mountain pine, lowland pine, and evergreen hardwood. Nicaragua's largest remaining timber resources, in the evergreen hardwood zone, are largely inaccessible. Nicaragua is the southernmost area of natural North American pine lands. The most well-known cloud forest in Nicaragua is Selva Negra (Black Forest), in the Matagalpa region. In 1997, roundwood production totaled 3,874,000 cu m, with 94% burned as fuel wood. Sawn wood production was about 148,000 cu m that year.

26MINING

Mining contributed less than 1% to the country's GDP in 1997. In the mid-20th century, Nicaragua ranked roughly 15th among the world's gold producers, and the development of gold mining was emphasized during the Sandinista years, when the entire mining industry was nationalized. Gold exports reached $39.9 million in 1980. In 1982, they had fallen to $15 million, and they were suspended thereafter through 1985. After a long period of low production, gold output more than doubled between 1996 and 1997, from 1,500 kg to 3,400 kg.

A 1996 law revised the tax structure of the mining industry and concessions policies and revisions in 1997 lifted a ban on new concessions. The Corporación Nicaragüense de Minas (INMINE), a subsidiary of the government holding company, controls most of the mineral exploration and production in the country. Gold and silver mines are located in León Department, Zelaya Department, and Chontales Department. Mineral production for 1997 included silver, 5,600 kg; marine salt, 15,000 tons; gypsum, 13,000 tons; and cement, 360,000 tons. Deposits of iron, copper, lead, antimony, and zinc have also been uncovered.

27ENERGY AND POWER

The National Light and Power Co. (Empresa Nacional de Luz y Fuerza—ENALUF) is responsible for most of the electricity generated in Nicaragua. Production of electricity increased from 77 million kWh in 1948 to 2,714 million kWh in 1998. Nicaragua had a net capacity of 446,000 kW, of which approximately 20% was hydroelectric and 15% was geothermal. In August 1983, a geothermal electrical generating plant was opened at the foot of the Momotombo volcano; its generating capacity of 70,000 kW provided about 30% of Nicaragua's electricity generation in 1994. A new 40-MW diesel plant was completed in 1998. In 1999 Nicaragua's electricity consumption was the lowest in Central America.

Since the US removed its economic embargo against Nicaragua in 1990, Nicaragua has been seeking to attract international exploration interests, especially along its Caribbean coast.

28INDUSTRY

Nicaraguan industry expanded during the 1970s but was severely disrupted by the civil war and nationalization in 1979. In 1980, the manufacturing sector began to recuperate, and modest growth continued through 1984. In 1985, however, net output again declined, by an estimated 5%. In the mid 1980s, there were still many state enterprises, some of them created by nationalization; in 1985, the government announced plans for a mixed economy. All state monopolies except for public utilities have been eliminated; price controls have ended; and more than 300 state enterprises have been privatized since 1990.

In 1998, the industrial sector contributed approximately 22% to the GDP and employed approximately 24% of the labor force. Industrial production grew by 4.6% in 1998. Among the most important industries are processed food, chemicals, metal products, textiles, clothing, petroleum refining and distribution, beverages, and shoes. The services sector has become the major player in the country's economy since the reforms instituted by the Chamorro government. Services account for 44% of GDP and include commerce, financial services, transportation, energy and construction.

29SCIENCE AND TECHNOLOGY

Among Nicaragua's scientific learned societies and research institutes are the Geophysical Observatory, founded in 1980, the Nicaraguan Society of Psychiatry and Psychology, founded in 1962, and the National Center of Agricultural Information and Documentation, founded in 1984, as part of the Ministry of Agriculture; all three are in Managua. Nicaragua has six universities and colleges offering degrees in agricultural studies and other scientific studies. In 1987–97, science and engineering students accounted for 33% of college and university enrollments. The National Museum of Nicaragua, founded in 1896 in Managua, has exhibits concerning archaeology, ceramics, zoology, botany, and geology.

At last estimate, total research and development expenditures amounted to c$989 million cordobas; 302 technicians and 725 scientists and engineers were engaged in research and development.

30DOMESTIC TRADE

Managua is the principal trading and distribution center, and all importers and exporters have offices there. Exporters, except those concerned with cotton, coffee or lumber, are usually importers also. Managua has a variety of retail establishments, including department stores and numerous general stores; many small shops are in private homes. Managua also has a central market to which merchants come daily with all types of produce and domestic and imported consumer goods. Retail sales are mainly for cash.

The usual business hours are from 8 AM to noon and from 2:30 to 5:30 PM, Monday through Friday, with a half-day on Saturday. Banking hours on weekdays are from 8:30 AM to noon and from 2 to 4 PM; on Saturday, from 8:30 to 11:30 AM.

31FOREIGN TRADE

Nicaragua's total trade volume grew considerably during the 1970s because of the country's membership in the CACM and because of worldwide inflation. Following the Sandinista revolution and the virtual collapse of the CACM because of political instability in the region, Nicaragua's imports and exports fell by more than half from 1976 to 1985.

By 1986, Latin America and EEC member countries, particularly Germany, accounted for the bulk of Nicaragua's trade volume; and the Communist bloc had filled the breach opened by the shutting down of US commerce. The Chamorro government changed Nicaragua's trading partners as it reduced trade barriers in 1991. The government issued export promotion incentives with special tax benefits for products sold outside Central America. The Communist bloc was discarded in favor of the US and South American countries, but Germany remained an important partner. By the Law of Free Trade Zones, Nicaragua waived all duties for imports used in the free zones. The result was widespread availability of US goods in several newly established Managua supermarkets.

One of the key engines of economic growth has been production for export. Although traditional products such as coffee, meat, and sugar continue to lead the list of Nicaraguan exports, during the late 1990s the fastest growth came in nontraditional exports: maquila goods (apparel), bananas, gold, seafood, and new agricultural products such as sesame, melons, and onions.

The most important commodity export from Nicaragua is coffee (23%), followed by meat (14%), and shell fish (13%). Other exports include office supplies and machines (7.0%), oil seeds (4.8%), and sugar (4.0%).

In 1997 Nicaragua's imports were distributed among the following categories:

Consumer goods	13.6%
Food	12.7%
Fuels	12.1%
Industrial supplies	32.5%
Machinery	16.1%
Transportation	12.5%
Other	0.5%

Principal trading partners in 1998 (in millions of US dollars) were as follows:

COUNTRY	EXPORTS	IMPORTS	BALANCE
United States	429	370	59
Honduras	183	77	106
El Salvador	61	74	-13
Germany	60	19	41
Costa Rica	23	158	-135
Mexico	14	63	-49
Guatemala	8	101	-93
Japan	5	88	-83
Venezuela	n.a.	131	
Taiwan	n.a.	63	

32BALANCE OF PAYMENTS

An adverse balance of trade with Nicaragua's major trading partners is the major factor in its deficit. Incoming capital in the form of public and private loans, as well as foreign capital investment and tourism, traditionally offset amortization and interest payments abroad. The current account balance has sustained a deficit averaging 30% of GDP throughout the 1990s.

The US Central Intelligence Agency reports that in 1997 the purchasing power parity of Nicaragua's exports was $704 million while imports totaled $1,450 million resulting in a trade balance of -$746 million.

The International Monetary Fund (IMF) reports that in 1998 Nicaragua had exports of goods totaling $579 million and imports totaling $1,384 million. The services credit totaled $182 million and debit $272 million. The following table summarizes Nicaragua's balance of payments as reported by the IMF for 1998 in millions of US dollars.

Current Account		-607
Balance on goods	-804	
Balance on services	-90	
Balance on income	-151	
Current transfers	438	
Capital Account		...
Financial Account		193
Direct investment in Nicaragua	184	
Other investment assets	49	
Other investment liabilities	-40	
Net Errors and Omissions		14
Reserves and Related Items		401

33 BANKING AND SECURITIES

The banking system, nationalized in July 1979, is under the supervision of the comptroller general. The National Bank of Nicaragua, established in 1912, has been government-owned since 1940. In 1979, the bank was reorganized to become the National Development Bank. The Central Bank of Nicaragua (Banco Central de Nicaragua), established in 1961, is the bank of issue and also handles all foreign exchange transactions. As of 1979, deposits in foreign banks were prohibited, but in May 1985, the establishment of private exchange houses was permitted. In 1990, legislation was passed that allowed for the establishment of private banks. There are no state-owned commercial banks in Nicaragua.

By 2000, there were at least 11 private banks operating. Commercial banks included the Banco Mercantil, the Banco de la Producción, the Banco Caley Dagnall, the Banco de América Central, the Banco de Crédito Centroamericano, the Banco de Finanzas, Banco Intercontinental, the Banco de Exportación, the Banco del Café, the Banco Européo de Centroamérica, and the Banco Nicaraguense de Industria y Comercio. Total assets of the Nicaraguan financial system reached $1.6 billion in 1998.

A small stock market began operations in the late 1990s.

34 INSURANCE

In 1979, the Nicaraguan Institute of Insurance and Reinsurance took over all domestic insurance companies. There were five domestic insurance companies operating in 2000, including the government-owned Iniser; and Seguros America, Seguros Centroamericanos, Seguros Metropolitana, and Seguros Pacificano. All private insurance companies were majority owned by Nicaraguan banks.

35 PUBLIC FINANCE

Since the mid-1960s, government spending has consistently exceeded revenues. During the Sandinista regime, detailed public finance budgets were not a priority. The government budget deficit shrank from 18% of GDP in 1987 to 4% in 1998, while government revenues consistently reflected almost one-third of GDP.

The US Central Intelligence Agency (CIA) estimates that in 1996 Nicaragua's central government took in revenues of approximately $389 million and had expenditures of $551 million including capital expenditures of $206 million. Overall, the government registered a deficit of approximately $162 million. External debt totaled $6 billion.

The following table shows an itemized breakdown of government revenues and expenditures. The percentages were calculated from data reported by the International Monetary Fund. The dollar amounts (millions) are based on the CIA estimates provided above.

REVENUE AND GRANTS	100%	389
Tax revenue	70.2%	273
Non-tax revenue	4.4%	17
Capital revenue	1.4%	5
Grants	24.0%	93
EXPENDITURES	100%	551
General public services	9.7%	53
Defense	5.8%	32
Public order and safety	8.0%	44
Education	15.5%	85
Health	13.4%	74
Social security	14.7%	81
Housing and community amenities	3.3%	18
Recreation, cultural, and religious affairs	1.3%	7
Economic affairs and services	11.4%	63
Other expenditures	2.4%	13
Interest payments	14.6%	80

36 TAXATION

In 1999, the individual income tax ranged up to 25%, and the corporate income tax rate was 25%. Other taxes included a 15% sales tax; a luxury tax generally lower than 15%; a 1% municipal tax levied on sales; a 1% tax on net worth; and a real estate tax at 1% of assessed value.

37 CUSTOMS AND DUTIES

In 1990, the government's liberalized import schedule allowed private sector imports for the first time in 11 years. Import licenses are only required for the import of sugar. Nicaragua follows the CACM common import tariff schedule with rates ranging from 5% to 15%. Duties are set on an ad valorem basis, and there is a specific consumption (less than 15%) and sales tax (15%). There are also a few prohibitive import duties, like that of chicken at 190%. An Industrial Free Zone operates at Las Mercedes near the Managua international airport. Employment in the Zone more than doubled from 1995 to 1998. There are also two private free zones, and construction of four others was authorized in 1999.

Nicaragua has free trade agreements with Mexico and the Dominican Republic; and is a member of the Central American Common Market (CACM). The country is also a Caribbean Basin Initiative beneficiary.

38 FOREIGN INVESTMENT

Until the 1979 revolution, Nicaragua encouraged private investment. Virtually no restrictions were imposed on the remittance of profits or the repatriation of capital. The economic and political climate for foreign investors in the 1980s was bleak, despite the claim that the Sandinista government was prepared to offer more favorable investment terms (including 100% foreign ownership and repatriation of profits) than the Somoza government had provided. As of 1984, direct US investment in Nicaragua had stopped completely.

As of 1994, Nicaragua has recovered some of the international credibility lost in the previous decade. Under the New Foreign investment Law, the government of Nicaragua has concentrated most of its efforts on the expansion and promotion of foreign and national investment. This law, among other things, guarantees the repatriation of invested capital and generated capital. Also, it allows for 100% foreign ownership in all areas.

Foreign private capital inflows doubled from $97 million in 1996, to $184 million in 1998. The US is Nicaragua's largest trading partner by far—the source of 32% of its imports and the destination for 42% of its exports. About 25 wholly or partly owned subsidiaries of US companies operate in Nicaragua. The largest investments are in the energy, communications, manufacturing, fisheries, and shrimp farming sectors. Good opportunities exist for further investments in those same sectors, as well as in tourism, construction, services, mining, and agriculture.

39 ECONOMIC DEVELOPMENT

The Somoza government's 1975–79 National Reconstruction and Development Plan had as its major objective the improvement in living conditions through increased employment, continuing reconstruction of Managua, reduction in the economy's dependence on the external sector, acceleration of regional development, and strengthening of the country's role in CACM. The plan was disrupted by the civil strife in the late 1970s.

After the 1979 revolution, the government nationalized banking, insurance, mining, fishing, forestry, and a number of industrial plans. Although the government officially favored a mixed economy, in practice the private sector took second place in a development strategy that focused on public investment and control.

In response to the macroeconomic problems that arose in 1992, a series of measures were adopted by the Chamorro administration aimed at consolidating the stabilization process, increasing the competitiveness of exports and establishing a base for the promotion of growth.

Nicaragua now appears poised for rapid economic growth. However, long-term success at attracting investment, creating jobs, and reducing poverty depend on its ability to comply with an International Monetary Fund (IMF) program, resolve the thousands of Sandinista-era property confiscation cases, and open its economy to foreign trade.

The Alemán government was faced with poverty (over 70%), unemployment and underemployment (over 50%), one of the highest per capita debt ratios in the world ($6 billion) and one of the highest population growth rates of the hemisphere (2.8%); in 1999. The new president signed an IMF Structural Adjustment Program for Nicaragua in 1998 that aimed at cutting the fiscal deficit, continuing liberalization, and maintaining monetary stability. Nicaragua received at least $2.5 billion for reconstruction in the aftermath of the hurricane, debt deferral until 2001, and debt forgiveness through the Highly Indebted Poor Country (HIPC) program.

40 SOCIAL DEVELOPMENT

Nicaragua's basic social welfare system was established during the Somoza period. A social insurance law enacted in 1956 provides for national compulsory coverage of employees against risks of maternity, sickness, employment injury, occupational disease, unemployment, old age, and death. These programs are financed by contributions from employers, employees and the government, and provide coverage for paid employees. Family allowance legislation enacted in 1982 provides benefits for the children of employees under the age of 15, but are provided on an earnings-tested basis.

There is no official discrimination against women, and a number of women hold government positions. However, women continue to suffer de facto sex discrimination in many segments of society. They tend to hold traditionally low-paid jobs in the health, education, and textile sectors while occupying few management positions in the private sector. In 1995, however, women held both the presidency and the vice-presidency. As of 1996, 9 of 93 members of Parliament were women. Domestic and sexual violence are common, and the perpetrators are seldom prosecuted. In 1997, the stepdaughter of Sandinista leader and former president Daniel Ortega filed charges accusing Ortega of having sexually molested her from the age 11. She led an effort to rescind Ortega's immunity from prosecution as a National Assembly deputy; the matter was still pending at the end of 1998.

Dire economic circumstances force many children to work to contribute to household income. Labor laws prohibit children under the age of 12 from working, and limit children aged 12–16 to working six hours a day. Many children work for low wages on banana or coffee plantations, while in urban areas, children often work as vendors in the streets. The Child and Family Act that took effect in late 1998 barred juveniles from being held in adult correction facilities and extended other types of protection to minors.

Human rights abuses have declined since 1995, but there were continued reports of the mistreatment of detainees, although torture is punishable by law.

41 HEALTH

Slow progress in health care was made from the 1960s through the 1980s, as the crude death rate dropped from 19 per 1,000 population in 1960 to 6.8 in 1990-95; during 1996, the infant mortality rate was 47 per 1,000 live births, and average life expectancy was 68.4 years in 1998. The maternal mortality rate was 124 per 100,000 live births in 1997. However, malnutrition and anemia remained common, poliomyelitis and goiter were endemic, and intestinal parasitic infections (a leading cause of death) afflicted over 80% of the population. The prevalence of child malnutrition was 12% of children under 5 in 1989–95. The goiter rate was 4.3 per 100 school age children. There were 2,836 reported cases of tuberculosis in 1990–95. Immunization rates for children up to one year old in 1997 were as follows: tuberculosis (99%); diphtheria, pertussis, and tetanus (94%); polio (99%); and measles (94%). Total health care expenditures for 1995 were $35 per capita.

Safe water is available to 61% of the Nicaraguan population in 1990–95. In 1997, according to UNICEF, the maternal mortality rate was 124 per 100,000 live births. The fertility rate was 5 per 1,000 people in 1990–95. The 1990–95 birthrate was 3.9 births per woman, with 44% of married women (ages 15 to 49) using some form of contraception in 1997. In 1995, there were 11 hospital beds per 1,000 inhabitants. In 1997 there were 7 doctors per 10,000 people.

The HIV-1 seroprevalence was 0.2 per 100 adults in 1997. A total of only 114 AIDS cases had been reported by 1995. Common diseases reported in Nicaragua were malaria (70,235 cases in 1995), cholera (2,979 in 1996), and tuberculosis (2,836 in 1990–95).

42 HOUSING

Both urban and rural dwellers suffer from a dire lack of adequate housing. As a result of the 1972 earthquake, approximately 53,000 residential units were destroyed or seriously damaged in the Managua area. The Sandinistas launched housing-construction and tree-planting programs, but were hampered by a shortage of hard currency to pay for the construction equipment required. An estimated 69% of dwellings are detached houses; 19% are rural homes called ranchos; and 9% are cuartes, or private units with some common facilities. Over 60% of all housing is owner occupied and 20% is rented.

43 EDUCATION

After the Sandinista takeover, a literacy campaign (with the help of 2,000 Cuban teachers) was launched in 1980. At the end of the campaign, the government claimed that the adult illiteracy rate, which was 50% in 1975, had been reduced to 13%. For the year 2000, the rate of adult illiteracy has been estimated at 35.7% (males, 35.8%; females, 35.6%).

Primary and secondary education is free and compulsory between the ages of 6 and 13. In 1998, 783,002 pupils attended 7,224 primary schools. Also in 1998, 287,476 students were enrolled in secondary schools, with approximately 6,000 teachers. In 1997, there were a total of 56,558 students enrolled in institutions of higher learning, with 3,840 teachers.

The National Autonomous University of Nicaragua offers instruction in 10 faculties: medicine, law and social sciences, dentistry, chemistry, and humanities in León; and agriculture, education, economics, physical and mathematical sciences, and humanities in Managua. The Central American University, affiliated with Georgetown University, opened in Managua in 1961, and the privately controlled Polytechnic University of Nicaragua, also in Managua, attained university status in 1977. Some others include the Central American Institute for Business Management, affiliated with the Harvard Business School, the University of Mobile, affiliated with Mobile College, Alabama; Nicaraguan Catholic University, and the National Engineering University. There were a total of 14 universities in Nicaragua in 1998.

44 LIBRARIES AND MUSEUMS

The National Library in Managua is the largest library in the country, holding a collection of 80,000 volumes. The National

Autonomous University of Nicaragua in Leon holds the largest university collection with 36,700 volumes. In 1990, Nicaragua had 13 branch public libraries holding a total of 187,000 volumes. The largest branch is in Leon, and holds 32,000 volumes. There is a Central American Institute in Managua with 39,000 volumes focusing on the social and economic conditions of the region. The National Museum, founded in 1896, is in Managua. There is an archeological museum in Granada and three provincial historical and archeological museums.

45 MEDIA

Postal, telegraph, and telephone facilities are government-owned. Since 1990, TELCOR, the national communications company, has invested over $100 million on upgrading its facilities. Telephone service is limited to the heavily populated west coast and, except for Managua (where there is an automatic dial system), is inadequate. In 1995 there were 66,800 telephone lines. Radiotelephone circuits allow communication between the west and east coasts. As of 1999 there were 45 AM radio stations, no FM stations, and 3 TV stations. Radio Católica, a Roman Catholic station, was closed by the government in 1986 but was reopened in 1987 in accordance with the democratic freedoms outlined in the Arias peace plan. The Voice of Nicaragua is the government station. In 1997, 283 radios, 190 television sets, and 2 mobile phones were in use per 1,000 population.

There were four daily newspapers in 1999 including *Nuevo Diario,* with a circulation of 50,000, and the *Barricada* with 95,000. *La Prensa,* a harsh critic of Somoza rule and of the Sandinista regime, was closed in 1986 but, in accordance with the Arias peace plan, was allowed to resume publication in 1987; its 1999 circulation was 75,000. Press censorship ended with the departure of the Sandinista government. The constitution provides for freedom of speech and the press, and the government is said to be supportive of these rights in practice. The privately owned print media and the broadcast media openly discuss diverse viewpoints without government interference.

As of 1996, there were 295 Internet hosts in Nicaragua. Online access is extremely limited, with approximately one Internet host per 1,000 population in 1998.

46 ORGANIZATIONS

In 1993 there were three cooperative organizations including one for cotton growers and one for shoemakers and leather workers. There were four employers' organizations as of that year. Of the employers' associations, the most important was the Higher Council of Private Enterprise (Consejo Superior de la Empresa Privada—COSEP).

47 TOURISM, TRAVEL, AND RECREATION

Although Nicaragua has beaches on two oceans, magnificent mountain and tropical scenery, and the two largest lakes in Central America, a decade of military conflict retarded the development of the tourist industry. In 1997, 358,000 tourists arrived in Nicaragua and tourist revenues reached $74 million. In that year there were 2,217 hotel rooms with 4,002 beds and an occupancy rate of 65%. All visitors must have a valid passport. US citizens can obtain 30-day visas. Baseball is the national sport. Basketball, cockfighting, bullfighting, and water sports are also popular.

According to 1999 UN estimates, the cost of staying in Managua ranges from $118 to $166 depending upon the choice of hotel.

48 FAMOUS NICARAGUANS

International literary fame came to Nicaragua with the publication of *Azul,* a collection of lyric poetry and short stories by Rubén Darío (Félix Rubén Garcia-Sarmiento, 1867–1916). Born in Metapa (renamed Ciudad Darío in his honor), Darío created a new literary style in Spanish, exemplified by "art for art's sake" and a revelry in the senses. Miguel Larreynaga (1771–1845) was an outstanding figure during the colonial period and later an ardent independence leader, teacher, jurist, and author. Santiago Arguëllo (1872–1940) was a noted poet and educator. Three modern poets are Fray Azarías Pallais (1885–1954), Alfonso Cortés (1893–1963), and Salomón de la Selva (1893–1959). Luis Abraham Delgadillo (1887–1961), a writer, educator, and musical conductor, was also Nicaragua's leading composer.

The Somoza family, which ruled Nicaragua from 1934 to 1979, included Anastasio Somoza García (1896–1956), president during 1937–47 and again during 1950–56; his oldest son, Luis Somoza Debayle (1922–67), president during 1956–63; and a younger son, Anastasio Somoza Debayle (1925–80), president during 1967–72 and again from 1974 until the 1979 revolution. The Sandinistas, who overthrew the Somoza dynasty, take their name from the nationalist Gen. Augusto César Sandino (1895–1934). José Daniel Ortega Saavedra (b.1946) emerged as the leading figure in the junta that governed Nicaragua from 1979 to 1990.

49 DEPENDENCIES

Nicaragua has no territories or colonies.

50 BIBLIOGRAPHY

Borge, Tomás, et al. *The Sandinistas Speak: Speeches and Writings of Nicaragua's Leaders.* New York: Pathfinder, 1982.

Brentlinger, John. *The Best of What We Are: Reflections on the Nicaraguan Revolution.* Amherst, Mass.: University of Massachusetts Press, 1995.

Dijkstra, Geske. *Industrialization in Sandinista Nicaragua: Policy and Practice in a Mixed Economy.* Boulder, Colo.: Westview, 1992.

Kagan, Robert. *A Twilight Struggle: American Power and Nicaragua, 1977-1990.* New York: Free Press, 1996.

Luciak, Ilja A. *The Sandinista Legacy: Lessons from a Political Economy in Transition.* Gainesville: University Press of Florida, 1995.

Nicaragua: A Country Study. 2d ed. Edited by James D. Rudolph. Washington, D.C.: Government Printing Office, 1994.

Nolan, David. *The Ideology of the Sandinistas and the Nicaraguan Revolution.* Miami: University of Miami North-South Center, 1984.

Norsworthy, Kent. *Nicaragua: A Country Guide.* 2d ed. Albuquerque, N.M.: Inter-Hemispheric Education Resource Center, 1990.

Paths to Central American Prehistory. Edited by Frederick W. Lange. Niwot, Colo.: University Press of Colorado, 1996.

Pezzullo, Lawrence. *At the Fall of Somoza.* Pittsburgh: University of Pittsburgh Press, 1993.

The Rise and Fall of the Nicaraguan Revolution. New York: Pathfinder, 1994.

Spalding, Rose J. (ed.). *The Political Economy of Revolutionary Nicaragua.* Boston: Allen & Unwin, 1987.

Stanislawski, Dan. *The Transformation of Nicaragua.* Berkeley: University of California Press, 1983.

Vanden, Harry E. *Democracy and Socialism in Sandinista Nicaragua.* Boulder, Colo.: L. Rienner, 1993.

Walker, Thomas W. (ed.). *Nicaragua in Revolution.* New York: Praeger, 1982.

——. (ed.). *Revolution & Counterrevolution in Nicaragua.* Boulder, Colo.: Westview, 1991.

——. *Nicaragua, the Land of Sandino.* 3rd ed. Boulder, Colo.: Westview, 1991.

Woodward, Ralph Lee, Jr. *Central America: A Nation Divided.* 2d ed. New York: Oxford University Press, 1985.

PANAMA

Republic of Panama
República de Panamá

CAPITAL: Panama City (Panamá).

FLAG: The national flag is divided into quarters. The upper quarter next to the staff is white with a blue star; the upper outer quarter is red; the lower quarter next to the staff is blue; and the lower outer quarter is white with a red star.

ANTHEM: *Himno Nacional,* beginning "Alcanzamos por fin la victoria" ("We reach victory at last").

MONETARY UNIT: The balboa (B) of 100 centésimos is the national unit of account. Panama issues no paper money, and US notes are legal tender. Panama mints coins of 0.05, 0.10, 0.25, 0.50, 1 and 5 balboas which are interchangeable with US coins. B1=$1.00 (or $1=B1.00)

WEIGHTS AND MEASURES: The metric system is official, but British, US, and old Spanish units are also used.

HOLIDAYS: New Year's Day, 1 January; Martyrs' Day, 9 January; Labor Day, 1 May; National Revolution Day, 11 October; National Anthem Day, 1 November; All Souls' Day, 2 November; Independence from Colombia, 3 November; Flag Day, 4 November; Independence Day (Colón only), 5 November; First Call of Independence, 10 November; Independence from Spain, 28 November; Mother's Day and Immaculate Conception, 8 December; Christmas, 25 December. Movable religious holidays are Shrove Tuesday and Good Friday.

TIME: 7 AM = noon GMT.

¹LOCATION, SIZE, AND EXTENT

The Republic of Panama, situated on the Isthmus of Panama, has an area of 78,200 sq km (30,193 sq mi). Comparatively, the area occupied by Panama is slightly smaller than the state of South Carolina. The Canal Zone (1,432 sq km/553 sq mi), over which the US formerly exercised sovereignty, was incorporated into Panama on 1 October 1979, with the US retaining responsibility for operation of the Panama Canal and the use of land in the zone for maintenance of the canal until the year 2000.

Panama extends 406 km (252 mi) ESE-WNW and 280 km (174 mi) NNE-SSW west of the Panama Canal and 345 km (214 mi) ESE-WNW and 167 km (104 mi) NNE-SSW east of the canal. Bordered on the N by the Caribbean Sea, on the E by Colombia, on the S by the Pacific Ocean, and on the W by Costa Rica, Panama has a total boundary length of 3,045 km (1,892 mi).

Panama's capital city, Panama City, is located where the Panama Canal meets the Gulf of Panama.

²TOPOGRAPHY

Panama is a country of heavily forested hills and mountain ranges. The two principal ranges are in the eastern and western sections of the country, and a third, minor range extends southward along the Pacific coast into Colombia. The eastern Serranía del Darién parallels the Caribbean coastline, while the Serranía de Tabasará ascends westward, culminating in the Barú volcano (3,475 m/11,401 ft), formerly known as Chiriquí. Between these ranges, the land breaks into high plateaus, ridges, and valleys. The Panama Canal utilizes a gap in these ranges that runs northwest to southeast and averages only 87 m (285 ft) in altitude. Panama has more than 300 rivers, most of which flow into the Pacific, with only the Tuira River in Darién Province of any commercial importance. Both coasts of the isthmus have deep bays, but the Gulf of Panama is especially well provided with deepwater anchorages. Panama also has more than 1,600 islands, including the Amerindian-inhabited San Blas Islands in the

Caribbean (366) and the Pearls Archipelago in the Gulf of Panama (over 100). Its largest island is the penal colony Coiba, which is south of the Gulf of Chiriquí.

³CLIMATE

Panama is tropical, but temperatures vary according to location and altitude. The annual average temperature on both coasts is 27°C (81°F), and it ranges from 10° to 19°C (50 to 66°F) at various mountain elevations. There is little seasonal change in temperature, with warm days and cool nights throughout the year. Humidity is quite high, however, averaging 80%. Rainfall averages 178 cm (70 in) in Panama City and 328 cm (129 in) in Colón. The period of lightest rainfall is from January to March.

⁴FLORA AND FAUNA

Most of Panama is a thick jungle, with occasional patches of savanna or prairie. On the wet Caribbean coast, the forest is evergreen, while on the drier Pacific side the forest is semi-deciduous. Species of flowering plants exceed 2,000 and include the national flower, the Holy Ghost orchid. Mammals inhabiting the isthmus are the anteater, armadillo, bat, coati, deer, opossum, peccary, raccoon, tapir, and many varieties of monkey. Reptiles, especially alligators, are numerous along the coasts. Bird life is rich and varies according to the presence of migratory species. Fish abound, and the Pacific coast is a favored region for sport fishing.

⁵ENVIRONMENT

Soil erosion and deforestation are among Panama's most significant environmental concerns. Soil erosion is occurring at a rate of 2,000 tons per year. During the late 1980s and early 1990s, Panama lost 139 sq mi of its forests. Air pollution is also a problem in urban centers due to emissions from industry and transportation. In the mid-1990s, industrial carbon dioxide emissions totaled 4.2 million metric tons, a per capita level of

1.69 metric tons. Water pollution directly affects 73% of rural dwellers who do not have pure drinking water. Pesticides, sewage, and pollution from the oil industry cause much of the pollution. Agencies with environmental responsibilities include the Ministry of Health and Ministry of Rural Development. The Smithsonian Tropical Research Institute, in Balboa, conducts studies on the conservation of natural resources. The nation's fish resources are threatened by water pollution. Thirteen of Panama's mammal species are endangered. Fourteen of the nation's bird species are also endangered. Of the nation's plant species, a total of 549 are threatened with extinction. Endangered or extinct species include the red-backed squirrel monkey, tundra peregrine falcon, spectacled caiman, American crocodile, and four species of sea turtle (green sea, hawksbill, olive ridley, and leatherback).

6 POPULATION

The population of Panama in 2000 was estimated at 2,821,085. An estimated 5.3% of the population is 65 years of age or older. The projected population for the year 2005 is 3,030,000, assuming a crude birthrate of 20 per 1,000 population and a death rate of 5, resulting in a natural rate of change of 1.4% for the period 2000–2005. The population rate of change between 1995 and 2000 was 1.6%. The population density in 1998 was 37 per sq km (96 per sq mi).

It was estimated that 58% of the population lived in urban areas in 2000, up from 50% in 1980. The capital, Panama City, had a 2000 metropolitan population of 1,088,000. Other major cities include Colón, 140,908; and David, 102,678.

7 MIGRATION

Immigration and emigration have been roughly in balance in recent years. In the 1990s, there were 61,400 foreign-born persons in Panama, of which 13,644 were Colombians. In 1999, UNHCR urged Panamanian authorities to take a more flexible approach toward Colombians who arrived after February 1998 and are under a Temporary Protection plan. UNHCR also made possible the voluntary repatriation of some 40 individuals in 1999. A decree was drafted to facilitate the change of the migratory status of long-stay refugees, which will benefit Salvadorans and Nicaraguans. In 1999, the net migration rate was estimated at -1.22 migrants per 1,000 population.

8 ETHNIC GROUPS

The racial and cultural composition of Panama is highly diverse. According to recent estimates, some 70% of the inhabitants are mestizo (mixed Amerindian and white) or mulatto (mixed white and black); 14% are Amerindian and mixed (West Indian); 10% are white (mostly Europeans); and 6% are Amerindian. There is also a Chinese community of about 100,000. About 100,000 Amerindians live in isolation in eastern Panama and on the San Blas Islands.

9 LANGUAGES

Spanish, the official language of Panama, is spoken by over 90% of the people, but English is a common second language, spoken by most Panamanian professionals and businesspeople. The Amerindians use their own languages. Many Panamanians are bilingual.

10 RELIGIONS

Although Roman Catholicism is recognized by the constitution of 1972 as the majority religion, the constitution also guarantees religious freedom, as well as separation of church and state. In 1998, an estimated 82% of the people were Roman Catholic; 10% were evangelical; and 3% were unaffiliated with any religious group. There were small groups of Latter-Day Saints (Mormons), Seventh-Day Adventists, Jehovah's Witnesses, Episcopalians, and other Christians. Buddhists, Jews, Muslims, and Baha'is also had small communities. Panama is home to one of the world's seven Baha'i Houses of Worship.

11 TRANSPORTATION

Motor vehicles transport most agricultural products. In 1999 there were 11,100 km (6,898 mi) of roads, of which about 3,730 km (2,318 mi) were paved, including 30 km (19 mi) of expressways. The principal highway is the National (or Central) Highway—the Panamanian section of the Pan American Highway—which runs from the Costa Rican border, via Panama City and Chepo, to the Colombian border. The 80-km (50-mi) Trans-Isthmian Highway links Colón and Panama City. Panama's rugged terrain impedes highway development, and there are few good roads in the republic's eastern sections. In 1995 there were 140,900 registered passenger cars and 79,000 trucks and buses.

Railway lines total 355 km (220 mi) of track, all government-run. The Panama Railroad parallels the canal for 77 km (48 mi) between Colón and Panama City. Other lines connect Pedregal, David, Puerto Armuelles, and Boquete and unify Bocas del Toro Province.

In 1998, the Panamanian merchant marine registered 4,632 ships, totaling 98,433,972 GRT. Most of the ships are foreign-owned but are registered as Panamanian because fees are low and labor laws lenient. International shipping passes almost entirely through the canal ports of Cristóbal, which serves Colón, and Balboa, which is the port for Panama City.

Panama is a crossroads for air travel within the Americas. In 1998 there were an estimated 110 airports, 43 of which had paved runways. The most widely used domestic airline is Compañía Panameña de Aviación (COPA), which also flies throughout Central America. Air Panama International serves passenger traffic to the US and South America, and Internacional de Aviación (INAIR) is an international passenger and cargo carrier. The main airfield is Omar Torrijos International Airport, 19 km (12 mi) east of Panama City. In 1997, 772,000 passengers were carried on scheduled domestic and international airline flights.

The Panama Canal—built during 1904–14 by the US Army Corps of Engineers, under Col. George Washington Goethals—traverses the isthmus and is 82 km (51 mi) in length from deep water to deep water. The great technical feat involved in constructing the canal was to cut through the mountains that span the region, dam the Chagres Lake, and then design and build the three sets of double locks that raise and lower ships the 26 m (85 ft) between lake and sea levels. The first passage through the canal was completed by the S.S. Ancon on 15 August 1914. When the US-Panama treaties went into effect on 1 October 1979, the canal was administered by the joint Panama Canal Commission, on which the US had majority representation through the end of 1989. The US turned over complete control of the canal to Panama on 31 December 1999. The canal takes ships of up to 67,000 tons. An oil pipeline across the isthmus was opened in 1982 to carry Alaskan oil; its capacity is 830,000 barrels per day. The Bridge of the Americas across the canal at the Pacific entrance unites eastern and western Panama as well as the northern and southern sections of the Pan American Highway. Panama, the US, and Japan have commissioned a $20-million study to search for alternatives to the canal. The feasibility of building a new canal at sea level is to be examined; alternatively, the Panama Canal Commission has indicated its intention to increase the width of the Gaillard Cut (Corte Culebra), since larger ships are restricted to one-way daylight passage, due to the narrowness. Panama also plans to consolidate the ports of Balboa on the Pacific and Cristóbal on the Caribbean into a single container terminal system.

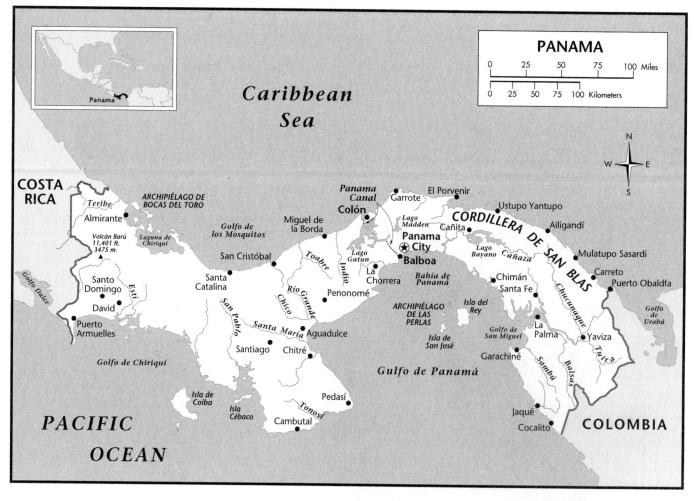

LOCATION: 7°12′9″ to 9°37′ 57″N; 77°9′24″ to 83°3′7″W. **BOUNDARY LENGTHS:** Caribbean coastline, 624 km (388 mi); Colombia, 266 km (165 mi); Pacific coastline, 1,188 km (738 mi); Costa Rica, 363 km (266 mi). **TERRITORIAL SEA LIMIT:** 200 mi.

12 HISTORY

The isthmian region was an area of economic transshipment long before Europeans explored it. It was also the converging point of several significant Amerindian cultures. Mayan, Aztec, Chibcha, and Caribs had indirect and direct contact with the area. The first European to explore Panama was the Spaniard Rodrigo de Bastidas in 1501. In 1502, Columbus claimed the region for Spain. In 1513, Vasco Nuñez de Balboa led soldiers across the isthmus and made the European discovery of the Pacific Ocean. Despite strong resistance by the Cuna Amerindians, the settlements of Nombre de Dios, San Sebastián, and, later, Portobelo were established on the Caribbean coast, while Panama City was founded on the Pacific coast. In 1567, Panama was made part of the viceroyalty of Peru. English buccaneers, notably Sir Francis Drake in the 16th century and Henry Morgan in the 17th, contested Spanish hegemony in Panama, burning and looting its ports, including Panama City in 1671.

From the 16th until the mid-18th century, the isthmus was a strategic link in Spanish trade with the west coast of South America, especially the viceregal capital of Lima. In 1740, the isthmus was placed under the jurisdiction of the newly recreated viceroyalty of New Granada.

Panama declared its independence from Spain in 1821 and joined the Republic of Gran Colombia, a short-lived union of Colombia, Venezuela, and Ecuador, founded in 1819. In 1826, it was the seat of the Pan American Conference called by the Liberator, Simón Bolívar. When Gran Colombia was dissolved in 1829–30, Panama still remained part of Colombia. Secessionist revolts took place in 1830 and 1831, and during 1840–41.

The discovery of gold in California in 1848 brought the isthmus into prominence as a canal site linking the Atlantic and Pacific oceans. After the French failed to build one in the 1880s, they sold those rights to the US for $40 million. The US then negotiated the Hay-Herrán Treaty with Colombia in 1903. After Colombia refused to ratify the treaty, Panama seceded from Colombia and, backed by US naval forces, declared its independence on 3 November 1903. Panama then signed a canal agreement with the US and received a lump sum of $10 million and an annual rent of $250,000. The Hay-Bunau-Varilla Treaty (1903) granted the US in perpetuity an 8-km (5-mi) strip of land on either side of the canal and permitted the US to intervene to protect Panamanian independence, to defend the canal, and to maintain order in the cities of Panama and Colón and in the Canal Zone.

The US intervened to establish order in 1908—while the canal was under construction—and, after the canal had opened to traffic, in 1917 and again in 1918. In 1936, however, the US adopted a policy of nonintervention, and in 1955, the annuity was raised to $1,930,000.

During the postwar decades, the question of sovereignty over the Canal Zone was a persistent irritant in Panamanian politics. On 9 January 1964, riots broke out in the Canal Zone as Panamanians protested US neglect of a 1962 joint Panama-US flag-flying agreement. On the following day, Panama suspended relations with the US and demanded complete revision of the Canal Zone treaty. Thereafter, Panama sought sovereignty over the Canal Zone and the elimination of the concept of perpetuity on any future arrangement. Diplomatic relations were restored in April, but negotiations went slowly thereafter.

The Panamanian government turned to dictatorship in October 1968, when National Guard Brig. Gen. Omar Torrijos Herrera deposed the elected president and established a dictatorship.

Final agreement on the future of the canal and the Canal Zone came on 7 September 1977, when Gen. Torrijos and US President Jimmy Carter signed two documents at OAS headquarters in Washington, D.C. The first document, the Panama Canal Treaty, abrogated the 1903 Hay-Bunau-Varilla accord, recognized Panama's sovereignty over the Canal Zone (which ceased to exist as of 1 October 1979), and granted the US rights to operate, maintain, and manage the canal through 31 December 1999, when ownership of the canal itself would revert to Panama. Panama would receive a fixed annuity of $10 million and a subsidy of $0.30 (to be adjusted periodically for inflation) for every ton of cargo that passed through the canal, plus up to $10 million annually from operating surpluses. The second document, the so-called Neutrality Treaty, guaranteed the neutrality of the canal for "peaceful transit by the vessels of all nations" in time of both peace and war. An additional provision added in October denied the US the right of intervention into Panamanian affairs. The treaties were ratified by plebiscite in Panama on 23 October 1977 and, after prolonged debate and extensive amendment, by the US Senate in March and April 1978. When both treaties came into force in 1979, about 60% of the former Canal Zone's total area immediately came under Panama's direct control, including 11 of 14 military bases, the Panama City-Colón railway, and ports at both ends of the canal.

The Torrijos regime was populist, with a wide appeal to the neglected lower and lower middle classes of Panama. Moreover, Torrijos established nationalist credentials by standing up to the US and demanding recognition of Panama's positions on the Canal Zone. Torrijos resigned as head of government in 1978 but continued to rule behind the scenes as National Guard commander until his death in a plane crash on 31 July 1981. Over the next few years, the National Guard, now renamed the Panama Defense Forces (PDF), came under the influence of Gen. Manuel Noriega.

On the civilian side, Aristedes Royo was elected president by the Assembly in October 1978, and was forced out of office in July 1982. His successor was the vice-president, Ricardo de la Espriella, who resigned in February 1984, just three months before scheduled presidential elections. In those elections, the economist and former World Bank official Nicolás Ardito Barletta, the military's approved candidate, won a close victory over former president Arnulfo Arias Madrid (running for the fifth time), in an election marked by voting irregularities and fraud. Barletta soon lost the confidence of the military and was forced out in September 1985. Vice-President Eric Arturo Delvalle assumed power.

By 1987, Noriega had been accused by close associates and the US of falsifying the 1984 election results, plotting the deaths of prominent opposition leaders and Gen. Torrijos, drug trafficking, giving aid to the Colombian radical group M-19 and Salvadoran rebels, and providing intelligence and restricted US technology to Cuba. Opposition forces, including the Roman Catholic Church, intensified and the government responded by banning public protest. The US Senate approved legislation cutting off aid to Panama in December 1987. In February 1988, following indictments of Noriega in US courts for drug trafficking, President Delvalle announced Noriega's dismissal. Noriega refused to step down, and the Legislative Assembly voted to remove Delvalle from office and replace him with Manuel Solís Palma, the minister of education. Delvalle went into hiding, and Panama entered a two-year period of instability and conflict.

Domestically, Noriega suffered from a lack of support. In March 1987, a general strike occurred for several weeks. Emboldened by US efforts to remove Noriega, opposition forces coalesced, even as the government became more repressive. In elections held in May 1989, opposition candidates scored overwhelming victories, forcing Noriega to annul the elections and rely on intimidation and force.

Noriega also had problems within the PDF. Dissident military leaders, with either tacit or direct US approval, attempted coups in March 1988 and in October 1989. Unable to rely on the loyalty of the PDF, Noriega created his own paramilitary force, called the "Dignity Batallions," which were nothing more than free-lance thugs called in at the dictator's whim.

Finally, the US was engaged in a series of moves calculated to bring down the Noriega regime, which eventually led to a showdown. In March 1988, President Reagan suspended preferential trade conditions and withheld canal-use payments. In April, Reagan froze US-held Panamanian assets and suspended all private payments to Panama. Negotiations to allow Noriega to step down dissolved in May, when Noriega refused to abide by an agreement between the US and Noriega's assistants. The administration of President Bush continued pressure on Noriega, but itself came under criticism for its inability to resolve the problem. Finally, in December 1989, Noriega played his final card, declaring war on the US and ordering attacks on US military personnel.

President Bush responded quickly, ordering the US military into Panama. The troops remained for a week, delayed when Noriega sought sanctuary in the residence of the Papal Nuncio. Noriega surrendered, and was returned to the US for trial. Immediately, the Panamanian Electoral Tribunal declared the 1989 elections valid and confirmed the results. Guillermo Endara became president, Ricardo Arias Calderón first vice-president, and Guillermo "Billy" Ford second vice-president. Legislative elections were confirmed for most Legislative Assembly seats, and in January 1991 a special election filled the remaining seats. Under President Endara, Panama made some strides toward economic recovery, but these were only impressive because the situation under Noriega had become so desperate. Politically, Endara lacked nationalist credentials, especially since he was installed by US military might. His administration was widely criticized for the continuing poor economic conditions. In May 1994, a new president, Ernesto Pérez Balladares, was elected in the country's first free and fair elections since 1968. Balladares's Democratic Revolutionary Party (PRD) was closely associated with the Noriega dictatorship but the new president identified himself with the populist Torrijos regime and included both independents and opposition figures as well as PRD members in his cabinet. In 1995 government reform of the country's labor code touched off widespread strikes and rioting, including a 10-day general strike in August. Balladares's economic reforms, including lowered tariffs and reductions in the public sector, failed to produce significant improvements by 1996, with economic growth remaining low and unemployment high (between 13% and 15%). In addition, both PRD and the other political parties faced allegations that they had accepted money from drug traffickers, including a leading figure in Colombia's Cali cartel. With Panama's notorious Defense Forces disbanded and the wide public availability of weapons, street crime and kidnappings increased.

As the end of the decade neared, the country prepared for the withdrawal of the US military on 31 December 1999, under the terms of the Panama Canal Treaty. Panamanian President Mireya Moscoso officiated the formal ceremony where the United States relinquished power over the Canal. On 31 December 1999, the Panama Canal was officially handed over to Panamanian rule; this marked an end to 80 years of US occupation. Though the accompanying ceremony took place a week prior to the historic date due to potential complications with millennium celebrations, the significance was nonetheless grand. The ceremony, officiated by Moscoso and former United States President Jimmy Carter, also included King Juan Carlos of Spain and several Latin American leaders. Carter, who began the process to granting Panama control over the waterway more than 20 years ago under a treaty with then-president General Omar Torrijos, signed over the United States rule. President Bill Clinton declined invitations to attend the ceremony. The celebrations that ensued were overshadowed somewhat by concerns from US conservative politicians that the Canal will not be secure in Panamanian hands. However, President Clinton pledged continued collaboration with Panama to ensure the Canal's security.

13GOVERNMENT

Under the constitution of 1972, Panama is a republic in which the president, assisted by a cabinet, exercises executive power. Reforms adopted in April 1983 changed the election of the president from an absolute majority of the National Assembly of Municipal Representatives to a direct popular vote, and a second vice-president was added. The president and the two vice-presidents must be at least 35 years of age and native Panamanians; they serve for five years and are not eligible for immediate reelection.

Legislative power is vested in the unicameral Legislative Assembly, which replaced the National Assembly of Municipal Representatives in 1984. The 72 members are elected for five-year terms by direct popular vote. Regular sessions are from 11 October to 11 November annually, and special sessions may be called by the president. Suffrage is universal for Panamanians 18 years of age or over.

The 1972 constitution conferred extraordinary decision-making powers upon the commander of the Panama Defense Forces (PDF), who was allowed to participate in sessions of all executive and legislative organs, to direct foreign policy, to appoint Supreme Court magistrates, and to appoint and remove ministers of state, among other responsibilities.

The PDF was subsequently converted into a civilian group called the Public Forces. Following a purge of PDF senior officials, the Public Forces were placed under the cabinet-level Minister of Government and Justice.

14POLITICAL PARTIES

Personalities rather than ideological platforms tend to be the dominating force in Panamanian politics. The traditional political parties were the Liberals and the Conservatives, and their differences lay initially in the issue of church and state power. More recently, parties tended to be coalitions of the many splinter groups that had formed around local leaders. Military interventions frequently led to the banning of political parties. Such interruptions have led to an extremely splintered party system, which held together only insofar as they opposed the military regimes.

The coalition that came to power in 1990 consisted of President Endara's Arnulfista Party, led by Dr. Arnulfo Escalona, the National Liberal Republican Movement (MOLIRENA), led by second vice-president Guillermo Ford and the Christian Democratic Party (PDC), led by first vice president Ricardo Arias.

Subsequently, Arias broke from the coalition, and the PDC, which held a plurality of seats in the Legislative Assembly, became the leader of the opposition.

With the election of Ernesto Pérez Balladares to the presidency in May 1994, the Democratic Revolutionary Party (PRD), which had been closely linked to the country's former military regime, was returned to power, as part of a coalition that also included the Liberal Republican Party (PLR) and the Labor Party (PALA). This coalition gained effective control of the National Assembly as well as the executive branch.

Opposition parties included MOLIRENA, the PDC, the Authentic Liberal Party (PLA), the Arnulfista Party (PA), the Solidarity Party (PS), the Liberal Party (PL), and others.

The years of Pérez Balladeres rule were characterized by a multi-party cabinet that included several members who publicly denounced former dictator Manuel Noriega. Peréz Balladeres set in motion various economic reforms and continued close collaboration with the United States to implement treaties regarding the eventual turnover of the Panama Canal to Panamanian rule [which occurred 31 December 1999, see History]. A new law ratified in 1997 created the Canal Authority to administer the Canal after the United States relinquished control in 1999. Though Pérez Balladeres worked to pass a referendum to allow his reelection, it failed. Presidential campaigns ensued. The PRD, with its majority in Congress, campaigned fiercely with its candidate Martin Torrijos Espino, son of the late dictator. The main opposition was the Arnulfista Party, named for former President Arnulfo Arias. It's candidate and widow of Arias, Mireya Moscoso, swept the elections on 2 May 1999 and became not only the new Panamanian president, but also the first woman to take the office. Moscoso, who lost to Pérez Balladeres in the 1994 elections, defeated Torrijos in what is considered a fair election; 75% of the country's 2.7 million citizens voted. Moscoso took office on 1 September 1999.

Mireya Moscoso was born to a poor family in Panama City on 1 July 1946. Moscoso's family originated from Pedasi, a town in the province of Los Santos, where she grew up and attended primary school. Moscoso, whose father was a teacher, studied high school in Panama City. Moscoso was first introduced to Arnulfo Arias in 1964 during her work on his campaign for president; soon after she became sales manager at one of his companies. Moscoso the became Arias' assistant and exiled to the United States with him after a coup attempt. Though he was 45 years her senior, the couple married in 1969. In 1974, Moscoso received a degree in interior design from Miami Dade Community College. Arias died in 1988, and in 1990 Moscoso returned to Panama, pledging to continue his political ideals in his honor. She formed the Arnulfista party and after losing the elections in 1994; she spent the next few years strengthening her party.

As the new president, Moscoso faces numerous contentions from her opposition regarding her lack of experience. Further, her new title does not grant the Arnulfista party automatic control of congress—as the PRD holds the majority of seats in the country's Parliament. Further complicating matters, Moscoso is facing pressure to do something about the increasing levels of unemployment, poverty, and worsening social services in Panama. She will need a strong congressional coalition to pass the necessary legislation to combat such problems. Moscoso is also challenged to oversee a peaceful management of the Panama Canal, which is set to be renovated in 2020 and which is experiencing increased traffic each year. Therefore, President Moscoso will need to establish herself as a respected national leader capable of unifying opposition politicians and ensuring Panama's role in the world economy throughout the new millennium.

[15] LOCAL GOVERNMENT

Panama is divided into nine administrative provinces, each headed by a governor appointed by the president, and one Amerindian territory. The provinces are subdivided into 67 municipal districts, each of which is governed by a mayor and a municipal council of at least five members, including all that district's representatives in the National Assembly. There are 511 municipal subdistricts in all.

[16] JUDICIAL SYSTEM

Judicial authority rests with the Supreme Court, composed of nine magistrates and nine alternates, all appointed by the president (subject to approval by the Legislative Assembly) for 10-year terms. The Supreme Court magistrates appoint judges of the superior courts who in turn appoint circuit court judges in their respective jurisdictions. There are 4 superior courts, 18 circuit courts (one civil and one criminal court for each province), and at least one municipal court in each district.

At the local level, two types of administrative judges, "corregidores" and "night" (or "police") judges hear minor civil and criminal cases involving sentences under one year. Appointed by the municipal mayors, these judges are similar to Justices of the Peace. Their proceedings are not subject to the Code of Criminal Procedure and defendants lack procedural safeguards afforded in the regular courts.

The Constitution guarantees a right to counsel for persons charged with crimes and requires the provision of public defenders for indigent criminal defendants. Trial by jury is afforded in some circumstances.

The 1996 amendment to the constitution abolished the standing military and contains a provision for the temporary formation of a "special police force" to protect the borders. The Judicial Technical Police perform criminal investigations in support of public prosecutors. The constitution also provides for an independent judiciary; however, the judiciary is susceptible to corruption.

The legal system is based on the civil law system. Panama accepts the compulsory jurisdiction of the International Court of Justice with reservation.

[17] ARMED FORCES

The Panamanian Defense Force disappeared with the US intervention in 1989. The new National Police Force numbers approximately 11,800, supported by a maritime service (400 staff, 7 patrol boats) and air service (400 staff, 33 aircraft and helos). In 1990 Panama spent $132 million on defense or 1.6% of GDP.

[18] INTERNATIONAL COOPERATION

Panama is a charter member of the UN, having joined on 13 November 1945, and participates in ECLAC and all the nonregional specialized agencies. Panama belongs to G-77, IADB, and OAS, and is a signatory to the Law of the Sea and a member of the WTO. With Colombia, Mexico, and Venezuela, Panama in 1987 was seeking to mediate the conflicts in El Salvador and Nicaragua as a member of the so-called Contadora group, but it did not join in the signing of the peace plan proposed by Costa Rican President Oscar Arias Sánchez in that year.

[19] ECONOMY

Panama depends largely on its privileged geographical position: the economy is based on a well-developed services sector, including the Panama Canal, banking, insurance, government, the trans-Panamanian oil pipeline, and the Colon Free Zone. The Panama Canal and the monetary regime anchored in the use of the US dollar as legal tender spurred the rapid development of the service economy which offset markedly unfavorable terms of trade. The unique monetary system played a significant role in the creation of an International Banking Center and the Colon Free Zone.

Whereas many countries were characterized by a growing protectionism in the late 1940s, Panama launched the Colon Free Zone (the second largest Free Zone in the world after Hong Kong). Panama also earned substantial rents through the construction of the trans-Panamanian oil pipeline and by the licensing of the Panamanian flag to merchant ships from around the world. Another important, but shrinking economic sector is agriculture, which accounted for 8% of GDP in 1997. Main primary products include bananas, rice, corn, coffee, sugar, vegetables, meat, and shrimp.

The economy generated growth of more than 6% a year over 1950–81. However, economic growth stagnated to 1.9% annually over 1977–87, caused by the aftermath of the second oil shock and the debt crisis. In the early 1990s, Panama rebounded from an excruciating recession brought about by a US embargo and subsequent military invasion. The US objective was the capture of General Manuel Noriega, who had installed puppet governments and was responsible for an increase in drug trafficking and money laundering. After Noriega was captured, extradited and condemned at a Miami federal court, Guillermo Endara assumed office. Nevertheless, his administration was widely criticized for not fulfilling Panamanians' hope for a rapid and bountiful recovery.

In May 1994, Armando Perez Balladares was elected president. The economy continued to grow, but a slower pace during the first half of the 1990s. Panama's main engines of economic growth (the Panama Canal, the Colon Free Zone, and International Banking Center) continued to loose competitiveness in the context of an open economy throughout the world. The Balladares Administration responded in 1996 with a solid program of economic reforms. These included the privatization of two seaports (Cristobal and Balboa), the promulgation of an antimonopoly law, the renegotiating of foreign debt with commercial banks, the privatization of the electricity and water companies, and a banking reform law. These economic reforms were accompanied with the recovery of the majority of traditional sectors, with the exception of the construction sector.

Between 1988 and 1998, the economy grew at 5% annually. In 1999, Ms. Mireya Moscoso was elected to the presidency. She did not intend to privatize the few remaining state enterprises, and wanted to raise protectionist tariffs to help local farmers (but membership in the WTO forbade this action). In the same year, the Panama Canal and all American bases were returned to the Panamanian government, comprising 364,000 acres, and estimated to be worth $4 billion. The government expected a boom in industries setting up shop in the buildings vacated by American nationals near the canal and investment in the airport.

[20] INCOME

The US Central Intelligence Agency (CIA) reports that in 1998 Panama's gross domestic product (GDP) was estimated at $19.9 billion. The per capita GDP was estimated at $7,300. The annual growth rate of GDP was estimated at 2.7%. The average inflation rate in 1998 was 1.4%. The CIA defines GDP as the value of all final goods and services produced within a nation in a given year and computed on the basis of purchasing power parity (PPP) rather than value as measured on the basis of the rate of exchange. It was estimated that agriculture accounted for 8% of GDP, industry 18%, and services 74%.

The World Bank reports that for the same period per capita private consumption (in PPP terms) was $3,200. Private consumption includes expenditures of individuals, households, and nongovernmental organizations. It was estimated that between 1990 and 1998 private consumption grew at an annual rate of 5.3%. Approximately 22% of household consumption was spent on food, 18% on fuel, 14% on health care, and 4% on education. The richest 10% of the population accounted for approximately 36% of household consumption and the poorest 10% approximately 1.2%.

21LABOR

In 1998, the economically active population numbered 1,049,000. Of the employed work force of 903,133 Panamanians in 1998, government and services engaged 31.8%; commerce and hotels, 16.4%; agriculture, 26.8%; manufacturing/mining, 9.4%; construction, 3.2%; transportation and communications, 6.2%; and services and real estate, 4.3%. The unemployment rate rose from 11.8% in 1985 to 17% in 1990, and then declined to 13.9% by 1998.

In 1999, Panama had over 250 unions with about 80,000 private sector members, organized into 48 federations and seven confederations. The province of Panama is where more than two-thirds of the total number of unions are found. About 10% of the work force was unionized as of 1999. The Confederation of Workers of the Republic of Panama, formed in 1963, is an affiliate of the ICFTU, and the National Center of Panamerican Workers is affiliated with the WFTU.

The law provides for an eight-hour day, a six-day week, minimum wages, a month's vacation with pay, maternity benefits and equal pay for women, and restrictions on the employment of minors. The minimum wage ranged from $0.77 to $1.33 per hour in 1999. All employees are entitled to a one-month annual bonus in three equal installments, two of which the worker receives directly and one of which is paid into the Social Security Fund.

In March 1986, a package of laws was approved that was intended, among other things, to promote employment and productivity. Labor contracts were made more flexible by removing some guaranteed benefits for workers, particularly in small businesses. These measures were passed over labor's objections.

22AGRICULTURE

About 8.8% of the total land area was classified as arable in 1997. Farming methods are primitive, and productivity is low. The best lands are held by large owners. Agriculture contributes about 8% to GDP.

Panama is self-sufficient in bananas, sugar, rice, corn, and coffee, but imports large quantities of other foods. Bananas are the leading export product and the banana industry is an important source of rural employment; exports were valued at $179.9 million in 1997, about half were destined for the German market. Sugar and coffee exports in 1997 were valued at $28.7 million and $123.5 million, respectively. In 1998, crop production (in tons) included sugarcane, 2,033,000; bananas, 500,000; rice, 130,000; corn, 39,000; and coffee, 11,000.

23ANIMAL HUSBANDRY

The Panamanian livestock industry produces sufficient meat to supply domestic demand and provides hides for export. Most cattle and hogs are tended by small herders, and dairy farming has expanded in recent years. In 1998 there were 1,492,000 head of cattle, 245,000 hogs, and about 10 million chickens. Milk production in 1998 was reported at 157,000 tons. Panama imports a substantial amount of its dairy needs (powdered milk, butterfat, and cheese), primarily from New Zealand.

24FISHING

The offshore waters of Panama abound in fish and seafood, and fisheries are a significant sector of the national economy. There is freshwater fishing in the Chiriquí River and deep-sea fishing along the Pacific and Caribbean coasts for amberjack, barracuda, bonito, corbina, dolphinfish, mackerel, pompano, red snapper, sailfish, sea bass, and tuna.

In 1997, the fish catch totaled 169,718 tons, as compared with 131,514 tons in 1986. The main commercial species caught that year were Pacific anchoveta (77,726 tons), Pacific thread herring (26,266 tons), yellowfin tuna (9,495 tons), and skipjack tuna (7,002 tons). Exports of fish products were valued at nearly $102.4 million in 1997.

25FORESTRY

Forests and woodland cover about 44% of the country's area but have been largely unexploited because of a lack of transportation facilities. Nearly all forestland is government-owned. Hardwood, particularly mahogany, is produced for export in Darién and along the Pacific coast in Veraguas. Abacá fiber, which is obtained in Bocas del Toro and is used in the making of marine cordage, is a valuable forest product. Approximately 30% of Panama's natural forests are still unused. In order to protect and preserve native forests, the National Association for the Conservation of Nature has begun a vast reforestation program. Production of roundwood was 1,082,000 cu m in 1997, 91% used as fuel wood.

26MINING

Mining is limited, but there are known deposits of copper, manganese, iron, asbestos, gold, and silver. Gold mining included small-scale placer operations in Darién Province, along with the newer large capacity Santa Rosa and Remance mines in Veraguas Province. Salt, produced by evaporation of seawater at Aguadulce, is a major mineral product; the total salt output was an estimated 22,000 tons in 1997. Cement, clays, lime, limestone, and sand and gravel are produced in small operations. Production totals for 1997 (in tons) included cement, 750,000; clay, 40,112; lime, 3,246; limestone for cement, 263,338; sand and gravel, 3,000.

27ENERGY AND POWER

Installation of hydroelectric stations has enabled Panama to reduce its dependence on imported oil for energy from 40% of total imports in 1975 to 15% of total imports in 1991. Panama had a net installed electric capacity of 1,050,000 kW in 1998; production of electric power totaled 4,523 million kWh, 70% of it hydroelectric. In 1998, IRHE, the state-owned electricity company, was broken up into four generating and three distribution companies and sold. A geothermal region in southwest Panama has an estimated potential of 400,000 kW. Some energy is also obtained from fuel wood and biomass residues.

After years of unsuccessful exploration, two oil strikes—one off the San Blas Islands, the other a 500-million-barrel find about 100 km (62 mi) east of Panama City—were announced in 1980. Several companies hold concessions in the Gulf of Panama, but there was no commercial production in the mid-1980s. The inauguration in 1982 of a trans-Panamanian pipeline, operated by Petroterminal de Panamá, facilitates the shipment of Alaskan crude oil to the eastern US by allowing the loading and unloading of supertankers on both sides of the isthmus; the pipeline's maximum capacity is 830,000 barrels per day. The pipeline's contribution to GDP fell from 6.9% in 1987 to 3.4% in 1990 and to 2.5% in 1991, reflecting reduced demand for Alaskan oil on the US east coast. In 1992–93, new legislation created Petroleum Free Zones to take advantage of Panama's location as a transshipment location for crude oil and petroleum products. The PFZs allow crude oil to be imported tax-free and then stored, pumped, transferred, distributed, sold, and refined for subsequent export.

28 INDUSTRY

The performance of Panama's industry as a whole was negative during the 1980s, but garnered a 7% growth rate during the 1990s. Construction, manufacturing, mining, and utilities together accounted for 17% of GDP in 1998. Industry grew by only 1.6%, compared to 5% in 1997, affected by reduced tariffs. The construction industry, however, was the star performer during 1998. The government and the private sector invested large amounts in the construction of ports, roads, and bridges. Thus, construction activity rose 5% in 1998, while the production of construction-related materials rose by 23% and finished wood products by 38%.

Limited by a small domestic market, Panamanian manufacturing represents around 8% of GDP. Growth in production reached an average 1.1% annually between 1978 and 1988, rising to 5.4% between 1988 and 1998 due to an import-substitution high tariff regime which ended in 1998. Manufacturing of mainly nondurable goods consists principally of food-processing plants and firms for the production of: alcoholic beverages, sugar, ceramics, tropical clothing, cigarettes, hats, furniture, shoes, soap and edible oils. Other manufactured products include clothing, chemicals, and construction products for domestic consumption.

The mining industry was poised for growth in 1998, rising by 5% in 1998 due to high demand for construction materials. Two copper mines and one gold mine await a rebound in world market prices before jumping into action. Revenues from the Panama Canal rose by over 9%, because of a 1998 toll increase, but 1.8% fewer ships traveled through the canal.

29 SCIENCE AND TECHNOLOGY

Although the shipping technology of the Panama Canal is owned and operated by the US, technicians from the US who operated the canal's facilities were replaced gradually by Panamanian personnel before the canal was officially turned over to Panama. The National Academy of Sciences of Panama (founded in 1942) advises the government on scientific matters, and the National Research Center (1976) coordinates scientific and technological research. The Smithsonian Institution has had a tropical research institute in Balboa since 1923. The University of Panama, founded in 1935 in Panama City, has faculties of agriculture, medicine, sciences, dentistry, nursing, and pharmacy. Santa María La Antigua University, founded in 1965 at El Doradom Panama, has a department of technology and natural science. The Technological University of Panama, founded in 1984 at El Dorado, has colleges of civil, mechanical, industrial, electrical, and computer-science engineering. The Nautical School of Panama, founded in 1959 at Paitilla, Panama, offers courses in nautical engineering. In 1987–97, science and engineering students accounted for 29% of college and university enrollments. The Museum of Natural Sciences, founded in Panama in 1975, is concerned with natural history and the fauna of Panama and other countries.

30 DOMESTIC TRADE

Marketing and distribution are generally on a small scale, with direct merchant-to-customer sales. Many shops in Panama City and Colon sell both native handicrafts and imported goods. Luxury items are generally untaxed in order to attract tourist sales. There are also US-style variety stores. In rural districts, agricultural products and meat are sold at markets.

The usual business hours are 8 AM to 5 PM, Monday through Friday; and 8 AM to noon on Saturday. Government offices are open weekdays from 8:30 AM to 4:30 PM, Monday through Friday. Banking hours in Panamanian urban centers are generally from 8:00 AM to 3 PM, Monday through Friday, and most banks are open on Saturdays from 9 AM to 12 noon.

31 FOREIGN TRADE

The leading agricultural export is bananas, which is mainly controlled by foreigners, followed by shrimp. The decline in exports from 1997 to 1998 of almost 11% can be explained by quotas imposed on banana exports by the European Community (bananas represent more than one-third of all exports). Light industry exports (clothing and manufacturing textiles) have been increasing due to the Free Trade Zone; but competition from Mexico starting in 1996, and the reduction of protective tariffs in 1998 stunted growth. Goods produced and exported from the FTZ are not accounted for in the foreign trade accounts below, including petrochemicals.

All of Panama's main export commodities are foods, including bananas (38%), shrimp (16%), coffee (4.2%), fresh fish (3.4%), and sugar (3.2%).

In 1996 Panama's imports were distributed among the following categories:

Consumer goods	19.1%
Food	8.3%
Fuels	15.8%
Industrial supplies	27.0%
Machinery	15.4%
Transportation	14.3%

Principal trading partners in 1998 (in millions of US dollars) were as follows:

COUNTRY	EXPORTS	IMPORTS	BALANCE
United States	298	1,363	-1,065
Sweden	51	26	25
Costa Rica	46	102	-56
Spain	38	45	-7
Guatemala	18	56	-38
Columbia	10	65	-55
Ecuador	8	109	-101
Mexico	7	164	-157
Japan	4	304	-300
Korea	1	89	-88

32 BALANCE OF PAYMENTS

Panama's adverse balance of trade is largely made up by invisible foreign exchange earnings from sales of goods and services in the Colón Free Trade Zone and from the Panama Canal.

The US Central Intelligence Agency reports that in 1997 the purchasing power parity of Panama's exports was $6,680 million while imports totaled $7,380 million resulting in a trade balance of -$700 million.

The International Monetary Fund (IMF) reports that in 1998 Panama had exports of goods totaling $6,325 million and imports totaling $7,696 million. The services credit totaled $1,697 million and debit $1,173 million. The following table summarizes Panama's balance of payments as reported by the IMF for 1998 in millions of US dollars.

Current Account		-1,212
Balance on goods	-1,371	
Balance on services	525	
Balance on income	-525	
Current transfers	159	
Capital Account		51
Financial Account		879
Direct investment abroad	...	
Direct investment in Panama	1,206	
Portfolio investment assets	438	
Portfolio investment liabilities	-66	
Other investment assets	645	
Other investment liabilities	-1,345	
Net Errors and Omissions		-181
Reserves and Related Items		463

33BANKING AND SECURITIES

Panama was considered the most important international banking center in Latin America in the late 1980s. In 1970, 28 banks operated in Panama's international banking center; by 1987 there were 120, with assets of nearly $39 billion. Liberalized banking regulations and use of the dollar made Panama one of Latin America's major offshore banking centers.

Since 1983, the year of the onset of Latin America's financial crisis, the Panamanian banking sector has contracted, both in number of banks and total assets. In 1999 there were about 94 banks in Panama, holding $36.6 billion in total assets. Fifty-seven of the banks in Panama have general licenses, 26 banks have offshore licenses, 12 foreign banks have representative offices, and two banks are government owned. The National Bank of Panama (Banco Nacional de Panamá–BNP), founded in 1904, is the principal official (but not central) bank and also transacts general banking business. Banking activities are supervised by the National Banking Commission (Comisión Bancaria Nacional–CBN).

The balboa is fully convertible with the dollar at a fixed rate of 1:1. The government cannot, therefore, implement a monetary policy. Most monetary developments are exogenously determined by the balance of payments.

Panama's banking center has allegedly been the main money-laundering point for proceeds from international drug-trafficking. In March 1994, it was decreed that persons entering Panama had to declare money or financial instruments in excess of $10,000. For deposits and withdrawals in excess of this amount from local banking institutions, a form had to be completed, providing details about the person carrying out the transaction. In 1998, a banking law was enacted in order to modernize the banking system and increase government supervision.

Panama's international stock exchange, the Bolsa de Valores de Panama, began operations in June 1990. In 1995, there were a total of 102 listed companies, of which 96 were local and 6 foreign entities. Companies rarely issue stock on the stock market, and investment is small because of a 10% withholding tax. Panama's Central de Custodia de Valores (Panaclear) began operations in November 1996. A rating agency was expected to begin operations by early 1997.

34INSURANCE

There were about 41 national insurance companies in Panama in 1997. Domestic companies include the General Insurance Co., the International Insurance Co., and the International Life Insurance Co. For a firm to qualify as a national insurance company, 51% of the capital must be Panamanian.

35PUBLIC FINANCE

Panama does not issue its own currency, therefore government spending and investment are limited by taxes, customs, and foreign loans.

The US Central Intelligence Agency (CIA) estimates that in 1997 Panama's central government took in revenues of approximately $2.4 billion and had expenditures of $2.4 billion including capital expenditures of $341 million. External debt totaled $6.69 billion. The following table shows an itemized breakdown of government revenues and expenditures. The percentages were calculated from data reported by the International Monetary Fund. The dollar amounts (millions) are based on the CIA estimates provided above.

REVENUE AND GRANTS	100%	2,400
Tax revenue	70.3%	1,688
Non-tax revenue	26.8%	642
Capital revenue	0.1%	3
Grants	2.8%	67

EXPENDITURES	100%	2,400
General public services	7.4%	179
Defense	5.0%	121
Public order and safety	3.3%	79
Education	18.3%	440
Health	18.7%	449
Social security	20.5%	493
Housing and community amenities	5.1%	122
Recreation, cultural, and religious affairs	1.0%	23
Economic affairs and services	8.0%	193
Other expenditures	0.1%	2
Interest payments	12.5%	301

36TAXATION

Income tax is paid to the national government by individuals and corporations on all income earned in or derived from Panama. The progressive rate rises from 4% to 30% for personal income. Corporate taxes are levied at 30–34%.

A real property tax ranges from 1.4% to 2.1% of assessed valuation. Property improvements are tax-exempt for the first five years. Other levies include license fees, stamp taxes, various payroll taxes, a tax on the manufacture or importation of consumer goods, and a VAT at a rate of 5%.

37CUSTOMS AND DUTIES

In 1999, tariffs were reduced on most agricultural and industrial goods to a rate averaging 12%. The maximum tariff is 15%. However, higher rates apply to certain sensitive agricultural produces. There is also a 5% VAT on imports.

Panama has a free port in the Colón Free Trade Zone, the world's second largest free-trade zone, where foreign goods enter without going through customs. Goods may be stored, assembled, processed, or repackaged for sale or shipment to another country free of duty. Panama is a part of the Caribbean Basin Initiative, and has bilateral preferential trade agreements with Costa Rica, El Salvador, Honduras, Guatemala, Nicaragua, and the Dominican Republic. The country also has special arrangements with Mexico, Colombia, and Chile.

38FOREIGN INVESTMENT

Increased private sector investment and inflows from lending agencies should offset lower public expenditure and help to stimulate economic growth. The government sold the electricity generation and distribution utilities in 1996. In addition, the government partially sold the telephone company. The UK's Cable and Wireless bought a 49% stake in INTEL, the national telecommunications monopoly. Privatization of the state water utility was put on hold in 1998 due to violent protests, which president Moscoso promised not to sell. Other parastatal sales included the transisthmian railroad, both canal ports, two sugar companies, a casino, a cement company, a fruit company, and a horse racetrack.

The government encourages industrialization by granting special tax concessions to new enterprises and imposing protective duties on competing foreign manufacturers. The Industrial Development Bank, equivalent to the US Small Business Administration, promotes small industries and facilitates credit on a long term basis. A 1986 law on industrial incentives grants industrial investors a wide range of benefits, the foremost of which is tax exceptions that vary according to whether all or part of the output is earmarked for the export or domestic market.

Foreign direct investment in 1998 reached 40% of GDP, the majority in the transport, storage, services, and communication sectors. Major investors included the US (40%), UK (23%), Mexico (19%), and Taiwan (8%).

³⁹ECONOMIC DEVELOPMENT

The Panamanian economy is the most stable, and among the most prosperous in the region. But the economy is highly segmented between its dynamic, internationally oriented service sector and the domestically oriented sector, which is beset with policy-induced rigidities and low productivity. Factor markets are also segmented by policies that drive up the cost of labor and lower the cost of capital. About 14% of the labor force is unemployed despite the preponderance of services in the economy, low growth of the economically active population and relatively slow rural-urban migration. The protected poor performance of the economy has impeded job creation, and contributed to high poverty levels and income inequality.

Despite Panama's relatively high per capita income, distribution of the wealth is highly skewed and had become progressively more evident in the 1990s. In 1979, the poorest 20% of the population received 4% of income; in the early 1990s that share had plunged to 2%, leaving Panama with one of the most unequal distributions in the hemisphere. The government's strategy for mitigating poverty and inequality rests primarily on reviving sustainable growth; its economic program emphasizes reforms that will mitigate the bias against employment creation (unemployment was 13% in 1998), increase agricultural productivity, and reduce the high cost of the basic consumption basket.

⁴⁰SOCIAL DEVELOPMENT

The Social Security Fund, established by the government in 1941, provides medical service and hospitalization, maternity care, pensions for disability or old age, and funeral benefits. Retirement is set at age 62 for men, or age 57 for women. This program is financed by an alcohol tax, in addition to employee and employer contributions. Employed women receive 14 week of maternity leave at 100% pay. Compulsory workers' compensation legislation covers employees in the public and private sectors. This program is funded entirely by employer contributions.

Children are cared for through a child welfare institute, which operates under the Ministry of Labor and Social Welfare. The government has made efforts to integrate the Amerindian population of the San Blas area through land grants, basic education, and improved transportation.

Despite Constitutional equality, women generally do not enjoy the same opportunities as men. While Panama has a relatively high rate of female enrollment in higher education, many female graduates are still forced to take low-paying jobs. As of 1999, women's wages were, on average, 20% lower than those of men. Until 1995, communal assets were not recognized in marriage, and many divorced women were left economically destitute. Women also face sexual harassment in the workplace, and in 1994 the Legislative Assembly failed to approve a bill that would penalize sexual harassment. In 1998 the Ministry of Women, Youth, Family, and Childhood was established, helping focus national attention on social issues affecting women and families.

Women remain underrepresented in politics. In 1999, 7 of 71 members of the Legislative Assembly were women.

Indigenous peoples in Panama are increasingly demanding more participation in decisions that affect their land. Semiautonomous status has been given to some tribal groups. Despite these provisions, many indigenous groups feel that existing reserves are too small. The Ngobe-Bugle group claims that government is allowing private landowners to encroach on tribal lands. This conflict erupted in violence in 1995. In 1999 members if the Ngobe-Bugle voted for their own local representatives in newly formed representative districts.

Human rights abuses include prolonged pretrial detention, poor prison conditions, and internal prison violence. It was estimated that in 1995, nearly 78% of all prisoners had not yet received a trial. In 1999, a $27 million judiciary reform program was launched to combat corruption and inefficiency in the justice system.

⁴¹HEALTH

Public health services are directed by the Ministry of Health, whose program includes free health examinations and medical care for the needy, health education, sanitation inspection, hospital and clinic construction, and nutrition services. Public expenditures for health care totaled $547 million, or 6.9% of the GDP.

In 1997, Panama had 4,434 physicians, 1,397 dentists, and 3,923 registered nurses (including nursing assistants). There were 12 physicians per 10,000 people and there were 18 hospital beds per 1,000 inhabitants.

Proceeds from a national lottery support state hospitals, asylums, and public welfare. Assistance has been received from such organizations as WHO, the US Institute of Inter-American Affairs, the Pan American Sanitary Bureau, the Institute of Nutrition of Central America and Panama, and UNICEF.

During the first two decades of the 20th century, when the Panama Canal was being built, the major health threats were yellow fever, malaria, smallpox, typhoid, dysentery, and intestinal parasites. Through the efforts of Col. William Crawford Gorgas, a US military surgeon and sanitary officer, malaria was controlled and the yellow-fever mosquito was virtually eliminated. Today, the principal causes of death are cancer, heart disease, cerebrovascular disease, pneumonia and bronchopneumonia, and enteritis and diarrhea. There were 476 malaria cases in 1996. Col. Gorgas pioneered in providing Panama City and Colón with water and sewer systems; in some areas of Panama, poor sanitation, inadequate housing, and malnutrition still constitute health hazards. In 1990–95, 93% of the population had access to safe water and 83% had adequate sanitation. However, in 1989–95, 7% of children under 5 years old were considered malnourished. The government of Panama is currently increasing distribution of vitamin A capsules to populations with high risk of vitamin A deficiency, mostly the Indians in the western region of Panama. Immunization rates for children up to one year old in 1997 were tuberculosis (99%); diphtheria, pertussis, and tetanus (95%); polio (99%); and measles (92%). Polio, measles, and neonatal tetanus were at extremely low numbers during 1994. Goiter was present in 13.2% of school age children during 1996.

Panama's 1998 birth rate was 22 per 1,000 people. The fertility rate was 2.6 children per woman surviving her childbearing years in 1997. The general mortality rate was 4.2 per 1,000 people in 1998, and the infant mortality rate was 16 per 1,000 live births in 1996. Maternal mortality was 84 per 1,000 live births in 1997. Average life expectancy in 1998 was 74 years.

The HIV-1 seroprevalence rate was 0.6 per 100 adults in 1997. As of 1997 there were 9,000 cases of AIDS in Panama.

⁴²HOUSING

Housing in urban areas has been a permanent problem since US construction in the Canal Zone brought a great influx of migrant laborers into Colón and Panama City. The government-established Bank of Urbanization and Rehabilitation began to build low-cost housing in 1944, and by 1950, it had built more than 1,500 units to house 8,000 people near Panama City. The Panamanian Institute of Housing estimated in 1970 that the national housing deficit of 76,000 units would increase by 7,700 units annually unless corrective measures were taken.

A 1973 housing law, designed to encourage low-income housing construction, banned evictions, froze all rents for three years, and required banks to commit half their domestic reserves to loans in support of housing construction projects. By the early 1980s, however, the shortage of low-income housing remained acute, particularly in Colón. A construction boom in the early 1980s was mainly confined to infrastructural projects and office space. According to the latest available information, total housing units numbered 448,000 with 4.9 people per dwelling.

43EDUCATION

For the year 2000, adult illiteracy was estimated at 8.1% of the population (males, 7.4%; females, 8.7%). Education is free and compulsory for children ages 6 through 15. At secondary, vocational, and university levels, fees may be charged for the development of libraries and laboratories. Primary education lasts six years. In 1996 there were 2,849 primary schools with 371,250 students. Secondary education has two stages, each lasting three years. In 1996, secondary schools enrolled 221,022 students, taught by 12,239 teachers. A major school construction program began in 1999, and the percentage of students completing the sixth grade is projected to rise from 78% in 1997 to 90% by the year 2002.

The leading institution, the state-run University of Panama, was founded in Panama City in 1935. A Catholic university, Santa María la Antigua, was inaugurated in May 1965, with an initial enrollment of 233. In 1996, at all institutions of higher learning, there were 4,979 teaching staff with 80,980 students enrolled. Approximately 16.3% of the central government budget was allocated to education in the period between in the latter half of the 1990s.

44LIBRARIES AND MUSEUMS

The National Library of Panama, located in Panama City, was founded in 1892 as Biblioteca Colón and reorganized as the National Library in 1942. It is a branch of the Ministry of Education's public library system and has over 200,000 volumes. There are more than 40 other public libraries and branches. The National Archives, established in 1924, contain historical documents, books, and maps, as well as administrative papers of government agencies and a judicial section with court records. The Simon Bolivar library at the University of Panama has holdings of over 267,000 volumes. The Smithsonian Tropical Research Institute in Balboa has 44,000 volumes.

The Instituto Panameño de Arte, founded in 1964, displays excellent collections of pre-Columbian art. Newer museums in Panama City include the Museum of Nationhood (dedicated in 1974); the Museum of Colonial Religious Art (1974); the Museum of the History of Panama (1977), which exhibits documents and objects of historical value; and the Museum of Panamanian Man (1976), with archaeological, ethnographic, and folkloric displays.

45MEDIA

The Instituto Nacional de Telecomunicaciones (INTEL) operates Panama's telephone and telegraph systems. In 1995 there were more than 273,000 telephones, mainly in the Panama City area. Telegraph cables link Panama to the US, to Central and South America, and to Europe. As of 1999 there were 91 AM commercial radio broadcasting stations and 9 television channels. In 1997 there were 299 radios, 187 television sets, and 6 mobile phones per 1,000 population.

There were six major daily newspapers in 1999. With their estimated 1999 circulations, they are as follows:

	CIRCULATION
La Prensa	45,000
Crítica Libre (m)	23,000
El Siglo	36,000
La Estrella de Panamá (m)	17,000
El Panama America	25,000
The Star and Herald	17,000
Diario Itoy	12,000

The constitution provides for freedom of speech and the press, and the government is said to respect these rights in practice.

Online access is extremely limited, with approximately one Internet host per 1,000 population in 1998.

46ORGANIZATIONS

The cooperative movement in Panama is limited. Producers' organizations are small, local, uncoordinated groups concerned mainly with practical education in techniques to improve production. The Chamber of Commerce, Industry, and Agriculture is in Panama City.

47TOURISM, TRAVEL, AND RECREATION

Visitors to Panama must have a valid passport and visa. Visitors who possess a valid passport can obtain a tourist visa from a Panamanian consul or buy a tourist card from a transportation company; both card and visa are valid for up to 90 days. Visas are available free of charge to US citizens.

The government encourages tourism through the Panamanian Tourist Bureau and is promoting investment in some of the most remote parts of the country, including Coiba Island, Rio Hato, and Amador. In 1997, 418,846 tourists arrived in Panama, over 90% of them from the Americas. Revenues from tourism totaled an estimated $369 million. That year there were 11,452 hotel rooms with 22,949 beds and an occupancy rate of 52%.

According to 1999 UN estimates, the cost of staying in Panama City is $152 per day. Hotel charges account for approximately 64% of daily expenditure. Estimated expenses in Colón are estimated at $90.

Travel facilities within Panama are good; Panama City and Colón are only one hour apart by road or rail. In addition to the Panama Canal itself, tourist attractions include Panama City, beach resorts in the Pearls Archipelago and San Blas Islands, the ruins of Portobelo, and the resort of El Valle in the mountains. Water sports, tennis, golf, and horse racing are popular.

48FAMOUS PANAMANIANS

Outstanding political figures of the 19th century include Tomás Herrera (1804–54), the national hero who led the first republican movement, and Justo Arosemena (1817–96), a writer and nationalist. The international lawyer Ricardo J. Alfaro (1882–1971) and the rector of the University of Panama, Dr. Octavio Méndez Pereira (1887–1954), were well-known Panamanian nationalists. The most important political leader of the 20th century was Omar Torrijos Herrera (1929–81), who ruled Panama from 1969 until his death and successfully negotiated the Panama Canal treaties of 1979 with the US.

Important poets were Tomás del Espíritu Santo (1834–62), the nationalist Amelia Denis de Icaza (1836–1910), Federico Escobar (1861–1912), Darío Herrera (1870–1914), and Ricardo Miró (1888–1940). Panamanian-born José Benjamin Quintero (b.1924) is a noted stage director in the US. Narciso Garay (1876–1953) founded the National Conservatory of Music and served as a foreign minister. Harmodio Arias (1886–1962) was the prominent owner of the newspaper El Panamá-America. Leading Panamanian painters include Epifanio Garay (1849–1903), Roberto Lewis (1874–1949), Sebastián Villalaz (1879–1919), and Humberto Ivaldi (1909–47). Noteworthy among Panamanian athletes is the former world light- and welter-weight boxing champion Roberto Durán (b.1949); the former baseball star Rod (Rodney) Carew (b.1945) is also of Panamanian birth.

49DEPENDENCIES

Panama has no territories or colonies.

50 BIBLIOGRAPHY

Conniff, Michael. *Black Labor on a White Canal: Panama*. Pittsburgh, Pennsylvania: University of Pittsburgh Press, 1985.

Flanagan, E. M. *Battle for Panama: Inside Operation Just Cause*. Washington, D.C.: Brassey's (US), Inc., 1993.

Greene, Graham. *Getting to Know the General*. New York: Simon & Schuster, 1984.

Guevara Mann, Carlos. *Panamanian Militarism: A Historical Interpretation*. Athens, Ohio: Ohio University Center for International Studies, 1996.

Hedrick, Basil C., and Anne K. Hedrick. *Historical Dictionary of Panama*. Metuchen, N.J.: Scarecrow, 1970.

Hogan, J. Michael. *The Panama Canal in American Politics: Domestic Advocacy and the Evolution of Policy*. Carbondale: Southern Illinois University Press, 1986.

LaFeber, Walter. *The Panama Canal: The Crisis in Historical Perspective*. New York: Oxford University Press, 1989.

Major, John. *Prize Possession: The United States and the Panama Canal, 1903–1979*. New York: Cambridge University Press, 1993.

McCullough, David G. *The Path Between the Seas: The Creation of the Panama Canal, 1870–1914*. New York: Simon & Schuster, 1977.

Meditz, Sandra W., and Dennis M. Hanratty (eds.). *Panama: A Country Study*. 4th ed. Washington, D.C.: Library of Congress, 1989.

Moffet, George D. *The Limits of Victory: The Ratification of the Panama Canal Treaties*. Ithaca, N.Y.: Cornell University Press, 1985.

Richard, Alfred Charles. *The Panama Canal in American National Consciousness, 1870–1990*. New York: Garland, 1990.

US Department of State. *The Panama Canal Treaties and Associated Agreements and Documents*. Washington, D.C.: Government Printing Office, 1979.

Watson, Bruce W., and Peter G. Tsouras (eds.). *Operation Just Cause: The U.S. Intervention in Panama*. Boulder, Colo.: Westview Press, 1991.

Zencey, Eric. *Panama*. New York: Farrar, Straus, and Giroux, 1995.

Zimbalist, Andrew S. *Panama at the Crossroads: Economic Development and Political Change in the Twentieth Century*. Berkeley, Calif.: University of California Press, 1991.

PARAGUAY

Republic of Paraguay
República del Paraguay

CAPITAL: Asunción.

FLAG: The national flag, officially adopted in 1842, is a tricolor of red, white, and blue horizontal stripes. The national coat of arms appears in the center of the white stripe on the obverse, and the Treasury seal in the same position on the reverse.

ANTHEM: *Himno Nacional,* beginning "Paraguayos, república o muerte" ("Paraguayans, republic or death").

MONETARY UNIT: The guaraní (G) is a paper currency of 100 céntimos. There are notes of 1, 5, 10, 50, 100, 500, 1,000, 5,000, and 10,000 guaraníes. G1 = $0.00029 (or $1 = G3493.75) as of 31 March 2000.

WEIGHTS AND MEASURES: The metric system is the legal standard.

HOLIDAYS: New Year's Day, 1 January; San Blas Day, 3 February; National Defense Day, 1 March; Labor Day, 1 May; Independence Days, 14–15 May; Peace Day, 12 June; Founding of Asunción, 15 August; Constitution Day, 25 August; Victory Day (Battle of Boquerón), 29 September; Columbus Day, 12 October; All Saints' Day, 1 November; Our Lady of Caacupé, 8 December; Christmas, 25 December. Movable religious holidays are Holy Thursday, Good Friday, and Corpus Christi.

TIME: 8 AM = noon GMT.

¹LOCATION, SIZE, AND EXTENT

One of South America's two landlocked countries, Paraguay has a total area of 406,750 sq km (157,047 sq mi). Comparatively, the area occupied by Paraguay is slightly smaller than the state of California. The western 246,925 sq km (95,338 sq mi) of the country constitute a dry, sparsely populated region known as the Chaco, while the remaining 159,827 sq km (61,709 sq mi) lie in the more verdant east. Paraguay extends 992 km (616 mi) SSE-NNW and 491 km (305 mi) ENE-WSW. Bounded on the NE and E by Brazil, on the SE, S, and W by Argentina, and on the NW and N by Bolivia, Paraguay has a total boundary length of 3,920 km (2,436 mi).

Paraguay's capital city, Asunción, is located in the southwestern part of the country.

²TOPOGRAPHY

The eastern part of Paraguay contains luxuriant hills, meadows, and forests. The western three-fifths is a waterless, brackish prairie covered with dry grass and sparsely dotted with shadeless trees. The southward-flowing Paraguay River, the nation's most important waterway, divides the two sections; this river, which for a long time was Paraguay's principal contact with the outside world, rises in southwestern Brazil and extends for a total length of 2,549 km (1,584 mi). The Pilcomayo River, which rises in the mountains of southern Bolivia and extends about 1,600 km (1,000 mi), flows southeast, forming the southwestern border between Argentina and Paraguay, and joins the Paraguay near Asunción.

The eastern sector of Paraguay comprises the western part of the great Paraná Plateau, varying from 300 to 610 m (1,000 to 2,000 ft) in altitude. The Paraná River—called Upper (Alto) Paraná in Paraguay—flows southward from south-central Brazil through the center of the plateau, dropping in the Guairá Falls at the easternmost point in the Paraguay-Brazil frontier. Between the Guairá Falls and the confluence with the Paraguay River at the

southwestern tip of the country, the Paraná passes through a deep canyon that forms the eastern and southern frontier with Argentina.

Just west of the plateau is an area of gently rounded hills descending to the low plains that stretch westward to the Paraguay River. These hills occur in two series, one extending northwestward to the Paraguay River just north of Concepción, and the other meeting the river at Asunción. The remaining territory east of the Paraguay River is composed of lowland plain, much of it subject to annual floods.

West of the Paraguay River is the Chaco, part of the larger Gran Chaco, which includes portions of Argentina, Bolivia, and Brazil. The Gran Chaco, a vast alluvial plain composed of unconsolidated sands and clays, is crossed by the Pilcomayo and Bermejo rivers, but over much of the area there are no surface streams. The water table, however, is only a few feet below the surface, and patches of alkali frequently appear during the long dry season. In many places the groundwater is salty.

³CLIMATE

Two-thirds of Paraguay is within the temperate zone, one-third in the tropical zone. The climate varies from mild to subtropical. During the autumn and winter months (roughly April through September), temperatures generally range from 10° to 21°C (50° to 70°F); nights are occasionally colder. During the spring and summer (October through March), temperatures range from about 26° to 37°C (79° to 99°F), with extremes of 43°C (109°F) and above. Paraguay is open to dry, cold polar winds from the south and to hot, humid north winds from southwestern Brazil; sudden sharp drops in temperatures are not uncommon. Rainfall averages about 200 cm (80 in) a year along the eastern frontier with Brazil, gradually diminishing toward the west to an average of 119 cm (47 in) along the Paraguay River and 81 cm (32 in) in the Chaco. Asunción has an annual average of about 130 cm (50 in), which is moderate for its latitude. There is no definite rainy season, although violent thunderstorms sometimes occur in the summer.

⁴FLORA AND FAUNA

The vegetation, like the rainfall, is concentrated in the Paraná Plateau and diminishes toward the west. Tall broadleaf trees, some evergreen and some deciduous, cover eastern Paraguay, thinning out on the red sandy soils of the hilly perimeter. Scrub woodland and palm also dot the sandy plateau areas. Between the semideciduous forest and the Paraguay River, the vegetation is mostly the savanna type mixed with scattered palms. In contrast, the Chaco supports primarily deciduous scrub woodlands, luxuriant along the Paraguay River but becoming more and more xerophytic as the rainfall decreases toward the west.

The eastern forests abound in hardwoods, including indigenous varieties, such as urunday, cedron, curupay, and lapacho. Softwoods are scarce. In the northern Chaco, along the Paraguay River, there are scattered stands of quebracho and many large, spreading trees, such as the ceiba. Medicinal herbs, shrubs, and trees abound, as well as some dyewoods. Yerba maté, a holly popularly used in tea, grows wild in the northeast.

Animals found in Paraguay include the jaguar (especially numerous in the Chaco), wild boar, capybara, deer, armadillo, anteater, fox, brown wolf, carpincho, and tapir. Paraguay abounds with crocodiles along its watercourses, and the boa constrictor thrives in the west. The carnivorous piranha is common.

⁵ENVIRONMENT

Agencies responsible for environmental protection include the National Environmental Health Service, the Ministry of Public Health, and the Ministry of Public Works and Communications. Nearly all forests are privately owned, and little was done to develop a national forest policy until the establishment in 1973 of the National Forest Service. Paraguay's forests are currently threatened by the expansion of agriculture. At most recent estimate, about a third of the nation's forest and woodland area has been lost. The absence of trees contributes to the loss of soil through erosion. Water pollution is also a problem. Its sources include industrial pollutants and sewage. The nation has 22.6 cu mi of reusable water. Seventy-eight percent of the water supply is used to support farming and 7% is used for industrial purposes. Thirty-nine percent of the city dwellers and 91% of the rural people do not have pure drinking water. The nation's cities produce 0.4 million tons of solid waste per year. Some of Paraguay's cities have no facilities for waste collection. In 1994 there were five endangered mammal species. Thirty-four bird species and 15 plant species are also endangered. Endangered or extinct species include the black-fronted piping guan, glaucous macaw, black caiman, spectacled caiman, and broad-nosed caiman.

⁶POPULATION

The population of Paraguay in 2000 was estimated at 5,579,503. An estimated 3.5% of the population is 65 years of age or older. The projected population for the year 2005 is 6,340,000, assuming a crude birthrate of 30 per 1,000 population and a death rate of 5, resulting in a natural rate of change of 2.5% for the period 2000–2005. The population rate of change between 1995 and 2000 was 2.6%. The population density in 1998 was 13 per sq km (34 per sq mi).

Over 98% of the population is located in the eastern two-fifths of the country; the vast western Chaco region is virtually uninhabited. It was estimated that 56% of the population lived in urban areas in 2000, up from 42% in 1980. The capital city, Asuncion, had a 2000 metropolitan population of 1,262,000. Other leading cities include Ciudad del Este, 98,591; Pedro Juan

Caballero, 41,475; Encarnación, 31,445; Pilar, 26,352; and Concepción, 25,607. Paraguay's next census is scheduled to take place in 2002.

⁷MIGRATION

Emigration has long been a problem for Paraguay. During 1955–70, some 650,000 Paraguayans emigrated, mainly to Argentina; more recently, the net loss from emigration has averaged an estimated 5,000–6,000 a year. Most of these emigrants live in Argentina, Uruguay, or Brazil. Much of the labor force of agricultural regions in Argentine border provinces is made up of Paraguayan nationals. The greatest exodus occurred after the 1947 civil war, but in the 1960s there were new waves of political emigration.

Immigration to Paraguay was limited to a few thousand Europeans during the 19th century. A major attempt by the Paraguayan government to encourage new settlers led to negotiations with Japan in 1959 for the immigration of 85,000 Japanese by 1990, but only about 8,000 arrived. An immigration agreement was signed with the Republic of Korea (ROK) in 1966. In 1985, the immigrant population totaled 199,500; the leading immigrant groups were Germans, Japanese, Koreans, Chinese, Brazilians, and Argentines. (It was believed, however, that the actual number of Brazilians was 300,000 to 350,000.) As of September 1999, Paraguay was hosting 26 asylum-seekers from Eastern Europe and Latin America. The net migration rate in 1999 was -0.09 migrants per 1,000 population.

⁸ETHNIC GROUPS

According to estimates reported in 1998, some 95% of the population is mestizo, principally a mixture of Spanish and Guaraní Amerindian. The others are pure Amerindian (1–3%), black, or of European or Asian immigrant stock. However, another estimate puts mestizos at 76% and Europeans at 20%. During the late 1950s, Japanese settlement began in the region between Encarnación and Caazapá. Korean settlement began in 1966.

The Guaraní Amerindians, belonging to the Tupi-Guaraní linguistic group, had spread throughout a large area of South America east of the Andes before the Spaniards arrived. Within Paraguay, extensive intermarriage between the races resulted in almost complete assimilation.

⁹LANGUAGES

Paraguay is a bilingual nation. Spanish, the dominant language, is taught in the schools and is spoken by slightly more than half of the people. However, the great majority of Paraguayans speak Guaraní, an Amerindian language that evolved from the southern dialect of the Tupi-Guaraní group. It is also the language of widely esteemed literature, drama, and popular music.

¹⁰RELIGIONS

The constitution of provides for freedom of conscience and recognizes no official religion. Roman Catholicism is the dominant religion, but all people are free to follow whichever faith they choose. In 1998, the total population was reportedly about 90% Roman Catholic. The remaining 10% consisted of mainline Protestant, evangelical Christian, Jewish, Mormon, Muslim, and Baha'i groups. There were also substantial Mennonite communities, whose practitioners originally came to the country in several waves between 1880 and 1950 in order to avoid religious persecution.

¹¹TRANSPORTATION

Inadequate transportation facilities have been a major impediment to Paraguay's development. For a long time, some 3,100 km (1,925 mi) of domestic waterways provided the chief means

PARAGUAY

| 0 | 50 | 100 | 150 | 200 Miles |
| 0 | 50 | 100 | 150 | 200 Kilometers |

BOLIVIA

BRAZIL

CHACO BOREAL

CHACO CENTRAL

ARGENTINA

Villazon

General Eugenio A. Garay

Mayor Pablo Lagerenza

Cerro León 3,281 ft. 1000 m.

Fortín Madrejón

Doctor Pedro P. Peña

Maríscal Estigarribia

Filadelfia

Misión Estero

Pozo Colorado

Fortín Gral. Delgado

Fuerte Olimpo

Pôrto Murtinho

Puerto La Victoria

Bella Vista

Pedro Juan Caballero

Ponta Porã

AMAMBAY MTS.

Concepción

San Pedro

Rosario

Estancia Villa Rey

Villa Hayes

Asunción

San Lorenzo

Caacupé

Coronel Oviedo

Paraguarí

Villarrica

Caazapá

Ciudad del Este

Salto del Guairá

Guaíra

Santa Helena

Cataratas del Iguazu (Iguazu Falls)

Pilar

San Juan Bautista

Encarnación

Corrientes

BRAZIL

Pilcomayo *Tueco* *Bermejo* *Paraguay* *Verde* *Monte Lindo* *Pilcomayo* *Apa* *Ypané* *Jejuí-Guazú* *Acaray* *Tebicuary* *Paraguay* *Paraná* *Alto Paraná*

Paraguay

LOCATION: 19°17′ to 27°30′s; 54°30′ to 62°28′w. **BOUNDARY LENGTHS:** Brazil, 1,339 km (832 mi); Argentina, 1,699 km (1,056 mi); Bolivia, 756 km (470 mi).

of transportation, with most vessels owned by Argentine interests. Hampered by the high costs and slow service of Argentine riverboats transporting cargo to and from Buenos Aires, the Paraguayan government put its own fleet of riverboats in operation. This remedy, however, did not solve the underlying problems of Paraguayan transport. Drought conditions frequently affect navigation, and while the Paraguay is open to river traffic as far as Concepción (about 290 km/180 mi north of Asunción), passage is sometimes hazardous to vessels of even

medium draft. The inland waterways and the Rio de la Plata handle more than half of Paraguay's foreign trade with Argentina, Brazil, Chile, Europe, Japan, and the US.

Asunción, the chief port, and Concepción can accommodate oceangoing vessels. In 1998, Paraguay had 21 merchant vessels, with a total capacity of 30,287 GRT. In addition, Paraguay has been given free port privileges at Santos and Paranaguá, Brazil. More than 90% of Paraguay's foreign trade passes to Asunción through ports in Argentina and Uruguay. A four-year project begun in 1967 substantially improved Asunción's cargo-handling capacity.

Road construction is another critical focus of development. In 1999, highways totaled an estimated 29,500 km (18,331 mi); of these roads, however, only 2,803 km (1,742 mi) were asphalted. Two major road projects of the 1960s were the Friendship Bridge on the Brazilian border in the Iguaçu Falls area, inaugurated in 1961, and the 770-km (480-mi) all-weather Trans-Chaco Road, which extends from Asunción to Bolivia. The Friendship Bridge permits highway travel from Asunción to the Brazilian Atlantic port of Paranaguá. A bridge over the Paraguay River, linking the western and eastern parts of the country, was inaugurated in 1978. All-weather roads connecting Asunción with Buenos Aires and Puerto Presidente Stroessner with Paranaguá have also been completed. In 1995, 75,000 passenger cars and 50,000 commercial vehicles were in use.

In 1961, the 441-km (274-mi) British-owned Paraguayan Central Railroad was sold to Paraguay for $560,000; it was subsequently renamed Ferrocarril Presidente Carlos Antonio López. There is a direct line between Asunción and Buenos Aires. Altogether there are some 971 km (603 mi) of trackage, including narrow-gauge industrial lines in the Chaco.

In 1998 there were an estimated 941 airports and airfields, only 10 of which had paved runways. S. Pettirossi is the principal airport at Asuncion. Paraguayan Air Lines (Líneas Aéreas Paraguayas—LAP) provides both domestic and international service. Three carriers provide domestic service. In 1997, 196,000 passengers were carried on scheduled domestic and international airline flights.

12 HISTORY

The original inhabitants of present-day Paraguay were Guaraní Amerindians of the Tupi-Guaraní language family. As many as 150,000 Amerindians may have been living in Paraguay at the time of the earliest European contacts. The first European known to have explored Paraguay was the Italian Sebastian Cabot, sailing from 1526 to 1530 in the service of Spain. The first permanent Spanish settlement, Nuestra Señora de la Asunción (Our Lady of the Assumption, present-day Asunción), was founded at the confluence of the Paraguay and Pilcomayo rivers on Assumption Day, 15 August 1537.

Paraguay's next two centuries were dominated by Jesuit missionaries, whose efforts to protect the Amerindians from Portuguese slave traders and Spanish colonists resulted in one of the most remarkable social experiments in the New World. Shortly after the founding of Asunción, missionary efforts began. The priests organized Guaraní families in mission villages (reducciones) designed as self-sufficient communes. Amerindians were taught trades, improved methods of cultivation, and the fine arts, as well as religion. Above all, they were protected from exploitation by the Spanish colonists, who sought to exploit them. As the settlements prospered and grew in number to around 30 (with over 100,000 Amerindians), the jealousy of the colonists sparked a campaign to discredit the Jesuits. Eventually, the King of Spain became convinced that the order was trying to set up a private kingdom in the New World, and in 1767, he expelled the Jesuits from the New World. Once they had left, the reducciones disappeared. As for the Spanish colony at Asunción, it dominated the area of the Río de la Plata throughout this period. However, in 1776, when Buenos Aires became the capital of the new viceroyalty of La Plata, Asunción was reduced to an outpost.

In achieving independence, Paraguay first had to fight the forces of Argentina. Buenos Aires called on Paraguay in 1810 to follow its lead in a virtual declaration of independence. Paraguay declared independence from Spain but rejected the leadership of Buenos Aires. An Argentine expedition was decisively defeated, and Paraguay completed its move toward independence by deposing the last of its royal governors in 1811.

Since then, Paraguay has been dominated by dictatorships or near-dictatorships. The first and most famous of the dictators was José Gaspar Rodríguez de Francia (known as "El Supremo"), originally a member of the five-man junta elected in 1811 to govern the newly independent nation. He was granted full dictatorial powers for three years in 1814 and thereafter had the term extended for life. Francia attempted to cut Paraguay off from all contact with the outside world. Commerce was suspended, foreigners were expelled, relations with the papacy were broken off, and an anticlerical campaign was begun. All criticism was stifled, and a widespread spy network was developed. However, at the same time, Francia was honest and tireless in his devotion to his personal concept of the country's welfare. Francia governed until his death in 1840. Today, he is regarded as Paraguay's "founding father."

The next dictator was Carlos Antonio López. López loosened the ties of dictatorship only slightly, but reversed Francia's paranoid isolationism. He reestablished communications with the outside world and normalized relations with the papacy. López encouraged road and railway building, improved education somewhat, and became the largest landowner and the richest man in Paraguay. He made his son Francisco Solano López commander-in-chief of the army, thereby ensuring the younger López's succession to power in 1862, when the elder López died.

During his dictatorship, Francisco Solano López provoked quarrels with Argentina, Brazil, and Uruguay, who allied and attacked Paraguay. The War of the Triple Alliance (1865–70), sometimes called the Paraguayan War, was the bloodiest in Latin American history. López, who fancied himself a Latin Napoleon, drafted virtually every male in Paraguay over the age of 12, with no upper age limit, and insisted that his troops never surrender. The war was a disaster for Paraguay, which lost two-thirds of all its adult males, including López himself. Paraguay's population fell from about 600,000 to about 250,000. The war also cost Paraguay 55,000 square miles of territory, its economic well-being, and its pride.

For the next 50 years, Paraguay stagnated economically. The male population was replaced by an influx from Italy, Spain, Germany, and Argentina. Politically, there was a succession of leaders, alternating between the Colorado and Liberal parties. Then, a long-smoldering feud with Bolivia broke into open warfare (1932–35) after oil was discovered in the Chaco, a desolate area known as the "green hell." Although outnumbered three to one, the Paraguayans had higher morale, were brilliantly led, and were better adapted to the climate of the region. Moreover, they regarded the conflict as a national undertaking to avenge the defeat of 1870. Paraguayans conquered three-fourths of the disputed territory, most of which they retained following the peace settlement of 1938.

Although President Eusebio Ayala emerged victorious from the Chaco War, he did not last long. The war produced a set of heroes, all of whom had great ambitions. One such man, Col. Rafael Franco, took power in February 1936. In 1939, after two more coups, Gen. José Felix Estigarribía, commander-in-chief during the Chaco War, was elected president. Estigarribía was killed in an airplane crash only a year later, and Gen. Higinio Morínigo, the minister of war, was appointed president by the cabinet. Through World War II, Morínigo received large amounts of aid from the US, even though he allowed widespread Axis activity in the country. Meanwhile, he dealt harshly with domestic critics.

Morínigo retired in 1948, but was unable to find a successor. After a one-year period of instability, Federico Chávez seized control, and ruled from 1949 until 1954. In May 1954, Gen. Alfredo Stroessner, commander-in-chief of the armed forces, used his cavalry to seize power. He had himself elected president as the candidate of the Colorado Party, and then was reelected in another single-slate election in 1958, although he did permit the Liberal Party to hold its first convention in many years. With US help, he brought financial stability to an economy racked by runaway inflation, but he used terrorist methods in silencing all opposition. Exiles who invaded Paraguay simultaneously from Argentina and Brazil in December 1959 were easily routed. Six other small invasions during 1960 were also repulsed. Stroessner won a third presidential term in February 1963, despite the constitutional stipulation that a president could be reelected only once.

In August 1967, a constitutional convention approved a new governing document that not only provided for a bicameral legislature but also established the legal means for Stroessner to run for reelection. Stroessner did so in 1968, 1973, 1978, 1983, and 1988, all with only token opposition permitted. On 17 September 1980, the exiled former dictator of Nicaragua, Anastasio Somoza Debayle, who had been granted asylum by the Stroessner government, was assassinated in Asunción, and Paraguay broke off relations with Nicaragua.

During the 1980s, Stroessner relaxed his hold on Paraguay. The state of siege, which had been renewed every three months since 1959 (with a partial suspension from February 1978 to September 1980), was allowed to lapse in April 1987. Opponents of the regime gave credit for the ending of the state of siege to the US, which had kept pressure on the Stroessner administration. However, allegations of widespread human rights abuses continued to be made. In April 1987, Domingo Laíno, an opposition leader exiled in December 1982, who had tried unsuccessfully to enter the country on five earlier occasions, was allowed to return to Paraguay. Part of this liberalization may have been in response to mounting criticism from the Roman Catholic Church, whose position moved closer to that of the various dissident groups.

On 3 February 1989 Stroessner's 35-year dictatorship came to an end at the hand of Gen. Andrés Rodríguez, second in command of the Paraguayan military. Immediately after the coup, Rodríguez announced that elections would be held in May. With only three months to prepare, little opposition beyond Domingo Laíno was mounted, and Rodríguez won easily with 75.8% of the vote. There followed an immediate easing of restrictions on free speech and organization. Labor unions were recognized and opposition parties allowed to operate freely. Rodríguez promised and delivered elections in 1993. In those elections, Colorado candidate Juan Carlos Wasmosy was elected to the presidency, the first time a civilian had become president through popular election since 1954. Paraguay had experienced an unprecedented transfer of political power through a constitution from one elected government to another. Wasmosy began to push for economic liberalization, including the sale of state-owned enterprises, but it was unclear whether the military was willing to support such measures. In April 1996, General Lino Cesar Oviedo staged a brief rebellion when asked by Wasmosy to resign his post as army commander, but a coup was averted and Oviedo was eventually acquitted of charges of armed insurrection. Oviedo, now a civilian, has become the leader of an opposing faction of Wasmosy's Colorado Party. Other than Oviedo's short-lived rebellion, however, no serious threats to Wasmosy's economic and political reforms have been offered. In fact, the more democratic environment was tested and proven in 1993 by the first general labor strike in 35 years. Although the government responded with some force to this first strike, subsequent strikes have been met with a much gentler governmental hand. Unfortunately, the economy itself has been slow to respond to the new reforms. In the 1990s, Paraguay experienced 0% economic growth.

In the 1998 presidential elections, Raúl Cubas of the Colorado Party became president with 55.3% of the vote, but a year later he had to resign after the assassination of vice-president Luis Argaña. Cubas was closely associated with General Oviedo and the later was linked to the political assassination. Upon Cubas' resignation, the president of the Senate, Luis González Macchi was sworn in as president. Cubas sought exile in Brazil and Oviedo sought refugee in Argentina. It is unclear what policies González will pursue but many consider him as a caretaker until new elections are held in 2003.

One attempt to bolster the economy through increased trade possibilities has met with marked resistance from conservationists. The proposed Hidrovia project, which would create a 3,200-km (2,000-mi) waterway from Brazil to Uruguay suitable for large cargo ships, could seriously endanger the Pantanal wetlands in Brazil (the largest wetlands area in the world). Although the five-country consortium initiating the project claims it will wait for the results of an environmental impact study before proceeding, Paraguay said it would begin blasting on the Paraguay River in June 1996. Ecologists, however, continue to battle any progress on the project while the environmental study is completed.

[13]GOVERNMENT

Under the constitution of 25 August 1967, Paraguay was a republic, with substantial powers conferred on the executive. The Constituent Assembly revised the constitution on 20 June 1992, but kept most of the structure from the previous document, while limiting many of the powers Stroessner used during his administration. The judicial system was also slated for overhaul.

The president is directly elected for a five-year term. The president is commander-in-chief of the military forces and conducts foreign relations. He appoints the 11-member cabinet, most administrators, and justices of the Supreme Court. He is advised by the Council of State, consisting of the cabinet ministers, the president of the National University, the archbishop of Asunción, the president of the Central Bank, and representatives of other sectors and the military.

The 1967 constitution provided for a bicameral legislature, consisting of the 45-member Senate and the 80-member Chamber of Deputies. By formula, two-thirds of the seats in each house are guaranteed to the party receiving the highest total vote in a general election. The remaining one-third is distributed proportionately among opposing political groups. Representatives must be at least 25 years of age and are elected for five-year terms.

Voting is by secret ballot and is compulsory for all citizens between 18–60 years of age. Women were first allowed to vote in 1963.

[14]POLITICAL PARTIES

Since the end of the War of the Triple Alliance, two parties have dominated politics—the National Republican Association (Asociación Nacional Republicana), generally known as the Colorado Party, and the Liberal Party. Both parties have exemplified the uncompromising nature of Paraguayan politics and used their position to stifle the opposition. Consequently, changes of administration have been effected principally by armed revolt.

The Colorado Party governed from its founding in 1887 until 1904, and again after 1947. Conservative and nationalistic, the Colorados split during the 1950s into two factions: the "officialist" Colorados supported the Stroessner dictatorship, while the People's Colorado Movement (Movimiento Popular Colorado—MOPOCO) styled itself a supporter of "representative democracy." Most of the MOPOCO leadership chose exile in 1959. In the 1980s the Colorados became even more divided. Three groups emerged: a "militant" pro-Stroessner faction; "traditionalists," pushing for Stroessner to step down; and a reformist "ethical" faction, which is interested in cleaning up government corruption.

The 1989 coup was engineered by a leader of the "traditionalist" faction. Wasmosy, the first freely elected civilian president, who took office in 1993, is more reformist in his approach. Raúl Cubas was elected party president in 1998. He ran against his fellow party member president Wasmosy and was supported by General Lino Oviedo, who had attempted a military coup against Wasmosy in 1995. After the assassination of Colorado Party vice-president Luis Argaña in 1999, Cubas had to resign. Senate president Luis González, also from the Colorado Party, became president. Cubas and Oviedo are sought by the Paraguayan police to face charges related to Argaña's assassination. Even with the hefty parliamentary majority— 45 out of 80 seats in the Chamber and 24 out of 45 seats in the Senate—the Colorados remain badly split and in disrepair.

The Liberal Party, like the Colorados, appeared in 1887. They seized power in 1904 and governed until 1936. Banned in 1942, the Liberals were reconstituted during the 1960s. There has never been a recognizable ideological distinction between the Liberals and Colorados, but the two parties are similar in their disunity. Liberals had, by 1982, split into three factions: the Authentic Radical Liberal Party (Partido Liberal Radical Auténtico— PLRA), the Liberal Teeté Party (Partido Liberal Teeté—PLT), and the Radical Liberal Party (Partido Liberal Radical—PLR). After 1989, the PLRA and the PLR reemerged to compete for votes, with the PLRA considerably stronger. The PLRA, led by Domingo Laíno, was the largest opposition party in 1996. In the 1998 presidential and parliamentary elections Laíno obtained 43.9% of the vote and his party secured 27 out of 80 seats in the Chamber of Deputies and 13 out of 45 seats in the Senate.

A new party, National Encounter (PEN), was formed in recent years. It consists of an alliance of several smaller parties and civic organizations and appeals to the urban middle class. The PEN won eight seats in the Senate and nine seats in the Chamber of Deputies in the 1993 elections. Finally, the White Party, a center-right movement, one seat in the Senate in 1998.

Electoral reform has purged the voter rolls of the deceased (who usually "voted" for Colorado Party members), made voting more than once in an election a punishable crime, and established a tribunal to oversee the electoral process. These reforms appear to be working so far, as evidenced by fair municipal elections in 1996 and presidential and parliamentary elections in 1998.

15 LOCAL GOVERNMENT

Paraguay is divided into 17 departments, which are subdivided into districts, which, in turn, comprise municipalities (the minimum requirement for a municipality is 3,000 persons) and rural districts (partidos). A governor, elected by popular vote, runs each department. Municipal government is exercised through a municipal board, chosen by direct election, and an executive department. In the principal cities and capitals, the executive department is headed by a mayor appointed by the minister of the interior; in other localities, the mayor is appointed by the presidents of the municipal boards. Police chiefs are appointed by the central government.

16 JUDICIAL SYSTEM

The five-judge Supreme Court exercises both original and appellate jurisdiction. There are four appellate tribunals: civil/commercial, criminal, labor, and juvenile. There are special appellate chambers for civil and commercial cases and criminal cases. Each rural district (partido) has a judge appointed by the central government to settle local disputes and to try accused persons and sentence those found guilty. Federal judges and magistrates are appointed by the executive for a term of five years coinciding with the presidential term, so that the judges of the

Supreme Court and lesser tribunals are always named by the president in power. The Council of State must approve the appointment of members of the Supreme Court and may remove them by impeachment. Justices of the peace deal with minor cases.

The 1992 Constitution provides for selection of judges by an independent body working with the Congress and the executive. As of 1997 based on recommendations from the Magistrates Council, the Supreme Court nominated 215 lower court judges and magistrates. There is also a military court system for the armed forces. The judicial system is based on civil law, mainly influenced by French and Argentine codes.

17 ARMED FORCES

Paraguay's armed forces were reported to number 20,200 (12,900 conscripts) as of 2000, about 14,900 in the army, 3,600 in the navy (including 900 marines), and 1,700 in the air force, with 28 combat aircraft and no armed helicopters. Paraguay has compulsory military service of 12–24 months for all males between the ages of 18 and 20. Expenditures of the Ministry of Defense were $125 million in 1998, or 1.4% of gross domestic product. There is a paramilitary police service of 14,800. Reservists number 164,500.

18 INTERNATIONAL COOPERATION

Paraguay is a charter member of the UN, having joined on 24 October 1945. It participates in ECLAC and all the nonregional specialized agencies except IMO. Paraguay also participates in G-77, IADB, LAIA, OAS, and the WTO, and has signed the Law of the Sea.

19 ECONOMY

Landlocked Paraguay has a limited economy based predominantly on agriculture (cotton and soy), livestock production, forestry, and the basic processing of materials. Agriculture accounts for roughly 27% of GDP. Mineral resources are negligible. In recent years, the relative importance of agriculture has declined, and the value of services has risen; however, cattle raising remains a key economic activity. The large informal sector consists of the reexport of consumer goods from Asia and the US to neighboring countries, and many small street vendors and businesses that provide services.

Paraguay suffered for years from runaway inflation. The IMF joined the US government in 1957 in providing for stabilization loans that enabled Paraguay to establish a free exchange system and accelerate the pace of public investment. During the 1960s, inflation ranged between 2% and 3%, but the rate increased during the following decade to 28.2% in 1979. The rate was an estimated 30–40% through the 1980s, fueled by rapid expansion of the money supply. Inflation was at 7% in 1997, but rose to 14.6% in 1998 because of a devaluation of the local currency.

During the 1980s, construction of the Itaipú hydroelectric project (which was finished in 1982) stimulated Paraguay's economic expansion. The end of the Itaipú building boom, currency devaluations in Argentina and Brazil (and thus the relative overvaluation of the guaraní), and declining international market prices for Paraguay's agricultural products led to an economic slowdown which was exacerbated by the impact of adverse weather on the agricultural sector.

An economic reform package instituted in the early 1990s included judicial reform, a macro-economic stabilization program featuring fiscal austerity, liberalization of the exchange rate, and efforts to privatize state-owned enterprises. A banking crisis in 1995 required a government bailout and sent shock waves through the economy causing a sharp drop in commercial sales. Progress on the reforms were continuing in 1996 although at a slow pace due to stiff political opposition, and reforms were all but abandoned in 1997 and 1998. Integration into Mercosur (Southern Cone Common Market), which should help the economy grow through foreign investment and increased exports. The economy grew at a rate of 2.7% between 1988 to 1998, but GDP contracted by 0.50% in 1998 alone, due in part to El Nino crop damage. In 1999, the economy shrunk by at least 3%, due to politically motivated violence.

20INCOME

The US Central Intelligence Agency (CIA) reports that in 1998 Paraguay's gross domestic product (GDP) was estimated at $19.8 billion. The per capita GDP was estimated at $3,700. The annual growth rate of GDP was estimated at -0.5%. The average inflation rate in 1998 was 14.6%. The CIA defines GDP as the value of all final goods and services produced within a nation in a given year and computed on the basis of purchasing power parity (PPP) rather than value as measured on the basis of the rate of exchange. It was estimated that agriculture accounted for 27% of GDP, industry 30%, and services 43%.

Private consumption includes expenditures of individuals, households, and nongovernmental organizations. It was estimated that between 1990 and 1998 private consumption grew at an annual rate of 2.5%. The richest 10% of the population accounted for approximately 47% of household consumption and the poorest 10% approximately 0.7%.

21LABOR

In 1996, there were 1,190,000 employed persons in Paraguay. Agriculture, animal husbandry, and forestry employed 5.2% of the work force; manufacturing and commerce, 21%; and construction, 6.9%.

The 1992 constitution provides Paraguayans in both the public and private sector the freedom to form and join unions without government interference. The constitution also protects fundamental worker rights, including the right of association. There also are provisions for antidiscrimination, employment tenure, severance pay, collective bargaining, and the right to strike. As of 1999, 15% of the labor force, or about 121,000 workers, belonged to unions, which numbered approximately 1,600.

Labor laws provide for a maximum workweek of 48 hours for day work and 42 for night work, with one day of rest. The law also provides for an annual bonus of one month's salary. The minimum wage was $179 per month in 1999. However, only 30% to 50% of eligible workers receive the minimum wage.

The minimum working age is 15, although minors as young as 12 may work in family enterprises. In reality these provisions are not effectively enforced and thousands of children work both on farms and in urban areas.

22AGRICULTURE

Cultivation utilizes about 5.7% of Paraguay's total land area. The total area under cultivation rose from 245,636 hectares (606,976 acres) in 1940–41 to an estimated 2,285,000 hectares (5,646,000 acres) in 1997. Primary agriculture accounts for 32% of GDP and about 35% of employment. The principal areas of cultivation are in the clearings around Asunción and Encarnación. Arable land outside these regions is sparsely settled, and inhabitants there rely principally on livestock and forestry for a living.

The two most widely cultivated crops are manioc (cassava) and corn, which, with meat, are the staples of the Paraguayan diet. Cotton, tobacco, and sugarcane are among the leading cash and export crops. A national wheat program increased production from 7,000 tons in 1965 to 23,000 tons in 1973, 55,000 tons in 1981, and 550,000 tons in 1998, eliminating the need for wheat imports. Enough beans, lentils, sweet potatoes,

peanuts, coffee, and fruits are grown for home use, and slightly more than enough rice. Crops yielding edible oils are widely grown, and yerba maté is cultivated on plantations. Production of principal crops for 1998 (in tons) included sugar cane, 2,800,000; manioc, 3,300,000; soybeans, 2,856,000; corn, 874,000; cotton, 88,000; and tobacco, 14,000. Cotton exports generated $76 million in 1997; soybeans, $316 million.

23ANIMAL HUSBANDRY

During the 1960s and 1970s, the meat-packing industry developed appreciably, with meat and related products constituting Paraguay's most important single export. Since the late 1970s, however, market conditions for beef exports have deteriorated, and the value of exported meat products has declined significantly. Exports of livestock and livestock products typically account for 7% of total exports and in some years comprise as much as 14%. In 1997, livestock sector exports (live animals, meat and dairy products, eggs, hides, and animal fats and oils) amounted to almost $105 million. About 70–80% of beef exports are sent to Mercosur countries.

In 1998, livestock totaled 9,794,000 head of cattle, 2,525,000 hogs, 387,000 sheep, and 370,000 horses. There were also an estimated 15 million chickens that year. Beef production was about 226,000 tons. Other livestock products in 1998 included 352,000 tons of cow's milk and 47,000 tons of eggs.

24FISHING

Paraguay has no appreciable fishing industry, and the consumption of fresh fish is low. The country has potential resources for fisheries, however. Dorado weighing up to 18 kg (40 lb) are caught in the Upper Paraná River, and the Paraguay River yields salmon, surubí, pacú, boga, and mandi. The catch was 28,000 tons in 1997. Aquacultural production that year included 210 tons of tilapia.

25FORESTRY

Although forest resources are immense, exploitation is limited by lack of roads and mechanized transport facilities. About 29% of Paraguay's total land area consists of forest and woodland (11.5 million hectares/28.5 million acres in 1995). However, much of that lies in the western Chaco, the forest resources of which have never been exploited. Roundwood cuttings totaled 10.4 million cu m in 1997, with 63% used for fuel wood.

Exportation of logs was banned in 1973 in order to encourage the domestic lumber industry; forest products earned $97.6 million on the export market during 1997.

The chief forest products are quebracho, various cabinet and other tropical hardwoods, and oil of petitgrain. Quebracho, the source of the tannin used by the leather-tanning industry, is the wood of the greatest commercial importance. Paraguay is the world's largest producer of petitgrain oil, a perfume base distilled from the leaves and shoots of the bitter orange tree. Since wood and charcoal are the only fuels produced in Paraguay, about two-thirds of all wood cut is used for burning.

26MINING

Paraguay's mining potential has been restricted by limited exploration, inadequate infrastructure, large fiscal and trade deficits, scarcity of foreign exchange, and limited private investment. In 1997 mining accounted for less than 1% of the GDP. There are small deposits of iron ore, and a few mines were worked before 1865, but there had been no evidence, until recently, of any metallic mineral deposits of commercial value. Lateritic iron ore deposits along the Paraná River near Encarnación were estimated at 300 million tons with 35% iron. Manganese deposits are known to exist near the Guairá Falls. Excellent limestone, found in large quantities along the Paraguay River north of Concepción, is quarried for the cement industry. Sandstone, mica, copper, kaolin, clay, and salt have been exploited modestly, and there are known deposits of azurite, barite, gypsum, lignite, malachite, mica, peat, pyrite, pyrolusite, soapstone, and uranium. Production of mineral commodities is predominantly for domestic consumption. Production estimates for 1997 included 66,700 tons of kaolin, 10 million tons of sand, 4.5 million tons of gypsum, and 600,000 tons of limestone.

Under Paraguayan law, all mineral rights belong to the government, which has sought to encourage mining development by the privatization of some state-owned companies. In 1997 it completed a major mineral concession contract with Yamana Resources of Canada, and there is ongoing exploration throughout the country by other foreign companies.

27 ENERGY AND POWER

Until 1968, Paraguay relied almost entirely on thermoelectric power. In that year, however, the first turbine was inaugurated at a major hydroelectric project at the juncture of the Acaray and Monday rivers. Planned jointly with Brazil and completed by an Italian company, this first stage of the project had a capacity of 45 MW; by 1976, the project was completed, with a capacity of 190 MW.

In 1973, Paraguay and Brazil agreed on the joint construction of the Itaipú power plant, the world's largest hydroelectric project. The plant, which came onstream in 1984, has a generating capacity of 12,600 MW. By the end of 1982, the total cost (shared by the two countries) exceeded $20 billion; construction of the power plant and auxiliary facilities employed a peak force of 39,000 Paraguayan workers. Itaipú produces about 70% of Paraguay's electricity. Paraguay is entitled to 50% of Itaipú's output, but can sell unused power to Brazil; Itaipú produces about 75 billion kWh of electricity per year. As of 1999, plans were under way for the addition of two new 700-MW turbines.

Another 1973 agreement, with Argentina, called for the joint construction on the Alto Paraná River of the Yacyretá hydroelectric plant (320 km/200 mi downstream from Itaipú), with an installed capacity of 4,000 MW. The final agreement was signed in 1979, but construction was delayed because of Argentina's economic crisis and disputes over contract awards, exacerbated by reports of cost overruns and high-level corruption. In 1986 and 1987, however, construction work on the project was speeded up, due largely to the securing of 85% of the project's $6.5-billion cost. By 1995, the Yacyretá-Apipé complex was onstream. The Corpus hydroelectric project, another joint Argentine-Paraguayan venture, which would add another 6,000 MW of generating capacity, has been postponed, due largely to budgetary constraints in Argentina.

The National Electrical Administration manages the entire power system, which was nationalized in 1947. Total power production grew from 598 million kWh in 1975 to 50.3 billion kWh in 1998, when installed capacity was 7,283 million kW.

It is generally assumed that the Paraguayan Chaco contains oil, but explorations, which in the mid-1980s involved several international companies, have thus far proved fruitless.

28 INDUSTRY

The average annual growth of manufacturing output was 3.3% between 1977 and 1987, and 1.3% during 1988–98. In 1998, manufacturing accounted for 15.3% of GDP. Processing of agricultural, animal, and forestry products, mainly for export, and small-scale manufacture of consumer goods for local needs are of greatest importance. Most manufacturing is done in the Asunción area; some plants, however, are near the source of their respective raw materials. Import-substitution industries

encouraged by the government include petroleum refining, foodstuffs, wood processing, and chemicals.

Industries include two cement plants, at Vallemí and Itapucumi, and a Paraguayan-Brazilian steel mill at Villa Hayes. Food-processing plants include slaughterhouses; flour mills; sugar mills; oil mills producing cottonseed and peanut oils for domestic consumption, as well as castor, tung, cocoa, and palm oils for export; related industries that process the by-products of oil extraction; and mills that produce yerba maté. There are numerous sawmills. A considerable but decreasing number of hides are also produced for export. Although there is a considerable textile industry, imports still run high. Products for domestic consumption include pharmaceutical and chemical goods, finished wood and furniture, brick and tiles, cigars and cigarettes, candles, shoes, matches, soap, and small metal goods.

29 SCIENCE AND TECHNOLOGY

In 1993 there were eight scientific and technological research institutes and learned societies in Paraguay, all of them located in Asunción. Notable among them are the Paraguayan Scientific Society, founded in 1921, and the South American Union of Engineers' Associations, established in 1935. The "Nuestra Senora de la Asunción" Catholic University, founded in 1960 at Asunción, has a faculty of science and technology. The National University of Asunción, founded in 1889, has faculties of medicine, dentistry, chemistry, exact and natural sciences, physical sciences and mathematics, veterinary sciences, and agricultural engineering. The Higher School of Philosophy, Sciences and Education, also in Asunción, was founded in 1944. In 1987–97, science and engineering students accounted for 20% of college and university enrollments.

30 DOMESTIC TRADE

Offices of foreign concerns and most important retail establishments are in Asunción, the only significant commercial center. Most retail trade is in small shops dealing in a limited variety of goods.

Legislation in 1961 provided for governmental and private commercial credit companies to aid in the development of agricultural, livestock, and industrial activities. Consumer credit facilities have been expanding. Many of the larger Asunción stores offer installment credit.

There is a large informal urban economy that some business groups claim is just as large as Paraguay's $20 billion formal economy. The informal sector features thousands of small enterprises and urban street vendors, along with reexports of imported consumer goods (electronics, whiskeys, perfumes, cigarettes, and office equipment).

31 FOREIGN TRADE

Paraguay has a foreign trade typical of an agricultural country, but the reexport trade on the black market is the largest foreign exchange earner. About a quarter each of Paraguay's reported commodity export returns come from cotton (24%) and oil seeds (23%). Other exports include wood and plywood (9.1%), meat (7.5%), leather (6.6%), and vegetable oil (6.6%).

In 1996 Paraguay's imports were distributed among the following categories:

Consumer goods	29.1%
Food	11.0%
Fuels	8.0%
Industrial supplies	20.2%
Machinery	18.9%
Transportation	12.6%
Other	0.2%

Principal trading partners in 1998 (in millions of US dollars) were as follows:

COUNTRY	EXPORTS	IMPORTS	BALANCE
Brazil	349	1,249	-900
Argentina	318	604	-286
Netherlands	190	11	179
Japan	59	103	-44
Chile	58	74	-16
United States	33	786	-753
Italy	25	86	-61
Uruguay	15	84	-69
China (inc. Hong Kong)	6	357	-351
Germany	5	67	-62

32BALANCE OF PAYMENTS

The US Central Intelligence Agency reports that in 1997 the purchasing power parity of Paraguay's exports was $1.1 billion while imports totaled $2.5 billion resulting in a trade balance of -$1.4 billion.

The International Monetary Fund (IMF) reports that in 1998 Paraguay had exports of goods totaling $3,824 million and imports totaling $3,938 million. The services credit totaled $489 million and debit $562 million. The following table summarizes Paraguay's balance of payments as reported by the IMF for 1998 in millions of US dollars.

Current Account		-106
Balance on goods	-114	
Balance on services	-73	
Balance on income	46	
Current transfers	35	
Capital Account		5
Financial Account		376
Direct investment abroad	...	
Direct investment in Paraguay	256	
Portfolio investment assets	-11	
Portfolio investment liabilities	...	
Other investment assets	-63	
Other investment liabilities	193	
Net Errors and Omissions		-174
Reserves and Related Items		-100

33BANKING AND SECURITIES

The Central Bank of Paraguay (BCP) was founded in 1952 as a state-owned, autonomous agency charged with establishing the government's monetary credit and exchange policies. Recommendations in early 1961 by an economic mission of the IDB and IBRD led to the establishment of the National Development Bank to provide an effective source of medium- and long-term agricultural and industrial credits. Savings and loan institutions are regulated by the superintendent of banks. There are two state-owned banks, some locally owned banks, and nine foreign banks. Foreign-owned banks account for 82% of total deposits and 78% of all loans, and the two largest banks—Banco de Asunción and Citibank—are foreign-owned.

In 1995, there were 35 banks operating in Paraguay, of which nine had opened since 1990. During the same period the number of finance companies nearly doubled to 68. The increase in the number of banks and finance companies, out of all proportion to the size of the economy, was generally believed to be related to the rapid increase in "hot money" flows through Paraguay associated with drug smuggling. In late 1995, the Central Bank announced a freeze on the opening of new banks and finance companies on the grounds that the local market was saturated. In the same year, a currency crisis caused the collapse of ten institutions, requiring $400 million in government subsidies. The 1996 Banking Law strengthened supervision of the banking system; in

1997 Banco Union was liquidated, as were two of the largest public banks due to poor performance.

Paraguay's first stock market began trading in October 1993. There are 60 local companies traded on the exchange. All companies have a minimum paid-up capital of $50,000. However, the tradition of family ownership and almost universal practice of "double accounting" for tax evasion purposes places limits on the growth of a capital market. In 1998, the stock market handled approximately $10 to $15 million per a month in transactions.

34INSURANCE

All insurance business in Paraguay is regulated by the government through the superintendent of banks. Foreign companies are permitted to operate in the country but are under stringent requirements calling for the investment of capital and reserves. In 1995 there were 40 insurance companies operating in Paraguay.

35PUBLIC FINANCE

The Paraguayan government depends upon import duties for revenue, especially from the reexport trade. The government is the largest employer, and the budget represents 40% of GDP. The majority of the budget (80%) goes to public employee salaries, 15% to servicing the foreign debt, and 5% for investment. The current account balance deficit was 3.1% of GDP in 1998.

The US Central Intelligence Agency (CIA) estimates that in 1995 Paraguay's central government took in revenues of approximately $1.25 billion and had expenditures of $1.66 billion including capital expenditures of $357 million. Overall, the government registered a deficit of approximately $410 million. External debt totaled $2.33 billion.

The following table shows an itemized breakdown of government revenues and expenditures. The percentages were calculated from data reported by the International Monetary Fund. The dollar amounts (millions) are based on the CIA estimates provided above.

REVENUE AND GRANTS	100%	1,250
Tax revenue	64.3%	804
Non-tax revenue	35.4%	443
Grants	0.2%	3

EXPENDITURES	100%	1,660
General public services	14.9%	247
Defense	10.7%	177
Public order and safety	5.8%	97
Education	22.1%	366
Health	7.3%	122
Social security	16.2%	270
Housing and community amenities	0.4%	7
Economic affairs and services	16.5%	274
Interest payments	6.0%	100

36TAXATION

The tax administration is marginally effective, characterized by cumbersome procedures and widespread tax evasion. There is no income tax on individual earnings from employment.

The basic corporate tax rate is 30%, but is reduced to 10% for companies that sell equity on the stock market and implement transparent accounting practices. A reduced rate of 25% applies to agricultural and cattle activities. A further reduced rate of 3% is applied to small companies. There is no excess profits tax or tax on dividends received by stockholders, except that stock dividends for nonresidents are subject to a withholding tax of 10%. Capital gains on all assets are taxed at 30%. A VAT is levied on goods and services at 10%. A 95% income tax exemption for five years is available for income sources in investments made, and the corporate tax on reinvested profits is 10%.

37CUSTOMS AND DUTIES

In general, Paraguayan customs duties have been viewed as a source of revenue and a means of conserving foreign exchange, with relatively few of the high duties being intended as protection for manufactured products. Tariff rates, under the MERCOSUR agreement, range from 0% for raw materials to 20% for automobiles. Import duties are specific, ad valorem, or both. Import pressures are such that the government has not kept a tight control on the purchase of nonessentials.

Paraguay has free port privileges at the Brazilian ports of Paranaguá, Santos, and Rio Grande do Sul; at the Argentinian ports of Buenos Aires and Rosario; in Chile at Antogagasta; and in Uruguay in Montevideo and Nueva Palmira. Most trade is done through the Brazilian ports.

38FOREIGN INVESTMENT

Paraguay's economy historically has been dominated by foreign interests, in particular by those of wealthy Argentines, Britons, and Brazilians. Nevertheless, the Paraguayan government has encouraged foreign investment in recent years, as a means of developing the country. Investors willing to start or to expand needed industries receive highly favorable concessions, including freedom from many import restrictions plus special rights to retain much of the foreign exchange earned. Foreign direct investment in Paraguay was approximately $100 million per year in 1993 and 1994. These were the most up-to-date figures in 2000.

39ECONOMIC DEVELOPMENT

To a considerable extent, Paraguay has a government-controlled economy; government agencies fix prices, control distribution, regulate production and exportation, and exercise monopolistic rights over much of the economy. In recent decades, and particularly since the IMF stabilization program went into effect in the late 1950s, some controls have been loosened. In the wake of the free exchange system have come moves to eliminate government subsidies, such as that for wheat. In agriculture there is an annual plan for acreage quotas, but the principal problem has been one of meeting the quotas rather than of the surpluses. The establishment of the National Development Bank has created a source of medium and long-term credits favorable to agriculture and industry. Price controls and marketing quotas are particularly significant to the cattle industry. Paraguay has sought to develop closer economic ties with Brazil, the US, and Western European nations, largely to reduce the country's dependence on trade with Argentina.

Economic planning is the responsibility of the Technical Planning Secretariat for Economic and Social Development, established in 1962. The first national plan covered 1965–66; the second, 1967–68. The third plan, a medium-term, five-year program for 1969–73, was replaced by a 1972–77 development scheme calling for a 26% increase in public investment in agriculture. Regional development, also given high priority, was to be accomplished through Paraguay's utilization of its water resources in the Itaipú hydroelectric project; a parallel development program for the Alto Paraná region was retarded by delays in the Yacyretá power project. The 1977–81 development plan aimed to achieve a more equitable distribution of social resources. A plan announced in September 1986 provided for comprehensive reform in exchange rates and in investment and fiscal policies. Government economic reforms during the 1990s were generally subsumed by opposition parties. Reforms in 1999 centered on a diversification of the economy, away from the reexportation business, and on fighting corruption, which the government's Comptroller office estimated to have cost $2.3 billion in 1997.

40SOCIAL DEVELOPMENT

Social insurance was legally established in 1943, when the Social Security Institute was created under the Ministry of Public Health. The original law, providing for medical care and sick benefits, was modified in 1951, when health insurance became obligatory for salary and wage earners of any age who work under a written or oral contract and for apprentices not receiving wages. Legislation in 1973 authorized the institute to establish a pension plan. Self-employed persons and workers who have no contract of employment are not required to carry social insurance but may do so voluntarily by applying to the institute; coverage of foreign workers is compulsory. The program provides for free medical, surgical, and hospital care (not always available) for the worker and dependents, maternity care and cash benefits, sickness and accident benefits, retirement pensions between the ages of 55 and 60, and funeral benefits. Unemployment insurance does not exist, but severance pay is provided. Social security contributions in 1991 included 9% of the gross salary withheld from the employee, 12% of payroll paid by the employer, and a government contribution equal to 1.5% of employee earnings.

Although women have full legal rights, in practice they face discrimination in education and employment, and their literacy rates are much lower than those of men. Domestic violence and workplace sexual harassment remain serious problems for women and have been targeted as key issues by both the government and nongovernmental organizations. Women are underrepresented in politics and in 1998 only 10 women served in Congress.

Human rights abuses have diminished since the return to civilian rule and improvement continued after Luis Gonzalez Macchi assumed the presidency in 1999. International observers, however, have continued to cite the use of prolonged detention and the mistreatment of prisoners. The civilian government has taken some steps to punish those responsible for human rights violations during the Stroessner regime. Prison conditions remained poor, but nongovernment organizations were allowed to visit and monitor their conditions.

41HEALTH

Hospital and medical facilities are generally concentrated in Asunción and other towns. In 1995 there was 1 hospital bed for every 762 people. There were 3,730 doctors, 1,279 dentists, and 433 nurses in 1995. In 1997 there were 5 doctors per 10,000 people. In 1990, total health care expenditures were $85 per capita.

Average life expectancy in 1998 was 70 years; the infant mortality rate averaged 36 per 1,000 live births in 1996. Overall mortality was 5.5 per 1,000 inhabitants in 1990–95 and maternal mortality was 123 per 100,000 live births in 1997. Almost half of the married women 15-44 used contraceptives between 1989–90. The principal causes of death are bacillary dysentery and other intestinal diseases, heart disease, pneumonia, and cancer. In 1990-96, only 42% of the population had access to safe water and 41% had adequate sanitation. Malaria cases remained below 1,000 from 1995 through 1998. The incidence of tuberculosis was 37.2 per 100,000 people in 1996. Immunization rates in 1997 for children up to one year old: tuberculosis (87%); diphtheria, pertussis, and tetanus (82%); polio (82%); and measles (60%). About 4% of children under 5 years old were considered malnourished in 1989-95.

The birth rate was 31 per 1,000 people in 1998. The HIV-1 seroprevalence rate was 0.1 per 100 adults in 1997, and 3,200 cases of AIDS had been diagnosed as of 1997.

42HOUSING

As of the 1982 census, there were an estimated 582,700 housing units in Paraguay; 38.4% of all dwellings had electricity and

59.4% had toilets. The average number of people per household was 5.2. At last estimate, the number of housing units rose to 755,000 with five people per dwelling. A government agency, the Paraguayan Housing and Urban Institute, was created in 1964 with an IBRD loan of $3.4 million to aid in the construction of living units for low-income families. In 1973, a National Housing Bank was established to finance low-income housing development. South Africa provided a $2-million loan in 1975 for the same purpose. Budgetary allocations to the Ministry of Housing during totaled about 12% of central government current expenditures.

43EDUCATION

For the year 2000, projected adult illiteracy rates stood at 6.7%, (males, 5.6%; females, 7.8%). Elementary education is compulsory and free between the ages of 7 and 14 (ages 9 and 14 in rural areas). Primary education lasts for six years followed by secondary education in two phases of three years each. In 1997 there were 905,813 students in primary schools. In that same year, there were 327,775 students and approximately 18,000 teachers at the secondary level.

The National University of Paraguay is located in Asunción, the capital city. Nuestra Señora de la Asunción Catholic University, a private institution, was founded in 1960. Total university and higher institution enrollment in 1996 was 42,302 students. Approximately 19.8% of the central government budget was allocated to education in the latter half of the 1990s.

44LIBRARIES AND MUSEUMS

Paraguay's modest cultural life is centered in Asunción, which has the nation's principal libraries and museums. The National Library and Archives, established in 1869, are located in Asunción and hold 44,000 volumes. The National University of Asunción holds 26,100 volumes, and the Natural and Ethnographic History Museum, also in Asunción, holds 30,000 volumes.

Asunción is the site of nine historical, scientific, and art museums. Prominent art museums include the National Museum of Fine Arts and Antiquities; the Andrés Barbero Ethnographic Museum, devoted to Amerindian art; the Julián de la Herrería Ceramics and Fine Arts Museum; and the Museum of Modern Art of the Ministry of Education. There is an historic house museum in Yaguarón.

45MEDIA

Since nationalization of the International Telephone Co. in 1947, a government monopoly, the National Telecommunications Administration (Administración Nacional de Telecommunicaciones—ANTELCO), has controlled the communications system. As of 1995 there were 111,514 telephones in use, most of them in Asunción. ANTELCO operates the national telegraph system; telephone, telex, and cable links have been established with most other countries. There were 40 AM radio stations in Paraguay as of 1999, including the official stations, Radio Nacional de Asunción and Radio Encarnación, and the Catholic Radio Caritas. Paraguay also has 10 television stations. In 1997, radio sets in use numbered 182 per 1,000 population, television receivers, 101, and mobile phones, 17.

There are five daily papers in circulation. Newspaper readership is among the lowest in Latin America. *Patia/Union* (circulation 8,000 in 1997), founded in 1946, is the organ of the Colorado Party. *Diario Hoy* began publication in 1967 and in 1999 had an estimated circulation of 125,000; the circulation of *Ultima Hora*, also founded in 1977, was 45,000. *El Diario Noticias* had a circulation of 35,000.

At present, the constitutionally guaranteed freedom of speech and the press is said to be respected by the government to a greater degree than any time in the country's recent history. An increasing amount of the media is independently owned.

Online access is extemely limited, with approximately one Internet host per 1,000 population in 1998.

46ORGANIZATIONS

Several chambers of commerce promote local and international trade. Active trade associations include the Federation of Production, Industry, and Commerce, an importers' association, and various organizations of particular trades. Professional and cultural organizations also are active.

The Paraguayan Atheneum sponsors lectures, concerts, and recitals, as well as courses in foreign languages, art, and music. The Paraguayan-American Cultural Center and the Argentine-Paraguayan Institute are important binational centers. Other organizations include the Women's Center and the Youth Atheneum. Paraguay has an Academy of Language and several organizations devoted primarily to Guaraní culture, including the Academy of Guaraní Culture and the Indian Association of Paraguay.

47TOURISM, TRAVEL, AND RECREATION

Foreign tourists entering Paraguay are required to present a valid passport; visas are not normally required for stays of less than 90 days. Visitors are urged to take precautions against tetanus, typhoid-paratyphoid, and malaria. In 1997 there were 395,058 tourist arrivals Paraguay and tourist receipts totaled $197 million. That year there were 4,843 rooms in hotels and other facilities with 10,388 beds and a 58% occupancy rate.

The monuments, museums, and parks of Asunción are the main tourist attractions. Also of interest are the Amerindian markets in and around the capital; at the famous market of Itauguá, about 30 km (18 mi) from Asunción, the makers of ñandutí lace sell their wares. Other popular tourist attractions include the world famous Iguazu Falls at Paraguay's borders with Brazil and Argentina, the San Bernardino resort, on Lake Ypacarai, and the modern boom town of Puerto Presidente Stroessner, the headquarters for construction of the Itaipú power project. Football (soccer) is Paraguay's national sport, with some 30 clubs in Asunción alone. Tennis, horse racing, boxing, basketball, and rugby football are also popular.

According to 1999 UN estimates, the cost of staying in Asunción is $177 per day. Elsewhere in the country, travel expenses average $54 per day.

48FAMOUS PARAGUAYANS

Paraguay acclaims—despite their reputations as dictators—the first three leaders of the independent nation: José Gaspar Rodríguez de Francia (El Supremo, 1761?–1840), his nephew Carlos Antonio López (1790–1862), and the latter's son Francisco Solano López (El Mariscal, 1827–70). Of nearly equal prominence is José Felix Estigarribia (1888–1940), president and Chaco War commander. Manuel Gondra (1872–1927), twice president of Paraguay, was a literary critic, educator, and diplomat. Eusebio Ayala (1875–1942), another president, was an authority on political economy and international law. Alfredo Stroessner (b.1912) was president of Paraguay from 1954 to 1989.

Leading writers include Juan Silvano Godoi (1850–1926), Manuel Domínguez (1869–1935), Pablo Max Ynsfrán (b.1894), Justo Pastor Benítez (1895–1962), former president Juan Natalicio González (1897–1966), Gabriel Casaccia (1907-80), Augusto Roa Bastos (b.1917), and Hugo Rodríguez Alcalá (b.1918). Pablo Alborno (1877–1958) and Juan Domínguez Samudio (1878–1936) were noted artists, while in music, José Asunción Flores (b.1904) is best known.

⁴⁹DEPENDENCIES
Paraguay has no territories or colonies.

⁵⁰BIBLIOGRAPHY

Hanratty, Dennis M., and Sandra W. Meditz (eds.). *Paraguay, a Country Study.* 2d ed. Washington, D.C.: Library of Congress, 1990.

Haverstock, Nathan A. *Paraguay in Pictures.* Minneapolis: Lerner Publications, 1987.

Lewis, Paul H. *Paraguay Under Stroessner.* Chapel Hill: University of North Carolina Press, 1980.

———. *Political Parties and Generations in Paraguay's Liberal Era, 1869–1940.* Chapel Hill: University of North Carolina Press, 1993.

Miranda, Carlos R. *The Stroessner Era: Authoritarian Rule in Paraguay.* Boulder, Colo.: Westview Press, 1990.

Nickson, R. Andrew. *Historical Dictionary of Paraguay.* 2d ed. Metuchen, N.J.: Scarecrow Press, 1993.

———. *Paraguay.* Santa Barbara, Calif.: Clio, 1987.

Roett, Riordan. *Paraguay.* Boulder, Colo.: Westview, 1986.

Warren, Harris Gaylord. *Rebirth of the Paraguayan Republic: The First Colorado Era, 1878–1904.* Pittsburgh: University of Pittsburgh Press, 1985.

Williams, John H. *The Rise and Fall of the Paraguayan Republic, 1800–70.* Latin American Monographs No. 48. Austin: University of Texas Press, 1979.

PERU

Republic of Peru
República del Perú

CAPITAL: Lima.

FLAG: The national flag consists of red, white, and red vertical stripes, with the coat of arms centered in the white band.

ANTHEM: *Himno Nacional,* beginning "Somos libres, seámoslo siempre" ("We are free; let us remain so forever").

MONETARY UNIT: The nuevo sol (ML), a paper currency of 100 céntimos, replaced the inti on 1 July 1991 at a rate of I1,000,000 = ML1, but, in practice, both currencies are circulating. There are coins of 1, 5, 10, 20, and 50 céntimos and 1 nuevo sol, and notes of 10, 20, 50, and 100 nuevos soles and 10,000, 50,000, 100,000, 500,000, 1,000,000, and 5,000,000 intis. ML1 = $0.28818 (or $1 = ML3.47) as of 31 March 2000.

WEIGHTS AND MEASURES: The metric system is the legal standard.

HOLIDAYS: New Year's Day, 1 January; Labor Day, 1 May; Day of the Peasant, half-day, 24 June; Day of St. Peter and St. Paul, 29 June; Independence Days, 28–29 July; Santa Rosa de Lima (patroness of Peru), 30 August; Battle of Anzamos, 8 October; All Saints' Day, 1 November; Immaculate Conception, 8 December; Christmas, 25 December. Movable holidays include Holy Thursday and Good Friday.

TIME: 7 AM = noon GMT.

¹LOCATION, SIZE, AND EXTENT

Peru is South America's third-largest country, with an area of 1,285,220 sq km (496,226 sq mi), extending about 1,290 km (800 mi) SE-NW and 560 km (350 mi) NE-SW. Comparatively, the area occupied by Peru is slightly smaller than the state of Alaska. It is bounded on the N by Ecuador and Colombia, on the E by Brazil and Bolivia, on the S by Chile, and on the W by the Pacific Ocean, with a total boundary length of 9,354 km (5,812 mi). A border dispute with Ecuador led to armed hostilities in January 1981; by 20 February, a 14-km (9-mi) demilitarized zone had been established along the disputed line.

Various offshore islands, chiefly the Chincha Islands off Pisco in southern Peru, are uninhabited, but at least 21 of these are important to the Peruvian economy and are protected by the government's guano monopoly.

Peru's capital city, Lima, is located on the Pacific coast.

²TOPOGRAPHY

Peru is divided into three contrasting topographical regions: the coast (costa), the highlands (sierra), and the eastern jungle (selva). The coastline is a narrow ribbon of desert plain from 16 to 160 km (10 to 100 mi) broad. It is scored by 50 rivers, which water some 40 oases. Only a few of these rivers, which have their source in the Andean snowbanks, reach the sea in all seasons. Although the coastal region constitutes only 12% of the national territory, it contains the ports and chief cities of Peru. Inland, the low costa rises through the steep wastes of the high costa (760–2,000 m/ 2,500–6,500 ft), then ascends abruptly to the western cordillera (Cordillera Occidental) of the Andes, which, with its ridge of towering peaks, runs parallel to the coast and forms the Peruvian continental divide. The less regular Cordillera Central and Cordillera Oriental merge in central Peru with the Cordillera Occidental. They branch off to the southeast, meeting a transverse range that becomes a crescent of peaks forming the drainage basin of the 8,300 sq km (3,200 sq mi) Lake Titicaca, the highest large navigable lake in the world (about 3,800 m/ 12,500 ft high), which is bisected by the Peruvian-Bolivian border. Of the 10 Peruvian peaks that rise above 5,800 m (19,000 ft), Huascarán, 6,768 m (22,205 ft), is the highest.

The intermontane basins, deep-gashed canyons, and high treeless plateaus (punas) of the Andes form the sierra and constitute 27% of the country's surface. The most important rivers draining the Andes on the Atlantic watershed, such as the Marañón, Huallaga, and Ucayali, flow north or south and eventually east to form the Amazon Basin. The selva covers 61% of Peru and consists of the low selva (the Amazon rain forest) and the high selva, a steeply sloping transition zone about 100–160 km (60–100 mi) wide between the sierra and the rain forest.

³CLIMATE

Although Peru's seaboard is situated well within the tropical zone, it does not display an equatorial climate; average temperatures range from 21°C (70°F) in January to 10°C (50°F) in June at Lima, on the coast. At Cuzco, in the sierra, the range is only from 12°C (54°F) to 9°C (48°F), while at Iquitos, in the Amazon region, the temperature averages about 32°C (90°F) all year round. The cold south–north Humboldt (or Peruvian) Current cools the ocean breezes, producing a sea mist with the inshore winds on the coastal plain. Only during the winter, from May to October, does this sea mist (garúa) condense into about 5 cm (2 in) of rain.

Latitude has less effect upon the climate of the sierra than altitude. The rainy season in the Andes extends from October to April, the reverse of the coastal climate. Temperatures vary more from day to night than seasonally. The snow line ranges from 4,700 to 5,800 m (15,500 to 19,000 ft). In the eastern jungle, precipitation is heavy, from 190 to 320 cm (75 to 125 in) annually; rain falls almost continuously between October and April.

A warm Pacific west-to-east current called El Niño appears near the Peruvian coast every five or six years around Christmastime (whence its name, for the Christ child), occasionally causing serious weather disturbances. During the first half of 1983, after the strongest such current ever recorded, more than 250 cm (100 in) of rain fell on Peru's northwestern plains.

4 FLORA AND FAUNA

Peru's several climates and contrasting surface features have produced a rich diversity of flora and fauna. Where the coastal desert is not barren of life, there are sparse xerophytic shrub, cactus, and algarroba, and a few palm oases along the perennially flowing rivers from the Andes. Where the sea mist (garúa) strikes against the rising slopes between 800 and 1,400 m (2,600 and 4,600 ft), a dense belt of lomas, flowering plants, and grasses (important for grazing) grows. Perennial shrubs, candelabra cacti, and intermontane pepper trees account for much of the western slope vegetation in the higher altitudes, and forests of eucalyptus have been planted. High-altitude vegetation varies from region to region, depending on the direction and intensity of sunlight. Tola grows in profusion at 3,400 m (11,000 ft) in the southern volcanic regions; bunch puna grasses may be found at 3,700 m (12,000 ft). On the brow (ceja) of the eastern slopes, mountain tall grass and sparse sierra cactus and low shrub give way at 900 m (3,000 ft) to rain forests and subtropical vegetation. As the eastern slopes descend, glaciers are remarkably close to tropical vegetation. The 601,000 sq km (232,000 sq mi) of eastern selva, with 18 rivers and 200 tributaries, contain the dense flora of the Amazon basin. Such native plants as sarsaparilla, barbasco, cinchona, coca, ipecac, vanilla, leche caspi, and curare have become commercially important, as well as the wild rubber tree, mahogany, and other tropical woods.

For centuries, vast colonies of pelicans, gannets, and cormorants have fed on the schools of anchovies that graze the rich sea pastures of the Humboldt Current and have deposited their excrement on the islands to accumulate, undisturbed by weather, in great quantities of guano. This natural fertilizer was used by the pre-Inca peoples, who carried it on their backs to the sierra. Forgotten during the days of colonial gold greed, guano attracted the attention of scientists in 1849, when its rich nitrogen content was analyzed as 14–17%. For 40 years thereafter, Peru paid many of its bills by exporting guano to exhausted croplands of Europe. Guano has since been largely replaced in the international market by synthetic fertilizers.

The rich marine plant life off the Peruvian coast attracts a wealth of marine fauna, the most important of which are anchoveta, tuna, whale, swordfish, and marlin. Characteristic of the Andes are the great condor, ducks, and other wild fowl. The vizcacha, a mountain rodent, and the chinchilla are well known, as is the puma, or mountain lion. Peru is famous for its American members of the camel family—the llama, alpaca, huarizo, and guanaco—all typical grazing animals of the highlands. The humid forests and savannas of eastern Peru contain almost half the country's species of fauna, including parrots, monkeys, sloths, alligators, paiche fish, piranhas, and boa constrictors, all common to the Amazon Basin.

5 ENVIRONMENT

Peru's principal environmental problems in the mid-1990s are air pollution, water pollution, soil erosion and pollution, and deforestation. Air pollution is a problem, especially in Lima, due to industrial and vehicle emissions. Carbon dioxide emissions from industrial sources totaled 22.2 million metric tons, a per capital level of 0.99 metric tons. Water pollution is another of Peru's environmental concerns. Its sources are industrial waste, sewage, and oil-related waste. The nation has 9.6 cu mi of water. Seventy-two percent is used to support farming and 9.0% is used for industrial activity. Twenty-five percent of city dwellers and 76% of the rural population do not have pure drinking water. The

nation's cities produce 3.0 million tons of solid waste per year. Soil erosion has resulted from overgrazing on the slopes of the costa and sierra.

The National Office for the Evaluation of Natural Resources is the principal policymaking body for resource development, while the General Department of the Environment, part of the Ministry of Health, deals with control of pollution problems; water, forest, and wildlife resources are the province of the Ministry of Agriculture. Numerous environmental protection measures have been passed, but enforcement is lax and hampered by inefficient management and scarce fiscal resources. A major environmental challenge for Peru in the 1980s has been opening the selva for agricultural development without doing irreparable harm to the ecology of the Amazon Basin.

In the mid-1990s, 29 of the nation's mammal species and 75 of its bird species were endangered. Three-hundred and sixty of its plant species were also endangered. Endangered or extinct species include the yellow-tailed woolly monkey, black spider monkey, puna rhea, tundra peregrine falcon, white-winged guan, arrau, green sea turtle, hawksbill turtle, olive ridley turtle, leatherback turtle, spectacled caiman, black caiman, Orinoco crocodile, and American crocodile.

6 POPULATION

In the 1990s, in order to decrease the rate of growth, the government set as a target a growth rate of 2% per year and a population size of 26.9 million by 2000. However, by 2000 the population of Peru was estimated at 27,135,689. An estimated 4.4% of the population is 65 years of age or older. The projected population for the year 2005 is 29,659,000, assuming a crude birthrate of 23 per 1,000 population and a death rate of 5, resulting in a natural rate of change of 1.8% for the period 2000–2005. The population rate of change between 1995 and 2000 was 1.7%. The population density in 1998 was 19 per sq km (49 per sq mi).

Some 53% of the inhabitants live in the coastal region; the Andean sierra has 36% of the population; the eastern jungle has 11%. It was estimated that 73% of the population lived in urban areas in 2000, up from 65% in 1980. The capital city, Lima, had a 2000 metropolitan population of 7,443,000. Other important cities, with estimated populations, are Trujillo, 531,000; Arequipa, 634,000; and Chiclayo, 426,000.

7 MIGRATION

During the guano boom in the 1860s and 1870s, the Peruvian government imported Chinese laborers to mine the guano deposits, build railroads, and work on cotton plantations. Since then, Peru has not attracted large numbers of immigrants, although there are Japanese as well as Chinese enclaves in the coastal cities. In 1991, 377,485 Peruvians left the country, and 309,136 returned. The US was the leading country of destination (38%), with Chile second. Arrivals by foreigners outnumbered departures by 7,789. In 1999, Peru continued to produce more refugees than it received, due particularly to human rights violations. As of September 1999, there were 433 recognized refugees, most of them from Latin American countries.

Recent governments have encouraged the movement of people into the empty areas of the eastern Andean slopes (the high selva) in order to bring the eastern provinces into the national economic mainstream. Since the 1950s, however, the main trend has been in the reverse, from the sierra to the coastal cities. Lima has received the bulk of rural migrants, and by the mid 1990s the metropolitan area of Lima supported nearly one-third of the total national population.

In 1999, the net migration rate was -1.13 migrants per 1,000 population.

LOCATION: 0°1′ to 18°20′s; 68°39′ to 81°19′w. **BOUNDARY LENGTHS:** Ecuador, 1,529 km (950 mi); Colombia, 1,506 km (936 mi); Brazil, 2,823 km (1,754 mi); Bolivia, 1,047 km (651 mi); Chile, 169 km (105 mi); Pacific coastline, 2,334 km (1,450 mi). **TERRITORIAL SEA LIMIT:** 200 mi.

⁸ETHNIC GROUPS

According to the latest estimates, about 45% of the inhabitants are Amerindian, 37% mestizo (of mixed Spanish and Amerindian ancestry), 15% white, and 3% black, Asian, or other.

Of the 4–7 million sierra Amerindians under Inca domination, fewer than one million were left when the first colonial census was taken in 1777. A failing food supply and new diseases, such as smallpox, scarlet fever, and measles, were lethal to the young. Despite continuing disease and poverty found among the Amerindians today, they have increased to more than eight million. The main groups are the Quechua- and Aymará-speaking tribes, but there are also some other small tribes in the highlands. Peru's lowland forest Amerindians were never subjugated by Incas or by Spaniards and continue to be fishermen, hunters, and foragers. In the mid-1980s, at least 225,000 jungle Indians were grouped in 37 tribes. A 20-year plan announced in 1968 called for the full social, economic, and political integration of Peru's Amerindian population. Nevertheless, in the 1980s, sociocultural distinctions based on ethnic background were endemic to Peruvian society, with whites (especially the criollos, those of early Spanish descent) at the top of the hierarchy, mestizos and cholos (acculturated Amerindians) below them, and monolingual Quechua- or Aymará-speaking Amerindians at the bottom.

Small groups of Germans, Italians, and Swiss are important in commerce, finance, and industry. Chinese and Japanese operate small businesses, and some Japanese have been successful in agriculture.

9LANGUAGES

Spanish is spoken, as in all Latin America, without the use of the sound represented by *th* in *thing* characteristic of Castilian. The majority of the population speaks only Spanish. At least seven million Amerindians, as well as many mestizos, speak Quechua, the native tongue of the Inca peoples, the use of which was outlawed following an Amerindian revolt in 1780. A decree of 27 May 1975 granted Quechua the status of an official language, along with Spanish. Some words in modern English usage derived from Quechua are *alpaca, condor, pampa, coca, guano, Inca, llama, guanaco, vicuña, puma,* and *quinine*. Aymará is spoken by at least 700,000 people, especially in the department of Puno and around Lake Titicaca, and various other languages are spoken by tribal groups in the Amazon Basin.

10RELIGIONS

The constitution guarantees religious freedom, but it also recognizes the Roman Catholic Church as an "important element in the historical, cultural, and moral development" of the country. Although the population is about 88.9% Roman Catholic, the practice of Catholicism in Peru is imbued with Amerindian elements. About 7.3% are non-Catholic Christians, including evangelical Christians (Lutherans, Calvinists, Anglicans, Methodists, Baptists, Presbyterians, Pentecostals, members of the Assemblies of God, the Christian Missionary Alliance, The Evangelical Church of Peru, and the Church of God) and non-evangelical Christians (Mormons, Seventh-Day Adventists, Jehovah's Witnesses, and Israelites). Approximately 0.3% of the populace are members of non-Christian religions, including Jews, Muslims, Buddhists, and Shintoists. Atheists and agnostics account for 1.4%; the remainder have no religious affiliation. Reports indicate that evangelical Christians are the fastest-growing segment within the religious population.

11TRANSPORTATION

The system of highways that was the key to the unification of the Inca Empire was not preserved by the Spanish conquerors. The lack of an adequate transportation system is still a major obstacle to economic integration and development.

Peru's railroad system, consisting of 2,041 km (1,268 mi) of track in 1997, nationalized in 1972, is subject to landslides and guerrilla attacks. The two principal railway systems, the Central and Southern railways, were built during the second half of the 19th century and were at one time owned and operated by British interests. The Central Railway, the world's highest standard-gauge railroad, connects Lima-Callao with the central sierra. The Southern Railway links Arequipa and Cuzco with the ports of Mollendo and Matarani and runs to Puno on Lake Titicaca, where steamers provide cross-lake connections with Bolivia. The Tacna-Arica Railway, totaling 62 km (39 mi) and linking Peru with Chile, is also a part of the nationalized system.

In 1998, of the estimated 72,146 km (44,832 mi) of existing roads, only 7,353 km (4,569 mi) were paved. The nation's highways are deteriorating, especially in the mountains, where landslides and guerrilla attacks often occur. The two primary routes are the 3,000 km (1,864 mi) north-south Pan American Highway, connecting Peru with Ecuador, Bolivia, and Chile, and the Trans-Andean Highway, which runs about 800 km (500 mi) from Callao to Pucallpa, an inland port on the Ucayali River. The 2,500-km (1,550-mi) Jungle Edge Highway, or Carretera Marginal de la Selva, spans most of Peru along the eastern slopes of the Andes and through the selva. In 1995, there were 472,000 automobiles and 264,000 commercial vehicles. About 60% of inland freight and 90% of all passengers are carried by road.

The Amazon River with its tributaries, such as the Marañón and the Ucayali, provides a network of waterways for eastern Peru. Atlantic Ocean vessels go 3,700 km (2,300 mi) up the Amazon to Iquitos and, at high water, to Pucallpa. Peru has 11 deepwater ports, and in 1998, its merchant fleet consisted of seven vessels over 1,000 tons, with a total GRT of 51,518. Only Peruvian ships may engage in coastal shipping. Callao, Peru's chief port, and Salaverry, Pisco, and Ilo have been expanded.

Much of Peru would be inaccessible without air transport. In 1998 there were an estimated 244 airports, 44 of which had paved runways. The two principal airports are Col. Fco. Secada at Iquitos and Jorge Chavez at Lima. Faucett Airlines is the older of the two main domestic air carriers, which serve 40 airports and landing fields. The recently privatized Aeroperú, created in May 1973, provides both domestic and international services. In 1997, 2,725,000 passengers were carried on scheduled domestic and international flights. The Peruvian Air Force also operates some commercial freight and passenger flights in jungle areas.

12HISTORY

Archaeological evidence indicates that Peru has been inhabited for at least 12,000 years. Perhaps as early as 6,000 years ago, the first primitive farmers appeared. Between 500 BC and AD 1000 at least five separate civilizations developed. The Paracas, on the southern coast, produced elaborately embroidered textiles. The Chavín, in the highlands, were noted for their great carved stone monoliths. The Mochica on the north coast, produced realistic pottery figures of human beings and animals. The Nazca in the south were noted for the giant figures of animals in the ground that can be seen only from the sky. The Chimú were the most developed of these groups.

The Quechua Empire, whose emperors had the title Sapa Inca, was established in the 13th century. During the next 300 years, the extraordinary empire of the Incas, with its capital at Cuzco, spread its spiritual and temporal power to northern Ecuador, middle Chile, and the Argentine plains. By means of a system of paved highways, the small Cuzco hierarchy communicated its interests to a population of 8–12 million. The intensive agriculture of scarcely tillable lands, held in common and controlled by the state, created a disciplined economy. The *ayllu,* a kinship group that also constituted an agrarian community, was the basic unit of the Inca Empire, economically and spiritually. The Incas were sun worshipers and embalmed their dead. Their advanced civilization used a calendar and a decimal system of counting, but never developed a wheel.

Francisco Pizarro's small band of Spaniards arrived in 1532, shortly after a civil war between the Inca half-brothers Huáscar and Atahualpa. The empire collapsed in 1533. Lima was established in 1535 and promptly became the opulent center of the Viceroyalty of Peru. It held jurisdiction over all Spanish South America except Venezuela. The Spanish imperial economy, with its huge land grants given by the crown and its tribute-collecting encomiendas, brought vast wealth and a new aristocracy to Peru. To Spain, Peru was a gold bank. Mines were exploited, and overworked Indians perished by the millions as food supplies declined.

Peru remained a Spanish stronghold into the 19th century, with little internal agitation for independence. One notable exception was the abortive revolt led by a mestizo known as Tupac Amaru II in 1780. Otherwise, Peruvian royalists helped the crown suppress uprisings in Peru and elsewhere. In the end, Peru was liberated by outsiders—José de San Martín of Argentina and Simón Bolívar of Venezuela. San Martín landed on Peruvian shores in 1820 and on 28 July 1821 proclaimed Peru's independence. The royalists were not quelled, however, until the Spaniards were defeated by forces under Bolívar at Junín and under Antonio José de Sucre at Ayacucho in 1824. The victory at Ayacucho on 9 December put an end to Spanish domination on the South American continent, although the Spanish flag did not cease to fly over Peru until 1826.

Between 1826 and 1908, Peruvian presidents ruled an unstable republic plagued by rivalries between military chieftains (caudillos) and by a rigid class system. Marshal Ramón Castilla, president from 1845 to 1851 and from 1855 to 1862, abolished Amerindian tributes and introduced progressive measures. Between the 1850s and the mid-1880s, Peru experienced an economic boom financed by sales of guano in Europe. A program of road building was implemented, and an American entrepreneur, Henry Meiggs, was hired by the government to build a railroad network in the Andes. In 1866, a Spanish attempt to regain possession of Peru was frustrated off Callao. An 1871 armistice was followed in 1879 by the formal recognition of Peruvian independence by Spain. The War of the Pacific (1879–84) followed, in which Chile vanquished the forces of Peru and Bolivia and occupied Lima from 1881 to 1883. Under the Treaty of Ancón, signed in October 1883, and subsequent agreements, Peru was forced to give up the nitrate-rich provinces of Tarapacá and Arica.

Peru entered the 20th century with a constitutional democratic government and a stable economy. This period of moderate reform came to an end in 1919, when a businessman, Augusto Leguía y Salcedo, who had served as constitutionally elected president during 1908–12, took power in a military coup and began to modernize the country along capitalistic lines. It was in opposition to Leguía's dictatorship, which had the backing of US bankers, that a Peruvian intellectual, Víctor Raúl Haya de la Torre, founded the leftist American Popular Revolutionary Alliance (APRA). In 1930, after the worldwide depression reached Peru, Leguía was overthrown by Luis M. Sánchez-Cerro, who became Peru's constitutional president in 1931 after an election which the Apristas (the followers of APRA) denounced as fraudulent. An Aprista uprising in 1932 was followed by the assassination of Sánchez-Cerro in April 1933, but the military and its conservative allies maneuvered successfully to keep APRA out of power. Manuel Prado y Ugartache served as president during World War II, a period that also brought the eruption of a border war with Ecuador in 1941. The 1942 Protocol of Rio de Janeiro, which resolved the conflict on terms favorable to Peru, was subsequently repudiated by Ecuador.

In 1945, Prado permitted free elections and legalized APRA. Haya de la Torre and the Apristas supported José Luis Bustamante y Rivera, who won the elections, and APRA (changing its name to the People's Party) received a majority in Congress. In 1948, military leaders charged the president with being too lenient with the Apristas and dividing the armed forces. A coup led by Gen. Manuel A. Odría ousted Bustamante, and APRA was again outlawed. Several hundred Apristas were jailed, while others went into exile. In January 1949, Haya de la Torre found refuge in the Colombian embassy, where he lived for the next five years. Under the rule of Odría and his military board of governors, the Peruvian economy flourished. Agriculture, industry, and education were stimulated by modernizing measures, and foreign trade prospered. Odría announced his

retirement in 1956, and promoted his own candidate for the presidency. In a free election, the opposition candidate, former President Prado (tacitly supported by the outlawed APRA) returned to office.

Peru under the Prado regime was characterized by deep-rooted social unrest and political tension. Prado himself faded into the background, allowing Premier Pedro Beltrán to rule. Beltrán's economic moves stabilized Peru's financial picture, but the political problems remained. The election of 1962 was a three-way race between Haya de la Torre; Odría, back from retirement; and Fernando Belaúnde Terry, leader of the Popular Action Party (AP). Although Haya de la Torre got the most votes, he did not receive the constitutionally required one-third of the votes cast. The parties then went into negotiations, and a deal was struck giving Odría the presidency with an APRA cabinet. The military thereupon intervened, annulled the vote, and suspended the newly elected Congress. The governing junta then announced new elections for July 1963, and the same candidates ran. This time, Belaúnde received 39% of the votes cast to become president.

Belaúnde embarked on a program of agrarian reform, as well as tax incentives to promote manufacturing. However, he was caught in a crossfire between the Odriístas, who considered him a radical, and the Apristas, who believed he was not doing enough. Belaúnde's AP formed a coalition with the Christian Democratic Party to control the senate, but APRA and the Odría National Union controlled the Chamber of Deputies. On top of all this, Belaúnde had to deal with two separate leftist insurgencies in Peru's highlands. As Peru approached new presidential elections, the AP began to quarrel, and opposition parties continued to sabotage Belaúnde's programs. Then a scandal concerning the granting of oil concessions to the International Petroleum Co., a subsidiary of Standard Oil of New Jersey, rocked the government. A military junta exiled Belaúnde on 3 October 1968 in a bloodless coup.

In 1969, the military government, under the presidency of Gen. Juan Velasco Alvarado, began enacting a series of social and economic reforms. This time, they did not worry about opposition, ruling instead by decree. By 1974 they had converted private landholdings into agricultural cooperatives, nationalized a number of basic industries, and had mandated profit-sharing schemes for industrial workers. A government-sponsored social mobilization agency, the National System for Support of Social Mobilization (Sistema Nacional de Apoyo a la Movilización Social—SINAMOS) was established in 1971. The military also reached out to Peru's long-neglected Amerindian population, making Tupac Amaru a national symbol, and recognizing Quechua as an official national language.

In August 1975, Velasco, whose health and political fortunes had both declined, was removed from office in a bloodless coup and replaced by Gen. Francisco Morales Bermúdez Cerruti, formerly his prime minister. The new regime moved to liberalize the system, declaring a general amnesty for post-1968 political exiles and the legalization of some previously banned publications. They subsequently announced a return to civilian government and the creation of a "fully participatory social democracy." Some state-controlled enterprises were sold, worker-participation programs were scaled down, and SINAMOS was dismantled. A Constituent Assembly was elected, and under the leadership of the perennial candidate Haya de la Torre they drew up a new constitution in 1979. New elections were held in 1980, and the AP and Belaúnde returned to power.

Belaúnde's second term was even less a success than his first. Adverse weather conditions and the world recession accompanied ill-conceived policies that led to triple-digit inflation. Austerity programs caused increased rates of unemployment, and currency problems pinched the Peruvian middle-class. Perhaps most disturbing of all, a small Maoist guerrilla group, Sendero Luminoso (Shining Path) was operating openly in the Andes, especially around Ayacucho. Despite passage of an antiterrorist law in 1981, terrorist activities intensified. During the first four months of 1983, more than 450 people lost their lives. The government's campaign against terrorism, beginning in May 1983 and continuing through 1985, resulted in the disappearance of thousands, charges of mass killings, and the granting of unlimited power to the armed forces. Meanwhile, the AP's tenuous hold on the government was slipping. The AP won only 15% of the vote in the 1983 municipal elections. By 1985, with Peru on the brink of an economic collapse, the AP received a mere 7% of the vote.

The election of 1985 was historic in two ways: it was the first peaceful transfer of power in 40 years, and it brought the first president from APRA since the party's founding in 1928. Alán García Pérez, secretary-general of APRA, won with 53% of the vote, and brought with him an APRA majority in both houses. The new president pursued populist economic policies, aimed at controlling inflation, stimulating the economy, and limiting external debt repayments. To get inflation under control, García established a strict set of price controls, dropping inflation precipitously. Salaries were then allowed to increase, which led to a dramatic surge in the production of industrial and consumer goods. García also announced that external debt service would be set at 10% of export earnings, when several times that amount would have been required to keep up with interest payments alone.

While initially successful, these programs eventually ran aground. The IMF, a constant target of García, declared Peru ineligible for any further borrowing because of the size of Peru's external debt. After its initial boom, industrial production began to sag. Food shortages became common as suppliers refused to produce with artificially low prices. By 1990, inflation had climbed to four-digit levels.

García had some success in dealing with Peru's democratic left, but the militant left was another story. By increasing the stridency of his rhetoric, especially against the US, García was able to capture leftist votes, seriously damaging the power of the United Left (Izquierda Unida—IU). However, Sendero escalated its attacks, coming down out of the mountains and striking at urban and suburban targets around Lima and Callao. In addition, the Tupac Amaru Revolutionary Movement (MRTA) merged with the Movement of the Revolutionary Left (MIR), and struck with increasing intensity. Although García had promised to get the military under control, it was soon clear that he could not function without them, and authorized a set of brutal counter-insurgent campaigns.

By 1990, Peruvians began to cast about for someone to deliver the country from its economic and social woes. Neither APRA nor the AP had any credibility. In a surprise, Alberto Fujimori, the son of Japanese immigrants, defeated conservative novelist Mario Vargas Llosa by 57% to 34%. Other candidates totaled a little over 9%. Fujimori immediately imposed a draconian set of austerity measures designed to curb inflation. These measures caused a great deal of economic dislocation, but did reduce inflation to pre-1988 levels.

Fujimori moved aggressively to combat Sendero and the MRTA-MIR. He organized and armed rural peasants to counter the increased guerrilla presence, and gave the military a broad mandate to crack down on the insurgents. The capture of Abimaél Guzmán, leader of Sendero Luminoso, was hailed as a major blow against the movement, but the violence continued. Human rights continued to deteriorate, and the military became stronger.

Domestic opposition increased as Fujimori became increasingly isolated politically. Then, in April 1992, Fujimori shut down Congress and refused to recognize any judicial decisions. The autogolpe ("self-coup") received widespread popular approval and, most significantly, the military supported Fujimori's moves. In 1992, elections were held to create a Constituent Assembly charged with making constitutional reforms, including allowing Fujimori to run for a second five-year term in 1995. Both APRA and AP refused to participate, and Fujimori's New Majority/Change 90 group took a majority of seats. With full executive powers and a legislature full of supporters, Fujimori was able to enact whatever reforms he deemed necessary to improve Peru's economic and social situations.

A border war with Ecuador in early 1995 (in which both sides claimed victory) boosted Fujimori's popularity to a level that enabled him to win his unprecedented second-consecutive presidential election by a landslide, roundly defeating former UN secretary general Javier Perez de Cuellar. In May 1999, Fujimori and Ecuadorian President Jamil Mahuad formally ended the border dispute that dated from 1941. The accord gave Ecuador a small piece of Peruvian territory and navigation rights on some Peruvian rivers. In Ecuador, the peace treaty was considered a capitulation, turning the army against Mahuad.

Fujimori continued to rule by martial law, and took decisive steps to end terrorist opposition and violence in Peru. In 1996, the second-highest leader of Sendero, Elizabeth Cardenas Huayta, was arrested. The Tupac Amaru rebel movement was decimated in April 1997 when military commandos stormed the Japanese Embassy, where the rebels had been holding hostages since December 1996, and killed all 14 of the Tupac Amaru guerillas who had carried out the siege (only one hostage died in the raid, from a heart attack as a result of a gunshot wound).

Although the success of the embassy raid and the end of the hostage crisis at first raised Fujimori's popularity, it soon began to decline as Peruvians wearied of Fujimori's strong-arm tactics. Government attacks on the press and on certain members of the business community created a mounting dissatisfaction with the Fujimori regime. When Fujimori fired three Constitutional Tribunal judges for rejecting his claim to a third consecutive presidential term, Peruvians' tolerance was pushed beyond its breaking point and protests erupted. Continuing widespread poverty (despite recent years of economic growth), coupled with governmental abuses of power and persistent guerilla violence eroded Fujimori's popular support. As the April 2000 elections came near, Fujimori at first remained silent on whether he would seek a third term. Yet political maneuvering by his supporters had ensured that no viable candidate would rise to face him. Opposition parties also were weak and divided. Former President Alan Garcia, who fled the country in 1992, and faces corruption charges, became a possible candidate. Fujimori's supporters in Congress quickly approved a law banning any former office-holder facing criminal charges from running for election. Yet, Fujimori remained vulnerable. A two-year recession and widespread unemployment had left one of two Peruvians living in poverty by mid-1999. Fujimori also was under a great deal of international pressure to rectify undemocratic conduct. In June 1999, members of the US House of Representatives said they were concerned at the "erosion of democracy and the rule of law" in Perú. A Senate subcommittee said it should be consulted before the White House gave any more American intelligence to Perú. Later that year, the Inter-American Court of Human Rights rejected Peru's bid to withdraw from its jurisdiction, saying it would continue to summon Peruvian officials to declare in reported abuses.

Within weeks of the April 2000 elections, Fujimori seemed all but certain of winning the presidency for a third term. Yet, a virtual unknown had suddenly become a viable candidate, winning support from throughout the country. Alejandro Toledo, a 54-year-old business school professor, was soon ahead of other challengers trying to defeat Fujimori. The US-educated Toledo had a modest upbringing. His father was a bricklayer, and his mother sold fish at a street market. Of strong Indian features, Toledo quickly gained an important following in Perú's Amerindian communities, where Fujimori had found support. The election was held on 9 April, with several international organizations monitoring polling stations. It soon became clear that Fujimori's supporters were trying to steal the election. There were unexplained delays in revealing the results, and widespread reports of voter fraud. The United States, the Organization of American States, the Atlanta-based Carter Center, and several other international organizations monitoring the election agreed that widespread fraud had tainted the elections and demanded a second presidential election between Fujimori and Toledo. Tens of thousands of Peruvians marched in peaceful protests demanding a second round. The other presidential candidates backed Toledo. Three days after the election, the electoral office said Fujimori had obtained 49.8% of the vote, not enough to capture the 50% plus one he needed to avoid a second round. Toledo was given 40.3 percent of the vote. A second election was called for June 2000.

13GOVERNMENT

Prior to the military coup in 1968, Peru was governed under the constitution of 1933, which declared Peru to be a republic with a centralized form of government. Legislative powers were vested in a Senate and a Chamber of Deputies, of variable number. Both senators and deputies served their electoral districts for a period of six years. Under the constitution, executive power was held by the president, who, with two vice-presidents, was elected for a six-year term, with a minimum of one-third of the vote, but could not be reelected until an intervening term had passed. Voting was obligatory for all literate Peruvian citizens aged 21 to 60.

The military leaders who seized control of the government in 1968 immediately disbanded the bicameral Congress. For the following decade, Peru was ruled by a military junta consisting of the president and the commanders of the three armed forces. The return to civilian rule began with the election of a Constituent Assembly in June 1978 and the promulgation of a new constitution on 12 July 1979. Presidential elections were held in May 1980, and Peru's first civilian government in 12 years took office in July.

Under the 1979 constitution, the president was popularly elected for a five-year term and could not be reelected to a consecutive term. The winning candidate had to win at least 50% of the vote, or face a runoff election against the second-place candidate. The National Congress consisted of a 60-member Senate and a 180-member Chamber of Deputies. All elected legislators had five-year terms. The 1979 constitution eliminated literacy as a qualification for voting, and made suffrage universal at age 18.

After the autogolpe in 1992, the constitution was suspended. The Constituent Assembly soon amended the 1979 constitution to allow a president to run for a second consecutive term. The document is still under revision.

The current Congress is unicameral, consisting of 120 elected members.

14POLITICAL PARTIES

Throughout most of Peru's modern political history, personalities and power politics have counted for more than party platforms. There are nevertheless several parties with origins at least as far back as the 1950s.

The American Popular Revolutionary Alliance (Alianza Popular Revolucionaria Americana—APRA) was begun in 1924 by Víctor Raúl Haya de la Torre as a movement of and for Latin American workers. The five planks in its original platform were opposition to "Yankee imperialism," internationalization of the Panama Canal, industrialization, land reform, and solidarity among the world's oppressed. Controlling most of unionized labor, APRA was anti-Communist and anti-imperialist. Outlawed in 1931 and again in 1948, APRA was legalized in 1956. APRA has been historically opposed to the military, and political conditions in Peru from the 1930s until the mid-1980s have been dominated by hostility between APRA and armed forces leaders. After the death of Haya de la Torre in 1979, APRA was weakened by internal dissension. By 1985, new leadership and the failure of the Belaúnde government allowed APRA its first experience in power. APRA is currently boycotting any political arrangement under Fujimori.

The Popular Action Party (Partido de Acción Popular, or AP) was founded in 1956. Originally a reform party, it competed with APRA for the support of those favoring change in Peru. After an impressive campaign in 1956, the AP won the presidency in 1963, thanks to the military's hatred of APRA. In the 1980 presidential election, Belaúnde received 45.4% of the votes cast, compared with 27.4% for APRA candidate Armando Villanueva del Campo.

The Popular Christian Party (Partido Popular Cristiano—PPC) left the Christian Democratic Party in 1966 while the latter was allied with Belaúnde's AP government. The PPC now defines the right in Peruvian politics. The party placed third in the 1980 and 1985 elections under Luis Bedoya Reyes, former mayor of Lima. The PPC is participating in the Fujimori government, and holds eight seats in the Constituent Assembly.

After the dissolution of Congress by the 1968 military coup, political parties continued to exist, although they were denied any role in government until the late 1970s. Ideologically, the military rulers between 1968 and 1980 reflected both strong socialist and nationalist principles.

The left has undergone a number of changes, partly as a result of military intervention, and most recently has been undermined by the activities of leftist guerrillas. The Peruvian Communist Party (Partido Comunista Peruano) was formed in 1929. Outlawed in 1948, it changed its name to the Revolutionary Labor Party (Partido Obrero Revolucionario—POR), which split in the 1980s into a number of small factions. The United Left (Izquierda Unida—IU), formed to support the candidacy of Alfonso Barrantes Lingán, took 21.3% of the 1985 ballot. Barrantes was mayor of Lima until APRA unseated him in 1986, whereupon Barrantes resigned as IU president and the coalition dissolved.

The largest active guerrilla party is Sendero Luminoso (Shining Path), a Maoist group founded in 1964. Its founder, Abimaél Guzmán, a former college professor, was captured by the government and is still imprisoned. Sendero's strength is concentrated around Ayacucho, in the sierra southeast of Lima. Its program includes not only attacks on bridges, power lines, and urban centers but also attempts to organize highland peasants. Sendero collects tribute from peasants in exchange for protection, and encourages peasants not to sell their food crops to the cities.

A smaller group, the Tupac Amaru Revolutionary Movement (Movimiento Revolucionario Tupac Amaru—MRTA), merged with the Movement of the Revolutionary Left (MIR) to form a group that has been increasingly active. The MRTA-MIR is more urban-oriented and follows a more orthodox Marxist line than the eccentric Sendero.

President Alberto Fujimori came to office in 1990 as an independent, calling his party Change 90-New Majority. In the 1995 elections, Fujimori was reelected in a landslide victory, and his party took 67 of the 120 congressional seats, giving it a clear majority (the next-highest number of seats, 17, went to the Union for Peru party, led by former UN secretary general Javier Perez de

Cuellar who came in second in the presidential election). Fujimori's popularity declined during his term because of his oppressive political tactics, and although he was reelected on 9 April 2000, the results of the election are being challenged as fraudulent.

15 LOCAL GOVERNMENT

In March 1987, President García promulgated a regionalization law that would replace the nation's 24 departments (and the constitutional province of Callao) with 12 regions having economic and administrative autonomy. Each region was to have an assembly of provincial mayors, directly elected members, and representatives of various institutions. However, due to inadequate funding and an uncertain political picture, these regions are not functioning, and currently exist alongside the departmental structure, which was never dismantled. The 148 provincial subdivisions remained intact.

The 1979 constitution confirms the legal status of about 5,000 Indian communities. The first local elections since 1966 took place in November 1980 and occur at three-year intervals.

16 JUDICIAL SYSTEM

The Peruvian legal system is based generally on the Napoleonic Code. The 1979 constitution guarantees the independence of the judiciary. Peru's highest judicial body, the 16-member Supreme Court, sits at Lima and has national jurisdiction. The 9-member Court of Constitutional Guarantees has jurisdiction in human rights cases. Superior courts, sitting in the departmental capitals, hear appeals from the provincial courts of first instance, which are divided into civil, penal, and special chambers. Judges are proposed by the National Justice Council, nominated by the president, and confirmed by the Senate; they serve permanently until age 70. Justices of the peace hear misdemeanor cases and minor civil cases.

The 1979 constitution abolished the death penalty (except for treason in time of war) and limited the jurisdiction of military tribunals; it also established the Public Ministry, including an independent attorney general, to serve as judicial ombudsman. Despite such reforms, the Peruvian judicial system still suffers from overcrowded prisons and complex trial procedures. Many accused persons (especially those accused of drug trafficking or terrorism) may spend months or even years in prison before they are brought to trial.

Although the judicial branch has never attained true independence, provisions of the 1993 constitution establish a new system for naming judges which may lead to greater judicial autonomy in the future. As of 1993, however, approximately 70% of incumbent judges and prosecutors were provisionally appointed by President Fujimori after his declaration of extraconstitutional powers in 1992. These appointees were never confirmed by Congress. The 1993 constitution also provides for a human rights ombudsman (the Office of the Defender of the People), a Tribunal of Constitutional Guarantees empowered to rule on the constitutionality of legislation and government actions, a National Judiciary Council, and a Judicial Academy to train judges and prosecutors. The Tribunal of Constitutional Guarantees has seven members; three of them are in some way associated with the President or his party. To declare a law unconstitutional, at least six of the judges must agree.

17 ARMED FORCES

Two years of military service is obligatory and universal, but only a limited number of men between the ages of 20 and 25 are drafted. After active service in the army, soldiers spend five years in the first or second reserve and 20 years in the national guard. There are 188,000 army reservists.

The total strength of the armed forces in 2000 was 115,000 (including 64,000 conscripts). Army personnel numbered 75,000, navy 25,000 (including 3,000 marines), and air force 15,000, with 114 combat aircraft and 23 armed helicopters. The navy mans 8 submarines, 2 cruisers, 1 destroyer, 4 frigates, and 11 smaller combatants. Naval aviation (7 combat planes, 9 armed helicopters) is land based or deployed in an ASW role. About 66,000 men make up the national police, under the direction of the Ministry of Interior and Police. In 1998, the defense establishment received approximately $913 million or 1.4% of GDP. The armed forces faces as many as 2,000 armed guerrillas of the Maoist Sendero Luminoso and some 600 terrorists of the Tupac Amaru movement.

18 INTERNATIONAL COOPERATION

Peru is a charter member of the UN, having joined on 31 October 1945, and belongs to ECLAC and all the nonregional specialized agencies. Peru also belongs to G-77 and the WTO, and cooperates with various foreign countries in cultural, scientific, trade, industrial, and health matters. A member of IADB, LAIA, and OAS, Peru is also the seat of the five-nation Andean Group.

19 ECONOMY

Since World War II, the Peruvian economy has developed rapidly, exhibiting a rate of growth that has been among the highest in Latin America. The strength of Peru's economy lies in the diversity of its natural resources. Silver and gold were the prized commodities of colonial Peru. In more recent times, lead, cooper, zinc, iron ore, and since the late 1960s, petroleum have become important export earners. Fishing, including the production of fish meal, has become a major undertaking. Agriculture, which occupies about 4.9% of the work force, is sharply divided between two sectors: small-scale farming, producing food crops for subsistence and the domestic market, and export-oriented production.

Policies from 1960 to 1990 aimed at social reform but worsened and perpetuated poverty. Repeated experiments in social engineering created economic and institutional uncertainty and a prolonged decline in governance. Government spending grew steadily in the 1980s—until it collapsed in 1989—but spending in the production of public services fell. As a result, there was a steady degradation of the civil service and the provision of public goods that undermined productivity, fostered anarchy and public turmoil, and, ultimately, made poverty reduction impossible.

By 1990 per capita income was below that of 1966; political violence was claiming 3,000 lives each year; tax collections were less than 5% of GDP; and prices had increased by a factor of 27 million over three decades. In fact, Peru's economy had all but collapsed. It was the finale of 30 years of misguided policies, economic mismanagement, and since 1980 rampant and escalating terrorism.

Since 1990 and the Fujimori regime, the government has pursued a bold reform agenda. It has strengthened the authority of the state throughout the country, defeating terrorism and fighting drug trafficking. It liberalized interest rates, the exchange rate, and international capital flows. It established the independence of the central bank and eliminated credit from the central bank to the government. It increased competition by opening the economy to trade with the rest of the world and eliminating public monopolies and price controls. It improved labor market efficiency by addressing tenure regulations and establishing more flexible terms for probationary periods and fixed-term contracts. It facilitated private ownership of land and developed a vast privatization program. It eliminated the state monopoly in social security and established the framework for a private pension fund system. And it eliminated public development banks and state intervention in the allocation of credit.

Since the reform program, Peru has enjoyed macroeconomic success, but the reforms have done little to alleviate poverty. Between 1993 and 1996, Peru's economy grew by 32%, in part due to the privatization of state companies; but thousands of Peruvians lost their jobs as a result. The rate of inflation fell steadily as a result of stringent monetary and fiscal measures. It dropped from over 7,650% in 1990 to about 40% in 1993; and 4% in 2000, one of the lowest inflation rates in Latin America. The Peruvian economy grew by 7.3% in 1997, but in 1998 and 1999 growth slowed to an estimated 1.8% and 3.8% respectively. A combination of El Niño weather that hurt the fishing and agricultural industries, and the Asian financial crisis which depressed metal prices, contributed to the Peruvian economic downturn. Growth for 2000 was forecast at over 5%.

20INCOME

The US Central Intelligence Agency (CIA) reports that in 1998 Peru's gross domestic product (GDP) was estimated at $112 billion. The per capita GDP was estimated at $4,300. The annual growth rate of GDP was estimated at 1.8%. The average inflation rate in 1998 was 33.7%. The CIA defines GDP as the value of all final goods and services produced within a nation in a given year and computed on the basis of purchasing power parity (PPP) rather than value as measured on the basis of the rate of exchange. It was estimated that agriculture accounted for 7% of GDP, industry 37%, and services 56%.

The World Bank reports that for the same period per capita private consumption (in PPP terms) was $2,800. Private consumption includes expenditures of individuals, households, and nongovernmental organizations. It was estimated that between 1990 and 1998 private consumption grew at an annual rate of 4.7%. Approximately 26% of household consumption was spent on food, 17% on fuel, 13% on health care, and 5% on education. The richest 10% of the population accounted for approximately 35% of household consumption and the poorest 10% approximately 1.6%.

21LABOR

In 1999, the employed labor force was estimated at 8.5 million. In 1998, 4.9% of the population was employed in agriculture, 13.3% in industry; 5.6% in construction; 29.4% in commerce; and 7.5% in education. According to official statistics, the unemployment rate was 7.7% in 1998.

About 5% of the total labor force was unionized in 1999; unions have played an important role in Peruvian politics in recent decades, but membership has declined as the informal labor sector grows. Began in 1944 under Communist domination, the Workers' Confederation of Peru was reorganized in 1956 as the national central labor organization, now known as the Peruvian Revolutionary Workers' Center (Central de Trabajadores de la Revolución Peruana—CTRP). In 1980, this organization was incorporated into the Democratic Trade Union Front, which also includes the Communist-led General Confederation of Peruvian Workers, the National Workers' Confederation, and the APRA-affiliated General Confederation of Peruvian Workers (Confederación General de Trabajadores Peruanos—CGTP), which dates from 1944. In 1999, the CGTP called a one-day general strike, supported by 400,000 transit workers and other public-sector employees, that paralyzed normal activity in Peru's major cities.

Legal machinery allows for conciliation or arbitration of disputes by government decree through the Ministry of Labor. An 8-hour day and a 48-hour week are the maximum in Peru, with shorter hours for women and minors. Legislation has been uneven, but the law requires in most cases that employers create healthy and safe working conditions. Dangerous and night work are regulated. The civil code prohibits labor by minors under 14; nevertheless, a recent study indicated that 8% of the work force was between the ages of 8 and 16. Peru's labor stability laws provide that after three months of employment a worker may be dismissed only for a "serious offense." As of 1999, the minimum wage was $104 a month.

22AGRICULTURE

Only 4.2 million hectares (10.4 million acres), or 3.3% of the total land, was under cultivation in 1997. The area of available agricultural land per capita is one of the lowest in the nonindustrialized world. The major portion of the coastal farmland is devoted to the raising of export crops, while the sierra and the selva are used primarily for the production of food for domestic consumption. In various communities, the Inca system of cooperative labor and land use still remains; fields are communally planted and harvested, and the produce or the profits divided.

The Agrarian Reform Law (ARL) of 1969 profoundly affected the whole of Peruvian agriculture. By 1973, most of Peru, except for the jungle on the eastern side of the Andes, was brought under the reform program. Large private landholdings were abolished. Contrary to the expectations of farm workers, however, the appropriated land was not redistributed in small individual parcels. The large estates expropriated by the government were instead reorganized into cooperatives that maintained their administrative unity and were often incorporated into still larger units, known as social-interest agricultural societies, through which they were linked on a cooperative basis. By 1980, the expropriation and redistribution of land were largely complete. Out of the nine million hectares (22.2 million acres) of cropland and pasture originally expropriated, 8.8 million hectares (21.7 million acres) were allocated to 379,000 families. In addition, 2.9 million hectares (7.2 million acres) reverted to the state, and 1.1 million hectares (2.7 million acres) were distributed to 10,706 families in the selva. The bulk of land went to cooperatives, and only about 43,000 families received land, totaling 683,000 hectares (1,688,000 acres), in the form of private holdings. The government justified this program by arguing that the supply of arable land in inhabited zones of Peru is so small that equal distribution of the land would permit an allotment of less than 0.5 hectares (1.2 acres) per rural inhabitant; that community ownership of land accords with Peruvian traditions, especially the proto-socialist Inca heritage; and that improved equipment and technique are more easily implemented in larger enterprises. As it turned out, inadequate distribution systems and lack of technical expertise limited the productivity of the cooperatives, and by 1981, about 80% of them were operating at a loss. The free market policies of President Fujimori played an important role in Peruvian agriculture during the 1990s, virtually undoing the expropriative and redistributive policies of the ARL. In 1996, the Land Tenure Law was instituted, which was a step toward allowing land to be titled and used as collateral. The Water Law no longer ties water usage with land area, and mandates that farmers must pay for their use of water. Water is an extremely expensive commodity in the coastal valleys.

Peru's agriculture is highly diversified but not well integrated. In an irrigated section of the coastal desert lowlands, more than 1,270,000 hectares (3,138,000 acres) are cultivated with cotton, sugar, rice, soybeans, pulses, fruits, tobacco, and flowers. Modern methods are widely used in this area, and as a result, output has risen at a much faster rate than population growth. The sierra, in contrast, is relatively dormant, its lands being inferior or impractical to till. The selva contributes cocoa, fruits and nuts, tea, coffee, tobacco, and forest products.

Staples are potatoes and corn, grown throughout Peru, but with very low yields. The leading commercial crops are rice, cotton, sugar, and barley. The principal agricultural deficiencies—wheat, livestock and meat, animal and vegetable fats, and oils—are covered by imports. Production of major crops (in thousands of tons) in 1998 included rice, 1,549; corn, 933; coffee, 120; wheat, 146; and beans and pulses, 223. Sugar cane and potato production in 1998 amounted to 7.1 million tons and 2.4 million tons, respectively.

In the 1980s, a combination of weak financing, heavy overseas borrowing, poor pricing policy, bad weather, and outmoded equipment contributed to a serious deterioration in the performance of the sugar industry. In 1996, the sugar industry's twelve collective farms were forced to change their management and ownership structure. Most had been inefficient, overloaded with administrative workers, and together owed the government $250 million in back taxes and social security payments. Some of the collective farms have begun selling portions of their capital to the private sector.

23ANIMAL HUSBANDRY

The cattle, sheep, hogs, goats, horses, and poultry brought by the Spaniards to Peru were strange to the Amerindians, whose only domestic animals were the hunting dog and the American members of the camel family—the llama, alpaca, and their hybrids—which served as carriers and for food, clothing, and fuel. Only recently domesticated, the vicuña is protected by law, and limited quantities of its fine fleece are marketed. Most Amerindians of the southern highlands are herders.

The southern Andes contain the major cattle ranges. Brown Swiss, zebu, and Holstein have been imported, and agronomists are crossbreeding stock to attain herds of greater weight or of more milk on less feed. Although 27.1 million hectares (66.9 million acres), or 21% of Peru's land area, are permanent natural pasture and meadow, areas suitable for dairy cattle are few. In 1998, the livestock population included 13,558,000 sheep, 4,657,000 head of cattle, 2,547,000 hogs, and 2,023,000 goats. There were also 2,755,000 alpacas and 1,074,000 llamas in 1995. Livestock output in 1998 included 124,000 tons of beef, 91,000 tons of pork, 23,000 tons of mutton, 490,000 tons of poultry, 154,000 tons of eggs, and 998,000 tons of milk.

24FISHING

Commercial deep-sea fishing off of Peru's coastal belt of over 3,000 km (1,860 mi), is a major enterprise. Peruvian waters normally abound with marketable fish: bonito, mackerel, drum, sea bass, tuna, swordfish, anchoveta, herring, shad, skipjack, yellowfin, pompano, and shark. More than 50 species are caught commercially. There are over 40 fishing ports on the Peruvian coast, Paita and Callao being the most important centers.

The Peruvian fishing industry, primarily based on the export of fish meal, used in poultry feed, is among the largest in the world. Peru's fishing sector led the world during the mid-1960s, although production since then has fluctuated radically. In the 1970s, overfishing nearly lead to the disappearance of the anchovy resource. The fish meal and fish-processing industry is managed by Pescaperú, which was founded in 1973.

The key to Peru's fishing industry in any given year is the presence or absence of El Niño; this warm ocean current displaces the normally cool waters deep in the Pacific, thereby killing the microorganisms upon which other marine life depends. The recurrence of El Niño in 1982/83 caused the disappearance of anchoveta until 1985 and a sharp fall in the catch of other species. The average annual catch during 1994–97 was 9,587,594 tons. The total catch in 1997 was 7,877,416 tons, second highest in the world after China. That total included 5,927,599 tons of anchoveta, 625,143 tons of South American pilchard, and 649,571 tons of Chilean jack mackerel. Exports of fish products in 1997 amounted to $1.34 billion.

To suppress invasion of their rich fishing grounds by foreign powers, Peru made formal agreements with Chile and Ecuador to extend the rights to their coastal waters out to 200 nautical mi. Violations of the proclaimed sovereignty by Argentine and US fishing fleets in 1952 and 1954 gave rise to shooting incidents. Since then, US fishing boats have occasionally been seized and fined or required to purchase fishing licenses; after eight US tuna boats were taken in November 1979, the US retaliated by imposing a temporary embargo on Peruvian tuna.

25FORESTRY

About 66% of Peru's land area, or approximately 84.8 million hectares (209.5 million acres), is covered by tropical rain forests. Most of Peru's exploitable timberlands lie on the eastern slopes of the Andes and in the Amazon Basin; the arid Pacific watershed cannot support forestlands. The trees of commercial importance on the coastal plain are amarillo, hualtaco, and algarroba (cut for railway ties and for charcoal fuel). Lumber from planted eucalyptus is used locally in the sierra for ties and for props by the mining industry. Eastern Peru, however, with its abundance of rain, consists of approximately 70 million ha (173 million acres) of forestland (more than half the country's area), most of it uncut. A precise indication of Peru's volume of standing timber has never been ascertained. The selva contains Peru's only coniferous stand, where ulcumano is logged. Cedar, mahogany, moena, tornillo, and congona (broadleaf hardwoods) are also logged. The rain forests of the Amazon lowlands contain cedar, mahogany, rubber (wild and plantation), and leche caspi (a chewing-gum base). Commercially important are tagua nuts, balata, coca, fibers, and a wide range of medicinal plants. Cultivation for illicit purposes of the coca leaf (the source of cocaine), which has long been used habitually and ritually by Andean Amerindians, was regarded as a growing problem by the Peruvian government and by the International Narcotics Control Board in the 1980s.

Lumbering is conducted chiefly in the selva, where Pucallpa and Iquitos are the main sawmill centers. Mahogany is now the principal lumber export product, sent mainly to the US and Europe; mahogany and Spanish cedar trees supply about half of Peru's lumber output, which falls far short of the nation's needs. In 1997, production of roundwood totaled 7,742,000 cu m.

26MINING

Peru has long been famous for the wealth of its mines, some of which have been worked extensively for more than 300 years. Through modern techniques and equipment, a vast potential of diverse marketable minerals is gradually becoming available from previously inaccessible regions. Because many of the richest mines are found in the central Andes, often above 4,300 m (14,000 ft), their operations have been wholly dependent on the Andean Indians' adaptation to working at high altitudes.

Copper, iron, lead, and zinc, the leading metals, are mined chiefly in the central Andes, where all refining is done at the metallurgical center of La Oroya. Copper production more than tripled in 1960 with the opening of the Southern Peru Copper Corp. mine at Toquepala. The completion of a 296 km (184 mi) rail line connecting the concentrator plant at Toquepala with the port of Ilo was the last major step in the $234 million Toquepala blister-copper project. Two large mines, at Cuajone and Cerro Verde, were opened in 1977, boosting copper production by 78%. Another large mine opened at Tintaya, 247 km (153 mi) South of Cuzco, in 1985, but slumping world prices, unfavorable exchange rate policies, and labor strife kept its production and that of other mines down. In 1997, Peru's copper output was 502,970 tons (up 3.9% from 1996), valued at $1.09 billion.

Production of iron ore reached 4,439,000 tons in 1997 (down from a near-record high of 7,430,000 in 1994). Exploitation of iron ore, centered in southern Peru, was exclusively for export until the steel mills at Chimbote began operations in 1958. Zinc production in 1997 stood at 865,000 tons (up from 760,563 tons in 1996), and lead at 258,189 (up from 248,787 in 1996). Minor industrial metals, such as tungsten, molybdenum, bismuth, and antimony, are extracted in various parts of Peru. There are huge phosphate deposits in the Sechura Desert.

In 1997, Peru was the world's second-largest producer of mine silver after the US and Mexico, producing 2,077 tons of the refined metal. Medium-sized companies accounted for 1,534 tons; large mining companies, 528; and small companies produced the remainder.

Of the 30 industrial minerals mined commercially in Peru, the most important ones are salt, gypsum, marble, limestone, and anthracite. Bituminous coal deposits, in immense reserves throughout the Andes, have not been extensively developed because of difficult access.

Peru's minerals (including petroleum) accounted for 40% of the total value of exports in 1997, and 8.7% of GDP. Mineral deposits were traditionally the property of the state, while development has been left largely to foreign concessions. After the 1968 junta, the government pursued a steady program of nationalization, which began in earnest in 1968 with expropriation of the Peruvian holdings of Standard Oil of New Jersey. In 1971, state mining rights were assigned to Mineroperú, a government enterprise that also represented the government's commercial interests in the mining sector. With the sweeping privatization process of the early 1990s in Peru, legal procedures to obtain mining rights were made easier with the enactment of new legislation in 1992. Privatization of the remaining state-owned mining assets was under way as of 1998. The government no longer has exclusive control over exploration, mining, smelting, and refining of metals and fuel minerals. Individuals and private companies are now allowed to hold mining permits.

27 ENERGY AND POWER

Of the electric power produced in Peru in 1996, about 80% was hydroelectric; the balance was thermal, mostly from diesel fuel, gasoline, and natural gas. The hydroelectric potential has been estimated at 60 million kW. Between 1960 and 1998, installed generating capacity increased from 841,000 kW to 5,179,000 kW. Production increased from 2,656 million kWh to 18,280 million kWh in 1998. Consumption of electricity in 1996 was 16.2 billion kWh, low by Latin American standards. Electrification was at 65% as of 1999.

In 1972, the government assumed control of electricity production and distribution through Electroperú, a newly created state authority. Peru's electric development plan called for the expenditure during the 1980s of some $6 billion on new generating plants and $3 billion on distribution and transmission facilities. A 1992 law reversed the decision to nationalize Electroperú, and it was broken up into three parts by the end of 1996. As of 1999, however, much of the electric sector was still government controlled. Demand for electric power is growing rapidly; annual investments of $300–$350 million are expected through 2000 to keep pace with population and economic growth.

In the 1970s, Peru's Upper Amazon Basin was developed into a major petroleum source; the nation's petroleum export revenues increased from $52.2 million in 1977 to $646 million in 1985. The 853 km (530 mi) trans-Andean pipeline, with a capacity of 200,000 barrels a day, was completed in 1977. Peru's petroleum fields are located in the northwestern parts of Piura and Tumbes, where oil was known in pre-Columbian days, and first produced in 1896. Peru's proven oil reserves amounted to 355 million barrels in early 2000. Production amounted to 107,000 barrels per day in 1999. Natural gas reserves in 2000 were estimated at 254 billion cu m, and production in 1999 amounted to about 566 million cu m. In 1969, the development of oil resources fell under the direction of the state-owned company Petroperú, which was partially privatized in 1993. Its successor is Perupetro.

28 INDUSTRY

Manufacturing in Peru began with the establishment of consumer goods industries, which still dominate the sector. Smelting and refining are among Peru's most important industrial enterprises. As part of a long-term industrial program through hydroelectric power development, the Chimbote steel mills began to function in 1958; by 1965, capacity reached 350,000 ingot tons. A number of foundries, cement plants, automobile assembly plants, and installations producing sulfuric acid and other industrial chemicals have also come into operation. The expansion of the fish meal industry necessitated the construction of new plants as well as the establishment of many subsidiary industries: boatyards, repair and maintenance installations, and factories for the production of tinplate and cans, paper, jute nags, and nylon fishnet. Once a major guano exporter, Peru now produces synthetic fertilizers high in nitrogen and related industrial chemicals.

The country's sustained economic growth has been the result of a well diversified economic base. In 1996, the most dynamic area was agriculture, with crop production rising by 7% due to substantial increases in industrial crops like cotton, soy bean, tea and asparagus. Other industries showing important growth during the late 1990s were the mining of metals, petroleum, and construction. The mining sector accounts for at least 11% of GDP. In 1998, it was estimated that an average of 11 new oil wells would be drilled per a year until 2003, but in 1999 oil exploration slowed when a couple of dry wells were drilled. There are five oil refineries operating in Peru. Growth in construction during 1998 skyrocketed by 12%, with projects related to the repair of an estimated $1 billion in El Niño damage, and road building projects. However, revenues from manufacturing production fell by 3%, because of low agricultural production and low world metals prices.

29 SCIENCE AND TECHNOLOGY

The Lima Academy of Exact, Physical, and Natural Sciences, in Lima, was founded in 1939. In 1996, Peru had 18 other scientific and technological learned societies and 15 scientific and technological research institutes. The Natural History Museum of the National University of San Marcos, founded in 1918, and the Geological Museum of the National University of Engineering are both located in Lima. In 1996, Peru had 34 universities that offered courses in basic and applied sciences. In 1987–97, science and engineering students accounted for 34% of college and university enrollments. According to the Industrial Law of 1982, enterprises may invest up to 10% of their income tax-free in research and development projects approved by the National Council of Science and Technology and carried out by the national universities. In 1987–97, 233 scientists and engineers and 10 technicians per million people were engaged in research and development.

30 DOMESTIC TRADE

A disproportionate amount of Peru's purchasing power is concentrated in the Lima-Callao area, where selling practices increasingly follow the pattern of more commercially developed Western countries. In the highlands, where more than 60% of the population lives, retailing is done at the market level. Only about 17% of Peruvians shop in supermarkets. The fiesta day, or weekly market, for the Andes Amerindian is an important social commercial affair, where objects made at home are bartered. Barter is also the method of exchange among the first Amerindians of the Amazon Basin. Cooperative retail outlets have been established in the large mining concerns and agricultural estates. Installment sales are increasing on vehicles, refrigerators, television sets, and agricultural and industrial equipment.

Shops and some businesses are open from 10:00 AM to 1 PM, and 4 to 8 PM, Monday through Saturday; banks transact public business from 8:30 AM to 4:00 PM. Business hours are normally 9 AM to 5:30 PM, Monday through Friday. In the provinces, openings and closings are usually one hour earlier. Business is generally done in Spanish.

³¹FOREIGN TRADE

In general, Peru exports raw materials and imports capital goods and manufactures. The US is Peru's largest trading partner, and exports include mineral fuel oil, refined silvery and jewelry, lead ore and concentrated coffee. Main imports from the US include cereals, refined oil, machinery parts, chemicals and electrical machinery.

Peru's major export commodities are copper (19%), animal feed (15%), lead (13%), and gold (8.2%). Other exports include coffee (5.0%), refined petroleum products (3.1%), zinc (2.9%), and refined silver (2.2%).

In 1997 Peru's imports were distributed among the following categories:

Consumer goods	11.6%
Food	11.5%
Fuels	10.3%
Industrial supplies	28.3%
Machinery	27.6%
Transportation	10.7%
Other	0.1%

Principal trading partners in 1998 (in millions of US dollars) were as follows:

COUNTRY	EXPORTS	IMPORTS	BALANCE
United States	1,852	2,512	-660
Switzerland	363	95	268
China (inc. Hong Kong)	282	136	146
Japan	220	326	-106
Germany	216	325	-109
Brazil	187	345	-158
Spain	161	514	-353
Colombia	155	295	-140
Chile	137	474	-337
Mexico	121	277	-156

³²BALANCE OF PAYMENTS

Peru's export earnings depend heavily on world market prices in metals and fish meal. Peru maintained a favorable balance of trade from 1966 to 1973; but a surge in the price of oil imports, a decline in world copper prices, and a drop in fishing exports reversed this trend. The trade balance began to improve in 1976 and 1977, but rising interest payments kept current accounts at a loss. An austerity program was adopted in 1978; by the end of the year, Peru had reduced the deficit on current accounts, thanks in part to IMF loans. The surplus rose in 1979 and 1980 because of an extremely favorable trade performance and an additional infusion of public-sector capital. During the 1980s, however, Peru's export position was negatively affected by the worldwide recession and by lower world mineral prices, resulting in a negative trade balance, which, together with rising interest payments on the foreign debt to the IMF, led once again to an overall payments deficit.

During 1990, Peru experienced a trade and capital surplus, but a deficit in the current account. Exports fell, while imports grew largely due to overvalued exchange and because government subsidies promoting exports were eliminated. With the reforms of the Fujimori government during the 1990s, trade liberalization more than doubled the overall trade volume during the decade.

Unfortunately, the current account balance remained low; between 1992 and 1999 the balance of payments deficit was over 5% of GDP.

The US Central Intelligence Agency reports that in 1997 the purchasing power parity of Peru's exports was $6.8 billion while imports totaled $10.3 billion resulting in a trade balance of -$3.5 billion.

The International Monetary Fund (IMF) reports that in 1998 Peru had exports of goods totaling $5,735 million and imports totaling $8.2 billion. The services credit totaled $1,753 million and debit $2,294 million. The following table summarizes Peru's balance of payments as reported by the IMF for 1998 in millions of US dollars.

Current Account		-3,800
Balance on goods	-2,465	
Balance on services	-541	
Balance on income	-1,484	
Current transfers	690	
Capital Account		-107
Financial Account		1,333
Direct investment abroad	...	
Direct investment in Peru	1,930	
Portfolio investment assets	18	
Portfolio investment liabilities	-348	
Other investment assets	-126	
Other investment liabilities	-141	
Net Errors and Omissions		423
Reserves and Related Items		2,151

³³BANKING AND SECURITIES

The Central Reserve Bank, the sole bank of issue, was established in Lima in 1931 to succeed the old Reserve Bank. Also created in 1931 was the Superintendency of Banks and Insurance, an agency of the Ministry of Finance, which defines procedure and obligations of banking institutions and has control of all banks. The government-owned National Bank (Banco de la Nación) not only acts as the government's tax collector and financial agent, but also is Peru's largest commercial bank. Another government agency, the Caja de Ahorros, provides secured loans to low-income borrowers. The government-owned development bank is COFIDE. There are at least 25 commercial banks in Peru.

Peru's banking sector has grown rapidly as a result of the economic recovery and capital inflows into the financial system. A decade ago, in 1987, the president of Peru was contemplating nationalizing the entire system. Shortly after his election, Mr. Fujimori decreed the abolition of the state's development and mortgage credit banks. Today, only COFIDE offers state-regulated development assistance, but as a second-tier bank channeling funds from other institutions and without the powers to raise financing on its own account. Along with the subsidized state development banks, a host of savings and loans cooperatives have disappeared, victims of financial mismanagement, hyperinflation, and embezzlement. With them went the savings of many lower and middle-class Peruvians, who have been left with a distrust of the financial system.

Financial operations and assets remain concentrated: four banks account for over 60% of all loans, and almost three-quarters of all deposits in the system. During 1997, commercial bank loan portfolios grew by approximately one-third. Total assets of the banking system amounted to $22.5 billion in 1998. Peru is severely underbanked.

The privately owned Lima Stock Exchange (Bolsa de Valores de Lima—BVL) regulates the sale of listed securities. Securities exchanges actually began in Lima in 1860, but the stock exchange in its current form was founded in 1971. There was a long bull run in 1992 as the economy stabilized after the coup and progress towards pacification was made. After falling by 17% in dollar terms in 1995, the dollar value of the index grew in

1996 until the third quarter. The gains, however, were almost completely wiped out by the hostage crisis at the end of the year. At the end of 1996, 234 companies were listed on the BVL, and the market capitalization was $13.7 billion. In 1997, the Lima Stock Exchange registered a general index growth of 25.5%, and the blue chip index rose by 32%. From 1997 to 1999, those indexes fell by about 11%.

34INSURANCE

Insurance companies are controlled through the Superintendency of Banks and Insurance of the Ministry of Finance. According to a law of 1952, branches controlled by foreign insurance companies may not be established in Peru, although foreign insurers may operate through Peruvian subsidiaries in which they hold only minority interest. A majority of stockholders and directors of locally incorporated stock companies must be Peruvian nationals. The National Bank assumes exclusive control of all foreign reinsurance operations, as well as the writing of export credit insurance. Both life and non-life insurance exist.

35PUBLIC FINANCE

The central government publishes an annual budget representing the government's consolidated accounts (including budgetary and extrabudgetary transactions). Indirect taxes, including import and export duties, constitute the major source of government revenues. In the early 1970s, the number of state enterprises increased rapidly, which led to increased public-sector spending. As the revenues from state enterprises lagged behind expenditures, the budget deficit increased to about 10% of GDP during 1975–77, as compared to 1.7% during 1970–72. As a result of a fiscal stabilization program, the deficit was reduced to 6.5% of GDP in 1978, and to 2.5% in 1985.

In 1990, the Fujimori administration began to pursue tighter fiscal policies and attempted to avoid domestic financing of the deficit. The consolidated public sector deficit, which in 1990 was 6.5% of GDP, fell to 2.5% by 1992, despite the suspension of most foreign financing after the 5 April coup. The IMF program allowed a foreign-financed deficit of 2.9% of GPD in 1993 for increased social sector spending and investment in infrastructure. However, with lower than expected foreign financing and tax collection, the deficit that could be maintained while meeting the public sector external debt obligations was only equivalent to about 2% of GDP. The privatization of state enterprises fattened the government's coffers between 1992 and 2000. The budget deficit for 2000 was 2.5% of GDP due to a rise in public sector wages of 16%, and lower than expected revenues from privatization that year.

The US Central Intelligence Agency (CIA) estimates that in 1996 Peru's central government took in revenues of approximately $8.5 billion and had expenditures of $9.3 billion including capital expenditures of $2 billion. Overall, the government registered a deficit of approximately $800 million. External debt totaled $32.4 billion.

The following table shows an itemized breakdown of government revenues and expenditures. The percentages were calculated from data reported by the International Monetary Fund. The dollar amounts (millions) are based on the CIA estimates provided above.

REVENUE AND GRANTS	100%	8,500
Tax revenue	85.1%	7,235
Non-tax revenue	14.3%	1,217
Capital revenue	0.6%	47
EXPENDITURES	100%	9,300

36TAXATION

There are four main levies: income tax, excise tax, VAT, and social-security contributions. Personal income tax rates range from 15–30%. The corporate income tax is calculated on the basis of a tax unit (UIT), which is recalculated annually to account for the effects of inflation. Corporate income tax is 30%. Corporate income tax in the Amazon region ranges from only 5% to 10%. The VAT is applied to all goods and services at a single rate of 18%. Luxury goods are subject to an excise tax with rates ranging form 2% to 118%.

37CUSTOMS AND DUTIES

Import licenses are not required on most products. Ad valorem duties are levied at 12% (on 95% of products) or 20% (on textiles, footwear, and agricultural products) c.i.f. There is a 5% over rate charged on a list of 5% of total items that are agricultural in nature. Tariffs range from a total of 12–25%, averaging 13%.

Export processing free zones offer investors exemptions from customs duties for imports and exports. Peru does not adhere to the CET of the Andean Community, but is a member of the group, which opened a Free Trade Zone with MERCOSUR in 2000. The Free Trade Area of the Americas is scheduled for 2005.

38FOREIGN INVESTMENT

The British were the first to gain prominence as investors in Peru, when they took power the railways in payment of debt to Peruvian bondholders in 1890. They developed oil fields and a long distance telephone and cable service. In the mid-1950s, Swiss, German, and Canadian interests became active in the transportation and communication services. Private US interests ventured capital and technical aid to all sectors, especially the oil and mining industries. The fishing industry from the beginning was fostered by the US. Private companies operated tuna fleets in Peruvian waters, as well as canneries.

Between 1959 and 1961, following passages of industrial development laws and the signing of an investment guarantee treaty with the US, under which private US investors could obtain federal risk insurance against currency inconvertibility, total foreign investment almost doubled, rising from $686 million to $1,274 million. US investments continued their rapid growth rate until the 1968 coup, after which Peru's military rulers pursued a nationalist course, characterized by selective expropriation of foreign-held interests in sectors such as mining, finance, and infrastructure. In addition, a variety of strictures were placed on the uses of foreign capital, as well as on the relative proportion of foreign-to-local control. US-linked firms were the hardest struck by these measures, causing a strain in relations. In February 1974, a US-Peruvian agreement provided a compensation schedule for properties taken over during 1968–73. At the end of 1973, the US investment column stood at $793 million, less than half of the total a decade earlier. Private investments in the 1970s continued to lag, although some new funding was being advanced in mining and petroleum. From 1977 through 1980, net direct capital investment totaled only $177 million, or less than the total for 1981 ($263 million), the first year after the restoration of civilian rule. In 1984 and 1985, after the economic slump, net direct investment was $89 million and $53 million, respectively.

After 1980, the official attitude toward foreign investment changed substantially. The 1979 constitution guarantees protection of private property, whether Peruvian or foreign, and permits foreign jurisdiction for international financial contracts. The agency responsible for foreign investment is the National Commission of Foreign Investment and Technology (Comite Nacional de Inversion Extranjera y Tecnologia, or CONITE). In late 1986, the Andean Group relaxed its regulations on foreign investment; this change was expected to benefit Peru. About

1,000 foreign companies were represented in Peru in the 1980s, either directly or through subsidiaries or affiliates.

The trade and investment climate in Peru has improved significantly since President Fujimori assumed office in July 1990. Foreign investor confidence in Peru should be maintained with Fujimori as the key element in sustaining capital inflows. The Foreign Investment Promotion Law, and the Framework Law for Private Investment Growth outlined the government's support for privatization and foreign investment in 1991. From 1991 to 1997, privatization sales totaled over $7 billion, most of which came from foreign investors. There are no restrictions on remittances, but there is a mandatory affirmative action program for Peruvian employees. Activities in Export Processing Zones are tax and customs duty exempt for 15 years. Foreign direct investment rose by $317 million to $7.3 billion in 1998. One-third of that investment came from Spain in telecommunications, 21% from the US, and 15% from the UK (in the energy and industry and mining sectors). In 1999, FDI reached $8.5 billion, a 10% increase from 1998.

[39]ECONOMIC DEVELOPMENT

After World War II, President Odria discontinued import licensing and certain price controls and enacted the Mining Code of 1950, the Petroleum Law of 1952, and the Electrical Industry Law of 1955, all with a view to reassuring sources of foreign and domestic capital of reasonable taxation and an adequate rate of earnings under liberal exploitation concessions. Given this stimulus to capital ventures, the economy expanded, and new exports, such as iron and coal, were developed.

After the coup of 1968, Peru's military rulers sought a profound restructuring of the country's economic life. The overall objectives were the establishment of effective state control of natural resources; and redistribution of foreign participation; creation of manageable balance among governmental, private, and foreign sectors; and redistribution of productive sources more broadly throughout the population. Nationalization, coupled with a redistribution of ownership and management authority in major enterprises, was the cornerstone of the new policy from its incipient stages in 1968 though 1975. After a five year plan was announced in December 1968, emphasizing a reorientation from an agricultural to an industrial economy and stressing the expropriation of large estates, with redistribution of land to peasants in the sierra. In early 1969, tax and credit incentives for the formation of cooperatives and the consolidation of smaller landholding were enacted. In nonagricultural sectors, the government began, in 1969, selective nationalization of major foreign holding in the mining, petroleum, and infrastructure sectors. In several areas, a government presence was asserted through the creation of state-owned commercial enterprises, the most notable of which included Induperu, in industry; Mineroperu, in mining; Pescaperu, in fishing; Petroperu, in petroleum; Entelperu, in telecommunications; and COFIDE (Corporacion Financiera de Desarrollo), in investment.

Industrial enterprises in general were required to adopt profit-sharing and co-ownership schemes for their employees. Although strict limits were placed on foreign participation in Peruvian industry, such as investments were not ruled out in principle, and in 1974, the government acted to guarantee fair settlement for US holdings expropriated during 1968–73.

On 28 July 1974, the government announced its Inca Plan (which may actually have been drawn up before the 1969 coup), a master plan that envisioned eventual transformation of all economic entities along prescribed socialist lines. Three types of enterprises were to be permitted to operate in Peru: state-owned enterprises, worker-owned collectives (industrial communities), and social-property companies (entities managed by workers but financed by the state). In late 1975, the Central Bank set up a line of credit to aid the formation of social-property companies through the National Fund for Social Property. The Agrarian Bank, which had been created in July, was authorized to handle the credit requirements of the reorganized agricultural sector, as well as to ease the transformation of cooperatives and farmers' associations, many of which had existed for only a few years, into social-property entities. The order of priorities for industry placed basic industries—notably steel, nonferrous metals, chemicals, fertilizers, cement, and paper—at high rung, followed by manufacturers of capital good, such as machine tools, and industrial research. Reinvestment of profits was stressed throughout.

In the mid-1970s, the regime began to moderate the rigid price control system instituted in its formative years. The prices of petroleum and basic consumer goods were increased, while wage increases were fixed and agricultural subsidies removed. In September 1975, the sol was devalued and financial controls were imposed to help stem inflation (reaching 40% in 1975) and to ease the trade imbalance. The Tupac Amaru Development Plan, announced in 1977, limited the structural reforms of the Inca Plan, calling for economic decentralization and encouragement of foreign investment. In the late 1970s, a number of state-controlled enterprises were sold, and worker participation was curtailed. The civilian leaders who came to power in 1980 sought to reduce government participation in the economy and to improve the efficiency of state enterprises. Import tariffs and export taxes were reduced, and a new investment program for 1980–85 emphasized power and irrigation projects and the construction of housing and health care facilities. These attempts to revitalize the economy were hampered by the worldwide recession and by the soft market of Peru's commodity exports. In response, the Garcia Administration reverted to an interventionist policy, imposing import controls and regulating foreign-exchange availability, as well as influencing the financial sector by threatening to nationalize the banks.

The decade of the 1990s, with an Administration in favor of a market economy, has attracted more investment into Peru's economy. With foreign capital flowing in recent years, Peru was poised for economic recovery. Privatization and the rapidly growing economy are providing the government with funds to spend on infrastructure and social programs.

In August of 1990, the government implemented an economic program based on an (1) economic stabilization plan, (2) a structural reform program and (3) a set of initiatives aimed at reintegrating the Peruvian economy into the international economic system. As a direct result economic growth in the 1990s was quite strong.

The economic stabilization plan focused on achieving an inflation rate comparable to international levels, and to foster an environment favorable for savings, investment and sustained economic growth. The plan was based on strict fiscal discipline in accordance with an austere monetary policy. The inflation rate was about 6% in 1999. Structural reforms resulted in capital amounting to $7 billion between 1991 and 1999, resulting in a massive inflow of foreign investment. The reinsertion of Peru into the international financial system, beginning in 1991, was intended to restore normal relations between the country and its international creditors. Peru normalized its relations with multilateral bodies and the Paris Club and with the commercial banks.

[40]SOCIAL DEVELOPMENT

A modern system of social security (referred to as SNP) has evolved from initial legislation provided in the 1933 constitution. Coverage and benefits were substantially broadened after the 1968 coup. Workers were entitled to receive benefits covering disability, medical attention, hospitalization, maternity, old age, retirement, and widows and orphans. In 1991, the government introduced a new system of individualized capitalization through private pensions (SPP), which exists along side the national social security system.

The original program is administered by the Ministry of Labor, while the private system is supervised by the Superintendency of Pension Fund Administrators. Social insurance is compulsory for all employees up to the age of 60. The national social security and pension funds (SNP) are endowed by 13% of employee earnings, with the balance of funds supplied by the government. The private system is funded entirely by contributions from employees amounting to 10% of earnings. Sickness and maternity benefits are funded by 9% of employer payroll, with a special credit for employers who use the newer private system. Workers are entitled to treatment from public hospitals or partial refund of expenses in private facilities. Working mothers are entitled to maternity leave of 90 days at 100% pay.

Women are often kept from leadership roles in the public and private sectors by the force of tradition, although they are equal under the constitution. As of 1997, 26 of 240 members of Parliament were women. In 1999, a government-supported program to provide credit to female entrepreneurs served 37,600 clients and had a portfolio valued at $13.3 million. Domestic abuse and violence against women is a widespread problem. There are some special police stations that are staffed by women to assist female victims of violence. Legislations enacted in 1997 facilitated the prosecution of domestic violence cases.

There were also reports of children being drafted into the army to serve in the border conflict with Ecuador. Until 1995, minors were tried as adults in cases of suspected terrorism. Current legislation now mandates that these minor be sent to juvenile detention centers.

Human rights violations have been committed by the government, Shining Path terrorists, and the Tupac Amaru Revolutionary Movement. There are restrictions on freedom of speech and of the press. Prison conditions are poor, and the physical abuse of prisoners is common. In 1995, the government passed an Amnesty Law that absolved members of the security forces who committed human rights abuses between 1980 and 1995. There is still a lack of accountability for both the armed forces and police, and the judicial system remains inefficient, with lengthy delays between arrest and trial.

Although the activities of the Shining Path have continued to decline, its members continue to torture and murder opponents.

41HEALTH

Although Peru has made significant advances toward reducing epidemic disease, improving sanitation, and expanding medical facilities, much remains to be done. The infant mortality rate in 1996 was estimated at 43 per 1,000 live births, while the general mortality rate in 1990–95 was 6.9 per 1,000 people. Maternal mortality in 1997 was high at 265 per 100,000 live births. Average life expectancy in 1998 was estimated at 68.5 years.

Leading causes of death in 1998 included acute respiratory infections (16.3%), intestinal infectious diseases (7.7%), circulatory system and cardiovascular disease (5.4%), tuberculosis (5%), and other causes. There were about 26,000 war-related deaths in Peru from 1983 to 1992. Serious Vitamin A deficiency was documented in 22% of children ages 4 and under in 1992 and a 1993 census found 48% of all children aged 6–9 suffering from malnutrition. Goiter rates in school age children during 1986–87 were high (35.8%). In 1994–95, still only 60% of the population had access to safe water and 47% had adequate sanitation. Peru has repeatedly reported the highest number of yellow fever cases in the Americas. The total number of cases in Peru was 503 with a 39% fatality rate in 1995. Other common diseases included malaria (211,561 cases in 1996) and tuberculosis (33,925 cases in 1995). Immunization rates for children up to one year old in 1997 were: tuberculosis (98%); diphtheria, pertussis, and tetanus (98%); polio (97%); and measles (95%).

Health services are concentrated around metropolitan Lima. A health care plan initiated in 1981 called for the establishment of 100 health centers in rural areas and shantytowns. The central administration of all health services lies with the Ministry of Health. A General Health Law enacted in 1997 restructured and reformed the health care sector. In 1997 there were 11 physicians per 10,000 people. Health care expenditures in 1995 were $128 per capita. In 1995, there were 13 hospital beds per 1,000 people. A total of 5.5% of gross domestic product went to health expenditures in 1995.

The birth rate in 1998 was 24.7 per 1,000 people. Some 64% of married women used contraception during 1997.

The HIV-1 seroprevalence rate was 0.6 per 100 adults in 1997. As of that year, 72,000 AIDS cases had been reported.

42HOUSING

Successive governments since the 1950s have recognized the importance of slum clearance and public housing programs in combating disease and high mortality rates. Most housing development programs carried out by the government and by private enterprise have been in the Lima area. In Lima and other towns, several "neighborhoods" (unidades vecinales) have been completed through government efforts since the early 1960s. Each such housing complex is designed to be a self-sufficient community. A typical neighborhood is built to house 6,000 persons at moderate rentals. In rural areas, however, a conservative estimate of the housing shortage runs to a minimum of 700,000. A 1970 earthquake tremendously increased the number of homeless, displacing some 500,000 persons. The total housing stock numbered 4,906,000 at latest estimate.

One of the revolutionary government's early decrees gave the Housing Bank control over financing low-cost housing. Construction grew rapidly during 1970–73, to the point of depleting local cement supplies. By 1983, however, only 18% of the rural population had access to safe water; the figure for the urban population was 73%. Sewerage facilities are nearly nonexistent in rural areas. Eighty-eight percent of all housing units were detached or semi-detached houses; 4% were apartments; 4% were vecindads, or semi-private dwellings; and 3% were villas. Owners occupied 73% of all dwellings, 15% were rented, and 7% were occupied by usufructus, households legally living in a dwelling belonging to another. Mud houses comprised 47% of all dwellings, 31% were constructed of bricks, 7% were clay, 7% were wood, and 5% were of stone and mud.

43EDUCATION

Education is nominally free and compulsory for children ages 7 to 16. For the year 2000, the adult illiteracy rate was estimated at 10.1% (males, 5.3%; females, 14.6%). The government has been responsible for public education since 1905; free secondary education began in 1946, but with far too few public schools to meet the need. Several long-term projects have been initiated to increase literacy and raise living standards among the adults of the remote sierra and selva areas. In March 1972, new education legislation enhanced the central authority of the Ministry of Education, granting the government control over all teaching appointments in the public schools and increasing its authority over the private sector. The legislation provided for adult literacy instruction and instituted the concept of a fully staffed six-grade "nuclear" school to serve the rural population. The 1972 law also established Quechua and Aymará as languages of instruction for non-Spanish-speaking Amerindians, especially in the lowest grades.

As of the early 1980s, the educational system consisted of three levels: nurseries and kindergartens; basic education, consisting of primary and secondary schools; and higher education (pre-university and university). In 1998 there were 4,185,489 pupils enrolled in primary schools. The number of secondary school students in 1997 was 1,969,501 students, with 106,614 teachers. Institutions of higher education had 45,443 teachers and enrolled 657,586 students in 1997. There is a national university in virtually every major city; the oldest is the National University of San Marcos of Lima, originally founded in 1551. The National University of Engineering and the National University of Agriculture are specialized governmental institutions. The University of San Cristóbal de Huamanga in Ayacucho, founded in the 17th century, was reopened in 1960 and offers mainly technical training. Peru's hard-pressed universities can accept only a fraction of each year's applicants.

44LIBRARIES AND MUSEUMS

The National Library in Lima, with 3.89 million volumes, is the largest in Peru. More than 450,000 volumes may be found in the various libraries of the University of San Marcos. The library at the National University of San Augustín at Arequipa contains over 430,000 volumes. The Library at the Pontifical Library has over 350,000 items. There are nearly 200 public libraries in Peru, the largest of them in Callao, Arequipa, and Lima.

Peru has endeavored to restore and maintain the aesthetic and historical evidences of its pre-Columbian and colonial civilizations in more than 250 public and private museums.

The City Hall in Lima contains a full record of the city's official acts since its founding. The Cathedral of Lima, with its silver-covered altars and carved stalls, contains priceless historical and religious relics. A chapel near the entrance contains the alleged remains of Francisco Pizarro. Two colonial residences, the Palacio Torre Tagle and the Quinta de Presa, have been maintained to exhibit antiques and to serve as examples of the architecture of traditional Lima. There is no law protecting old houses, however, and many have been removed to make way for new downtown buildings. Some have been privately restored, such as the headquarters of the Association of Amateur Artists, the Institute Riva Aguero, the Associated Electrical Companies, the Bullfight Museum, and the Oquendo Mansion. In the Quinta de Presa is a museum with the possessions of the actress La Perricholi, the famous favorite of the 18th-century Viceroy Amat. At Pueblo Libre in Lima are the National Museum of Archaeology and Anthropology, with exhibits of pre-Columbian civilizations, and the Museum of the Republic, a historical museum. The Rafael Larco Herrera Museum in Lima (housing the former collection of the Chiclín plantation near Trujillo) is a private museum with a vast collection of notable antiquities from the pre-Inca Chimú culture. The University of Trujillo has a museum with specimens of early Peruvian cultures. Lima's Museum of Art exhibits Peru's national art from the pre-Columbian era to the contemporary period. There are regional museums throughout the country, including the Frederico Galvez Durand Archeological Museum in Huancayo featuring artifacts from the Nazca peoples.

45MEDIA

Peru's major telecommunications systems were developed privately by Swedish, US, and Swiss enterprises. In 1970, however, the government nationalized the Lima Telephone Co. and announced plans to take over the entire telecommunications system through its wholly owned company Entelperú. A joint Peruvian-Chilean firm operates a system in southern Peru and Arica, Chile. In 1995, there were 779,300 telephones, more than two-thirds of them in Lima. The government's Bureau of Mails and Telecommunications operates the domestic telegraph system, using radio to reach communities not served by land lines. As of 1999, there were 273 radio stations and 13 television broadcast stations. In 1997, there were 271 radios, 143 television sets, and 18 mobile phones per 1,000 population

The leading Lima dailies—among them *El Comercio* (1999 circulation 140,000), *Ojo* (100,000), and *Expreso* (80,000)—are the most important newspapers and are flown daily to provincial towns. The official government organ is *El Peruano* (75,000), a daily gazette in which laws, decrees, and brief government announcements are published. Special-interest periodicals are published by learned societies, agricultural groups, and business associations.

During the period of military rule between 1968 and 1980, the press in Peru was under strict government control. The law provided severe penalties for criticizing government officials and required newspapers to publish reports from the president and cabinet ministers. In 1974, the government shut down *Caretas,* the last remaining independent political magazine, and all remaining private national newspapers with circulations of more than 20,000 were expropriated. When civilian rule returned in 1980, the press was returned to private control. However, freedom of the press has once again been restricted since the political crackdown by President Fujimori in April 1992, and journalists have been arrested by the government. As of 1999, journalists were subject to harassment and intimidation, and practiced self-censorship. The government is said also to exert control over the media through the purchasing of advertising to promote government views and pro-government opinion.

As of 1996, there were over 135,000 personal computers. Online access is extremely limited, with about one Internet host per 1,000 population in 1998.

46ORGANIZATIONS

Although Congress had earlier authorized an organic cooperative law, nothing was done until 1941, when a number of agricultural cooperatives were created by the Ministry of Agriculture. During the early years of the military junta, cooperatives were seen as a primary device for restructuring the agricultural sector. Most expropriated commercial estates were converted to cooperative farms, while smaller holdings were consolidated into units collectively owned by farmers' associations. Subsequent reform programs, culminating in the Inca Plan of 1974, pointed toward the restructuring of Peruvian society, with the social-property company as a basic unit. However, this corporatist idea was gradually deemphasized, and when the civilian government took over in 1980, most of the reforms of the previous decade were scaled down or abandoned.

The national Society of Industries, founded in 1896, coordinates the branches of organized industry. The Office of Small Industry and the Institute for the Development of Manual Arts were established in 1946 to revive the weaving and spinning skills of Incas and to coordinate the handicraft workers in textile and other industries, such as gold and silver crafts. Numerous chambers of commerce continue to function. Of Peru's many learned societies, perhaps the most important is the Academia Peruana, affiliated with the Royal Spanish Academy of Madrid.

47TOURISM, TRAVEL, AND RECREATION

Citizens of most Western European and Latin American countries, Canada, the US, and Japan do not need visas; for visits of up to 60 days. As part of a program to encourage foreign tourism, the government has built and manages, through its Peruvian Hotel Co., several hotels or inns and a variety of tourist services. To help increase foreign exchange earnings from tourism, Peru consolidated all government agencies dealing with tourism into an autonomous corporation in 1964. The Fund for the Promotion of Tourism was established in 1979. In the early 1980s, the government outlined new tax incentives for investment in the tourist sector.

Tourists, as well as scholars, are especially drawn to the wealth of archaeological remains on the coast and in the sierra. Chan Chan, the center of the Chimú civilization, stands in adobe ruins near Trujillo. The ruins of the 9th century coastal city of Pachacamac are just south of Lima. Inca ruins may be seen at Cuzco, Sacsahuamán (on the northern edge of Cuzco), Ollantaytambo, and Machu Picchu, as well as on Lake Titicaca islands.

The northern coastal waters are famous for big-game fishing, and the abundant resources of the sierra waters are maintained by fish culture stations. Lakes and streams have been stocked with trout throughout Peru. In Lake Titicaca, trout average 10 kg (22 lb); trout weighing as much as 21 kg (46 lb) have been caught. Other tourist attractions include beaches and water sports; several state parks offer mountain climbing, cross-country skiing, and white-water rafting. The most popular sports are football (soccer), baseball, basketball, and bullfighting. Fiestas, especially the annual celebrations of patron saints, include both Catholic and Indian rites; bands of musicians, or conjuntos, are an important part of each fiesta.

In 1997, 2,098,150 tourists visited Peru; earnings from tourism were $805 million. There were 63,817 hotel rooms with 111,461 beds and an occupancy rate of 32% in 1993.

In 1999 the UN estimated the cost of staying in Lima at $213 per day. Travel expenses for Cusco were $162 and Puno were $123.

48FAMOUS PERUVIANS

The Inca Huayna Capac (1450?–1525) reigned from 1487 and extended the Inca Empire, encouraging public works and fine arts. On his death he left the empire to his two sons, Huáscar (1495?–1533) and Atahualpa (1500?–1533); Huáscar was executed by his half-brother, and Atahualpa, the last of the great Incas, was executed by the Spanish conquistador Francisco Pizarro (1470?–1541). Acknowledged as America's first great writer, Garcilaso de la Vega (El Inca, 1539?–1616), son of a Spanish conquistador and an Inca princess, preserved in his *Royal Commentaries of the Incas* authentic descriptions of his ancestral empire and its traditions. Manuel de Amat (fl.18th century), viceroy from 1762 to 1776, was a patron of the colonial theater and of the famous actress Micaela Villegas, known as La Perricholi. Tupac Amaru II (José Gabriel Condorcanqui, 1742–81), partly descended from the Incas, led a revolt against Spanish rule in 1780 in which he was defeated, captured, and executed.

Dr. José Hipólito Unnúe (1758–1833), a statesman and scientist, founded Lima's medical school in 1808 and reformed Peruvian education. The hero of the War of Independence, Mariano Melgar (1792–1815), was also a poet and composer whose regional songs *(yaravís)* are still popular. Marshal Ramón Castilla (1797–1867) distinguished himself in two great presidential terms (1845–51, 1855–62), introducing railways and the telegraph, emancipating the slaves, abolishing Amerindian tribute, modernizing Lima, and developing the important guano industry. Ricardo Palma (1833–1919) is considered Peru's greatest literary figure; a critic, historian, and storyteller, he originated the genre called tradición, and wrote the 10-volume *Tradiciones Peruanas*. José María Valle-Riestra (1858–1925) was an important composer.

In the modern era, the work of an erudite Amerindian, Julio Tello (1880–1947), became internationally known in archaeological circles. Jorge Chávez (1887–1910) made the first solo flight across the Alps in 1910. Santos Chocano (1875–1934), César Vallejo (1895–1938), and José María Eguren (1882–1942) are considered Peru's finest modern poets. Established prose writers are Víctor Andrés Belaúnde (1883–1966), Jorge Basadre (1903–80), and Ciro Alegría (1909–67); the novelist Mario Vargas Llosa (b.1936) was the first Latin American president of PEN, an international writers' organization. Peru's best-known

contemporary painter is Fernando de Szyszlo (b.1925). Other noted Peruvians include Ventura García Calderón (1866–1959), a writer; José Sabogal (1888–1956), a painter; Honorio Delgado (b.1892), a scientist; and José Carlos Mariátegui (1895–1930), a political essayist. Yma Sumac (b.1928) is an internationally known singer.

Víctor Raúl Haya de la Torre (1895–1979) originated APRA in 1924 as a Latin American workers' movement; it became Peru's most significant political force. Gen. Juan Velasco Alvarado (1910–77), who led the military coup of 1968, ruled as president of Peru until his own ouster by a bloodless coup in 1975. Gen. Francisco Morales Bermúdez Cerruti (b.1921), president during 1975–80, prepared the country for a return to civilian rule. Fernando Belaúnde Terry (b.1913), founder of the Popular Action Party, served as president during 1963–68 and again during 1980–85. Alán García Pérez (b.1949) was elected president in 1985. In 1982, Javier Pérez de Cuéllar (b.1920) became secretary-general of the UN.

49DEPENDENCIES

Peru has no territories or colonies.

50BIBLIOGRAPHY

Alisky, Marvin. *Historical Dictionary of Peru*. Metuchen, N.J.: Scarecrow, 1979.

Becker, David G. *The New Bourgeoisie and the Limits of Dependency: Mining, Class and Power in "Revolutionary" Peru*. Princeton, N.J.: Princeton University Press, 1983.

Bingham, Hiram. *Lost City of the Incas: The Story of Machu Picchu and Its Builders*. New York: Duell, Sloan & Pearce, 1949.

Cleaves, Peter S., and Martin J. Scurrah. *Agriculture, Bureaucracy, and Military Government in Peru*. Ithaca, N.Y.: Cornell University Press, 1980.

Collier, David. *Squatters and Oligarchs: Authoritarian Rule and Policy Change in Peru*. Baltimore: Johns Hopkins University Press, 1976.

Descola, Jean. *Daily Life in Colonial Peru, 1710–1820*. New York: Macmillan, 1968.

Dobyns, Henry F., and Paul L. Doughty. *Peru: A Cultural History*. New York: Oxford University Press, 1976.

Figueroa, Adolfo. *Capitalist Development and the Peasant Economy of Peru*. New York: Cambridge University Press, 1984.

Fisher, John Robert. *Peru*. Santa Barbara, Calif.: Clio Press, 1989.

Garcilaso de la Vega. *Royal Commentaries of the Incas and General History of Peru*. 2 vols. Austin: University of Texas Press, 1966.

Goodsell, Charles T. *American Corporations and Peruvian Politics*. Cambridge, Mass.: Harvard University Press, 1974.

Gootenberg, Paul Eliot. *Between Silver and Guano: Commercial Policy and the State in Postindependence Peru*. Princeton, N.J.: Princeton University Press, 1989.

———. *Imagining Development: Economic Ideas in Peru's "Fictitious Prosperity" of Guano, 1840–1880*. Berkeley: University of California Press, 1993.

Griffiths, Nicholas. *The Cross and the Serpent: Religious Repression and Resurgence in Colonial Peru*. Norman, Okla.: University of Oklahoma Press, 1996.

Haas, Jonathan, Shelia Pozorski, and Thomas Pozorski (eds.). *The Origins and Development of the Andean State*. New York: Cambridge University Press, 1987.

Health Care in Peru: Resources and Policy. Boulder, Colo.: Westview Press, 1988.

Hemming, John. *The Conquest of the Incas*. New York: Harcourt Brace Jovanovich, 1970.

Herzog, Kristin. *Finding Their Voice: Peruvian Women's Testimonies of War.* Valley Forge, Pa.: Trinity Press International, 1993.

Hudson, Rex A. (ed.). *Peru in Pictures.* Minneapolis: Lerner, 1987.

Keatinge, Richard W. (ed.). *Peruvian Prehistory: An Overview of Pre-Inca and Inca Society.* New York: Cambridge University Press, 1988.

Lockhart, James. *Spanish Peru, 1532–1560: A Social History,* 2nd ed. Madison, Wisconsin.: University of Wisconsin Press, 1994.

Lowenthal, Abraham F. (ed.). *The Peruvian Experiment: Continuity and Change Under Military Rule.* Princeton, N.J.: Princeton University Press, 1975.

Martin, Luis. *The Kingdom of the Sun: A Short History of Peru.* New York: Scribner, 1974.

Mauceri, Philip. *State under Siege: Development and Policy Making in Peru.* Boulder, Colo.: Westview, 1996.

Moseley, Michael Edward. *The Incas and their Ancestors: the Archaeology of Peru.* New York: Thames and Hudson, 1992.

Palmer, David Scott. *Peru: The Authoritarian Legacy.* New York: Praeger, 1980.

Prescott, William Hickling. *History of the Conquest of Peru.* Rev. ed. New York: New American Library, 1981 (orig. 1847).

Peru: A Country Study. 4th ed. Edited by Rex A. Hudson. Washington, D.C.: Library of Congress, Federal Research Division, 1993.

The Peruvian Economy and Structural Adjustment: Past, Present, and Future. Edited by Efraín Gonzales de Olarte. Boulder, Colo.: L. Rienner, 1996.

The Peru Reader: History, Culture, Politics. Edited by Carlos Ivan Degregori, Robin Kirk, and Orin Starn. Durham, N.C.: Duke University Press, 1995.

St. John, Ronald Bruce. *The Foreign Policy of Peru.* Boulder, Colo.: L. Rienner, 1992.

The Shining Path of Peru. New York: St. Martin's Press, 1992.

Stepan, Alfred C. *The State and Society: Peru in Comparative Perspective.* Princeton, N.J.: Princeton University Press, 1978.

Stokes, Susan Carol. *Cultures in Conflict: Social Movements and the State in Peru.* Berkeley, Calif.: University of California Press, 1995.

Thorp, Rosemary. *Economic Management and Economic Development in Peru and Colombia.* Pittsburgh, Pa.: University of Pittsburgh Press, 1991.

Werlich, David P. *Admiral of the Amazon: John Randolph Tucker, his Confederate Colleagues, and Peru.* Charlottesville: University Press of Virginia, 1990.

ST. KITTS AND NEVIS

Federation of Saint Kitts and Nevis

CAPITAL: Basseterre.

FLAG: Two thin diagonal yellow bands flanking a wide black diagonal band separate a green triangle at the hoist from a red triangle at the fly. On the black band are two white five-pointed stars.

ANTHEM: *National Anthem,* beginning "O land of beauty."

MONETARY UNIT: The East Caribbean dollar of 100 cents, pegged to the US dollar, is the national currency. There are coins of 1, 2, 5, 10, and 25 cents and 1 East Caribbean dollar, and notes of 5, 10, 20, and 100 East Caribbean dollars. EC$1 = US$0.37037 (US$1 = EC$2.70).

WEIGHTS AND MEASURES: The imperial system is used.

HOLIDAYS: New Year's Day, 1 January; Labor Day, 1st Monday in May; Bank Holiday, 1st Monday in August; Independence Day, 19 September; Prince of Wales's Birthday, 14 November; Christmas, 25 December; Boxing Day, 26 December; Carnival, 30 December. Movable religious holidays include Good Friday and Whitmonday.

TIME: 8 AM = noon GMT.

1 LOCATION, SIZE, AND EXTENT

St. Kitts lies about 8 km (5 mi) SE of the Netherlands Antilles and 72 km (45 mi) NW of Antigua, in the Leeward Islands. It is 37 km (23 mi) long and 8 km (5 mi) across at its widest point, with a total area of 269 sq km (104 sq mi). Comparatively, the area occupied by St. Kitts and Nevis is slightly more than 1.5 times the size of Washington, D.C. Nevis lies about 3.2 km (2 mi) SE of St. Kitts, across a channel called the Narrows; it is 13 km (8 mi) long and 10 km (6 mi) wide, with a land area of 93 sq km (36 sq mi). Together the islands have a coastline of 135 km (84 mi).

The capital city, Basseterre, is located on St. Kitts.

2 TOPOGRAPHY

St. Kitts and Nevis are of volcanic origin. In the northwest of St. Kitts is Mt. Liamuiga, the island's highest peak at 1,156 m (3,793 ft); to the south and west of Mt. Liamuiga are 210-m (700-ft) cliffs that drop straight to the sea. On the southern arm of the island lies the Great Salt Pond. Nevis's highest elevation is the central peak of Mt. Nevis, at 985 m (3,232 ft); it is usually capped in clouds. There is a black sand beach on the northwest coast.

3 CLIMATE

Temperatures range from 20°C (68°F) to 29°C (84°F) all year long. Northeast tradewinds are constant. Rain usually falls between May and November, averaging 109 cm (43 in) a year. High humidity characterizes the summer months.

4 FLORA AND FAUNA

The upper slopes of Mt. Nevis are well wooded; coconut palms, poincianas, and palmettos are profuse. Lemon trees, bougainvillea, hibiscus, and tamarind are common on both islands. There are some black-faced vervet monkeys on Monkey Hill in St. Kitts.

5 ENVIRONMENT

Deforestation, erosion, and water pollution are among the most significant environmental problems in St. Kitts and Nevis.

Deforestation has affected the nation's wildlife population and contributed to soil erosion. The erosion of the soil produces silt, which affects the living environment for marine life on the coral reefs.

Water pollution results from uncontrolled dumping of sewage into the nation's waters. Another contributing factor is pollution from cruise ships which support the nation's tourist trade. In an effort to establish a framework for the regulation of environmental issues, the government has introduced legislation. The National Conservation and Environmental Protection Act, along with the Letter Act, are aimed at monitoring the nation's most pressing environmental concerns.

6 POPULATION

The population of St. Kitts and Nevis in 2000 was estimated at 43,441, with the majority living on St. Kitts. An estimated 6.3% of the population is 65 years of age or older. The projected population for the year 2005 is 47,000, assuming a crude birthrate of 21 per 1,000 population and a death rate of 6, resulting in a natural rate of change of 1.5% for the period 2000–2005. In 1996, the estimated population density overall was 115 per sq km (298 per sq mi), with the density of St. Kitts twice that of Nevis.

It was estimated that 34% of the population lived in urban areas in 2000. Basseterre, the capital on St. Kitts, had a 2000 metropolitan population of 12,000. Charlestown is the largest urban settlement on Nevis.

7 MIGRATION

There is less emigration in the current period than there was during the mid-20th century, largely because the economy enjoys almost full employment during the tourist and harvest seasons. During the off-season, some people migrate to other islands in search of work. In 1999, the net migration rate was -1.05 migrants per 1,000 population.

⁸ETHNIC GROUPS

The population is mainly of black African descent. Only about 5% of the population are mulatto, 3% Indo-Pakistani, and 1.5% European.

⁹LANGUAGES

English, sprinkled with local expressions, is the universal language.

¹⁰RELIGIONS

Christianity is the dominant religion. The Anglican Church, the largest church on the island, claims more than a third of all adherents. Other principal Christian groups are the Church of God, Methodists, Moravians, Baptists, Seventh-Day Adventists, and Roman Catholics. Religious freedom is guaranteed by the constitution, and there are non-Christian practitioners, most notably the small Baha'i community.

¹¹TRANSPORTATION

A light, narrow-gauge railway of 58 km (36 mi) on St. Kitts is operated by the government to transport sugarcane from fields to factory and processed sugar to the pier at Rawlins Bay. In 1998 there were 320 km (199 mi) of roads on the islands, of which 136 km (85 mi) were paved; the main roads circle each island. Basseterre and Charlestown are the principal ports. A state-run motorboat service is maintained between St. Kitts and Nevis. In 1998 there were two airports, both with paved runways. Golden Rock International Airport is a modern facility serving Basseterre; several small airlines fly to a landing strip at Newcastle, on Nevis.

12 HISTORY

Arawak Indians, followed by Caribs, were the earliest known inhabitants of the islands. Discovered by Columbus in 1493 and named St. Christopher, St. Kitts was the first of the British West Indies to be settled. Sir Thomas Warner established a settlement on St. Kitts in 1623, later leading colonial expeditions to Nevis in 1628 and Antigua in 1632. For a short while during this period there were French settlements at both ends of St. Kitts, and the French settlers cooperated with the British to repel a Spanish invasion. By the 1660s there were some 4,000 Europeans engaged in the sugar trade, based on a plantation system with slaves imported from Africa. The French gained control in 1664 but lost it to the British in 1713, under the Peace of Utrecht. The French besieged the British garrison in the Brimstone Hill fortress in 1782 and once more gained control of the island, but the Treaty of Versailles (1783) returned St. Kitts again to Britain. By the late 18th century, the thermal baths at Charlestown, Nevis, attracted thousands of international tourists. Although the slaves were emancipated in 1834, many of the ex-slaves continued to work on the sugar plantations, so the sugar-based economy did not decline as rapidly as elsewhere in the West Indies.

St. Kitts, Nevis, and Anguilla (the most northerly island of the Leeward chain) incorporated with the British Virgin Islands in 1816. The territorial unit of St. Kitts-Nevis-Anguilla became part of the Leeward Islands Federation in 1871 and belonged to the Federation of the West Indies from 1958 to 1962. In 1967, the three islands became an associated state with full internal autonomy under a new constitution. After the Anguilla islanders rebelled in 1969, British paratroopers intervened, and Anguilla seceded in 1971, an arrangement formally recognized on 19 December 1980.

There have been regular general elections in St. Kitts and Nevis since 1971. A 1982 white paper on independence provoked stormy debate over the form of the constitution, spilling over into civil unrest in 1982 and 1983. Nevertheless, St. Kitts and Nevis

became an independent federated state within the Commonwealth on 19 September 1983. Under the arrangement, Nevis developed its own legislature and gained the power to secede from the federation. Elections in June 1984 produced a clear majority for the People's Action Movement/Nevis Reformation Party coalition. In June 1996, Nevis premier Vance Amory announced plans for Nevis to secede from the federation as detailed in the constitution. Elections for the Nevis Island Assembly held in February 1997 returned Amory to power. The CCM retained its three seats, and the NRP held its two seats. Nevis's assembly voted unanimously for secession in 1997. However, a referendum on succession in July 1998 was unsuccessful when it failed to gain the approval of two-thirds of the electorate (61.8% in favor).

In the 21 March 1989 elections, 11 of 14 members of the National Assembly were elected, six from the People's Action Movement Party (PAM), two from St. Kitts and Nevis Labor Party (SKNLP), two from the Nevis Reformation Party (NRP), and one from the Concerned Citizens Movement (CCM). In the 29 November 1993 elections, no major party won the most seats and no coalition government emerged. The governor-general invited a minority government to form. In response, the Labour Party demonstrated, which led to serious disturbances, causing a 21-day state of emergency in December 1993.

The 3 July 1995 elections gave the SKNLP seven seats, PAM kept one seat, NRP, one seat, and the CCM, two seats. Denzil L. Douglas, leader of the Labour Party, became prime minister. Elections in March 2000 resulted in SKNLP winning all eight seats in St. Kitts, returning Douglas for a second five-year term as prime minister. The CCM retained two seats in Nevis, and NRP kept one seat. The PAM won no seats.

¹³GOVERNMENT

St. Kitts-Nevis is a federation of the two constituent islands. Under the constitution passed at independence in 1983, the British monarch is head of state and is represented by a governor-general, who is required to act upon the advice of the cabinet, and a deputy governor-general for Nevis.

The nation is governed under a parliamentary system, with legislative power vested in the unicameral House of Assembly, consisting of the speaker, three senators (two appointed on the advice of the prime minister and one on the advice of the leader of the opposition), and eleven elected members elected from each of eleven constituencies for up to five years. The cabinet, collectively responsible to the Assembly, consists of the prime minister (who must be able to command the support of a legislative majority), the attorney general (ex officio), and other ministers. The prime minister could call for an early election if the people request it in a voted referendum, though it has yet to happen. The Nevis Island Assembly and the Nevis Island Administration (headed by the British monarch represented by the deputy governor-general) operate similarly to the federation government.

Suffrage is universal for all citizens 18 or older.

¹⁴POLITICAL PARTIES

There are four political parties that have held seats in the House of Assembly. Although the Labour Party (also known as the Workers' League) dominated the political scene from the 1950s until 1980, it was supplanted after independence by the People's Action Movement. The PAM, led by Prime Minister Kennedy A. Simmonds won six seats, a clear majority, in both 1984 and 1989. The Labour Party held two seats in 1984 and 1989. The Nevis Reformation Party, founded in 1970 and led by Simeon Daniel, took three seats in 1984 and 2 seats in 1989, all of which were from constituencies on Nevis. The Concerned Citizen's Movement, under Vance Amory, took one Nevisian seat in 1989. In 1993, the Labour Party and PAM each had four seats. CCM

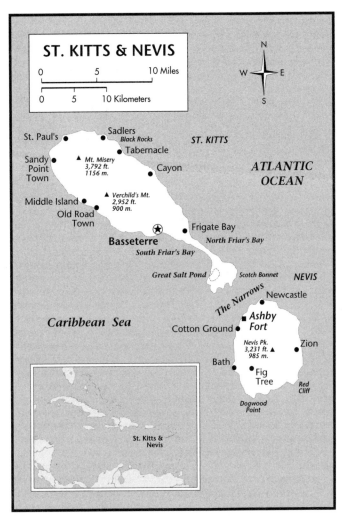

ST. KITTS & NEVIS

St. Paul's • Sadlers • Black Rocks
• Tabernacle
ST. KITTS

Sandy Point Town • ▲ Mt. Misery 3,792 ft. 1156 m.
Cayon •

ATLANTIC OCEAN

Middle Island • ▲ Verchild's Mt. 2,952 ft. 900 m.
Old Road Town •

⊛ Frigate Bay •
Basseterre   North Friar's Bay
South Friar's Bay

Great Salt Pond   Scotch Bonnet
NEVIS

The Narrows   Newcastle •

Caribbean Sea

Ashby Fort ■
Cotton Ground •   Nevis Pk. 3,231 ft. ▲ 985 m.   Zion •
Bath •   • Fig Tree   Red Cliff

Dogwood Point

St. Kitts & Nevis

LOCATION: 17°10' to 17°20'N; 62°24' to 62°45'w.
TOTAL COASTLINE: 135 km (84 mi). **TERRITORIAL SEA LIMIT:** 12 mi.

attorney general is the government's principal legal adviser. An appeal may be taken to the organization of Eastern Caribbean States Court of Appeal and a final appeal may be taken to the Privy Council in the UK. There are no military or political courts.

The judiciary has a reputation for independence and integrity. The system provides legal assistance to indigent criminal defendants.

17ARMED FORCES

St. Kitts and Nevis participates in the Eastern Caribbean Regional Security System created jointly with Antigua and Barbuda, Dominica, Grenada, St. Lucia, and St. Vincent and the Grenadines in 1985.

18INTERNATIONAL COOPERATION

St. Kitts and Nevis became a member of the UN on 23 September 1983 and belongs to FAO, IBRD, IMF, UNESCO, UNIDO, and WHO. It also belongs to CARICOM, OECS, the Commonwealth of Nations, G-77, OAS, and the WTO and is a signatory of the Law of the Sea.

19ECONOMY

Before 1987, The economy was based on agriculture, particularly on sugar, which generated over half of export revenues. During the 1990s, tourism and related industries became the most important source of revenue in St. Kitts and Nevis. The country still produces sea island cotton, coconuts, and sugar; but the more than 400,000 visitors per year are the most important sources of jobs and earnings. The government has also been making efforts to diversify the economy industrially, to expand tourism, and to improve local food production (the country imports most of its food needs). The country has had success with the development of its light manufacturing industries—mainly garments and electronics assembly, data entry, the expansion of non sugar agricultural production and tourism. The average annual GDP between 1988 and 1998 was 4.8%.

Decreasing world prices have hurt the sugarcane industry in recent years, as have hurricanes. The newly elected government has undertaken a program designed to revitalize the faltering sugar sector. Tourism and export-oriented manufacturing are assuming larger roles.

20INCOME

The US Central Intelligence Agency (CIA) reports that in 1997 St. Kitts and Nevis's gross domestic product (GDP) was estimated at US$235 million. The per capita GDP was estimated at US$6,000. The annual growth rate of GDP was estimated at 6.3%. The average inflation rate in 1997 was 2.9%. The CIA defines GDP as the value of all final goods and services produced within a nation in a given year and computed on the basis of purchasing power parity (PPP) rather than value as measured on the basis of the rate of exchange. It was estimated that agriculture accounted for 5.5% of GDP, industry 22.5%, and services 72%.

The World Bank reports that for the same period per capita private consumption (in PPP terms) was US$5,445. Private consumption includes expenditures of individuals, households, and nongovernmental organizations. Approximately 33% of household consumption was spent on food, 11% on fuel, 5% on health care, and 13% on education.

21LABOR

A 1995 estimate placed the labor force at 18,172. Manufacturing employed 31% and services 69%. The St. Kitts and Nevis Trades and Labour Union, established in 1940, is associated with the Labour Party and is the major workers' labor organization.

took two seats and the NRP took one seat. In 1995, the Labour Party won seven seats, the PAM, one seat, and the CCM, two seats. In 2000, the Labour Party won all eight seats from St. Kitts. The CCM held its two seats, and the NRP held its single seat.

15LOCAL GOVERNMENT

There are nine parishes in St. Kitts: St. George Basseterre, St. Peter Basseterre, St. Mary Cayon, Christ Church Nichola Town, St. John Capisterre, St. Paul Capisterre, St. Anne Sandy Point, St. Thomas Middle Island, and Trinity Palmetto Point. Nevis has five parishes: St. Paul Charlestown, St. John Figtree, St. George Gingerland, St. James Windward, and St. Thomas Lowland. Under the 1983 constitution, Nevis has its own legislative assembly and the right to secede under certain conditions.

16JUDICIAL SYSTEM

The Eastern Caribbean Supreme Court, established on St. Lucia, administers the judicial system, which is based on English common law and statutory acts of the House of Assembly. A puisne judge of the Court is responsible for St. Kitts and Nevis and presides over the Court of Summary Jurisdiction. Magistrates' courts deal with petty criminal and civil cases. The

Unemployment fluctuates due to slack periods in the tourist, sugar, and cotton seasons; in 1997, the unemployment rate was 4%. The sugar industry and civil service are the largest employers, with tourism gaining importance, especially on Nevis.

Unions have the right to organize and bargain collectively. The right to strike is not codified by law but is well established and respected.

The minimum working age is 14 years and this is effectively enforced. The government sets and enforces basic worker health and safety laws. The minimum wage varies by job classification and skill level of the wage earner. In 1999, it was US$56.18 per week for a full-time domestic worker and US$74.91 per week for a skilled worker.

22 AGRICULTURE

Of the islands' total land area, about 39% is devoted to crops. The principal agricultural product of St. Kitts is sugarcane; peanuts are now the second crop. On Nevis, sea island cotton and coconuts are the major commodities. Sweet potatoes, onions, tomatoes, cabbages, carrots, and breadfruit are grown for local consumption on both islands, mostly by individual smallholders. From 1992 to 1997, agricultural products on average accounted for about 14.4% of total imports by value; the government has embarked on a program to substitute for food imports.

Sugar estate lands were nationalized in 1975, and the sugar factory was purchased by the government the following year. The output of raw sugar slumped between 1986 and 1989, and as a result the government entered into a management agreement with Booke and Tate of Great Britain in August 1991; a World Bank loan of US$1.9 million was utilized to provide financial stability. Sugar production in 1998 was estimated at 244,000 tons.

23 ANIMAL HUSBANDRY

Pasture areas are small, covering some 2.7% of the islands. Pangola and Bermuda grasses provide the bulk of the fodder. Estimates of livestock in 1998 were sheep, 15,000; goats, 11,000; cattle, 4,000 head; and pigs, 3,000.

24 FISHING

Fishing is a traditional occupation that has not expanded to any great extent; the catch in 1997 was 165 tons (down from 620 tons in 1990). Some exports (primarily lobsters) are made to the Netherlands Antilles and Puerto Rico; fisheries exports totaled US$69,000 in 1997.

25 FORESTRY

Both islands have small stands of virgin tropical forest, with palms, poincianas, and palmettos. About 17% of the land area consists of forests. Imports of forest products nearly reached US$1.8 million in 1997.

26 MINING

Salt raking is done from time to time. Local quarrying of some materials is used to supplement the construction industry. In 1997, production totals included sand and gravel, 50,000 tons, and crushed stone, 105,000 tons. Beach sand mining was authorized by the 1987 National Conservation and Environmental Protection Act.

27 ENERGY AND POWER

The government-owned electricity station supplies power to Basseterre and all rural areas. Net installed capacity was 16,000 kW in 1998, when 85 million kWh were produced, entirely from conventional sources. St. Kitts and Nevis has no fossil fuels, and all petroleum products must be imported. Imports of refined petroleum products in 1994 averaged about 680 barrels per day.

28 INDUSTRY

The principal manufacturing plant and largest industrial employer is the St. Kitts Sugar Manufacturing Corp., a government enterprise; it grinds and processes sugarcane for export. A brewery on St. Kitts makes beer for local consumption, and cotton is ginned and baled on Nevis. Electronic plants produce switches, calculators, car radios, and pocket radios. Other industries are clothing and shoe manufacturing

The manufacturing sector grew by almost 19% in 1997, but declined by almost 5% in 1998 due to Hurricane Georges. As a result of diversification and expansion, St. Kitts and Nevis has transformed small electronic plants into the largest electronics assembly industry in the Eastern Caribbean. Its apparel assembly industry has also become very successful in recent years.

There were four major industrial sites in St. Kitts and Nevis in 2000: C. A. Paul Southwell Industrial Park, Bourkes Industrial Estate, Canada Industrial Estate, and Prospect Industrial Estate. Porte Zante is the main seaport.

29 SCIENCE AND TECHNOLOGY

St. Kitts and Nevis is dependent on outside resources both for industrial technology and for advanced scientific and technical education. The government is currently developing post-secondary education; a technical school was in operation in 1987.

30 DOMESTIC TRADE

General business is conducted every day except for Sunday, generally from 8 AM to noon, and 1 to 4 PM; on Thursday and Saturday shops close at noon. Normal banking hours are 8 AM to noon; banks are also open from 3 to 5 PM on Friday.

31 FOREIGN TRADE

The government of St. Kitts and Nevis has expanded trade incentives in recent years. Doing business in the country is virtually tax-free.

Most exports go to the US (69%), the UK (22%), and CARICOM (5.5%). About two-thirds of the sugar crop is exported to the US. Other exports include machinery, food, electronics, beverages, and tobacco.

The majority of imports come from the US (43%), CARICOM (17%), and the UK (11%). In 1997 St. Kitts and Nevis's imports were distributed among the following categories:

Consumer goods	19.9%
Food	18.4%
Fuels	7.4%
Industrial supplies	27.1%
Machinery	18.8%
Transportation	7.6%
Other	0.8%

32 BALANCE OF PAYMENTS

Earnings from tourism and overseas remittances largely offset the trade deficit. From 1988 to 1990, the current account deficit increased from 21% of GDP to nearly 35% of GDP, but went down to about 20% in 1998.

The US Central Intelligence Agency reports that in 1997 the purchasing power parity of St. Kitts and Nevis's exports was US$43.7 million while imports totaled US$129.6 million resulting in a trade balance of -US$85.9 million.

The International Monetary Fund (IMF) reports that in 1994 St. Kitts and Nevis had exports of goods totaling US$29 million and imports totaling US$98 million. The services credit totaled us$92 million and debit us$46 million. The following table summarizes St. Kitts and Nevis's balance of payments for 1994 in millions of US dollars.

Current Account		-26
Balance on goods	-69	
Balance on services	46	
Balance on income	-13	
Current transfers	9	
Capital Account		2
Financial Account		26
Direct investment abroad	...	
Dir. invest. in St. Kitts and Nevis	15	
Portfolio investment assets	...	
Portfolio investment liabilities	...	
Other investment assets	3	
Other investment liabilities	7	
Net Errors and Omissions		1
Reserves and Related Items		-2

33BANKING AND SECURITIES

St. Kitts and Nevis has a relatively simple system of public and private financial institutions, which the government wishes to expand. As a member of the Organization of Eastern Caribbean States (OECS); it has as its central monetary authority the Eastern Caribbean Central Bank (ECCB), headquartered in Basseterre. The Eastern Caribbean Home Mortgage Bank is also located in St. Kitts and Nevis.

The two islands had eight banks in 2000, including both foreign and domestic concerns. Barclays Bank, the Royal Bank of Canada, and the Bank of Nova Scotia represent foreign interests, whereas domestic interests include the St. Kitts and Nevis National Bank, the Development Bank of St. Kitts and Nevis, and the Nevis Cooperative Bank.

Securities transactions on international exchanges are performed by the banks.

34INSURANCE

International, regional, and local insurance companies or agents offer life and property insurance. There are five insurance companies in St. Kitts and Nevis, including Barbados Mutual Life and Assurance Society, British American Insurance, Colonial Life Insurance (Trinidad), St. Kitts and Nevis Insurance, and National Caribbean Insurance.

35PUBLIC FINANCE

The US Central Intelligence Agency (CIA) estimates that in 1997 St. Kitts and Nevis's central government took in revenues of approximately us$64.1 million and had expenditures of us$73.3 million including capital expenditures of us$10.4 million. Overall, the government registered a deficit of approximately us$9.2 million. External debt totaled us$66 million.

The following table shows an itemized breakdown of government revenues and expenditures. The percentages were calculated from data reported by the International Monetary Fund. The dollar amounts (millions) are based on the CIA estimates provided above.

REVENUE AND GRANTS	100%	64.1
Tax revenue	76.8%	49
Non-tax revenue	21.5%	14
Capital revenue	0.4%	0.25
Grants	0.9%	1
EXPENDITURES	100%	73.3

36TAXATION

There is no personal income tax for residents of St. Kitts and Nevis. Corporations are taxed at the rate of 38% of income, but the Fiscal Incentives Act offers generous development and tax concessions. Profit remittances are taxed at a 10% rate; there is also a land tax and a house tax. There is a capital gains tax of 20%.

37CUSTOMS AND DUTIES

St. Kitts and Nevis is bound by the common external tariff of CARICOM and requires an import license for certain durable and nondurable products. CARICOM members have reduced rates to a maximum of 35%.

38FOREIGN INVESTMENT

Like most Caribbean microstates, St. Kitts and Nevis has an investment incentives program. Joint ventures and labor-incentive industries are specially welcome. Official development assistance and resource flows from commercial sources totaled us$25 million in 1997.

Foreign investment incentives include the following: a tax holiday of up to 15 years; tax rebates of up to 5 years; and exemption from custom duties on machinery deemed necessary to establish and update an enterprise.

39ECONOMIC DEVELOPMENT

The government has attempted to halt the decline of the sugar industry by restructuring the sector, and has encouraged agricultural diversification and the establishment of small industrial enclaves linked to the international export market. Four industrial estates have been developed. The tourist industry has received considerable government support. The Development and Finance Corporation is the principal development agency.

The country's immediate plans continue to be aimed at diversifying the economy. Construction projects in the private and public sector are expected to contribute substantially to the moderate economic growth that St. Kitts and Nevis should experience in the near future. A plan to double livestock production by the year 2000 with the development of additional lands was launched in 1996. In addition, the tourism industry is expected to keep growing as a result of successful promotions.

40SOCIAL DEVELOPMENT

Housing shortages place a continuing strain on the government's ability to establish and fund social welfare programs. Effective 1978, a social security system replaced the existing provident fund as the provider of old age, disability, survivor, sickness, and maternity benefits. The original 1977 law governing social security was amended in 1996; the same year additional regulations governing self-employment went into effect. Coverage is compulsory for employed persons, with provisions for voluntary coverage where applicable. In 1999, this system is funded by 5% contributions from employers and employees. Qualifying conditions for receiving an old-age pension include an age of 62 and 500 weeks of paid contributions.

The Ministry of Women's Affairs was created by the government to promote women's rights and provide counseling for abused women. A special police unit works closely with the Ministry to investigate domestic violence and rape cases and, since 1997, there has been a special training program to educate police and school guidance counselors in dealing with domestic violence, sex crimes, and child abuse. Most of the provisions of the UN Convention on the Rights of the Child have been incorporated into domestic law. As of 1995, 2 of the nation's 15 legislators were women.

Human rights are generally well respected, although prison conditions are poor. Facilities are overcrowded, and in the past has led to prison riots.

41 HEALTH

In 1995, there were 64 hospital beds per 1,000 people. There were 12 doctors per 10,000 people in 1997. In 1988 there were 190 nurses. Hygienic education is the primary concern of the Central Board of Health. The infant mortality rate was 9.2 per 1,000 people in 1995. The under 5 mortality rate was 24 children per 1,000 live births in 1996. Average life expectancy in 1988 was 67.6 years. There were 27 cases of dengue fever in 1995. Altogether, 14 confirmed AIDS cases were reported between 1992 and 1995. The country's health care expenditures in 1995 were estimated at US$289 per capita. In 1995 there were 50 AIDS cases reported. Polio and measles appeared to be absent from these islands in 1994–95.

42 HOUSING

The government has placed emphasis on planned housing development in order to conserve agricultural lands. The Central Housing Authority began a program of low-cost home construction in 1977. The water supply, which comes from mountain springs and deep wells, is controlled by the Water Department. In the early 1980's, roughly four-fifths of all dwellings were detached houses, with apartments and commercial buildings making up most of the remainder. Over half of all dwellings were owner occupied, and about one-third were rented privately; the remainder were occupied rent free or rented from the government. The most common construction materials for housing were wood (50%), wood and concrete combined (25%), and concrete (20%).

In 1996, the newly established National Housing Corporation and the Social Security Board have signed a US$30.6 million loan for the construction of houses for low income earners.

43 EDUCATION

The literacy rate is over 90%. Education is free and compulsory for 12 years. Elementary education lasts for seven years followed by four years of secondary education at the first level and two at the second level.

A National Committee on Education was established in 1991 to examine all aspects of the education system at the primary and secondary level. Issues under consideration included introducing technical and vocational education and training; economic trends and the education system; administration and management of the education system; and teachers and their work conditions.

In 1993, there were 7,068 students at the primary level. Secondary-level schools employed 322 teachers and enrolled 4,402 students in the same year. By 1998 there were a total of 68 primary and secondary schools, with a combined enrollment of 21,946.

Well known for its higher education is the College of Further Education. The St. Kitts Technical College, a division of the College of Further Education, specializes in technical education. At the post-secondary level, there were 51 teachers and 394 students enrolled in 1993.

44 LIBRARIES AND MUSEUMS

There is a public library in Charlestown. The Old Court House in Basseterre houses a museum, and there is a museum of Lord Nelson memorabilia on Nevis.

45 MEDIA

The telephone system (12,200 main telephone lines) is operated by the government, while international cable and wireless services are operated privately. ZIZ Radio and Television is owned and operated by the government; Radio Paradise broadcasts from Basseterre; and Trinity Broadcasting is based on Nevis. Radio broadcasting began in 1961, and television broadcasting in 1972. As of 1999, there were 2 AM radio stations and 1 television station. In 1997 there were 575 radios and 273 television sets in use per 1,000 population. There are two newspapers: the *Labour Spokesman*, founded in 1957, is published twice weekly and had a 1999 circulation of 6,000, and the *Democrat*, which is published weekly, with a 1999 circulation of 3,500.

The constitution provides for freedom of speech and the press, and the government is said to generally respect these rights. However, because the government owns the only radio and TV stations, these media are said to inadequately cover opposition rallies and other events.

46 ORGANIZATIONS

The St. Kitts and Nevis Chamber of Commerce has its headquarters in Basseterre, and the Nevis Cotton Growers' Association has its office in Charlestown. Many US charitable organizations have operations in the islands, including the 4-H Foundation, Planned Parenthood, Heifer Project International, Operation Crossroads Africa, and Project Concern.

47 TOURISM, TRAVEL, AND RECREATION

Visitors from the US, the UK, and Canada need proof of citizenship and an onward ticket; nationals of most Commonwealth countries need passports but not visas. The chief historic attraction on St. Kitts is Brimstone Hill fortress, which towers 230 m (750 ft) above the Caribbean, took 100 years to build, and is partially restored. Beautiful beaches and the Georgian architecture of Basseterre also attract tourists. Nevis has many beaches and relic plantations and a quaint atmosphere reminiscent of the 18th century. In 1997, approximately 88,000 stayover tourists arrived on the islands, and tourism revenue was US$72 million. There were 1,759 hotel rooms that year. The government has dredged the main harbor on St. Kitts to accommodate cruise ships.

The cost of traveling in St. Kitts and Nevis varies according to the season. Between December and April, estimated daily expenses are approximately US$248 per day. During other times of the year, travel expenses are estimated at US$111.

48 FAMOUS KITTSIANS AND NEVISIANS

Sir Thomas Warner (d.1649) established the first colony on each island. US statesman Alexander Hamilton (1757–1804) was born in Charlestown.

49 DEPENDENCIES

St. Kitts and Nevis has no territories or colonies.

50 BIBLIOGRAPHY

Cox, Edward L. *Free Coloreds in the Slave Societies of St. Kitts and Grenada, 1763–1833.* Knoxville: University of Tennessee Press, 1984.

Hamshere, Cyril. *The British in the Caribbean.* Cambridge, Mass.: Harvard University Press, 1972.

Lowenthal, David. *West Indian Societies.* London: Oxford University Press, 1972.

Merrill, Gordon Clark. *The Historical Geography of St. Kitts and Nevis, the West Indies.* Mexico: Editorial Fournier, 1958.

Moll, V.P. *St. Kitts-Nevis.* Santa Barbara, Calif.: Clio, 1995.

Olwig, Karen Fog. *Global Culture, Island Identity: Continuity and Change in the Afro-Caribbean Community of Nevis.* Philadelphia: Harwood, 1993.

Richardson, Bonham C. *Caribbean Migrants: Environment and Human Survival on St. Kitts and Nevis.* Knoxville: University of Tennessee Press, 1983.

Sherlock, Sir Philip M. *West Indian Nations: A New History.* New York: St. Martin's, 1973.

Williams, Eric Eustace. *From Columbus to Castro: The History of the Caribbean, 1492–1969.* London: Deutsch, 1970.

ST. LUCIA

CAPITAL: Castries.

FLAG: On a blue background is a yellow triangle surmounted by a black arrowhead whose outer edges are bordered in white.

ANTHEM: *Sons and Daughters of St. Lucia.*

MONETARY UNIT: The East Caribbean dollar (EC$) of 100 cents, pegged to the US dollar, is the national currency. There are coins of 1, 2, 5, 10, and 25 cents and 1 dollar, and notes of 5, 10, 20, and 100 East Caribbean dollars. EC$1 = US$0.37037 (or US$1 = EC$2.70).

WEIGHTS AND MEASURES: The metric system has been introduced, but imperial measures are still commonly employed.

HOLIDAYS: New Year's Day, 1 January; Carnival, 8–9 February; Independence Day, 22 February; Labor Day, 1 May; Queen's Official Birthday, 5 June; Bank Holiday, 1st Monday in August; Thanksgiving Day, 1st Monday in October; St. Lucia Day, 13 December; Christmas Day, 25 December; Boxing Day, 26 December. Movable religious holidays include Good Friday, Easter Monday, Whitmonday, and Corpus Christi.

TIME: 8 AM = noon GMT.

¹LOCATION, SIZE, AND EXTENT

The Caribbean island of St. Lucia, part of the Windward Islands group of the Lesser Antilles, is 43 km (27 mi) N–S by 23 km (14 mi) E–W and has a total area of 620 sq km (239 sq mi). Comparatively, the area occupied by St. Lucia is slightly less than 3.5 times the size of Washington, D.C. Situated between Martinique to the N and St. Vincent to the SW, St. Lucia has a total coastline of 158 km (98 mi). The capital city, Castries, is located on St. Lucia's northwest coast.

²TOPOGRAPHY

St. Lucia is a volcanic island, the younger part of which is the mountainous southern half, and the older the hilly but more nearly level northern half. The highest mountain, Mt. Gimie, rises 959 m (3,145 ft) above sea level. Better known are the two peaks on the southern coast, Grand Piton (798 m/2,619 ft) and Petit Piton (750 m/2,461 ft), which together form one of the scenic highlights of the West Indies. The lowlands and valleys of the island have fertile soil and are irrigated by many streams. The island has beautiful beaches, some with black volcanic sand.

³CLIMATE

The average yearly temperature on St. Lucia is 26°C (79°F); the warmest month is usually September, and the coolest January. The average rainfall at sea level is 231 cm (91 in) a year; on the mountain peaks, more than 380 cm (150 in). Like the rest of the West Indies, St. Lucia is vulnerable to hurricanes, which hit the Caribbean in the late summer months.

⁴FLORA AND FAUNA

Tropical sunlight, heavy rainfall, and fertile soil combine to produce an abundance of tropical flora, including hibiscus, poinciana, frangipani, orchids, jasmine, and bougainvillea. There are no large mammals on St. Lucia. Bats are common, and there are several species of small snakes. The central highlands provide nesting places for many birds, including flycatchers, humming-

birds, pigeons, and about a hundred other species. The surrounding sea contains lobster, turtle, and conch, as well as an abundance of fish.

⁵ENVIRONMENT

Densely populated, St. Lucia has been shorn of much of its protective woodland by agricultural and commercial interests, except for limited areas in the south-central rain forest. The loss of forest cover contributes to the erosion of the soil, particularly in the drier, northern part of the island. The nation does not have the financial resources to develop an adequate water purification system and the population is at risk from contamination of the water supply by agricultural chemicals and sewage. Two small areas have been set aside as nature preserves, but population pressure prevents the government from expanding them. Principal responsibility for the environment is vested in the Ministry of Agriculture's Lands, Fisheries, and Cooperatives Forestry Division and the National Trust Fund. Excessive use of herbicides and pesticides threaten the wildlife population in St. Lucia and the eastern Caribbean states in general. Endangered or threatened species include the St. Lucia parrot and St. Lucia white-breasted thrasher.

⁶POPULATION

The population of St. Lucia in 2000 was estimated at 155,678. An estimated 5.4% of the population is 65 years of age or older. The projected population for the year 2005 is 164,000, assuming a crude birthrate of 19 per 1,000 population and a death rate of 5, resulting in a natural rate of change of 1.3% for the period 2000–2005. In 1996, the nation's population density was 258 persons per sq km (669 per sq mi).

It was estimated that 38% of the population lived in urban areas in 2000. The capital city, Castries, had a 2000 population of 53,000, about 34% of the population.

[7] MIGRATION

Emigration has provided an escape valve for population pressure. Neighbors such as Trinidad, Guyana, and the French Caribbean islands have received the bulk of emigrants from St. Lucia, with lesser numbers going to the UK, Canada, and the US. In 1999 the net migration rate was -5.19 migrants per 1,000 population. Despite the high emigration rate, the population is still growing at 1.09% per year, according to 1999 estimates.

[8] ETHNIC GROUPS

Reliable statistics on ethnic groups are unavailable. It is estimated, however, that 90% of the population consists of descendants of slaves brought from Africa in the 17th and 18th centuries. Some 6% is mulatto, and 3% East Indian. Approximately 1% of the population is of European descent.

[9] LANGUAGES

English is the official language of St. Lucia. Nearly 20% of the population cannot speak it, however. Language outreach programs are seeking to integrate these people into the mainstream of society. Almost all the islanders also speak a French patois based on a mixture of African and French grammar and a vocabulary of mostly French with some English and Spanish words.

[10] RELIGIONS

The vast majority of the population is Christian. About 90% of the populace are Roman Catholic. However, there is a substantial Protestant community comprised of Anglicans, Pentecostals, Seventh-Day Adventists, Baptists, and Methodists. The constitution guarantees freedom of religion, and there are practicing non-Christian groups, most notably Baha'is, Hindus, and Muslims.

[11] TRANSPORTATION

Direct flights to New York, Miami, Toronto, London, and Frankfurt operate out of Hewanorra International Airport, on the southern tip of the island at Vieux-Fort. The smaller Vigie Airport, located near Castries, is used for flights to and from neighboring Caribbean islands. St. Lucia has two important ports: Castries, in the north, with a cargo-handling capacity of 365,000 tons per year; and Vieux Fort, at the southern tip of the island, from which ferries link St. Lucia with St. Vincent and the Grenadines.

All of the island's towns, villages, and main residential areas were linked by 1,147 km (713 mi) of all-purpose roads in 1998, of which 63 km (39 mi) were paved. Motor vehicles numbered 12,157 in 1995, including 11,399 passenger cars and 758 commercial vehicles.

[12] HISTORY

Arawak and Carib Amerindians were the earliest known inhabitants of what is now St. Lucia. There is no hard evidence for the folklore that Columbus sighted St. Lucia on St. Lucy's Day in 1498, but in keeping with the tradition, 13 December is still celebrated as the date of the island's discovery. It was not settled until the mid-17th century because the Caribs defended the islands successfully for years. The French settled the islands, but the natural harbor at Castries brought English interest. The island changed hands between the British and the French no fewer than 14 times, until in 1814, the British took permanent possession. In 1838, St. Lucia came under the administration of the Windward Islands government set up by Great Britain.

Unlike other islands in the area, sugar did not monopolize commerce on St. Lucia. Instead, it was one product among many others including tobacco, ginger, and cotton. Small farms rather than large plantations continued to dominate agricultural

production into the 20th century. A total of 10,328 slaves were freed when slavery was abolished in 1834. To replace the slave labor, East Indian indentured workers were brought to the island during the late 1800s.

St. Lucia has a democratic tradition which began in 1924 when a few elected positions were added to the appointed legislative council. St. Lucia became an associated state with full internal self-government in 1967 and on 22 February 1979 became an independent member of the Commonwealth.

The first three years of independence were marked by political turmoil and civil strife, as leaders of rival political parties fought bitterly. In 1982, the conservative United Workers' Party (UWP) won 14 of 17 seats in the House of Assembly. Party leader and prime minister John Compton, who had been premier of the island since 1964, became prime minister at independence.

The UWP dominance was eroded in 1987, when the party won only 9 seats. Prime Minister Compton called for new elections almost immediately, but received the same result. In 1992, the UWP increased its majority to 11 seats, as the SLP won 6 seats. The SLP, which had been out of office for 15 years, won the April 1997 elections in a landslide, and its leader, Kenny Anthony, replaced Compton as prime minister.

St. Lucia suffered back-to-back tropical storms in 1994 and 1995 that caused losses of about 65% and 20% of each of those years' banana crops, respectively. In the late 1990s, the country's heavy reliance on bananas posed an additional economic threat as the US challenged the preferential treatment accorded by several European nations to their former colonies in the Caribbean. In February 1999, a ruling by the World Trade Organization allowed the US to impose trade penalties on Europe in response to these banana import policies. St. Lucia joined with its Caribbean neighbors in lobbying against the ruling.

[13] GOVERNMENT

St. Lucia became independent in 1979. Under its constitution, the British monarch continues to be the titular head of government, appointing, upon recommendation of the local leaders, a governor-general to represent the crown. Executive power is effectively exercised by the prime minister and cabinet. There is a bicameral parliament consisting of a Senate with 11 members and a House of Assembly with 17 representatives. The House of Assembly has the important legislative functions. The Senate is an appointed body with little political power. The Senate has 11 members. Six of the members are appointed on the advice of the prime minister, three are appointed on the advice of the opposition leader, and two are appointed after consultation with religious, economic, and social groups.

Members of the lower house are elected for a maximum period of five years. Suffrage on St. Lucia has been universal for those 18 and older since 1951, before St. Lucia achieved independence.

Under the constitution, the government could call for elections at any time. Under the current schedule, elections are held by secret ballot and at least every five years.

[14] POLITICAL PARTIES

After sweeping the 1997 parliamentary elections by gaining 16 out of 17 seats, the left-of-center St. Lucia Labour Party (SLP), led by Kenny Anthony, became the majority party, ending 15 years of dominance by the United Workers' Party (UWP). Following the UWP's electoral defeat, its leader, Vaughan Lewis, resigned, and former leader and prime minister John Compton, resumed leadership of the party in its new role as opposition party. The UWP was the party in power at the time of independence, lost power in 1979, and regained it in 1982. It is by reputation the more conservative party.

The Progressive Labour Party (PLP), under the leadership of Jon Odlum, has no representation. It is an offshoot of the SLP.

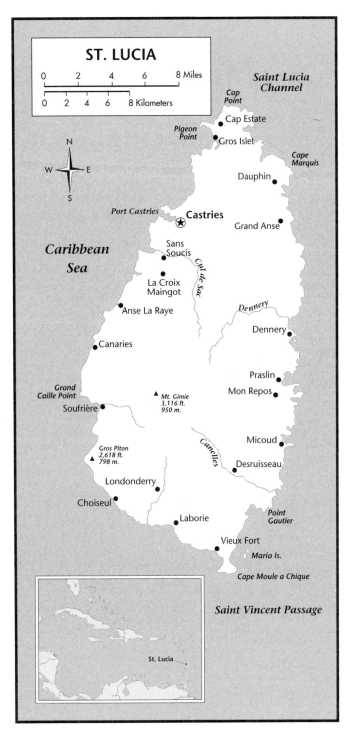

ST. LUCIA

Saint Lucia Channel

Cap Point
Cap Estate
Pigeon Point
Gros Islet
Cape Marquis
Dauphin
Port Castries
★ Castries
Grand Anse
Sans Soucis
Cul de Sac
La Croix Maingot
Anse La Raye
Dennery
Dennery
Canaries
Praslin
Mon Repos
Grand Caille Point
▲ Mt. Gimie
3,116 ft.
950 m.
Soufrière
Canelles
Micoud
Gros Piton
2,618 ft.
798 m.
Desruisseau
Londonderry
Choiseul
Laborie
Point Gautier
Vieux Fort
Maria Is.
Cape Moule a Chique

Caribbean Sea

Saint Vincent Passage

St. Lucia

LOCATION: 13°53′N; 60°58′W. **TOTAL COASTLINE:** 158 km (98 mi).
TERRITORIAL SEA LIMIT: 12 mi.

15 LOCAL GOVERNMENT

St. Lucia is divided into eight administrative regions. Local governments are elected by popular vote.

16 JUDICIAL SYSTEM

The legal system is based on English common law and "Code Napoleon". The highest judicial body is the Privy Council of the United Kingdom. Both common law and statute law govern St.

Lucia. The lowest court is the district or magistrate's court, above which is the Court of Summary Jurisdiction. Seated in Castries, the Eastern Caribbean Supreme Court (known as the West Indies Associated States Supreme Court upon its founding in 1967, and as the Supreme Court of Grenada and the West Indies Associated States from 1974 until 1979) has jurisdiction in St. Lucia, Anguilla, Antigua and Barbuda, the British Virgin Islands, Dominica, Montserrat, St. Kitts and Nevis, and St. Vincent and the Grenadines. It consists of the High Court, made up of a chief justice and seven puisne judges, and the Court of Appeal, made up of the chief justice and two other appellate justices. In exceptional cases, appeals may be carried to the UK Privy Council.

The constitution guarantees a public trial before an independent and impartial court. Legal counsel is afforded to indigent defendants in cases involving capital punishment.

17 ARMED FORCES

As of 2000 there were no armed forces other than those of the police force and coast guard. The Eastern Caribbean Regional Security System, formed in 1985, includes Antigua and Barbuda, Barbados, Dominica, Grenada, Jamaica, St. Kitts and Nevis, and St. Vincent and the Grenadines, as well as St. Lucia, and provides for joint coast-guard operations, military exercises, and disaster contingency plans.

18 INTERNATIONAL COOPERATION

St. Lucia became a member of the UN on 12 September 1979 and belongs to ECLAC and all the nonregional specialized agencies except IAEA. It is also a member of the Commonwealth of Nations, as well as the Caribbean Development Bank, CARICOM, G-77, the OAS, the OECS, and the Windward Islands Banana Growers' Association. St. Lucia is a signatory to the Law of the Sea and a member of the WTO.

19 ECONOMY

Agriculture is the main economic activity on St. Lucia, which is the leading producer of bananas in the Windward Islands group. Tourism, with direct flights from Europe and North America, has recently become an equally important economic activity. St. Lucia's manufacturing sector has grown steadily, with the construction of many light manufacturing and assembly plants that produce for local or export markets.

Though foreign investment in manufacturing and information processing in recent years has increased St. Lucia's industrial base, the economy remains vulnerable due to its heavy dependence on banana production, which is subject to periodic droughts and tropical storms. Indeed, the destructive effect of Tropical Storm Iris in mid-1995 caused the loss of 20% of the year's banana crop, and the agriculture sector recorded its sixth year of decline in 1998. Increased competition from Latin American bananas will probably further reduce market prices, intensifying St. Lucia's need to diversify its economy in coming years by expanding tourism, manufacturing, and construction.

20 INCOME

The US Central Intelligence Agency (CIA) reports that in 1997 St. Lucia's gross domestic product (GDP) was estimated at US$625 million. The per capita GDP was estimated at US$4,100. The annual growth rate of GDP was estimated at 2.2%. The average inflation rate in 1997 was 2.5%. The CIA defines GDP as the value of all final goods and services produced within a nation in a given year and computed on the basis of purchasing power parity (PPP) rather than value as measured on the basis of the rate of exchange. It was estimated that agriculture accounted for 10.7% of GDP, industry 32.3%, and services 57%.

The World Bank reports that for the same period per capita private consumption (in PPP terms) was US$3,376. Private consumption includes expenditures of individuals, households, and nongovernmental organizations. Approximately 40% of household consumption was spent on food, 11% on fuel, 4% on health care, and 17% on education. The richest 10% of the population accounted for approximately 33% of household consumption and the poorest 10% approximately 2.0%.

21LABOR

In 1998, the labor force was estimated at 73,660. Some 13% of the labor force was engaged in commerce, 7.5% in tourism, 23% in agriculture, and 9% in manufacturing. Unemployment was unofficially estimated at 22% in 1998.

As of 1999 there were seven labor unions in St. Lucia, representing about 20% of the work force. The largest trade union grouping, the Industrial Solidarity Pact, includes the National Workers' Union, the St. Lucia Civil Service Association, the Prison Officers' Association, and the St. Lucia Teachers' Union.

The law provides for a minimum working age of 14 and occupational safety and health regulations. The government enforces these provisions effectively. There is no national legislated workweek, although the common practice is to work 40 hours a week spread over 5 days. Special legislation covers hours which shop assistants, agricultural workers, domestics and young industrial employees work.

There is a minimum wage for office clerks only. It was US$300 per month in 1999.

22AGRICULTURE

Agriculture accounts for about 14% of GDP. The production of bananas, St. Lucia's most important crop, fluctuates as a result of climatic conditions and plant disease; it has gone from a low of 32,000 tons in 1975 to 160,000 tons in 1990 (48% of the Windward Islands' banana production that year) to 77,000 tons in 1998. Almost the entire production is exported. The second most important crop is coconuts, exported as oil and copra; about 12,000 tons of coconuts were produced in 1998. The production of vegetables and fruits for local consumption increased steadily since 1979, as the government sought to achieve self-sufficiency in tomatoes, onions, carrots, cabbages, and breadfruit. In 1997, the value of exported agricultural products amounted to US$33.6 million, down from US$85.7 million in 1990.

23ANIMAL HUSBANDRY

Production in almost every category of animal husbandry is insufficient to satisfy local demand. There are only 12,000 head of cattle on the island, mostly grazing in the middle altitudes of the central mountain region; milk production covers only about 25% of local demand. There were also an estimated 13,000 sheep, 15,000 pigs, and 10,000 goats on island in 1998. St. Lucia has attained self-sufficiency in pork and egg production. Egg production was about 1,000 tons in 1998.

24FISHING

The establishment of the St. Lucia Fish Market Corp. in 1985, with a US$2.5-million grant from Canada, provided local fishermen with processing, storage, and marketing facilities, enabling St. Lucia to become self-sufficient in fresh fish production. In 1997, the total catch was 1,313 tons. Dolphinfish, wahoo, and yellowfin tuna accounted for 455, 224, and 109 tons, respectively, in 1997.

25FORESTRY

A small timber industry processes mahogany, pine, and blue mahoe; expansion of cultivation is planned at the rate of 40 hectares (100 acres) annually. About 13% of total available land consists of forest and woodlands. Legislation is in force to protect against deforestation. Imports of forest products amounted to US$11.7 million in 1997.

26MINING

There is no regular commercial mining in St. Lucia. A few quarrying operations produce gravel, pumice, and sand for construction purposes.

27ENERGY AND POWER

St. Lucia Electricity Services is responsible for the generation and supply of electricity throughout the island. In 1998, net installed capacity was 22,000 kW, electrical production 110 million kWh. St. Lucia's requirements are met through an island-wide grid serviced by two main diesel generating centers, which utilize oil imported from Venezuela and Trinidad and Tobago. The Sulfur Springs in Soufrière on the west coast, have been confirmed as a source of geothermal energy, with a potential generating capacity of 10 MW.

28INDUSTRY

St. Lucia's manufacturing sector is the largest and most diversified in the Windward Islands, with many light manufacturing or assembly plants producing apparel, electronic components, plastic products, and paper and cardboard boxes. Agricultural manufacturing includes lime and coconut processing.

Recently, the government has devoted its efforts to the improvement of economic activity as well as development of the major export markets. With the formation of the Eastern Caribbean Stated Export Development Agency (ECSEDA) in 1990, the performance of local manufacturers was expected to be significantly enhanced in the future. Several industrial estates and free trade zones were established during the 1990s, including a goods distribution free zone that opened in 2000. The site included 11 factory-style warehouses, and one administration center. Many large-scale industrial projects were funded by foreign investors in 2000, including port reconstruction, housing construction, a national stadium, banana trade subsidies, and a fisheries industry upgrade.

In 1998, the country experienced a decline of 9% in its industrial production growth rate, in part because of drought. The manufacturing sector experienced sluggish growth during most of the 1990s, but an increased government budget that focused on capital projects in the construction industry during the fiscal year 1999/2000 stimulated growth.

29SCIENCE AND TECHNOLOGY

The government of St. Lucia has established a Science and Technology Division within the government's Central Planning Unit (CPU). As of 1987, three scientists were employed with the CPU. The Windward Islands Banana Growers' Association (WINBAN) maintains a research laboratory in St. Lucia serving the needs of banana growers in the region. The St. Lucia National Trust, headquartered in Castries, is responsible for the wildlife, seabirds, rare plants, and geology on Pigeon, Fregate, and Maria islands. In 1984, total expenditures on research and development amounted to US$12 million; 86 technicians and 53 scientists and engineers were engaged in research and development.

30DOMESTIC TRADE

Local produce markets are found in all the small villages and towns; they are usually most active in the early morning hours to avoid the midday heat and the afternoon tropical showers. Normal business hours are 8 AM to 12 noon and 1 to 4 PM on weekdays, except for Wednesday, when shops close early. Banks are open from 8 AM to 1 PM on weekdays and on Fridays from 3 to 6 PM.

[31] FOREIGN TRADE

The economy of St. Lucia is highly dependent on foreign trade. Agriculture is the major export earner. Foreign trade continues to be crucial to St. Lucia and a variety of duty exemption and tax credits are implemented for trade inducements. Nevertheless, some traders complain of the countries protectionist attitude towards selected goods.

For the most part, St. Lucia exports bananas and other fruits (59%), and clothes (15%). Other export commodities include paper (7.5%), small mechanical parts (5.6%), and alcoholic beverages (5.36).

In 1996 St. Lucia's imports were distributed among the following categories:

Consumer goods	18.9%
Food	24.8%
Fuels	8.3%
Industrial supplies	27.4%
Machinery	11.1%
Transportation	9.4%
Other	0.2%

St. Lucia's exports go primarily to the UK (50%), the US (24%), and other CARICOM countries (16%). Imports come from the US (36%), CARICOM countries (22%), the UK (11%), and Japan (5%).

[32] BALANCE OF PAYMENTS

St. Lucia has had a negative balance of trade every year since independence; this annual deficit has been counterbalanced in part by inflows from tourism and direct investment.

The US Central Intelligence Agency reports that in 1997 the purchasing power parity of St. Lucia's exports was US$70.1 million while imports totaled US$292.4 million resulting in a trade balance of -US$222.3 million.

The International Monetary Fund (IMF) reports that in 1996 St. Lucia had exports of goods totaling US$86 million and imports totaling US$271 million. The services credit totaled US$270 million and debit US$143 million. The following table summarizes St. Lucia's balance of payments for 1996 in millions of US dollars.

Current Account		-80
Balance on goods	-184	
Balance on services	127	
Balance on income	-37	
Current transfers	14	
Capital Account		9
Financial Account		61
Direct investment abroad	...	
Direct investment in St. Lucia	23	
Portfolio investment assets	...	
Portfolio investment liabilities	-1	
Other investment assets	23	
Other investment liabilities	16	
Net Errors and Omissions		3
Reserves and Related Items		7

[33] BANKING AND SECURITIES

In early 1981, the government-owned St. Lucia National Bank and the St. Lucia Development Bank were opened. There were eight commercial banks as of 2000, including the St. Lucia Cooperative Bank, the Bank of Nova Scotia, Barclays, CIBC Caribbean, Caribbean Banking Corporation, the Republic Bank, the Royal Bank of Canada. St. Lucia is a member of the Eastern Caribbean Central Bank, which is responsible for the administration of the country's monetary policies, the regulation of exchange control and supervision of commercial banks and other financial institutions for the islands belonging to the Organization of Eastern Caribbean States. The Central Bank has special

arrangements for discounting loans made by commercial banks to productive sectors, such as tourism, agriculture, and manufacturing. The interest rates are normally below the commercial banks' lending rates. In 1999, the St. Lucia National Commercial Bank offered public shares for the first time, receiving investment of over US$11 million.

[34] INSURANCE

As of 1997, there were at least 18 companies registered to transact insurance business in St. Lucia.

[35] PUBLIC FINANCE

The US Central Intelligence Agency (CIA) estimates that in 1998 St. Lucia's central government took in revenues of approximately US$141.2 million and had expenditures of US$146.7 million including capital expenditures of US$25.1 million. Overall, the government registered a deficit of approximately US$5.5 million. Revenues in 1998 equaled 30% of GDP. External debt totaled US$184 million. In 1999, the St. Lucia government allocated 44.4% of total expenditures of approximately US$275 million to capital works, while 51% of the budget went to public sector worker wages.

[36] TAXATION

Individual income tax rates in St. Lucia range from 10% to 30%. There are no local taxes on income. Resident corporations and branches of foreign companies are taxed at the same flat rate of 33.33%. There are no other corporate taxes. Hotel companies and other industries receive a tax holiday of up to 15 years in St. Lucia.

[37] CUSTOMS AND DUTIES

Duties on imported goods such as alcoholic beverages, motor vehicles, cigarettes, and gasoline and oil continue to be major sources of government income. Most imports except those from CARICOM nations are subject to import duties, which consist of a customs duty, a consumption tax, and a service charge. The CARICOM CET ranges up to a maximum of 35%. To facilitate industrial development, the government has in specific cases negotiated the complete elimination of both import and export duties. In 2000, the government implemented a consumption tax retooling that involved a rebate of 20% for electronics producers, 40% for most other small manufactures, and 60% on the production of food and beverages.

[38] FOREIGN INVESTMENT

Firms based in Canada, the US, the UK, and other EC members, Venezuela, Hong Kong, and the Republic of Korea are the principal investors in St. Lucia. Two free-trade zones operate on the island, and a goods distribution free zone was opened in 2000.

The government, through the St. Lucia National Development Corporation, set up five industrial zones in order to attract foreign investment in manufacturing and assembly type operations. A Data Entry Park was built to attract information processing operations to St. Lucia. Development incentives are available in the form of tax concessions of up to 15 years in industries prescribed as beneficial to St. Lucia, namely in the manufacturing and tourist industries.

In 1996, St. Lucia was granted a US$955 thousand loan from the Caribbean Development Bank (CDB). The money was used to partly finance a project to help poor households in rural districts diversify agricultural production in order to decrease dependence on the banana industry. The banana industry was highly subsidized during 1999 and 2000 by the EC through the Banana Industry Trust Company, despite the need for diversification. Other investment in 2000 came from the Japanese government to encourage growth of the fishing industry, and from the Chinese government in construction and manufacturing.

39ECONOMIC DEVELOPMENT

Since the establishment the National Development Corp. in 1971, St. Lucia has succeeded in diversifying its economy. St. Lucia has the most highly developed infrastructure of all the Windward Islands, with an international airport, a highway system that connects the important coastal and agricultural areas with the political and commercial centers, and a fully automated telephone system with direct dialing to most parts of the world.

At the end of 1996, the Lewis government unveiled a job-creating budget aimed at boosting his party's flagging fortunes. A US$242 million package devoted US$136 million to current expenditure and US$104 million to capital items. With the unemployment rate standing at 25%, the Prime Minister pledged to create 10,000 jobs by the end of the 1997/98 fiscal year. The 2.9% GDP of 1998 was a marked improvement from previous years, with average growth below 2%. Unemployment was down to about 15% in 1999, and the government had plans to spend half of its budget on capital projects to foster the growing economy.

40SOCIAL DEVELOPMENT

In 1979, the government established the National Insurance Scheme to provide all workers from age 16 to 60 with old age, disability, survivor, sickness, and maternity coverage, as well as workers' compensation. The program is financed by 5% contributions from employers and employees. Retirement pensions begin at age 60, provided that 10 years of contributions have been made. Those lacking the necessary years of contributions are entitled to an old-age grant equivalent to a refund of contributions with interest, plus 7.5% of earnings for each year of contribution.

There are no legal restrictions on the rights of women, but social discrimination is not uncommon. The Minister for Women's Affairs promotes and protects the rights of women, and addresses employment discrimination complaints. As of 1997, 4 of 29 members of Parliament were women. As part of increased awareness of violence against women, battering and sexual harassment are included as curriculum topics in some secondary schools. The St. Lucia Crisis Center, established in Castries in 1988, opened a second facility in Vieux Fort in 1999. Both centers monitor abuse and act as advisors and advocates for women on a number of issues. Plans to establish a shelter for battered women and homeless girls were still pending as of 1999.

Human rights are generally well respected in St. Lucia, although there were reports of mistreatment of prisoners and generally poor prison conditions.

41HEALTH

There were 2 general hospitals, 1 psychiatric hospital and 2 district hospitals on St. Lucia in 1998. The main hospital, with over 200 beds, is located in Castries. In addition, there are 34 health centers scattered throughout the island. In 1995 there were an estimated 33 hospital beds per 1,000 people. In the same year, there were 71 doctors, 401 nurses; 15 pharmacists, and 7 dentists. Total health care expenditures for 1995 were estimated at US$167 per capita.

Malnutrition and intestinal difficulties are the main health problems. Tuberculosis, once widespread, has been brought under control (82 cases were reported in 1992–95). The total fertility rate in 1994 was 3.1 children born to a woman during her childbearing years. The death rate in 1995 was estimated at 6.7 per 1,000 population. The infant mortality rate in 1996 was 15 per 1,000 live births, and the rate for children under 5 years of age was 18.5. In 1997, 95% of children were immunized against measles. The average life expectancy is 70 years in 1998.

42HOUSING

The demand for private ownership of homes far exceeds the supply. In the 1980s, about four-fifths of dwellings were detached houses and most of the rest were apartments. Over half were owner occupied, and about a quarter were rented privately; others were occupied rent free or rented from the government. The majority of housing units (about three-quarters) were built of wood, with a smaller number built of either concrete, or wood and concrete.

43EDUCATION

In 1993, the literacy rate was estimated at over 72%. Education, free and compulsory for 10 years, is allocated 25% of the total annual budget. Elementary schooling lasts for seven years, followed by three years of lower secondary education and another two years of upper secondary education. In 1997 there were 89 primary schools with 1,214 teaching staff and 31,615 students enrolled. The student-to-teacher ratio stood at 26 to one. At the secondary level, there were 682 teachers and 11,753 students. An education complex in Castries maintains a teacher-training center, a technical school, a secretarial training center, and a branch of the University of the West Indies. The Sir Arthur Lewis Community College is to be upgraded into a full-fledged campus of the University of the West Indies.

In 1996, institutions of higher learning had 157 teaching staff and 2,760 students.

44LIBRARIES AND MUSEUMS

The government provides free library service. The Central Library of St. Lucia with 106,000 volumes is located in Castries, and other, smaller public libraries are located in villages throughout the island. St. Lucia has a historical and natural history museum on Pigeon Island, founded in 1994. The country also had four zoos and botanical gardens. Specific information about these institutions was unavailable.

45MEDIA

Three newspapers are published in St. Lucia. *The Voice of St. Lucia* (1999 circulation 15,000) appears on Wednesday and Saturday; two weeklies, the *Crusader* (4,000) and the *Star* (6,000), are published on Saturday. The telephone system is fully automatic, with an estimated 26,000 telephones in service in 1995. In the same year there were 4 AM and 1 FM radio station and 1 TV station. In 1997 there were 668 radios and 167 TV sets in use per 1,000 population. Television programs consist of some local programming, videotapes, and live broadcasts originating in Barbados; television transmissions from Martinique are also received.

The government is said to generally respect constitutionally provided free speech and free press, though occasionally it has shown open hostility toward both the print media and radio. Newspapers, radio and television carry a wide spectrum of opinion, including that which is directly critical of the government.

46ORGANIZATIONS

There is a chamber of commerce, which meets in Castries. Other organizations include the St. Lucia Hotel Association, the St. Lucia Manufacturing Association, and the St. Lucia Historical Society.

47TOURISM, TRAVEL, AND RECREATION

Tourists come by air directly from Europe, Canada, and the US, and on cruise ships sailing through the West Indies out of North

American and European ports. Some 248,406 tourists visited St. Lucia in 1997 and tourist receipts totaled US$282 million. In that year there were 6,382 beds available in the island's 3,701 hotel rooms. The hotel occupancy rate was 71%. Dramatic tropical scenery, beautiful beaches, and excellent water-sports facilities are St. Lucia's principal tourist attractions. Of special interest are the Piton Mountains and the Sulphur Springs (the world's only drive-in volcano). Visitors, except citizens of the US, the UK, Canada and the Windward Islands, need a valid passport and may need a visa if their government has no exemption agreement with St. Lucia.

According to 1999 UN estimates, the cost of staying in St. Lucia is US$237 per day between December and April, and US$193 per day at other times of the year.

48FAMOUS ST. LUCIANS

John G. M. Compton (b.1926), trained as a barrister and one of the founders of the United Workers' Party, was prime minister from 1982–96. The writer Derek Walcott (b.1930) is best known for his epic autobiographical poem *Another Life*.

49DEPENDENCIES

St. Lucia has no territories or colonies.

50BIBLIOGRAPHY

Breen, Henry Hegart. *St. Lucia: Historical, Statistical, and Descriptive*. London: F. Cass, 1970.

Eggleston, Hazel. *St. Lucia Diary*. Greenwich, Conn.: Devin-Adair, 1977.

Momsen, Janet Henshall. *St. Lucia*. Santa Barbara, Calif.: Clio, 1996.

ST. VINCENT AND THE GRENADINES

CAPITAL: Kingstown.

FLAG: Three vertical bands of blue, yellow, and green; centered on the yellow band are three green diamonds arranged in a v-pattern.

ANTHEM: *National Anthem*, beginning "St. Vincent! Land so beautiful."

MONETARY UNIT: The East Caribbean dollar (EC$) of 100 cents, pegged to the US dollar, is the national currency. There are coins of 1, 2, 5, 10, and 25 cents and 1 dollar, and notes of 5, 10, 20, and 100 East Caribbean dollars. EC$1 = US$0.37037 (US$1 = EC$2.70).

WEIGHTS AND MEASURES: The imperial measures are used.

HOLIDAYS: New Year's Day, 1 January; Labor Day, 1 May; CARICOM Day, 5 July; Carnival, 6 July; Bank Holiday, 1st Monday in August; Independence Day, 27 October; Christmas Day, 25 December; Boxing Day, 26 December. Movable religious holidays include Good Friday, Easter Monday, and Whitmonday.

TIME: 8 AM = noon GMT.

¹LOCATION, SIZE, AND EXTENT

Located in the Windward Islands group of the Lesser Antilles, St. Vincent and the Grenadines is 34 km (21 mi) sw of St. Lucia and about 160 km (100 mi) w of Barbados. Scattered between St. Vincent and Grenada to the sw are more than 100 small islands called the Grenadines, half of which belong to St. Vincent and the other half to Grenada. The Grenadines belonging to St. Vincent include Union Island, Mayreau, Canouan, Mustique, Bequia, and many other uninhabited cays, rocks, and reefs. The land area of St. Vincent is 347 sq km (134 sq mi), and the coastline is 84 km (52 mi). Bequia, the largest of the Grenadines belonging to St. Vincent, has an area of 18 sq km (7 sq mi). The total land area of the country is 340 sq km (131 sq mi). Comparatively, the area occupied by St. Vincent and the Grenadines is slightly less than twice the size of Washington, D.C.

The capital city, Kingstown, is located on the southeast coast of the island of St. Vincent.

²TOPOGRAPHY

St. Vincent is a rugged island of volcanic formation, and the Grenadines are formed by a volcanic ridge running north–south between St. Vincent and Grenada. The highest peak on St. Vincent is Soufrière, an active volcano with an altitude of 1,234 m (4,048 ft); it has a crater lake 1.6 km (1 mi) wide. In the center of the island Richmond Peak rises to a height of 1,079 m (3,539 ft). Only 5% of the island's surface has slopes of less than 5°. The low-lying Grenadines have wide beaches and shallow bays and harbors, but most have no source of freshwater except rainfall. The highest point in the Grenadines is on Union Island, with an altitude of 308 m (1,010 ft).

³CLIMATE

The islands enjoy a pleasant tropical climate all year round, with a yearly average temperature of 26°C (79°F). The warmest month is September, with an average temperature of 27°C (81°F); the coolest is January, with an average temperature of 25°C (77°F).

The average yearly rainfall on St. Vincent is 231 cm (91 in), but in the mountainous areas the average rainfall is more than 380 cm (150 in) a year. May or June through December is the rainy season.

⁴FLORA AND FAUNA

The shallow waters of the Grenadines abound with marine life. Lobsters, conch, fish of all varieties, and turtles can be found in such areas as the Tobago Cays, which lie north of Prune (Palm) Island. Whales are frequently sighted off Petit Nevis, and large iguana can be found on some of the waterless rocks and cays.

In Kingstown, on St. Vincent, there is a famous botanical garden where the breadfruit tree was introduced to the West Indies from South Pacific islands in 1793. Some of the many birds found in St. Vincent are the Caribbean eleania, the trembler, the bananaquit, and the Antillean crested hummingbird.

⁵ENVIRONMENT

The principal recurrent threat to the environment comes from the Soufrière volcano, which erupted violently on 7 May, 1902, destroying much of northern St. Vincent and claiming 1,565 lives. After another eruption, on 13 April, 1979, the volcano remained active for weeks, spewing over much of the island a pall of volcanic ash, which covered mountains, forests, and plantation fields. Forests are threatened by farming development and use of wood for commercial purposes.

Pollution from pleasure yachts and other sources has seriously affected the eastern shorelines of all the major islands of the Grenadines. In Bequia's Admiralty Bay, the pollution is so severe that swimming is dangerous. The main contributing factors are toxic chemicals used in farming and sewage. Fresh water resources are also limited. The nation's tourist trade increases the need for water even more. The nation's coast is particularly vulnerable to pollution from industrial sources.

The central highlands of St. Vincent have been set aside as a natural preservation area for nesting of the St. Vincent parrot, the St. Vincent wren, and the St. Vincent solitaire, all endangered or rare species. In the Grenadines, the hawksbill, green sea, and leatherback turtles have been declared endangered. The Tobago Cays have been proposed as a nature preserve, but aside from a

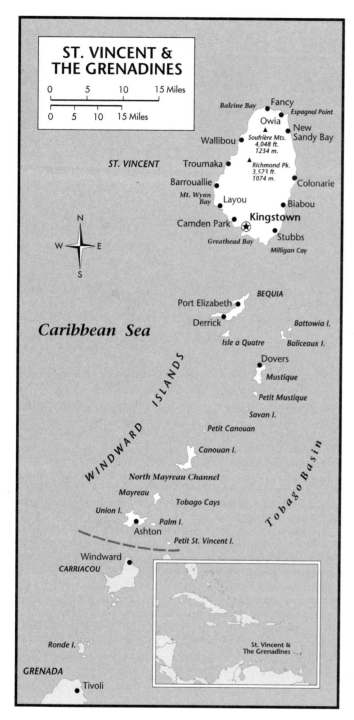

ST. VINCENT & THE GRENADINES

0   5   10   15 Miles

0   5   10   15 Miles

Baleine Bay • **Fancy**
Espagnol Point
Owia ▲
Wallibou • *Soufrière Mts.* **New**
4,048 ft. **Sandy Bay**
1234 m.
ST. VINCENT   **Troumaka** • ▲ *Richmond Pk.*
3,523 ft.
1074 m.
Barrouallie •   • **Colonarie**
Mt. Wynn **Layou**
Bay   • **Biabou**
★ **Kingstown**
Camden Park •
Greathead Bay   • **Stubbs**
Milligan Cay

BEQUIA
Port Elizabeth •

Caribbean Sea   **Derrick** •   *Battowia I.*

Isle a Quatre   *Baliceaux I.*

Dovers •
Mustique

Petit Mustique

Savan I.

Petit Canouan

Canouan I.

North Mayreau Channel

Mayreau
Tobago Cays
Union I.
Palm I.
Ashton
Petit St. Vincent I.

Windward
CARRIACOU

W I N D W A R D   I S L A N D S

Tobago Basin

Ronde I.

GRENADA
• *Tivoli*

St. Vincent & The Grenadines

LOCATION: St. Vincent—13°6′ to 14°35′ N; 61°6′ to 61°20′ w.
TOTAL COASTLINE: 84 km (52 mi). **TERRITORIAL SEA LIMIT:** 12 mi.

few sites on Union Island there are no protected areas in the Grenadines belonging to St. Vincent.

⁶POPULATION

The population of St. Vincent and the Grenadines in 2000 was estimated at 121,188, with the majority living on St. Vincent, the main island. An estimated 5.5% of the population is 65 years of age or older. The projected population for the year 2005 is 126,000, assuming a crude birthrate of 17 per 1,000 population and a death rate of 5, resulting in a natural rate of change of

1.2% for the period 2000–2005. Overall, the islands had a population density in 1996 of 349 per sq km (904 per sq mi).

It was estimated that 55% of the population lived in urban areas in 2000. The capital city, Kingstown, had a 2000 metropolitan population of 27,000. The next census in St. Vincent and the Grenadines is scheduled to take place in 2001.

⁷MIGRATION

Although no reliable statistics are available, emigration is known to take place to Trinidad, Guyana, Guadeloupe, and Martinique. In the past, the UK and US also accepted substantial numbers of migrants, and Canada is still receiving arrivals from the islands. In 1999 the net migration rate was -7.43 per 1,000 population.

⁸ETHNIC GROUPS

About 65% of the islanders are descendants of slaves brought from Africa. About 20% of the population is of mixed origin, and a small minority (3.5%) is of European descent. In the second half of the 19th century, 2,472 indentured laborers from Asia were brought to St. Vincent; their descendants, making up about 5.5% of the current population, are known as East Indians. About 2% of the people are Amerindians. Of the mixed group, about 1,000 persons, identified as Black Caribs, descend from the intermingling of Amerindians and Africans that occurred before European colonization.

⁹LANGUAGES

English is the official language of St. Vincent and the Grenadines. Some islanders speak a French patois, representing a mixture of African and French grammar, with a vocabulary drawing mostly upon French, along with some English and a few Spanish words. A few islanders speak French as their first language.

¹⁰RELIGIONS

Christianity is the dominant religion. The majority of the Christian population is Protestant, most notably Anglican, Methodist, and Seventh-Day Adventist; however, there is a significant Roman Catholic minority. Religious freedom is guaranteed by the constitution, and there are practicing members of non-Christian religions, including Baha'is, Hindus, and Muslims. There is also a sizable Rastafarian minority, some of whom claim discrimination by local police because their religion endorses the use of marijuana, which is illegal in the country.

¹¹TRANSPORTATION

St. Vincent is on the main air routes of the Caribbean, with direct flights to Trinidad and Barbados as well as the other islands to the north. In 1998 there were 6 airports and airfields, 5 of which had paved runways. The international airport is located on the southern tip of the island, near Kingstown; one of the much smaller airports is located on the east coast, north of Georgetown. Small airports are also located on Union, Canouan, and Mustique islands. In 1991, the construction industry and the infrastructure were given a minor boost with the government's announcement of an US$18.5 million airport improvement and road construction and upgrading program.

All of the Grenadines have excellent harbors served by a ferry service operating out of Kingstown. Wharf facilities were enlarged in the early 1980s, with financial support from the US, to include a deepwater pier. In 1998, the merchant fleet comprised 814 ships totaling 7,726,930 GRT. Although the main road of St. Vincent, going down the east coast and up the west coast, does not encircle the island, it does connect all the main towns with the capital. As of 1998, the islands had about 1,040 km (646 mi) of roads, of which 320 km (199 mi) were paved. About 8,110 vehicles were registered in 1995, including 4,935 passenger cars. There is approximately one vehicle for every 15 residents.

12 HISTORY

The Arawak Amerindians, who migrated from South America, are the earliest known inhabitants of St. Vincent and the Grenadines. Subsequently, the Caribs took control of the islands, and were there when Christopher Columbus reached St. Vincent on 22 January 1498.

St. Vincent was one of the last of the West Indies to be settled. Left to the Carib Amerindians by British and French agreement in 1660, the island continued to have a sizable Amerindian population until the first quarter of the 18th century. One of the results of this isolation from European influence was the evolution of the Black Caribs, who descend from the intermarriage of runaway or shipwrecked slaves with the Amerindians. The island was taken formally by the British in 1763, who ruled thereafter, except from 1779 to 1783 when it was in the hands of the French.

The island changed its ethnic character during the next century. When the Black Caribs and the remaining Amerindians rebelled against the British in 1795 at French instigation, most of the defeated insurgents were removed to the Bay of Honduras. Those who remained were decimated by an eruption of Soufrière in 1812. They were supplanted by African slaves, who were freed in 1834, Madeiran Portuguese, who immigrated in 1848 because of a labor shortage, and Asian indentured laborers who arrived in the latter half of the 19th century.

St. Vincent was administered as a crown colony within the Windward Islands group from 1833 until 1960, when it became a separate administrative unit linked with the Federation of the West Indies. The federation fell apart in 1962, and after lengthy discussion, St. Vincent became a self-governing state in association with the UK seven years later. On 27 October 1979, St. Vincent and the Grenadines achieved full independence as a member of the Commonwealth.

During the first months of independence, the young nation faced a rebellion on Union Island, its southernmost constituent, by a group of Rastafarians attempting to secede. The revolt was put down with military support from neighboring Barbados. In the end, 1 person was killed and 40 arrested. Otherwise, the political system has had few disruptions. The government at independence under the St. Vincent Labor Party gave way to the New Democratic Party (NDP) in 1984, with the NDP renewing its government in 1989.

In 1990, leaders of St. Vincent and the Grenadines, Dominica, Grenada, and St. Lucia formed the Regional Constituent Assembly to plan for a limited union. However, these talks have been halted since 1995 because the parties in power have changed in several of the countries. In the February 1994 election, the NDP won its third consecutive term in office. The NDP captured 12 seats in the House of Assembly and the ULP won three seats.

Tropical storms destroyed large portions of the islands' crops in 1994 and 1995.

The NDP retained its parliamentary majority by only one vote in early elections held in June 1998, winning 8 seats as opposed to 7 won by the opposition ULP led by Vincent Beache. Later that year, Prime Minister Mitchell invited opposition members to take part in talks on reforming the nation's 1979 constitution .

In spite of efforts at diversification, bananas remain the most important sector of the country's economy. However, the banana industry, like those of other Caribbean island nations, suffered a serious blow in early 1999 when the WTO ruled that the Lomé agreement giving preferential treatment to banana exports to EU countries by their former colonies violated international trade regulations. This ruling aroused strong protest as well as anti-American feeling, since it was initiated by the US in conjunction with Latin American banana producers.

13 GOVERNMENT

When the nation became independent in 1979, it kept the then British monarch as the nominal head of government, represented by a governor-general. The governor-general appoints the leader of the majority party to be prime minister. The cabinet is appointed by the governor-general on the advice of the prime minister. Executive power is in the hands of the prime minister and cabinet, who are members of the majority party in the legislature. The legislature is unicameral, a 21-seat House of Assembly. The House of Assembly consists of representatives elected from each of 15 constituencies for a maximum of five years, plus 6 senators appointed by the governor-general.

14 POLITICAL PARTIES

There are two major parties and three minor parties on the islands. The majority party is the New Democratic Party (NDP), led by Prime Minister James FitzAllen Mitchell. Founded in 1975, the party has, since 1984, held a parliamentary majority. In the elections of June 1998, the NDP's majority slipped from 12 to 8 out of 15 seats, giving it only a one-seat margin over the opposition SVLP.

The St. Vincent Labour Party (SVLP) was founded in 1955 and was in power at independence and governed the nation, under Robert Milton Cato, until the July 1984 elections. The SVLP held three elective seats until losing them in 1989. The current party leader is Dr. Ralph Gonsalves.

A left-wing coalition, the United People's Movement, embraces the Democratic Freedom Movement, the Youyou United Liberation Movement, and Arwee, a rural group. The Movement for National Unity, a moderate left-wing party, was founded in 1982 after the United People's Movement split. The National Reform Party, led by Joel Miguel, rounds out the list of these parties, which have never won an elected Assembly seat.

In 1994, the SVLP and MNU formed a coalition, the United Labor Party (ULP), which won 3 seats in the February 1994 elections.

15 LOCAL GOVERNMENT

In an attempt to decentralize the government, the nation has been subdivided into six parishes.

16 JUDICIAL SYSTEM

The islands are divided into three judicial districts, each with its own magistrate's court. Appeals may be carried to the East Caribbean Supreme Court, based in St. Lucia, and made up of the Court of Appeal and the High Court. In exceptional cases, appeals can be brought to the Judicial Committee of the UK Privy Council.

The constitution guarantees a public trial before an independent and impartial court. Legal counsel is afforded to indigent defendants in cases involving capital punishment. There are no separate security or military courts.

17 ARMED FORCES

There are no armed forces except those of the police force and coast guard. The Eastern Caribbean Regional Security System, which includes Antigua and Barbuda, Barbados, Dominica, Grenada, Jamaica, St. Kitts and Nevis, and St. Lucia, as well as St. Vincent and the Grenadines, provides for joint coast-guard operations, military exercises, and disaster contingency plans.

18 INTERNATIONAL COOPERATION

St. Vincent and the Grenadines became a member of the UN on 16 September 1980 and belongs to ECLAC, FAO, IBRD, ICAO,

IDA, IMF, IMO, UNESCO, UPU, and WHO. As a special member of the Commonwealth of Nations, it is not represented at meetings of the heads of government. St. Vincent and the Grenadines also belongs to the Caribbean Development Bank, CARICOM, G-77, the OAS, the OECS, and the Windward Islands Banana Association. It is a signatory to the Law of the Sea and a member of the WTO.

19ECONOMY

Agriculture is the mainstay of the economy of St. Vincent and the Grenadines, with bananas as the primary cash crop. Vegetable production for export grew significantly in the mid 1980s, as the market for arrowroot declined. Revenues from banana exports have fallen since 1990, but EU support after 1998 helped the industry. Tourism is particularly important in the Grenadines, where yachting is a principal pastime. Some of the smaller cays have been wholly acquired by private interests and developed into resorts for European and North American visitors. Some industrial development has begun in St. Vincent, but the government has been relatively unsuccessful at introducing new industries, and high unemployment rates of 35–40% continue. The continuing dependence on a single crop represents the biggest obstacle to economic development; tropical storms frequently disturb agricultural production.

20INCOME

The US Central Intelligence Agency (CIA) reports that in 1998 St. Vincent and the Grenadines's gross domestic product (GDP) was estimated at US$289 million. The per capita GDP was estimated at US$2,400. The annual growth rate of GDP was estimated at 4%. The average inflation rate in 1998 was 2.5%. The CIA defines GDP as the value of all final goods and services produced within a nation in a given year and computed on the basis of purchasing power parity (PPP) rather than value as measured on the basis of the rate of exchange. It was estimated that agriculture accounted for 10.6% of GDP, industry 17.5%, and services 71.9%.

The World Bank reports that for the same period per capita private consumption (in PPP terms) was US$2,955. Private consumption includes expenditures of individuals, households, and nongovernmental organizations. Approximately 27% of household consumption was spent on food, 8% on fuel, 2% on health care, and 13% on education.

21LABOR

Some 37,800 persons make up the work force. Unemployment, which was 30% in 1991, remained a serious problem at the end of the decade, reaching levels as high as 35–40%. One of the first authentic labor unions in the West Indies was formed in St. Vincent in 1935, during the Great Depression. From this initial Workingman's Association, the labor movement in St. Vincent has developed unions for agricultural workers, dockworkers, civil servants, and teachers. There is some poaching of members among competing trade unions, and the labor movement is gradually losing support. While workers have the right to form unions and strike, employers are not compelled to recognize a union or bargain collectively with them. Many employers do try to maintain good relations with their workers though, and strikes are rare. St. Vincent and the Grenadines joined the International Labor Organization in 1999.

The minimum working age is 16 and this is enforced by the government and respected by employers. Some children under 16 do work on family-owned banana plantations.

There is no statutory workweek, but most workweeks are 40 hours long in practice. The minimum wage varies by economic sector and level of employee skill. As of 1999, the minimum wage for agricultural workers was US$0.82 per hour (not including shelter); for skilled industrial workers, US$7.36 per day and for unskilled workers, US$3.68.

22AGRICULTURE

About half of St. Vincent is devoted to crop growing. Real growth in agriculture has been averaging 6.7% annually. Bananas constitute the main crop; vegetables, coconut, spices, and sugar are also important. Banana production was adversely affected by the eruption of Soufrière, which reduced exports from 30,414 tons in 1978 to 22,692 tons in 1979. Further damage was done by two hurricanes in 1979 and 1980; in the latter year, some 95% of the crop was destroyed. Production rebounded during 1981, and 83,000 tons were produced in 1982; in 1998, 55,000 tons were produced. Other crops in 1998 included coconuts, 23,000 tons; sugar cane, 20,000 tons; sweet potatoes, 2,000 tons; and plantains, 1,000 tons. Most of the agricultural products are grown on small farms; quality control is sometimes a problem, particularly in the production of bananas. There are approximately 5,000 banana growers on the island.

23ANIMAL HUSBANDRY

Estimates of the livestock population in 1998 include 13,000 sheep, 9,000 hogs, 6,000 head of cattle, 6,000 goats, and 100,000 poultry of all types. The island of St. Vincent does not produce enough meat, poultry, eggs, and milk to satisfy local demand.

24FISHING

At one time, St. Vincent and Bequia were the centers for a thriving whaling industry, but only six humpback whales were captured from 1982 to 1991. Since the New Kingston Fish Market opened in the late 1980s, the fish catch has rapidly increased. In 1997, the total catch amounted to 1,410 tons, down from 8,998 tons in 1990. Similarly, fisheries exports declined from US$19,603,000 to US$654,000 during that same period. Technical assistance and training to fisherman and fisheries staff is being sponsored by the Canadian Fisheries Development Project.

25FORESTRY

There is virtually no commercial forestry, although 36% of the land consists of forests and woodlands. Some local timber is used for residential and boat construction. Imports of forest products amounted to almost US$6.1 million in 1997.

26MINING

There is no commercial mining. Some sand is extracted for local construction projects, and on some of the smaller and drier Grenadines salt is produced on a small scale for local consumption.

27ENERGY AND POWER

The electric power facilities of St. Vincent and the Grenadines are being expanded and improved to meet the growing industrial demand. Two hydroelectric plants provide 34% of the electricity generated. In 1998, total power generation amounted to 64 million kWh, from a total capacity of 14,000 kW.

28INDUSTRY

A substantial amount of industrial activity centers on the processing of agricultural products. Because of depression in the sugar industry, sugar-processing facilities established in 1981/82 were shut down in 1985; in the same year, a beer factory began production. Nonagricultural industries include several garment factories, a furniture factory, an electronics plant, and a corrugated cardboard box plant. Manufacturing declined by almost

6% in 1998, but industry as a whole rose by almost the same figure.

The tourism industry has lagged in the 1990s because of difficult transportation access and the lack of white sand beaches on the main islands. However, the government has been putting more emphasis than ever on the promotion of the country as an upscale tourist destination. A new airport on Union island was opened in April 1993. A year earlier, a new airport, financed by a grant from the EC, opened on the island of Bequia. In 1996, a new cruise ship and berths came on line.

29SCIENCE AND TECHNOLOGY

St. Vincent seeks scientific expertise to deal with problems associated with its main agricultural products, especially bananas. The computer industry in the US and Europe has opened up a new demand for paper; with proper processing, arrowroot might be able to compete in this new market, but so far the technology is lacking. Experimentation on arrowroot waste as a source of biogas has also been undertaken. A National Council for Science and Technology was created late in 1981. St. Vincent also has an Appropriate Technology Center, established in 1982.

30DOMESTIC TRADE

Kingstown is the main commercial distribution center. Local produce markets exist in all the Grenadines and in the small villages on St. Vincent. Government offices on St. Vincent are open on weekdays from 8 AM to noon and from 1 to 4 PM. On Saturday afternoons, most shops are closed.

31FOREIGN TRADE

St. Vincent and the Grenadines is highly dependent on foreign trade. From the agricultural sector, bananas (39%) and vegetables are major foreign exchange earners. Other exports include eddoes and dasheen (taro), arrowroot starch, and tennis racquets.

In 1995 the country's imports were distributed among the following categories: consumer goods, 17.6%; Food, 22.1%; Fuels, 5.9%; Industrial supplies, 34.9%; Machinery, 13.1%; and Transportation, 6.1%.

Half of exports go to other CARICOM countries, and over one-third of imports come from the US. Principal trading partners in 1998 (in millions of US dollars) were as follows:

COUNTRY	EXPORTS	IMPORTS	BALANCE
United Kingdom	21	24	-3
Trinidad and Tobago	5	32	-27
St. Lucia	5	1	4
United States	3	77	-74
Barbados	3	8	-5
Antigua and Barbuda	3	n.a.	
Dominica	2	1	1
Canada	n.a.	5	
Japan	n.a.	5	
Italy	n.a.	8	

32BALANCE OF PAYMENTS

St. Vincent and the Grenadines has had an unfavorable balance of trade since the 1950s. Income from tourism, investments, and development assistance makes up the balance.

The US Central Intelligence Agency reports that in 1997 the purchasing power parity of the islands' exports was US$47.3 million while imports totaled US$158.8 million resulting in a trade balance of -US$111.5 million.

The International Monetary Fund (IMF) reports that in 1996 St. Vincent and the Grenadines had exports of goods totaling US$52 million and imports totaling US$127 million. The services credit totaled US$94 million and debit totaled US$56 million. The

following table summarizes the nation's balance of payments for 1996 in millions of US dollars.

Current Account		-35
Balance on goods	-75	
Balance on services	38	
Balance on income	-10	
Current transfers	11	
Capital Account		4
Financial Account		18
Direct investment abroad	...	
Direct investment in St. Vincent	18	
Portfolio investment assets	...	
Portfolio investment liabilities	-3	
Other investment assets	4	
Other investment liabilities	-	
Net Errors and Omissions		13
Reserves and Related Items		-

33BANKING AND SECURITIES

In the late 1980s, the nation's largest financial institution was the state-run National Commercial Bank, and various branches of Canadian banks were prominent in Kingstown. Commercial banks include Bank of Nova Scotia, Barclays, CIBC, Development Corp., First St. Vincent Bank, New Bank, Owens Bank, St. Vincent Cooperative Bank, and Republic Bank. The government has established arrangements for offshore banking corporations, with direct connections to Swiss banking facilities. There is no securities exchange, except for the common CARICOM exchange.

34INSURANCE

Local insurance companies are limited in scope and importance. Representatives of insurance corporations based in the UK, Canada, and the US operate on St. Vincent.

35PUBLIC FINANCE

Most of the government's income comes from customs duties and taxes. The leading categories of expenditures are education, public works, and health.

The US Central Intelligence Agency (CIA) estimates that in 1997 St. Vincent and the Grenadines's central government took in revenues of approximately US$85.7 million and had expenditures of US$98.6 million including capital expenditures of US$25.7 million. Overall, the government registered a deficit of approximately US$12.9 million. External debt totaled US$420 million.

The following table shows an itemized breakdown of government revenues and expenditures. The percentages were calculated from data reported by the International Monetary Fund. The dollar amounts (millions) are based on the CIA estimates provided above.

REVENUE AND GRANTS	100%	85.7
Tax revenue	78.0%	67
Non-tax revenue	8.7%	7
Capital revenue	2.1%	2
Grants	11.2%	10
EXPENDITURES	100%	98.6
General public services	19.2%	19
Public order and safety	5.8%	6
Education	12.8%	13
Health	9.6%	9
Social security	7.0%	7
Housing and community amenities	1.5%	1
Economic affairs and services	9.3%	9
Other expenditures	6.2%	6
Adjustments	28.6%	28

36TAXATION

The government of St. Vincent and the Grenadines levies a progressive personal income tax (ranging from 10% to 55%), a corporate tax of 45% of net income, inheritance taxes, and a social security contribution of 2.5% of gross salary up to a maximum of US$41.75 per month.

37CUSTOMS AND DUTIES

By far the most important customs revenues are from import duties. There is a duty on exported goods, but the revenue earned is relatively small. By agreement with certain private corporations, the government waives customs duties on specific items in order to stimulate industrial development. Under an October 1992 CARICOM agreement, St. Vincent and the Grenadines have eliminated import licensing. St. Vincent has adopted CARICOM's Common External Tariff, which ranges from 0% to 35%.

38FOREIGN INVESTMENT

The government has encouraged foreign investment by establishing industrial estates, including both factories and homes for laborers, as well as by offering favorable tax conditions for the investors. A large multinational company handles the marketing of most banana production, and a US firm has established a children's garment factory. The government has allowed the sale of some small islands in the Grenadines, notably Mustique, owned by a Scotsman, and Prune, bought by a US family and now called Palm Island by its entrepreneur owner. Petit St. Vincent and much of Canouan are being developed by the government for tourism.

St. Vincent is still eager to receive foreign investment, while providing special incentives and credit tailored to the needs of the investors. St. Vincent is eligible for trade benefits under Caribcan (Canada), the Caribbean Basin Initiative (CBI), and the Lomé Convention (Europe—although these have been challenged by the WTO).

The government is targeting offshore services as means of diversification away from bananas and tourism. The Offshore Finance Authority was set up in December 1996 to regulate bank and company registration, and the island is to be marketed in Puerto Rico, London, Hong Kong, New York and Miami.

39ECONOMIC DEVELOPMENT

A 1982 loan from the Caribbean Development Bank was designed to stimulate and redirect agricultural production, support the tourist industry, and contribute to the creation of the infrastructure necessary for industrial development. Loans and government incentives have since focused on supporting the banana trade, improving infrastructure, and stimulating tourism.

40SOCIAL DEVELOPMENT

In 1986, legislation established a social security system, replacing the provident fund that had been in existence since 1970. Workers contribute 2.5% of earnings, while employers pay 3.5% of payroll distributions. Benefits are provided for old age, disability, death, sickness, and maternity, and have been expanded to cover the self-employed. Employers fund a compulsory workers' compensation program. The worker is eligible for a pension at age 60, or earlier if incapacitated. Maternity benefits are provided at a rate of 65% of average earnings for a period of 13 weeks. Workers' compensation is provided through compulsory employer liability insurance with a private carrier.

St. Vincent also has an extensive program of community development, which stimulates the formation of cooperatives and self-help programs in the rural communities. A national family planning program has been introduced as part of the government's maternal and child welfare services. A food distribution program was initiated in 1984.

A law mandating that women receive equal pay for equal work went into effect in 1990. In 1995, a Domestic Violence Law was passed that established a family court to handle cases of spousal abuse. The penalty for rape is usually 10 or more years in prison. Women are underrepresented in politics and in government. In 1998, only one of the 21 members of Parliament was a woman.

Human rights violations reported in 1999 included the use of physical force to extract confessions and inadequate prison conditions.

41HEALTH

As of 1998, Kingstown's general hospital, with 209 beds, was the country's only government-run acute care hospital. There were 5 rural hospitals, including one located on the east coast of St. Vincent, the second on the west coast, and the third on Bequia. There are also hospitals for the aged and a 120-bed Mental Health Center. Approximately 38 outpatient clinics provide medical care to 9 health districts throughout the nation. In 1990 there were an estimated 2.7 hospital beds per 1,000 inhabitants. In 1995 there were 53 doctors and 231 nurses.

The fertility rate in 1994 was 2.4 children per woman. Gastrointestinal diseases continue to be a problem, although they are less so than in the past. There were an average of 7 new cases of tuberculosis each year from 1992 to 1995. The immunization rates for a child under one were as follows: diptheria, pertussis and tetanus (99%), measles (99%), polio (99%), and tuberculosis (98%). The death rate in 1992–95 was 6.5 per 1,000 population. Infant mortality in 1996 was 18 per 1,000 live births. Life expectancy at birth in 1998 was 73.4 years. In 1995, there were 6 new AIDS cases reported. Estimated per capita health care expenditures were US$125 million in 1995.

42HOUSING

Among other efforts to eliminate substandard housing conditions, the government has undertaken housing renewal projects in both rural and urban areas and has sought to provide housing for workers on industrial estates. Another government program supplies building materials at low cost to working people. In the 1980s, a majority of dwellings were detached houses; apartments accounted for less than 10%. In the same period, over half of all housing units were owner occupied, with smaller percentages either rented or occupied rent free. Dwellings were constructed primarily of either wood or concrete, with a smaller number constructed of both wood and concrete, or stone.

43EDUCATION

Primary education, which lasts for seven years, is free but not compulsory. In 1994, there are 65 primary schools, enrolling 21,386 students, with 1,080 teaching staff. In general secondary schools the same year, there were 9,870 students and 395 teachers. Secondary education at the first stage is for five years, followed by two more years at the second stage. The government-assisted School for Children with Special Needs serves handicapped students.

At the postsecondary level there are a teachers' training college, affiliated with the University of the West Indies, and a technical college. Adult education classes are offered by the Ministry of Education. Vocational training is available through the Department of Public Works, and agricultural training is offered by the Ministry of Agriculture. Literacy is estimated at 85%. In 1989, students at the university and all higher-level institutions numbered 677 with 96 teaching staff. Nearly 68% of these higher level students were women.

44LIBRARIES AND MUSEUMS

The government maintains a free public library system with 100,000 volumes. The main library is in Kingstown, and there are 16 branches located throughout St. Vincent and on the larger Grenadine islands. There were two libraries affiliated with institutions of higher education in 2000, with combined collections of nearly 20,000 volumes. The small National Museum in Kingstown houses ancient Indian clay pottery. The Botanical Garden in Kingstown is open to the public.

45MEDIA

The internal telephone system of St. Vincent and the Grenadines, fully automatic, is operated by Cable and Wireless (West Indies) Ltd., which also provides telegraph, telex, and international telephone services. There were 24,200 main telephones lines on the islands in 1995. There is one main newspaper, the *Voice of St. Lucia,* appearing three times per week, with a circulation of 9,000. There are 2 AM radio stations, no FM stations, and 1 television station. In 1997 there were 627 radios and 170 television sets per 1,000 population.

Constitutionally provided free speech and free press are respected by the government, with no reports of interference or censorship.

46ORGANIZATIONS

A chamber of commerce meets in Kingstown. Among the important commercial organizations is the St. Vincent Hotel Association.

47TOURISM, TRAVEL, AND RECREATION

Tourism is oriented toward yachting, with havens located on most of the Grenadines and also at Young Island, off the southern tip of St. Vincent. Posh resorts have been created on many of the smaller Grenadines, with villas and cottages built alongside small private beaches. In 1997 there are a total of 1,272 hotel rooms with 2,544 beds. The number of tourist arrivals totaled 65,143 that year, and tourist expenditures totaled an estimated us$70 million.

According to 1999 UN estimates, the cost of staying in St. Vincent is us$233 per day between December and April, and us$200 per day at other times of the year.

48FAMOUS ST. VINCENTIANS

Robert Milton Cato (b.1915), prime minister from independence until 1984, was one of the founders of the SVLP. James FitzAllen Mitchell (b.1931), prime minister since 1984, was one of the founders of the NDP. Sir Fred Albert Phillips (b.1918) is a specialist on constitutional and international law.

49DEPENDENCIES

St. Vincent and the Grenadines has no territories or colonies.

50BIBLIOGRAPHY

John, Sir Rupert. *Pioneers in Nation-building in a Caribbean Mini-state.* New York: United Nations Institute for Training and Research, 1979.

Potter, Robert B. *St. Vincent and the Grenadines.* Santa Barbara, Calif.: Clio, 1992.

Shephard, Charles. *An Historical Account of the Island of Saint Vincent.* London: F. Cass, 1971.

St. Vincent and the Grenadines. Washington, D.C.: U.S. Dept. of Commerce, International Trade Administration, n.d.

Young, Virginia Heyer. *Becoming West Indian: Culture, Self, and Nation in St. Vincent.* Washington, D.C.: Smithsonian Institution Press, 1993.

SURINAME

Republic of Suriname
Republiek Suriname

CAPITAL: Paramaribo.

FLAG: A yellow star is at the center of five stripes: a broad red band in the middle, two white bands, and a green stripe at the top and bottom.

ANTHEM: The *Surinaams Volkslied (National Anthem)* begins "God zij met ons Suriname" ("God be with our Suriname").

MONETARY UNIT: The Suriname guilder (Sf) is a paper currency of 100 cents. There are coins of 1, 5, 10, and 25 cents, and notes of 5, 10, 25, 100, and 500 guilders. Sf1 = $0.00073 (or $1 = Sf1365.00) as of 31 March 2000.

WEIGHTS AND MEASURES: The metric system is used.

HOLIDAYS: New Year's Day, 1 January; Revolution Day, 25 February; Labor Day, 1 May; National Union Day, 1 July; Independence Day, 25 November; Christmas, 25 December; Boxing Day, 26 December. Movable religious holidays include Holi Phagwah, Good Friday, Easter Monday, and 'Id al-Fitr.

TIME: 8:30 AM = noon GMT.

¹LOCATION, SIZE, AND EXTENT

Situated on the northeast coast of South America, Suriname is the smallest independent country on the continent, with a total area of 163,270 sq km (63,039 sq mi). Comparatively, the area occupied by Suriname is slightly larger than the state of Georgia. The nation has an extension of 662 km (411 mi) NE–SW and 487 km (303 mi) SE–NW. Suriname is bordered on the N by the Atlantic Ocean, on the E by French Guiana, on the S by Brazil, and on the W by Guyana, with a total boundary length of 2,093 km (1,301 mi). Suriname also claims about 15,000 sq km (5,800 sq mi) of southeastern Guyana and some 5,000 sq km (1,900 sq mi) of southwestern French Guiana.

Suriname's capital city, Paramaribo, is located on the Atlantic coast.

²TOPOGRAPHY

Suriname is composed of thick forests, unexplored mountains, and swampy plains. Approximately 80% of the territory is classified as tropical rain forest. Several geologically old rivers, including the Maroni in the east and the Courantyne, flow northward to the Atlantic Ocean from the southern highlands near the Brazilian border; there, numerous rapids and waterfalls bar boat passage.

The coastal plain is flat and sometimes as much as 1.5 m (5 ft) below sea level, necessitating a system of sea defenses. The soils of the coastal plain are relatively fertile. A forest belt, 48–72 km (30–45 mi) wide, lies to the south, interspersed with grassy savannas. Farther south are jungle and higher ground.

³CLIMATE

The climate is tropical and moist. Daytime temperatures range from 28° to 32°C (82–90°F). At night the temperature drops as low as 21°C (70°F) because of the moderating influence of the northeast trade winds, which blow in from the sea all year. The annual rainfall in Paramaribo is about 230 cm (90 in). May to

August is the main rainy season, with a lesser rainy season from November to February.

⁴FLORA AND FAUNA

Dominated by rain forest, Suriname contains many flowers but is most famous for water lilies and orchids. Tropical shrubs include hibiscus, bougainvillea, and oleander. There are over 184 species of mammals. Among the reptiles are the tortoise, iguana, caiman, and numerous snakes. Tropical birds abound, especially the white egret.

⁵ENVIRONMENT

In general, Suriname's environment and wildlife are protected from the destructive influences that threaten the majority of the world's nations. However, deforestation is becoming a concern, as foreign interests obtain timber concessions from the government. Suriname's eight nature reserves are managed by the Foundation for Nature Preservation, founded in 1969. The Suriname Wildlife Rangers Club, consisting mainly of students 15–20 years old, assists in various nature preservation activities. National responsibility for environmental matters is vested in the Ministry of Health and Environment and the Ministry of Natural Resources and Energy. The nation has 48.0 cubic miles of water. Eighty-nine percent is used for farming activities and 5% for industrial purposes. Eighteen percent of Suriname's city dwellers and 44% of all rural dwellers do not have pure drinking water. Pollutants from the country's mining industry affect the purity of the water. Salinization of the water supply is becoming a problem for the coastal areas.

Due to the preservation of Suriname's tropical rain forest, the nation's wildlife flourishes. Eleven of the country's 184 mammal species and six of its 670 bird species are endangered. Sixty-eight types of plants are also endangered. Endangered or extinct species in Suriname include the tundra peregrine falcon, five species of turtle (South American river, green sea, hawksbill, olive ridley, and leatherback), the Caribbean manatee, and the spectacled caiman.

⁶POPULATION

According to the census of 1 July 1980, Suriname had a population of 352,041, a decrease of 7.6% from 1972, largely because of emigration to the Netherlands. By 2000, the population of Suriname was estimated at 434,093. An estimated 6.0% of the population is 65 years of age or older. The projected population for the year 2005 is 446,000, assuming a crude birthrate of 18 per 1,000 population and a death rate of 6, resulting in a natural rate of change of 1.3% for the period 2000–2005. The population rate of change between 1995 and 2000 was 1.2%. Average estimated population density in 1996 was 2.7 per sq km (7 per sq mi).

It was estimated that 52% of the population lived in urban areas in 2000. The capital city, Paramaribo, had a 2000 population estimated at 112,000.

⁷MIGRATION

About 90,000 Surinamese resided in the Netherlands by the mid-1970s, and the number had reached some 200,000 by 1985. Emigration was about 12,000 per year in the early 1970s, but it accelerated as the date of independence approached and again after the coup of February 1980. An estimated 8,000 Surinamese fled to neighboring French Guiana by 1987, seeking refuge from a guerrilla conflict raging in the northeast. Democracy was restored in 1987, and a repatriation movement began in 1988. In 1991, the refugees still living in French Guinea took part in that year's elections. Repatriation was completed with the return of most refugees by the end of 1993. In 1999, the net migration rate was -8.92 migrants per 1,000 population.

⁸ETHNIC GROUPS

Suriname has one of the most cosmopolitan populations in the world. The largest ethnic group is the Hindustani (also known locally as "East Indians"), whose ancestors emigrated from northern India in the latter part of the 19th century, with 37% of the total population. Ranking a close second is the Creole community (mixed white and black), with 31%. The Javanese constitute about 15.3%. "Maroons," whose African ancestors were brought to the country in the 17th and 18th centuries as slaves but escaped to the interior lands, make up 10.3%. Amerindians, Suriname's original inhabitants, form 2.6% of the population and include the Arawak, Carib, and Warrau groups along the riverbanks and coastal plains, and Trios, Akurios, and Wyanas along the upper reaches of the rivers. Chinese account for 1.7% of the populace; whites for 1%; and other groups for the remaining 1.1%.

⁹LANGUAGES

The official language is Dutch, but English is widely spoken, and the local people use a lingua franca known as Sranang-Tongo or Takki-Takki, a mixture of Dutch, African, and other languages. Hindustani (a dialect of Hindi), Javanese, and several Chinese, Amerindian, and African languages and dialects are also spoken.

¹⁰RELIGIONS

Religious freedom is guaranteed by the constitution, and there is no state or dominant religion. According to government statistics, 48% of the population is Christian. Approximately 22.8% are Roman Catholic, and some 25.2% are Protestant, of whom 16% are Moravian and the rest of other denominations, including Lutheran, Dutch reformed, and the Evangelical Churches. Hindu is practiced by 27.4% of the inhabitants, and Islam by 19.6%. Indigenous tribal religionists make up 5% of the populace.

¹¹TRANSPORTATION

Suriname has 1,200 km (746 mi) of navigable waterways. A ferry service across the Corantijn River to Guyana began operating in 1990. There are 166 km (103 mi) of single-track railway, 86 km (53 mi) government owned and the rest industrial. Paramaribo can be reached from any town or village on the coastal plain by good all-weather roads. As of 1998, there were an estimated 4,530 km (2,815 mi) of roadways. State-owned and private companies operate regular bus services, both local and long distance. In 1995, there were 49,315 passenger cars and 17,000 commercial vehicles. Total number of airports stood at 46 in 1998, only 5 of which had paved runways. Zanderij International Airport near Paramaribo can handle jet aircraft, and there are small airstrips throughout the interior. The government-owned Suriname Airways offers regularly scheduled service to the Netherlands and Curaçao. In 1997 it carried 279,000 passengers.

Military operations involving the Jungle Commando and the national army badly damaged Albina and the road connecting Moengo to the eastern border. Overall lack of proper maintenance on roads, canals, and port facilities has resulted in a degraded infrastructure and higher local transportation costs.

¹²HISTORY

Spaniards came to Suriname in the 16th century in search of gold, but did not stay when they found none. The first large-scale colonization took place under Francis, Lord Willoughby, the English governor of Barbados, who sent an expedition to Suriname in 1650 under Anthony Rowse. In 1660, the British crown granted Willoughby official rights, and it became a flourishing agricultural colony. Settlers included English colonists, African slaves, and Jewish immigrants from the Netherlands, Italy, and Brazil. In the Peace of Breda between England and the United Netherlands in 1667, Suriname became a Dutch colony.

The English held Suriname again between 1799 and 1802 and from 1804 to 1816, when the Dutch resumed control over the colony under the Treaty of Paris. With the final abolition of slavery in 1863, workers were imported from India, Java, and China. In 1954, a new Dutch statute provided for full autonomy for Suriname, except in foreign affairs and defense. A commission was set up on 5 January 1972 to prepare alternatives to the existing legal framework. In May 1974, the terms for Suriname's independence were agreed on, and Suriname became an independent country on 25 November 1975.

For five years, Suriname was a parliamentary republic under prime minister Henk Arron. On 25 February 1980, the government was overthrown in a military coup led by Désiré Bouterse. Parliament was dissolved and the constitution suspended, and in 1981 the new government declared itself a Socialist republic. Relations with the US became strained as the Bouterse government moved closer to Cuba. In December 1982, as a result of the government's execution of 15 political opponents, the Netherlands and the US suspended all aid to Suriname.

The military and Bouterse continued to rule through a succession of nominally civilian governments. Still, pressure mounted for a return to genuine civilian rule. A separate challenge to the government came from a guerrilla movement under the leadership of Ronny Brunswijk. The Surinamese Liberation Army (SLA), also known as the Maroon or Bush Negro insurgency, began operating in the northeast in July 1986. It struck various economic targets, including the Suriname Aluminium Company. The government responded with repression, killing civilians suspected of supporting the insurgency.

The military allowed for elections on 25 November 1987. An anti-Bouterse coalition, the Front for Democracy, won 80% of the vote and 40 of the 51 seats in the newly constituted National these elections marked the first time in independent Suriname's history that power passed peacefully from one democratically elected government to another.

Wijdenbosch did not prove to be a popular president. His close association with Bouterse hurt him, both at home and abroad, as did the failure of his administration to improve Suriname's faltering economy, which continued to struggle with high inflation and unemployment, a major budget deficit, and the virtual collapse of its currency. A plan to privatize the oil and banana industries met with widespread protests culminating in a five-day general strike in the first part of June 1999. By the end of that month, popular discontent with the government had become so strong that Wijdenbosch called for early elections (which took months to arrange but still took place earlier than the normally scheduled date in 2001). In the meantime, Bouterse, sought by human rights groups for abuses during his time in power, was tried in absentia in the Netherlands for cocaine trafficking and convicted in July 1999.

The opposition New Front coalition, supported by former president Venetiaan, swept the May 2000 elections, winning 32 of the 51 contested parliamentary seats, just short of the two-thirds majority needed to select a new president. The Democratic National Platform 2000 of President Wijdenbosch sustained a staggering loss, winning only 3 seats, while Millennium Combination, a separate party formed by Desi Bouterse, won 10 seats.

¹³GOVERNMENT

Between 1954 and 1975, Suriname was administered by a governor appointed by and representing the Dutch crown, with a cabinet appointed by the governor and an elected Parliament (Staten van Suriname). Under the constitution adopted by Parliament on 21 November 1975, Suriname is a republic. However, that constitution, which provided for a unicameral, 39-member Parliament directly elected for a four-year term by universal suffrage, was suspended on 15 August 1980 and Parliament was dissolved. Bouterse then ruled through a series of appointed governments, whose members represented the military, industry, trade unions, business, and political parties. In September 1987, a popular referendum approved a new constitution, which is still in effect.

The constitution provides for a unicameral 51-member National Assembly directly elected for a five-year term. The executive branch consists of the president, vice president, and prime minister, all selected by the legislature. There is also a cabinet and an appointed Council of State. The judicial system is ineffective and in need of reform.

¹⁴POLITICAL PARTIES

Suriname's political parties tend to represent particular ethnic groups. The National Party of Suriname (NPS), led by former president Ronald Venetiaan, draws support from the Creole population. The Progressive Reform Party (VHP), led by Jaggernath Lachmon, is East Indian; and the Party of National Unity and Solidarity, formerly the Indonesian Peasant's Party (KTPI), led by Willy Soemita, is more tied in name to its constituency. All three parties allied in the coalition National Front for Democracy in 1987 to defeat Bouterse's National Democratic Party (NDP). In 1991, these three parties and the Suriname Labor Party (SPA) formed the New Front (NF) and won a solid victory, gaining 30 of 51 Assembly seats, while Bouterse's NDP took 10 seats. Another coalition formed during the 1991 elections was called Democratic Alternative '91. It included four non-ethnic parties representing a variety of white-collar concerns. They took 9 of the remaining 11 seats in the Assembly, with the other 2 going to minor parties.

After four years as an opposition party, following the 1996 elections, the New Front regained its parliamentary majority in

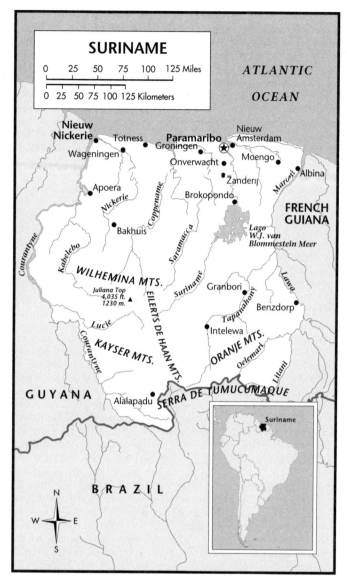

LOCATION: 2° to 6°N; 54° to 58°W. **BOUNDARY LENGTHS:** Atlantic coastline, 364 km (226 mi); French Guiana, 467 km (290 mi); Brazil, 593 km (369 mi); Guyana, 726 km (451 mi). **TERRITORIAL SEA LIMIT:** 12 mi.

Assembly, but a new appointive State Council, rather than the elective National Assembly, was given law-making authority. The new president, Ramsewak Shankar, remained in office from 25 January 1988 until 24 December 1990, when the military once again took over. International pressure mounted, and the military soon relented, allowing for elections on 25 May 1991. Again, an anti-military coalition, called the New Front (NF), swept the election. The leader of the coalition, Ronald Venetiaan, was chosen president on 6 September 1991. Bouterse was forced to resign his post as army commander in 1992, but he retained his political influence by becoming president of the National Democratic Party (NDP).

Although Venetiaan managed to remain in office throughout his five-year term, severe economic difficulties leading to increased poverty for the majority of Suriname's citizens caused his popular support to decline. In the May 1996 elections, NDP candidate Jules Wijdenbosch was elected president, effectively returning Bouterse—as NDP president—to power. Nevertheless, early elections called for May 2000, winning a total of 32 seats (Suriname National Party, 14; Progressive Reform Party, 9; the Javan Pertjajah Luhur party, 7; Suriname Labor Party, 2) to 10 for Desi Bouterse's Millennium Combination and only 3 for President Wijdenbosch's Democratic National Platform 2000.

15 LOCAL GOVERNMENT

The republic is divided into 10 districts, which include the urban district of Paramaribo. Administration is centralized, and there are no recognized municipalities.

16 JUDICIAL SYSTEM

The Constitution provides the right to a fair public trial before a single judge, the right to counsel, and the right to appeal. There is a Supreme Court, whose six members are nominated for life, and there are three Cantonal Courts.

Military personnel fall under military jurisdiction and are generally not subject to civilian criminal law. Military courts follow the same procedural rules as do the civil courts with military trials held before a judge and two military personnel.

The 1987 constitution calls for the establishment of an independent constitutional court. However, as of 1997, there was no effort taken by the government to create such an institution.

17 ARMED FORCES

The Suriname National Army consists of army, air force, and naval components, with a strength of about 1,800 in 2000 (army 1,400, navy 240, and air force 160). The army included one infantry battalion, one mechanized cavalry squadron, and one military police brigade. The navy mans three patrol craft, and the air force operates four combat aircraft and no armed helicopters. The defense budget was $8.5 million in 1997 or 1.6% of GDP.

18 INTERNATIONAL COOPERATION

Suriname was admitted to the UN on 4 December 1975 and is a member of ECLAC and all the nonregional specialized agencies except IAEA, IDA, and IFC. It also belongs to G-77, IADB, and OAS. Suriname is a signatory of the Law of the Sea and a member of the WTO.

19 ECONOMY

The bauxite and alumina industries traditionally set the pace for Suriname's economy, accounting for about 15% of GDP and 70% of exports. Two companies, Suriname Aluminum Co. (Suralco), a wholly-owned Alcoa subsidiary, and Billiton, owned by Royal Dutch/Shell, account for about one-third of government revenue and employ nearly 4,000 workers. Current mining areas will be depleted in ten years.

Although agriculture is the chief means of subsistence and second-largest employer after the government; plantation agriculture is the weakest sector of the economy, with the notable exception of rice growing. Suriname is self-sufficient in rice, and exports large amounts; however, Suriname is a net food importer. Imports account for more than 80% of consumption. Agricultural products accounted for only 10% of GDP in 1996, with rice, bananas, palm kernels, coconuts, plaintains, and peanuts the principal crops.

Next to bauxite, foreign aid is the mainstay of the country's economy. Suriname was once a colony of the Netherlands, and thus the Dutch government continues to provide economic aid. When Suriname's economic and political problems escalated, the Netherlands suspended aid between 1982 and 1991, and in 1997. Aid was resumed, from both the Netherlands and the US, once reforms were initiated.

In February 1987, guerrilla destruction of electricity pylons to the bauxite mines closed the industry while repairs were made. The collapse of world prices for bauxite in 1987 was another

severe blow for the economy. Despite high expectations, the civilian government inaugurated in early 1988 proved unable to address the country's considerable economic problems and was overthrown by the military on 24 December 1990. A year later, civilian government, under the leadership of President Ronald Venetiaan, came back to power.

The new government inherited a formidable array of economic problems. In 1992, real GDP fell by 5% and average inflation accelerated to 44%, compared to 26% in 1991. Foreign exchange reserves had reached a record low, unemployment was high, and climate for foreign investment was bad. The government implemented a structural adjustment program (SAP), which included the legalization of the parallel foreign exchange market, reduced government spending, privatization of key sectors of the economy, and revision of the country's investment code. By 1994, the inflation rate had reached over 400%, but thereafter the SAP kicked in and reduced inflation to less than 1% in 1996. In 1997, relations with the Netherlands soured when Suriname ended the SAP and replaced it with an ambiguous National Reconstruction Plan, and the government failed to implement necessary austerity measures. Inflation reached almost 21% in 1999, and growth had slowed to 2%.

20 INCOME

The US Central Intelligence Agency (CIA) reports that in 1998 Suriname's gross domestic product (GDP) was estimated at $1,480 million. The per capita GDP was estimated at $3,500. The annual growth rate of GDP was estimated at 2%. The average inflation rate in 1998 was 20%. The CIA defines GDP as the value of all final goods and services produced within a nation in a given year and computed on the basis of purchasing power parity (PPP) rather than value as measured on the basis of the rate of exchange. It was estimated that agriculture accounted for 10% of GDP, industry 32%, and services 58%.

21 LABOR

In 1994, there were 26,591 employed wage earners in Suriname. As of 1996, about 70% were engaged in services, 8.3% in manufacturing, 17% in commerce, 5.9% in agriculture, and 7.8% in transport and communications. Overall, agriculture accounts for about one-third of national civilian employment. About 9.25% of the total labor force was unemployed in 1994.

Suriname has numerous small unions, representing individual workplaces or enterprises, organized into six union federations. Among them are the General Confederation of Trade Unions, sometimes called the Moederbond (Mother Union); the Progressive Workers Organization, whose members are predominantly from the commercial and banking sectors; the Centrale 47, which includes bauxite and sugar unions; and the Central Organization for Civil Service Employees. Nearly 60% of the workforce is organized and about one-half are covered by collective bargaining agreements. Workers, with the exception of civil servants, are freely allowed to strike and do so often. Antiunion discrimination is illegal.

The minimum working age is 14 but this is not sufficiently enforced and many children work, especially in the informal sector. There is no minimum wage. The lowest wage for civil servants was $56 per month in 1999. The standard work week is 45 hours and time worked in excess of that requires overtime pay.

22 AGRICULTURE

The chief crops are rice, sugar, plantains and bananas, citrus fruits, coffee, coconuts, and palm oil, in addition to staple food crops. With the exception of rice, the main export crop, plantation agriculture has suffered the consequences of absentee ownership. Rice production was 213,000 tons in 1998. Sugar production dropped so substantially in the 1980s that imports were required to meet local demand. Under union pressure, the government in early 1987 agreed to a national sugar plan to improve machinery and housing, and to create employment. Production of sugar cane in 1998 was 90,000 tons; of bananas, 48,000 tons; of plantains, 12,000 tons; of oranges, 12,000 tons; and of coconuts, 9,000 tons.

Since its creation in 1945, the Commission for the Application of Mechanized Techniques to Agriculture in Suriname has worked to reactivate several old plantations and bring new land under cultivation. The successful control of diseases and pests, introduction of water storage and irrigation schemes, and the development of new quick-growing varieties of rice have also increased total agricultural production.

23ANIMAL HUSBANDRY

Livestock numbers are relatively small, since breeding is done primarily by small farmers who own only a few animals each. The government has tried to reduce the import of eggs, dairy products, and meat by undertaking projects to cross Dutch and local breeds of cattle and poultry. Estimated livestock numbers in 1998 included 89,000 head of cattle, 20,000 hogs, 8,000 goats, 7,000 sheep, and 2 million chickens.

24FISHING

Fishing has become increasingly important, both on inland waterways and at sea. The chief commercial catch is shrimp, which is exported. In 1997, the freshwater catch was 151 tons, and marine landings amounted to 12,850 tons. Shrimp production totaled 245 tons that year. The Fisheries Service, founded in 1947, has worked to develop the fishing industry. Exports of fish and fish products in 1997 amounted to nearly $12.7 million. Japan is the largest market for Surinamese shrimp.

25FORESTRY

Approximately 94% of Suriname is covered by tropical rain forest, but existing forest resources have scarcely been touched. Initial exploitation has been confined to the more accessible strips along the riverbanks. The Suriname Forestry Service, under an FAO technical assistance program, has undertaken to survey and open up the forests for commercial use. Roundwood production was about 204,000 cu m in 1998. In August 1992, a peace agreement between the central government and insurgent groups from the interior (where timber is found) was signed. Since the fighting ended, logging has increased. The trade surplus in forest products was $5.25 million for 1997.

26MINING

Bauxite and alumina accounted for 70% (about $300 million) of foreign exchange earnings in 1997. Mining accounts for about 4% of GDP. Suriname is one of the 10 largest producers of bauxite in the world. The total quantity of bauxite mined in 1997 was some 4 million tons (up from 3.5 million tons in 1995). Suriname's bauxite industry has suffered in recent years from a weak market, foreign competition, and the effects of the guerrilla war, but new mines with higher grade bauxite are replacing older depleted mines. The alumina industry, however, is threatened by the deterioration of the international alumina market. Suriname's privately owned multinational companies mine the bauxite and process alumina and aluminum. The Suriname Aluminum Company (SURALCO), has estimated bauxite reserves at 575 million tons.

Gold has been mined in Suriname since the second half of the 19th century. Since 1992, mine production has been about 300 kg per year. Gold concessions are negotiated with N.V. Grassalco, the state-owned gold company. Gold is produced by numerous small operators and sold to the government. Mine production in 1997 was 300 tons.

27ENERGY AND POWER

Electricity, primarily for industry, is supplied by the 189-MW hydroelectric power station at Afobaka, south of Brokopondo. The plant, which was built by Alcoa, is owned and operated by the Suriname Aluminum Company (Suralco). Suriname's energy sector and bauxite industry are closely linked. Suralco also owns and operates a 47 MW oil-fired turbine plant. Total installed generating capacity was 314 MW in 1998; total production was 2,008 million kWh.

Gas and electricity for the city of Paramaribo are supplied by the Overseas Gas and Electric Co. Electric service throughout the rest of the country is the responsibility of the Ministry of Local Government and Decentralization. In 1990, the government-owned oil company, Staatsolie, increased production by 2.8% to 4,500 barrels per day; production in 1998 was 7,000 barrels per day. In 1992, Staatsolie completed construction of a 60-km (37-mi) pipeline between the oil fields and distribution facilities. The Dutch government also has promised $15 million toward the construction of a new refinery. Staatsolie is also seeking joint venture partners to conduct exploration and eventual exploitation of oil reserves in western Suriname.

28INDUSTRY

The major industries are bauxite and gold mining, alumina and aluminum production, lumber, and food processing. Industrial production grew by 6.4% in 1994.

The bauxite industry, which accounts for about 15% of GDP, has developed into a complex of factories, workshops, power stations, laboratories, hospitals, recreational facilities, residential areas, and sports grounds. The bauxite refinery near Paramaribo produced 1.6 million tons of alumina and 32,000 tons of aluminum in 1995. Depressed world prices for bauxite and alumina in recent years have reduced the industry's development.

The long-term future of the mining industry depends on the companies' ability to keep production costs low and competitive, the availability of financing to exploit new reserves, and on the consolidation of peace in the country's interior. Because mineral rights are still vested in the state, exploration rights are granted by the government. The Canadian company Golden Star started mining for gold in Suriname in 1992. Proven and probable oil reserves in Suriname are estimated at 166 billion barrels. The State Oil Company of Suriname, or Staatsolie, produced 12,500 barrels per day in 1999.

29SCIENCE AND TECHNOLOGY

Research centers and scientific societies in Suriname include the Center for Agricultural Research in Suriname (founded 1965), Geological Mining Service (founded 1943), and the Agricultural Experiment Station of the Ministry of Agriculture, Animal Husbandry, and Fisheries (founded 1903), all in Paramaribo. The University of Suriname, founded in 1968 at Paramaribo, has faculties of medicine and technology.

30DOMESTIC TRADE

There are a few supermarkets and department stores, but most urban trade is conducted in small shops. Business hours are, Monday–Saturday, 8 AM to 4 PM. Banks are open weekdays from 6 AM to 12:30 PM, and on Saturdays 8–11 AM. Most trade in rural areas is conducted in open markets. Advertisements appear on radio and television and in the newspapers.

31FOREIGN TRADE

In 1995, exports of bauxite and alumina contributed $300 million, or about 80%, to total exports earnings. Other exports include rice, shrimp, wood products, and bananas. On the black market, Suriname is a large exporter of cocaine, especially to the

Netherlands. In 1995 Suriname's imports were distributed among the following categories:

Consumer goods	9.6%
Food	13.0%
Fuels	11.8%
Industrial supplies	31.0%
Machinery	19.8%
Transportation	14.6%

The US is Suriname's most important trading partner. In 1998, US exports to Suriname totaled $130 million. Principal trading partners in 1998 (in millions of US dollars) were as follows:

COUNTRY	EXPORTS	IMPORTS	BALANCE
Netherlands	98	141	-43
Norway	90	n.a.	
United States	84	204	-120
Canada	45	5	40
France	39	3	36
Japan	18	31	-13
Trinidad and Tobago	11	55	-44
United Kingdom	8	7	1
Netherlands Antilles	4	31	-27
Brazil	1	9	-8

32BALANCE OF PAYMENTS

Suriname runs a persistent deficit on current accounts, which has generally been offset by a surplus on capital accounts deriving from development aid, mainly from the Netherlands. Remittances from some 200,000 Surinamese expatriates in the Netherlands are not apparent in the balance of payments because they are usually exchanged in the parallel market.

In 1989, lower profitability in the bauxite sector led to a decline in remittances which was not offset by investment inflows, resulting in the first capital account surplus in many years. Foreign exchange reserves grew by 110%; from $10 million in 1989 to $21 million in 1990. Unfortunately, these reserves were squandered by the interim government during its nine-month rule and had fallen close to zero by July 1993. Suriname had a surplus of $66 million by 1996, but this figure declined to $25 million in 1997 and a deficit in 1998 due to a lack of development aid.

The US Central Intelligence Agency reports that in 1997 the purchasing power parity of Suriname's exports was $548.84 million while imports totaled $551.8 million resulting in a trade balance of -$2.96 million.

33BANKING AND SECURITIES

The Central Bank of Suriname has acted as a bank of issue since 1 April 1957. Other banks include the ABN-AMRO (Dutch), De Surinaamsche Bank (majority-owned by the ABN-AMRO), Hakrinbank, Volkscredietbank, and the Landbouwbank.

In 1998, the exchange rate separated into multiple rates, leading to a 40% currency devaluation in January 1999. According to the government, cocaine sold by Surinamese shippers was confiscated by Dutch authorities, causing a currency flow problem.

34INSURANCE

Both Dutch and foreign insurance companies operate in Suriname.

35PUBLIC FINANCE

For years the Suriname budget operated with a deficit. Government revenues increased following the introduction of a new bauxite levy in 1974. In 1979 and 1980 there were budget surpluses. During the 1980s, however, the military regime in power increased government intervention and participation in the

economy, causing public employment and budget deficits to soar. The return to civilian government in 1991 enticed the Dutch government to resume its development aid program, which amounted to $200 million by 1996. Reforms enacted included the reduction of deficit spending, the renunciation of monetary creation as a means of financing deficits, and the deregulation of trade and business licensing systems. After the Netherlands halted development aid in 1997, over half of the labor force was on the government payroll, and government spending was equal to 41% of GNP.

The US Central Intelligence Agency (CIA) estimates that in 1997 Suriname's central government took in revenues of approximately $393 million and had expenditures of $403 million including capital expenditures of $34 million. Overall, the government registered a deficit of approximately $10 million. Total external debt is estimated at over $200 million.

36TAXATION

Direct taxes provide only a small portion of governmental revenues, and payments have been in arrears for years. By far the greatest tax sources are the bauxite-related industries. Companies are taxed on the sum of all net profits. The corporate income tax has a flat rate of 38%, and the dividend tax is 25%. All the operating costs of a company are tax deductible, at set rates for certain equipment.

37CUSTOMS AND DUTIES

Suriname became a full member of CARICOM in 1995. There is a CET, ranging from 5% to 25%. Import tariffs from non-CARICOM countries range between 0% and 40%, averaging 30% to 40%. Duty-free import of various goods is offered by the National Development Incentives program. The government has offered full and partial exemption from import duties to new businesses. Suriname's trade licensing system is outdated and time-consuming, and is in fact a trade barrier in itself. There are no free trade zones.

38FOREIGN INVESTMENT

Suriname does not have a foreign investment code. In an effort to attract new investment, the government negotiates each investment project individually, offering incentives such as special tax holidays, depending on the project. Economic and business relations with the US are very important to this nation. US firms operating in Suriname include Suralco, the bauxite company, Exxon, Texaco, IBM, and the insurance firm, Alico. In addition, Suriname is highly dependent on relations with the Dutch government.

Foreign investment during the 1990s included gold mining by the Canadian company Golden Star, and Japanese shrimp farming by the company Sujafi.

39ECONOMIC DEVELOPMENT

In wholesale, retail, and foreign trade, the government has been highly interventionist. Quota restrictions or outright bans on many imported items considered nonessential or in competition with local products have been announced. The government forced price rollbacks on domestic items and imposed price controls on essential imports, resulting in some shortages.

Although the government has been Socialist in principle since 1981, it refrained from nationalizing key industries, although it did increase its participation in them. The Action Program announced by the government in May 1982 called for the encouragement of small-scale industry, establishment of industrial parks, development of rural electrification and water supply projects, liberalization of land distribution, and worker participation in management of government enterprises.

In 1975, the Netherlands promised Suriname $110 million annually in grants and loans, for a period of 10–15 years. This aid program and $1.5 million in aid authorized by the US in September 1982 were suspended following the killings of prominent Surinamese in December 1982. In 1983, Brazil and Suriname reached agreement on a trade and aid package, reportedly underwritten by the US. By 1986, Suriname had signed trade agreements with several countries, among them the Netherlands.

As of 1994, Suriname was undergoing a comprehensive structural adjustment program (SAP). This program, recommended by the EC, was designed to establish the conditions for sustained growth of output and employment with relative stability of prices, a viable balance of payments, and protection of the low-income population. However, as of the end of 1996, only minimal progress toward restructuring had been accomplished. Enacting the full SAP in its proper sequence was hoped to improve the prospects for the Surinamese economy and living conditions in the late 1990s. Unfortunately, the SAP was abandoned in late 1996 in favor of a National Reconstruction Plan that remains unclear. A volatile exchange rate, high public spending, and continued government intervention in commerce conspire to stilt economic development.

40 SOCIAL DEVELOPMENT

Organized welfare programs are conducted largely by private initiative, through ethnic or religious associations. However, the government has begun to establish a social welfare system designed eventually to include a free national health service.

Women have full legal rights under the law, but discrimination in hiring and salary practices persist. Opportunities for women remain limited as a result of traditional attitudes that encourage women to stay at home. In 1996, there were 8 women in the National Assembly, out of 51 members. Spousal abuse and other forms of violence against women is a widespread social problems.

Amerindians in Suriname have traditionally played only a limited role in decisions affecting their land and culture. The government has negotiated with timber and gold companies operating in the region without any input from Maroon and Amerindian groups. In recent years, these groups have become more effective in expressing their demands to government. In 1995, the government appointed a Consultative Council for the Development of the Interior, which includes representatives from these indigenous groups. In 1996 Maroon and Amerindian tribal leaders held the second of two summit meetings to promote solidarity in their demands for a greater voice in issues pertaining to land use.

Although Suriname's human rights record has improved, some abuses continue to be committed. These include the mistreatment of detainees, the abuse of prisoners, and overcrowding of jails. Pretrial detainees still constitute a large percentage of all prisoners. Nongovernmental organizations are permitted to monitor the conditions of prisons.

41 HEALTH

Tuberculosis, malaria, and syphilis, once the chief causes of death, have been controlled. In 1995, there were 72 cases of tuberculosis reported. Safe water was available to 89% of the population in 1995.

In 1998, Suriname's birthrate was 21.5 per 1,000 people. In 1998, average life expectancy was 71.6 years. The total fertility rate was 2.6 in 1994. The infant mortality rate was 25.1 per 1,000 live births in 1996, and the mortality rate for children under 5 years of age was 8.7 per 1,000). Overall mortality was 5.8 per 1,000 in 1990–95. In 1997, there were 2.5 doctors per 1,000 people. In 1990, there were an estimated 2.7 hospital beds

per 1,000 people. In 1994 health care expenditures totaled 5% of GDP.

The immunization rates for a child under one in 1997 were as follows: diphtheria, pertussis and tetanus (85%), polio (81%), and measles (81%). No polio nor tuberculosis was documented in 1995 and malaria incidence has decreased. In 1996, malaria deaths totaled 14. At the end of 1996 there had been 597 cases of HIV/AIDS reported in Suriname.

42 HOUSING

Housing programs are supervised by the Department of Social Affairs. As of 1 July 1980 there were 68,141 inhabited houses in Suriname and 8,208 huts; 82.3% of living quarters had electricity. Between 1988 and 1990, 82% of the urban and 94% of the rural population had access to a public water supply, while 64% of urban dwellers and 36% of rural dwellers had sanitation services.

43 EDUCATION

In 1993, there were 87,882 pupils in primary schools. Secondary schools had 16,511 pupils and 2,487 teachers. Education is compulsory and free for all children ages 6 through 16. While primary education lasts for six years, secondary education has two phases—four years followed by three years. Free primary education is offered by the government and by Roman Catholic and Protestant mission schools. The official school language is Dutch. The adult illiteracy rate for the year 2000 was estimated at 5.8% (males, 4.1%; females, 7.4%).

Higher education is provided by five teacher-training colleges, five technical schools, and the University of Suriname, with its Law School and a Medical Science Institute. In 1990, all higher level institutions reported 495 teaching staff with 4,319 students enrolled. Higher education is free of charge to citizens.

44 LIBRARIES AND MUSEUMS

The main public library is at the Suriname Cultural Center in Paramaribo, with 500,000 volumes, seven branches, and two bookmobiles. The Anton de Kom University in Paramoribo has 51,000 volumes. The Suriname State Museum and the Natural History Museum are in Paramaribo, and there is an open-air museum in Nieuw Amsterdam, with historical exhibits based at an 18th century fort.

45 MEDIA

Nearly all the towns and villages have telephone connections. There were 46,900 telephones in 1995. As of the same year there were 5 AM radio stations, 32 FM stations and 3 state-run television stations. In 1997, 668 radios and 137 television receivers were in use. There are two daily newspapers, the Dutch-language *De Ware Tijd* (circulation 10,000), and *Dagblad de West* (circulation 15,000).

The constitution provides for freedom of speech and of the press, and the government is said to generally respect these rights.

46 ORGANIZATIONS

International organizations in Suriname include the YWCA, Girl Scouts, Boy Scouts, and Red Cross. The Bouterse government established the National Women's Organization and the Suriname Youth Union.

47 TOURISM, TRAVEL, AND RECREATION

Most visitors need a valid passport and an onward ticket, but no visa. In 1997, there were approximately 61,000 tourist arrivals in Suriname with receipts totaling $43 million. Hotel rooms numbered 1,276 that year.

In 1999, the UN estimated the cost of staying in Suriname at $131 per day.

⁴⁸FAMOUS SURINAMESE
Lt. Col. Désiré ("Desi") Bouterse (b.1945) led the coup of February 1980.

⁴⁹DEPENDENCIES
Suriname has no territories or colonies.

⁵⁰BIBLIOGRAPHY

Binnendijk, Chandra van. *Sranan: Cultuur in Suriname.* Amsterdam: Koninklijk Instituut voor de Tropen, 1992.

Brown, Enid. *Suriname and the Netherlands Antilles: An Annotated English-Language Bibliography.* Metuchen, N.J.: Scarecrow Press, 1992.

Chin, Henk E. *Surinam: Politics, Economics, and Society.* New York: F. Pinter, 1987.

Dew, Edward M. *The Trouble in Suriname, 1975-1993.* Westport, Conn.: Praeger, 1994.

Goslinga, Cornelis C. *A Short History of the Netherlands Antilles and Surinam.* Norwell, Mass.: Kluwer Academic Press, 1978.

Hoefte, Rosemarijn. *Suriname.* Santa Barbara, Calif.: Clio Press, 1990.

Hoogbergen, Wim S. M. *The Boni Maroon Wars in Suriname.* New York: Brill, 1990.

Price, Richard (ed.). *Maroon Societies.* 3rd ed. Baltimore, Md.: John Hopkins University Press, 1996.

Sedoc-Dahlberg, Betty (ed.). *The Dutch Caribbean: Prospects for Democracy.* New York: Gordon and Breach, 1990.

Wooding, Charles J. *Evolving Culture: A Cross-cultural Study of Suriname, West Africa, and the Caribbean.* Washington, D.C.: University Press of America, 1981.

TRINIDAD AND TOBAGO

Republic of Trinidad and Tobago

CAPITAL: Port-of-Spain.

FLAG: On a red field, a black diagonal stripe with a narrow white border on either side extends from top left to bottom right.

ANTHEM: Begins, "Forged from the love of liberty, in the fires of hope and prayer."

MONETARY UNIT: The Trinidad and Tobago dollar (TT$) is a paper currency of 100 cents. There are coins of 1, 5, 10, 25, and 50 cents, and 1 dollar, and notes of 1, 5, 10, 20, and 100 dollars. TT$1 = US$0.15949 (US$1 = TT$6.270) as of 31 March 2000.

WEIGHTS AND MEASURES: The metric system is official, but some imperial weights and measures are still used.

HOLIDAYS: New Year's Day, 1 January; Carnival, 14–15 February; Emancipation Day, 1st Monday in August; Independence Day, 31 August; Republic Day, 24 September; Christmas, 25 December; Boxing Day, 26 December. Movable holidays include Carnival, Good Friday, Easter Monday, Whitmonday, Corpus Christi, 'Id al-Fitr, and Dewali.

TIME: 8 AM = noon GMT.

¹LOCATION, SIZE, AND EXTENT

Situated off the northeast coast of South America at the extreme southern end of the Lesser Antilles, the islands of Trinidad and Tobago cover an area of 5,130 sq km (1,981 sq mi), with a length of 210 km (130 mi) NE–SW and a width of 93 km (58 mi) NW–SE. Comparatively, the area occupied by Trinidad and Tobago is slightly smaller than the state of Delaware. Trinidad, the main island, rectangular in shape, has an area of 4,828 sq km (1,863 sq mi), extending 143 km (89 mi) N–S and 61 km (38 mi) E–W. Cigar-shaped Tobago, 31 km (19 mi) northeast of Trinidad, has an area of 300 sq km (116 sq mi), a length of 42 km (26 mi) NE–SW, and an average width of 12 km (7.5 mi) NW–SE. Sixteen small islands are found off the coasts. The Atlantic Ocean is to the E and the Caribbean Sea to the W. Venezuela lies only 11 km (7 mi) SW across the shallow Gulf of Paria.

Trinidad and Tobago have a coastline length of 362 km (225 mi). The capital city of Trinidad and Tobago, Port-of-Spain, is located on Trinidad's Gulf of Paria coast.

²TOPOGRAPHY

Trinidad is geologically part of South America, and its topography is similar to that of the adjoining Orinoco section of Venezuela. Three hill ranges, trending east–west, cross the island roughly through the northern, central, and southern parts, respectively. The Northern Range, a continuation of the mountains of the Paria Peninsula of Venezuela, is the most extensive and rugged of the three and has peaks rising above 900 m (3,000 ft). The highest peaks on Trinidad are El Cerro del Aripo (940 m/3,084 ft) and El Tucuche (936 m/3,071 ft). Hills in the Central Range rise just over 300 m (1,000 ft). Those in the Southern Range are somewhat lower. In between these hill ranges is level or gently rolling flatland, dissected by small streams flowing from the hills. Extensive swamp areas, some of them mangrove, are found along the east, south, and west coasts. Trinidad has the world's largest natural asphalt bog, the 46-hectare (114-acre) Pitch Lake, on the southwestern coast.

Tobago is geologically part of the Lesser Antilles, and its topography, generally more irregular and rugged than Trinidad's, resembles that of Grenada, St. Vincent, and other volcanic islands to the north. A central volcanic hill core rising to over 550 m (1,800 ft) fills most of the island and reaches the sea in many places. Patches of a narrow coastal plain are scattered here and there; much of the island's limited level land is concentrated in its southwestern tip.

³CLIMATE

There is little variation in temperature conditions through the year. The mean annual temperature for the entire nation is 21°C (70°F). In Port-of-Spain the annual average is 25°C (77°F), with an average minimum of 20°C (68°F) and an average maximum of 30°C (86°F) in January; the July range is 23–31°C (73–88°F). Increasing elevation in Trinidad's Northern Range causes a corresponding decrease in temperature. Nights are generally cool.

In the northern and central hill areas and on Tobago, annual rainfall exceeds 250 cm (100 in) and probably exceeds 380 cm (150 in) in specific areas. Most hilly sections receive 200 cm (80 in) or more, while in the lowlands the average drops below 165 cm (65 in) and in certain sections below 125 cm (50 in). There is a relatively dry season from about January to May and a wet season from June to December. The dry period is not, however, a season of drought, for rain still falls every few days in most areas.

⁴FLORA AND FAUNA

The plant and animal life of Trinidad, like the geology of the island, resembles that of neighboring Venezuela. Tobago, by contrast, shows in its flora and fauna its connection with the volcanic Lesser Antillean arc. There are distinct altitudinal variations in indigenous plant life on both islands. The natural vegetation includes wild flowers, many flowering shrubs and trees, palms, giant aroids, and large broad-leaved varieties. Natural animal life includes a few species of mammals, monkeys among them, and many reptiles and birds.

⁵ENVIRONMENT

Among environmental problems, pollution from oil spills is the most serious. Water pollution is also caused by mining by-products, pesticides, fertilizers, sewage, and saltwater. The nation has 1.2 cu mi of water, with 35% used for farming and 38% used for industrial purposes. Twelve percent of the people living in rural areas do not have pure water. The nation's cities produce 0.2 million tons of solid waste per year. Soil erosion has occurred, in part, because of the clearing of land for farming. Environmental responsibility is vested in the Ministry of Energy and Natural Resources. In 1989, the Ministry of the Environment and National Service was formed to regulate the nation's treatment of its natural environment.

On the west coast of Trinidad is the Caroni Bird Sanctuary, famed for its marshland and mangroves, where flocks of scarlet ibis roost. Little Tobago is reputed to be the only place aside from New Guinea where the bird of paradise lives in the wild. Endangered or extinct species on Trinidad include the Trinidad piping guan, tundra peregrine falcon, loggerhead turtle, and red siskin.

⁶POPULATION

The population of Trinidad and Tobago in 2000 was estimated at 1,086,908, with the majority living on Trinidad. An estimated 6.2% of the population is 65 years of age or older. The projected population for the year 2005 is 1,033,000 assuming a crude birthrate of 14 per 1,000 population and a death rate of 9 resulting in a natural rate of change of 0.01% for the period 2000–2005. The population rate of change between 1995 and 2000 was 0.8%. The population density in 1996 was 248 per sq km (642 per sq mi).

It was estimated that 74% of the population lived in urban areas in 2000, up from 72% in 1995. Port-of-Spain, the capital since 1783, had a 2000 metropolitan population estimated at 52,000. The second most important town is San Fernando, with a population of 33,600. An almost continuous urban area extends from Port-of-Spain eastward to Tunapuna, westward, and northward into the Northern Range. About one-third of the population lives in Port-of-Spain or its suburbs or within 16 km (10 mi) of them. The remainder of Trinidad and virtually all of Tobago are sparsely settled. Scarborough, the main town of Tobago, has a population of approximately 4,000.

⁷MIGRATION

Lack of opportunity has encouraged the migration of numbers of people to the UK, US, and occasionally to other places abroad. In 1990 there were 119,000 people in the US who had been born in Trinidad and Tobago, up from 66,000 in 1980. This movement, however, has been counterbalanced by immigration from other islands in the Lesser Antilles, mainly from Grenada and St. Vincent, where lack of opportunity is far more critical. Some of this immigration has been legal, some not. Migration from Tobago to Trinidad is common also, and there are as many native Tobagonians living on Trinidad as on Tobago. In 1999, the net migration rate was -19.8 migrants per 1,000 population.

As of September 1999 Trinidad and Tobago did not host any refugees or asylum-seekers. However, the lack of a national refugee law is a cause for concern as Trinidad and Tobago are likely to experience increased numbers of asylum-seekers due to increased extra-regional migration and migrant trafficking through the Caribbean.

⁸ETHNIC GROUPS

The population is mainly comprised of blacks (the descendants of former slaves), East Indians (originally brought to the island as contract laborers from northern India), whites, and Chinese, many of whom are racially and culturally intermixed. The total population is estimated at 40% black, 40.3% East Indian, 14% mixed, 1% white, 1% Chinese, and 3.7% other. Tobago is predominantly black.

While blacks and East Indians on Trinidad are economically interdependent, each community retains its cultural individuality: this is a life that has been called coexistence without assimilation. Intermarriage is rare, and facial and other bodily characteristics still separate the two groups, as do occupation, diet, religion, residence, agricultural landscape, sometimes dress, and often politics. Blacks are dominant in the urban areas, in the oil fields, in the poorer agricultural areas of the north, east, and southeast, and on Tobago. East Indians are dominant in the best agricultural regions. Although outnumbered in Port-of-Spain and San Fernando, urban East Indians are apt to be economically better off than the urban blacks and tend to be highly involved in commerce, industry, and the professions.

⁹LANGUAGES

English is the official language; an English patois, characterized by numerous foreign words and the special pronunciations of the islands, is understood everywhere. Here and there, a French patois and Spanish are used. In rural village areas, notably in the southern part of Trinidad, East Indians, especially of the older generation, use Hindi and, less frequently, Urdu, Tamil, and Telegu.

¹⁰RELIGIONS

Complete freedom and equality are enjoyed by all religious groups. Christian churches are found on both islands; Hindu temples and Muslim mosques in the recognizable architectural styles of southern Asia are found on Trinidad. According to statistics published in 1999, the population is roughly 32.2% Roman Catholic, 24.3% Hindu, 14.4% Anglican, 14% other Protestant, 6% Muslim, and 9.1% other or nonaffiliated.

¹¹TRANSPORTATION

In 1998 there were an estimated 8,320 km (5,170 mi) of roads, of which 4,252 km (2,642 mi) were paved. The more densely settled sections of both islands are served by reasonably adequate roads, but large sections of Tobago either have no motorable roads or are connected by narrow, tortuous, and poorly surfaced ones. In 1995, registered motor vehicles included 126,764 passenger cars and 25,830 commercial vehicles. The Public Service Transport Corp. is responsible for road transport. Trinidad's lone remaining railway, from Port-of-Spain to San Juan, was closed down in 1968.

The largest port installation for passengers and cargo is at Port-of-Spain. Brighton is an important port for oil and asphalt loading, and there are also oil terminals at Chaguaramas, Pointe-à-Pierre, and Point Fortin. A deep-water port at Point Lisas accommodates energy-based industries at the Point Lisas industrial estate. Numerous steamship lines regularly schedule freight and passenger services from Europe and the Americas. Regularly scheduled coastal vessels connect Port-of-Spain with Scarborough. The main shipping line is the West Indies Shipping Service. In 1998, Trinidad and Tobago had 1 merchant ship with a total of 1,336 GRT.

Air facilities are concentrated at Piarco International Airport, about 26 km (16 mi) southeast of Port-of-Spain. There is a secondary main airport at Crown Point, on the western tip of Tobago. In 1998 there were an estimated six total airports and airfields, three of which had paved runways. Trinidad and Tobago Airways, owned by the government and formed by the merger of British West Indian Airways (BWIA) International and Trinidad and Tobago Air Services in 1980, operates domestic, regional, and international services. In 1997, 807,000 passengers were carried on scheduled domestic and international airline flights.

TRINIDAD & TOBAGO

0 10 20 30 Miles

0 10 20 30 Kilometers

Charlotteville

Plymouth

Canaan   Scarborough

TOBAGO

Caribbean Sea

Blanchisseuse   Matelot   Toco

Maracas

El Cerro
del Aripo
3,084 ft.
940 m.

TRINIDAD

Port-of-Spain   Tunapuna   Sangre
Grange

Coroni   *Oropuche*

*Gulf
of
Paria*

Couva

**ATLANTIC
OCEAN**

Rio Claro

San Fernando

Pierreville

Brighton

Oropuche

Fullarton   Siparia   Moruga   Guayaguayare

San
Francique

VENEZUELA

N
W   E
S

Trinidad &
Tobago

LOCATION: 10°2′ to 11°21′N; 60°30′ to 61°56′W.
TOTAL COASTLINE: 470 km (292 mi). **TERRITORIAL SEA LIMIT:** 12 mi.

12 HISTORY

Arawak Indians inhabited what they knew as "Land of the Hummingbird" before the arrival on 31 July 1498 of Christopher Columbus, who called the island La Trinidad, or "The Trinity." The Spanish took little interest in the island and did not appoint a governor until 1532. Thereafter, Spanish colonists gradually came, but skirmishes with local Indians and raids by other Europeans, including Sir Walter Raleigh, made it difficult for the Spanish to obtain a foothold there. During the early European period, the island acted as a supply and transshipment center for Spanish traders and fortune seekers in South America. In time, colonists established plantations and imported slave labor from West Africa. The Europeans eventually wiped out the native Indians.

In 1797, a British expedition from Martinique captured Trinidad, which Spain ceded formally to Great Britain in 1802 by the Treaty of Amiens, and Trinidad became a crown colony. During the late Spanish period and through most of the 19th century, sugar dominated as the island's main agricultural product. The emancipation of slaves in 1834 brought severe labor shortages, and between 1845 and 1917, the colonial government brought in more than 150,000 contract workers, mostly Hindus and some Muslims from India, to the island as 'cheap labor' to replace the slaves. With added labor supplies and new techniques, the cocoa industry thrived, and by the late 19th century cocoa had joined sugar as a major export crop. The discovery of petroleum on south Trinidad in 1910 led to its addition as an important export, and since then it has assumed increasing economic importance.

Columbus also discovered Tobago in 1498, and it too received little attention from Europeans for many years. British from Barbados first colonized the island in 1616, but the local Carib Indians soon drove this group out. Other colonists followed shortly, however, and during the next 200 years the island changed hands many times among the Dutch, French, and British. Finally, in 1814, the British crown gained possession, which it maintained for a century and a half. The British first ruled Tobago as a separate colony, but during much of the 19th century administered the island from the Windward Islands government. It became a crown colony in 1877 and in 1888 amalgamated with Trinidad under the colony name of Trinidad and Tobago. In 1958, Jamaica, Barbados, and the British Windward and Leeward Islands formed the Federation of the West Indies. but Jamaica and Trinidad and Tobago withdrew in 1961, and the federation collapsed.

On 31 August 1962, Trinidad and Tobago became independent. The country retained membership in the Commonwealth as a British dominion. Eric Williams, the founder of the People's National Movement (PNM), became prime minister in 1961 and held the office till his death in 1981.

In 1976, Trinidad and Tobago declared itself a republic, and a president replaced the British monarch as chief of state. In 1980, Tobago attained a degree of self-government when it was granted its own House of Assembly. Williams's successor as majority party leader and prime minister was George Chambers, former deputy leader of the PNM. Following the victory of the National Alliance for Reconstruction (NAR) in the December 1986 elections, A.N.R. Robinson, leader of the NAR, became prime minister.

In July 1991, the government ratified a treaty with Venezuela on maritime boundaries that extended Trinidad and Tobago's nautical boundaries by 150 nautical miles. Also in 1991, the PNM returned to power under Prime Minister Patrick Augustus Mervyn Manning. However, at the end of 1995, a prime minister of Indian descent came to power for the first time when members of the Parliament elected Basdeo Panday. Panday's party, the UNC, formed a coalition with the PAR to overtake the PNM. There has been a long history of racial friction and discord. In July 1990, the Jamaat al-Muslimeen, a black fundamentalist group, made a failed coup attempt in July 1990 that killed 23 people and injured 250 more during a week-long siege of parliament. Beginning in 1992, the government has laid the foundations for a market-based economy, as opposed to a state-controlled economy. In 1993, the government began floating the Trinidad and Tobago dollar. The government has courted foreign investors, dismantled trade barriers, and started privatizing a large number of state-owned companies.

In an attempt to reduce tensions, Prime Minister Panday has nominated multi-ethic cabinets during his term. More symbolically, recent carnivals have seen the growth of Indian-influenced music such as 'chutney.' The 1995 election also saw an increase in the number of women elected to Parliament and the nomination of three women to Panday's first cabinet. In February 1997 the first contested presidential election was won by ANR Robinson, the former prime minister and leader of the NAR. He was sworn in for a five-year term, succeeding Noor Hassanali, who retired after serving two terms.

The murder of councillor Hansraj Sumairsingh in January 2000 brought the question of corruption in the ruling party into public scrutiny. No one has accused or believes Prime Minister Panday is involved in the case, but Sumairshing's colleagues believe his stand against corruption and his refusal to resign as both a councillor and Chairman of the Mayaro/Rio Claro Regional Corporation led to his death.

Trinidad and Tobago is a member of the Association of Caribbean States (ACS), which formed in 1995. The 38 members of ACS have a combined population of 200 million. The ACS promotes cooperation and exploring opportunities in economic development, trade, tourism, transportation, and the environment. Trinidad & Tobago's economy, the most highly industrialized in the Caribbean, has liberalized for several years and applied to become a member of NAFTA in 1997. Also in 1997, Trinidad signed a bilateral trade agreement with India, and held discussions on trade and investment with Cuba, as well as other South American countries. Trinidad has the second-largest amount of US direct investment on a per capita basis in the Western Hemisphere, excluding offshore finance centers. US investment reached $4 billion for the years 1996–99, according to the US Embassy in Port of Spain.

13GOVERNMENT

In 1976, Trinidad and Tobago amended its 1961 constitution. The 1976 draft preserved the bicameral legislature but replaced the crown-appointed governor-general with a ceremonial president chosen by parliament.

The House of Representatives is the more important of the two houses. Its 36 members are elected for five-year terms, but new elections can be called by the prime minister or by the house itself in a vote of "no confidence" in the cabinet. The party with a majority of seats in the House forms the government. The Senate consists of 31 members all appointed by the president, 16 on the advice of the prime minister, six on the advice of the leader of the opposition, and nine discretionary, based on consultation with various religious, economic, and social groups.

The head of the government is the prime minister, who is leader of the majority party. The current prime minister, Basdeo Panday, was elected in 1995. Cabinet ministers are appointed primarily from the House of Representatives by the president, acting on the prime minister's recommendations.

Active participation in government by the nonwhite (black and East Indian) population began in 1925, when for the first time elected representatives were included in the otherwise appointed Legislative Council that ruled the colony. Over the years the proportion of elected members increased, and a fully electoral self-government came in December 1961. In 1976, suffrage was lowered to the age of 18.

14POLITICAL PARTIES

The People's National Movement (PNM), formed in 1956 by Eric Williams, dominated politics in Trinidad and Tobago until 1995. After winning the 1961 elections, the opposition became disorganized. The PNM won all 36 seats in the House of Representatives in an election on 24 May 1972, which the opposition boycotted. When two members of the House of Representatives broke ranks to form a splinter party in June 1972, the PNM monopoly.

In the 1976 elections, the first held under the republican constitution, the PNM won 24 seats, and the new United Labour Front (ULF), a trade unionist party, took 10. The Democratic Action Congress (DAC) elected the two representatives from Tobago.

In the election of 1981, the PNM continued its dominance with 26 seats. The opposition ULF, the DAC, and the Tapia House Movement formed a coalition party, the Trinidad and Tobago National Alliance, and took 10 seats. The Organization for National Reconstruction (ONR), founded in 1980, took 22.3% of the vote but won no seats.

In 1986, the opposition coalition incorporated the ONR and, under the National Alliance for Reconstruction, took 33 seats to the PNM's three in the December elections. In 1991, the PNM returned to office, winning 21 of 36 seats. The NAR received only two seats, and the United National Congress, under Basdeo Panday, won 13 seats.

In 1995, the UNC formed a coalition with the NAR to take control of the House from the PNM. The PNM and UNC each had 17 seats, and the NAR had two seats in the House of Representatives. The next elections are scheduled by December 2000.

Party membership has been to a large extent based on race and region. The PNM is the party of the blacks. The NAR has been more powerful on the island of Tobago, where it has controlled the local assembly. Whites, Chinese, and other minorities have traditionally been anti-PNM. The UNC is made up of predominantly Indians. The other political parties are the Movement for Social Transformation (MOTION), National Joint Action Committee (NJAC), Republican Party, National Development Party (NDP), and the Movement for Unity and Progress (MUP).

15LOCAL GOVERNMENT

Elected county councils with certain executive powers govern the eight counties of Trinidad. The three major cities, Port-of-Spain, San Fernando, and Arima, each have a mayor and a city council. In 1980, Tobago was granted its own House of Assembly, which sits for four years and consists of 12 elected members and three members chosen by the majority party. In January 1987, Tobago gained full internal self-government. In the 1992 elections, the National Alliance of Reconstruction won 11 seats and the People's National Movement won one seat.

16JUDICIAL SYSTEM

The judicial system follows the model of the UK, with some local variations. The Supreme Court of Judicature consists of the High Court of Justice and the Court of Appeal. The former includes a chief justice and 10 puisne judges. Its jurisdiction and its practices and procedures follow closely those of the High Court of Justice in England. Civil actions and proceedings are usually heard by only one High Court judge but may be tried by a jury of nine members. A High Court judge with a jury of 9–12 members tries criminal offences. The Court of Appeal consists of the chief justice and three other justices. There is a limited right of appeal to the Privy Council, seated in London. Minor offenses are handled by district courts, including traffic courts. The judicial system also includes the Industrial Court and Tax Appeal Board, and a system of magistrate courts. All criminal cases are first sent to a magistrate's court. Appeals may be made to the Court of Appeal and then to the Privy Council in London.

The judiciary is independent of the other branches and free from outside interference. Criminal defendants are presumed innocent and are afforded the right to representation by counsel. In practice, the civil and criminal dockets are badly backlogged due to inadequate resources and inefficiency.

In an ongoing dispute about using the death penalty, the government of Trinidad and Tobago withdrew as a party to the American Convention on Human Rights but remained obligated until May 1999 to the Organization of American States to afford all of the rights set out within the American Declaration. In June 1999 the government carried out five executions, the first to take place in the country in five years.

[17]ARMED FORCES

The Trinidad and Tobago Defense Force number an estimated 2,700 in one reinforced battalion. The army, which numbers 2,000, consists of two infantry battalions and one support battalion. The navy mans 10 patrol craft and has an air wing equipped with five aircraft. There is also a coast guard of 700 (10 patrol craft). Under lend-lease agreements with the UK signed early in 1941, the US acquired several Caribbean bases, including one on Trinidad, on a 99-year lease. After local agitation over a number of years, Trinidad reclaimed the last remaining foreign base in June 1967. Two US tracking and navigation stations were closed in 1971 and 1980. Defense cost $88 million, or around 1.4% of GDP.

[18]INTERNATIONAL COOPERATION

Trinidad and Tobago became a UN member on 18 September 1962, and it belongs to ECLAC and all the nonregional specialized agencies except IAEA. Trinidad and Tobago also belongs to the Commonwealth of Nations, G-77, IADB, and OAS, and is a signatory to the Law of the Sea and a member of the WTO. The nation joined CARIFTA in 1968 and its replacement, CARICOM, in 1973; it is a member of the nonaligned movement. Oil revenues in recent years have enabled Trinidad and Tobago to contribute to regional lending agencies, such as the Caribbean Development Bank.

[19]ECONOMY

Trinidad and Tobago is a twin island state whose economy is oriented toward trade and tourism. The largest island, Trinidad, is more heavy industrialized; while Tobago is dominated by tourism and agriculture. The country can not feed itself and must look abroad not only for its food staple, but also for the bulk of manufactured goods. Import payments are met by the export of petroleum and products, invisible exports, tourism, and the trans-shipment trade. Specialized tropical crops are produced for export, but exploitation of petroleum reserves and refining of local and imported oils and their subsequent export are the dominant factors of the country's economy. Although by far the most prosperous of Caribbean nations, the country's high degree of dependence on oil revenues has made it exceedingly vulnerable to falling oil prices. Over the past three decades, its economic fortunes have followed closely the world price of oil, its major export commodity. Oil revenue windfall after 1973 brought unprecedented prosperity. However, this prosperity was not sustained when oil prices began to fall in 1982. Only after a further steep decline in the price of oil in 1986 did the government face the challenge of a fundamental adjustment in economic policy and initiate a program supported by the World Bank and the IMF. The country began the difficult transition from an oil dependent, public sector dominated economy, to a more diversified, market-oriented, private sector-led one.

Real GDP grew by 2.4% in 1995, after a decade of almost uninterrupted economic decline. Economic growth increased to 4.3% in 1998. The government's efforts to stabilize the macro-economic situation have yielded results, but in 1997 and 1998 the current account balance registered a deficit equal to 10% of GDP. A surge in imports related to a boom in the hydrocarbons sector helped to incur the debt. Inflation fell from 13.5% in 1993 to 3.6% in 1997 but had increased to 5.6% in 1998. Lower inflation rates were the result of a tight monetary policy achieved by raising the banks' required reserve ratio and prudent fiscal policies. The government is actively pursuing an ambitious privatization program and trade liberalization.

[20]INCOME

The US Central Intelligence Agency (CIA) reports that in 1998 Trinidad and Tobago's gross domestic product (GDP) was estimated at $8,850 million. The per capita GDP was estimated at $8,000. The annual growth rate of GDP was estimated at 4.3%. The average inflation rate in 1998 was 6.9%. The CIA defines GDP as the value of all final goods and services produced within a nation in a given year and computed on the basis of purchasing power parity (PPP) rather than value as measured on the basis of the rate of exchange. It was estimated that agriculture accounted for 2.2% of GDP, industry 44%, and services 53.8%.

The World Bank reports that for the same period per capita private consumption (in PPP terms) was $5,660. Private consumption includes expenditures of individuals, households, and nongovernmental organizations. It was estimated that between 1990 and 1998 private consumption grew at an annual rate of -2.4%. Approximately 20% of household consumption was spent on food, 23% on fuel, 5% on health care, and 13% on education. The richest 10% of the population accounted for approximately 30% of household consumption and the poorest 10% approximately 2.1%.

[21]LABOR

The economically active population in 1997 was estimated at 541,000 persons, of whom approximately 64.1% were engaged in services; 12.4% in construction and electricity, gas, and water supply; 14% in mining, quarrying, and manufacturing; and 9.5% in agriculture, forestry, hunting, and fishing. Unemployment averaged 13% in the early 1970s and had risen to 17% by 1973; in 1981, the rate was about 10%, after which it rose to 22% by 1989, but fell back to 14% in 1998.

The principal national labor federation is the Trinidad and Tobago Labour Congress. Of nonaffiliated unions, the largest is the National Union of Government and Federated Workers. As of 1996, about 20–28% of the work force was organized into 14 labor unions.

There is little protective labor legislation; work rules are subject to labor-management negotiation. Strikes are illegal in essential service industries. The normal workday is eight to nine hours, five days a week. Vacation periods vary from two to five weeks a year, depending on length of service.

A minimum wage of $1.10 per hour was established in 1998, but it is considered insufficient to support a family. Children between the ages of 12 and 14 may work in family businesses, otherwise until the age of 18 minors may only work during daylight hours. There is no organized exploitation of children, but they do occasionally serve in the informal economy such as working as street vendors.

[22]AGRICULTURE

About 28% of the total land area was arable in 1997, most of it on Trinidad. There are two distinct types of agricultural operations—the large estate or plantation that is managed by a specialist and employs large numbers of laborers, and the small farm cultivated by the owner (or tenant) and family. The small farms grow mainly for the home market. Crops include corn, rice, peas, beans, potatoes, other vegetables, and a wide variety of fruits. Lowland rice is grown almost entirely by Indian farmers. The large estates are interested mainly in commercial export crops, although the small farmers also grow some export crops. Agriculture accounted for only 2% of GDP in 1998. During the 1970s and early 1980s, agriculture's traditional labor force was lured away by the booming energy sector, with foreign exchange plentiful enough to import food. By the late 1980s, however, this trend was being reversed.

The value of crops grown for the domestic market is believed to be considerably greater than that of the export crops. Sugar, the main commercial crop, is grown on a few large company-owned estates and by thousands of small farmers; modern methods allow the estates to produce about two-thirds of the sugar crop. Normally, 80% or more of the islands' production is exported. Sugar production declined from 250,000 tons in 1961 to 213,200 tons in 1971 and some 65,000 tons in 1984, the lowest output in four decades; 1998 production was 100,000 tons. The second major export crop, cocoa, is cultivated in the hill sections of both Trinidad and Tobago. Estates produce considerably more cocoa than smallholdings, owing to better agricultural practices and to the fact that small farmers intercrop bananas, coffee, and other crops with cocoa. Cocoa production has been in decline since 1970; the output in 1998 was 2,000 tons. Coffee is grown in much the same hill areas as cocoa, and there is about the same proportion of estate-grown to small-farmer-grown coffee. Both cocoa and coffee have been described as sick industries because of inefficiency, crop disease, and uncertain world market conditions. In 1998, coffee production was less than 1,000 tons, down from 2,361 tons in 1985.

Some 90 acres (36 hectares) of ornamental flowers are also cultivated for export. Rice, citrus, corn, cassava, peanuts, and pigeon peas are now being grown to diversify agricultural output.

23 ANIMAL HUSBANDRY

Livestock plays only an incidental role in the agricultural pattern. The water buffalo, adept at turning heavy, water-laden soils, has been brought from India by Indian farmers and is the major draft animal in rice cultivation and probably the most productive animal in the country. Cattle are kept by some small farmers, but the best stock is that on estates and government farms or in large dairies. Poor animals and poor breeding and feeding methods keep meat and milk quantity and quality low and prices high. Trinidad and Tobago relies heavily on dairy imports from Europe to satisfy domestic demand.

In 1998, the livestock population included an estimated 10,000,000 poultry, 39,000 head of cattle, 59,000 goats, 28,000 hogs, 12,000 sheep, and 5,000 water buffalo. Animals slaughtered at abattoirs run by the government and by municipalities yielded an estimated 25,000 tons of poultry meat, and 2,000 tons of pork in 1998.

24 FISHING

The fishing industry has great potential, but current production does not begin to meet local demands, and large quantities of fish must be imported. Shrimp and mackerel make up one-third of the total annual catch, with shrimp the leading fisheries export. In 1997, Trinidad and Tobago exported $10.2 million in fish and fish products, up from $2.4 million in 1990. In 1986, the Archipelagic Waters and Exclusive Economic Zone Act defined the sovereign fishing jurisdiction around the nation, which has created new opportunities for marine fishing off the east coast of Trinidad. The harvest in 1997 was about 15,012 tons, up from 3,730 tons in 1986.

25 FORESTRY

Approximately 31%, or 161,000 hectares (398,000 acres), of the land is forested. Roughly four-fifths of the forestland is government owned or administered; however, much of the state forestland is in hill areas, inaccessible for exploitation. Several dozen small sawmills are in operation. Roundwood production in 1997 was about 96,000 cu m, 23% used for fuel.

26 MINING

Petroleum and natural gas are the country's most important mineral resources. Trinidad and Tobago is the world's second-largest exporter of ammonia, after Russia. It also has the world's largest supply of natural asphalt. Southwest of San Fernando is the island's famous Pitch Lake, a 46-hectare (114-acre) deposit of oozing black asphalt; it has been mined commercially since the 19th century. The annual yield has declined from an average of 200,000 tons in the 1960s to 15,400 tons in 1997. Iron ore deposits of commercial value are reported to have been discovered in Trinidad's Northern Range. Quarrying operations on the islands produced 1.6 million tons of limestone and 652,500 tons of cement in 1997.

27 ENERGY AND POWER

Petroleum is the main source of energy and since the 1940s has been the principal industry. Petroleum and petroleum products provided 68% of export earnings and 22% of government revenue in 1995. However, production of petroleum has been steadily decreasing since 1978, and its contribution to the GDP (including asphalt extraction and refining) decreased from about 35% in 1980 to about 25% in 1999.

Commercial petroleum operations began in 1911 and increased substantially since that time. Current mining and exploration leases cover almost 90% of the land area and the bulk of all Trinidad and Tobago's territorial waters. Natural gas reserves were estimated at 566 billion cu m in early 2000. Foreign capital has sponsored most exploration, mining, and processing. The oil fields are in the south of Trinidad and offshore in the Gulf of Paria; roughly 75% of production is from offshore wells.

Trinidad's oil production peaked at 245,000 barrels a day in 1977 and fell to 162,000 barrels a day in 1998. Proved crude oil reserves exceed 500 million barrels; several untapped offshore fields in the southeast were under exploration. Subsidiaries of Shell and Texaco built the two largest refineries. In August 1974, the government took over Shell (Trinidad), paying compensation of us$45 million. In 1985, it acquired Texaco's onshore fields and oil refinery. That year the government also acquired ownership of another major oil company, Trinidad-Tesoro Petroleum, which it renamed the Tesoro Petroleum Company. As of 1995, the government-owned petroleum company, now called the Petroleum Company of Trinidad and Tobago (Petrotrin) operated two of the four major production facilities and had 66% equity in one of the remaining two. As of 2000, Trinidad and Tobago is one of the world's leaders in natural gas production and uses natural gas for electricity, and in the petrochemical and other industries. Exports of LNG, from a plant built by an ARCO-led consortium, began in 1999. Plans are under way to triple the plant's capacity, making it the world's fourth-largest LNG facility. Natural gas production in 1995 was 7.2 billion cu m, 80% of which was produced by Amoco. All natural gas produced is used domestically. About 70% is piped to ammonia, methanol, and urea plants; the state-owned steel mill; and the Trinidad and Tobago electric utility sector.

The Trinidad and Tobago Electricity Commission has been carrying out electrification throughout the islands, and generation as well as domestic, commercial, and industrial use of electric power is well ahead of other areas in the former British West Indies. More than 95% of the current total generating capacity is publicly owned and operated by the commission; the remainder is installed mainly in oil refineries and sugar factories. In 1998, total electrical energy production by public utilities was 4,763 million kWh. Net installed capacity was 1,253,000 kW, all of it in conventional thermal facilities. A submarine cable provides Tobago with electricity from Trinidad.

28 INDUSTRY

Long-established industries are those processing raw materials of the farm, forest and sea; foremost are sugar, molasses, and rum, followed by fish, lumber, fats and oils, and stock feed. Manufacturing products include matches, angostura bitters, soap, and confectionery and clay products. Newer industries include petroleum refining, petrochemicals, concrete products, canned citrus, bottled drinks, glass, drugs, chemicals, clothing, building materials, and metal goods.

The most important industrial center is found at the port at Point Lisas. Many new industrial plants have been established under the benefits of the country's New Companies Act (1997). The manufacturing sector has contributed a substantial share of GDP since the 1970s, which amounted to 8% in 1998. After the establishment of the free zone program in 1993, manufacturing investment soared. Caroni Inc., the government-owned sugar company and the largest employer on Trinidad, undertook a major revitalization project in 1998, yet had persistent problems paying employees in 1999.

Due to a decrease in drilling activities and the maturation of existing wells, the petroleum sector registered sharp declines during the 1990s. The government attempted to increase oil exploration and production by giving contracts to US companies. One of the most ambitious projects was the $935 million Atlantic LNG plant, in which the US's Amoco had the largest stake, of 34%, and another US company, Cabot, had a 10% share. The other foreign participants were British Gas (26%) and Spain's Repsol (10%). The petroleum sector, which more than doubled its growth rate to 1.8% in 1996, fell by 1.1% in 1997 due to a continuation of declining oil production. Diversification of the petrochemicals industry and investments in other heavy industry and manufacturing may broaden the export base; but hydrocarbons will continue to provide at least 25% of foreign exchange earnings.

29 SCIENCE AND TECHNOLOGY

Among the research centers and learned societies of Trinidad and Tobago are the Commonwealth Institute of Biological Control, the Agricultural Society of Trinidad and Tobago, the Tobago District Agricultural Society, the Pharmaceutical Society of Trinidad and Tobago, and the Sugar Manufacture Association of Trinidad and Tobago. The University of the West Indies has a campus in St. Augustine (founded 1948) with faculties of agriculture, engineering, medical sciences, and natural sciences. In 1987–97, science and engineering students accounted for 58% of college and university enrollments.

30 DOMESTIC TRADE

Trinidad and Tobago's wholesale trade is highly organized and highly competitive; much of its is controlled by a few managing agencies located in Port-of-Spain. These agencies are direct importers in bulk and have exclusive wholesale rights for sales in the islands, and often in other Caribbean nations and territories.

In small communities, in rural areas, on Tobago, and in less developed parts of Port-of-Spain and San Fernando, the general retail store carries a wide variety of commodities. Many of these stores are family enterprises and most are small. Business hours are generally from 8 AM to 4 PM, Monday through Friday, with a lunch break from noon to 1 PM. Shops are often open from 8 AM to 4 PM, except on Fridays (till 6 PM) and Saturdays (till noon). Banks stay open from 8 AM to 2 PM, Monday through Thursday, and from 8 AM to 1 PM and from 3 PM to 5 PM each Friday.

31 FOREIGN TRADE

The foreign trade of Trinidad and Tobago is very large for a country of its size, a fact attributable mainly to its petroleum processing industry, whereby crude oil is imported and then re-exported as gasoline, kerosene, and other petroleum products. The economy's prosperity is thus tied closely to trade which, in turn, is closely linked to the price and demand structure of the world petroleum market.

Up to 1992, the government prohibited the importation of some manufactured products without a license. The government replaced this list with supplemental tariffs, which coupled with the CARICOM Common External Tariff (CET), reached nearly 100%. These supplemental tariffs were reduced to CET levels by 1995, alleviating high prices on foreign goods. By 1996, quantitative restrictions were eliminated, as were surcharges and stamp duties on non-agricultural goods.

Trinidad and Tobago's main sources of commodity export income are refined petroleum products (29%), crude petroleum (17%), and chemicals (11%). Other exports include manufactured fertilizers (3.5%), natural and manufactured gas (2.2%), and sugar (1.7%).

In 1996 Trinidad and Tobago's imports were distributed among the following categories:

Consumer goods	8.2%
Food	11.8%
Fuels	19.1%
Industrial supplies	28.7%
Machinery	21.4%
Transportation	10.2%
Other	0.5%

Principal trading partners in 1998 (in millions of US dollars) were as follows:

COUNTRY	EXPORTS	IMPORTS	BALANCE
United States	974	1,216	-242
Jamaica	209	18	191
France	141	46	95
Guyana	110	15	95
Spain	74	46	28
Germany	64	99	-35
United Kingdom	59	175	-116
Venezuela	58	298	-240
Colombia	42	188	-146
Japan	4	119	-115

32 BALANCE OF PAYMENTS

Between 1974 and 1981, largely because of the huge increase in the value of petroleum exports, Trinidad and Tobago's payments balance was favorable. With the weakening of the market for the country's petroleum and oil refinery products in 1982, however, a deficit was recorded for the first time since the early 1970s. Foreign exchange reserves, which had reached $3.3 billion in 1981 were depleted rapidly through the 1980s, as expenditures reduced revenues (caused by lower oil prices). By 1988, foreign exchange reserves had plummeted to –$5.7 million, forcing the government to reschedule its commercial and official debt. During the 1990s, Trinidad ran a balance of payments surplus from 1992 until 1997 due to a rise in foreign direct investment, but ran a deficit after 1997 because of low oil prices, and high industrial imports.

The US Central Intelligence Agency reports that in 1997 the purchasing power parity of Trinidad and Tobago's exports was $2.4 billion while imports totaled $3.3 billion resulting in a trade balance of -$900 million.

The International Monetary Fund (IMF) reports that in 1998 Trinidad and Tobago had exports of goods totaling $2,258 million and imports totaling $5,999 million. The services credit totaled $67,137 million and debit $255 million. The following table summarizes Trinidad and Tobago's balance of payments as reported by the IMF for 1998 in millions of US dollars.

Current Account		-644
Balance on goods	-3,741	
Balance on services	66,882	
Balance on income	-341	
Current transfers	22	
Capital Account		...
Financial Account		472
Direct investment abroad	...	
Direct investment in Trinidad and Tobago	730	
Portfolio investment assets	-	
Other investment assets	1	
Other investment liabilities	-259	
Net Errors and Omissions		252
Reserves and Related Items		-80

33 BANKING AND SECURITIES

The Central Bank of Trinidad and Tobago (established 1964) is the central regulatory institution and the sole bank of issue. The commercial banking business is well established and is operated chiefly by Canadian, British, and American interests. Monetary and fiscal developments have been closely linked with the fortunes of the oil industry.

There are six commercial banks operating in Trinidad and Tobago, with assets of over $25 billion. In 1997, bank CEO's formed a Banking Association. The largest is Republic Bank, formerly Barclays. Other commercial banks include the Bank of Nova Scotia, Citibank, First Citizens Bank, Intercommercial Bank, and Royal Bank of T&T. The Bank of Baroda, India's second largest bank, and the Bank of India, the third largest, have both expressed interest in entering the Trinidadian market. Offshore banking services were begun in the late 1990s by Republic Bank.

Workers and farmers make use of the Government Savings Bank offices. There are numerous agricultural credit societies, most of which are financed by the government's Agricultural Credit Bank. Credit unions are also common. The Trinidad and Tobago Development Finance Co., jointly owned by the government and the private sector, offers medium- and long-term financing to industry.

Since about 1948, limited liability companies with publicly issued share capital have become increasingly important. The West Indies Stock Exchange (succeeded by West Indies Stock Brokers, Ltd.) opened a branch in Port-of-Spain in 1964. The brokerage organization became a member of the Jamaica Stock Exchange in December 1970. The Trinidad and Tobago Stock Exchange began operating in 1981.

34 INSURANCE

Insurance firms include branches of UK and US companies and a few local companies. Their operations are highly competitive. A government-owned reinsurance company has been in operation since 1979. The Colonial Life Insurance Co. is the largest life insurance company in Trinidad.

35 PUBLIC FINANCE

After three years of deficit, the 1973 budget registered a surplus, primarily attributable to increased revenues resulting from higher petroleum prices. The budget generally remained in surplus until 1982, when a deficit was registered. The budget continued in deficit, although at decreasing levels, until 1990. In 1988, the government began an adjustment program which included currency devaluation, debt reschedulings, and the adoption of an austere budget that included public service wage reductions and decreased transfers to state enterprises. These reforms resulted in

an improved budget by 1994 which lasted until 1998, when expanded infrastructure and industrial projects drained revenues.

The US Central Intelligence Agency (CIA) estimates that in 1997 Trinidad and Tobago's central government took in revenues of approximately $1,590 million and had expenditures of $1,540 million including capital expenditures of $165.8 million. Overall, the government registered a surplus of approximately $50 million. External debt totaled $2.2 billion.

The following table shows an itemized breakdown of government revenues and expenditures. The percentages were calculated from data reported by the International Monetary Fund. The dollar amounts (millions) are based on the CIA estimates provided above.

REVENUE AND GRANTS	100%	1,590
Tax revenue	82.9%	1,318
Non-tax revenue	13.8%	220
Capital revenue	2.7%	43
Grants	0.6%	9
EXPENDITURES	100%	1,540
General public services	15.7%	242
Defense	1.8%	28
Public order and safety	7.0%	107
Education	13.7%	211
Health	8.4%	130
Social security	14.3%	220
Housing and community amenities	8.9%	137
Recreation, cultural, and religious affairs	0.9%	14
Economic affairs and services	11.7%	180
Interest payments	17.7%	272

36 TAXATION

Important sources of taxation are income taxes, a motor vehicle tax (25% to 30%), license duties, property and building taxes, customs and excise duties (including purchase taxes), and petroleum royalties and concessions.

The individual income tax is calculated on net chargeable income, from 28% up to $50,000; and 35% thereafter. A VAT of 15% is levied on many goods. The basic corporate tax rate is 35%. This rate is increased to 50% for petroleum companies, with a supplemental petroleum tax. Dividend and interest payments are taxed at 15% and royalties at 20%.

37 CUSTOMS AND DUTIES

Customs and duties are a significant source of government revenue. Most imported articles are subject to import duties, as well as a stamp tax, an import surcharge, a VAT (15%), and excise taxes on petroleum products, tobacco, and alcoholic beverages that are sold locally. Trinidad and Tobago applies the CARICOM Common External Tariff to most goods. The rates range from 5% to 20%.

Free Trade Zones were authorized by law in 1988; the first FTZ was established in the Point Lisas Industrial Estate. Trinidad and Tobago is a member of CARIBCAN, is a signatory to the Lome Convention, and has special trade agreements with Venezuela, the UK, Ireland, France, and the US. The country benefits from the Caribbean Basin Initiative (CBI), which allows duty-free entry of many products into the US.

38 FOREIGN INVESTMENT

Foreign investment in Trinidad and Tobago, particularly from British, Canadian, US and Dutch sources, has played a major role in the development of all major manufacturing and processing industries, as well as most large agricultural enterprises. Several private banking institutions have provided development loans through the Industrial Development Corporation, established by the government in 1959 to act as a liaison between investors and various government departments.

Starting in 1970, the government required foreign investment in Trinidad and Tobago to be conducted in a joint venture basis, with majority domestic participation most often in a 60:40 ratio. The government has emphasized foreign investment with a privatization program allowing foreign companies to own the majority of the shares. In 2000, investment in publicly-held companies required a 70:30 ratio. Investment in other sectors may be 100% foreign owned.

Oil and gas exploration continues to attract inflows of foreign capital, boosting economic growth and strengthening public finances. The US is the major investor, followed by the UK, Canada, Germany, India, and Norway. Inflows of over $3 billion in foreign investment between 1997 and 2000 strengthened the balance of payments and permitted the relaxation of policies. Total US direct investment averaged $1 billion per year in 1997 and 1998. US investment is traditionally in hydrocarbons and petrochemicals; while Canada has investments in ammonia/urea, Germany in methanol and iron, India in iron and steel, and Norway in ammonia.

39 ECONOMIC DEVELOPMENT

To diversify the economy and raise the national standard of living, foreign capital and technical assistance are actively solicited. Major incentives are duty-free imports of equipment and raw materials, income tax holidays, accelerated depreciation allowances, unlimited carryover of losses, and repatriation of capital and profits. To encourage diversification toward non-oil/gas sectors, the government has undertaken comprehensive reforms in the trade and exchange rate regimes, and the investment environment. A major downsizing and refocusing of the public sector with an extensive program of divestment and reduction of public employment has occurred.

Nonetheless, the country remains largely an oil economy even though oil reserves are being depleted. While the natural gas sector will benefit the economy in the future, it will not solve the country's most crucial economic problems. Only by diversifying into more labor intensive export industries and services will Trinidad and Tobago generate employment and growth and minimize its external vulnerability. The key ingredients for development are a buildup of reserves consistent with the maintenance of a competitive exchange rate; the use of monetary policy to contain inflation and sterilize reserve accumulation, and the strengthening of fiscal balances to reduce government debt and lower interest rates.

40 SOCIAL DEVELOPMENT

All employees aged 16 through 64 are required to become members of the National Insurance System. Employers contribute 5.6% of payroll, according to 12 wage classes, and employees normally contribute 2.8% of earnings. The program covers employed persons, including agricultural and domestic workers. In addition, a social insurance scheme is funded by the government and extends benefits to those with limited means. The system provides old age, retirement, and disability pensions; maternity, sickness, and survivors' benefits; and funeral grants. A compulsory system of workers' compensation for injury is also in place, financed entirely by employer contributions. A food stamp program was introduced in 1978. Public work programs are introduced in areas where seasonal unemployment in agriculture is a major problem.

The Constitution mandates human rights and freedoms to all citizens regardless of sex. Women are active in the labor force, but few rise to senior management positions. There is no law that mandates equal pay for equal work. In 1995, four of 36 members of the House of Representatives and nine of 31 Senators were female. A new domestic violence law providing easier access to police went into effect in 1999.

Human rights organizations operate freely. A human rights ombudsman has been established by the government to investigate allegations of human rights violations. Poor prison conditions and lengthy pre-trial detention remain a problem.

41 HEALTH

The general health of the population has been improving; substantial decreases have been recorded in the death rates for malaria, tuberculosis, typhoid, and syphilis. Immunization rates for children up to one year old in 1997 were diphtheria, pertussis, and tetanus (90%); polio (81%); and measles (88%).

Government health facilities include general hospitals in Port-of-Spain and San Fernando, small district hospitals, several major health centers, dental service centers, a mental hospital, and a nurses' training school. In the mid-1990s, there were more than 900 physicians, about 560 pharmacists, and over 100 dentists. The population per physician was 1,200 in 1998. There were 38 hospital beds per 1,000 people in 1995.

Improvements in sanitation have reaped impressive health benefits. During 1990–96, 97% had access to safe water and 79% had access to proper sanitation. As a result, reported cases of dysentery and hookworm have declined dramatically.

The 1998 birth rate was 16.7 per 1,000 people, and average life expectancy was 73.8 years. Infant mortality was 16.2 per 1,000 live births in 1996; maternal mortality was 75 per 1,000 live births in 1997; and general mortality was 6.1 per 1,000 people in 1990–95.

There were 2,083 AIDS cases reported in late 1995, a great increase from the 149 cases reported early that same year. The HIV-1 seroprevalence rate was 0.9 per 100 adults in 1997.

42 HOUSING

There is an acute shortage of adequate housing, and high rents have contributed to inflation. Industrial construction has outpaced residential building in recent years. A typical rural home for a large family consists of one to three rooms plus an outside kitchen. Slums and tenements are typical of urban life. Nearly all private dwellings, urban or rural, have toilets and piped-in water. At last estimate, more than 75% of all housing units were detached houses; nearly 20% were flats; and less than 5% were duplexes. Owners occupied 65% of all dwellings; nearly 25% were rented; and less than 10% were occupied rent free.

43 EDUCATION

For the year 2000, adult illiteracy rates were estimated at 1.8% (males, 1.0%; females, 2.5%). In 1997, the islands had 476 primary schools with 7,311 teachers and 181,030 students. Secondary schools enrolled 104,349 pupils and employed 5,070 teachers in that same year. Many schools are run jointly by the state and religious bodies. Education is free at primary and secondary levels and compulsory for seven years. Elementary education lasts for seven years, followed by five years of secondary education.

At the post-secondary level, government technical vocational schools and teachers colleges are free for qualified students. There are four small, government-run technical colleges, five teachers colleges, and two polytechnic institutes. The University of the West Indies has a faculty of engineering, arts, and agriculture at its Trinidad campus. John F. Kennedy College, a liberal arts school outside Port-of-Spain built with a US$30-million grant from the Agency for International Development (AID), has teaching facilities for about 600 students. The Trinidad and Tobago Hotel School offers courses for the hotel, catering, and travel industries. The Eastern Caribbean Institute of Agriculture and Forestry is located in St. Augustine. In 1997, 6,007 students were estimated to be enrolled at the universities and equivalent institutions.

⁴⁴LIBRARIES AND MUSEUMS

The National Library of Trinidad and Tobago, with 442,000 volumes, and the Port-of-Spain Public Library, with 70,000 volumes, are both in Port-of-Spain. In San Fernando, the Carnegie Free Library functions as regional headquarters for rural library services to the south. The University of the West Indies main library in St. Augustine has more than 395,000 volumes. The National Museum and Art Gallery is located in Port-of-Spain, as is the Royal Victoria Institute Museum (1892), a general museum featuring local flora and fauna, crafts of the indigenous people, and a sampling of moon dust.

⁴⁵MEDIA

Postal and internal telegraph services throughout the islands are operated by the government. As of 1995, there were 192,500 main telephone lines. Commercial cable communication and radiotelephone services are maintained between Trinidad and all major countries of the world. Radio broadcasting is provided by the National Broadcasting Service (public) and the Trinidad Broadcasting Co., a subsidiary of Rediffusion International of London. Founded in 1962 and state-owned since 1969, the Trinidad and Tobago Television Service emphasizes school and adult-education programs. There were one AM and 10 FM radio stations and four TV stations as of 1999. In 1997, there were 332 television sets, 517 radios, and 14 mobile phones in use per 1,000 population.

There are three daily newspapers. The *Trinidad Guardian,* a morning and Sunday paper, had an average daily circulation of 46,700 in 1999. The *Daily Express,* published daily and Sunday, had a daily circulation of 51,000. *Newsday,* also published daily and Sunday, had a daily circulation of 25,000.

Freedom of the press is both constitutionally guaranteed and respected in practice.

As of 1996, there were almost 25,000 personal computers. There were 12 Internet hosts per 1,000 population in Trinidad and Tobago.

⁴⁶ORGANIZATIONS

Producers of agricultural crops for export are organized into associations for solving common problems, as well as for social purposes. Among these are the Cocoa Planters Association, Cooperative Citrus Growers Association, and Sugar Manufacturers Association. Nonagricultural associations are many and varied and include the Law Society, Medical Board, Petroleum Association, Shipping Association, and Trinidad Chamber of Commerce.

⁴⁷TOURISM, TRAVEL, AND RECREATION

The government offers fiscal and other incentives for the development of hotels and other tourist facilities. As of 1997, hotels and similar establishments on the islands had a total of 3,652 rooms with a 49% occupancy rate. Tourist arrivals that year totaled 324,293 and tourism revenues reached US$193 million.

Outstanding tourist attractions include the mountainous areas, beaches, and reefs on both islands. Entertainment includes calypso and steel band music, both of which originated in Trinidad. Festive events include Carnival, held annually on the two days before Ash Wednesday; the Muslim festival of Hosein, which begins 10 days after the new moon in the month of Muharram; and the Hindu festival of lights, Dewali, which occurs in October or November. Cricket and football (soccer) are the most popular sports.

According to 1999 UN estimates, the cost of staying in Trinidad is approximately US$158 per day. Tobago daily costs are seasonal, averaging between US$148 and US$196.

⁴⁸FAMOUS TRINIDADIANS AND TOBAGO-NIANS

Eric Eustace Williams (1911–81), the main political figure of his time and the leader of Trinidad and Tobago's major political party, was instrumental in his country's achievement of independence in 1962; he was prime minister from 1961 until his death. His successor was George Michael Chambers (b.1928). A.N.R. Robinson (b.1926) became prime minister in 1986. Notable writers include Samuel Selvon (b.1923) and V.S. (Vidiadhur Surajprasad) Naipaul (b.1932).

⁴⁹DEPENDENCIES

Trinidad and Tobago has no territories or colonies.

⁵⁰BIBLIOGRAPHY

Bereton, Bridget. *A History of Modern Trinidad.* Portsmouth, N.H.: Heinemann Educational Books, 1981.

Hintzen, Percy C. *The Costs of Regime Survival: Racial Mobilization, Elite Domination, and Control of the State in Guyana and Trinidad.* New York: Cambridge University Press, 1989.

John, A. Meredith. *The Plantation Slaves of Trinidad, 1783–1816: A Mathematical and Demographic Enquiry.* New York: Cambridge University Press, 1988.

Magid, Alvin. *Urban Nationalism: A Study of Political Development in Trinidad.* Gainesville: University of Florida Press, 1988.

Oxaal, Iva. *Black Intellectuals and the Dilemmas of Race and Class in Trinidad.* Cambridge, Mass.: Schenkman, 1982.

Reddock, Rhoda. *Women, Labour & Politics in Trinidad & Tobago: A History.* London: Zed Books, 1994.

Singh, Chaitram. *Multinationals, the State, and the Management of Economic Nationalism: The Case of Trinidad.* New York: Praeger, 1989.

Stuempfle, Stephen. *The Steelband Movement: The Forging of a National Art in Trinidad an Tobago.* Philadelphia, Pa.: University of Pennsylvania Press, 1995.

Winer, Lise. *Trinidad and Tobago.* Philadelphia, Pa.: J. Benjamins, 1993.

Yelvington, Kevin A. (ed.). *Trinidad Ethnicity.* Knoxville: University of Tennessee Press, 1993.

BERMUDA

Bermuda is a colony consisting of some 300 coral islands (20 of them inhabited), situated in the Atlantic Ocean, 933 km (580 mi) east of Cape Hatteras (US) at 32°19′N and 64°35′W. Their total area is about 54 sq km (21 sq mi). The US leases a 5.8-sq-km (2.2-sq-mi) area of land reclaimed from the sea for military purposes. The largest island, Bermuda (sometimes called Main) Island, is about 23 km (14 mi) long and has an average width of 1.6 km (1 mi). The islands are mostly flat and rocky, with luxuriant semitropical vegetation. Because Bermuda lies in the Gulf Stream, the climate is generally mild and humid, with a mean annual temperature of 21°C (70°F) and average rainfall of 147 cm (48 in). The resident civilian population in mid-1999 was 62,472, of which about 61% was black and 39% white (mainly of English or Portuguese descent) and other.

Most of the 240 km (149 mi) of roads are surfaced. Public transportation is largely by bus. Hamilton, the capital, has a deepwater harbor. Kindley Field, near St. George, the former capital, is Bermuda's international airport.

The oldest British colony, the islands were uninhabited when discovered in 1503 by the Spaniard Juan de Bermúdez. Bermuda was first settled by a group of British colonists under Sir George Somers, who were wrecked there while en route to Virginia in 1609. Bermuda was acquired from a chartered company by the crown in 1684. Under the 1968 constitution, the governor, representing the sovereign, is advised by a cabinet of legislators appointed at the recommendation of the prime minister. The bicameral legislature consists of an appointed Senate of 11 members and a 40-member House of Assembly (elected by universal suffrage from 20 electoral districts). The Bermuda dollar of 100 cents is equal in value to the US dollar, which circulates freely.

Tourism is the islands' largest employer, providing about half the total national income and two-thirds of foreign exchange. Bermuda does not impose income or corporate taxes which has led to a substantial offshore financial sector. By the end of 1994, 8,200 international companies were registered in Bermuda, contributing $500 million to the economy and employing 2,214 people. A failed referendum on independence in late 1995 was partially attributed to concerns that independence would drive away foreign firms. Also important to the economy are goods and services supplied to the UK and US armed forces stationed in Bermuda. Light industries produce pharmaceuticals and essences, brass electrical contacts, and cut flowers for export. Per capita GDP in 1997 was $30,000, among the highest in the world. In August 1995, Hurricane Felix inflicted $2.5 million in damages to Bermuda.

The chief imports are food, textiles, furniture, motor vehicles, and fuel. In 1996, import partners were the US (73%), the UK (5%), and Canada (4%); export partners were Netherlands (50%), Brazil (13%), and Canada (6%). Visible trade balances are unfavorable, although trade in invisibles, primarily tourism and international business, more than offsets the commodity trade deficit. Imports of timber alone in 1995 amounted to over $9 million. Exports in 1997 were estimated at $57 million; imports, $617 million. There is a free port at Ireland Island.

Medical services are private. King Edward VII Hospital, with 233 beds, receives government support. Education is compulsory between the ages of 5 and 16. There are 18 primary and 14 secondary schools, 12 government preschools, and 5 private schools. A major education program between 1996 and 2002 will add five middle schools and two high schools. Bermuda College provides post-secondary vocational courses and an associate degree program.

In 1993 there were over 54,000 telephones on the island. The Bermuda Broadcasting Co., Ltd., runs the three commercial television stations and five of the six radio stations. There is one daily newspaper, the *Royal Gazette*.

BRITISH ANTARCTIC TERRITORY

Created on 3 March 1962 from former Falkland Islands dependencies, the British Antarctic Territory (BAT) lies south of 60°S and between 20° and 80°W, and consists of the South Shetlands, 4,662 sq km (1,800 sq mi); the South Orkneys, 622 sq km (240 sq mi); and Graham Land on the Antarctic continent. The territory is governed by a UK-appointed high commissioner, who also serves as governor of the Falklands. Three British Antarctic Survey stations are inhabited year-round: Signy on the South Orkneys, Rothera on Adelaide Island, and Halley V on moving ice along the Caird coast. Their personnel varies from 50 in the winter to 150 during the summer. The bases of 12 other Antarctic Treaty nations lie within the BAT claim on the Antarctic continent, with an estimated population of 1,000 in winter to 2,500 in the summer.

BRITISH VIRGIN ISLANDS

The British Virgin Islands consist of some 50 Caribbean islands and islets, totaling 153 sq km (59 sq mi), at about 18°25′N and 64°30′W. Until 1 July 1956, they were administered as part of the Leeward Islands. The mid-1996 population was 13,195, almost 90% of African descent. About 40% of the population consists of immigrants from St. Kitts and Nevis or from St. Vincent and the Grenadines. Road Town (population about 2,500 in 1992) on the island of Tortola is the capital. The climate is pleasantly subtropical. At least 164.5 km (99 mi) of roads are motorable. There are several airstrips on the islands.

Under the constitution of 1968, as revised in 1977, the government is headed by a British-appointed administrator, who is assisted by an Executive Council and a Legislative Council of 13 members.

The economy is interdependent with that of the US Virgin Islands, which lie to the west. The US dollar is the legal currency. Livestock raising, farming, and fishing are the principal economic activities. Light industries include distilleries for alcoholic beverages, a concrete block factory, boat building, and handicrafts. Offshore financial services have also become a prominent part of the economy; in 1994 there were 130,000 company registrations, and many companies have recently moved to the islands from Panama. Imports come predominantly from the US Virgin Islands, Puerto Rico, or the US and include foodstuffs, apparel, cotton piece goods, timber, and machinery. The overwhelmingly adverse balance of trade is offset by remittances from migrant workers and an expanding tourist industry. Tourism accounts for about 45% of the islands' annual income; in 1993 there were an estimated 395,000 visitors. Most of the tourists were from the US mainland, Puerto Rico, and Canada. Principal export partners include the Virgin Islands (US), Puerto Rico, and the US. Per capita GDP was $10,000 in 1997.

The infant mortality rate—22.17 per 1,000 live births in 1999—has been reduced from 78.9 per 1,000 live births in 1960. In 1990 there were 1,056 inhabitants per physician and 246 per hospital bed.

Primary education is provided by the state between the ages of 5 and 15 and compulsory up to the age of 13. In 1994/95 there were 20 primary schools with 2,625 students. There are also and 3 public and private high schools in the British Virgin Islands. Scholarships are available for students to attend a university in the Caribbean, the US, or the UK. The sole newspaper, the *Island Sun*, is published weekly.

CAYMAN ISLANDS

The three low-lying Cayman Islands—Grand Cayman, Little Cayman, and Cayman Brac, with a total area of 262 sq km (101 sq mi)—are situated between 79°44′ and 81°27′w and 19°15′ and 19°45′n, about 290 km (180 mi) wnw of Jamaica, of which they were formerly a dependency. Grand Cayman, flat, rockbound, and protected by coral reefs, is about 32 km (20 mi) long and 6 to 11 km (4–7 mi) broad; George Town, on Grand Cayman, is the capital and chief town. The other two islands are about 145 km (90 mi) to the ne. The mid-1999 population was estimated at 39,335, about 90% of whom resided on Grand Cayman. Cayman Airways is the main air carrier; the principal international airport is on Grand Cayman.

The islands were discovered in 1503 by Columbus, who named them Las Tortugas, from the turtles with which the surrounding seas abound. They were never occupied by Spaniards and were colonized from Jamaica by the British. They were a dependency of Jamaica until 1959, but severed all constitutional links with Jamaica when the latter became independent in 1962.

The 1972 constitution empowers the crown-appointed governor to make laws with the advice and consent of the Legislative Assembly. The Executive Council consists of 4 members chosen by the Assembly from among its 12 elected members, and 3 Assembly members appointed to the Council by the governor. The Legislative Assembly includes 3 ex officio members, 12 elected members, and the governor. Elections, in which all adult British residents may vote, are held every three years. Local administration is in the hands of justices of the peace and vestrymen.

The Cayman Islands dollar (ci$) is linked to the US dollar at the rate of ci$1 = us$1.20 (or us$1 = ci$0.835). Customs, duties, license and company fees, and postage and stamp taxes are the principal source of government revenue. The absence of taxes on income, capital gains, real estate, and inheritances attracts overseas investors to the region; international financial services and tourism have become principal sectors of the economy. At the end of 1993, 380 insurance licenses were registered in the Caymans, and 537 bank and trust companies were represented. Tourism has grown rapidly: in 1993, 892,000 people visited the Caymans. Tourism accounts for about 70% of GDP and 75% of foreign exchange earnings. Although the soil is fertile and there is some farming, the agricultural sector remains small; the catching of turtles, sharks, and sponges also provides some employment. The total fish catch in 1994 was 710 tons, and fisheries exports were valued at $13.7 million that year. In 1996, total exports were valued at $2.65 million, while imports amounted to $379.4 million. Remittances from Caymanian seamen serving on foreign ships contribute to the economy as well. The government-owned

Cayman Turtle Farm, unique in the world, produces turtle meat for local consumption; exports have waned in recent years due to restrictions by the Convention on International Trade of Endangered Species of Wild Fauna and Flora.

The islands have 2 hospitals with a total 70 beds, 10 of them for extended care. Education is compulsory between the ages of 4 and 16, and provided cost-free for Caymanians. There are also some private church schools.

FALKLAND ISLANDS

The Falkland Islands (Islas Malvinas), a British crown colony in the South Atlantic, lie some 772 km (480 mi) northeast of Cape Horn, between 51° and 53°s and 57° and 62°w, and have an area of 12,173 sq km (4,700 sq mi). The two main islands, East Falkland and West Falkland, consist chiefly of hilly moorlands. The population (estimated at 2,758 in mid-1999) is almost exclusively of British origin. Stanley, on East Falkland, the capital and only town, has about 1,000 inhabitants. There are no railways and few surfaced roads beyond the vicinity of Stanley. Shipping service to and from the islands is slight. There is internal air service but no international service.

The Falklands were sighted in 1592 by John Davis, an English navigator. The French founded the first colony on East Falkland, in 1764, transferring it two years later to Spain, which renamed it Soledad. The British took possession of West Falkland in 1765. Both islands were eventually abandoned. In 1820, Argentina (then the United Provinces of La Plata) colonized East Falkland. British troops occupied the islands in 1832–33, but Argentina has continued to dispute Britain's claim to the Falklands. On 2 April 1982, Argentine troops invaded the islands, precipitating a conflict with the British that cost over 1,000 lives. The UK recaptured the islands on 14 June, and some 4,300 British soldiers remain in the Falklands following the conflict.

Under a new constitution which came into effect in October 1985, the colony is administered by an appointed governor, with an Executive Council of 5 members: 3 chosen by the 10-member Legislative Council, and 2 ex officio members, the chief executive and the financial secretary. The currency unit is the Falkland Island Pound (f£), which is equal to the pound sterling.

There is no commercial agriculture. Most households in Stanley and the outlying areas grow their own vegetables. Sheep farming, the traditional industry, is directed primarily to the production of wool, hides, and skins, and the manufacture of tallow. All land is divided into large sheep farms; there were some 717,000 sheep on the islands in 1995. Wool production (greasy) that year was 2,414 tons. Most commodities needed by the territory and its dependencies are imported. In 1987, the government began selling fishing licenses to foreign trawlers operating within the islands' exclusive economic zone. These licenses generate about $40 million per year, and support the local health, education, and welfare system. There are also substantial oil reserves offshore. In 1995, an agreement between Argentina and the UK helped to soften the ongoing tensions regarding licensing and sovereignty that would inhibit foreign interest in developing the potential oil reserves. Exports, (mostly wool), were valued at us$7.6 million in 1995. Trade is principally with the UK.

All medical services are public. The islands has three physicians. The only civilian hospital was destroyed by fire in 1984; temporary facilities were used, with support from the British Military Hospital, while a replacement was constructed. Education is free and compulsory for children from 5 to 15 years of age. Students unable to attend the schools in Stanley are taught by traveling teachers and by radio and correspondence. In 1994, 34 students were studying abroad.

Dependencies include South Georgia and the South Sandwich Islands, some 1,300 km (800 mi) e of the Falklands, with an area

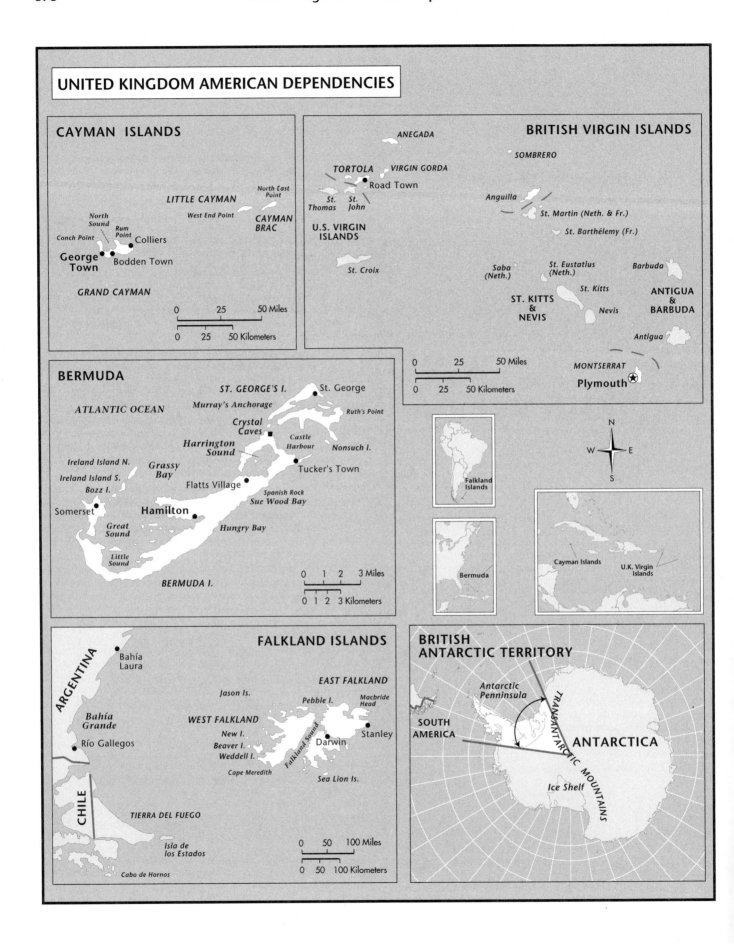

UNITED KINGDOM AMERICAN DEPENDENCIES

CAYMAN ISLANDS

LITTLE CAYMAN
North East Point
West End Point
CAYMAN BRAC
North Sound
Rum Point
Conch Point
Colliers
George Town
Bodden Town
GRAND CAYMAN

0   25   50 Miles
0   25   50 Kilometers

BRITISH VIRGIN ISLANDS

ANEGADA
SOMBRERO
TORTOLA   VIRGIN GORDA
Road Town
St. Thomas   St. John
U.S. VIRGIN ISLANDS
Anguilla
St. Martin (Neth. & Fr.)
St. Barthélemy (Fr.)
St. Croix
Saba (Neth.)
St. Eustatius (Neth.)
Barbuda
St. Kitts
ST. KITTS & NEVIS
Nevis
ANTIGUA & BARBUDA
Antigua
MONTSERRAT
Plymouth ⊛

0   25   50 Miles
0   25   50 Kilometers

BERMUDA

ST. GEORGE'S I.   St. George
ATLANTIC OCEAN
Murray's Anchorage
Ruth's Point
Crystal Caves
Castle Harbour
Harrington Sound
Nonsuch I.
Ireland Island N.
Grassy Bay
Ireland Island S.
Bozz I.
Flatts Village
Tucker's Town
Somerset
Spanish Rock
Sue Wood Bay
Hamilton
Great Sound
Hungry Bay
Little Sound
BERMUDA I.

0   1   2   3 Miles
0   1   2   3 Kilometers

Falkland Islands

Bermuda

Cayman Islands   U.K. Virgin Islands

N
W   E
S

FALKLAND ISLANDS

ARGENTINA
Bahía Laura
EAST FALKLAND
Jason Is.
Pebble I.
Macbride Head
Bahía Grande
WEST FALKLAND
New I.
Beaver I.
Stanley
Río Gallegos
Weddell I.
Darwin
Cape Meredith
Falkland Sound
CHILE
Sea Lion Is.
TIERRA DEL FUEGO
Isla de los Estados
Cabo de Hornos

0   50   100 Miles
0   50   100 Kilometers

BRITISH ANTARCTIC TERRITORY

Antarctic Peninnsula
SOUTH AMERICA
TRANSANTARCTIC MOUNTAINS
ANTARCTICA
Ice Shelf

of 4,092 sq km (1,580 sq mi). Whaling and sealing are the main industries.

LEEWARD ISLANDS

The Leeward Islands, part of the Lesser Antilles island chain, lie east and south of Puerto Rico and north of the Windward group. Of the four territorial units that constitute the Leeward Islands, two—Antigua and Barbuda, and St. Kitts and Nevis—are independent nations covered elsewhere in this volume. The other two—Anguilla and Montserrat—retained the status of UK dependencies as of early 1988.

ANGUILLA

Anguilla, the most northerly of the Leeward chain, lies at approximately 18°N and 63°W, and has an area of 90 sq km (35 sq mi). The island is long, flat, dry, and covered with scrub; its rolling hills reach a peak elevation of 65 m (213 ft) above sea level. The average annual temperature is 27°C (81°F), with July–October being the hottest period and December–February the coolest. Rainfall averages 89 cm (35 in) a year, but there is considerable variation both from season to season and from year to year. The hurricane season, marked by occasional thunderstorms and sudden squalls, lasts from July to October.

The population was estimated at 11,510 in mid-1999. Most Anguillans are of African descent, with an admixture of European (especially Irish) ancestry. The population is overwhelmingly Christian: Anglicans and Methodists predominate, but there are also Seventh-Day Adventist, Baptist, Roman Catholic, and Church of God congregations. English is the official language, spoken in a distinctive island patois. Anguilla has no official capital, but The Valley serves as an administrative center. Anguilla has about 105 km (65 mi) of roads, 65 km (41 mi) of them paved. Road Bay is the main harbor, and there is daily ferry service between Blowing Point and the French-Dutch island of St. Martin (Sint Maarten), about 8 km (5 mi) away. Air service to and from Wallblake Airport is provided by the privately owned Air Anguilla and two other interisland airways.

Although sighted by Columbus in 1496, Anguilla was not settled by Europeans until 1650, when British colonists arrived from St. Kitts. From 1671, Anguilla was governed as part of the Leeward Islands, and between 1871 and 1956 the island formed (with St. Kitts and, from 1882, Nevis) part of the Leeward Islands Federation. All the Leeward Islands were consolidated into a single territory in 1956 and, as such, were incorporated into the Federation of the West Indies two years later. With the breakup of the West Indies Federation in 1962, St. Kitts–Nevis–Anguilla reverted to colonial status. On 17 February 1967, St. Kitts–Nevis–Anguilla acquired self-government within the newly formed West Indies Associated States. After Anguilla declared its independence of the Associated States in 1969, some 300 British paratroopers temporarily took command of the island. On 10 February 1976, the UK recognized Anguilla's status as a dependency distinct from St. Kitts and Nevis, which achieved independence in 1983.

Under the Anguilla Constitution Order of 1982, the crown is represented by a governor, who presides over an appointed Executive Council and an elected House of Assembly. The Executive Council consists of the chief minister, three other ministers selected by the governor from among the members of the House of Assembly, and the attorney general and permanent secretary for finance, who serve ex officio both on the council and in the legislature. The governor also appoints two members of the House of Assembly, the remaining seven being elected to five-year terms by universal adult suffrage. In the election of March 1984, the Anguilla People's Party took two seats while the Anguilla National Alliance won four. Justice is administered by a magistrate's court, a Court of Appeal, and a High Court, whose sitting judge is provided by the Eastern Caribbean Supreme Court on St. Lucia.

The mainstays of the economy have traditionally been animal husbandry, salt production, fishing, and boat building, but tourism and offshore banking have played an increasingly important role in recent years. The principal crops are pigeon peas, corn, and sweet potatoes; sheep, goats, hogs, cattle, and poultry are raised. Salt is extracted by evaporation from two briny ponds, and live lobsters are exported to neighboring islands. Tourism, construction, and a developing offshore banking sector have become the most prominent economic sectors in recent years. The East Caribbean dollar (EC$) is used; EC$1 = US$0.3704 (or US$1 = EC$2.70). The GDP was estimated at $81 million in 1997, or $7,300 per capita. The economy, especially tourism, suffered damage from Hurricane Luis in 1995.

Education is provided by the state and is compulsory between the ages of 5 and 14 years. The government maintains six primary schools and one secondary school; total school enrollment exceeds 2,200. A 36-bed cottage hospital offers limited services. International telephone, telegraph, and telex services are available, and the government-run Radio Anguilla is on the air for more than 10 hours a day; a privately owned religious station, Caribbean Beacon Radio, operates from The Valley.

Dependencies of Anguilla include numerous offshore islets and cays, as well as Sombrero Island (5 sq km/2 sq mi), about 56 km (35 mi) to the northwest.

MONTSERRAT

Situated at 16°45′N and 62°10′W, Montserrat has an area of 103 sq km (40 sq mi). The island, which lies between Nevis and Guadeloupe, about 43 km (27 mi) southeast of Antigua, has a mountainous terrain, with two peaks rising higher than 900 m (3,000 ft). Montserrat is wholly volcanic in origin, and there are seven active volcanoes. Mean temperatures range from a minimum of 23°C (73°F) to a maximum of 31°C (88°F); June–November, the hurricane season, is the warmest time of the year, and December–March is the coolest. There is no clearly defined rainy season, although rainfall tends to be more abundant during the second half of the year; the annual average is 157 cm (62 in).

In mid-1999, an estimated 12,853 people lived on the island, of whom 3,500 lived in Plymouth, the capital and sole port. The threat of a volcanic eruption first started in 1995. Since then, the British government has developed three contingency plans concerning the population, depending on the amount of the volcano's destruction: moving the southern population to the north; total evacuation to neighboring islands (Antigua and Barbuda, and Guadeloupe); and permanent settlement elsewhere should the island become uninhabitable. When destructive pyroclastic lava flows came in mid-1997, much of Montserrat's population was evacuated to the northern tip of the island, and about half of the population left the island.

Most residents of Montserrat are of African ancestry. Anglicans, Methodists, Roman Catholics, and Pentecostals make up the great majority of the population. English, the official language, is spoken in an island patois. Montserrat has about 269 km (168 mi) of main surfaced roads. Blackburne Airport, about 15 km (9 mi) from the capital, has a surfaced runway of 1,030 m (3,380 ft), which opened to traffic in 1967. Montserrat Aviation Services, in cooperation with Leeward Islands Air Transport (LIAT), maintains regular flights to and from Antigua, Nevis, and St. Kitts.

Christopher Columbus, who sighted the island in November 1493, gave it the name Montserrat because its rugged terrain reminded him of the site of the Abbey of Montserrat in the Spanish highlands near Barcelona. English and Irish colonists from St. Kitts settled on the island in 1632, and the first African slaves arrived 32 years later. Throughout the 18th century, the British and French warred for possession of Montserrat, which was finally confirmed as a British possession by the Treaty of Versailles (1783). By the early 19th century, Montserrat had a plantation economy, but the abolition of slavery in 1834, the elimination of the apprentice system, the declining market for sugar, and a series of natural disasters brought the downfall of the sugar estates. In the mid-19th century, Joseph Sturge of Birmingham, England, organized a company that bought up the abandoned estates, planted them with limes (a product for which Montserrat is still famous), and sold plots of land to small farmers. From 1871 to 1956, Montserrat formed part of the Federation of the Leeward Islands, and after two years as a separate colony it became part of the Federation of the West Indies (1958–62). Since the breakup of the Federation, Montserrat has been separately administered, under a constitution effective 1 January 1960.

The crown is represented by an appointed governor, who presides over an Executive Council structured like that of Anguilla. There is also a Legislative Council which, like Anguilla's, includes two appointed and two ex officio members. The seven elected members of the legislature are chosen from single-member constituencies by universal adult suffrage at age 18. The legislators serve terms of up to five years. In elections held in November 1978, the People's Liberation Movement, headed by John Osborne, swept all seven elective seats; the party was returned to power in the February 1983 general election, though with a reduced majority of five seats, two having been captured by the Progressive Democratic Party. Montserrat's judicial system consists of a magistrate's court and a Court of Summary Jurisdiction; appeals are to the Eastern Caribbean Supreme Court on St. Lucia.

Tourism accounts for about one-fourth of the annual GDP; the island had some 17,000 visitors in 1992. Important crops include hot peppers (mostly for export), limes and other orchard fruits, tomatoes, and vegetables. Exports of live cattle and leather are significant, as are such light industrial exports as plastic bags, cotton garments, and electronic parts. Montserrat uses the East Caribbean dollar. In 1997, GDP was US$36 million. Exports that year were US$8.2 million; imports, chiefly of industrial goods, foodstuffs, and mineral fuels, totaled some US$26.1 million. Governmental revenues in 1996 were US$31.4 million; expenditures, US$31.6 million. Effective corporate income tax rates are 20–40%; the maximum personal income tax rate is 30%. A property tax is also levied.

The principal health facility is a 67-bed general hospital maintained by the government; provisions for social welfare include a family planning association and an old people's welfare association. Free dental care is provided by the government for all schoolchildren, elderly persons, and expectant or nursing mothers. Education is free and compulsory up to age 14. The government maintains 15 schools: 1 infant school (ages 5–7), 9 primary schools (ages 5–12), 2 all-age schools (ages 5–15), and 3 secondary schools (ages 10–19). As of 1997, radio service was provided by 8 AM and 4 FM stations, including the government-owned Radio Montserrat, and Radio Antilles and Gem; one television service is provided by relay from elsewhere in the Caribbean and transmitted locally by Antilles Television and cable stations. There are two weekly newspapers, the *Montserrat Times* and the *Montserrat Reporter*.

TURKS AND CAICOS ISLANDS

Archaeological expeditions have found Arawak implements and utensils on Turks and Caicos Islands. When Juan Ponce de León arrived in 1512, Lucayan Indians had come to inhabit the islands. There is some speculation that Columbus may have made his landfall on Grand Turk or East Caicos on his first voyage of

discovery in 1492. The first settlements were by Bermudians, who established solar salt pans in the 1670s. Bahamian, Bermudan, Spanish, French, and British rivalry over the prospering salt trade resulted in numerous invasions and evictions through the first half of the 18th century. In 1787, Loyalists fleeing the American Revolution established settlements and cotton and sisal plantations on several of the larger Caicos Islands. Ten years later, the islands came under the jurisdiction of the Bahamas colonial government. Slavery was abolished in 1834. In 1848, the Turks and Caicos islanders were granted a charter of separation from the Bahamas after they complained of Bahamian taxes on their salt industry.

From 1848 to 1873, the islands were largely self-governing, under the supervision of the governor of Jamaica. Following the decline of the salt industry, the islands became a Jamaican dependency until 1958, when they joined the Federation of the West Indies. When the federation dissolved and Jamaica achieved independence in 1962, Turks and Caicos became a crown colony administered by the British Colonial Office and a local council of elected and appointed members. In 1965, the governor of the Bahamas was also appointed governor of Turks and Caicos, but with the advent of Bahamian independence in 1973, a separate governor was appointed. A new constitution maintaining the status of crown colony and providing for ministerial government was introduced in September 1976. Although independence for Turks and Caicos in 1982 had been agreed upon in principle in 1979, a change in government brought a reversal in policy. The islands are still a crown colony.

The islands were shaken by scandals in the mid-1980s. In March 1985, Chief Minister Norman B. Saunders and two other ministers were arrested in Florida on drug charges and later convicted and sentenced to prison. In July 1986, a commission of inquiry found that Chief Minister Nathaniel Francis and two other ministers had been guilty of "unconstitutional behavior, political discrimination, and administrative malpractice." The governor thereupon ended ministerial government in July 1986 and, with four members of the former Executive Council, formed an Advisory Council to govern until new elections. The islands have returned to their previous form of government, and remain a dependent territory of the UK.

Situated in the Atlantic Ocean SE of the Bahamas, E of Cuba, and N of Hispaniola, the Turks and Caicos Islands consist of two island groups separated by the Turks Island Passage, 35 km (22 mi) across and about 2,100 m (7,000 ft) deep. The Turks group comprises two inhabited islands, Grand Turk and Salt Cay, six uninhabited cays, and numerous rocks surrounded by a roughly triangular reef bank. The Caicos group encompasses six principal islands (North Caicos, Middle Caicos, East Caicos, South Caicos, West Caicos, and Providenciales), plus numerous rocky islets, all surrounded by the Caicos Bank, a triangular shoal. The total land area of the Turks and Caicos Islands is 430 sq km (166 sq mi), with extensions of about 120 km (75 mi) E–W and 80 km (50 mi) N–S. Comparatively, the area occupied by the Turks and Caicos Islands is slightly less than 2.5 times the size of Washington, D.C. The Turks and Caicos Islands have a coastline length of 389 km (242 mi). The capital city, Grand Turk, is in the Turks Islands.

The Turks Islands are low and flat, and surrounded by reefs, sunken coral heads, and boilers. The land mass is limestone, well weathered with pockets of soil; the coastlines are indented with shallow creeks and mangrove swamps. The Caicos Bank is a triangular shoal about 93 km (58 mi) long on its northern side and 90 km (56 mi) long on its eastern and western sides. The highest elevation is only 50 m (163 ft) above sea level on Providenciales. On the north coast of Middle Caicos (which is also known as Grand Caicos) are limestone cave formations.

Days are sunny and dry and nights are cool and clear throughout the year. Temperatures on the islands range from a low of 16°C (61°F) to a high of 32°C (90°F), with the hottest period generally occurring between April and November. There are almost constant tradewinds from the east. Rainfall averages 53 cm (21 in) per year, and hurricanes are a frequent occurrence. Major hurricanes struck the islands in 1866, 1873, 1888, 1908, 1926, 1928, 1945, 1960, and 1985.

The ground cover is scrubby and stunted tropical vegetation, with sea oats, mangrove, casuarina, and palmetto. There is little natural wildlife other than birds and butterflies. West Caicos island is especially noted as a sanctuary for birds, and Penniston, Gibb, and Round cays are known for their extensive varieties of butterflies. Spiny lobster, conch, clams, bonefish, snapper, grouper, and turtle are plentiful.

Fresh water is a scarce commodity, and most islanders rely on private cisterns. Underground water is present on North and Middle Caicos, but surface water collected in ponds after rainfall becomes brackish. There have been some complaints of actual or potential ecological damage resulting from the expansion of tourist facilities on Providenciales. The government has identified the absence of environmental education as a potential problem for the preservation of the nation's natural heritage in the future. It has also introduced the National Physical Development Plan for the period from 1987 to 1997, emphasizing the need for preservation of the nation's resources. By 1992, the government had developed legislation that would create 12 national parks, 8 nature reserves, 5 sanctuaries, and 9 historic sites.

The population of the Turks and Caicos Islands in 2000 was estimated at 17,000. In the 1990s, most people were living on Grand Turk, South Caicos, and North Caicos islands. The projected population for the year 2005 is 19,000, assuming a crude birthrate of 13 per 1,000 population and a death rate of 5. The 1996 population density was 33 per sq km (86 per sq mi).

It was estimated that 72% of the population lived in urban areas in 2000. The capital, Grand Turk, had a 2000 population estimated at 4,000. Cockburn Harbour is the major town on South Caicos.

About 90% of the population is of black African descent, the remainder being of mixed, European, or North American origin. The official and universal language of the Turks and Caicos Islands is English, interspersed with a number of local colloquialisms. Most islanders are Christian; the main denominations are Baptist (41.2%), Methodist (18.9%), and Anglican (18.3%). Other Protestant groups and the Roman Catholic Church are also represented.

There are about 121 km (75 mi) of roads on the islands. The main roads on Grand Turk and South Caicos are paved. Some secondary roads are surfaced with scale from the salinas (salt ponds); otherwise, the roads are merely dirt and sand tracks.

The main seaports are at Grand Turk, Cockburn Harbour on South Caicos, Providenciales, and Salt Cay. An offshore registry program with the UK enables British merchant ships to register with the Turks and Caicos Islands in order to cut crew costs while enabling the vessels to fly the Red Ensign of the UK. There are seven airports and four paved runways of more than 1,220 m (4,000 ft) on Grand Turk, South Caicos, and Providenciales; in addition, there are three small unpaved landing strips among the other inhabited islands.

Tourism and lobster fishing have replaced salt raking as the main economic activity of the islands, which are very poor. Fishing and subsistence farming are the principal occupations; underemployment and unemployment are estimated at over 40%. Important sources of income include tourism and offshore financial services. The closing of the last US military base in 1983

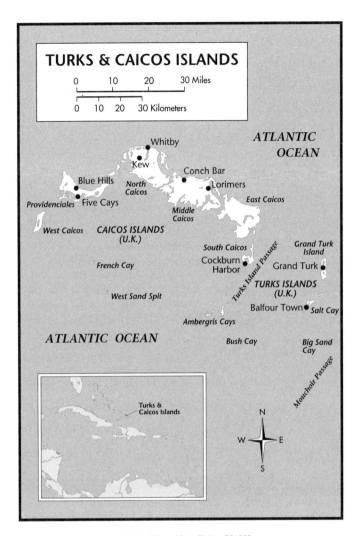

TURKS & CAICOS ISLANDS

LOCATION: 21° to 22°N; 71° to 72°30′W.

resulted in the loss of rental payments that accounted for 10% of government revenue. Most of the retail trade on the islands consist of imported goods. Tourism has been boosted by the advent of service by American Airlines, and new hotel, resort and casino openings. Visitors are attracted by the beautiful beaches and by opportunities for snorkeling, diving, and sport fishing. The windmills and salinas on Salt Cay and the 19th-century architecture on Grand Turk, along with horse carriages, provide a quaint setting.

Most food for domestic consumption is imported; there is some subsistence farming—mainly corn, cassava, citrus, and beans—on the Caicos Islands. Major sources of government revenue include fees from offshore financial activities and customs receipts as the Islands rely on imports for nearly all consumption and capital goods.

A modern cottage hospital (30 beds) and an outpatient and dental clinic are located on Grand Turk, and there are 11 outpatient and dental clinics on South, Middle, and North Caicos, Providenciales, and Salt Cay. In 1992, there were 1.25 doctors per 1,000 people. The infant mortality rate was 21.11 deaths per live births in 1999, down from 25 per 1,000 live births in 1993.

UNITED STATES OF AMERICA

CAPITAL: Washington, D.C. (District of Columbia).

FLAG: The flag consists of 13 alternate stripes, 7 red and 6 white; these represent the 13 original colonies. Fifty 5-pointed white stars, representing the present number of states in the Union, are placed in 9 horizontal rows alternately of 6 and 5 against a blue field in the upper left corner of the flag.

ANTHEM: *The Star-Spangled Banner.*

MONETARY UNIT: The dollar ($) of 100 cents is a paper currency with a floating rate. There are coins of 1, 5, 10, 25, and 50 cents and 1 dollar, and notes of 1, 2, 5, 10, 20, 50, and 100 dollars. Although issuance of higher notes ceased in 1969, a limited number of notes of 500, 1,000, 5,000, and 10,000 dollars remain in circulation. A gold-colored 1 dollar coin featuring Sacagawea was introduced in 2000.

WEIGHTS AND MEASURES: The imperial system is in common use; however, the use of metrics in industry is increasing, and the metric system is taught in public schools throughout the US. Common avoirdupois units in use are the avoirdupois pound of 16 oz or 453.5924277 gm; the long ton of 2,240 lb or 35,840 oz; and the short ton, more commonly used, of 2,000 lb or 32,000 oz. (Unless otherwise indicated, all measures given in tons are in short tons.) Liquid measures: 1 gallon = 231 cu in = 4 quarts = 8 pints. Dry measures: 1 bushel = 4 pecks = 32 dry quarts = 64 dry pints. Linear measures: 1 ft = 12 in; 1 statute mi = 1,760 yd = 5,280 ft. Metric equivalent: 1 m = 39.37 in.

HOLIDAYS: New Year's Day, 1 January; Birthday of Martin Luther King, Jr., 3d Monday in January; Lincoln's Birthday, 12 February (only in the northern and western states); Washington's Birthday, 3d Monday in February; Memorial or Decoration Day, last Monday in May; Independence Day, 4 July; Labor Day, 1st Monday in September; Columbus Day, 2d Monday in October; Election Day, 1st Tuesday after the 1st Monday in November; Veterans or Armistice Day, 11 November; Thanksgiving Day, 4th Thursday in November; Christmas, 25 December.

TIME: Eastern, 7 AM = noon GMT; Central, 6 AM = noon GMT; Mountain, 5 AM = noon GMT; Pacific (includes the Alaska panhandle), 4 AM = noon GMT; Yukon, 3 AM = noon GMT; Alaska and Hawaii, 2 AM = noon GMT; western Alaska, 1 AM = noon GMT.

---

¹LOCATION, SIZE, AND EXTENT

Located in the Western Hemisphere on the continent of North America, the US is the fourth-largest country in the world. Its total area, including Alaska and Hawaii, is 9,372,607 sq km (3,618,773 sq mi). The conterminous US extends 4,662 km (2,897 mi) ENE–WSW and 4,583 km (2,848 mi) SSE–NNW. It is bordered on the N by Canada, on the E by the Atlantic Ocean, on the S by the Gulf of Mexico and Mexico, and on the W by the Pacific Ocean, with a total boundary length of 17,563 km (10,913 mi). Alaska, the 49th state, extends 3,639 km (2,261 mi) E–W and 2,185 km (1,358 mi) N–S. It is bounded on the N by the Arctic Ocean and Beaufort Sea, on the E by Canada, on the S by the Gulf of Alaska, Pacific Ocean and Bering Sea, and on the W by the Bering Sea, Bering Strait, Chukchi Sea, and Arctic Ocean, with a total boundary length of 13,161 km (8,178 mi). The 50th state, Hawaii, consists of islands in the Pacific Ocean extending 2,536 km (1,576 mi) N–S and 2,293 km (1,425 mi) E–W, with a general coastline of 1,207 km (750 mi).

²TOPOGRAPHY

Although the northern New England coast is rocky, along the rest of the eastern seaboard the Atlantic Coastal Plain rises gradually from the shoreline. Narrow in the north, the plain widens to about 320 km (200 mi) in the south and in Georgia merges with the Gulf Coastal Plain that borders the Gulf of Mexico and extends through Mexico as far as the Yucatán. West of the

Atlantic Coastal Plain is the Piedmont Plateau, bounded by the Appalachian Mountains. The Appalachians, which extend from southwest Maine into central Alabama—with special names in some areas—are old mountains, largely eroded away, with rounded contours and forested, as a rule, to the top. Few of their summits rise much above 1,100 m (3,500 ft), although the highest, Mt. Mitchell in North Carolina, reaches 2,037 m (6,684 ft).

Between the Appalachians and the Rocky Mountains, more than 1,600 km (1,000 mi) to the west, lies the vast interior plain of the US. Running south through the center of this plain and draining almost two-thirds of the area of the continental US is the Mississippi River. Waters starting from the source of the Missouri, the longest of its tributaries, travel almost 6,450 km (4,000 mi) to the Gulf of Mexico. The eastern reaches of the great interior plain are bounded on the north by the Great Lakes, which are thought to contain about half the world's total supply of fresh water. Under US jurisdiction are 57,441 sq km (22,178 sq mi) of Lake Michigan, 54,696 sq km (21,118 sq mi) of Lake Superior, 23,245 sq km (8,975 sq mi) of Lake Huron, 12,955 sq km (5,002 sq mi) of Lake Erie, and 7,855 sq km (3,033 sq mi) of Lake Ontario. The five lakes are now accessible to oceangoing vessels from the Atlantic via the St. Lawrence Seaway. The basins of the Great Lakes were formed by the glacial ice cap that moved down over large parts of North America some 25,000 years ago. The glaciers also determined the direction of flow of the Missouri

River and, it is believed, were responsible for carrying soil from what is now Canada down into the central agricultural basin of the US. The great interior plain consists of two major subregions: the fertile Central Plains, extending from the Appalachian highlands to a line drawn approximately 480 km (300 mi) west of the Mississippi, broken by the Ozark Plateau; and the more arid Great Plains, extending from that line to the foothills of the Rocky Mountains. Although they appear flat, the Great Plains rise gradually from about 460 m (1,500 ft) to more than 1,500 m (5,000 ft) at their western extremity.

The Continental Divide, the Atlantic-Pacific watershed, runs along the crest of the Rocky Mountains. The Rockies and the ranges to the west are parts of the great system of young, rugged mountains, shaped like a gigantic spinal column, that runs along western North, Central, and South America from Alaska to Tierra del Fuego, Chile. In the continental US, the series of western ranges, most of them paralleling the Pacific coast, are the Sierra Nevada, the Coast Ranges, the Cascade Range, and the Tehachapi and San Bernardino mountains. Between the Rockies and the Sierra Nevada–Cascade mountain barrier to the west lies the Great Basin, a group of vast arid plateaus containing most of the desert areas of the US, in the south eroded by deep canyons. The coastal plains along the Pacific are narrow, and in many places the mountains plunge directly into the sea. The most extensive lowland near the west coast is the Great Valley of California, lying between the Sierra Nevada and the Coast Ranges. There are 71 peaks in these western ranges of the continental US that rise to an altitude of 4,267 m (14,000 ft) or more, Mt. Whitney in California at 4,418 m (14,494 ft) being the highest. The greatest rivers of the Far West are the Colorado in the south, flowing into the Gulf of California, and the Columbia in the northwest, flowing to the Pacific. Each is more than 1,900 km (1,200 mi) long; both have been intensively developed to generate electric power, and both are important sources of irrigation.

Separated from the continental US by Canadian territory, the state of Alaska occupies the extreme northwest portion of the North American continent. A series of precipitous mountain ranges separates the heavily indented Pacific coast on the south from Alaska's broad central basin, through which the Yukon River flows from Canada in the east to the Bering Sea in the west. The central basin is bounded on the north by the Brooks Range, which slopes down gradually to the Arctic Ocean. The Alaskan Peninsula and the Aleutian Islands, sweeping west far out to sea, consist of a chain of volcanoes, many still active. The state of Hawaii consists of a group of Pacific islands formed by volcanoes rising sharply from the ocean floor. The highest of these volcanoes, Mauna Loa, at 4,168 m (13,675 ft), is located on the largest of the islands, Hawaii, and is still active.

The lowest point in the US is Death Valley in California, 86 m (282 ft) below sea level. At 6,194 m (20,320 ft), Mt. McKinley in Alaska is the highest peak in North America. These topographic extremes suggest the geological instability of the Pacific Coast region. Major earthquakes destroyed San Francisco in 1906 and Anchorage, Alaska, in 1964, and the San Andreas Fault in California still causes frequent earth tremors. Washington State's Mt. St. Helens erupted in 1980, spewing volcanic ash over much of the Northwest.

³CLIMATE

The eastern continental region is well watered, with annual rainfall generally in excess of 100 cm (40 in). It includes all of the Atlantic seaboard and southeastern states and extends west to cover Indiana, southern Illinois, most of Missouri, Arkansas, Louisiana, and easternmost Texas. The eastern seaboard is affected primarily by the masses of air moving from west to east across the continent rather than by air moving in from the

Atlantic. Hence its climate is basically continental rather than maritime. The midwestern and Atlantic seaboard states experience hot summers and cold winters; spring and autumn are clearly defined periods of climatic transition. Only Florida, with the Gulf of Mexico lying to its west, experiences moderate differences between summer and winter temperatures. Mean annual temperatures vary considerably between north and south: Boston, 11°C (51°F); New York City, 13°C (55°F); Charlotte, N.C., 16°C (61°F); Miami, Fla., 24°C (76°F). The Gulf and South Atlantic states are often hit by severe tropical storms originating in the Caribbean in late summer and early autumn.

The prairie lands lying to the west constitute a subhumid region. Precipitation usually exceeds evaporation by only a small amount; hence the region experiences drought more often than excessive rainfall. Dryness generally increases from east to west. The average midwinter temperature in the extreme north—Minnesota and North Dakota—is about –13°C (9°F) or less, while the average July temperature is 18°C (65°F). In the Texas prairie region to the south, January temperatures average 10–13°C (50–55°F) and July temperatures 27–29°C (80–85°F). Rainfall along the western border of the prairie region is as low as 46 cm (18 in) per year in the north and 64 cm (25 in) in the south. Precipitation is greatest in the early summer—a matter of great importance to agriculture, particularly in the growing of grain crops. In dry years, the prevailing winds may carry the topsoil eastward (particularly from the southern region) for hundreds of miles in clouds that obscure the sun.

The Great Plains constitute a semiarid climatic region. Rainfall in the southern plains averages about 50 cm (20 in) per year and in the northern plains about 25 cm (10 in), but extreme year-to-year variations are common. The tropical air masses that move northward across the plains originate on the fairly high plateaus of Mexico and contain little water vapor. Periods as long as 120 days without rain have been experienced in this region. The rains that do occur are often violent, and a third of the total annual rainfall may be recorded in a single day at certain weather stations. The contrast between summer and winter temperatures is extreme throughout the Great Plains. Maximum summer temperatures of over 43°C (110°F) have been recorded in the northern as well as in the southern plains. From the Texas panhandle north, blizzards are common in the winter, and tornadoes at other seasons. The average minimum temperature for January in Duluth, Minn., is –19°C (–3°F).

The higher reaches of the Rockies and the mountains paralleling the Pacific coast to the west are characterized by a typical alpine climate. Precipitation as a rule is heavier on the western slopes of the ranges. The great intermontane arid region of the West shows considerable climatic variation between its northern and southern portions. In New Mexico, Arizona, and southeastern California, the greatest precipitation occurs in July, August, and September, mean annual rainfall ranging from 8 cm (3 in) in Yuma, Ariz., to 76 cm (30 in) in the mountains of northern Arizona and New Mexico. Phoenix has a mean annual temperature of 22°C (71°F), rising to 33°C (92°F) in July and falling to 11°C (52°F) in January. North of the Utah-Arizona line, the summer months usually are very dry; maximum precipitation occurs in the winter and early spring. In the desert valleys west of Great Salt Lake, mean annual precipitation adds up to only 10 cm (4 in). Although the northern plateaus are generally arid, some of the mountainous areas of central Washington and Idaho receive at least 152 cm (60 in) of rain per year. Throughout the intermontane region, the uneven availability of water is the principal factor shaping the habitat.

The Pacific coast, separated by tall mountain barriers from the severe continental climate to the east, is a region of mild winters and moderately warm, dry summers. Its climate is basically maritime, the westerly winds from the Pacific Ocean moderating

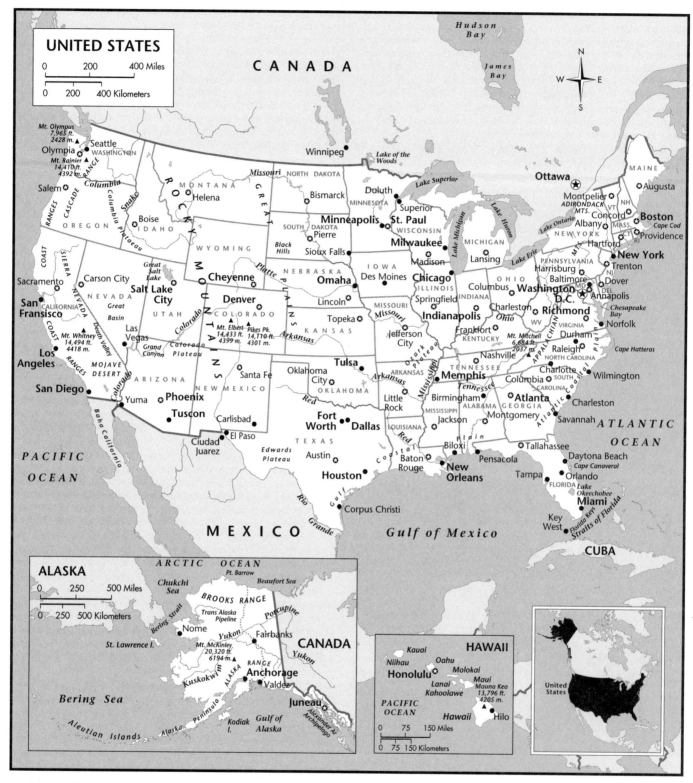

LOCATION: Conterminous US: 66°57′ to 124°44′w; 24°33′ to 49°23′n. Alaska: 130°w to 172°28′e; 51° to 71°23′n. Hawaii: 154°48′ to 178°22′w 18°55′ to 28°25′n.
BOUNDARY LENGTHS: Conterminous US: Canada, 6,416 km (3,987 mi); Atlantic Ocean, 3,330 km (2,069 mi); Gulf of Mexico coastline, 2,625 km (1,631 mi); Mexico, 3,111 km (1,933 mi); Pacific coastline, 2,081 km (1,293 mi). Alaska: Arctic Ocean coastline, 1,706 km (1,060 mi); Canada, 2,475 km (1,538 mi); Pacific coastline, including the Bering Sea and Strait and Chukchi coastlines, 8,980 km (5,580 mi). Hawaii: coastline, 1,207 km (750 mi).

the extremes of both winter and summer temperatures. Los Angeles in the south has an average temperature of 13°C (56°F) in January and 21°C (69°F) in July; Seattle in the north has an average temperature of 4°C (39°F) in January and 18°C (65°F) in July. Precipitation in general increases along the coast from south to north, extremes ranging from an annual average of 4.52 cm (1.78 in) at Death Valley in California (the lowest in the US) to more than 356 cm (140 in) in Washington's Olympic Mountains.

Climatic conditions vary considerably in the vastness of Alaska. In the fogbound Aleutians and in the coastal panhandle strip that extends southeastward along the Gulf of Alaska and includes the capital, Juneau, a relatively moderate maritime climate prevails. The interior is characterized by short, hot summers and long, bitterly cold winters, and in the region bordering the Arctic Ocean a polar climate prevails, the soil hundreds of feet below the surface remaining frozen the year round. Although snowy in winter, continental Alaska is relatively dry.

Hawaii has a remarkably mild and stable climate with only slight seasonal variations in temperature, as a result of northeast ocean winds. The mean January temperature in Honolulu is 23°C (73°F); the mean July temperature 27°C (80°F). Rainfall is moderate—about 71 cm (28 in) per year—but much greater in the mountains; Mt. Waialeale on Kauai has a mean annual rainfall of 1,168 cm (460 in), highest in the world.

The lowest temperature recorded in the US was –62°c (–79.8°F) at Prospect Creek Camp, Alaska, on 23 January 1971; the highest, 57°c (134°F) at Greenland Ranch, in Death Valley, Calif., on 10 July 1913. The record annual rainfall is 1,878 cm (739 in) recorded at Kukui, Maui in 1982; the previous record for a one-year period was 1,468 cm (578 in) recorded at Fuu Kukui, Maui, in 1950; in 1 hour, 30 cm (12 in), at Holt, Mo., on 22 June 1947, and on Kauai, Hawaii, on 24–25 January 1956.

⁴FLORA AND FAUNA

Including Alaska and Hawaii, about 29% of the US is forestland, 26% is grassland pasture, 20% is arable cropland, 2% is irrigated land, and the remaining 25% encompass military, urban, and designated recreational and wilderness areas, among other lands.

At least 7,000 species and subspecies of indigenous US flora have been categorized. The eastern forests contain a mixture of softwoods and hardwoods that includes pine, oak, maple, spruce, beech, birch, hemlock, walnut, gum, and hickory. The central hardwood forest, which originally stretched unbroken from Cape Cod to Texas and northwest to Minnesota—still an important timber source—supports oak, hickory, ash, maple, and walnut. Pine, hickory, tupelo, pecan, gum, birch, and sycamore are found in the southern forest that stretches along the Gulf coast into the eastern half of Texas. The Pacific forest is the most spectacular of all because of its enormous redwoods and Douglas firs. In the southwest are saguaro (giant cactus), yucca, candlewood, and the Joshua tree.

The central grasslands lie in the interior of the continent, where the moisture is not sufficient to support the growth of large forests. The tall grassland or prairie (now almost entirely under cultivation) lies to the east of the 100th meridian. To the west of this line, where rainfall is frequently less than 50 cm (20 in) per year, is the short grassland. Mesquite grass covers parts of west Texas, southern New Mexico, and Arizona. Short grass may be found in the highlands of the latter two states, while tall grass covers large portions of the coastal regions of Texas and Louisiana and occurs in some parts of Mississippi, Alabama, and Florida. The Pacific grassland includes northern Idaho, the higher plateaus of eastern Washington and Oregon, and the mountain valleys of California.

The intermontane region of the Western Cordillera is for the most part covered with desert shrubs. Sagebrush predominates in the northern part of this area, creosote in the southern, and saltbrush near the Great Salt Lake and in Death Valley.

The lower slopes of the mountains running up to the coastline of Alaska are covered with coniferous forests as far north as the Seward Peninsula. The central part of the Yukon Basin is also a region of softwood forests. The rest of Alaska is heath or tundra. Hawaii has extensive forests of bamboo and ferns. Sugarcane and pineapple, although not native to the islands, now cover a large portion of the cultivated land.

Small trees and shrubs common to most of the US include hackberry, hawthorn, serviceberry, blackberry, wild cherry, dogwood, and snowberry. Wildflowers bloom in all areas, from the seldom-seen blossoms of rare desert cacti to the hardiest alpine species. Wildflowers include forget-me-not, fringed and closed gentians, jack-in-the-pulpit, black-eyed Susan, columbine, and common dandelion, along with numerous varieties of aster, orchid, lady's slipper, and wild rose.

An estimated 1,500 species and subspecies of mammals characterize the animal life of the continental US. Among the larger game animals are the white-tailed deer, moose, pronghorn antelope, bighorn sheep, mountain goat, black bear, and grizzly bear. The Alaskan brown bear often reaches a weight of 1,200–1,400 lbs. Some 25 important furbearers are common, including the muskrat, red and gray foxes, mink, raccoon, beaver, opossum, striped skunk, woodchuck, common cottontail, snowshoe hare, and various squirrels. Human encroachment has transformed the mammalian habitat over the last two centuries. The American buffalo (bison), millions of which once roamed the plains, is now found only on select reserves. Other mammals, such as the elk and gray wolf, have been restricted to much smaller ranges.

Year-round and migratory birds abound. Loons, wild ducks, and wild geese are found in lake country; terns, gulls, sandpipers, herons, and other seabirds live along the coasts. Wrens, thrushes, owls, hummingbirds, sparrows, woodpeckers, swallows, chickadees, vireos, warblers, and finches appear in profusion, along with the robin, common crow, cardinal, Baltimore oriole, eastern and western meadowlarks, and various blackbirds. Wild turkey, ruffed grouse, and ring-necked pheasant (introduced from Europe) are popular game birds.

Lakes, rivers, and streams teem with trout, bass, perch, muskellunge, carp, catfish, and pike; sea bass, cod, snapper, and flounder are abundant along the coasts, along with such shellfish as lobster, shrimp, clams, oysters, and mussels. Garter, pine, and milk snakes are found in most regions. Four poisonous snakes survive, of which the rattlesnake is the most common. Alligators appear in southern waterways, and the Gila monster makes its home in the Southwest.

Laws and lists designed to protect threatened and endangered flora and fauna have been adopted throughout the US. Generally, each species listed as protected by the federal government is also protected by the states, but some states may list species not included on federal lists or on the lists of neighboring states. (Conversely, a species threatened throughout most of the US may be abundant in one or two states.) As of June 2000, the US Fish and Wildlife Service listed 961 endangered US species (up from 751 listed in 1996), including 63 mammals (64 in 1996), 90 birds (77 in 1996), 105 fish (69 in 1996), and 593 plants (432 in 1996); and 271 threatened species (209 in 1996), including 142 plants (94 in 1996). The agency listed another 519 endangered and 39 threatened foreign species by international agreement.

Threatened species, likely to become endangered if recent trends continue, include such plants as Lee pincushion cactus. Among the endangered floral species (in imminent danger of extinction in the wild) are the Virginia round-leaf birch, San Clemente Island broom, Texas wild-rice, Furbish lousewort, Truckee barberry, Sneed pincushion cactus, spineless hedgehog cactus, Knowlton cactus, persistent trillium, dwarf bear-poppy, and small whorled pogonia. Species formerly listed as threatened or endangered that have been removed from the list include (with delisting year and reason) Rydberg milk-vetch (1987, new information); and Lloyd's hedgehog cactus (1999, taxonomic revision).

Endangered mammals included the red wolf, black-footed ferret, jaguar, and Sonoran pronghorn. Endangered species of rodents included the Delmarva Peninsula fox squirrel, beach mouse, salt-marsh harvest mouse, 7 species of bat (Virginia and Ozark big-eared Sanborn's and Mexican long-nosed, Hawaiian hoary, Indiana, and gray), and the Morro Ba, Fresno, Stephens', and Tipton Kangaroo rats and rice rat.

Endangered species of birds included the California condor, bald eagle, 3 species of falcon (American peregrine, tundra peregrine, and northern aplomado), Eskimo curlew, 2 species of crane (whooping and Mississippi sandhill), 3 species of warbler (Kirtland's, Bachman's, and golden-cheeked), dusky seaside sparrow, light-footed clapper rail, least tern, and San Clemente loggerhead shrike. Endangered amphibians included 4 species of salamander (Santa Cruz long-toed, Shenandoah, desert slender, and Texas blind), Houston and Wyoming toad, and 6 species of turtle (green sea, hawksbill, Kemp's ridley, Plymouth and Alabama red-bellied, and leatherback). Endangered reptiles included the American crocodile, (blunt nosed leopard and island night), and San Francisco garter snake.

Aquatic species included the shortnose sturgeon, Gila trout, 8 species of chub (humpback, Pahranagat, Yaqui, Mohave tui, Owens tui, bonytail, Virgin River, and Borax lake), Colorado River squawfish, 5 species of dace (Kendall Warm Springs, and Clover Valley, Independence Valley, Moapa and Ash Meadows speckled), Modoc sucker, cui-ui, Smoky and Scioto madtom, 7 species of pupfish (Leon Springs, Gila Desert, Ash Meadows Amargosa, Warm Springs, Owens, Devil's Hole, and Comanche Springs), Pahrump killifish, 4 species of gambusia (San Marcos, Pecos, Amistad, Big Bend, and Clear Creek), 6 species of darter (fountain, watercress, Okaloosa, boulder, Maryland, and amber), totoaba, and 32 species of mussel and pearly mussel. Also classified as endangered were 2 species of earthworm (Washington giant and Oregon giant), the Socorro isopod, San Francisco forktail damselfly, Ohio emerald dragonfly, 2 species of beetle (Kretschmarr Cave, Tooth Cave, and giant carrion), Belkin's dune tabanid fly, and 10 species of butterfly (Schaus' swallowtail, lotis, mission, El Segundo, and Palos Verde blue, Mitchell's satyr, Uncompahgre fritillary, Lange's metalmark, San Bruno elfin, and Smith's blue).

Several species on the federal list of endangered and threatened wildlife and plants are found only in Hawaii. Endangered bird species in Hawaii included the Hawaiian dark-rumped petrel, Hawaiian gallinule, Hawaiian crow, 3 species of thrush (Kauai, Molokai, and puaiohi), Kauai 'o'o, Kauai nukupu'u, Kauai 'alialoa, 'akiapola'au, Maui 'akepa, Molokai creeper, Oahu creeper, palila, and 'o'u.

Endangered plants (and number of species) in the US include: aster, 32; cactus, 19; pea, 18; mustard, 14; mint, 12; mallow, 11; bellflower and pink family, 9 each; snapdragon, 8; and buckwheat, 6.

Threatened fauna include the grizzly bear, southern sea otter, Newell's shearwater, eastern indigo snake, bayou darter, several southwestern trout species, and Schaus swallowtail butterfly. Among endangered fauna are the Indiana bat, key deer, black-footed ferret, northern swift fox, San Joaquin kit fox, jaguar, jaguarundi, Florida manatee, ocelot, Florida panther, Utah prairie dog, Sonoran pronghorn, Delmarva Peninsula fox squirrel, gray wolf (except in Minnesota, where it is threatened), red wolf, numerous whale species, bald eagle (endangered in most states, but only threatened in the Northwest and the Great Lakes region), Hawaii creeper, Everglade kite, California clapper rail, red-cockaded woodpecker, bluntnosed leopard lizard, American crocodile, desert slender salamander, Houston toad, humpback chub, several species of pupfish, 17 US species of pearly mussel, Socorro isopod, Kentucky cave shrimp, and mission blue butterfly. Species formerly listed as threatened or endangered that have been removed from the list include (with delisting year and reason) American alligator (1987, recovered); coastal cutthroat

trout (2000, taxonomic revision); Bahama swallowtail butterfly (1984, amendment); gray whale (1994, recovered); brown pelican (1984, recovered); and Tecopa pupfish (1983, believed extinct).

[5] ENVIRONMENT

The Council on Environmental Quality, an advisory body contained within the Executive Office of the President, was established by the National Environmental Policy Act of 1969, which mandated an assessment of environmental impact for every federally funded project. The Environmental Protection Agency (EPA), created in 1970, is an independent body with primary regulatory responsibility in the fields of air and noise pollution, water and waste management, and control of toxic substances. Other federal agencies with environmental responsibilities are the Forest Service and Soil Conservation Service within the Department of Agriculture, the Fish and Wildlife Service and the National Park Service within the Department of the Interior, the Department of Energy, and the Nuclear Regulatory Commission. In addition to the 1969 legislation, landmark federal laws protecting the environment include the Clean Air Act Amendments of 1970 and 1990, controlling automobile and electric utility emissions; the Water Pollution Act of 1972, setting clean-water criteria for fishing and swimming; and the Endangered Species Act of 1973, protecting wildlife near extinction. A measure enacted in December 1980 established a $1.6-billion "Superfund," financed largely by excise taxes on chemical companies, to clean up toxic waste dumps such as the one in the Love Canal district of Niagara Falls, N.Y. In 1998, there were 1,245 hazardous waste sites on the Superfund's national priority list.

In 2000, the expenditure estimate for the Environmental Protection Agency was $7.2 billion. In 1999, the EPA employed 18,375 workers.

The most influential environmental lobbies include the Sierra Club (founded in 1892; 600,000 members in 1998) and its legal arm, the Sierra Club Legal Defense Fund. Large conservation groups include the National Wildlife Federation (1936; 4,400,000), the National Audubon Society (1905; 600,000), and the Nature Conservancy (1917; 705,000). Greenpeace USA (founded in 1979) has gained international attention by seeking to disrupt hunts for whales and seals.

Among the environmental movement's most notable successes have been the inauguration (and mandating in some states) of recycling programs; the banning in the US of the insecticide dichlorodiphenyltrichloroethane (DDT); the successful fight against construction of a supersonic transport (SST); and the protection of more than 40 million hectares (100 million acres) of Alaska lands (after a fruitless fight to halt construction of the trans-Alaska pipeline); and the gradual elimination of chlorofluorocarbon (CFC) production by 2000.

Outstanding problems include acid rain (precipitation contaminated by fossil fuel wastes); inadequate facilities for solid waste disposal; air pollution from industrial emissions (the US leads the world in carbon dioxide emissions from the burning of fossil fuels); the contamination of homes by radon, a radioactive gas that is produced by the decay of underground deposits of radium and can cause cancer; runoffs of agricultural pesticides, pollutants deadly to fishing streams and very difficult to regulate; continued dumping of raw or partially treated sewage from major cities into US waterways; falling water tables in many western states; the decrease in arable land because of depletion, erosion, and urbanization; the need for reclamation of strip-mined lands and for regulation of present and future strip mining; and the expansion of the US nuclear industry in the absence of a fully satisfactory technique for the handling and permanent disposal of radioactive wastes.

⁶POPULATION

At the time of the first federal census, in 1790, the population of the United States was 3,929,214. Between 1800 and 1850, the population almost quadrupled; between 1850 and 1900, it tripled; and between 1900 and 1950, it almost doubled. During the 1960s and 1970s, however, the growth rate slowed steadily, declining from 2.9% annually in 1960 to 2% in 1969 and to less than 1% in the 1980s. The population was estimated at 263,064,000 in mid-1995. The median age of the population increased from 16.7 years in 1820 to 22.9 years in 1900 and to 34.3 years in 1995.

By 2000, the population of United States was estimated at 274,943,496. An estimated 12.3% of the population is 65 years of age or older. The projected population for the year 2005 is 286,291,000, assuming a crude birthrate of 14 per 1,000 population and a death rate of 9, resulting in a natural rate of change of 0.5% for the period 2000–2005. The population rate of change between 1995 and 2000 was 0.8%. The population density in 1998 was 29 per sq km (75 per sq mi).

It was estimated that 77% of the population lived in urban areas in 2000, up from 74% in 1980. Suburbs have absorbed most of the shift in population distribution since 1950. The capital city, Washington, D.C., had a 2000 metropolitan population of 3,927,000. Other major metropolitan areas, with their 2000 population counts, include the following: New York, 16,626,000; Los Angeles, 13,129,000; Chicago, 6,945,000; Dallas, 3,912,000; Houston, 3,365,000; Philadelphia, 2,607,000; San Diego, 2,983,000; and Phoenix, 2,607,000.

⁷MIGRATION

Between 1840 and 1930, some 37 million immigrants, the overwhelming majority of them Europeans, arrived in the US. Immigration reached its peak in the first decade of the 20th century, when nearly 9 million came. Following the end of World War I, the tradition of almost unlimited immigration was abandoned, and through the National Origins Act of 1924, a quota system was established as the basis of a carefully restricted policy of immigration. Under the McCarran Act of 1952, one-sixth of 1% of the number of inhabitants from each European nation residing in the continental US as of 1920 could be admitted annually. In practice, this system favored nations of northern and western Europe, with the UK, Germany, and Ireland being the chief beneficiaries. The quota system was radically reformed in 1965, under a new law that established an annual ceiling of 170,000 for Eastern Hemisphere immigrants and 120,000 for entrants from the Western Hemisphere; in October 1978, these limits were replaced by a worldwide limit of 290,000, which was lowered to 270,000 by 1981. A major 1990 overhaul set a total annual ceiling of 700,000 (675,000 beginning in fiscal 1995), of which 480,000 would be family sponsored and 140,000 employment based.

In 1998, 660,466 immigrants entered the US, 598,787 of them subject to the numerical ceiling. Some 219,696 were from Asia; 252,996 were from North America; 45,394 were from South America; 90,793 from Europe; 40,660 from Africa, and 3,935 from Oceania. A direct result of the immigration law revisions has been a sharp rise in the influx of Asians (primarily Chinese, Filipinos, Indians, Japanese, and Koreans), of whom 2,738,157 entered the country during 1981–90, as compared with 153,249 during the entire decade of the 1950s.

Since 1961, the federal government supported and financed the Cuban Refugee Program; in 1995, new accords were agreed to by the two countries. More than 500,000 Cubans were living in southern Florida by 1980, when another 125,000 Cuban refugees arrived; by 1990, 4% of Florida's population was of Cuban descent. Between 1975 and 1978, following the defeat of the US-backed Saigon (Vietnam) government, several hundred thousand Vietnamese refugees came to the US. Under the Refugee Act of 1980, a ceiling for the number of admissible refugees is set annually; in fiscal 1998, 54,709 immigrants were admitted under the various refugee acts. Since Puerto Ricans are American citizens, no special authorization is required for their admission to the continental US. The ceiling for refugees in 1996 was 90,000. The population of refugees, asylees, resettled refugees, and asylum-seekers with pending claims was estimated at 1,146,400 in 1998. During the same year, the Immigration and Naturalization Service (INS) received 35,038 applications for asylum, a decline of more than 50% from 1997, with an approval rate of 20%. UNHCR reports the US as the leading destination of refugees, accounting for half of all resettlement worldwide. The US authorized admission for approximately 78,000 refugees in 1999. The net migration rate in 1999 was 3 migrants per 1,000 population.

Large numbers of aliens—mainly from Latin America, especially Mexico—have illegally established residence in the US after entering the country as tourists, students, or temporary visitors engaged in work or business. In November 1986, Congress passed a bill allowing illegal aliens who had lived and worked in the US since 1982 the opportunity to become permanent residents. By the end of fiscal year 1992, 2,650,000 of a potential 2,760,000 eligible for permanent residence under this bill had attained that status. In 1996 the number of illegal alien residents was estimated at 5 million, of which 2 million were believed to be in California.

The major migratory trends within the US have been a general westward movement during the 19th century; a long-term movement from farms and other rural settlements to metropolitan areas, which showed signs of reversing in some states during the 1970s; an exodus of southern blacks to the cities of the North and Midwest, especially after World War I; a shift of whites from central cities to surrounding suburbs since World War II; and, also during the post–World War II period, a massive shift from the North and East to the Sunbelt region of the South and Southwest.

⁸ETHNIC GROUPS

The majority of the population of the US is of European origin, with the largest groups having primary ancestry traceable to the UK, Germany, and Ireland; many Americans report multiple ancestries. Major racial and national minority groups include blacks (either of US or Caribbean parentage), Chinese, Filipinos, Japanese, Mexicans, and other Spanish-speaking peoples of the Americas. In 2000, it was estimated that whites comprised 82.2% of the US population; blacks, 12.8%; Asians and Pacific Islanders, 4%; Native Americans (Amerindians—more commonly known as Indians, Eskimos, and Aleuts), 0.9%. Responding to a census question that cut across racial lines, 9% of Americans in 1990 described themselves as of Hispanic origin; in 2000, it was estimated that 11.8% of the population was of Hispanic origin. Inequality in social and economic opportunities for ethnic minorities became a key public issue in the post–World War II period.

Some Indian societies survived warfare with land-hungry white settlers and retained their tribal cultures. Their survival, however, has been on the fringes of North American society, especially as a result of the implementation of a national policy of resettling Indian tribes on reservations. In 1890, according to the official census count, there were 248,253 Indians; in 1940, 333,909; and in 1990, 1,959,234 (including also Eskimos and Aleuts). The estimated American Indian population in 2000 was 2,431,000. Groups of Indians are found most numerously in the southwestern states of Oklahoma, Arizona, New Mexico, and California. The 1960s and 1970s saw successful court fights by Indians in Alaska, Maine, South Dakota, and other states to regain tribal lands or to receive cash settlements for lands taken from them in violation of treaties during the 1800s.

The black population in 1998 was estimated at 35,268,000, with the majority still residing in the South, the region that absorbed most of the slaves brought from Africa in the 18th and 19th centuries. Two important regional migrations of blacks have taken place: (1) a "Great Migration" to the North, commencing in 1915, and (2) a small but then unprecedented westward movement beginning about 1940. Both migrations were fostered by wartime demands for labor and by postwar job opportunities in northern and western urban centers. More than three out of four black Americans live in metropolitan areas, notably in Washington, D.C., Atlanta, Detroit, New Orleans, Newark, Baltimore, and New York City, which had the largest number of black residents. Large-scale federal programs to ensure equality for blacks in voting rights, public education, employment, and housing were initiated after the historic 1954 Supreme Court ruling that barred racial segregation in public schools. By 1966, however, in the midst of growing and increasingly violent expressions of dissatisfaction by black residents of northern cities and southern rural areas, the federal Civil Rights Commission reported that integration programs were lagging. Throughout the 1960s, 1970s, and 1980s, the unemployment rate among nonwhites in the US was at least double that for whites, and school integration proceeded slowly, especially outside the South.

Also included in the US population are a substantial number of persons whose lineage can be traced to Asian and Pacific nationalities, chiefly Chinese, Filipino, Japanese, Indian, Korean, and Vietnamese. The Chinese population is highly urbanized and concentrated particularly in cities of over 100,000 population, mostly on the West Coast and in New York City. The Japanese population has risen steadily from a level of 72,157 in 1910. Hawaii has been the most popular magnet of Japanese emigration. Most Japanese in California were farmers until the outbreak of World War II, when they were interned and deprived of their landholdings; after the war, most entered the professions and other urban occupations.

Mexican settlement is largely in the Southwest. Spanish-speaking Puerto Ricans, who often represent an amalgam of racial strains, have largely settled in the New York metropolitan area, where they partake in considerable measure of the hardships and problems experienced by other immigrant groups in the process of settling in the US. Since 1959, many Cubans have settled in Florida and other eastern states.

9LANGUAGES

The primary language of the US is English, enriched by words borrowed from the languages of Indians and immigrants, predominantly European. Spanish is also spoken by a sizable minority.

When European settlement began, Indians living north of Mexico spoke about 300 different languages now held to belong to 58 different language families. Only 2 such families have contributed noticeably to the American vocabulary: Algonkian in the Northeast and Aztec-Tanoan in the Southwest. From Algonkian languages, directly or sometimes through Canadian French, English has taken such words as *moose, skunk, caribou, opossum, woodchuck,* and *raccoon* for New World animals; *hickory, squash,* and *tamarack* for New World flora; and *succotash, hominy, mackinaw, moccasin, tomahawk, toboggan,* and *totem* for various cultural items. From Nahuatl, the language of the Aztecs, terms such as *tomato, mesquite, coyote, chili, tamale, chocolate,* and *ocelot* have entered English, largely by way of Spanish. A bare handful of words come from other Indian language groups, such as *tepee* from Dakota Siouan, *catalpa* from Creek, *sequoia* from Cherokee, *hogan* from Navaho, and *sockeye* from Salish, as well as *cayuse* from Chinook.

Professional dialect research, initiated in Germany in 1878 and in France in 1902, did not begin in the US until 1931, in connection with the *Linguistic Atlas of New England* (1939–43). This kind of research, requiring trained field-workers to interview representative informants in their homes, subsequently was extended to the entire Atlantic Coast, the north-central states, the upper Midwest, the Pacific Coast, the Gulf states, and Oklahoma. The New England atlas, the *Linguistic Atlas of the Upper Midwest* (1973–76), and the first two fascicles of the *Linguistic Atlas of the Middle and South Atlantic States* (1980) have been published, along with three volumes based on Atlantic Coast field materials. Also published or nearing publication are atlases of the north-central states, the Gulf states, and Oklahoma. In other areas, individual dialect researchers have produced more specialized studies. The definitive work on dialect speech, the American Dialect Society's monumental *Dictionary of American Regional English,* began publication in 1985.

Dialect studies confirm that standard English is not uniform throughout the country. Major regional variations reflect patterns of colonial settlement, dialect features from England having dominated particular areas along the Atlantic Coast and then spread westward along the three main migration routes through the Appalachian system. Dialectologists recognize three main dialects—Northern, Midland, and Southern—each with subdivisions related to the effect of mountain ranges and rivers and railroads on population movement.

The Northern dialect is that of New England and its derivative settlements in New York; the northern parts of Ohio, Indiana, Illinois, and Iowa; and Michigan, Wisconsin, northeastern South Dakota, and North Dakota. A major subdivision is that of New England east of the Connecticut River, an area noted typically by the loss of /r/ after a vowel, and by the pronunciation of *can't, dance, half,* and *bath* with a vowel more like that in *father* than that in *fat.* Generally, however, Northern speech has a strong /r/ after a vowel, the same vowel in *can't* and *cat,* a conspicuous contrast between *cot* and *caught,* the /s/ sound in *greasy, creek* rhyming with *pick,* and *with* ending with the same consonant sound as at the end of *breath.*

Midland speech extends in a wide band across the US: there are two main subdivisions, North Midland and South Midland. North Midland speech extends westward from New Jersey, Delaware, and Pennsylvania into Ohio, Illinois, southern Iowa, and northern Missouri. Its speakers generally end *with* with the consonant sound that begins the word *thin,* pronounce *cot* and *caught* alike, and say *cow* and *down* as /caow/ and /daown/. South Midland speech was carried by the Scotch–Irish from Pennsylvania down the Shenandoah Valley into the southern Appalachians, where it acquired many Southern speech features before it spread westward into Kentucky, Tennessee, southern Missouri, Arkansas, and northeast Texas. Its speakers are likely to say *plum peach* rather than *clingstone peach* and *snake doctor* rather than *dragonfly.*

Southern speech typically, though not always, lacks the consonant /r/ after a vowel, lengthens the first part of the diphthong in *write* so that to Northern ears it sounds almost like *rat,* and diphthongizes the vowels in *bed* and *hit* so that they sound like /beuhd/ and /hiuht/. *Horse* and *hoarse* do not sound alike, and *creek* rhymes with *meek. Corn bread* is *corn pone,* and *you-all* is standard for the plural.

In the western part of the US, migration routes so crossed and intermingled that no neat dialect boundaries can be drawn, although there are a few rather clear population pockets.

The majority of Spanish speakers live in the Southwest, Florida, and eastern urban centers. Refugee immigration since the 1950s has greatly increased the number of foreign-language speakers from Latin America and Asia.

Very early English borrowed from neighboring French speakers such words as *shivaree, butte, levee,* and *prairie;* from German, *sauerkraut, smearcase,* and *cranberry;* from Dutch, *stoop, spook,* and *cookie;* and from Spanish, *tornado, corral, ranch,* and *canyon.* From various West African languages, blacks have given English *jazz, voodoo,* and *okra.*

Educational problems raised by the presence of large blocs of non-English speakers led to the passage in 1976 of the Bilingual Educational Act, enabling children to study basic courses in their first language while they learn English. A related school problem is that of black English, a Southern dialect variant that is the vernacular of many black students now in northern schools.

10RELIGIONS

US religious traditions are predominantly Judeo-Christian, and most Americans identify themselves as Protestants (of various denominations), Roman Catholics, or Jews. As of 1995, 163 million Americans, about 63% of the total population, reported affiliation with a religious group. The largest Christian denomination is the Roman Catholic Church, with 1995 membership estimated at 59.9 million in 19,787 local congregations with some 50,000 clergy. Immigration from Ireland, Italy, Eastern Europe, French Canada, and the Caribbean accounts for the predominance of Roman Catholicism in the Northeast, Northwest, and some parts of the Great Lakes region, while Hispanic traditions and more recent immigration from Mexico and other Latin American countries account for the historical importance of Roman Catholicism in California and throughout most of the sunbelt. More than any other US religious body, the Roman Catholic Church maintains an extensive network of parochial schools.

Jewish immigrants settled first in the Northeast, where the largest Jewish population remains; at last estimates, nearly 6 million Jews (or 3.7% of those reporting religious affiliation in the US) were affiliated with over 3,400 local congregation served by 6,500 clergy.

According to reported statistics, 94,612,579 persons in the US reported affiliation with a Protestant denomination. Baptists predominate below the Mason-Dixon line and west to Texas. By far the nation's largest Protestant group, the Southern Baptist Convention had 15,892,000 adherents by 1997 estimates; the American Baptist Churches in the USA claimed some 1,503,000 adherents in 1996. A concentration of Methodist groups extends westward in a band from Delaware to eastern Colorado; the largest of these groups, the United Methodist Church had 8,646,595 adherents. Lutheran denominations, reflecting in part the patterns of German and Scandinavian settlement, are most highly concentrated in the north-central states, especially Minnesota and the Dakotas. Two Lutheran synods, the Lutheran Church in America and the American Lutheran Church, merged in 1987 to form the Evangelical Lutheran Church in America, with more than 5,185,000 adherents in 1997. In June 1983, the two major Presbyterian churches, the northern-based United Presbyterian Church in the USA and the southern-based Presbyterian Church in the US, formally merged as the Presbyterian Church (USA), ending a division that began with the Civil War. This group claimed 3,611,000 adherents in 1997. Other Protestant denominations and their estimated adherents (by year) include the Episcopal Church 2,365,000 (1996); Churches of Christ 1,800,000 (1997); and the United Church of Christ 1,438,000 (1997). One Christian group, the Church of Jesus Christ of Latter-Day Saints (Mormon), with 4,923,000 members (1997), was organized in New York in 1830 and, since migrating westward has played a leading role in Utah's political, economic, and religious life. Notable during the 1970s and early 1980s was a rise in the fundamentalist, evangelical, and Pentecostal movements. In the first half of the 1990s, Pentecostal churches

reported 10,281,559 adherents, representing over 6% of the population reporting religious affiliation.

Several million Muslims followers of various Asian religious, a multiplicity of small Protestant groups, and a sizable number of cults also participate in US religious life.

11TRANSPORTATION

Railroads have lost not only the largest share of intercity freight traffic, their chief source of revenue, but passenger traffic as well. Despite an attempt to revive passenger transport through the development of a national network (Amtrak) in the 1970s, the rail sector has continued to experience heavy losses and declining revenues. In 1998 there were 9 Class I rail companies in the US, down from 13 in 1994, with a total of 178,222 employees and operating revenues of $32.2 billion. In 1998, Amtrak carried 21 million passengers.

The most conspicuous form of transportation is the automobile, and the extent and quality of the US road-transport system are without parallel in the world. Over 204 million vehicles—a record number—were registered in 1997, including more than 128.5 million passenger cars. In 1997, there were some 3.8 million motorcycles registered as well.

The US has a vast network of public roads, whose total length as of 1998 was 6.42 million km (3.99 million mi). Of that total, about 3,903,360 km (2,425,548 mi) were paved, including 88,400 km (54,932 mi) of expressways. In 1998, about $46.8 billion was spent annually on highway construction, and $25.6 billion on highway maintenance and services.

Major ocean ports or port areas are New York, the Delaware River areas (Philadelphia), the Chesapeake Bay area (Baltimore, Norfolk, Newport News), New Orleans, Houston, and the San Francisco Bay area. The inland port of Duluth on Lake Superior handles more freight than all but the top-ranking ocean ports. The importance of this port, along with those of Chicago and Detroit, was enhanced with the opening in 1959 of the St. Lawrence Seaway. Waterborne freight consists primarily of bulk commodities such as petroleum and its products, coal and coke, iron ore and steel, sand, gravel and stone, grains, and lumber. The US merchant marine industry has been decreasing gradually since the 1950s. In 1998, the US had a merchant shipping fleet of 385 vessels of more than 1,000 gross registered tons with a combined GRT of 11,123,848.

In 1998, the US had an estimated 14,459 airports, of which 5,167 had paved runways. Principal airports include Hartsfield at Atlanta, Logan International at Boston, O'Hare International at Chicago, Dallas-Fort Worth at Dallas, Detroit Metropolitan at Detroit, Honolulu International at Honolulu, Houston Intercontinental at Houston, Los Angeles International at Los Angeles, John F. Kennedy, La Guardia, and Newark International at New York, Philadelphia International at Philadelphia, Orlando International at Orlando, Miami International at Miami, San Francisco International at San Francisco, L. Munoz Marin at San Juan, Seattle-Tacoma at Seattle, and Dulles International at Washington. Revenue passengers carried by the airlines in 1940 totaled 2.7 million; by 1997, the figure exceeded 590 million. US domestic and international carriers performed some 964,533 million passenger-km (599,361 million passenger-mi) of service in 1997, along with 25,479 million freight ton-km (15,833 million freight ton-mi).

12HISTORY

The first Americans—distant ancestors of the American Indians—probably crossed the Bering Strait from Asia at least 12,000 years ago. By the time Christopher Columbus came to the New World in 1492 there were probably no more than 2 million Native Americans living in the land that was to become the US.

Following exploration of the American coasts by English, Portuguese, Spanish, Dutch, and French sea captains from the late 15th century onward, European settlements sprang up in the latter part of the 16th century. The Spanish established the first permanent settlement at St. Augustine in the future state of Florida in 1565, and another in New Mexico in 1599. During the early 17th century, the English founded Jamestown in Virginia Colony (1607) and Plymouth Colony in present-day Massachusetts (1620). The Dutch established settlements at Ft. Orange (now Albany, N.Y.) in 1624, New Amsterdam (now New York City) in 1626, and at Bergen (now part of Jersey City, N.J.) in 1660; they conquered New Sweden—the Swedish colony in Delaware and New Jersey—in 1655. Nine years later, however, the English seized this New Netherland Colony and subsequently monopolized settlement of the East Coast except for Florida, where Spanish rule prevailed until 1821. In the Southwest, California, Arizona, New Mexico, and Texas also were part of the Spanish empire until the 19th century. Meanwhile, in the Great Lakes area south of present-day Canada, France set up a few trading posts and settlements but never established effective control; New Orleans was one of the few areas of the US where France pursued an active colonial policy.

From the founding of Jamestown to the outbreak of the American Revolution more than 150 years later, the British government administered its American colonies within the context of mercantilism: the colonies existed primarily for the economic benefit of the empire. Great Britain valued its American colonies especially for their tobacco, lumber, indigo, rice, furs, fish, grain, and naval stores, relying particularly in the southern colonies on black slave labor.

The colonies enjoyed a large measure of internal self-government until the end of the French and Indian War (1745–63), which resulted in the loss of French Canada to the British. To prevent further troubles with the Indians, the British government in 1763 prohibited the American colonists from settling beyond the Appalachian Mountains. Heavy debts forced London to decree that the colonists should assume the costs of their own defense, and the British government enacted a series of revenue measures to provide funds for that purpose. But soon, the colonists began to insist that they could be taxed "only with their consent," and the struggle grew to become one of local versus imperial authority.

Widening cultural and intellectual differences also served to divide the colonies and the mother country. Life on the edge of the civilized world had brought about changes in the colonists' attitudes and outlook, emphasizing their remoteness from English life. In view of the long tradition of virtual self-government in the colonies, strict enforcement of imperial regulations and British efforts to curtail the power of colonial legislatures presaged inevitable conflict between the colonies and the mother country. When citizens of Massachusetts, protesting the tax on tea, dumped a shipload of tea belonging to the East India Company into Boston harbor in 1773, the British felt compelled to act in defense of their authority as well as in defense of private property. Punitive measures—referred to as the Intolerable Acts by the colonists—struck at the foundations of self-government.

In response, the First Continental Congress, composed of delegates from 12 of the 13 colonies—Georgia was not represented—met in Philadelphia in September 1774, and proposed a general boycott of English goods, together with the organizing of a militia. British troops marched to Concord, Mass., on 19 April 1775 and destroyed the supplies that the colonists had assembled there. American "minutemen" assembled on the nearby Lexington green and fired "the shot heard round the world," although no one knows who actually fired the first shot that morning. The British soldiers withdrew and fought their way back to Boston.

Voices in favor of conciliation were raised in the Second Continental Congress that assembled in Philadelphia on 10 May 1775, this time including Georgia; but with news of the Restraining Act (30 March 1775), which denied the colonies the right to trade with countries outside the British Empire, all hopes for peace vanished. George Washington was appointed commander in chief of the new American army, and on 4 July 1776, the 13 American colonies adopted the Declaration of Independence, justifying the right of revolution by the theory of natural rights.

British and American forces met in their first organized encounter near Boston on 17 June 1775. Numerous battles up and down the coast followed. The British seized and held the principal cities but were unable to inflict a decisive defeat on Washington's troops. The entry of France into the war on the American side eventually tipped the balance. On 19 October 1781, the British commander, Cornwallis, cut off from reinforcements by the French fleet on one side and besieged by French and American forces on the other, surrendered his army at Yorktown, Va. American independence was acknowledged by the British in a treaty of peace signed in Paris on 3 September 1783.

The first constitution uniting the 13 original states—the Articles of Confederation—reflected all the suspicions that Americans entertained about a strong central government. Congress was denied power to raise taxes or regulate commerce, and many of the powers it was authorized to exercise required the approval of a minimum of nine states. Dissatisfaction with the Articles of Confederation was aggravated by the hardships of a postwar depression, and in 1787—the same year that Congress passed the Northwest Ordinance, providing for the organization of new territories and states on the frontier—a convention assembled in Philadelphia to revise the articles. The convention adopted an altogether new constitution, the present Constitution of the United States, which greatly increased the powers of the central government at the expense of the states. This document was ratified by the states with the understanding that it would be amended to include a bill of rights guaranteeing certain fundamental freedoms. These freedoms—including the rights of free speech, press, and assembly, freedom from unreasonable search and seizure, and the right to a speedy and public trial by an impartial jury—are assured by the first 10 amendments to the constitution, adopted on 5 December 1791; the constitution did however recognize slavery, and did not provide for universal suffrage. On 30 April 1789 George Washington was inaugurated as the first president of the US.

During Washington's administration, the credit of the new nation was bolstered by acts providing for a revenue tariff and an excise tax; opposition to the excise on whiskey sparked the Whiskey Rebellion, suppressed on Washington's orders in 1794. Alexander Hamilton's proposals for funding the domestic and foreign debt and permitting the national government to assume the debts of the states were also implemented. Hamilton, the secretary of the treasury, also created the first national bank, and was the founder of the Federalist Party. Opposition to the bank as well as to the rest of the Hamiltonian program, which tended to favor northeastern commercial and business interests, led to the formation of an anti-Federalist party, the Democratic-Republicans, led by Thomas Jefferson.

The Federalist Party, to which Washington belonged, regarded the French Revolution as a threat to security and property; the Democratic-Republicans, while condemning the violence of the revolutionists, hailed the overthrow of the French monarchy as a blow to tyranny. The split of the nation's leadership into rival camps was the first manifestation of the two-party system, which has since been the dominant characteristic of the US political scene. (Jefferson's party should not be confused with the modern Republican Party, formed in 1854.)

The 1800 election brought the defeat of Federalist President John Adams, Washington's successor, by Jefferson; a key factor in Adam's loss was the unpopularity of the Alien and Sedition Acts (1798), Federalist-sponsored measures that had abridged certain freedoms guaranteed in the Bill of Rights. In 1803, Jefferson achieved the purchase from France of the Louisiana Territory, including all the present territory of the US west of the Mississippi drained by that river and its tributaries; exploration and mapping of the new territory, notably through the expeditions of Meriwether Lewis and William Clark, began almost immediately. Under Chief Justice John Marshall, the US Supreme Court, in the landmark case of *Marbury v. Madison,* established the principle of federal supremacy in conflicts with the states and enunciated the doctrine of judicial review.

During Jefferson's second term in office, the US became involved in a protracted struggle between Britain and Napoleonic France. Seizures of US ships and the impressment of US seamen by the British navy led the administration to pass the Embargo Act of 1807, under which no US ships were to be put out to sea. After the act was repealed in 1809, ship seizures and impressment of seamen by the British continued, and were the ostensible reasons for the declaration of war on Britain in 1812 during the administration of James Madison. An underlying cause of the War of 1812, however, was land-hungry Westerners' coveting of southern Canada as potential US territory.

The war was largely a standoff. A few surprising US naval victories countered British successes on land. The Treaty of Ghent (24 December 1814), which ended the war, made no mention of impressment and provided for no territorial changes. The occasion for further maritime conflict with Britain, however, disappeared with the defeat of Napoleon in 1815.

Now the nation became occupied primarily with domestic problems and westward expansion. Because the US had been cut off from its normal sources of manufactured goods in Great Britain during the war, textiles and other industries developed and prospered in New England. To protect these infant industries, Congress adopted a high-tariff policy in 1816.

Three events of the late 1810s and the 1820s were of considerable importance for the future of the country. The federal government in 1817 began a policy of forcibly resettling the Indians, already decimated by war and disease, in what later became known as Indian Territory (now Oklahoma); those Indians not forced to move were restricted to reservations. The Missouri Compromise (1820) was an attempt to find a nationally acceptable solution to the volatile dispute over the extension of black slavery to new territories. It provided for admission of Missouri into the Union as a slave state but banned slavery in territories to the west that lay north of 36°30′. As a result of the establishment of independent Latin American republics and threats by France and Spain to reestablish colonial rule, President James Monroe in 1823 asserted that the Western Hemisphere was closed to further colonization by European powers. The Monroe Doctrine declared that any effort by such powers to recover territories whose independence the US had recognized would be regarded as an unfriendly act.

From the 1820s to the outbreak of the Civil War, the growth of manufacturing continued, mainly in the North, and was accelerated by inventions and technological advances. Farming expanded with westward migration. The South discovered that its future lay in the cultivation of cotton. The cotton gin, invented by Eli Whitney in 1793, greatly simplified the problems of production; the growth of the textile industry in New England and Great Britain assured a firm market for cotton. Hence, during the first half of the 19th century, the South remained a fundamentally agrarian society based increasingly on a one-crop economy. Large numbers of field hands were required for cotton

cultivation, and black slavery became solidly entrenched in the southern economy.

The construction of roads and canals paralleled the country's growth and economic expansion. The successful completion of the Erie Canal (1825), linking the Great Lakes with the Atlantic, ushered in a canal-building boom. Railroad building began in earnest in the 1830s, and by 1840, about 3,300 mi (5,300 km) of track had been laid. The development of the telegraph a few years later gave the nation the beginnings of a modern telecommunications network. As a result of the establishment of the factory system, a laboring class appeared in the North by the 1830s, bringing with it the earliest unionization efforts.

Western states admitted into the Union following the War of 1812 provided for free white male suffrage without property qualifications and helped spark a democratic revolution. As eastern states began to broaden the franchise, mass appeal became an important requisite for political candidates. The election to the presidency in 1928 of Andrew Jackson, a military hero and Indian fighter from Tennessee, was no doubt a result of this widening of the democratic process. By this time, the US consisted of 24 states and had a population of nearly 13 million.

The relentless westward thrust of the US population ultimately involved the US in foreign conflict. In 1836, US settlers in Texas revolted against Mexican rule and established an independent republic. Texas was admitted to the Union as a state in 1845, and relations between Mexico and the US steadily worsened. A dispute arose over the southern boundary of Texas, and a Mexican attack on a US patrol in May 1846 gave President James K. Polk a pretext to declare war. After a rapid advance, US forces captured Mexico City, and on 2 February 1848, Mexico formally gave up the unequal fight by signing the Treaty of Guadalupe Hidalgo, providing for the cession of California and the territory of New Mexico to the US. With the Gadsden Purchase of 1853, the US acquired from Mexico for $10 million large strips of land forming the balance of southern Arizona and New Mexico. A dispute with Britain over the Oregon Territory was settled in 1846 by a treaty that established the 49th parallel as the boundary with Canada. Thenceforth the US was to be a Pacific as well as an Atlantic power.

Westward expansion exacerbated the issue of slavery in the territories. By 1840, abolition of slavery constituted a fundamental aspect of a movement for moral reform, which also encompassed woman's rights, universal education, alleviation of working class hardships, and temperance. In 1849, a year after the discovery of gold had precipitated a rush of new settlers to California, that territory (whose constitution prohibited slavery) demanded admission to the Union. A compromise engineered in Congress by Senator Henry Clay in 1850 provided for California's admission as a free state in return for various concessions to the South. But enmities dividing North and South could not be silenced. The issue of slavery in the territories came to a head with the Kansas-Nebraska Act of 1854, which repealed the Missouri Compromise and left the question of slavery in those territories to be decided by the settlers themselves. The ensuing conflicts in Kansas between northern and southern settlers earned the territory the name "bleeding Kansas." in 1860, the Democratic Party, split along northern and southern lines, offered two presidential candidates. The new Republican Party, organized in 1854 and opposed to the expansion of slavery, nominated Abraham Lincoln. Owing to the defection in Democratic ranks, Lincoln was able to carry the election in the electoral college, although he did not obtain a majority of the popular vote. To ardent supporters of slavery, Lincoln's election provided a reason for immediate secession. Between December 1860 and February 1861, the seven states of the Deep South— South Carolina, Mississippi, Florida, Alabama, Georgia, Louisiana, and Texas—withdrew from the Union and formed a separate government, known as the Confederate States of America, under the presidency of Jefferson Davis. The secessionists soon began to confiscate federal property in the South. On 12 April 1861, the Confederates opened fire on Ft. Sumter in the harbor of Charleston, S.C., and thus precipitated the US Civil War. Following the outbreak of hostilities, Arkansas, North Carolina, Virginia, and Tennessee joined the Confederacy.

For the next four years, war raged between the Confederate and Union forces, largely in southern territories. An estimated 360,000 men in the Union forces died of various causes, including 110,000 killed in battle. Confederate dead were estimated at 250,000, including 94,000 killed in battle. The North, with great superiority in manpower and resources, finally prevailed. A Confederate invasion of the North was repulsed at the battle of Gettysburg, Pa. in July 1863; a Union army took Atlanta in September 1864; and Confederate forces evacuated Richmond, the Confederate capital, in early April 1865. With much of the South in Union hands, Confederate Gen. Robert E. Lee surrendered to Gen. Ulysses S. Grant at Appomattox Courthouse in Virginia on 9 April.

The outcome of the war brought great changes in US life. Lincoln's Emancipation Proclamation of 1863 was the initial step in freeing some 4 million black slaves; their liberation was completed soon after the war's end by amendments to the Constitution. Lincoln's plan for the reconstruction of the rebellious states was compassionate, but only five days after Lee's surrender, Lincoln was assassinated by John Wilkes Booth as part of a conspiracy in which US Secretary of State William H. Seward was seriously wounded.

During the Reconstruction era (1865–77), the defeated South was governed by Union Army commanders, and the resultant bitterness of southerners toward northern Republican rule, which enfranchised blacks, persisted for years afterward. Vice President Andrew Johnson, who succeeded Lincoln as president, tried to carry out Lincoln's conciliatory policies but was opposed by radical Republican leaders in Congress, who demanded harsher treatment of the South. On the pretext that he had failed to carry out an act of Congress, the House of Representatives voted to impeach Johnson in 1868, but the Senate failed by one vote to convict him and remove him from office. It was during Johnson's presidency that Secretary of State Seward negotiated the purchase of Alaska (which attained statehood in 1959) from Russia for $7.2 million.

The efforts of southern whites to regain political control of their states led to the formation of terrorist organizations like the Ku Klux Klan, which employed violence to prevent blacks from voting. By the end of the Reconstruction era, whites had reestablished their political domination over blacks in the southern states and had begun to enforce patterns of segregation in education and social organization that were to last for nearly a century.

In many southern states, the decades following the Civil War were ones of economic devastation, in which rural whites as well as blacks were reduced to sharecropper status. Outside the South, however, a great period of economic expansion began. Transcontinental railroads were constructed, corporate enterprise spurted ahead, and the remaining western frontier lands were rapidly occupied and settled. The age of big business tycoons dawned. As heavy manufacturing developed, Pittsburgh, Chicago, and New York emerged as the nation's great industrial centers. The Knights of Labor, founded in 1869, engaged in numerous strikes, and violent conflicts between strikers and strikebreakers were common. The American Federation of Labor, founded in 1886, established a nationwide system of craft unionism that remained dominant for many decades. During this period, too, the woman's rights movement organized actively to secure the vote (although woman's suffrage was not enacted nationally until 1920), and groups outraged by the depletion of forests and wildlife in the West pressed for the conservation of natural resources.

During the latter half of the 19th century, the acceleration of westward expansion made room for millions of immigrants from Europe. The country's population grew to more than 76 million by 1900. As homesteaders, prospectors, and other settlers tamed the frontier, the federal government forced Indians west of the Mississippi to cede vast tracts of land to the whites, precipitating a series of wars with various tribes. By 1890, only 250,000 Indians remained in the US, virtually all of them residing on reservations.

The 1890s marked the closing of the US frontier for settlement and the beginning of US overseas expansion. By 1892, Hawaiian sugar planters of US origin had become strong enough to bring about the downfall of the native queen and to establish a republic, which in 1898, at its own request, was annexed as a territory by the US. The sympathies of the US with the Cuban nationalists who were battling for independence from Spain were aroused by a lurid press and by expansionist elements. A series of events climaxed by the sinking of the USS *Maine* in Havana harbor finally forced a reluctant President William McKinley to declare war on Spain on 25 April 1898. US forces overwhelmed those of Spain in Cuba, and as a result of the Spanish-American War, the US added to its territories the Philippines, Guam, and Puerto Rico. A newly independent Cuba was drawn into the US orbit as a virtual protectorate through the 1950s. Many eminent citizens saw these new departures into imperialism as a betrayal of the time-honored US doctrine of government by the consent of the governed.

With the marked expansion of big business came increasing protests against the oppressive policies of large corporations and their dominant role in the public life of the nation. A demand emerged for strict control of monopolistic business practice through the enforcement of antitrust laws. Two US presidents, Theodore Roosevelt (1901–9), a Republican and Woodrow Wilson (1913–21), a Democrat, approved of the general movement for reform, which came to be called progressivism. Roosevelt developed a considerable reputation as a trustbuster, while Wilson's program, known as the New Freedom, called for reform of tariffs, business procedures, and banking. During Roosevelt's first term, the US leased the Panama Canal Zone and started construction of a 42-mi (68-km) canal, completed in 1914.

US involvement in World War I marked the country's active emergence as one of the great powers of the world. When war broke out in 1914 between Germany, Austria-Hungary, and Turkey on one side and Britain, France, and Russia on the other, sentiment in the US was strongly opposed to participation in the conflict, although a large segment of the American people sympathized with the British and the French. While both sides violated US maritime rights on the high seas, the Germans, enmeshed in a British blockade, resorted to unrestricted submarine warfare. On 6 April 1917, Congress declared war on Germany. Through a national draft of all able-bodied men between the ages of 18 and 45, some 4 million US soldiers were trained, of whom more than 2 million were sent overseas to France. By late 1917, when US troops began to take part in the fighting on the western front, the European armies were approaching exhaustion, and US intervention may well have been decisive in ensuring the eventual victory of the Allies. In a series of great battles in which US soldiers took an increasingly major part, the German forces were rolled back in the west, and in the autumn of 1918 were compelled to sue for peace. Fighting ended with the armistice of 11 November 1918. President Wilson played an active role in drawing up the 1919 Versailles peace treaty, which embodied his dream of establishing a League of Nations to preserve the peace, but the isolationist bloc in the Senate was able to prevent US ratification of the treaty.

In the 1920s, the US had little enthusiasm left for crusades, either for democracy abroad or for reform at home; a rare instance of idealism in action was the Kellogg-Briand Pact (1928), an antiwar accord negotiated on behalf of the US by Secretary of State Frank B. Kellogg. In general, however, the philosophy of the Republican administrations from 1921 to 1933 was expressed in the aphorism "The business of America is business," and the 1920s saw a great business boom. The years 1923–24 also witnessed the unraveling of the Teapot Dome scandal: the revelation that President Warren G. Harding's secretary of the interior, Albert B. Fall, had secretly leased federal oil reserves in California and Wyoming to private oil companies in return for gifts and loans.

The great stock market crash of October 1929 ushered in the most serious and most prolonged economic depression the country had ever known. By 1933, an estimated 12 million men and women were out of work; personal savings were wiped out on a vast scale through a disastrous series of corporate bankruptcies and bank failures. Relief for the unemployed was left to private charities and local governments, which were incapable of handling the enormous task.

The inauguration of the successful Democratic presidential candidate, Franklin D. Roosevelt, in March 1933 ushered in a new era of US history, in which the federal government was to assume a much more prominent role in the nation's economic affairs. Proposing to give the country a "New Deal," Roosevelt accepted national responsibility for alleviating the hardships of unemployment; relief measures were instituted, work projects were established, the deficit spending was accepted in preference to ignoring public distress. The federal Social Security program was inaugurated, as were various measures designed to stimulate and develop the economy through federal intervention. Unions were strengthened through the National Labor Relations Act, which established the right of employees' organizations to bargain collectively with employers. Union membership increased rapidly, and the dominance of the American Federation of Labor was challenged by the newly formed Congress of Industrial Organizations, which organized workers along industrial lines.

The depression of the 1930s was worldwide, and certain nations attempted to counter economic stagnation by building large military establishments and embarking on foreign adventures. Following German, Italian, and Japanese aggression, World War II broke out in Europe during September 1939. In 1940, Roosevelt, disregarding a tradition dating back to Washington that no president should serve more than two terms, ran again for reelection. He easily defeated his Republican opponent, Wendell Willkie, who, along with Roosevelt, advocated increased rearmament and all possible aid to victims of aggression. The US was brought actively into the war by the Japanese attack on the Pearl Harbor naval base in Hawaii on 7 December 1941. The forces of Germany, Italy, and Japan were now arrayed over a vast theater of war against those of the US and the British Commonwealth; in Europe, Germany was locked in a bloody struggle with the Soviet Union. US forces waged war across the vast expanses of the Pacific, in Africa, in Asia, and in Europe. Italy surrendered in 1943; Germany was successfully invaded in 1944 and conquered in May 1945; and after the US dropped the world's first atomic bombs on Hiroshima and Nagasaki, the Japanese capitulated in August. The Philippines became an independent republic soon after the war, but the US retained most of its other Pacific possessions, with Hawaii becoming the 50th state in 1959.

Roosevelt, who had been elected to a fourth term in 1944, died in April 1945 and was succeeded by Harry S Truman, his vice president. Under the Truman administration, the US became an active member of the new world organization, the United Nations. The Truman administration embarked on large-scale programs of military aid and economic support to check the expansion of communism. Aid to Greece and Turkey in 1948 and the Marshall Plan, a program designed to accelerate the economic recovery of Western Europe, were outstanding features of US postwar foreign policy. The North Atlantic Treaty (1949) established a defensive alliance among a number of West European nations and the US. Truman's Point Four program gave technical and scientific aid to developing nations. When, following the North Korean attack on South Korea on 25 June 1950, the UN Security Council resolved that members of the UN should proceed to the aid of South Korea. US naval, air, and ground forces were immediately dispatched by President Truman. An undeclared war ensued, which eventually was brought to a halt by an armistice signed on 27 June 1953.

In 1952, Dwight D. Eisenhower, supreme commander of Allied forces in Europe during World War II, was elected president on the Republican ticket, thereby bringing to an end 20 years of Democratic presidential leadership. In foreign affairs, the Eisenhower administration continued the Truman policy of containing the USSR and threatened "massive retaliation" in the event of Soviet aggression, thus heightening the Cold War between the world's two great nuclear powers. Although Republican domestic policies were more conservative than those of the Democrats, the Eisenhower administration extended certain major social and economic programs of the Roosevelt and Truman administrations, notably Social Security and public housing. The early years of the Eisenhower administration were marked by agitation (arising in 1950) over charges of Communist and other allegedly subversive activities in the US—a phenomenon known as McCarthyism, after Republican Senator Joseph R. McCarthy of Wisconsin, who aroused much controversy with unsubstantiated allegations that Communists had penetrated the US government, especially the Army and the Department of State. Even those who personally opposed McCarthy lent their support to the imposition of loyalty oaths and the blacklisting of persons with left-wing backgrounds.

A major event of the Eisenhower years was the US Supreme Court's decision in *Brown v. Board of Education of Topeka* (1954) outlawing segregation of whites and blacks in public schools. In the aftermath of this ruling, desegregation proceeded slowly and painfully. In the early 1960s, sit-ins, "freedom rides," and similar expressions of nonviolent resistance by blacks and their sympathizers led to a lessening of segregation practices in public facilities. Under Chief Justice Earl Warren, the high court in 1962 mandated the reapportionment of state and federal legislative districts according to a "one person, one vote" formula. It also broadly extended the rights of defendants in criminal trials to include the provision of a defense lawyer at public expense for an accused person unable to afford one, and established the duty of police to advise an accused person of his or her legal rights immediately upon arrest.

In the early 1960s, during the administration of Eisenhower's Democratic successor, John F. Kennedy, the Cold War heated up as Cuba, under the regime of Fidel Castro, aligned itself with the Soviet Union. Attempts by anti-Communist Cuban exiles to invade their homeland in the spring of 1961 failed despite US aid. In October 1962, President Kennedy successfully forced a showdown with the Soviet Union over Cuba in demanding the withdrawal of Soviet-supplied "offensive weapons"—missiles—from the nearby island. On 22 November 1963, President Kennedy was assassinated while riding in a motorcade through Dallas, Texas; hours later, Vice President Lyndon B. Johnson was inaugurated president. In the November 1964 elections, Johnson overwhelmingly defeated his Republican opponent, Barry M. Goldwater, and embarked on a vigorous program of social legislation unprecedented since Roosevelt's New Deal. His "Great

Society" program sought to ensure black Americans' rights in voting and public housing, to give the underprivileged job training, and to provide persons 65 and over with hospitalization and other medical benefits (Medicare). Measures ensuring equal opportunity for minority groups may have contributed to the growth of the woman's rights movement in the late 1960s. This same period also saw the growth of a powerful environmental protection movement.

US military and economic aid to anti-Communist forces in Viet-Nam, which had its beginnings during the Truman administration (while Viet-Nam was still part of French Indochina) and was increased gradually by presidents Eisenhower and Kennedy, escalated in 1965. In that year, President Johnson sent US combat troops to South Viet-Nam and ordered US bombing raids on North Viet-Nam, after Congress (in the Gulf of Tonkin Resolution of 1964) had given him practically carte blanche authority to wage war in that region. By the end of 1968, American forces in Viet-Nam numbered 536,100 men, but US military might was unable to defeat the Vietnamese guerrillas, and the American people were badly split over continuing the undeclared (and, some thought, ill-advised or even immoral) war, with its high price in casualties and materiel. Reacting to widespread dissatisfaction with his Viet-Nam policies, Johnson withdrew in March 1968 from the upcoming presidential race, and in November, Republican Richard M. Nixon, who had been the vice president under Eisenhower, was elected president. Thus, the Johnson years—which had begun with the new hopes of a Great Society but had soured with a rising tide of racial violence in US cities and the assassinations of civil rights leader Martin Luther King, Jr., and US Senator Robert F. Kennedy, among others—drew to a close.

President Nixon gradually withdrew US ground troops from Viet-Nam but expanded aerial bombardment throughout Indochina, and the increasingly unpopular and costly war continued for four more years before a cease-fire—negotiated by Nixon's national security adviser, Henry Kissinger—was finally signed on 27 January 1973 and the last US soldiers were withdrawn. The most protracted conflict in American history had resulted in 46,163 US combat deaths and 303,654 wounded soldiers, and had cost the US government $112 billion in military allocations. Two years later, the South Vietnamese army collapsed, and the North Vietnamese Communist regime united the country.

In 1972, during the last year of his first administration, Nixon initiated the normalization of relations—ruptured in 1949—with the People's Republic of China and signed a strategic arms limitation agreement with the Soviet Union as part of a Nixon-Kissinger policy of pursuing détente with both major Communist powers. (Earlier, in July 1969, American technology had achieved a national triumph by landing the first astronaut on the moon.) The Nixon administration sought to muster a "silent majority" in support of its Indochina policies and its conservative social outlook in domestic affairs. The most momentous domestic development, however, was the Watergate scandal, which began on 17 June 1972 with the arrest of five men associated with Nixon's reelection campaign, during a break-in at Democratic Party headquarters in the Watergate office building in Washington, D.C. Although Nixon was reelected in 1972, subsequent disclosures by the press and by a Senate investigating committee revealed a complex pattern of political "dirty tricks" and illegal domestic surveillance throughout his first term. The president's apparent attempts to obstruct justice by helping his aides cover up the scandal were confirmed by tape recordings (made by Nixon himself) of his private conversations, which the Supreme Court ordered him to release for use as evidence in criminal proceedings. The House voted to begin impeachment proceedings, and in late July 1974, its Judiciary Committee approved three articles of impeachment. On 9 August, Nixon became the first president to resign the office. The following year, Nixon's top aides and former attorney general, John N. Mitchell, were convicted of obstruction and were subsequently sentenced to prison.

Nixon's successor was Gerald R. Ford, who in October 1973 had been appointed to succeed Vice President Spiro T. Agnew when Agnew resigned following his plea of *nolo contendere* to charges that he had evaded paying income tax on moneys he had received from contractors while governor of Maryland. Less than a month after taking office, President Ford granted a full pardon to Nixon for any crimes he may have committed as president. In August 1974, Ford nominated Nelson A. Rockefeller as vice president (he was not confirmed until December), thus giving the country the first instance of a nonelected president and an appointed vice president serving simultaneously. Ford's pardon of Nixon, as well as continued inflation and unemployment, probably contributed to his narrow defeat by a Georgia Democrat, Jimmy Carter, in 1976.

President Carter's forthright championing of human rights—though consistent with the Helsinki accords, the "final act" of the Conference on Security and Cooperation in Europe, signed by the US and 34 other nations in July 1974—contributed to strained relations with the USSR and with some US allies. During 1978–79, the president concluded and secured Senate passage of treaties ending US sovereignty over the Panama Canal Zone. His major accomplishment in foreign affairs, however, was his role in mediating a peace agreement between Israel and Egypt, signed at the camp David, Md., retreat in September 1978. Domestically, the Carter administration initiated a national energy program to reduce US dependence on foreign oil by cutting gasoline and oil consumption and by encouraging the development of alternative energy resources. But the continuing decline of the economy because of double-digit inflation and high unemployment caused his popularity to wane, and confusing shifts in economic policy (coupled with a lack of clear goals in foreign affairs) characterized his administration during 1979 and 1980; a prolonged quarrel with Iran over more than 50 US hostages seized in Tehran on 4 November 1979 contributed to public doubts about his presidency. Exactly a year after the hostages were taken, former California Governor Ronald Reagan defeated Carter in an election that saw the Republican Party score major gains throughout the US. The hostages were released on 20 January 1981, the day of Reagan's inauguration.

Reagan, who survived a chest wound from an assassination attempt in Washington, D.C. in 1981, used his popularity to push through significant policy changes. He succeeded in enacting income tax cuts of 25%, reducing the maximum tax rate on unearned income from 70% to 50%, and accelerating depreciation allowances for businesses. At the same time, he more than doubled the military budget, in constant 1985 dollars, between 1980 and 1989. Vowing to reduce domestic spending, Reagan cut benefits for the working poor, reduced allocations for food stamps and Aid to Families With Dependent Children by 13%, and decreased grants for the education of disadvantaged children. He slashed the budget of the Environmental Protection Agency and instituted a flat rate reimbursement system for the treatment of Medicare patients with particular illnesses, replacing a more flexible arrangement in which hospitals had been reimbursed for "reasonable charges."

Reagan's appointment of Sandra Day O'Connor as the first woman justice of the Supreme Court was widely praised and won unanimous confirmation from the Senate. However, some of his other high-level choices were extremely controversial—none more so than that of his secretary of the interior, James G. Watt, who finally resigned on October 1983. To direct foreign affairs, Reagan named Alexander M. Haig, Jr., former NATO supreme commander for Europe, to the post of secretary of state; Haig, who clashed frequently with other administration officials, resigned in June 1982 and was replace by George P. Shultz. In framing his foreign and defense policy, Reagan insisted on a military buildup as a precondition for arms-control talks with the USSR. His administration sent money and advisers to help the government of El Salvador in its war against leftist rebels, and US advisers were also sent to Honduras, reportedly to aid groups of Nicaraguans trying to overthrow the Sandinista government in their country. Troops were also dispatched to Lebanon in September 1982, as part of a multinational peacekeeping force in Beirut, and to Grenada in October 1983 to oust a leftist government there.

Reelected in 1984, President Reagan embarked on his second term with a legislative agenda that included reduction of federal budget deficits (which had mounted rapidly during his first term in office), further cuts in domestic spending, and reform of the federal tax code. In military affairs, Reagan persuaded Congress to fund on a modest scale his Strategic Defense Initiative, commonly known as Star Wars, a highly complex and extremely costly space-based antimissile system. In 1987, the downing of an aircraft carrying arms to Nicaragua led to the disclosure that a group of National Security Council members had secretly diverted $48 million that the federal government had received in payment from Iran for American arms to rebel forces in Nicaragua. The disclosure prompted the resignation of two of the leaders of the group, Vice Admiral John Poindexter and Lieutenant Colonel Oliver North, as well as investigations by House and Senate committees and a special prosecutor, Lawrence Walsh. The congressional investigations found no conclusive evidence that Reagan had authorized or known of the diversion. Yet they noted that because Reagan had approved of the sale of arms to Iran and had encouraged his staff to assist Nicaraguan rebels despite the prohibition of such assistance by Congress, "the President created or at least tolerated an environment where those who did know of the diversion believed with certainty that they were carrying out the President's policies."

Reagan was succeeded in 1988 by his vice president, George Bush. Benefiting from a prolonged economic expansion, Bush handily defeated Michael Dukakis, governor of Massachusetts and a liberal Democrat. On domestic issues, Bush sought to maintain policies introduced by the Reagan administration. His few legislative initiatives included the passage of legislation establishing strict regulations of air pollution, providing subsidies for child care, and protecting the rights of the disabled. Abroad, Bush showed more confidence and energy. While he responded cautiously to revolutions in Eastern Europe and the Soviet Union, he used his personal relationships with foreign leaders to bring about comprehensive peace talks between Israel and its Arab neighbors, to encourage a peaceful unification of Germany, and to negotiate broad and substantial arms cuts with the Russians. Bush reacted to Iraq's invasion of Kuwait in 1990 by sending 400,000 soldiers to form the basis of a multinational coalition which he assembled and which destroyed Iraq's main force within seven months.

One of the biggest crises that the Bush administration encountered was the collapse of the savings and loan industry in the late eighties. Thrift institutions were required by law to pay low interest rates for deposits and long-term loans. The creation of money market funds for the small investor in the eighties which paid higher rates of return than savings accounts prompted depositors to withdraw their money from banks and invest it in the higher yielding mutual funds. To finance the withdrawals, banks began selling assets at a loss. The deregulation of the savings and loan industry, combined with the increase in federal deposit insurance from $40,000 to $100,000 per account, encouraged many desperate savings institutions to invest in high-

risk real-estate ventures, for which no state supervision or regulation existed. When the majority of such ventures predictably failed, the federal government found itself compelled by law to rescue the thrifts. It is estimated that this will cost to taxpayers $345 billion, in settlements that will continue through 2029.

In his bid for reelection in 1992, Bush faced not only Democratic nominee Bill Clinton, Governor of Arkansas, but also third-party candidate Ross Perot, a Dallas billionaire who had made his fortune in the computer industry. In contrast to Bush's first run for the presidency, when the nation had enjoyed an unusually long period of economic expansion, the economy in 1992 was just beginning to recover from a recession. Although data released the following year indicated that a healthy rebound had already begun in 1992, the public perceived the economy during election year as weak. Clinton took advantage of this perception in his campaign, focusing on the financial concerns of what he called "the forgotten middle class." He also took a more centrist position on many issues than more traditional Democrats, promising fiscal responsibility and economic growth. Clinton defeated Bush, winning 43 percent of the vote to Bush's 38 percent. Perot garnered 18 percent of the vote.

At its outset, Clinton's presidency was plagued by numerous setbacks, most notably the failure of his controversial health care reform plan, drawn up under the leadership of first lady Hillary Rodham Clinton. Major accomplishments included the passage, by a narrow margin, of a deficit-reduction bill calling for tax increases and spending cuts and Congressional approval of the North American Free Trade Agreement, which removed or reduced tariffs on most goods moving across the borders of the United States, Canada, and Mexico. Although supporters and critics agreed that the treaty would create or eliminate relatively few jobs—two hundred thousand—the accord prompted heated debate. Labor strenuously opposed the agreement, seeing it as accelerating the flight of factory jobs to countries with low labor costs such as Mexico, the third largest trading partner of the US. Business, on the other hand, lobbied heavily for the treaty, arguing that it would create new markets for American goods and insisting that competition from Mexico would benefit the American economy.

By the fall of 1994, many American workers, still confronting stagnating wages, benefits, and living standards, had yet to feel the effects of the nation's recovery from the recession of 1990/91. The resulting disillusionment with the actions of the Clinton administration and the Democrat-controlled Congress, combined with the widespread climate of social conservatism resulting from a perceived erosion of traditional moral values led to an overwhelming upset by the Republican party in the 1994 midterm elections. The GOP gained control of both houses of Congress for the first time in over 40 years, also winning 11 gubernatorial races, for control of a total of 30 governorships nationwide. The Republican agenda—increased defense spending and cuts in taxes, social programs, and farm subsidies—had been popularized under the label "Contract with America," the title of a manifesto circulated during the campaign.

The ensuing confrontation between the nation's Democratic president and Republican-controlled Congress came to a head at the end of 1995, when Congress responded to presidential vetoes of appropriations and budget bills by refusing to pass stop gap spending measures, resulting in major shutdowns of the federal government in November and December. The following summer, however, the president and Congress joined forces to reform the welfare system through a bill replacing Aid to Families with Dependent Children with block grants through which welfare funding would largely become the province of the states.

The nation's economic recovery gained strength as the decade advanced, with healthy growth, falling unemployment, and moderate interest and inflation levels. Public confidence in the economy was reflected in a bull market on the stock exchange, which gained 60% between 1995 and 1997. Bolstered by a favorable economy at home and peace abroad, Clinton's faltering popularity rebounded and in 1996 he became the first Democratic president elected to a second term since Franklin D. Roosevelt in 1936, defeating the Republican candidate, former Senate majority leader Robert Dole, and Independent Ross Perot, whose electoral support was greatly reduced from its 1992 level. The Republicans retained control of both houses of Congress. In 1997, President Clinton signed into law a bipartisan budget plan designed to balance the federal budget by 2002 for the first time since 1969, through a combination of tax and spending cuts. In 1998–99, the federal government experienced two straight years of budget surpluses.

In 1998, Special Prosecutor Kenneth Starr submitted a report to Congress that resulted in the House of Representatives passing four articles of impeachment against President Clinton. In the subsequent trial in the Senate, the articles were defeated.

Regulation of the three large financial industries underwent significant change in late 1999. The Gramm-Leach-Bliley Act, (also known as the Financial Modernization Act) passed by Congress in November 1999. It cleared the way for banks, insurance companies, and securities companies to sell each other's services and to engage in merger and acquisition activity. Prior to the Act's passage, activities of the banking, insurance and securities industries were strictly limited by the Glass Steagall Act of 1933, which Gramm-Leach-Bliley repealed.

Health care issues were receiving significant attention as of 2000. On 23 November 1998, 46 states and the District of Columbia together reached a settlement with the large US tobacco companies over compensation for smoking-related health-care costs incurred by the states. Payments to the states, totaling $206 billion, were scheduled to be made over 25 years beginning in 1999. As of 2000, 44 states and the District of Columbia had passed Patients' Rights legislation; 39 passed legislation allowing Medicaid to pay for assisted-living care in qualifying cases; and all 50 states and the District of Columbia passed Children's Health Insurance Programs (CHIP) legislation to provide health care to children in low-income families.

The ongoing strong economy continued through the late 1990s and into 2000. Economic expansion set a record for longevity, and—except for higher gasoline prices during summer 2000, stemming from higher crude oil prices—inflation continued to be relatively low. By 2000, there was additional evidence that productivity growth had improved substantially since the mid-1990s, boosting living standards while helping to hold down increases in costs and prices despite very tight labor markets.

13 GOVERNMENT

The Constitution of the United States, signed in 1787, is the nation's governing document. In the first 10 amendments to the Constitution, ratified in 1791 and known as the Bill of Rights, the federal government is denied the power to infringe on rights generally regarded as fundamental to the civil liberties of the people. These amendments prohibit the establishment of a state religion and the abridgment of freedom of speech, press, and the right to assemble. They protect all persons against unreasonable searches and seizures, guarantee trial by jury, and prohibit excessive bail and cruel and unusual punishments. No person may be required to testify against himself, nor may he be deprived of life, liberty, or property without due process of law. The 13th Amendment (1865) banned slavery; the 15th (1870) protected the freed slaves' right to vote; and the 19th (1920) guaranteed the franchise to women. In all, there have been 26 amendments, the last of which, in 1971, reduced the voting age to 18. The Equal Rights Amendment (ERA), approved by Congress in 1972, would have mandated equality between the sexes; only 35 of the required 38 states had ratified the ERA by the time the ratification deadline expired on 30 June 1982.

The US has a federal form of government, with the distribution of powers between the federal government and the states constitutionally defined. The legislative powers of the federal government are vested in Congress, which consists of the House of Representatives and the Senate. There are 435 members of the House of Representatives. Each state is allotted a number of representatives in proportion to its population as determined by the decennial census. Representatives are elected for two-year terms in every even-numbered year. A representative must be at least 25 years old, must be a resident of the state represented, and must have been a citizen of the US for at least seven years. The Senate consists of two senators from each state, elected for six-year terms. Senators must be at least 30 years old, must be residents of the states from which they are elected, and must have been citizens of the US for at least nine years. One-third of the Senate is elected in every even-numbered year.

Congress legislates on matters of taxation, borrowing, regulation of international and interstate commerce, formulation of rules of naturalization, bankruptcy, coinage, weights and measures, post offices and post roads, courts inferior to the Supreme Court, provision for the armed forces, among many other matters. A broad interpretation of the "necessary and proper" clause of the Constitution has widened considerably the scope of congressional legislation based on the enumerated powers.

A bill that is passed by both houses of Congress in the same form is submitted to the president, who may sign it or veto it. If the president chooses to veto the bill, it is returned to the house in which it originated with the reasons for the veto. The bill may become law despite the president's veto if it is passed again by a two-thirds vote in both houses. A bill becomes law without the president's signature if retained for 10 days while Congress is in session. After Congress adjourns, if the president does not sign a bill within 10 days, an automatic veto ensues.

The president must be "a natural born citizen" at least 35 years old, and must have been a resident of the US for 14 years. Under the 22nd Amendment to the Constitution, adopted in 1951, a president may not be elected more than twice. Each state is allotted a number of electors based on its combined total of US senators and representatives, and, technically, it is these electors who, constituted as the electoral college, cast their vote for president, with all of the state's electoral votes customarily going to the candidate who won the largest share of the popular vote of the state (the District of Columbia also has three electors, making a total of 538 votes). Thus, the candidate who wins the greatest share of the popular vote throughout the US may, in rare cases, fail to win a majority of the electoral vote. If no candidate gains a majority in the electoral college, the choice passes to the House of Representatives.

The vice president, elected at the same time and on the same ballot as the president, serves as ex officio president of the Senate. The vice president assumes the power and duties of the presidency on the president's removal from office or as a result of the president's death, resignation, or inability to perform his duties. In the case of a vacancy in the vice-presidency, the president nominates a successor, who must be approved by a majority in both houses of Congress. The Congress has the power to determine the line of presidential succession in case of the death or disability of both the president and vice president.

Under the Constitution, the president is enjoined to "take care that the laws be faithfully executed." In reality, the president has a considerable amount of leeway in determining to what extent a law is or is not enforced. Congress's only recourse is impeachment, to which it has resorted only twice, in proceedings against presidents Andrew Johnson and Richard Nixon. Both the president and the vice president are removable from office after impeachment by the House and conviction at a Senate trial for "treason, bribery, or other high crimes and misdemeanors." The president has the power to grant reprieves and pardons for offenses against the US except in cases of impeachment.

The president nominates and "by and with the advice and consent of the Senate" appoints ambassadors, public ministers, consuls, and all federal judges, including the justices of the Supreme Court. As commander in chief, the president is ultimately responsible for the disposition of the land, naval, and air forces, but the power to declare war belongs to Congress. The president conducts foreign relations and makes treaties with the advice and consent of the Senate. No treaty is binding unless it wins the approval of two-thirds of the Senate. The president's independence is also limited by the House of Representatives, where all money bills originate.

The president also appoints as his cabinet, subject to Senate confirmation, the secretaries who head the departments of the executive branch. As of 2000, the executive branch included the following cabinet departments: Agriculture (created in 1862), Commerce (1913), Defense (1947), Education (1980), Energy (1977), Health and Human Services (1980), Housing and Urban Development (1965), Interior (1849), Justice (1870), Labor (1913), State (1789), Transportation (1966), Treasury (1789), and Veterans' Affairs (1989). The Department of Defense—headquartered in the Pentagon, the world's largest office building—also administers the various branches of the military: Air Force, Army, Navy, defense agencies, and joint-service schools. The Department of Justice administers the Federal Bureau of Investigation, which originated in 1908; the Central Intelligence Agency (1947) is under the aegis of the Executive office. Among the several hundred quasi-independent agencies are the Federal Reserve System (1913), serving as the nation's central bank, and the major regulatory bodies, notably the Environmental Protection Agency (1970), Federal Communications Commission (1934), Federal Power Commission (1920), Federal Trade Commission (1914), and Interstate Commerce Commission (1887).

Regulations for voting are determined by the individual states for federal as well as for local offices, and requirements vary from state to state. In the past, various southern states used literacy tests, poll taxes, "grandfather" clauses, and other methods to disfranchise black voters, but Supreme Court decisions and congressional measures, including the Voting Rights Act of 1965, more than doubled the number of black registrants in Deep South states between 1964 and 1992. In 1960, only 29.1% of the black voting-age population was registered to vote; by the mid-1990s, that percentage had risen to over 65%.

14POLITICAL PARTIES

Two major parties, Democratic and Republican, have dominated national, state, and local politics since 1860. These parties are made up of clusters of small autonomous local groups primarily concerned with local politics and the election of local candidates to office. Within each party, such groups frequently differ drastically in policies and beliefs on many issues, but once every four years, they successfully bury their differences and rally around a candidate for the presidency. Minority parties have been formed at various periods in US political history, but most have generally allied with one of the two major parties, and none has achieved sustained national prominence. The most successful minority party in recent decades—that of Texas billionaire Ross Perot in 1992—was little more than a protest vote. Various extreme groups on the right and left, including a small US Communist Party, have had little political significance on a national scale; in 1980, the Libertarian Party became the first minor party since

1916 to appear on the ballot in all 50 states. Independent candidates have won state and local office, but no candidate has won the presidency without major party backing. In the 1998 gubernatorial election in Minnesota, Jesse Ventura won as the candidate of the Reform Party.

Traditionally, the Republican Party is more solicitous of business interests and gets greater support from business than does the Democratic Party. A majority of blue-collar workers, by contrast, have generally supported the Democratic Party, which favors more lenient labor laws, particularly as they affect labor unions; the Republican Party often (though not always) supports legislation that restricts the power of labor unions. Republicans favor the enhancement of the private sector of the economy, while Democrats generally urge the cause of greater government participation and regulatory authority, especially at the federal level.

Within both parties there are sharp differences on a great many issues; for example, northeastern Democrats in the past almost uniformly favored strong federal civil rights legislation, which was anathema to the Deep South; eastern Republicans in foreign policy are internationalist-minded, while midwesterners of the same party constituted from 1910 through 1940 the hard core of isolationist sentiment in the country. More recently, "conservative" headings have been adopted by members of both parties who emphasize decentralized government power, strengthened private enterprise, and a strong US military posture overseas, while the designation "liberal" has been applied to those favoring an increased federal government role in economic and social affairs, disengagement from foreign military commitments, and the intensive pursuit of nuclear-arms reduction.

President Nixon's resignation and the accompanying scandal surrounding the Republican Party hierarchy had a telling, if predictable, effect on party morale, as indicated by Republican losses in the 1974 and 1976 elections. The latent consequences of the Viet-Nam and Watergate years appeared to take their toll on both parties, however, in growing apathy toward politics and mistrust of politicians among the electorate. As of 1992, Democrats enjoyed a large advantage over Republicans in voter registration, held both houses of congress, had a majority of state governorships, and controlled most state legislative bodies. The centers of Democratic strength were the South and the major cities; most of the solidly Republican states were west of the Mississippi. Ronald Reagan's successful 1980 presidential bid cut into traditional Democratic strongholds throughout the US, as Republicans won control of the US Senate and eroded state and local Democratic majorities. On the strength of an economic recovery, President Reagan won reelection in November 1984, carrying 49 of 50 states (with a combined total of 525 electoral votes) and 58.8% of the popular vote; the Republicans retained control of the Senate, but the Democrats held on to the House. Benefiting from a six-year expansion of the economy, Republican George Bush won 54% of the vote in 1988. As Reagan had, Bush successfully penetrated traditionally Democratic regions. He carried every state in the South as well as the industrial states of the north.

Bush's approval rating reached a high of 91% in March of 1991 in the wake of the Persian Gulf War. By July of 1992, however, that rating had plummeted to 25%, in part because Bush appeared to be disengaged from domestic issues, particularly the 1991 recession. Bill Clinton, governor of Arkansas and twenty years younger than Bush, presented himself to the electorate as a "New Democrat." He took more moderate positions than traditional New Deal Democrats, including calling for a middle-class tax cut, welfare reform, national service, and such traditionally Republican goals as getting tough on crime. The presidential race took on an unpredictable dimension with the entrance of Independent Ross Perot, a Texas billionaire. Perot, who attacked the budget deficit and called for shared sacrifice, withdrew from the race in July and then re-entered it in October. Clinton won the election with 43% of the vote, Bush received 38%, and Perot captured 18%, more than any third-party presidential candidate since Theodore Roosevelt in 1912. The Republicans gained nine seats in the House of Representatives while the Democrats picked up one seat in the Senate. In 1996 Bill Clinton became the first Democratic president since Franklin Roosevelt to be elected to a second term, with 49% of the popular vote to 41% for Republican Bob Dole, and 8% for Ross Perot, who once again ran as an Independent. Republicans retained control of the House and Senate.

Aided by a growing climate of conservatism on moral issues and popular discontent with the pace of economic recovery from the recent recession, the Republicans accomplished an historic upset in the 1994 midterm elections, gaining control of both houses of Congress for the first time since 1952. They gained 52 seats in the House, for a majority of 230–204, and 8 seats in the Senate, for a majority that came to 53–47 once Democrat Richard Shelby of Alabama changed parties shortly after the election. The Republicans also increased their power at the state level, winning 11 governorships, for a national total of 30. The number of state legislatures under Republican control increased from 8 to 19, with 18 controlled by the Democrats and 12 under split control. After the 1998 election, the Republican majority had eroded slightly in the House, with the 106th Congress including 223 Republicans, 210 Democrats, and 2 Independents; the Senate included 55 Republicans and 45 Democrats.

The 1984 election marked a turning point for women in national politics. Geraldine A. Ferraro, a Democrat, became the first female vice-presidential nominee of a major US political party; no woman has ever captured a major-party presidential nomination. As of 2000, 9 women served in the US Senate, and 58 women held seats in the US House of Representatives.

The 1984 presidential candidacy of Jesse L. Jackson, election, the first black ever to win a plurality in a statewide presidential preference primary, likewise marked the emergence of black Americans as a political force, especially within the Democratic Party. In 1992 a black woman, Democrat Carol Moseley Braun of Illinois, won election to the Senate, becoming the first black senator; Moseley Braun lost her reelection bid in 1998. There were 39 blacks and 17 Hispanics in the House as of 2000.

The candidates in the 2000 presidential were Republican George W. Bush, son of former president George Herbert Walker Bush; his vice-presidential running mate was Dick Cheney. The Democratic candidate was Vice President Al Gore, Jr. (Clinton Administration 1992–2000). Gore chose Joseph Lieberman, senator from Connecticut, as his running mate. Lieberman, an Orthodox Jew, became the first Jew to run for national office.

15LOCAL GOVERNMENT

Governmental units within each state comprise counties, municipalities, and such special districts as those for water, sanitation, highways, parks. and recreation. There are more than 3,000 counties in the US; more than 19,000 municipalities, including cities, villages, towns, and boroughs; nearly 15,000 school districts; and at least 31,000 special districts. Additional townships, authorities, commissions, and boards make up the rest of the nearly 85,000 local governmental units.

The states are autonomous within their own spheres of government, and their autonomy is defined in broad terms by the 10th Amendment to the US Constitution, which reserves to the states such powers as are not granted to the federal government and not denied to the states. The states may not, among other restrictions, issue paper money, conduct foreign relations, impair the obligations of contracts, or establish a government that is not republican in form. Subsequent amendments to the Constitution and many Supreme Court decisions added to the restrictions

placed on the states. The 13th Amendment prohibited the states from legalizing the ownership of one person by another (slavery); the 14th Amendment deprived the states of their power to determine qualifications for citizenship; the 15th Amendment prohibited the states from denying the right to vote because of race, color, or previous condition of servitude; and the 19th, from denying the vote to women.

Since the Civil War, the functions of the state have expanded. Local business—that is, business not involved in foreign or interstate commerce—is regulated by the state. The states create subordinate governmental bodies such as counties, cities, towns, villages, and boroughs, whose charters they either issue or, where home rule is permitted, approve. States regulate employment of children and women in industry, and enact safety laws to prevent industrial accidents. Unemployment insurance is a state function, as are education, public health, highway construction and safety, operation of a state highway patrol, and various kinds of personal relief. The state and local governments still are primarily responsible for providing public assistance, despite the large part the federal government plays in financing welfare.

Each state is headed by an elected governor. State legislatures are bicameral except Nebraska's, which has been unicameral since 1934. Generally, the upper house is called the senate, and the lower house the house of representatives or the assembly. Bills must be passed by both houses, and the governor has a suspensive veto, which usually may be overridden by a two-thirds vote.

The number, population, and geographic extent of the more than 3,000 counties in the US—including the analogous units called boroughs in Alaska and parishes in Louisiana—show no uniformity from state to state. The county is the most conspicuous unit of rural local government and has a variety of powers, including location and repair of highways, county poor relief, determination of voting precincts and of polling places, and organization of school and road districts. City governments, usually headed by a mayor or city manager, have the power to levy taxes; to borrow; to pass, amend, and repeal local ordinances; and to grant franchises for public service corporations. Township government through an annual town meeting is an important New England tradition.

From the 1960s into the 21st century, a number of large cities began to suffer severe fiscal crises brought on by a combination of factors. Loss of tax revenues stemmed from the migration of middle-class residents to the suburbs and the flight of many small and large firms seeking to avoid the usually higher costs of doing business in urban areas. Low-income groups, many of them unskilled blacks and hispanic migrants, came to constitute large segments of city populations, placing added burdens on locally funded welfare, medical, housing, and other services without providing the commensurate tax base for additional revenues.

16JUDICIAL SYSTEM

The Supreme Court, established by the US Constitution, is the nation's highest judicial body, consisting of the chief justice of the US and eight associate justices. All justices are appointed by the president with the advice and consent of the Senate. Appointments are for life "during good behavior," otherwise terminating only by resignation or impeachment and conviction.

The original jurisdiction of the Supreme Court is relatively narrow; as an appellate court, it is open to appeal from decisions of federal district courts, circuit courts of appeals, and the highest courts in the states, although it may dismiss an appeal if it sees fit to do so. The Supreme Court, by means of a writ of certiorari, may call up a case from a district court for review. Regardless of how cases reach it, the Court enforces a kind of unity on the decisions of the lower courts. It also exercises the power of judicial review, determining the constitutionality of state laws, state constitutions, congressional statutes, and federal regulations, but only when these are specifically challenged.

The Constitution empowers Congress to establish all federal courts inferior to the Supreme Court. On the lowest level and handling the greatest proportion of federal cases are the district courts—including one each in Puerto Rico, Guam, the Virgin Islands, the Northern Mariana Islands, and the District of Columbia—where all offenses against the laws of the US are tried. Civil actions that involve cases arising under treaties and laws of the US and under the Constitution, where the amount in dispute is greater than $5,000, also fall within the jurisdiction of the district courts. District courts have no appellate jurisdiction; their decisions may be carried to the courts of appeals, organized into 13 circuits. These courts also hear appeals from decisions made by administrative commissions. For most cases, this is usually the last stage of appeal, except where the court rules that a statute of a state conflicts with the Constitution of the US, with federal law, or with a treaty. Special federal courts include the Court of Claims, Court of Customs and Patent Appeals, and Tax Court.

State courts operate independently of the federal judiciary. Most states adhere to a court system that begins on the lowest level with a justice of the peace and includes courts of general trial jurisdiction, appellate courts, and, at the apex of the system, a state supreme court. The court of trial jurisdiction, sometimes called the county or superior court, has both original and appellate jurisdiction; all criminal cases (except those of a petty kind) and some civil cases are tried in this court. The state's highest court, like the Supreme Court of the US, interprets the constitution and the laws of the state.

The grand jury is a body of from 13 to 24 persons that brings indictments against individuals suspected of having violated the law. Initially, evidence is presented to it by either a justice of the peace or a prosecuting county or district attorney. The trial or petit jury of 12 persons is used in trials of common law, both criminal and civil, except where the right to a jury trial is waived by consent of all parties at law. It judges the facts of the case, while the court is concerned exclusively with questions of law. The US accepts the compulsory jurisdiction of the International Court of Justice with reservations.

17ARMED FORCES

The armed forces of the United States of America in 2000 numbered 1.37 million on active duty and 1.27 million in the Ready Reserve, a category of participation that allows regular training with pay and extended active duty periods for training. The Standby and Retired Reserve includes about 28,700 experienced officers and NCOs who can be recalled in a national emergency. Membership in all of these forces is voluntary and has been since 1973 when conscription expired as the Viet Nam war was winding down. The active duty force includes 199,900 women, who serve in all grades and all occupational specialties except direct ground combat units and some aviation billets.

In the 1990s, the armed forces reduced their personnel numbers and force structure because of the diminished threat of a nuclear war with the former Soviet Union or a major conflict in central Europe. Despite the interlude of the Gulf War, 1990–91, the force reductions continued throughout the decade, forcing some restructuring of the active duty forces, with emphasis on rapid deployment to deter or fight major regional conflicts much like the Gulf War, in Korea, elsewhere in the Middle East, or Latin America (e.g. Cuba). The conventional force debate centered on whether the US could or should maintain forces to fight two regional conflicts simultaneously. In the spring of 1999, the US took part in the NATO air campaign in response to the crisis in Kosovo, and the ensuing US participation in peace-

keeping operations in the region brought with it the prospect of another long-term overseas deployment.

For the purposes of administration, personnel management, logistics, and training, the traditional four military services in the Department of Defense remain central to strategic planning. The US Army numbers 469,300 (71,000 women) soldiers on active duty, divided roughly between 6 heavy (armored or mechanized) divisions, 4 light (infantry airborne, airmobile) divisions, and three independent infantry battalions as well as three armored cavalry regiments, five aviation brigades, and 11 air defense battalions. Army special operations missions go to Special Forces groups, an airborne ranger regiment, an aviation group, and a psychological warfare group with civil affairs and communications support units. The Army has 7,684 main battle tanks, 6,715 infantry fighting vehicles, 17,800 other tracked vehicles, almost 6,000 towed or self-propelled artillery, some 249 aircraft, and about 4,923 armed and transport helicopters. The Army National Guard (362,400; 35,700 women) emphasizes the preparation of combat units up to division size for major regional conflicts while the Army Reserve (421,500; 49,700 women) prepares individuals to fill active units or provide combat support or service support/technical/medical units upon mobilization. In addition, the National Guard retains a residual state role in suppressing civil disturbances and providing disaster relief.

The US Navy (369,800; 52,800 women) has shifted from its role in nuclear strategic deterrence and control of sea routes to Europe and Asia to the projection of naval power from the sea. Naval task forces normally combine three combat elements: air, surface, and subsurface. The Navy mans 24 nuclear-powered attack submarines with one configured for special operations; most of these boats can launch cruise missiles at land targets.

Naval aviation is centered on 12 carriers (9 nuclear-powered) and 11 carrier aircraft wings. Including its armed ASW helicopters and armed long-range ASW patrol aircraft—as well as a large fleet of communications and support aircraft—the Navy controls 1,510 aircraft and 506 armed helicopters. Naval aviation reserves provide additional wings for carrier deployment. The surface force includes 27 cruisers (22 with advanced anti-air suites), 54 destroyers, 37 frigates, 42 amphibious ships, 27 mine warfare ships, and 21 patrol and coastal combatants. More ships are kept in ready reserve or are manned by surface line reserve units. The fleet support force also includes specialized ships for global logistics that are not base-dependent.

The Marine Corps, a separate naval service, is organized into three active divisions and three aircraft wings of the Fleet Marine Force, which also include 3 Force Service Support groups. The Marine Corps (171,000; 9,800 women) emphasizes amphibious landings but trains for a wide-range of contingency employments. The marines have 403 main battle tanks, 1,321 amphibious armored vehicles, and about 1,000 towed artillery pieces.

The US Air Force (361,400; 66,300 women) has focused on becoming rapidly deployable rather than US-based. Almost all its aircraft are now dedicated to nonstrategic roles in support of forward deployed ground and naval forces. The Air Force stresses the missions of air superiority and interdiction with complementary operations in electronic warfare and reconnaissance, but it also includes 28 transport squadrons. Air Force personnel manage the US radar and satellite early-warning and intelligence effort. The Air Force Reserve and Air National Guard (roughly 106,300 active reserves) provides a wide range of flying and support units, and its flying squadrons have demonstrated exceptional readiness and combat skills on contingency missions. Air Force reserves, for example, provide the backbone of the air refueling and transport fleets.

The armed forces are deployed in functional unified or specified commands for actual missions. The Strategic Command controls the strategic nuclear deterrence forces: 550 ICMBs, 18 Navy fleet ballistic missile submarines, and 178 operational long-range bombers. These forces have undergone reduction to conform with the START arms limitation treaty of 1991, as amended in 1992, so that by the year 2003 the US will have only 500 ICMBs, 1,728 SLBMs, and 95 nuclear-armed bombers. Strategic Command is complemented by Space Command/North American Air Defense Command. The conventional forces are assigned to a mix of geographic and functional commands: Atlantic Command, European Command, Central Command, Southern Command, and Pacific Command, as well as Transportation Command and Special Operations Command. The Army also maintains a Forces Command for ground forces in strategic reserve in the US. Major operational units are deployed to Germany, Korea, and Japan as part of collective security alliances. About one-third of active duty personnel are assigned to overseas billets (1–3 years) or serve in air, naval, and ground units that serve short tours on a rotational basis. Peacekeeping forces are stationed in Bosnia, Croatia, Egypt, Saudi Arabia, and Turkey; observers are stationed in Georgia, Iraq, Kuwait, and the Western Sahara region.

Patterns of defense spending reflect the movement away from Cold War assumptions and confrontation with the former Soviet Union and the People's Republic of China. During the 1980s when defense spending hovered around $300 billion a year and increased roughly 30% over the decade, defense spending absorbed roughly 6% of the gross domestic spending, 25% of federal spending, and 16% of net public spending. In the early 1990s, when the defense budget slipped back to the $250–$260 billion level, the respective percentages were 4.5, 18, and 11, the lowest levels of support for defense since the Korean War (1950). In 1997, the defense budget was $267.2 million or 3.4% of GDP. US military assistance abroad shows similar trends. From 1981 to 1991 the US sold $118 billion in arms abroad and provided some outright grants, military training, and other support services, most in dollar value to its NATOs allies, Sauʻdi Arabia, Israel, South Korea, and Japan. This spending also declined in the 1990s. However, when the Czech Republic, Hungary, and Poland become full members of NATO (slated to occur between 2002 and 2005), US defense costs are expected to rise in order to support these countries' efforts to meet NATO military standards.

The Clinton administration's defense budget for 2000 called for a $112 billion rise in military spending in the first five years of the 21st century. Particular target areas for increased funds included military pay (the largest increase since 1982), equipment modernization and readiness, and budgeting for unforeseen contingencies. Purchases of new weapons were slated to reach almost $62 billion in 2001.

18INTERNATIONAL COOPERATION

The US, whose failure to join the League of Nations was a major cause of the failure of that body, is a charter member of the UN, having joined on 24 October 1945. The US participates in ECE, ECLAC, ESCAP, and all the nonregional specialized agencies except UNESCO, from which it withdrew at the end of 1984, charging the agency with mismanagement and with bias against Western nations; there are also policy differences between the US and several other UN agencies. The US share of the total funds required for the upkeep of the UN is about 25% of the total, far more than any other nation; however, the US withheld its payments during the 1990s. The US participates in more than 70 intergovernmental organizations, including the Asian Development Bank, OECD, the IMF and IBRD (World Bank), and international councils and commissions on various industries. The US also participates actively in the Permanent Court of

Arbitration. Hemispheric agencies include the Inter-American Committee on the Alliance for Progress, IADB, and OAS.

NATO is the principal military alliance to which the US belongs. The ANZUS alliance is a mutual defense pact between Australia, New Zealand, and the US; in 1986, following New Zealand's decision to ban US nuclear-armed or nuclear-powered ships from its ports, the US renounced its ANZUS treaty security commitments to New Zealand. The nation is a member of the WTO but refused to sign the Law of the Sea because of unwillingness to relinquish rights over seabed mining; in keeping with international practice, however, the US does maintain a 200-mi coastal economic zone. In 1992, the US, Canada, and Mexico signed the North American Free Trade Agreement (NAFTA), creating a free-trade zone among the three countries. It was ratified by all three governments in 1993 and took effect the following year. In 1986, the US approved the 1948 UN convention against genocide.

19ECONOMY

In variety and quantity, the natural resources of the US probably exceed those of any other nation, with the possible exception of the former Soviet Union. The US is among the world's leading exporters of coal, wheat, corn, and soybeans. However, because of its vast economic growth, the US depends increasingly on foreign sources for a long list of raw materials including oil.

By the middle of the 20th century, the US was a leading consumer of nearly every important industrial raw material. The industry of the US produced about 40% of the world's total output of goods, despite the fact that the country's population comprised about 6% of the world total and its land area about 7% of the earth's surface. In recent decades, US production has continued to expand, though at a slower rate than that of most other industrialized nations.

In absolute terms the US far exceeds every other nation in the size of its gross national product (GNP), which more than tripled between 1970 and 1983 to $3.3 trillion. In 1998 the nation's gross domestic product (GDP) reached a record $8.5 trillion in current dollars, with per capita GDP reaching $31,500.

Inflation has not been as significant factor in the US economy in the 1990s as it was in the 1970s and 1980s. The US inflation rate tends to be lower than that of the majority of industrialized nations. For the period 1970–78, for example, consumer prices increased by an annual average of 6.7%, less than in every other Western country except Austria, Luxembourg, Switzerland, and West Germany, and well below the price increase in Japan. The double-digit inflation of 1979–81 came as a rude shock to most Americans, with economists and politicians variously blaming international oil price rises, federal monetary policies, and US government spending.

The following table shows the erosion of the purchasing power of the dollar between 1950 and 1995:

	PRODUCER PRICES (1982=$1.00)	CONSUMER PRICES (1982–84=$1.00)
1950	3.546	4.151
1955	3.279	3.732
1960	2.994	3.373
1965	2.933	3.166
1970	2.545	2.574
1975	1.718	1.859
1980	1.136	1.215
1985	0.955	0.928
1990	0.839	0.766
1992	0.812	0.713
1995	0.760	0.656

The US entered the post–World War II era with the world's largest, and strongest, economy. Public confidence in both business and government was strong, the nation enjoyed the largest peacetime trade surplus in its history, and the gross national product grew to a record $482.7 billion by the end of the 1950s. In the sixties the country enjoyed the most sustained period of economic expansion it had known, accompanied by rising productivity and low unemployment. Real income rose 50% during the decade, and US investment in foreign countries reached $49 billion in 1965, up from $11.8 billion in 1950. Big business and big government were both powerful forces in the economy during this period, when large industrial corporations accounted for vast portions of the national income, and the federal government expanded its role in such areas as social welfare, scientific research, space technology, and development of the nation's highway system.

After two decades of prosperity, Americans experienced an economic downturn in the 1970s, a period known for the unprecedented combination of lagging economic growth and inflation that gave birth to the term *stagflation*. Foreign competitors in Japan and Europe challenged the global dominance of American manufacturers, and oil crises in 1973–74 and 1979 shook public confidence in the institutions of both government and business. The forced bailouts of Chrysler and Lockheed were symbolic of the difficult transition to a new economic era, marked by the growing importance of the service sector and the ascendancy of small businesses.

During Ronald Reagan's first presidential term, from 1980 to 1984, the nation endured two years of severe recession followed by two years of robust recovery. The inflation rate was brought down, and millions of new jobs were created. The economic boom of the early and mid-eighties, however, coincided with a number of alarming developments. Federal budget deficits, caused by dramatic increases in the military budget and by rising costs of entitlement programs such as Medicaid and Medicare, averaged more than $150 billion annually. By 1992, the total deficit reached $290 billion, or $1,150 for every American. In addition, corporate debt rose dramatically, and household borrowing grew twice as fast as personal income. The eighties also witnessed a crisis in the banking industry, caused by a combination of factors, including high inflation and interest rates, problem loans to developing countries, and speculative real-estate ventures that caused thousands of banks to fail when the real-estate boom of the early eighties collapsed. In 1998, the federal budget showed a surplus of $69 billion.

The disparity between the affluent and the poor widened in at the end of the 20th century. The share of the nation's income received by the richest 5% of American families rose from 18.6% in 1977 to 24.5% in 1990, while the share of the poorest 20% fell from 5.7% to 4.3%. Externally, the nation's trade position deteriorated, as a high level of foreign investment combined with an uncompetitive US dollar to create a ballooning trade deficit. In 1990, the American economy plunged into a recession. Factors contributing to the slump included rising oil prices following Iraq's invasion of Kuwait, a sharp increase in interest rates, and declining availability of credit. Output fell 1.6% and 1.7 million jobs were cut. Unemployment rose from 5.2% in 1989 to 7.5% in 1991, but had fallen to 4.5% by 1998.

The recovery that began in March 1991 inaugurated a sustained period of expansion that, as of mid-2000, was the third longest since World War II, characterized by moderation in the key areas of growth, inflation, unemployment, and interest rates. Real GDP growth, which fluctuated between 2% and 3.5% throughout the period, was 3.9% for 1998. After peaking at 7.5%, unemployment declined steadily throughout the early and mid-1990s, falling to 5.6% in 1995, 5.3% at the end of 1996, and, as of 1998, remaining below 5%. After 1993/94, inflation mostly remained under 3%. One exception to the generally moderate character of the economy was the stock market, which rose 60% between 1995 and 1997, buoyed by the combination of low unemployment and low inflation, as well as strong corporate earnings. By 1999/2000, stock market growth had slowed somewhat. Further cause for optimism was the bipartisan balanced-budget legislation enacted and signed into law in 1997. The plan, combining tax and spending cuts over a five-year period, was aimed at balancing the federal budget by 2002 for the first time since 1969.

At the beginning of the 21st century, significant economic concerns—aside from the inevitable worry over how long the boom could last without an eventual downturn—included the nation's sizable trade deficit, the increasing medical costs of an aging population, and the failure of the strong economy to improve conditions for the poor. Since 1975, gains in household income were experienced almost exclusively by the top 20% of households. However, in the late 1990s and early 2000, productivity was continuing to grow, inflation was relatively low, and the labor market was tight.

20 INCOME

The US Central Intelligence Agency (CIA) reports that in 1998 the United States's gross domestic product (GDP) was estimated at $8.5 trillion. The per capita GDP was estimated at $31,500. The annual growth rate of GDP was estimated at 3.9%. The average inflation rate in 1998 was 1.6%. The CIA defines GDP as the value of all final goods and services produced within a nation in a given year and computed on the basis of purchasing power parity (PPP) rather than value as measured on the basis of the rate of exchange. It was estimated that agriculture accounted for 2% of GDP, industry 23%, and services 75%.

The World Bank reports that for the same period per capita private consumption (in PPP terms) was $21,515. Private consumption includes expenditures of individuals, households, and nongovernmental organizations. It was estimated that between 1990 and 1998 private consumption grew at an annual rate of 3.0%. Approximately 13% of household consumption was spent on food, 9% on fuel, 4% on health care, and 6% on education. The richest 10% of the population accounted for approximately 31% of household consumption and the poorest 10% approximately 1.8%.

21 LABOR

About 139,368,000 persons constituted the country's civilian labor force in 1999. During 1998, the unemployment rate was 4.5%. A federal survey in January 1997 revealed the following nonfarm employment patterns:

	EMPLOYEES	AVE. HOURLY EARNINGS (EST.)
Agricultural services	3,036,000	n/a
Mining	553,000	$16.18
Construction	7,792,000	$15.69
Manufacturing	20,591,000	$13.07
Durable goods	12,467,000	n/a
Nondurable goods	8,124,000	n/a
Transportation and public utilities	8,724,000	$14.76
Wholesale and retail trade	25,892,000	
Wholesale trade	4,824,000	$13.15
Retail trade	21,068,000	$8.22
Finance, insurance, and real estate	8,007,000	$13.04
Services, of which:	46,073,000	$12.21
Private households	946,000	n/a
Other service industries	45,127,000	n/a
Professional services	30,923,000	n/a
Public administration	5,715,000	n/a

As of 1999, agriculture engaged 3,281,000 Americans. Earnings of workers vary considerably with type of work and section of country. In 1999, the national average wage was $13.24 per hour for nonagricultural workers, with an average workweek of 34.5 hours. Workers in manufacturing had a national average wage of $13.91, with the longest average workweek of all categories of workers at 41.7 hours.

There were 39 national labor unions with over 100,000, the largest being the National Educational Association with 2.5 million members as of 2000. The most important federation of organized workers in the US is the American Federation of Labor–Congress of Industrial Organizations (AFL–CIO), whose affiliated unions had 13 million members as of 2000, down from 14.1 million members in 1992. The major independent industrial and labor unions and their estimated 2000 memberships are the International Brotherhood of Teamsters, 1,500,000, and the United Automobile Workers, 760,000 (407,00 of whom work for General Motors, Ford, and Daimler-Chrysler). Most of the other unaffiliated unions are confined to a single establishment or locality. US labor unions exercise economic and political influence not only through the power of strikes and slowdowns but also through the human and financial resources they allocate to political campaigns (usually on behalf of Democratic candidates) and through the selective investment of multibillion-dollar pension funds.

The National Labor Relations Act of 1935 (The Wagner Act), the basic labor law of the US, was considerably modified by the Labor-Management Relations Act of 1947 (the Taft-Hartley Act) and the Labor-Management Reporting and Disclosure Act of 1959 (the Landrum-Griffin Act). Closed-shop agreements, which require employers to hire only union members, are banned. The union shop agreement, however, is permitted; it allows the hiring of nonunion members on the condition that they join the union within a given period of time.

As of 2000, 21 states had right-to-work laws, forbidding the imposition of union membership as a condition of employment. Under the Taft-Hartley Act, the president of the US may postpone a strike for 90 days in the national interest. The act of 1959 requires all labor organizations to file constitutions, bylaws, and detailed financial reports with the secretary of labor, and stipulates methods of union elections. The National Labor Relations Board seeks to remedy or prevent unfair labor practices and supervises union elections, while the Equal Employment Opportunity Commission seeks to prevent discrimination in hiring, firing, and apprenticeship programs.

The number of work stoppages and of workers involved reached a peak in the late 1960s and early 1970s, declining steadily thereafter. In 1999 there were 17 major stoppages involving 73,000 workers resulting in 1,996 workdays idle, compared with 1995, when there were 31 major stoppages involving 191,500 workers resulting in 5,771 days idle; a major stoppage was defined as one involving 1,000 workers or more for a minimum of one day or shift.

22AGRICULTURE

In 1998, the US produced a substantial share of the world's agricultural commodities, including soybeans, 47%; corn for grain (maize), 41%; cotton, 16%; wheat, 12%; and tobacco, 10%. Much US farm produce is exported. Agricultural exports reached $62.5 billion in 1997.

Between 1930 and 1998, the number of farms in the US declined from 6,546,000 to an estimated 2,190,000. The total amount of farmland increased from 399 million hectares (986 million acres) in 1930 to 479 million hectares (1.18 billion acres) in 1959 but declined to 386 million hectares (954 million acres) in 1998. From 1930 to 1998, the size of the average farm tripled from 61 to 136 hectares (from 151 to 435 acres), a result of the

consolidation effected by large-scale mechanized production. The farm population, which comprised 35% of the total US population in 1910, declined to 25% during the Great Depression of the 1930s, and dwindled to less than 2% by 1998.

A remarkable increase in the application of machinery to farms took place during and after World War II. Tractors, trucks, milking machines, grain combines, corn pickers, and pickup bailers became virtual necessities in farming. In 1920 there were less than one tractor in use for every 400 hectares (1,000 acres) of cropland harvested; by 1997 there were 5 tractors per 400 hectares. Two other elements essential to US farm productivity are chemical fertilizers and irrigation. In 1997, $10.9 billion allocated to fertilizers and lime represented more than 6% of farm operating expenses. Arable land under irrigation amounted to 12% of the total in 1997.

Substantial quantities of corn, the most valuable crop produced in the US, are grown in almost every state; its yield and price are important factors in the economies of the regions where it is grown. The following table reports figures for production of selected US crops in 1998, and their percent of world production:

	PRODUCTION (1,000 METRIC TONS)	US AS PERCENT OF WORLD
Wheat	69,410	11.7
Corn	247,943	41.0
Rice	8,530	1.5
Soybeans	75,028	47.4
Cotton	3,004	16.4

In 1997, the total farm cash receipts of $208.7 billion were made up of the following (in millions): feed crops, $27,638; oil-bearing crops, $19,911; cotton (lint and seed), $6,515; tobacco, $2,886; vegetables and melons, $15,086; fruits and tree nuts, $12,790; and livestock $95,568. In 1998, the United States had 23,758 horticultural facilities, with sales of $10.6 billion.

23ANIMAL HUSBANDRY

The livestock population at the end of 1998 included an estimated 98.5 million head of cattle, 62.2 million hogs, and 7.2 million sheep and lambs. That year, there were 1.7 billion chickens, and 95 million turkeys. Milk production totaled 71.4 million metric tons in that year, with Wisconsin, California, and New York together accounting for much of the total. Wisconsin, Minnesota, and California account for more than half of all US butter production, which totaled 491,000 metric tons in 1998; in that year, the US was the world's largest producer of cheese, with more than 3.4 million metric tons (28% of the world's total). The US produced an estimated 17% of the world's meat supply in 1998. In 1997, meat animals accounted for 52% of the value of livestock products; dairy products, 22%; poultry and eggs, 23%; and other products, 3%.

24FISHING

The 1997 commercial catch was 5.5 million tons. Food fish make up 78% of the catch, and nonfood fish, processed for fertilizer and oil, 22%.

Alaska pollock, with landings of 1,139,642 tons, was the most important species in quantity among the commercial fishery landings in the US in 1997. Other leading species by volume included Gulf menhaden, 597,565 tons; Atlantic menhaden, 322,239 tons; Pacific cod, 299,970 tons; channel catfish, 238,115 tons; North Pacific hake, 226,616 tons; and American cupped oyster, 178,100 tons. In 1997, exports of fish products totaled $2,912.9 million (third after Norway and China). The leading species by export value that year included (in millions): frozen Pacific salmon, $252.2; fresh or chilled lobsters, $177.6; frozen Alaska pollock, $162.4; sea urchin, $87; frozen soles, $86;

canned sockeye salmon, $69.8; frozen squid, $67.2; and frozen sablefish, $64.

In 1997, the total value of aquacultural production was $771.2 million, consisting mostly of catfish, oysters, trout, and crayfish. In 1998, there were 1,810 aquacultural farms in the US, with sales of $179.8 million.

Pollution is a problem of increasing concern to the US fishing industry; dumping of raw sewage, industrial wastes, spillage from oil tankers, and blowouts of offshore wells are the main threats to the fishing grounds. Overfishing is also a threat to the viability of the industry in some areas, especially Alaska.

[25]FORESTRY

US forestland covered about 212.5 million hectares (525 million acres) in 1995, or 23% of the land area. Major forest regions include the eastern, central hardwood, southern, Rocky Mountain, and Pacific coast areas. The National Forest Service lands account for approximately 19% of the nation's forestland. Extensive tracts of land (4 million acres or more) are under ownership of private lumber companies in Alabama, Arkansas, Florida, Georgia, Maine, Oregon, and Washington.

Domestic production of roundwood during 1997 amounted to 490.7 million cu m, of which softwoods accounted for roughly 60%. Other forest products in 1997 included 60.5 million metric tons of wood pulp, 86.3 million metric tons of paper and paperboard (excluding newsprint), and 38.5 million cu m of wood-based panels. Rising petroleum prices in the late 1970s sparked a revival in the use of wood as home heating fuel, especially in the Northeast. Fuelwood and charcoal production amounted to 74.6 million cu m in 1997.

Throughout the 19th century, the federal government distributed forestlands lavishly as a means of subsidizing railroads and education. By the turn of the century, the realization that the forests were not inexhaustible led to the growth of a vigorous conservation movement, which was given increased impetus during the 1930s and again in the late 1960s. Federal timberlands are no longer open for private acquisition, although the lands can be leased for timber cutting and for grazing. In recent decades, the states also have moved in the direction of retaining forestlands and adding to their holdings when possible.

[26]MINING

Rich in a variety of mineral resources, the US is a world leader in the production of many important mineral commodities, such as aluminum, cement, copper, pig iron, lead, molybdenum, phosphates, potash, salt, sulfur, uranium, and zinc. The leading mineral-producing states are Arizona (copper, construction sand and gravel, portland cement, molybdenum); California (portland cement, construction sand and gravel, gold, boron); Michigan (iron ore, portland cement, construction sand and gravel, magnesium compounds); Georgia (clays, crushed and broken stone, portland and masonry cement, construction sand and gravel); Florida (phosphate rock, crushed and broken stone, portland cement, construction sand and gravel); Utah (copper, gold, magnesium metal, construction sand and gravel); Texas (portland cement, crushed and broken stone, magnesium metal, and construction sand and gravel); and Minnesota (iron ore, construction and industrial sand and gravel, crushed and broken stone). Oklahoma, and New Mexico are important for petroleum and natural gas, and Kentucky, West Virginia, and Pennsylvania, important for coal. Iron ore supports the nation's most basic nonagricultural industry, iron and steel manufacture; the major domestic sources are in the Lake Superior area, with Minnesota and Michigan leading all other states in iron ore yields.

[27]ENERGY AND POWER

The US, with about 4.6% of the world's population, consumed 24.3% of the world's energy in 1995. The US is also the world's leading energy producer, accounting for about 19.1% of the world's primary energy production in 1995. In 1999, US coal production was 1.10 billion short tons, ranking second only to China in the world. Natural gas production was 18.7 trillion cu ft; and crude oil production was 5.93 million barrels per day (about 9% of world total). Coal supplied about 22% of energy consumed (Btu basis) in 1999; nuclear sources, 8%; natural gas, 23.4%; hydroelectric power, 3.6%; petroleum, 39%; and geothermal, wind, photovoltaic, and wood and waste, 4%. Increased use of natural gas was the most spectacular development in the commercial marketing of fuel after World War II; between 1950 and the peak in 1975, its share of total US energy production doubled from 20% to 40%; since then, production has stabilized at just under 30%.

Mineral fuel production in the US dates to the early 1800s; by 1810–19 US coal production was about 230,000 tons, and fuelwood production equivalent to 26 million tons of coal. In 1854, a refinery opened in Brooklyn, New York, to process shale and coal to kerosene. In 1859, the US recorded its first oil production, and in 1870, John D. Rockefeller established the Standard Oil Company in Cleveland, Ohio, which controlled 90% of the Western oil market from 1880 to 1910, and was split into 33 independent companies in 1911 under the Sherman Antitrust Act. In 1957, the nuclear portion of domestic electricity generation accounted for less than 0.05% of the nation's total; it represented about 20% in the mid-1990s, but by 1999 had declined to 8%.

Proved reserves of crude oil totaled an estimated 22.5 billion barrels at the start of 1999. Reserves of natural gas were about 167 trillion cu ft (4.7 trillion cu m) in 1996, equivalent to more than 3% of the world's proved reserves. Recoverable coal reserves amounted to 275.1 billion tons at the end of 1998 (46% anthracite and bituminous), more than 20% of the world's total. Mineral fuel production in 1995 included an estimated 636.1 million tons of hard coal (2d after China) and 393.5 million tons of lignite (1st); 538.5 billion cu m (18.9 trillion cu ft) of natural gas (2d after Russia), and 382.5 million tons of crude oil (2d after Saudi Arabia). The 1973 Arab oil embargo and subsequent fuel shortages prompted a host of governmental measures aimed at increasing development of oil and gas resources, including an easing of restrictions on oil drilling on the continental shelf.

In 1998, public utilities and private industrial plants generated 3,619.6 billion kWh of electricity. Conventional steam and internal combustion plants produced most of the electricity. Coal-fired generation accounted for 50.9%; natural gas, 14.8%; and oil, 2.3%. Nuclear power and hydroelectricity contributed 20% and 9.1%, respectively. Other sources of electricity generation in 1995 included wood/waste, 1.9%; geothermal, 0.5%; other gaseous fuels, 0.4%; and wind/solar power, 0.1%. Installed generating capacity at electric utilities totaled 778.5 million kW in 1998. In 1995, nuclear-powered generators in operation had an estimated total capability of 1,165 million kW and generated 673.4 billion kWh of electricity (up from 51.8 million kW and 251.1 billion kWh in 1980). Because of cost and safety problems, the future of the nuclear power industry in the US was in doubt in the late 1980s. The number of operable nuclear power units peaked at 112 units in 1990, and had declined to 109 in 1995. As of 1999, no new nuclear power plants had begun operation.

During the 1980s, some attention was focused on the development of solar power, synthetic fuels, geothermal resources, and other energy technologies. Such energy conservation measures as mandatory automobile fuel-efficiency standards and tax incentives for home insulation were promoted by the federal government, which also decontrolled oil and gas prices in the expectation that a rise in domestic costs to world-market levels would provide a powerful economic incentive for consumers to conserve fuel. Since the mid-1980s, net petroleum imports have risen from 4.29 million barrels per day in 1985 to 9.76 million barrels daily in 1998, exceeding the record level of 8.56 million barrels per day set in 1977.

28INDUSTRY

Although the US remains one of the world's preeminent industrial powers, manufacturing no longer plays as dominant a role in the economy as it once did.

Between 1979 and 1998, manufacturing employment fell from 20.9 million to 18.7 million, or from 21.8% to 14.8% of national employment. Throughout the 1960s, manufacturing accounted for about 29% of total national income; by 1987, the proportion was down to about 19%. In 1993, manufacturing, with a gross product o $1,118 in current dollars, accounted for about 17.6% of GDP.

In 1997 shipments by US manufacturers amounted to $3.9 trillion, an increase of almost 32% over 1992.

Industrial activity within the US has been expanding southward and westward for much of the 20th century, most rapidly since World War II. Louisiana, Oklahoma, and especially Texas are centers of industrial expansion based on petroleum refining; aerospace and other high technology industries are the basis of the new wealth of Texas and California, the nation's leading manufacturing state. The industrial heartland of the US is the east–north–central region, comprising Ohio, Indiana, Illinois, Michigan, and Wisconsin, with steelmaking and automobile manufacturing among the leading industries. The Middle Atlantic states (New Jersey, New York, and Pennsylvania) and the Northeast are also highly industrialized; but of the major industrial states in these two regions, Massachusetts has taken the lead in reorienting itself toward such high-technology industries as electronics and information processing.

Large corporations are dominant especially in sectors such as steel, automobiles, pharmaceuticals, aircraft, petroleum refining, computers, soaps and detergents, tires, and communications equipment. In 1998, sales of the 500 largest firms, as ranked by *Fortune* magazine, grew by 4% over 1997, and profit margins declined for the 4th year in a row, from 4.9% to 4.4%. Eleven companies had revenues exceeding $50 billion in 1998, led by General Motors ($7.51 billion); Ford, $144.42 billion; Wal-Mart Stores, $139.2 billion; Exxon, $100.7 billion; General Electric, $100.5 billion; International Business Machines (IBM), $81.7 billion; Citigroup, $76.4 billion; Philip Morris, $57.8 billion; Boeing, $56.2 billion; AT&T, $53.6 billion; and Bankamerica Corp., $50.8 billion. In the late 1990s, *Fortune* magazine also ranked the top Internet companies. As of 1998, these were, with profits and sales: Ebay, with profits of $2.4 million on sales of $47.4 million; At Home, losses of $144.2 million, sales $48.0 million; Yahoo, profits $25.6 million, sales $203.3 million; CMGI, profits $16.6 million, sales $91.5 million; Lycos, losses $96.9 million, sales $56.1 million; Infoseek, losses $109.7 million, sales $80.9 million; and Amazon.com, losses $124.5 million, sales $610.0 million. The growth of multinational activities of US corporations has been rapid in recent decades.

The history of US industry has been marked by the introduction of increasingly sophisticated technology in the manufacturing process. Advances in chemistry and electronics have revolutionized many industries through new products and methods: examples include the impact of plastics on petrochemicals, the use of lasers and electronic sensors as measuring and controlling devices, and the application of microprocessors to computing machines, home entertainment products, and a variety of other industries. Science has vastly expanded the number of metals available for industrial purposes, notably such light metals

as aluminum, magnesium, and titanium. Integrated machines now perform a complex number of successive operations that formerly were done on the assembly line at separate stations. Those industries have prospered that have been best able to make use of the new technology, and the economies of some states—in particular California and Massachusetts—are largely based on it. In the 1980s and 1990s, the US has been the world leader in computer manufacturing, although the industry declined somewhat in the early 1990s, due to a global recession and growing saturation of the computer market. However as of 1992, the world's top five manufacturers were all American; they controlled 80% of the global computer market and 90% of the domestic market. In contrast, certain long-established industries—especially clothing and steelmaking—have suffered from outmoded facilities that (coupled with high US labor costs) have forced the price of their products above the world market level. In 1997, the US was the world's 3d-leading steel producer (after China and Japan) at nearly 100 million metric tons. Employment in the steel industry fell from 521,000 in 1974 to 190,000 in 1992. Automobile manufacturing was an ailing industry in the 1980s, but has rebounded in the 1990s. The "Big Three" US automakers—General Motors, Ford, and Daimler-Chrysler— manufactured over 60% of the passenger cars sold in the US in 1995. Passenger car production, which had fallen from 7.1 million units in 1987 to 5.4 million in 1991, rose to 6.3 million by 1995 and to 8.3 million in 1999. In 1999, a total of 16.9 million motor vehicles were sold in the US. The estimated trade deficit in motor vehicles was $4 billion in 1993, an increase of 12% over the previous year.

29SCIENCE AND TECHNOLOGY

In 1998, an estimated $227 billion was spent on research and development. Since 1980, industry's share of funding for research and development has grown to exceed the share provided by the federal government; the proportions in 1995 were 46% from industry and 54% from the federal government; in 1998, 66% came from industry, with 30% from the federal government, and the remainder coming from academic institutions.

In 1998 NASA's budget was $9.9 billion. In 1960 NASA spent only $1.1 billion. Launching of the space shuttle orbiter *Columbia* began in 1981; a fleet of four reusable shuttles, which would replace all other launch vehicles was planned. However, the January 1986 *Challenger* disaster, in which seven crew members died, cast doubt on the program. The three remaining shuttles were grounded, and the shuttles were redesigned for increased safety. A new shuttle, *Endeavour*, was built to take the place of *Challenger*. President Reagan, following the *Challenger* disaster, banned the shuttle from commercial use for nine years. The shuttles' return to space began with the launch of the shuttle *Atlantis* in September 1988.

An estimated 3,676 scientists and engineers per million people participated in research and development in 1987–97. In 1998, national expenditures on research and development were 2.67% of GDP. The National Science Foundation (founded 1950) is one of the chief government agencies funding scientific research. The American Association for the Advancement of Science (founded 1848) promotes public understanding of science and technology. The National Academy of Sciences (founded 1863) and the National Academy of Engineering (founded 1964) are both headquartered in Washington, DC. In 1996, more than 95,000 students in the US earned master's degrees in science and engineering.

30DOMESTIC TRADE

Retail sales in the US exceeded $2.995 trillion in 1999, with California, Texas, Florida, and New York leading in volume. Sales by durable goods stores, led by automotive dealers, totaled

$936.2 billion. Sales by retailers of nondurable goods, led by grocery and department stores, totaled $1.4 trillion. The growth of great chains of retail stores, particularly in the form of the supermarket, was one of the most conspicuous developments in retail trade following the end of World War II. Nearly 100,000 single-unit grocery stores went out of business between 1948 and 1958; the independent grocer's share of the food market dropped from 50% to 30% of the total in the same period. With the great suburban expansion of the 1960s emerged the planned shopping center, usually designed by a single development organization and intended to provide different kinds of stores in order to meet all the shopping needs of the particular area. Between 1974 and 2000, the square footage occupied by shopping centers in the US grew at a far greater rate than the nation's population.

Sales in 1999 by Wal-Mart, the top discount department store chain, totaled $166.8 billion; other leading retail chains in 1999, were KMart ($45.4 billion); Kroger ($45.35 billion); Sears ($41.1 billion); and Dayton Hudson, which changed its name to Target in January 2000 ($33.7 billion).

Installment credit is a major support for consumer purchases in the US. Most US families own and use credit cards, and their frequency of use has grown significantly in the 1990s with aggressive marketing by credit card companies which have made cards available to households that didn't qualify in the past. The number of cards in circulation rose 68% between 1990 and 1995, to total 450 million, or 4.9 cards per household. The number of credit cards projected to be in circulation by 2000 was 1.5 billion. Credit cards accounted for 36% of the consumer installment debt by the end of 1996, up from 13% in 1985.

The US advertising industry is the world's most highly developed. Particularly with the expansion of television audiences, spending for advertising has increased almost annually to successive record levels. Advertising expenditures in 1996 nearly reached an estimated $173.22 billion, up from $66.58 billion in 1982 and $11.96 billion in 1960. Of the 1996 total, an estimated 59% was spent in national media and 41% in local media. Newspaper advertising accounted for 22.3%, television advertising 22.7%, and radio advertising 7.0%. Direct mail advertising (chiefly letters, booklets, catalogs, and handbills) accounted for 20%, magazines 5.3%, and other media 22.7%.

In 1997 wholesale trade was conducted by 453,470 establishments, with 5.8 million employees and combined total sales of $4.06 trillion.

31 FOREIGN TRADE

The foreign trade position of the United States deteriorated in the 1980s as the US became a debtor nation with a trade deficit that ballooned from $24 billion to over $100 billion by the end of the decade of the 1980s; by 1998, the trade deficit had reached an estimated $249 billion by 1998. In 1998, exports, made up that year of automobiles, industrial supplies and raw materials, consumer goods, and agricultural products, up from $393.6 billion in 1990. General imports for 1998 were valued at $912 billion, a record high. California led the nation in value of exports originating in the state, followed by Texas, and New York.

The United States's imports and exports for 1999 (in millions of US dollars) are distributed among the following categories:

ITEM (1)	EXPORTS	IMPORTS
Balance of Payment Basis	684,358	1,029,917
Net Adjustments	-11,439	5,299
Total Census Basis (2)	695,797	1,024,618
Manufactured goods (3)	565,490	882,013
Agricultural commodities (3)	47,091	36,681
Mineral fuels (3)	9,880	75,803

EXPORTS AND IMPORTS (CONTINUED)		
ITEM (1)	EXPORTS	IMPORTS
Selected commodities (3)		
ADP equipment; office mach	40,787	84,430
Airplane parts	15,141	5,827
Airplanes	32,665	9,222
Alcoholic bev.,distilled	432	2,618
Aluminum	3,564	6,269
Animal feeds	3,372	564
Artwork/antiques	1,148	4,890
Basketware, etc.	2,872	4,378
Cereal flour	1,308	1,620
Chemicals - cosmetics	4,853	3,148
Chemicals - dyeing	3,620	2,633
Chemicals - fertilizers	2,921	1,501
Chemicals - inorganic	4,632	5,167
Chemicals - medicinal	11,203	13,497
Chemicals - n.e.s.	11,068	5,084
Chemicals - organic	15,376	21,896
Chemicals - plastics	16,832	9,279
Cigarettes	3,226	151
Clothing	7,962	56,412
Coal	2,268	665
Coffee	9	2,534
Copper	1,068	3,460
Cork, wood, lumber	4,253	8,925
Corn	5,126	156
Cotton, raw and linters	968	148
Crude fertilizers	1,536	1,268
Crude oil	772	50,890
Electrical machinery	75,249	88,620
Fish and preparations	2,742	8,910
Footwear	694	14,064
Furniture and bedding	4,343	16,181
Gem diamonds	312	9,885
General industrial mach	29,882	31,467
Glass	2,119	2,038
Glassware	730	1,811
Gold, nonmonetary	5,226	3,032
Hides and skins	1,020	100
Iron and steel mill prod	4,989	13,369
Jewelry	1,070	5,691
Lighting, plumbing	1,298	4,330
Liquified propane/butane	299	859
Live animals	652	1,642
Meat and preparations	6,506	3,259
Metal manufactures, n.e.s.	11,185	14,414
Metal ores; scrap	3,484	3,647
Metalworking machinery	5,268	6,782
Mineral fuels, other	2,633	1,241
Natural gas	218	6,669
Nickel	321	846
Oils/fats, vegetable	1,147	1,201
Optical goods	2,231	3,077
Paper and paperboard	9,863	13,400
Petroleum preparations	3,414	14,183
Photographic equipment	3,624	6,111
Plastic articles, n.e.s.	6,362	7,013
Platinum	503	3,613
Pottery	109	1,680
Power generating mach.	30,894	31,551
Printed materials	4,581	3,323
Pulp and waste paper	3,528	2,597
Records/magnetic media	5,802	4,703
Rice	942	187
Rubber articles, n.e.s.	1,401	1,791
Rubber tires and tubes	2,400	4,638
Scientific instruments	25,644	17,658
Ships, boats	1,632	1,127
Silver and bullion	214	630
Soybeans	4,569	29
Spacecraft	641	245
Specialized ind. mach.	24,941	21,596
Sugar	4	557

EXPORTS AND IMPORTS (CONTINUED)

ITEM (1)	EXPORTS	IMPORTS
Selected commodities (3)		
Television, VCR, etc.	24,404	50,936
Textile yearn, fabric	9,245	13,578
Tobacco, unmanufactured	1,312	753
Toys/games/sporting goods	3,315	18,987
Travel goods	329	4,148
Vegetables and fruits	7,152	9,259
Vehicles	54,299	145,927
Watches/clocks/parts	334	3,258
Wheat	3,578	273
Wood manufactures	1,739	7,089
Re-exports	50,969	(X)
Agricultural commodities	1,314	(X)
Manufactured goods	49,011	(X)
Mineral fuels	132	(X)

(-) Represents zero or less than one half unit of measurement shown.
(X) Not applicable.
(1) Detailed data are presented on a census basis. The information needed to convert to a BOP basis is not available.
(2) Total exports (Domestic and Foreign)
(3) Domestic exports

The following countries represent 70% of U.S. imports, and 65% of U.S. exports in goods: Argentina, Australia, Belgium, Canada, China, Egypt, Germany, France, Hong Kong, Italy, Japan, Republic of Korea, Malaysia, Mexico, Netherlands, Saudi Arabia, Singapore, Spain, Switzerland, Taiwan, United Arab Emirates, United Kingdom, Venezuela.

Principal trading partners in 1998 (in millions of US dollars) were as follows:

COUNTRY	EXPORTS	IMPORTS	BALANCE
Canada	154,152	178,048	-23,896
Mexico	79,010	96,078	-17,068
Japan	57,888	125,091	-67,203
United Kingdom	39,070	35,721	3,349
China (inc. Hong Kong)	27,182	86,044	-58,862
Germany	26,642	51,283	-24,641
Taiwan	18,157	34,343	-16,186
France	18,071	24,746	-6,675
Korea	16,538	24,805	-8,267
Singapore	15,673	18,654	-2,981

US exports to and imports from the countries and dependences of the world are povided in the table that follows together with their rankings.

32BALANCE OF PAYMENTS
Since 1950, the US has generally recorded deficits in its overall payments with the rest of the world, despite the fact that it had an unbroken record of annual surpluses up to 1970 on current-account goods, services, and remittances transactions. The balance of trade, in the red since 1975, reached a record deficit of $249 billion in 1998.

The nation's stock of gold declined from a value of $22.9 billion at the start of 1958 to $10.5 billion as of 31 July 1971, only two weeks before President Nixon announced that the US would no longer exchange dollars for gold. From 1990–98, the value of the gold stock has been stable at $11 billion. On 12 February 1973, pressures on the US dollar compelled the government to announce a 10% devaluation against nearly all of the world's major currencies. US international gold reserves thereupon rose from $14.4 billion in 1973 to $15.9 billion at the end of 1974; as of 1999, US gold reserves stood at $75 billion, down from $102 billion in 1990.

The US Central Intelligence Agency reports that in 1998 the purchasing power parity of the United States's exports was $663

billion while imports totaled $912 billion resulting in a trade balance deficit of $249 billion.

The International Monetary Fund (IMF) reports that in 1998 the United States had exports of goods totaling $672 billion and imports totaling $917 billion. The services credit totaled $262 billion and debit $181 billion. The following table summarizes the United States's balance of payments as reported by the IMF for 1998 in billions of US dollars.

Current Account		-221
Balance on goods	-245	
Balance on services	81	
Balance on income	-12	
Current transfers	-44	
Capital Account		1
Financial Account		217
Direct investment abroad	-133	
Direct investment in United States	193	
Portfolio investment assets	-103	
Portfolio investment liabilities	267	
Other investment assets	-50	
Other investment liabilities	42	
Net Errors and Omissions		11
Reserves and Related Items		-7

33BANKING AND SECURITIES
The Federal Reserve Act of 1913 provided the US with a central banking system. The Federal Reserve System dominates US banking, is a strong influence in the affairs of commercial banks, and exercises virtually unlimited control over the money supply.

Each of the 12 federal reserve districts contains a federal reserve bank. A board of nine directors presides over each reserve bank. Six are elected by the member banks in the district: of this group, three may be bankers; the other three represent business, industry, or agriculture. The Board of Governors of the Federal Reserve System (usually known as the Federal Reserve Board) appoints the remaining three, who may not be officers, directors, stockholders, or employees of any bank and who are presumed therefore to represent the public.

The Federal Reserve Board regulates the money supply and the amount of credit available to the public by asserting its power to alter the rediscount rate, by buying and selling securities in the open market, by setting margin requirements for securities purchases by altering reserve requirements of member banks in the system, and by resorting to a specific number of selective controls at its disposal. The Federal Reserve Board's role in regulating the money supply is held by economists of the monetarist school to be the single most important factor in determining the nation's inflation rate. Money supply, as measured by M2, totaled $3,725 billion in the first quarter of 1996.

Member banks increase their reserves or cash holdings by rediscounting commercial notes at the federal reserve bank at a rate of interest ultimately determined by the Board of Governors. A change in the rediscount rate, therefore, directly affects the capacity of the member banks to accommodate their customers with loans. Similarly, the purchase or sale of securities in the open market, as determined by the Federal Open Market Committee, is another device whereby the amount of credit available to the public is expanded or contracted. The same effect is achieved in some measure by the power of the Board of Governors to raise or lower the reserves that member banks must keep against demand deposits. Credit tightening by federal authorities in early 1980 pushed the prime rate—the rate that commercial banks charge their most creditworthy customers—above 20% for the first time since the financial panics of 1837 and 1839, when rates reached 36%. As federal monetary policies eased, the prime rate dropped below 12% in late 1984; as of 2000 it was below 10%. The financial sector is dominated by commercial banks, insurance companies, and mutual funds. There was little change in the

Exports, Imports, and Balance of Goods by Selected Countries for 1999

In millions of dollars. Details may not equal totals due to rounding. (-) Represents zero or less then half unit of measure. (X) Not applicable.

COUNTRY	EXPORTS	EXPORTS RANK	IMPORTS	IMPORTS RANK	TRADE BALANCE	TRADE BALNACE RANK
Afganistan	18.0	164	9.3	162	8.8	143
Albania	24.8	155	9.0	164	15.8	153
Algeria	458.8	67	1,824.4	49	-1,365.5	31
Andorra	7.8	182	0.1	213	7.7	141
Angola	252.0	82	2,418.3	44	-2,166.3	24
Anguilla	22.2	157	2.3	188	19.9	156
Antigua and Barbuda	95.2	112	1.8	189	93.4	191
Argentina	4,949.9	26	2,598.3	43	2,351.5	223
Armenia	51.2	129	15.3	150	35.9	174
Aruba	307.2	74	674.8	64	-367.6	44
Australia	11,818.4	15	5,280.1	29	6,538.2	226
Austria	2,588.2	35	2,909.3	38	-321.1	50
Azerbaijan	54.8	127	26.3	136	28.6	169
Bahamas	842.0	55	195.3	97	646.7	216
Bahrain	347.8	71	225.4	91	122.3	192
Bangladesh	274.2	81	1,918.2	47	-1,644.0	26
Barbados	304.9	75	58.9	120	246.0	205
Belarus	26.1	150	93.6	112	-67.6	75
Belgium	12,381.4	14	9,196.1	22	3,185.4	225
Belize	135.8	103	80.6	114	55.2	182
Benin	31.4	147	17.8	147	13.5	149
Bermuda	343.8	72	24.6	138	319.2	210
Bhutan	0.7	217	0.4	202	0.3	111
Bolivia	298.3	76	223.7	92	74.6	186
Bosnia-Hercegovina	43.7	136	14.9	151	28.8	170
Botswana	33.4	146	17.0	148	16.5	154
Brazil	13,202.6	11	11,313.8	16	1,888.8	220
British Indian Ocean Terr	0.9	213	0.3	205	0.6	114
British Virgin Islands	60.1	124	22.3	142	37.8	175
Brunei	66.7	118	388.7	73	-322.0	49
Bulgaria	102.8	110	198.8	95	-96.0	69
Burkina	10.9	171	2.8	184	8.1	142
Burma (Myanmar)	8.6	179	232.1	87	-223.5	57
Burundi	2.6	201	6.1	171	-3.5	95
Cambodia	19.9	160	592.6	67	-572.7	41
Cameroon	37.0	142	77.4	116	-40.4	82
Canada	166,600.0	1	198,711.1	1	-32,111.1	3
Cape Verde	7.5	184	0.1	214	7.4	140
Cayman Islands	368.8	69	9.4	161	359.4	211
Central African Republic	3.7	196	2.3	187	1.4	121
Chad	2.7	200	6.9	169	-4.3	94
Chile	3,078.3	32	2,953.1	37	125.2	193
China	13,111.0	12	81,788.2	4	-68,677.2	2
Christmas Island	1.5	206	0.1	216	1.4	122
Cocos (Keeling) Island	0.5	219	0.2	207	0.3	112
Colombia	3,559.5	30	6,259.0	27	-2,699.4	21
Comoros	0.2	220	1.7	190	-1.5	100
Congo (Brazzaville)	47.0	133	414.6	72	-367.6	45
Congo (Kinshasa)	21.0	159	229.0	89	-207.9	59
Cook Islands	1.1	211	0.6	199	0.4	113
Costa Rica	2,380.6	37	3,967.8	35	-1,587.2	27
Croatia	107.5	107	110.0	107	-2.5	96
Cuba	4.5	192	0.6	198	3.8	134
Cyprus	191.7	89	31.4	130	160.2	196
Czech Republic	609.7	60	753.6	61	-143.9	63
Denmark	1,725.6	44	2,818.7	40	-1,093.1	35

Exports, Imports, and Balance of Goods by Selected Countries for 1999 (Continued)

In millions of dollars. Details may not equal totals due to rounding. (-) Represents zero or less then half unit of measure. (X) Not applicable.

COUNTRY	EXPORTS	EXPORTS RANK	IMPORTS	IMPORTS RANK	TRADE BALANCE	TRADE BALNACE RANK
Djibouti	26.4	149	0.1	215	26.3	167
Dominica	38.6	140	19.1	145	19.5	155
Dominican Republic	4,100.4	28	4,286.7	32	-186.3	60
Ecuador	909.9	53	1,821.3	50	-911.4	37
Egypt	3,000.8	33	617.6	65	2,383.2	224
El Salvador	1,519.1	47	1,605.0	54	-85.9	70
Equatorial Guinea	221.2	84	43.3	124	177.9	199
Eritrea	3.9	195	0.5	201	3.4	131
Estonia	162.9	98	237.0	86	-74.0	73
Ethiopia	163.5	97	30.2	133	133.3	194
Falkland Islands	0.1	224	1.2	193	-1.1	102
Faroe Islands	5.3	191	22.4	141	-17.1	87
Federal Republic of Germany	26,800.2	5	55,228.4	5	-28,428.2	4
Fedrated States of Micronesia	25.0	153	10.1	158	14.9	151
Fiji	126.4	105	99.8	109	26.6	168
Finland	1,668.8	46	2,907.7	39	-1,238.9	33
France	18,877.4	9	25,708.6	9	-6,831.2	12
French Guiana	194.2	88	4.2	179	190.0	201
French Polynesia	93.5	114	42.7	125	50.9	179
French Southern and Antarctic Lands	1.1	210	(-)	225	1.1	118
Gabon	45.4	134	1,543.2	55	-1,497.8	29
Gambia	9.6	174	0.2	209	9.4	145
Gaza Strip Administered by Israel	1.3	209	0.2	211	1.1	119
Georgia	83.5	116	18.3	146	65.3	184
Ghana	232.7	83	208.6	94	24.1	161
Gibraltar	4.1	193	9.5	160	-5.5	93
Greece	995.5	51	563.1	68	432.3	212
Greenland	3.1	197	13.3	153	-10.1	90
Grenada	66.2	119	19.8	144	46.4	178
Guadeloupe	63.2	122	2.8	183	60.4	183
Guatemala	1,811.9	42	2,265.2	45	-453.2	43
Guinea	54.6	128	116.9	105	-62.4	77
Guinea-Bissau	0.8	214	0.1	218	0.7	117
Guyana	145.1	101	120.5	104	24.5	164
Haiti	613.8	59	301.1	81	312.7	208
Heard and McDonald Islands	(-)	226	(-)	226	(-)	106
Honduras	2,369.8	38	2,713.3	41	-343.5	46
Hong Kong	12,651.8	13	10,527.9	18	2,123.9	222
Hungary	504.1	64	1,892.6	48	-1,388.5	30
Iceland	297.6	77	303.7	80	-6.0	92
India	3,687.8	29	9,070.8	23	-5,383.0	14
Indonesia	2,038.3	40	9,525.4	21	-7,487.0	11
Iran	48.1	131	2.4	186	45.7	177
Iraq	9.5	175	4,226.4	33	-4,216.9	17
Ireland	6,383.6	22	10,994.3	17	-4,610.7	16
Israel	7,690.8	20	9,864.3	19	-2,173.5	23
Italy	10,090.6	16	22,356.5	10	-12,265.9	8
Ivory Coast	104.0	109	350.2	77	-246.1	55
Jamaica	1,292.9	49	678.1	63	614.8	215
Japan	57,465.7	3	130,863.9	2	-73,398.2	1
Jordan	275.6	80	30.9	131	244.7	204
Kazakhstan	179.5	93	229.1	88	-49.6	79
Kenya	189.2	91	106.3	108	82.8	188
Kiribati	6.8	188	1.4	192	5.4	136
Korea, South	22,958.4	6	31,178.6	8	-8,220.2	10
Kuwait	864.4	54	1,439.2	56	-574.9	40

Exports, Imports, and Balance of Goods by Selected Countries for 1999 (Continued)

In millions of dollars. Details may not equal totals due to rounding. (-) Represents zero or less then half unit of measure. (X) Not applicable.

COUNTRY	EXPORTS	EXPORTS RANK	IMPORTS	IMPORTS RANK	TRADE BALANCE	TRADE BALNACE RANK
Kyrgyzstan	22.8	156	0.5	200	22.3	159
Laos	1.6	205	12.7	154	-11.1	88
Latvia	218.2	85	228.8	90	-10.6	89
Lebanon	356.5	70	51.4	122	305.1	207
Lesotho	0.7	216	110.8	106	-110.1	67
Liberia	44.7	135	30.3	132	14.4	150
Libya	(-)	(X)	(-)	(X)	(-)	(X)
Liechtenstein	9.1	177	276.8	82	-267.8	52
Lithuania	66.0	120	96.8	110	-30.8	84
Luxembourg	983.4	52	313.9	79	669.5	217
Macao	41.9	137	1,124.4	59	-1,082.5	36
Macedonia (Skopje)	56.2	126	136.5	101	-80.3	71
Madagascar	105.8	108	80.3	115	25.5	165
Malawi	7.4	185	72.5	118	-65.1	76
Malaysia	9,060.0	17	21,424.3	11	-12,364.3	7
Maldives	8.5	180	54.9	121	-46.4	80
Mali	29.8	148	9.0	165	20.8	157
Malta	190.4	90	325.0	78	-134.6	64
Marshall Islands	35.8	143	9.8	159	26.0	166
Martinique	34.9	144	0.8	196	34.1	173
Mauritania	25.2	152	0.8	195	24.4	162
Mauritius	39.0	139	259.3	85	-220.3	58
Mexico	86,908.9	2	109,720.6	3	-22,811.6	5
Moldova	10.6	172	87.1	113	-76.6	72
Monaco	12.6	168	14.3	152	-1.7	99
Mongolia	10.1	173	60.8	119	-50.7	78
Montserrat	4.0	194	0.3	204	3.7	132
Morocco	565.8	62	386.4	74	179.5	200
Mozambique	34.8	145	10.3	156	24.5	163
Namibia	195.6	87	29.7	134	165.9	197
Nauru	0.9	212	0.2	208	0.7	116
Nepal	21.2	158	177.6	98	-156.4	62
Netherlands	19,436.6	7	8,475.0	24	10,961.6	227
Netherlands Antilles	597.4	61	384.3	75	213.1	203
New Caledonia	41.7	138	8.6	166	33.0	172
New Zealand	1,923.4	41	1,748.2	51	175.2	198
Nicaragua	373.7	68	495.2	70	-121.5	66
Niger	18.5	162	12.1	155	6.4	138
Nigeria	627.8	58	4,385.1	31	-3,757.3	20
Niue	0.1	223	0.1	219	0.1	107
Norfolk Island	2.6	202	0.4	203	2.2	126
North Korea	11.3	170	(-)	223	11.2	148
Norway	1,439.4	48	4,042.6	34	-2,603.2	22
Oman	188.2	92	219.5	93	-31.3	83
Pakistan	496.7	65	1,740.7	53	-1,244.0	32
Palau	14.6	165	15.8	149	-1.1	101
Panama	1,742.3	43	364.8	76	1,377.5	219
Papua New Guinea	37.1	141	144.5	100	-107.3	68
Paraguay	514.7	63	48.1	123	466.6	213
Peru	1,696.5	45	1,928.4	46	-231.9	56
Philippines	7,222.1	21	12,352.8	14	-5,130.6	15
Pitcairn Island	0.2	221	(-)	224	0.2	110
Poland	826.2	56	816.2	60	10.0	147
Portugal	1,091.8	50	1,355.8	57	-264.0	54
Qatar	145.5	100	272.2	84	-126.7	65
Republic of Yemen	157.0	99	23.6	139	133.4	195

Exports, Imports, and Balance of Goods by Selected Countries for 1999 (Continued)

In millions of dollars. Details may not equal totals due to rounding. (-) Represents zero or less then half unit of measure. (X) Not applicable.

COUNTRY	EXPORTS	EXPORTS RANK	IMPORTS	IMPORTS RANK	TRADE BALANCE	TRADE BALNACE RANK
Reunion	2.4	203	0.1	217	2.3	127
Romania	176.0	94	442.4	71	-266.4	53
Russia	2,059.8	39	5,920.8	28	-3,861.0	18
Rwanda	47.5	132	3.7	180	43.8	176
San Marino	8.0	181	6.0	172	2.0	124
Sao Tome and Principe	0.5	218	2.7	185	-2.2	97
Saudi Arabia	7,911.9	19	8,253.5	25	-341.6	47
Senegal	63.4	121	9.2	163	54.3	181
Seychelles	7.6	183	5.2	175	2.4	128
Sierra Leone	13.2	167	10.3	157	2.8	130
Singapore	16,247.3	10	18,191.4	12	-1,944.1	25
Slovakia	127.2	104	169.3	99	-42.1	81
Slovenia	114.2	106	275.8	83	-161.6	61
Solomon Islands	1.5	207	0.8	194	0.7	115
Somalia	2.8	199	0.2	210	2.6	129
South Africa	2,585.5	36	3,194.4	36	-609.0	39
Spain	6,133.4	23	5,059.2	30	1,074.2	218
Sri Lanka	167.1	96	1,742.2	52	-1,575.1	28
St Helena	1.5	208	0.2	206	1.2	120
St Kitts and Nevis	48.3	130	32.8	129	15.5	152
St Lucia	98.1	111	28.0	135	70.1	185
St Pierre and Miquelon	2.9	198	4.9	177	-2.0	98
St Vincent and the Grenadines	92.1	115	8.2	168	83.8	189
Sudan	8.8	178	0.1	220	8.8	144
Suriname	143.8	102	122.9	103	20.9	158
Svalbard, Jan Mayen Island	0.8	215	0.7	197	0.1	108
Swaziland	9.4	176	37.7	126	-28.3	85
Sweden	4,250.5	27	8,102.7	26	-3,852.2	19
Switzerland	8,371.3	18	9,538.6	20	-1,167.4	34
Syria	173.1	95	94.9	111	78.2	187
Taiwan	19,131.4	8	35,204.4	7	-16,073.1	6
Tajikistan	13.8	166	22.7	140	-8.9	91
Tanzania	68.4	117	35.4	128	33.0	171
Thailand	4,984.6	25	14,329.9	13	-9,345.3	9
Togo	25.7	151	3.2	182	22.5	160
Tokelau	5.5	190	5.7	173	-0.2	103
Tonga	6.7	189	5.0	176	1.7	123
Trinidad and Tobago	785.3	57	1,286.7	58	-501.4	42
Tunisia	280.2	79	74.6	117	205.6	202
Turkey	3,217.1	31	2,629.4	42	587.7	214
Turkmenistan	18.4	163	8.5	167	9.9	146
Turks and Caicos Islands	94.8	113	6.3	170	88.5	190
Tuvalu	(-)	227	(-)	227	(-)	104
Uganda	25.0	154	20.3	143	4.7	135
Ukraine	204.6	86	528.9	69	-324.3	48
United Arab Emirates	2,707.8	34	714.3	62	1,993.5	221
United Kingdom	38,407.1	4	39,237.2	6	-830.1	38
Uruguay	494.5	66	198.6	96	295.9	206
Uzbekistan	339.0	73	25.6	137	313.4	209
Vanuatu	7.3	186	1.7	191	5.6	137
Vatican City	2.2	204	0.2	212	2.0	125
Venezuela	5,353.5	24	11,334.5	15	-5,981.0	13
Vietnam	291.5	78	608.3	66	-316.8	51
Wallis and Futuna	0.2	222	(-)	221	0.1	109
West Bank	7.0	187	3.3	181	3.8	133
Western Sahara	(-)	225	(-)	222	(-)	105

Exports, Imports, and Balance of Goods by Selected Countries for 1999 (Continued)

In millions of dollars. Details may not equal totals due to rounding. (-) Represents zero or less then half unit of measure. (X) Not applicable.

COUNTRY	EXPORTS	EXPORTS RANK	IMPORTS	IMPORTS RANK	TRADE BALANCE	TRADE BALNACE RANK
Western Samoa	12.4	169	5.3	174	7.0	139
Yugoslavia	58.6	125	4.5	178	54.1	180
Zambia	19.8	161	37.7	127	-17.8	86
Zimbabwe	60.9	123	132.8	102	-71.9	74

nature of the sector between the 1930s, when it was rescued through the creation of regulatory bodies and deposit insurance, and the 1980s, when the market was deregulated. In the 1980s, the capital markets underwent extensive reforms. The markets became increasingly internationalized, as deregulationallowed foreign-owned banks to extend their operations. There was also extensive restructuring of domestic financial markets—interest-rate ceilings were abolished and competition between different financial institution intensified, facilitated by greater diversification.

Commercial and investment banking activities are separated in the US by the Glass Steagall Act, which was passed in 1933 in the wake of the Great Depression. Fears that investment banking activities put deposits at risk led to a situation where commercial banks were unable to deal in non-bank financial instruments. This put them at severe commercial disadvantage, and the pressure for reform became so strong that the Federal Reserve Board has allowed the affiliates of commercial banks to enter a wide range of securities activities since 1986. Attempts to repeal the act were unsuccessful until November 1999, when the Gramm-Leach-Bliley Act (also known as the Financial Modernization Act) was passed by Congress. The Gramm-Leach-Bliley Act repeals Glass-Steagall and allows banks, insurance companies, and stock brokers and mutual fund companies to sell each other's products and services; these companies are also now free to merge or acquire one another.

The expansion and diversification in financial services was facilitated by information technology. Financial deregulation led to the collapse of many commercial banks and savings and loan associations in the second half of the 1980s. In the 1990s, change has continued in the form of a proliferation of bank mergers; with the passage in 1999 of Gramm-Leach-Bliley, further consolidation of the industry was predicted.

Prior to 1994 the banking system was highly fragmented; national banks were not allowed to establish branches at will, as they were subject to the banking laws of each state. Within states, local banks faced similar restraints on their branching activities. In 1988, only 22 states permitted statewide banking of national banks, while 18 allowed limited banking and ten permitted no branches. Consequently in 1988 over 60% of US commercial banks had assets of less the $150 million, while only 3% had assets valued at $500 million or more.

Such regulation rendered US banks vulnerable to merger and acquisition. Acquisitions have generally taken place through bank holding companies, which then fall under the jurisdiction of the Federal Reserve System. This has allowed banks to extend their business into non-bank activities such as insurance, financial planning, and mortgages, as well as opening up geographical markets. The number of such holding companies is estimated at 6,500. These companies are believed to control over 90% of total bank assets.

The Riegle-Neal Interstate Banking and Branching Efficiency Act of 1994 removed most of the barriers to interstate bank acquisitions and interstate banking. The new act allowed banks to merge with banks in other states although they must operate them as separate banks. In addition, banks are allowed to establish branches in neighboring states. Restrictions on branching activity were lifted as of June 1997. The legislation allowed banks to lessen their exposure to regional economic downturns. It also ensured a continuing stream of bank mergers. Liberalization has encouraged a proliferation of in-store banking at supermarkets. International Banking Technologies, Inc., reported that the number of supermarket bank branches rose to 7,100 in 1998, up from 2,191 in 1994. In the mid-1990s, the number of supermarket branch banks grew at an annual rate of around 30%, but growth from 1997 to 1998 slowed to just over 10%.

Under the provisions of the Banking Act of 1935, all members of the Federal Reserve System (and other banks that wish to do so) participate in a plan of deposit insurance (up to $100,000 for each individual account as of 2000) administered by the Federal Deposit Insurance Corporation (FDIC).

Savings and loan associations are insured by the Federal Savings and Loan Insurance Corporation (FSLIC). Individual accounts were insured up to a limit of $100,000. Savings and loans failed at an alarming rate in the 1980s. In 1989 the government signed legislation that created the Resolution Trust Corporation. The RTC's job is to handle the savings and loans bailout, expected to cost taxpayers $345 billion through 2029. Approximately 30 million members participated in thousands of credit unions chartered by a federal agency; state-chartered credit unions had over 20 million members.

When the New York Stock Exchange (NYSE) opened in 1817, its trading volume was 100 shares a day. On 17 December 1999, 1.35 billion shares were traded, the record high for shares traded in a single day. Record-setting trading volume occurred for 1999 as a whole, with 203.9 billion shares traded (a 20% increase over 1998) for a total value of $8.9 trillion, up from $7.3 trillion in 1998. In 1996, 51 million individuals and 10,000 institutional investors owned stocks or shares in mutual funds traded on the NYSE. The two other major stock markets in the US are the American Stock Exchange (AMEX) and the NASDAQ (National Association o Securities Dealers). The NASD (National Association of Securities Dealers) is regulated by the SEC (Securities and Exchange Commission).

34INSURANCE

The number of life insurance companies has shrunk in recent years. Between 1985 and 1995 the number fell from 2,261 to 1,840; in 1998, there were 51 life insurance mergers and acquisition. Life insurance premiums in 1998 totaled $355.3 billion, representing growth of 88% since 1989. Competition between financial institutions has been healthy and premium income has risen steadily. The overwhelming majority of US families have some life insurance with a legal reserve company the Veterans Administration, or fraternal, assessment, burial, or savings bank organization. The passage in 1999 of the Gramm-Leach-Bliley Act allowed insurance companies, banks, and securities firms to sell each other's products and services; restrictions were also lifted on cross-industry mergers and acquisitions.

Hundreds of varieties of insurance may be purchased. Besides life, the more important include accident, fire, hospital and medical expense, group accident and health, automobile liability, automobile damage, workers' compensation, ocean marine, and inland marine. Americans buy more life and health insurance than any other group except Canadians and Japanese. During the 1970s, many states enacted a "no fault" form of automobile insurance, under which damages may be awarded automatically, without recourse to a lawsuit.

35PUBLIC FINANCE

Under the Budget and Accounting Act of 1921, the president is responsible for preparing the federal government budget. In fact, the budget is prepared by the Office of Management and Budget (established in 1970), based on requests from the heads of all federal departments and agencies and advice from the Board of Governors of the Federal Reserve System, the Council of Economic Advisers, and the Treasury Department. The president submits a budget message to Congress in January. Under the Congressional Budget Act of 1974, the Congress establishes, by concurrent resolution, targets for overall expenditures and broad functional categories, as well as targets for revenues, the budget deficit, and the public debt. The Congressional Budget Office monitors the actions of Congress on individual appropriations bills with reference to those targets. The president exercises fiscal control over executive agencies, which issue periodic reports subject to presidential perusal. Congress exercises control through the comptroller general, head of the General Accounting Office, who sees to it that all funds have been spent and accounted for according to legislative intent. The fiscal year runs from 1 October to 30 September.

The public debt, subject to a statutory debt limit, rose from $43 billion in 1939/40 to more than $3.3 trillion in 1993. In fiscal year 1991/92, the federal deficit reached $290 million, a record high. Pressured by Congressional Republicans, President Clinton introduced a taxing and spending plan to reduce the rate of growth of the federal deficit when he began his term in 1993. The Clinton Administration calculated the package of tax increases and spending would cut the deficit by $500 billion over a four year period; in fiscal year 1997/98, the budget experienced an estimated surplus of $69 billion.

The US Central Intelligence Agency (CIA) estimates that in 1998 the United States's central government took in revenues of approximately $1.722 trillion and had expenditures of $1.653 trillion. Overall, the government registered a surplus of approximately $69 billion.

The following table shows an itemized breakdown of government revenues and expenditures. The percentages were calculated from data reported by the International Monetary Fund. The dollar amounts (millions) are based on the CIA estimates provided above.

REVENUE AND GRANTS	100%	1,722,000
Tax revenue	93.3%	1,607,354
Non-tax revenue	6.2%	106,938
Capital revenue	0.4%	7,708
EXPENDITURES	100%	1,653,000
General public services	9.2%	152,853
Defense	15.4%	253,938
Public order and safety	1.5%	25,226
Education	1.8%	29,767
Health	20.5%	339,175
Social security	28.7%	474,540
Housing and community amenities	2.9%	47,551
Recreation, cultural, and religious affairs	0.5%	8,806
Economic affairs and services	5.1%	83,997
Interest payments	14.6%	242,002
Adjustments	-.3%	-4,856

36TAXATION

Measured as a proportion of the GDP, the total US tax burden is less than that in most industrialized countries. Federal, state, and local taxes are levied in a variety of forms. The greatest source of revenue for the federal government is the personal income tax, which is paid by citizens and resident aliens on their worldwide income.

The Tax Reform Act of 1986, which took full effect in 1988, reduced 14 graduated tax brackets, ranging from 11% to 50%, to two brackets, 15% and 28%, in taxing individual income. In 1996, there were five tax brackets, ranging from 15% to 39.6%. The 1986 law also eliminated the capital gains exclusion, reduced other deductions, and curtailed the number of value of tax shelters. The top corporate tax rate was reduced from 46% to 34%, and the investment tax credit was eliminated. In 1996, corporate tax rates range from 15% to 39%. Generally, corporations are required to prepay 100% of estimated tax liability (including regular tax, alternative minimum tax, and environmental tax). Other corporate taxes include an accumulated earnings tax and a personal holding company tax. Excise taxes are levied on certain motor vehicles, personal air transportation, some motor fuels (excluding gasohol), alcoholic beverages, tobacco products, tires and tubes, telephone charges, and gifts and estates.

37CUSTOMS AND DUTIES

Under the Trade Agreements Extension Act of 1951, the president is required to inform the US International Trade Commission (known until 1974 as the US Tariff Commission) of contemplated concessions in the tariff schedules. The commission then determines what the "peril point" is; that is, it informs the president how far the tariff may be lowered without injuring a domestic producer, or it indicates the amount of increase necessary to enable a domestic producer to avoid injury by foreign competition. Similarly, the act provides an "escape clause,"—in effect, a method for rescinding a tariff concession granted on a specific commodity if the effect of the concession, once granted, has caused or threatens to cause "serious injury" to a domestic producer. The Trade Expansion Act of 1962 grants the president the power to negotiate tariff reductions of up to 50% under the terms of GATT.

In 1974, Congress authorized the president to reduce tariffs still further, especially on goods from developing countries. As the cost of imported oil rose in the mid-1970s, however, Congress became increasingly concerned with reducing the trade imbalance by discouraging "dumping" of foreign goods on the US market. The International Trade Commission is required to impose a special duty on foreign goods offered for sale at what the commission determines is less than fair market value.

Most products are dutiable under most-favored-nation (MFN) rates or general duty rates. The import tariff schedules contain over 10,000 classifications, most of which are subject to interpretation. Besides duties, the US imposes a 17% "user fee" on all imports. Excise taxes and harsher maintenance fees are also imposed on certain imports. Under the terms of the North American Free Trade Agreement (NAFTA), which was approved by Congress in 1993, tariffs on goods qualifying as North American under the rules of origin will be phased out over a 15-year period.

38FOREIGN INVESTMENT

From the end of World War II through 1952, US government transfers of capital abroad averaged about $5,470 million annually, while private investments averaged roughly $730 million. Portfolio investment represented less than $150 million a year, or only 2.5% of the annual aggregate.

After 1952, however, direct private investment began to increase and portfolio investment rose markedly. In the late 1950s, new private direct investment was increasing yearly by $2 billion or more, while private portfolio investment and official US government loans were climbing by a minimum annual amount of $1 billion each. During the 1960–73 period, the value of US-held assets abroad increased by nearly 12% annually. From the mid-1970s through the early 1980s, it rose most years by at least 15%, and doubled between 1980 and 1990. Direct investments abroad had a book value of $711.6 billion in 1995, over half of which was invested in Europe, with the single greatest concentration ($119.9 billion) in the United Kingdom. Asia and the Pacific Islands had the 2d-largest regional total ($126 billion), with Japan ($39.1 billion) the leading country.

Direct foreign investments in the US have risen rapidly, from $6.9 billion in 1960 to $27.7 billion in 1975 and an estimated $182.95 billion at the end of 1985. As of 1995, foreign direct investment in the US was valued at $560 billion of which $363.5 billion originated in Europe ($119.9 billion in the United Kingdom). Asian and the Pacific was the other major source of direct foreign investment, of which close to 90% ($108.6 billion) came from Japan. Total foreign assets in 1994 (current cost) were over $3.16 trillion. Over one-third of the investment volume is in manufacturing.

[39] ECONOMIC DEVELOPMENT

By the end of the 19th century, regulation rather than subsidy had become the characteristic form of government intervention in US economic life. The abuses of the railroads with respect to rates and services gave rise to the Interstate Commerce Commission in 1887, which was subsequently strengthened by numerous acts that now stringently regulate all aspects of US railroad operations.

The growth of large-scale corporate enterprises, capable of exercising monopolistic or near-monopolistic control of given segments of the economy, resulted in federal legislation designed to control trusts. The Sherman Antitrust Act of 1890, reinforced by the Clayton Act of 1914 and subsequent acts, established the federal government as regulator of large-scale business. This tradition of government intervention in the economy was reinforced during the Great Depression of the 1930s, when the Securities and Exchange Commission and the National Labor Relations Board were established. The expansion of regulatory programs accelerated during the 1960s and early 1970s with the creation of the federal Environmental Protection Agency, Equal Employment Opportunity Commission, Occupational Safety and Health Administration, and Consumer Product Safety Commission, among other bodies. Subsidy programs were not entirely abandoned, however. Federal price supports and production subsidies remained a major force in stabilizing US agriculture. Moreover, the federal government stepped in to arrange for guaranteed loans for two large private firms—Lockheed in 1971 and Chrysler in 1980—where thousands of jobs would have been lost in the event of bankruptcy.

During this period, a general consensus emerged that, at least in some areas, government regulation was contributing to inefficiency and higher prices. The Carter administration moved to deregulate the airline, trucking, and communications industries; subsequently, the Reagan administration relaxed government regulation of bank savings accounts and automobile manufacture as it decontrolled oil and gas prices. The Reagan administration also sought to slow the growth of social-welfare spending and attempted, with only partial success, to transfer control over certain federal social programs to the states and to reduce or eliminate some programs entirely. Ironically, it was a Democrat, Bill Clinton, who, in 1996, signed legislation that replaced Aid to Families with Dependent Children with a system of block grants

that would enable the states to design and run their own welfare programs.

Some areas of federal involvement in social welfare, however, seem safely entrenched. Old age and survivors' insurance, unemployment insurance, and other aspects of the Social Security program have been accepted areas of governmental responsibility for decades. With the approach of the 21st century, the government faced the challenge of keeping the Medicare program solvent as the postwar baby-boomer generation reached retirement age. Federal responsibility has also been extended to insurance of bank deposits, to mortgage insurance, and to regulation of stock transactions. The government fulfills a supervisory and regulatory role in labor-management relations. Labor and management customarily disagree on what the role should be, but neither side advocates total removal of government from this field.

Since the Reciprocal Trade Agreement Act of 1934, government regulation of foreign trade has tended toward decreased levels of protection, a trend maintained by the 1945 Trade Agreements Extension Act, the 1962 Trade Expansion Act, and the 1974 Trade Act. The goals of free trade have also been furthered since World War II by US participation in the International Monetary Fund (IMF), the World Bank, and the General Agreement on Tariffs and Trade (GATT). With the formation in 1995 of the World Trade Organization (WTO), most-favored-nation policies were expanded to trade in services and other areas.

In 1993, Congress approved the North American Free Trade Agreement, which extended the Free Trade Agreement between Canada and the United States to include Mexico. NAFTA, by eliminating tariffs and other trade barriers, created a free trade zone with a combined market size of $6.5 trillion and 370 million consumers. The effect on employment was uncertain—estimates varied from a loss of 150,000 jobs over the next ten years to a net gain of 200,000. Labor intensive goods-producing industries, such as apparel and textiles, were expected to suffer, while it was predicted that capital goods industries would benefit. It was anticipated that US automakers would benefit in the short run by taking advantage of the low wages in Mexico and that US grain farmers and the US banking, financial, and telecommunications sectors would gain enormous new markets. As of 2000, the pros and cons of NAFTA were still being hotly debated. Spokespersons for organized labor claimed that the agreement had resulted in a net loss of 420,000 jobs, while advocates of free trade insisted that 311,000 new jobs had been created to support record US exports to Canada and Mexico, with only 116,000 workers displaced—a net gain of 195,000 jobs.

[40] SOCIAL DEVELOPMENT

Social welfare programs in the US depend on both the federal government and the state governments for resources and administration. Old age, survivors', disability, and the Medicare (health) programs are administered by the federal government; unemployment insurance, dependent child care, and a variety of other public assistance programs are state administered, although the federal government contributes to all of them through grants to the states. State and local public expenditures for all social welfare programs—including social insurance, health, education, and welfare services—reached $617 billion in 1995. Federal expenditures on social welfare rose to $888 billion in the same year. During the Reagan presidency, eligibility requirements for many social programs were tightened, operating budgets were slashed, and some programs—notably public-sector employment under the Comprehensive Employment and Training Act (CETA)—were eliminated entirely.

Between the early 1960s and 1993, the number of welfare (AFDC) recipients rose to 4 million families in spite of efforts to get clients "off the welfare rolls and into the payrolls." In 1996, President Clinton signed into law a groundbreaking welfare reform act that turned nearly the entire responsibility for the welfare system over to the states in the form of block grants. It also set a two-year limit on continuous welfare payments and a five-year cap on all payments over the mother's lifetime. As of 1999, the new system had been highly successful in reducing the number of recipients and in encouraging them to make the transition from "welfare to work." However, critics attributed at least some of the program's success to the booming economy during this period.

The Food and Nutrition Service of the US Department of Agriculture oversees several food assistance programs. Eligible Americans take part in the food stamp program, and eligible pupils participate in the school lunch program. The federal government also expends money for school breakfasts, nutrition programs for the elderly, and in commodity aid for the needy. The present Social Security program differs greatly from that created by the Social Security Act of 1935, which provided that retirement benefits be paid to retired workers aged 65 or older. Since 1939, Congress has attached a series of amendments to the program, including provisions for workers who retire at age 62, for widows, for dependent children under 18 years of age, and for children who are disabled prior to age 18. Disabled workers between 50 and 65 years of age are also entitled to monthly benefits. Other measures increased the number of years a person may work; among these reforms was a 1977 law banning mandatory retirement in private industry before age 70. The actuarial basis for the Social Security system has also changed. In 1935 there were about nine US wage earners for each American aged 65 or more; by the mid–1990s, however, the ratio was closer to three to one.

In 1940, the first year benefits were payable, $35 million was paid out. By 1983, Social Security benefits totaled $268.1 billion, paid to more than 40.6 million beneficiaries. The average monthly benefit for a retired worker with no dependents in 1960 was $74; in 1983, the average benefit was $629.30. Under legislation enacted in the early 1970s, increases in monthly benefits were pegged to the inflation rate, as expressed through the Consumer Price Index. Employers, employees, and the self-employed are legally required to make contributions to the Social Security fund. In 1999, 6.2% of employee earnings (12.4% of self-employed earnings) went toward old-age, disability, and survivor benefits. Wage and salary earners pay Social Security taxes under the Federal Insurance Contributions Act (FICA). As the amount of benefits and the number of beneficiaries have increased, so has the maximum FICA payment. In 1990, Social Security Taxes leveled off at 7.65% on earnings up to $51,300. Among workers with many dependents, the Social Security tax deduction can now exceed the federal income tax deduction.

In January 1974, the Social Security Administration assumed responsibility for assisting the aged, blind, and disabled under the Supplemental Security Income program. In 1998, the Social Security system paid out $375 billion in monthly and lump sum benefits, including $232.3 billion in monthly retirement benefits and $43.5 billion in disability benefits. Medicare, another program administered under the Social Security Act, provides hospital insurance and voluntary medical insurance for persons 65 and over, with reduced benefits available at age 62. Medicaid is a program that helps the needy meet the costs of medical, hospital, and nursing-home care.

The laws governing unemployment compensation originate in the states. Therefore, the benefits provided vary from state to state in duration (generally from 26 to 39 weeks) and amount (about 50% of earnings); the average employer contribution to Workers' Compensation in 1995 was 2% of payroll; which covered all or most costs, depending on the state.

Private philanthropy plays a major role in the support of relief and health services. The private sector plays an especially important role in pension management.

The federal agency Corporation for National and Community Service, established in October 1993, absorbed most of the programs of ACTION, established in 1971. CNCS coordinates three principal US volunteer service efforts: AmeriCorps, which has 40,000 volunteers placed in programs such as Habitat for Humanity and Volunteers in Service to America (VISTA); Learn and Serve America; and the National Senior Service Corporation, enlisting senior Americans persons to work with children and others who have special physical, mental, or emotional needs.

41 HEALTH

The US health care system is among the most advanced in the world. In 1995, health expenditures reached $988.5 billion, equivalent to 13.6% of GDP. Escalating health care costs resulted in several proposals for a national health care program in the 1970s, early 1980s, and early 1990s. During 1991, the US Census Bureau estimated that 35.4 million US residents (14% of the population) were without any form of health insurance. At the end of 1991, over 40 such proposals had been aired by politicians, medical and business groups, labor unions, and academicians. Most reform measures relied either on market-oriented approaches designed to widen insurance coverage through tax subsidies, on a federally controlled single-payer plan, or on mandatory employer payments for insurance coverage. From 1987 to 1996, enrollment in health maintenance organizations (HMOs) doubled.

Life expectancy for someone born in 1998 was a US record high 76.8 years. Males could expect to live 73.5 years, females 80.2 years. Infant mortality has fallen from 3,830 per 100,000 live births in 1945 to 848.7 in 1992. In 1996 it was 7 per 1,000 live births. In 1990, 1,429,577 legal abortions were obtained in the US, for a rate of 24 per 1,000 women ages 15–44 and a ratio of 345 per 1,000 live births.

The overall death rate is comparable to that of most nations—8.8 per 1,000 people in 1999. Leading causes of death (number, rate per 100,000 people) in 1998 were: heart disease (724,859, 268.2); cancer (537,400, 200.8); cerebrovascular diseases (158,448, 58.5); chronic obstructive pulmonary diseases (112,584, 41.7); accidents and adverse effects (97,835, 36.2); pneumonia and influenza (88,400, 33.0); diabetes mellitus (64,751, 24.0); motor vehicle accidents (43,501, 16.1); suicide (30,575, 11.3); Alzheimer's disease (22,725, 8.4); and homicide and legal intervention (18,272, 6.8). Cigarette smoking has been linked to heart and lung disease; about 20% of all deaths in the US were attributed to cigarette smoking in 1990. Smoking has decreased overall since the late 1980s. The overall trends in smoking mortality point to a decrease for males since the 1960s, but an increase in mortality for females. On 23 November 1998, the Master Settlement Agreement was signed, the result of a lawsuit brought by 46 states and the District of Columbia against tobacco companies for damages related to smoking. Payments from the settlement, totaling $206 billion, began in 1999.

First identified in 1981, HIV infection (resulting in acquired immune deficiency syndrome—AIDS) has risen; by 1992, there were just under 250,000 AIDS cases reported in the US, and by December 1999, the number of people living with HIV/AIDS was estimated at 650,000–900,000, with the number of new HIV infections estimated at 40,000 annually. AIDS continued to affect racial and ethnic minorities disproportionately. In 1999, the breakdown of men reporting new HIV infections was 50% black, 20% Hispanic, 30% white. The breakdown for new cases among women was 64% black, 18% Hispanic, 18% white. As of 1999, 50% of new infections (of men) were men who engaged in sex with other men, and 25% were injecting drug users.

Medical facilities in the US included 6,097 hospitals in 1997, with 1,035,000 beds. There were 756,700 physicians as of 1 January 1997. Between 1990 and 1997, there were 2.5 physicians and 4.1 hospital beds in the US per 1,000 people. Of the total number of active classified physicians, the largest areas of activity were internal medicine, 81,400; general and family practice, 62,000; pediatrics, 36,800; obstetrics and gynecology, 30,100; and general surgery, 27,900. As of the end of 1996, there were 2,162,000 registered nurses. Dentists numbered approximately 196,000 in 1996.

Per capita health care expenditures rose from $247 in 1967 to about $3,380 in 1993. Between 1990 and 1997, health care expenditures totaled 14.1% of GDP. National health care spending reached $1 trillion in 1996 and is projected to rise to $1.8 trillion by 2005. Hospital care represented 34% of national health care spending in 1997. Hospital costs amounted to over $371 billion in 1997. In 1996, services provided for Medicaid recipients required $147.7 billion in federal expenditures, while Medicare enrollees received benefit payments of $203.1 billion. Medicare payments have lagged behind escalating hospital costs. Meanwhile, the elderly population in the US is projected to increase to 18% of the total population by 2020, thus exacerbating the conundrum of health care finance. As of June 1999, 39 states had adopted policies enabling Medicaid funds to be used to cover medical services for qualified individuals requiring services provided by assisted-living facilities.

[42]HOUSING

The housing resources of the US far exceed those of any other country, with 106.6 million housing units in 1993, 94.7 million (nearly 90%) of which were occupied. That same year, 61.3 million (57.5%) of all US homes were occupied by their owners; 33.4 million (31.3%) were rented; 8.8 million (8.3%) were vacant; and 3 million (2.8%) were occupied seasonally. Home ownership rates lagged among single-person households; in 1998, only about 50% owned their homes. Households of persons under 35 years of age was under 40% during the same period.

About 70 million housing units (66%) were single-unit structures. The majority of rental tenants are found in the large metropolitan areas. As of 1990, an estimated 94 million year-round households possessed and used electrical appliances. Of these, 90.3% had color television sets; 71.7% had washing machines; 64.7% had clothes dryers; 42.7% had electric dishwashers; 29.1% had room air conditioners; and 36.6% had central air conditioning. As of 1980, about 22% of all housing units in the US had been built before 1940; 8% during 1940–49; 13% during 1950–59; 15% from 1960 to 1969; 23% during 1970–79; and 19% since 1980. The median construction year was 1964.

In 1993, the median age of US housing structures was 28 years. The median number of rooms per house that year was 5.3, with about 32% having two bedrooms, and 39% having three bedrooms. Nearly half of all housing units have one full bathroom. Houses being built in the 1990s were significantly larger than those built in the 1970s. The average area of single-family housing built in 1993 was 180.88 sq m (1,947 sq ft), compared to 139.35 sq m (1,500 sq ft) in 1970.

[43]EDUCATION

Education is compulsory in all states and a responsibility of each state and the local government. However, federal funds are available to help meet special needs at primary, secondary, or higher levels. Generally, formal schooling begins at the age of six and continues up to age 17. Each state specifies the age and circumstances for compulsory attendance.

"Regular" schools which educate a person towards a diploma or degree include both public and private schools. Public schools are controlled and supported by the local authorities, as well as

state or federal governmental agencies. Private schools are controlled and supported by religious or private organizations. Elementary schooling is from grade 1 through grade 8. High schools cover grades 9 through 12. Colleges include junior or community colleges, offering two-year associate degrees; regular four-year colleges and universities; and graduate or professional schools. The school year begins in September and ends in June.

The enrollment rate of three- to five-year-olds in preprimary schools was 37% in 1970. It went up to 56% in 1991. Persons 25 years old and over completing college education was 11% in 1970 and 21% in 1992. By 1994, approximately 46.5% of the adult population had attended a post-secondary institution.

The total number of children enrolled in public and private elementary and secondary schools in 1996 was 51.7 million; that year, public schools had 45.8 million, and private schools, 8.9 million. It was projected that by the year 2000, public schools would have 47.7 million students and private schools 6 million students. Students in grades 1–8 numbered 24,045,967 in 1996, with 1,499,697 teachers and a student-to-teacher ratio of 16 to one. Students in grades 9– 12 numbered 21,473,692 in 1996, with 1,394,080 teachers. Colleges had 14,261,778 students enrolled, with 915,321 teaching staff. In 1994–95, there were 3,688 higher education institutions, 1,473 of which were two-year and 2,215 were four-year colleges and universities. The literacy rate is estimated to be 98% (males 97% and females 98%).

[44]LIBRARIES AND MUSEUMS

Of the 32,852 libraries in the US in 2000, 9,837 were public, with 6,376 branches; 4,723 were academic; 1,874 were government; 1,906 were medical; and a number were religious, military, legal, and specialized independent collections. The country's vast public library system is administered by municipality. The largest of these is the New York Public Library system with a total of 33.6 million items, including 17.7 million bound volumes. Other major public library systems include the Miami-Dade Public Library System with 3.9 million volumes, the Los Angeles Public Library (5.8 million), and the Chicago Public Library (6.5 million).

The foremost library in the country is the Library of Congress, with holdings of more than 26 million books and pamphlets in 2000. Other great libraries are the public libraries of Philadelphia, Boston, Cleveland, and Baltimore, and the John Crerar and Newberry libraries in Chicago. Noted special collections are those of the Pierpont Morgan Library in New York; the Huntington Library in San Marino, Calif.; the Folger Shakespeare Library in Washington, D.C.; the Hoover Library at Stanford University; and the rare book divisions of Harvard, Yale, Indiana, Texas, and Virginia universities. Among the leading university libraries, as judged by the extent of their holdings in 2000, are those of Harvard, Yale, Illinois (Urbana-Champaign), Michigan (Ann Arbor), California (Berkeley), Columbia, Stanford, Cornell, California (Los Angeles), Chicago, Wisconsin (Madison), and Washington (Seattle). In 1997, Cleveland, Chicago, and San Francisco all opened new, multi-million dollar libraries.

There are about 5,000 nonprofit museums in the US. The most numerous type is the historic building, followed in descending order by college and university museums, museums of science, public museums of history, and public museums of art. Eminent US museums include the American Museum of Natural History, the Metropolitan Museum of Art, the Museum of Modern Art, the Guggenheim Museum, the Whitney Collection of American Art, the Frick Collection, and the Brooklyn Museum, all in New York City; the National Gallery of Art and the Smithsonian Institution in Washington, D.C.; the Boston Museum of Fine Arts; the Art Institute of Chicago and the Chicago Museum of Natural

History; the Franklin Institute and Philadelphia Museum of Art, both in Philadelphia; and the M. H. de Young Memorial Museum in San Francisco. Also of prominence are the Cleveland Museum of Art, the St. Louis Museum of Art, and the Baltimore Museum of Art. In 2000 the Hayden Planetarium at the American Museum of Natural History reopened after a six-year, $210 million renovation.

45MEDIA

All major electric communications systems are privately owned but regulated by the Federal Communications Commission. The US uses wire and radio services for communications more extensively than any other country in the world. In 2000 over 98% of all US households had telephones, utilizing some 148 million main telephone lines.

Radio serves a variety of purposes other than broadcasting. It is widely used by ships and aircraft for safety; it has become an important tool in the movement of buses, trucks, and taxicabs. Forest conservators, fire departments, and the police operate with radio as a necessary aid; it is used in logging operations, surveying, construction work, and dispatching of repair crews. In 1999, broadcasting stations on the air comprised over 10,000 radio stations (both AM and FM) and more than 1,500 television stations. Nearly 1,000 stations were affiliated with the five major networks. As of 1997 the US had some 9,000 cable television systems. In the same year, there were 2,115 radios, 847 television sets, and 206 mobile phones per 1,000 population. In 2000 over 98% of all US households owned at least one TV set.

The Post Office Department of the US was replaced on 1 July 1971 by the US Postal Service, a financially autonomous federal agency. In addition to mail delivery, the Postal Service provides registered, certified, insured, express and COD mail service, issues money orders, and operates a postal savings system. Since the 1970s, numerous privately owned overnight mail and package delivery services have been established.

In 1995 there were 1,586 daily newspapers in the US, with a combined circulation of over 60 million. Twenty large newspaper chains account for almost 60% of the total daily circulation. The US daily newspapers with the largest circulations as of 30 September 1998 were as follows:

	CIRCULATION
Wall Street Journal	1,740,450
USA Today	1,652,428
Los Angeles Times	1,067,540
New York Times	1,066,658
Washington Post	759,122
New York Daily News	723,143
Chicago Tribune	673,508
Long Island/New York Newsday	572,444
Houston Chronicle	550,763
Chicago Sun-Times	485,666
Dallas Morning News	479,863
San Francisco Chronicle	475,324
Boston Globe	470,825
New York Post	437,467
Arizona Republic	435,330
Philadelphia Inquirer	428,895
Star-Ledger (Newark)	407,026
Cleveland Plain Dealer	382,933
Union-Tribune (San Diego)	378,112
Register (Orange County)	356,953

Modern Maturity, published bimonthly by AARP, had a circulation of 20 million in 2000. The two general circulation magazines that appealed to the largest audiences were *Reader's Digest* (about 17 million), and *TV Guide* (about 15 million).

Time and *Newsweek* were the leading news magazines, with a weekly circulation of 4,630,140 and 3,100,000 respectively.

The US book-publishing industry consists of the major book companies (mainly in the New York metro area), nonprofit university presses distributed throughout the US, and numerous small publishing firms. In 1994, 51,863 book titles were published in the US.

The US Constitution provides for freedom of speech and of the press in its Bill of Rights, and the government supports these rights. Citizens enjoy a wide range of opinions in all media, where debate, editorial opinion, and government opposition viewpoints are represented in some form or another. Nearly all media are privately owned.

As of 1996, there were some 85 million personal computers; in 1998 there were 976 Internet hosts per 1,000 population.

46ORGANIZATIONS

The 1997 Census of Service Industries counted 65,943 membership organizations, embracing 36,099 civic, social, and fraternal associations; 15,238 business associations; 7,239 professional associations, and 7,367 other bodies.

A number of industrial and commercial organizations exercise considerable influence on economic policy. The National Association of Manufacturers and the US Chamber of Commerce, with numerous local branches, are the two central bodies of business and commerce. Various industries have their own associations, concerned with cooperative research and questions of policy alike.

Practically every profession in the US is represented by one or more professional organizations. Among the most powerful of these are the American Medical Association, comprising regional, state, and local medical societies; the American Bar Association, also comprising state and local associations; the American Hospital Association; and the National Education Association. The most prestigious scientific and technical institution s are the National Academy of Sciences (founded 1863) and the National Academy of Engineering (1964).

Many private organizations are dedicated to programs of political and social action. Prominent in this realm are the National Association for the Advancement of Colored People (NAACP), the Urban League, the American Civil Liberties Union (ACLU), Common Cause, and the Anti-Defamation League. The League of Women Voters, which provides the public with nonpartisan information about candidates and election issues, began sponsoring televised debates between the major presidential candidates in 1976. The National Organization for Women, and the National Rifle Association have each mounted nationwide lobbying campaigns on issues affecting their members. There are thousands of political action committees (PACs) that disburse funds to candidates for the House and Senate and other elected offices.

The great privately endowed philanthropic foundations and trusts play an important part in encouraging the development of education, art, science, and social progress in the US. Prominent foundations include the Carnegie Corporation and the Carnegie Endowment for International Peace, the Ford Foundation, the Guggenheim Foundation, the Mayo Association for the Advancement of Medical Research and Education, and the Rockefeller Foundation. Private philanthropy was responsible for the establishment of many of the nation's most eminent libraries, concert halls, museums, and university and medical facilities; private bequests were also responsible for the establishment of the Pulitzer Prizes. Merit awards offered by industry and professional groups include the "Oscars" of the Academy of Motion Picture Arts and Sciences, the "Emmys" of the National Academy of Television Arts and Sciences, and the "Grammys" of the National Academy of Recording Arts and Sciences.

Funds for a variety of community health and welfare services are funneled through United Way campaigns, which raise funds annually. The American Red Cross has over 3,000 chapters, which paid for services and activities ranging from disaster relief to blood donor programs. Private organizations supported by contributions from the general public lead the fight against specific diseases.

The Boy Scouts of America, the Girl Scouts of the USA, rural 4–H Clubs, and the Young Men's and the Young Women's Christian Associations are among the organizations devoted to recreation, sports, camping, and education.

The largest religious organization in the US is the National Council of the Churches of Christ in the USA, which embraces 32 Protestant and Orthodox denominations, whose adherents total more than 42 million. Many organizations, such as the American Philosophical Society, the American Association for the Advancement of Science, and the National Geographic Society, are dedicated to the enlargement of various branches of human knowledge. National, state, and local historical societies abound, and there are numerous educational, sports, and hobbyist groups.

The larger veterans' organizations are the American Legion, the Veterans of Foreign Wars of the US, the Catholic War Veterans, and the Jewish War Veterans. Fraternal organizations, in addition to such international organizations as the Masons, include indigenous groups such as the Benevolent and Protective Order of Elks, the Loyal Order of Moose, and the Woodmen of the World. Many, such as the Ancient Order of Hibernians in America, commemorate the national origin of their members. One of the largest fraternal organizations is the Roman Catholic Knights of Columbus.

47TOURISM, TRAVEL, AND RECREATION

Foreign visitors to the US numbered 46,395,419 in 1998. Of these visitors, 13,421,832 came from Canada, 9,276,000 from Mexico, and 4,885,369 from Japan. Travelers to the US from all foreign countries spent $73.3 billion in 1997. With a few exceptions, such as Canadians entering from the Western Hemisphere, all visitors to the US are required to have passports and visas.

Among the most striking scenic attractions in the US are the Grand Canyon in Arizona; Carlsbad Caverns in New Mexico; Yosemite National Park in California; Yellowstone National Park in Idaho, Montana, and Wyoming; Niagara Falls, partly in New York; and the Everglades in Florida. The US has a total of 49 national parks. Popular coastal resorts include those of Florida, California, and Cape Code in Massachusetts. Historical attractions include the Liberty Bell and Constitution Hall in Philadelphia; the Statue of Liberty in New York City; the White House, the Capitol, and the monuments to Washington, Jefferson, and Lincoln in the District of Columbia; the Williamsburg historical restoration in Virginia; various Revolutionary and Civil War battlefields and monuments in the East and South; the Alamo in San Antonio; and Mt. Rushmore in South Dakota. Among many other popular tourist attractions are the movie and television studios in Los Angeles; the cable cars in San Francisco; casino gambling in Las Vegas and in Atlantic City, N.J.; thoroughbred horse racing in Kentucky; the Grand Ole Opry in Nashville, Tenn.; the many jazz clubs of New Orleans; and such amusement parks as Disneyland (Anaheim, Calif.) and Walt Disney World (near Orlando, Fla.). For abundance and diversity of entertainment—theater, movies, music, dance, and sports—New York City has few rivals. In April 1993, Amtrak began the country's first regularly scheduled transcontinental passenger service, from Los Angeles to Miami.

Americans' recreational activities range from the major spectator sports—professional baseball, football, basketball, ice hockey, and soccer, horse racing, and collegiate football and basketball—to home gardening. Participant sports are a favorite form of recreation, including jogging, aerobics, tennis, and golf. Skiing is a popular recreation in New England and the western mountain ranges, while sailing, power boating, rafting, and canoeing are popular water sports.

The cost of traveling in the US varies from city to city. According to 1999 UN estimates, daily expenses were approximately $263 in Chicago, $275 in New York, $235 in Washington, and $213 in Miami. Costs are lower in smaller cities and rural areas.

48FAMOUS AMERICANS

Printer, publisher, inventor, scientist, statesman, and diplomat, Benjamin Franklin (1706–90) was America's outstanding figure of the colonial period. George Washington (1732–99), leader of the colonial army in the American Revolution, became first president of the US and is known as the "father of his country." Chief author of the Declaration of Independence, founder of the US political party system, and third president was Thomas Jefferson (1743–1826). His leading political opponents were John Adams (1735–1826), second president, and Alexander Hamilton (b.West Indies, 1755–1804), first secretary of the treasury, who secured the new nation's credit. James Madison (1751–1836), a leading figure in drawing up the US Constitution, served as fourth president. John Quincy Adams (1767–1848), sixth president, was an outstanding diplomat and secretary of state.

Andrew Jackson (1767–1845), seventh president, was an ardent champion of the common people and opponent of vested interests. Outstanding senators during the Jackson era were John Caldwell Calhoun (1782–1850), spokesman of the southern planter aristocracy and leading exponent of the supremacy of states' rights over federal powers; Henry Clay (1777–1852), the great compromiser, who sought to reconcile the conflicting views of the North and the South; and Daniel Webster (1782–1852), statesman and orator, who championed the preservation of the Union against sectional interests and division. Abraham Lincoln (1809–65) led the US through its most difficult period, the Civil War, in the course of which he issued the Emancipation Proclamation. Jefferson Davis (1808–89) served as the only president of the short-lived Confederacy. Stephen Grover Cleveland (1837–1908), a conservative reformer, was the strongest president in the latter part of the 19th century. Among the foremost presidents of the 20th century have been Nobel Peace Prize winner Theodore Roosevelt (1858–1919); Woodrow Wilson (1856–1924), who led the nation during World War I and helped establish the League of Nations; and Franklin Delano Roosevelt (1882–1945), elected to four terms spanning the Great Depression and World War II. The presidents during the 1961–88 period have been John Fitzgerald Kennedy (1917–63), Lyndon Baines Johnson (1908–73), Richard Milhous Nixon (1913–94), Gerald Rudolph Ford (Leslie Lynch King, Jr., b.1913), Jimmy Carter (James Earl Carter, Jr., b.1924), and Ronald Wilson Reagan (b.1911).

Of the outstanding US military leaders, four were produced by the Civil War: Union generals Ulysses Simpson Grant (1822–85), who later served as the eighteenth president, and William Tecumseh Sherman (1820–91); and Confederate generals Robert Edward Lee (1807–70) and Thomas Jonathan "Stonewall" Jackson (1824–63). George Catlett Marshall (1880–1959), army chief of staff during World War II, in his later capacity as secretary of state under President Harry S Truman (1884–1972), formulated the Marshall Plan, which did much to revitalize Western Europe. Douglas MacArthur (1880–1964) commanded the US forces in Asia during World War II, oversaw the postwar occupation and reorganization of Japan, and directed UN forces in the first year of the Korean conflict. Dwight D. Eisenhower (1890–1969) served as supreme Allied commander during World War II, later becoming the thirty-fourth president.

John Marshall (1755–1835), chief justice of the US from 1801 to 1835, established the power of the Supreme Court through the principle of judicial review. Other important chief justices were Edward Douglass White (1845–1921), former president William Howard Taft (1857–1930), and Earl Warren (1891–1974), whose tenure as chief justice from 1953 to 1969 saw important decisions on desegregation, reapportionment, and civil liberties. The justice who enjoyed the longest tenure on the court was William O. Douglas (1898–1980), who served from 1939 to 1975; other prominent associate justices were Oliver Wendell Holmes (1841–1935), Louis Dembitz Brandeis (1856–1941), and Hugo Lafayette Black (1886–1971).

Indian chiefs renowned for their resistance to white encroachment were Pontiac (1729?–69), Black Hawk (1767–1838), Tecumseh (1768–1813), Osceola (1804?–38), Cochise (1812?–74), Geronimo (1829?–1909), Sitting Bull (1831?–90), Chief Joseph (1840?–1904), and Crazy Horse (1849?–77). Other significant Indian chiefs were Hiawatha (fl. 1500), Squanto (d.1622), and Sequoya (1770?–1843). Historical figures who have become part of American folklore include pioneer Daniel Boone (1734–1820); silversmith, engraver, and patriot Paul Revere (1735–1818); frontiersman David "Davy" Crockett (1786–1836); scout and Indian agent Christopher "Kit" Carson (1809–68); James Butler "Wild Bill" Hickok (1837–76); William Frederick "Buffalo Bill" Cody (1846–1917); and the outlaws Jesse Woodson James (1847–82) and Billy the Kid (William H. Bonney, 1859–81).

Inventors and Scientists

Outstanding inventors were Robert Fulton (1765–1815), who developed the steamboat; Eli Whitney (1765–1825), inventor of the cotton gin and mass production techniques; Samuel Finley Breese Morse (1791–1872), who invented the telegraph; and Elias Howe (1819–67), who invented the sewing machine. Alexander Graham Bell (b.Scotland, 1847–1922) gave the world the telephone. Thomas Alva Edison (1847–1931) was responsible for hundreds of inventions, among them the long-burning incandescent electric lamp, the phonograph, automatic telegraph devices, a motion picture camera and projector, the microphone, and the mimeograph. Lee De Forest (1873–1961), the "father of the radio," developed the vacuum tube and many other inventions. Vladimir Kosma Zworykin (b.Russia, 1889–1982) was principally responsible for the invention of television. Two brothers, Wilbur Wright (1867–1912) and Orville Wright (1871–1948), designed, built, and flew the first successful motor-powered airplane. Amelia Earhart (1898–1937) and Charles Lindbergh (1902–74) were aviation pioneers. Pioneers in the space program include John Glenn (b.1921), the first US astronaut to orbit the earth, and Neil Armstrong (b.1930), the first man to set foot on the moon.

Benjamin Thompson, Count Rumford (1753–1814), developed devices for measuring light and heat, and the physicist Joseph Henry (1797–1878) did important work in magnetism and electricity. Outstanding botanists and naturalists were John Bartram (1699–1777); his son William Bartram (1739–1832); Louis Agassiz (b.Switzerland, 1807–73); Asa Gray (1810–88); Luther Burbank (1849–1926), developer of a vast number of new and improved varieties of fruits, vegetables, and flowers; and George Washington Carver (1864–1943), known especially for his work on industrial applications for peanuts. John James Audubon (1785–1851) won fame as an ornithologist and artist.

Distinguished physical scientists include Samuel Pierpont Langley (1834–1906), astronomer and aviation pioneer; Josiah Willard Gibbs (1839–1903), mathematical physicist, whose work laid the basis for physical chemistry; Henry Augustus Rowland (1848–1901), who did important research in magnetism and optics; and Albert Abraham Michelson (b.Germany, 1852–1931),

who measured the speed of light and became the first of a long line of US Nobel Prize winners. The chemists Gilbert Newton Lewis (1875–1946) and Irving Langmuir (1881–1957) developed a theory of atomic structure.

The theory of relativity was conceived by Albert Einstein (b.Germany, 1879–1955), generally considered the greatest mind in the physical sciences since Newton. Percy Williams Bridgman (1882–1961) was the father of operationalism and studied the effect of high pressures on materials. Arthur Holly Compton (1892–1962) made discoveries in the field of X rays and cosmic rays. The physical chemist Harold Clayton Urey (1893–1981) discovered heavy hydrogen. Isidor Isaac Rabi (b.Austria, 1898–1988), nuclear physicist, did important work in magnetism, quantum mechanics, and radiation. Enrico Fermi (b.Italy, 1901–54) created the first nuclear chain reaction, in Chicago in 1942, and contributed to the development of the atomic and hydrogen bombs. Also prominent in the splitting of the atom were Leo Szilard (b.Hungary, 1898–1964), J. Robert Oppenheimer (1904–67), and Edward Teller (b.Hungary, 1908). Ernest Orlando Lawrence (1901–58) developed the cyclotron. Carl David Anderson (1905–91) discovered the positron. Mathematician Norbert Wiener (1894–1964) developed the science of cybernetics.

Outstanding figures in the biological sciences include Theobald Smith (1859–1934), who developed immunization theory and practical immunization techniques for animals; the geneticist Thomas Hunt Morgan (1866–1945), who discovered the heredity functions of chromosomes; and neurosurgeon Harvey William Cushing (1869–1939). Selman Abraham Waksman (b.Russia, 1888–1973), a microbiologist specializing in antibiotics, was codiscoverer of streptomycin. Edwin Joseph Cohn (1892–1953) is noted for his work in the protein fractionalization of blood, particularly the isolation of serum albumin. Philip Showalter Hench (1896–1965) isolated and synthesized cortisone. Wendell Meredith Stanley (1904–71) was the first to isolate and crystallize a virus. Jonas Edward Salk (1914–95) developed an effective killed-virus poliomyelitis vaccine, and Albert Bruce Sabin (1906–93) contributed oral, attenuated live-virus polio vaccines.

Adolf Meyer (b.Switzerland, 1866–1950) developed the concepts of mental hygiene and dementia praecox and the theory of psychobiology; Harry Stack Sullivan (1892–1949) created the interpersonal theory of psychiatry. Social psychologist George Herbert Mead (1863–1931) and behaviorist Burrhus Frederic Skinner (1904–90) have been influential in the 20th century.

A pioneer in psychology who was also an influential philosopher was William James (1842–1910). Other leading US philosophers are Charles Sanders Peirce (1839–1914); Josiah Royce (1855–1916); John Dewey (1859–1952), also famous for his theories of education; George Santayana (b.Spain, 1863–1952); Rudolf Carnap (b.Germany, 1891–1970); and Willard Van Orman Quine (b.1908). Educators of note include Horace Mann (1796–1859), Henry Barnard (1811–1900), and Charles William Eliot (1834–1926). Noah Webster (1758–1843) was the outstanding US lexicographer, and Melvil Dewey (1851–1931) was a leader in the development of library science. Thorstein Bunde Veblen (1857–1929) wrote books that have strongly influenced economic and social thinking. Also important in the social sciences have been sociologists Talcott Parsons (1902–79) and William Graham Sumner (1840–1910) and anthropologist Margaret Mead (1901–78).

Social Reformers

Social reformers of note include Dorothea Lynde Dix (1802–87), who led movements for the reform of prisons and insane asylums; William Lloyd Garrison (1805–79) and Frederick Douglass (Frederick Augustus Washington Bailey, 1817–95), prominent abolitionists; Elizabeth Cady Stanton (1815–1902) and Susan Brownell Anthony (1820–1906), leaders in the women's suffrage movement; Clara Barton (1821–1912), founder of the American Red Cross; economist Henry George (1839–97), advocate of the single-tax theory; Eugene Victor Debs (1855–1926), labor leader and an outstanding organizer of the Socialist movement in the US; Jane Addams (1860–1935), who pioneered in settlement house work; Robert Marion La Follette (1855–1925), a leader for progressive political reform in Wisconsin and in the US Senate; Margaret Higgins Sanger (1883–1966), pioneer in birth control; Norman Thomas (1884–1968), Socialist Party leader; and Martin Luther King, Jr. (1929–68), a central figure in the black civil rights movement and winner of the Nobel Peace Prize in 1964.

Religious leaders include Roger Williams (1603–83), an early advocate of religious tolerance in the US; Jonathan Edwards (1703–58), New England preacher and theologian; Elizabeth Ann Seton (1774–1821), the first American canonized in the Roman Catholic Church; William Ellery Channing (1780–1842), a founder of American Unitarianism; Joseph Smith (1805–44), founder of the Church of Jesus Christ of Latter-day Saints (Mormon) and his chief associate, Brigham Young (1801–77); and Mary Baker Eddy (1821–1910), founder of the Christian Science Church. Paul Tillich (b.Germany, 1886–1965) and Reinhold Niebuhr (1892–1971) were outstanding Protestant theologians of international influence.

Famous US businessmen include Éleuthere Irénée du Pont de Nemours (b.France, 1771–1834), John Jacob Astor (Johann Jakob Ashdour, b.Germany, 1763–1848), Cornelius Vanderbilt (1794–1877), Andrew Carnegie (b.Scotland, 1835–1919), John Pierpont Morgan (1837–1913), John Davison Rockefeller (1839–1937), Andrew William Mellon (1855–1937), Henry Ford (1863–1947), and Thomas John Watson (1874–1956).

Literary Figures

The first US author to be widely read outside the US was Washington Irving (1783–1859). James Fenimore Cooper (1789–1851) was the first popular US novelist. Three noted historians were William Hickling Prescott (1796–1859), John Lothrop Motley (1814–77), and Francis Parkman (1823–93). The writings of two men of Concord, Mass.—Ralph Waldo Emerson (1803–82) and Henry David Thoreau (1817–62)—influenced philosophers, political leaders, and ordinary men and women in many parts of the world. The novels and short stories of Nathaniel Hawthorne (1804–64) explore New England's Puritan heritage. Herman Melville (1819–91) wrote the powerful novel *Moby-Dick,* a symbolic work about a whale hunt that has become an American classic. Mark Twain (Samuel Langhorne Clemens, 1835–1910) is the best-known US humorist. Other leading novelists of the later 19th and early 20th centuries were William Dean Howells (1837–1920), Henry James (1843–1916), Edith Wharton (1862–1937), Stephen Crane (1871–1900), Theodore Dreiser (1871–1945), Willa Cather (1873–1947), and Sinclair Lewis (1885–1951), first US winner of the Nobel Prize for literature (1930). Later Nobel Prize–winning US novelists include Pearl Sydenstricker Buck (1892–1973), in 1938; William Faulkner (1897–1962), in 1949; Ernest Hemingway (1899–1961), in 1954; John Steinbeck (1902–68), in 1962; Saul Bellow (b.Canada, 1915), in 1976; and Isaac Bashevis Singer (b.Poland, 1904–91), in 1978. Among other noteworthy writers are James Thurber (1894–1961), Francis Scott Key Fitzgerald (1896–1940), Thomas Wolfe (1900–1938), Richard Wright (1908–60), Eudora Welty (b.1909), John Cheever (1912–82), Norman Mailer (b.1923), James Baldwin (1924–87), John Updike (b.1932), and Philip Roth (b.1933).

Noted US poets include Henry Wadsworth Longfellow (1807–82), Edgar Allan Poe (1809–49), Walt Whitman (1819–92), Emily Dickinson (1830–86), Edwin Arlington Robinson (1869–1935), Robert Frost (1874–1963), Wallace Stevens (1879–1955), William Carlos Williams (1883–1963), Marianne Moore (1887–1972), Edward Estlin Cummings (1894–1962), Hart Crane (1899–1932), and Langston Hughes (1902–67). Ezra Pound (1885–1972) and Nobel laureate Thomas Stearns Eliot (1888–1965) lived and worked abroad for most of their careers. Wystan Hugh Auden (b.England, 1907–73), who became an American citizen in 1946, published poetry and criticism. Elizabeth Bishop (1911–79), Robert Lowell (1917–77), Allen Ginsberg (1926–97), and Sylvia Plath (1932–63) are among the best-known poets since World War II. Robert Penn Warren (1905–89) won the Pulitzer Prize for both fiction and poetry and became the first US poet laureate. Carl Sandburg (1878–1967) was a noted poet, historian, novelist, and folklorist. The foremost US dramatists are Eugene (Gladstone) O'Neill (1888–1953), who won the Nobel Prize for literature in 1936; Tennessee Williams (Thomas Lanier Williams, 1911–83); Arthur Miller (b.1915); and Edward Albee (b.1928). Neil Simon (b.1927) is among the nation's most popular playwrights and screenwriters.

Artists

Two renowned painters of the early period were John Singleton Copley (1738–1815) and Gilbert Stuart (1755–1828). Outstanding 19th-century painters were James Abbott McNeill Whistler (1834–1903), Winslow Homer (1836–1910), Thomas Eakins (1844–1916), Mary Cassatt (1845–1926), Albert Pinkham Ryder (1847–1917), John Singer Sargent (b.Italy, 1856–1925), and Frederic Remington (1861–1909). More recently, Edward Hopper (1882–1967), Georgia O'Keeffe (1887–1986), Thomas Hart Benton (1889–1975), Charles Burchfield (1893–1967), Norman Rockwell (1894–1978), Ben Shahn (1898–1969), Mark Rothko (b.Russia, 1903–70), Jackson Pollock (1912–56), Andrew Wyeth (b.1917), Robert Rauschenberg (b.1925), and Jasper Johns (b.1930) have achieved international recognition.

Sculptors of note include Augustus Saint-Gaudens (1848–1907), Gaston Lachaise (1882–1935), Jo Davidson (1883–1952), Daniel Chester French (1850–1931), Alexander Calder (1898–1976), Louise Nevelson (b.Russia, 1899–1988), and Isamu Noguchi (1904–88). Henry Hobson Richardson (1838–86), Louis Henry Sullivan (1856–1924), Frank Lloyd Wright (1869–1959), Louis I. Kahn (b.Estonia, 1901–74), and Eero Saarinen (1910–61) were outstanding architects. Contemporary architects of note include Richard Buckminster Fuller (1895–1983), Edward Durell Stone (1902–78), Philip Cortelyou Johnson (b.1906), and Ieoh Ming Pei (b.China, 1917). The US has produced many fine photographers, notably Mathew B. Brady (1823?–96), Alfred Stieglitz (1864–1946), Edward Steichen (1879–1973), Edward Weston (1886–1958), Ansel Adams (1902–84), and Margaret Bourke-White (1904–71).

Entertainment Figures

Outstanding figures in the motion picture industry are D. W. (David Lewelyn Wark) Griffith (1875–1948), Sir Charles Spencer "Charlie" Chaplin (b.England, 1889–1978), Walter Elias "Walt" Disney (1906–66), and George Orson Welles (1915–85). John Ford (1895–1973), Howard Winchester Hawks (1896–1977), Frank Capra (b.Italy, 1897–1991), Sir Alfred Hitchcock (b.England, 1899–1980), and John Huston (1906–87) were influential motion picture directors; Mel Brooks (Kaminsky, b.1926), George Lucas (b.1944), and Steven Spielberg (b.1947) have achieved remarkable popular success. Woody Allen (Allen Konigsberg, b.1935) has written, directed, and starred in comedies on stage and screen. World-famous American actors and actresses include the Barrymores, Ethel (1879–1959) and her brothers Lionel (1878–1954) and John (1882–1942); Humphrey Bogart (1899–1957); James Cagney (1899–1986); Spencer Tracy (1900–1967); Helen Hayes Brown (1900–93); Clark Gable

(1901–60); Joan Crawford (Lucille Fay LeSueur, 1904–77); Cary Grant (Alexander Archibald Leach, b.England, 1904–86); Greta Garbo (Greta Louisa Gustafsson, b.Sweden, 1905–90); Henry Fonda (1905–82) and his daughter, Jane (b.1937); John Wayne (Marion Michael Morrison, 1907–79); Bette (Ruth Elizabeth) Davis (1908–89); Katharine Hepburn (b.1909); Judy Garland (Frances Gumm, 1922–69); Marlon Brando (b.1924); Marilyn Monroe (Norma Jean Mortenson, 1926–62); and Dustin Hoffman (b.1937). Among other great entertainers are W. C. Fields (William Claude Dukenfield, 1880–1946), Al Jolson (Asa Yoelson, b.Russia, 1886–1950), Jack Benny (Benjamin Kubelsky, 1894–1974), Fred Astaire (Fred Austerlitz, 1899–1987), Bob (Leslie Townes) Hope (b.England, 1903), Bing (Harry Lillis) Crosby (1904–78), Frank (Francis Albert) Sinatra (1915–98), Elvis Aaron Presley (1935–77), and Barbra (Barbara Joan) Streisand (b.1942). The first great US "showman" was Phineas Taylor Barnum (1810–91).

Composers and Musicians

The foremost composers are Edward MacDowell (1861–1908), Charles Ives (1874–1954), Ernest Bloch (b.Switzerland, 1880–1959), Virgil Thomson (1896–89), Roger Sessions (1896–1985), Roy Harris (1898–1979), Aaron Copland (1900–90), Elliott Carter (b.1908), Samuel Barber (1910–81), John Cage (1912–92), and Leonard Bernstein (1918–90). George Rochberg (b.1918), George Crumb (b.1929), Steve Reich (b.1936), and Philip Glass (b.1937) have won more recent followings. The songs of Stephen Collins Foster (1826–64) have achieved folksong status. Leading composers of popular music are John Philip Sousa (1854–1932), George Michael Cohan (1878–1942), Jerome Kern (1885–1945), Irving Berlin (Israel Baline, b.Russia, 1888–1989), Cole Porter (1893–1964), George Gershwin (1898–1937), Richard Rodgers (1902–79), Woody Guthrie (1912–67), Stephen Joshua Sondheim (b.1930), Paul Simon (b.1941), and Bob Dylan (Robert Zimmerman, b.1941). Preeminent in the blues traditions are Leadbelly (Huddie Ledbetter, 1888–1949), Bessie Smith (1898?–1937), and Muddy Waters (McKinley Morganfield, 1915–83). Leading jazz figures include the composers Scott Joplin (1868–1917), James Hubert "Eubie" Blake (1883–1983), Edward Kennedy "Duke" Ellington (1899–1974), and William "Count" Basie (1904–84), and performers Louis Armstrong (1900–1971), Billie Holiday (Eleanora Fagan, 1915–59), John Birks "Dizzy" Gillespie (1917–93), Charlie "Bird" Parker (1920–55), John Coltrane (1926–67), and Miles Davis (1926–91).

Many foreign-born musicians have enjoyed personal and professional freedom in the US; principal among them were pianists Artur Schnabel (b.Austria, 1882–1951), Arthur Rubinstein (b.Poland, 1887–1982), Rudolf Serkin (b.Bohemia, 1903–91), Vladimir Horowitz (b.Russia, 1904–89), and violinists Jascha Heifetz (b.Russia, 1901–87) and Isaac Stern (b.USSR, 1920). Among distinguished instrumentalists born in the US are Benny Goodman (1909–86), a classical as well as jazz clarinetist, and concert pianist Van Cliburn (Harvey Lavan, Jr., b.1934). Singers Paul Robeson (1898–1976), Marian Anderson (1897–1993), Maria Callas (Maria Kalogeropoulos, 1923–77), Leontyne Price (b.1927), and Beverly Sills (Belle Silverman, b.1929) have achieved international acclaim. Isadora Duncan (1878–1927) was one of the first US dancers to win fame abroad. Martha Graham (1893–91) pioneered in modern dance. George Balanchine (b.Russia, 1904–83), Agnes De Mille (1905–93), Jerome Robbins (1918–98), Paul Taylor (b.1930), and Twyla Tharp (b.1941) are leading choreographers; Martha Graham (1893–1991) pioneered in modern dance.

Sports Figures

Among the many noteworthy sports stars are baseball's Tyrus Raymond "Ty" Cobb (1886–1961) and George Herman "Babe" Ruth (1895–1948); football's Samuel Adrian "Sammy" Baugh (b.1914), Jim Brown (b.1936), Francis A. "Fran" Tarkenton (b.1940), and Orenthal James Simpson (b.1947); and golf's Robert Tyre "Bobby" Jones (1902–71) and Mildred "Babe" Didrikson Zaharias (1914–56). William Tatum "Bill" Tilden (1893–1953) and Billie Jean (Moffitt) King (b.1943) have starred in tennis; Joe Louis (Joseph Louis Barrow, 1914–81) and Muhammad Ali (Cassius Marcellus Clay, b.1942) in boxing; William Felton "Bill" Russell (b.1934) and Wilton Norman "Wilt" Chamberlain (1936–99) in basketball; Mark Spitz (b.1950) in swimming; Eric Heiden (b.1958) in speed skating; and Jesse Owens (1913–80) in track and field.

49 DEPENDENCIES

As of January 1988, US dependencies, in addition to those listed below, included American Samoa, Guam, Midway, Wake Island, and the Northern Mariana Islands; see the *Asia* volume. Sovereignty over the Panama Canal Zone was transferred to Panama on 1 October 1979; the canal itself reverted to Panamanian control until 31 December 1999.

Navassa

Navassa, a 5-sq-km (2-sq-mi) island between Jamaica and Haiti, was claimed by the US under the Guano Act of 1856. The island, located at 18°24′N and 75°1′W, is uninhabited except for a lighthouse station under the administration of the coast guard.

Puerto Rico

Puerto Rico—total area 8,897 sq km (3,435 sq mi)—is the smallest and most easterly of the Greater Antilles, which screen the Caribbean Sea from the Atlantic proper. It lies between 17°51′ and 18°31′N and 65°13′ and 67°56′W, being separated from the Dominican Republic on the island of Hispaniola to the W by the Mona Passage, 121 km (75 mi) wide, and from the Virgin Islands on the E by Vieques Sound and the Virgin Passage. Roughly rectangular, the main island of Puerto Rico extends 179 km (111 mi) E–W and 58 km (36 mi) N–S. It is crossed from east to west by mountain ranges, the most prominent being the Cordillera Central, rising to nearly 1,338 m (4,390 ft). The coastal plain is about 24 km (15 mi) wide at its broadest point, and approximately one-third of the island's land is arable. About 50 short rivers flow rapidly to the sea. Islands off the coast include Mona and Desecheo to the W and Vieques and Culebra to the E. The mildly tropical climate is moderated by the surrounding sea, and seasonal variations are slight. The prevailing winds are the northeast trades. In San Juan on the northern coast, mean temperatures range from 24°C (75°F) for January to 27°C (81°F) for July. Mean annual rainfall varies from 74 cm (29 in) on the south coast to 150 cm (59 in) in San Juan and may total more than 380 cm (150 in) on the northern mountain slopes in the interior. Tropical fruits and other vegetation abound. As of 1991, endangered species on the island included the Puerto Rican plain pigeon, Puerto Rican parrot, Puerto Rican boa, giant anole, and hawksbill, leatherback, olive ridley, and green sea turtles.

The official census figure for 1990 was 3,522,039; the 1999 estimate was 3,887,652. In 1990, San Juan, the capital, had a population of 415,000, with a metropolitan area of more than 1 million. The population has more than doubled since 1930, despite extensive migration to the US mainland. Improved economic conditions on the island and diminishing opportunities in the US had slowed the trend by 1970; net out-migration was -2.31 migrants per 1000 population in 1999. Over three million Puerto Ricans reside in the US. Thousands commute annually between Puerto Rico and the US.

Many Puerto Ricans are of mixed black and Spanish ancestry; nearly all of the Amerindian inhabitants were exterminated in the 16th century. Spanish is the official language, but many Puerto Ricans also speak English, which is required as a second language in the schools. The Roman Catholic religion is predominant, but evangelical Protestant sects also have wide followings.

San Juan is the busiest commercial air center in the Caribbean, and there is excellent air service to New York, Miami, other points in the Caribbean, and Latin America. More than 40 steamship companies provide overseas freight and passenger service; San Juan, Ponce, and Mayagüez are the principal ports. In 1998 there were 14,400 km (9,020 mi) of paved highway; trucks carry the bulk of overland freight.

Archaeological finds indicate that at least three Amerindian cultures settled on the island now known as Puerto Rico, long before its European discovery by Christopher Columbus on 19 November 1493. The first group, belonging to the Archaic Culture, are believed to have come from Florida. Having no knowledge of agriculture or pottery, they relied on the products of the sea; their remains have been found mostly in caves. The second group, the Igneri, came from northern South America. Descended from South American Arawak stock, the Igneri brought agriculture and pottery to the island; their remains are found mostly in the coastal areas. The third culture, the Taíno, also of Arawak origin, combined fishing with agriculture. A peaceful, sedentary tribe, the Taíno were adept at stonework and lived in many parts of the island; to these Amerindians, the island was known as Borinquén.

Columbus, accompanied by a young nobleman named Juan Ponce de León, landed at the western end of the island—which he called San Juan Bautista (St. John the Baptist)—and claimed it for Spain. Not until colonization was well under way would the island acquire the name Puerto Rico ("rich port"), with the name San Juan Bautista applied to the capital city. The first settlers arrived on 12 August 1508, under the able leadership of Ponce de León, who sought to transplant and adapt Spanish civilization to Puerto Rico's tropical habitat. The small contingent of Spaniards compelled the Taíno, numbering perhaps 30,000, to mine for gold; the rigors of forced labor and the losses from rebellion reduced the Taíno population to about 4,000 by 1514, by which time the mines were nearly depleted. With the introduction of slaves from Africa, sugarcane growing became the leading economic activity.

Puerto Rico was briefly held by the English in 1598, and San Juan was besieged by the Dutch in 1625; otherwise, Spanish rule continued until the latter part of the 19th century. The island was captured by US forces during the Spanish-American War, and under the Treaty of Paris (December 1898) Puerto Rico was ceded outright to the US. It remained under direct military rule until 1900, when the US Congress established an administration with a governor and an executive council, appointed by the US president, and a popularly elected House of Delegates. In 1917, Puerto Ricans were granted US citizenship.

In 1947, Congress provided for popular election of the governor, and in 1948, Luis Muñoz Marín was elected to that office. A congressional act of 1950, affirmed by popular vote in the island on 4 June 1951, granted Puerto Rico the right to draft its own constitution. The constitution was ratified by popular referendum on 3 March 1952. Puerto Rico's new status as a free commonwealth voluntarily associated with the US became effective on 25 July. The commonwealth status was upheld in a plebiscite in 1967, with 60.5% voting for continuation of the commonwealth and 38.9% for Puerto Rican statehood. In 1993 the plebiscite vote drew nearly 1.7 million voters or 73.6 percent of those eligible. The voters choose to keep the commonwealth status 48.4% to 46.2% for statehood, and 4.4% for independence.

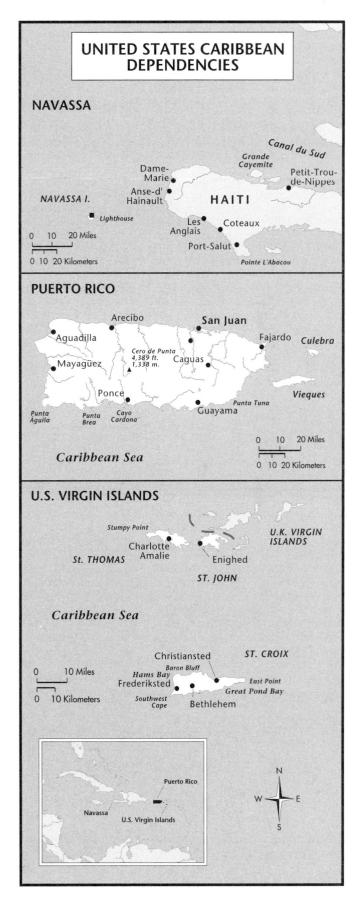

UNITED STATES CARIBBEAN DEPENDENCIES

The Commonwealth of Puerto Rico enjoys almost complete internal autonomy. The chief executive is the governor, elected by popular vote to a four-year term. The legislature consists of a 27-member Senate and 51-member House of Representatives elected by popular vote to four-year terms. The Supreme Court and lower courts are tied in with the US federal judiciary, and appeals from Puerto Rican courts may be carried as far as the US Supreme Court.

The Popular Democratic Party (PDP) was the dominant political party until 1968, when Luis A. Ferré, a New Progressive Party (NPP) candidate, who had supported the statehood position in the 1967 plebiscite, won the governorship. The NPP also won control of the House, while the PDP retained the Senate. The PDP returned to power in 1972 but lost to the NPP in 1976 and again, by a very narrow margin, in 1980; in 1984, it took roughly two-to-one majorities in both houses. The pro-commonwealth PDP remained in control of the government in every election from 1984–92, when Pedro Rosselló, a New Progressive and supporter of statehood, was elected governor; Rosselló was reelected in 1996. There is a small but vocal independence movement, divided into two wings: the moderates, favoring social democracy, and the radicals, supporting close ties with the Fidel Castro regime in Cuba.

For more than 400 years, the island's economy was based almost exclusively on sugar. Since 1947, agriculture has been diversified, and a thriving manufacturing industry has been established; since 1956 there has been increasing emphasis on hotel building to encourage the expansion of the tourist industry. By 1998, the gross commonwealth domestic product reached $34.7 billion, up from $15.8 billion in 1986. The leading industrial products were pharmaceuticals, electronics, apparel, food products, and tourism. Sugar processing, once the dominant industry, now plays a lesser role. In 1952, there were only 82 labor-intensive plants on the island. By 1990 there were 2,000 plants—most capital intensive—in Puerto Rico.

US taxes do not apply in Puerto Rico, since the commonwealth is not represented in Congress. New or expanding manufacturing and hotel enterprises are granted exemptions of varying lengths and degrees from income taxes and municipal levies. In 1940, when annual income per capita was $118, agricultural workers made as little as 6 cents an hour, and the illiteracy rate was 70%. By 1990/91, however, personal income per capita was $6,330, and by 1998, had increased to $9,000.

In 1998, Puerto Rico's exports totaled $30.3 billion, imports totaled $21.8 billion. In the 1990s, an estimated 4 million tourists visited Puerto Rico annually.

In 1995/96, 621,370 pupils were enrolled in public schools. Enrollment in the 14 institutions of higher education was 156,439 in 1994/95; the main state-supported university is the University of Puerto Rico, with its main campus at Rico Piedras. Other institutions of higher learning are the Catholic University of Puerto Rico in Ponce, and the Inter-American University with campuses at Hato Rey, San Germán, and elsewhere.

In 1997, there were an estimated 1.39 million telephone lines on the island; that year, the government was negotiating the sale of the Puerto Rico Telephone Co. to private entities. As of 1995, 118 radio stations (65 AM, 53 FM) were operation. In 1997, there were 18 television stations, six cable television service companies, and three stations of the US Armed Forces Radio and Television Service. The three largest Spanish-language daily newspapers, all from San Juan, are *El Vocero de Puerto Rico* (259,129 daily circulation in 1992), *El Nuevo Día* (228,685), and *El Mundo* (97,236).

Virgin Islands of the United States

The Virgin Islands of the United States lie about 64 km (40 mi) n of Puerto Rico and 1,600 km (1,000 mi) sse of Miami, between 17°40′ and 18°25′n and 64°34′ and 65°3′n. The island group extends 82 km (51 mi) n–s and 80 km (50 mi) e–w with a total area of at least 353 sq km (136 sq mi). Only 3 of the more than 50 islands and cays are of significant size: St. Croix, 218 sq km (84 sq mi) in area; St. Thomas, 83 sq km (32 sq mi); and St. John, 52 sq km (20 sq mi). The territorial capital, Charlotte Amalie, on St. Thomas, has one of the finest harbors in the Caribbean.

St. Croix is relatively flat, with a terrain suitable for sugarcane cultivation. St. Thomas is mountainous and little cultivated, but it has many snug harbors. St. John, also mountainous, has fine beaches and lush vegetation; about two-thirds of St. John's area has been declared a national park. The subtropical climate, with temperatures ranging from 21° to 32°c (70–90°f) and an average temperature of 25°c (77°f), is moderated by northeast trade winds. Rainfall, the main source of fresh water, varies widely, and severe droughts are frequent. The average yearly rainfall is 114 cm (45 in), mostly during the summer months.

The population of the US Virgin Islands was 96,569 at the time of the 1980 census, about triple the 1960 census total of 32,099, and was estimated at 119,827 in 1999. St. Croix has two principal towns: Christiansted and Frederiksted. Economic development has brought an influx of new residents, mainly from Puerto Rico, other Caribbean islands, and the US mainland. Most of the permanent inhabitants are descendants of slaves who were brought from Africa in the early days of Danish rule, and about 80% of the population is black. English is the official and most widely spoken language.

Some of the oldest religious congregations in the Western Hemisphere are located in the Virgin Islands. A Jewish synagogue there is the second oldest in the New World, and the Lutheran Congregation of St. Thomas, founded in 1666, is one of the three oldest congregations in the US. As of 1999, Baptists made up an estimated 42% of the population, Roman Catholics 34%, and Episcopalians 17%.

In 1998 there were 856 km (531.6 mi) of roads in the US Virgin Islands. Cargo-shipping services operate from Baltimore, Jacksonville, and Miami via Puerto Rico. In addition, weekly shipping service is available from Miami. Both St. Croix and St. Thomas have airports, with St. Croix's facility handling the larger number of jet flights from the continental US and Europe.

Excavations at St. Croix in the 1970s uncovered evidence of a civilization perhaps as ancient as AD 100. Christopher Columbus, who reached the islands in 1493, named them for the martyred virgin St. Ursula. At this time, St. Croix was inhabited by Carib Indians, who were eventually driven from the island by Spanish soldiers in 1555. During the 17th century, the archipelago was divided into two territorial units, one controlled by the British, the other (now the US Virgin Islands) controlled by Denmark. The separate history of the latter unit began with the settlement of St. Thomas by the Danish West India Company in 1672. St. John was claimed by the company in 1683, and St. Croix was purchased from France in 1733. The holdings of the company were taken over as a Danish crown colony in 1754. Sugarcane, cultivated by slave labor, was the backbone of the islands' prosperity in the 18th and early 19th centuries. After brutally suppressing several slave revolts. Denmark abolished slavery in the colony in 1848. A long period of economic decline followed, until Denmark sold the islands to the US in 1917 for $25 million. Congress granted US citizenship to the Virgin Islanders in 1927. In 1931, administration of the islands was transferred from the Department of the Navy to the Department of the Interior, and the first civilian governor was appointed. In the late 1970s, the Virgin Islands government began to consider ways to expand self-rule. A UN delegation in 1977 found little interest in independence, however, and a locally drafted constitution was voted down by the electorate in 1979.

The chief executive of the Virgin Islands is the territorial governor, elected by direct popular vote (prior to 1970, territorial governors were appointed by the US president). Constitutionally, the US Congress has plenary authority to legislate for the territory. Enactment of the Revised Organic Act of the Virgin Islands on 22 July 1954 vested local legislative power—subject to veto by the governor—in a unicameral legislature. Since 1972, the islands have sent one nonvoting representative to the US House of Representatives. Courts are under the US federal judiciary; the two federal district court judges are appointed by the US president. Territorial court judges, who preside over misdemeanor and traffic cases, are appointed by the governor and confirmed by the legislature. The district court has appellate jurisdiction over the territorial court.

Tourism, which accounts for approximately 70% of both GDP and employment is the islands' principal economic activity. The number of tourists rose dramatically throughout the late 1960s and early 1970s, from 448,165 in 1964 to over 2 million per year in the 1990s. Rum remains an important manufacture, with petroleum refining (on St. Croix) a major addition in the late 1960s. Economic development is promoted by the US-government-owned Virgin Islands Corp. In 1987 the national product per capita was $12,500. The unemployment rate was 6.2% in 1994. Exports for 1992 totaled $1.8 billion while imports totaled $2.2 billion. The island's primary export is refined petroleum products. Raw crude oil constitutes the Virgin Island's principal import. Between 1970 and 1989 economic aid from the nations of the world totaled $42 million. In 1990, median family income was $24,036. The total operating budget of the Virgin Islands government in 1994 was $364.4.

The territorial Department of Health provides hospital and medical services, public health services, and veterinary medicine. Education is compulsory. The College of the Virgin Islands is the territory's first institution of higher learning. There are 60,000 telephones, 66,000 televisions, and 105,000 radios in use on the islands. The Virgin Islands had 12 radio stations (4 AM, 8 FM) and 2 television stations in 1997.

[50]BIBLIOGRAPHY

Ahlstrom, Sydney E. *A Religious History of the American People.* New Haven: Yale University Press, 1972.

America's Century: Year by Year from 1900–2000. London: Dorling Kindersley, 2000.

Ayres, Stephen M. *Health Care in the Unites States: The Facts and the Choices.* Chicago: American Library Association, 1996.

Bacchi, Carol Lee. *The Politics of Affirmative Action: 'Women', Equality, and Category Politics.* London: Sage, 1996.

Bailey, Richard. *Nineteenth Century English.* Ann Arbor, Mich.: University of Michigan Press, 1996.

Barone, Michael. *The Almanac of American Politics.* Washington, D.C.: National Journal, 1992.

Becker, Carl Lotus. *The Declaration of Independence: A Study in the History of Political Ideas.* New York: Knopf, 1960.

Bennett, Lerone. *Before the Mayflower: A History of Black America.* 6th ed. New York: Penguin, 1993.

Brown, Richard Maxwell. *No Duty to Retreat: Violence and Values in American History and Society.* New York: Oxford University Press, 1991.

Chambers, S. Allen. *National Landmarks, America's Treasures: the National Park Foundation's Complete Guide to National Historic Landmarks.* New York: J. Wiley & Sons, 2000.

Commager, Henry Steele (ed.). *Documents of American History.* Englewood Cliffs, N.J.: Prentice-Hall, 1988.

Davies, Philip John. (ed.) *An American Quarter Century: US Politics from Vietnam to Clinton.* New York: Manchester University Press, 1995.

Donaldson, Gary. *America at War since 1945: Politics and Diplomacy in Korea, Vietnam, and the Gulf War.* Westport, Conn.: Praeger, 1996.

Glassborow, Jilly, Gillian Freeman (eds.). *Atlas of the United States.* New York: Macmillan, 1986.

Hart, James David (ed.). *Oxford Companion to American Literature.* 6th ed. New York: Oxford University Press, 1995.

Harvard Encyclopedia of American Ethnic Groups. Cambridge: Harvard University Press, 1980.

Hummel, Jeffrey Rogers. *Emancipating Slaves, Enslaving Free Men: A History of the Civil War.* Chicago: Open Court, 1996.

Josephy, Alvin M., Jr. *Now that the Buffalo's Gone: A Study of Today's American Indians.* Norman, Okla.: University of Oklahoma Press, 1984.

Kammen, Michale (ed.). *The Origins of the American Constitution: A Documentary History.* New York: Penguin, 1986.

———. *People of Paradox: An Inquiry Concerning the Origins of American Civilization.* New York: Oxford University Press, 1980.

Kaplan, Edward S. *American Trade Policy, 1923–1995.* Westport, Conn.: Praeger, 1996.

Martis, Kenneth C. *The Historical Atlas of Political Parties in the United States Congress 1789–1989.* New York: Macmillan, 1989.

McNickle, D'Arcy. *Native American Tribalism: Indian Survivals and Renewals.* New York: Oxford University Press, 1993.

Morison, Samuel Eliot. *The Oxford History of the American People.* New York: New American Library, 1972.

Nevins, Allan. *Ordeal of the Union.* New York: Collier Books, 1992.

Reed, Carroll E. *Dialects of American English.* Amherst: University of Massachusetts Press, 1977.

Rein, Meiling, Nancyc R. Jacobs, Maek S. Siegel (eds.). *Immigration and Illegal Aliens: Burden or Blessing?* Wylie, Tex.: Information Plus, 1999.

Robinson, Cedric J. *Black Movements in America.* New York: Routledge, 1997.

Sinclair, Andrew. *A Concise History of the United States.* Rev. ed. Stroud: Sutton, 1999.

Tocqueville, Alexis de. *Democracy in America.* New York: Knopf, 1994.

United States Government Manual. Washington, D.C.: US Government Printing Office, 1935-date.

US Bureau of the Census. *Historical Statistics of the United States, Colonial Times to 1970.* Washington, D.C.: US Government Printing Office, 1879-date.

Who's Who in America: A Biographical Dictionary of Notable Living Men and Women. Chicago: Marquis, 1899—.

URUGUAY

Oriental Republic of Uruguay
República Oriental del Uruguay

CAPITAL: Montevideo.

FLAG: The flag, approved in 1830, has four azure blue horizontal stripes on a white background; on a white canton is a golden sun with 16 rays (sometimes 20 rays are shown), alternately straight and wavy. This "Sun of May" symbolizes Uruguay's independence.

ANTHEM: *Himno Nacional,* which begins "Orientales, la patria o la tumba" ("Easterners [Uruguayans], our country or death").

MONETARY UNIT: The Uruguayan peso (UP), of 100 centésimos replaced the new peso in 1993 at the rate of UP1=1,000 new pesos. There are coins of 10, 20, and 50 centésimos and 1, 2, 5, and 10 new pesos, and notes of 1, 5, 10, 20, and 50 Uruguayan pesos. UP1 = $0.08525 ($1 = UP11.73) as of 31 March 2000.

WEIGHTS AND MEASURES: The metric system is the legal standard, but some traditional measures are also used.

HOLIDAYS: New Year's Day, 1 January; Epiphany, 6 January; Landing of the 33, 19 April; Labor Day, 1 May; Battle of Las Piedras, 18 May; Birthday of Artigas, 19 June; Constitution Day, 18 July; Independence Day, 25 August; Columbus Day, 12 October; All Souls' Day, 2 November; Blessing of the Waters, 8 December; Christmas Day, 25 December.

TIME: 9 AM = noon GMT.

¹LOCATION, SIZE, AND EXTENT

The second-smallest South American country, Uruguay is situated in the southeastern part of the continent. It has an area of 176,220 sq km (68,039 sq mi), extending 555 km (345 mi) NNW–SSE and 504 km (313 mi) ENE–WSW. Comparatively, the area occupied by Uruguay is slightly smaller than the state of Washington. Bounded on the N and NE by Brazil, on the SE and S by the Atlantic Ocean, and on the W by Argentina, Uruguay has a total boundary length of 2,063 km (1,279 mi). The Uruguay River and the Río de la Plata separate Uruguay from Argentina. The Cuareim and Yaguarón rivers and the Laguna Merín separate it from Brazil.

Uruguay's capital city, Montevideo, is located in the southern part of the country on the Atlantic coast.

²TOPOGRAPHY

The general character of the land is undulating hills, with a few forest areas along the banks of the numerous streams. Southern Uruguay consists mostly of rolling plains and is an eastward extension of the Argentine pampas. The Atlantic coastline is fringed with tidal lakes and sand dunes. Low, unbroken stretches of level land line the banks of the two border rivers, the Uruguay and the Plata. The northern section is broken by occasional ridges and low ranges (cuchillas), alternating with broad valleys, and is a southern extension of Brazil. The highest point in the country, Mirador Nacional, near Montevideo, is 501 m (1,644 ft) above sea level. The most noteworthy feature of the northwest landscape is the Cuchilla de Haedo. The Cuchilla Grande runs northeastward from the southern region to the Brazilian border. The Negro, which rises in Brazil, crosses Uruguayan territory and flows into the Uruguay River, which separates Uruguay from Argentina.

³CLIMATE

The climate is temperate; the average temperature in June, the coolest month, is about 15°C (59°F), and the average for January, the warmest month, is 25°C (77°F). The weather is transitional between the weather of the humid Argentine pampas and that of southern Brazil. Rainfall is evenly distributed throughout the year; it averages about 109 cm (43 in), varying from 97 cm (38 in) in Montevideo to nearly 127 cm (50 in) farther north. There are from 120 to 180 sunny days a year. Frost is virtually unknown.

⁴FLORA AND FAUNA

Uruguay is primarily a grass-growing land, and the vegetation is essentially a continuation of the Argentine pampas. Forest areas are relatively small. The most useful hardwoods are algarobo, guayabo, quebracho, and urunday; other hardwoods include arazá, coronilla, espinillo, lapacho, lignum vitae, and nandubay. The acacia, alder, aloe, eucalyptus (imported from Australia), ombú, poplar, and willow are common softwoods. Palms are indigenous to the valleys. Rosemary, myrtle, scarlet-flowered ceibo, and mimosa are common. Most of the valleys are covered with aromatic shrubs, and the rolling hills with white and scarlet verbena.

Large animals have virtually disappeared from the eastern regions. The carpincho (water hog), fox, deer, nutria, otter, and small armadillo roam the northern foothills. On the pampas are the hornero (ovenbird), quail, partridge, and crow. The avestruz (a small ostrich similar to the Argentine rhea), swan, and royal duck are found at lagoons. Fish include pompano, salmon, and corvina. The principal reptiles are cross vipers and tortoises. Seals are found on Lobos Island, near Punta del Este.

5ENVIRONMENT

Air and water pollution are environmental concerns in Uruguay. Air pollution, which is worse in the larger population centers, is caused primarily by Uruguay's own industries and by an energy plant in neighboring Brazil. Water pollution from mining and industrial sources threatens the nation's water supply, especially pollution from the meat packing and tannery industry. Uruguay has 14.2 cu mi of water with 91% used for farming activity and 3% for industrial purposes. Ninety-five percent of the nation's rural people do not have pure water. Natural hazards to the environment include drought, flooding, and fires. Erosion of the soil affects the nation's agricultural productivity. The nation's cities produce 0.5 million tons of solid waste per year. Forty percent of the urban population does not have adequate waste disposal facilities. Government agencies with environmental responsibilities include the Division of Environmental Health, within the Ministry of Public Health; the Ministry of Agriculture; and the Interior Ministry. As of the mid-1990s, five of Uruguay's mammal species and 11 of its bird species were endangered. Fourteen types of plants were threatened with extinction. Endangered or extinct species included the tundra peregrine falcon, glaucous macaw, two species of turtle (green sea and leatherback), and two species of crocodile (spectacled caiman and broad-nosed caiman).

6POPULATION

The population of Uruguay in 2000 was estimated at 3,332,782. An estimated 12.4% of the population is 65 years of age or older. The projected population for the year 2005 is 3,459,000, assuming a crude birthrate of 16 per 1,000 population and a death rate of 9, resulting in a natural rate of change of 0.8% for the period 2000–2005. The population rate of change between 1995 and 2000 was 0.6%. The population density in 1998 was 19 per sq km (49 per sq mi), about double that of South America as a whole.

It was estimated that 91% of the population lived in urban areas in 2000, up from 85% in 1980. The capital city, Montevideo, had a 2000 metropolitan population of 1,325,000.

7MIGRATION

The basic sources of immigration to Uruguay were Spain and Italy. English, French, German, Slavic, and Swiss immigrants also settled in various departments (provinces). In the 1930s, restrictions were placed on immigration, and the importation of seasonal farm workers was stopped. There were 103,002 foreign-born people in 1985. Substantial emigration by Uruguayans for political or economic reasons occurred during the mid-1970s and early 1980s. Official figures suggest that about 180,000 Uruguayans left between 1963 and 1975 and 150,000 between 1975 and an estimated 500,000 between 1975–95. Argentina and Brazil were the main destinations.

As of September 1999, Uruguay hosted some 160 refugees, most coming from Russia (51%) and other Eastern European countries (30%). The net migration rate in 1999 was -0.78 migrants per 1,000 population.

8ETHNIC GROUPS

The inhabitants of Uruguay are primarily (about 88%) white and of European origin, mostly Spanish and Italian; a small percentage is descended from Portuguese, English, and other Europeans. Mestizos (those of mixed white and Amerindian lineage) represent 8% of the population, and mulattoes and blacks about 4%. The indigenous Charrúa Amerindians were virtually wiped out early in the colonial era.

9LANGUAGES

Spanish is the official language. Uruguayan Spanish, like Argentine Spanish, has been somewhat modified by the Italians who migrated in large numbers to both countries. In general, the language of Uruguay is softer than that of Castile, and some words are different from those commonly used in Spain. The gauchos have influenced the language, particularly in words dealing with their way of life. Brazilero, a Portuguese-Spanish mix, is spoken on the Brazilian frontier.

10RELIGIONS

Since 1919, church and state have been separated, and the constitution, as revised in 1966, guarantees religious freedom. Uruguay is the only Latin American nation that approaches religious pluralism. Contrasting with the 90% formal Roman Catholic affiliation in other Latin American countries, only about 52% of Uruguayans identify themselves as Roman Catholic. Approximately 16% of the population is Protestant or other Christian, and 2.4% are Jewish. As many as 30% are members of other religions or profess no religious faith whatsoever.

11TRANSPORTATION

After World War II, the Uruguayan government purchased the British-owned railroads and nationalized the entire system. The railroads are run by the State Railway Administration. Four main lines connect the western and northern areas with Montevideo. In 1997, there were 2,994 km (1,860 mi) of track, 2,073 km (1,288 mi) of which were standard-gauge, government-owned track.

Highways have surpassed railroads as the principal means of conveyance of passengers and freight. In 1998, there were an estimated 8,420 km (5,232 mi) of roads, of which 7,578 km (4,709 mi) were paved. The Investment and Economic Development Commission's 10-year plan (1965–74) provided about $87 million for highway construction and improvement. A five-year plan for transport and public works, covering the years 1983–87 and partly financed by the IBRD and IDB, provided for construction of 10,000 km (6,200 mi) of new roads. In 1986, the IDB approved a loan of $36 million to help finance a highway development project. Two sections of highway (Routes 1 and 5) in addition to a main artery funneling traffic into Montevideo were scheduled for improvement. In 1995, there were 491,000 motor vehicles, of which 444,800 were passenger cars.

Montevideo is the major Uruguayan port. Colonia and Nueva Palmira are free ports. There are some 1,600 km (994 mi) of inland waterways, of which the most important are the Plata and the Uruguay; the latter has a depth of 4.3 m (14 ft) as far as Paysandú. There were two vessels in the merchant fleet in 1998, both oil tankers, with a GRT of 44,042.

There were 65 airports in 1998, 15 of which had paved runways. Carrasco, an airport 19 km (12 mi) from the center of Montevideo, is used by most international carriers between Europe, Brazil, and Argentina. Frequent air service links Buenos Aires with Montevideo. The state-owned Primeras Líneas Uruguayas de Navegación Aérea (PLUNA) offers service to the principal departmental capitals as well as international flights. In 1997, 544,000 passengers were carried on scheduled domestic and international airline flights.

12HISTORY

During the 16th century, only a few Spanish expeditions landed on the Banda Oriental, or east bank of the Uruguay River. Most of them were driven off by the native Charrúa Amerindians. Jesuit and Franciscan missionaries landed in 1624, and formed permanent settlements. By 1680, Portuguese from Brazil had founded Colonia do Sacramento as a rival to Buenos Aires, on the opposite bank of the estuary. Thereafter, the area was a focal point for Spanish-Portuguese rivalry.

URUGUAY

0   40   80   120 Miles

0   40   80   120 Kilometers

LOCATION: 30°06′ to 35°02′s; 53°05′ to 59°29′w. **BOUNDARY LENGTHS:** Brazil, 1,003 km (623 mi); Atlantic coastline, 565 km (351 mi); Argentina, 495 km (308 mi). **TERRITORIAL SEA LIMIT:** 200 mi.

Montevideo was founded in 1726, and Uruguay became part of the viceroyalty of La Plata, which the Spaniards established in Buenos Aires in 1776. During the Napoleonic Wars, the British invaded the region of La Plata and captured Buenos Aires and Montevideo (1806–7), but they were forced out in 1807. After Buenos Aires refused to give Uruguay autonomy, the Uruguayan national hero, José Gervasio Artigas, declared Uruguay independent in 1815. A year later, Brazilians attacked Montevideo from the north, but Artigas led a revolutionary movement against them. The struggle continued from 1816 to 1820, when the Portuguese captured Montevideo and Artigas had to flee to Paraguay. Uruguay was annexed to Brazil in 1821 and was known as the Cisplatine Province.

On 25 August 1825, Juan Antonio Lavalleja, at the head of a group of patriots called the "treinta y tres orientales" ("33 Easterners"), issued a declaration of independence. After a three-

year fight, a peace treaty signed on 28 August 1828 guaranteed Uruguay's independence. Disappointed in his hopes for the presidency, Lavalleja launched a series of rebellions. During this period of political turmoil and civil war, the two political parties around which Uruguayan history has traditionally revolved, the Colorados (reds) and the Blancos (whites), were founded. Uruguay's first president, Gen. José Fructuoso Rivera, an ally of Artigas, founded the Colorados. The second president, Brig. Gen. Manuel Oribe, a friend of Lavalleja, founded the Blancos.

The 19th century was largely a struggle between the two factions. Some measure of national unity was achieved in the 1860s. In 1865, Uruguay allied with Brazil and Argentina to defeat Paraguay in the Paraguayan War (1865–70), also known as the War of the Triple Alliance and the Triguarantine War. However, it was not until the election of José Batlle y Ordóñez as president in 1903 that Uruguay matured as a nation.

The Batlle administrations (1903–7, 1911–15) marked the period of greatest progress. A distinguished statesman, Batlle initiated the social welfare system codified in the Uruguayan constitution. From then on, Uruguay's social programs, funded primarily by earnings of beef and wool in foreign markets, gave Uruguay the sobriquet "Switzerland of South America."

After World War II, the Colorados ruled, except for an eight-year period from 1958–66. It was during the administration of President Jorge Pacheco Areco (1967–72) that Uruguay entered a political and social crisis. As wool declined in world markets, export earnings no longer kept pace with the need for greater social expenditures. Political instability resulted, most dramatically in the emergence of Uruguay's National Liberation Movement, popularly known as the Tupamaros. This well-organized urban guerrilla movement mounted a campaign of kidnapping, assassination, and bank robbery while espousing Marxist and nationalist ideals.

In November 1971, Colorado candidate Juan María Bordaberry Arocena was elected president, and the Colorados retained control of the Senate and Chamber of Deputies. After Bordaberry assumed office in March 1972, the Tupamaros ended a temporary truce and returned to the offensive. Their activities, coupled with the worsening economic situation, exacerbated Uruguay's political uncertainty. Gradually, the military assumed a greater role in government, and by 1973 was in control of the system. By the end of 1973, the Tupamaros had been crushed.

Military officers were named in 1974 to head all state-run enterprises, including the Central Bank. The 1966 constitution was suspended, and political activity was banned. Military leaders ousted Bordaberry from the presidency in 1976, because of his refusal to restore constitutional rule, and they named a new president, Aparicio Méndez Manfredini. The OAS and other international organizations denounced Uruguay for human rights violations; in 1979, Amnesty International estimated the number of political prisoners at 6,000. In mid-1981, the military government began to negotiate with leaders of the traditional parties, and in September 1981, a "transitional" president, Georgio Álvarez Armellino, was installed.

Intraparty elections took place in November 1982, followed by legislative and presidential voting in November 1984. The moderate government of Colorado candidate Julio María Sanguinetti Cairolo took office in March 1985. Lacking a majority in Congress, Sanguinetti worked closely with other political leaders to reach a consensus on major issues.

One of the first acts of the new government was to release all political prisoners. Another was to declare amnesty for former military and police leaders accused of human rights violations. In an attempt to reconcile warring factions, the government initiated a "social dialogue" with employers and union leaders to reduce social tension. However, slow progress on the economic front led to the 1989 election of the Blanco candidate, Luis Alberto Lacalle.

Lacalle engaged in an ambitious attempt to liberalize the Uruguayan economy. He emphasized deficit reduction, reforms in education, labor, and the civil service, as well as the privatization of state enterprises. However, these plans were dealt a serious blow in 1993, when a plebiscite failed to ratify a set of proposals for liberalization. In November 1994, Sanguinetti was returned to office in the closest elections ever recorded in Uruguay's history. The three-way race between the Colorado, Blanco, and Broad Front (a leftist coalition) parties ended in just a slight majority for Sanguinetti and the Colorados. Both the Blanco and Broad Front candidates were only a few votes behind. It was the first time the Broad Front party had come within reach of the presidency. The Broad Front also gained the municipal government of Montevideo, Uruguay's capital, in 1989 and again in 1994. In the 1990s, the left had discarded revolutionary rhetoric and become more moderate and more appealing to centrist voters. At the same time, many Uruguayans had grown more critical of the traditional parties.

Sanguinetti himself immediately embarked on a program of economic reforms, including a long-range plan for cutting back on Uruguay's historically generous social programs and benefits, including 20 days of vacation after a year of work, paid maternity leave, and a generous retirement package. As a member of Mercosur, Uruguay faced growing pressure to liberalize its economy during the 1990s, as economic giants, and Mercosur partners Brazil and Argentina, had done. Yet voters had twice rejected privatization of state-owned companies, some of which were profitable, and often even competitive. The economy also had done well, with the GDP averaging 4.2% growth between 1992–98. By 1999, the country's economic picture had changed. The troubled Argentinean and Brazilian economies affected Uruguay, where the economy contracted by 2%. Instead of panicking and clamoring for a cut in social benefits and privatization of state industries, presidential candidates from the right and left called for a cautious approach to economic reforms as they neared the October 1999 elections. Tabaré Ramon Vazquez, the former socialist mayor of Montevideo and candidate representing the Broad Front, finished first in the presidential election, with 39% of the vote. He had appealed for caution, gaining the largest number of votes for a leftist coalition in the country's history. But Vazquez failed to gain a 51% majority, forcing a presidential runoff. The Colorado candidate, Jorge Batlle Ibáñez, had unsuccessfully run for the presidency four times and finished second with 31% in the October election. The Blanco candidate, Luis Lacalle, had finished third with 21.5%.

The 72-year-old Batlle, whose great-uncle had built the country's social programs, was not about to dismantle them. He positioned his party as a moderate alternative to Vazquez's leftist coalition. But ultimately, he persevered at the polls by aligning the Colorados with their historic foes: the Blancos. The Blancos aligned themselves with Batlle in exchange for political concessions, and ministerial posts. In the November runoff election, Batlle gained 54.1% of the vote to Vazquez's 45.9%. Batlle was inaugurated in March 2000 and named five Blancos to his cabinet. The Blancos and the Colorados also held a slim majority in the Senate, with 17 of 31 seats, and a majority in the lower house, with 54 of 99 seats. Faced with a shrinking economy, Batlle has not distanced himself from campaign promises. While unemployment had reached 11% by 2000, and the country expected more economic turmoil, Batlle called for a conservative course that promises to leave most state-run companies untouched.

13 GOVERNMENT

The constitution of 1830 underwent numerous revisions, notably in 1917, 1934, 1952, and 1966. This constitution provided for a republican government, divided into three branches: executive, legislative, and judicial. From 1951 to 1966, the executive consisted of a colegiado, or council, of nine ministers, six from the majority party and three from the minority. In the 1966 elections, however, the electorate reinstated the positions of president and a vice-president, popularly elected for a five-year term, together with a council of ministers.

According to the constitutional revision of 1966, the Congress (or General Assembly) consisted of the Senate and the Chamber of Deputies. The Senate had 30 popularly elected senators, plus the vice-president of the republic as the thirty-first voting member. The Chamber of Deputies had 99 deputies, popularly elected by departments (provinces). The right to vote was extended to all citizens 18 years of age or older, with female suffrage in local elections as early as 1919 and in national elections in 1934.

From June 1973, when President Bordaberry dissolved the Assembly and suspended the constitution, until March 1985, Uruguay was ruled by executive decree, subject to veto by the military, with legislative functions carried out by the 25-member Council of State, appointed by the executive. A new constitution, providing for the permanent participation of the armed forces in government by means of a National Security Council, was drafted by the Council of State but rejected by 57.2% of the voters in a referendum on 30 November 1980. In March 1985, democracy was restored under President Sanguinetti; in July, the government set up a National Constituent Assembly to devise constitutional reforms that would be submitted to the electorate for ratification. In the elections of November 1994, the proposed reform of 14 articles of the constitution was again rejected, this time by 63% of Uruguayan voters.

14 POLITICAL PARTIES

Uruguay has Latin America's oldest two-party system. The Colorados (reds) and Blancos (whites), formed during the conflicts of the 1830s and 1840s, persisted into the 1990s. The Colorados are traditional Latin American liberals, representing urban business interests, and favoring limitation on the power of the Catholic Church. The Blancos (officially called the National Party) are conservatives, defenders of large landowners and the Church.

For more than 90 years, until the 1958 elections, the executive power was controlled by the Colorados. Under such leaders as Batlle, the party promulgated a progressive program advocating public education, advanced labor laws, government ownership of public utilities, and separation of church and state. After eight years of Blanco government, the Colorado party regained power in the 1966 election.

The results of the November 1971 balloting were so close that the final tabulation took more than two months to ascertain; the Colorados won 36.3% of the vote; the Blancos, 35.7%; and the Broad Front (Frente Amplio, a left-wing coalition that included the Tupamaros), 16.6%. These three groups, plus the Christian Democratic Party (Partido Democrático Cristiano—PDC), formed in 1962 from the former Catholic Civic Union, made up the Uruguayan party system at the time of the military takeover.

Political activities were suspended following the constitutional crisis of June 1973, and in December 1973 the Communist and Socialist parties were outlawed. In June 1980, the military began to liberalize, as they permitted political meetings of nonleftist groups. In November 1982, they allowed for intraparty elections in each of three parties: the Colorados, the National Party (Blancos), and the small Civic Union (an outgrowth of the Christian Democrats). In the voting, party candidates who had campaigned against the military's proposed constitution in 1980 took more than 60% of the vote.

Neither Blanco leader Wilson Ferreira Aldunate nor Broad Front leader Líber Seregni Mosquera was allowed to participate in the elections, but both retained their party posts. In the November 1984 elections, Colorado candidate Julio María Sanguinetti Cairolo won the presidency with 38.6% of the vote. The Colorados also won pluralities in the Chamber of Deputies and the Senate. Aldunate and Seregni frequently consulted with President Sanguinetti, and previously outlawed parties were legalized. In 1985, the PDC and FIDEL belonged to the Broad Front, and the National Liberation Movement (Movimiento de Liberación Nacional—MLN), also known as the Tupamaros, reconstituted years after their destruction in 1973, announced their intention to give up violence and join the Broad Front as a legal party.

In 1989, Blanco candidate Lacalle took 37% of the vote. Jorge Batlle, of the Colorado party, unable to capitalize on name recognition, received 29%, while Liber Seregni Mosquera of the Broad Front received 20%. The Blancos also carried a plurality in each house of the legislature, followed respectively by the Colorados, the Broad Front, and the "New Space (or Sector)" Coalition, which consists of the PDC and the Civic Union. As more people grow disenchanted with market reforms in Latin America, leftist coalitions have become more palatable to voters. In Argentina and Chile, the center-left was in power in 2000. In Uruguay, the Broad Coalition candidate Tabaré Vazquez made an impressive show at the polls, finishing first with 39% of the vote in the October 1999 presidential election. His success forced historic foes Blancos and Colorados to back Jorge Batlle in the November runoff election. While Batlle persevered, the leftist coalition managed to increase its total vote behind Vazquez (45.9%).

15 LOCAL GOVERNMENT

Uruguay territorially is divided into 19 departments (provinces). Under the 1966 constitutional revision, each department had a unicameral legislature, but all 19 legislatures were dissolved by President Bordaberry on 28 June 1973. Following the installation of the democratic government in 1985, the departments returned to their pre-1973 status of limited autonomy under the central government.

16 JUDICIAL SYSTEM

Most of the nation's legal system was suspended in 1973, but in 1981, the military government restored the independence of the civilian judiciary. In that year, a Supreme Judicial Council was empowered to name Supreme Court justices and supervise the judiciary. Below the Supreme Court are appellate courts and lower civil and criminal courts, justices of the peace, electoral and administrative courts, and an accounts court. A parallel military court system operates under its own procedure. When the Supreme Court hears cases involving the military, two military justices join the Court. Civilians are tried in the military court only in time of war or insurrection. The judiciary is structurally independent of the executive and this separation of powers is respected in practice.

The constitution prohibits the arbitrary interference with privacy, family, home, or correspondence, and the government authorities respect these provisions in practice.

The legal system is based on Spanish civil law. Uruguay accepts the compulsory jurisdiction of the international court of justice.

17 ARMED FORCES

The armed forces numbered 25,600 in 2000. The active army consists of volunteers between the ages of 18 and 45 who contract for one or two years of service. The army numbered 17,600, organized in four regional divisions of 10 brigades; the navy (including naval air force and infantry) numbered 5,000 with three frigates and 10 patrol and coastal combatants. The air force had 3,000 men and 27 combat aircraft. Since 1985, the military has redirected its attention to traditional concerns of national defense and to reducing its size from 32,000 to under 25,000. Defense spending was $172 million (1998). Uruguay participates in UN peacekeeping and has troops and observers stationed in six regions.

18 INTERNATIONAL COOPERATION

Uruguay is a charter member of the UN, having joined on 18 December 1945, and belongs to ECLAC and all the non-regional specialized agencies except IDA. It is also a member of the G-77, IADB, OAS, and WTO. In 1927, the Inter-American Child Institute was established in Montevideo as a center for social action, study, and information in the Americas. Under the direction of the OAS, it has given particular attention to health and nutrition. In 1961, Montevideo became the seat of the Latin American Free Trade Association, which was superseded by LAIA in 1981. Uruguay is also a signatory of the Law of the Sea and the Treaty for the Prohibition of Nuclear Weapons in Latin America (1967).

Uruguay and Argentina signed an agreement in 1973 guaranteeing free passage in perpetuity on the Río de la Plata. In 1985, the presidents of the two countries signed an agreement "to promote the economic and social integration of the two countries." In 1995, Uruguay became a founding member (with Brazil, Argentina, and Paraguay) of the Southern Cone Common Market, known as Mercosur.

19 ECONOMY

Uruguay's economy was based on the production and processing of agricultural commodities until the services sector, especially tourism and financial services, took over. The services sector accounts for over 60% of GDP. Agriculture, however, is still important, particularly livestock production, which produces products for export and consumption as well as for inputs for other sectors of the economy. Industry (agro-industry, chemicals, and consumer goods for local consumption) has declined in recent years as the service sector has expanded. There is a mixture of private and state enterprises with the economy generally open to foreign trade and investment.

Owing partly to the need for industrial products generated by World War II and the Korean War and also to government efforts to attain a fair degree of economic self-sufficiency and to improve foreign trade, the value of Uruguay's industrial output doubled between 1936 and 1960. Between 1960 and 1970, the industrial growth rate leveled off, as the limitations of an import-substitution strategy became apparent. Encouragement of non-traditional manufactured exports led to industrial production increases averaging 6% annually during 1973–79. The lack of natural resources obliges Uruguay to import most raw materials needed by its industries.

In the early 1980s, the economic situation was characterized by an uninterrupted fall in real output, low levels of investment, high unemployment, mounting inflation, a severe imbalance in public finance, and a massive accumulation of arrears in private-sector debt to the domestic banking system, which in turn caused a potentially critical situation in the country's financial institutions. In mid-1985, the government negotiated agreements with the IMF and creditor banks that produced a standby credit from the fund, a renegotiation of debt with foreign banks, and an economic-financial program with the IMF intended to reduce the public-sector deficit, inflation, and the money supply and to remedy the balance-of-payments disequilibrium.

Since 1990, the government has pursued a program of economic liberalization which has included lowering tariffs, Southern Common Market (Mercosur) integration, reducing deficit spending, controlling inflation, and downsizing government. Growth in GDP averaged 3.7% between 1988 and 1998 but experienced a negative growth rate of approximately 2% in 1999, due to reduced competitiveness of Uruguayan exports in MERCOSUR countries, the Brazilian currency devaluation, and a run against the Argentine Peso. On a positive note, the inflation rate decreased from 130% in 1990 to 4% in 1999.

20 INCOME

The US Central Intelligence Agency (CIA) reports that in 1998 Uruguay's gross domestic product (GDP) was estimated at $28.4 billion. The per capita GDP was estimated at $8,600. The annual growth rate of GDP was estimated at 3%. The average inflation rate in 1998 was 8.6%. The CIA defines GDP as the value of all final goods and services produced within a nation in a given year and computed on the basis of purchasing power parity (PPP) rather than value as measured on the basis of the rate of exchange. It was estimated that agriculture accounted for 8% of GDP, industry 26%, and services 66%.

The World Bank reports that for the same period per capita private consumption (in PPP terms) was $5,910. Private consumption includes expenditures of individuals, households, and non-governmental organizations. It was estimated that between 1990 and 1998 private consumption grew at an annual rate of 5.9%. Approximately 22% of household consumption was spent on food, 14% on fuel, 11% on health care, and 30% on education. The richest 10% of the population accounted for approximately 33% of household consumption and the poorest 10% approximately 2.1%.

21 LABOR

About 1,239,400 Uruguayans, or an estimated 47% of the population, were in the civilian labor force in 1998. In that year, manufacturing and construction accounted for 19.9% of the labor force; agriculture, 3.8%; and services, 76.3%. The unemployment rate rose from 8.94% in 1991 to 10.1% in 1998.

The eight-hour day and 48-hour week were instituted in 1915. The law provides for one day of rest after every six days of work and grants holidays with pay, plus an annual vacation bonus.

In 1943, industrial wage boards with seven members (three for the government, two for the employers, and two for the employees) were established to fix minimum wages and settle wage disputes. Because the wage boards (consejos de salarios) were slow in reaching decisions, the Uruguayan labor force tended to use the strike as a first resort rather than as a last one, to force the initiation of negotiations. Since December 1968, wages and prices have been controlled by the Price and Wage Commission. Unemployment and dismissal compensation, old age and liability pensions, workers' accident compensation, and family allowances are provided by law.

In July 1973, the National Workers' Convention, which claimed 400,000 members, was declared illegal. Laws enacted in August 1974 restricted trade-union membership to "free and nonpolitical" trade unions. Political activity by union officials was banned, as were strikes in the public sector, health, and commerce. Labor conditions returned to pre-1973 conditions with the 1985 government changeover. The sudden release of years of frustration triggered some 250 strikes in the ensuing year. As of March 1993, seven general strikes had occurred within the previous three years, for a ratio of one hour of general strike for every 114 worked. Uruguay's sole labor confederation is the Inter-Union Workers Assembly-National Federation of Workers (PIT-CNT), which organized a one-day general strike in 1999. In the same year, an estimated 13% of the work force belonged to unions.

The standard workweek is 48 hours in industry and 44 hours in commerce. The minimum wage was $90 per month in 1999, but it functions in practice as an index for calculating wage rates rather than a measure of a minimum subsistence wage. The minimum working age is 15, and it is generally enforced although the number of children working in the informal economy as street vendors is increasing.

22 AGRICULTURE

Uruguay has a primarily agricultural and pastoral economy, but the importance of these sectors has been declining. The formation of the Mercosur common market in 1995 had a significant effect on Uruguayan agriculture by providing preferential access to neighboring countries, particularly Brazil. Agriculture and animal husbandry together contributed 8% of the GDP in 1998. About 40% of the agriculture's contribution to GDP comes from crops, the rest is from animal husbandry. About 77% of Uruguay's land area is devoted to stock raising and 7.4% to the cultivation of crops. In pasturage, large farms predominate, with farms of more than 1,000 hectares (2,500 acres) accounting for two-thirds of all farmland. Crops are grown mainly on small farms of less than 100 hectares (250 acres).

The principal crops (in thousands of tons) are listed below:

	1997	1998
Rice	1,035	865
Wheat	124	145
Barley	199	250
Corn	162	226
Sorghum	130	97
Sunflower seeds	114	86
Oats	36	45
Apples	66	50
Peaches	27	25

23 ANIMAL HUSBANDRY

Livestock is the basis of the economy. The production costs of stock raising are low, and the quality of the product is generally high. Hereford, Shorthorn, and Aberdeen Angus breeds account for 90% of all beef cattle, with Hereford the most numerous. Corriedale represents about 70% of the sheep stock, followed by Ideal (11%).

Uruguay is especially suited to the raising of sheep and cattle. In 1998, Uruguay had 17,800,000 sheep, second in South America after Brazil. There were also 10,475,000 head of cattle, 500,000 horses, 270,000 pigs, 15,000 goats, and 12 million chickens in 1998. Milk production has been expanding rapidly in recent years, reaching 1,432,000 tons in 1998. The preferential duties provided under Mercosur have given Uruguay a great advantage in selling its dairy products to Brazil. In 1997, Uruguay's exports of dairy products totaled more than $138 million. The main products exported are cheese, whole and nonfat dry milk, and butter. Meat production in 1998 included 454,000 tons of beef and 53,000 tons of mutton. Beef consumption in Uruguay was about 60 kg per person in 1998, one of highest rates in the world. Leading exports of animals and animal products by value (in million of dollars) in 1997 were: wool, $43.5; beef, $363.8; live animals, $37.8; hides, $5.3; and mutton, $32.6.

The Ministry of Agriculture and Fisheries is responsible for stock raising and breeding, control of animal diseases, and improvement of existing grassland and arable resources. The National Meat Board acts as consultant to the government. The meat-packing industry, taken over by the government in 1958, has been restored to the private sector. The government encourages local production through a system of special licenses or customs documents for imported meat and livestock. Furthermore, imports of bull semen and embryos are numerically restricted and must comply with animal health requirements.

24 FISHING

Fishing underwent rapid growth in the 1970s. The government-promoted fishing industry made an average annual catch of about 6,000 tons in the 1960s; the catch increased to 20,600 tons in 1972 and, despite temporary setbacks, to 143,170 tons by 1991. In 1997, the total catch was 136,912 tons. Fish exports in 1997 amounted to $109.6 million.

There are three fishing zones on the southern coast: the low zone, from Colonia to Piriápolis; the middle zone, from Piriápolis to Punta del Este, which is considered one of the finest fishing areas in the world; and the high zone, from Punta del Este to the Brazilian border. Principal commercial species include Argentine hake, whitemouth croaker, and striped weakfish. Other important sea fish are corvina negra (a kind of bass), mullet, sole, anchovy, mackerel, whiting, and shark. The finest freshwater fish is the dorado, a type of salmon.

25 FORESTRY

Uruguay has some 930,000 hectares (2,298,000 acres) of forestland. About 8,200 hectares (20,300 acres) were reforested annually from 1981 to 1986. The principal species cultivated are eucalyptus and pine; domestic woods are used primarily for windbreaks, fence posts, and firewood. Lumber suitable for building and construction is imported. Roundwood removals totaled 4,099,000 cu m in 1997, with 75% used as fuel wood.

26 MINING

Mining is limited to the extraction of clay, granite, gravel, and limestone, with minor production of semiprecious stones and agates. There are deposits of manganese, iron, lead, and copper, and in the Rivera Department, gold is mined in small quantities. Commercial gold production began in 1997 at the San Gregorio gold mine. Agates, opals, and onyx are found in Salto and Artigas. Various types of clay are mined for producing brick, pipe, tile, and whiteware. Talc is mined for use in the paper industry and in ceramics, cosmetics, insecticides, and pharmaceuticals. Feldspar is mined for the ceramics industry and glass. Production amounts in 1997 included (in tons): sand, 1,768,000; limestone, 1,118,000; clays, 59,400; gypsum, 183,383; feldspar, 12,579; talc, 1,133; agate, 74; and amethyst, 49. Sand, common stone, and talcum are exported. Mining accounts for about 0.5% of GDP, and all products of the subsoil belong to the state.

27 ENERGY AND POWER

Uruguay's power is provided by hydroelectric and diesel-generating plants. Supplying electricity for light, power, and traction has been a state monopoly since 1897. Uruguay's installed capacity was 2,184,000 kW in 1998; total output was 9,474 million kWh, of which about 90% came from hydroelectric sources. In the mid-1970s, the government imposed a mandatory program to curb power consumption because of rising fuel import costs. As of 1999, 50% of total energy consumption came from imported oil.

The first hydroelectric plant, at the site of the Rincón del Bonete Dam on the Río Negro, was completed in 1949 and has a capacity of 128 MW. The dam created the Lago Artificial del Río Negro, the largest artificial lake in South America. In 1960, a generating plant with a capacity of 108 MW was completed at Rincón de Baygorría, also on the Río Negro. Several large hydroelectric projects were under way in the early 1980s. The Salto Grande Dam on the Río Uruguay, built with Argentina and having a potential capacity of 1,890 MW, began producing electricity in 1979; as a result, Uruguay became a net exporter of electricity to Argentina in the mid-1980s. The 300-MW Palmar hydroelectric power station, financed and built by Brazil, started production in 1981 and was completed by the mid-1980s. In the mid-1980s there were also plans for a 150-MW plant at Isla González on the Río Negro and another 150-MW plant on the Río Cebollatí in eastern Uruguay.

By a bilateral agreement signed with the US, Uruguay is entitled to receive atomic equipment and to lease nuclear fuels. Negotiations on contracts with four US oil companies for offshore oil exploration were concluded by the Uruguayan government in February 1975, but no commercially exploitable resources were found. The Administración Nacional Combustibles, Alcohol, y Portland (ANCAP) refines 80% of Uruguay's fuel energy requirements at its Teja plant in Montevideo. In 1995, the state-owned refinery processed 3.6 million barrels of distillate fuel oil, three million barrels of residual fuel oil, and 2.1 million barrels of gasoline. Consumption included 38,000 barrels per day of crude and refined petroleum in 1998.

At the beginning of the 21st century, Uruguay was planning to shift much of its energy dependence from hydroelectric power to natural gas with the projected installation of some 850 MW of gas-fired generating capacity over a 10-year period. In late 1998, the first natural gas pipeline from Uruguay to Argentina was completed, at a cost of $8 million. Construction of a second, 133-mile pipeline began in 1999.

28 INDUSTRY

Although foreign trade depends mainly on agricultural production, the production of industrial goods for domestic consumption is increasing, primarily in the fields of textiles, tires, shoes, leather apparel, cement, petroleum refining, and wine. World War II spurred the industrial growth of Uruguay, and now local industry supplies most of the manufactured products used. Most industry is concentrated in and around Montevideo.

Manufacturing output declined by an average of 1.3% annually between 1977 and 1987, and declined by an average 0.10% per year during 1988–98. In 1998 alone, manufacturing grew by 2.3%, and accounted for 18% of GDP. Growth was led by oil refining, car production, and food production. However, the manufacturing sector declined by 6.1% in the first half of 1999. Reduction of domestic demand and a decrease in exports to Brazil and Argentina have contributed to the overall decline. Sectors showing overall production decreases included textiles, vehicles, machinery, chemicals, paper, processed meat, and sugar.

The manufacturing sector still has severe structural problems as a legacy of the protectionist policies that stressed import substitution during the 1970s. With the Mercosur trade bloc, the domestic market for manufactured goods has opened to strong competition from Argentina and Brazil. Some industries, like textiles, may expand because they are already internationally competitive. Others, like petrochemical refining, chemicals, pharmaceuticals, and tires are reasonably competitive and should do well with new investment. The automotive, electronic, and machinery sectors will probably continue to decline because of competition among Mercosur partners.

29 SCIENCE AND TECHNOLOGY

The UNESCO Regional Office for Science and Technology in Latin America and the Caribbean is located in Montevideo. Learned societies include the Pediatrics Society, the Association of Uruguayan Engineers, and the Chemical and Pharmaceutical Association, the Odontological Association, and the Surgical Society, all headquartered in Montevideo. The University of the Republic, founded in 1849 at Montevideo, has faculties of agronomy, sciences, engineering, medicine, dentistry, chemistry, and veterinary medicine. The Institute of Higher Studies, founded in 1928 at Montevideo, offers courses in biological climatology, geomorphology, palaeontology, and mathematics. The Higher Institute of Electrical Engineering, Electronics, and Computing was founded in 1922 at Montevideo. In 1987–97, science and engineering students accounted for 32% of college and university enrollments. In 1997, 2,093 scientists and engineers were engaged in research and development.

³⁰DOMESTIC TRADE

Although the Uruguayan population is small, it has a relatively high purchasing power. Wholesale and retail trade accounted for 12.4% of GDP in 1996. The reasonably good transportation system allows easy shipment of agricultural products to the capital. Chambers of commerce and other trade associations play an active role in interpreting local market demands. Normal business hours are 9 AM to 12 noon and 2 to 7 PM, Monday through Friday, and 9 AM to 2 PM, Saturday. Banks open to the public on weekdays from 1 to 5 PM.

³¹FOREIGN TRADE

Uruguay traditionally relies on foreign sales of wool, hides, and meat and meat products for its export revenues, which have been increasing over the past several years. Export revenues from goods and services annually increased by an average of 3.3% during 1977–87, and by 8.2% between 1988 and 1998. The value of imports fell by an average 1.7% per year during the 1980s, but have increased by an average of 17.1% annually during 1990–95. In 1998, exports increased by 1.4%, and imports rose 2.8%.

Imports have been stimulated by falling tariffs, the ongoing implementation of Mercosur agreements, revaluation of the Uruguayan peso, and gradual liberalization of the economy. Rising imports of consumer goods reflect pent up demand, while increased imports of capital goods reflect the need to upgrade industrial facilities to meet foreign competition. Exports were overtaken by imports in 1999; in the first half of 1999, Uruguay's exports declined by 25%. The nation's trade deficit nearly doubled between 1998 and 1999, hit by the international financial recession.

Uruguay's major commodity exports are meat (12%), textile yarn (9.8%), and rice (7.8%). Other exports include leather (7.0%) and automobiles (5.8%).

In 1997 Uruguay's imports were distributed among the following categories: consumer goods, 16.4%; food, 9.1%; fuels, 9.1%; industrial supplies, 31.5%; machinery, 19.7%; and transportation, 14.2%.

Trade with Brazil and Argentina accounts for more than half of Uruguay's trade. Principal trading partners in 1998 (in millions of US dollars) were as follows:

COUNTRY	EXPORTS	IMPORTS	BALANCE
Brazil	935	793	142
Argentina	513	839	-326
United States	160	461	-301
China (inc. Hong Kong)	122	124	-2
Germany	112	125	-13
United Kingdom	94	59	35
Italy	79	176	-97
Chile	73	59	14
Spain	55	141	-86
Japan	22	93	-71
France	21	178	-157

³²BALANCE OF PAYMENTS

Balance of payments deficits are common in Uruguay, owing to fluctuating world markets for agricultural exports and a high dependency on imports for raw materials and fuels. Traditionally, multilateral assistance, income from tourism, and inflow of capital from other Latin American countries have tended to offset the negative trade picture. The balance of payments in the 1980s and 1990s was affected by the continued weakening of international prices of Uruguay's exports.

The US Central Intelligence Agency reports that in 1997 the purchasing power parity of Uruguay's exports was $2.7 billion while imports totaled $3.7 billion, resulting in a trade balance of -$1 billion.

The International Monetary Fund (IMF) reports that in 1998 Uruguay had exports of goods totaling $2,832 million and imports totaling $3,594 million. The services credit totaled $1,393 million and debit $913 million. The following table summarizes Uruguay's balance of payments as reported by the IMF for 1998 in millions of US dollars.

Current Account		-400
Balance on goods	-762	
Balance on services	480	
Balance on income	-185	
Current transfers	67	
Capital Account		...
Financial Account		679
Direct investment abroad	...	
Direct investment in Uruguay	164	
Portfolio investment assets	...	
Portfolio investment liabilities	424	
Other investment assets	-433	
Other investment liabilities	524	
Net Errors and Omissions		81
Reserves and Related Items		-360

³³BANKING AND SECURITIES

The Bank of the Republic (Banco de la República Oriental del Uruguay—BRDU), established in 1896, is a state bank with a government-appointed director. It operates as both a public and a private bank. It is the financial agent of the government; it also acts as an autonomous agency and, as a commercial bank, makes loans and receives deposits. It participates in determining financial policies and the allocation of foreign exchange for imports. One of its main functions is to provide rural credit.

The 1966 constitutional revision created a Central Bank (Banco Central del Uruguay—BCU), which is responsible for currency circulation, thus permitting the Bank of the Republic to concentrate on public and private credit. The third state bank is the Mortgage Bank (Banco Hipotecario del Uruguay—BHU). There are 21 private banks operating in Uruguay, 10 financial institutions, 11 offshore banks, and six savings and loans organizations.

In the early 1980s, economic recession produced a flood of bad debts, prompting the BCU to introduce a refinancing scheme in 1983, under which it took over the non-performing loans of some financial institutions. This improved the liquidity of the financial system, but shifted the burden onto public finances. In 1999, the IMF criticized Uruguay's two large public banks as being less efficient and profitable than private banks, calling for banking reforms.

A policy of regular minidevaluations was introduced in mid-1975; currency stability was established in the late 1970s, but in November 1982, the peso, regarded as overvalued, was allowed to float freely. The peso has fallen against the dollar since that time. As of 1999, about 90% of the private sector's deposits in the banking system were dollar-denominated, and 75% of the overall credit to the private sector was in dollars. Most purchases were made in dollars. Net foreign reserves equaled $2.43 billion at the end of 1998.

The Montevideo Stock Exchange is supplemented by its Internet based partner, the Bolsa Electrónica de Valores (BEVSA). The number of firms raising risk capital through the stock exchange is very small, and only 19 companies are quoted on it. In 1999, practically no shares were traded in the stock market.

34INSURANCE

The State Insurance Bank (Banco de Seguros del Estado—BSE), launched early in 1912 by a bond issue, was granted a monopoly on all insurance in 1919; however, private insurance companies were allowed to continue issuing life, fire, and marine insurance if they had been in business prior to creation of the state bank. An October 1993 law demonopolized the insurance industry, and Brazilian, UK, and Spanish companies now participate in the market.

35PUBLIC FINANCE

Under the inflationary pressures of the 1990s, budgetary expenditures generally exceeded revenues, although greater fiscal austerity caused a decrease in annual the budget deficit. In 1998, the number of government offices was reduced by one-third. The 1998 budget deficit was 0.90% of GDP, mostly financed by external loans ($685 million). Because of falling tax revenues and increased spending, the deficit was expected to rise in 1999.

The US Central Intelligence Agency (CIA) estimates that in 1997 Uruguay's central government took in revenues of approximately $4 billion and had expenditures of $4.3 billion including capital expenditures of $385 million. Overall, the government registered a deficit of approximately $300 million. External debt totaled $6.8 billion.

The following table shows an itemized breakdown of government revenues and expenditures. The percentages were calculated from data reported by the International Monetary Fund. The dollar amounts (millions) are based on the CIA estimates provided above.

REVENUE AND GRANTS	100%	4,000
Tax revenue	92.5%	3,702
Non-tax revenue	7.1%	285
Capital revenue	0.4%	16
EXPENDITURES	100%	4,300
General public services	7.4%	318
Defense	3.9%	168
Public order and safety	3.3%	140
Education	7.0%	299
Health	5.8%	249
Social security	61.4%	2,641
Housing and community amenities	1.5%	63
Recreation, cultural, and religious affairs	0.3%	14
Economic affairs and services	5.9%	253
Other expenditures	1.1%	49
Interest payments	4.7%	203
Adjustments	-2.3%	-98

36TAXATION

Personal income and inheritance taxes were repealed in 1974; the only individual direct taxes are a levy on farm profits and a net worth tax. The most important indirect tax is the value-added tax, which consists of a basic rate of 23%, and 14% on necessities. Corporate tax is imposed on industrial and commercial income at a rate of 30%. A 30% withholding tax is imposed on dividends. Other taxes include a commissions tax of 9% and a capital tax of 15%.

37CUSTOMS AND DUTIES

Uruguay's traditionally protectionist policies were relaxed as a result of the economic reforms of 1974. Average tariff rates fell from 139% in 1976 to 36% in 1982. As of 2000, the CET ranged from 6–20%. Excise taxes ranged from 10% to 30% on soft drinks, cosmetics, and motor vehicles; to 70% on tobacco, 80% on alcohol, and 133% for gasoline. Almost all goods can be imported into Uruguay without restrictions or licenses.

Effective January 1995, Brazil, Argentina, Uruguay, and Paraguay formed the Southern Common Market (MERCOSUR).

This agreement allows duty-free trade between the four countries. Tariff preferences are also given to members of the LAFA. Uruguay also has a large number of bilateral investment agreement, mostly with EU countries.

Free Trade Zones operate in Colonia, Florida, Nueva Helvecia, Nueva Palmira, Rio Negro, Rivera, San Jose, and Montevideo.

38FOREIGN INVESTMENT

The Foreign Investment Law of 28 March 1974 closed certain industries to foreign investors: public water and drainage services; railroads; alcohol and petroleum refineries; electric, telephone, local telegraph, mail, and port services; insurance; and issuance of mortgage bonds. Private investment in other sectors was generally welcome.

The 1998 Investment Promotion and Protection Law declared that foreign and national investments would be treated the same, and that investment would be allowed without government regulation. If a foreign company is considered to be of national benefit, it is entitled to extra benefits such as credit assistance and tax exemptions. Complete foreign ownership was allowed in most sectors except for oil and telecoms. The state-owned oil company ANCAP is the only importer and refiner of petroleum products in Uruguay, and ANTEL controls telecommunications. From 1992 to 1998, foreign direct investment amounted to about $150 million annually, which reflected a relatively low pace of privatization. Main investors included Canada and the EU. FDI hardly experienced any growth during the 1990s, even though the government promoted investment in the mining, tourism, hydrocarbons, forestry, printing, and media sectors.

39ECONOMIC DEVELOPMENT

Monopolies are permitted in the fields of banking and insurance, postal services, ports, water, light and power, telephone services, and fuels. Industrial and commercial activities of the state must be organized as "autonomous entities." Other public services may be organized as autonomous entities, as decentralized services, or as divisions under a ministry. Exceptions to this policy are state-operated postal and telephone services, customs houses, port administration, and public health.

The Committee on Investment and Economic Development, established in 1960, published a 10-year plan for 1965–75 for production, investment, and consumption. The plan, stressing industrial development and external financing, was superseded in April 1973 by the National Development Plan for 1973–77, prepared by the Planning and Budget Office. This plan projected an annual growth rate of 3.8% in real GDP, or 2.5% per capita; increases in exports and imports were projected at 10.1% and 14.9%, respectively. Domestic investment was to rise at an annual rate of 15.1%—a projection quite remote from the actual average annual increase of 3.2% realized during 1966–72.

After the severe slump of the early 1980s, the decisive actions by the new government injected life into the economy. In particular, restructuring the heavy domestic debt burden of the industrial and agricultural sectors increased confidence in the economy. Domestic investment rose sharply with some industries at full capacity.

The Lacalle administration continued the fiscal adjustment program in 1990 to reduce the budget deficit. A state enterprises reforms law passed in September 1991 permitted partial privatization of certain state-owned enterprises. Uruguay also became an important trade partner and provider of services to MERCOSUR countries. The flip side of this relationship was Uruguay's dependency on and vulnerability to economic developments in its neighboring countries. A slowdown in Brazilian growth and a recession in Argentina caused Uruguay's economy to slip into recession in 1995 and in 1998.

The Sanguinetti government continued the reforms of the previous administration. It also instituted a three-stage stabilization program in 1994. The plan increased consumption and payroll taxes, instituted a program designed to downsize government, and planned for long-term social security reform. This plan continued into the late 1990s with moderate success, but a recession hit in 1999 that exacerbated the problems of a state-monopolized economy dependent upon exports to Argentina and Brazil, and dependent on US dollars for the currency.

40SOCIAL DEVELOPMENT

Uruguay has frequently been referred to as South America's first welfare state. The social reform movement began under the leadership of José Batlle y Ordóñez in the early 1900s. Social legislation now provides for a day of rest in every week (plus Saturday afternoon), holidays with pay, minimum wages, annual cash and vacation bonuses, family allowances, compensation for unemployment or dismissal, workers' accident compensation, retirement pensions for rural and domestic workers, old age and disability pensions, and special consideration for working women and minors. The state also provides care for children and mothers, as well as for the blind, deaf, and mute. Free medical attention is available to the poor, as are low-cost living quarters for workers.

The government's social security system is divided into six main funds: civil service and teachers, industrial and commercial, rural workers and domestic servants, family allowances, banking, and the professions. For pension coverage, employers withhold 15% of each employee's gross earnings and contribute 12.5% of payroll to the appropriate fund. Employer and employee contributions for other benefits vary.

In 1995, women made up nearly half of the work force but tended to be concentrated in lower paying jobs. Nevertheless, many attend the national university and pursue professional careers. In 1999, 12 legislators were female. The air force and army military academies began admitting women in, respectively, 1997 and 1998. Spousal abuse is a serious social problem which is receiving greater attention by nongovernmental organizations. In 1999 a government study predicted that within five years domestic violence would rank as the second most serious public health threat, surpassed only by traffic accidents. The number of reported cases has increased dramatically, reflecting a greater willingness by women to confront the problem.

Black minorities, accounting for 6% of the population, are severely underrepresented in politics and in the professions. They face considerable discrimination in education and employment. There are no black Uruguayans in the legislature.

Occasional reports of the use of excessive force by police are reported each year, and judicial delays can result in lengthy pretrial detention. Human rights organizations operate freely in Uruguay.

41HEALTH

The government traditionally has placed great emphasis on preventive medicine and on the sociological approach to public health problems. The US Institute of Inter-American Affairs and the Uruguayan Ministry of Public Health created the Inter-American Cooperative Public Health Service, which built four health centers and clinics. For the region, life expectancy is high (72.9 years in 1998); infant mortality is low (17.5 per 1,000 live births in 1996); and the ratios of doctors and beds to the population are exceptionally good. In 1997 there were 3.7 doctors per 1,000 people. In 1995 there were 45 hospital beds per 1,000 people.

The Commission for the Fight against Tuberculosis is under the jurisdiction of the Ministry of Health; as a result of its efforts, tuberculosis is almost unknown in Uruguay today. In 1995, the incidence of tuberculosis was 19.3 per 100,000. No polio or neonatal tetanus were reported in 1995. The commission also deals with the social and economic effects of various diseases. The major causes of death are heart diseases, cancer, and digestive disorders. Degenerative diseases rank higher as a cause of death in Uruguay than in most other Latin American countries. The general mortality rate was 9.9 per 1,000 people in 1995, and maternal mortality was 19 per 1,000 live births that same year. The birth rate in Uruguay was 17.1 per 1,000 in 1997. Contraceptive use was high, with nearly 85% of married women in Uruguay using some method of birth control in 1989–90.

In 1995, 89% of the population had access to safe water. Immunization rates in 1997 for children up to one year old were tuberculosis (99%); diphtheria, pertussis, and tetanus (88%); polio (88%); and measles (80%). Total health care expenditures in 1995 were $516 per capita.

The HIV-1 seroprevalence rate was 0.3 per 100 adults in 1997. By the end of 1997, 851 AIDS cases had been reported.

42HOUSING

The housing situation is more favorable in Uruguay than in most Latin American countries. Housing construction, dominated by the public sector, is financed in large part by the Mortgage Bank. The National Institute of Low-Cost Housing builds low-cost dwellings for low-income workers and pensioners. At last estimate, 98% of all housing units were made of durable materials including stone masonry, wood, zinc, or concrete. Owners occupied more than 55% of all dwellings; nearly 25% were rented; less than 20% were occupied by usufructus (households legally inhabiting someone else's living quarters); and about 1% were occupied by members of housing cooperatives. Of all housing units, more than 90% had private toilet facilities, and nearly 75% had water piped indoors.

43EDUCATION

Adult illiteracy for the year 2000 was estimated at 2.2% (males, 2.6% and females, 1.8%), among the lowest in Latin America. Education in elementary, secondary, and technical schools and at the University of the Republic in Montevideo is free. Elementary education, which lasts six years, is compulsory. Secondary education is in two stages of three years.

In 1996 there were 2,415 primary schools, with 16,868 teachers and 345,573 students. Student-to-teacher ratio stood at 20 to one. There were 269,826 students in secondary schools in the same year.

There are two major universities, one of which is state run, the University of the Republic, and one is private, the Catholic University. The institutions of higher learning had a total of 9,907 teachers and 79,691 students in 1996.

44LIBRARIES AND MUSEUMS

The National Library, founded in 1816, contains over 900,000 volumes, primarily modern but including a sizable historical collection. Other major collections are found in the special libraries of the Council of Secondary, Basic, and Higher Education (110,000 volumes), and the Museum of Natural History (200,000), and at the Pedagogic Library (118,000). The University of the Republic in Montevideo (1849) holds nearly one million volumes.

The National Historical Museum exhibits artifacts of local Amerindian cultures and of Uruguayan historical development. The National Museum of Fine Arts has paintings by prominent Uruguayan artists, including Juan Manuel Blanes and Joaquín Torres García. Both are in Montevideo, as are the Museum of Industrial Arts, the Pedagogical Museum, and the Museum of the Discovery, a unique public affairs institution chronicling the impact of the European encounter with the new world. There are regional museums in Mercedes, Salto, San José de Mayo, and Tacuarembo.

45MEDIA

The state owns the telegraph and telephone services. In 1997, there were 767,300 telephones, most of them in the metropolitan Montevideo area. As of 1999, Uruguay had 72 AM radio stations and 26 television stations; color television broadcasting was introduced in 1981. In 1997 the number of radio receivers was 610 per 1,000 population; the number of television sets was 242 per 1,000 population, and the number of mobile phones was 46.

In 1999, there were six daily newspapers in Montevideo, with their affiliations and circulations as follows:

	AFFILIATION	CIRCULATION
El Diario (e)	Conservative	170,000
El País (m)	Conservative	100,000
La Mañana (m)	NA	40,000
La Republica	NA	NA
Últimas Noticias	NA	25,000
El Observador Economico	NA	10,000

The first newspaper in the Banda Oriental was the *Southern Star,* published by the British in 1807 during their brief occupation of Montevideo. *El Día,* founded by José Batlle y Ordóñez in 1886, helped lay the foundation for the social reforms of the first two decades of the 20th century. Under the military regime established in 1973, periodicals were forbidden to report on internal security matters. Censorship was imposed, and more than 30 newspapers and periodicals were closed down; many newspapers were harassed with suspensions of one day or more. In November 1974, *Marcha,* a weekly read throughout Latin America and Uruguay's last remaining opposition periodical, was shut down. Press censorship was relaxed in the late 1970s, but the military government still reserved the right to detain and question editors and reporters and to suspend publication for four or more issues. Press freedom was restored in 1985.

As of 1996, there were about 69,600 personal computers; in 1998 there were 50 Internet hosts per 1,000 population.

46ORGANIZATIONS

The two most important organizations of livestock farmers are the Rural Association and the Rural Federation, both founded by large landowners. Other employers' organizations include the Importers' and Wholesalers' Association and the Uruguayan Exporters' Union. The Chamber of Industries is a powerful organization, with a representative on the Export and Import Control Commission.

47TOURISM, TRAVEL, AND RECREATION

Tourism, one of Uruguay's major enterprises, enjoys government support. The state owns many hotels along the coast, especially in the area of Punta del Este, 145 km (90 mi) east of Montevideo and one of the more sophisticated resorts in South America. Montevideo has been promoted as the "city of roses" because of its many parks and gardens.

A visitor must have a valid passport; for most visitors, no visa is required. The maximum stay is three months, plus an extension for another three months. In 1997, 2,258,616 tourists visited Uruguay and tourism receipts totaled $759 million. That year there were 14,957 hotel rooms with 36,140 beds.

The most popular sport in Uruguay is soccer; there is an intense rivalry between supporters of the two major teams, the Peñarol and the Nacional. Other popular sports include basketball, cycling, tennis, pelota, golf, and water sports.

Uruguayan soccer teams won the World Cup in 1930 and 1950; the first World Cup competition was hosted by Uruguay in 1930.

According to 1999 UN estimates, the cost of staying in Montevideo is $153 per day; elsewhere the average is about $111.

48FAMOUS URUGUAYANS

The national hero of Uruguay is José Gervasio Artigas (1764–1850), who led the fight for independence against Brazil and Portugal. Juan Antonio Lavalleja (1786?–1853) directed the uprising that established Uruguay's independence in 1828. The nation's first two presidents were Gen. José Fructuoso Rivera (1790?–1854) and Brig. Gen. Manuel Oribe (1796?–1857), the founders of the Colorados and Blancos, respectively. One of Uruguay's greatest citizens was José Batlle y Ordóñez (1856–1929), who served twice as president of the country. José Pedro Varela (1845–79) was Uruguay's chief educational reformer.

One of the most respected defenders of Latin America's cultural tradition was José Enrique Rodó (1872–1917), whose *Ariel* and *Motivos de Proteo* fostered the idea of the superiority of Latin American culture. Juan Zorrilla de San Martín (1855–1933) was a 19th-century romantic poet whose finest work, *Tabaré,* describes Uruguay at the time of the Spanish conquest. Eduardo Acevedo Díaz (1851–1924) won fame as the writer of a gaucho novel, *Soledad* (1894). Other significant novelists are Carlos Reyles (1868–1938) and Javier de Viana (1872–1925). Horacio Quiroga (1878–1937) is regarded as one of Latin America's foremost short-story writers. The poets Julio Herrera y Reissig (1875–1910) and Juana de Ibarbourou (1895–1979) have attained a devoted audience beyond the borders of Uruguay. Emir Rodríguez Monegal (1921–85) is considered a leading writer and literary scholar.

The painter Juan Manuel Blanes (1830–1901) is best known for his *Episode of the Yellow Fever.* Pedro Figari (1861–1938) painted vivid scenes of early 19th-century Uruguay. Joaquín Torres García (1874–1949) founded his painting style on the principles of universalism and constructivism. Eduardo Fabini (1883–1951) is Uruguay's best-known composer. Francisco Curt Lange (b.Germany, 1903), Latin America's foremost musicologist, founded various inter-American institutions and publications for the promotion of music of the Americas.

49DEPENDENCIES

Uruguay has no territories or colonies.

50BIBLIOGRAPHY

Finch, Martin H. J. *A Political Economy of Uruguay Since 1870.* New York: St. Martin's, 1982.

Finch, Martin. *Uruguay.* Santa Barbara, Calif.: Clio, 1989.

Gillespie, Charles. *Negotiating Democracy: Politicians and Generals in Uruguay.* New York: Cambridge University Press, 1991.

Gonzalez, Luis E. *Political Parties and Democracy in Uruguay.* Notre Dame, Ind.: Helen Kellogg Institute for International Studies, 1991.

Hudson, Rex A., and Sandra W. Meditz (eds.). *Uruguay, a Country Study.* 2d ed. Washington, D.C.: Dept. of the Army, 1992.

Sosnowski, Saul, and Louise B. Popkin (eds.). *Repression, Exile, and Democracy: Uruguayan Culture.* Durham, N.C.: Duke University Press, 1993.

Weinstein, Martin. *Uruguay, Democracy at the Crossroads.* Boulder, Colo.: Westview, 1988.

VENEZUELA

Republic of Venezuela
República de Venezuela

CAPITAL: Caracas.

FLAG: The national flag, adopted in 1930, is a tricolor of yellow, blue, and red horizontal stripes. An arc of seven white stars on the blue stripe represents the seven original states.

ANTHEM: *Himno Nacional,* beginning "Gloria al bravo pueblo" ("Glory to the brave people").

MONETARY UNIT: The bolívar (B) is a paper currency of 100 céntimos. There are coins of 5, 25, and 50 céntimos and 1, 2, and 5 bolívares, and notes of 5, 10, 20, 50, 100, 500, and 1,000 bolívares. B1 = $0.00151 (or $1 = B661.00) as of 31 March 2000.

WEIGHTS AND MEASURES: The metric system is the legal standard.

HOLIDAYS: New Year's Day, 1 January; Declaration of Independence and Day of the Indian, 19 April; Labor Day, 1 May; Army Day and Anniversary of the Battle of Carabobo, 24 June; Independence Day, 5 July; Bolívar's Birthday, 24 July; Civil Servants Day, 4 September; Columbus Day, 12 October; Christmas, 25 December; New Year's Eve, 31 December. Movable holidays are Carnival (Monday and Tuesday before Ash Wednesday), Holy Thursday, Good Friday, and Holy Saturday. Numerous other bank holidays and local festivals are observed.

TIME: 8 AM = noon GMT.

¹LOCATION, SIZE, AND EXTENT

Venezuela, located on the northern coast of South America, covers an area of 912,050 sq km (352,144 sq mi), extending 1,487 km (924 mi) WNW–ESE and 1,175 km (730 mi) NNE–SSW. Comparatively, the area occupied by Venezuela is slightly more than twice the size of the state of California. It is bordered on the N by the Caribbean Sea and the Atlantic Ocean, on the E by Guyana, on the S by Brazil, and on the W by Colombia, with a total boundary length of 7,609 km (4,718 mi). There are 72 offshore islands.

Venezuela claims more than 130,000 sq km (50,000 sq mi) of Guyanese territory west of the Essequibo River, constituting over three-fifths of Guyana. In 1985, UN mediation was requested by both countries. Conflicting maritime claims with Colombia in the Gulf of Venezuela remain unresolved, despite negotiations since 1970. Demarcation of the land boundary between the two nations began in February 1982. In August 1987, a Colombian naval vessel entered the disputed area in an apparent attempt to pressure Venezuela to be more flexible.

Venezuela's capital city, Caracas, is located in the northern part of the country on the Caribbean Sea coast.

²TOPOGRAPHY

Venezuela has four principal geographical divisions. In the north emerges a low extension of the Andes chain; to the west lies the hot basin of Lake Maracaibo; to the southeast spread the great plains (llanos) and forests; and south of the Orinoco River lie the unoccupied and largely unexplored Guiana Highlands, accounting for about half the country's total area. The Orinoco, which is more than 2,900 km (1,800 mi) long and has over 70 mouths and a delta of nearly 23,300 sq km (9,000 sq mi), drains four-fifths of Venezuela. There are more than 1,000 other rivers. About 90% of the nation's population is concentrated between the northeastern plateau of the Andes, on which is located the capital, Caracas, and another Andean extension to the west along

the Venezuela-Colombia border, covering approximately one-fourth of the total national area.

Outstanding geographical features include Angel Falls (979 m/3,212 ft high) in the Guiana Highlands of southeastern Venezuela, the highest waterfall in the world; the navigable Lake Maracaibo in the west, which is about 80 km (50 mi) wide and 210 km (130 mi) long and is accessible to ocean shipping; and Pico Bolívar in the Sierra Nevada de Mérida, the highest peak in Venezuela (5,007 m/16,427 ft).

³CLIMATE

Although Venezuela lies entirely within the torrid zone, generally there are four climatic regions, based mainly on altitude: tropical, up to 760 m (2,500 ft) in elevation; subtropical, from 760 to 1,830 m (2,500 to 6,000 ft); temperate, from 1,830 to 2,740 m (6,000 to 9,000 ft); and cold, above 2,740 m (9,000 ft). In the tropical region, including the cities of Maracaibo and Ciudad Bolívar, mean annual temperatures range from 24° to 35°C (75° to 95°F). In the subtropical region, where Caracas is situated, the means range from 10° to 25°C (50° to 77°F). In January, in Caracas, the average minimum and maximum temperatures are 15°C (59°F) and 26°C (79°F), respectively; the range in July is 17–26°C (63–79°F). During the wet season (May to October), the llanos and forest areas are swampy, green, and lush. Upon the advent of the dry season, the same areas become dry, brown, and parched. There is perpetual snow on several peaks of the Cordillera de Mérida.

⁴FLORA AND FAUNA

The natural vegetation of the tropical zone varies from the rain forest regions of the lower Maracaibo Basin to the grasslands of the llanos. In the areas of insufficient rainfall are found xerophytic plants, as well as mimosa. The subtropical zone, tierra templada, was originally almost covered by a luxuriant forest and is now the nation's principal agricultural region. In the temperate region, only a small portion of the total land area, wild vegetation is sparse and scrubby. In the páramo region, from about 2,740 to 4,880 m (9,000 to 16,000 ft) in elevation, vegetation becomes even thinner and barely affords an existence for the few sheep and cattle raised by the local Amerindian population. Above 3,050 m (10,000 ft), the only vegetation seen is the espeletia, similar to the century plant, which grows to a height of 1.8–2.1 m (6–7 ft).

The wild animals of Venezuela are abundant because of their relative isolation from human disturbance. The forests are populated with tapirs, sloths, anteaters, and a variety of monkeys. In the mountains are puma, margay, vampire bats, and deer. Semiwild horses, donkeys, and cattle are found in the plains. The forests are rich in tropical birds such as the cacique, crested coquette, heron, umbrella bird, manakin, cock-of-the-rock, parrot, macaw, and aigrette. Aquatic fowl include the pelican, heron, flamingo, and a muscovy duck weighing up to 9.1 kg (20 lb). More than 32 species of eagles are found in Venezuela. There are numerous reptiles, including the rattlesnake, coral snake, bushmaster, anaconda, and boa. Crocodiles are found in the lowland rivers. Fish, shellfish, tortoises, and sand tortoises are also plentiful.

5ENVIRONMENT

Pressing environmental problems—such as urbanization, the unrestricted use of pesticides, the pollution of waterways with untreated industrial wastes, increasing air pollution and gasoline consumption by automobiles, and the uncontrolled exploitation of soil and forest resources—led the government in 1976 to establish the Ministry of Environment and Renewable Natural Resources. The basic legislative instrument is the Organic Law of the Environment; other laws govern the protection of soils, forests, and water supplies, regulate public sanitation, and seek to prevent the contamination of waterways by oil. Incentives are offered to industry to avoid environmental damage. Air pollution results from the activity of power plants and from industrial and vehicle exhaust emissions In 1992, industrial carbon dioxide emissions totaled 116.4 million metric tons, a per capita level of 5.75 metric tons. Water pollution is caused by contaminants from the oil industry, mining activity, and industrial chemicals. The nation's cities also produce 3.6 million tons of solid waste per year. Venezuela has 205.4 cu mi of water. Forty-six percent is used for farming activity and 11% for industrial purposes. As of 1995, 20% of urban dwellers and 25% of the rural population lacked access to safe drinking water. Between 1983 and 1993, the nation lost 8.2% of its forest and woodland. Measures designed to prevent forest depletion include suspension of logging permits and a large-scale afforestation program. In the Andes area, Venezuela loses up to 300 tons of soil per hectare due to land erosion by rivers. A shrinking oil market reduced funding for the Ministry of Environment in the 1980s to the detriment of its reputation as a model for the third world.

In the mid-1990s, 19 of the nation's mammal species and 34 bird species were endangered. Also 106 plant types were also endangered. Endangered or extinct species in Venezuela include the tundra peregrine falcon, red siskin, giant otter, five species of turtle (green sea, hawksbill, olive ridley, leatherback, and South American river), and three species of crocodile (spectacled caiman, American, and Orinoco).

6POPULATION

The 1990 census placed the total population of Venezuela at 18,105,265, 17% above the 1981 census figure. By 2000, the population of Venezuela was estimated at 23,595,822. An estimated 4.2% of the population is 65 years of age or older. The projected population for the year 2005 is 25,504,000, assuming a crude birthrate of 19 per 1,000 population and a death rate of 5, resulting in a natural rate of change of 1.5% for the period 2000–

2005. The population rate of change between 1995 and 2000 was 2.0%. The population density in 1998 was 26 per sq km (67 per sq mi); in the relatively populous northwest, the density is more than twice the national average.

Nevertheless, Venezuela remains one of the least densely populated countries in the Western Hemisphere. The Amazon River area (nearly 20% of the total) averages only about 0.3 population per sq km (0.8 per sq mi). It was estimated that 87% of the population lived in urban areas in 2000, up from 79% in 1980. The capital city, Caracas, had a 2000 metropolitan population estimated at 3,153,000. Other large cities, with their 2000 metropolitan population counts, include Maracaibo, 1,857,000; Valencia, 1,817,000; Maracay, 1,077,000; and Barquisimeto, 914,000.

7MIGRATION

For a time, Venezuela encouraged large-scale immigration in the hope that the newcomers would help increase the nation's food production. Although the yearly totals of foreigners entering Venezuela were high, a large portion of these immigrants remained only briefly. In the decades immediately before and after World War II, nearly 500,000 Europeans—mostly from Italy, Spain, and Portugal—came to Venezuela. By 1990, however, only 5.7% of the resident population was of foreign birth. In 1989 there were 18,893 immigrants and 9,643 emigrants. An estimated 300,000 illegal immigrants, most of them Colombians, were living in Venezuela in 1985. Internal migration in the 1980s was chiefly from the federal district to adjoining areas and eastward from the state of Zulia, in the far northwest. Between 1990–97, 1,630 persons were given refugee status by the UNHCR in Venezuela. As of September 1999, government sources reported at least 1,500,000 Colombians in Venezuela, of whom only 500,000 were legal residents. In June 1999 alone, some 3,500 Colombians entered the country following a paramilitary offensive in the Colombian area of La Gabarra. In the same year, there were 166 recognized refugees, of whom only 27 were Colombians. The net migration movement in 1999 was -0.23 migrants per 1,000 population.

8ETHNIC GROUPS

The original inhabitants of Venezuela were Amerindians, predominantly Caribs and Arawaks. The majority (about 68%) of the present population is mestizo (mixed race). Approximately 21% are European, primarily Spanish, Italian, Portuguese, and German. Blacks account for an estimated 8–10%, and Amerindians for about 2%. Arab peoples are also represented in the overall populace.

9LANGUAGES

The official language is Spanish. It is fairly standardized throughout the country among the educated population, but there are marked regional variations. Numerous indigenous dialects are also spoken.

10RELIGIONS

Venezuelans are constitutionally guaranteed freedom of religion provided that a faith is not contrary to public order or good custom. According to the latest government statistics, an estimated 75% of the population are Roman Catholic. Protestants constitute 18%, and the remaining 7% profess other religions or are atheists. Of the other religions, there are small but influential Muslim and Jewish communities. Caracas, the capital city, has a large mosque. According to government reports in 1998, Protestant churches are Venezuela's most rapidly growing segment of the religious population.

LOCATION: 0°35′ to 12°11′N; 60°10′ to 73°25′W. **BOUNDARY LENGTHS:** Total coastline, 2,816 km (1,750 mi); Guyana, 743 km (462 mi); Brazil, 2,000 km (1,243 mi); Colombia, 2,050 km (1,274 mi). **TERRITORIAL SEA LIMIT:** 12 mi.

¹¹TRANSPORTATION

The most important mode of domestic cargo and passenger transport is shipping over the country's more than 16,000 km (9,900 mi) of navigable inland waterways, which include 7,100 km (4,410 mi) navigable to oceangoing vessels. A large percentage of Venezuelan tonnage is carried by ships of the government-owned Venezuelan Navigation Co. In 1998, the merchant fleet had 32 vessels of over 1,000 gross tons, for a total GRT of 535,882. Shallow-draught ships are able to reach Colombian river ports in the wet season. Shallow-draught river steamers are the principal means of transportation from the eastern llanos to Puerto Ordaz, which, thanks to constant dredging, is also reached by deep-draught oceangoing vessels. Dredging operations also are maintained in Lake Maracaibo to allow the entry of oceangoing tankers. The government has

invested substantially in the port of La Guaira, hoping to make it one of the most modern in the Caribbean area. Puerto Cabello handles the most cargo, and Maracaibo is the main port for oil shipments.

Highway and railroad construction is both costly and dangerous because of the rough mountainous terrain in the areas of dense population. Nevertheless, the government has undertaken massive highway construction projects throughout the country. Major ventures include the completion of the Caracas-La Guaira Autopista, which links the capital with its airport at Maiquetía and its seaport at La Guaira, and a section of the Pan-American Highway connecting Carora with the Colombian border. The General Rafael Urdañeta Bridge crosses the narrow neck of water connecting Lake Maracaibo with the Gulf of Venezuela and provides a direct surface link between Maracaibo and the east. By 1998, Venezuela had 84,300 km (52,384 mi) of highway, of which 33,214 km (20,639 mi) were paved. In 1995 there were 1,485,000 passenger cars and 511,800 commercial vehicles in Venezuela.

Venezuela's two railroads carry mostly freight. Rail transportation is concentrated in the northern states of Lara, Miranda, Carabobo, Aragua, and Yaracuy, with branches connecting the principal seaports with the important cities of the central highlands. There were 584 km (362 mi) of track in 1998, 336 km (208 mi) of which were owned and operated by the government. Much of the equipment is antiquated, and the linking of lines is difficult because of the different gauges in use. The government planned in the early 1980s to build a 3,900-km (2,420-mi) railroad network by the end of the decade; however, the financial crisis that began in 1983 has scaled the program down to 2,000 km (1,200 mi) over 20 years. The first 7.2-km (4.5-mi) section of a government-financed metro line in Caracas was opened in 1983.

Cities and towns of the remote regions are linked principally by air transportation. In 1998 there were an estimated 371 airports, 122 of which had paved runways. Venezuela has three main airlines, the government-owned Aerovías Venezolanas S.A. (AVENSA), Línea Aeropostal Venezolana (LAV), and Venezolana Internacional de Aviación, S.A. (VIASA); VIASA, an overseas service, is jointly run by AVENSA and LAV. A new airline, Aeronaves del Centro, began domestic flights in 1980. The government has expanded Simón Bolívar International Airport at Maiquetía, near Caracas, to accommodate heavy jet traffic. In 1997, 4,020,000 passengers were carried on scheduled domestic and international airline flights.

12HISTORY

As many as 400,000 Amerindians were living in the land now known as Venezuela when Christopher Columbus landed at the mouth of the Orinoco in August 1498, on his third voyage of discovery. The nation received its name, meaning "Little Venice," from Alonso de Ojeda, who sailed into the Gulf of Venezuela in August 1499 and was reminded of the Italian city by the native huts built on stilts over the water.

The first Europeans to settle Venezuela were Germans. Holy Roman Emperor Charles V granted the Welsers, a German banking firm, the right to colonize and develop Venezuela in exchange for the cancellation of a debt. Lasting a little less than 20 years, the administration of the Welsers was characterized by extensive exploration and organization of the territory but also by brutality toward the native population. In 1546, the grant was rescinded, and Venezuela was returned to the Spanish crown.

Under the Spanish, Eastern Venezuela was governed under the audiencia (region under a royal court) of Santo Domingo, and the western and southern regions became a captaincy-general under the viceroyalty of Peru. Settlement of the colony was hampered by constant wars with the Amerindians, which did not stop until after a smallpox epidemic in 1580. Meanwhile, the province was carved into encomiendas (hereditary grants), which were given to the conquistadores as rewards. By the end of the century, however, the encomienda system was abandoned, and existing grants were declared illegal. The cabildos, or town councils, won more authority, and a national consciousness began to develop. In 1717, the western and southern provinces were incorporated into the viceroyalty of New Granada, and in 1783, the area of present-day Venezuela became a captaincy-general of Caracas.

The war for independence against Spain began in 1810. Francisco de Miranda ("El Precursor"), a military adventurer, was named leader of the Congress of Cabildos, which declared the independence of Venezuela on 5 July 1811. Royalist factions rallied to overthrow the new republic, which was weakened when an earthquake destroyed revolutionary strongholds and left royalist centers virtually untouched. Miranda was captured and sent to die in a dungeon in Cádiz, but Simón Bolívar, a native of Caracas who had served under Miranda, was able to flee to Colombia. He then led an army across the Andes into Venezuela, declaring "War to the death and no quarter to Spaniards." In August 1812, he entered Caracas and assumed the title of Liberator ("El Libertador"). He was defeated and forced to flee to Jamaica, as the royalists again took control of the capital. In December 1816, Bolívar, after landing in eastern Venezuela, established his headquarters in Angostura, now Ciudad Bolívar. He was aided by Gen. José Antonio Páez. The Congress of Angostura convened in October 1818 and in February 1819 elected Bolívar president of the Venezuelan republic. In the spring, he crossed the Andes, and in July, he entered Tunja, Colombia, with about 3,000 men and, after defeating the Spaniards at Boyacá, entered Bogotá. Under Bolívar's leadership, Gran Colombia (Greater Colombia) was formed from Colombia, Ecuador, and Venezuela, with Bolívar as its president and military dictator. The end of the Venezuelan war of independence came with Bolívar's victory at Carabobo in June 1821.

In 1830, Venezuela seceded from Gran Colombia. A period of civil wars lasted from 1846 to 1870, when the caudillo Antonio Guzmán Blanco assumed power. Guzmán was overthrown in 1888, and a few years later, Joaquín Crespo, a former puppet president of Guzmán, seized power. The next dictator, Cipriano Castro (1899–1908), was a colorful, if controversial, figure. A drunkard and a libertine, Castro also put Venezuela deeply into debt. When Castro refused to repay its outstanding loans, Germany, Great Britain, and Italy sent gunboats to blockade the Venezuelan coast. After mediation by the US and a decision favorable to the European creditors by the Permanent Court of Arbitration at The Hague, Venezuela met its obligations by 1907. The next year, Castro sought medical care in Paris, leaving Venezuela in the hands of Juan Vicente Gómez. Gómez (1908–35) promptly seized power and ruled as dictator until his death. Although uneducated and practically illiterate, Gómez had a mind for business and proved a capable administrator. During his dictatorship, agriculture was developed and oil was discovered, making Venezuela one of the richest countries in Latin America. Oil concessions attracted US, British, and Dutch companies, initiating an era of oil wealth that continues today.

After the death of Gómez, Venezuela began to move toward democracy. During two military governments, opposition parties were permitted, allowing the Democratic Action (Acción Democrática—AD) to organize. In 1945, the military scheduled an election, but many feared a fraudulent outcome. The AD deposed the military, and a junta named AD leader Rómulo Betancourt provisional president. Betancourt set elections for 1947, and conducted the first free election for president in Venezuelan history. The AD candidate Rómulo Gallegos, a distinguished novelist, was elected overwhelmingly, but the military intervened in November 1948. A bloodless army coup replaced Gallegos with a military junta that ruled for four years. In December 1952, during the scheduled presidential election Marcos Pérez Jiménez seized power and became an absolute dictator.

Venezuela took its last steps toward full democracy after January 1958, when a popular revolt with military backing drove Pérez Jiménez from power. An interim government consisting of a military junta held elections in December 1958, and Betancourt was chosen president. Venezuela has had fair and free elections ever since.

The Betancourt government (1959–64) instituted modest programs for fiscal and agrarian reform, school construction, the elimination of illiteracy, and diversification of the economy. However, a depression beginning in 1960 trammeled these efforts and aggravated dissatisfaction with the regime. Betancourt was challenged by political instability coming from several fronts. The military, looking for a chance to return to power, engaged in several attempts to overthrow the government. Betancourt also opposed Fidel Castro, and allied with the US against him. Castroites in Venezuela responded with a guerrilla campaign under the FALN (Armed Forces for National Liberation). Betancourt charged the Castro government with attempting to subvert his government by supporting the FALN. In February 1964, the OAS formally charged Cuba with an act of aggression against Venezuela as a result of the discovery of an arms shipment to guerrillas in November 1963.

The AD was reelected in December 1964, when Raúl Leoni won the presidency over five other candidates. In 1966, supporters of Pérez Jiménez staged an unsuccessful military uprising. In the same year, in a drive against continued Castro-supported terrorism, President Leoni suspended constitutional guarantees and empowered the police to make arrests without warrants, to hold suspects without bail for an indefinite period, and to enter the quarters of suspected terrorists without judicial permission.

In 1968, Venezuela passed another test of democracy by transferring power peacefully from AD to the opposition Social Christian Party. The victor, Rafael Caldera Rodríguez, governed along the same lines as his AD predecessors, maintaining a set of social programs and benefiting from increasing oil revenues. At this point, Venezuela's future seemed assured, and public expenditures increased. The AD returned in 1973 with the victory of Carlos Andrés Pérez. By 1976, Pérez had brought about complete nationalization of the oil and iron industries. In the December 1978 elections, Luis Herrera Campíns, leader of the Social Christian Party, won the presidency. The next year, Venezuela received its first rude awakening, when the oil market dropped, thus threatening the foundations of the Venezuelan economic and political systems. There was soon a financial crisis, as Venezuela struggled to make payments on its overextended debt. The crisis culminated in the devaluation of the national currency, the bolívar, which dropped to one-third of its previous value against the dollar. Venezuelan consumers responded angrily, and the early 1980s were years of unrest. In the elections of December 1983, the AD returned to power behind presidential candidate Jaime Lusinchi.

Lusinchi's tenure was marred by scandal and trouble in the midst of the world petroleum crisis. While the economy floundered through the 1980s, the government maintained public confidence by stressing a "social pact" with guarantees of housing, education, and public health. Some progress was made in boosting non-oil exports, particularly in agriculture and mining, and the government promoted import substitution, particularly in food and manufacturing.

The 1988 elections brought back Carlos Andrés Pérez, who had been elected president 15 years earlier. Pérez immediately imposed austerity measures, removing government subsidies on a number of consumer goods, including gasoline. Prices rose and Caracas was rocked by rioting on a scale not seen since the uprising of 1958. The military was called in to quell the disturbances, but when the trouble finally died down, thousands had been killed or injured. The situation continued to deteriorate, and in 1992 Venezuela was shocked by two military coup attempts. The leader of the coup was an obscure and young military leader named Hugo Rafael Chavez Friaz. Venezuelans could not have guessed that Chavez within a short few years would be leading the nation.

Pérez seemed unmoved by the coup attempts, and his administration continued business as usual. A major scandal, with allegations of embezzlement and theft in office, brought him down. Pérez was suspended from office and later sentenced to 28 months in prison, and Ramón José Velásquez was named interim president until the regularly scheduled elections in December 1993.

In that election, Venezuelans chose Rafael Caldera, who ran under a coalition of four parties. The election of Caldera, who had been president during the brighter years of 1968–73, demonstrated the level of impasse in the Venezuelan system. Unable to produce new leadership, former presidents were being returned to office. Even though Venezuela remained one of the wealthiest countries in Latin America, instability was rapidly increasing. The Venezuelan economy fell into a recession in 1993, which continued to worsen over the next four years. In order to enforce emergency economic measures, President Caldera suspended a number of civil rights in 1994–95.

The Venezuelan middle class plunged into poverty as inflation soared to 103% by 1995. Doctors, university professors, and national telephone company workers all went out on strike during 1997, and several other groups threatened to strike as well. Within this fragile political atmosphere, Chavez reappeared in the political scene. Backed by the new party Movement for the Fifth Republic, Chavez quickly established himself as a major contender in the 1998 presidential election. A charismatic populist, Chavez appealed to the nation's poor. The traditional parties that had ruled the country for some 40 years had impoverished the nation and pillaged its resources, he said, promising to end the avarice and poverty. In December 1998, he gained 57% of the votes to become president.

During his inauguration speech in February 1999, Chavez unveiled his intentions to dramatically change the political and social fabric of the nation. He swore allegiance to the 1961 constitution, but he stressed it was a moribund document and vowed to replace it. He promised a "peaceful democratic revolution." To some Venezuelans and international observers, Chavez's leftist rhetoric was alarming. Some saw a caudillo in the making, a man who reminded them too much of Cuba's Fidel Castro. But Castro, a close friend, said he and Chavez did not share the same political ideology, even though Chavez had become a vocal opponent of free-market economics. Chavez called for a new constitution, and in April, voters approved a 131-member National Constitutional Assembly (ANC) to rewrite the document. Backers of Chavez won 121 of the 131 seats in July elections. In December, 46% of the country's 11 million eligible voters went to the polls to decide the fate of the proposed constitution. Approved by 71% of those who voted, the new document, the country's 26th constitution, came into effect on 30 December 1999. The new constitution is expected to bring dramatic changes to all branches of government as laws are changed to meet its demands.

The new constitution eliminated the Senate and replaced it with a unicameral National Assembly. It gave the nation a new name to honor Bolívar: Republica Bolivariana de Venezuela (Bolivarian Republic of Venezuela). It consolidated power in the executive branch, extended the presidential term from five to six years, and eliminated a restriction that prevented the president from serving two consecutive terms. It banned the privatization of social security, health care, the oil industry, and other key state-owned enterprises. In January 2000, the ANC concluded its work and selected a 21-member National Commission to help rule the country until elections for the new National Assembly could be held sometime in May 2000. Nearly all national, regional and local offices will be up for grabs during the May "mega-elections," including the presidential office. While Chavez said he would not campaign, he is a formidable candidate with no serious opposition.

13 GOVERNMENT

The transitional 21-member National Commission that took office in February 2000 was expected to reform as many as 60 laws in preparation for the May 2000 elections, when members of the new National Assembly are elected. Under the new constitution of 1999, Venezuela remained a republic. The new document stresses social, economic, and political rights similar to the previous document, but critics of President Hugo Chavez believe it concentrates too much power in the presidency.

The constitution also allows the state to play a greater role in the economy, reducing the autonomy of the Central Bank. It also reduces civilian oversight of the military.

The president is elected by direct popular vote for a six-year term, and the president can seek consecutive terms. In the previous constitution, a president could not run for reelection until 10 years after the completion of a term. The president must be a native citizen, at least 30 years of age, and a "layman." Presidential duties include the selection and removal of cabinet ministers and all other administrative officers and employees of the national government, as well as the appointment of state governors. The president is commander-in-chief of the armed forces, directs foreign affairs, and may make and ratify international treaties, conventions, and agreements. In the former document, there was no vice-president, but the new constitution created the vice-presidential office.

14POLITICAL PARTIES

Before the formation of the existing political parties, political conflict in Venezuela was confined to the traditionally Latin American centralist-federalist debate, with few actual differences in governments. Since the late 1950s, however, a stable party system evolved. Each political group had its own ballot with its own distinctive color and symbol, so that illiteracy was not a barrier to political participation. Constitutional provisions barring the military from political involvement further ensured the stability of the party system and the continuity of elected civilian leadership. But Chavez came into office promising to dismantle the party system that dominated Venezuelan politics for more than four decades. While his left-of-center coalition remained firmly in control in 1999 and early 2000, it was not known how the new constitution and political reforms would affect other parties in the long run. All parties will be allowed to compete for national, regional, and municipal posts in the proposed May 2000 elections.

Since 1958, the dominant force in Venezuelan politics was the Democratic Action Party (Acción Democrática—AD). It grew out of the socialist movement, which unified under the National Democratic Party (PDN). That party splintered, with a Moscow-oriented group forming the Communist Party of Venezuela (PCV) and the nationalist and democratic-socialist faction creating the AD.

The left has been fragmented throughout modern Venezuelan politics. After the split between AD and the PCV, the advent of Fidel Castro in Cuba caused further fragmentation. A group of AD members left the party to form the Movement of the Revolutionary Left (Movimiento de Izquierda Revolucionaria—MIR). The Armed Liberation Forces (Fuerzas Armadas de Liberación Nacional—FALN) took to the field and attempted a guerrilla uprising. The PCV remained loyal to Moscow and at times battled the FALN openly. All of these movements were denounced by the AD, and in 1962 the MIR and PCV were barred from political activity. The FALN, which never bothered with legal political action, was subdued, and with it hopes of a Castroite takeover died. The most recent development from the left has been the emergence of the Movement for Socialism (Movimiento al Socialismo—MAS), which took 10% of the vote for the Chamber of Deputies in 1988. MAS is an attempt to rejuvenate the left by a faction of the old PCV.

The right has been characterized by small parties without much chance of electoral success alone. Some have been able to form coalitions with larger parties to achieve some success within the system. One such party, the Democratic Republican Union (Unión Republicana Democrática—URD), has been a governing partner with the AD during the Leoni government (1963–68). The Committee for Free Elections (Comité de Organización Política Electoral Independiente—COPEI), also known as the Social Christian Party (Partido Social-Cristiano), is a Christian Democratic party, with the center-right implications of that movement. It has succeeded as an opposition party to the AD, occasionally taking advantage of splits in the AD's governing coalition or within the AD itself.

In 1947, the AD won the first free elections ever held in Venezuela. The PCV also fielded a candidate, as did COPEI. These three parties were outlawed during the dictatorship of Pérez Jiménez, and carried on their activities clandestinely. In December 1958, after Pérez Jiménez had been driven from power, free elections were held. The presidential victor, Rómulo Betancourt, formed a coalition government of the AD, COPEI, and URD.

The AD and COPEI reached several agreements over the years to cooperate with each other and to exclude the more leftist parties from the Venezuelan system. After the COPEI victory in 1968, Venezuela became a more competitive two-party system, with AD and COPEI competing for power. Agreements between AD and COPEI in 1970 and 1973 called for cooperation in appointive posts, so the competition has been controlled. AD and COPEI have dominated the system since, although the 1994 election of Caldera as the candidate of a four-party coalition, the National Convergence (Convergencia), suggested a movement away from the two-party arrangement. Chavez, who came to power backed by the leftist Patriotic Pole, a coalition of parties that includes the Communist Party of Venezuela, has dramatically changed the power structure in the country.

15LOCAL GOVERNMENT

Venezuela is divided into 21 states, 1 federal territory (Amazonas), the Federal District, and 72 offshore islands. All of the islands, except for the Isla de Margarita and adjacent islands (which together constitute a state), are classified as federal dependencies. As of 1985, the states were subdivided into 156 districts and 613 municipalities.

State government has been traditionally weak, with the state governor being the agent of the federal government directed to enforce national laws and decrees, as well as state legislation. Governors (including the governor of the Federal District) are appointed by the president and may be removed by him. According to the constitution the states are autonomous and are guaranteed the right to regulate their own affairs. They are given all powers not reserved to the nation or the municipalities. In reality, these powers are very few, since control of elections, education, health, agriculture, and labor is delegated to the national government. The state legislatures are unicameral.

Municipalities are autonomous in the election of their officials, in all matters within their competence, and in action regarding the collection, creation, and expenditure of their revenues. City councils vary from 5 to 22 members according to population. The council is popularly elected and, in turn, selects the mayor. According to the constitution, elections for state and municipal offices may not be held more often than once every two years or less often than once every five years. As with the other branches of government, the power structure of local government was expected to change radically with the new constitution.

16JUDICIAL SYSTEM

In August 1999, the National Constitutional Assembly (ANC) declared a judicial emergency to reform the highly discredited judiciary. The ANC immediately dismissed 16 judges. By the end of the year, 200 judges had been fired, mostly for corruption.

While the judicial system was independent, it was corrupt and inefficient. Most crimes in Venezuela went unpunished, and citizens often have taken the law into their own hands. In the prisons, more than 70% of inmates have never been formally charged with a crime, and they languish behind bars for years before their cases are heard. Prisons have been criticized for inhumane conditions.

The ANC approved the new Organic Code of Criminal Procedures in 1999, replacing the inquisitorial system with an open court system. For the first time, trials were open to the public, with oral proceedings and verdicts by juries or panels of judges. The new system introduced presumption of innocence and prevented police from arbitrarily detaining persons for up to eight days without charges. Judges no longer act as investigators. Now they are arbiters of law, presiding court sessions where prosecutors and defense attorneys argue cases in open court. Police investigators now work under the supervision of prosecutors. While judicial reforms were applauded by human rights organizations, it was uncertain how they would affect the judicial system in the long run. Intensive training will be required for judges, attorneys and police.

The Supreme Court of Justice remains the nation's highest tribunal and court of final appeal. The Prosecutor General provides opinions to the courts, investigates violations of constitutional rights of prisoners, and criminal conduct of public employees. The Ministry of Justice oversees the lower court system, selects and trains judges. The lower courts are made up of district and municipal courts, and trial and appeal courts that hear civil and criminal cases.

[17]ARMED FORCES

Venezuela's armed forces are professional and well equipped. In principle, all male Venezuelans 18 years of age are required to serve two years (or 30 months in the navy) and then to remain in the reserve until the age of 45. In practice, however, many males, including workers in essential occupations, students, and heads of households, are exempted from service.

Total armed strength in 2000 was 79,000, including 23,000 volunteers in the Fuerzas Armados de Cooperacion, an internal security force. The army had 34,000 regulars, including six infantry divisions and 12 specialized brigades. The navy had 15,000 members, including 5,000 marines; naval strength included two submarines and six frigates. The air force had 7,000 personnel, 124 combat aircraft, and 31 armed helicopters.

Defense expenditures in 1998 were $1.1 billion, or 1% of the GDP.

[18]INTERNATIONAL COOPERATION

Venezuela is a charter member of the UN, having joined on 15 November 1945, and participates in ECLAC and all the nonregional specialized agencies except the IDA. The nation is also a member of G-77, IADB, LAIA, OAS, and OPEC. On 31 December 1973, Venezuela entered the Andean Pact. In June 1974, Caracas hosted the third UN Conference on the Law of the Sea; as of late 1987, however, it had declined to endorse the Law of the Sea treaty. Venezuela was instrumental in the creation of the 25-member Latin American Economic System in October 1975. Venezuela is a member of the WTO.

Venezuela reportedly played an important role in supporting the Sandinistas in their successful effort to win power in Nicaragua. After the Sandinista takeover, Venezuela sought to reduce tensions between Nicaragua on one side and Honduras and the US on the other.

[19]ECONOMY

During the colonial era and until the development of petroleum resources, the exportation of coffee and cocoa and the raising of cattle and goats provided the main support for the economy. However, agriculture now accounts for only about 4% of the GDP. For over 40 years the economy has been completely dominated by the petroleum industry; in the mid-1980s, oil exports accounted for 90% of all export value, and in 1998 petroleum accounted for over 25% of the GDP (one-third of export revenues). The Venezuelan economy is therefore greatly influenced by petroleum market conditions and by OPEC pricing policies. The second most important mineral product is iron, and Venezuela's mineral wealth is augmented almost daily by discoveries of additional reserves. Industrial development is fostered by government policy.

The average annual GDP growth during 1970–80 was 5%, with a peak of 7.2% during 1974–77. In the late 1970s, the economy began to stagnate, and the GDP growth rate declined from 3.2% in 1978 to zero in 1979, with a negative rate of 1.5% recorded in 1980. Weakening world oil prices contributed to further economic stagnation in the 1980s when Venezuela had difficulty meeting its obligations on short-term loans accumulated by state-owned enterprises. Soft markets for oil, iron ore, and aluminum aggravated Venezuela's financial problems in 1982; the GDP declined during 1983–85. During 1980–90, average annual GDP growth was only 1.1%.

After severe adjustments experienced during 1989 and 1990, the main economic indicators improved considerably in 1991 and 1992. Real GDP was 10.4% and 7.3% respectively. Growth was led by expansion of the petroleum sector due mainly to the Persian Gulf War. Growth was also a result of the liberalization of the economy, including a privatization program initiated in 1990 and restructuring of the public sector enterprises. However, growth slowed down and real GDP contracted by 1.0% in 1993. In April 1996, President Caldera announced a shift towards a more free market orientation coupled with fiscal austerity to revitalized the economy. The government devalued the currency, eliminated exchange controls, and raised gasoline prices 369–862%. These moves were taken to reduce trade and fiscal deficits. Instead, they induced inflation, which was already at 60% in 1995 and rose to 103% in 1996.

During 1988–98, average annual GDP growth was 2.5%. Inflation remained stubbornly high; between 1990 and 1996, consumer prices rose by an average of about 50% per year. The inflation rate was at 30% in 1998. A recession during 1998 due to low oil prices triggered a steep rise in the cost of living and halted economic growth.

[20]INCOME

The US Central Intelligence Agency (CIA) reports that in 1998 Venezuela's gross domestic product (GDP) was estimated at $194.5 billion. The per capita GDP was estimated at $8,500. The annual growth rate of GDP was estimated at -0.9%. The average inflation rate in 1998 was 30%. The CIA defines GDP as the value of all final goods and services produced within a nation in a given year and computed on the basis of purchasing power parity (PPP) rather than value as measured on the basis of the rate of exchange. It was estimated that agriculture accounted for 4% of GDP, industry 63%, and services 33%.

The World Bank reports that for the same period per capita private consumption (in PPP terms) was $3,685. Private consumption includes expenditures of individuals, households, and nongovernmental organizations. It was estimated that between 1990 and 1998 private consumption grew at an annual rate of 0.8%. Approximately 30% of household consumption was spent on food, 17% on fuel, 16% on health care, and 13% on education. The richest 10% of the population accounted for approximately 37% of household consumption and the poorest 10% approximately 1.3%.

21 LABOR

Venezuela's economically active population in 1997 was 9,507,000. The distribution of employment among major economic sectors was as follows: services, 64%; industry, 23%; and agriculture, 13%. The unemployment rate was 11.4% as of 1997.

The Venezuelan labor movement, for all practical purposes, had its inception in 1928 with the formation of the Syndicalist Labor Federation of Venezuela. The movement, stunted by the Gómez dictatorship, grew rapidly after his death. After the election of Betancourt, the Confederation of Venezuelan Workers (Confederación de Trabajadores de Venezuela—CTV), which had been founded between 1945 and 1948 but outlawed by Pérez Jiménez, was reconstituted. Another major labor federation, the National Movement of Workers for Liberation (Movimiento Nacional de Trabajadores para la Liberación—MONTRAL), was formed in 1974. CTV has remained Venezuela's major labor confederation. In 1996, about 25% of the labor force was unionized.

There are fiscal controls over union funds. A strike may not be called before a conciliation attempt is made. Voluntary arbitration is encouraged, but arbitration may be ordered by the Ministry of Labor; awards are binding on all parties for a period of not less than six months. If no agreement is reached, a strike may be called 120 hours after the government labor inspector has been notified.

The comprehensive Labor Code enacted in 1990 extends to all public sector and private sector employees (except members of the armed forces) the right to form and join unions of their choosing. The Code also lowered the maximum workweek to 44 hours; the constitution provides for a minimum wage, the right to strike, and the right of labor to organize into unions. Labor laws include provisions for an eight-hour day, a paid vacation of at least 15 workdays a year, compulsory profit sharing, severance pay, death and disability payments, medical services, and social security.

The monthly minimum wage was $201 in the private sector for urban workers and $165 for rural workers. Minimum wage workers in the private sector received mandatory food and transport bonuses amounting to $65 per month.

Until the age of 16, minors may work only with restrictions as to hours and working conditions. The labor ministry effectively enforces this restriction in the formal economic sector but as many as one million children were believed to be working in the informal economy in 1996.

22 AGRICULTURE

In 1998, agriculture accounted for 4% of the GDP, engaging 8.8% of the economically active population. Venezuela continues to rely heavily on food and agricultural imports. Despite abundant resources favorable to agricultural production, 70% of cereals and 98% of oilseeds consumed in Venezuela are imported.

Venezuela does not have the rich soil of many other Latin American countries. In 1997, 3,490,000 hectares (8,624,000 acres), or 4% of the total land area, were used for temporary or permanent crops. The most highly developed agricultural region is the basin of Lake Valencia, west of Caracas and inland from Puerto Cabello. The principal crop of this area is coffee. Before oil came to dominate the economy, coffee accounted for 40–60% of all income from exports.

The main field crops are sugarcane, rice, corn, and sorghum, and the chief fruits are bananas, plantains, oranges, coconuts, and mangoes. The most important agricultural items for indus-trial use are cotton, tobacco, and sisal. Two varieties of tobacco grow in Venezuela, black and Virginia blond; the latter is used for the most part to make certain popular brands of US cigarettes under license. Sisal is grown and widely used to make cordage and bags for sacking grains and coffee. Thin strings of the fiber are also employed in hammocks, household bags, doormats, hats, and sandals. Agricultural production in 1998 (in tons) included sugarcane, 7,233,000; bananas, 1,135,000; corn, 938,000; rice, 673,000; sorghum, 386,000; plantains, 509,000; oranges, 528,000; potatoes, 349,000; cotton, 12,000; tobacco, 14,000; sisal, 14,000; and tomatoes, 292,000.

Under an agrarian reform law of 1960, three kinds of land are subject to expropriation by the government: uncultivated lands; lands worked indirectly through renters, sharecroppers, and other intermediaries; and lands suitable for cultivation that are being devoted to livestock raising. Compensation is paid for expropriated lands. Between 1960 and 1980, 8,467,000 hectares (20,922,295 acres) of land were distributed to 155,200 farming families who had never previously owned property. However, the land reform was adversely affected by mass migration of rural people to the cities.

23 ANIMAL HUSBANDRY

Since colonial days, cattle raising has been the dominant livestock industry in Venezuela. Chiefly criollos, or Spanish longhorns, the cattle are raised on the unfenced ranges of the llanos. Cross-breeding with shorthorns has been going on since the last half of the 19th century and with zebu since 1915. The government has made considerable progress in eradicating tick and other infestations and hoof and mouth disease. It buys breeding stock from the US, and finances programs to improve cattle production, processing, and distribution. The government also offers a subsidy for pasteurized milk, thereby helping to expand and improve the dairy industry.

Venezuela's livestock population in 1998 included 15,367,000 head of cattle, 3,200,000 goats, 4,756,000 hogs, 820,000 sheep, 500,000 horses, 440,000 burros, and 72,000 mules. Beef production increased from 147,000 tons in 1963 to 363,000 tons in 1998. In 1998, pork production was 105,000 tons; goat meat, 5,000 tons; mutton, 2,000 tons; and poultry, 495,000 tons. One of the few areas in which Venezuela is self-sufficient is beef, which is largely grass fed. Although significant amounts of pork and poultry are produced, they rely on imported feeds and other imported inputs. Fluid milk production reached 1498,000 tons in 1998, up 1.6% from 1997. Around 50% of the total fluid milk production is processed into cheese, 36% into powdered milk, 12% into pasteurized milk, and 2% into other dairy products. Venezuela relies on imports for 50% of its milk consumption.

24 FISHING

With its 2,816 km (1,750 mi) of open coast, Venezuela has vast fishing potential. Fish and fish products currently play a relatively minor role in Venezuela's international trade, but fish are extremely important domestically. Venezuela has the highest per capita fish consumption in Latin America, about three times that of the US. The principal fishing areas are La Guaira, the Paraguaná peninsula, and the Cariaco-Margarita-Carúpano area. The total catch in 1997 was 502,764 tons, up from 284,235 tons in 1986.

The fish-canning industry, begun in the 1940s, has had diffi-culty finding a market, since there has long been a preference for imported canned fish of higher quality. In recent years, however, exports to the US, the Netherlands Antilles, and other countries have increased. Tariff protection and improvements in quality have helped the industry.

25FORESTRY

Forest and woodlands covered about 50% of the land area in 1995. Partly because of the inaccessibility of forest areas, Venezuela's high-quality wood is very much underdeveloped. It is also misused by small farmers, who clear land for farming by burning trees without replacing them. The greatest concentration of forests lies south of the Orinoco, but the areas currently utilized are in the states of Portuguesa and Barinas. Cedar and mahogany are the principal trees cut; rubber, dividivi, mangrove bark, tonka beans, oil-bearing palm nuts, and medicinal plants are also produced. Roundwood output was 2,197,000 cu m in 1997, with 43% used as fuel wood. Sawn wood production was 224,000 cu m that year. Virtually all sectors of the forest products industry rely on domestic output to meet domestic demand.

26MINING

Principal commodities produced are aluminum, cement, diamonds, ferroalloys, gold, and iron ore. The most important metal mined in Venezuela is iron. Venezuela is Latin America's second-largest producer of iron ore (after Brazil), and the world's largest producer of direct-reduced iron. Iron ore production peaked at 26.4 million tons in 1974 before declining to 9.4 million tons in 1983, mainly because of the worldwide recession and the consequent lessening of the demand for steel. Average 1987–91 annual production amounted to 19,338,000 tons, for a relative ranking of tenth highest in the world. Production of iron ore in 1995 was 19,484,000 tons, and by 1997 it had declined to 18,359,000 tons.

Iron mining was developed mainly by the Orinoco Mining Co., a subsidiary of US Steel, and by Iron Mines of Venezuela, a subsidiary of Bethlehem Steel. The industry was nationalized as of 1 January 1975 when a state-owned regional development corporation assumed control. Late in 1975, a new state enterprise, the Orinoco Ferrominerals Co., was established to run the nationalized concerns.

Gold, the first metal found in Venezuela, reached its production peak in 1890. Gold was exported until 1950, but thereafter it became necessary to import small amounts. Production rose from 570 kg in 1981 to 7,259 kg in 1995. Then it more than tripled, to 22,322 by 1997. Since about 1930, both industrial and gem diamonds have been mined in the Gran Sabana region in the southern part of the state of Bolívar. Diamond production in 1974 had an extraordinary increase of 468,200 carats over 1973, to a total of 1,249,000 carats, but output has since fallen to 158,260 carats in 1997. Deposits of high-grade bauxite, estimated at 300 million tons in 1991, were discovered at Los Pijiguaos, in the northern part of the state of Bolívar. Today Venezuela is the world's seventh-largest producer of bauxite and alumina. Bauxite production was 4,967,000 tons in 1997; alumina production was 1,730,000 tons.

Other minerals extracted are sulfur, gypsum, limestone, salt (produced as a government monopoly), granite, clay, and phosphate rock. Minerals known to exist but not yet exploited are manganese (with deposits estimated at several million tons), mercury, nickel, magnesite, cobalt, mica, cyanite, and radioactive materials.

27ENERGY AND POWER

With vast petroleum deposits, extensive waterways, and an abundance of natural gas, Venezuela possesses great electric power potential. The country is 90% electrified, one of the highest rates in Latin America. In 1998, net installed capacity was 22,533 MW; total electrical output in 1998 was an estimated 70,390 million kWh. Until 1975, the electric power companies were privately owned, with the exception of the government-run Maracay Electric. In March 1975, President Pérez announced that all electrical generating companies would be taken over by the state by the end of the year and merged into a single enterprise. Privatization of many government-owned enterprises began in 1991. The electricity sector in 1996 was a hybrid of state-owned and private companies which used a fully integrated system of 875 kv, 400 kv, 230 kv, and 115 kv transmission lines. The largest private utility, Electricidad de Caracas, serves one million customers in the Caracas metropolitan area and is the largest private company in Venezuela.

In 1964, a regional development agency, the Corporación Venezolana de Guayana, began construction of one of the world's largest hydroelectric power plants. Constructed across the Caroní River, which flows out of the Guiana Highlands, the Guri Dam began operations in November 1968, generating 525,000 kW of power. The capacity of the Guri project increased to 14.5 million kW in 1982. About 75% of total electric generating capacity is hydropower. Hydropower generation is expected to grow as Venezuela adds 8,000 MW during 1996–2006. Hydroelectric potential is estimated at 70,000–80,000 MW or more.

Venezuela is among the world's 10 leading oil producers. Together with Mexico and the North Sea area, Venezuela is among the most important producers of oil for the Western world outside of the Middle East, with a net exportable capacity of about two million barrels of oil per day (including 1.3 million barrels per day to the US). Venezuela's proven oil reserves are the largest outside the Middle East. In early 2000, proven oil reserves were estimated at 72.6 billion barrels. The Orinoco tar belt has potential in-place reserves of 1.2 trillion barrels inside a region about 434 km (270 mi) by 64 km (40 mi) in eastern Venezuela. About 72% of Venezuela's reserves are heavy or extra-heavy. Venezuela will soon need more advanced refineries to process heavy crude into more marketable products.

Petroleum production in Venezuela began in 1917, when 120,000 barrels were produced. Until the early 1960s, Venezuela was the world's third-largest producer of oil after the US and the USSR. Output rose to a peak daily volume of 3,700,000 barrels a day in 1970, but in 1974, President Pérez began a conservation program, resulting in cutbacks to 2,400,000 barrels a day by mid-1975. The 1986 collapse of oil prices eventually forced OPEC producers to set production quotas, which cut Venezuela's output to 1.5 million barrels per day for the first half of 1987. At the end of 1999, OPEC's crude oil production quota for Venezuela was about 2.7 million barrels per day, but production capacity was around 3.3 million barrels per day. Production rose from 1,902,000 barrels per day in 1988 to an estimated 3,300,000 barrels per day in 1998.

The output of natural gas was an estimated 28,310 million cu m in 1998. Proven reserves totaled 4 trillion cu m in early 2000. The long-awaited Cristobal Colon liquefied natural gas (LNG) export project received congressional approval in August 1993. The $4.9-billion multinational project plans to eventually export up to six million tons of LNG annually, supplied by four offshore Caribbean fields utilizing 77 km (48 mi) of pipelines. As of 1996, the project was being delayed due to the forecasted low prices for natural gas.

Venezuela's present production of crude oil is confined mostly to the western part of the country. The eastern shore and floor of Lake Maracaibo produce about 50% of the total oil extracted. A plan to develop the Orinoco tar belt was reactivated in the late 1980s after having been postponed in 1982 because of petroleum price cuts. Production in the initial phases is to be directed to the thermoelectric sector as a substitute for coal and conventional oil.

On 29 August 1975, President Pérez signed into law the Oil Industry Nationalization Act, under which all concessions to private oil companies were rescinded as of 31 December 1975. A state holding company, Petroleum of Venezuela (Petróleos de

Venezuela—Petrovén), was established in September 1975 with an initial capitalization of $465 million. Petrovén obtained a 50-year renewable monopoly over Venezuelan petroleum production, beginning 1 January 1976. Initial compensation of B1.9 billion was paid in December 1975; total compensation was to exceed B5 billion, of which B3.9 billion was to be paid in tax-free five-year bonds, at 6% interest, redeemable only in Venezuelan oil. Within a few years, Petrovén's 16 original operating companies were combined into four: Lagovén, the largest subsidiary, formerly the Creole Petroleum Corp., an Exxon affiliate; Maravén, formerly a Royal Dutch/Shell subsidiary; Menevén, formerly Mene Grande, a Gulf subsidiary; and Corpovén, including the former Mobil Oil subsidiary. In 1986, the state holding company (now referred to as Petróleos de Venezuela, S. A.—PdVSA) was reorganized. Menevén was absorbed into Corpovén, and the new operating company ceded its operations in Zulia and Falcón states to Maraven and Lagovén. PdVSA's reputation has developed into what may be considered the best-managed state oil company in the world; the company has major refinery, pipeline, and service station networks in Europe, the US, and elsewhere in the Caribbean.

In July 1995, Venezuela's oil sector was opened to limited foreign participation in exploration and production. Congressional support also indicates support for the eventual limited privatization of PdVSA, which was the world's second largest oil company in 1995, with profits of over $3 billion. Two decades after nationalizing its oil industry, Venezuela is now trying to establish strategic alliances with foreign oil companies. Production sharing contracts signed in July 1996 guarded rights in eight promising oil regions estimated to contain over seven billion barrels of crude oil.

28INDUSTRY

Since the economy was largely dependent on oil, Venezuela neglected other domestic industries for decades in favor of importing goods to satisfy Venezuelan consumer needs. The government has encouraged industrial diversification and development through protective tariffs and tax exemptions for reinvestment. Industrial output grew by 1.6% on average during the 1980s and by 3.8% annually during the 1990s. Manufacturing industries grew by an average of 4.3% annually during the 1980s and 1.7% per year between 1988 and 1998. In 1998, manufacturing accounted for an estimated 15% of GDP.

Although much of Venezuela's petroleum is exported in crude form, petroleum refining is a major industry. Refinery production capacity amounted to about three billion barrels per day in 1999. The steel industry operates at about 48% of capacity. The Venezuelan metal engineering industry produces auto body parts, valves, boilers, piping, wire mesh, and many other cast products. By 1983, Venezuela had the largest aluminum-smelting capacity in Latin America, with a total of 400,000 tons a year. Bauxite is processed in plants owned by the three state companies—Bauxalum, Venalum, and Alcasa. Other industries include shipbuilding, automobile assembly, and fertilizer manufacture.

The government is involved in a massive decentralization project to relocate industries in the peripheral cities and the interior. Valencia, the capital of Carabobo State, is a major new industrial center. A second major industrial development scheme has made Ciudad Guayana the hub of a vast industrial area with a 160-km (100-mi) radius. Puerto Ordaz was founded on the basis of the Cerro Bolívar iron ore deposits. West of Puerto Ordaz are the Matanzas steel mill, with a yearly capacity of 750,000 tons, and the Bauxalum bauxite-processing installation.

29SCIENCE AND TECHNOLOGY

The National Council of Scientific and Technological Research (founded in 1967) and the State Ministry for Science and Technology direct and coordinate research activities. Among the principal research institutes, academies, and learned societies are the National Academy of Medicine (1904), the Academy of Physical, Mathematical, and Natural Sciences (1917), and the Venezuelan Association for the Advancement of Science (1950). Major research institutes include the Institute of Experimental Medicine (1940), the Venezuelan Scientific Research Institute (1959), and the Center for Investigation of Petroleum Technology (1979). All of these societies and institutes are located in Caracas. Venezuela has 20 universities and colleges that offer courses in basic and applied sciences. In 1987–97, science and engineering students accounted for 26% of college and university enrollments. In 1987–97, research and development expenditures amounted to 0.5% of GNP; 32 technicians and 209 scientists and engineers per million people were engaged in research and development.

30DOMESTIC TRADE

The three primary distribution centers for import trade are the Caracas area, the Maracaibo area, and an area that centers on Ciudad Bolívar and serves the vast inland llanos region and the Guiana Highlands. In Caracas are located the main offices of the national and foreign banks, many of the important industries, and the largest commercial houses. Wholesale importers and distributors in Caracas cover the entire country by means of branch offices, stores, and traveling salespeople. The most common and widespread form of retail selling used to be door-to-door, but the number of large shopping centers and supermarkets has risen in recent years. Supermarkets handle over half of all retail food sales, with the rest mostly from bodegas (delicatessens) and abastos (small family-operated shops). There are also numerous farmers' markets throughout Caracas and the rest of Venezuela.

Stores are usually open from 9 AM to 1 PM and from 3 to 7 PM, Monday through Saturday. Normal banking hours are from 8:30 to 11:30 AM and from 2 to 4:30 PM on weekdays only.

31FOREIGN TRADE

Since 1950, Venezuelan foreign trade has gone through a number of bust and boom phases linked with oil prices. The first, between 1950 and 1957, was marked by the maturation of the new oil industry and high demand. The second, from the late 1950s through the 1960s, was characterized by a decline in world petroleum prices and a general drop in investment; during this period, exports of iron ore became increasingly important. The third phase, beginning in the early 1970s, featured a fivefold rise in petroleum prices and a staggering increase in the value of Venezuela's petroleum exports, despite declining output. The 1986 plunge in world oil prices was followed by a sustained period of growth in the sector, that lost momentum in 1998.

Crude petroleum (47%) and refined petroleum products (29%) are the main commodity exports of Venezuela, with refined petroleum products accounting for 6.1% of the world's total exports. Other exports include aluminum (4.6%), automobiles (1.2%), iron and steel (2.8%), and gold (1.1%).

In 1996 Venezuela's imports were distributed among the following categories:

Consumer goods	10.6%
Food	10.8%
Fuels	0.8%
Industrial supplies	38.6%
Machinery	27.4%
Transportation	11.6%
Other	0.2%

Principal trading partners in 1998 (in millions of US dollars) were as follows:

COUNTRY	EXPORTS	IMPORTS	BALANCE
United States	9,157	6,520	2,637
Colombia	1,570	958	612
Dominican Republic	878	3	875
Brazil	791	706	85
Canada	569	442	127
Mexico	303	546	-243
Spain	269	385	-116
Germany	264	698	-434
Japan	242	655	-413
Italy	196	740	-544

32 BALANCE OF PAYMENTS

Venezuela has enjoyed an enviable balance-of-payments position for many years. Although the country was forced to import goods to satisfy the demand for many industrial, construction, and household items, its income from exports has more than equaled its expenditures for imports.

Venezuela experienced foreign exchange problems throughout the 1990s, largely because of the fluctuation of world oil prices. Venezuela's balance of payments position deteriorated from its strong performance of 1991. In 1992, the merchandise trade surplus fell to $1.6 billion, a drop of 66% from 1991, primarily due to the economic recovery program and a decline in exports. The current account balance rose from –3.7% of GDP in 1993 to an estimated 11.5% in 1996, but fell by 2.8% in 1998.

The US Central Intelligence Agency reports that in 1998 the purchasing power parity of Venezuela's exports was $16.9 billion while imports totaled $12.4 billion resulting in a trade balance of $4.5 billion.

The International Monetary Fund (IMF) reports that in 1998 Venezuela had exports of goods totaling $17,564 million and imports totaling $14,816 million. The services credit totaled $1,457 million and debit $5,054 million. The following table summarizes Venezuela's balance of payments as reported by the IMF for 1998 in millions of US dollars.

Current Account		-2,562
Balance on goods	2,748	
Balance on services	-3,597	
Balance on income	-1,559	
Current transfers	-154	
Capital Account		...
Financial Account		844
Direct investment abroad	-267	
Direct investment in Venezuela	4,435	
Portfolio investment assets	806	
Portfolio investment liabilities	239	
Other investment assets	-3,630	
Other investment liabilities	-739	
Net Errors and Omissions		-1,226
Reserves and Related Items		2,944

33 BANKING AND SECURITIES

The Central Bank of Venezuela (Banco Central de Venezuela–BCV, founded in 1939) is the fiscal agent of the government, responsible for fixing the rediscount rates, holding the country's gold and foreign exchange reserves, making collections and payments on behalf of the Treasury, and buying foreign exchange acquired from the oil companies and from exporters and reselling it to the government or to commercial banks. It also cooperates with government departments and other institutions in the work of special commissions, and is the sole note-issuing agency.

The state banking system consists of the Central Bank, the Industrial Bank of Venezuela, the Workers' Bank, seven regional and development banks controlled by the Venezuelan Development Corp., and the Agricultural Bank. In the private sector there are commercial banks, investment banks, mortgage banks, and savings and loan associations. The country's first mortgage bank, the Mortgage Bank of Urban Credit, initiated operations in Caracas in 1958.

The government has traditionally played a key role in the financial system, not so much because of budget financing needs (which until recently were modest by Latin American standards) but because of its involvement in medium- and long-term credit institutions which were set up to meet deficiencies in the system of financial intermediation, and also to channel the high oil revenues into productive sectors. The commercial banking system is, however, almost entirely privately owned. In 1994 there were 33 commercial banks, 16 mortgage banks providing long-term loans for construction, land acquisition, or real estate development, and 29 financieras.

Until 1972, Caracas was the only city in Latin America with two stock exchanges: the Commercial Exchange of Caracas (founded in 1947, although informal trading in stocks has taken place in Caracas since 1805), controlled by the Caracas Chamber of Commerce, and the Commercial Exchange of Miranda State (founded in July 1958). The two exchanges were merged under the terms of the 1972 Capital Markets Law, which regulates the trading of securities and the activities of brokerage houses. There is also an exchange in Valencia. The National Securities Commission, established in 1973, oversees public securities transactions. Not all the securities of Venezuelan corporations are listed on the exchanges, and new securities are constantly added.

Venezuela's stock market was among the best performing in the world in 1996 because of restored confidence in economic policy and currency stability. The index of the Caracas stock exchange closed the year at 6,690.06, a 135% increase in dollar terms from the low base at the start of the year. In 1999, the index closed at 5,418.01. The average number of trades decreased in 1999 by 33% from 1998, due to problems in the financial sector.

34 INSURANCE

All insurance companies operating in Venezuela are under the direction of the Ministry of Development. The insurance industry is an important source of investment capital. It is regulated by the Superintendent of Insurance.

35 PUBLIC FINANCE

Petroleum provided about 67% of total revenues in 1992, while personal and corporate income taxes represented only 29% of total current revenues that year. Although revenues increased greatly in the 1980s, expenditures grew at an even faster rate, mainly because of heavy spending to combat the nation's pressing social and industrial problems. Falling oil prices in the mid-1980s caused a severe deterioration in the deficit. In 1994, subsidies and other current transfers accounted for 32% of the federal government's expenditures; goods and services (including wages for government employees), 30%; interest payments, 21%; and capital expenditure, 14%.

Budget surpluses were recorded in 1990 and 1991 (0.4% and 0.8% of GDP, respectively), due neither to fiscal restraint nor enhanced tax collections, but largely to privatization revenues. In 1992, however, the government recorded a deficit equivalent to 6.1% of GDP. According to the Central Bank, the central government's deficit in 1994 amounted to 6.8% of GDP, but it declined to 2.8% in 1998. Petroleum revenues accounted for about half of the government budget in 1999, but amounted to only about 3.9% of total GDP.

The US Central Intelligence Agency (CIA) estimates that in 1996 Venezuela's central government took in revenues of approximately $11.99 billion and had expenditures of $11.48 billion including capital expenditures of $3 billion. Overall, the government registered a surplus of approximately $510 million. External debt totaled $36.9 billion in 1998.

The following table shows an itemized breakdown of government revenues and expenditures. The percentages were calculated from data reported by the International Monetary Fund. The dollar amounts (millions) are based on the CIA estimates provided above.

REVENUE AND GRANTS	100%	11,990
Tax revenue	73.6%	8,826
Non-tax revenue	26.4%	3,164
EXPENDITURES	100%	11,480

36 TAXATION

Almost all forms of taxation are the responsibility of the federal government; it apportions federal tax revenue to the states, which, in turn, allocate a portion to the municipalities. Cities may levy taxes on such items as water and other municipal services and the exploitation of community lands.

The basic personal income tax is progressive and ranges from 6% to 34%. However, different rates apply to income from special sources, including oil and other minerals and proceeds from gambling or lotteries. Corporate income tax ranges from 15% to 34%. Oil income is taxed at a flat rate of 67.7%. Exemptions are available for income from new industries or from agriculture, livestock, reforestation, and fishing.

Municipal license fees range from 0.25% to 10% of gross revenue. There are also inheritance and gift taxes, a real estate tax, an entertainment and advertising tax (in the Federal District), and minor excise taxes on liquor, tobacco, cigarettes, and petroleum products. A value-added tax became effective in 1993 and is presently levied at a rate of 12.5% to 20%. A 34% tax on dividends was implemented for foreign companies in 2000.

37 CUSTOMS AND DUTIES

Duties on imports are calculated ad valorem, according to government classifications. At the government's discretion, export duties may also be levied. Transit duties are required on certain goods, including hides, cocoa, coffee, cotton, and plumes. The government may also increase duties on items coming in from certain countries; in addition, it may establish import quotas or subject imports to licensing to protect domestic industry.

In 1967, Venezuela joined LAFTA, which became LAIA in 1981. The ad valorem duty system was adopted in 1973 to harmonize Venezuela's tariff structure with that of the other members of the Andean Pact. As of 1996, Venezuela adheres to the Andean Pact's Common External Tariff, which ranges from 5% to 20%. The average tariff rate is 10% except for automobiles, which carry a duty of 35%. Venezuela has three free trade zones: the Isla de Margarita, the Paraguaná Peninsula Industrial Zone, and the Port of La Guaira.

After several years of negotiations, the Group of Three (Colombia, Mexico, and Venezuela) signed a free-trade agreement in Cartagena. The agreement went into effect at the beginning of 1995 and commits the countries to lifting most trade restrictions by 2007. In 1995, Venezuela also implemented an Andean Pact with Colombia and Ecuador that established common external tariffs. Venezuela also has a preferential agreement with the Caribbean Common Market (CARICOM) which started tariff reductions in 1998. Venezuela also has a free trade accord with the Southern Cone Common Market (Mercosur).

38 FOREIGN INVESTMENT

Before the 1970s, over 97% of the total foreign investment in Venezuela was made by firms representing the US and the UK. In 1972, total foreign investment in Venezuela was $5.5 billion, of which 85% was in oil. Of the total, 68% came from US sources, 9% from the Netherlands, and 7% from the UK. Until the mid-1970s, Venezuela imposed few restrictions on foreign investment. Beginning in 1974, however, new foreign investors were required to obtain advance authorization from the Superintendency of Foreign Investment (Superintendencia de Inversiones Extranjeras—SIEX). After the nationalization of petroleum companies on 1 January 1976, the total foreign investment in Venezuela declined sharply; by the end of 1984, registered US direct investment was $1.7 billion, or approximately 55% of all foreign holdings in Venezuela.

The economic reforms started in 1989 stripped away many barriers to trade and investment. The government has been opening up production activities of the petroleum sector to foreign participation on a contract basis. In 1995, Venezuela's oil sector was opened to limited foreign participation in exploration and production, and political support has grown for a limited privatization of PdVSA, the state-owned oil company. Foreigners may now buy shares in national or mixed companies, but repatriation of dividends and their reinvestment of profits is restricted. Beginning in 2000, a 34% tax on dividends was levied on foreign companies that had not sufficiently reinvested in the country. Foreign direct investment totaled almost $3.5 billion in 1998, down from $4.5 billion in 1997.

39 ECONOMIC DEVELOPMENT

The Venezuelan economy has been directed by government policy since the 1970s. The iron and petroleum industries were nationalized in 1974–75, and the electrical generating industry was also a state enterprise. The government operated the salt and match industries; set the prices of pharmaceuticals, petroleum products, milk, meat, and other consumer goods and services; and controlled rents. The terms of Andean Pact membership also obligated the government to keep a tight rein on foreign trade and foreign investment.

Development policy from the 1950s through the late 1970s stressed import substitution, industrialization, and foreign investment. A new policy, inaugurated in 1979 and formulated in detail in the sixth national development plan (1981–85), was intended to eliminate price controls and reduce protectionism. The government also sought to reduce Venezuela's dependence on oil by industrial diversification, to pay more attention to agriculture, and to devote greater resources to social development, particularly housing, education, public services, and health. The economic crisis of the early 1980s led to a partial abandonment of the new policy. An economic adjustment program aimed at decreasing inflation, limiting imports, and cutting government spending was announced in April 1983, and further austerity measures were imposed in February 1984. In late 1986, the Lusinchi government announced a three-year plan to stimulate the economy through government spending.

Venezuela's economic reform program, initiated in 1989, focused on transforming the country from a traditionally state-dominated, oil driven economy, toward a more market-oriented, diversified, and export-oriented economy. However, the financial crisis persisted and the administration assumed direct control over the banking system. Much of the liquidity created by the support for the financial sector was soaked up by the Central Bank. The government confirmed its commitment to selling off state enterprises. The bolivar was in free-fall before the government announced exchanged controls.

In April 1996, the Caldera administration adopted an economic stabilization program with the backing of the IMF. The fundamental goal of the plan was to reduce inflation by maintaining a surplus in consolidated public sector finances. The program also encouraged real growth in the non-oil economy.

Deficit reduction through fiscal policy was also defined as a goal. The government increased general sales taxes, improved tax administration, and increased fuel prices. The program also called for the elimination of price controls on most goods and services.

The 1999–2000 economic plan called for reduced inflation, increased privatization, and higher taxes on foreign operations in Venezuela. An increase of the public budget was supposed to reduce inflation, as in the 1996 plan, but the traditional overspending of the government (one report claimed $24,000 per month for pension plans in the state-run oil company) may undermine this plan. The dividends tax on foreign investment in Venezuela offsets any privatization plans by reducing the flow of capital from other countries. The country remains dependent upon oil revenues.

40 SOCIAL DEVELOPMENT

The social security system was originally implemented in 1940, and was revised and amended by law in 1966, 1989, and 1991. The system covers medical care, maternity benefits, incapacity and invalidity, retirement and survivors' pensions, burial costs, and a marriage bonus. The employer is assessed about 5% on average of each employee's salary, with the worker paying about 2%. Old age pensions are provided at age 60 for men and age 55 for women, with early retirement permitted for those in arduous occupations. Medical coverage is financed by an additional contribution of about 2% from employees and about 3.5% by employers. Unemployment benefits are paid for a period of 26 weeks. These programs exclude temporary and casual workers; self-employed; and domestic workers.

In July 1982, a reform of the Venezuelan civil code extended women's rights, but women are still underrepresented in political and economic life. Women are protected by legislation that prohibits discrimination in pay or working conditions, but these are not always observed in practice. In 2000, there were 12 female deputies. The Law Against Violence Toward Women and Children went into effect in 1999.

Approximately 25 indigenous ethnic groups exist in Venezuela. They have limited decision-making power on issues that directly affect their land. Few have been granted legal title to their lands. The territory of the Yanomami is continuously encroached upon by Brazilian gold miners and in 1993, 16 Yanomami were killed by miners. As of 1998, the government was still working toward a mediated resolution of charges stemming from the incident.

The human rights situation is poor, with reports of extrajudicial killings, arbitrary detentions, and the abuse of detainees. Human rights organizations operate openly. Prisons are regularly the sites of murderous violence. In 1994, Amnesty International declared that Venezuela's prisons were the most dangerous in Latin America. In 1999 the national assembly declared a prison emergency and took steps to remedy conditions in the nation's prisons.

41 HEALTH

Despite strenuous government efforts in the field of public health, Venezuela lacks a sufficient number of physicians for its booming population. The birthrate was 24.7 per 1,000 people in 1998. In 1997 there were 2.4 physicians per 1,000 inhabitants.

Great strides have been made in improving public health conditions. The death rate was reduced from 21.4 per 1,000 population in 1915 to 10.8 in 1950 and 4.7 in 1990–95. The infant mortality rate, 50.2 per 1,000 live births in 1971, fell to 22 in 1996. Life expectancy rose to an average of 72.9 years in 1998. Commonly reported diseases included malaria (14,610 cases in the first half of 1997); and tuberculosis (3,056 cases in 1995). Leading causes of death per 100,000 people in 1994 were:

communicable diseases (79.5); neoplasms (100.1); injuries (74.6) and diseases of the circulatory system (257.9). Venezuela is virtually free of typhoid and yellow fever. To maintain this status, the Department of Health and Social Welfare continues its drainage and mosquito control programs. It also builds aqueducts and sewers in towns of fewer than 5,000 persons. In 1995, 79% of the population had access to safe water. From 1989–95, about 6% of children under five years old were considered malnourished. Venezuela currently fortifies maize flour with iron and vitamin A. Immunization rates for children up to one year old in 1997 were tuberculosis (98%); diphtheria, pertussis, and tetanus (60%); polio (76%); and measles (68%). Health care expenditures per capita were $229 in 1995 and equaled 7.6% of the Venezuelan gross domestic product.

The HIV-1 seroprevalence rate in 1997 was 0.7 per 100 adults. In 1996 there were 226 new AIDS cases.

42 HOUSING

In 1928, the Workers' Bank was founded as a public housing agency of the federal government. Between 1959 and mid-1966, 23,881 low-cost units (houses and apartments) were constructed by the Workers' Bank throughout the country. By spending 75% of housing funds in rural areas and 25% in the cities, reversing the earlier ratio, the government hoped to cut down the exodus of peasants to Caracas and to maintain the nation's essential agricultural labor force. A housing program was initiated in 1958 to build low-cost rural homes to replace the existing mud and thatch huts with homes built of cement and earthen blocks with asbestos roofs. The average cost of each home came to an estimated B4,450, payable in 20 years at a rate of B20 monthly. By 1969, the government had built 104,598 cheap and comfortable homes for lower-income groups, 57,675 in cities and 46,923 in rural areas.

Construction of low-cost housing units during the early 1970s proceeded at a rate of about 100,000 a year. During 1977–81, the public sector built 167,325 housing units, and the private sector 71,922. In 1981, the government introduced new low-interest housing loans, but that policy did not prevent a housing slump that persisted from 1982 through 1986 as a result of the general recession; housing units built by the public sector in 1986 totaled 91,666. The total number of housing units in the mid-1990s exceeded three million.

In the mid-1990s, more than 60% of all housing units were detached or semi-detached houses; nearly 20% were apartments; and over 15% were improvised living quarters. Owners occupied 75% of all dwellings, and almost 20% were rented.

43 EDUCATION

Venezuela has made considerable progress in education in recent years. An extensive literacy campaign has been conducted by the Venezuelan business community since 1980. For the year 2000, adult illiteracy was estimated at 7.0% (males, 6.7%; females, 7.3%). Public education from kindergarten through university is free, and education is compulsory for children ages 6 through 15. Approximately 20% of the national budget is assigned to education.

Preprimary schools are being established throughout the country by the government. After nine years of elementary school, children undergo two to three years of secondary school, which comes in two stages: the first is designed to provide a general education in the sciences and the humanities; the second prepares students for the university and offers specialization in philosophy and literature, physical science and mathematics, or biological science. In 1997, there were 4,262,221 students enrolled in elementary schools, with 202,195 teachers. Also in 1997, secondary schools enrolled 377,984 students and employed approximately 34,000 teachers. Technical and vocational schools provide instruction in industry and commerce, the trades, nursing, and social welfare.

There are 14 universities, both national and private, including the University of Venezuela (founded in 1725), Los Andes University (1785), Simón Bolívar University (1970), and the Open University (1977). Leading private institutions were the Andrés Bello Catholic University (1953), Santa María University (1953), and the Metropolitan University of Caracas (1970). Over 47 institutes of higher learning, colleges, and polytechnic institutes exist where students pursue at least 180 different fields or professions. As of 1998, all universities had a combined enrollment that exceeded 300,000, representing a 40% increase over the last decade.

44LIBRARIES AND MUSEUMS

Venezuela's largest library is the National Library, which was founded in 1833 and has over two million volumes. In 1958, the family of Pedro Manuel Arcaya donated his library of 100,000 rare volumes to the National Library. Both the National Library and National Archives are in Caracas, as are many of the largest libraries in the country. Other libraries include the Library of the Venezuelan Institute for Scientific Research (500,000 volumes), the National Academy of History (100,000), the Central University of Venezuela (280,000), Los Andes University in Mérida (500,000), the Andrés Bello Catholic University in Caracas (116,000), and public libraries and reading rooms in most state capitals.

Bolívar Museum, founded in 1911, has about 1,500 exhibits dealing with the life of Simon Bolívar and his fellow patriots in the independence movement. The National Pantheon, located in the restored Church of the Holy Trinity (dating from 1744), contains the ashes of Bolívar and the remains of other national heroes. The Birthplace of Bolívar (Bolívar's house) is also a national museum. The Fine Arts Museum, founded in 1938, contains paintings and sculpture by Venezuelan and foreign artists. The Natural Science Museum contains about 30,000 scientific exhibits. Other notable institutions include the Phelps Ornithological Collection, containing exhibits of thousands of Venezuelan birds, the Museum of Colonial Art, and the National Gallery of Art. All the preceding museums are located in Caracas, as are the Fine Arts Museum of Caracas, the Museum of Folklore, and the Pedagogical Museum of Art History. In Ciudad Bolívar are the Talavera Museum, with pre-Columbian and colonial exhibits, and the Jesus Soto Museum of Modern Art, founded in 1971; in Maracaibo are the Natural Science Museum and Urdaneta Museum of Military History; and in Trujillo is the Cristóbal Mendoza Museum.

45MEDIA

Venezuela is covered by a network of telephone, telegraph, and radiotelephone services and is also served by international cable and radiotelephone systems. In 1991, the government sold 40% of the state-owned CANTV to a consortium led by GTE. In 1995 there were 2,082,800 telephones in use. As of 1999, there were 181 AM radio stations and 66 television stations. In 1997 there were 471 radios, 172 television sets, and 46 mobile phones in use per 1,000 population.

Leading Venezuelan newspapers (all published in Caracas, except as noted), with their 1999 circulations, are as follows:

Diario Ultimas Noticias	285,000
Meridiano	300,000
El Nacional	200,000
El Mundo	270,000
Diario 2001	120,000
El Universal	180,000
Panorama (Maracaibo)	125,000

During the Gómez dictatorship, there was no freedom of the press whatsoever; suppression of newspapers was again practiced under the dictatorship of Marcos Pérez Jiménez. With the overthrow of his regime in January 1958, complete press freedom was proclaimed. Restrictions were imposed again during the second Betancourt administration. Since the late 1960s, however, the press has been generally open and free.

As of 1996, there were some 357,000 personal computers in Venezuela; in 1998, there were three Internet hosts per 1,000 population.

46ORGANIZATIONS

Organization membership for the vast majority of Venezuelans is confined to labor unions and professional societies. Industrial, commercial, and agricultural management associations—including the National Association of Merchants and Industrialists, the Industrial Chamber of Caracas, the National Confederation of Associations of Agricultural Producers, and the National Association of Metallurgical Industries and Mining—are represented nationally by the Federation of Chambers, which is influential in shaping foreign and domestic trade policy.

47TOURISM, TRAVEL, AND RECREATION

Since the early 1970s, Venezuela has sought foreign investors for the construction, rehabilitation, and management of top-ranking hotels. As Venezuela's economic restructuring progresses, the tourism sector is expected to undergo privatization. Angel Falls in Bolívar, the highest waterfall in the world, is a major tourist attraction for travelers to Venezuela. The number of foreign visitors in 1998 was an estimated 837,061. Tourism receipts totaled $1.1 billion in 1997. That year there were 71,737 hotel rooms with 154,547 beds.

According to 1999 UN estimates, the cost of staying in Caracas is $278 per day. Approximately 60% of daily expenses are accounted for by hotel charges. The cost of staying elsewhere is estimated at $90 per day.

A valid passport and visa issued by a Venezuelan consulate are required for entry into the country. Tourist attractions include Angel Falls, the many remembrances of Bolívar, numerous beach resorts, and the duty-free shopping and superb water sports facilities of the Isla de Margarita.

The most popular sports are baseball, football (soccer), bullfighting, cockfighting, horse racing, and water-related activities. Cultural life in the national capital offers, among other attractions, the Ballet Nuevo Mundo de Caracas.

48FAMOUS VENEZUELANS

No participant in the drama of Venezuelan history is as well known, both nationally and internationally, as the great Liberator of the South American revolution, Simón Bolívar (1783–1830). Renowned for his military genius and his ability to lead and to inspire, Bolívar also wrote brilliantly and prophetically on government and international politics. Among the greatest Venezuelan literary figures was Andrés Bello (1781–1864), outstanding in journalism, history, law, literary criticism, philology, and philosophy. Francisco de Miranda (1750–1816) is credited with bringing the first printing press to Venezuela and publishing the first newspaper, *La Gaceta de Caracas;* he was also an adventurer who, for a three-month period in 1812, held dictatorial powers in Venezuela. For most of the period since independence was achieved, a series of dictators held power, including Antonio Guzmán Blanco (1829–99), Cipriano Castro (1858?–1924), Juan Vicente Gómez (1857?–1935), and Marcos Pérez Jiménez (b.1914). Rómulo Betancourt (1908–81) was a leading political leader in the decades after World War II.

Simón Rodríguez (1771–1854), called the "American Rousseau," was the leading liberal scholar of the prerevolutionary period. Other writers of note were Rafael María Baralt (1810–60) and Juan Vicente González (1811–66), known as the father of Venezuelan national literature. Fermín Toro (1807–74) introduced the Indianist movement into Venezuelan romantic poetry. José Antonio Calcaño (1827–97) was referred to as "the Nightingale" for the flowing beauty of his verse. A noted poet and educator was Cecilio Acosta (1831–81), who was also Venezuela's first corresponding member of the Spanish Royal Academy and the author of the Venezuelan penal code. Juan Antonio Pérez Bonalde (1846–92) is considered Venezuela's greatest romantic novelist of the 19th century. The outstanding writers of the later 19th century were Manuel Díaz Rodríguez (1868–1927) and Manuel Fombona Palacio (1857–1903). The most famous contemporary writer, Rómulo Gallegos (1884–1969), gained world renown almost overnight with the publication of his *Doña Bárbara* in 1929. Other prominent contemporary writers include the poet, novelist, and playwright Mariano Picón Salas (1901–65); the novelist Ramón Díaz Sánchez (1903–68); the economist, historian, and novelist Arturo Uslar-Pietri (b.1906); and the poet Juan Liscano (b.1915).

Father Pedro Palacios y Sojo (fl.18th cent.) founded the Chacao Conservatory. Among his students were José Cayetano Carreño (1774–1836), José Angel Lamas (1775–1814), and Juan José Landaeta (1780–1812). Teresa Carreño (1853–1917) won world fame as a concert pianist. Leading contemporary composers are Vicente Emilio Sojo (1887–1974), Juan Bautista Plaza (1898–1965), Juan Lecuna (1898–1954), and María Luisa Escobar (b.1903).

The first painter of note in Venezuela was Juan Llovera (1785–1840). His son Pedro Llovera (fl.19th cent.) became the teacher of the first generation of 19th-century Venezuelan painters. Important Venezuelan painters of the 19th century were Martín Tovar y Tovar (1828–1902) and Arturo Michelena (1863–98). The best-known 20th-century painter is Tito Salas (b.1889).

The outstanding pioneer of Venezuelan science was José María Vargas (1786–1854). The first university courses in mathematics and physics were introduced by Vargas's contemporary Juan Manuel Cajigal (1802–56). Modern scientists include Gaspar Marcano (1850–1910), famous for his investigations of blood; Luis Razetti (1862–1932), biologist and physician; and Arnoldo Gabaldón (b.1909), director of an antimalaria campaign from 1945 to 1948.

⁴⁹DEPENDENCIES

The small, sparsely inhabited Caribbean islands off the Venezuelan coast are federal dependencies, with a total area of 120 sq km (46 sq mi). The chief economic activity in the region is fishing and pearl diving.

Venezuela has two territories, Delta Amacuro and Amazonas. Delta Amacuro, with an area of 40,200 sq km (15,521 sq mi), is located in the northeastern corner of Venezuela, bordering Guyana, and had an estimated population of 93,000 as of the mid-1990s. The capital city of Tucupita is situated on Caño Mánamo, one of the principal channels of the Orinoco Delta. It is a commercial center for the petroleum-producing area to the west and is also a loading port for cocoa exports. The remote Amazonas territory, located in the southern corner of Venezuela and bordered by Colombia and Brazil, is larger in area, with 175,750 sq km (67,857 sq mi). Its population was estimated at 80,000 in the mid-1990s, and its capital, Puerto Ayacucho, is scarcely more than a trading post.

⁵⁰BIBLIOGRAPHY

Baloyra, Enrique, and John Martz. *Political Attitudes in Venezuela.* Austin: University of Texas Press, 1979.

Betancourt, Rómulo. *Venezuela, Oil, and Politics.* Boston: Houghton Mifflin, 1979.

Blank, David E. *Venezuela: Politics in a Petroleum Republic.* New York: Praeger, 1984.

Bond, Robert D. (ed.). *Contemporary Venezuela and Its Role in International Affairs.* New York: New York University Press, 1977.

Boue, Juan Carlos. *Venezuela: The Political Economy of Oil.* New York: Oxford University Press, 1993.

Ewell, Judith. *Venezuela and the United States: From Monroe's Hemisphere to Petroleum's Empire.* Athens: University of Georgia Press, 1996.

Fox, Geoffrey. *The Land and People of Venezuela.* New York: Harper Collins, 1991.

Gall, Norman. *Oil and Democracy in Venezuela.* Hanover, N.H.: American Universities Field Staff, 1973.

Gilmore, Robert L. *Caudillism and Militarism in Venezuela, 1810–1910.* Athens: Ohio University Press, 1964.

Haggerty, Richard A. (ed.). *Venezuela: A Country Study.* 4th ed. Washington, D.C.: Library of Congress, 1993.

Hellinger, Daniel. *Venezuela: Tarnished Democracy.* Boulder, Colo.: Westview Press, 1991.

Lessons of the Venezuelan Experience. Edited by Louis W. Goodman et al. Washington, D.C.: Woodrow Wilson Center, 1995.

Levine, Daniel H. *Conflict and Political Change in Venezuela.* Princeton, N.J.: Princeton University Press, 1973.

Lombardi, John V. *Venezuela: The Search for Order, the Dream of Progress.* New York: Oxford University Press, 1982.

——. *Venezuelan History: A Comprehensive Bibliography.* Boston: G. K. Hall, 1977.

Naim, Moises. *Paper Tigers and Minotaurs: The Politics of Venezuela's Economic Reforms.* Washington, D.C.: Carnegie Endowment for International Peace, 1993.

Oropeza, Luis. *Venezuela's Tutelary Pluralism: A Critical Approach to Venezuelan Democracy.* Cambridge, Mass.: Harvard University Press, 1984.

Petras, James F., et al. *The Nationalization of Venezuelan Oil.* New York: Praeger, 1977.

Pollak-Eltz, Angelina. *Black Culture and Society in Venezuela.* Caracas, Venezuela: Public Affairs Dept. of Lagoven, 1994.

Rudolph, Donna K., and G. A. Rudolph. *Historical Dictionary of Venezuela.* 2d ed. Lanham, Md.: Scarecrow, 1996.

Salazar-Carrillo, J. *Oil in the Economic Development of Venezuela.* Stanford, Calif.: Stanford University Press, 1976.

Silva Michelena, José A. *The Illusion of Democracy in Dependent Nations: The Politics of Change in Venezuela,* Vol. 3. Cambridge, Mass.: MIT Press, 1971.

Smith-Perera, Roberto. *Energy and the Economy in Venezuela.* Cambridge, Mass.: Harvard University, 1988.

Tugwell, Franklin. *The Politics of Oil in Venezuela.* Stanford, Calif.: Stanford University Press, 1975.

Venezuela in Pictures. Minneapolis: Lerner, 1987.

Waddell, D. A. G. (David Alan Gilmour). *Venezuela.* Oxford, England, and Santa Barbara, Calif.: Clio Press, 1990.

INDEX TO COUNTRIES AND TERRITORIES

This alphabetical list includes countries and dependencies (colonies, protectorates, and other territories) described in the encyclopedia. Countries and territories described in their own articles are followed by the continental volume (printed in *italics*) in which each appears. Country articles are arranged alphabetically in each volume. For example, Argentina, which appears in *Americas*, is listed this way: Argentina—*Americas*. Dependencies are listed here with the title of the volume in which they are treated, followed by the name of the article in which they are dealt with. In a few cases, an alternative name for the same place is given in parentheses at the end of the entry. The name of the volume *Asia and Oceania* is abbreviated in this list to *Asia*.

Adélie Land—*Asia:* French Pacific Dependencies: French Southern and Antarctic Territories
Afars and the Issas, Territory of the—*Africa:* Djibouti
Afghanistan—*Asia*
Albania—*Europe*
Algeria—*Africa*
American Samoa—*Asia:* US Pacific Dependencies
Andaman Islands—*Asia:* India
Andorra—*Europe*
Angola—*Africa*
Anguilla—*Americas:* UK American Dependencies: Leeward Islands
Antarctica—*United Nations:* Polar Regions
Antigua and Barbuda—*Americas*
Arctic—*United Nations:* Polar Regions
Argentina—*Americas*
Armenia—*Europe*
Aruba—*Americas:* Netherlands American Dependencies: Aruba
Ashmore and Cartier Islands—*Asia:* Australia
Australia—*Asia*
Austria—*Europe*
Azerbaijan—*Asia*
Azores—*Europe:* Portugal

Bahamas—*Americas*
Bahrain—*Asia*
Bangladesh—*Asia*
Barbados—*Americas*
Basutoland—*Africa:* Lesotho
Bechuanaland—*Africa:* Botswana
Belarus—*Europe*
Belau—*Asia:* Palau
Belgium—*Europe*
Belize—*Americas*
Benin—*Africa*
Bermuda—*Americas:* UK American Dependencies
Bhutan—*Asia*
Bolivia—*Americas*
Bonin Islands—*Asia:* Japan (Ogasawara Islands)
Borneo, North—*Asia:* Malaysia
Bosnia and Herzegovina—*Europe*
Botswana—*Africa*
Bouvet Island—*Europe:* Norway
Brazil—*Americas*
British Antarctic Territory—*Americas:* UK American Dependencies

British Guiana—*Americas:* Guyana
British Honduras—*Americas:* Belize
British Indian Ocean Territory—*Africa:* UK African Dependencies
British Virgin Islands—*Americas:* UK American Dependencies
Brunei Darussalam—*Asia*
Bulgaria—*Europe*
Burkina Faso—*Africa*
Burma—*Asia:* Myanmar
Burundi—*Africa*

Caicos Islands—*Americas:* UK American Dependencies
Cambodia—*Asia*
Cameroon—*Africa*
Canada—*Americas*
Canary Islands—*Europe:* Spain
Cape Verde—*Africa*
Caroline Islands—*Asia:* Federated States of Micronesia; Palau
Carriacou—*Americas:* Grenada
Cayman Islands—*Americas:* UK American Dependencies
Central African Republic—*Africa*
Ceuta—*Europe:* Spain
Ceylon—*Asia:* Sri Lanka
Chad—*Africa*
Chile—*Americas*
Chilean Antarctic Territory—*Americas:* Chile
China—*Asia*
Christmas Island (Indian Ocean)—*Asia:* Australia
Christmas Island (Pacific Ocean)—*Asia:* Kiribati
Cocos Islands—*Americas:* Costa Rica
Cocos (Keeling) Islands—*Asia:* Australia
Colombia—*Americas*
Columbus, Archipelago of—*Americas:* Ecuador (Galapagos Islands)
Comoros—*Africa*
Congo—*Africa*
Congo, Democratic Republic of (former Zaire)—*Africa*
Cook Islands—*Asia:* New Zealand
Coral Sea Islands—*Asia:* Australia
Corn Islands—*Americas:* Nicaragua
Costa Rica—*Americas*
Côte d'Ivoire—*Africa*
Croatia—*Europe*
Cuba—*Americas*
Curaçao—*Americas:* Netherlands American Dependencies: Netherlands Antilles
Cyprus—*Asia*

ISBN 0-7876-0514-X

90000

9 780787 605148

Antigua and Barbuda

Argentina

Bahamas

Barbados

Chile

Colombia

Costa Rica

Cuba

Grenada

Guatemala

Guyana

Haiti

Panama

Paraguay

Peru

St. Kitts and Nevis

Turks and
Caicos Islands

United States
of America

Uruguay

Venezuela